EDITORIAL BOARD

ROBERT C. CLARK
DIRECTING EDITOR
Distinguished Service Professor and Austin Wakeman Scott
Professor of Law and Former Dean of the Law School
Harvard University

DANIEL A. FARBER
Sho Sato Professor of Law and Director, Environmental Law Program
University of California at Berkeley

SAMUEL ISSACHAROFF
Bonnie and Richard Reiss Professor of Constitutional Law
New York University

HERMA HILL KAY
Barbara Nachtrieb Armstrong Professor of Law and
Former Dean of the School of Law
University of California at Berkeley

HAROLD HONGJU KOH
Sterling Professor of International Law and
Former Dean of the Law School
Yale University

SAUL LEVMORE
William B. Graham Distinguished Service Professor of Law and
Former Dean of the Law School
University of Chicago

THOMAS W. MERRILL
Charles Evans Hughes Professor of Law
Columbia University

ROBERT L. RABIN
A. Calder Mackay Professor of Law
Stanford University

CAROL M. ROSE
Gordon Bradford Tweedy Professor Emeritus of Law and Organization and
Professorial Lecturer in Law
Yale University
Lohse Chair in Water and Natural Resources
University of Arizona

UNIVERSITY CASEBOOK SERIES®

INSURANCE LAW AND REGULATION

CASES AND MATERIALS

SIXTH EDITION

by

KENNETH S. ABRAHAM
David and Mary Harrison Distinguished Professor of Law
University of Virginia

DANIEL SCHWARCZ
Professor of Law
University of Minnesota

The publisher is not engaged in rendering legal or other professional advice, and this publication is not a substitute for the advice of an attorney. If you require legal or other expert advice, you should seek the services of a competent attorney or other professional.

University Casebook Series is a trademark registered in the U.S. Patent and Trademark Office.

© 1990, 1995, 2000 FOUNDATION PRESS
© 2005 THOMSON REUTERS/FOUNDATION PRESS
© 2010 by THOMSON REUTERS/FOUNDATION PRESS
© 2015 LEG, Inc. d/b/a West Academic
    444 Cedar Street, Suite 700
    St. Paul, MN 55101
    1-877-888-1330

Printed in the United States of America

ISBN: 978-1-60930-401-0

Mat #41487717

For Katherine and Michael

and

For Tamar, Orly, Tova, and Esther

PREFACE

Publication of this sixth edition of the casebook brings with it a major change: Professor Daniel Schwarcz of the University of Minnesota Law School has become a co-author. The casebook has now been in continuous use for twenty-five years. Professor Schwarcz brings a new perspective and adds considerable expertise to the work of revision.

In the years since the earlier editions of this casebook were published, interest in insurance law has continued to grow within law schools, across the practicing bar, and in the domain of public policy. Once an obscure specialty, the issues that arise in modern insurance law have become part of the mainstream, and a mature body of legal doctrine has grown up around them. However, both the structure of the casebook and its emphases remain the same.

Organization by Type of Insurance. The first three chapters of the casebook crosscut different types of insurance, examining issues that arise in all types of insurance. Thus, Chapter One takes up doctrines governing applications for insurance and representations made by the applicant, Chapter Two examines the law governing contract formation, meaning, and damages, and Chapter Three addresses the regulation of insurance. Beyond these chapters, however, the structure of the casebook is not determined by general themes, but by types of insurance. Consequently, Chapters Four through Nine are devoted to property, life, health, disability, liability, auto, and reinsurance. This organization reflects the fact that it is extremely difficult to understand a particular insurance law problem without also understanding the kind of insurance the problem involves.

At the same time, the basic legal and regulatory concepts examined in the casebook's first three chapters provide an indispensible foundation for the coverage-line specific material that follows. This is perhaps obvious for Chapters One and Two, as the contract law foundations covered in these chapters reflect the primacy of the insurance policy in defining insurers' and policyholders' rights and obligations. Even more so than in the past, however, the regulatory concepts covered in Chapter Three also provide an essential base for the subsequent materials. This reflects the increasing importance of statutes and regulation in insurance law, as most clearly exemplified by the transformation of health insurance law by the Affordable Care Act (i.e. "Obamacare") and the wave of federal and state regulations that have been promulgated in its wake.

A Focus on Insurance Policies and Policy Language. The starting point for the study of any contractual relationship should be the terms of the contract itself. In insurance, that contract is the insurance policy. Although cases typically focus on individual policy provisions, the meaning and functions of those provisions are deeply informed by their place in the larger contract. Consequently, at the beginning of the Chapters on Property, Liability, and Auto Insurance, and in the material in Chapter Six on Directors & Officers Insurance (a specialized form of liability insurance), we have set out complete copies of insurance policies providing these forms of coverage. An entire insurance policy is a forbidding document to the uninitiated; but the ability to read an insurance policy is a skill that every insurance lawyer must master. As students proceed through the book, they should become familiar with the structure and organization of each sample policy: the terms of its Insuring Agreement, the location and general focus of the Exclusions, the nature of the Conditions of coverage, and so forth. Then, as each case or problem is addressed, students should consider how, if at all, their analysis would be impacted if the sample policy governed.

Equal Emphasis on Commercial and Personal Insurance. We believe that the traditional emphasis in insurance law courses on personal insurance, and especially on automobile and homeowners insurance, gives law students a misleading impression of the nature of the subject and of the shape of insurance law doctrines. Consumer protection concerns are much stronger in personal than in commercial insurance law, and nowhere is this more evident than in automobile insurance disputes. Consequently, we have tried throughout the casebook to provide a representative mix of personal and commercial insurance issues and cases, and we have chosen to treat automobile insurance issues in a separate chapter devoted exclusively to the very special problems of this field.

A Sustained Examination of Insurance Regulation. As we noted above, Chapter Three is devoted entirely to an examination of the administrative and statutory regulation of insurance. Virtually all of insurance law, however, directly or indirectly regulates insurance. Consequently, running through this entire casebook is a concern about the nature of insurance regulation. We place particular emphasis on considering when and why the law should intervene in insurance markets. Because the purpose of insurance regulation is to influence insurance activity, we also emphasize the possible impacts of different forms of regulation on that activity. Throughout the casebook, we often consider these issues from an economic perspective. At the same time, we frequently consider alternative, noneconomic ways of looking at the issues examined.

The Use of Descriptive Introductions and Essays. As with many casebooks, judicial opinions figure prominently in the casebook, as they often do a good job of describing the law, applying it to particular situations, and considering its policy implications. However, we have not hesitated to supplement cases with introductory or explanatory text. Moreover, in many instances we have opted to rely more extensively on our own descriptive text than on judicial opinions, particularly on subjects such as insurance regulation and health insurance reform, where the caselaw is either under-developed or typically addresses very narrow issues. This approach reflects the overall strategy of the casebook, which is to provide the easiest possible access to descriptive material, so that the hard work of thinking about what has been described can take priority. Consistent with this approach, we have heavily edited some cases, often omitting references to the record in the case, string citations, and footnotes, and renumbering the latter in consecutive order, all without specific notation that we have done so. This makes the excerpted opinions more readable and the underlying analysis more transparent. At a few points where reference to leading cases in the field on a given issue are useful, we have retained string citations.

No work of this scope can be prepared entirely alone. Our fellow insurance law teachers at other law schools have generously commented on aspects of the book that they have found useful or difficult. We received very capable research assistance from Emily Riff, University of Virginia Law School Class of 2016, Lokys Gust, University of Minnesota Law School Class of 2015, and Samuel Posnick, University of Minnesota Law School Class of 2016. Our colleagues at UVA and Minnesota have enriched our ability to think about legal issues, including insurance law, in countless ways over the years.

Finally, we thank the Insurance Services Office, Inc., for permission to reprint the Homeowners, Commercial General Liability Insurance, and Automobile Insurance policies set out in Chapters Four, Six, and Eight, respectively; and the Chubb Insurance Companies for permission to reprint the D&O insurance policy included in Chapter Six. The Insurance Services Office, Inc., requires that the following statement be included: Information which is copyrighted by and proprietary to Insurance Services Office, Inc. ("ISO Material") is included in this publication. Use of the ISO Material is limited to ISO Participating Insurers and their Authorized Representatives. Use by ISO Participating Insurers is limited to use in those jurisdictions for which the insurer has an appropriate participation with ISO. Use of the ISO Material by Authorized Representatives is limited to use solely on behalf of one or more ISO Participating Insurers.

KENNETH S. ABRAHAM

DANIEL SCHWARCZ

Charlottesville and Minneapolis
January 2015

SUMMARY OF CONTENTS

PREFACE V

TABLE OF CASES XIX

Chapter One. Introduction 1
A. The History and Functions of Insurance 1
B. The Problems of Adverse Selection and Moral Hazard 6

Chapter Two. Insurance Contract Formation, Meaning, and Damages 33
A. The Role of Standardized Forms 33
B. The Role of Intermediaries 63
C. Bad Faith 81
D. Public Policy Restrictions on Contract Terms 94

Chapter Three. Insurance Regulation 107
A. The Allocation of Regulatory Powers 107
B. State Insurance Regulation 111
C. Federal Regulation 151
D. International Regulation of Insurance 179

Chapter Four. Property Insurance 183
A. Sample Homeowners Policy 183
B. The Requirement of an Insurable Interest in Property Insurance 210
C. Trigger and Occurrence Issues 217
D. Business Interruption Coverage 223
E. Exclusions 229
F. The Measure of Recovery 260
G. Subrogation 266
H. Limited Interests 273

Chapter Five. Life, Health, and Disability Insurance 291
A. Life Insurance 291
B. Health Insurance 343
C. Disability Insurance 421

Chapter Six. Liability Insurance: Indemnity 435
A. General Liability Insurance 435
B. Claims-Made Policies 534

Chapter Seven. Liability Insurance: Defense, Settlement, and Excess Coverage 577
A. The Duty to Defend and the Consequences of Breach 577
B. Settlement 609
C. The Rights and Obligations of Excess Insurers 617

Chapter Eight. Automobile Insurance **637**
A. Sample Personal Automobile Insurance Policy 638
B. Auto Liability Insurance 651
C. Collision and Comprehensive Coverage 686
D. Uninsured Motorists Coverage 693
E. Auto No-Fault 710

Chapter Nine. Reinsurance **717**
A. Nature and Functions 717
B. The Duty of Utmost Good Faith 721
C. "Follow-the-Fortunes" Clauses 728
D. Insolvency Clauses 745
E. Set-Offs in Insolvency 751

INDEX 759

TABLE OF CONTENTS

PREFACE..V

TABLE OF CASES.. XIX

Chapter One. Introduction 1
A. The History and Functions of Insurance 1
B. The Problems of Adverse Selection and Moral Hazard 6
    1. Breach of Warranty... 9
        Vlastos v. Sumitomo Marine & Fire Insurance Company 9
        Notes and Questions 13
    2. The Transformation of Warranty Law: The Modern Law of Misrepresentation and Non-Disclosure 15
        Notes and Questions 20
        Neill v. Nationwide Mutual Fire Insurance Company 22
        Notes and Questions 24
        MacKenzie v. Prudential Insurance Company of America 27
        Notes and Questions 29

Chapter Two. Insurance Contract Formation, Meaning, and Damages.. 33
A. The Role of Standardized Forms 33
    1. The Policy Standardization Process.................................. 33
    2. Binders and Policyholder Assent to Standardized Forms 38
    3. Construing Ambiguities Against the Insurer................... 40
        Vargas v. Insurance Company of North America 41
        Notes and Questions 45
        Stone Container Corporation v. Hartford Steam Boiler Inspection and Insurance Company................................. 47
        Notes and Questions 52
    4. Honoring the Reasonable Expectations of the Insured 53
        Atwater Creamery Company v. Western National Mutual Insurance Company 54
        Notes and Questions 58
B. The Role of Intermediaries... 63
    1. The Authority of Intermediaries 64
    2. Intermediaries' Duties to Policyholders 65
        Langwith v. American National General Insurance Company 65
        Notes and Questions 71
    3. Waiver and Estoppel.. 74
        Roseth v. St. Paul Property & Liability Insurance Company 74
        Notes and Questions 77
    4. Group Insurance and ERISA... 78
C. Bad Faith... 81
    Silberg v. California Life Insurance Company....................... 82
    Notes and Questions 90

	D.	Public Policy Restrictions on Contract Terms 94

    D. Public Policy Restrictions on Contract Terms 94
         Hartford Casualty Insurance Company v. Powell 95
         Notes and Questions 97
         Strickland v. Gulf Life Insurance Company 99
         Notes and Questions 104

Chapter Three. Insurance Regulation 107
  A. The Allocation of Regulatory Powers 107
      Notes and Questions 110
  B. State Insurance Regulation 111
    1. The First Virtue of Insurance: Regulation to Assure
        Solvency 113
        a. Rationales for Solvency Regulation 113
            Notes and Questions 116
        b. The Tools of Solvency Regulation 117
            Notes and Questions 124
    2. Regulation of "Excessive" Rates 126
        Commissioner of Insurance v. North Carolina Rate Bureau 128
        Notes and Questions 131
    3. Regulation of "Unfairly Discriminatory" Rates 133
        Allstate Insurance Company v. Schmidt 135
        Notes and Questions 138
    4. Policy Form Regulation 142
        Notes and Questions 145
    5. Market Conduct Regulation 147
        Notes and Questions 148
    6. Residual Market Mechanisms 149
        Notes and Questions 150
  C. Federal Regulation 151
    1. Federal Regulation and Reverse Preemption 151
        Patrick O. Ojo v. Farmers Group, Inc. 152
        Notes and Questions 155
    2. Federal Antitrust Law and Insurance 157
        a. What Constitutes "The Business of Insurance"? 157
        b. What Constitutes "Regulation" by the States? 159
        c. What Constitutes "Boycott, Coercion, or Intimidation"? 160
            Hartford Fire Insurance Company v. California 161
            Notes and Questions 167
    3. Federal Role in Catastrophe Insurance 169
        Notes and Questions 170
    4. Federal Regulation of Insurance After the Dodd-Frank Act 171
        a. The AIG Bailout 171
            Notes and Questions 173
        b. Dodd-Frank's Insurance Reforms 174
            Notes and Questions 178
  D. International Regulation of Insurance 179
      Notes and Questions 182

Chapter Four. Property Insurance 183
A. Sample Homeowners Policy 183
  Notes and Questions 210
B. The Requirement of an Insurable Interest in Property Insurance 210
  Richard C. Gossett and Margaret D. Gossett v. Farmers Insurance Company of Washington 211
  Notes and Questions 215
C. Trigger and Occurrence Issues 217
  Port Authority of New York and New Jersey v. Affiliated FM Insurance Company 217
  Notes and Questions 221
D. Business Interruption Coverage 223
  Duane Reade, Inc. v. St. Paul Fire & Marine Insurance Company 223
  Notes and Questions 227
E. Exclusions 229
  1. The Problem of Intrinsic Loss 230
    Chute v. North River Insurance Company 230
    Notes and Questions 231
    Rosen v. State Farm General Insurance Company 232
    Notes and Questions 236
  2. The Problem of Causation 237
    State Farm Fire and Casualty Company v. Bongen 237
    Notes and Questions 240
    Liristis v. American Family Mutual Insurance Company 242
    Notes and Questions 246
    Broussard v. State Farm Fire and Casualty Company 247
    Notes and Questions 252
  3. The Problem of Increased Risk 253
    Langill v. Vermont Mutual Insurance Company 254
    Notes and Questions 259
F. The Measure of Recovery 260
  Zochert v. National Farmers Union Property & Casualty Company 260
  Notes and Questions 263
G. Subrogation 266
  Great Northern Oil Company v. St. Paul Fire and Marine Insurance Company 268
  Notes and Questions 272
H. Limited Interests 273
  1. Mortgages 274
    Northwest Farm Bureau Insurance Company v. Althauser 274
    Notes and Questions 276
  2. Leaseholds 277
    Alaska Insurance Company v. RCA Alaska Communications, Inc. 277
    Notes and Questions 281

	3. Real Estate Sales	282
	Paramount Fire Insurance Company v. Aetna Casualty and Surety Company	283
	Notes and Questions	288

Chapter Five. Life, Health, and Disability Insurance 291

A. Life Insurance 291
　　1. The Application 292
　　　　Gaunt v. John Hancock Mutual Life Insurance Company..........292
　　　　Notes and Questions 296
　　2. The Requirement of an Insurable Interest.............................298
　　　　Ryan v. Tickle 299
　　　　Notes and Questions 302
　　　　Mayo v. Hartford Life Insurance Company...........................305
　　　　Notes and Questions 308
　　3. Assignment of Life Insurance Policies....................................309
　　　　Grigsby v. Russell 309
　　　　Notes and Questions 311
　　4. Designating Beneficiaries..314
　　　　Engelman v. Connecticut General Life Insurance Company......315
　　　　Notes and Questions 320
　　5. Incontestability 321
　　　　Amex Life Assurance Company v. Superior Court 322
　　　　Notes and Questions 326
　　6. Negligence Actions Against the Insurer 327
　　　　Mauroner v. Massachusetts Indemnity and Life Insurance Company 327
　　　　Notes and Questions 332
　　7. Life Insurance Products and Securities Regulation 333
　　　　American Equity Investment Life Insurance Company, et al. v. Securities and Exchange Commission 333
　　　　Notes and Questions 341

B. Health Insurance 343
　　1. The Structure of Health Insurance Markets...............................343
　　2. The Need for Reform Prior to the ACA..346
　　　　a. Coverage, Cost and Quality Prior to the ACA......................346
　　　　b. Under-Insurance Prior to the ACA 348
　　　　　(1) Moral Hazard, Cost-Sharing and Consumer-Driven Health Care..348
　　　　　(2) Preexisting Condition Exclusions.................................349
　　　　　(3) Rescissions 350
　　　　　(4) Annual and Lifetime Coverage Limits..........................350
　　　　　(5) Loss of Employer-Sponsored Coverage 350
　　　　　　Notes and Questions 351
　　3. The ACA's Reform of Health Insurance 353
　　　　a. Reforms of Private Health Insurance 353
　　　　　(1) The ACA's Regulation of Insurers' Pricing, Offering, and Renewal of Coverage..353
　　　　　(2) The ACA's Regulation of the Content of Coverage........354

			(3)	The ACA's Creation of Health Insurance Exchanges 356

          b. Health Insurance Mandates, Subsidies, and Taxes Under the ACA 356
              (1) The Individual Mandate/Tax 356
              (2) Individual Subsidies 357
              (3) Employer Mandate/Tax 357
              (4) Cadillac Tax 357
              (5) Small Employer Subsidies 358
          c. Public Insurance Reforms Under the ACA 358
              (1) Medicaid Eligibility 358
              (2) Medicare and Medicaid Payment Reforms 358
          Notes and Questions 359
     4. Constitutional Challenges to the ACA 362
         National Federation of Independent Business et al. v. Sebelius 362
         Notes and Questions 371
     5. Employer-Sponsored Coverage After the ACA 372
         McGann v. H & H Music Company 373
         Notes and Questions 379
     6. Managed Care and the Definition of "Medically Necessary" 383
         Fuja v. Benefit Trust Life Insurance Company 384
         Notes and Questions 388
     7. Challenging Coverage Denials Under ERISA 390
         Pilot Life Insurance Company v. Dedeaux 390
         Notes and Questions 396
         Aetna Health Inc. v. Davila 398
         Notes and Questions 405
     8. Coordination of Coverage 406
         Harris Corporation v. Humana Health Insurance Company of Florida, Inc. 407
         Notes and Questions 413
         Associated Hospital Service of Philadelphia v. Pustilnik 415
         Notes and Questions 418

C. Disability Insurance 421
    Mossa v. Provident Life and Casualty Insurance Company 422
    Notes and Questions 427
    Heller v. Equitable Life Assurance Society of the United States 429
    Notes and Questions 433

Chapter Six. Liability Insurance: Indemnity 435
A. General Liability Insurance 435
     1. Sample CGL Policy 437
     2. The Insuring Agreement 455
         a. The Meaning of "Damages," "Property Damage," and "Bodily Injury" 455
            A.Y. McDonald Industries, Inc. v. Insurance Company of North America 455
            Notes and Questions 461

				Eyeblaster, Inc. v. Federal Insurance Company 463

				Eyeblaster, Inc. v. Federal Insurance Company 463

Eyeblaster, Inc. v. Federal Insurance Company 463
Notes and Questions 466
Heacker v. Safeco Insurance Company of America 466
Notes and Questions 468

b. The Trigger and Allocation of Coverage 469
American Home Products Corporation v. Liberty Mutual Insurance Company 469
Notes and Questions 475
In re Silicone Implant Insurance Coverage Litigation 477
Notes and Questions 485

c. The Number of Occurrences 487
Metropolitan Life Insurance Company v. Aetna Casualty & Surety Company 488
Notes and Questions 493

3. Exclusions and Conditions 495
    a. Expected or Intended Harm 495
Stonewall Insurance Company v. Asbestos Claims Management Corporation 496
Notes and Questions 500
Unigard Mutual Insurance Company v. Argonaut Insurance Company 502
Notes and Questions 505

    b. The Business Risk Exclusions 507
Weedo v. Stone-E-Brick, Inc. 507
Notes and Questions 514

    c. The Pollution Exclusion 516
American States Insurance Co. v. Koloms 516
Notes and Questions 525

    d. Notice Conditions 528
West Bay Exploration v. AIG Specialty Agencies 528
Notes and Questions 532

B. Claims-Made Policies 534
  1. Sample Directors and Officers Policy 538
  2. Selected Claims-Made Exclusions and Conditions 555
Alstrin v. St. Paul Mercury Insurance Company 555
Notes and Questions 561
Federal Insurance Company v. Raytheon Company 563
Notes and Questions 567
Thoracic Cardiovascular Associates, Ltd. v. St. Paul Fire and Marine Insurance Company 568
Notes and Questions 574

Chapter Seven. Liability Insurance: Defense, Settlement, and Excess Coverage 577

A. The Duty to Defend and the Consequences of Breach 577
  1. The Scope of the Duty 578
Beckwith Machinery Company v. Travelers Indemnity Company 578
Notes and Questions 584

		2.	"Mixed" Claims and Conflicts of Interest 587

        2.   "Mixed" Claims and Conflicts of Interest 587
            Gray v. Zurich Insurance Company 588
            Notes and Questions 592
            Shoshone First Bank v. Pacific Employers Insurance
                Company 595
            Notes and Questions 600
            Parsons v. Continental National American Group 601
            Notes and Questions 607
B.   Settlement 609
        Crisci v. Security Insurance Company of New Haven,
            Connecticut 610
        Notes and Questions 614
C.   The Rights and Obligations of Excess Insurers 617
        1.   Exhaustion 618
            Comerica, Inc. v. Zurich American Insurance Company 618
            Notes and Questions 622
        2.   Primary Insurers' Duty to Excess Insurers to Settle 624
            Commercial Union Assurance Companies v. Safeway Stores,
                Inc. 624
            Notes and Questions 629
        3.   Drop-Down Liability 630
            Mission National Insurance Company v. Duke Transportation
                Company 630
            Notes and Questions 635

Chapter Eight. Automobile Insurance 637
A.   Sample Personal Automobile Insurance Policy 638
B.   Auto Liability Insurance 651
        1.   The Scope of Compulsory Insurance Requirements 651
            St. Paul Fire & Marine Insurance Company v. Smith 651
            Notes and Questions 656
        2.   The Omnibus Clause 658
            Curtis v. State Farm Mutual Automobile Insurance
                Company 658
            Notes and Questions 664
        3.   "Use" of the Vehicle 665
            Farm Bureau Mutual Insurance Company v. Evans 665
            Notes and Questions 668
        4.   Notice and Cooperation Conditions 669
            State Farm Mutual Automobile Insurance Company v.
                Davies 669
            Notes and Questions 673
            Miller v. Shugart 674
            Notes and Questions 679
        5.   Other Insurance Clauses 679
            Carriers Insurance Company v. American Policyholders'
                Insurance Company 679
            Notes and Questions 685

C.	Collision and Comprehensive Coverage	686
	Allison v. Iowa Mutual Insurance Company	687
	Rodemich v. State Farm Mutual Automobile Insurance Company	690
	Notes and Questions	693
D.	Uninsured Motorists Coverage	693
	Allstate Insurance Co. v. Boynton	693
	Notes and Questions	700
	Simpson v. Farmers Insurance Company, Inc.	701
	Notes and Questions	706
	Taft v. Cerwonka	706
	Notes and Questions	709
E.	Auto No-Fault	710
	1. Mandatory No-Fault	711
	2. "Add-on" No-Fault	714
	3. "Choice" No-Fault	714

Chapter Nine. Reinsurance 717

A.	Nature and Functions	717
B.	The Duty of Utmost Good Faith	721
	Allendale Mutual Insurance Company v. Excess Insurance Co. Limited	721
	Notes and Questions	726
C.	"Follow-the-Fortunes" Clauses	728
	Travelers Casualty & Surety Company v. Certain Underwriters at Lloyd's of London	728
	Travelers Casualty & Surety Company v. Gerling Global Reinsurance Corporation of America	735
	Notes and Questions	744
D.	Insolvency Clauses	745
	Ainsworth v. General Reinsurance Corporation	745
	Notes and Questions	749
E.	Set-Offs in Insolvency	751
	O'Connor v. Insurance Company of North America	751
	Notes and Questions	757

INDEX 759

TABLE OF CASES

The principal cases are in bold type.

56 Assocs. ex rel. Paolino v. Frieband 281
80 Broad St. Co. v. U.S. Fire Ins. Co. 221
525 Main Street Corp. v. Eagle Roofing Co. Inc. 510
A.Y. McDonald Industries, Inc. v. Insurance Company of North America 455
ABB Power T & D Co., Inc. v. Gothaer Versicherungsbank VVAG 215
Abbott v. Western Nat. Indem. Co. 590
Ackerman v. Foster 45
Adams Tree Service Inc. v. Hawaiian Insurance & Guaranty Co. Ltd. 511
Adams v. Jefferson-Pilot Life Ins. Co. 321
Addison Ins. Co. v. Fay 494
Adelphia Commc'n Corp., In re 536
AES Corp. v. Steadfast Ins. Co. 436, 526
Aetna Cas. & Surety Co. v. Cartmel 689
Aetna Cas. & Surety Co. v. Commonwealth 461
Aetna Cas. & Surety Co. v. Hanna 459, 462
Aetna Health Inc. v. Davilla 398
Aetna Ins. Co. v. Aaron 527
Aetna Ins. Co. v. Pete Wilson Roofing & Heating Co., Inc. 514
Aetna Life and Casualty Co. v. McCabe 581, 582, 583
Aetna Life Ins. Co. v. France 311
Aetna Life Ins. Co. v. Hartford National Bank & Trust Co. 318
Aetna Life Ins. Co. v. Industrial Acc. Comm. 89
Aetna Life Ins. Co. v. Moses 269
Aggio v. Estate of Aggio 527
Agra-By-Products, Inc. v. Agway, Inc. 282
Aguiar v. Generali Assicurazioni Ins. Co. 256
AIG Hawai'i Ins. Co. v. Caraang 657
Alaska Civil Liberties Union v. State of Alaska & Municipality of Anchorage 382
Alaska Insurance Company v. RCA Alaska Communications, Inc. 277
Albany Ins. Co. v. United Alarm Servs., Inc. 272
Alessi v. Raybestos-Manhattan, Inc. 392, 399
Alf v. State Farm Fire & Casualty Co. 238, 239
Allen v. Prudential Prop. & Cas. Ins. Co. 53
Allen v. Scottsdale Insurance Co. 525
Allendale Mutual Insurance Company v. Excess Insurance Co. Limited 721
Alliance Mutual Casualty Co. v. Boston Insurance Co. 666
Allied Mut. Ins. Co. v. Heiken 267
Allied Prop. & Cas. Ins. Co. v. Good 25
Allis-Chalmers Corp. v. Lueck 392, 402
Allison v. Fire Insurance Exchange 247
Allison v. Iowa Mutual Insurance Company 687
Allmerica Fin. Cor. v. Certain Underwriters at Lloyd's, London 630
Allstate Ins. Co. v. American Home Assurance Co. 744
Allstate Ins. Co. v. Boynton 693
Allstate Ins. Co. v. Dana Corp. 475, 486, 630
Allstate Ins. Co. v. Gillespie 668
Allstate Ins. Co. v. Huston 30
Allstate Ins. Co. v. Keillor 62
Allstate Ins. Co. v. LaRandeau 276
Allstate Ins. Co. v. Loester 674
Allstate Ins. Co. v. Maglish 708, 709
Allstate Ins. Co. v. Schmidt 135
Allstate Life Ins. Co. v. Miller 326
Alm v. Hartford Fire Insurance Co. 663
Alstrin v. St. Paul Mercury Insurance Company 555
Altimari v. John Hancock Variable Life Ins. Co. 298
AM International, Inc. v. Graphic Management Associates, Inc. 51
America Online, Inc. v. St. Paul Mer. Ins. Co. 465, 466
America States Ins. Co. v. Ridco, Inc., Riddles Jewelry, Inc., and Ken B. Berger 599

American & Foreign Ins. Co. v.
 Jerry's Sport Ctr., Inc. 600
American Access Cas. Co. v.
 Reyes 656
American Bankers Ins. Co. of Florida
 v. Inman 155
American Bankers Ins. Co. v.
 Northwestern Natl. Ins. Co. 735
American Bumper & Mfg. Co. v. Nat.
 Union Fire Ins. Co. 500
American Cas. Co. v. Myrick 49,
 663
American Cas. Co. v. Rose 302
American Contract Bridge v.
 Nationwide Mutual Fire Insurance
 Co. 580, 581, 583
American Economy Ins. Co. v. Fort
 Deposit Bank 468
American Electric Power Co. v.
 Connecticut 526
American Empire Surplus Lines
 Insurance Co. v. Hathaway 507
American Employers' Ins. Co. v.
 Swiss Reinsurance Am.
 Corp. 741, 742, 743
**American Equity Investment Life
 Insurance Company, et al. v.
 Securities and Exchange
 Commission 333**
American Family Insurance Co. v.
 Walser 505
American Fire & Casualty Co. v.
 Boyd 695
American Home Assurance Co. v.
 International Ins. Co. 533
American Home Assurance Co. v.
 Safway Steel Products Co. 498
**American Home Products Corp.
 v. Liberty Mutual Ins.
 Co.** **469**, 475
American Income Life Ins. Co. v.
 Hollins 65
American Medical Int'l, Inc. v. Nat'l
 Union Fire Ins. Co. 562
American Motorists Ins. v. E.R.
 Squibb & Sons 471
American Mut. Fire Ins. Co. v.
 Durrence 257
American National Fire Ins. Co. v.
 Rose Acre Farms, Inc. 51
American Physicians Ins. Exch. v.
 Garcia 615
American Red Cross v. Travelers
 Indemnity Co. of Rhode
 Island 493
American States Insurance Co. v.
 Kiger 521
**American States Insurance Co. v.
 Koloms** **516**
American United Life Ins. Co. v.
 Martinez 313

**Amex Life Assurance Company v.
 Superior Court** **322**
Anderson v. Aul 574
Anderson v. Continental Insurance
 Co. 93
Anderson v. Kemper Ins. Co. 530
Anspach v. United of Omaha Life Ins.
 Co. 326
Appalachian Insurance Co. v. Liberty
 Mutual Insurance Co. 500
Archer-Daniels-Midland Company v.
 Phoenix Assurance Company of
 New York 228
Arcos Corp. v. Am. Mut. Liab. Ins.
 Co. 516
Arenson v. National Auto. & Cas.
 Ins. Co. 592
Arizona Governing Comm. v.
 Norris 142, 154
Aronson v. Servus Rubber, Div. of
 Chromalloy 376, 377
Arrow Trucking Co. v. Continental
 Insurance Co. 750
Arroyo-Melecio v. Puerto Rican
 American Insurance
 Company 159
Asermely v. Allstate Ins. Co. 615
Associated Aviation Underwriters v.
 Wood 468
**Associated Hospital Service of
 Philadelphia v. Pustilnik** **415**,
420
AT&T v. Clarendon Am. Ins.
 Co. 561
Atlantic Mut. Ins. Co. v. Equinox Ins.
 Co. 617
**Atwater Creamery Company v.
 Western National Mutual
 Insurance Company** **54**
Atwood v. Hartford Accident &
 Indemnity Co. 61
Automobile Insurance Company of
 Hartford v. Springfield Dyeing
 Company 681
Avco Corp. v. Machinists 400
Avery v. Diedrich 71
Awbrey v. Pennzoil Co. 386, 388
Axis Reinsurance Co. v. Telekenex,
 Inc. 477
Babcock & Wilcox Co. v. Arkwright-
 Boston Mfg. Mutual Ins. Co. 491
Bachrach v. Herrup 318
Bacich v. Homeland Ins. Co. 269,
270
Bacon v. Federal Kemper Life
 Assurance Co. 332
Baesler v. Globe Indemnity
 Co. 662, 663
Bailey v. Blue Cross & Blue Shield of
 Virginia 388
Bailey v. General Insurance
 Co. 662

Bajwa v. Metropolitian Life Ins. Co. 332, 333
Bakowski v. Mountain States Steel, Inc. 272
Bank of Miss. v. Miss. Life and Health Ins. Guar. Ass'n 123
Baptist Memorial Hosp. v. Pan American Life Ins. Co. 408, 409, 410, 411, 412
Bareno v. Employers Life Ins. Co. 88
Bartholomew v. Appalachian Insurance Co. 499
Bartlett v. Allstate Ins. Co. 213
Baugh-Belarde Constr. Co. v. College Utilities Corp. 279
BCS v. Big Thyme Enterprises 575
Beckwith Machinery Company v. Travelers Indemnity Company **578**
Bedoya v. Illinois Founders Ins. Co. 598
Bell v. Progressive Direct Ins. Co. 59
Bellefonte Reins. Co. v. Aetna Cas. & Sur. Co. 734
Belt Painting Corp. v. TIG Insurance Co. 525
Belton v. Cincinnati Ins. Co. 216
Benjamin Moore & Co. v. Aetna Cas. & Sur. Co. 62
Bennett v. Life & Cas. Ins. Co. 100
Bering Strait Sch. Dist. v. RLI Ins. Co. 239
Berkshire Life Ins. Co. v. Owens 27
Bernhardt v. Hartford Fire Insurance Co. 517, 520
Bertot v. School District No. 1 ..... 660, 662
Beryllium Corp. v. American Mutual Liability Ins. Co. 436
Biebel Bros., Inc. v. United States Fidelity & Guar. Co. 511, 514
Bi-Econ. Mkt., Inc. v. Harleysville Ins. Co. of N.Y. 81, 229
Bigley v. Pacific Standard Life Ins. Co. 318
Bill Binko Chrysler-Plymouth, Inc. v. Compass Ins. Co. 570
Bill Brown Constr. Co., Inc. v. Glens Falls Ins. Co. 77
Bilodeau v. Lumbermens Mut. Cas. Co. 255
Bilsten v. Porter 661
Bituminous Casualty Corp. v. Sand Livestock Systems, Inc. 525
Bituminous Insurance Cos. v. Pennsylvania Manufacturers' Association Insurance Co. 581
Blodgett v. Holden 366
Blue Cross & Blue Shield Ass'n, State of Maryland v. 159

Blue Cross & Blue Shield of Kansas v. Riverside Hospital 413
Blue Ridge Insurance Co. v. Jacobsen 616
Blume v. Evans Fur Co. 273
Board of Trustees of First Congregational Church of Austin v. Cream City Mutual Ins. Co. 269
Bogle v. Conway 606
Bolin v. Bolin 304
Bondox Int'l, Inc. v. Hartford Accident & Indem. Co. 477
Bonney v. Citizens' Mut. Auto. Ins. Co. 89
Boston Gas Co. v. Century Indem. Co. 485
Boston Ins. Co. v. Beckett 214
Bowers v. Kushnick 321
Boyd Motors Inc. v. Employers Ins. of Wausau 227
Boyd v. Nationwide Mutual Ins. Co. 98
Boyes v. Continental Ins. Co. 100
Boynton v. Allstate Ins. Co. 693, 696
Breaux v. Government Employees Insurance Co. 709
Breed v. Insurance Co. of North America 470
Brennan v. Hall 24
British & Foreign Marine Insurance Co., Ltd. v. Gaunt 231
Britt v. Travelers Ins. Co. 250
Brohawn v. Transamerica Ins. Co. 607
Broussard v. State Farm Fire & Casualty Company **247**
Brown v. Superior Court 627
Brugnoli v. United National Insurance Co. 581
Bryant v. Nationwide Mutual Fire Insurance Co. 30
Buckeye Countrymark, Inc., In re 560
Buntin v. Continental Insurance Co. 11
Burd v. Sussex Mutual Insurance Co. 593
Burgess v. American Fidelity Fire Ins. Co. 530
Burne v. Franklin Life Ins. Co. 101
Burton v. Government Employees Insurance Company 430
Burwell v. Hobby Lobby Stores, Inc. 355
Bushey v. Allstate Ins. Co. 90
Butler Brothers v. American Fidelity Co. 678
C & J Fertilizer, Inc. v. Allied Mutual Insurance Co. 57

C. Raymond Davis & Sons, Inc. v. Liberty Mutual Insurance Co. 581
Cadwallader v. New Amsterdam Casualty Co. 581
Caldwell Freight Lines, Inc. v. Lumbermen's Mut. Cas. Co., Inc. 635
Camara v. Agsalud 137
Cameron Mut. Ins. Co. v. Ward 667
Canron, Inc. v. Federal Insurance Co. 533
Capece v. Allstate Ins. Co. 509
Carboline Co. v. Home Indem. Co. 514
Carmichael v. Nationwide Life Ins. Co. 23
Carpenter Plastering Co. v. Puritan Insurance Co. 500
Carriers Insurance Company v. American Policyholders' Insurance Company 679
Carrington v. St. Paul Fire & Marine Ins. Co. 709
Castillo v. Bickley 694
Catalina Enter. v. Hartford Fire Ins. Co. 256
Caterpillar Inc. v. Williams 401, 402
Catucci v. Greenwich Ins. Co. 236
Cedar Rapids, City of v. Northwestern Nat'l Ins. Co. 461
Celley v. Mutual Benefit Health & Accident Association 11
Centennial Insurance Co. v. Wallace 693
Center for Creative Studies v. Aetna Life & Casualty Co. 521
Central Illinois Light Co. v. Home Ins. Co. 462
Central Illinois Pub. Serv. Co. v. Agric. Ins. Co. 629
Central States Pension Fund v. Hartlage Truck Serv. 385
Certain Underwriters at Lloyd's London v. Home Ins. Co. 727
Certain Underwriters at Lloyd's of London v. Superior Court 232, 462
Champion International Corp. v. Continental Casualty Co. 472, 490
Chandler v. Illinois Central R.R. Co. 654
Charter Oak Fire Ins. Co. v. Interstate Mech., Inc. 674
Charter Oil Co. v. American Employers' Ins. Co. 51
Chawla v. Transamerica Occidental Life Ins. Co. 26

Checkrite Ltd., Inc. v. Illinois Nat'l Ins. Co. 567
Cheeves v. Anders 308
Chelini v. Nieri 614
Chemical Waste Management, Inc. v. Armstrong World Indus., Inc. 456
Chevron U.S.A., Inc. v. Natural Res. Def. Council, Inc. 153, 338
Chicago Title Ins. Co. v. Wash. State Office of Ins. Comm'r 72
Chism v. Protective Life Ins. Co. 25
Christ Gospel Temple v. Liberty Mut. Ins. Co. 213
Christiania Gen. Ins. Corp. v. Great Am. Ins. Co. 723, 725, 726, 734
Chronister v. State Farm Mut. Auto. Ins. Co. 661
Chute v. North River Insurance Company 230
Cicio v. Does 404
CIGNA Corp. v. Amara 81
Cincinnati Ins. Co. v. Am. Alternative Ins. Corp. 685
Cincinnati Ins. Co. v. Grand Pointe, LLC 600
Cincinnati Ins. Co. v. Wills 607
Cinergy Corp. v. Associated Elec. & Gas Ins. Servs., Ltd. 463, 526
Citizens Ins. Co. of Am. v. Leiendecker 467
Clarendon Am. Ins. Co. v. S. States Plumbing, Inc. 526
Clarke v. Mannheim Ins. Co. 231
Clausen v. Standard Ins. Co. 427
Claussen v. Aetna Cas. & Sur. Co. 526
Clay v. Independence Mutual Insurance Co. 749
Clayton v. Alliance Mutual Casualty Co. 704
CNA Ins. Co. v. McGinnis 506
Coblentz v. American Security Co. of New York 677
Cobra Products Inc. v. Federal Ins. Co. 218
Cochran v. MFA Mutual Insurance Co. 55
Cole v. U.S. Auto. Assoc. 668
Collegiate Mfg. Co. v. McDowell's Agency, Inc. 67
Collister v. Nationwide Life Ins. Co. 297
Colony Insurance Co. v. G & E Tires & Service, Inc. 600
Colorado Pool Systems, Inc. v. Scottsdale Ins. Co. 506
Colson v. Lloyd's of London 461
Comerica, Inc. v. Zurich American Insurance Company 618

Commercial Union Assurance Companies v. Safeway Stores, Inc. **624**
Commercial Union Ins. Co. v. Byrne 251, 252
Commercial Union Ins. Co. v. Flagship Marine Servs., Inc. 16
Commercial Union Ins. Co. v. Pittsburgh Corning Corp. 581
Commissioner of Insurance v. Munich Am. Reinsurance Co. 757
Commissioner of Insurance v. North Carolina Rate Bureau **128**, 129, 130, 131
Commonwealth Life Ins. Co. v. Goodknight's Adm'r 28
Comunale v. Traders & General Ins. Co. 86
Conex Freight Sys., Inc. v. Ga. Ins. Insolvency Pool 123
Connecticut General Life Insurance Co. v. Gulley 315
Connecticut Mut. L. Ins. Co. v. Schaefer 311
Consolidated Edison Co. of New York, Inc. v. Allstate Ins. Co. 485, 501
Continental Casualty Co. v. Darch 709
Continental Casualty Co. v. Howard Hoffman Assocs. 567
Continental Insurance Co., v. State 486
Continental Marble & Granite v. Canal Insurance Co. 633
Convenient Food Mart #350 v. Cincinnati Ins. Co. 60
Cook v. Equitable Life Assur. Soc. of U.S. 321
Cooper v. Insurance Company 670
Cooperative Health Insurance Fund v. Blue Cross & Blue Shield 413
Copeland Oaks v. Haupt 421
Cora Pub, Inc. v. Cont'l Cas. Co. 20
Coram Healthcare Corp. v. Wal-Mart Stores, Inc. 389
Corban v. United Servs. Auto. Ass'n 252
Corbitt v. Fed. Kemper Ins. Co. 65
Cosentino v. William Penn Life Ins. Co. of New York 302
Costabile v. Metro. Prop. & Cas. Ins. Co. 184
Cotter Corp. v. Am. Empire Surplus Lines Ins. Co. 587
Cotton States Mut. Ins. Co. v. Daniel 506
Courtemanche v. Lumbermens Mut. Cas. Co. 709
Crawford v. Am. Title Ins. Co. 159

Crawford v. Equitable Life Assurance Soc'y of U.S. 326
Crawfordsville Square, LLC. v. Monroe Guar. Ins. Co. 222
Crider v. Ga. Life & Health Ins. Guar. Ass'n 123
Crisci v. Security Ins. Co. of New Haven, Conn. 86, **610**
Critz v. Farmers Ins. Group 611, 613
Crowell v. Benson 367
Crum v. Anchor Casualty Company 606
Crump v. Northwestern Nat. Life Ins. Co. 324
Culhane v. W. Nat'l Mut. Ins. Co. 687
Cullen v. Valley Forge Life Ins. Co. 25
Cunningham v. Commissioner of Banks 756
Cunningham v. Metropolitan Life Ins. Co. 418
Curtis v. State Farm Mut. Auto. Ins. Co. **658**
Cutter & Buck, Inc. v. Genesis Ins. Co. 536
D'Ambrosio v. Pennsylvania National Mutual Casualty Insurance Co. 583
Dairyland Insurance Co. v. Concrete Products Co. 667
Dairyland Insurance Co. v. Drum 684
Dairyland Insurance Co. v. State Farm Mut. Auto. Ins. Co. 655
Dakota, Minn. & Eastern R.R. Corp. v. Acuity 92
Dalrymple v. Royal-Globe Ins. Co. 277
Danbeck v. Am. Family Mut. Ins. Co. 620, 621
Dang v. Northwestern Mut. Life Ins. Co. 428
Darby, United States v. 365
Darcy v. Hartford Insurance Co. 533
Darner Motor Sales v. Universal Underwriters 76
Davenport Peters Co. v. Royal Globe Insurance Co. 56
Davenport v. Harry N. Abrams, Inc. 397
Davidson v. Cincinnati Ins. Co. 557
Davis v. Combes 321
Davy v. Public National Ins. Co. 611
Dayton Independent School District v. National Gypsum Co. 515
De Hahn v. Hartley 14
Deepwater Horizon, In re 52

Deeter v. Indiana Farmers Mut. Ins. Co. 276
Deevy v. Tassi 614
DeJonge v. Mutual of Enumclaw 77
DeLeon v. Lloyd's London, Certain Underwriters 308, 309
Delta Holdings, Inc., In re 751
Department of Ins. v. Ins. Serv. Office 139
Desert Mountain Ltd. P'ship v. Liberty Mut. Fire Ins. Co. 462
Desrochers v. New York Cas. Co. 459, 462
Detroit Water Team Joint Venture v. Agricultural Ins. Co. 462
Dibble v. Reliance Life Ins. Co. 322
Diehl v. Cumberland Mut. Fire Ins. Co. 668
DiFelice v. Aetna U.S. Healthcare 404
Dike v. Valley Forge Ins. Co. 264
DiMare v. Cresci 611, 614
DiOrio v. New Jersey Manufacturers Insurance Co. 512
Doe (Jane, John) v. Prudential Insurance Co. 332
Doe v. Great-West Life & Annuity Ins. Co. 428
Doe v. Shaffer 507
Dominion Ins. Co., Ltd. v. State 266
Donegal Mut. Ins. Co. v. Baumhammers 506
Donovan v. Commercial Union Insurance Co. 506
Dora Twp. v. Indiana Insurance Company 431
Douglas v. United States Fidelity & Guar. Co. 626
Draft Systems, Inc. v. Alspach 581
Drane v. Jefferson Standard Life Ins. Co. 306, 308
Dreis & Krump Mfg. Co. v. Phoenix Insurance Co. 514
Dresser Industries, Inc. v. Underwriters at Lloyd's, London 486
Droegkamp v. Langdon 526
Drummond v. Hartford Fire Ins. Co. 258, 259
Dryden v. Continental Baking Co. 614
Duane Reade, Inc. v. St. Paul Fire & Marine Ins. Co.............. 223, 224
Eads v. Marks 613
Eagle-Picher Indus., Inc. v. Liberty Mutual Ins. Co. 476
Econ. Premier Assur. Co. v. W. Nat. Mut. Ins. Co. 53
Edgerton, City of v. General Casualty Co. of Wisconsin 461
Edgington v. Equitable L. Assur. Soc. 301
Ekleberry, Inc. v. Motorists Mutual Insurance Co. 521
Elberon Bathing Co., Inc. v. Ambassador Ins. Co., Inc. 261, 262
Ellis Court Apartments Ltd. P'ship ex rel. Woodside Corp. v. State Farm Fire & Cas. Co. 222
Ellmex Constr. Co., Inc. v. Republic Ins. Co. 258
Elmer Tallant Agency, Inc. v. Bailey Wood Products, Inc. 64
Emond v. State Farm Mut. Auto. Ins. Co. 104
Emons Industries, Inc. v. Liberty Mutual Fire Insurance Co. 487
Empire Life Ins. Co. of America v. Moody 306, 307, 308
Employers Casualty Company v. Tilley 606
Employers Liability Assur. Corp. v. Morse 269
Employers Mutual Cas. Co. v. Nelson 674
Employers Mutual Liability Insurance Co. of Wisconsin v. Melcher 417
Employers Mutual Liability Insurance Co. of Wisconsin v. Pacific Indemnity Company 681
Employers Reinsurance Corp. v. Massachusetts Mut. Life Ins. Co. 745
Endicott Johnson Corp. v. Liberty Mutual Ins. Co. 491
EnergyNorth Natural Gas, Inc. v. Underwriters at Lloyd's 475
Engelman v. Connecticut General Life Insurance Company 315
Erie Ins. Exch. v. Lansberry 587
Erie Ins. Exch. v. Szamatowicz 528
Esfeld Trucking, Inc. v. Metropolitan Insurance Co. 666, 667
Essex Ins. Co. v. BloomSouth Flooring Corp. 222, 514
Essex Ins. Co. v. Tri-Town Corp. 519
Eugene S. v. Horizon Blue Cross Blue Shield of N.J. 81
Excess Underwriters at Lloyd's, London v. Frank's Casing Crew & Rental Tools, Inc. 616
Exploration Place, Inc. v. Midwest Drywall Co. 123
Eyeblaster, Inc. v. Federal Insurance Company 463
F&H Construction v. ITT Hartford Insurance Co. of the Midwest 466

Fairfield Insurance Company v. Stephens Martin Paving 98
Fairview Hosp. and Health Care Serv. v. St. Paul Fire & Marine Ins. Co. 478
Fantis Foods, Inc. v. N. River Ins. Co. 236
Farm Bureau Mut. Auto. Ins. Co. v. Preferred Acc. Ins. Co................ 681
Farm Bureau Mut. Ins. Co. v. Evans 665
Farm Bureau Mut. Ins. Co. v. Waugh.. 682
Farmers Mut. Auto. Ins. Co. v. Bechard... 76
Farmers Mut. Ins. Co. of Nebraska v. Kment... 505
Fayad v. Clarendon Nat. Ins. Co. 46
Federal Ins. Co. v. CompUSA, Inc. 574
Federal Ins. Co. v. HPSC, Inc. 17
Federal Ins. Co. v. Infoglide Corp... 562
Federal Ins. Co. v. Raytheon Company 563
Federal Ins. Co. v. Travelers Cas. & Sur. Co. 630
Federal Trade Commission v. National Cas. Co................ 156, 159
Federated Mut. Ins. Co. v. Grapevine Excavation Inc. 81
Ferguson v. Phoenix Assurance Co. of New York 55
Fidelity & Deposit Co. of Maryland v. Zandstra..................................... 562
Filor, Bullard & Smyth v. Insurance Co. of North America........... 42, 473
Financial Indus. Corp. v. XL Specialty Ins. Co......................... 574
Finci v. American Cas. Co............. 562
Fioretti v. Massachusetts Gen. Life Ins. Co. 326
Fireman's Fund Ins. Co. of Wisconsin v. Bradley Corp........................... 533
Fireman's Fund Ins. Co. v. Gen. Reinsurance Corp. 727
Fireman's Fund Ins. Co. v. Holland Am. Line-Westours, Inc............. 228
Firestone Tire & Rubber Co. v. Bruch 396, 400
First Colony Life Ins. Co. v. Sanford.. 298
First Fin. Ins. Co. v. Bugg 467
First Fin. Ins. Co. v. Jetco Contracting Corp. 534
First Ins. Co. of Hawaii, Inc. v. State, by Minami.................................. 599
FL Aerospace v. Aetna Casualty Sur. Co. 531
Fletcher v. Western National Life Ins. Co. 86

Flores v. Arroyo 87
Florida Farm Bureau Insurance Co. v. Martin 267
Fluke Corp. v. Hartford Accident & Indem. Co. 98
FMC Corp. v. Holliday 420
Fontenot v. Marquette Casualty Co... 750
Ford v. Ford 304
Foremost Dairies v. Industrial Acc. Com. 86
Forrester v. State Farm Mut. Auto. Ins. Co. 703
Foster v. Hurley................................ 321
Fowler v. Berry Seed Co.................. 68
Fraley v. Allstate Ins. Co. 92
Franklin v. Healthsource of Arkansas 420
Franks v. City and County of Honolulu..................................... 137
Free Enterprise Fund v. Public Company Accounting Oversight Bd. 365
Friez v. Nat'l Old Line Ins. Co. 30
Fuja v. Benefit Trust Life Insurance Company.......383, 388
Furia v. Philadelphia 417
Gamble Farm Inn v. Selective Insurance Co. 520
Garden Sanctuary, Inc. v. Insurance Co. of N.Am. 459
Garman v. New York Life Insurance Company 431
Garvey v. State Farm Fire & Casualty Co. 240
Gaspers v. Minneapolis Elec. Steel Castings Co. 479
Gasquet v. Commercial Union Ins. Co. 620
Gaunt v. John Hancock Mutual Life Insurance Company 292
Gedeon v. State Farm Mut. Auto. Ins. Co. 580, 582, 583, 584
Gee v. AAA Life Ins. Co.................... 30
General Accident Ins. Co. of Am. v. Safety Nat'l Cas. Corp. 630
General Agents Ins. Co. v. Midwest Sporting Goods Co. 600
General Agents Ins. Co. v. St. Paul Ins. Co. 23
General Mills v. Goldman 270
General Reinsurance Corp. v. Missouri General Ins. Co.......... 748, 749
Georgia Life & Health Ins. Co. v. Sewell 100
Gerber, People ex rel. v. Central Casualty Co.................................. 754
Gerson v. Industrial Acc. Com. 86
Gillen v. Globe Indemnity Co........ 662
Giustra v. Unum Life Insurance Co. of America 427

Given v. Commerce Ins. Co. 687
Golden Rule Ins. Co. v. Hopkins 27
Goldstein v. Milton Brokerage
　Ass'n 65
Goodyear Tire & Rubber Co. v. Aetna
　Casualty & Surety Co. 486
Government Employees Insurance
　Co. v. Lammert 662
Government Employees Insurance
　Co. v. Melton 667
Government Employees Insurance
　Co. v. Welch 657
Graham v. Public Employees Mutual
　Insurance Co. 239
Graham v. Rockman 278
Grange Mut. Cas. Co. v. W. Bend
　Mut. Ins. Co. 485
Grant v. Emmco Insurance Co. 689
Grant-Southern Iron & Metal Co. v.
　CNA Ins. Co. 531
Gray v. Nationwide Mutual
　Insurance Co. 583
**Gray v. Zurich Insurance
　Company** **588**, 598
Great Northern Ins. Co. v. Benjamin
　Franklin Sav. & Loan Ass'n 220
**Great Northern Oil Company v.
　St. Paul Fire & Marine Ins.
　Co.** **268**
Greater Palm Beach Symphony Ass'n
　v. Hughes 98
Great-West Life & Annuity Ins. Co.
　v. Knudson 404, 421
Griffin v. McCoach 306
Grigsby v. Russell **309**
Grimes v. Concord General Mutual
　Insurance Co., N.H. 708, 709
Grinnell Mutual Reinsurance Co. v.
　Shierk 600
Gros v. Houston Fire & Casualty
　Insurance Co. 633
Group Life & Health Ins. Co. v. Royal
　Drug Co. 158
Gruenberg v. Aetna Ins. Co. 86, 92
GTE Corp. v. Allendale Mut. Ins.
　Co 237
Guebara v. Allstate Ins. Co. 92, 616
Gulf Chemical & Metallurgical Corp.
　v. Associated Metals & Minerals
　Corp. 499
Gulf Ins. Co. v. Dolan, Fertig &
　Curtis 570, 572, 573
Gulf Transportation Co. v. Fireman's
　Fund Ins. Co. 231
H.E. Butt Grocery Co. v. National
　Union Fire Ins. Co. of Pittsburgh,
　Pa. 494
Hahn v. Sargent 378
Hailey v. Cal. Physicians' Serv. 26
Hakim v. Massachusetts Ins.
　Insolvency Fund 527
Halbig v. Burwell 372

Hamilton Die Cast, Inc. v. United
　States F. & G. Co. 514
Hamilton Life Ins. Co. v. Republic
　National Life Ins. Co. 393
Hammerstone v. Indiana Insurance
　Co. 46
Hanson v. Hamnes 282
Hardy v. Progressive Specialty
　Insurance Co. 710
Harr v. Allstate Ins. Co. 76
Harrington v. Agricultural Ins.
　Co. 214
**Harris Corporation v. Humana
　Health Insurance Company of
　Florida, Inc.** **407**
Harris v. Gulf Ins. Co. 562
Harris v. Harvard Pilgrim Health
　Care, Inc. 421
Harris v. Prudential Prop. & Cas.
　Ins. Co. 674
Harry's Cadillac-Pontiac-GMC Truck
　Co., Inc. v. Motors Ins. Corp. 227
Hart v. Orion Ins. Co. 393
Harter v. American Eagle Fire Ins.
　Co. 269
Hartford Accident & Indem. Co. v.
　Civil Serv. Emp. Ins. Co. 668
Hartford Accident & Indem. Co. v.
　Insurance Comm'r 139
**Hartford Casualty Insurance
　Company v. Powell** **95**
**Hartford Fire Ins. Co. v.
　California** **161**
Hartford Fire Ins. Co. v. Chicago, M.
　& St. P. Ry. Co. 269
Hartford Fire Ins. Co. v. Davis 664
Hartline v. Hartline 658
Hathaway Dev. Co. v. Illinois Union
　Ins. Co. 514
Haugan v. Home Indem. Co. 513,
514
Hawaiian Elec. Co., In re 138
Hawkinson Tread Tire Serv. Co. v.
　Indiana Lumbermens Mut. Ins.
　Co. 226
**Heacker v. Safeco Insurance
　Company of America** **466**
Health Cost Controls, Inc. v.
　Gifford 420
Health Ins. Ass'n of America v.
　Shalala 408
Heer v. State 262
Heirs of Boisdoré, United States
　v. 394
**Heller v. Equitable Life Assur.
　Soc.** 386, 388, **429**
Henderson v. Lawyers Title Ins.
　Corp. 39
Henkel Corp. v. Hartford Accident &
　Indemnity Corp. 477
Henningsen v. Bloomfield Motors,
　Inc. 509

TABLE OF CASES   xxvii

Hershberger v. Young 302
Herzog v. National American
  Insurance Co. 62
Hicks v. Cary 301
Higginbotham v. Am. Family Ins.
  Co. 264
Hilker v. Western Automobile Ins.
  Co. 626
Hill v. Gateway 2000 Inc. 38
Hillery v. Allstate Indem. Co. 25
Hionis v. N. Mut. Ins. Co. 60
Hobson v. Metropolitan Life Ins.
  Co. 428
Hodgson v. Chin 509
Hoffert v. Commercial Ins. Co. of
  Newark 424, 425, 426
Holloway v. Nationwide Mutual
  Insurance Co. 708, 709
Homan v. Employers Reinsurance
  Corp. 749
Home Ins. Co. v. Adler 288
Home Ins. Co. v. Greene 250
Home Ins. Co., Village of Constantine
  v. 215
Hooper v. California 367
Hooters of Augusta, Inc. v. Am.
  Global Ins. Co. 98
Hoover v. Neff & Son 673
Horace Mann Insurance Co. v.
  Barbara B. 506
Houghton v. American Life Insurance
  Co. 11
Housing Fin. and Dev. Corp. v.
  Castle 137
Howell v. State Farm Fire & Cas.
  Co. 238
Huberman v. John Hancock Mut.
  Life Ins. Co. 332
Humana Inc. v. Forsyth 153, 155
Illinois Automobile Insurance
  Exchange v. Braun 417
Imperial Cas. and Indem. Co. v.
  State 557
INA Insurance Co. v. Commonwealth
  Ins. Dept. 101
Independent School Dist. No. 877 v.
  Loberg Plumbing & Heating
  Co. 270
Index Fund, Inc. v. Insurance
  Company of North America 42
Industrial Enterprises, Inc. v. Penn
  American Insurance Co. 463
Industrial Indem. Co. v.
  Goettl 244
Ingalls v. Paul Revere Life Insurance
  Group 93
Ingersoll-Rand Co. v.
  McClendon 375, 400, 403
Insurance Antitrust Litigation,
  In re 164, 168
Insurance Brokerage Antitrust
  Litigation, In re 159

Insurance Co. of North America v.
  Alberstadt 285
Insurance Co. of North America v.
  Forty-Eight Insulations,
  Inc. 471, 472
Insurance Co. of North America v.
  State Farm Mut. Auto. Ins.
  Co. 239
Insurance Co. of Texas v. Employers
  Liability Assurance Corp. 680,
683
Integon Gen. Ins. Corp. v.
  Gibson 212
Intel Corp. v. Am. Guar. & Liab. Ins.
  Co. 622
International Surplus Lines Inc. Co.
  v. Certain Underwriters &
  Underwriting Syndicates at Lloyd's
  of London 734, 735, 744
Interstate Fire Ins. Co. of
  Chattanooga, Tenn. v. Ingram 23
Ivy v. Pacific Automobile Ins.
  Co. 626, 627
J.C. Penney Cas. Ins. Co. v.
  M.K. 506
J.H. France Refractories Co. v.
  Allstate Ins. Co. 486
James v. Fulcrod 95
Jebian v. Hewlett-Packard 397
Jeffries v. Stewart 707
Jenoff, Inc. v. N.H. Ins. Co. 478
Jerry v. Kentucky Cent. Ins.
  Co. 256
Jiminez v. Sears, Roebuck & Co. 88
Johansen v. California State
  Automobile Association Inter-
  Insurance Bureau 616
John Hancock Mutual Life Insurance
  Company v. Spurgeon 432
Johnson Controls, Inc. v. Employers
  Insurance of Wassau 461
Johnson v. Trustmark Insurance
  Company 428
Johnson v. Westhoff Sand Co.,
  Inc. 528
Johnstown, City of v. Bankers
  Standard Ins. 497, 502
Jones v. Farm Bureau Mutual Ins.
  Co. 530
Jones v. Horace Mann Ins. Co. 62
Jones v. Medox, Inc. 685
Jones v. Robbins 581, 582
Joslin v. Mitchell 709
Jostens, Inc. v. Mission Ins.
  Co. 630
Judge v. Metropolitan Life Ins.
  Co. 428
Julian v. Hartford Underwriters Ins.
  Co. 241
Julio L., In re 246
Jupiter Aluminum Corp. v. Home
  Ins. Co. 229

Juvland v. Plaisance 676
K.C. Working Chemical Co. v. Eureka-Sec. Fire & Marine Ins. Co. 324
K2 Inv. Grp., LLC v. Am. Guar. & Liab. Ins. Co. 586
KAAPA Ethanol, LLC v. Affiliated FM Ins. Co. 236
Kahriger, United States v. 367
Kaiser Foundation Hospitals v. North Star Reinsurance Corp. 628
Kangas v. Aetna Casualty Co. 667
Karl v. New York Life Ins. Co. 101
Katrina Canal Breaches Litig., In re 252
Kazi v. State Farm Fire & Casualty Co. 235
Keene Corp. v. Ins. Co. of N. Am. 62
Keeton, Estate of v. Cherry 320
Kelly v. Robinson 394
Kemp v. Allstate Ins. Co., Mont. 708, 709
Kennedy v. Dashner 530
Kentucky Ass'n of Health Plans v. Miller 382
Kentucky Cent. Life Ins. Co. v. McNabb 303
Kenyon v. Security Insurance Co. 520
Kessler Export Corp. v. Reliance Insurance Co. 44
Kilpatrick v. Hartford Fire Ins. Co. 212
Kimmel v. Western Reserve Life Assur. Co. of Ohio 297, 332
King v. Burwell 372
King v. Dunlap 282
Klamath-Lake Pharm. Ass'n v. Klamath Med. Serv. Bureau 159
Klapp v. United Ins. Group Agency 621
Klos v. Mobil Oil Co. 60
Knickerbocker L. Ins. Co. v. Norton 310
Knight v. U.S. Fire Ins. Co. 723, 724
Knight v. United States Fidelity & Guar. Co. 258
Kobold v. Aetna U.S. Healthcare, Inc. 80
Koehler v. Aetna Health Inc. 397
Koikos v. Travelers Ins. Co. 494
Kolling v. Blue Cross & Blue Shield of Michigan 381
Kooker v. Benefit Ass'n of Ry. Employees 426
Koppers Co., Inc. v. Aetna Casualty & Surety Co. 218, 486, 730
Kovacs v. Zurich Am. Ins. Co. 327

Kraus v. Allstate Ins. Company 667
Krebsbach v. Miller 662
Kretschmer's House of Appliances, Inc. v. United States Fidelity & Guar. Co. 55
Kulmacz v. New York Life Ins. Co. 319
L.A. Dep't of Water & Power v. Manhart 142
La Franca, United States v. 368
Lachs v. Fidelity & Casualty Co. of N.Y. 42, 60, 473
Laing v. Occidental Life Ins. Co. 89
Lamb v. Belt Casualty Co. 590
Lamb-Weston, Inc. v. Oregon Auto. Ins. Co. 683
Laminate Kingdom, LLC, In re 537
Lamoureux v. New York Cent. Mut. Fire Ins. Co. 257
Lampe Market Co. v. Alliance Ins. Co. 262
Langill v. Vermont Mutual Insurance Company **254**
Langlois v. Metropolitan Life Ins. Co. 81
Langwith v. American National General Insurance Company **65**
Lapeka, Inc. v. Security Nat'l Ins. Co. 467
Laurentis v. United Servs. Autom. Ass'n 223
Lavanant v. General Accident Ins. Co. of Am. 468
Lazenby v. Universal Underwriters Ins. Co. 97
Leafland Group-II v. Insurance Co. of North America 220
League of Minnesota Cities Insurance Trust v. City of Coon Rapids 519, 520
Lee v. Aetna Casualty & Surety Co. 581, 587
Le Gierse v., Helvering 335
Leonard v. Nationwide Mutual Ins. Co. 145, 248
LeRette v. American Med. Sec., Inc. 92
Level 3 Commcns. v. Fed. Ins. Co. 562
Lever Bros. Co. v. Atlas Assurance Co. 49
Lewis v. New York State Dep't of Civil Services 382
Lexington Ins. Co. v. Unity/Waterford–Fair Oaks, Ltd. 526
Liberty Mut. Ins. Co. v. Altfillisch Constr. Co. 627, 628
Liberty Mut. Ins. Co. v. Pacific Indemnity Co. 580

Liberty Nat. Life Ins. Co. v. Weldon 298
Life Ins. Co. of N. Am. v. Ortiz 320
Life Prod. Clearing, LLC v. Angel 314
Limbaugh v. Columbia Ins. Co. of N.Y. 258
Limberis v. Aetna Casualty & Surety Co. 55, 682
Linderer v. Royal Globe Insurance Co. 709
Lipsky v. Commonwealth United Corp. 44
Liquidation of Integrity Insurance Co., In re 751
Liquidation of Union Indemnity Ins. Co., In re 723, 724, 728, 729
Liristis v. American Family Mutual Insurance Company **242**
Lititz Mut. Ins. Co. v. Boatner..... 251, 252
Liverpool & London & Globe Ins. Co., Ltd. v. Bolling 215
Livingston Parish Sch. Bd. v. Fireman's Fund Am. Ins. Co. 573
Loblaw, Inc. v. Employers' Liability Assurance Corp. 472
London Market Ins. v. Superior Court 493
Longobardi v. Chubb Ins. Co. of N.J. 31
Lopes v. Metropolitan Life Ins. Co. 427
Lopez v. Massachusetts Mutual Life Ins. Co. 319
Lopez, United States v. 365
Lowing v. Allstate Ins. Co. 706
Luria Bros. & Co. v. Alliance Assurance Co. 617
Macalco, Inc. v. Gulf Insurance Co. 633
MacKenzie v. Prudential Insurance Company of America **27**
Maddux v. Philadelphia Life Ins. Co. 320
Maine Mut. Fire Ins. Co. v. Gervais 500
Malone v. White Motor Corp. 392
Mann v. Metropolitan Life Ins. Co. 319
Marcy v. Sun Mutual Ins. Co. 231
Marin Gen. Hosp. v. Modesto & Empire Traction Co. 420
Mario v. P & C Food Markets, Inc. 388, 396
Markham v. Nationwide Mut. Fire Ins. Co. 267
Marlin v. Wetzel Cnty. Bd. of Educ. 77

Martin v. Allianz Life Ins. Co. of N. Am. 104
Martinonis v. Utica Nat'l Ins. Grp. 266
Marx v. Hartford Accident & Indem. Co. 575
Maslin v. Columbian Nat'l Life Ins. Co. 326
Mason v. Loyal Protective Life Ins. Co. 426
Massachusetts Mutual Life Ins. Co. v. Russell 395, 398, 399, 400, 404
Massachusetts Mutual Life Ins. Co. v. Woodall 97
Mastellone v. Lightning Rod Mut. Ins. Co. 223
Mastro Plastics Corp. v. NLRB 394
Mathewson v. Aloha Airlines, Inc. 137
Mauroner v. Massachusetts Indemnity and Life Insurance Company **327**
Max True Plastering Co. v. U.S. Fid. & Guar. Co. 59
Mayo v. Hartford Life Insurance Company **305**
Mayor & City Council of Baltimore v. Utica Mut. Ins. Co. 485
Mayor v. Wedding 700
Mazon v. Farmers Insurance Exchange 667
McCabe v. Allstate Ins. Co. 259
McDill, Estate of 625
McDonald v. Great American Insurance Company 667
McDonald v. Mianecki 509
McGrail v. Equitable Life Assurance Society 472
McKay v. State Farm Mut. Auto. Ins. Co. 693
McKnight v. USAA Cas. Ins. Co. 526
McLachlan v. New York Life Ins. Co. 332
Meirthew v. Last 606
Melco System v. Receivers of Trans-America Ins. Co. 756
Mendlein v. United States Fidelity & Guaranty Co. 699
Mendoza v. Rivera-Chavez 657
Mercer v. Perez 87
Merchants Indemnity Corp. v. Eggleston 606
Mertens v. Hewitt Associates 404
Metropolitan Life Ins. Co. v. Aetna Casualty & Surety Company **488**
Metropolitan Life Ins. Co. v. Glenn 396
Metropolitan Life Ins. Co. v. Jackson 100

Metropolitan Life Ins. Co. v.
  Massachusetts 381, 391,
  392, 393
Metropolitan Life Ins. Co. v.
  Taylor 397, 400, 402
Metropolitan Mortg. & Sec. Co.,
  In re 537
Michigan Chemical Corp. v.
  American Home Assurance
  Co. 494
Michigan Mutual Liability Company
  v. Hoover Brothers Inc. 431
Midland Ins. Co., In re 728
Mighty Midgets, Inc. v. Centennial
  Ins. Co. 528
Millar v. State Farm Fire & Cas.
  Co. 244
Miller v. Hartford Life Ins. Co. 90
Miller v. Shugart 594, 617, **674**
Mills v. Reserve Life Ins. Co.,
  Ky. 28
Minerva Enterprises, Inc. v.
  Bituminous Casualty Corp. 521
Minter v. Great Am. Ins. Co. 665
**Mission National Insurance
  Company v. Duke
  Transportation Company 630**
Missouri, K. & T. Ry. v. Carter 96
Mitchell v. Allstate Ins. Co. 665
Molina v. U.S. Fire Ins. Co. 632,
  634
Montanez v. Irizarry-
  Rodriguez 608
Monterey Corp. v. Hart 278, 280
Montoya v. Dairyland Insurance
  Company 705
Montrose Chem. Corp. of California
  v. Superior Court 587, 598
Montrose Chem. Corp. v. Admiral
  Ins. Co. 502
Moore v. CapitalCare, Inc. 421
Moore v. Metropolitan Life Ins.
  Co. 376, 378
Moots v. Bankers Life
  Company 428
Moradi-Shalal v. Fireman's Fund Ins.
  Cos. 148
Moreau, Town of v. Orkin
  Exterminating Co. 497
Morgan v. Patrons Mutual Insurance
  Association 216
Morton Int'l, Inc. v. Gen. Accident
  Ins. Co. of Am. 521, 526
Morton v. Blue Ridge Insurance
  Co. 689
**Mossa v. Provident Life and
  Casualty Insurance
  Company** **422**
Motorists Mutual Insurance Co. v.
  RSJ, Inc. 520, 521
Motorola, Inc. v. Associated Indem.
  Corp. 468
Mowry v. Badger State Mutual
  Casualty Company 594
Mt. Hope Inn v. Travelers Indemnity
  Company 509
Muller v. First Unum Life Ins.
  Co. 397
Munich Reinsurance Am., Inc. v. Am.
  Nat'l Ins. Co. 727
Murphy v. Allstate Ins. Co. 626,
  627
Mutual Benefit Insurance Co. v.
  Goschenhoppen Mutual Insurance
  Co. 288
Mutual Benefit Life Insurance Co. v.
  JMR Electronics Corp. 21
Mutual Life Inssurance Co. v.
  Armstrong 311
National Cable & Telecomm. Ass'n v.
  Brand X Internet Servs. 339
National Century Fin. Enters. v. Gulf
  Ins. Co. 537
National Family Ins. Co. v.
  Boyer 667
**National Federation of
  Independent Business et al. v.
  Sebelius** 358, **362**, 363
National Fire Insurance Co. of
  Hartford v. Lewis 575
National Pride at Work, Inc. v.
  Governor of Michigan 382
National Sav. Life Ins. Co. v.
  Dutton 92
National Screen Service Corp. v.
  United States Fidelity & Guar.
  Co. 473
National Surety Co. v. Silberberg
  Bros. 55
National Union Fire Ins. Co. v.
  Continental Ill. Corp. 556
National Union Fire Ins. Co. v.
  Grimes 269
Nationwide Mutual Ins. Co. v. State
  Farm Mut. Auto. Ins. Co. 684
Nationwide Mutual Ins. Co. v.
  Webb 668
Nautilus Insurance Co. v. 1735 W.
  Diversey, LLC 507
**Neill v. Nationwide Mutual Fire
  Insurance Company** **22**
Nelson v. Davidson 71
Netherlands Ins. Co. v. Main Street
  Ingredients, LLC 515
New Amsterdam Casualty Co. v.
  Kelly 582
New Castle County v. Hartford
  Accident & Indemnity Co. 522
New England Mut. Life Ins. Co. v.
  Caruso 326
New England Mut. Life Ins. Co. v.
  Null 312
New Ponce Shopping Ctr., S.E. v.
  Integrand Assurance Co. 216

TABLE OF CASES   xxxi

New York Life Ins. Co. v. Gay 29
New York State Conference of Blue Cross & Blue Shield Plans v. Travelers Ins. Co. 381
New York Times Co. v. Sullivan..... 98
Newcomb v. Meiss................ 605, 606
Nichols v. Am. Casualty Co. 581
Nichols v. Am. Risk Mgm't, Inc. 727
Niglio v. Omaha Prop. & Cas. Ins. Co. 668
Nobel Ins. Co. v. Austin Power Co. 600
Nolan v. First Colony Life Ins. Co. 332
Norfolk & Western Ry. Co. v. Accident & Casualty Ins. Co. of Winterthur................................. 493
Norfolk S. Corp. v. California Union Ins. Co. 527
Norgaard v. Nodak Mutual Insurance Company 667
North Carolina Rate Bureau, v. State ex rel. Comr. of Insurance 128
North East Ins. Co. v. Young........... 25
North River Insurance Co. v. ACE American Reinsurance Co. 736, 738, 739, 740, 741, 742, 743
Northbrook Insurance Co. v. Kuljian Corp. 11
Northville Indus. Corp. v. National Union Fire Ins. Co. 733
Northwest Airlines, Inc. v. Transport Workers....................................... 395
Northwest Farm Bureau Insurance Company v. Althauser 274
Northwestern Mut. Ins. Co. v. Farmers' Ins. Group 626
Northwestern Mut. Life Ins. Co. v. Yoe's Ex'r 28
Northwestern Nat'l Cas. Co. v. McNulty 97
Northwestern Nat'l Ins. Co., Carlsbad, City of........................ 214
Norwest Bank, N.A. v. Fed. Kemper Life Ins. Co.................................. 332
Novo v. Employers' Liability Assurance Corp. 662
O'Connor v. Insurance Company of North America..................... 751
O'Hare v. Pursell........................... 748
O'Neill v. Long............................... 665
Oade v. Jackson Nat'l Life Ins. Co. of Mich. 21
Oakes v. Manufacturers' F. & M. Ins. Co. 310
O'Connell v. Brady 318, 319
Odolecki v. Hartford Accident & Indem. Co..................................... 665

Odum v. Nationwide Mutual Ins. Co..657
Offshore Logistics, Inc. v. Tallentire 394
Ohio Casualty Insurance Co. v. Stanfield......................................709
Ohio National Life Assurance Corp. v. Crampton 428
Ojo v. Farmers Group, Inc. 152, 155
Old American County Mutual Fire Insurance Co. v. Renfrow 664
Old Line Life Ins. Co. v. Superior Court 21
Old Reliable Fire Ins. Co. v. Castle Reinsurance Co., Ltd. 727
Oliver B. Cannon & Son v. Fidelity and Casualty Co. of New York..584
Olson v. Bankers Life Ins. Co. 25
Omaha Sky Divers Parachute Club, Inc. v. Ranger Insurance Co. 19
One Beacon Ins. Co. v. Aviva Ins. Ltd. 745
Oritani Sav. & Loan Ass'n v. Fid. & Deposit Co. of Md..........................62
Orleans Parish Sch. Bd. v. Lexington Ins. Co..247
Otero v. Hartford Life & Accident Ins..80
Ott v. All-Star Insurance Corp. 750
Outboard Marine Corp. v. Liberty Mutual Ins. Co. 49, 502, 523
Owens-Corning Fiberglas Corp. v. Malone..96
Owens-Illinois, Inc. v. United Insurance Co..................................486
Pacific Employers Ins. Co. v. Servco Pacific, Inc.....................................534
Pacific Employers Ins. Co. v. Superior Court 571
Pacific Indem. Co. v. Acel Delivery Service, Inc....................................607
Pacific Indem. Co. v. Federated Am. Ins. Co. 683
Page v. Mountain W. Farm Bureau Mut. Ins. Co. 658
Palisades Safety & Insurance Ass'n v. Bastien 17
Pallozzi v. Allstate Life Ins. Co..381
Palmer v. Financial Indem. Co. 611
Pan American World Airways, Inc. v. Aetna Casualty & Surety Co.......43, 470
Paradigm Ins. Co. v. Langerman Law Offices..607
Paramount Fire Insurance Company v. Aetna Casualty and Surety Company............ 283
Parsons v. Bedford........................366

Parsons v. Continental National American Group **601**
Parsons v. Smithey........................603
Patout, Estate of v. City of New Iberia..502
Patrick O. Ojo v. Farmers Group, Inc. **152**
Patrons Oxford Insurance Co. v. Harris 665, 679
Patrons Oxford Mutual Ins. Co. v. Marois 461
Paul v. Virginia 107
Pekin Ins. Co. v. Hugh 468
Peninsular Life Ins. Co. v. Wade 76
Penn. Estate of, v. Amalgamated General Agencies 626
Pepsico, Inc. v. Winterthur International America Company 221
Perkoski v. Wilson.................581, 606
Perry v. United Food and Commerical Workers District Unions 408, 411, 412
Peter v. Schumacher Enters., Inc. 70
Petrosky v. Brasner.......................332
Phen v. Progressive N. Ins. Co. 710
Phillips & Assocs., P.C. v. Navigators Ins. Co. 616
Phillips Home Builders, Inc. v. Travelers Ins. Co. 244
PHL Variable Ins. Co. v. Fulbright McNeill, Inc...................................29
PHL Variable Ins. Co. v. Price Dawe 2006 Ins. Trust, ex rel. Christiana Bank & Trust Co.........................326
Phoenix Assurance Co. v. Latta................................660, 662
Phoenix Mut. L. Ins. Co. v. Bailey 311
Pickett v. Lloyds.............................90
Pierce v. Oklahoma Property & Casualty Insurance Co. 655
Pile Foundation Constr. Co. v. Investors Ins. Co. of Am. 528
Pilot Life Insurance Company v. Dedeaux................................154, **390**
Pintlar Corp. v. Fidelity and Cas. Co. of N.Y. (In re Pintlar Corp.) 560
Pipefitters Welfare Educational Fund v. Westchester Fire Insurance Co. 520
Pirie v. Federal Ins. Co. 220
Pittsburgh Plate Glass Co.............581
Pittsburgh, C, C & St. L.R. Co. v. Kinney...102
Plastics Engineering Co. v. Liberty Mutual Insurance Co.........486, 493
Plaxco v. U. S. Fidelity & Guaranty Co. 667

PM Group Life Insurance Company v. Western Growers Assurance Trust 414
PMI Mortg. Ins. Co. v. Am. Int'l Specialty Lines Ins. Co. 561
Pokol v. E.I. du Pont de Nemours & Company......................................427
Poland v. Fisher's Estate...............301
Popich Bros. Water Transp., Inc. v. Gulf Coast Marine, Inc. 151
Port Authority of New York and New Jersey v. Affiliated FM Insurance Company............... **217**
Powell v. Blue Cross & Blue Shield of Alabama 420
Powerine Oil Co., Inc. v. Superior Court..................................462, 534
Powers v. Travelers' Insurance Co. 689
PPG Industries, Inc. v. Transamerica Insurance Co. 616
Prahm v. Rupp Construction Co. 676
Pre-Cast Concrete Products, Inc. v. Home Ins. Co..................................49
Primax Recoveries v. State Farm Mutual..414
Primerica Life Ins. Co. v. Skinner...298
Principal Life Ins. Co. v. Lawrence Rucker 2007 Ins. Trust..............314
ProCD v. Zeidenberg 38
Providence Washington Ins. Co. v. Adler..231
Provident Mutual Life Ins. Co. v. Ehrlich...319
Prudential Ins. Co. of America v. Lampley...28
Prudential Ins. Co. of America v. SEC 335
Prudential Lines, Inc., In re.........491, 493
Prudential-LMI Commercial Insurance v. Superior Court......222
Pruett v. Precision Plumbing........692
Pryzbowski v. U.S. Healthcare, Inc. 401
Public Serv. Mut. Ins. Co. v. Goldfarb..98
Pum v. Wisconsin Physicians Service Insurance Corp...............................25
Purefoy v. Pacific Automobile Indem. Exchange 531
Puritan Ins. Co. v. Canadian Universal Ins. Co., Ltd. 629
Puritan Life Ins. Co. v. Guess 297
Purkey v. American Home Assurance Co. 657
QBE Ins. Corp. v. Chalfonte Condo. Apartment Ass'n, Inc. 53

TABLE OF CASES   xxxiii

Qualcomm, Inc. v. Certain Underwriters at Lloyd's, London 622
R.T. Vanderbilt Co., Inc. v. Continental Casualty Co. 534
Race v. Nationwide Mut. Fire Ins. Co. 668
Raischell & Cottrell, Inc. v. Workmen's Comp. App. Bd. 89
Ramsdell v. Insurance Company of North America 285
Randall v. State Mutual Ins. Co. 100
Ranger Ins. Co. v. United States Fire Ins. Co. 570
Rawlings v. Apodaca 92
Raze v. Mueller 479
Red Giant Oil Co. v. Lawlor 617
Regional Bank v. St. Paul Fire & Marine Insurance Co. 520
Reich v. Tharp 266
Reid v. State Farm Fire & Casualty Co. 696
Reilly v. Ozzard 512
Reliance Co. of Illinois v. Weis 560
Reliance Insurance Co. v. Certain Member Companies 723, 724
Reliance Insurance Co. v. East-Lind Heat Treat, Inc. 282
Reliance Insurance Co. v. Kinman 103
Reliance Insurance Co. v. Moessner 520, 521
ReliaStar Life Ins. Co. v. IOA Re, Inc. 745
Reorganized CF & I Fabricators of Utah, Inc., United States v. 368
Reserve Insurance Co. v. Pisciotta 633, 635
Residential Mgmt. (N.Y.) Inc. v. Fed. Ins. Co. 236
Retail Clerks v. Schermerhorn 392
Rhead v. Hartford Ins. Co. of the Midwest....................................... 215
Rhodes v. Farmers Ins. Co. 264
Rhone-Poulenc Inc. v. International Ins. Co. 50, 51
Richard C. Gossett and Margaret D. Gossett v. Farmers Insurance Company of Washington.............................. **211**
Richardson v. Commissioner of Internal Revenue 296
Richardson v. Employers Liab. Assur. Corp... 86
Richland Knox Mutual Insurance Company v. Kallen 667
Rick Franklin Corp. v. State ex rel. Dep't of Transp. 630
Rigby v. Underwriters at Lloyds, London 563
Riley Stoker Corp. v. Fidelity and Guar. Ins. Underwriters, Inc...598
Rimes v. State Farm Mut. Auto. Ins. Co...420
River Ins. Co. v. Emp'rs Reinsurance Corp..745
Rizzuto v. Morris 278, 280, 281
RJC Realty Holding Corp. v. Republic Franklin Insurance Co. 501
Roark v. Humana, Inc. 399
Robroy Land Co. v. Prather 213
Rock Island Bank v. Time Ins. Co...431
Rock Springs Realty, Inc. v. Waid 278
Rockgate Management Co. v. CGU Insurance, Inc. 467
Rodemich v. State Farm Mut. Auto. Ins. Co. **690**
Rodriguez v. McGraw-Hill Cos. 427
Rohm & Haas Co. v. Continental Cas. Co...502
Roman Catholic Diocese of Brooklyn v. National Union Fire Ins. Co...494
Romero v. Pough............................65
Rose Acre Farms, Inc. v. Columbia Cas. Co. 436
Rosen v. State Farm General Insurance Company.............. **232**
Rosenthal v. American Bonding Co. of Baltimore 55
Roseth v. St. Paul Property & Liability Insurance Company **74**
Roth v. Shell Oil Co. 87
Rova Farms Resort, Inc. v. Investors Ins. Co. of Am...............................615
Royal Ins. Co. of Am. v. KSI Trading Corp..52
Royal Maccabees Ins. Co. v. James 91
RSUI Indem. Co. v. Discover P&C Ins. Co. 629
Ruan Transport Corp. v. Truck Rentals, Inc. 683
Rubenstein v. Mutual Life Insurance Co. of New York 303
Rubi, In re.....................................245
Russell v. Prudential Insurance Co. of America 431
Russo v. Rochford 630
Rust Tractor Co. v. Consolidated Constructors, Inc. 692
Rusthoven v. Commercial Standard Insurance Co. 46
Rutgers Council of AAUP Chapters v. Rutgers, The State University 382
Ryan v. Andrewski 301
Ryan v. Tickle............................ **299**

Ryder Truck Rental, Inc. v. Schapiro & Whitehouse, Inc. 683
Sacks v. Dallas Gold & Silver Exch., Inc. 96
Sade v. Northern Natural Gas Co. 662
Safeco Insurance Co. v. Hirschmann 238, 240
Sahloff v. Western Casualty & Surety Co. 699
Saint Consulting Group v. Endurance American Specialty Insurance Co. 575
Salomaa v. Honda Long Term Disability Plan 427
Samuel N. Zarpas, Inc. v. Morrow 570
Samuelson v. Chicago, Rock Island & Pacific R. Co. 678
San Diego Navy Federal Credit Union v. Cumis Insurance Society, Inc. 594
Sanchez, United States v. 368
Sandbulte v. Farm Bureau Mut. Ins. Co. 67, 71
Santisas v. Goodin 235
Scala v. Jerry Witt & Sons, Inc. 87
Scherer v. Wahlstrom 315
Schering Corp. v. Home Insurance Co. 473
Schnitzer Inv. Corp. v. Certain Underwriters at Lloyd's of London 527
Schoolcraft v. Ross 276
Schorsch v. Reliance Standard Life Ins. Co. 397
Schultz v. Erie Ins. Group 246
Scott v. Gallacher 617
Scott v. Northwestern Agencies 276
Scott v. Underhill 506
Scottsdale Ins. Co. v. Knox Park Constr., Inc. 635
Scottsdale Ins. Co. v. MV Transp. Co. 600
SCSC Corp. v. Allied Mut. Ins. Co. 480, 481, 482, 484
Seaboard Industries, Inc. v. Monaco 581
SEC v. Life Partners 314
SEC v. Mut. Benefits Corp 314
SEC v. United Benefit Life Ins. Co. 334, 335, 338, 339, 340
SEC v. Variable Annuity Life Ins. Co. of Am. (VALIC) 156, 333, 334, 335, 337, 338, 339, 342, 343, 368
Secor v. Pioneer Foundry 301
Security Mutual Casualty Company v. Century Casualty Co. 728
Security Mutual Insurance Co. v. Acker-Fitzsimons Corp. 532
Seidler v. Georgetown Life Insurance Co. 30

Senn v. United Dominion Indust, Inc. 386, 388
Sentinel Mgmt. Co. v. Aetna Cas. & Surety Co. 219
Sentinel Mgmt. Co. v. New Hampshire Ins. Co. 219
Sereboff v. Mid Atlantic Medical Services, Inc. 421
Sewell v. Great N. Ins. Co. 71
SFI Ltd. P'ship 8 v. Carroll 281
Shabotzky v. Equitable Life Assur. Soc. 425
Shade Foods, Inc. v. Innovative Products Sales & Marketing, Inc. 466
Shalimar Contractors, Inc. v. American States Insurance Co. 525
Shamblin v. Nationwide Mutual Insurance Co. 615
Shapero v. Allstate Ins. Co 627
Shaw v. Delta Air Lines, Inc. 377, 392
Shelter Mut. Ins. Co. v. See 665
Sher v. Lafayette Ins. Co 228, 232
Sherwood Brands, Inc. v. Great Am. Ins. Co. 574
Shinabarger v. Citizens Mutual Ins. Co. 667
Shipp v. Connecticut Indem. Co. 670
Shoshone First Bank v. Pacific Employers Insurance Company 595
Sigma Fin. Co. v. Am. Int'l Speciality Lines Ins. Co. 574
Signo Trading Int'l, Inc., State v. 527
Silberg v. California Life Insurance Company 82
Silicone Implant Ins. Coverage Lit., In re 477
Silverstein v. Metropolitan Life Ins. Co. 327
Simon Wrecking Co., Inc. v. AIU Insurance Co. 534
Simpson v. Farmers Insurance Company, Inc. 701
Simpson v. Phoenix Mut. Life Ins. Co. 326
Sinclair Oil Corp. v. Republic Ins. Co. 600
Sincoff v. Liberty Mutual Fire Insurance Co. 42
Singsaas v. Diederich 478
Sintros v. Hamon 69
Skandia America Reinsurance Corp. v. Schenck 44
SL Industries, Inc. v. American Motorists Insurance Co. 505
Slagle v. ITT Hartford Ins. Grp. 159

Slater v. Lawyers' Mut. Ins. Co. 572, 573
Smith v. Jim Dandy Markets 285
Smith v. Lumbermen's Mut. Ins. Co. 258, 259
Smith v. Travelers Ins. Co. 331
Smith v. Westland Life Ins. Co. 298
Snethen v. Oklahoma State Union of the Farmers Educational and Cooperative Union of America 216
Snodgrass v. State Farm Mut. Auto. Ins. Co. 616
Snyder v. Ridge Hill Memorial Park 102
Sonzinsky v. United States 368
South Carolina Insurance Co. v. Fidelity & Guaranty Insurance Underwriters, Inc. 407
South-Eastern Underwriters Association, United States v. 108
Southtrust Bank v. Export Ins. Servs., Inc. 77
Sovereign Life Ins. Co. of Cal. v. Rewald 17
Sparks v. Republic National Life Insurance Co. 92
Spencer v. Hawkeye Security Ins. Co. 677
Speziale v. Kohnke 667
Sphinx International, Inc. v. National Union Fire Insurance Co. of Pittsburgh, Pennsylvania 562
Spirt v. Teachers Ins. and Annuity Ass'n 154
SR Int'l Bus. Ins. Co. v. World Trade Ctr. Properties, LLC 40
St. Paul Fire & Marine Ins. Co. v. Barry 166
St. Paul Fire & Marine Ins. Co. v. Coss 513
St. Paul Fire & Marine Ins. Co. v. Smith............................ 651
St. Vincent's Hospital & Medical Center v. Insurance Co. of North America 634
Stargatt v. Fid. and Cas. Co. of New York 620
State Auto Prop. & Cas. Ins. Co. v. Midwest Computers & More 466
State Automobile Casualty Underwriters v. Ruotsalainen 76
State Farm Auto Ins. Co. v. Rowland 615
State Farm Fire & Casualty Co. v. Bongen 237
State Farm Fire & Casualty Co. v. Muth............................ 505
State Farm Fire & Casualty Co. v. Tringali 656
State Farm Gen. Ins. Co. v. Frake............................ 506

State Farm Gen. Ins. Co. v. Stewart 288
State Farm Ins. Co. v. Shaffer 689
State Farm Mut. Auto. Ins. Co. v. Bridges 24
State Farm Mut. Auto. Ins. Co. v. Campbell 94
State Farm Mut. Auto. Ins. Co. v. Centennial Ins. Co. 667
State Farm Mut. Auto. Ins. Co. v. Cook............................ 663
State Farm Mut. Auto Ins. Co. v. Daprato 657
State Farm Mut. Auto. Ins. Co. v. Davies 669
State Farm Mut. Auto. Ins. Co. v. Fisher 653
State Farm Mut. Auto. Ins. Co. v. General Mut. Ins. Co. 683
State Farm Mut. Auto. Ins. Co. v. Mabry 687
State Farm Mut. Auto. Ins. Co. v. Secrist............................ 673
State Farm Mut. Auto. Ins. Co. v. Sewell 100
State Farm Mut. Auto. Ins. Co. v. Smith 652, 653
State Farm Mut. Auto. Ins. Co. v. Strang 661
State Farm Mut. Auto. Ins. Co. v. Travelers Insurance Co. 681
State Farm Mut. Auto. Ins. Co. v. Universal Underwriters Group............................ 653
State Farm Mut. Auto. Ins. Co. v. Washington 655
State Farm Mut. Auto. Ins. Co. v. Wertz 657
State Farm Mut. Ins. Co. v. Sewell 100
State Mut. Life Assurance Co. of Am. v. Hampton 304
Steelworkers v. Rawson 402
Steil v. Humana Kansas City, Inc............................ 389
Steinke v. Safeco Ins. Co. of Am. 420
Stephan v. Unum Life Ins. Co. of Am. 145
Stephens v. Pension Ben. Guar. Corp............................ 397
Steven v. Fid. & Cas. Co. 60
Stevens Shipping & Terminal Co. v. Japan Rainbow II MV............... 249, 250
Stillwagoner v. Travelers Ins. Co............................ 306, 308, 365
Stine v. Continental Casualty Co............................ 570
Stipcich v. Metropolitan Life Ins. Co............................ 29

Stone Container Corporation v. Hartford Steam Boiler Inspection and Insurance Company 47
Stonewall Ins. Co. v. Asbestos Claims Management Corp. 491
Stonewall Ins. Co. v. Webb 530
Stoney Run Co. v. Prudential–LMI Commercial Insurance Co. 525
Strickland v. Gulf Life Ins. Co. **99**
Sullins v. Allstate Ins. Co. 521
Sullivan Financial Group, Inc. v. Wrynn 73
Sumitomo Mar. & Fire Ins. Co. v. Cologne Reins. Co. 728
Sunbeam Corp. v. Liberty Mutual Ins. Co. 526
Sutton v. Jondahl 280, 281
Swentusky v. Prudential Ins. Co. of America 296
Swihart v. Universal Underwriters Life Ins. Co. 18
Sylva, State v. 137
Taft v. Cerwonka **706**
Tamez v. Certain Underwriters at Lloyd's, London 306, 308
Tauriello v. Aetna Insurance Co. 285
Taylor v. Leonard 96
Teague-Strebeck Motors, Inc. v. Chrysler Ins. Co. 216
Textron, Inc. v. Aetna Cas. & Sur. Co. 526
The Birth Center v. St. Paul Cos., Inc. 615
The Maccabees v. Covert 28
Thomas J. Lipton, Inc. v. Liberty Mutual Insurance Co. 473
Thoracic Cardiovascular Associates, Ltd. v. St. Paul Fire & Marine Ins. Co. **568**
Tiedtke v. Fidelity & Casualty Company of New York 606
TIG Ins. Co. of Michigan v. Homestore, Inc. 536
Timberline Equipment Co., Inc. v. St. Paul Fire & Marine Ins. Co. 597
Time Ins. Co. v. Graves 23
Tomerlin v. Canadian Indemnity Co. 592
Torgeson v. Unum Life Ins. Co. of America 428
Town & Country Management Corp. v. Comcast Cablevision 518
Towns v. Northern Security Ins. Co. 485
Transit Casualty Co. v. Selective Ins. Co. of the Southeast 757
Transit Casualty Co. v. Spink Corp. 624, 629
Transport Ins. Co. v. Lee Way Motor Freight, Inc. 494
Transportation Ins. Co. v. Moriel 96
Travelers Casualty & Surety Company v. Certain Underwriters at Lloyd's of London **728**
Travelers Casualty & Surety Company v. Gerling Global Reinsurance Corporation of America **735**
Travelers Casualty & Surety Company v. Ins. Co. of N. Am. 727
Travelers Ins. Co. v. Pac. 709
Travelers Ins. Co. v. Pratt 100, 103
Travelers Ins. Co. v. Weatherford 663
Travelers Property Cas. of Am. v. Hillerich & Bradsby Co., Inc. 616
Trinity Evangelical Lutheran Church & School-Freistadt v. Tower Ins. Co. 92
Trinity Homes LLC v. Ohio Cas. Ins. Co. 623
Trinity Universal Ins. Co. v. Cowan 468
Trinity Universal Ins. Co. v. General Accident, Fire & Life Assurance Corp. 682
TS Indus., Inc., In re 560
Tschida v. Continental Cas. Co. 424
Tublitz v. Glens Falls Ins. Co. 216
Tucker v. Fireman's Fund Insurance Co. 518
Tucker v. Government Employees Insurance Co. 707, 708
Tyree v. General Ins. Co. 213
Underwriters at Lloyds, London, State v. 239
Unified Western Grocers v. Twin City Fire Insurance Co. 563
Unigard Ins. Co. v. Studer 663
Unigard Mutual Insurance Company v. Argonaut **502**
Unigard Security Ins. Co. v. North River Ins. Co. 724, 734, 737, 744
Union Flights, Inc. v. Administrator, FAA 138
Union Labor Life Ins. Co. v. Pireno 393
United Auto Insurance Co. v. Buckley 673
United Co-op. v. Frontier FS Co-op 527
United Fidelity Life Ins. Co. v. Emert 324
United Services Automobile Association v. Elitzky 505

United Services Automobile Association v. Preferred Accident Insurance Co. 660
United States Automobile Association v. Markosky 674
United States Aviex Co. v. Travelers Ins. Co. 458, 461
United States Department of the Treasury v. Fabe........................ 155
United States Fidelity & Guar. Co. v. Am. Re-Insurance Co. 745
United States Fidelity & Guar. Co. v. Bramwell...................................... 276
United States Fidelity & Guar. Co. v. Farm Bureau Mut. Ins. Co. 666
United States Fidelity & Guar. Co. v. Thomas Solvent Co..................... 463
United States Fidelity & Guar. Co. v. Wilkin Insulation Co. 515
United States Fidelity & Guar. Co. v. Woodward 55
United States Gypsum v. Admiral Ins. Co. 494
United Tech. Corp. v. American Home Assurance Co. 216
UNUM Life Insurance Co. of America v. Ward.. 79
Upshaw v. Trinity Cos. 710
Utica Mutual Insurance Co. v. Prudential Property and Casualty Insurance Co. 497
Valdez v. Metro. Prop. & Cas. Ins. Co. 155
Valentine v. Aetna Ins. Co. 626
Van Dyke v. White 606
Van Hoozer v. Farmers Insurance Exchange..................................... 704
Vantage Development Corp. v. American Environment Technologies Corp. 523
Vargas v. Insurance Co. of North America.................................. **41**, 473
Villella v. Public Employees Mutual Insurance Co. 238, 240
Vlastos v. Sumitomo Marine & Fire Insurance Company **9**
Vogel v. Independence Federal Sav. Bank... 376
Vogel v. Northern Assurance Co. 285, 288
Wachovia Bank & Trust Co. v. Westchester Fire Insurance Co. 689
Waldman v. Mutual Life Ins. Co. of New York 425
Walker v. UnumProvident Corp... 428
Wall v. Swilley............................... 250
Wanzek Construction, Inc. v. Employers Insurance of Wassau.. 515
Ward v. Durham Life Ins. Co. 25

TABLE OF CASES   xxxvii

Warnock v. Davis.......................... 311
Washington Nat. Ins. Corp. v. Ruderman 52
Washoe County v. Transcontinental Ins. Co. 494
Waste Management of Carolinas, Inc. v. Peerless Insurance Co. 524
Watson v. Watson.......................... 667
Waupaca Foundry, Inc. v. Gehlhausen 397
Waxse v. Reserve Life Insurance Co. 26
Weaver Brothers, Inc. v. Chappel 533
Weaver v. Prudential Ins. Co. of America 80
Weaver v. Royal Insurance Co. of America 521, 523
Weber v. Weber 216
Weedo v. Stone-E-Brick, Inc.... **507**
Wehner v. Foster 530
Weller v. Cummins........................ 530
Wells v. John Hancock Mut. Life Ins. Co... 332
Wendel v. Swanberg...................... 530
Wenthe v. Hospital Service, Incorporated, of Iowa................... 89
West American Insurance Co. v. Tufco Flooring East, Inc. 523, 524, 525
West Bay Exploration v. AIG Specialty Agencies **528**
West Coast Life Ins. Co. v. Hoar..... 25
West Homeowners' Assn. v. American Guarantee & Liability Ins. Co. 234
West v. McNamara......................... 662
Westchester Fire Insurance Co. v. City of Pittsburg 519, 522
Westchester Fire Insurance Co. v. Gulf Coast Rod, Reel & Gun Club... 502
Western Fire Ins. Co. v. First Presbyterian Church 220
Western Reserve Life Assurance Co. of Ohio v. ADM Assocs., LLC... 326
Western World Ins. Co. v. Stack Oil, Inc... 725
Westfield Ins. Co. v. Tech Dry, Inc... 500
Westview Associates v. Guaranty National Insurance Co............... 525
Weyerhaeuser v. Aetna Cas. & Sur. Co. 462
White v. American Cas. Ins. Co.. 668
Wickman v. Northwestern National Ins. Co. 327
Wilburn Boat Co. v. Fireman's Fund Ins. Co. 16

Wilkie v. Auto-Owners Ins. Co. 53
Will Realty Corp. v. Transportation Ins. Co. 256
Wilson v. Maryland Casualty Co. 581
Winner v. Ratzlaff 696, 697, 703
Wirth v. Maryland Casualty Company 667
Wischmeyer v. Paul Revere Life Ins. Co. 323, 324
Wm. Skinner & Sons Ship-Building and Dry-Dock Co. v. Houghton 285
Wolfsen v. Hathaway 87
Wood v. Duckworth 530
Woodling v. Garrett Corp. 497
Woods v. Cloyd W. Miller Co. 369
Woods v. Nationwide Mutual Insurance Co. 688, 689
World Trade Center Properties, L.L.C. v. Hartford Fire Insurance Co. 40
Wright-Ryan Constr., Inc. v. AIG Ins. Co. of Canada 685
Wurtz v. Rawlings Co., LLC 420
Wyoming Farm Bureau Mutual Insurance Co. v. May 662, 663
Yates v. Estate of Ferguson 685
Yount v. Maisano 598
Zachary Trading, Inc. v. Northwestern Mutual Life Ins. Co. 27
Zamora v. Dairyland County Mutual Insurance Co. 655
Zeig v. Massachusetts Bonding & Ins. Co. 619, 620, 621
Zeitz v. Zurich General Accident Liability Insurance Co. 580
Zochert v. National Farmers Union Property & Casualty Company **260**
Zuckerman v. National Union Fire Ins. Co. 572
Zurich Am. Ins. Co. v. ABM Indus., Inc. 228
Zurich General Accident & Liability Insurance Co. v. Clamor 682

UNIVERSITY CASEBOOK SERIES®

INSURANCE LAW AND REGULATION

CASES AND MATERIALS

SIXTH EDITION

CHAPTER ONE

INTRODUCTION

A. THE HISTORY AND FUNCTIONS OF INSURANCE

We live in a risky world and we are increasingly aware of it. The events of the early 21st century have confirmed that disaster is never far away. Hurricanes, epidemics of new disease, terrorism, financial panics, forest fires, earthquakes, exposure to hazardous chemicals, industrial accidents, and transportation calamities may cause significant injury or death, property damage, and economic loss. We are also at risk of suffering loss because of events that are statistically more mundane but nonetheless personally tragic, such as illnesses, home fires, traffic accidents, and medical mistakes. At the same time, new information technologies and the globalization of markets have made it possible to deal with these and other risks more systematically than ever before. Insurance is one method of addressing these risks.

A Brief History

Although insurance is a modern method of managing risk, it has ancient roots. For example, using a practice called "bottomry," Phoenician merchants transported separate portions of their goods on different ships in order to reduce their risk of loss. Demosthenes, writing in the 4th century B.C., tells of the Greeks loaning money on ships and cargoes, with the loans to be repaid only if the ships were not lost. Both were primitive forms of insurance. The origins of modern insurance contracts can be traced at least as far back as 14th century Italy and Flanders.

By the 16th century the practice of insuring ships and their cargo had spread to London. Late in the 17th century much of this "marine" insurance business was being transacted in a gathering place called Lloyds Coffee House, which ultimately evolved into the modern Lloyds of London. After the Great Fire of London in 1666, people recognized the need for fire insurance and new companies started to offer it for sale. Shortly thereafter a market in life insurance began to develop. For a considerable period the common law played a minimal role in regulating insurance, but from the time of Lord Mansfield's mid-18th century appointment as Lord Chief Justice, insurance contracts were increasingly governed by the common law and insurance disputes were resolved in the common law courts.

Although marine, fire, and life insurance were all sold in the United States in the 18th century, marine insurance was the dominant form of coverage until the 1840's, when it was overtaken by fire insurance. As wealth accumulated and individuals recognized that they had something to protect, life insurance also became more widespread. After the Civil War the pace of industrialization quickened and accidental injury in factories and on railroads and other forms of transportation became more common. Tort liability then became a serious threat. Beginning in the 1880's, liability insurance was introduced to meet this concern. For discussion of the history of insurance and its relation to the development of tort liability, see Kenneth S. Abraham, The Liability Century: Insurance and Tort Law from the Progressive Era to 9/11 (2008).

The 20th century was a period of enormous growth in all forms of insurance in the United States. Health insurance was introduced as a fringe benefit of employment during World War Two and spread rapidly after that. Various new forms of liability insurance were also marketed to deal with the expansion of tort liability. Auto liability, products liability, medical malpractice liability, and directors and officers liability insurance are representative examples. As homeownership grew, demand for protection of individuals' investments and lenders' collateral resulted in the development of homeowners insurance—a combination of property and liability insurance. In recent years, employers have moved away from providing fixed pensions and financial markets have been roiled by turmoil, creating new demand for life insurance and annuity products that protect against financial and longevity risk (the risk of living longer than anticipated). Today ordinary people as well as virtually all businesses typically are covered by a number of these different forms of insurance.

The Contemporary Insurance System

As we progress through the second decade of the 21st century, insurance has become pervasive. Premiums paid for private insurance in the United States exceed $1.8 trillion per year. The cost of social insurance such as Social Security and Medicare provided by various levels of government adds over $1 trillion more each year to total national expenditures on insurance. Insurance protecting individuals and businesses is an essential feature of our economic system because it helps to provide the security necessary to reduce risk, cushion economic hardship, and encourage productive investment. And globally, insurance is proliferating, with Japan spending over $500 billion per year on private insurance, and half a dozen other countries spending over $100 billion a year. China, which was not in the top 25 countries in insurance spending in 1980, now ranks fourth, spending over $270 billion per year on private insurance. Swiss Re, Sigma: World Insurance in 2013: Steering Towards Recovery (2014). In parallel with these developments, international entities like the International Association of Insurance Supervisors (IAIS) and the European Union are increasingly influencing U.S. insurance regulation.

There is no terribly satisfactory all-purpose definition of insurance. If we think of insurance as a risk-distribution arrangement for the compensation of damages or loss that is entered into by one party as its business, rather than as an incident of another business transaction, we have a definition that is good enough to get us started. The principal sellers of insurance are *stock* and *mutual* companies, although a few unusual forms of operation that are holdovers from an earlier age, such as *reciprocals* and *fraternal benefit societies*, still exist. The owners of stock companies are shareholders; the owners of mutual companies are policyholders, or "insureds"—the individuals or institutions that have purchased insurance from the company. Notwithstanding this difference in corporate form and ownership, stock and mutual companies compete with each other in virtually all markets, the products they sell are similar, and the body of insurance law governing them does not depend on the kind of company involved. Companies can sell coverage directly to policyholders, through exclusive agents, or through independent agents who represent more than one company. Once again, these differences in distribution—except for the law governing the different kinds of agency involved—have little practical significance for the rights of policyholders or for the obligations of insuring companies.

The distinction between *property/casualty* and *life and health* insurance, however, is of some significance. The two terms represent roughly what they suggest—that insurance against loss of property and legal liability falls into a category separate from insurance against risks to one's body, such as loss of life, ill health, and disability. It was common in the 19th century for insurers to sell one category of coverage or the other. It is now typical for large insurers to sell both, sometimes through subsidiaries owned by a holding company and specializing in a particular category. Thus, it is common to see references to The Travelers "group" of companies and the "Chubb Group of Insurance Companies." Many other companies still specialize in one category of coverage or the other, and many specialize in selling only certain forms of coverage, or *lines* of insurance. Some companies sell only health insurance, for example, and others only auto and homeowners insurance.

How Insurance Works

In the simplest sense, the function of insurance is to protect the policyholder in the event of a future loss. A more sophisticated description, however, recognizes three separate insurance functions. The first is *risk-transfer* from comparatively risk-averse to less risk-averse or risk-neutral parties. A risk-neutral party is indifferent as between a small risk of suffering a large loss and greater risk of suffering a small loss, when each risk has the same *expected value*—the probability of a loss multiplied by its magnitude if it occurs. In contrast, a risk-averse party would prefer the large risk of suffering a small loss to a smaller risk of suffering the large loss.

For example, a 1 percent chance of suffering a $10,000 loss and a 10 percent chance of suffering a $1000 loss each have the same expected value, -$100. A risk-neutral party is indifferent between the two risks, but a risk-averse party would tend to prefer the latter. Consequently, the risk-averse party is likely to be willing to pay a sum exceeding the expected value of a given risk in order to transfer that risk to another party. In the above example, the party transferring a 1 percent chance of suffering a $10,000 loss might be willing to pay a $105, $110, or even $150 premium to transfer the risk of loss, depending on the degree of risk-aversion involved. In this sense, insurance transforms a small risk of suffering a large loss into a large risk (100 percent) of paying a smaller sum—the insurance premium.

Individuals (and most business entities) are generally risk-averse with respect to low-probability, high-magnitude losses, such as the prospect of a home burning down. Economists explain this as a function of the diminishing marginal utility of wealth. This concept reflects the intuition that events substantially diminishing a person's wealth will generally have a *disproportionately* large impact on that person's well-being relative to smaller losses of wealth. Building on the example above, a $10,000 loss might well be more than 10 times worse for a poor law student than a $1,000 loss. In the former case, the law student could have to drop out of law school, for instance, whereas in the latter case the poor law student might simply be forced to work extra hours as a research assistant.

The second function of insurance is *risk-pooling,* or diversification. Insurance companies are not intrinsically risk-neutral. Rather, by insuring a large number of insureds posing similar and independent risks, an insurer can transform these risks into a highly predictable set of obligations. This is an application of the law of large numbers. To illustrate, if one flips a coin 10 times, the likelihood that the flips will produce 3, 4, 5, 6, or 7 flips of heads (i.e. conform to the expected distribution of heads and tails) is about 90%. But if one flipped a coin 100 times, the likelihood that between 30 and 70 of these flips would be heads would be much greater than 90%, or even 99%. In other words, as one increases the number of coin flips, the distribution of heads and tails becomes more and more likely to reflect the expected distribution of 50% heads and 50% tails. Insurance operates in the same way: the pooling of individual risks largely eliminates uncertainty, as reflected by the fact that each year a relatively predictable and stable number of individuals get into car accidents, experience house fires, and are sued for negligence. Insurance is thus a vehicle by which risk-averse parties combine to share and thereby reduce their collective risk. The insurance company's profits constitute payment for providing this service to its policyholders and for bearing the residual risk that losses will vary beyond the range predicted.

In order for the risk-pooling function of insurance to operate properly, the underlying risks insured must be independent, or "uncorrelated." In the example above, the likelihood that one flip will come up heads is completely unrelated to whether the coin previously came up heads, thus satisfying this condition. By contrast, when risks are correlated, a single event may result in losses among a large number of policyholders. For instance, the likelihood that an earthquake damages one building is highly correlated to the likelihood an earthquake damages neighboring buildings. When risks are correlated in this fashion, eliminating them through pooling becomes much more difficult.

The third function of insurance is *risk-allocation.* Insurers not only accept the transfer of risks and then pool them. In charging for the coverage they provide, insurers attempt to set a price that is proportional to the degree of risk posed by each insured. Insurers thereby allocate risk to groups of insureds posing similar or identical degrees of risk. Different methods of risk classification measure risk in different ways. But by classifying risks and then pricing coverage in accordance with those classifications, insurers can create incentives for insureds to appropriately limit the degree of risk they pose. For instance, by charging more for health insurance to those who smoke cigarettes, insurers may encourage smokers to quit.

Any given insurance arrangement accomplishes these three functions in varying degrees. For example, a particular insurance policy will transfer some but by no means all the risks faced by the insured. In addition, because an insurer's effort at risk diversification through pooling is always imperfect, insurers inevitably face a greater or lesser degree of risk themselves. Finally, obtaining the information necessary to classify risks and price accordingly is not cost-free; consequently, risk-allocation normally can proceed only to the point at which further refinement is not worthwhile. Insurance law can help or hinder these functions, sometimes with justification and sometimes without it.

The Social Functions of Insurance

Insurance not only performs the direct economic functions of risk transfer, risk pooling, and risk allocation. Because over time insurance has come to occupy such an important place in our way of life, insurance also plays a number of social roles. Arguably in both positive and negative ways, insurance constrains and in a sense helps constitute social life. For example, insurance affects our norms. When health insurance covers contraception or mental health needs, these services gradually come to be seen as appropriate forms of medical treatment. And when homeowners insurance premiums are reduced because a home contains smoke detectors, it becomes irresponsible not to have them installed. Insurance sometimes is also a surrogate regulator or instrument of governance. In most states it is unlawful to drive a car without liability insurance. Drivers who cannot obtain liability insurance at tolerable cost because of their accident records are effectively prohibited from driving, though admittedly they still may drive in violation of law and at considerable financial risk to themselves and their potential victims. Similarly, physicians who cannot obtain malpractice insurance may be denied hospital admitting privileges and marginalized in their medical practices. Finally, insurance is a kind of equalizer. It takes money from the lucky and gives it to the unlucky. In so doing it smooths out some of the differences among people that would otherwise result from bad luck. I may still suffer if I become ill and can no longer work, but if I have disability insurance my income will be maintained.

These sorts of insights have been developed by a group of "insurance and society" scholars whose work has shed new light on the way that insurance operates in practice. See, e.g., Richard V. Erickson et al., Insurance as Governance (2003); Embracing Risk (Tom Baker & Jonathan Simon eds., 2002). One of the long-term legal implications of these insights is that insurance can often operate as a substitute for government regulation of safety. See Omri Ben-Shahar & Kyle D. Logue, Outsourcing Regulation: How Insurance Reduces Moral Hazard, 111 Mich. L. Rev. 197 (2012). Another, even broader, implication may be that insurance does not fit comfortably within the public-private dichotomy. Private insurers are not agents of government, and therefore are not subject to the standards that restrict the scope of the government's discretion. Insurers, for example, are not and probably should not be required to accord their applicants and policyholders with full-blown due process and equal protection. But given the social role and importance of insurance, we may need standards for regulating the behavior of private insurers that recognize their unique public role. See Kenneth S. Abraham, Four Conceptions of Insurance, 161 U. Pa. L. Rev. 653 (2013).

B. THE PROBLEMS OF ADVERSE SELECTION AND MORAL HAZARD

If insurance markets functioned perfectly, law would have a much less important role to play in regulating insurance than it does in practice. Among other things, consumers of insurance would know exactly what they wanted and what was offered to them, insurers would know what to charge for each form of coverage, and the purchase of insurance by one party would have no impact on anyone else. The ideal of the perfectly functioning market, however, is never achieved in practice.

Insurance markets are especially susceptible to two well-known market failures: adverse selection and moral hazard. Both of these market failures arise from policyholders having better information than insurers regarding their risk levels. Of course, quite often the tables are turned, and insurers possess better information than policyholders about relevant information, such as the content of insurance policies. For now though, we focus on adverse selection and moral hazard, which are fundamental to understanding insurance products and market practices in addition to the law that governs them.

Adverse Selection. Other things being equal, a party facing a high risk of loss is more likely to seek insurance than a party facing a low risk. If potential policyholders know better than insurers whether they pose comparatively high or low risk prior to acquiring insurance, then adverse selection may occur: when insurers charge each party the same price for coverage, then high-risk parties elect to be insured in greater proportion than low-risk parties, and insurers are forced to raise the price of coverage. As a result of the increased price, some of the comparatively low-risk parties that had previously been insured decline to purchase coverage or purchase less of it, the average degree of risk posed by the insurer's policyholders rises, and the insurer is forced to raise prices again, thus restarting the cycle of adverse selection.

For example, suppose that an insurer has five policyholders, and it knows that they pose an average risk of 7. But the insurer does not know the risk posed by any individual policyholder. Individually, the risks posed are 5, 6, 7, 8 and 9, and each individual knows the risk he poses. If the insurer charges each policyholder a premium of 7 (plus an increment for costs and profit that can be ignored here), then coverage is a good buy for two of the policyholders (those whose risk is 8 or 9), a less good buy for two policyholders (those whose risk is 5 or 6), and actuarially fair for one policyholder (the one whose risk is 7). When the time comes for renewing coverage, the policyholder whose risk is 5 may decide not to buy coverage, or to buy less coverage than before. Suppose that this policyholder decides not to buy coverage at all. At the end of the policy year, the insurer will find that its average loss was 7.5, and will therefore have to raise premiums for the next year. When it does so, however, the policyholder who poses a risk of 6 may decide not to buy coverage. Then the insurer will find at the end of the next year that its average loss was 8, and raise premiums. At that point the policyholder who poses a risk of 7 may decide not to buy coverage.

Eventually the insurer's risk pool either unravels completely, or an equilibrium is reached in which some low-risk parties purchase less coverage than they would otherwise desire and others purchase none. In either case, low-risk parties buy less coverage and high-risk parties buy more coverage than they would if insurers could distinguish between the risks posed by different policyholders. For classic economic expositions of the problem, see Michael D. Rothschild & Joseph E. Stiglitz, Equilibrium in Competitive Insurance Markets: An Essay on the Economics of Imperfect Information, 90 Quart. J. Econ. 629 (1976); George Akerloff, The Market for "Lemons": Quality Uncertainty and the Market Mechanism, 84 Quart. J. Econ. 488 (1970).

Moral Hazard. The term moral hazard originated in insurance as a description of the risk that an insured or insurance beneficiary would deliberately destroy the subject matter that was insured in order to obtain payment of an insurance benefit. For example, in 18th century England it was possible to purchase insurance on the lives of strangers. This was a form of gambling rather than true insurance. As in ordinary gambling, when the insured death occurred, the policyholder would not merely avoid a loss, but would actually obtain a gain. Moreover, because of this prospect it was in the policyholder's interest for the party whose life was insured to die sooner rather than later. The policyholder therefore had an incentive to cause the insured death to occur. Because of this moral hazard, eventually (as we will see in Chapters Four and Five) the practice of insuring without an "insurable interest" in the insured subject matter—an interest engendered by love and affection or an economic relationship—was prohibited. The term moral hazard now often refers more generally to the tendency of any insured party to exercise less care to avoid an insured loss than would be exercised if the loss were not insured.

Like adverse selection, moral hazard is fundamentally an information asymmetry problem: if insurers could costlessly monitor the ongoing behavior of their insureds, insurance would not be plagued by moral hazard. Because premiums could be charged in proportion to the level of care actually exercised by the insured, there would be no incentive for insured parties to exercise less care than those who were uninsured. But of course insurers cannot costlessly monitor the levels of care their insureds exercise. Consequently, because of this imperfect information, moral hazard is a common threat to the functioning of insurance.

Combating Threats to the Insurance Function. Insurers attempt to combat adverse selection and moral hazard with a variety of devices. They engage in "underwriting," the process of screening and evaluating applications to determine the degree of risk posed by prospective insureds; they classify insureds based on the degree of risk posed and set premium levels accordingly; they experience-rate, or charge premiums for coverage renewals based in part on the insured's loss experience during the previous policy period; they include deductible, coinsurance, and dollar limits of coverage in policies so that all losses are not fully insured; they do not let people buy insurance on the lives of strangers, or on property in which the prospective policyholder has no interest; and they fashion the terms of coverage so that unusual risks are not insured by standard policies and so that the results of inordinately dangerous behavior are not insured. Sometimes insurance law confirms the validity of these devices, but often it intervenes to prohibit or regulate them.

Although the threat posed by adverse selection should not be underestimated, neither should it be exaggerated. See Peter Siegelman, Adverse Selection in Insurance Markets: An Exaggerated Threat, 113 Yale L.J. 1223 (2004). But see George L. Priest, The Current Insurance Crisis and Modern Tort Law, 96 Yale L.J. 1521 (1987). In certain respects insurers know more about applicants than the applicants know themselves. Insurers maintain data about the characteristics that affect risk levels, for example, that individuals do not possess. Applicants may think that they pose higher or lower risks than they actually pose, or may have no intuition about the issue. In these situations adverse selection is likely to be weak or nonexistent. In addition, risk-aversion prompts demand for insurance in the first place. Risk-averse insureds have a tendency to become and to remain insured even if they are charged somewhat more for coverage than perfect actuarial calculations would dictate. The result is an often-tolerable level of cross-subsidization from low-risk individuals to high-risk individuals within any given risk pool. In this sense every risk classification involves some redistribution of risk, up to the point where the factors that prevent adverse selection begin to dissolve.

Similarly, different forms of insurance are subject to moral hazard in different respects, and some more than others. Insurance is less likely to lead to moral hazard, for instance, when individuals do not have substantial control over loss-producing behavior or when money cannot fully compensate for a loss. See Tom Baker, On the Genealogy of Moral Hazard, 75 Tex. L. Rev. 237 (1996). Thus, having health insurance probably does not significantly influence a policyholder's incentive to stay healthy, although it may increase the tendency to seek health care after a policyholder becomes sick or suffers injury. And given drivers' instinct for self-protection, having auto liability insurance probably does not significantly influence driving behavior. On the other hand, having products liability insurance, or any other form of insurance involving behavior that does not affect the policyholder's own risk of suffering injury, may well involve more substantial moral hazard.

Two devices involved in combating adverse selection and moral hazard are examined in the following pages. One device, the insurance warranty, is a creation of the insurance market, but is now subject to legal regulation that limits its effect. The other device, the voiding of a policy because of a misrepresentation by the insured in the application process, is a creation of insurance law. In both instances, the law must determine how far the insurer can go in obtaining reliable information to decide whether to insure a prospective insured and under what terms.

1. Breach of Warranty

Vlastos v. Sumitomo Marine & Fire Insurance Company

United States Court of Appeals, Third Circuit, 1983.
707 F.2d 775.

■ ADAMS, CIRCUIT JUDGE.

Evelyn Vlastos appeals from a judgment denying her recovery on an insurance policy for a fire that occurred in a commercial building that she owned. Applying Pennsylvania law, the district court declared that Vlastos had unambiguously warranted that the third floor of her building was occupied exclusively as a janitor's residence. Based on this ruling by the court, the jury found that Vlastos had breached the warranty, and the court declined to set aside the jury verdict. Inasmuch as we hold that it was error to determine that the warranty clause in question is unambiguous, the order of the district court will be vacated and the case remanded for further proceedings.

I.

Vlastos owned a 20' × 80' four-story building at 823 Pennsylvania Avenue, Pittsburgh, Pennsylvania. Prior to a fire on April 23, 1980, Vlastos and her son operated a luncheonette and a bar on the first floor of the building. The second and third floors were leased to Spartacus, Inc., which conducted a massage parlor on the second floor. Evidence was introduced at trial tending to show that the massage parlor also utilized at least a portion of the third floor. At the rear of the third floor there was a section variously described as a padlocked room or a section partitioned off from the remainder of the floor. It was in this area that Philip "Red" Pinkney, Vlastos' handyman and janitor, is alleged to have lived. Vlastos kept supplies on the fourth floor, and maintained a small office there as well. She occasionally remained overnight on the fourth floor rather than return to her residence. Vlastos was not staying there the night of the fire, but two friends of hers were residing there temporarily and were killed. A third person was also killed in the fire.

All of Vlastos' insurance matters were handled by her broker, John Mitchell. Mitchell obtained insurance for Vlastos from a group of European insurance companies through two sub-brokers. The policy in question, dated November 22, 1979, provided $345,000 of fire insurance with a $1,000 deductible provision. It contained a section, Endorsement No. 4, expressly incorporated into the policy, which stated in part: "Warranted that the 3rd floor is occupied as Janitor's residence."

After the building and its contents were destroyed by the fire, the insurers refused to pay the claim, citing an alleged breach of the warranty. Vlastos filed a complaint based on diversity jurisdiction. The jury trial was bifurcated as to liability and damages; the parties agreed that Pennsylvania law is applicable. During the trial on liability, the district court ruled that the insurers were not required to produce evidence that the warranty was material to the risk insured against, holding that materiality was irrelevant. At the conclusion of the evidence, the court denied Vlastos' motion for a directed verdict, and proceeded to charge the jury that the warranty regarding the third floor was breached if a massage parlor occupied any significant portion of the floor, regardless of whether the janitor had a residence there as well. The jury was also instructed that if the third floor was totally unoccupied this too would have constituted a breach of the warranty. The sole question put to the jury was: "Have the defendants proved by a preponderance of the evidence that the plaintiff breached the warranty?" The jury answered affirmatively. Vlastos' motions for judgment notwithstanding the verdict or a new trial were denied in a memorandum opinion and order. Vlastos has appealed, raising numerous points, including the contention that the jury was incorrectly instructed that the warranty was unambiguous.

II.

Vlastos objects that "no proof was offered that the provision in Endorsement No. 4 actually was a warranty." Reply Br. 1. Although her brief does not specify an alternate characterization of the provision, presumably she means to assert that it was a representation. If, as Vlastos implied, it was a representation, then the insurers would be under an obligation to show that the provision was material to the risk insured against in order for the insurers to avoid their obligations under the contract.

A representation, unlike a warranty, is not part of the insurance contract but is collateral to it. If a representation is not material to the risk, its falsity does not avoid the contract. On the other hand, the materiality of a warranty to the risk insured against is irrelevant; if the fact is not as warranted, the insurer may deny recovery. * * * In case of doubt, courts normally construe a statement in an insurance contract as a representation rather than a warranty. *See* 12A V. Appleman & J. Appleman, Insurance Law and Practice § 7342 (1981); 43 Am. Jur. 2d, *Insurance* §§ 1027, 1028 (1982). But no reason has been advanced for doubting that the provision in question here—which by its terms "warrant[s]" a fact and is part of the insurance contract—is a warranty. Accordingly, we cannot hold that it was improper for the trial judge to read this provision as a warranty. The district court therefore did not err in ruling that evidence of materiality would not have been relevant to the question whether Vlastos can recover on the policy.

The parties agree that the provision in question concerned a state of affairs existing at the time the contract was signed, and was not a promise that a janitor *would* occupy the third floor in the future. In other words, the provision is satisfied if a janitor occupied the floor on Nov. 22, 1979, the date the policy was issued, even if the situation had changed by the time of the fire several months later. The district court erroneously instructed the jury on this issue at two points. It stated that Vlastos agreed that the floor "*would be* occupied as a janitor's residence" (App. 389, emphasis added) and that the warranty was breached if "*at the time of the fire*" a massage parlor occupied any significant portion of the floor (App. 390, emphasis added). If the district court on remand decides that the case must be retried (*see infra* Part III), then it should instruct the jury that the relevant time for purposes of the warranty is the time at which the parties entered into the contract.

III.

Having established that Vlastos did warrant that at the time she entered into the contract "the 3rd floor [was] occupied as Janitor's residence," it must be determined what the language of the warranty should be construed to mean. For the reasons set forth below, the provision must be read in Vlastos' favor, as warranting merely that a janitor occupied some portion of the third floor.

Under Pennsylvania law, the question "whether a written contract is ambiguous is one for the court to decide as a matter of law. * * * Our review therefore is plenary." *Northbrook Insurance Co. v. Kuljian Corp.,* 690 F.2d 368, 371 (3d Cir.1982). "[T]he language of the policy may not be tortured to create ambiguities where none exist." *Houghton v. American Life Insurance Co.,* 692 F.2d 289, 291 (3d Cir.1982); see *Northbrook,* 690 F.2d at 372. If any ambiguity exists, however, it is well-settled that the ambiguity "*must* be construed against the insurer, and in a manner which is more favorable to coverage." *Houghton,* 692 F.2d at 291 (quoting *Buntin v. Continental Insurance Co.,* 583 F.2d 1201, 1207) (3d Cir.1978) (emphasis in original).

"A provision of an insurance policy is ambiguous if reasonably intelligent [persons] on considering it in the context of the entire policy would honestly differ as to its meaning." *Northbrook,* 690 F.2d at 372 (quoting *Celley v. Mutual Benefit Health & Accident Association,* 229 Pa.Super. 475, 481–82 (1974)). * * * In determining whether there is any ambiguity, the court need not confine its attention to the "four corners" of the contract but may consider external evidence. *Northbrook,* 690 F.2d at 371–72. *Celley,* 229 Pa.Super. at 482, states that the court may consider "whether alternative or more precise language, if used, would have put the matter beyond reasonable question."

Applying Pennsylvania law to the facts of this case, we conclude that the warranty here was ambiguous. Although the view of the insurance companies—that Vlastos stated that the floor was to be the janitor's exclusive province—is a possible construction, a reasonable person could have understood Vlastos to have warranted merely that her janitor lived on the third floor.

Even if one takes the warranty clause in isolation, it is questionable that the reading proffered by the insurance companies is the only plausible one. If Pinkney resided on the third floor, then it is not simply and unambiguously false to say that he occupied that floor, even assuming the existence of a significant competing or concurrent use. In response to the query "does a janitor occupy the third floor?" a categorical "no" surely would be misleading at best, and even a qualified "no" ("no, he occupies only part of it" or "no, a massage parlor occupies it as well") is strained. It seems that the most appropriate reply, making the relevant factual assumptions, would be a qualified affirmative ("yes, although he occupies it along with a massage parlor").

When the relevant language is examined in the context of the remainder of the policy, and in light of the alleged purposes for the insertion of the warranty, it becomes even more difficult to say that Vlastos unambiguously warranted that her janitor alone occupied the third floor.

It is significant that the warranty was not made in the course of a description of the various uses to which the building was being put. The policy did not make any warranties as to any other floors of the building. Thus, it would be reasonable to infer that the warranty evinced a concern that there be a resident janitor rather than an intent that the various floors of the building, such as the third floor, be put to relatively safe uses.

Although the actual reasons for the insertion of the warranty are not clear from the record, the insurers represented at trial that one reason was that a resident janitor decreases the risk of losses due to fire. See App. at 358, 372. This purpose of the provision would be fulfilled if Pinkney lived on the third floor, regardless of the proportion of this floor that was reserved for his sole use. Occupancy of the premises by a janitor might increase the likelihood that fire hazards would be taken care of promptly. It also might mean that there is a good chance that if a fire were to begin a responsible person would be on the scene to put it out or call the fire department, thus minimizing the damage from fires that do occur. A full-time resident janitor might also deter prowlers and vandals from entering the building. For reasons such as these, Vlastos could have assumed that the insurance companies looked kindly upon her having a resident janitor, without understanding that the insurance companies had any interest in whether the janitor occupied all or only part of the floor.

It is true that a second reason has been proposed for the insertion of the warranty. If a janitor occupied all of the third floor, then no occupant more dangerous—as a massage parlor perhaps is—would be there. Viewed in light of this possible motive, the warranty would have been intended to contemplate the occupancy of the entire third floor. Although this suggestion as to the purpose of the warranty is plausible, it is less obvious than the first suggested reasons, especially when it is recalled that the insurers did not request any assurance that extremely dangerous usages were absent from the other three floors of the building.

The conclusion that the warranty is ambiguous is buttressed by the consideration that the insurers easily could have precluded doubt by the addition of one word. Had the provision read: "Warranted that the 3rd Floor is occupied solely as Janitor's residence," then the question whether there would be a breach if a massage parlor operated in some of the space would have been unlikely to arise. Cf. *Celley, supra,* 229 Pa.Super. at 482.

Because the provision is ambiguous, under Pennsylvania law it must be construed in a manner favorable to insurance coverage. We therefore hold that Vlastos warranted only that a janitor resided on the third floor, not that there was no other occupancy of the floor.

If any jury issue existed at all, it was simply whether or not a janitor resided on the third floor at the time of the contract. The district court at several points indicated that the insurers had presented no evidence that Pinkney did not live on the third floor, and that it would not let the insurers go to the jury on this question.[1] On the other hand,

---

[1] *See* App. 357 ("You [the insurers] haven't produced any evidence that he [Pinkney] was not there or that he was not a janitor in the ordinary sense of the word * * * [the insurers']

the district court did instruct the jury that it could find "that nothing occupied the space at all. * * *" App. 391. There also is some uncertainty whether the district court, in considering the sufficiency of the evidence that Pinkney did not occupy the third floor, focused on the time of the fire as distinguished from the time that the parties entered into the contract. *See supra,* Part II. Accordingly, on remand the district court should clarify whether, in its view, there was a jury question whether Pinkney lived on the third floor at the time the contract was made. If it determines that there was sufficient evidence to go to the jury on this issue, then a new trial on the liability issue should be held. If there is no jury question, then under the facts of this case a new trial would be unwarranted, and the district should enter judgment for Vlastos on liability. * * *

NOTES AND QUESTIONS

1. *The History of Warranties.* Warranties first became prominent during the 18th century in marine insurance. For over one hundred years it had been the practice of shipowners and men of means to gather at Lloyds Coffee House in London, to arrange for insurance of ships and the cargo they carried. The shipowner would circulate a statement of the subject of the insurance and the amount of coverage desired on a *slip,* and each individual willing to insure a portion of the total coverage requested would write his name under this statement. Thus the insurers became known as *underwriters.* Often those who sought insurance for one voyage participated as underwriters of other voyages. As indicated earlier, eventually the process of screening and evaluating applications for coverage came to be known as "underwriting." See generally Antony Brown, Hazard Unlimited: The Story of Lloyds of London (1978).

As part of these insurance agreements, insureds often made statements or promises about certain characteristics of the ship or voyage in question, in order to inform the underwriters of the nature of the risks they were being asked to insure. In a series of decisions during this period, Lord Mansfield made it clear that the terms of an insurance *warranty*—a statement or promise by the policyholder in the policy itself—must be strictly complied with, or the policy is void:

> There is a material distinction between a warranty and a representation. A representation may be equitably and substantially answered; but a warranty must be strictly complied with. Supposing a warranty to sail on the first of August, and the ship did not sail until the second, the warranty would not be complied with. A warranty in a policy of insurance is a condition or a contingency, and unless that be performed, there is no contract. It is perfectly immaterial for what purpose a warranty is introduced; but being inserted, the contract does not exist unless it be literally complied with. Now, in the present case, the

---

only substantial contention * * * is that there was a massage parlor there"); App. 360 ("The only evidence I think that you've introduced, at least the evidence that I'm letting you go to the Jury on, is that there may have been a massage parlor there."). *See also* App. 358, 359. The insurers have not questioned that they bear the burden of proof.

condition was the sailing of the ship with a certain number of men; which not being complied with, the policy is void.

De Hahn v. Hartley, 1 T.R. 323 (1786). This strict approach likely reflected the expectations of those involved in the marine insurance business at that time. These parties were "repeat players" who dealt with each other on a frequent basis; and they were insuring ships and cargo that might be far away. The underwriters had to take the policyholder's word for what was being covered. The warranty was a method of disclosing the nature of the risk to be insured. And, of course, the nature of the risk in question was critical to the underwriters' decision whether to insure and what premium to charge. For these reasons, it would not be surprising if completely accurate disclosure of all the risks entailed in a particular voyage was expected.

2. *Immateriality?* The significance of Mansfield's warranty decisions was that the policyholder's breach of a warranty voided the policy even if that breach did not contribute to the loss in question, and even if it did not increase the risk that a loss would occur. Under the circumstances that gave rise to these warranties, however, the latter would rarely be true. Why? Consequently, the real issue in the cases Mansfield decided was whether a breach of warranty voided a policy when, although the breach increased the risk taken by the underwriters, it did not in fact contribute to the loss that occurred. For example, suppose that breach of a warranty that a ship is copper sheathed had nothing to do with its actual loss due to piracy. Does it seem appropriate to deny coverage in such a case?

Though it may seem inappropriate to take a "strict" approach and deprive a policyholder of coverage for an "immaterial breach," there are several arguments supporting the approach Mansfield took. First, the rule may well have reflected the moral code of those who frequented Lloyd's. Mansfield would simply have been honoring their expectations. Second, determining whether the breach of a warranty actually contributed to loss typically would be difficult—the loss often occurred at a distance, the damaged subject matter could be at the bottom of the ocean and unavailable for inspection, and often witnesses would have perished with the ship and cargo. On the other hand, almost any breach of warranty would have increased the risk of loss; why else include the warranty in the policy? Third, the cost of coverage for all would be reduced by a rule that created strong incentives to comply with warranties, particularly because monitoring compliance with warranties would be difficult. A rule requiring strict compliance might therefore have been necessary in order to minimize incentives for the occasional renegade to cheat, especially as the marine insurance business grew and the tight community of Lloyds began to dissolve.

In other words, Mansfield's strict approach to warranties helped to combat adverse selection and moral hazard. A policyholder who breached a warranty from the outset had adversely selected—i.e., posed a higher risk than he had represented that he posed. Similarly, the rule discouraged policyholders from reducing safety levels in a manner that breached a warranty because breach meant that coverage was voided even if the reduction in safety was not the cause of loss. In this way the rule helped to combat moral hazard.

2. THE TRANSFORMATION OF WARRANTY LAW: THE MODERN LAW OF MISREPRESENTATION AND NON-DISCLOSURE

Whatever may be said in favor of Mansfield's strict approach to warranties when applied to marine insurance, the argument for this approach is weaker in cases where the policyholder is not a sophisticated purchaser, insurers have multiple avenues for assessing policyholders' risk levels, or the parties' expectations about the significance of the insured's representations differ. The argument for the strict approach is of course weakest where the breach of warranty does not even increase the risk of loss. For example, a homeowner who purchases fire insurance and does not read the fine print of his policy might be astounded to learn that he had warranted that chamber music concerts would not be permitted on the premises, and that his breach of this warranty voided coverage even though that breach was not responsible for the destruction of his property. His situation is quite different from the shipowner who warrants the condition of his vessel.

The Emergence of Modern-Day Legislative Regulation of Warranties. Beginning in the 19th century, courts employed various common law strategies to mitigate the harshness of the law of warranties. See William Reynolds Vance, The History of the Development of the Warranty in Insurance Law, 20 Yale L.J. 523, 534 (1911). One approach—which presaged the dominant strategy today—was to interpret what might be a warranty as a "mere" representation by the policyholder. This approach—which the *Vlastos* court rejected in light of the policy's use of the term "warrant[s]"—would treat breached warranties as akin to factually incorrect statements made by one party in the bargaining process preceding a contact. Under ordinary contract law principles, such misrepresentations by one party only allow the other party to void the contract when the misrepresentation is material or fraudulent and induced justifiable reliance by the other party. See Restatement (Second) of Contracts, § 164(1) ("If a party's manifestation of assent is induced by either a fraudulent or a material misrepresentation by the other party upon which the recipient is justified in relying, the contract is voidable by the recipient.").

Courts also adopted a variety of other common law approaches to mitigating the harshness of the law governing warranties. Some courts, as exemplified in *Vlastos,* held that policyholders had in fact complied with warranties, which should be strictly construed against the insurer. Another approach also invoked by the *Vlastos* court, was to interpret warranties that seem to relate to future facts ("promissory warranties") as relating only to present facts ("affirmative warranties"). Under this approach, the warranty need only be complied with at the time it is made. For elaboration on these and other judicial strategies of interpretation, see Robert H. Jerry II & Douglas R. Richmond, Understanding Insurance Law 754–58 (5th ed. 2012); Robert E. Keeton & Alan I. Widiss, Insurance Law 665–67 (2d ed. 1988).

Today, the regulation of warranties is almost entirely a product of state statutory law. Virtually every state has enacted a statute governing the effect of insurance warranties. Susan Koehler Sullivan & David A. Ring, Recurring Issues in Rescission Cases, 42 Tort Trial &

Ins. Prac. L.J. 51 (2006). Although the statutes vary, their effect is generally to collapse the distinction between warranties and representations, so that breach of a warranty is treated no differently than an incorrect answer on an insurance application or any other misrepresentation by the policyholder. The result, as noted above, is that both breached warranties and misrepresentations render a policy voidable only if the breach or misrepresentation is material or fraudulent and the insurer justifiably relied on the misrepresentation in providing coverage. If employed in *Vlastos*, this approach would have allowed the policyholder to defeat rescission by showing that the partial use of the third floor by the massage parlor did not materially impact the risk insured or that the insurer did not in fact rely on the third floor being occupied exclusively by the janitor in issuing coverage.

State statutes governing insurance warranties vary in their scope. Some statutes apply to all forms of insurance, others limit the forms to which they apply; and some apply only to statements made in applications, while others apply to statements in policies as well as in applications. In some states the strict compliance rule still applies in marine insurance while in others it has been limited even in that field. Compare *Wilburn Boat Co. v. Fireman's Fund Ins. Co.*, 348 U.S. 310 (1955) (applying the liberal Texas rule rather than the "literal performance" requirement of federal admiralty law), with *Commercial Union Ins. Co. v. Flagship Marine Servs., Inc.*, 190 F.3d 26, 31–32 (2d Cir. 1999) (discussing New York's strict warranty rule without any requirement of materiality for maritime insurance contracts).

The future of the law governing misrepresentation and warranties—as well as numerous other features of insurance law—may be substantially influenced by the ongoing (as of 2015) American Law Institute's ("ALI") Restatement of the Law of Liability Insurance ("RLLI") project. The RLLI seeks to clearly describe the law of liability insurance as it presently stands or might plausibly be stated by a court. Although the RLLI is focused on liability insurance, it also addresses various more general features of insurance law, including the law of warranties and misrepresentations. The RLLI mirrors most state statutes in collapsing the distinction between breached warranties and misrepresentations and imposing materiality and reliance requirements. See RLLI § 7. But as we will see below, preliminary versions of the RLLI also break some new ground on various elements of this issue.

The Meaning of the Materiality Requirement. As described above, in general insurers can only void coverage on the basis of either a breached warranty or misrepresentation if the breach or misrepresentation was material or fraudulent. But state statutes vary in how they define what exactly "material" means. Many statutes provide that a breach is material if it *increases the risk* of loss—that is, makes the overall risk posed by the applicant greater than it would have been if the representation had been true, regardless of whether this particular risk was involved in the actual loss. See, e.g., Mich. Comp. Laws Ann. § 500.2218. By contrast, a minority of states require that the breach *contribute to loss*—that the risk which actually materialized in loss be the one about which there was a misrepresentation. See, e.g., Kan. Stat. Ann. § 40–418. Under this approach, a ship owner who falsely represented that his ship was copper sheathed and subsequently suffered a loss due to piracy would be entitled to coverage. Similarly, this approach would not permit a life insurer to rescind coverage of a policyholder who misrepresented his age on his application but was then killed in an airplane crash. Some statutes sidestep this issue by simply requiring that the breach be "material" without defining that term. See, e.g., Wis. Stat. Ann. § 631.11.

The Meaning of the Reliance Requirement and Its Relationship to Materiality. Another issue that commonly arises in misrepresentation and warranty cases is whether an objective or subjective approach should be used to assess the closely related elements of materiality and justifiable reliance. Since the party allegedly victimized by a misrepresentation is the insurer, the issue here is whether the insurer should be able to prevail if it shows that the misrepresented fact was material to it and that it relied on this misrepresentation in issuing coverage, or whether it should have to show that the misrepresented fact would have been material to an objectively reasonably insurer, which would have relied on that fact. In most settings the difference will be negligible, but in some cases the insurer's underwriting or rating standards may be sufficiently more exacting than the norm that the choice will be significant. The classic case on the issue is *Penn Mutual Life Insurance Co. v. Mechanics' Savings Bank & Trust Co.,* 72 Fed. 413 (6th Cir.1896), which adopted an objective test in an opinion written by Judge (later President and still later Chief Justice) Taft. For recent applications, see *Federal Insurance Co. v. HPSC, Inc.,* 480 F.3d 26, 33 (1st Cir. 2007); *Palisades Safety & Insurance Ass'n v. Bastien,* 175 N.J. 144 (2003). See generally Jeffrey E. Thomas, 3–16 New Appleman on Insurance Law Library Edition § 16.03[1][d] (Lexis 2012). The RLLI explicitly adopts an objective standard. RLLI § 9. Does an objective test treat the insurer fairly, particularly when it may have more exacting standards than others in the industry? On the other hand, if a subjective test is adopted, there may not be much left of the distinction between materiality and reliance.

The Degree of Materiality and/or Reliance Required. Another common issue involves the strength of the materiality and reliance requirements, rather than their definitions. At one extreme, the insurer might be required to show that the risk misrepresented was so central to the coverage provided that under no circumstances would a policy have been issued if the insured had made an accurate disclosure. At the other extreme, the insurer might be required to show merely that the fact misrepresented increased the insurer's risk and that knowledge of that fact would have been relevant to the decision about whether to issue a policy, or whether to issue it on the terms and at the rate offered. The RLLI takes an intermediate position on this issue, defining materiality to require that a reasonable insurer would not have issued the policy, or would have issued the policy on substantially different terms, in the absence of the misrepresentation. RLLI § 9.

Occasionally the issue can be sidestepped with something like a statutory or judicial presumption. For example, it is well-settled that a few recurring kinds of misrepresentations normally are material. See, e.g., *Sovereign Life Ins. Co. of Cal. v. Rewald,* 601 F. Supp. 1489 (D.

Haw. 1985) (misrepresentation of the applicant's net worth on a life insurance application); *Swihart v. Universal Underwriters Life Ins. Co.*, 669 N.W.2d 260 (Iowa Ct. App. 2003) (applicant signed application stating that he was not under care of physician but in fact had seen a physician several times in the past 12 months).

Unintentional Misrepresentations, Disproportionate Forfeiture, and Proportional Remedies. Under ordinary contract law principles, a material misrepresentation permits the affected party to void a contract even if the misrepresentation was entirely unintentional and non-negligent. See Restatement (Second) of Contracts, § 162. This can result in "disproportionate forfeiture" to a policyholder, particularly when the misrepresentation, while material, would not have completely changed the nature of the coverage offered or price charged. In such cases, the policyholder may forfeit all of the benefits of coverage due to an innocent mistake on the insurance application that, while material, might still have made only a small difference in the policy received or price charged.

Consider, for instance, a person who told her life insurance agent, in response to an application question, that she had not been diagnosed with a disease or condition in the past five years. Assume that she forgot that she had, in fact, been diagnosed as having a non-serious skin disease three years earlier. Assume also that people having that skin disease have an elevated risk of experiencing heart trouble at some point in their life and that, for that reason, the insurer's practice is to charge 10% higher premiums to individuals with this particular skin condition. The traditional approach to such a case would result in the insurer maintaining the right to void coverage and refuse to pay any proceeds to the policyholder's beneficiary if she died. But the result seems to impose a disproportionate forfeiture on the policyholder (and her beneficiaries), who are left without any recovery despite an innocent and seemingly minor mistake.

The *value* of preventing disproportionate forfeiture influences a number of insurance law doctrines, including the law of misrepresentation. See Bob Works, Excusing Nonoccurrence of Insurance Policy Conditions in Order to Avoid Disproportionate Forfeiture: Claims-Made Formats as a Test Case, 5 Conn. Ins. L.J. 505 (1999); Eugene R. Anderson, Richard G. Tuttle & Susannah Crego, Draconian Forfeitures of Insurance: Commonplace, Indefensible, and Unnecessary, 65 Fordham L. Rev. 825 (1996). Technically, though, the *doctrine* of disproportionate forfeiture is formally only applicable when a policyholder fails to comply with an express condition of coverage, a situation that is not implicated by most misrepresentation disputes. See Restatement (Second) of Contracts § 229 ("To the extent that the non-occurrence of a condition would cause disproportionate forfeiture, a court may excuse the non-occurrence of that condition unless its occurrence was a material part of the agreed exchange.").

The strongest response to the concern that the traditional approach to warranties and misrepresentations creates a risk of disproportionate forfeiture is to require that a misrepresentation/breached warranty involve some sort of intentional or reckless behavior on the part of the policyholder in order for the insurer to be able to void the policy on that basis. For instance, a provision in federal healthcare reform (i.e.

"Obamacare" or "The Affordable Care Act") preempts all state law on misrepresentations and warranties with respect to health insurance and prohibits the rescission of health insurance policies unless the policyholder engaged in fraud or an intentional misrepresentation of a material fact. See Patient Protection and Affordable Care Act § 2712, 42 U.S.C. § 300gg–12.

An alternative approach is to employ a more proportional remedy than rescission in the case of certain unintentional misrepresentations. Under an early draft of § 11 of the RLLI, for instance, in the case of misrepresentations that are (i) neither intentional nor reckless, and (ii) where the insurer would have issued the policy at a higher premium in the absence of the misrepresentation, the insurer must pay the claim in full, but may deduct from the payout the premiums that would have been charged had the policyholder accurately represented the facts. The United Kingdom recently embraced a similar approach to this issue, in the Consumer Insurance (Disclosure and Representations) Act of 2012. Like the RLLI, the UK Act provides that, in the case of a careless but innocent misrepresentation, where the insurer would have issued the same policy at a different premium, the insurer must pay the claim and cannot rescind coverage. Unlike the RLLI approach, however, the UK Act permits insurers to reduce claims payouts by the ratio of the discounted premium paid to the actual premiums that would have been paid in the absence of a misrepresentation. Id. Which approach is more policyholder friendly?

All of these approaches deviate from the conventional approach to misrepresentation and warranties when the policyholder commits an honest or merely negligent error. Should proportional remedies also be available in cases where the policyholder intentionally or recklessly misrepresents a fact to the insurer, but the fact would not have been sufficiently important to the carrier that it would have completely refused to issue coverage? A number of state statutes provide for proportional remedies in just such a case: in some states, when the insured has misrepresented her age in an application for life insurance, the policy is not voided, but the beneficiary is entitled only to the benefit that would have been payable if the decedent's age had been accurately stated. See, e.g., Va. Code Ann. § 38.2–3306.

Distinguishing Warranties and Misrepresentations from Coverage Provisions. Some statutes apply to warranties and representations, but not to what are typically referred to as *coverage provisions*—conditions and exclusions that specify the terms of coverage. As a result, it may still be possible for an insurer to phrase a prerequisite to coverage as a condition or exclusion that achieves the same purpose as a warranty, and thereby avoid any materiality or reliance requirements at all. A key question in this circumstance is how to distinguish between warranties and representations (which are subject to materiality and reliance requirements) on the one hand, and coverage provisions (which are not) on the other. Unfortunately, that distinction is sometimes elusive. Each of these different provisions in some sense state conditions precedent to coverage or constitute descriptions of the risk insured. Some courts therefore look to see whether the provision in question is in the verbal form of a warranty, as distinguished, for example, from a condition precedent, and reach a decision on this basis. For instance, in *Omaha*

Sky Divers Parachute Club, Inc. v. Ranger Insurance Co., 189 Neb. 610 (1973), the court construed a clause in the policy excluding coverage of loss "occurring while the aircraft is operated in flight by other than the pilot or pilots" as a coverage provision. A different approach holds that warranties and representations apply to *potential* causes of loss, whereas coverage provisions apply to *actual* causes. See N.Y. Ins. Law § 3106. Under this approach, a policy provision that there is no coverage against loss by fire *while* gasoline is stored on the insured premises would constitute a warranty, no matter how phrased; and a provision that there is no coverage against loss by fire *caused* by the ignition of gasoline stored on the premises would constitute a coverage provision.

Non-Disclosure. The problem of non-disclosure of material facts, as distinguished from affirmative misrepresentation, poses slightly different issues. Outside of the context of marine insurance—where a more stringent obligation to disclose material information still tends to prevail—insurers can only void a contract on the basis of non-disclosure by demonstrating *scienter*. See, e.g., *Cora Pub, Inc. v. Cont'l Cas. Co.*, 619 F.2d 482, 487 (5th Cir. 1980). In effect, innocent failure to disclose does not make the policy voidable. See Restatement (Second) of Contracts, §§ 161 & 164 (generally requiring lack of good faith or similar forms of scienter for non-disclosure of a fact to allow the other party to void a contract on that basis). An insurer may be able to sidestep this problem by inquiring about the subject matter, and thereby either eliciting a knowingly false answer (and therefore an affirmative misrepresentation) or at least putting the applicant on notice that the subject of the inquiry is material.

Under the modern practice of asking relatively detailed questions on insurance applications, the difficulty of proving knowing non-disclosure of a material fact rather than innocent but affirmative misrepresentation can be reduced in this way. This problem cannot be completely eliminated, however, because there may still be gaps between the cracks of questions asked, and material facts may fall into these cracks. Moreover, fashioning applications to produce misrepresentation rather than non-disclosure may require a lengthy, potentially off-putting series of questions on applications. Yet, incomplete answers to open-ended questions may be more easily forgiven than false answers to detailed questions. In close cases the common sense morality of a jury may well be more likely to find an affirmative misrepresentation to be blameworthy than the failure to fully and completely answer a question that the insurer could have phrased to elicit a complete response.

NOTES AND QUESTIONS

1. *Proving or Disproving Materiality.* An applicant (now deceased) had answered "no" to a question on a life insurance application that asked, "Have you been treated by a physician during the last five years?", when in fact he had been treated for high blood pressure on two occasions during the period. In a jurisdiction with a statute making a misrepresentation material if it "increases the risk assumed by the insurer," as counsel for the insurer how would you go about proving materiality and reliance? As counsel for the insured, how would you attempt to refute the insurer's proofs? What kinds of information would you want to discover from the

insurer's files? How would your answers to these questions change if the jurisdiction's statute defined a statement to be material only if it "contributed to the loss"?

2. *Rationale for Increase-in-Risk Test.* Should application of the increase-of-risk test to innocent misrepresentations be regarded as risking disproportionate forfeiture, as an overinclusive but useful method of combating adverse selection, as an incentive to applicants to ensure that what they say on an application is accurate, or as an inducement to say as little as possible? See C. Edgar Sentell, The Misrepresentation Defense in Life and Disability Insurance Cases: The Issue of Causation, 52 Fed'n Def. & Corp. Couns. Q. 277 (2002). In light of your consideration of these issues, do you think the increase-in-risk test or the contributed-to-loss test is a better approach to defining materiality?

3. *Issuance for a Greater Premium.* An applicant (now deceased) had answered "no" to a question on a life insurance application that asked, "Do you smoke cigarettes?", when in fact she smoked two packs of cigarettes per day. The insurer issued a policy at the no-smoker premium rate. A "misrepresentation" is defined by statute in that jurisdiction as a false "statement as to past or present fact, made to the insurer . . . at or before the making of the insurance contract as an inducement to the making thereof." The statute provides that the contract may be rescinded if the misrepresentation is "material," and provides that it is material if "knowledge by the insurer of the facts misrepresented would have led to a refusal by the insurer to make such contract." The insured argues that the misrepresentation is not material, because the insurer would have issued a policy (though for a higher premium) even if the misrepresentation had not been made. How should the case be resolved? How would it be resolved under the RLLI approach?

In *Mutual Benefit Life Insurance Co. v. JMR Electronics Corp.*, 848 F.2d 30 (2d Cir.1988), the court confronting these facts denied recovery to the policyholder. The court reasoned that a policy issued at a higher rate would have been a different contract and therefore would not satisfy the "such contract" requirement of the statute. The courts of other states tend increasingly to interpret their statutes this way as well, holding that a misrepresentation that would have resulted in issuance of the same policy for a higher premium is material. See, e.g., *Oade v. Jackson Nat'l Life Ins. Co. of Mich.*, 465 Mich. 244 (2001); *Old Line Life Ins. Co. v. Superior Court*, 229 Cal. App. 3d 1600 (1991).

4. *Rationale for a* Scienter *Requirement for Misrepresentation.* To what extent should the law require some sort of intentional misconduct by policyholders before allowing insurers to rescind or cancel coverage on the basis of a misrepresentation? For example, should a policyholder who genuinely forgets that he consulted a physician about chest pains two and one-half years before applying for life insurance and therefore falsely answers a question on the application be denied coverage completely? Do policyholders appreciate the potential that such innocent misstatements on their applications may have such draconian results? Does placing risk on policyholders that unintentional misrepresentations may result in non-coverage in the event of loss unduly expose them to the very risk they were seeking to avoid in purchasing coverage? On the other hand, what do you think insurers' main objection would be to imposing a *scienter* requirement for rescinding coverage? How would insurers go about proving that a

particular misrepresentation was intentional and not innocent or merely negligent? To what extent does the RLLI's proportional remedies approach address this problem?

Neill v. Nationwide Mutual Fire Insurance Company

Court of Appeals of Arkansas, 2003.
81 Ark. App. 67.

■ ANDREE LAYTON ROAF, JUDGE.

Appellant Lamar Neill's home was damaged by a fire, and he filed a claim with his homeowners' insurance company, appellee Nationwide Mutual Fire Insurance Company. After finding out that Neill had previous fire losses that were not disclosed in his application, Nationwide denied Neill's claim and filed an action for declaratory relief, seeking to void the policy. Neill counterclaimed for breach of contract and bad faith. The trial court granted summary judgment in favor of Nationwide based on the misrepresentation in the application and voided the policy. On appeal, Neill argues that the trial court erred in granting summary judgment to Nationwide and voiding the policy. We reverse and remand.

On November 18, 1993, Neill met with a Nationwide agent, Leon Anderson, to apply for homeowners' insurance for a mobile home. According to Neill, Anderson asked him several questions and typed in Neill's answers on the computer, such as whether he had ever been sued and whether he had ever filed bankruptcy. Neill testified in his deposition that Anderson did not ask him about any previous fire losses, or if he did ask him, Neill stated that he must not have understood the question because he would not have replied that he had no prior losses. After Anderson finished asking the questions, the application for insurance was printed out, and Neill testified that he signed it without reading it, as he assumed that it contained the answers he had given to Anderson. Above his signature, the application contained a clause that Neill declared that the facts in the application were true and that he was requesting the company to issue the policy in reliance thereon. It is undisputed that on that application, under a section titled "Past Losses," the answer "None" was typed.

On April 16, 1997, Neill's home was severely damaged by fire, and he made a claim for insurance benefits with Nationwide. In the course of its investigation, Nationwide learned from Neill that he had had three previous fire losses. Nationwide denied Neill's claim, stating that he made a material misrepresentation in his application, and filed a complaint for declaratory judgment, seeking to have the policy declared void *ab initio*. The trial court granted summary judgment to Nationwide based on the misrepresentation, and Neill appeals from that ruling. * * *

It is a well-settled proposition that where the facts have been truthfully stated by an insured to the soliciting agent, but by fraud, negligence, or mistake, the facts are misstated in the application to the insurer, the insurer cannot rely on the misstatements in avoidance of liability, if the agent was acting within his real or apparent authority, and there is no fraud or collusion on the part of the insured. *Interstate Fire Ins. Co. of Chattanooga, Tenn. v. Ingram,* 256 Ark. 986 (1974); *General Agents Ins. Co. v. St. Paul Ins. Co.,* 22 Ark.App. 46 (1987); *Time Ins. Co. v. Graves,* 21 Ark.App. 273 (1987). However, in *Carmichael v. Nationwide Life Ins. Co.,* 305 Ark. 549 (1991), the court also stated that a person is bound under the law to know the contents of the papers he signs and that he cannot excuse himself by saying that he did not know what the papers contained.

In *Graves, supra,* an insurance agent, who knew the Graveses and knew that Mrs. Graves had been operated on for cancer, told the insureds that he could provide her with coverage for her pre-existing condition. The Graveses testified that the agent filled out the application and that they truthfully answered each question asked by the agent, but that they did not read the application before they signed it. One question asked on the application, whether the insured had previously been treated for cancer, was left unanswered. Subsequently, an amendment to the application was received by the agent containing the unanswered question. The amendment already had the word "no" typed on it, and the agent testified that he got Mr. Graves to sign it. The amendment stated that Mr. Graves hereby amends "my application." Mr. Graves testified that the amendment contained his signature, but that he did not remember signing it. The court stated that the jury could have found that his signature did not constitute an untruthful statement as to Mrs. Graves's pre-existing condition. *Id.*

In *Ingram, supra,* the agent asked Ingram questions and filled out the application, which Ingram signed. Although there were several questions answered incorrectly, Ingram testified that he answered each question that the agent asked correctly, so that the agent must have inaccurately recorded his answers. The court stated that Interstate was not entitled to a directed verdict under the evidence in that case and that there was no error in instructing the jury that where the facts were truthfully stated to an agent, but by fraud, negligence, or mistake, the agent misstated the information, the company cannot avoid liability if the agent had authority and there is no fraud or collusion on the part of the insured. *Id.*

In *Carmichael, supra,* the insured's beneficiary appealed from an order of summary judgment in favor of the insurer. The evidence showed that the agent asked questions and recorded Mr. Carmichael's answers on the application. Mr. Carmichael then signed the application. Based on misrepresentations in the policy that Mr. Carmichael did not suffer from diabetes, the insurer refused to pay the benefits under the policy. The appellant, Mrs. Carmichael, argued that the agent must have failed to ask her husband the question or that the agent must have inaccurately recorded his answer, because her husband had suffered from diabetes for many years and would not have responded negatively to the question. However, the court stated that there was no evidence to sustain Mrs. Carmichael's allegations and that the only person with personal knowledge of what transpired was the agent, because Mr. Carmichael had died. *Id.* The agent, in his affidavit, averred that he had asked every question on the application and that he had correctly recorded Mr. Carmichael's answers. The court noted that Mr. Carmichael had signed a certification that the information in the application was true and stated that this was at least probative evidence of his misrepresentation. *Id.* Because Mrs. Carmichael offered no evidence to rebut any of the assertions made by the insurer, the court found that summary judgment was appropriate. *Id.*

Nationwide relies heavily on *Carmichael, supra,* in support of its argument that summary judgment was properly granted to them in this case. However, in *Carmichael,* the insured was not alive to testify as to the circumstances surrounding the application process, the agent testified that he had asked every question and correctly recorded the insured's answers, and the appellant offered no other evidence to rebut the insurer's assertion that the insured misrepresented a material fact in the application. As noted by the court, the appellant "would have the jury consider the credibility of a witness whose testimony is uncontroverted." 305 Ark. at 553. Here, Neill is able to testify and has testified that he was not asked about prior losses by the agent. In contrast, Nationwide has not presented evidence by its agent that the question was asked and answered incorrectly by Neill.

Pursuant to the foregoing authorities, we find that there is a fact question as to whether Nationwide asked and correctly recorded Neill's answer about previous losses. The fact that Neill signed the certification that the information was true is merely probative evidence of his misrepresentation and not dispositive of the case. Thus, summary judgment in this instance was not appropriate, and we reverse and remand.

Reversed and remanded.

NOTES AND QUESTIONS

1. *A Duty to Read?* On the one hand, the court in *Neill* seems to accept the rule that the applicant cannot excuse himself by saying that he did not know the contents of the papers he signs. On the other hand, the court reverses the lower court's grant of summary judgment to the insurer, even though the application contained a false statement. Are these two positions consistent? Can they be reconciled by the rule that if the applicant answers the agent's questions truthfully, the insurer cannot rely on the agent's misstatements, unless there is also fraud or collusion by the applicant? Consider the following scenarios: a) The applicant is not asked about the fact at issue, the agent completes the application with a false answer, and the applicant signs but does not read the completed application. This is apparently what the applicant contended had occurred in *Neill,* and what the court seemed to hold would have excused Neill if it were proved to be true. See *State Farm Mut. Auto. Ins. Co. v. Bridges*, 36 So. 3d 1142 (La. App. 2 Cir. 2010); RLLI § 9, reptr. note c ("In the insurance context, it has long been held that false information entered into an insurance application by agent of the insurer will be imputed to the insurer unless the insured has reason to know that the agent is attempting to defraud the insurer."). But see *Brennan v. Hall*, 904 N.E.2d 383, 387 (Ind. Ct. App. 2009) (holding that a material misrepresentation in an application entitles the insurer to rescind coverage even if the policyholder answers truthfully and the error is the fault of the agent, so long as the policyholder has had an opportunity to review and sign the application). b) The applicant is asked about the fact at issue and answers truthfully, the agent says "that won't matter," completes the application with a false answer,

and the applicant signs and does not read the completed application. See *Ward v. Durham Life Ins. Co.*, 90 N.C. App. 286 (1988). c) The applicant reads the completed application, comments on the false answer, and is told that it is "not important." See *Olson v. Bankers Life Ins. Co.*, 63 Wash. 2d 547 (1964).

On the other hand, sometimes the applicant completes the application himself and the agent fails to read it carefully. In *Pum v. Wisconsin Physicians Service Insurance Corp.*, 298 Wis. 2d 497 (Ct. App. 2006), the court held that the agent might be liable to the applicant for negligence in this situation if the insurer were permitted to rescind the policy for misrepresentation.

2. *Mistakes in Applications by Insurance Agents.* It is obvious why a policyholder such as Neill might have had an incentive to lie in his insurance application about the previous fire losses he had experienced. But why might the insurance agent in *Neill* have had an incentive to fabricate the insurance application, as alleged by the policyholder? Even in the absence of any such intent, insurance agents may of course make mistakes in filling out applications and accurately transcribing policyholder responses to questions. How well can judges and juries distinguish between cases where insurance agents incorrectly fill out insurance applications, and cases in which policyholders incorrectly state material facts to their agents? The case law is replete with such disputes. See, e.g., *N.E. Ins. Co. v. Young*, 26 A.3d 794 (Sup. Jud. Ct. Me. 2011); *Hillery v. Allstate Indem. Co.*, 705 F. Supp. 2d 1343 (S.D. Ala. 2010); *Chism v. Protective Life Ins. Co.*, 290 Kan. 645 (2010).

3. *Post-Claim Underwriting.* Why might an insurer have an incentive to conduct a relatively cursory review of an application at the time it is submitted, but a more thorough review after a claim is made? Some commentators have charged that, after a large claim is made, insurance companies sometimes look hard for inaccuracies on an application for coverage in order to develop a misrepresentation defense, a strategy termed post-claim underwriting. See Thomas C. Cady & Georgia Lee Gates, Post Claim Underwriting, 102 W. Va. L. Rev. 809 (2000). A prominent investigation and hearing by the House Committee on Energy and Commerce in 2009 found numerous instances of such post-claim underwriting in health insurance. Terminations of Individual Health Policies by Ins. Companies: Hearing Before the Subcomm. on Oversight and Investigations of the Comm. on Energy and Commerce, 111th Cong. (2009). This finding was used to buttress the aforementioned provision in Obamacare prohibiting rescissions except in the case of fraud or intentional misrepresentation of a material fact.

If an insurer could easily have discovered a false answer or half-truth in an insurance application at the time it was filed, should a misrepresentation defense still be available at the time a claim is submitted? The "inquiry notice" rule provides that, if the insured furnishes reasonably complete answers that would lead an objectively reasonable insurer to the information it seeks through diligent follow-up search, then there has been no misrepresentation or concealment. See, e.g., *Allied Prop. & Cas. Ins. Co. v. Good*, 938 N.E.2d 227, 232 (Ind. Ct. App. 2010); *Cullen v. Valley Forge Life Ins. Co.*, 161 N.C. App. 570 (2003); *W. Coast Life Ins. Co. v. Hoar*, 558 F.3d 1151, 1159–60 (10th Cir. 2009). How should this result be reached—by a holding that there has been no misrepresentation, or that although there has been, the insurer has not justifiably relied upon it? Note, however, that not all courts have adopted the inquiry notice rule, and that some apply it only where the application contains "suspicious information." See, e.g., *Chawla v. Transamerica Occidental Life Ins. Co.*, 440 F.3d 639 (4th Cir. 2006). Some courts have gone further than the inquiry-notice rule, holding that a policyholder may be able to press a tort claim of intentional infliction of emotional distress against her insurer on the basis of alleged post-claim underwriting. See *Hailey v. Cal. Physicians' Serv.*, 158 Cal. App. 4th 452 (2007).

State legislatures and regulators have also played a role in limiting the perceived risk of post-claim underwriting. For instance, numerous states require by regulation certain forms of up-front underwriting by long-term care insurers and disclosures that coverage may be rescinded on the basis of material misrepresentations. See Nat'l Ass'n of Ins. Comm'rs, Long-Term Care Ins. Model Regulation 641 (2010). And, as we will study in more detail in Chapter Five, special incontestability rules designed to limit the risk of post-claim underwriting apply in the context of life insurance. Does the court's discussion of the *Carmichael* case provide any insight into why legislatures and regulators have devoted special attention to the risk of post-claim underwriting in the context of life and long-term care insurance?

Why is post-claim underwriting generally viewed as problematic? Is there an argument that it is efficient for insurers to limit their costly efforts to verify the accuracy of insurance applications to cases where the outcome of such an investigation will actually be consequential? And, in any event, don't insurers have a legitimate interest in denying coverage based on material misrepresentations that they only discover once a claim is made. See Gary Schuman, Post-Claim Underwriting: A Life & Health Insurer's Right to Investigate or Bad Faith?, 45 Tort Trial & Ins. Prac. L.J. 697 (2010). Or is there something wrong with insurers accepting premiums and purporting to provide coverage, but only undertaking efforts to confirm relevant information once it matters to their bottom line?

4. *HIV and the Law of Misrepresentation*. In order to limit the risk of adverse selection, life insurers have long attempted to screen out individuals who have been exposed to the Human Immunodeficiency Virus (HIV), which causes AIDS. See Alan I. Widiss, To Insure or Not to Insure Persons Infected with the Virus That Causes AIDS, 77 Iowa L. Rev. 1617 (1992). States generally permit such testing, subject to certain procedural safeguards, such as requiring that results be kept confidential and precluding the use of sexual orientation as the basis for determining which applicants are required to submit to HIV testing. See, e.g., Cal. Ins. Code §§ 799–799.09; Fla. Stat. Ann. § 627.429; N.Y. Pub. Health Law §§ 2780–87.

In addition to administering their own blood tests as a condition of coverage, insurers often ask questions in the insurance application that relate to potential exposure to HIV. The case law generally suggests that insurers must ask highly targeted questions if they want to reserve their right to rescind coverage due to a misrepresentation. For example, in *Waxse v. Reserve Life Insurance Co.*, 248 Kan. 582 (1991), the applicant did not disclose that he had tested HIV positive in response to a question asking whether he had any blood disorder or knew of any "impairment" of his health or physical condition. The court held that this answer was not a misrepresentation because being HIV positive was not an impairment of health and granted summary judgment against the insurer. How would you evaluate the argument that the insurer was entitled to rescind the policy on the basis of non-disclosure? What, if anything, would you need to know about his state of mind to answer this question? How likely is it that such information will be available?

There is little doubt that a false answer to the question whether the applicant has tested positive for HIV, assuming proof of materiality, will void coverage. See, e.g., *Golden Rule Ins. Co. v. Hopkins*, 788 F. Supp. 295 (S.D. Miss. 1991). Is it appropriate, however, to require an insurer to ask questions as precisely as the court in *Waxse* apparently would in order to generate a finding of misrepresentation by the applicant? Other courts are more willing to permit a finding of material misrepresentation in cases involving HIV, at least when the misrepresentation is clear. See, e.g., *Berkshire Life Ins. Co. v. Owens*, 910 F. Supp. 132 (S.D.N.Y. 1996); *Zachary Trading, Inc. v. Nw. Mutual Life Ins. Co.*, 668 F. Supp. 343 (S.D.N.Y. 1987). But outcomes tend to turn on the nature of the questions asked and answered on the application. Asking whether the applicant currently has a "disease" is much less likely to elicit an answer that the courts will permit a jury to find false than asking whether the applicant has visited a physician during the last year or asking what blood testing has been done during that period. Similarly, asking whether the applicant is in good health to the best of his knowledge is much less likely to elicit an answer that a court will find clearly false than asking whether the applicant suffers from an immune system deficiency.

MacKenzie v. Prudential Insurance Company of America

United States Court of Appeals, Sixth Circuit, 1969.
411 F.2d 781.

■ COMBS, CIRCUIT JUDGE.

Plaintiff-appellant was beneficiary under an insurance policy written by defendant-appellee on the life of her decedent, Jerome F. MacKenzie. After Mr. MacKenzie's death in August, 1966,[1] Prudential refused to pay over the proceeds of the policy, contending that MacKenzie had in legal effect made material misrepresentations concerning his health when he accepted delivery of the policy. This action was brought in state court in Louisville, Kentucky, but was removed to the United States District Court by reason of diversity of citizenship. The district court granted summary judgment for the defendant, and the plaintiff appeals. We affirm. * * *

On August 10, 1964, MacKenzie made initial application with Prudential for a $40,000 decreasing term life insurance policy. The application was completed and signed by MacKenzie in the presence of Dr. Robert McGrath, who had examined MacKenzie at Prudential's request.

The application called for MacKenzie to disclose whether he had ever been treated for or had any known indication of "heart trouble or

---

[1] The cause of death was pulmonary embolus which developed after decedent was injured in a fall from a bicycle.

murmur, high blood pressure, or abnormal pulse?" To this, he answered, "No." He was also asked to disclose any visits to physicians in the preceding five years. In answering this question, MacKenzie listed three visits to doctors, two of which were for routine physical examinations and the other for removal of a cyst. The application provided that no insurance would take effect unless "all of the answers to the questions in Part 1 and Part 2 of the application continue to be true and complete answers as of the date of the delivery of the policy * * *."

So far as is known, the above representations were true when MacKenzie signed the application. Dr. McGrath found his blood pressure to be 140/78 (within normal limits). However, sometime before September 17, 1964, the date the policy was delivered, MacKenzie suffered a chest bruise. This was apparently a minor injury, but he sought medical assistance from another doctor on September 16. Upon examining MacKenzie, the doctor found that his blood pressure was 170/100 (higher than normal). He was given a prescription for Naturetin, a diuretic prescribed to decrease blood pressure, and advised to get a complete check-up.

When the policy was delivered to MacKenzie by Prudential's agent on the evening of September 17, he said nothing about his recent visit to a doctor or the increase in his blood pressure. He did have the policy decreased to $20,000 because of anticipated difficulty in paying premiums, but no further statement was made concerning the application.[2]

The affidavits and answers to interrogatories appended to Prudential's motion for summary judgment establish without contradiction that Prudential accepted the risk in reliance upon the truthfulness of the answers in the application and that, if MacKenzie had volunteered the truth about his blood pressure, the policy would not have been delivered. One of Prudential's underwriters stated in interrogatories that, if the change in MacKenzie's condition had been divulged, the company either would have refused to issue the policy or would have increased the premium.

Under Kentucky law, which under the *Erie* doctrine is controlling here, misrepresentations sufficient to prevent recovery on an insurance policy must be material to the risk *or* fraudulently made. Ky.Rev.Stat. § 304.656 (1962); *Mills v. Reserve Life Ins. Co.,* Ky., 335 S.W.2d 955 (1960); *The Maccabees v. Covert,* 302 Ky. 481 (1946); *Prudential Ins. Co. of America v. Lampley,* 297 Ky. 495 (1944). Prudential contends and we hold that, since the increase in the blood pressure reading was obviously material, no fraud need be shown. The Kentucky court held in *Maccabees, supra,* that "[t]he standard by which materiality is to be determined is the action which insurance companies generally would have taken on the application, when acting in accordance with their usual practice and usage, if the truth had been told." See also *Northwestern Mut. Life Ins. Co. v. Yoe's Ex'r,* 283 Ky. 406 (1940); *Commonwealth Life Ins. Co. v. Goodknight's Adm'r,* 212 Ky. 763 (1926).

---

[2] Prudential's agent who delivered the policy, Irvin G. Walter, said that he asked about health changes, but this was contradicted by Mrs. MacKenzie. For the purpose of this appeal, we construe the facts in favor of appellant.

So, the decisive question is whether MacKenzie had a duty to divulge his change in health the breach of which would amount to a material misrepresentation. The Supreme Court has spoken on this question in *Stipcich v. Metropolitan Life Ins. Co.,* 277 U.S. 311, 316–317 (1928):

> "[E]ven the most unsophisticated person must know that, in answering the questionnaire and submitting it to the insurer, he is furnishing the data on the basis of which the company will decide whether, by issuing a policy, it wishes to insure him. If, while the company deliberates, he discovers facts which make portions of his application no longer true, the most elementary spirit of fair dealing would seem to require him to make a full disclosure. If he fails to do so the company may, despite its acceptance of the application, decline to issue a policy, [cases cited] or, if a policy has been issued, it has a valid defense to a suit upon it." [Citations omitted.]

Although the Kentucky Court of Appeals has not considered this specific issue, the rule of *Stipcich* has received rather universal acceptance—and we have no reason to believe Kentucky would not adhere to it. See *New York Life Ins. Co. v. Gay,* 36 F.2d 634 (6th Cir.1929). Accordingly, Mr. MacKenzie's failure to divulge his high blood pressure reading must be regarded as a material misrepresentation sufficient to void the policy.

Judgment affirmed.

NOTES AND QUESTIONS

1. *A Duty to Disclose?* Recent decisions confirm the continued authority of the *MacKenzie* rule. See, e.g., *PHL Variable Ins. Co. v. Fulbright McNeill, Inc.*, 519 F.3d 825 (8th Cir. 2008) (duty to disclose substantial change in health condition that occurred after completing application). See also Restatement (Second) of Contracts, §§ 161 & 164 (non-disclosure of fact that "is necessary to prevent some previous assertion from being a misrepresentation or from being fraudulent" may allow the other party to void a contract on that basis). Suppose that the applicant expects the policy to arrive by mail. To what lengths should he be required to go in order to make disclosure? Would it matter whether he had applied through an intermediary such as an agent or broker whom he could telephone? Should the applicant be expected to make a materiality determination based on his memory of the questions asked in the application, or based on some other standard? Suppose the policy comes up for renewal and the insurer includes the following printed language on the renewal bill: "Subject to the continued accuracy of answers provided on the original application"?

2. *Rationale for a Duty to Disclose Updated Information.* Does the *MacKenzie* rule appropriately allocate risk between the insurer and the policyholder? Consider the policyholder's perspective first. Is it as clear as the court suggests that MacKenzie actually appreciated his duty to disclose the updated medical information to his insurer? To what extent does the fact that Mackenzie apparently decreased his coverage limits after learning of his high blood pressure indicate that he did not realize that this information might have a material impact on his riskiness? Next consider

the insurer's perspective. Over the long run, should it make any difference to an insurer whether applicants in MacKenzie's position disclose the occurrence of new and material facts that develop during the application period? A rule that imposed no duty to disclose would merely create insurance against the risk that facts would change during the application period. Does the answer depend on the nature of the new facts? For example, in fashioning a rule to govern the issue, would it make sense to distinguish what happened in *MacKenzie* from the decision of an applicant for fire insurance to begin storing large amounts of gasoline in her basement the day after completing an application? What reasons might there be for ignoring this distinction?

3. *Alternatives.* Would it be preferable to hold that there is no affirmative duty to disclose changes in health or other material conditions unless the insurer or its agent makes a specific inquiry? In *Seidler v. Georgetown Life Insurance Co.,* 82 Ill. App. 3d 361 (1980), the insured signed an application containing a provision that coverage would not take effect unless the health of the insured remained as described in the application. He submitted to a physical examination, but then (before the policy was issued) suffered a heart attack whose occurrence he did not disclose to the insurer. The practice of the insurer's agent (actually a reinsurer) was to require the insured to complete a special form at the time the policy was delivered indicating whether there had been a change in health; but for some reason the form was not completed in Seidler's case. The court held that the insured's failure to disclose was not dispositive.

Instead of asking policyholders whether there has been a change in their health at the time of policy delivery, insurers sometimes attempt to include language in their applications creating a duty to provide updated information. Such language may provide that no insurance will take effect unless all of the answers continued to be true and complete as of the date of delivery of the policy, unless the insured is in good health at the time of policy delivery, or unless there has been no change in the policyholder's insurability at the time of policy delivery. These types of clauses obviously raise difficult factual and definitional issues that may limit their usefulness. See, e.g., *Friez v. Nat'l Old Line Ins. Co.*, 703 F.2d 1093 (9th Cir. 1983); *Gee v. AAA Life Ins. Co.*, 847 So.2d 103 (La. App. 2003). But assuming these difficulties can be overcome, do these provisions, in effect, create a duty to disclose, and thereby render moot the question whether there would be a duty to disclose even in the absence of such provisions?

4. *Misrepresentation after Loss.* Many property/casualty insurance policies contain provisions that purport to bar coverage where the insured has made a knowing misrepresentation after a loss has occurred. See, e.g., *Allstate Ins. Co. v. Huston*, 123 Wash. App. 530 (2004). Such provisions are generally intended to protect the insurer against policyholder fraud with respect to the nature or magnitude of a claimed loss. Should the same test for materiality and reliance be applied to post-loss misrepresentations as is applied to pre-loss misrepresentations? Or do post-loss misrepresentations raise distinctive issues because of the risk of policyholder forfeiture, such that both intent to deceive and detrimental reliance by the insurer (something like contribution to loss) should be required?

The issue arises in cases such as *Bryant v. Nationwide Mutual Fire Insurance Co.,* 67 N.C. App. 616 (1984), in which the insured house was destroyed by fire. In the course of the insurer's investigation, the insured misrepresented the size of his debts. Since the desire to capture the benefit of insurance on mortgaged property might create moral hazard, some courts hold that a misrepresentation of the size of the insured's debts on an insurance *application* is material. If such a misrepresentation after loss would discourage an insurer from conducting an arson investigation, is it material? Should the answer depend on whether in fact there was arson? If so, is there any need for a post-loss misrepresentation defense? See also *Longobardi v. Chubb Ins. Co. of N.J.*, 121 N.J. 530 (1990) (misrepresentation provision is applicable to post-loss fraud even if such fraud does not prejudice the insurer).

CHAPTER TWO

INSURANCE CONTRACT FORMATION, MEANING, AND DAMAGES

Because insurance policies are contracts, they are subject to ordinary principles of contract law. Contract law, of course, is a matter of state law and it therefore varies in its particulars across states. But a variety of basic contract law principles are virtually universally accepted, both in the insurance context and more broadly. For instance, insurance contracts, as with all contracts, are formed through mutual assent, which often takes the form of offer and acceptance. Similarly, the meaning of an insurance policy, as with all contracts, generally depends on the objectively reasonable meaning of the parties' agreement.

Although insurance policies are indeed contracts, they are distinctive types of contracts. This results in certain doctrines of contract law taking on outsized importance in insurance law. And in some cases, it even results in insurance law doctrines that are in substantial tension with principles of contract law. As with ordinary contract law, however, insurance-specific contract rules are a matter of state, rather than federal, law. Federal cases resolving insurance disputes therefore do so pursuant to their understanding of the relevant state's law.

The state-based nature of insurance law means that insurance disputes often implicate conflict of law questions. For instance, should California or Nevada insurance law apply when a Los Angeles resident who purchased his coverage in California gets into a car accident with a Nevada citizen in Nevada? In general, the applicable law in insurance disputes is determined by the principal location of the insured risk during the term of the policy (in the case of property/casualty insurance) or by the domicile of the policyholder when she applied for coverage (in the case of life insurance). Restatement (Second) of Conflict of Laws §§ 192, 193 (1971). In the hypothetical above, then, California law would presumably govern. However, conflict of law is a notoriously complicated subject, as reflected by an exception to the above principles for cases in which "some other state has a more significant relationship" to the dispute. Id. For this reason, parties involved in insurance disputes must be attuned to possible conflict of law issues.

A. THE ROLE OF STANDARDIZED FORMS

1. THE POLICY STANDARDIZATION PROCESS

Virtually all insurance policies are standard-form contracts. Contract law has long recognized the special problems posed by such contracts. Indeed, a seminal article on contracts of adhesion cited insurance contracts as a principal example. See Friedrich Kessler, Contracts of Adhesion—Some Thoughts About Freedom of Contract, 43 Colum. L. Rev. 629 (1943). For several generations of scholars and judges, these "take-it-or-leave-it" offers have warranted greater judicial and legislative regulation than contracts whose terms are individually negotiated by parties dealing at arms length with equal resources and information.

More attention seems to have been paid to the advantages and disadvantages of standardized contracts, however, than to the process by which these contracts actually become standard. Although the fact that insurance policies are contracts of adhesion is important to understanding the law governing their operation, it is equally important that all insurance companies use either an industry-standard contract or a company-specific variant of the industry-standard contract. Thus, standardization in insurance not only involves a take-it-or-leave-it offer of the same policy by one company to all its customers, but (in the extreme case) a take-it-or-leave-it offer of the same policy, to all customers, by all companies.

Some Useful Background

The development of standardization in property/casualty insurance helps to shed light on its current advantages and disadvantages. A brief and only slightly caricatured history of fire insurance is illustrative. Early fire insurance companies encountered two problems. First, they had no reliable statistics on the probability of loss from fire because they were just beginning to operate. They knew intuitively that brick structures are less likely to burn than wood ones, but quantified probabilities of loss were unavailable. Second, this lack of data meant that insurers didn't know what to charge for coverage. As a result, they were potentially very shaky enterprises. The first virtue of any insurance company is its solvency. If I buy a fire insurance policy from a shaky insurer, I can lose the entire value of my house. No matter how attractive the terms and price of a policy, it is worthless if the insurer is not around to pay losses when they occur. In fact, from this perspective low premiums are not a virtue at all. The less an insurer charges for coverage, the less likely it is that the insurer will be able to pay claims when losses occur.

What happened next in the development of fire insurance is no surprise. The absence of loss probability data, the forces of competition, and human nature, combined to produce price wars. Unsure of what an accurate premium would be, and eager to capture market share, insurers sometimes competed premiums down to levels below what later proved to be necessary to cover their costs. Not only were these price wars bad for insurers, they were bad for policyholders, who could not be assured of their carriers' solvency. This, in turn, reduced policyholder demand for insurance, further undermining insurers' interests.

As we will see in Chapter Three, the modern solution to this predicament is solvency regulation, which is designed to ensure that insurers have adequate capital, invest their assets prudently, make accurate disclosure of their financial condition, and participate in a guaranty fund that protects policyholders whose insurers are insolvent. But it was to be many decades before anything like this approach developed. In the meantime, insurers found a way to address the problem of "destructive competition" on their own: they began to pool data on their claims experiences in order to create a broader, more statistically reliable database. The more data they had on the characteristics of losses and claims, the more accurate their estimates of loss probabilities were, and the more confident they could be of the premiums they would need to charge in order to be able to pay claims.

But useful as this was, it was only part of what insurers needed to do to solve their problem. Pooled data can be meaningful only if it is data about the same thing. If I insure against fire caused by lightning, and you insure against fire caused by defective chimneys, pooling our claims data will not enable either of us to price our coverage more accurately. We will be pooling data about apples and oranges. Unless we both actually would prefer to insure fruit salad, the effort will be pointless. So the fire insurers eventually learned that, to make predictions about their own individual expected losses based on pooled data, each insurer had to promise to pay its policyholders on essentially the same terms.

This marked the birth of the modern standard-form insurance policy. Each insurer had to sell the same standard-form coverage in order for all insurers to capture the benefits of data pooling. Insurers would compete over price and reliability of service, but not over the terms of coverage. Their price competition would be informed by their pooled data, and would be subject to the constraint that unduly low prices would risk producing insolvency. The public got enhanced financial stability from insurers, but at the cost of constrained price competition and loss of product differentiation.

That may seem like a reasonable tradeoff, and it might have been, if there were no more to the story. But there were downsides to all of this industry collaboration. In early fire insurance, as in most industries, there were always a few renegades who thought that they could do their job better at a lower price than their competitors, and there were some shady characters who charged low premiums without any intention of being around when the time came for paying claims. In addition, some insurers offered policies with unusually narrow coverage without informing their policyholders of this fact. In response to these developments, insurers set up organizations to receive and pool claims data and to prepare standard-form policies to be used by insurers so that the pooled data was meaningful. But these organizations did not stop there. To guard against price wars, the insurers who controlled these organizations, which came to be known as "rate bureaus," sometimes provided that they would supply pooled data only to insurers that agreed to charge the rates that the bureau dictated. Naturally, the resulting rates were set at above-competitive levels. Insolvencies tended to be avoided, but at the cost of uncompetitive pricing.

When liability insurance came on the scene in the early 1880's in the form of "Employers Liability Insurance," it did not take long before liability insurers adopted the same approach, for largely the same reasons and with the same results. They formed rate bureaus to pool data and prepare standard policies, and sometimes they also required that anyone taking advantage of their services charge the rates they specified. As new forms of liability insurance developed in the late 19th and early 20th centuries, they followed the same pattern. So for many decades the insurance industry achieved enhanced solvency through industry price-fixing.

Standardization Today

Much data pooling and preparation of standard policy forms now occurs under the umbrella of an entity known as the Insurance Services Organization, or "ISO," which was formed in 1971 as a superbureau successor to the rate bureaus. Other similar organizations also perform this function. As recently as the late 1980's, ISO was still preparing what it called "advisory rates" for insurers to use if they wished—a practice that facilitated parallel pricing, although in many markets there was nonetheless vigorous price competition. This last vestige of the old rate bureau system of inhibiting competition thus died away only recently, and even now the core purposes for which the bureau system was founded—the pooling of data and promulgation of standard forms—continue to be served by ISO, although ISO divested insurers' control of the organization in 1994 and became an independent, for-profit corporation in 1997.

The vast majority of property and liability insurance policies are now written on versions of standard forms prepared by ISO. However, individual insurance carriers vary significantly in how closely their individual policies replicate ISO standard policy forms. See Daniel Schwarcz, Reevaluating Standardized Insurance Policies, 78 U. Chi. L. Rev. 1263 (2011) (systemically reviewing different carriers' homeowners policies and cataloguing substantial differences in coverage provisions). Many insurers—particularly smaller carriers—take the standard ISO policy form, place their own logos on it, and may even tweak the language here and there. But all the important coverage provisions and exclusions are the same. Increasingly, however, some carriers substantially alter key terms of the ISO policies in their own policy forms. In most cases, but certainly not all, these changes limit coverage or address policy terms that courts have found to be ambiguous. Even in these cases, however, the basic structure, and much of the core language, of the resulting policies closely resembles the corresponding ISO policy.

The continued importance of industry-standard insurance policies stems from the importance of ISO data for many companies. For example, as of 2006, ISO provided data on prospective loss costs, rules, and policy forms for more than 1100 classes of Commercial General Liability (CGL) insurance, ranging from hardware stores to mines. It cost ISO about $11 million per year to produce these products. But a typical insurer operating in 25 states with annual CGL premium volume of $50 million paid only about $75,000 for all of ISO's CGL products. This is less than two tenths of one cent for every dollar of CGL premiums that the insurer receives. The result is that barriers to entry into sub-markets for particular kinds of insurance probably are significantly reduced. Implications of Repealing ISO's Antitrust Exemption: Hearing on the McCarran-Ferguson Act Before the S. Comm. on the Judiciary, 109th Cong. 140–152 (2006) (statement of Kevin B. Thompson, Senior Vice President, Insurance Services Office).

To see how the ISO's standard policy forms and data might reduce barriers to entry into an insurance market, suppose that "Newby

Insurance Company" wants to start selling homeowners insurance in Minnesota. Like the early fire insurers, Newby will have little idea of the loss rate for homes in Minnesota, and hence little idea how to price its coverage. ISO, of course, will have this data, and (for a fee) Newby can obtain it. But Newby will find this data meaningful only if it sells the ISO policies on which this data is based. Thus, ISO allows for easier entry into the market, but only for companies selling policies identical or substantially similar to ISO forms.

While smaller companies still substantially rely on ISO data, technological developments and a rich store of historical data have reduced large companies' dependence on ISO data. This helps explain why some large companies have recently been willing to depart substantially from industry standard forms. Because they can rely on their own data, they do not need to adhere rigidly to ISO forms.

Just as it is to the advantage of small, and even some large, insurers to employ ISO standard forms, in some ways it is also to the advantage of policyholders when insurers do so. Policy standardization across companies allows policyholders to shop for price, service, and financial strength, without also worrying about coverage differences. Additionally, standardized policy language has a well developed meaning that may reduce the risk of coverage disputes. For many of the same reasons, the increasing tendency of some insurers to employ divergent policy forms can produce substantial policyholder protection issues, particularly because many policyholders assume that all insurance policies are the same, and market and regulatory structures are largely premised on this assumed reality. See Daniel Schwarcz, Transparently Opaque: Understanding the Lack of Transparency in Insurance Consumer Protection, 61 UCLA L. Rev. 394 (2014).

Unlike what is sometimes said of contracts of adhesion, however, the importance of ISO policy forms is not mainly a "bargaining power" issue. Although you and I have no power to persuade Newby Insurance Company to sell us a customized policy, major corporations have enough bargaining power to draft their own customized policy language and put it out for bid. However, the additional drafting and uncertainty costs to both these businesses and the insurers who might bid on that coverage apparently outweigh the advantage that could be gained by tailoring coverage precisely to each business's needs, from the ground up. Customization like that simply doesn't happen very often, because it is too expensive for both policyholders and insurers, and would result in policy language whose meaning and application would be insufficiently predictable. And when customization does occasionally occur, changes are made incrementally, through the attachment of "endorsements" to standard policies that change only the portion of standardized coverage that needs to be changed. These days, even endorsements are highly standardized.

In contrast to property and liability insurance, there is much less standardization in life and health insurance. Because there has long been fairly reliable data about mortality, life insurers never experienced the same pressure to standardize that property-casualty insurers felt, and never banded together to form the rate bureaus that gave rise to standard-form property and liability insurance. Life insurance policies are also contracts of adhesion—life insurers will not draft policy language to suit your particular needs—but different insurers sell policies containing different language and terms. Health insurers also never had incentives to pool their data or standardize coverage. In large part, this is because claims in health insurance vary substantially among different pools of policyholders, as a result of geographic variations in the cost of medical care and potential differences in healthcare needs among different groups. Consequently, pooling data for health insurers would provide limited value even if coverage were standardized. Additionally, policyholders' desired terms of health insurance are quite variable relative to their desired terms of property-casualty insurance.

There is a different force that promotes standardization in both the property-casualty and life-and-health sides of the insurance market. Increasingly, statutory and regulatory mandates require insurers to provide certain forms of coverage. Perhaps the most prominent recent examples are federal coverage mandates in the Affordable Care Act, which require health insurance policies to include a variety of benefits. Similarly, by statute or regulation, most states require the inclusion of certain standard provisions and coverages in auto insurance policies. Conversely, specific provisions are often prohibited by statute or regulation. By operation of law all these different kinds of mandates and prohibitions have a standardizing effect, locating the source of some policy provisions (and the absence of others) outside the four corners of the policy itself.

2. BINDERS AND POLICYHOLDER ASSENT TO STANDARDIZED FORMS

Unlike in the case of most contracts, and even most contracts of adhesion, policyholders do not typically agree to their insurance policies at the time they purchase them. Due principally to custom and industry practice, policyholders generally receive their actual insurance policy several weeks after they purchase or apply for coverage. Policyholders are deemed to assent to these terms of coverage by retaining the policy and failing to cancel coverage. Thus, policyholder agreement to standardized policy terms operates in the same way as consumer agreement to "shrinkwrap" terms that are included within the contents of a tangible product that consumers receive. See *ProCD v. Zeidenberg*, 86 F.3d 1447 (7th Cir. 1996) (holding that consumers agree to shrinkwrap terms that they receive after the point of purchase when they do not return the product); *Hill v. Gateway 2000 Inc.*, 105 F.3d 1147 (7th Cir. 1997) (similar). Contract law scholars have long debated whether such "rolling contracts" present enhanced consumer protection concerns. See Robert A. Hillman, Rolling Contracts, 71 Fordham L. Rev. 743 (2002); Florencia Marotta-Wurgler, Are "Pay Now, Terms Later" Contracts Worse for Buyers? Evidence from Software License Agreements, 38 J. Legal Stud. 309 (2009).

Although it is well established that policyholders assent to standard insurance policies by failing to cancel coverage after they receive their policies, it is less clear that policyholders assent to non-standard policy language in the same manner. Because of the history of insurance policy standardization, insurance markets, consumer shopping behavior, and regulatory protections are all substantially structured around the assumption that insurance policies are completely standardized across companies. Given this context, to what extent does it make sense to understand a policyholder to have agreed to non-standard terms that reduce coverage and that were not disclosed, or even available to policyholders, at the point of sale? See Daniel Schwarcz, Reevaluating Standardized Insurance Policies, 78 U. Chi. L. Rev. 1263, 1343-44 (2011); *Henderson v. Lawyers Title Ins. Corp.*, 843 N.E.2d 152 (Ohio 2006) (concluding that an arbitration term in a title insurance policy was unenforceable because the policyholder did not receive the policy until after purchase and the arbitration clause was not a "usual and customary term[ ]").

The fact that insurance policies are not issued immediately upon purchase or application can raise complications for prospective policyholders who need coverage immediately. To deal with this need, insurers and their agents often execute a "binder." A binder obligates the insurer to provide coverage if there is a loss before the insurer issues a policy, and specifies, expressly or by reference, the basic terms and conditions of coverage. Binders are thus temporary and incomplete contracts, intended to be replaced by the terms of the actual policy, once it is issued. Given this distinctive structure, it is not surprising that questions regarding the legal effect of binders are not uncommon.

By far the most famous example of this involves property insurance for the World Trade Center ("WTC") towers in the wake of the 9/11 attacks. In the summer of 2001, the owner of the WTC towers purchased approximately $3.5 billion "per occurrence" of property insurance from a coalition of different insurance carriers. (Why did no single insurance carrier want to issue the entire amount of coverage?) Although all of the insurers had agreed to provide coverage through binders prior to 9/11, most of them had not issued the final insurance policy by 9/11. In the wake of the attacks, it was clear that the owner of the WTC was entitled to the $3.5 billion that the coalition of carriers had agreed to provide in their binders, even though most had not issued a final policy. What was not clear was whether the plane strikes on each of the two WTC towers constituted two "occurrences" or a single "occurrence." Because the coverage limit in the binders was $3.5 billion per occurrence, much turned on this question. If the attacks constituted two occurrences, then the coalition of insurers owed a total of $7 billion in insurance proceeds rather than just $3.5 billion for a single occurrence, as the property damage to the WTC towers likely exceeded $7 billion.

Resolution of this issue turned on the meaning of the term "occurrence." But because the insurers had provided coverage through temporary binders rather than through a final policy, it was not even clear where the court should look for the meaning of this term. The binders of the insurance companies did not define the term "occurrence." But at least one draft policy form that the various insurers had reviewed in the course of negotiating coverage with the insurance broker, Willis, did include the following definition of an occurrence:

> "[A]ll losses or damages that are attributable directly or indirectly to one cause or to one series of similar causes. All such losses will be added together and the total amount of such

losses will be treated as one occurrence irrespective of the period of time or area over which such losses occur.

The draft policy containing this definition was referred to as the Wilprop form, as it was the insurance broker Willis's draft property insurance form.

In *World Trade Center Properties, L.L.C. v. Hartford Fire Insurance Co.*, 345 F.3d 154 (2d Cir. 2003), the court first addressed the coverage obligations of the insurers that had reviewed only the Wilprop form in the course of the negotiations leading up to the issuance of their binders. The appellate court affirmed the district court's holding that "each of the insurers had issued a binder that incorporated the terms of the WilProp form and that under the WilProp form's definition of 'occurrence' there was only one occurrence on September 11, 2001." The court explained that, for these insurers, the definition of an "occurrence" contained in a policy that was actually issued by another insurer (Travelers) on 9/14 was irrelevant, regardless of whether "the parties might have agreed to ultimately issue policies tracking [this] policy."

The court then addressed the coverage obligations of Travelers, which had submitted "its own specimen policy form (the 'Travelers form') during the course of negotiating the terms of coverage." Unlike the Wilprop form, the Travelers form explicitly left the term "occurrence" undefined. The court first held that the Travelers binder incorporated the terms of the Travelers form, and thus that this binder did not contain any specific definition of "occurrence." The court next turned to the question whether it was proper under the parol evidence rule to consider extrinsic evidence regarding the meaning of the undefined term "occurrence" in the Travelers binder. Under New York's version of that rule, courts can only examine extrinsic evidence when a contract is ambiguous on its face. The court concluded that the undefined term "occurrence" was indeed ambiguous, and thus that the parties could submit extrinsic evidence to help resolve its meaning.

On remand, a jury decided that there were two occurrences under the Travelers binder. This result was affirmed on appeal. *SR Int'l Bus. Ins. Co. v. World Trade Ctr. Properties, LLC*, 467 F.3d 107 (2d Cir. 2006). Insurance companies ultimately made total claims payments of $4.55 billion to the WTC owner.

3. Construing Ambiguities Against the Insurer

Insurance policies are subject to many of the general principles of contract interpretation. For example, interpretation is typically a matter for the court. The purpose of interpretation is to determine the parties' intent, as reflected by the objectively reasonably meaning of their contract. In some jurisdictions, such as New York in the 9/11 cases, this means that extrinsic evidence is not admissible unless the written contract is ambiguous. In other jurisdictions, extrinsic evidence is always admissible to determine the meaning of the parties' agreement in context, but is not admissible to contradict or supplement the final written agreement. An insurance policy is to be read as a whole, with reference to the relation among its provisions; whenever possible, the same terms in different parts of the policy are to be interpreted consistently. All the provisions in the policy are to be given effect, if possible.

Several principles of interpretation, however, figure particularly prominently in insurance law. First, the insuring agreement, or affirmative grant of coverage in a policy, is broadly construed, whereas exclusions from or limitations on coverage are narrowly construed. Second, policyholders generally bear the burden of proof in demonstrating that a particular loss comes within a coverage grant, while insurers bear the burden of proof in demonstrating that an exclusion limits coverage. Third, policy provisions ordinarily are not given a hyper-technical meaning, but are instead interpreted as they would be understood by the typical policyholder of that kind of policy.

The most frequently employed principle of interpretation, however, is *contra proferentem*, which roughly translated means "against the drafter" or "against the offeror." This is the rule that an ambiguous provision in an insurance policy—one that is subject to two reasonable interpretations—is interpreted against the drafter. Since the drafter of an insurance policy is almost always the insurer, for practical purposes this translates into a rule that ambiguous policy language is interpreted in favor of coverage. Literally thousands of reported decisions have applied this rule.

If post-modernism has taught us anything, however, it is that language is an imperfect instrument for communicating meaning. Many of the provisions in an insurance policy are at least potentially ambiguous in one context or another. So the puzzle is why and how so many policy provisions whose meaning has been placed at issue in insurance disputes have been held to be unambiguous. What is it that makes a policy provision sufficiently clear that it avoids *contra proferentem*?

Vargas v. Insurance Company of North America

United States Court of Appeals, Second Circuit, 1981.
651 F.2d 838.

■ SOFAER, DISTRICT JUDGE:

This is an appeal from a grant of summary judgment to defendant-appellee Insurance Company of North America ("INA") in a declaratory judgment action brought to determine whether INA is liable under an aviation insurance policy issued to Joseph Khurey for his single-engine Piper Arrow. The policy, issued on December 13, 1977, provided in part that it would apply "only to occurrences, accidents or losses which happen * * * within the United States of America, its territories or possessions, Canada or Mexico." An endorsement, added to the policy on December 14, 1977, extended the territorial limits to include the Bahama Islands.

On December 23, 1977, Khurey, his wife, and his daughter were killed when the plane crashed into the sea approximately twenty-five miles west of Puerto Rico. The family had been traveling from New York to Puerto Rico, and they had stopped in Miami and Haiti to rest and refuel. The crash occurred on the last leg of the trip, while the

Khureys were en route from Haiti to Puerto Rico. Puerto Rico is a "territory" of the United States. 48 U.S.C. § 731 (1976).

INA denied insurance coverage on the ground that the loss did not occur "within" the United States, its territories, or its possessions. INA claims that the policy covers losses that occur only in the enumerated areas or in territorial waters within three miles adjacent to the coasts of such areas. Appellants read the language more broadly, to include coverage for losses that occur while the plane is traveling between two points that are both within areas expressly covered.

Under New York law, which governs this case, an ambiguous provision in an insurance policy is construed "most favorably to the insured and most strictly against the insurer." *Index Fund, Inc. v. Insurance Company of North America,* 580 F.2d 1158, 1162 (2d Cir.1978). The insurer bears a heavy burden of proof, for it must "'establish that the words and expressions used [in the insurance policy] not only are susceptible of the construction sought by [the insurer] but that it is the only construction which may fairly be placed on them.'" *Filor, Bullard & Smyth v. Insurance Company of North America,* 605 F.2d 598, 602 (2d Cir.1978) (quoting *Lachs v. Fidelity & Casualty Co. of New York,* 306 N.Y. 357, 365–66 (1954)). The insurer is "obliged to show (1) that it would be unreasonable for the average man reading the policy to [construe it as the insured does] and (2) that its own construction was the only one that fairly could be placed on the policy." *Sincoff v. Liberty Mutual Fire Insurance Co.,* 11 N.Y.2d 386, 390 (1962). Thus, the question in this case is narrow: is the insurer's interpretation of the contract the only reasonable and fair construction as a matter of law? * * *

The policy is readily susceptible of a reasonable and fair interpretation that would cover the flight at issue in this case. The policy was for an airplane, which is not merely an object but also a mode of transportation, capable of long-distance travel over water as well as land. The parties knew that the plane would fly substantial distances as it transported the insured and various passengers to their contemplated destinations. The policy, moreover, provided coverage for losses both within the continental United States and within territories more than three miles beyond the continental United States. It is reasonable to construe this coverage of United States territories (some of which are ocean islands), not as restricted to the airspace immediately above them, but rather as including destinations to and from which the plane could travel without forfeiting coverage. Appellants' construction is more consistent with the realities of airplane travel. So long as the plane is on a reasonably direct course from and to geographic areas covered by the policy, the plane could reasonably be said to be within the contemplated territorial limits. Coverage of "ordinary and customary" routes has frequently been implied in analogous marine insurance contracts. *See, e.g.,* 9 Couch on Insurance, § 37:1476 (2d ed. 1962). If the plane were flown on an unreasonable course between two covered points, coverage could be lost.

Appellants' construction is supported by the language of the policy. The territory clause limits coverage to occurrences "within the United States of America, its territories or possessions, Canada or Mexico." The word "within" can reasonably be construed to mean "inside the borders" of the places specified. On the other hand, the term can also reasonably be construed to mean "inside an area that includes the places specified as well as such area as must be crossed in passing to and from the places specified." The policy's "Extension of Territorial Limits Endorsement" is consistent with the latter construction. The endorsement is phrased, not in terms of specific places, but rather in terms of "geographical limits"; and the controlling clause provides that the "limits set forth in the [c]onditions of this policy * * * are extended to include" the places covered by the endorsement. Thus, the "limits" may be read as describing the outside boundaries of an area within which flights, on reasonable routes, are covered.

Appellee concedes that this construction is appropriate with respect to specific places covered by an Extension of Territorial Endorsement. It acknowledges that the insured "requested an endorsement to cover flights *to* the Bahamas." * * * The extension was not explicitly drafted to include the Bahama Islands *and* the route over which a plane would have to fly to get to and return from the Bahamas. Yet, the addition of "The Bahama Islands" to the covered territory reasonably implied that trips to and from those islands, on reasonable routes, would also be covered. Otherwise, an insured would be forced to ship his plane to and from places covered by the policy, although those places are well within the aircraft's known range and capacity. If inclusion of "The Bahama Islands" carries with it inclusion of any reasonable route to and from those islands, then the policy itself should be construed to include reasonable routes to and from any location covered by the policy's territory clause, and within the aircraft's known capacity.

Appellee argues that the terms of the insurance contract are so clear that the court need not resort to rules of construction. The coverage provision of the contract is in fact ambiguous, and the insurer could have avoided that ambiguity by defining the territorial limits with more precision. Had appellee wished to preclude coverage for trips to and from places included in the territory provision, language to accomplish that objective was readily available. As Judge Frankel stated in *Pan American World Airways, Inc. v. Aetna Casualty & Surety Co.*, 368 F.Supp. 1098 (S.D.N.Y.1973), *aff'd,* 505 F.2d 989 (2d Cir.1974):

> Where the risk is well known and there are terms reasonably apt and precise to describe it, the use of substantially less certain phraseology, upon which dictionaries and common understanding may fairly differ, is likely to result in interpretations favoring coverage rather than exclusion.

368 F.Supp. at 1118. * * *

In support of its position that its construction is the only reasonable one, appellee contended at oral argument that flights over waters beyond the territorial limits pose special dangers, for which insureds should be required to pay extra premiums; and it notes that Khurey had rejected an offer to cover the entire Caribbean. This ostensible appeal to commercial commonsense does not withstand analysis. The fact that coverage of the entire Caribbean, including the ocean areas, cost only an additional fifty dollars undermines the argument that substantial additional risks are involved. Moreover, INA offers no evidence that over-water flights between covered locations are more dangerous than flights over points anywhere within the United

States, Canada, Alaska, and Mexico—areas that are expressly covered by the policy and that include vast mountain ranges, lakes, deserts, and urban centers with heavy air traffic. Commonsense and experience contradict INA's assertion that over-water flights add materially to these explicitly covered risks.

In fact, it is appellee's construction that appears unreasonable in terms of aviation practice. If the policy excluded coverage for all flights over waters beyond the territorial limits, then flights between certain points within the continental United States would have to stay within the territorial limits in order to remain covered. Yet the most direct routes between many points within the continental United States pass over waters beyond the territorial limits; for example, the most direct route from New York City to Miami takes aircraft more than three miles beyond the coast. The same is true of many other routes, including routes between points within the territorial United States and points in Mexico, Canada, or Alaska, all of which are areas covered by the policy. Were INA's construction accepted, a pilot would be required to follow a less-direct route to avoid losing coverage, and the economic and air-safety consequences of utilizing indirect routes are likely to be far more significant than the cost of covering routes between areas expressly covered, as suggested by INA's price quotation for coverage for the Caribbean. Moreover, inducing aircraft to fly within three miles of the coast, or to risk losing coverage, might well be inconsistent with air-safety practices and rules. The record is barren of evidence as to the likely effects of INA's construction upon, for example, landing patterns at coastal airports that can take planes more than three miles off the coast. INA's assertion that its construction is supported by the reduced safety of flights beyond the territorial limits must be weighed against safety implications of using indirect routes in lieu of more direct, over-water routes.

Another factor that undermines appellee's case for summary judgment is the intent of the parties. *See, e.g., Lipsky v. Commonwealth United Corp.,* 551 F.2d 887, 896 (2d Cir.1976); *Skandia America Reinsurance Corp. v. Schenck,* 441 F.Supp. 715, 723–24 n. 13 (S.D.N.Y.1977); *Kessler Export Corp. v. Reliance Insurance Co.,* 207 F.Supp. 355, 358 (E.D.N.Y.1962), *aff'd,* 310 F.2d 936 (2d Cir.1962). In this case, Khurey revealed in his original insurance application his intention to fly the insured aircraft outside the United States. He responded affirmatively to a question on the application, "Will aircraft be used outside Continental United States?"; and to the request for details, he replied, "for vacations." It was in fact on a flight outside the continental United States, during a Christmas vacation, that Khurey and his family were killed. In addition, appellants allege that Khurey's wife came from Puerto Rico and that the family expected to vacation there occasionally. Appellants have not had an opportunity to prove this allegation or to establish that INA agents knew of Khurey's intentions. But the purported intention is entirely consistent with a belief on Khurey's part that the insurance policy covered flights between the United States and Puerto Rico.

Because appellee failed to prove that its construction of the insurance policy was the only fair and reasonable one, the decision granting it summary judgment is reversed. On the present record, the

appellants, rather than the appellee, are entitled to summary judgment on the coverage issue. INA may, however, raise factual questions that would render summary judgment in appellants' favor inappropriate. This and other issues will be for the trial court to determine on remand.
* * *

NOTES AND QUESTIONS

1. *You Get What You Pay For.* The insurer in *Vargas* argued that flights beyond territorial limits pose special dangers for which the insured should pay extra premiums. How persuasive was the court's refutation of this argument? Does the fact that coverage for flights over the entire Caribbean would have cost only an additional $50 tell you anything significant without your knowing the total premium paid? Should courts be in the business of determining the meaning of policy language by reference to the price that was paid for coverage?

2. *Identifying Ambiguity.* Given the centrality of *contra proferentem* in insurance coverage disputes, much turns on the process that courts employ to determine whether or not the underlying policy language is ambiguous. Most courts frame this question by asking whether the policy language at issue is reasonably susceptible to an interpretation that would cover the specific coverage dispute at issue in the case. A logical byproduct of this approach is that a specific policy term can be ambiguous in one coverage dispute but unambiguous in another. See RLLI § 4, cmt. A. Using this approach, the policy language in *Vargas* might be deemed to unambiguously exclude coverage in a case where the plane crashed en route to Haiti when Haiti was the policyholder's final destination.

By contrast, some courts have suggested that *contra proferentem* requires them to determine in the abstract whether the relevant policy language is susceptible to only one reasonable meaning. If so, then *contra proferentem* is not implicated, even if it is unclear how that meaning should be applied to the specific case at issue. For instance, in *Ackerman v. Foster*, 974 P.2d 1 (Colo. App. 1998), the court was required to determine whether the defendant—who lived in a different state from her father while she was completing military training—was covered under her father's auto insurance policy as a "resident" of his "household." The lower court determined that the policy language was ambiguous because it was not clear how it applied in that particular case. However, the appellate court rejected this logic, reasoning that a policy "term's meaning does not vary according to the facts surrounding a particular accident." After concluding that the terms "resident" and "household" have clear and unambiguous meanings in the abstract, it held that "an 'ambiguity' does not reappear merely because, when that meaning is *applied* in the circumstances surrounding the accident and injuries in question, coverage is 'unclear.'"

Does the *Ackerman* approach to assessing ambiguity seem viable? To what extent is it really possible to determine whether policy language is ambiguous in the abstract? Does the fact that most words can be given a single definition suggest that the *Ackerman* approach substantially limits the potential scope of the ambiguity rule?

3. *Contradictions in Coverage Provisions and Ambiguity.* One setting in which courts often conclude that a policy is ambiguous is when it contains seemingly contradictory terms with respect to whether a

particular loss is covered. For instance, in *Hammerstone v. Indiana Insurance Co.*, 986 N.E.2d 841 (Ind. App. 2013), the court confronted a liability insurance policy that simultaneously indicated (i) that it provided $2 million of coverage for liability arising out of completed operations and (ii) excluded all coverage for liability arising out of completed operations. These conflicting provisions, the court ruled, automatically triggered *contra proferentem*, and a ruling in favor of the policyholder. To what extent are these seemingly conflicting provisions any different than the typical approach of an insurance policy, which contains some terms that grant coverage and other terms that carve out exclusions to those coverage grants?

4. *Limits on* Contra Proferentem? Decisions such as *Vargas* could be read to impose limits on the scope of *contra proferentem* even when the relevant policy language is ambiguous. In particular, the case arguably suggests that the ambiguity doctrine should be invoked only if the policy language could reasonably have been drafted more clearly and the insured could reasonably have expected the coverage at issue. See Kenneth S. Abraham, A Theory of Insurance Policy Interpretation, 95 Mich. L. Rev. 531 (1996). In contrast, some decisions seem to reject these limits and impose liability as a kind of penalty. See, e.g., *Rusthoven v. Commercial Standard Insurance Co.*, 387 N.W.2d 642 (Minn. 1986), in which the court held that, because of contradictory policy provisions, an employee of a company that had purchased uninsured motorist coverage of $25,000 "per person" was entitled to $25,000 for each vehicle the company owned, for a total $1,675,000 of coverage. It seems unlikely that the employer expected that it had purchased and paid for over a million dollars worth of uninsured motorist coverage for each of its employees. Should this fact have affected the result in the case?

5. *Rationales for* Contra Proferentem. The principal argument for *contra proferentem* is that, as the drafter of the policy, the insurer has control of its language and therefore the capacity to make it clear. By interpreting ambiguities against the drafter, courts can therefore encourage insurers to clarify the scope of their coverage. The implication of this argument, however, is that clearer policy language would make a difference. Is this likely to be true for most policyholders, who do not read their policies at the time of purchase at all, much less with the care that would be necessary to respond to the elimination of potential ambiguities? Or is the benefit of clearer drafting that it better equips policyholders to clearly determine the scope of coverage after a loss has occurred? Alternatively, perhaps clearer drafting might benefit the public by limiting the need for costly litigation to resolve coverage disputes.

In any event, the extent to which *contra proferentem* does in fact result in less ambiguous policy language is contestable. In some cases, courts' repeated application of *contra proferentem* has indeed caused insurers to redraft their policy language to clarify the scope of coverage. For instance, in response to judicial decisions concluding that exclusions in property insurance policies for "earth movement" might not apply to earth movement caused by human, rather than natural, forces, see *Fayad v. Clarendon Nat. Ins. Co.*, 899 So.2d 1082 (Fla. 2005), some insurers altered their policies to exclude earth movement from "human or animal forces or any act of nature." But in other cases, insurers have seemingly been more reluctant to alter policy language that courts have consistently found to be ambiguous. Michelle Boardman has argued that this is because the very process of finding a policy term to be ambiguous provides it with a fixed (albeit pro-policyholder) meaning that insurers can price. Michelle E. Boardman, *Contra Proferentem*: The Allure of Ambiguous Boilerplate, 104 Mich. L. Rev. 1105 (2006); Michelle Boardman, Penalty Default Rules in Insurance Law, 40 Fla. St. U. L. Rev. 305 (2013).

Even if *contra proferentem* does reduce ambiguity in insurance policies, is it clear that this will improve the comprehensibility of that language for policyholders? In light of the complex nature of the coverage people need and the variety of losses to be covered, reducing ambiguity in insurance policy language can often lead to increasing the complexity and length of policy language. For example, can you draft a provision for the policy in *Vargas* that is easily understandable, but also provides coverage for trips to Puerto Rico while excluding the loss that actually occurred? Is the problem a matter of drafting technique or a contradiction in what the INA policy purported to cover?

An alternative explanation for *contra proferentem* is that its pro-policyholder orientation is an appropriate counter-weight to the fact that insurers enjoy superior bargaining power and sophistication over policyholders. Insurers may be able to exploit this position to draft excessively restrictive coverage provisions. The weakness of this rationale is that there is a limited nexus between the potential problem (unfair policy exclusions) and the underlying doctrine. In other words, there is little reason to suspect that insurance policy terms that are ambiguous align well with those terms that may be unfair or inefficient. Michael B. Rappaport, The Ambiguity Rule and Insurance Law: Why Insurance Contracts Should Not Be Construed Against the Drafter, 30 Ga. L. Rev. 171 (1995).

Stone Container Corporation v. Hartford Steam Boiler Inspection and Insurance Company

United States Court of Appeals, Seventh Circuit, 1999.
165 F.3d 1157.

■ POSNER, CHIEF JUDGE.

The plaintiff in this insurance suit, Stone Container Corporation, is a large manufacturer of pulp, paper, and paper products. It makes the pulp in huge steel tanks called "pulp digesters." Wood chips are placed in the tank along with chemicals. The tank is then sealed and its contents subjected to heat and pressure from steam piped into the tank, causing the chips to decompose into pulp fiber. One of the tanks in one of Stone's plants exploded when a thin area of its steel shell ruptured during the high-pressure operation of the tank. The explosion blew a 28-ton chunk into the air; it landed more than 200 feet away with disastrous results. Besides much property damage, several workers were killed. The plant was forced to shut down for months. Stone Container incurred total losses in excess of $80 million.

Stone had an "all-risks" insurance policy from Lloyd's that, the parties agree, covered an accident of this kind. But it also had a "boiler and machinery insurance" policy from Hartford Steam Boiler Inspection and Insurance Company. Lloyd's believed that Hartford's policy was primary and that Lloyd's should have to pay on its own policy only if

Hartford was determined not to be legally obligated to pay for Stone's losses. Because the accident caused liquidity problems for Stone, Lloyd's was able to make a deal whereby Stone agreed to sue Hartford (which had denied coverage) and in exchange Lloyd's lent Stone one-half of the insurance proceeds to which Stone would be entitled if it won the suit against Hartford. It is unclear to us what incentive Stone had to press such a suit vigorously, the dispute really being between the insurance companies; but it has done so.

The Hartford policy is limited to accidents to particular enumerated "objects" in Stone's plants. The enumeration covers a broad range of different types of machinery, but there is an exclusion for losses caused by "explosions." There is also an exception to the exclusion. The exception is "for loss caused by or resulting from an explosion of an 'object' of a kind described below. . . . Explosion of any: (1) Steam boiler; (2) Electric steam generator; (3) Steam piping; (4) Steam turbine; (5) Steam engine; (6) Gas turbine; or (7) Moving or rotating machinery [if the explosion is] caused by centrifugal force or mechanical breakdown." Anything within the exception is covered by Hartford's policy. If, therefore, either the accident to the pulp digester was not an "explosion," and so was not within the exclusion, or it was an explosion of "an 'object' of a kind described" in the list in the exception to the exclusion, and so was within the exception, then Hartford's policy covers the accident; otherwise it does not.

The district judge granted summary judgment for Stone. He held that although the accident was indeed an explosion, the policy is ambiguous as to whether a pulp digester is an object "of a kind" described in the list of kinds of machinery excepted from the exclusion, and an ambiguity in an insurance contract is, under Illinois law, which governs the substantive issues in this diversity suit, to be resolved in favor of the insured. He refused to allow Hartford to present evidence to disambiguate the ambiguity.

Hartford has appealed, arguing that the policy unambiguously excludes pulp digesters; in the alternative it asks for a remand to enable it to present evidence of drafting history and the like to show that the parties intended to exclude pulp digesters. Stone [argued as] an alternative ground for affirmance of the judgment to the district court [that] what happened to the pulp digester was not an explosion.
* * *

We shall take up the alternative ground for affirmance first. Stone argues that "explosion" means, for exclusion purposes at any rate, a sudden and violent release of energy (which of course we have here) caused by combustion or some other chemical reaction (which we don't have here). The qualification "for exclusion purposes" is noteworthy. Stone believes that the same word should be read narrowly when it appears in an exclusion from coverage, and broadly when it appears in an exception to an exclusion, even if the context is the same. Thus, "explosion" might mean a sudden and violent release of energy caused by combustion or some other chemical reaction in the exclusion clause but in the exception to the exclusion clause might mean any rupture. Stone offers no support for this suggestion, in cases or other recognized legal authorities, beyond the principle that ambiguities in insurance contracts should be resolved in favor of the insured: the principle of "*contra proferentem*," well discussed in Jeffrey W. Stempel, *Interpretation of Insurance Contracts: Law and Strategy for Insurers and Policyholders* § 5.2 (1994), which Illinois applies even where, as in this case, the insured is a large and sophisticated firm, provided it didn't actually negotiate over the terms of coverage. *Outboard Marine Corp. v. Liberty Mutual Ins. Co.*, 154 Ill.2d 90 (Ill.1992); see generally Stempel, *supra*, ch. 23. Stone's suggestion would make insurance contracts even more complex, esoteric, and inscrutable than they are already.

In any event, the proposed definition of "explosion" is not only narrow, but weirdly narrow. It seems to exclude the explosion of an atomic bomb, since a nuclear reaction is not a form of combustion or a chemical reaction, at least in the usual senses of these words. It would certainly exclude volcanic explosions, as well as the "explosion" of a tire caused by a blowout, the explosion of a melon caused by a bullet, and, to take an example very close to home, the explosion of a boiler as a result of the failure of a valve to open. All these are commonplace examples of the use of the word "explosion" in ordinary speech. None involves stretching the ordinary meaning. And likewise a blast that blows 28 tons of steel and concrete more than 200 feet away is the ordinary person's idea of an explosion, whatever the precise cause of the explosion. The Hartford policy does not define the word or scatter any clues that it is being used in other than its normal sense; even the engineering firm that Stone hired to investigate the accident called it an explosion—a "Boiling Liquid Expanding Vapor Explosion (BLEVE) of a large, steam-pressurized vessel."

And Stone has cited no case that impresses an artificial definition on the term. The case law, fatally to Stone on this issue, gives the word "explosion" when it appears without a definition in an insurance contract its ordinary-language meaning. *Pre-Cast Concrete Products, Inc. v. Home Ins. Co.*, 417 F.2d 1323 (7th Cir.1969) (discussing and applying Illinois law); *Lever Bros. Co. v. Atlas Assurance Co.*, 131 F.2d 770, 775–76 (7th Cir.1942); *American Casualty Co. v. Myrick*, 304 F.2d 179, 182–83 (5th Cir.1962). Stone's argument is at root that if a term is not defined in an insurance contract, the insured can impress any definition on it that will establish coverage. "You wrote it, you lose" is not the insurance law of Illinois.

It is a slightly closer question whether the pulp digester is "of a kind" listed in the list of objects that are excepted from the exclusion of accidents caused by explosions, that is, that are covered by the boiler and machinery policy. Clearly the pulp digester is not any of the listed "objects." It is closest to a steam boiler, because it employs steam under pressure. But a steam boiler creates steam by boiling water. In the pulp digester the steam is generated outside and fed into the digester; the digester does not create steam. Its function and mode of operation are thus completely different from those of a steam boiler. In engineering lingo, the steam boiler is a "fired pressure vessel," the pulp digester an "unfired pressure vessel." Had the pipe that carried the steam to the digester exploded, the explosion would have been covered by Hartford's policy, because steam piping is one of the objects enumerated in the exception to the exclusion. But it is the digester itself that, as a result of the rupture in its wall, blew up.

The pulp digester is, then, certainly not a steam boiler or even a kind of steam boiler; but might it be "of a kind" with a steam boiler? If so, the explosion exclusion from the policy is hopelessly ambiguous and probably illusory, for when pressed at argument for examples of explosions that Stone's reading of the Hartford policy would exclude, Stone's lawyer could suggest only the explosion of the gasoline tank of a truck that was in the plant. The objects covered by the policy include air-conditioning units. Suppose one exploded. Is an air-conditioning unit "of a kind" with the seven objects enumerated in the explosion exclusion? A boiler heats water; an air conditioner cools air; these could be thought analogous functions (heat exchange). An *industrial* air conditioner, the kind presumably found in Stone's plants, uses water as an intermediary between the refrigerant and the air, and the water changes temperature.

Even if the essential commonality of the objects embraced by the exception to the exclusion (setting aside the last and most clearly irrelevant type of object, moving machinery) is the use of steam, does this mean that an espresso machine, the radiator of a motor vehicle, a Sauna bath, a dishwasher, a steam iron, a humidifier, and a teapot are all "of a kind" with a steam boiler? We think not. Stone's error is its refusal to read "of a kind" contextually. The term introduces a list of kinds of object. "Steam boiler" denotes a class of objects, not a single object. A class is a kind; the phrase "of a kind" introduces the various kinds or classes of object subject to the explosion exclusion. Steam boilers are one kind; steam pipes another; and so on. Pulp digesters are a kind of object, but not one of the kinds in the list. The distinction between fired and unfired pressure vessels helps to show this. These are two different kinds of pressure vessel. One includes steam boilers but not pulp digesters; the other includes pulp digesters but not steam boilers. One is covered by the boiler and machinery insurance policy; the other is not.

This is clear enough to compel judgment for Hartford without an evidentiary hearing. We agree with Stone that it is desirable to resolve insurance disputes where possible without a trial likely to drain the resources of the insured. *Rhone-Poulenc Inc. v. International Ins. Co.*, 71 F.3d 1299, 1305 (7th Cir.1995) (Illinois law). We also agree with Stone that ambiguities are to be resolved in favor of the insured. That is not only the rule in Illinois, but the rule everywhere. 2 Eric Mills Holmes, *Holmes's Appleman on Insurance*, 2d § 6.1, p. 134 and n. 4 (1996); see also 2 Lee R. Russ, *Couch on Insurance* 3d § 22:14, p. 22–31 n. 23 (1997). But we do not think that "of a kind," read in context as all contractual language must be read, is ambiguous. Read as Stone would have us read it, it would introduce radical ambiguity into an exclusion designed to be mechanically applicable and would expand coverage beyond its intended scope. The form in which the insurance policy extends coverage to boiler explosions, that is, by means of an exception to an exclusion, obscures what is at issue here. This is a *boiler* and machinery policy, which gives a manufacturer or other user of a narrow range of industrial equipment in which Hartford specializes additional protection for accidents involving the enumerated items, which besides moving or rotating machinery consist of steam boilers and closely related, specifically enumerated types of equipment. Stone wants to convert it to an "all risks" policy.

There are, we conclude, compelling reasons to reject Stone's reading of "of a kind" without need for a trial. But we add, lest our silence on the point mislead, that we disagree with Stone that when a term in an insurance contract is ambiguous, the insured is entitled to judgment in its favor without the insurance company's being allowed to present evidence to disambiguate the ambiguity. As we held in *Rhone-Poulenc Inc. v. International Ins. Co., supra,* 71 F.3d at 1305, applying Illinois law, the rule that ambiguities in insurance contracts are to be resolved in favor of the insured comes into play only after the insurance company has had an opportunity to present evidence designed to dispel the ambiguity. *Rhone-Poulenc* does not, as Stone argues, stand alone. There is a legion of similar holdings. * * * It is also worth noting that the rule that ambiguities in insurance contracts are to be resolved against the insurer is an application of the broader rule of contract law (also called *contra proferentem*, though the rule has greater force in the insurance setting, see Stempel, *supra*, ch. 5—as if to "insure" the insured against the risk of losing coverage because of ambiguous language in the policy) that ambiguities in a contract are to be resolved against the party that drafted the contract, and that in that setting as well the drafting party is entitled to present extrinsic evidence (that is, evidence outside the contract itself) to disambiguate the ambiguity. * * *

Courts in a minority of jurisdictions, it is true (but not Illinois), distinguish between "patent" and "latent" ambiguities in insurance contracts and hold that extrinsic evidence can be used only to disambiguate the latter. See, e.g., *American National Fire Ins. Co. v. Rose Acre Farms, Inc.*, 107 F.3d 451, 457–58 (7th Cir.1997) (Indiana law); *Charter Oil Co. v. American Employers' Ins. Co.*, 69 F.3d 1160, 1163 (D.C.Cir.1995) (Missouri law). Stone seems to be appealing to this rule in arguing that even if "of a kind" is ambiguous, Hartford has no right to present evidence about its meaning.

The distinction between the two types of ambiguity, though not the twist that the minority rule gives to it, is not peculiar to insurance law. A patent ambiguity in a contract is one that is apparent from just reading the contract. A latent ambiguity arises when, although the contract is clear "on its face," anyone knowing the background would know that it didn't mean what it seems to mean. *AM International, Inc. v. Graphic Management Associates, Inc.*, 44 F.3d 572 (7th Cir.1995) (Illinois law). A latent ambiguity thus requires extrinsic evidence to establish, as well as to resolve, and only objective evidence may be used for these purposes. The minority rule for insurance contracts seems to be based on the idea that if a term in an insurance contract obviously is ambiguous, the insured should be able to rely upon that meaning within the range of possible meanings that confers coverage. As Illinois does not have this rule, and anyway neither "explosion" nor "of a kind" is ambiguous in the context of Hartford's boiler and machinery policy, there is no need for us to opine on the merits or demerits of the minority rule.

The judgment is reversed with directions to enter judgment in favor of Hartford.

REVERSED.

NOTES AND QUESTIONS

1. *The Limits of* Contra Proferentem *and Extrinsic Evidence.* As *Stone Container* illustrates, courts can draw on a number of factors to determine that policy language unambiguously precludes coverage in a particular case. This includes the words surrounding contested policy language, the structure of the policy document, and the purpose of the underlying policy coverage. Additionally, although it does not ultimately end up considering it, the court explicitly holds that extrinsic evidence can be used to show that the meaning of a policy term is not ambiguous. Is this appropriate if the primary goal of *contra proferentem* is understood to be encouraging less ambiguous drafting? Some courts have explicitly refused to consider extrinsic evidence to resolve an ambiguity on the basis that doing so would undermine the insurer's responsibility for making the scope of the coverage clear in the policy itself. See *Washington Nat. Ins. Corp. v. Ruderman*, 117 So.3d 943 (Fla. 2013). According to some commentators, many other courts implicitly adopt this approach. See David S. Miller, Note, Insurance as Contract: The Argument for Abandoning the Ambiguity Doctrine, 88 Colum. L. Rev. 1849 (1988).

Relevant extrinsic evidence in an insurance coverage case can include pre-contractual negotiations, drafting history, expert testimony on industry custom, and regulatory filings, to name a few. A court's consideration of extrinsic evidence when policy language is ambiguous does not implicate the parol evidence rule, which permits the use of extrinsic evidence to help resolve the meaning of ambiguous contract language. Should insurers be allowed to admit extrinsic evidence to "disambiguate" policy language even if the policyholder could not reasonably have known about that extrinsic evidence at the time of purchase? According to the RLLI, a court should only consider extrinsic evidence when a reasonable policyholder in the policyholder's position could reasonably be expected to be aware of that evidence. RLLI § 3.

A related question is whether policyholders should be allowed to introduce extrinsic evidence to show that seemingly clear policy language is, in fact, ambiguous. As *Stone Court* notes, this is often described as a "latent ambiguity." Resolution of this issue often turns on the specific jurisdictions' version of the parol evidence rule, which may explicitly forbid the consideration of extrinsic evidence when a written, final and complete contract is unambiguous on its face.

2. *The Sophisticated Insured. Stone Container* expresses a willingness to apply the ambiguity rule even when the underlying policyholder is a large and presumably sophisticated corporate entity. A number of courts have endorsed this view. See, e.g., *Royal Ins. Co. of Am. v. KSI Trading Corp.*, 563 F.3d 68, 74–77 (3d Cir. 2009). Others have expressed uncertainty. In one recent high-profile case involving coverage in connection with the Deepwater Horizon Disaster, for instance, a Fifth Circuit panel certified the issue to the Texas Supreme Court. See *In re Deepwater Horizon*, 728 F.3d 491, 499 (5th Cir. 2013) (noting that while Texas has never recognized a sophisticated insured exception to *contra proferentem*, it has long recognized that this rule is "partially derivative of the unequal bargaining power typical in many negotiations over insurance contracts," which might justify such an exception). What are the arguments for and against this view? Should it matter if the insurer in fact drafted any

of the relevant policy language, or simply used the standard policy language available from the ISO?

3. *Coverage Disputes Between Two Insurers.* To what extent is it relevant that the real parties at interest in *Stone Container* were two insurers, one which had issued an all-risks policy and the other which had issued a narrower boiler and machinery policy? A number of courts have held that *contra proferentem* should not be available in coverage disputes between two insurers. See, e.g., *Econ. Premier Assur. Co. v. W. Nat. Mut. Ins. Co.*, 839 N.W.2d 749 (Minn. Ct. App. 2013). What rationale can you offer for this view? How might this help explain why Lloyds gave a short-term loan to Stone Container to pursue the coverage case against Hartford rather than paying coverage to Stone Container and then pursuing indemnification from Hartford on its own behalf?

4. HONORING THE REASONABLE EXPECTATIONS OF THE INSURED

Even when the meaning of an insurance policy or a provision in it is not ambiguous, it may be difficult for the layperson to read, or contain surprising limitations on coverage. Many of the cases finding a policy provision to be ambiguous and then construing it against the insurer may in fact be dealing with one of these problems, rather than a simple ambiguity. Beginning several decades ago, some courts began to be more candid about this phenomenon. By 1971 there were enough cases for Professor (later Judge) Robert Keeton to recognize a principle behind these decisions. He called it "honoring the reasonable expectations of the insured." Robert E. Keeton, Insurance Rights at Variance with Policy Provisions, 83 Harv. L. Rev. 961 (1970).

Some courts followed Keeton's lead, and some commentators take the position that about ten jurisdictions now explicitly employ the expectations principle. The doctrine is formulated differently in different jurisdictions, however, and applied somewhat selectively in other jurisdictions. And many courts probably are influenced by the principle even though they have not adopted it. Quantifying the number of jurisdictions that have adopted or sometimes follow the doctrine is therefore difficult. Nonetheless, it would certainly be fair to say that the majority of jurisdictions have not squarely adopted the expectations principle. See, e.g., *QBE Ins. Corp. v. Chalfonte Condo. Apartment Ass'n, Inc.*, 94 So.3d 541 (Fla. 2012); *Wilkie v. Auto-Owners Ins. Co.*, 469 Mich. 41 (2003); *Allen v. Prudential Prop. & Cas. Ins. Co.*, 839 P.2d 798 (Utah 1992) (all three rejecting the reasonable expectations doctrine). For a thorough analysis, see the articles in a Symposium on reasonable expectations in 5 Conn. Ins. L.J. 1 (1998–99); see also Roger C. Henderson, The Doctrine of Reasonable Expectations in Insurance Law After Two Decades, 51 Ohio St. L.J. 823 (1990). One author of this casebook has described the expectations principle as the vehicle through which "judge made insurance" is created. Kenneth S. Abraham, Distributing Risk: Insurance, Legal Theory, and Public Policy 100–32 (1986). Does the following case support this description or contradict it?

Atwater Creamery Company v. Western National Mutual Insurance Company

Supreme Court of Minnesota, 1985.
366 N.W.2d 271.

■ WAHL, JUSTICE.

Atwater Creamery Company (Atwater) sought a declaratory judgment against its insurer, Western National Mutual Insurance Company (Western), seeking coverage for losses sustained during a burglary of the creamery's storage building. * * * The Kandiyohi County District Court granted a directed verdict for Strehlow because Atwater failed to establish an insurance agent's standard of care by expert testimony. The trial court then dismissed the jury for lack of disputed issues of fact and ordered judgment in favor of the insurer, concluding that the burglary insurance policy in effect defined burglary so as to exclude coverage of this burglary. We affirm the directed verdict for Strehlow but reverse as to the policy coverage.

Atwater does business as a creamery and as a supplier of farm chemicals in Atwater, Minnesota. It was insured during the time in question against burglary, up to a ceiling of $20,000, by Western under Mercantile Open Stock Burglary Policy SC10–1010–12, which contained an "evidence of forcible entry" requirement in its definition of burglary. The creamery had recovered small amounts under this policy for two separate burglaries prior to the events in this case. * * *

Sometime between 9:30 p.m., Saturday, April 9, and 6 a.m., Monday, April 11, 1977, one or more persons made unauthorized entry into the building, took chemicals worth $15,587.40, apparently loading them on the truck that had been parked outside and driving away after loosening the turnbuckles on the east door and closing it. The truck was later found parked near the town dump, with the key still in the ignition.

Larry Poe, the plant manager at the Soil Center, had left at 9:30 p.m. on Saturday, after making sure everything was properly secured. On Monday morning, the north side doors were locked securely, but two of the three doors to the storage bin were ajar. Their padlocks were gone and never found. The turnbuckles had been loosened on the east sliding door so that it could be easily opened or closed.

An investigation by the local police, the Kandiyohi County Sheriff's Department, and the Minnesota Bureau of Criminal Investigation determined that no Atwater Creamery employees, past or present, were involved in the burglary. Suspicion settled on persons wholly unconnected with the creamery or even with the local area, but no one has been apprehended or charged with the crime.

Atwater filed a claim with Western under the burglary policy. Western denied coverage because there were no visible marks of physical damage to the exterior at the point of entrance or to the interior at the point of exit, as required by the definition of burglary in the policy. The creamery then brought suit against Western for the $15,587.40 loss, $7,500 in other directly related business losses and costs, disbursements and reasonable attorney fees.

Charles H. Strehlow, the owner of the Strehlow Insurance Agency in Willmar, Minnesota, and Western's agent, testified that he is certain he mentioned the evidence-of-forcible-entry requirement to Poe and members of the Atwater Board of Directors but was unable to say when the discussion occurred. Poe and the board members examined do not remember any such discussion. None of the board members had read the policy, which is kept in the safe at the main plant, and Poe had not read it in its entirety. He stated that he started to read it but gave up because he could not understand it.

The issues on appeal are

* * * 2. whether the reasonable expectations of the insured as to coverage govern to defeat the literal language of the policy * * *

2. Application of the Policy Definition of Burglary.

The definition of burglary in this policy is one used generally in burglary insurance. Courts have construed it in different ways. It has been held ambiguous and construed in favor of coverage in the absence of visible marks of forcible entry or exit. *United States Fidelity & Guaranty Co. v. Woodward,* 118 Ga.App. 591 (1968). We reject this analysis because we view the definition in the policy as clear and precise. It is not ambiguous.

In determining the intent of the parties to the insurance contract, courts have looked to the purpose of the visible-marks-of-forcible-entry requirement. These purposes are two: to protect insurance companies from fraud by way of "inside jobs" and to encourage insureds to reasonably secure the premises. See 5 Appleman § 3176 at 517. As long as the theft involved clearly [is] neither an inside job nor the result of a lack of secured premises, some courts have simply held that the definition does not apply. *Limberis v. Aetna Casualty & Surety Co.,* 263 A.2d 83 (Me.1970); *Kretschmer's House of Appliances, Inc. v. United States Fidelity & Guaranty Co.,* 410 S.W.2d 617 (Ky.1966).

In the instant case, there is no dispute as to whether Atwater is attempting to defraud Western or whether the Soil Center was properly secured. The trial court found that the premises were secured before the robbery and that the law enforcement investigators had determined that it was not an "inside job." To enforce the burglary definition literally against the creamery will in no way effectuate either purpose behind the restrictive definition. We are uncomfortable, however, with this analysis given the right of an insurer to limit the risk against which it will indemnify insureds.

At least three state courts have held that the definition merely provides for one form of evidence which may be used to prove a burglary and that, consequently, other evidence of a burglary will suffice to provide coverage. *Ferguson v. Phoenix Assurance Co. of New York,* 189 Kan. 459 (1962); *National Surety Co. v. Silberberg Bros.,* 176 S.W. 97 (Tex.Civ.App.1915); *Rosenthal v. American Bonding Co. of Baltimore,* 124 N.Y.S. 905 (N.Y.Sup.Ct.1910). The Nebraska Supreme Court recently rejected this argument in *Cochran v. MFA Mutual Insurance Co.,* 201 Neb. 631 (1978). The *Cochran* court held that the definition is not a rule of evidence but is a limit on liability, is unambiguous and is applied literally to the facts of the case at hand. We, too, reject this view of the definition as merely a form of evidence. The policy attempts to comprehensively define burglaries that are covered by it. In essence, this approach ignores the policy definition altogether and substitutes the court's or the statute's definition of burglary. This we decline to do, either via the conformity clause or by calling the policy definition merely one form of evidence of a burglary.

Some courts and commentators have recognized that the burglary definition at issue in this case constitutes a rather hidden exclusion from coverage. Exclusions in insurance contracts are read narrowly against the insurer. Running through the many court opinions refusing to literally enforce this burglary definition is the concept that the definition is surprisingly restrictive, that no one purchasing something called burglary insurance would expect coverage to exclude skilled burglaries that leave no visible marks of forcible entry or exit. Professor Robert E. Keeton, in analyzing these and other insurance cases where the results often do not follow from the rules stated, found there to be two general principles underlying many decisions. These principles are the reasonable expectations of the insured and the unconscionability of the clause itself or as applied to the facts of a specific case. Keeton, Insurance Law Rights at Variance with Policy Provisions, 83 Harv.L.Rev. 961 (1970). Keeton's article and subsequent book, Basic Text on Insurance Law (1971), have had significant impact on the construction of insurance contracts.

The doctrine of protecting the reasonable expectations of the insured is closely related to the doctrine of contracts of adhesion. Where there is unequal bargaining power between the parties so that one party controls all of the terms and offers the contract on a take-it-or-leave-it basis, the contract will be strictly construed against the party who drafted it. Most courts recognize the great disparity in bargaining power between insurance companies and those who seek insurance. Further, they recognize that, in the majority of cases, a lay person lacks the necessary skills to read and understand insurance policies, which are typically long, set out in very small type and written from a legalistic or insurance expert's perspective. Finally, courts recognize that people purchase insurance relying on others, the agent or company, to provide a policy that meets their needs. The result of the lack of insurance expertise on the part of insureds and the recognized marketing techniques of insurance companies is that "[t]he objectively reasonable expectations of applicants and intended beneficiaries regarding the terms of insurance contracts will be honored even though painstaking study of the policy provisions would have negated those expectations." Keeton, 83 Harv.L.Rev. at 967.

The traditional approach to construction of insurance contracts is to require some kind of ambiguity in the policy before applying the doctrine of reasonable expectations. Several courts, however, have adopted Keeton's view that ambiguity ought not be a condition precedent to the application of the reasonable-expectations doctrine.

As of 1980, approximately ten states had adopted the newer rule of reasonable expectations regardless of ambiguity. *Davenport Peters Co. v. Royal Globe Insurance Co.,* 490 F.Supp. 286, 291 (D.Mass.1980). Other states, such as Missouri and North Dakota, have joined the ten since then. Most courts recognize that insureds seldom see the policy until the premium is paid, and even if they try to read it, they do not comprehend it. Few courts require insureds to have minutely examined the policy before relying on the terms they expect it to have and for which they have paid.

The burglary definition is a classic example of a policy provision that should be, and has been, interpreted according to the reasonable expectations of the insured. *C & J Fertilizer, Inc. v. Allied Mutual Insurance Co.*, 227 N.W.2d 169 (Iowa 1975). *C & J Fertilizer* involved a burglary definition almost exactly like the one in the instant case as well as a burglary very similar to the Atwater burglary. The court applied the reasonable-expectations-regardless-of-ambiguity doctrine, noting that "[t]he most plaintiff might have reasonably anticipated was a policy requirement of visual evidence (abundant here) indicating the burglary was an 'outside' not an 'inside' job. The exclusion in issue, masking as a definition, makes the insurer's obligation to pay turn on the skill of the burglar, not on the event the parties bargained for: a bona fide third party burglary resulting in loss of plaintiff's chemicals and equipment." *Id.* at 177. The burglary in *C & J Fertilizer* left no visible marks on the exterior of the building, but an interior door was damaged. In the instant case, the facts are very similar except that there was no damage to the interior doors; their padlocks were simply gone. In *C & J Fertilizer,* the police concluded that an "outside" burglary had occurred. The same is true here.

Atwater had a burglary policy with Western for more than 30 years. The creamery relied on Charles Strehlow to procure for it insurance suitable for its needs. There is some factual dispute as to whether Strehlow ever told Poe about the "exclusion," as Strehlow called it. Even if he had said that there was a visible-marks-of-forcible-entry requirement, Poe could reasonably have thought that it meant that there must be clear evidence of a burglary. There are, of course, fidelity bonds which cover employee theft. The creamery had such a policy covering director and manager theft. The fidelity company, however, does not undertake to insure against the risk of third-party burglaries. A business that requests and purchases burglary insurance reasonably is seeking coverage for loss from third-party burglaries whether a break-in is accomplished by an inept burglar or by a highly skilled burglar. Two other burglaries had occurred at the Soil Center, for which Atwater had received insurance proceeds under the policy. Poe and the board of the creamery could reasonably have expected the burglary policy to cover this burglary where the police, as well as the trial court, found that it was an "outside job."

The reasonable-expectations doctrine gives the court a standard by which to construe insurance contracts without having to rely on arbitrary rules which do not reflect real-life situations and without having to bend and stretch those rules to do justice in individual cases. As Professor Keeton points out, ambiguity in the language of the contract is not irrelevant under this standard but becomes a factor in determining the reasonable expectations of the insured, along with such factors as whether the insured was told of important, but obscure, conditions or exclusions and whether the particular provision in the contract at issue is an item known by the public generally. The doctrine does not automatically remove from the insured a responsibility to read the policy. It does, however, recognize that in certain instances, such as where major exclusions are hidden in the definitions section, the insured should be held only to reasonable knowledge of the literal terms and conditions. The insured may show what actual expectations he or she had, but the factfinder should determine whether those expectations were reasonable under the circumstances. * * *

In our view, the reasonable-expectations doctrine does not automatically mandate either pro-insurer or pro-insured results. It does place a burden on insurance companies to communicate coverage and exclusions of policies accurately and clearly. It does require that expectations of coverage by the insured be reasonable under the circumstances. Neither of those requirements seems overly burdensome. Properly used, the doctrine will result in coverage in some cases and in no coverage in others.

We hold that where the technical definition of burglary in a burglary insurance policy is, in effect, an exclusion from coverage, it will not be interpreted so as to defeat the reasonable expectations of the purchaser of the policy. Under the facts and circumstances of this case, Atwater reasonably expected that its burglary insurance policy with Western would cover the burglary that occurred. Our holding requires reversal as to policy coverage.

NOTES AND QUESTIONS

1. *The Theory Behind the Expectations Principle.* There are a number of ways to justify honoring the reasonable expectations of the insured notwithstanding policy language that negates coverage. One is that the insurer in some way has misrepresented what is in the policy; another is that the insurer is estopped to deny coverage because it has allowed the insured to labor under a misimpression about the policy's contents. For an elaboration of these theories, see Kenneth S. Abraham, Distributing Risk: Insurance, Legal Theory, and Public Policy 104–09 (1986).

Under the *misrepresentation* and *estoppel* theories, some proof of the insured's reliance on his misimpression about coverage would seem to be necessary; yet there does not seem to be any such requirement in *Atwater Creamery,* or for that matter in most expectations cases. Possibly something like a presumption of reliance is operating where the kind of coverage the insured reasonably expects is available elsewhere. But neither the misrepresentation nor estoppel theories can be called upon for support where the expected coverage is unavailable in the market, for then there has been no detrimental reliance. Do you think a finding that all burglary insurance policies sold at the time contained a visible marks clause would have, or should have, influenced the *Atwater Creamery* decision?

Another theory that may underlie the expectations principle is that there is something *unconscionable* about omitting coverage that an insured reasonably expects. Is this an adequate explanation of the result in *Atwater Creamery*? That is, is it substantively unfair to provide burglary coverage that does not cover burglaries where no visible marks of forced entry appear on the exterior of the premises? Does this depend in part on what the insured pays for his coverage? When there is no detrimental reliance, no substantive unfairness inherent in an omission of a particular kind of coverage from a policy, and when the insurer has not created the insured's expectation that the policy does contain that coverage, is it ever appropriate to honor the insured's expectation, even if it is reasonable? Put another way, in such a situation there are two sets of reasonable expectations: a) the insured's, derived independently of anything misleading or unconscionable on the part of the insurer; and b) the insurer's, based on what the policy language states. The issue is which meaning should then be given priority, the one derived from the policy language or the one derived from extrinsic sources? Given the difficulty of making this choice, it should not be surprising that the courts have divided about whether to adopt the expectations principle.

Finally, it may be that principles similar to those that underlie the law of products liability are operating here. Insurance policies, after all, are not merely contracts, but intangible products. It would not be surprising, then, if the same concerns that result in liability for harm caused by "defective" products also operated in insurance law to help correct "defective language." In particular, it may be that the producers of insurance policies do not always take sufficient care in crafting policy language to avoid consumer harms, precisely because consumers are ill-informed about the quality of coverage language. If so, doctrines such as the reasonable expectations rule may have a role to play in inducing insurers to take more care to craft policy language that can reasonably accomplish their goals without unduly harming innocent policyholders. See, e.g., Daniel Schwarcz, A Products Liability Theory of the Judicial Regulation of Insurance Policies, 48 Wm. & Mary L. Rev. 1389 (2007); Jeffrey W. Stempel, The Insurance Policy as Thing, 44 Tort Trial & Ins. Prac. L.J. 813 (2009).

2. *Reasonable Expectations and Ambiguity.* Many courts have limited the scope of the reasonable expectations doctrine to cases in which the relevant policy language is ambiguous. See, e.g., *Bell v. Progressive Direct Ins. Co.*, 407 S.C. 565, 581 (2014) ("[W]hile we now hold that reasonable expectations may be used as another interpretive tool, the doctrine cannot be used to alter the plain terms of an insurance policy."); *Max True Plastering Co. v. U.S. Fid. & Guar. Co.*, 912 P.2d 861, 870 (Okla. 1996) (the reasonable expectations doctrine only applies "to cases in which policy language is ambiguous and to situations where, although clear, the policy contains exclusions masked by technical or obscure language or hidden exclusions"). Under this approach, to what extent does the doctrine of reasonable expectations have the ironic effect of limiting the scope of coverage for policyholders?

3. *Policyholders' Actual Coverage Expectations.* Are you satisfied that the insured in *Atwater Creamery* had the expectations the court thought he had? Suppose that the insured testified that he thought he would have coverage against the claim in question, but admitted on cross examination that he would not have been surprised to find a series of "fine print" exclusions that limited his rights. Alternatively, suppose that Atwater Creamery's insurance agent not only mentioned the evidence-of-forcible-entry requirement, but explained that the specific contours of the requirement were laid out in the policy. Should either of these facts alter the result in *Atwater Creamery*?

Although the cases are often unclear regarding the role to be played by the actual expectations of policyholders, they generally suggest that this is one component of the analysis. For example, courts sometimes suggest that provisions that the insured would not expect should be pointed out or made conspicuous. See, e.g., *Hionis v. N. Mut. Ins. Co.,* 230 Pa. Super. 511 (1974). The implication is that the insured's expectations are no longer reasonable if he is aware of a policy provision negating them. Similarly, some of the early expectations cases involved automated marketing or solicitation by mail, where there is no practical way for the insured to inquire as to the scope of coverage, or for the insurer to dispel inaccurate expectations. See, e.g., *Lachs v. Fid. & Cas. Co.,* 306 N.Y. 357 (1954) (flight insurance); *Steven v. Fid. & Cas. Co.,* 58 Cal. 2d 862 (1962) (flight insurance); *Klos v. Mobil Oil Co.,* 55 N.J. 117 (1969) (life insurance solicitation by mail).

How often do you think policyholders have any expectations about coverage that are specific and reliable enough to provide meaningful guidance in reasonable expectations cases? According to one review of various empirical sources, in most cases "insureds do not rationally evaluate insurance information or arrive at specific expectations of coverage." Jeffrey E. Thomas, An Interdisciplinary Critique of the Reasonable Expectations Doctrine, 5 Conn. Ins. L.J. 295, 333 (1998). Moreover, consumers often have expectations of coverage that are clearly and stubbornly incorrect. For instance, according to one recent survey, a majority of consumers mistakenly believe that their homeowners policies cover vehicles stolen from or damaged on their property, as well as damage caused by a break in their water supply line. See Press Release, NAIC, What Isn't Covered by Your Homeowners Insurance? (June 4, 2007). Similarly, approximately 1/3 of policyholders believe that their homeowners policies provide flood insurance, notwithstanding massive public education efforts by entities like FEMA. See Michelle Boardman, Insuring Understanding: The Tested Language Defense, 95 Iowa L. Rev. 1075 (2010) (reviewing these and other sources of consumer misperceptions regarding coverage). Even assuming that policyholders do have specific coverage expectations, how are courts supposed to figure out the content of these expectations?

4. *When are Coverage Expectations Reasonable?* Courts applying the reasonable expectations doctrine generally focus on the reasonableness of proffered coverage expectations. In *Atwater Creamery*, for instance, the court emphasized the name of the insurance policy, the "hidden" nature of the coverage restriction, and the purpose of the exclusion to conclude that an expectation of coverage was reasonable. But to what extent does this allow courts to simply create insurance coverage when they are so inclined? And how well equipped are courts to perform this role in ways that don't unduly interfere with insurance markets?

For instance, the court in *Atwater Creamery* determined that the purposes of the evidence-of-forcible-entry requirement were to prevent fraud by way of inside jobs and to encourage insureds to secure the insured premises (i.e. to prevent moral hazard). The policyholder's expectation of coverage was reasonable because, in that particular case, it was clear that the burglary was not the result of moral hazard. Other courts have echoed this reasoning when confronting visible marks clauses, in some cases finding that the requirement is merely an evidentiary condition, and that proof that the burglary was not an inside job may come in other ways as well. See *Convenient Food Mart #350 v. Cincinnati Ins. Co.,* 114 Ohio App. 3d 649 (1996) (finding that a forcible-entry requirement was satisfied when thieves forced their way into a locked office and then used a key to a safe that was left near it); Eric M. Holmes, Interpreting an Insurance Policy in

Georgia: The Problem of the Evidentiary Condition, 12 Ga. L. Rev. 783 (1978).

But to what extent does this framing ignore the fact that the evidence-of-forcible-entry requirement also serves (as do all *per se* rules) to reduce administrative and litigation costs? In other words, the exclusion limits the insurer's need to investigate whether a burglary was an inside job or a result of a failure to secure the insured premises. This may reduce the costs of providing coverage, and thus the price of coverage for policyholders. It may also reduce the risk of moral hazard because treating the exclusion as an evidentiary condition is likely to result in some moral hazard going unidentified by the insurer. Decisions such as *Atwater Creamery* may implicitly suggest that it is objectively unreasonable for insurers to provide coverage with these cost-saving benefits. Is it clear that this reflects policyholders' real preferences?

If a significant portion of the insured population would be willing to pay extra for the form of coverage created in *Atwater Creamery,* then why would not some insurers already have found it in their interest to offer such coverage? One answer is that the insured population believes that it already has such coverage, and is therefore already paying the price it is willing to pay in order to have such coverage. Another possible answer is that the cost of marketing both kinds of burglary insurance—i.e., the cost of having agents explain the two options and the benefits of each—are prohibitively high, given the size of the competitive edge that could be obtained by selling two different forms of coverage. The former answer may justify decisions such as *Atwater Creamery*, but the latter answer does not necessarily. And it is far from clear which answer is factually correct. Certainly trials in cases like *Atwater Creamery* do not involve evidence as to this factual question.

Perhaps the message of *Atwater Creamery* is merely that if insureds are not being provided with all-purpose burglary insurance, they are entitled to disclosure of this fact. If in fact it is too costly for insurers to explain the choice between the two forms of coverage, however, it will also be too costly to point out the evidence-of-forcible-entry requirement in policies that contain it, because the explanation in the two situations is the same, even if no choice is provided. Consequently, it will be too costly to dispel the "reasonable" expectation that there is coverage for all burglaries. As a result, the broader form of coverage will in effect be incorporated by law into all burglary policies, even though many (perhaps most) insureds would prefer narrower, less expensive coverage. The choice is thus between a result that in effect mandates the purchase of coverage that some insureds do not want, and a result that denies all insureds coverage that some of them do want. *Atwater Creamery* seems to choose the former.

5. *Reasonable Expectations and the Completed Operations Exclusion.* Another well-known context in which courts have invoked the reasonable expectations doctrine to find coverage disclaimed in the underlying policy involves the "completed operations exclusion" in liability insurance policies. This clause excludes coverage when liability results from bodily injury or property damage taking place after an insured contractor's work has been completed or abandoned. For instance, in *Atwood v. Hartford Accident & Indemnity Co.*, 116 N.H. 636 (1976), an insurer denied coverage to an electrician on the basis of a completed operations exclusion after he was sued due to an alleged failure to properly fix a thermostat, which

contributed to the death of a baby from heat prostration the next day. Emphasizing that the exclusion was buried within a long and complex policy document and that the policyholder's agent never informed him of the exclusion, the court concluded that the policyholder reasonably expected coverage. To what extent is the setting in *Atwood* a more compelling case than *Atwater Creamery* for invocation of the reasonable expectations doctrine? What do you make of the contention that virtually all electricians in Atwood's situation would want to buy products/completed operations coverage, whereas the preferences of policyholders for broad or narrow burglary coverage may vary?

6. *Unreasonable Expectations.* Even in jurisdictions that have squarely adopted the expectations principle, there are of course decisions denying an insured's claim that she is entitled to coverage notwithstanding contrary policy provisions. Some of these decisions suggest that an insured's expectation of coverage is less reasonable if that coverage can be purchased through an alternative type of policy. For example, in *Herzog v. National American Insurance Co.*, 2 Cal. 3d 192 (1970), the court held that the insured could not reasonably expect coverage for liability arising out of the operation of a motor bike under the liability provisions of a homeowners policy because motor vehicle insurance was available. See also *Jones v. Horace Mann Ins. Co.*, 937 P.2d 1360 (Alaska 1997) (coverage of liability arising out of snowmobile being operated on a public road not reasonably expected); *Allstate Ins. Co. v. Keillor*, 450 Mich. 412 (1995) (coverage of liability arising out of use of motor vehicle not reasonably expected under a homeowners policy). Other decisions, however, honor an insured's expectations even when the coverage expected is separately available elsewhere. Should proof of such availability at least be admissible on the reasonableness issue? Should the unavailability of the expected coverage be admissible in the insured's favor?

7. *A Sophisticated Insured Exception?* Although most of the expectations decisions still involve ordinary individuals who have purchased personal insurance, some decisions invoke the expectations principle even when the insured is a sizeable commercial enterprise. See, e.g., *Keene Corp. v. Ins. Co. of N. Am.*, 667 F.2d 1034 (D.C. Cir. 1981). On the other hand, some decisions explicitly reject application of the principle to cases involving sophisticated insureds. See, e.g., *Benjamin Moore & Co. v. Aetna Cas. & Sur. Co.*, 179 N.J. 87, 102 (2004); *Oritani Sav. & Loan Ass'n v. Fid. & Deposit Co. of Md.*, 989 F.2d 635 (3d Cir. 1993). Should there be a "sophisticated insured" exception to *contra proferentem* or the expectations principle? See Hazel Glenn Beh, Reassessing the Sophisticated Insured Exception, 39 Tort Trial & Ins. Prac. L.J. 85 (2003); Jeffrey W. Stempel, Reassessing the "Sophisticated" Policyholder Defense in Insurance Coverage Litigation, 42 Drake L. Rev. 807 (1993); James M. Fischer, Why Are Insurance Contracts Subject to Special Rules of Interpretation?: Text Versus Context, 24 Ariz. St. L.J. 995 (1992).

Although the RLLI does not adopt the reasonable expectations doctrine, it does specify that a number of policy terms are "mandatory" and cannot be altered by the insurer. But the RLLI contains an exception in the case of "large commercial policyholders," which it defines as policyholders having assets reaching a threshold from federal securities laws (presently $10 million) at the time of policy purchase. RLLI § 1(6). For these policyholders, virtually all insurance policy terms are "defaults" that insurers can change if they are so inclined. See generally Tom Baker & Kyle Logue, Mandatory Rules and Default Rules in Insurance Contracts, in The Law and Economics of Insurance (Daniel Schwarcz & Peter Siegelman eds., 2015).

B. THE ROLE OF INTERMEDIARIES

To consumers uneducated about insurance, the prospect of purchasing a policy that appropriately covers their needs can be a daunting task. Even for a sophisticated business, making direct, individual contact with the variety of insurers who can provide the many different forms of coverage the business needs would be onerous. For this reason, much insurance is purchased through intermediaries who can assess a prospective customer's exposure to risk and help to secure insurance adequate to that customer's needs. Nevertheless, a number of insurers sell the most common types of policies, such as auto or homeowners, directly over the phone or internet. Such *direct writers* (who include State Farm, Allstate, Nationwide, and GEICO) can often offer lower rates than companies selling only through intermediaries, and are therefore attractive to many consumers. However, purchasers of insurance who forego intermediaries must decide for themselves what their insurance needs are and how to meet them. The purchase of insurance through intermediaries is therefore likely to continue in the future for many consumers, notwithstanding the importance of direct writers.

Numerous types of insurance intermediaries (who are also often referred to as "producers") exist in today's insurance market places. Often they are sub-divided into two broad categories: brokers and agents. Insurance brokers operate primarily on behalf of individuals and entities seeking coverage. By contrast, insurance agents are generally understood to be the representatives of insurance companies, who authorize them to solicit and prepare coverage applications. However, the distinction between brokers and agents is much more fluid than this dichotomy suggests. For instance, insurers can authorize brokers to issue endorsements or process claims on their behalf. Meanwhile, insurers may authorize agents to temporarily "bind" coverage for applicants during the underwriting stage, but they do not always do so. Both insurance brokers and agents are principally compensated through commissions on policyholder premiums, which are generally calculated as a simple percentage of premiums.

Insurance agents are themselves often subdivided into captive and independent agents. Captive agents sell coverage exclusively from a single carrier. They can be either an employee of the insurer or an independent contractor. Independent agents sell coverage from multiple carriers and are always independent contractors. These agents typically have considerable discretion to determine which company their clients should apply to for coverage. In addition to ordinary commissions, both brokers and independent agents may be compensated in part by bonuses for referring a substantial amount of business to a particular carrier, a payment often labeled as a "contingent commission."

As all this suggests, the distinctions among different types of insurance intermediaries are slippery indeed. For this reason, the law governing insurance intermediaries rarely turns solely on an intermediary's label as an independent agent, captive agent, or broker. Instead, it turns on the specific character of the underlying relationships at issue. As you study the following cases and materials, consider whether this approach results in excessive uncertainty, and whether a legal and regulatory approach that attempted to more closely hew to market-based distinctions would be more sensible. Also consider whether the existing legal and regulatory approach to regulating insurance intermediaries ends up replicating market-based distinctions in the end anyway. To the extent this is so, do the results always make sense from a policy perspective?

1. THE AUTHORITY OF INTERMEDIARIES

The law governing insurance intermediaries of all types is substantially influenced by basic agency law principles, which you likely have encountered either in contract law or corporate law classes. According to the Restatement (Third) of Agency § 1.01, "[a]gency is the fiduciary relationship that arises when one person (a 'principal') manifests assent to another person (an 'agent') that the agent shall act on the principal's behalf and subject to the principal's control, and the agent manifests assent or otherwise consents so to act." As this definition suggests, agency relationships often arise out of contractual agreements that the agent shall act on behalf of the principal.

Agency law determines when an agent can bind a principal to a contract. When a principal grants an agent "actual authority" to enter into contracts on its behalf, the agent can bind the principal to these contracts in the same way as if the principal itself entered into the contract. Agents can also contractually bind principals if doing so is implicit within the agent's actual authority or necessary or incidental to achieving the principal's objectives. Additionally, agents can bind principals even in the absence of any actual authority when they possess "apparent authority" from their principal, which requires that the principal has done or said something that would lead a third party to reasonably believe that the agent has actual authority to enter into the contract at issue on behalf of the principal.

Agency law has important implications for an agent's authority to act on behalf of insurance companies or policyholders. For instance, as described above, policyholders often wish to "bind" coverage during the period of time when their policy application is being reviewed by an insurance company. Recall the significance of the binder in the *World Trade Center* case—until a policy is actually issued, the binder may be the only source of coverage rights. But an insurance agent may or may not have contractual authority to "bind" an insurance company and provide immediate coverage, sometimes subject to later rejection by the company and sometimes not. Indeed, the cases and treatises are replete with references to the different levels of authority possessed by different kinds of agents. General agents are said to have authority to bind the company (except in life insurance, where the home office alone makes binding decisions), but soliciting agents and local agents do not.

Even when agents do not possess actual authority to bind insurers, they may nonetheless end up doing so because they possess apparent authority. For instance, in *Elmer Tallant Agency, Inc. v. Bailey Wood*

Products, Inc., 374 So.2d 1312 (Ala. 1979), an independent agent possessed actual authority to bind a Workers Compensation carrier to coverage. However, the carrier limited this authority when the applicant's coverage had previously been cancelled, denied, or non-renewed or when the applicant ran certain types of businesses, such as a sawmill business. A sawmill business that had been denied coverage in the recent past applied for coverage through the agent, and the agent informed the business that coverage was bound with the carrier. An employee of the business then suffered a workplace injury before the carrier had a chance to deny the insurance application. The carrier refused to pay the claim because the agent had acted outside of the scope of his authority in binding coverage. The court, however, ruled that the agent did indeed bind the principal and thus that the carrier must pay for the loss. Despite its lack of actual authority to bind coverage in this case, the agent possessed apparent authority to do so because the insurer's restriction on the agent's authority was not reasonably apparent to the applicant.

Numerous cases similarly find that agents clothed with apparent authority can bind insurers notwithstanding insurer-imposed restrictions on an agent's authority. See, e.g., *Am. Income Life Ins. Co. v. Hollins,* 830 So.2d 1230 (Miss. 2002); *Romero v. Pough,* 532 So.2d 279 (La. App. 1988); *Goldstein v. Milton Brokerage Ass'n,* 632 F. Supp. 285 (E.D. Pa. 1986); *Corbitt v. Fed. Kemper Ins. Co.,* 594 S.W.2d 728 (Tenn. App. 1979). When this occurs, an insurer is likely to have a cause of action against the agent for violating the terms of their contract. The insurer's ability to recoup from the agent its payment to the policyholder would depend on the extent of the agent's assets, including any liability insurance (Errors and Omissions coverage or a Surety Bond) protecting the agent.

2. Intermediaries' Duties to Policyholders

Langwith v. American National General Insurance Company

Supreme Court of Iowa, 2010.
793 N.W.2d 215.

■ Ternus, Chief Justice.

The primary issue presented by this appeal is the scope of liability of an insurance agent to her clients. The appellants, Dennis Langwith and his son, Ben Langwith, sued Dennis's insurance agent, appellee Janet Fitzgerald, alleging she breached a duty of reasonable care, which resulted in their partially uninsured exposure on a personal injury claim filed against them. The Langwith plaintiffs contend appellees American National General Insurance Company and American National Property and Casualty Co. (collectively American National) are vicariously liable for the actions of Fitzgerald, American National's captive agent.

The district court granted summary judgment to Fitzgerald and American National, ruling Fitzgerald did not owe a duty beyond a "general duty to procure the insurance requested by the Langwiths," and therefore, Fitzgerald had no duty to advise Dennis Langwith with respect to the coverage provided by Dennis's umbrella liability policy or to render risk-management advice to her client, as alleged by the plaintiffs. * * * We reverse the district court's summary judgment ruling insofar as it determined the defendants had demonstrated they were entitled to judgment as a matter of law with respect to the claim that Fitzgerald should have advised the plaintiffs on the status of their coverage under the umbrella liability policy. * * *

I. Background Facts and Proceedings

Fitzgerald is a self-employed captive agent for American National doing business under the name of American National Janet Fitzgerald Insurance Services. Prior to the events giving rise to this lawsuit, Dennis and his wife, Susan Langwith (hereinafter the Langwiths), had purchased substantially all of their insurance through Fitzgerald. During this time, they had consistently carried an automobile liability insurance policy with limits of $250,000 and an umbrella policy with $3,000,000 limits, both issued by American National. These policies also covered the Langwiths' two children, including Ben.

In December 2003, Ben's driver's license was suspended, which prompted American National to cancel Ben's coverage under the automobile liability policy. American National also sought to cancel the umbrella policy, but did not do so after Dennis and Susan signed a form agreeing to a driver exclusion for Ben. (This exclusion precluded coverage under the umbrella policy for any insured for any loss sustained while the vehicle was being operated by Ben.) When Ben's driver's license was reinstated, Susan spoke with Fitzgerald regarding insurance coverage for Ben. As a result of that conversation, Fitzgerald procured a high-risk policy from American National that covered Ben when driving the Langwiths' vehicles. This policy had limits of $250,000. The Langwiths assumed Ben was once again covered by the umbrella policy since Ben's driver's license had been reinstated and he had obtained the required underlying liability coverage. Contrary to this understanding, the driver exclusion for Ben remained on the Langwiths' umbrella policy.

On July 16, 2006, Ben was in an accident when driving a Chevrolet Suburban titled in Dennis's name. Corey Shannon, a passenger in Ben's vehicle, was severely injured. Shannon sued Ben based on Ben's alleged negligent operation of the Suburban, and he sued Dennis under the owner-liability statute. *See* Iowa Code § 321.493 (2005) (imposing liability on the owner of a vehicle for damages caused by a consent driver). American National acknowledged coverage for these claims under the automobile liability policy issued to the Langwiths and has provided a defense to Dennis and Ben in the Shannon lawsuit pursuant to its obligations under this policy. American National has denied any liability under the umbrella policy, however, based on the driver exclusion for Ben.

Dennis and Ben filed this suit alleging, after various amendments, that Fitzgerald breached a duty of care to them by (1) failing to disclose that the driver exclusion in the umbrella policy continued after Ben's license was reinstated, and (2) failing to advise the Langwiths that Dennis could avoid all personal liability for Ben's driving by transferring title to the Suburban to Ben. The plaintiffs sought to hold the insurers vicariously liable for Fitzgerald's breach of duty. * * *

Fitzgerald filed a motion for summary judgment requesting that the court rule as a matter of law that informing the Langwiths that the driver exclusion continued on the umbrella policy and advising them that title to the Suburban should be transferred to Ben so Dennis could avoid legal liability for Ben's negligent driving "are outside the scope of Fitzgerald's duty as an insurance agent." American National joined in Fitzgerald's motion for summary judgment. As noted earlier, the district court granted the motion filed by Fitzgerald and denied the plaintiffs' motions for partial summary judgment. The plaintiffs appealed. * * *

III. Defendant's Motion for Summary Judgment

A. Duty of Insurance Agent. The district court granted Fitzgerald's motion for summary judgment on the ground that Fitzgerald had no duty to advise the Langwiths with respect to umbrella coverage on Ben or with respect to avoiding Dennis's vicarious liability for Ben's negligent driving. In reaching this conclusion, the court relied on settled Iowa law restricting the obligation of insurance agents to their clients. *See Sandbulte v. Farm Bureau Mut. Ins. Co.*, 343 N.W.2d 457, 464–65 (Iowa 1984); *Collegiate Mfg. Co. v. McDowell's Agency, Inc.*, 200 N.W.2d 854, 857–58 (Iowa 1972). We begin our discussion with a review of these cases.

In *Collegiate Manufacturing Co.*, the plaintiff sued its insurance agent, claiming the agent negligently failed to provide adequate coverage for the plaintiff's business inventory. 200 N.W.2d at 856. After an adverse jury verdict, the plaintiff appealed, asserting error in the trial court's instructions. *Id.* at 856–57. Specifically, the plaintiff objected to an instruction that stated in part:

> You are instructed that there is a duty upon the owner of insurable property to familiarize himself with the quantity and value of such property, its insurability, the kinds and amounts of insurance available, and in general the terms and conditions of the insurances issued upon his property.

As applied to this case, it was the duty of the plaintiff to advise Stoll [the insurance agent], generally, as to the quantity and value of the property to be insured and the kinds and amounts of insurance desired, and then it was the duty of Stoll to use due diligence to procure the insurance and at all times to keep the plaintiff advised and informed as to the insurances available and procured.

This court rejected the plaintiff's challenge to this instruction, noting the relationship between an insured and an insurance agent is one of principal/agent. *Id.* at 858. Consistent with the nature of this relationship, we held an insurance agent "owes his principal the use of such skill as is required *to accomplish the object of his employment.*" *Id.* at 857 (emphasis added). Acknowledging that an agent's duties may be limited or enlarged "by agreement of the parties," *id.*, we concluded there was no evidence showing "the burden of deciding for plaintiff both the type and amount of insurance to be provided" had been delegated to the insurance agent. *Id.* at 859.

In our subsequent decision in *Sandbulte*, we discussed the circumstances under which an insurance agent's "general duty . . . to use reasonable care, diligence, and judgment in procuring the insurance requested by an insured" could be enlarged. 343 N.W.2d at 464. We stated:

> An expanded agency agreement, arrangement or relationship, sufficient to require a greater duty from the agent than the general duty, generally exists when the agent holds himself out as an insurance specialist, consultant or counselor and is receiving compensation for consultation and advice apart from premiums paid by the insured.

Id. We rejected the notion that such an expanded agency relationship could be established solely by proof of a long-standing relationship between the insurance agent and his client. *Id.* at 465. * * *

[T]he import of our decisions in *Collegiate Manufacturing Co.* and *Sandbulte* was to limit an insurance agent's obligation to procurement of the coverage requested by the client, relieving the agent of any duty to advise his client of the kinds and amounts of insurance that would protect his client's insurable interests unless there was evidence of an expanded agency agreement. Moreover, the circumstances under which an expanded agency agreement could arise were narrowly circumscribed in *Sandbulte*: "the agent holds himself out as an insurance specialist, consultant or counselor and is receiving compensation for consultation and advice apart from premiums paid by the insured." 343 N.W.2d at 464. Although this court cited some authority for its holding in *Sandbulte*, we gave no rationale for such a restrictive approach.

Our examination of the general principles governing agency relationships convinces us that a more flexible method of determining the undertaking of an insurance agent is appropriate. The Restatement (Third) of Agency ties the duty of the agent to the agent's contractual undertaking. Restatement (Third) of Agency § 8.07, at 334 ("An agent has a duty to act *in accordance with the express and implied terms of any contract* between the agent and principal." (Emphasis added.)); *id.* § 8.07 cmt. a, at 334 ("This section makes the basic point that an agent's duties of performance to the principal are subject to the terms of any contract between them."). As the authors of the Restatement note in a comment to section 8.08, "The specific skills that an agent must possess to be competent depend on the nature of the service *that the agent undertakes to provide* and the circumstances under which it will be provided. . . ." *Id.* § 8.08 cmt. c, at 345–46 (emphasis added); * * *

The defendants have advanced no reason, nor have we identified one, that would justify the limitations placed on the circumstances that might be considered in determining the duty undertaken by an insurance agent, as stated in *Sandbulte*. Therefore, we hold that it is for the fact finder to determine, based on a consideration of all the circumstances, the agreement of the parties with respect to the service to be rendered by the insurance agent and whether that service was performed with the skill and knowledge normally possessed by insurance agents under like circumstances. *See Fowler v. Berry Seed Co.*, 248 Iowa 1158, 1165 (1957) (stating extent of agency is a fact question). Some of the circumstances that may be considered by the fact finder in determining the undertaking of the insurance agent include the nature and content of the discussions between the agent and the client; the prior dealings of the parties, if any; the knowledge and sophistication of the client; whether the agent holds himself out as an insurance specialist, consultant, or counselor; and whether the agent receives compensation for additional or specialized services. * * *

The client bears the burden of proving an agreement to render services beyond the general duty to obtain the coverage requested. *Murphy*, 682 N.E.2d at 976. In the absence of circumstances indicating the insurance agent has assumed a duty beyond the procurement of the coverage requested by the client, the insurance agent has no obligation to advise a client regarding additional coverage or risk management. *See Sintros v. Hamon*, 810 A.2d 553, 555 (2002) ("A majority of courts that have considered the issue have held that an insurance agent owes clients a duty of reasonable care and diligence, but absent a special relationship, that duty does not include an affirmative, continuing obligation to inform or advise an insured regarding the availability or sufficiency of insurance coverage."). We think this analytical framework respects the principal/agent relationship, yet accounts for the diverse undertakings of an insurance agent that can vary from the simple procurement of the particular insurance coverage requested by the client to a full risk assessment to anything in-between. In light of our abandonment of the restrictive requirements for an expanded agency duty, we overrule our *Sandbulte* decision to the extent it limits an expanded duty to those cases in which the agent holds himself out as an insurance specialist, consultant, or counselor and receives compensation for additional or specialized services.

B. Application of Summary Judgment Standard. Applying the principles announced above, we now examine the defendants' contention they are entitled to judgment as a matter of law. The plaintiffs claim Fitzgerald was negligent in two respects: (1) failing to disclose that the driver exclusion in the umbrella policy continued after Ben's license was reinstated, and (2) failing to advise the Langwiths that Dennis could avoid all personal liability for Ben's driving by transferring title to the Suburban to Ben. We must examine the record, in the light most favorable to the plaintiffs, to determine whether there are facts that would support a finding of an "agreement between the parties, interpreted in light of the circumstances under which it is made," that obligated Fitzgerald to advise the Langwiths that the driver exclusion on the umbrella policy continued and that Dennis could avoid liability for Ben if he put the title to the Suburban in Ben's name.

The summary judgment record shows the Langwiths had purchased nearly all their insurance policies through Fitzgerald for ten to twelve years. Dennis Langwith had several conversations with Fitzgerald over the years with respect to property insurance and general liability insurance on his business and his business properties, as well as with respect to liability insurance on his business vehicles. Dennis testified in his deposition that Fitzgerald recommended the appropriate coverage to meet his insurance needs, advice that he usually, but not always, followed.

Susan had the most contact with Fitzgerald with respect to family insurance matters and testified in her deposition that their relationship was based solely upon the Langwiths' "insurance liability and needs." Susan also stated that Fitzgerald gave the Langwiths advice on insurance matters, which they would usually follow. When Ben lost his driver's license, Susan called Fitzgerald to have Ben removed from their automobile liability policy. At that time, Fitzgerald asked the Langwiths to sign an exclusion on their umbrella policy for any liability arising from Ben's operation of any vehicle in order to avoid cancellation of that policy. The Langwiths signed the requested form and were aware the exclusion precluded coverage under the umbrella policy for claims arising from Ben's driving.

After Ben's license was reinstated, Susan met with Fitzgerald at Fitzgerald's office and asked Fitzgerald "what we could do about Ben." Susan testified she meant "how can we cover him? How can we provide liability coverage that protects him and all of us?" Susan said she "was asking for [Fitzgerald's] professional advice." Fitzgerald told her they could get a high-risk policy for Ben with limits of $250,000, which Fitzgerald did. Although Susan and Fitzgerald did not discuss the umbrella coverage, Susan and Dennis assumed the umbrella policy covered Ben's driving once his license was reinstated. Fitzgerald did not inform the Langwiths that the driver's exclusion had been removed from the umbrella policy, nor did she tell them it had not been removed. The parties disagree as to whether the Langwiths should have known the exclusion continued based on the declarations pages they periodically received.

Dennis testified they had never asked Fitzgerald for advice on matters other than those that involved insurance. * * *

We conclude the record shows a genuine issue of material fact with respect to the plaintiffs' first claim of negligence, namely, that Fitzgerald should have told the Langwiths that the driver exclusion remained on the umbrella policy. A fact finder could conclude from Susan's inquiry regarding "what [they] could do about Ben" that she was seeking Fitzgerald's "professional guidance" regarding "liability coverage that [would] protect [ ] him and [the Langwiths]," as Susan testified. A fact finder could also conclude that Fitzgerald understood or should have understood the nature of this request and that she responded by finding an automobile liability policy to insure Ben. Accordingly, a fact finder could find that the parties had an implied agreement that Fitzgerald would advise the Langwiths with respect to the liability coverage that could or should be put in place to protect Ben and his parents, including umbrella liability coverage. *Cf. Fitzpatrick*, 67 Cal.Rptr.2d at 452 (stating duty may arise if "there is a request or inquiry by the insured for a particular type or extent of coverage"); *Murphy*, 682 N.E.2d at 976 (noting jurisdictions have recognized "an additional duty of advisement . . . where, for example . . . there was some interaction regarding a question of coverage, with the insured relying on the expertise of the agent"); 4 Couch on Insurance 3d § 55:5, at 55–12 (1996) (stating "although insurer's agents are not required under a general duty of care to advise the insured regarding the sufficiency of coverage limits . . . , once they elect to respond to his or her inquiries, a special duty arises requiring them to use reasonable care"). * * * Therefore, we reverse that part of the district court's summary judgment ruling granting judgment to the defendants on the claim Fitzgerald negligently failed to advise the Langwiths regarding coverage under the umbrella policy. *See Peter v. Schumacher Enters., Inc.*, 22 P.3d 481, 487 (Alaska 2001) (stating whether client made inquiry that required insurance agent to advise client on available levels of coverage for UM/UIM coverage is a fact question to be resolved at trial).

We reach a contrary conclusion with respect to the allegation that Fitzgerald should have advised the Langwiths to transfer title on the vehicle driven by Ben from Dennis to Ben. It is undisputed there was no express agreement that Fitzgerald would assess the Langwiths' liability risk with respect to Ben and advise them on how to avoid that risk. Fitzgerald did not hold herself out as a specialist, consultant, or counselor, nor did the Langwiths compensate her for consultation and advice apart from the premiums they paid. Moreover, there were no prior dealings between these parties in which Fitzgerald was ever requested to give advice outside of the proper insurance policy to ensure a particular risk. As Susan testified, Fitzgerald had never given them advice in the past "about matters other than insurance." The fact that the parties had a long-standing relationship through which Fitzgerald gained knowledge of the "family dynamics" is not sufficient evidence from which a fact finder could find that there was an implied agreement to expand Fitzgerald's undertaking from advising how risk could be *insured* to advising how risk could be *avoided*. Cf. *Nelson v. Davidson*, 456 N.W.2d 343, 347 (1990) ("The mere allegation that a client relied upon an agent and had great confidence in him is insufficient to imply the existence of a duty to advise."), superseded on other grounds by statute, Wis. Stat. § 632.32(4m) (1995), as recognized in *Avery v. Diedrich*, 734 N.W.2d 159, 165 (2007). There is a material distinction between insuring risk and avoiding risk, and there are no circumstances present here that support a finding the parties agreed Fitzgerald would advise the Langwiths on risk avoidance. * *

* * * Therefore, we affirm that part of the district court's summary judgment ruling granting judgment to the defendants on the plaintiffs' claim Fitzgerald was negligent in failing to advise the Langwiths to put title to the Suburban in Ben's name alone. See *Sewell v. Great N. Ins. Co.*, 535 F.3d 1166, 1171 (10th Cir.2008) (affirming summary judgment for insurance agent, finding no facts to show agent assumed any responsibilities for personal risk-management services). * * *

NOTES AND QUESTIONS

1. *Repudiated by Statute.* Within a year of *Langwith*, the Iowa legislature passed a statute overruling the case and reinstating the very narrow standard for insurance agents' duties to policyholders previously established in *Sandbulte v. Farm Bureau Mut. Ins. Co.*, 343 N.W.2d 457 (Iowa 1984). The Iowa legislature's swift repudiation of *Langwith* reveals some of the political forces that tend to restrict insurance agents' legal obligations to policyholders in many states.

2. *Predictability v. Flexibility.* Although *Langwith* was repudiated by statute, its flexible approach to identifying the cases in which insurance intermediaries may have a duty to advise policyholders about coverage is the dominant approach. See Douglas R. Richmond, 1–2 New Appleman on Insurance Law Library Edition § 2.05 (2012). As illustrated by *Langwith*, however, this approach seems to create substantial uncertainty regarding whether an insurance intermediary owes a particular policyholder a duty that extends beyond simply securing the coverage that a policyholder has

requested. See Hazel Beh & Amanda M. Willis, Insurance Intermediaries, 15 Conn. Ins. L.J. 571 (2009) (noting that outcomes in these cases "are fact-driven and unpredictable"). Based on the evidence reviewed in *Langwith*, did the Langwiths do enough to seek the agent's "professional guidance" regarding coverage such that it would be appropriate to place special obligations on the agent? And how reliable is testimony regarding the precise discussions between agents and policyholders likely to be?

3. *Dual Agency.* Note that *Langwith* locates insurance intermediaries' limited obligation to procure requested coverage in an agency relationship between insurance agents and policyholders. This agency relationship generally co-exists with the insurance intermediary's agency relationship with the insurer. Insurance intermediaries are thus often described as dual agents: agents of insurers for some purposes and agents of policyholders for other purposes.

4. *Insurers' Liability for Agent Misconduct.* The Langwiths attempted to hold their insurer, American National, liable for the alleged failings of its insurance agent. Under basic agency law principles, principals can often be held vicariously liable for the acts of agents when those acts are in furtherance of the agency relationship. See, e.g., *Chicago Title Ins. Co. v. Wash. State Office of Ins. Comm'r,* 309 P.3d 372 (Wash. 2013). How might holding insurers liable for the misconduct of agents impact insurers' monitoring of agents? Are insurers in a better position than policyholders to police agents for misconduct?

5. *The Character of Intermediaries' Advice.* Remarkably little evidence exists regarding the quality of the advice that insurance intermediaries provide to policyholders, or the extent to which they seek to provide such guidance in the first place. See Daniel Schwarcz & Peter Siegelman, Insurance Agents in the 21st Century: The Problem of Biased Advice, in The Law and Economics of Insurance (Daniel Schwarcz & Peter Siegelman eds., 2015) (reviewing the extant literature). Of course, the answer depends significantly on context. Large insurance brokers, for instance, clearly provide extensive guidance to customers on risk management, potential insurance program structures, and the merits of different carriers. Moreover, the relative sophistication of the policyholders that these insurance intermediaries serve (often large commercial enterprises with risk managers) probably means that large insurance brokers typically provide high-quality advice. Even here, however, there are some very notable counter-examples. For instance, in the late 1990s and early 2000s, the largest commercial insurance broker in the world, Marsh & McLennan, steered some of its customers to insurers predominantly on the basis of which pairings would produce the greatest amount of commission revenue for Marsh. Marsh's elaborate scheme—which included concocting phony bids to create the illusion of competition by insurers for potential policyholders—resulted in extensive regulatory action, litigation, and even several criminal convictions. Sean M. Fitzpatrick, The Small Laws: Eliot Spitzer and the Way to Insurance Market Reform, 74 Fordham L. Rev. 3041, 3064 (2006).

The character of insurance agents' advice in more consumer-oriented markets is even less clear. Such agents are required to acquire a license in every state, though states vary in the types of licenses they offer and the requirements they impose for obtaining one. See U.S. Gov't Accountability Office, Rep. No. GAO–09–372, Insurance

Reciprocity and Uniformity: NAIC and State Regulators Have Made Progress in Producer Licensing, Product Approval, and Market Conduct Regulation, but Challenges Remain (2009). In most states, though, individuals must pass an insurance exam and background check to acquire a license, and they can lose this license if they are found to have engaged in misconduct. Little evidence exists, however, regarding the extent to which this licensing regime contributes to more reliable and informed guidance from insurance intermediaries.

6. *Conflicts of Interest.* Many insurance intermediaries may face financial incentives to act in ways that are not in policyholders' interests. For instance, insurance agents generally receive a single commission at the time of sale in connection with a policyholder's purchase of a life insurance product. This can create strong incentives for insurance agents to sell policyholders inappropriate replacement policies in order to generate new commissions. See Douglas Richmond, Liability Issues in the Sale of Life Insurance, 40 Tort Trial & Ins. Prac. L.J. 877 (2005) (describing excessive replacement of life insurance policies among some insurance agents in order to generate new commissions). Similarly, in many insurance markets, independent insurance agents and brokers receive contingent commissions, which are bonuses from an insurer to an intermediary for reaching pre-specified benchmarks with respect to the business they direct to the insurer. As in the case of Marsh, this can create strong incentives for brokers and independent agents to direct customers to insurers on the basis of which pairings will maximize revenue, rather than on the basis of which carriers are best for the individual customer. See Daniel Schwarcz, Beyond Disclosure: The Case for Banning Contingent Commissions, 25 Yale L. & Pol'y Rev. 289, 290 (2007). The NAIC has approved a model law requiring the disclosure of producer compensation, but it applies only when intermediaries are paid a fee by the policyholder or otherwise "represent" the policyholder in the placement (i.e. when the intermediary is a broker). See Producer Licensing Model Act, NAIC, Model Laws, Regulations, and Guidelines 218 § 18 (2005). New York recently went further, requiring all insurance intermediaries to provide customers with a disclosure of their potential conflict of interest. See N.Y. Ins. Reg. 194, codified at 11 NYCRR part 30. In *Sullivan Financial Group, Inc. v. Wrynn*, 939 N.Y.S.2d 761 (N.Y. App. 2012), the court held that this regulation was a lawful exercise of the New York Insurance Department's broad authority to license and discipline insurance intermediaries. Are such disclosures likely to help address any problems created by intermediaries' conflicts of interest?

7. *Increasing Intermediaries' Legal Obligations?* To what extent do the limited obligations imposed on most insurance agents make sense? Should ordinary insurance agents have a duty to advise policyholders on coverage irrespective of the existence of a special relationship? Note that one oddity of the predominant approach to these issues, which is articulated in *Langwith*, is that insurance intermediaries owe very limited obligations to most ordinary insurance consumers, but tend to have relatively robust legal obligations when it comes to sophisticated commercial enterprises. Arguably, this approach has it exactly backwards, as ordinary consumers are much more likely than sophisticated commercial

entities to need good advice about their insurance needs, and legal assurances that they will receive such advice.

8. *Suitability Requirements.* Insurance intermediaries who sell certain types of policies—generally those that are also deemed to be securities as well as insurance, such as variable annuities—face enhanced obligations to policyholders as a result of state and federal statutes. In particular, they are generally required to sell products that are "suitable" for the particular purchaser. See, e.g., Suitability in Annuity Transactions Model Regulation, NAIC, Model Laws, Regulations, and Guidelines 275 (2010). By contrast, suitability rules are universally applied to the sale of securities by broker/dealers. Similarly, mortgage brokers and credit card companies are legally required to ensure that consumers have "a reasonable ability to repay" loans or credit limits that are extended to them. Why don't similar rules apply to the sale of all insurance products? Should insurance agents be required to determine, for instance, that the limits and coverage selected by policyholders are suitable for their individual needs?

3. WAIVER AND ESTOPPEL

In addition to the construction of ambiguities against the insurer and the principle that the reasonable expectations of the insured should be honored, insureds commonly rely on the doctrines of waiver and estoppel to combat the insurer's defense that a claim is not covered by the language of a policy. In contrast to the first two approaches, however, these doctrines tend to turn on actions taken or not taken by an agent of the insurer. Waiver is the voluntary relinquishment of a known right or conduct that would reasonably be regarded by another party as such a relinquishment. Whether there has been a waiver is normally a question of fact. Waiver claims can frequently arise when a carrier or agent accepts late premium payments or notice of a claim, thereby (arguably) waiving its right to insist on strict compliance with policy conditions. Estoppel, in contrast, results from a change of position by the insured as a consequence of some representation or act by the insurer. Because this is a somewhat vague notion, claims of estoppel often raise perplexing legal questions.

Roseth v. St. Paul Property & Liability Insurance Company

Supreme Court of South Dakota, 1985.
374 N.W.2d 105.

■ WOLLMAN, JUSTICE.

This is an appeal by St. Paul Property & Liability Insurance Company (St. Paul) from a judgment entered by the trial court in favor of Jerry Roseth, d/b/a Philip Livestock Express. We reverse.

On November 12, 1979, a livestock trailer owned by Roseth and leased to Richard Miller was involved in an accident on U.S. highway 83 near Mission, South Dakota. Miller was transporting 109 calves for the 720 Cattle Company of Idaho, to a buyer in O'Neill, Nebraska, when the accident occurred. Eleven of the cattle were killed at the scene of the accident and two were missing. Miller immediately contacted Roseth by telephone and informed him of the accident.

Miller was transporting the calves from Idaho to Nebraska pursuant to an agreement with Roseth. Under this agreement, Miller would haul livestock for Philip Livestock Express using Roseth's trailer, with Roseth receiving twenty percent of the trucking charge.

On either the day of the accident or the day after, Roseth reported the accident to the Black Hills Agency (Black Hills). Roseth had purchased a cargo insurance policy from St. Paul through Black Hills' agent David Brinkman in 1977. The policy insured against the risk of livestock mortality only, specifically excluding coverage of "any animal able to walk from the conveyance or able to walk after unloading therefrom."

On November 14, 1979, St. Paul adjuster, James Wattleworth, was notified of the mishap by the Black Hills Agency. Wattleworth called Roseth that same day. Roseth informed Wattleworth that the surviving calves, which had been moved to Philip by Roseth, were generally "stiff," "gaunt," and "in pretty tough shape." Roseth also told Wattleworth that he had an all-risk policy that would cover the injured calves. Wattleworth stated to Roseth that he did not have a copy of the policy before him, but assured Roseth that St. Paul would perform in accordance with the provisions of the policy.

Wattleworth and Roseth then discussed alternatives concerning disposition of the surviving calves. Wattleworth advised Roseth that he had a duty to minimize his loss. Both parties agreed that this could best be accomplished by selling the calves the next day at an auction sale scheduled at Roseth's sale barn. Accordingly, the injured calves were sold the next day for approximately $20.00 to $22.00 per hundred weight less than the amount brought by similar, but uninjured, calves. The difference between the net value of the calves prior to the accident and the net value obtained from the sale was $8,865.98.

St. Paul issued payment under the policy for only fourteen calves, which included the eleven dead at the scene, one that later died, and the two that were missing. St. Paul denied coverage for the injured calves pursuant to the exclusion in the policy. Roseth brought an action against St. Paul and Black Hills Agency for recovery of the loss he sustained ($8,865.98) in selling the injured calves for less than their market value.

[The action against the Agency alleged negligence in failing to procure coverage against the kind of loss suffered. The court held that there could be no such action in this case, because the Agency had procured the maximum coverage available on the market at that time, which limited coverage to livestock mortality.] * * *

Roseth's second claimed basis for recovery was that St. Paul should be estopped from denying coverage on the basis of the exclusion contained in the policy for the reason that Wattleworth had failed to correct his misconception that the policy covered the injured calves. Roseth contended that Wattleworth had reinforced his misconception by instructing him to sell the injured calves immediately, and that he sold the calves on the assumption that St. Paul would reimburse him for the diminishing value of the injured calves. Roseth testified that had he been informed that the injured calves were not covered, he would have nurtured them back to a healthier condition and sold them later to obtain a better price. * * *

With respect to Roseth's claim against St. Paul, the trial court held that St. Paul should be estopped from defending on the basis of the exclusion contained in the policy.

The trial court found that Roseth had told Wattleworth that he believed he had an all-risk policy and that the decrease in value of the livestock would be covered under his policy; that Wattleworth thought at the time that St. Paul did not have an all-risk cargo policy; that Wattleworth nevertheless allowed Roseth to go on thinking that the coverage existed because Wattleworth did not want to antagonize Roseth; and that Wattleworth told Roseth that he thought it was a good idea to sell the cattle the next day to minimize the loss. The trial court held that it would be inequitable to allow St. Paul to claim the exclusion under the policy.

St. Paul contends on appeal that the trial court erred in applying the doctrine of estoppel to provide coverage for a risk not covered by the policy where there was no clear and convincing evidence of any misrepresentation or concealment of material fact by Wattleworth. We need not decide this question. Rather, we hold that the doctrine of equitable estoppel is not applicable under the facts of this case.

In *Farmers Mutual Automobile Ins. Co. v. Bechard,* 80 S.D. 237, 246 (1963), this court held:

> [A]n insurance company which in its policy has written the generally broad coverage may be estopped to defend by reason of an exclusionary clause not within the terms the insured ordered and coverage which he was led to believe was contained therein.

This holding was followed in *State Automobile Casualty Underwriters v. Ruotsalainen,* 81 S.D. 472 (1965). The *Bechard-Ruotsalainen* rule is contrary to the majority rule, which provides that estoppel is not available to bring within the coverage of a policy those risks not covered by its terms or expressly excluded by the policy. * * *

In adopting the minority rule, the New Jersey Supreme Court held that

> [w]here an insurer or its agent misrepresents, even though innocently, the coverage of an insurance contract, or the exclusions therefrom, to an insured *before or at the inception of the contract,* and the insured reasonably relies thereupon to his ultimate detriment, the insurer is estopped to deny coverage after a loss on a risk from a peril actually not covered by the terms of the policy.

Harr v. Allstate Insurance Co., 54 N.J. 287, 306–307 (1969) (emphasis added). *See also Darner Motor Sales v. Universal Underwriters,* 682 P.2d 388, 400 n. 10 (1984) (adopting rule of *Harr*); *Peninsular Life Ins. Co. v. Wade,* 425 So.2d 1181, 1183 (Fla.App.1983).

The requirement that the estopping conduct occur "before or at the inception of the policy" is consistent with the underlying rationale of the minority rule. The minority rule was born out of the inequities which result where an insured relies to his detriment on an insurer's superior knowledge in purchasing a policy of insurance and consequently is deprived of the opportunity to purchase the desired coverage elsewhere. *Harr, supra.*

In both *Bechard* and *Ruotsalainen,* the insureds sought specific coverage for which they gave consideration based on assurances that such coverage was provided for in the policy. Under the facts of the case before us, Wattleworth at most indirectly perpetuated a misconception held by Roseth concerning the nature of his coverage. We hold that under these facts the remedy of estoppel is not available to expand the terms of the policy.

The judgment is reversed.

NOTES AND QUESTIONS

1. *The Purpose of the Exclusion.* Why do you think the policy contained the exclusion that created Roseth's problem?

2. *Commission or Omission?* Do you agree with the court that "Wattleworth at best indirectly perpetuated a misconception held by Roseth"? In light of the court's rationale, was this language mere dictum, or does it cast doubt on what the holding was? Suppose that Roseth had not said that he thought he was covered, but had merely asked what Wattleworth thought he should do with the cattle, and Wattleworth had replied that Roseth should minimize his losses? Would any other result in *Roseth* have required Wattleworth to deny any assistance or advice to Roseth until he could inspect Roseth's policy? Would that be a realistic requirement?

3. *Waiver in* Roseth*?* Why didn't Roseth argue that St. Paul had waived the policy exclusion? Would Roseth have had a plausible waiver claim if Wattleworth had told him that St Paul always pays for cattle that have been injured in an accident? What if Wattleworth had told Roseth about the policy exclusion for non-fatally injured cattle, but indicated that St Paul never actually enforces that clause?

4. *Expanding Coverage Through Waiver and Estoppel.* As indicated in *Roseth,* many courts have held that neither waiver nor estoppel can create coverage that was not provided for by the policy to begin with: these doctrines can negate defenses, but cannot create additional coverage. At least in the case of statements or conduct that occur prior to issuance of the policy, this approach is sometimes justified on the basis of the parol evidence rule. See, e.g., *DeJonge v. Mut. of Enumclaw,* 315 Or. 237 (1992). That rule provides that extrinsic evidence cannot be used to supplement or contradict a final and complete written agreement.

However, the minority rule originating in *Harr v. Allstate Insurance Co.,* cited by the court, is growing in influence and was explicitly endorsed in the RLLI. RLLI §§ 5–6. The courts seem to be increasingly willing to allow waiver and estoppel not only to prevent the forfeiture of coverage afforded by the policy (e.g., because the policyholder gave late notice of a covered claim), but to create coverage not explicitly provided for as well. See, e.g., *Marlin v. Wetzel Cnty. Bd. of Educ.,* 212 W. Va. 215 (2002); *Southtrust Bank v. Export Ins. Servs., Inc.,* 190 F. Supp. 2d 1304 (M.D. Fla. 2002); *Bill Brown Constr. Co., Inc. v. Glens Falls Ins. Co.,* 818 S.W.2d 1 (Tenn. 1991) (an insurer whose agent said the applicant would have "full coverage" for transportation of "large cargo" is estopped to rely on a policy provision limiting coverage to "collision of the conveyance with any other vehicle or object" when cargo riding on a truck, but not the truck carrying it, collided with an overhead bridge).

5. *Estoppel and Post-Contract Conduct.* *Roseth* categorically states that conduct occuring after the inception of the contract cannot generate estoppel. This rule presumably relates to the fact that detrimental reliance—a key element of estoppel—is much less likely to occur on the basis of post-contract statements, because there is nothing the policyholder can do to alter coverage. But the facts of *Roseth* suggest that this presumption may not always be accurate. For instance, suppose that Roseth indicated to Wattleworth that selling the cattle at auction was a bad idea, but Wattleworth insisted in pursuing this approach. If Roseth could show that the price his cattle fetched at auction was much lower than the true value of the cattle, why shouldn't he be able to recover on an estoppel claim?

6. *Explanations for Limitations on Waiver and Estoppel.* Professor Morris has argued that limitations on the scope of waiver and estoppel in insurance law result from a generalized concern by the courts that these rather flexible notions might otherwise carry the process of favoring consumers too far. See Clarence Morris, Waiver and Estoppel in Insurance Policy Litigation, 105 U. Pa. L. Rev. 925 (1957). Could another concern be that the words and conduct that may constitute a waiver or estoppel are likely to have taken place months or years before loss, and in any event to be unrecorded and therefore highly susceptible to fraudulent proof? How much support for its defense can an insurer expect from the testimony of an agent that he simply "cannot remember" the words or conduct that the insured claims created a waiver or estoppel? What incentives might independent agents have not to remember?

7. *Mitigation of Damages.* Virtually every insurance policy contains a requirement that policyholders mitigate the extent of damage after a loss has occurred. Roseth argued that he would have nursed the cattle he sold back to good health if he had known that he had no coverage for them. If this were true, by selling the cattle immediately was he not violating any duty he had to the insurer to mitigate his damages? Should policyholders have an obligation to mitigate damages even after an insurer has breached the contract? For an affirmative argument on this question, see James M. Fischer, Does an Insured Have A Duty to Mitigate Damages When the Insurer Breaches?, 20 Conn. Ins. L.J. 89 (2013).

4. GROUP INSURANCE AND ERISA

Health, life, disability, and long-term care insurance are often provided as fringe benefits of employment. Employers frequently pay a portion of the premiums for such coverage, with the remaining premiums deducted from the employee's paycheck. Group insurance can provide a number of advantages. First, because the group insurer's marketing costs are greatly reduced, it can offer coverage at a lower price. Second, other administrative costs may be reduced by allocating certain record-keeping tasks to the employer, which may be able to perform them less expensively because it has easy access to employees and to records that already are maintained for other purposes. This economy may produce still lower premiums. Third, group insurance may improve policyholder shopping because the employer can screen different carriers and plans to find options that provide favorable combinations of price and coverage.

Two other advantages depend on the degree to which a plan is contributory, i.e., financed by payroll deductions. First, adverse selection in group insurance may be less severe than in non-group insurance. This may be the case even when a plan is wholly paid for by employees, because the pool from which eligible applicants self-select is comprised of a group of persons healthy enough to be employed. But to the extent that employers contribute to premiums, adverse selection is further reduced, because such payments offset the costs that low-risk employees incur in paying for coverage that cross-subsidizes higher-risk employees. Under these circumstances the employer may have an incentive to screen out high-risk applicants for employment, since the employer's premiums may be experience-rated. Second, employer-sponsored insurance enjoys a number of tax benefits that are linked to its financing. Most importantly, employers' contributions to insurance premiums are often not taxable to the employee as income, and, in certain cases, employees' can pay their premiums using pre-tax dollars.

The law and regulation of insurance provided to policyholders through employer-sponsored insurance is importantly different from the rules governing insurance purchased directly from insurers and/or agents. This is principally a result of the Employee Retirement Income Security Act of 1974, or ERISA, 29 U.S.C. § 1001 *et seq.* ERISA is the central federal statute regulating "employee benefit plans," which include all insurance provided as a fringe benefit of employment. ERISA regulates the manner in which employee benefit plans are administered, but it does not substantially regulate or prescribe the terms and conditions of such plans. It also provides a federal cause of action for violations of the statute.

Perhaps even more importantly, ERISA preempts a substantial amount of state insurance law and regulation. ERISA preemption is a notoriously difficult and complicated concept, one that we shall examine in some detail in Chapter 5. For now, we review only the basics. There are two types of ERISA preemption. The first, which is often called "express preemption," is based upon ERISA § 514. This provision preempts all state laws that "relate to" employee benefit plans, but exempts from this preemption any state law that "regulates insurance." The second form of ERISA preemption, which is based on § 502(a) and is frequently labeled "complete preemption," preempts state laws and regulations relating to remedies for denied insurance benefits.

The Employer as Agent of the Insurer. Because employers often perform some of the insurer's functions in group insurance plans, the question whether the employer is an agent of the employee or of the insurer has often arisen. In *UNUM Life Insurance Co. of America v. Ward*, 526 U.S. 358 (1999), the Supreme Court held that ERISA preempts state agency law on this question. In *UNUM*, the employee was denied disability insurance benefits by his carrier because he provided the carrier with late notice of his disability under the terms of the policy. The policyholder argued that he had given the requisite notice to his employer in a timely fashion, and the employer was the insurer's agent for the purpose of receiving notice under California law.

The Supreme Court concluded that California agency law was expressly preempted by ERISA, because it "relates to" an employee benefit plan. As the court explained:

> [D]eeming the policyholder-employer the agent of the insurer would have a marked effect on plan administration. It would "forc[e] the employer, as plan administrator, to assume a role, with attendant legal duties and consequences, that it has not undertaken voluntarily"; it would affect "not merely the plan's bookkeeping obligations regarding to whom benefits checks must be sent, but [would] also regulat[e] the basic services that a plan may or must provide to its participants and beneficiaries."

Id. at 379.

Although the Supreme Court made clear that federal law governs the extent to which an employer operates as an agent of an insurer providing a group plan, it did not clarify the content of federal law on this topic. Since *UNUM*, courts have reached varying conclusions on this subject. Some courts have held that federal common law governs this issue and that, under that law, an employer can be an agent of the insurer under many of the same principles of state agency law. See *Kobold v. Aetna U.S. Healthcare, Inc.*, 258 F. Supp. 2d 1317 (M.D. Fla. 2003). Others have resisted this approach on the grounds that it could undermine ERISA's goal of facilitating plan administration for employers, and have concluded that, at the very least, it has no application where the employer acts as a decision maker, rather than a messenger. *Otero v. Hartford Life & Accident Ins.*, No. CIV 06–1035 MCA/RHS, 2007 WL 6624118 (D.N.M. Aug. 27, 2007). Still other courts have concluded that plan documents specifying that the employer does not act as an agent of the insurer are enforceable notwithstanding ordinary agency principles. *Weaver v. Prudential Ins. Co. of Am.*, 763 F. Supp. 2d 930 (M.D. Tenn. 2010).

The Employer's Fiduciary Obligations to Beneficiaries. One of ERISA's primary protections for beneficiaries of group insurance policies is that it imposes fiduciary obligations on anyone who has any discretionary authority in the administration of the plan. There are a number of ways in which employers can have discretion over the administration of a group insurance policy, and thus owe beneficiaries fiduciary duties. For instance, employers generally owe plan beneficiaries a fiduciary duty in selecting a carrier, which involves the use of discretion. Similarly, to the extent that the employer is involved in the resolution of beneficiaries' claims, it owes a fiduciary duty here as well. One important exception to these rules is that the employer does not owe any fiduciary duties to beneficiaries with respect to decisions to establish a plan or to determine the benefit package, as the employer is understood to be making business decisions in these cases rather than administering the plan.

What Document Is Binding? One problem that is largely independent of agency questions is how to identify the contract that binds the insurer. The typical group insurance policy—the contract executed by the insurer and the employer—is likely to be much longer and more detailed than a standard individual policy. This Master Policy is kept on file by the employer, and each employee is issued a certificate of insurance that summarizes the terms of coverage and incorporates the Master Policy by reference. Similarly, often the insurer prepares a promotional brochure that describes the terms of coverage in language that is even simpler than the individual certificate of insurance. When the Master Policy contains limitations on coverage that are not described in the brochure or other summaries of coverage, which should control?

In *CIGNA Corp. v. Amara*, 131 S. Ct. 1866 (2011), the Supreme Court addressed this issue, concluding that "the summary documents, important as they are, provide communication with beneficiaries *about* the plan, but . . . their statements do not themselves constitute the *terms* of the plan." Since *CIGNA*, however, courts have held that summary documents can indeed be enforceable when they are themselves made part of the group document due to language so indicating in the summary itself or in other plan documents. See *Eugene S. v. Horizon Blue Cross Blue Shield of N.J.*, 663 F.3d 1124 (10th Cir. 2011). Other courts have concluded that summary plan documents may be enforceable if they do not conflict with the master policy or certificate of insurance. See *Langlois v. Metro. Life Ins. Co.*, 833 F. Supp. 2d 1182 (N.D. Cal. 2011).

C. BAD FAITH

Damages due to the breach of an insurance contract are, at least as an initial matter, subject to ordinary contract law damages principles. Thus, policyholders are entitled to expectation damages as a result of an insurer's breach, which generally consists of the amount necessary to place the policyholder in the position that he or she would have been in had the insurer not breached the policy in the first place. Typically, of course, this consists of the benefits owed under the policy. However, consequential damages for an insurer's breach of its policy obligations are also available to the extent that they were reasonably foreseeable to the insurer at the time it entered into the contract under the familiar rule of *Hadley v. Baxendale*. See *Bi-Econ. Mkt., Inc. v. Harleysville Ins. Co. of N.Y.*, 886 N.E.2d 127 (N.Y. 2008) (holding that policyholder who alleged breach of a business interruption policy could seek consequential damages for the failure of of its business, as this was a reasonably foreseeable consequence of the breach).

In some insurance coverage disputes, however, standard principles of contract law damages are substantially altered. For instance, policyholders in many states are entitled to recover their attorneys' fees when they successfully challenge a coverage denial, contrary to the usual default rule. See, e.g., N.H. Rev. Stat. Ann. § 491:22–b; *Federated Mut. Ins. Co. v. Grapevine Excavation Inc.*, 241 F.3d 396, 398 (5th Cir. 2001) (applying Texas law). Even more importantly, in many states, policyholders who demonstrate that an insurer delayed or denied coverage benefits in "bad faith" may be able to recover emotional distress damages and potentially even punitive damages. We now turn to the law governing such bad faith insurer liability.

Two important caveats are in order before we explore bad faith in more detail. First, as a result of ERISA complete preemption (which, you may recall, preempts state laws relating to remedies for denied insurance benefits), enhanced damages due to bad faith, and even ordinary consequential damages, are not available for breaches of group insurance policies. See Brendan Maher, The Affordable Care Act, Remedy, and Litigation Reform, 63 Am. U. L. Rev. 649 (2014). We will examine this issue more closely in Chapter Five, which focuses on coverage lines that are generally provided via group insurance. Second, while bad faith claims can arise in connection with denials of liability insurance coverage, such claims are relatively uncommon because they are overshadowed by related doctrines involving liability insurers' duties to defend and settle, both of which we will study in some detail in Chapter Seven.

Silberg v. California Life Insurance Company
Supreme Court of California, 1974.
11 Cal.3d 452.

■ MOSK, JUSTICE.

We are called upon to interpret the provisions of an insurance policy issued to plaintiff by defendant company and the scope of defendant's duty to make payment thereunder. The policy provided that defendant would pay the cost of hospital care, including surgeon's fees, up to a limit of $5,000, with $100 deductible, and there was an exclusion for losses caused by injuries for which compensation was payable under any workmen's compensation law.

In July 1966, while the policy was in effect, plaintiff was seriously injured and as a result ultimately incurred $6,900 in medical charges. Defendant carrier refused to make any payments under the policy because plaintiff had filed a claim for workmen's compensation benefits on account of the injury. The company insisted there could be no final determination as to its liability under the policy until the workmen's compensation proceeding was concluded. At the same time, the workmen's compensation carrier denied liability because of defendant's questionable employment status. The compensation aspect was ultimately determined on April 30, 1968—nearly two years after the injury—when a compromise and release was approved by the Workmen's Compensation Appeals Board, settling the case for $3,700; of this recovery $1,100 was in payment of hospital bills through a lien filed by one hospital, the balance of $5,800 in hospital bills remaining unpaid. Defendant denied liability under the policy on the ground that the $3,700 paid under the compensation settlement rendered the exclusion applicable.

Plaintiff filed this action, alleging two causes of action: the first sought a declaration that defendant was liable under the policy, and the second sought damages for physical and mental distress. It was alleged that defendant was guilty of fraud, bad faith and malicious and oppressive conduct, and that plaintiff was entitled to both compensatory and punitive damages.

Initially, the trial court, sitting without a jury, determined in the declaratory relief count that the policy was ambiguous and that, therefore, defendant was obligated under the policy to pay $4,900 of plaintiff's medical costs (the policy limits minus the $100 deductible). A jury found for plaintiff on the second cause of action, and awarded

$75,000 compensatory damages and $500,000 punitive damages. After judgment on the verdict was rendered, the trial court granted defendant's motion for a new trial on the grounds of insufficiency of the evidence to support the verdict, errors in law, and excessive damages. Plaintiff appeals from the order granting the new trial, and defendant cross-appeals from the judgment. (Cal.Rules of Court, rule 3(c).)

The major issues involved in plaintiff's appeal from the order granting a new trial are whether the trial court abused its discretion in concluding that the evidence was insufficient to support a finding defendant was guilty of bad faith justifying an award of compensatory damages, or of fraud or oppression justifying an award of exemplary damages. We determine that the evidence demonstrates as a matter of law that defendant's failure to pay benefits under the policy constituted bad faith but that the trial court did not abuse its discretion in ruling that the evidence was insufficient to support an award of exemplary damages. In defendant's appeal from the judgment, our inquiry focuses primarily upon whether the trial court properly found in the first cause of action that the policy was ambiguous. We conclude the trial court judgment was correct in this regard.

Plaintiff's Appeal

At the time of the accident, plaintiff was 38 years old and the father of two minor children. He owned and operated a dry cleaning business, and earned a monthly income of $500. Plaintiff's landlord owned a laundromat adjacent to the dry cleaning premises. Although not entirely clear from the record, plaintiff apparently agreed with his landlord that, in return for a reduction in rent, he would perform incidental services in connection with the laundromat operation. On July 17, 1966, plaintiff noticed smoke in the laundromat area, and in order to locate its source he climbed onto a washing machine. The glass in the lid of the machine broke; plaintiff's right foot fell into the machine, which was in operation at the time. His foot was severed at the ankle but was surgically restored later that day.

Upon his admission plaintiff advised the hospital that he was insured by defendant, and he notified defendant of the accident within a few days. Defendant immediately sent a routine inquiry to an investigative bureau to determine whether plaintiff had ever previously sought insurance benefits. In the claim forms subsequently filed by plaintiff, he declared that he was self-employed and that he had instituted proceedings to obtain workmen's compensation benefits. Medical bills for the first hospitalization were received by defendant by early September.

Plaintiff developed an infection in his foot, and further surgery was required. On October 3 he entered another hospital. In his testimony at the trial he claimed that he was unable to return to the hospital where the prior surgery had been performed because its bill remained unpaid. Upon the second admission plaintiff again named defendant as his insurer, and the charges for hospital and surgical services were sent to defendant.

Defendant initially failed to explain to either plaintiff or the hospitals the cause of the delay in making payment, but wrote an adjuster in Los Angeles, requesting him to determine whether plaintiff was covered by workmen's compensation. The letter conceded that workmen's compensation coverage was questionable because plaintiff was the owner-operator of a cleaning plant. The adjuster was also instructed that, in the event workmen's compensation did not cover the injury, he should review plaintiff's medical history for the 10 years prior to the injury. Defendant explained that the purpose of the exhaustive inquiry was to determine if plaintiff might have been uninsurable at the time of the injury. That is, in the event plaintiff had falsified his application in any respect or omitted to mention that he had some prior serious illness such as heart trouble or cancer, defendant could, on the basis of the misrepresentation, rescind the policy, even though such illnesses were not involved in plaintiff's claim.

The adjuster replied in mid-November that the workmen's compensation carrier denied coverage on the ground plaintiff was not an employee at the time of the injury, and that a hearing would be held by the Workmen's Compensation Appeals Board in December to determine the issue. The December hearing was continued to February 1967.

Throughout this period, plaintiff and a representative of the insurance agency through which he had purchased the policy made persistent inquiries regarding his claim, and the hospitals at which he had been treated also expressed impatience with the delay in receiving payment. In November and December defendant informed plaintiff as well as the hospitals that there was a question whether plaintiff was covered by workmen's compensation at the time of the injury, and that until the matter was resolved his benefits under the policy would be withheld.

In April 1967, defendant forwarded its claim file to the Workmen's Compensation Appeals Board in response to a subpoena duces tecum. No further action was taken by defendant until April 1968, when plaintiff's attorney wrote defendant that the workmen's compensation proceeding had been settled by compromise and release because the evidence was in conflict as to whether plaintiff's injury occurred in the course of employment. The attorney stated that since no formal findings of workmen's compensation coverage had been made by the board, defendant was liable under the policy. Defendant denied liability on the ground that the exclusion was applicable because plaintiff had received payment under the workmen's compensation law. It offered to settle the claim for $200 "to avoid litigation." The offer was rejected.

Plaintiff's condition continued to deteriorate after his second hospitalization. In June 1967 he had a third operation, which was performed at the same hospital as the second surgery. The hospital refused to admit him unless he paid $500 of his previous bill. A fourth operation was performed in April 1968, this time at another hospital, since the hospital at which the second and third operations had been performed refused to accept plaintiff as a patient. Plaintiff was also compelled to engage a different surgeon because the surgeon who had previously operated on him had not been paid. In order to obtain the needed surgery plaintiff resorted to a ruse. He entered the hospital on a Saturday, the operation to be performed on Sunday, so that the hospital administrators would not be able to discover over the weekend whether insurance coverage existed. Plaintiff again named defendant as his insurer.[1]

Shortly after his injury plaintiff borrowed $2,000 to pay business expenses. Ultimately, he lost his business and could not borrow additional funds because unpaid hospital and medical bills established him to be a poor credit risk. He was compelled to change the place of his residence five times during this period because of lack of funds to pay rent. His utilities were turned off several times for nonpayment, his wheelchair was repossessed, and he had difficulty in affording medication to ease his constant pain. Ultimately, in 1969 plaintiff suffered two nervous breakdowns. A psychiatrist testified that plaintiff's concern over inability to meet medical expenses contributed to these episodes.

At the trial, the manager of defendant's claims department testified that defendant refused to pay the medical expenses plaintiff incurred in 1966 because it was awaiting the outcome of the workmen's compensation proceeding in order to determine whether there was liability under the policy.

The evidence was in sharp conflict as to the custom in the insurance industry regarding the payment of a claim for hospital benefits in these circumstances. Several witnesses for defendant testified that during pendency of a workmen's compensation proceeding, it was customary to deny benefits or to suspend judgment on an insured's claim under a hospital care policy until the question of workmen's compensation coverage was finally decided. A witness for plaintiff testified, on the other hand, that the prevailing practice was to pay the insured's claim if the workmen's compensation carrier denied liability and the insured had suffered severe injuries. Thus, he stated, if no workmen's compensation award was ultimately ordered the payments under the policy would have been properly made, and if benefits were awarded, the insurer could impose a lien on the sums to be paid in the workmen's compensation proceeding.[2]

Compensatory Damages

In its order granting a new trial, the trial court found, for the reasons set forth in the margin, that the evidence was insufficient to justify a finding of bad faith.[3] It is not necessary to analyze these

---

[1] When the hospital sent the bill for the fourth operation to defendant in April 1968, defendant wrote in response that plaintiff's policy had not been in force for more than a year. As we shall see, defendant took the position that it was not liable for the cost of plaintiff's hospitalization after January 1, 1967, because the policy had lapsed on that date for nonpayment of premiums. This contention will be discussed in the context of defendant's appeal from the judgment on the jury's verdict.

[2] Another alternative customarily utilized, according to plaintiff's witness, was for the insurer on the hospital benefit policy to attempt to reach an informal agreement for reimbursement with the workmen's compensation carrier.

[3] "The evidence was insufficient to support the verdict. The plaintiff was injured in July of 1966. A workmen's compensation claim was filed by him in August of 1966. That matter was pending until April 30, 1968, at which time it was settled by compromise and release. [¶] There was no evidence that at the time the policy was issued the defendant knew or should have known how a Court would rule on this set of facts or that they made any misrepresentation to him on which he relied. In researching the case neither counsel nor the Court found any case specifically on point that they would have been on notice of at the time of issuance of the policy. [¶] Similarly there was insufficient evidence of any custom or usage in the industry at that time to justify any such finding or to impose any duty on the defendant to

reasons in detail because, in our view, the evidence shows as a matter of law that defendant breached the covenant of good faith and fair dealing implied in every insurance contract by its failure to make payments under the policy and that, therefore, it was liable for the physical and mental distress proximately caused by its conduct.

The principle was firmly established in *Comunale v. Traders & General Ins. Co.* (1958) 50 Cal.2d 654, 658–660, and *Crisci v. Security Ins. Co.* (1967) 66 Cal.2d 425, 429–433, that the duty of an insurer to accept a reasonable settlement so as to absolve its insured of liability to a third person is implied in the covenant of good faith and fair dealing which exists in every insurance contract. The covenant requires that neither party will do anything to injure the right of the other to receive the benefits of the agreement, and an insurer is obligated to give the interests of the insured at least as much consideration as it gives to its own interests. Violation of the duty of the insurer sounds in tort, we held, and an insured may recover for all detriment resulting from such violation, including mental distress. These principles have been extended to cases in which the insurer unreasonably and in bad faith withholds payment of the claim of the insured. (*Gruenberg v. Aetna Ins. Co.* (1973) 9 Cal.3d 566, 575; *Richardson v. Employers Liab. Assur. Corp.* (1972) 25 Cal.App.3d 232, 239 (disapproved on another ground in *Gruenberg v. Aetna Ins. Co., supra*, 9 Cal.3d 566, at fn. 10, pp. 580–581); *Fletcher v. Western National Life Ins. Co.* (1970) 10 Cal.App.3d 376, 401.)

In the present case, the company's policy application declared in large, heavy type, "Protect Yourself Against the Medical Bills That Can Ruin You." Plaintiff's application, filed shortly before the accident, indicated that he had no other hospital or disability insurance and, indeed, the manager of defendant's claims department testified that the policy would not have been issued if plaintiff had other hospital insurance. Defendant was aware that plaintiff earned only a modest income and had incurred substantial medical and hospital bills. The company also knew that there was a serious question whether plaintiff would qualify for workmen's compensation benefits, and that the compensation carrier had consistently denied coverage on the ground that plaintiff was not an employee at the time of the accident.

There is no question that if defendant had paid the hospital charges and it was ultimately determined workmen's compensation covered the injury, defendant could have asserted a lien in the workmen's compensation proceeding to recover the payments it had made and it would have been entitled to payment from the proceeds of the award. (Lab.Code, § 4903, subd. (b); *Foremost Dairies v. Industrial Acc. Com.* (1965) 237 Cal.App.2d 560, 579; *Gerson v. Industrial Acc. Com.* (1961) 188 Cal.App.2d 735; see also Rules of Practice & Procedure, Workmen's Comp. App. Bd., art. 15 § 10886.) Indeed, some of the medical bills incurred by plaintiff were paid by the allowance of a lien

---

pay the proceeds of its policy and then assert a lien claim. [¶] There was no sufficient evidence for the jury to determine that the defendant asserted its claim of defense in bad faith, considering the language of the policy, or that the defendant was guilty of oppressive conduct, misrepresentation or bad faith."

from the settlement obtained in the workmen's compensation proceeding.

No explanation was advanced by defendant as to why it failed to adopt this course in order to vindicate the promise made in the application that the policy was intended to protect the insured against medical bills which could result in financial ruin. Defendant's attitude toward the payment of plaintiff's claim was expressed in the declaratory relief phase of the case: merely that it was entitled to wait until the pending compensation proceeding was concluded before it paid or denied the claim. The company failed to see a conflict with its express promise to protect against ruinous medical bills.

Although the evidence was in conflict on the issue whether it was customary in the insurance industry to make payments under the policy in these circumstances and the order granting a new trial declared there was insufficient evidence of such a custom, the failure to establish common practice in this regard cannot absolve the insurer. The scope of the duty of an insurer to deal fairly with its insured is prescribed by law and cannot be delineated entirely by customs of the insurance industry.

Under these circumstances defendant's failure to afford relief to its insured against the very eventuality insured against by the policy amounts to a violation as a matter of law of its duty of good faith and fair dealing implied in every policy. Thus, we conclude the trial court abused its discretion in granting a new trial on the ground that the evidence was insufficient to support a finding that plaintiff is entitled to compensatory damages.

In granting a new trial, the court also indicated that the damages were excessive. However, the order failed to state any reason for this ground other than the declaration that the evidence did not justify an award of $75,000 in compensatory damages "for the reasons stated above." Since "the reasons stated above" (see fn. 3, *ante*) did not refer to whether damages awarded by the jury were disproportionate to the injuries suffered by plaintiff but, rather, to whether the evidence justified a finding of bad faith or oppression, the reasons advanced by the trial court for finding the damages to be excessive are clearly inadequate. (See Code Civ.Proc., § 657; *Mercer v. Perez* (1968) 68 Cal.2d 104, 111 et seq.; *Scala v. Jerry Witt & Sons, Inc.* (1970) 3 Cal.3d 359, 363 et seq.) The trial court's order must be reversed insofar as it determines that plaintiff was not entitled to compensatory damages and that an award of $75,000 for such damages was excessive.

Exemplary Damages

It does not follow that because plaintiff is entitled to compensatory damages that he is also entitled to exemplary damages. In order to justify an award of exemplary damages, the defendant must be guilty of oppression, fraud or malice. (Civ.Code, § 3294.) He must act with the intent to vex, injure or annoy, or with a conscious disregard of the plaintiff's rights. (*Wolfsen v. Hathaway* (1948) 32 Cal.2d 632, 647 et seq. (overruled on another ground in *Flores v. Arroyo* (1961) 56 Cal.2d 492, 497); *Roth v. Shell Oil Co.* (1960) 185 Cal.App.2d 676, 682.) While we have concluded that defendant violated its duty of good faith and fair dealing, this alone does not necessarily establish that defendant acted with the requisite intent to injure plaintiff.

In granting a new trial the trial court stated that the evidence was insufficient to justify an award of punitive damages because defendant was not put on notice by cases previously decided that its interpretation of the policy was incorrect and because there was insufficient evidence of a practice in the insurance industry to pay a disputed claim and then file a lien in the workmen's compensation proceeding to recover the payments made. The trial court's conclusion that defendant was not guilty of oppressive conduct did not constitute a manifest and unmistakable abuse of discretion. (*Jiminez v. Sears, Roebuck & Co.* (1971) 4 Cal.3d 379, 387.) Therefore, the order granting a new trial must be affirmed insofar as it determines that the evidence was insufficient to justify the award of punitive damages. * * *

Defendant's Appeal

In its appeal from the judgment on the jury's verdict, defendant contends that the trial court erred in the declaratory relief phase of the case in finding the policy to be ambiguous and in awarding plaintiff $4,900 in benefits thereunder.

Two separate clauses of the policy are involved on the issue of liability. The first is the insuring clause. It provides "subject to the exceptions, limitations and provisions of this policy [defendant] promises to pay for loss, except losses covered by any Workmen's Compensation * * * Law * * * covered by this policy and sustained by the insured * * * resulting from injury or sickness; * * *"

The second relevant provision is the exclusionary clause, which states, "EXCLUSIONS. This policy does not cover any loss caused by or resulting from (1) injury or sickness for which compensation is payable under any Workmen's Compensation * * * Law."

Plaintiff contends, and the trial court found, that the insuring clause could be interpreted to mean that payments would be made under the policy even though plaintiff also recovered workmen's compensation benefits if workmen's compensation did not meet his total medical expenses. That is, defendant was required to pay hospital charges not covered by workmen's compensation payments. Defendant, on the other hand, claims that the insuring clause must be read in conjunction with the exclusionary clause, and that the latter provision makes it plain that if workmen's compensation benefits in any amount are received by the insured, then defendant is not required to make any payments whatever under the policy.

The trial court construed the policy in the light of the familiar rule that any ambiguities in an insurance policy must be read against the insurer. (*Bareno v. Employers Life Ins. Co.* (1972) 7 Cal.3d 875, 878.) It determined that the word "loss" in the insuring clause could mean compensable expense and, if so, defendant was required to pay hospital expenses not covered by workmen's compensation. The application for the policy declared in large, capital letters, "ALL BENEFITS PAYABLE IN FULL REGARDLESS OF ANY OTHER INSURANCE YOU MAY HAVE." This assurance implies at the very least that the receipt of workmen's compensation payments, comparable to "other insurance" payments, would not entirely vitiate defendant's liability under the policy.

Thus, the provision in the insuring clause that defendant would pay for "loss, except losses covered by * * * Workmen's Compensation" rationally means that defendant promised to pay such hospital expenses incurred by plaintiff as were not paid by workmen's compensation, up to the policy limits.

Defendant relies heavily upon the language of the exclusionary provision, which excludes liability for "any loss caused by or resulting from * * * injury * * * for which compensation is payable under any Workmen's Compensation * * * Law * * *" This provision does not clearly absolve defendant of liability if plaintiff receives any amount in workmen's compensation benefits, particularly since it must be read in conjunction with the insuring clause, which requires defendant to pay expenses not covered by workmen's compensation. At best, even acquiescence in defendant's interpretation of the exclusion would merely result in a conflict between the exclusionary and the insuring clauses. Under prevailing law that conflict must be resolved in plaintiff's favor.[4] Defendant relies upon a number of cases to support its assertion that the policy is not ambiguous. However, with one exception these decisions involved provisions at variance with those in the present case. (E.g., *Laing v. Occidental Life Ins. Co.* (1966) 244 Cal.App.2d 811; *Wenthe v. Hospital Service, Incorporated, of Iowa* (1960) 251 Iowa 765.) In *Bonney v. Citizens' Mut. Auto. Ins. Co.* (1952) 333 Mich. 435, the policy contained a provision similar to the exclusion here. But there was no inconsistency between that provision and another clause of the policy, as in the present case, and the decision merely held that the exclusion applied to persons eligible for workmen's compensation benefits whether or not they had actually received such benefits.

There is a penultimate problem involving the policy provisions: whether defendant's liability terminated as of January 1, 1967, because plaintiff did not pay the premium due on that date. The relevant provision states, "When as the result of injury or sickness and commencing while covered hereunder, any member * * * is necessarily confined in a hospital, the Company will pay, subject to the above limitation, [various specified expenses]." Defendant interprets this provision as meaning that the injury and the hospitalization must both occur while the policy is in effect in order to entitle the insured to benefits and that defendant was not liable for those expenses which were incurred by plaintiff after the policy lapsed for nonpayment of premium on January 1, 1967.

The trial court found that the provision meant that if the insured was injured while the policy was in effect defendant would pay hospital expenses during the term of the policy even though the actual

---

[4] The trial court found that the exclusionary clause did not apply where, as here, the workmen's compensation proceeding terminated by compromise and release. Defendant disputes this conclusion, asserting that payments under a compromise and release are "compensation" and are therefore within the ambit of the exclusion. (Citing *Raischell & Cottrell, Inc. v. Workmen's Comp. App. Bd.* (1967) 249 Cal.App.2d 991, 58 Cal.Rptr. 159, and *Aetna Life Ins. Co. v. Ind. Acc. Comm.* (1952) 38 Cal.2d 599, 241 P.2d 530.) We need not determine the merits of this claim in view of the conclusions we have reached above.

hospitalization or the injury occurred after the policy had been deemed to lapse for nonpayment.[5]

At best, the provision is ambiguous. It can reasonably be interpreted to mean that payments would be made if the *injury* commenced during the life of the policy. Under settled rules of construction, the provision must therefore be interpreted against defendant. * * *

The order granting a new trial is reversed insofar as it grants a new trial on defendant's liability for compensatory damages and the amount of compensatory damages, and in all other respects the order is affirmed. On defendant's cross-appeal, the judgment is affirmed insofar as it awards $75,000 in compensatory damages and $4,900 as benefits under the policy. Plaintiff is to recover costs on appeal.

■ WRIGHT, C.J., and MCCOMB, TOBRINER, BURKE and SULLIVAN, JJ., concur.

NOTES AND QUESTIONS

1. *The Rise of the Cause of Action.* Until the late 1960's, the common law action for bad-faith breach of a first-party insurance policy was virtually unheard of, but it is now accepted in one form or another in more than half the states. See, e.g., *Miller v. Hartford Life Ins. Co.*, 126 Haw. 165 (2011); *Bushey v. Allstate Ins. Co.*, 164 Vt. 399 (1995); *Pickett v. Lloyds*, 252 N.J. Super. 477 (1991). A number of other states have enacted statutes imposing liability for limited damages (e.g., for counsel fees, or for a multiple of the covered loss) on first-party insurers for bad-faith denial of claims. See, e.g., Ga. Code Ann. § 33–4–6; Ky. R. S. § 304.12–230. Many complaints in insurance coverage disputes now routinely include a separate count alleging bad-faith breach of the policy, and bad-faith litigation has become a recognized subspecialty that has spawned its own professional education programs and practitioners' treatises. See, e.g., Stephen S. Ashley, Bad Faith Actions: Liability and Damages (1997). For analysis of a whole range of issues associated with the cause of action, see Jay M. Feinman, The Law of Insurance Claim Practices: Beyond Bad Faith, 47 Tort Trial & Ins. Prac. L.J. 693 (2012); Marc S. Mayerson, "First Party" Insurance Bad Faith Claims: Mooring Procedure to Substance, 38 Tort Trial & Ins. Prac. L.J. 861 (2003); William T. Barker, Evidentiary Sufficiency in Insurance Bad Faith Suits, 6 Conn. Ins. L.J. 81 (1999); Symposium on the Law of Bad Faith in Contract and Insurance, 72 Tex. L. Rev. 1203 (1994).

2. *The Underdeterrence Problem.* If in the event of breach the insured is entitled only to the amount of his coverage plus any consequential damages that are contemplated by the parties under *Hadley v. Baxendale,* and the latter category does not include emotional distress, what incentives do insurers have to pay doubtful but legitimate claims?

---

[5] Defendant complains that the trial court misread the provision as though a comma had been printed after the word "When" and as if the word "and" had been deleted. That is, claims defendant, the court rewrote the sentence to read, "When, as the result of injury or sickness commencing while covered hereunder, any member * * * is necessarily confined" etc. The court interpreted the phrase "subject to the above limitations" to include, inter alia, the limitation that the policy was for a two-year term.

3. *The Prevalence of Bad Faith.* Little concrete evidence exists regarding the actual prevalence of bad faith, in part because it is so hard to define. Some commentators argue that reputation is a substantial constraint on the practice. See Alan O. Sykes, "Bad Faith" Breach of Contract by First-Party Insurers, 25 J. Legal Stud. 405 (1996). Others have suggested that reputation is unlikely to constrain insurer over-reaching for at least two reasons. First, virtually no concrete data is available to consumers or others in the market regarding the relative quality of different carriers' claims paying practices. See Daniel Schwarcz, Transparently Opaque: Understanding the Lack of Transparency in Insurance Consumer Protection, 61 UCLA L. Rev. 394 (2014). Second, many policyholders are unable to determine when they have been victims of bad faith. See Tom Baker, Constructing the Insurance Relationship: Sales Stories, Claims Stories, and Insurance Contract Damages, 72 Tex. L. Rev. 1395 (1994). Even when policyholders believe they have experienced insurer bad faith, it is extremely difficult for them to *verifiably* communicate this to other potential or actual policyholders.

4. *The Nature of the Cause of Action.* Courts have long struggled with whether bad faith is a contract or tort cause of action. Some courts consider the action to be in contract, for breach of an implied covenant of good faith. The issue then is, what measure of damages is available? Where the damages are economic, in many cases it is relatively easy to hold that they were within the contemplation of the parties—business disruptions, mortgage foreclosures, etc. If the only damages are noneconomic, however, then precedents denying damages for emotional distress resulting from breach of contract must be rejected in order to put teeth in the cause of action. Other courts—particularly during the initial development of the bad-faith cause of action—held that extra-contractual damages for breach can be awarded only if the breach also constitutes an independent tort, such as fraud or intentional infliction of emotional distress.

The dominant approach today is to hold that the cause of action sounds in tort, but that an independent tort is not necessary to its existence. Rather, the insurer commits a tort if its breach is in "bad faith." There is then a cause of action in tort for bad-faith breach of contract, and the rules governing recovery of damages in tort apply. Compensatory damages are not limited to those within the contemplation of the parties so long as they are proximately caused by the defendant's tortious action, emotional distress damages are generally available, and punitive damages may be awarded when the misbehavior is sufficiently blameworthy.

5. *What Constitutes "Bad Faith?"* It is extremely difficult to specify the kind of behavior that triggers the bad faith cause of action. Bad faith is not merely the absence of good faith; something more seems to be required. Mere negligence generally is not enough; the fact that the insurer should have known that the insured's claim was covered, or that it was careless in processing a claim, normally does not constitute bad faith. But see *Royal Maccabees Ins. Co. v. James*, 134 S.W.3d 906 (Tex. App. 2004) (holding that a cause of action for breach of the duty of good faith and fair dealing is established when an insurer has no reasonable basis for denying or delaying payment of a claim and the insurer knew or should have known this fact). In most cases, however, objective negligence, coupled with evidence that the insurer was probably aware at some point during the claim process that the claim was covered, may constitute bad faith. A

number of courts have developed a somewhat more precise test, holding that the denial of a claim is in bad faith if it is not "fairly debatable" whether the claim is covered. See, e.g., *Dakota, Minn. & E. R.R. Corp. v. Acuity,* 771 N.W.2d 623 (S.D. 2009); *LeRette v. Am. Med. Sec., Inc.*, 270 Neb. 545 (2005); *Trinity Evangelical Lutheran Church & School-Freistadt v. Tower Ins. Co.*, 261 Wis. 2d 333 (2003). Alternative but very similar tests are the directed-verdict rule, under which there is no bad faith unless the policyholder would have been entitled to a directed verdict in its coverage claim, see *National Savings Life Insurance Co. v. Dutton*, 419 So. 2d 1357 (Ala. 1982), and the genuine-issue doctrine, under which there is bad faith if there was no genuine issue as to coverage, see *Guebara v. Allstate Insurance Co.*, 237 F.3d 987 (9th Cir. 2001); *Fraley v. Allstate Insurance Co.*, 81 Cal. App. 4th 1282 (2000).

Beyond this, it may be that each case requires a judgment in context. Certainly many of the decisions in which there is a finding of bad faith involve unconventional situations, in which there is more than the straightforward presentation and denial of a claim. In *Rawlings v. Apodaca,* 151 Ariz. 149 (1986), the insured's fire insurer also provided liability insurance for the party allegedly responsible for the fire, and refused to supply the insured with an investigation report; in *Silberg* the insurer was aware of the dire circumstances in which its repeated denials of coverage placed the insured. Many other cases present similarly unusual facts. For example, in one of the earliest, *Gruenberg v. Aetna Insurance Co.,* 9 Cal. 3d 566 (1973), the insured's fire insurers allegedly encouraged authorities to bring arson charges against him, and then used his refusal to appear for a civil deposition during the pendency of the criminal action as a pretense for denying his claim. And in *Sparks v. Republic National Life Insurance Co.,* 132 Ariz. 529 (1982), a health insurer relying on an ambiguous policy provision terminated coverage, and refused to pay the continuing cost of treating injuries that the insured suffered while coverage was in force, because the insured had not paid subsequent premiums—premiums which the insurer might simply have deducted from the several hundred thousand dollars for which it was obligated. The lesson seems to be that a bad-faith claim has a much greater chance of succeeding where the insurer is guilty of considerably more than a merely unreasonable misinterpretation of the terms of a policy, or has become aware of more facts about the insured's claims than are present in a typical bare-bones claim file.

6. *Systematic Bad Faith.* In recent years, plaintiffs and commentators have increasingly alleged that insurer bad faith can result from a systemic strategy of certain insurance carriers, rather than just from an idiosyncratic mistake of a single claims-handler. See Kenneth S. Abraham, Liability for Bad Faith and a Principle Without a Name (Yet), 19 Conn. Ins. L.J. 1 (2012) (identifying this shift); Jay M. Feinman, Delay, Deny, Defend: Why Insurance Companies Don't Pay Claims and What you Can Do About It (2010) (reviewing evidence that Allstate systemically underpaid claims to increase profit); John H. Langbein, Trust Law as Regulatory Law: The Unum/Provident Scandal and Judicial Review of Benefit Denials Under ERISA, 101 Nw. U. L. Rev. 1315 (2007) (reviewing evidence that Unum/Provident systemically denied legitimate policyholder claims in bad faith and attributing this pattern, in part, to the company's protection from bad faith laws and other forms of state insurance law due to ERISA complete preemption).

7. *Punitive Damages.* Punitive damages also may be awarded in a bad-faith claim. If something more than negligence is required to support an action for "ordinary" bad faith, is the line dividing these actions from cases in which punitive damages also are available likely to exist more in theory than in practice? The court in *Rawlings,* supra, described the difference this way:

> Thus, we establish no new category of punitive damages for bad faith cases. Such damages are recoverable in bad faith tort actions when, *and only when,* the facts establish that defendant's conduct was aggravated, outrageous, malicious or fraudulent. *See Anderson v. Continental Insurance Co.,* 85 Wis.2d 675 (1978). Indifference to facts or failure to investigate are sufficient to establish the tort of bad faith but may not rise to the level required by the punitive damage rule. The difference is no doubt harder to articulate in legalistic terms than it is to differentiate on the facts. To obtain tort damages, for instance, plaintiff must prove only that defendant failed to ascertain the true facts and thus acted without or indifferent to the reasonable basis required for denying the claim. To obtain punitive damages, plaintiff must also show that the evil hand that unjustifiably damaged the objectives sought to be reached by the insurance contract was guided by an evil mind which either consciously sought to damage the insured or acted intentionally, knowing that its conduct was likely to cause unjustified, significant damage to the insured. * * * When defendant's motives are shown to be so improper, *or* its conduct so impressive, outrageous or intolerable that such an "evil mind" may be inferred, punitive damages may be awarded. Restatement (Second) of Torts § 908(2).

A more straightforward articulation of the test can be found in *Ingalls v. Paul Revere Life Insurance Group,* 1997 N.D. 43 (1997), which holds that an insurer who violates its duty of good faith and fair dealing may be held liable for punitive damages if it acted with the intent to vex, injure or annoy, or in conscious disregard of the plaintiff's rights.

8. *The Impact of Bad Faith Law.* Bad faith doctrine clearly has a substantial impact on insurer claims-handling practices. For instance, not surprisingly, insurers' settlements of claims are significantly larger when aggrieved policyholders can pursue a bad faith claim. See Mark J. Browne, Ellen S. Pryor, & Bob Puelz, The Effect of Bad-Faith Laws on First-Party Insurance Claims Decisions, 33 J. Legal Stud. 355 (2004); Danial P. Asmat & Sharon Tennyson, Does the Threat of Insurer Liability for "Bad Faith" Affect Insurance Settlements?, 81 J. Risk & Ins. 1 (2014). Whether this is a good thing or not is less clear. According to some, this effect is driven in substantial part by the fact that bad faith discourages insurers from conducting rigorous claims handling investigations, which increases the incidence of fraudulent insurance claiming. Sharon Tennyson & William J. Warfel, The Law and Economics of First-Party Insurance Bad Faith Liability, 16 Conn. Ins. L.J. 203 (2010). On the other hand, it may be that this effect is driven by a decrease in insurers' bad faith denial of claims because they are no longer able to opportunistically breach policies. In many cases, the line between these two interpretations is unclear because it may be that insurers who are too aggressive in trying to reduce insurance

fraud—which is indeed a substantial (though notoriously difficult to measure) problem—wrongly, and perhaps even unreasonably, deny claims.

9. *Constitutional Restrictions on Bad Faith Law.* Constitutional principles limit the availability of punitive damages in bad faith cases. In *State Farm Mutual Automobile Insurance Co. v. Campbell*, 538 U.S. 408 (2003), the U.S. Supreme Court addressed the constitutionality of a Utah state court award of $145 million in punitive damages for the insurer's bad faith denial of a claim in which compensatory damages for breach were $1 million. The court held that three factors placed limits on the amount of punitive damages that could be awarded under the Due Process clause of the Constitution: 1) the degree of reprehensibility of the defendant's conduct; 2) the disparity between the actual or potential harm suffered by the plaintiff and the punitive damages award; and 3) the difference between the punitive damages awarded and the civil penalties authorized or imposed in similar cases. Applying these factors, the Court reversed the award and remanded for further proceedings.

D. PUBLIC POLICY RESTRICTIONS ON CONTRACT TERMS

In addition to the doctrines that govern the *meaning* of provisions in insurance policies, the *validity* of those provisions is governed by the public policies of the states in which they are sold. Under ordinary contract law, state public policies—as embodied in constitutional, statutory, and perhaps even judicial sources—can render contracts void when there is no countervailing protectable interest embodied in the contract. Thus, a contract to sell illegal drugs would be void. If a contract term potentially implicates public policy but also serves a legitimate interest of the parties, then courts will typically employ a balancing test to determine whether the contract or term is void or should be limited by the court.

Insurance contracts can implicate a range of potential state public policies. These public policies are often embodied in state constitutions, statutes, and regulations. But they can also arise from more general judicial sensitivity to the differences between good and evil, fairness and unfairness, straight dealing and overreaching. Even when all other tests for the validity of insurance policy provisions have been exhausted, this residual category of restrictions on what may and may not be included in a policy remains.

Throughout this book we will encounter various public policy restrictions on insurance policy terms, such as the insurable interest requirement (Chapters 4 and 5) and the scope of Uninsured Motorist Coverage (Chapter 8). In this Section, we introduce these concepts with two cases. As you study the following cases, consider whether the principles that lie behind the decisions can be generalized beyond the subjects with which they deal, into a formula that might add predictability and structure to this area of insurance law. Are public policy restrictions on the validity of insurance policy provisions an undefinable and brooding omnipresence, or the result of a set of principles that can be articulated and applied in the same manner as other legal rules?

Hartford Casualty Insurance Company v. Powell
United States District Court, Northern District of Texas, 1998.
19 F.Supp.2d 678.

■ McBryde, District Judge.

* * *

I. Plaintiff's Complaint and Claims

Hartford seeks a declaration that it has no insuring obligation in relation to claims that have been made by Gann against defendant Eilene Jamie Powell ("Powell") under an insurance policy it had issued to Powell's employer. The allegations of Hartford that are pertinent to the memorandum opinion and order are that:

On July 7, 1995, Hartford issued a commercial auto coverage policy, Hartford Policy No. 45 CSE D62203 (E) ("policy"), to Powell's employer. On July 29, 1997, Powell was involved in an automobile collision with Gann while she was driving a vehicle that was covered by the policy. Gann filed suit against Powell in the 96th Judicial District Court of Tarrant County, Texas, ("the Tarrant County action") seeking recovery of actual damages he sustained because of bodily injuries and property damage he suffered as a result of the collision, and of punitive damages because of Powell's alleged gross negligence.

Hartford seeks a declaration that it does not have any insurance coverage under the policy for any claims resulting from the collision in question, or, alternatively, that it has no liability under the policy for any punitive damages that might be awarded Gann against Powell in the Tarrant County action. * * *

In his state court pleading, Gann described the conduct about which he complains as follows:

Defendant, EILENE JAMIE POWELL, was hopelessly intoxicated. She did not have control over the vehicle she was operating when she swerved to her left into the grassy median which separated the east and west bound lanes of traffic. Defendant then veered all the way to the right, across all the east bound lanes of traffic, striking the guard rail. After striking the guardrail, the Defendant then swerved all the way back left crossing all the east bound lanes of traffic and the grassy median into the west bound lanes of traffic where she, violently and without warning, slammed into Plaintiff's car which, then, thrust Plaintiff's vehicle into an 18-wheeler truck which had also been traveling in the west bound lanes of traffic.

* * *

At an early date the Texas Supreme Court declared "that contracts against public policy are void and will not be carried into effect by courts of justice are principles of law too well-established to require the support of authorities...." *James v. Fulcrod,* 5 Tex. 512, 520 (1851). So far as the court can determine, the Texas Supreme Court has never departed from those fundamental principles. A competing, but subservient, public policy also recognized by the Texas Supreme Court is that "contracts, when entered into freely and voluntarily, shall be held sacred, and shall be enforced by courts of justice." *Missouri, K. & T. Ry. v. Carter,* 68 S.W. 159, 164 (1902). "The power to make contracts is too valuable a right to be lightly swept away under the general declaration that such contracts are contrary to public policy, and we must come to some definite point of understanding what the public policy offended against consists of." Id.

The public policy of Texas is to be found in the unwritten or common-law restrictions, as well as in statutory limitations. *Taylor v. Leonard,* 275 S.W. 134, 135 (Tex. Civ. App.–Texarkana 1925, no writ). An intermediate appellate court of Texas has said that "in examining an agreement to determine if it is contrary to public policy[,] the court must look for a tendency to be injurious to the public good." *Sacks v. Dallas Gold & Silver Exch., Inc.,* 720 S.W.2d 177, 180 (Tex. App.–Dallas 1986, no writ).

Since the Texas Supreme Court decision in *Transportation Ins. Co. v. Moriel,* 879 S.W.2d at 19, 26, the conclusions are inescapable that under Texas law an award of punitive damages has as its sole purposes punishment of the wrongdoer and deterrence, and that the public policy of Texas is for the courts of Texas to ensure that defendants who deserve to be punished by punitive damages in fact receive an appropriate level of punishment. *Moriel,* 879 S.W.2d at 16–17. Any uncertainty that might previously have existed as to the status of the law of Texas on that subject was eliminated by the clear, concise, and unequivocal language of the Texas Supreme Court in *Moriel.* The conclusions that are forced by *Moriel* are supported by the analysis by the Texas Supreme Court in its *Owens-Corning Fiberglas Corp. v. Malone* opinion, 972 S.W.2d at 42, 48, of the kinds of evidence that are relevant to the issue of the amount of punitive damages to be awarded. These public policy interests were expressly recognized by the intermediate appellate court in *I-Gotcha, Inc. v. McInnis* when the court explained that "the public policy interest[ ] of using punitive damages as punishment rather than as compensation for the plaintiff" is best served by a rule that causes the punitive damage award to be the total amount of punitive damages found by the jury without reduction under the contributory negligence scheme. 903 S.W.2d at 840. Confirming that the public policy of Texas is that punitive damages serve as punishment of the wrongdoer is the legislative enactment of 1987, as modified in 1995. 903 S.W.2d at 840.

Thus, the principles of law declared by the Texas Supreme Court in *Fulcrod,* supra at 37, that contracts against public policy are void and will not be carried into effect by courts of justice would seem to lead to the conclusion that any insurance contract that prevents a punitive damage award from having its punishment effect is void and unenforceable by a court applying Texas law. And, in fact, that conclusion is now inescapable. The strong public policy of Texas that punitive damages serve to punish the wrongdoer overcomes any competing policy that a contract entered into freely and voluntarily shall be enforced. Contrary to the situation in the Carter case, 95 Tex. at 461, the Texas Supreme Court in *Moriel* provided a "definite point of understanding what public policy [is] offended" by insurance coverage that seeks to protect the wrongdoer from an obligation to pay punitive damages.

The precedent created by the Fifth Circuit opinion in *Northwestern Nat'l Cas. Co. v. McNulty,* 307 F.2d at 433, 434, is directly in point here. The Erie guess made by the Fifth Circuit in *McNulty* that the Supreme Courts of the States of Florida and Virginia would find that the public policies of those states would be offended by liability insurance covering punitive damages was based solely on the Court's determinations that in those states punitive damages are awarded for the purposes of punishment and deterrence and none other. The reasoning of the Fifth Circuit in *McNulty* would, when applied to Texas law as it now exists, lead to the conclusion that Texas public policy would be offended if Powell were to be protected by the policy from a punitive damage award recovered from her by Gann. Consequently, *McNulty* stands as persuasive authority for an Erie guess that the Texas Supreme Court would rule that public policy prevents Hartford from having coverage under the policy for the claim Gann has made for recovery of punitive damages from Powell.

On the other hand, the reasoning of the example given as expressive of the competing view, *Lazenby v. Universal Underwriters Ins. Co.,* 214 Tenn. at 645, 649, does not fit into the Texas legal landscape. The Texas Supreme Court and Texas Legislature seem to have no misgivings on the issue of whether an award of punitive damage against a wrongdoer will tend to deter. Moreover, under Texas law as it now exists the line between simple negligence and negligence upon which an award for punitive damages can be made is no longer, if it ever was, fine. Texas law makes clear that a strong public policy such as the Texas Supreme Court announced in *Moriel* will prevail over the subservient policy that private contracts be honored. Finally, the Texas Supreme Court and Texas Legislature have made pronouncements that establish in Texas that requiring a wrongdoer to suffer the sting of a punitive damage award is synonymous with public good, with the consequence that necessarily a private contract that would tend to diminish the punishment effect of a punitive damage award would harm or injure the public good. In these respects, the laws of Texas appear to be at variance with the laws of Tennessee as announced by the *Lazenby* court. * * *

The court's Erie guess is that the Texas Supreme Court would, if presented with the facts of this case, hold that the public policy of Texas would be offended if the coverage of the policy were to protect Powell from a punitive damage award recovered by Gann against Powell, and that, therefore, to whatever extent the coverage of the policy would literally extend to Gann's claim for punitive damages, the coverage is void and unenforceable under Texas law. Therefore, the motion is being granted. * * *

NOTES AND QUESTIONS

1. *Public Policy and Insurance against Intentional Wrongdoing and Punitive Damages.* Most courts hold that insurance against intentional wrongdoing violates public policy. This rule applies to all forms of liability insurance. See, e.g., *Mass. Mut. Life Ins. Co. v. Woodall,* 304 F. Supp. 2d 1364 (S.D. Ga. 2003) (holding that an insured who suffered from depression

resulting from the prospect of being disbarred from the practice of law because of intentional misconduct was not entitled to recover for lost income under his disability insurance policy). But cf. Christopher C. French, Debunking the Myth That Insurance Coverage Is Not Available or Allowed for Intentional Torts or Damages, 8 Hastings Bus. L.J. 65 (2012).

The implications of this principle for the insurability of punitive damages are unclear, however. As *Powell* notes, liability for punitive damages apparently may be imposed in some states for conduct that does not involve an actual, subjective intent to cause harm. See *Fairfield Ins. Co. v. Stephens Martin Paving*, 246 S.W.3d 653 (Tex. 2008) (holding that Texas law and public policy do not prohibit insurance of liability for punitive damages imposed for gross negligence). Moreover, in a variety of cases parties may be vicariously liable for punitive damages due to the intentional misconduct of another party. According to one review, approximately half of the states ultimately permit coverage for punitive damages in certain circumstances. See Catherine M. Sharkey, Revisiting the Noninsurable Costs of Accidents, 64 Md. L. Rev. 409, 423 (2005). For a detailed state by state survey of the insurability of punitive damages, see Robert G. Schloerb *et al.*, Punitive Damages: A Guide to the Insurability of Punitive Damages in the United States and Its Territories (3d ed. 2003).

The applicability of a state's prohibition on insurance against intentional wrongdoing can also create confusion in other contexts due to the fact that tort and insurance concepts are not completely congruent. For example, under certain circumstances, as a matter of federal constitutional law, a public official may not recover for libel or slander without proof that the defamatory statement was made with "actual malice." The U.S. Supreme Court has defined "actual malice" as knowledge that the statement is false or reckless disregard of whether the statement is true or false. See *N.Y. Times Co. v. Sullivan*, 376 U.S. 254 (1964). How would you determine whether allegations of libel brought by a public official against a newspaper fall within the *Powell* rule? See *Greater Palm Beach Symphony Ass'n v. Hughes*, 441 So. 2d 1171 (Fla. Dist. Ct. App. 1983), in which the insurer was required to defend a libel and slander action in which some counts of the complaint contained no allegations of malicious intent.

2. *Does the Policy Provide Coverage?* Aside from public policy, most liability and property insurance policies contain express exclusions of coverage (or limitations contained in the insuring agreement itself) for harm that is intentionally caused. The phrasing of these provisions varies; the most common excludes coverage of harm that is "either expected or intended from the standpoint of the insured." Does the decision in *Powell* provide any guidance regarding the relation between this sort of exclusion and the public policy against insuring for intentional harm? Do the two coincide, or is the latter broader than the former?

Where liability insurance covering alleged conduct is not barred by public policy, the courts are divided on the question whether a basic liability insurance policy that covers the insured against liability for "damages" includes liability for punitive damages. The majority of courts hold that the standard policy does provide such coverage. See, e.g., *Hooters of Augusta, Inc. v. Am. Global Ins. Co.*, 272 F. Supp. 2d 1365 (S.D. Ga. 2003); *Fluke Corp. v. Hartford Accident & Indem. Co.*, 102 Wash. App. 237 (2000); *Boyd v. Nationwide Mut. Ins. Co.*, 108 N.C. App. 536 (1993); *Public Serv. Mut. Ins. Co. v. Goldfarb*, 53 N.Y.2d 392 (1981). An express exclusion of coverage against liability for punitive damages will negate the inference that such coverage is intended, but most liability insurance policies do not contain such an exclusion. When ISO attempted to introduce such an exclusion into general liability policies in 1977, it was met with a storm of protest from the insurance industry, and the exclusion was withdrawn.

3. *The Merits of a Punitive Damages Exclusion.* A rule that punitive damages are not insurable would eliminate case-by-case determination of whether harm resulting in punitive damages was caused intentionally. But would such a *per se* rule be so overbroad as to preclude coverage of a range of liabilities that should be insurable? The issue has been addressed in detail in the literature. See, e.g., Catherine M. Sharkey, Revisiting the Noninsurable Costs of Accidents, 64 Md. L. Rev. 409 (2005); Tom Baker, Reconsidering Insurance for Punitive Damages, 1998 Wisc. L. Rev. 101; Michael A. Pope, Punitive Damages: When, Where and How They Are Covered, 62 Def. Couns. J. 539 (1995); Alan I. Widiss, Liability Insurance Coverage for Punitive Damages?, 39 Vill. L. Rev. 455 (1994); George L. Priest, Insurability and Punitive Damages, 40 Ala. L. Rev. 1009 (1989).

4. *Countervailing Public Policy.* Are there any public policy considerations that might counsel in favor of permitting liability insurance for punitive damages? Consider, for instance, the prospect that a tortfeasor would be unable to pay punitive damages from his or her personal funds. In that case, who does it actually impact if courts or insurance policies limit coverage for punitive damages? Might this explain why South Carolina apparently *requires* that certain auto liability insurance policies include coverage against liability for punitive damages? See S.C. Code Ann. § 38–77–30(4).

5. *Circumventing Public Policy Restrictions.* When states' public policy laws substantially limit the capacity of insurers to provide liability insurance that would cover punitive damages, sophisticated policyholders are often nonetheless able to secure liability coverage. They simply purchase such coverage "off-shore," in jurisdictions such as Bermuda that are not subject to U.S. insurance law and regulation. To what extent does the possibility of such work-arounds for sophisticated policyholders undermine the case for state laws restricting the insurability of punitive damages?

Strickland v. Gulf Life Insurance Company

Supreme Court of Georgia, 1978.
240 Ga. 723.

■ UNDERCOFLER, PRESIDING JUSTICE.

This is a certiorari. *Strickland v. Gulf Life Ins. Co.,* 143 Ga.App. 67 (1977). It involves a life-accident policy issued in 1946 which, among other things, insures against the loss of a leg. The policy provides coverage if within 90 days of the injury there is "dismemberment by severance." Strickland injured his right lower leg. Medical efforts to save the leg continued for 118 days. They proved unsuccessful and the leg was amputated. Gulf Life denied coverage because severance of the leg was beyond the 90 day limitation. The trial court granted Gulf Life's motion for summary judgment. The Court of Appeals affirmed. We reverse in order that the trial court may consider in the light of this opinion Strickland's pleadings that the condition requiring severance within 90 days is contrary to public policy.

The Court of Appeals, in considering Strickland's appeal from the trial court's grant of summary judgment in favor of the insurance company, relied on our case of *State Farm Mutual Automobile Ins. Co. v. Sewell,* 223 Ga. 31 (1967), which it had reluctantly followed earlier in *Travelers Ins. Co. v. Pratt,* 130 Ga.App. 331 (1973) and *Boyes v. Continental Ins. Co.,* 139 Ga.App. 609 (1976).

In *Sewell* and *Boyes,* the issue was whether the loss incurred was the loss covered by the policy. The plaintiff in *Sewell* had suffered partial loss of his vision; he could make out images and colors and retained some peripheral vision. The Court of Appeals, in *State Farm Mutual Ins. Co. v. Sewell,* 114 Ga.App. 331 (1966), and in *Georgia Life & Health Ins. Co. v. Sewell,* 113 Ga.App. 443 (1966), construed the policy language, "the irrecoverable loss of the entire sight," as meaning a loss of sight "for all practical purposes" and affirmed such a charge given in the trial court. This court reversed, holding that the word "entire" had to be construed as meaning entire.

Similarly in *Boyes,* supra, the Court of Appeals, following *Sewell,* 223 Ga. 31, supra, held that the total loss of use of the plaintiff's left arm was not covered by an insurance policy covering only a loss of a member by severance. This court denied certiorari.

A time limitation, as is involved in the case now before us, was presented to the Court of Appeals in *Pratt,* supra. The plaintiff's left foot had been injured in a hunting accident, but was not amputated for eighteen months. During this time he was under constant treatment to avoid the amputation. Although the leg as originally injured was completely useless, there remained the possibility that regeneration might occur. It did not, and amputation was eventually necessary. The policy covered a loss by severance within 90 days of the injury. At that point, the plaintiff's leg was still in a cast. The Court of Appeals, relying on *Sewell,* 223 Ga. 31, supra, held that, since the policy required severance within 90 days, rather than merely loss of use during that time, the insurance company was not liable for the loss. Certiorari was denied by a divided court.

The plaintiff raised the public policy argument regarding the time limitation now before us in *Pratt,* but the Court of Appeals denied the challenge on the authority of *Randall v. State Mutual Ins. Co.,* 112 Ga.App. 268 (1965) (death not within 90 days), *Metropolitan Life Ins. Co. v. Jackson,* 79 Ga.App. 263 (1949) (loss of sight not within 90 days) and *Bennett v. Life & Cas. Ins. Co.,* 60 Ga.App. 228 (1939) (death not within 30 days). In all of these cases, the Court of Appeals had held that time limitations in an insurance policy were "valid." This court has not directly ruled on this issue. However, "[s]tandardized contracts such as insurance policies, drafted by powerful commercial units and put before individuals on the 'accept this or get nothing' basis, are carefully scrutinized by the courts for the purpose of avoiding enforcement of 'unconscionable' clauses." Corbin, Contracts § 1376, p. 21.

Where loss of a limb is involved at an arbitrary point in time, here 90 days, the insured under these cases is confronted with the ugly choice whether to continue treatment and retain hope of regaining the use of his leg or to amputate his leg in order to be eligible for insurance benefits which he would forgo if amputation became necessary at a later time. We find an insurance limitation forcing such a gruesome choice may be unreasonable and thus may be void as against public policy.

Finding such a limitation unreasonable is not without precedent. In *Burne v. Franklin Life Ins. Co.,* 301 A.2d 799, 801 (1973), a pedestrian had been struck by an automobile and had lain in a vegetative state for 4½ years. The insurance company paid the life policy, but refused to pay the double indemnity accidental death benefits which were "payable only if ' * * * such death occurred * * * within ninety days from the date of the accident.' " * * *

[A] New Jersey court has also found this reasoning persuasive. "The rule in almost every jurisdiction which has considered the question is that the time limitations set forth in the policy are controlling and that recovery must be denied in a case such as the present one. See Appleman, Insurance Law and Practice (2d ed. 1963), § 612. However, a recent decision by the Supreme Court of Pennsylvania has held that such time limitations are unenforceable and has allowed recovery where death by accident occurred well after the period stipulated in the policy. [Cit. omitted.] Although it is presently very much a minority rule, I am persuaded that the rule announced in Burne is the better rule and should be followed." *Karl v. New York Life Ins. Co.,* 353 A.2d 564, 565 (1976). The court thus allowed the beneficiary of a man who had sustained a skull injury in a criminal assault to recover under the accidental double indemnity provisions in his two policies, which contained 90 and 120 day limitations, even though he died 11 months after the assault.

We note further that in *Karl, supra*, the court considered the question whether with the minimal cost of the accidental death benefit, it would be unfair to the insurance company to ignore these time limitations in light of the company's economic risk calculations. It concluded, however, that the real purpose of the time limitation was to limit disputes concerning the causal connection between the death and the accident rather than because of any economic relationship between the premium and the time limitation. Also, the court observed that the reason the cost of accidental death policies was so low was that relatively few deaths occur because of accidents.

In *INA Insurance Co. v. Commonwealth Ins. Dept.,* 376 A.2d 670 (Pa.Cmwlth.1977), the insurance company also argued that the causation problem was the main reason for these time limitations. That court rejected the argument, observing that the burden was on the claimant to establish the causative relationship, and held that causation was not a weighty enough problem to deny benefits arbitrarily to those surviving beyond the time limitation set out in the policy, who had died as a result of the accident. Following *Burne,* the court upheld the insurance commissioner's ruling that all similar time limitations in accident policies are arbitrary and unreasonable and thus against public policy.

"[I]t may be pointed out that 'liberty of contract' as that term is used by its admirers includes two very different elements. These are the privilege of doing the acts constituting the transaction and the power to make it legally operative. One does not have 'liberty of contract' unless organized society both forbears and enforces, forbears to penalize him for making his bargain and enforces it for him after it is made."

"This is the 'liberty of contract' that has so often been extolled as one of the great boons of modern democratic civilization, as one of the principal causes of prosperity and comfort. And yet the very fact that a chapter on 'legality' of contract must be written shows that we have never had and never shall have unlimited liberty of contract, either in its phase of societal forbearance or in its phase of societal enforcement. There are many contract transactions that are definitely forbidden by the law, forbidden under pains and penalties assessed for crime and tort; and there are many more such transactions that are denied judicial enforcement, even though their makers are not subjected to affirmative pains and penalties." Corbin, Contracts § 1376, p. 20.

Corbin, in his treatise on contracts, also observes that the declaration of public policy is the proper function of the courts, as well as of the legislature. "Constitutions and statutes are declarations of public policy by bodies of men authorized to legislate. It is the function of the courts to interpret and apply these, so far as they go and so far as they are understandable. Some judges have thought that they must look solely to constitutions and statutes and to earlier decisions interpreting and applying them as the sources from which they may determine what public policy requires. This is far from true, even though these are the sources that are first to be considered and that often may be conclusive."[1]

"In determining what public policy requires, there is no limit whatever to the 'sources' to which the court is permitted to go; and there is no limit to the 'evidence' that the court may cause to be produced, * * *" 6A Corbin, Contracts, § 1375, pp. 15–19. Then, the validity of the contract in question is one of law for the court.[2] 17A C.J.S. Contracts § 615 p. 1238.

Although we are impressed by the persuasive reasoning of the above authorities, we do not here reach the question of law whether all such policy limitations are void as against public policy, nor indeed whether the 90 days severance clause before us is unenforceable. The trial court granted summary judgment in favor of the insurance company on the authority of *Sewell, Pratt,* and *Boyes, supra,* and on the

---

[1] " 'Public policy is the cornerstone—the foundation of all constitutions, statutes, and judicial decisions, and its latitude and longitude, its height and its depth, greater than any or all of them. If this be not true, whence came the first judicial decision on matter of public policy? There was no precedent for it, else it would not have been the first.' *Pittsburgh, C, C & St. L.R. Co. v. Kinney,* 115 N.E. 505, 507, quoted and applied in *Snyder v. Ridge Hill Memorial Park,* 22 N.E.2d 559 (1938)." Corbin, Contracts, § 1375, p. 15, n. 12. [footnote in original].

[2] "When the validity of a contract is in issue before a court, the judge is obliged to make decision whatever the degree of his ignorance or wisdom. Before decision there should be some debate and much evidence; afterwards the decision is subject to criticism, by litigant and lawyer, by juryman and jurist, by the learner and the scholar. It is thus that the mores, the considered notions as to what makes for human welfare and survival are formed, to be constantly verified or altered in new cases, forever hammered on the anvil of life experience."

"The court can not postpone decision until all possible evidence is in. Sometimes the judge may properly take 'judicial notice' of what is common knowledge and generally held opinion. But it is never wise to jump to a conclusion or to disregard experience; and it is never necessary to decide an issue as to public policy without expert briefing of former decisions and without listening to the testimony of those whose interests are at stake and of disinterested and experienced observers." Corbin, Contracts § 1375, pp. 10–11. [Footnotes omitted].

basis of the pleadings, the contract of insurance and a stipulation of fact by counsel. The stipulated facts included only the date Strickland had been injured and the date over 90 days later that his right lower leg had been amputated, naming the doctor and place of the amputation. No evidence was produced on the issue, raised in Strickland's pleadings, that the contract was unreasonable, and thus void as against public policy. We are reluctant to make such an important pronouncement without further evidence. For example, medical evidence reported in *Reliance Ins. Co. v. Kinman,* 252 Ark. 1168 (1972), that it takes about 18 months for bone and nerve tissue to regenerate would be relevant to the reasonableness of the 90 day clause in this insurance policy. Other information important to the court's decision may include, for example, (1) the present state of medical science on rehabilitation of injured limbs; (2) whether the insured had a choice of other policies with other time limitations; (3) whether the time limitation is related to the economic risk of the insurance company and (4) whether there is a relationship between the time limitation and the difficulty of proving causation.

We reverse the Court of Appeals in order that the trial court may fully consider the public policy issue.

Judgment reversed. * * *

■ BOWLES, JUSTICE, dissenting.

As I read the opinion of the majority, I find only one conclusion reached—that the opinion of the Court of Appeals is reversed so that the matter may be referred back to the trial court to hear evidence, and *"fully consider"* the public policy issue.

Heretofore in Georgia, where the contract is unambiguous, our courts have been able to decide, without the benefit of evidentiary hearings, whether or not a given contract or clause in a given contract violates the public policy of this state. While I do not contend that it is impermissible for a trial judge to hear evidence to aid him in making such a decision, I conclude that the trial judge in this case made his determination based on his experience, common sense, general knowledge prevailing in his community regarding the habits and customs of his people, and prior decisions of our courts touching the question. He was not required by law to hear evidence.

Now, for the first time, we require the trial judge to receive or hear evidence on whether a given contract clause violates public policy. Having done so, he can again use his experience, common sense and general knowledge, and can again consider prior case law in making a determination as to whether or not the 90 day contract clause in question violates the public policy of this state. Thus, we are forcing him to do what he did not consider necessary in the first instance, in addition to his customary procedure.

The majority opinion does not specifically overrule *Travelers Insurance Co. v. Pratt,* 130 Ga.App. 331, which has heretofore decided the exact question contra to this position. But to support their argument the majority quotes approvingly from two decisions in other states representing the minority view in America and which are without precedent. The majority says, "An insurance limitation forcing such a gruesome choice may be unreasonable and thus may be void as against public policy." It also castigates "powerful commercial units" and suggests that the policy of insurance offered in this case may have been offered to the insured on an "accept this or get nothing basis."

The fundamental right of our citizens to legally contract; the fact that the right to contract is paramount public policy of our state and should not be interfered with lightly; and the fact that our appellate courts have heretofore ruled on the exact question one time, and similar questions many times, are disregarded. Unless there is some compelling reason to do so, we do the citizens of Georgia, the practicing lawyers and the lower courts an injustice when we attempt to overrule precedent without justification. I find no compelling reason, in this case, to deviate from the precedent laid down by this court in earlier cases.

I would affirm the opinion of the Court of Appeals without further ado.

I am authorized to state that Justice JORDAN joins in this dissent.

NOTES AND QUESTIONS

1. *Precedent.* Did the court adequately distinguish the holdings in its previous decisions in the *Sewell* and *Boyes* cases? Can you do so? Numerous courts have rejected *Stickland*, holding that provisions similar to the 90 day limitation in that case do not violate public policy. See, e.g., *Martin v. Allianz Life Ins. Co. of N. Am.*, 573 N.W.2d 823 (N.D. 1998).

2. *An Evidentiary Condition?* Did the court do anything more than hold that under certain circumstances, the 90 day requirement is merely a non-exclusive evidentiary condition? Are you more or less comfortable with this approach in *Strickland* than the court's approach in *Atwater Creamery*, supra (involving the forcible-entry requirement in a burglary insurance policy)? Why?

3. *Crazy Like a Fox?* At first glance the dissent's criticism of the court's remand in *Strickland* may seem well taken. Consider, however, what might have been entailed in fashioning a rule to govern all future cases. The logic of the opinion suggests that there may not be *any* time limit that is automatically valid, because all such limits may be open to challenge depending on the circumstances. But the opinion does not actually state such a rule. Rather than invalidate all such limits, or openly increase unpredictability by stating that such limits are sometimes valid but can always be questioned, the court sidestepped that issue by remanding. Do you support this approach, or would more candor have been preferable?

4. *Problem.* If you represented a disability insurer after the decision in *Strickland,* how (if at all) would you advise that future policies be redrafted? Consider in that regard *Emond v. State Farm Mutual Automobile Insurance Co.*, 175 Ga. App. 548 (1985), in which the court held that a provision limiting excess medical coverage to expenses incurred within one year of an accident was enforceable because the restriction did not force the insured into making a gruesome choice.

5. *A General Theory of Public Policy Restrictions?* After examining the cases on the issue in this Section, are you prepared to venture a principle or principles that are at the foundation of this field? Consider the following:

An insurance policy provision violates public policy when a constitution or statute expressly or impliedly prohibits the aim or effect of the provision, when the provision unduly encourages moral hazard, or when the provision would force the insured to engage in unreasonable behavior in order to preserve coverage.

What are the strengths and weaknesses of this formulation?

CHAPTER THREE

INSURANCE REGULATION

The existence of insurance regulation has been a given for a long time. But the question why insurance is heavily regulated remains. Many contracts transfer risk. Why do the types of risk-transferring contracts that qualify as "insurance" receive heavier regulation than ordinary risk-transfer contracts? There is no single answer to this question, in large part because insurance regulation takes so many different forms. But one common theme in virtually all justifications for insurance regulation (and, indeed, regulation more generally) is market imperfections. In idealized market conditions, where insurers and policyholders both possess perfect information and are completely rational, where insurance arrangements only impact the policyholder and insurer, and where numerous firms can freely enter and exit the marketplace, there is little need for insurance regulation. Of course, these idealized conditions are never met in any market. But for reasons that we will explore in the pages below, insurance markets are particularly susceptible to large deviations from these idealized market conditions. Although the reasons for these deviations vary, most of them involve information asymmetries between insurers and policyholders. These include both informational advantages that policyholders have over insurers—and which are responsible for moral hazard and adverse selection—and informational advantages that insurers have over policyholders.

Because of the prevalence of market failures in insurance, regulation may be able to improve outcomes through various strategies. For instance, insurance regulation can attempt to directly remedy the underlying market failure by improving information or decision-making among insurers or policyholders. More commonly, insurance regulation can attempt to replicate the outcomes that regulators believe would prevail in idealized market settings. But whatever strategy is employed, it is important to remember that regulation is itself both costly and imperfect. As you read through the materials that follow, you should therefore consider the significance of any underlying market failure, the effectiveness of regulation in addressing that failure, and the costs associated with implementing and complying with the chosen regulatory strategy.

A. THE ALLOCATION OF REGULATORY POWERS

Although most authority to regulate insurance directly is currently allocated to the states, the nature of that allocation is complex. In 1869, the United States Supreme Court held, in *Paul v. Virginia,* 75 U.S. (8 Wall.) 168, 183 (1869), that insurance is not "commerce" under the U.S. Constitution's Commerce Clause. As a result, Congress had no authority under the Commerce Clause to regulate insurance. *Paul* squelched an incipient effort to encourage federal rather than state regulation. It also limited the scope of future federal legislation. For instance, when the Sherman Act was enacted in 1890, *Paul* had already made clear that the Act's antitrust prohibitions could not be applied to insurance.

Authority to regulate insurance continued to rest exclusively at the state level for the next three-quarters of a century. Viewed from the present perspective, state regulation during this period was unsystematic. Over half the states established insurance departments and vested them with varying powers. In 1871 the National Association of Insurance Commissioners (NAIC) was formed to encourage cooperation among the states and promote more nearly uniform regulation. For detailed discussions of the history of insurance regulation, see Kenneth J. Meier, The Political Economy of Regulation: The Case of Insurance (1988); John G. Day, Economic Regulation of Insurance in the United States (1970); Spencer L. Kimball, The Purpose of Insurance Regulation: A Preliminary Inquiry in the Theory of Insurance Law, 45 Minn. L. Rev. 471 (1961).

Perhaps the most salient event in the history of insurance regulation during this period was the 1905 Armstrong Investigation of the life insurance industry in New York. Led by future Chief Justice of the United States Charles Evans Hughes, the investigation uncovered a series of abuses and ethical misconduct by major life insurers. In response, New York and other states enacted a number of regulatory reforms, including requiring detailed financial reporting by life insurers, limiting the amount of new business that could be written each year, imposing stricter regulation of agents' commissions, and imposing new controls on the investments life insurers were permitted to make. Morton Keller, The Life Insurance Enterprise, 1885–1910: A Study in the Limits of Corporate Power 245–59 (1963).

The period of a constitutionally-mandated federal absence from insurance regulation came to an abrupt end with the decision in *United States v. South-Eastern Underwriters Ass'n,* 322 U.S. 533 (1944), which overruled *Paul v. Virginia.* The case involved an indictment of a rating bureau and its member companies for violating the Sherman Act by agreeing to fix premium rates and boycott non-members. The Court held that insurance transactions such as this agreement are subject to federal regulation under the Commerce Clause:

> Not only, then, may transactions be commerce though non-commercial; they may be commerce though illegal and sporadic, and though they do not utilize common carriers or concern the flow of anything more tangible than electrons and information. These activities having already been held to constitute interstate commerce, and persons engaged in them therefore having been held subject to federal regulation, it would indeed be difficult now to hold that no activities of any insurance company can ever constitute interstate commerce so as to make it subject to such regulation—activities which, as part of the conduct of a legitimate and useful commercial enterprise, may embrace integrated operations in many states and involve the transmission of great quantities of money, documents, and communications across dozens of state lines.

322 U.S. at 549–50. The Supreme Court's decision threw the insurance industry into a near panic, for the Court held not only that Congress has the power to regulate insurance; in addition, the effect of the

holding was that Congress had already regulated insurance by enacting the Sherman Act and any number of other general statutes governing commerce among the states. Federal antitrust laws therefore applied immediately to the business of insurance. This new legal landscape was particularly distressing to property/casualty insurers, who, as described in Chapter 2, relied extensively on industry coordination in pooling data and drafting policy forms, activities that could be challenged under federal antitrust laws.

Nothing in *South-Eastern Underwriters,* however, either compelled Congress to exercise its power to regulate insurance or precluded it from allowing the states to exercise concurrent regulatory jurisdiction. The Court merely held that Congress could exercise this power and that to some extent it already had done so without knowing it, with the enactment of the Sherman Act. The insurance industry promptly supported legislation prepared by the National Association of Insurance Commissioners (NAIC) that would return regulatory authority to the states. Enacted by Congress in 1945, this legislation is known as the McCarran-Ferguson Act.

The McCarran-Ferguson Act, 15 U.S.C. §§ 1011–15

§ 1011. Declaration of policy [Section 1.]

Congress declares that the continued regulation and taxation by the several States of the business of insurance is in the public interest, and that silence on the part of the Congress shall not be construed to impose any barrier to the regulation or taxation of such business by the several States.

§ 1012. Regulation by State law; Federal law relating specifically to insurance; applicability of certain Federal laws after June 30, 1948 [Section 2.]

(a) The business of insurance, and every person engaged therein, shall be subject to the laws of the several States which relate to the regulation or taxation of such business.

(b) No Act of Congress shall be construed to invalidate, impair, or supersede any law enacted by any State for the purpose of regulating the business of insurance, or which imposes a fee or tax upon such business, unless such Act specifically relates to the business of insurance: *Provided,* That after June 30, 1948, the Act of July 2, 1890, as amended, known as the Sherman Act, and the Act of October 15, 1914, as amended, known as the Clayton Act, and the Act of September 26, 1914, known as the Federal Trade Commission Act, as amended, shall be applicable to the business of insurance to the extent that such business is not regulated by State law.

§ 1013. * * * Sherman Antitrust Act applicable to agreements to, or acts of, boycott, coercion, or intimidation [Section 3.] * * *

(b) Nothing contained in this chapter shall render the said Sherman Act inapplicable to any agreement to boycott, coerce, or intimidate, or act of boycott, coercion, or intimidation.

NOTES AND QUESTIONS

1. *The Structure of the Act.* Important as the McCarran-Ferguson Act is, it merely states some ground rules governing the allocation of federal and state regulatory powers. The Act itself does not regulate, nor does it require regulation by the states. Rather, it performs a quasi-constitutional function, by setting the terms under which legislative and administrative regulation may take place. Section 1 of the Act declares a broad federal policy in favor of state regulation of insurance. It also rejects any inference that the "dormant" commerce clause of the U.S. Constitution precludes state regulation. Katherine M. Jones, Law, Politics, and the Political Safeguards of Federalism: The Case of Insurance Regulation and the Commerce Clause, 1938–1948, 11 Conn. Ins. L.J. 345, 355–65 (2004). Section 2(b) contains the substantive heart of the Act. It first establishes a principle of "reverse preemption" under which general federal legislation does not preempt or override state insurance law unless the federal legislation makes specific reference to insurance. The second clause of Section 2(b) then creates a special exemption from various antitrust laws for insurance, at least to the extent that the business of insurance is regulated by state law. Finally, Section 3 of the Act limits the scope of the insurance antitrust exemption contained in Section 2(b). We will return to both reverse preemption and the antitrust provisions of the Act later in the Chapter when we focus on the scope of federal regulation of insurance.

2. *Express Federal Regulation.* Numerous federal statutes expressly regulate insurance, and thus "specifically relate" to insurance within the meaning of Section 2(b) of McCarran-Ferguson. The most prominent recent examples are the Patient Protection and Affordable Care Act ("Obamacare"), 42 U.S.C. § 18001 *et seq.* and the Dodd-Frank Wall Street Reform and Consumer Protection Act ("Dodd-Frank"), 12 U.S.C. § 5301 *et seq.* Another important example, which we have already encountered in Chapter 2, is the Employee Retirement Income Security Act of 1974 (ERISA), 29 U.S.C. § 1001 *et seq.* The core point is that the McCarran-Ferguson Act does not in any way limit the power of the federal government to regulate insurance when it explicitly decides to do so. Instead, it merely serves as a guide for how to understand federal law when Congress has not made its intent to regulate insurance clear.

3. *The Purpose of the Act.* One view of the core purpose of the McCarran-Ferguson Act is that it allocates power to regulate insurance as between the states and the federal government. See Spencer L. Kimball & Barbara P. Heaney, Emasculation of the McCarran-Ferguson Act: A Study in Judicial Activism, 1985 Utah L. Rev. 1. On this view, one might favor interpretations of the Act that assure that traditional forms of state insurance regulation are protected from federal interference absent clear federal intent to supplant such regulation. An alternative view is that the Act is less important as an allocation of powers than as an effort to recognize that the insurance business should be protected against certain antitrust rules that are generally applicable to the non-insurance world. On this view, the Act's meaning should perhaps depend on which source of regulatory authority—state or federal—can most effectively deal with the kind of issue involved. Certain kinds of problems (e.g., the sale of securities) may be handled best by federal agencies with national jurisdiction and special expertise in the field in question; others (e.g., regulation of the relations between insurers and health-care providers) may

be handled more effectively by state agencies that can investigate, supervise, and categorize these relations than by courts applying federal antitrust law.

B. STATE INSURANCE REGULATION

In the wake of the McCarran-Ferguson Act, every state enacted rate regulation legislation intended to ensure that insurance was "regulated by State law" under Section 2(b) of the Act, thus triggering the antitrust exemption. See Robert H. Jerry II & Douglas S. Richmond, Understanding Insurance Law 69 (4th ed. 2007). These statutes required state insurance departments to assure that insurance rates were not "excessive, inadequate, or unfairly discriminatory." Although these laws still persist and play an important role in many states' insurance regulation, the substance of modern state insurance regulation has grown substantially in its scope and complexity in the last eighty years. See The Future of Insurance Regulation in the United States (Martin F. Grace & Robert W. Klein eds., 2009).

Every state (as well as the District of Columbia and the five U.S. territories) has an office that is charged with regulating the business of insurance. These departments are headed by a "commissioner" or "director," who is either appointed by the Governor or elected. Either way, state insurance departments are subject to a variety of political pressures. Total staff in these departments varies from fewer than 100 in small states like Delaware to over 1,000 in large states like New York. See National Association of Insurance Commissioners, Insurance Department Resources Report (2013). All state insurance departments are subject to their state's administrative law rules. These rules track federal administrative law in their basics. For instance, states' administrative law generally (i) requires notice and comment procedures to promulgate rules, (ii) permits affected parties to challenge regulators' actions in court in some cases, and (iii) requires deferential judicial review of certain agency decisions. See Michael Asimow & Ronald M. Levin, State and Federal Administrative Law (3d ed. 2009).

By far the most important single player in state insurance regulation is the National Association of Insurance Commissioners (NAIC). See generally Susan Randall, Insurance Regulation in the United States: Regulatory Federalism and the National Association of Insurance Commissioners, 26 Fla. St. U. L. Rev. 625 (1999). The NAIC is not a regulator or even a public entity; it is a non-profit corporation with over 450 employees and an annual budget of approximately $80 million. Its Board of Directors is comprised of several state insurance commissioners, who are themselves elected by the commissioners of every jurisdiction. Broadly conceived, the NAIC has three major functions: it promotes uniformity in state insurance law and regulation, it facilitates coordination and cooperation among the states, and it directly provides services to state regulators and consumers.

Promoting Uniformity. Perhaps the primary goal of the NAIC is to promote uniform insurance law and regulation. For insurers who operate on a multi-state basis, differences in state insurance rules can create substantial administrative costs, even when those differences are not substantively significant. Insurance agents and brokers also have some interest in uniformity across states. Varying requirements for obtaining a state license can result in duplicative licensing fees and application standards in order to sell products across state lines. Even consumers have a direct interest in uniformity of state insurance regulations. For instance, regulatory uniformity may increase consumers' ability to learn about different coverage options using non-state specific resources. At the same time, uniformity is not without its downsides. Uniform laws and regulations limit the capacity of jurisdictions to develop rules that match the particular views of their population, and covered risks in certain lines of insurance—such as property/casualty and health—can vary significantly across different regions of the country.

The most important strategy that the NAIC uses to promote uniformity is drafting model insurance statutes and regulations. Like the Uniform Commercial Code, NAIC models do not themselves have the force of law. Rather, they serve as a template for state legislatures and regulators who are interested in harmonizing their insurance laws and regulations with other jurisdictions. Although NAIC models promote consistency, they do so imperfectly. Some state legislatures and regulators do not enact model laws and regulations while others enact model laws or regulations that deviate slightly from the national model. When researching state insurance statutes and regulations, it is often helpful to first determine whether an NAIC model exists on the relevant issue. All model laws and regulations are available for free online, at http://www.naic.org/store_model_laws.htm. For each model, the NAIC maintains an up to date list indicating which jurisdictions have enacted that model or a substantially similar version.

Facilitating Coordination and Cooperation. The efficiency and effectiveness of many regulatory activities can be enhanced when state regulators work collaboratively. In some cases, this may simply amount to states dividing up overlapping regulatory responsibilities so as to limit duplicative efforts. In other cases, state collaboration may be more active, allowing states to identify and respond to national regulatory issues, to learn from their varying experiences and perspectives, or to double-check each other's work in a form of "peer review." Therese M. Vaughan, The Implications of Solvency II for U.S. Insurance Regulation (Networks Fin. Inst., Policy Brief No. 3, 2009). The NAIC organizes individual state regulators into numerous working groups and committees to explore a wide range of regulatory issues. These committees collaborate during tri-annual NAIC meetings and regular conference calls to evaluate individual companies and produce white papers, bulletins, model laws, regulatory manuals, accounting forms, educational materials, and various other forms of regulatory work product. See, e.g., Timothy Stoltzfus Jost, Reflections on the National Association of Insurance Commissioners and Implementation of the Patient Protection and Affordable Care Act, 159 U. Penn. L. Rev. 2043 (2011) (discussing the NAIC's substantial role in fostering collaboration among the states and other stakeholders in the implementation of the Affordable Care Act).

Services for Insurance Regulators and Consumers. A third substantial role of the NAIC is to provide services to both state regulators and insurance consumers. State regulators rely extensively on the NAIC in performing their basic regulatory functions. For instance, the NAIC helps individual departments collect and analyze data, particularly in the solvency sphere. It also provides centralized research and logistical support for states. The NAIC offers some consumer services as well, such as the production of buyers' guides and the aggregation of relevant information, like consumer complaint data.

* * *

In general, the top priority of state insurance regulation is to ensure that carriers have the financial capacity to pay claims when they come due. However, state insurance regulation also devotes substantial resources to a number of additional functions, including preventing "excessive" or "unfairly discriminatory" rates; regulating the content of insurance policy forms; policing against market conduct abuses in claims payments, marketing, and sales; and operating residual markets that provide coverage to individuals who cannot secure insurance from private carriers. We explore each of these regulatory functions below.

1. THE FIRST VIRTUE OF INSURANCE: REGULATION TO ASSURE SOLVENCY

Solvency regulation is widely acknowledged to be the most important element of insurance regulation. As we will see, state insurance departments use a wide variety of tools to ensure that insurers have sufficient resources to pay policyholder claims when they come due. But before examining these tools, we must first understand why solvency regulation is so important in insurance.

a. RATIONALES FOR SOLVENCY REGULATION

The first virtue of an insurance company is its solvency. Insurance is unlike most tangible products, because the insured pays for the product immediately but receives in return only the insurer's promise to pay in the event that the insured suffers a future loss. That promise to pay is valuable only so long as the insurer making the promise is financially capable of performing when an insured loss actually occurs. Meanwhile, the policyholder often substantially relies on the insurer's promise to pay in the event of tragedy, engaging in risky activities that otherwise might be avoided and developing a broad financial plan that encompasses assumptions about the availability of insurance payouts in the future. The importance of insurer solvency is even further enhanced in the case of certain life insurance and annuity products, which effectively combine insurance with savings and investment products, as we will see in Chapter Five. Policyholders of such products who see their insurers fail may lose not only their protection from risk and their coverage for insured losses that have already occurred, but also much of their life savings as well.

If markets worked perfectly, policyholders would realize the importance of their insurer's financial health and would consequently purchase coverage from financially sound carriers that could credibly commit to maintaining their financial stability for as long as benefits on the underlying policy might be owed to the policyholder. But as illustrated by the early history of fire insurers described in Chapter

Two, unregulated markets often do a poor job of ensuring that insurers can pay claims when they come due. There are several explanations for this fact.

The most important explanation for insurers' tendency to take on excessive risk in unregulated markets involves the inability of insurers to commit to avoiding excessively risky practices after a policyholder has purchased coverage (a type of "principal/agent" problem, in economic terms). Once they have received policyholders' premiums, the owners and managers of insurance firms may face strong incentives to adopt risky investment, management, or business strategies. The reason is that increased risk generally results in the prospect of increased reward. Of course, increased risk also can result in large losses as well. But when increased risk pays off, all of this upside generally goes to insurers' managers and owners, who will receive increased bonuses and stock options (in the case of managers) or a more valuable company (in the case of owners). If, on the other hand, increased risk results in large losses, much of the resulting downside will be borne by policyholders because the insurer will not be able to pay their claims in full.

To illustrate, assume Peterson establishes Minnesota Insurance ("MI") and contributes $50,000 in capital to get the company started. The company sells coverage to 1,000 policyholders, who in total pay $950,000 in premiums. Because the risks insured are stable and uncorrelated, MI is confident that it will need to pay $900,000 in claims on these policies. Assume for simplicity that that all of these payments must be made exactly one year after the policies are purchased. In the meantime, MI will need to invest the $1 million in funds it holds, which consists of $950,000 in policyholder premiums and $50,000 in Peterson's start-up capital. Assume that it can invest in a low-risk strategy that will certainly return 10% in one year, or in a high-risk strategy that is equally likely to return either a 50% gain in a year or a 50% loss in a year.

MI's policyholders would strongly prefer that the company adopt the low-risk investment strategy. Doing so would mean that MI would have $1.1 million in assets to pay expected claims of $900,000, so all policyholders who experience losses would be paid in full. By contrast, under the high-risk strategy, there would be a 50% chance that MI would only have $500,000 to pay expected claims of $900,000 at year end, resulting in policyholders not getting paid in full. Peterson, on the other hand, is likely to favor the high-risk strategy. To be sure, if that strategy fails, then he will lose his $50,000 investment, as MI would be insolvent (with liabilities exceeding assets). But the bulk of the loss would be borne by policyholders whose claims wouldn't be paid in full. On the other hand, if the strategy succeeds, then Peterson will own a company that has increased in value by $500,000. The expected value to Peterson of the high-risk strategy is substantially higher than the expected value of the low-risk strategy.

This dynamic is similar to the conflicts of interest that face owners and lenders of ordinary corporations. Lenders generally prefer that borrowers avoid excessive risk, whereas borrowers may be inclined to take large risks to increase their potential rewards. But a key difference between the standard corporate setting and the insurance setting is that, for insurers, policyholders effectively take the place of lenders. This is due to the inverted production cycle of insurance—whereby policyholders pay premiums in exchange for the insurer's commitment of future funds. In the example of Minnesota Insurance, the company was able to offer almost $1 million in products with only $50,000 in start-up capital and no borrowing because it received $950,000 from policyholders well before it ever paid a claim. No other type of firm could have accomplished this.

Insurers' use of policyholders, rather than lenders, to fund their operations is important because, unlike lenders, policyholders are very poorly situated to prevent excessive risk taking by insurers. Lenders go to extraordinary lengths to prevent excessive risk taking by their borrowers. They routinely monitor borrowers' financial health and business outcomes while maintaining the ability to pursue a broad range of remedial options (depending on context) in the event they become concerned about borrowers' ability to repay. See generally Saul Levmore, Monitors and Freeriders in Commercial and Corporate Settings, 92 Yale L.J. 49 (1982). Policyholders do not, and cannot, protect themselves in these ways. Fundamentally, this is because insurers have numerous policyholders, each of whom makes up a small fraction of a carrier's funding base. This results in a classic "collective action problem": all policyholders would benefit from monitoring the insurer to prevent it from taking on excessive risk, but no individual policyholder has an incentive to do so because, for any individual policyholder, the costs of monitoring would outweigh the benefits. Additionally, policyholders are not in the business of understanding and monitoring financial risk: they purchase insurance for financial protection, not for investment purposes. See Guillaume Plantin & Jean-Charles Rochet, When Insurers Go Bust: An Economic Analysis of the Role and Design of Prudential Regulation (2007); M. Todd Henderson, Credit Derivatives Are Not "Insurance," 16 Conn. Ins. L.J. 1, 5 (2009).

Although this principal/agent problem is the most important rationale for solvency regulation, several others are also important. For instance, solvency regulation might be justified because many policyholders fail to fully understand or appreciate insurers' financial risk at the time they purchase coverage. The argument here focuses less on the ability of policyholders to continuously monitor and respond to increases in financial risk by their current insurers, and more on the limits of policyholders in making their initial decisions among insurers in a fashion that appropriately accounts for financial risk. If policyholders are not sufficiently sensitive to insurers' financial health when they initially purchase coverage, then insurers will have limited market incentive to adopt safe, but less profitable, financial and business strategies, as doing so will not win them more business from policyholders. This explanation is weakened by the fact that information about insurers' financial strength is relatively easy to find: several rating agencies—such as A.M. Best and Fitch—routinely assign an overall letter grade to each carrier on the basis of its financial strength. Nevertheless, this information does little if potential policyholders are unaware of it, or unaware of its importance, when they are making coverage decisions.

Another market failure explanation for solvency regulation focuses on state-mandated guaranty funds. We will examine state guaranty funds in more detail later in this Chapter, but in general they partially protect most policyholders from the consequences of their insurer being unable to pay claims. Like all insurance, however, this state-mandated insurance against one's insurer becoming insolvent creates moral hazard. Why should a policyholder take care to select a more financially secure insurer, and pay more for that privilege, if the state insures against the risk that his insurer will go bust? And why should insurers seek to maintain their financial strength when doing so interferes with maximizing profit, and policyholders will buy their coverage no matter what financial strategy they pursue? See David H. Downs & David W. Sommer, Monitoring, Ownership, and Risk-Taking: The Impact of Guaranty Funds, 66 J. Risk & Ins. 477 (1999). Of course, if guaranty funds provide a central rationale for solvency regulation, an alternative to solvency regulation would simply be to eliminate state guaranty funds.

A final potential rationale for solvency regulation that has become substantially more important since 2008 is that insurance companies' financial operations may have important implications for the broader financial system. See generally Daniel Schwarcz & Steven L. Schwarcz, Regulating Systemic Risk in Insurance, 81 U. Chi. L. Rev. 1569 (2014); J. David Cummins & Mary A. Weiss, Systemic Risk and Regulation of the U.S. Insurance Industry, 81 J. Risk & Ins. 489 (2014). To the extent that insurers are indeed systemically risky—meaning that their instability or operations could negatively impact the broader financial system or macro-economy—solvency regulation can be justified in much the same way as the regulation of pollution. In both cases, firms' operations impose costs on the broader public that are not "internalized" by the company or its policyholders. As a result, firms will generally take insufficient care to limit these risks. Whether insurers actually do pose systemic risks is quite controversial. We will return to this topic later in the Chapter when we examine federal regulation of insurance and AIG's role in the 2008 financial crisis.

NOTES AND QUESTIONS

1. *Alternatives to Solvency Regulation?* Although most modern countries maintain an extensive solvency regulation regime, there are exceptions. New Zealand imposes limited solvency requirements and does not maintain any insurance guaranty fund system. Instead, New Zealand requires insurers to acquire financial strength ratings from rating agencies and to publicly disclose these ratings to prospective policyholders. See Martin Eling & Ines Holzmüller, An Overview and Comparison of Risk-Based Capital Standards, 26 J. Ins. Reg. 31 (2008). What benefits does the New Zealand system offer relative to the U.S. system? What risks, if any, does the New Zealand system fail to account for? Why is it particularly important that New Zealand does not maintain a guaranty fund system, given its general approach to insurance solvency regulation? On balance, which regulatory approach is preferable? For an argument in favor of decreasing the stringency of U.S. solvency regulation, see Scott E. Harrington, Capital Adequacy in Insurance and Reinsurance, in Capital

Adequacy Beyond Basel: Banking, Securities, and Insurance (Hal S. Scott ed., 2005).

2. *Differing Levels of Solvency Regulation for Different Insurance Companies?* Most insurance solvency requirements apply in the same way to companies that sell coverage to different types of policyholders. Thus insurers that provide property/casualty coverage predominantly to large commercial enterprises with risk managers are subject to the same solvency requirements as insurers that predominantly sell homeowners and personal auto insurance policies. What can explain this uniformity in regulatory scrutiny, which, as we will see, does not persist when it comes to non-solvency forms of regulation? Relatedly, could it be that the New Zealand approach described above might be preferable for certain lines of coverage, where policyholders are relatively sophisticated, but that the U.S. system is preferable for insurance lines marketed principally to ordinary individuals?

3. *Mutual Insurance Companies.* Some studies have found that insurers organized as mutual companies are less likely to take large risks than companies organized as stock companies. See, e.g., Joan Lamm-Tennant & Laura T. Starks, Stock Versus Mutual Ownership Structures: The Risk Implications, 66 J. Bus. 29 (1993); J. David Cummins, Scott E. Harrington, & Robert Klein, Insolvency Experience, Risk-Based Capital and Prompt Corrective Action in Property-Liability Insurance, 19 J. Banking & Fin. 511 (1995); cf. Steven W. Pottier & David W. Sommer, Agency Theory and Life Insurer Ownership Structure, 64 J. Risk & Ins. 529 (1997). Mutual insurers differ from stock companies in that they are owned by their policyholders. Profits are typically returned to policyholders in the form of dividends or decreased future premiums. Why might mutual insurers be safer than insurers that are organized as stock companies?

b. THE TOOLS OF SOLVENCY REGULATION

Historically, the core tool of solvency regulation was the mandate that insurance rates be "adequate." Today, that is a historical relic. Modern insurance solvency regulation dates back to the mid-1990s. In the preceding years, state solvency regulation was subject to blistering criticism at the federal level, culminating in a 1990 U.S. House Energy and Commerce Committee report entitled "Failed Promises: Insurance Company Insolvencies." The report reviewed the prominent failures of several insurers in the 1980s and concluded that state insurance solvency regulation was "seriously deficient." In the face of this criticism, states developed a number of the current tools of U.S. solvency regulation. See generally Robert W. Klein, Insurance Regulation in Transition, 62 J. Risk & Ins. 363 (1995). These tools can be divided into the following categories: (i) the NAIC's Financial Standards and Accreditation Program, (ii) accounting and reporting, (iii) capital requirements, (iv) reserve requirements, (v) investment restrictions, (vi) financial monitoring, and (vii) state guaranty funds. For more detailed overviews of state solvency regulation, see NAIC, The U.S. National State-Based System of Insurance Regulation and the Solvency Modernization Initiative (2013); Elizabeth F. Brown & Robert W. Klein, Insurance Solvency Regulation: A New World Order?, in The Law and Economics of Insurance (Daniel Schwarcz & Peter Siegelman eds., 2015).

(i) *The NAIC's Financial Standards and Accreditation Program.* As we will see below, state solvency regulation is relatively well coordinated and uniform relative to other forms of insurance regulation. This is due almost entirely to the NAIC's Financial Standards and Accreditation Program, which is the backbone of state solvency regulation. Under this program, an NAIC committee comprised of state regulators certifies that individual state insurance departments' solvency regulation meets various minimum standards. Accredited state insurance departments must possess adequate authority under their state's laws and regulations, sufficient resources, and effective organizational and personnel practices. NAIC, Financial Regulation Standards and Accreditation Program (2014).

If only a small number of states were accredited, the NAIC's solvency accreditation program would not be noteworthy. In fact, though, every single state is currently accredited. The accreditation program accomplished this with an ingenious scheme of regulatory deference. Within the various model laws and regulations that states must adopt as a condition of accreditation are provisions *providing that accredited state insurance departments are permitted, but not required, to defer to the solvency regulation of an insurer's state of domicile, so long as that state of domicile is itself accredited*. An insurer's state of domicile is essentially its state of incorporation, and it need not be its principal place of business. Consider a concrete example. Assume that Minnesota Insurance is domiciled in Minnesota, but also sells insurance in Iowa and North Dakota. If all three states are accredited, then Iowa and North Dakota's regulators need not (and generally would not) directly scrutinize the financial health of Minnesota Insurance. Instead, they would defer to Minnesota's solvency regulation. This makes some sense: if Minnesota is accredited, then other states can (in theory) rest assured that it possesses adequate authority, resources, and expertise to conduct effective solvency regulation.

This scheme of state deference embedded within the solvency accreditation program creates enormous pressure for states to become and remain accredited. If a state is not accredited, then insurers will generally choose not to domicile in that state. Doing so would mean that the insurer would have to independently satisfy the state regulator of every state in which it sold coverage of its financial health. Returning to the example above, if Minnesota's insurance department were not accredited, but Iowa's and North Dakota's were, then Minnesota Insurance would likely shift its state of domicile to Iowa or North Dakota to avoid being subject to duplicative solvency regulation by all three. States and their insurance departments have strong incentives to encourage insurers to domicile in their states, including increased regulatory authority, fees, and taxes. In addition to promoting relatively uniform solvency regulation, the NAIC accreditation program helps allocate state regulatory resources efficiently. It would clearly be inefficient if every insurer's financial health were carefully scrutinized by every state in which it operated. The solvency accreditation program eliminates the need for such duplicative regulation.

(ii) *Accounting and Reporting.* Accounting and reporting rules provide the data on which the rest of state solvency regulation is premised. Insurers report financial data to regulators, via the NAIC, in standardized quarterly and annual financial reports. Companies prepare these reports using unique accounting rules, which are known as "statutory accounting principles" (SAP) because they are set by state insurance statutes. By contrast, the more commonly used Generally Accepted Accounting Principles (GAAP) framework is developed and set by the Financial Accounting Standards Board (FASB). SAP starts with GAAP rules, but makes a number of adjustments. The ostensible goal of SAP is to better reflect the capacity of a reporting insurer to pay off its commitments to policyholders. By contrast, GAAP's core purpose, according to FASB, is to provide "decision-useful information to investors and other users of financial reporting." See Robert F. Weber, Combatting Teleological Drift of Life Insurance Solvency Regulation: The Case for a Meta-Risk Management Approach to Principles-Based Reserving, 8 Berkeley Bus. L.J. 35, 53–63 (2011). To ensure the accuracy of reported financial data, regulators regularly conduct on-site financial exams of insurers, which operate much like audits.

(iii) *Capital Requirements.* The most fundamental element of state solvency regulation is capital requirements. See Kris DeFrain, U.S. Insurance Financial Regulatory Oversight and the Role of Capital Requirements, The Center for Insurance Policy & Research Newsletter (Jan. 2012). An insurer's regulatory capital consists (roughly) of its total assets minus its total liabilities. Equivalently, regulatory capital can be understood as the amount invested in the company by its owners as well as any retained earnings the company has accrued, but not paid to its owners. Regulatory capital is analogous to the equity that a homeowner has in his or her home, which consists of the homeowner's down payment plus any change in the value of the home since purchase.

Consider once again the example of Minnesota Insurance ("MI"). Recall that MI received a $50,000 investment from its owner and sold $950,000 in policies, on which it expected to pay $900,000 in one year. Using these figures, the company had $100,000 in capital, consisting of its $1 million in assets ($950,000 in premiums+$50,000 in startup cash) subtracted by its total liabilities of $900,000 (expected claims payouts). Visually, this financial position is depicted in MI's Balance Sheet A, below. The insurer's capital is represented by the box in the lower right, which corresponds to assets minus liabilities.

MINNESOTA INSURANCE BALANCE SHEET A

Assets of $1 Million, corresponding to $950,000 in premiums and $50,000 in startup cash	Liabilities of $900,000, consisting of reserves for anticipated claims payments
	Regulatory Capital of $100,000

Capital requirements are a crucial tool for solvency regulation for at least two reasons. First, capital requirements help protect policyholders against losses that are incurred by their insurance company. Recall that MI faced substantial insolvency risk if it invested its $1 Million in assets in a high-risk strategy, which was equally likely to increase assets by 50%, to a total of $1.5 Million, or to reduce assets by 50%, to a total of $500,000. In the latter scenario, the company would have had insufficient assets to pay its $900,000 in expected claims. Now suppose that regulators had insisted that MI maintain at least $1,000,000 in regulatory capital. This would have required Peterson to invest $950,000 in start-up capital rather than just $50,000. This scenario is represented visually in MI Balance Sheet B, below.

MINNESOTA INSURANCE BALANCE SHEET B

Assets of $1.9 Million, corresponding to $950,000 in premiums and $950,000 in startup cash.	Liabilities of $900,000, consisting of reserves for anticipated claims payments
To be invested in high-risk strategy (50% chance of 50% gain, 50% chance of 50% loss), or low-risk strategy (certain 10% gain).	Regulatory Capital of $1 Million, corresponding to $950,000 from owner and $50,000 in retained earnings

With this increased capital buffer, MI's policyholders would be paid in full even if the company pursued the high-risk strategy and fared poorly, losing 50% of its assets. In this case, the company would have $950,000 in assets remaining, more than its $900,000 in expected claims payments. MI's loss would thus be experienced entirely by its owner, Peterson, rather than its policyholders. To return to the home mortgage analogy, mortgage providers often require large downpayments by purchasers so that even if the value of the house decreases, the house's value still exceeds the amount owed and the lender can recoup the entire loan amount in the event of a borrower default.

Aside from protecting policyholders against large losses by their insurers, capital requirements provide an additional benefit to policyholders: they limit insurers' incentives to engage in high-risk strategies in the first place. Again consider the perspective of Peterson in the example where there is a $1 Million capital requirement, as illustrated in MI Balance Sheet B. Unlike the scenario depicted in Balance Sheet A, Peterson will now have a substantial incentive to choose the low-risk investment strategy. As a result of his higher capital contribution, Peterson now bears the entire downside of the high-risk strategy. The expected value to him of this strategy is therefore 0, obviously less than the sure thing 10% gain of the low-risk strategy.

Insurance capital requirements come in two basic varieties. The first is fixed capital requirements, which require a minimum amount of capital for all insurers operating within a particular coverage line. For instance, states often require between $500,000 and $6,000,000 in fixed capital, depending on the coverage line and state. See NAIC, http://www.naic.org/documents/industry_ucaa_chart_min_capital_surplus.pdf. (listing minimum capital requirements by state). Fixed capital requirements suffer from various important limitations, however. For instance, they provide much less protection for policyholders of larger companies than smaller companies, because the overall capital required becomes smaller as a percentage of assets as a company's total size increases. Additionally, fixed capital requirements do not differentiate among companies based on their risk levels.

The second, and much more important, type of capital requirement is Risk-Based Capital requirements (RBC). RBC links an insurer's required capital to its riskiness and size. States use several RBC formulas, depending on the type of insurance at issue, to determine required capital levels. All of these formulas attempt to measure the riskiness of carriers' assets. Thus, insurers incur no "capital charge" for assets that are considered completely safe, such as U.S. treasury bonds, but substantial "capital charges" for riskier assets, such as stocks and junk bonds. RBC formulas also attempt to measure some non-asset risks. For instance, life insurers' RBC requirements are substantially influenced by interest rate risk; life insurers face risk from unexpected interest rate changes due to the long-term nature of their commitments. For a detailed overview of the varying RBC formulas, see Robert W. Klein, The Growing Sophistication of Solvency Policing Tools, 19 J. Ins. Reg. 235 (2000).

State rules link insurers' RBC levels to specific regulatory responses. For instance, if an insurer has RBC in excess of 200% of its required amount, then regulators take no action. If RBC levels are between 150 to 200% of required levels, then the insurer must prepare a detailed plan for its regulator explaining how it will restore its capital levels. And if a company's RBC falls below 70% of its required amount, the regulator is required to take over the company. These "prompt corrective action" requirements are designed to prevent regulators from deferring remedial actions when insurers are experiencing financial trouble, a phenomenon known as regulatory forbearance. Regulatory forbearance can result in much larger losses to policyholders: as an insurer's regulatory capital decreases, both its incentive to engage in risky activities and policyholders' exposure to such risk increases. Can you see why? See J. David Cummins, Scott E. Harrington, & Robert Klein, Insolvency Experience, Risk-Based Capital and Prompt Corrective Action in Property-Liability Insurance, 19 J. Banking & Fin. 511 (1995).

(iv) *Reserve Requirements.* Most firms, and even most financial firms, have relatively transparent liabilities, which consist of the amounts they owe or may owe to others. Insurers' liabilities, however, are deeply opaque: it is impossible to know with absolute precision how much an insurer owes to policyholders and when it will owe this amount. See Howell E. Jackson, Regulation in a Multisectored Financial Services Industry: An Exploratory Essay, 77 Wash. U. L. Q. 319, 342 (1999). Although the law of large numbers can make an insurer's liabilities relatively predictable, they cannot eliminate uncertainty. Moreover, recall that the law of large numbers does not operate when insurers' exposures are correlated. Insurers vary in the extent to which they insure non-correlated risks, and, in some cases, correlations among insured risks can arise where they were unexpected. For instance, sudden drought conditions can lead to a sudden increase in fire losses in a state, even though correlations in insured fire losses are normally low.

For these reasons, state solvency rules extensively regulate how insurers must set "reserves" to pay for anticipated future policyholder claims. Because insurers' reserves are their primary liabilities, reserve requirements constrain insurers predominantly through their impact on insurer capital: increased reserves lead to decreased capital. The nature of regulatory reserve requirements varies dramatically by line of coverage. In property/casualty insurance, insurers have traditionally enjoyed substantial leeway in setting reserves, so long as they follow broad guidelines. By contrast, life insurers have historically faced formulaic rules for how they must set reserves, reflecting the relative uniformity of mortality rates and the enhanced solvency concerns at play in life insurance. However, over the last several years, state insurance regulators have begun designing and implementing a controversial "principles-based" approach to reserving that gives life insurers more flexibility in setting their reserves. See Robert F. Weber, Combatting Teleological Drift of Life Insurance Solvency Regulation: The Case for a Meta-Risk Management Approach to Principles-Based Reserving, 8 Berkeley Bus. L.J. 35 (2011).

(v) *Investment Restrictions.* Insurers also are subject to regulation of the composition of their investment portfolios. These regulations limit the percentage of their portfolios that insurers can hold in medium or low grade assets. The riskiness of different asset types is generally linked to private rating agencies' assessments, though a special office of the NAIC, the Securities Valuation Office ("SVO"), plays an important role in the assessment of certain investment types. See John Patrick Hunt, Credit Ratings in Insurance Regulation: The Missing Piece of Financial Reform, 68 Wash. & Lee L. Rev. 1667 (2011). Investment restrictions may also include diversification requirements, for example limiting investment in real property to 10% of assets. In some cases, investment restrictions may expressly prohibit or limit certain investments as well, such as foreign investment and hedging transactions.

(vi) *Financial Surveillance.* State insurance regulators also monitor insurers' financial health using the Insurance Regulatory Information System (IRIS), a suite of financial diagnostic tests developed and coordinated by the NAIC. The IRIS program calculates eleven measures of insurers' financial health based on such data as premiums received, investment yield, reserves, and surplus. For example, the *premium-to-surplus* ratio is a measure of the amount of capital available to an insurer in relation to its coverage obligations. Other things being equal, the higher the ratio, the greater the insurer's exposure. Insurers that do not meet specified standards for these ratios are designated for further review. The system is thus often described as an "early-warning" system.

(vii) *State Guaranty Funds.* Creditors normally bear the risk of a debtor's insolvency. Once secured creditors are paid, any remaining assets of the insolvent company normally are divided pro-rata among general creditors. By contrast, state guaranty funds provide most policyholders with special protections against the risk that their insurers will be unable to pay claims. In most states, these guaranty funds ensure that policyholders can recover up to $300,000 of claims irrespective of their insurers' financial health. However, the extent of guaranty fund protection varies by insurance product and state. Corporations with a net worth over a specified threshold are often excluded from protection via state guaranty funds. See NAIC, Property and Casualty Insurance Guaranty Association Model Act, Model Law 540 (2009). So too are other insurers. See, e.g., *Exploration Place, Inc. v. Midwest Drywall Co.*, 277 Kan. 898 (2004) (insurer's subrogation claim is precluded). Additionally, policyholders generally cannot collect against guaranty funds for anything other than insurance claims, including attorneys' fees and bad faith damages. See *Bank of Miss. v. Miss. Life & Health Ins. Guar. Ass'n*, 850 So. 2d 127 (Miss. Ct. App. 2003) (guaranty fund not liable for counsel fees even when an insurer would be); *Crider v. Ga. Life & Health Ins. Guar. Ass'n*, 188 Ga. App. 407 (1988) (guaranty fund was not obligated to satisfy judgment for bad-faith penalties and attorneys' fees against an insolvent insurer).

Guaranty funds are coordinated by the National Conference of Insurance Guaranty Funds (in the case of property/casualty insurance) and the National Organization of Life and Health Insurnace Guaranty Associations (in the case of life and health insurance). Both organizations are non-profit industry groups. Each state's enabling laws, which establish the authority and structure of the funds, generally require the claimant to be a resident of the state and the insurer to be licensed to do business in the state. See, e.g., Mass. Gen. Laws Ann. ch. 175D, § 1(1). Since policies are frequently held by businesses operating in many states, most funds will also allow recovery by non-residents when the interest insured is permanently located in the state. See, e.g., Ga. Code Ann. § 33–36–3(2)(B)(iv); *Conex Freight Sys., Inc. v. Ga. Ins. Insolvency Pool*, 254 Ga. App. 92 (2002).

State guaranty funds are financed by assessments on insurers licensed to do business in the state where the insolvent insurer operated. Insurers are assessed in proportion to their premium volume in the state. These assessments occur *after* an insurer is deemed insolvent. As a result, the only insurer that does not pay for the consequences of failure is the insurer that itself failed. By contrast, in banking regulation, banks are assessed insurance premiums in advance of their failure for the FDIC insurance that they and their customers enjoy. Moreover, these premiums are risk-rated, meaning that banks that face a larger risk of failing are generally required to pay higher premiums. See generally Richard Scott Carnell, Jonathan R. Macey & Geoffrey P. Miller, The Law of Banking and Financial Institutions (5th ed. 2013); J. David Cummins, Risk-Based Premiums for Insurance Guaranty Funds, 43 J. Fin. 823 (1988).

How may state guaranty funds create a kind of moral hazard on the part of policyholders? On the part of insurers themselves? For discussion, see Jonathan R. Macey & Geoffrey P. Miller, Costly Policies: State Regulation and Antitrust Exemption in Insurance Markets 84–91 (1993); Michael F. Aylward & Paul M. Hummer, When Insurers Go Belly Up: Implications for Insurers, Policyholders and Guaranty Funds, 70 Defense Couns. J. 448 (2003); Spencer W. Kimball & Noreen J. Parrett, Creation of the Guaranty Association System, 19 J. Ins. Reg. 259 (2000).

NOTES AND QUESTIONS

1. *Virginia Life Insurance.* Suppose that Virginia Life Insurance Company has $5 Million of assets. Of this, $2.5 Million is invested in risky high-tech stocks, $1.5 Million is invested in real estate, and $1 Million is invested in U.S. treasuries and short-term bonds. Virginia Insurance currently provides $100 Million in term life insurance coverage, but its internal models suggest that it will only end up paying out $3.5 Million in claims on these policies. However, state regulatory rules require it to reserve $4.5 Million for its exposures on these policies. Meanwhile, the relevant RBC formula indicates that the insurer must hold a minimum of $500,000 in regulatory capital.

   a. Does Virginia Life Insurance currently have the minimum amount of capital required? What might happen to the company if its capital levels deteriorate? How will its regulator respond to the company's current capital levels?

   b. Assume that Virginia Life decides to improve its RBC levels. What options might it have for accomplishing this? How could it accomplish this by shifting its investment strategy? What other options might be available to the company to increase its capital levels?

   c. Suppose that Virginia Life's regulators allow it to use a principles-based approach to setting its liabilities. How would that likely impact Virginia Life's capital levels?

   d. Is there a risk that Virginia Life might be in violation of relevant investment restrictions? If so, what options does the company have to rectify this? To what extent do these overlap with available strategies for remedying any capital deficiencies that the firm faces?

2. *The Propriety of the NAIC's Role in Solvency Regulation.* Because the NAIC is not a public entity, it is not subject to state or federal administrative law. Moreover, almost half of its budget comes from industry fees. In light of these facts, to what extent is it problematic for the NAIC's solvency accreditation program to play such a substantial role in solvency regulation? Consider, for instance, that many model laws and rules that are required as a condition of accreditation incorporate a variety of manuals and forms that are constantly maintained and updated by NAIC committees. See, e.g., NAIC, Standard Valuation Law, Model Law 820 (2010); NAIC, Annual Financial Reporting Model Regulation, Model Law 205 (2014). As a result, whenever an NAIC committee updates one of these cross-referenced forms or manuals, it ultimately alters the substance of state insurance regulation across the country with no governmentally-mandated procedural safeguards.

3. *Risks of the NAIC's Solvency Accreditation Program.* An important risk of the solvency accreditation program is that it may result in regulatory arbitrage, meaning that companies might be able to exploit the state regulatory system to reduce the stringency of the regulation they face. For instance, a state might offer less restrictive solvency regulation in order to induce insurers to domicile there. In theory, two features of the accreditation program limit this risk. First, state regulators are constrained in how much they can decrease the stringency of their solvency regulation because doing so might jeopardize their status as an accredited state. Second, if states become concerned that one of their peer states is watering down its regulation, they can opt not to defer to that state's

solvency regulation. This is because the accreditation program merely allows states to defer to an insurer's domiciliary regulator; it does not require them to do so.

The effectiveness of these safeguards against regulatory arbitrage is open to debate. An important federal report on modernizing U.S. insurance regulation—which we will examine in more depth later in this Chapter—recently questioned the effectiveness of the accreditation program in promoting uniformity and limiting the risk of regulatory arbitrage. Federal Insurance Office, How to Modernize and Improve the System of Insurance Regulation in the United States (2013). The report noted that "significant elements of non-uniformity remain" in states' solvency regulation. Id. at 29. In part, this is due to variations in state solvency laws: accreditation standards are often broad enough to permit multiple statutory schemes and, in any event, accredited states must only adopt laws and regulations that are "substantially equivalent" to the specified NAIC models. It is also attributable to "a range of discretionary decisions by state regulators" that are embedded within the process of solvency regulation. Id. at 31. To what extent could these problems be addressed by a federal system of insurance solvency regulation? Are they an inherent risk of any extensive regulatory system that maintains different offices and large numbers of employees?

4. *Continued Monitoring of Accredited States.* Once a state becomes accredited, it is re-assessed every five years for continued adherence to accreditation standards. No state has ever lost accreditation. What political and logistical pressures would the NAIC face if it attempted to de-accredit a state? Does this suggest that the accreditation program faces important limitations in its efforts to maintain or increase the effectiveness of state solvency regulation?

5. *The Accuracy of RBC Formulas.* State RBC formulas attempt to link an insurer's baseline capital requirements to its riskiness. But how well do the RBC formulas capture the risk posed by an insurance entity? A substantial economics literature addresses this question. See, e.g., J. David Cummins, Scott E. Harrington, & Robert Klein, Insolvency Experience, Risk-Based Capital and Prompt Corrective Action in Property-Liability Insurance, 19 J. Banking & Fin. 511 (1995). Because RBC measures risk imperfectly, some have argued that, instead of simple formulas, regulators should embrace more advanced modeling techniques to measure risk for purposes of setting capital requirements. J. David Cummins & Richard D. Phillips, Capital Adequacy and Insurance Risk-Based Capital Systems, 28 J. Ins. Reg. 25 (2009). What problems might such an approach pose? What costs are created by the relatively simplistic and crude approach to measuring risk that is currently employed in the RBC formulas? For evidence that insurers exploit RBC rules to "reach for yield" by investing in the riskiest bonds within broad categories of assets that are treated the same by RBC formulas, see Bo Becker, & Victoria Ivashina, Reaching for Yield in the Bond Market, J. of Finance (2015).

6. *The Rationale for Insurance Guaranty Funds.* FDIC deposit insurance is perhaps the key cog of banking regulation. The core logic of deposit insurance is that it prevents a run on a bank, where depositors lose confidence in a bank and rush to extract their funds. Such bank runs can become self-fulfilling prophecies, dooming even healthy banks and spreading chaos throughout the financial system. By assuring depositors that they will be paid by the federal government, FDIC deposit insurance

eliminates the incentive of depositors to run on banks. This, of course, creates substantial moral hazard among bank depositors and banks themselves. Much of prudential regulation in banking—which is analogous to solvency regulation in insurance—is premised on limiting bank risk taking that results from the moral hazard of deposit insurance.

In most cases, this logic does not apply to insurance companies. With the exception of certain life insurance and annuity products, most insurance policyholders are relatively powerless if they become concerned about the financial stability of their insurers. Unlike in the case of banks, they cannot simply withdraw funds on demand. Instead, they are generally contractually allowed to "withdraw" funds only if they suffer an insured loss, such as their property being destroyed or a policyholder dying. For this reason, insurers are generally much less susceptible to "runs" than are banks. Therefore, state guaranty funds are generally not needed to prevent self-reinforcing runs on insurance companies. Given this background, do state insurance guaranty funds make sense? Do they make enough sense to overcome the moral hazard that they inevitably generate?

7. *Limiting Moral Hazard of State Guaranty Funds.* In order to limit the risk that state guaranty funds may generate moral hazard, states generally maintain "gag rules" that forbid insurers from describing state guaranty fund protection in their marketing and advertising. See NAIC, Life and Health Insurance Guaranty Association Model Act, Model Law 520, § 19 (2009). Is this a good solution to the potential risk that guaranty funds might create moral hazard? See Daniel Schwarcz, Transparently Opaque: Understanding the Lack of Transparency in Insurance Consumer Protection, 61 UCLA L. Rev. 394, 441–43 (2014) (arguing that these gag rules undermine transparency, inhibiting the financial planning ability of policyholders).

8. *Insurance vs. Bank Capital Rules.* The basic definition of regulatory capital is similar in banking and insurance. However, insurance RBC rules differ from bank capital rules in important ways. For instance, different types of assets receive different capital charges in banking and insurance. In general, long-term assets (i.e. bonds where the principal is not due for 10 or 20 years) receive lower capital charges for insurers than banks, because, by matching long-term assets with long-term liabilities (i.e. insurance policies likely to pay out in 10 or 20 years), insurers can limit risk in ways that banks cannot. For instance, an insurer that promises to pay $10 million in coverage in 10 years can eliminate a substantial amount of risk by pairing this promise with a $10 million investment in 10-year bonds. Short-term movements in the price of the bonds should not impact the insurer's ability to repay, so long as the issuer of the bonds does not default. Long-term assets present much greater risks to banks because most of their liabilities—which consist of bank deposits—are extremely short term, in that they can be withdrawn at a moment's notice.

2. REGULATION OF "EXCESSIVE" RATES

Recall that in the wake of the McCarran-Ferguson Act most states passed statutes requiring insurance departments to assure that insurance rates are not "excessive, inadequate, or unfairly discriminatory." Many states continue to closely scrutinize whether insurance rates in certain coverage lines are "excessive." However, the nature of such regulation varies significantly by state and coverage line.

States can employ several different types of procedures for reviewing insurance rates. First, some states employ a "prior approval" system, under which insurers file proposed rate changes and supporting documentation with the insurance department, which must approve the new rates before they may be used. Even in prior approval systems, rates are often deemed to be approved if the insurance department does not respond to a filing within a specified time period. Second, some states employ a "file and use" procedure, under which rates become effective immediately upon filing, but may be disapproved within a specified period of time. A third approach, known as "flex-rating," is to employ prior approval review, but only for insurance rates that fall outside of a specified range.

Commentators often suggest that states with prior approval or flex rating regimes engage in relatively active rate review, whereas those with file and use review are less rigorous. From this perspective, approximately 20 states engage in "active" review of rates in automobile insurance, homeowners' insurance, medical malpractice insurance and individual health insurance. And almost 40 states actively regulate workers' compensation insurance rates. In all of these cases, prior approval is much more common than flex rating. See Sharon Tennyson, Efficiency Consequences of Rate Regulation in Insurance Markets, (Networks Fin. Inst., Policy Brief No. 3, 2007). For many state/coverage line combinations, insurance rates are not reviewed at all to determine whether they are excessive. For instance, many, if not most, states do not engage in even file and use review of rates for commercial insurance lines. And rate filings are not required by any state for life insurance.

States that do rigorously review insurance rates to determine whether they are excessive must complete a series of complicated tasks. First, rate-makers must examine insurers' (and the ISO's) statistical data on historical claims and losses. Second, they must adjust this historical data to account for known or anticipated changes in risk. This is particularly difficult when claims data from recent years is not complete because the underlying line of coverage is *long-tail*, meaning that claims against a single year's policies are not all made and paid until half-a-dozen or more years after a policy is issued. Third, rate-makers must estimate insurers' non-claims expenses in providing coverage, such as agent commissions and marketing costs. Fourth, they must assess the likely investment return that the insurer will earn on premiums held between the time policyholders pay them and the time a claim is paid, which is often referred to as the "float." This, in turn, is impacted by an estimate of both expected market returns and how long it will take to pay off claims in the underlying coverage line. Finally, rate-makers must consider what amount of profit can be built into rates in light of competitive conditions.

If there were no regulation of insurance rates, all this would merely be a description of some of the factors insurers take into account in setting rates. Any insurer that overestimated its future losses—deliberately or in error—might fool its shareholders for a short time, but ultimately other insurers would make more accurate projections and increase their market shares by underpricing the first insurer. But regulatory efforts to prevent excessive rates are not subject to such market pressures. And they often are subject to various political pressures, particularly when insurance rates are politically salient. The regulatory process of reviewing rates analyzed in the following case illustrates both how much potential there is for rate-setting mistakes to be made, whether by insurers or regulators, and how difficult it is to determine whether mistakes actually have been made until data on claims, losses, and the other factors affecting the appropriate premium rate accumulates in the years after a rate is set.

Commissioner of Insurance v. North Carolina Rate Bureau

Court of Appeals of North Carolina, 1996.
124 N.C.App. 674.

■ MCGEE, JUDGE.

On 1 February 1994, the North Carolina Rate Bureau (Bureau) filed a general request for increased rates for private passenger automobiles and motorcycles. The rate increase requested an increase of 10.8% for automobile rates and 22.4% for motorcycle rates. The Commissioner held a comprehensive hearing during the summer of 1994. The filing request was more than 1,500 pages in length; there were an additional 800 pages of responses by the Bureau to the Commissioner's requests for data to explain the filing; the hearing transcript is more than 3,500 pages in length and the evidence included more than 120 exhibits. The Commissioner's lengthy order of more than 500 pages, including calculations and exhibits, disapproved the Bureau's filing and ordered rate changes reducing rates for automobiles by 13.8% and increasing rates for motorcycles by 10.2%. The Bureau appealed from this order. * * *

I. STANDARDS OF REVIEW

A. Appellate Court Review

In reviewing orders of the Insurance Commissioner, the test is whether the Commissioner's conclusions of law are supported by material and substantial evidence in light of the whole record. *State ex rel. Comr. of Insurance v. N.C. Rate Bureau*, 75 N.C. App. 201, 208, disc. review denied, 314 N.C. 547 (1985). * * *

While this Court employs the "whole record" test in reviewing the Commissioner's orders, "it is not our function to substitute our judgment for that of the Commissioner when the evidence is conflicting." *State ex rel. Comr. of Insurance v. N.C. Rate Bureau*, 96 N.C. App. 220, 221, 385 S.E.2d 510, 511 (1989). The weight and sufficiency of the evidence as well as the credibility of the witnesses are determined by the Commissioner. Id. * * *

IV. UNDERWRITING PROFIT PROVISIONS

The Bureau next argues the Commissioner erred in reducing the filed underwriting profit provisions from .8% to -3.75% for liability coverage and from 5.4% to 1.75% for physical damage. * * *

A. Rate of Return

Essentially, the Bureau argues part of the methodology employed by the Commissioner in determining the underwriting profit provisions was faulty because the Commissioner used the more conservative accounting system known as SAP (statutory accounting principles) as opposed to the GAAP system (generally accepted accounting principles). The Bureau contends SAP, established by the National Association of Insurance Commissioners (NAIC), is inappropriate because its purpose is to measure the liquidation value of a company and it does not include all of a company's assets in its calculations. By contrast, the GAAP system measures the financial condition of a company as an ongoing concern, not its liquidation value. According to the Bureau, the more conservative SAP approach to measuring assets produced a chain of reactions: an understatement of the value of the aggregate insurance company and a smaller base upon which to apply the return, and ultimately resulted in a lower rate of return. Additionally, the Bureau contends the Commissioner's calculations are not supported by material and substantial evidence.

The Bureau has not cited any authority and we find nothing in the cases or statutes which prescribe the system the Commissioner must use, either SAP or GAAP, in calculating these profit provisions. In *Comr. of Insurance v. Rating Bureau,* 292 N.C. 471, 489 (1977), our Supreme Court said:

> The ultimate question for the Commissioner's determination is whether the proposed rates will, after provision for reasonably anticipated losses and operating expenses, leave for the insurers . . . *a fair and reasonable profit and no more.* The purpose of the entire statutory plan is to provide for the public, at reasonable cost, insurance in financially responsible companies. The public interest extends as truly to the financial responsibility of the insurer as it does to the reasonable cost of the insurance to the insured, and vice versa. (citations omitted (emphasis added).

The Commissioner is considered an expert in the field of insurance and his reliance on various "methods of analysis of the profit to which the insurance companies are entitled lies entirely within his discretion." *State ex rel. Comr. of Insurance v. N.C. Rate Bureau,* 96 N.C. App. at 223. The rates the Commissioner determines in his order are prima facie correct so long as there is substantial and material evidence to support the Commissioner's findings. G.S. 58–2–80; G.S. 58–2–90(e).

We find there is substantial and material evidence to support the Commissioner's use of SAP in calculating the profit provisions. Not only was there expert testimony that SAP was the appropriate method, but as the Commissioner pointed out in his order, even our statutes refer to the accounting practices set forth by the NAIC (i.e. SAP system) in requiring insurance companies to evaluate and make regular reports of their financial positions. N.C. Gen. Stat. § 58–2–165. Additionally, the Commissioner reasons that since SAP represents that level of financial commitment an insurance company is legally required to make to its policyholders, it is a logical foundation upon which to base a rate of return in determining "a fair and reasonable profit and no more." *Comr. of Insurance v. Rating Bureau,* 292 N.C. at 489. "As we do not find error in the Commissioner's judgment we cannot replace our judgment for his." *State ex rel. Comr. of Insurance v. N.C. Rate Bureau,* 96 N.C. App. at 223. * * *

VI. CURRENT COST AND EXPENSE TREND PROVISIONS

The Bureau next argues the Commissioner erred in disapproving the filed current cost and expense trend provisions and in ordering rates based on inadequate current cost and expense trend provisions.
* * *

After explaining the necessity of prospective loss and experience (trending) in insurance ratemaking cases, the Commissioner noted, "the evidence in this case was conflicting concerning trends that will most accurately predict the prospective loss and expense experience. . . ." He then made detailed and specific findings based on department witness O'Neil's "extensive analysis" on the issue of current cost and expense trend provisions, occasionally making general references to inconsistencies between the Bureau and O'Neil findings. The Commissioner ultimately chose to use O'Neil's trend selections in the calculation of the rate level change. As to the Bureau's trends, the Commissioner made the following findings of fact:

> 4. The Bureau trends were all selected by its committees. However, no testimony was offered by any member of these committees to explain the reasons for the selection of exponential curves as has been automatically made by the Bureau in all auto filings for many years. The mechanical process of calculating the pure premium and cost trend was briefly explained by the Bureau witness Woods, without independent evaluation, on pages 25 and 26 of RB–14. Woods was not a member of the Bureau committees.
>
> . . . [findings 5–10 discussed O'Neil's research and conclusions]
>
> 11. The trends selected by the Bureau will result in rates which are excessive in violation of the law of this state.
>
> 12. The trends selected by the Bureau committees and briefly explained by Woods were not determined upon the same thoughtful analysis as those derived by O'Neil and, thus, are found to be less credible, reasonable and reliable, and are rejected.
>
> 13. For the reasons set forth above, the trend selections derived by O'Neil are accepted as credible and reliable for use in the calculation of the rate level change in this proceeding, while the trends selected by the Bureau are found to lack credibility and are rejected.

O'Neil's analysis and findings are supported by the evidence in the record; however, the Commissioner's statements regarding the Bureau's evidence are conclusory and unsupported by specific evidence. While "there is no burden upon the Commissioner to disprove the filing," *Comr. of Insurance v. Rate Bureau,* 300 N.C. at 455, the statutes do compel the Commissioner to be specific in rejecting rate increases by stating " 'wherein and to what extent' the proposed filings are deemed improper." *Id.* at 456, 269. The Commissioner's recognition of conflicting evidence, but his failure to resolve the conflicts in precise detail along with his failure to specifically show he has given consideration to the material and substantial evidence the Bureau offered before rejecting the Bureau in favor of O'Neil's evidence require us to remand this issue to the Commissioner for more specific findings as to the Bureau's evidence. * * *

NOTES AND QUESTIONS

1. *North Carolina's Unique Rate Review System.* Judicial decisions on ratemaking issues are not common in most states. North Carolina is an exception. For a more recent example, see *Commissioner of Insurance v. North Carolina Rate Bureau,* 160 N.C. App. 416 (2003), upholding the Commissioner's decision regarding the proper way to account for investment income. North Carolina is also unique in that insurance rates are initially set by the North Carolina Rating Bureau, a non-profit entity that serves the industry and is similar to the ISO. It is for this reason that regulatory review of these rate determinations is so extensive, as illustrated by *North Carolina Rate Bureau.* Individual companies can apply to the North Carolina regulator for permission to deviate from these rates. This approach amounts to a flex-rating system, where the permitted range of rates is set through prior approval review of the Bureau's filing.

2. *Judicial Review of State Insurance Departments.* Judicial review of state regulatory actions is generally quite deferential, as illustrated in *North Carolina Rate Bureau.* The basic rationale for this approach is that administrative agencies possess expertise and, in any event, the legislature has delegated authority to them, rather than the courts. As a general principle of administrative law, this rationale is still accepted, but it is a bit tattered at the edges. Perhaps the primary reason for the tatters is the increased recognition that regulators are not merely experts divorced from the political process, but part of that process and subject to external influences similar to those that operate in legislatures and in the executive branch of government. Not only is the influence of lobbying and the possible "capture" of administrative agencies by the enterprises that are the very subjects of regulation a threat to disinterested decision-making; the "revolving door" phenomenon, under which regulators move from the regulated industry to the agency regulating it and back again to the industry, creates at least the appearance of conflicts of interest on the part of the regulators.

Insurance Commissioners are at least as susceptible to these influences as other regulators. For example, many insurance commissioners come from and return to the insurance industry after leaving office. In other cases, insurance commissioners may have political aspirations that impact their decision-making. See generally Martin F. Grace & Richard D. Phillips, Regulator Performance, Regulatory Environment and Outcomes: An Examination of Insurance Regulator Career Incentives on State Insurance Markets, 32 J. Banking & Fin. 116 (2008). In addition, in all but the largest states, the assumption of administrative expertise that underlies judicial deference may also be less warranted than might be supposed. For example, state insurance departments are notoriously understaffed, and are especially lacking in the key form of expertise necessary for rate regulation—actuarial analysis. Indeed, many states only have 1 or 2 actuaries on staff, in part because actuaries command a high salary on the private market. See NAIC, Insurance Department Resources Report (2013). Finally, while the insurance industry devotes significant resources to lobbying state insurance regulators, very few public interest groups lobby on insurance issues outside of the health insurance domain.

One approach to offsetting some of these forces is to develop consumer empowerment programs that directly enhance the capacity of consumer groups and representatives to participate in regulatory processes, thus attempting to amplify their voice and influence. Various insurance regulators, as well as the NAIC, have experimented with these efforts. For an overview and assessment of these efforts, see Daniel Schwarcz, Preventing Capture Through Consumer Empowerment Programs: Some Evidence from Insurance Regulation, in Preventing Regulatory Capture: Special Interest Influence and How to Limit It (Daniel Carpenter & David A. Moss eds., 2013).

3. *Rationales for Regulatory Review of Excessive Rates.* Historically, the primary rationale for regulatory review to prevent excessive rates was that property/casualty insurance inevitably involved some degree of monopolization, as reflected in industry pooling of claims data. Basic economic principles suggest that prices will tend to be excessive when markets are dominated by a single seller or by a group of sellers who coordinate their pricing decisions. To the extent that industry collaboration on pricing was necessary, it followed that regulators could promote the public interest by preventing excessive rates.

This historical rationale for using regulation to prevent excessive rates is much less convincing today in light of the current practices of the property/casualty industry. With limited exceptions (as in North Carolina), industry organizations such as the ISO no longer set rates, or even advisory rates, for the industry. Although the ISO does publish "advisory prospective loss costs"—estimates of future loss payments line-by-line and state-by-state—it long ago abandoned its practice of generating advisory rates that would account for competitive conditions, overhead and marketing, and investment conditions. Moreover, the large number of competing property/casualty carriers in most states and lines of coverage makes it virtually impossible that any implicit scheme of pricing coordination among carriers could survive. See generally Deregulating Property-Liability Insurance: Restoring Competition and Increasing Market Efficiency (J. David Cummins ed., 2002).

Although various alternative rationales for regulation designed to prevent excessive rates can be articulated, most are not convincing. For instance, as we will explore later, insurers' informational advantages over policyholders regarding the scope of coverage provided certainly remains an important problem in many insurance markets. But this hardly seems to justify regulating insurance rates: policyholders are very well informed about the premiums they are charged. That is precisely why most insurance advertising focuses on price. An alternative rationale for regulating excessive rates in property/casualty markets might focus on the fact that, unlike most products, the lion's share of an insurer's costs are unknown at the time it must set a price for coverage. Yet this difference between insurance and other products is sometimes exaggerated. Companies in other lines of business must also make decisions in the face of uncertainty about the future. For example, an auto manufacturer must decide whether to build a new plant, open a new assembly line, hire more employees, or design a new model vehicle before it knows what all of its costs will be and how future economic forces will affect demand for its product. Moreover, even if insurance really is unique in the extent to which costs are unpredictable at the time of sale, it is not clear why this suggests that regulation will tend to produce better estimates of cost than traditional competition.

4. *Economic Evidence on Regulation to Prevent Excessive Prices.* A substantial body of economic research suggests that regulation to prevent excessive rates in insurance markets is generally inefficient. For instance, states such as Illinois and South Carolina that deregulated rates in auto insurance markets generally experienced substantial decreases in prices and increases in insurance availability. See Stephen P. D'Arcy, Insurance Price Deregulation: The Illinois Experience, in Deregulating Property-Liability Insurance (J. David Cummins ed., 2002); Martin F. Grace, Robert W. Klein, & Richard D. Phillips, Auto Insurance Reform: Salvation in South Carolina, in Deregulating Property-Liability Insurance, supra. By contrast, several studies suggest that premiums in intensely price-regulated markets cycle between artificially low and artificially high levels, without decreasing consumer costs in the long term. See Scott E. Harrington, Effects of Prior Approval Rate Regulation of Auto Insurance, in Deregulating Property-Liability Insurance, supra. At the same time, intense price regulation often reduces the number of firms willing to offer insurance coverage in the first place. See Sharon Tennyson, The Impact of Rate Regulation on State Automobile Insurance, 15 J. Ins. Reg. 502 (1997). In Florida, for instance, regulators' refusal to ease up on price regulation has increasingly caused property insurers to leave the state, forcing a large percentage of homeowners to purchase their coverage from a state-run insurer. See Martin F. Grace & Robert W. Klein, The Perfect Storm: Hurricanes, Insurance and Regulation, 12 Risk Mgm't & Ins. Rev. 81, 105 (2009).

One notable exception to this evidence involves California, where economic studies have generally found that the state's automobile insurance premiums have increased at a slower rate than in any other state since it began intensely regulating rates in 1988. At the same time, the state has remained profitable for insurers and, for that reason, many carriers compete for consumers' business in the state. Interpretations of this evidence varies, ranging from claims that California's regulators are more competent than those of other states to arguments that California's experience is attributable to factors other than rate regulation, such as its contemporaneous adoption of new seatbelt laws. Dwight M. Jaffee & Thomas Russell, The Regulation of Automobile Insurance in California, in Deregulating Property-Liability Insurance, supra; J. Robert Hunter, State Automobile Insurance Regulation: A National Quality Assessment and In-Depth Review of California's Uniquely Effective Regulatory System (2008); Stephen D. Sugarman, California's Insurance Regulation Revolution: The First Two Years, 27 San Diego L. Rev. 683 (1990).

3. REGULATION OF "UNFAIRLY DISCRIMINATORY" RATES

In addition to prohibiting excessive and inadequate rates, the original post-McCarran-Ferguson Act state statutes prohibited "unfairly discriminatory" insurance rates. Why would an insurer ever engage in unfair discrimination? Indeed, why would an insurer bother to engage in any form of "discrimination," i.e., charge different policyholders different rates for the same coverage? In order to combat adverse selection and moral hazard. Even an insurer holding a monopoly would have to risk classify to some extent to avoid these problems. Otherwise, high-risk insureds might adversely select into the insurer's single risk pool and potentially cause it to unravel, as lower-risk insureds continually decided to self-insure all or part of the risks they would otherwise transfer to the insurer. Similarly, to the extent that policyholders had some control over a characteristic that impacted their riskiness and they were not charged on the basis of this trait, an insurer might well find that it continually paid more claims for larger sums than it had predicted. Those whom it insured would have less incentive to avoid losses than they would if their future premium levels depended on their current levels of precaution or losses.

When the monopoly assumption is relaxed and we suppose that there is competition in an insurance market, the advantages of risk classification become even more pronounced. Any insurer that does not risk classify, or whose classifications are insufficiently refined or accurate, will be at risk of finding that the low-risk insureds whom it is overcharging seek coverage from insurers who would charge them less. Simultaneously, high-risk insureds being charged more accurately by other insurers will adversely select into the first insurer's risk pool. For example, an insurer that charged police on SWAT teams the same price for life insurance as it charged law professors would find that it was besieged by applications from police, and quickly in danger of losing its low-risk law professor applicants. These forces can operate even when applicants for coverage do not themselves know how high-risk they are; so long as policyholders shop for low prices, it will pay for insurers to identify low-risk insureds and offer them correspondingly lower premiums. Thus, the development of risk classification is to be expected as a natural correlate of unregulated insurance markets.

Although discrimination by insurers is inevitable in unregulated markets, the magnitude and character of such discrimination is not always easy to predict. Risk classification is not costless. It generally requires insurers to develop and maintain information about characteristics correlated with expected losses and to secure reliable data on prospective policyholders' characteristics. At some point, the costs of such research and investigation outweigh the benefits. Consequently, insurers only classify risks up to the point that the additional competitive advantage gained from classifying equals its costs, but no further. Additionally, existing risk classification practices are path-dependent—they stand on the shoulders of those that have preceded them. As such, they may not be the most cost-effective practices that could have been developed. For example, suppose that insurers had never maintained data on the (hypothetically) useful classification variable of drivers' experience in playing video games that require eye-hand coordination. This classification variable might have been more cost-effective than others in automobile liability insurance, provided that data on its correlation to losses had been maintained for many years. But employing it now could require incurring prohibitively high start-up and data collection costs. And even if one insurer were interested in making such an investment, that insurer might have difficulty excluding other insurers from free-riding on these efforts. Classification schemes cannot be copyrighted easily, and perhaps not at all; the first insurer to use a new scheme might be able to gain a competitive edge for only a short time before other insurers also adopted it.

However insurers weigh the costs and benefits to them of varying risk classification practices, they will tend to ignore broader social values or costs implicated by such discrimination. But because insurer discrimination, like most other forms of discrimination, can implicate a broad array of social values and costs, regulation plays an important role in this domain.

Allstate Insurance Company v. Schmidt
Supreme Court of Hawai'i, 2004.
104 Hawai'i 261.

■ Opinion of the Court by DUFFY, J.

Appellants-appellants Allstate Insurance Company and Allstate Indemnity Company [hereinafter collectively, Allstate] appeal from the judgment of the first circuit court, the Honorable Eden Elizabeth Hifo presiding, in favor of appellee-appellee J.P. Schmidt, Insurance Commissioner, Department of Commerce and Consumer Affairs, State of Hawai'i (the Commissioner). * * *

This appeal involves the interpretation of Hawai'i Revised Statutes (HRS) § 431:10C–207 (1993).[1] The Commissioner contends that this statute prohibits an insurer from discriminating against an applicant for automobile insurance on the basis of that individual's length of driving experience; Allstate argues that this statute does prohibit discrimination in setting insurance rates, but does not prohibit an insurer from discriminating against an individual on the basis of length of driving experience in underwriting (*i.e.*, in determining whether to issue a policy to a particular individual).

Based on the following, we affirm the judgment of the circuit court and hold that HRS § 431:10C–207 prohibits discrimination on the basis of length of driving experience in underwriting.

I.   *BACKGROUND*

On August 9, 1996, Kaoru N. Reinertson filed a written complaint with the State of Hawai'i's Insurance Division, Department of Commerce and Consumer Affairs, regarding Allstate's calculation of her insurance premium. Initially, Allstate declined Ms. Reinertson's application: Allstate required an insured to hold a driver's license for more than one year, and Ms. Reinertson had held a driver's license for less than one year at the time of her application. Allstate explicitly stated that it based its rejection of Ms. Reinertson's application on the length of her driving experience. * * *

On November 18, 1996, the Chief Deputy Insurance Commissioner issued Allstate a Cease and Desist Order, instructing Allstate that it may not use the length of an applicant's driving experience as a basis for rejecting her or his application for insurance. The Order also

---

[1] HRS § 431:10C–207 provides: **Discriminatory practices prohibited.** No insurer shall base any standard or rating plan, in whole or in part, directly or indirectly, upon a person's race, creed, ethnic extraction, age, sex, length of driving experience, credit bureau rating, marital status, or physical handicap.

instructed Allstate to pay a penalty of $3,000.00 for violating HRS § 431:10C–207. Allstate timely requested a hearing on the Cease and Desist Order. The parties agreed to proceed on the basis of the legal briefs and stipulated facts rather than have a formal hearing.

1. The hearings officer's recommendations

The hearings officer issued her findings of fact, conclusions of law, and recommended order on June 15, 1999. The hearings officer recommended that the Insurance Commissioner vacate the Cease and Desist Order, concluding that HRS § 431:10C–207 applies only to rate making and not to underwriting. * * *

2. The Commissioner's order

The Commissioner reversed the hearings officer's recommended decision. The Commissioner concluded that the plain language of the statute—HRS § 431:10C–207's reference to "any standard or rating plan"—included Allstate's underwriting guidelines and standards: "Otherwise, insurers would be able to discriminate, via underwriting guidelines and standards, against a person applying for insurance on the basis of race, creed, ethnic extraction, age, sex, length of driving experience, credit bureau rating, marital status, or physical handicap." Allstate appealed to the circuit court on November 15, 1999.

3. The circuit court's determinations

On appeal to the circuit court, Allstate argued that the Commissioner erred because he (1) violated the statutory scheme by improperly applying HRS § 431:10C–207 to underwriting [and] (2) exceeded his authority by engaging in impromptu rulemaking * * *. On April 20, 2000, the circuit court issued its decision and order affirming the October 15, 1999 final order of the Commissioner. The circuit court determined that HRS § 431:10C–207 prohibits discrimination in underwriting and rate making, basing its decision on the language and context of HRS § 431:10C–207. * * *

II. *STANDARDS OF REVIEW*

Review of a decision made by the circuit court upon its review of an agency's decision is a secondary appeal. The standard of review is one in which this court must determine whether the circuit court was right or wrong in its decision, applying the standards set forth in HRS § 91–14(g) [(1993)] to the agency's decision. This court's review is further qualified by the principle that the agency's decision carries a presumption of validity and appellant has the heavy burden of making a convincing showing that the decision is invalid because it is unjust and unreasonable in its consequences. * * *

Upon review of the record the court may affirm the decision of the agency or remand the case with instructions for further proceedings; or it may reverse or modify the decision and order if the substantial rights of the petitioners may have been prejudiced because the administrative findings, conclusions, decisions, or orders are:

(1) In violation of constitutional or statutory provisions; or

(2) In excess of the statutory authority or jurisdiction of the agency; or

(3) Made upon unlawful procedure; or

(4) Affected by other error of law; or

(5) Clearly erroneous in view of the reliable, probative, and substantial evidence on the whole record; or

(6) Arbitrary, or capricious, or characterized by abuse of discretion or clearly unwarranted exercise of discretion.

III. *DISCUSSION*

A. *HRS § 431:10C–207 Applies to Both Underwriting and Rate Making.*

1. Principles of statutory construction

In determining whether HRS § 431:10C–207 prohibits discrimination in underwriting, we are mindful of the following canons of statutory construction:

> [T]he fundamental starting point is the language of the statute itself.... [W]here the language of the statute is plain and unambiguous, our only duty is to give effect to its plain and obvious meaning. When construing a statute, our foremost obligation is to ascertain and give effect to the intention of the legislature, which is to be obtained primarily from the language contained in the statute itself. And we must read statutory language in the context of the entire statute and construe it in a manner consistent with its purpose.

Mathewson v. Aloha Airlines, Inc., 82 Hawai'i 57, 71 (1996) (quoting *Housing Fin. and Dev. Corp. v. Castle*, 79 Hawai'i 64, 76–77 (1995)). "'When there is doubt, doubleness of meaning, or indistinctiveness or uncertainty of an expression used in a statute an ambiguity exists.'" *Franks v. City and County of Honolulu*, 74 Haw. 328, 335 (1993) (quoting *State v. Sylva*, 61 Haw. 385, 388 (1980)). When construing an ambiguous statute, we bear in mind "that courts are bound, if rational and practicable, to give effect to all parts of a statute, and that no clause, sentence, or word shall be construed as superfluous, void, or insignificant if a construction can be legitimately found which will give force to and preserve all words of the statute." *Camara v. Agsalud*, 67 Haw. 212, 215–16 (1984). If the language of the statute is ambiguous, courts may look to legislative history for assistance in construing the statute. *Franks v. City and County of Honolulu*, 74 Haw. at 335.

2. Applying these principles to the instant case

The plain language of HRS § 431:10C–207, referring to "any standard or rating plan" in prohibiting certain types of discrimination, is not entirely clear on its face. HRS chapter 431 does not define "standard"; therefore, whether "standard" includes underwriting standards, or whether "standard" means the same thing as "ratings plan," is unclear.

Reading this statute in context also does not lead to a clear result: although HRS § 431:10C–207 is contained in Part II of Article 10C (entitled "Rates and Administration"), which generally covers automobile insurance rates, several other statutory sections in Part II cover insurance practices other than rate making. *See, e.g.,* HRS §§ 431:10C–206.5 (Supp.2003) (entitled "Group insurance plans"),

431:10C–213 (1993 & Supp.2003) (entitled "Arbitration"). In other words, the statutory context of HRS § 431:10C–207 does not deal exclusively with rate making, such that HRS § 431:10C–207 is not necessarily restricted to rate making.

However, as stated *supra,* this court has held that "no clause, sentence, or word shall be construed as superfluous, void, or insignificant if a construction can be legitimately found which will give force to and preserve all words of the statute." *Camara,* 67 Haw. at 215–16. Allstate's contention—that the phrase "any standard or rating plan" refers only to rate making—would lead to the word "standard" being deemed superfluous. Therefore, we hold that HRS § 431:10C–207 applies to both "rating plan[s]" *and* "standard[s]," including underwriting standards, such that the Commissioner and the circuit court were correct in concluding that Allstate improperly denied Ms. Reinertson's application for insurance.

B. *The Commissioner Did Not Engage In "Impromptu Rule Making."*

In concluding that HRS § 431:10C–207 applies to underwriting, the Commissioner did not create a new rule. Instead, he applied the existing rule in HRS § 431:10C–207 to the facts of Ms. Reinertson's complaint. Furthermore, even if the Commissioner's determination did constitute new agency policy, the Commissioner's creation of policy through adjudication is not an abuse of discretion unless " 'an agency's sudden change of direction leads to undue hardship for those who had relied on past policy.' " *In re Hawaiian Elec. Co.,* 81 Hawai'i at 468 (quoting *Union Flights, Inc. v. Administrator, FAA,* 957 F.2d 685, 688 (9th Cir.1992)). Allstate does not allege any undue hardship from the Commissioner's ruling; therefore, we hold that the Commissioner did not abuse his discretion and did not engage in impromptu rulemaking.

* * *

NOTES AND QUESTIONS

1. *Discrimination in Underwriting and Risk Classification.* Is prohibiting unfair discrimination not only in risk classification but also in underwriting, as the court in *Schmidt* held the Hawaii statute did, necessary in order put normative teeth into the prohibition? Even if it is, violations of the former prohibition are likely to be much easier to detect than violations of the latter. An auto insurer that does not want to insure applicants with less than a year of driving experience, or a life insurer that does not want to insure applicants with a parent who died of Huntington's disease, for example, can make a series of "subjective," individual decisions not to insure such applicants without filing a rating plan with the Insurance Commissioner that uses these considerations as classification variables. Detecting and proving such violations may therefore involve considerable statistical work. If you were an Insurance Commissioner, how would you go about detecting insurers who engaged in such subterfuge?

2. *Actuarially Sound Classification and "Unfair Discrimination."* Virtually every jurisdiction continues to prohibit "unfair discrimination" in most forms of insurance. When regulators review insurers' rate filings, this review in theory includes an assessment of whether the filed rates are unfairly discriminatory (in addition to whether they are excessive). But

insurance regulators rarely deny proposed rate changes on the basis that they are unfairly discriminatory. Instead, as illustrated in *Schmidt*, statutes directed at particular classifications in particular lines of coverage play a much more prominent role in limiting insurer's risk-classification practices.

Limited and conflicting authority exists regarding the precise meaning of "unfair discrimination." At the very least, this prohibition seems to apply to classifications that are inaccurate or unsupported from an actuarial standpoint. See *Dept. of Ins. v. Ins. Serv. Office*, 434 So. 2d 908, 912–13 (Fla. Dist. Ct. App. 1983). In most cases, insurers have market-based reasons to ensure that their classification schemes are actuarially sound. Nonetheless, even this narrow understanding of "unfair discrimination" can have practical importance in some contexts. For instance, recent reports indicate that certain insurers are experimenting with pricing strategies that charge more for coverage to policyholders who are less likely to shop for alternative coverage. See Herb Weisbaum, Data Mining Is Now Used to Set Insurance Rates; Critics Cry Foul, CNBC, Apr. 16, 2014. If true, would this constitute "unfair discrimination?" Alternatively, would it constitute "unfair discrimination" if an insurer wanted to employ a new approach to classifying policyholders, which it only applied to new customers to limit the risk that existing customers would shop elsewhere?

3. *Objectionable Forms of "Actuarially Fair" Discrimination.* Some courts and commentators have suggested that unfair discrimination can also encompass discrimination that, while justified by actuarial data, is objectionable on other grounds. *Hartford Accident & Indem. Co. v. Ins. Comm'r*, 505 Pa. 571 (1984); Leah Wortham, Insurance Classification: Too Important to Be Left to the Actuaries, 19 U. Mich. J.L. Reform 349, 387–92 (1986). Consistent with this perspective, the Hawaii statute applied in *Schmidt* was presumably designed to prohibit actuarially justified discrimination, given that it is likely that, as a group, those with less than one year of driving experience are involved in more accidents than those with more driving experience. How should an insurance commissioner, legislature, or other policymaker determine whether a particular form of risk classification is unfairly discriminatory in this broader sense? Several potential considerations are relevant.

First, insurers' classifications may be objectionable because they explicitly use factors that are suspect for non-insurance reasons. Race, religion and national origin are the most obvious examples, gender is a very close second, and even genetic factors may be suspect, in light of the "eugenics" movement of the early twentieth-century and the genetic discrimination practiced in Nazi Germany. Other characteristics that may also be suspect include sexual orientation, age, or income.

Second, insurance classifications may be unfair because they perpetuate social inequalities by limiting access to insurance among historically oppressed or otherwise vulnerable groups. This can have broader economic consequences, because insurance is a prerequisite to many core economic activities, such as purchasing a home, driving a car, and owning a business. For instance, many automobile and homeowners insurers use information derived from policyholders' credit scores to price policies, because such information correlates with policyholders' expected losses and is relatively cheap for insurers to obtain. This practice has drawn criticism from some consumer groups, who argue it disproportionately harms low-income and minority populations because they have substantially lower credit scores than the rest of the population. Thus, insurers' use of credit-based information reinforces racial and economic inequalities. See generally Federal Trade Commission, Credit-Based Insurance Scores: Impacts on Consumers of Automobile Insurance (2007). These objections have had some success, as evidenced by the fact the insurer discrimination on the basis of credit information was prohibited by the Hawaii statute that figured in *Schmidt*. Several other states, such as California, also prohibit auto insurers from using credit scoring in their insurance pricing. However, most states permit insurers to use credit scoring, albeit with certain mandated consumer protections, such as a prohibition on considering medical bills sent to a debt collection agency.

Third, actuarially justified discrimination by insurers may be objectionable because it is non-causal. That is, the policyholder characteristic against which insurers discriminate may merely be correlated with the probability of loss because it is a proxy for something that is causally connected to risk. Lack of driving experience does not "cause" accidents; rather, it may tend to reflect factors that are more nearly causal—unfamiliarity with local road conditions, unrefined ability to recognize dangerous situations, or lack of physical dexterity in handling a vehicle, for example. Similarly, a driver's credit information obviously is not causally related to a driver's ability. Yet it might be a proxy for something causally related to driving risk, such as a general lack of care. See Patrick L. Brockett & Linda L. Golden, Biological and Psychobehavioral Correlates of Credit Scores and Automobile Insurance Losses: Toward an Explication of Why Credit Scoring Works, 74 J. Risk & Ins. 23 (2007). Insurers' reliance on non-causal risk factors raises the prospect that a policyholder characteristic predicts risk in part *because* it is correlated with an independently objectionable policyholder characteristic. Returning to the issue of credit-based insurance scores, some have claimed that the predictive power of credit information may actually be partially caused by its link to policyholder race or income. Unlike the disparate impact argument above, this claim suggests that the correlation between credit-based insurance scores and race/income is not merely an incidental side effect of insurers' risk classification practices, but rather a core reason that insurance scores predict risk in the first place. Additionally, non-causal rating factors raise the prospect that some individuals are paying more than they "should," if only insurers would examine their riskiness more carefully.

Fourth, even when classifications are both actuarially accurate and causal, they may be non-controllable. People with hemophilia, or with inherited genetic tendencies toward suffering from other disorders, for example, cannot control the increased risk that they may pose for health insurers. Should the results of the "natural lottery" for good health be a legitimate factor for insurers to take into account? Or, should law or regulation require insurers to spread these risks among the insured population at large? What is the relevance of the possibility that requiring insurers to force low-risk policyholders to cross-subsidize high-risk policyholders may result in the former being less likely to purchase insurance in the first place?

A final concern with actuarially fair discrimination by insurers is that it may unduly intrude on policyholder privacy. With the advent of increasingly extensive databases and accessible computer technology, insurers are now able to develop classifications based on information such as what magazines people read and what food they buy. See Jonathan L. Shreve, Analyze This, Best's Review 101–02 (October 2008). In some cases, privacy concerns may be allayed by requiring insurers to secure policyholder consent before accessing private data. But this strategy can end up discouraging policyholders from learning about information that they might wish to keep private in the future. For example, some people avoid genetic tests that may provide them with valuable information because they fear that insurers may inquire about the results of any such tests. For general discussion of discriminatory classification, see Ronen Avraham, Kyle D. Logue, & Daniel Schwarcz, Understanding Insurance Anti-discrimination Laws, 87 S. Cal. L. Rev. 195 (2014); Kenneth S. Abraham, Distributing Risk: Insurance, Legal Theory, and Public Policy 64–100 (1986); Deborah S. Hellman, Is Actuarially Fair Insurance Fair?: A Case Study in Insuring Battered Women, 32 Harv. Civ. Rights—Civ. Lib. L. Rev. 355, 361–69 (1997); Regina Austin, The Insurance Classification Controversy, 131 U. Pa. L. Rev. 517 (1983).

4. *Regulatory Adverse Selection.* A key question about any insurance anti-discrimination rule is whether it will generate adverse selection, a phenomenon that has been dubbed "regulatory adverse selection." Michael Hoy, Risk Classification and Social Welfare, 31 Geneva Papers on Risk & Ins. 245 (2006). Substantial amounts of adverse selection resulting from regulatory prohibitions on classification can undermine the very point of anti-discrimination regulation by limiting the cross-subsidization of risk across the population and, in extreme forms, limiting the availability of coverage for all. The actual risk of regulatory adverse selection depends on numerous potential factors, including the ability of policyholders to over-insure, the magnitude of the risk differentials between those with the prohibited characteristic and those without it, the percentage of the policyholder population with the high-risk characteristic, and general risk aversion among prospective policyholders. In a study of state insurance anti-discrimination law, a recent article concluded that the strength of state restrictions on insurer discrimination was substantially influenced by the prospect of regulatory adverse selection. See Ronen Avraham, Kyle D. Logue, & Daniel Schwarcz, Towards a Universal Framework for Anti-Discrimination Laws, 21 Conn. Ins. L.J. 1 (2014). For instance, discrimination by life insurers is generally much less regulated than discrimination by other types of insurers, in large part because of the capacity of policyholders to purchase large amounts of life insurance coverage and thereafter sell that coverage to investors, all of which greatly enhances the risk of regulatory adverse selection.

5. *Federal Regulation of Unfair Discrimination in Insurance.* The federal government has often taken an active role in regulating discrimination in insurance. The most important example is the Affordable Care Act, which prohibits most forms of risk classification by health insurers. We will study this scheme in detail in Chapter Five. Additionally, federal law prohibits health insurers from requesting or using individuals' personal genetic information in underwriting or risk-classification and prohibits employers from using that information in their hiring decisions. Genetic Information Nondiscrimination Act of 2008 ("GINA"), 42 U.S.C. § 2000ff *et seq.* GINA responds to several of the general insurance anti-discrimination concerns discussed above, including socially-suspect

classifications, policyholder control, and privacy. But it also responds to the prospect that genetic information may actually convert risk into certainty, thus transforming insurance from a risk-spreading mechanism into a savings vehicle for anticipated losses. See Deborah Hellman, What Makes Genetic Discrimination Exceptional, 29 Amer. J. L. & Med. 77 (2003); Robyn B. Nicoll, Long-Term Care Insurance and Genetic Discrimination—Get it While You're Young and Ignorant: An Examination of Current Discriminatory Problems in Long-Term Care Insurance Through the Use of Genetic Information, 13 Alb. L.J. Sci. & Tech. 751 (2003). Despite these concerns, insurers' use of genetic information is not generally prohibited in life insurance, long-term care insurance, or disability insurance.

Federal law also limits the ability of insurers that provide coverage through an employer group to discriminate on the basis of sex. Various insurers, particularly life insurers, have historically relied on sex in pricing their policies because women have a longer life expectancy than men. In two landmark cases, the U.S. Supreme Court made clear that this practice violates Title VII of the Civil Rights Act of 1964 when it occurs in the context of employer-sponsored insurance coverage. See *L.A. Dep't of Water & Power v. Manhart,* 435 U.S. 702 (1978) (pension plan requiring women to make 15 percent higher contributions than males violated the Act); *Ariz. Governing Comm. v. Norris,* 463 U.S. 1073 (1983) (retirement program financed by equal payments from males and females, but which paid men higher monthly benefits upon retirement because of their shorter life expectancy, violated the Act). These holdings do not, however, apply to insurance sold in individual markets outside of employment, where sex-based discrimination is generally permitted, especially in the context of life insurance. The literature on the application of Title VII to insurance is voluminous. See, e.g., Spencer L. Kimball, Reverse Sex Discrimination: *Manhart,* 1979 Am. Bar Found. Research J. 83; Leah Brilmayer, et al., Sex Discrimination in Employer-Sponsored Insurance Plans: A Legal and Demographic Analysis, 47 U. Chi. L. Rev. 505 (1980); George J. Benston, The Economics of Gender Discrimination in Employee Fringe Benefits: *Manhart* Revisited, 49 U. Chi. L. Rev. 489 (1982).

4. POLICY FORM REGULATION

The regulation of insurance policy forms dates back to well before the McCarran-Ferguson Act. Shortly after the Civil War, various fire insurers hollowed out their coverage in ways that were not fully (or even partially) understood by policyholders. In response, some states required fire insurers to use policy language laid out verbatim in state statutes. The most famous example was New York's two-page 1943 Standard Fire Insurance Policy, or "the 165 lines," as it is known in the trade. See Thomas L. Wenck, The Historical Development of Standard Policies, 35 J. of Risk & Ins. 537, 538–44 (1968). In some states, this standard policy is still on the books, and it operates as a mandatory coverage floor for fire insurance that is embedded within broader property insurance policies. See 1 Steven Plitt et al., Couch on Insurance § 149:3 (3d ed. 2009).

Today, the vast majority of states continue to regulate the content of insurance policies in consumer-oriented markets, including auto, homeowners, health, life, annuities, long-term care, and disability insurance. However, outside of the very narrow context of fire insurance, states do not mandate the use of specific policy forms or require that insurers' coverages exceed a comprehensive state-mandated bar. Instead, as with rate review, policy form regulation typically occurs through a prior approval process. Robert L. Tucker, Disappearing Ink: The Emerging Duty to Remove Invalid Policy Provisions, 42 Akron L. Rev. 519, 577 (2009). File and use is less common for the regulation of insurance policy forms than it is for insurance rates.

Modern form regulation can be subdivided into two broad categories. First, in many states, regulators are empowered to review policy forms to determine whether they are "unfair," "ambiguous," "unreasonable," "contrary to public policy" or some combination of these broad standards. See, e.g., Ala. Code § 27–14–9 (1975); Ga. Code Ann. § 33–24–10; Neb. Rev. Stat. § 44–7513. These forms of statutory authority give regulators broad discretion to disapprove of policy terms that they find objectionable. But, as with the prohibition against "unfair discrimination," most regulators generally do not invoke this broad authority in the vast majority of cases. Second, regulators review filed policy forms to ensure that they comply with various specific state rules. These rules vary significantly by state. One excellent resource for exploring their scope is available at: https://eapps.naic.org/prl/do/search/dialog.

In the context of property/casualty insurance, the most common specific policy form requirements restrict insurers' grounds for cancelling or non-renewing coverage, and require insurers to provide minimum amounts of notice to policyholders when they do cancel or non-renew coverage. Most states also require that insurance policies meet minimum "readability" requirements, which use word and sentence length to estimate the difficulty of comprehending a written document. See John Aloysius Cogan Jr., Readability, Contracts of Recurring Use, and the Problem of Ex Post Judicial Governance of Health Insurance Policies, 15 Roger Williams U. L. Rev. 93, 119 (2010). States often have various other policy form requirements—ranging from required coverage for innocent co-insureds to prohibitions on absolute pollution exclusions or mandatory arbitration provisions—that we will encounter throughout the remainder of the book. To cope with all of these state-specific rules, most property-casualty insurers operating in multiple states maintain a single "base" policy for each coverage line, and amend it with a state-specific endorsement for each state in which they operate. Regulation of policy forms in commercial property/casualty insurance markets is less common. For instance, in many states, filing of forms is not required when the coverage is intended for policyholders who have a risk manager or whose premiums, net worth, or workforce exceeds specific thresholds. See Ilana Hessing, The Partial Deregulation of Commercial Property and Casualty Insurance: Benefits and Challenges, 20 CPCU Soc'y Regulation & Legislation Interest Grp. Compliance Matters 3 (2013).

State policy content requirements in health insurance markets are often dubbed "mandated benefits." State-mandated health insurance benefits vary substantially, touching on topics such as rehabilitative services, gender-reassignment surgery, contraceptives, and fertility treatment. See generally Amy Monahan, Federalism, Federal

Regulation, or Free Market? An Examination of Mandated Health Benefit Reform, 2007 U. Ill. L. Rev. 1361 (discussing mandated state benefits). Such benefit mandates are substantially impacted by ERISA express preemption. Recall that ERISA preempts all state laws that "relate to" employee benefit plans, but exempts from this preemption any state law that "regulates insurance." The result of these provisions is that group insurance policies that employers purchase for their employees must comply with state mandated benefits. However, ERISA also includes a "deemer" provision that provides that "self-insured" employers should not be deemed to be insurers for purposes of ERISA. The effect of this provision is that employers who self-insure their employees' health insurance need not comply with state mandated benefit laws. See generally *Metro. Life Ins. v. Massachusetts*, 471 U.S. 724 (1985). We will explore these rules, as well as the ACA's impact on state mandated benefits, in more detail in Chapter Five.

Form regulation in the context of life, annuities, disability, and long-term care is distinctive in its own way. Life insurers have historically been vocal in their complaints about the cumbersome and duplicative state regulation of their products. These complaints have particular resonance when it comes to life insurance products, because there is no plausible argument that different state conditions should impact product requirements in these lines: people die, live, and become disabled in exactly the same ways across state lines. In response to these concerns, the NAIC established the Interstate Insurance Product Regulation Commission (IIPRC) in 2004 to conduct form regulation for these coverage lines according to a single set of rules and processes. The IIRPC achieves this result through an interstate compact. States that sign on to this compact agree that insurers can sell IIRPC-approved products in their state without going through the normal state regulatory process. The IIPRC began operating in 2006 and, as of September, 2014, 44 states had enacted legislation agreeing to the Compact, representing over 70% of national premium volume.

The IIPRC's review of policy forms is based on uniform rules that it promulgates. For all policy types, these rules include quantitative readability requirements and prohibitions on both mandatory arbitration clauses and no-assignment provisions. Beyond these general provisions, each product line has its own detailed requirements. For example, individual term life insurance policies must include a clause providing that if a policyholder misstates her age or gender, she will be entitled to the benefit she could have purchased with her premiums had she stated her correct age or gender. IIPRC product rules are initially devised by NAIC and IIPRC committees and subjected to a sixty-day public comment period. To be adopted, they must be approved by 2/3 of the IIPRC management committee, made up of 15 member states representing a cross-section of states, and then 2/3 of all member states. Even after adoption, individual states have the ability to opt out of any particular set of product rules they don't like. As of March 31st, 2014, the IIPRC had promulgated 93 Uniform Standards dealing with 21 different types of insurance and more than 125 various subtypes. The IIPRC reviews product filings in an average of under six weeks, as compared with as long as six to nine months in individual states. See Elizabeth F. Brown, Will the Federal Insurance Office Improve Insurance Regulation?, 81 U. Cin. L. Rev. 551, 563 (2012). For more information on the IIPRC, see the Interstate Insurance Product Regulation Commission's website at, http://www.insurancecompact.org/industry_resources.htm.

NOTES AND QUESTIONS

1. *The Relationship Between State Form Review and the Judicial Regulation of Insurance.* As we saw in Chapter Two, many judicial doctrines of insurance, including the reasonable expectations rule, *contra proferentem*, and public policy restrictions on coverage terms, potentially envision a role for courts to play in regulating insurance policies. What should be the relationship between such judicial regulation of insurance policies and the state administrative process of policy form regulation? For instance, what, if any, deference should the judiciary give to a policy form that has been approved by a state's insurance department?

Judicial opinions typically either scrutinize the reasonableness of policy language without mention of regulatory review, or else completely disclaim any role for courts to play in scrutinizing the fairness of particular policy terms. Compare *Leonard v. Nationwide Mut. Ins. Co.*, 438 F. Supp. 2d 684 (S.D. Miss. 2006) (rejecting relevance of regulatory review), with *Stephan v. Unum Life Ins. Co. of Am.*, 697 F.3d 917 (9th Cir. 2012) (stating that forms approved by the regulator are conclusively presumed to comply with California Law). And in academic literature, sustained treatment of this topic is notably lacking. But cf. Kenneth Abraham, The Expectations Principle as a Regulative Ideal, 5 Conn. Ins. L.J. 59 (1998) (arguing that safeguarding policyholders' reasonable expectations should inform administrative form regulation more than judicial scrutiny of insurance contracts); Susan Randall, Freedom of Contract in Insurance, 14 Conn. Ins. L.J. 107 (2008) (arguing that because insurance policies are regulated, the very idea of contractual intent should be disregarded, and interpretation should occur in view of the statutory and regulatory policies that dictate or constrain insurance policy provisions).

Courts and regulators may have different comparative advantages in scrutinizing the reasonableness of policy language. Regulators, in general, have more expertise than courts in both insurance markets and consumer literacy. See Russell Korobkin, The Efficiency of Managed Care Patient Protection Laws: Incomplete Contracts, Bounded Rationality, and Market Failure, 85 Cornell L. Rev. 2 (1999). They have access to insurance data, which may help explain or justify certain policy provisions. And they can also adjust their regulation over time and in response to policyholder and insurer feedback. At the same time, courts possess several important advantages over regulators in scrutinizing potentially confusing, ambiguous, or unfair policy terms. For instance, they focus on specific terms in the context of a concrete dispute. This is important, as policy language that may seem relatively unobjectionable in the abstract can conceivably present substantial concerns in specific cases. See Daniel Schwarcz, A Products Liability Theory of the Judicial Regulation of Insurance Policies, 48 Wm. & Mary L. Rev. 1389, 1422 (2007). Courts may also be less vulnerable to political forces and/or regulatory capture than regulators, which may allow them to exercise more effective scrutiny over the reasonableness of policy language.

2. *The Effectiveness of State Form Regulation.* No systematic empirical evidence exists on the effectiveness of state form regulation.

Historically, various commentators have claimed that such regulation is cursory and ineffective, though these criticisms are often implicitly or explicitly directed at property/casualty insurance. See Robert E. Keeton, Insurance Law Rights at Variance with Policy Provisions, 83 Harv. L. Rev. 961, 967 (1970). Recent evidence provides some modern support for this assessment. A 2011 study found that most state insurance departments do not have complete copies of different carriers' homeowners insurance policies in their records. Daniel Schwarcz, Reevaluating Standardized Insurance Policies, 78 U. Chi. L. Rev. 1263, 1323 (2011). The reason was that insurers typically only filed with regulators the specific policy language that they sought to change, but not the entire policy and all mandatory endorsements associated with the altered language. Given that the impact of policy language can only be well-understood in context, this evidence may suggest a "check the box" mentality among many state form regulators.

3. *The Costs of Form Review*. Although the IIPRC limits the costs of form review for certain products, it is an incomplete solution. Several of the biggest and most important states, including California and New York, have not joined the IIPRC over concern about the quality of its consumer protections. In property/casualty insurance, the NAIC helped develop an electronic filing system known as the System for Electronic Rate and Form Filing (SERFF) to facilitate the electronic submission of form and rate filings. But unlike the IIPRC, filings submitted through SERFF still must be individually reviewed and approved by each state in which policies will be sold. All of this regulatory red tape inevitably imposes substantial compliance costs on insurers, which, to varying degrees, will tend to result in higher prices for policyholders. Additionally, the patchwork nature of state form regulation may impede product innovation. To what extent would federal regulation of forms (and rates) limit these costs? Would federal regulation of property/casualty policies unduly limit states' ability to tailor their form review to their citizens' political views and risk exposures?

4. *Downsides of the IIPRC*. Does the IIPRC represent a problematic solution to the costs of state-based form review? One objection to the IIPRC is that it effectively empowers a non-public entity with legislative authority. The product rules adopted by the IIPRC are not passed via ordinary state law making procedures, nor are they subject to state administrative law. This may create an excessive risk of industry capture in addition to more general concerns regarding democratic accountability. Another objection is that the IIPRC creates the prospect of regulatory arbitrage, because it gives insurers the choice of submitting their forms either to the IIPRC or to individual state insurance departments. By allowing insurance companies to select between two competing form review regimes, the IIPRC may reduce consumer protections. See Fed. Ins. Office, How to Modernize and Improve the System of Insurance Regulation in the United States (2013).

5. *Mandatory Policy Forms*. Would it make sense to return to the use of mandatory policy forms in consumer-oriented insurance markets? This would reduce compliance costs, increase consumer understanding of the scope of coverage, and limit the risk of unfair or exploitative policy terms. Although this reform may seem radical, it mirrors the current approach to Medicare Supplement policies. In the wake of substantial

consumer protection problems associated with the sale of such policies, the federal government mandated that all Medicare Supplement policies must fit one of several standardized benefit designs. Today, eleven variations of these policies exist, all of which were designed by the NAIC. See Ctrs. for Medicare & Medicaid Services, Choosing a Medigap Policy: A Guide to Health Insurance for People with Medicare (2014).

5. Market Conduct Regulation

Market conduct regulation encompasses insurers' marketing and distribution of products and resolution of claims. Some also use the term to encompass rate and form regulation. Two NAIC model laws play a particularly important role in market conduct regulation and have been adopted in some form in virtually every state. First, the Model Unfair Claims Settlement Practices Act, Model Law 900 (1997), defines numerous "unfair claims practices," such as "[n]ot attempting in good faith to effectuate prompt, fair and equitable settlements of claims submitted in which liability has become reasonably clear" and "[r]efusing to pay claims without conducting a reasonable investigation." Second, the Model Unfair Trade Practices Act, Model Law 880 (2004), defines various "unfair trade practices," such as "[m]isrepresent[ing] the benefits, advantages, conditions, or terms of any policy" or disseminating any advertising or marketing that is "untrue, deceptive or misleading." Both model acts allow state regulators to take remedial action when, and only when, the unfair act or practice has been "committed flagrantly and in conscious disregard" of the law or has "been committed with such frequency to indicate a general business practice to engage in that type of conduct."

Insurance regulators use a variety of tools to monitor compliance with these and other market conduct rules. For instance, they require insurers to complete an annual Market Conduct Annual Statement (MCAS), which includes data on claims payment rates, speed of claim payment, and policy cancellations and non-renewals. Much like with financial solvency regulation, regulators can then use these data to identify potential outlier companies. Unlike the data that carriers report on their annual financial statements, insurers' MCAS data is not made publicly available. State insurance regulators also track consumer complaints about insurers' market conduct practices and routinely conduct market conduct exams of different carriers, which are analogous to on-site financial exams of carriers.

In contrast to solvency regulation, market conduct regulation is generally understood to be relatively non-uniform and uncoordinated. For instance, insurance companies often complain about enduring multiple and overlapping market conduct exams by different state insurance regulators. See Robert W. Klein & James W. Schacht, An Assessment of Insurance Market Conduct Surveillances, 20 J. Ins. Reg. 51 (2001). Additionally, the scope and rigor of different states' market conduct regulation is quite variable, as there is no formal process of accreditation for state market conduct regulation (in contrast to the financial standards accreditation program, described above). In part, this lack of coordination and uniformity reflects the fact that some market conduct issues are indeed local or regional: particular insurer offices or insurance agents may generate market conduct issues that do not extend company-wide. Another important explanation is that, in contrast to solvency regulation, states generally refuse to defer to other states with respect to market conduct regulation, because they understandably believe that other states would not be sufficiently responsive to market conduct issues predominantly impacting out-of-state consumers.

NOTES AND QUESTIONS

1. *The Relationship Between Market Conduct Regulation and Bad Faith Law.* As we saw in Chapter Two, the doctrine of insurer bad faith is designed to deter inappropriate insurer claims handling practices. Additionally, the reasonable expectations doctrine and doctrines relating to estoppel and waiver may also respond to misleading or deceptive marketing or sales practices by insurers or their agents. What should be the relationship between judicial and administrative regulation of insurers' market conduct? For instance, should the availability of the bad faith cause of action turn on the effectiveness of the relevant state's market conduct regulation? See, e.g., *Moradi-Shalal v. Fireman's Fund Ins. Cos.*, 758 P.2d 58 (Cal. 1988) (Mosk, J., dissenting) (suggesting that insurer bad faith cause of action should be permitted because the state insurance commissioner does little to regulate inappropriate market conduct). Similarly, to what extent should regulators use information from bad faith lawsuits in conducting market conduct regulation?

As with form regulation, the answers to these questions turn on the relative institutional competence of courts and state regulations in detecting and responding to inappropriate forms of market conduct. Many of the same basic institutional strengths and weaknesses discussed in the context of policy form regulation apply here as well: courts may have greater resources and less risk of capture, while regulators have more insurance expertise and capacity to adopt market-wide remedies that can be adjusted over time. But there also may be particular institutional advantages that play out differently with respect to market conduct regulation. For instance, the gap between the expertise of courts and the expertise of regulators may be greater when it comes to market conduct regulation than form regulation, given that form regulation ultimately involves the regulation of legal contracts. Similarly, judicial regulation of insurance policy terms may more naturally safeguard the interests of all consumers than judicial regulation of market conduct because precedent as to the permissibility of certain policy terms may be easier to enforce than precedent about impermissible forms of market conduct.

2. *Coordination of Market Conduct Regulation.* Why couldn't states simply replicate the successful solvency regulation accreditation program for market conduct regulation? What is the central difference between market conduct regulation and solvency regulation that makes this so difficult? Would federal regulation of insurers' market conduct help to solve this problem?

3. *Data for Market Conduct Regulation.* The MCAS was only developed recently, and it currently is only operational in a few lines of coverage, including life & annuity, homeowners, and private passenger auto. The specific data elements that are collected in each line are available through the NAIC, at http://www.naic.org/mcas_2013.htm. Can you think of any compelling public policy reasons for keeping this data confidential?

Could making this data publicly available help decrease the risk of market conduct violations? See Daniel Schwarcz, Transparently Opaque: Understanding the Lack of Transparency in Insurance Consumer Protection, 61 UCLA L. Rev. 394 (2014) (criticizing the lack of public disclosure of MCAS data).

6. RESIDUAL MARKET MECHANISMS

Insurance Information Institute, Residual Markets (2009)[*]

To make basic coverage more readily available to everyone who wants or needs insurance, special insurance plans, known as residual, shared or involuntary markets, have been set up by state regulators working with the insurance industry. * * * Many different programs have been established to assure that insurance is available to individuals and businesses having difficulty obtaining coverage in the "voluntary market," that is the risk that insurers voluntarily assume. * * *

[The most important residual market is The Automobile Residual Market] * * *As states began to pass laws requiring drivers to furnish proof of insurance, having auto liability insurance became a prerequisite for driving a car. Today, all 50 states and the District of Columbia use one of four systems to guarantee that auto insurance is available to those who need it. * * * [These consist of (i) assigned risk plans, (ii) Joint Underwriting Associations ("JUA"), (iii) Reinsurance Facilities, and (iv) State Funds. We will examine the first two, which are the two most important and widespread.]

[First,] the assigned risk plan, the most common type, currently found in 42 states and the District of Columbia, generally is administered through an office created or supported by the state and governed by a board representing insurance companies licensed in the state. * * * When agents or company representatives are unable to obtain auto insurance for an applicant in the voluntary market, they submit the application to the assigned risk plan office. These applications are distributed randomly by the automobile insurance plan to all insurance companies that offer automobile liability coverage in the state in proportion to the amount of their voluntary business. Thus, if on a given day the plan receives 100 applications from agents around the state, a company with 10 percent of that state's regular private passenger automobile insurance business will be assigned 10 of those applicants and will be responsible for all associated losses.

Generally, each insurer services the policyholders assigned to it just as it would the policyholders it insures in the voluntary market. * * * Assigned risk policies usually are more restricted in the coverage they can provide and have lower limits than voluntary market policies. In addition, premiums for assigned risk policies usually are significantly higher, although not always sufficiently high enough to cover the increased costs of insuring high-risk drivers.

[Second, automobile JUAs], found in four states, Florida, Hawaii, Michigan and Missouri, are state-mandated pooling mechanisms through which all companies doing business in the state share the

---

[*] Copyright 2009, Insurance Information Institute.

premiums of business outside the voluntary market as well as the profits or losses and expenses incurred. To simplify the policyholder distribution process, insurance agents and company representatives are generally assigned one of several servicing carriers (companies that have agreed for a fee to issue and service JUA policies). They submit applications to that company, which then issues the JUA policy. * * *

[Residual Market mechanisms are not limited to automobile insurance. For instance, at] various times, there have been JUAs for residential insurance. Florida's residential JUA became part of its Citizens Property Insurance Corporation in 2002. Florida also has a workers compensation JUA, which was established in 1993. A number of states have medical malpractice JUAs, most of which were set up in the 1970s or 1980s when the line was beset by high losses. However, in the 1990s, the market for medical malpractice insurance softened, as in other commercial sectors, and several JUAs were dissolved.

NOTES AND QUESTIONS

1. *The Purpose of Residual Market Mechanisms.* Residual market mechanisms are formed in response to shortages of coverage for specific sets of policyholders who insurers view as high-risk. Why do such shortages exist? One answer is that they are a byproduct of form and rate regulation, which limit the ability of insurers to offer sufficiently limited coverage or charge appropriately high premiums to high-risk policyholders. From this perspective, residual market mechanisms can be understood as an effort to force insurers to offer minimally robust coverage at below-market prices. Even so, coverage and premiums in residual markets are usually less favorable than they are in the voluntary market, as noted above. Under this view, it is no surprise that residual market mechanisms often run deficits, since in a sense that is precisely what they are designed to do. A second explanation for residual market mechanisms is that they respond to structural deficiencies in insurance markets, such as the arbitrariness of auto insurers' risk classification decisions or periodic overcautiousness by companies writing small-volume lines such as medical malpractice. From this perspective, residual market mechanisms combat these structural imperfections in the market by forcing insurers to write coverage at a fair price. Deficits must then be interpreted as resulting from improper management of the mechanism by the state or insurer-sponsored entity charged with this responsibility.

2. *Deficit Recoupment.* The deficits often run by residual market mechanisms can be made up in a variety of ways. In auto insurance, drivers in the voluntary market may be surcharged, directly or indirectly, to correct for the subsidy that runs to those in the assigned-risk pool. In medical malpractice and commercial liability JUA's, participating insurers in many states are permitted to surcharge policyholders in other lines, or to take a credit for their share of any deficit against future premium taxes owed to the state. Which approach seems most appropriate? What does your answer imply about who should bear the ultimate responsibility for assuring the affordability of each form of coverage?

3. *Withdrawal Restrictions.* When residual market mechanisms run deficits, some of the insurers bearing the cost of the deficits may conclude that they would be better off not selling the line of insurance subject to the residual market mechanism, since their profits on sales do not exceed their

share of the deficit. Withdrawal from the market, however, is not always so easy as it may seem. In the wake of the deficits that auto insurance assigned risk plans ran in the late 1980's and early 1990's, a number of states enacted restrictions on insurers' right to withdraw from the market. These restrictions were challenged on constitutional and other grounds, but were for the most part upheld. For discussion, see Richard A. Epstein, Exit Rights and Insurance Regulation: From Federalism to Takings, 7 Geo. Mason L. Rev. 293 (1999).

  4. *Excess and Surplus Lines.* An alternative option for prospective policyholders who find that insurance coverage is not available through ordinary insurance markets is to look to Excess and Surplus (E&S) lines of coverage, which are often also referred to as the "non-admitted" market. Unlike ordinary insurance markets ("admitted" markets), E&S insurers are not licensed by individual states and are exempt from many forms of insurance regulation, including rate and form regulation. They also do not participate in state guaranty funds. See generally Matthew Gaul et al., Recent Developments in Excess Insurance, Surplus Lines Insurance, 47 Tort Trial & Ins. Prac. L.J. 185 (2011). However, E&S insurers must nonetheless comply with certain basic regulatory rules. The most important of these rules ensure that E&S insurers are not writing coverage that is available in the admitted market. Regulations also generally make it extremely difficult, if not impossible, for policyholders purchasing through the non-admitted market to do so without the assistance of a licensed surplus-lines broker who certifies that the coverage cannot be obtained from the admitted market. See N.Y. Ins. Law § 2118(b)(1)–(3). As a consequence, the surplus-lines broker becomes a key intermediary in obtaining coverage from the non-admitted market, and may engage in at least some monitoring of the quality and solvency of individual insurers operating in that market. Cf. *Popich Bros. Water Transp., Inc. v. Gulf Coast Marine, Inc.*, 705 So. 2d 1267 (La. Ct. App. 1998) (surplus lines broker had no duty to investigate the financial soundness of a non-admitted insurer). In general, the E&S market tends to provide coverage for more sophisticated and wealthy policyholders than residual market mechanisms.

C. FEDERAL REGULATION

  Federal regulation of insurance has long been an extremely controversial topic. Regularly over the last 80 years—even since it became clear that federal regulation of insurance was constitutionally permissible—lawmakers, insurers, and commentators have debated the appropriate role of the federal government in insurance regulation. The McCarran-Ferguson Act itself retained a role for federal regulation of insurance by limiting the scope of both "reverse preemption" and the federal antitrust exemption for the business of insurance. Moreover, on numerous occasions, including after the 2008 global financial crisis, reformers have been partially successful in shifting additional elements of insurance regulation to the federal level.

1. FEDERAL REGULATION AND REVERSE PREEMPTION

  As noted at the start of this Chapter, the McCarran-Ferguson Act was substantially motivated by the concern that federal laws not specific to insurance, such as the Sherman Act, might interfere with long-standing state insurance regulation. Section 2(b) of the Act therefore established the unique principle of "reverse preemption" for insurance, whereby state laws specific to insurance trump federal laws of general applicability. As the following case makes clear, reverse preemption still leaves substantial scope for general federal law to influence insurance markets.

Patrick O. Ojo v. Farmers Group, Inc.

United States Court of Appeals, Ninth Circuit, 2010.
600 F.3d 1205.

■ PER CURIAM:

In this appeal we are asked to determine whether a disparate impact suit alleging the discriminatory provision of homeowner's insurance in violation of the federal Fair Housing Act ("FHA"), 42 U.S.C. §§ 3601–19, is reverse-preempted by the McCarran-Ferguson Act, 15 U.S.C. § 1012, because it invalidates, impairs, or supersedes Texas insurance law. In order to do so, we must answer two preliminary questions. First, we must decide whether the FHA prohibits discrimination in the denial and pricing of homeowner's insurance. Second, we must determine whether the reverse-preemption standard set forth in the McCarran-Ferguson Act applies to claims brought under latter-enacted civil rights statutes such as the FHA. We answer yes to both questions. Having resolved these issues, in a separate order filed concurrently with this opinion we certify to the Supreme Court of Texas the dispositive question of whether Texas law permits an insurance company to price insurance by using credit-score factors that have a racially disparate impact that, were it not for the McCarran-Ferguson Act, would violate the FHA.

I.

Plaintiff-Appellant Patrick O. Ojo is an African-American resident of Texas and the owner of a homeowner's property—and casualty policy issued by Farmers Group, Inc. ("Farmers"). Ojo sued Farmers and its affiliates, subsidiaries, and reinsurers (collectively "Defendants") in federal court on behalf of himself and other minorities. He claims that Defendants, acting in concert, use a number of "undisclosed factors" in their credit-scoring system that disparately impact minorities, in violation of the federal Fair Housing Act ("FHA"), 42 U.S.C. §§ 3601–19. Ojo does not claim that Defendants intentionally discriminated against any members of the putative plaintiff class.

Defendants moved to dismiss all claims pursuant to Federal Rules of Civil Procedure 12(b)(1) and 12(b)(6). The district court concluded that the Texas Insurance Code preempted Ojo's FHA claims under the reverse-preemption standard set forth in the McCarran-Ferguson Act, 15 U.S.C. § 1012. Ojo appealed, and a divided three-judge panel of our court initially reversed the district court, holding that Texas law does not reverse-preempt Ojo's FHA claim. *Ojo v. Farmers Group, Inc.*, 565 F.3d 1175 (9th Cir.2009). We ordered the case reheard en banc pursuant to Ninth Circuit Rule 35–3, and it is now pending before us.

II.

It is unlawful under the FHA "[t]o discriminate against any person in the terms, conditions, or privileges of sale or rental of a dwelling, or in the provision of services or facilities in connection therewith, because of race." 42 U.S.C. § 3604(b). This provision has been interpreted to prohibit not just intentional discrimination but also actions that have a discriminatory effect based on race (disparate-impact discrimination). * * *

We have not yet had occasion to decide whether or not the FHA applies to homeowner's insurance. We now hold that the FHA prohibits racial discrimination in both the denial and pricing of homeowner's insurance. * * *

Section 3604(a) of the FHA makes it unlawful to "otherwise make unavailable or deny" a dwelling because of race. 42 U.S.C. § 3604(a). Similarly, Section 3604(b) makes it unlawful to discriminate because of race "in the provision of services or facilities" in connection with "the terms, conditions, or privileges of sale or rental of a dwelling." *Id.* § 3604(b). The terms "make unavailable" and "service" are ambiguous. *See NAACP*, 978 F.2d at 298.

When statutory language is ambiguous, we defer to a "permissible construction" of that statute by the agency charged with administering that statute. *Chevron U.S.A., Inc. v. Natural Res. Def. Council, Inc.*, 467 U.S. 837, 842–43 (1984). Here, Congress has charged the Department of Housing and Urban Development ("HUD") with the duty to make rules to carry out the FHA. *See* 42 U.S.C. § 3614a. HUD in turn has determined explicitly that the FHA does indeed prohibit discrimination in the provision of homeowner's insurance. *See* 24 C.F.R. § 100.70(d)(4). The terms of the FHA reasonably can bear this construction. For example, the denial of homeowner's insurance can make housing unavailable: Mortgage lenders require prospective borrowers to obtain homeowner's insurance, so without insurance, there may be no loan, and without a loan, there may be no home available to a person who wants to buy the home. Homeowner's insurance can also be seen as a "service" connected to the sale of a dwelling. In sum, HUD's construction of the FHA is reasonable and *Chevron* requires us to defer to it. * * *

III.

The outcome of Ojo's appeal also depends on whether the McCarran-Ferguson Act is capable of "reversepreempting" claims brought under latter-enacted civil rights statutes such as the FHA. The McCarran-Ferguson Act states the following:

> No Act of Congress shall be construed to invalidate, impair, or supersede any law enacted by any State for the purpose of regulating the business of insurance, or which imposes a fee or tax upon such business, unless such Act specifically relates to the business of insurance. . . .

15 U.S.C. § 1012(b). Under the McCarran-Ferguson Act, state law preempts a federal statute if (1) the federal law does not specifically relate to insurance; (2) the state law is enacted for the purpose of regulating insurance; and (3) the application of federal law to the case might invalidate, impair, or supersede the state law. *Humana Inc. v.*

Forsyth, 525 U.S. 299, 307 (1999). Here, it is undisputed that the FHA does not specifically relate to insurance and that the relevant provisions of Texas law are enacted for the purpose of insurance regulation.

We hold that the FHA can indeed be reverse-preempted by the McCarran-Ferguson Act. By using the phrase "No Act of Congress," the text of McCarran-Ferguson could not be clearer. "'No Act of Congress' differs from 'no act on the books in 1946' or 'no act other than a civil rights statute.'" *NAACP*, 978 F.2d at 294. By its plain terms, the McCarran-Ferguson Act applies to the FHA.

Precedents are in accord with our interpretation. Although the McCarran-Ferguson Act predates Title VII of the Civil Rights Act of 1964, the Supreme Court has never expressed reluctance in applying McCarran-Ferguson to latter-enacted statutes. *See, e.g., Pilot Life Ins. Co. v. Dedeaux*, 481 U.S. 41 (1987) (applying McCarran-Ferguson to the Employee Retirement Income Security Act of 1974). Four justices of the Supreme Court have once already concluded that the McCarran-Ferguson Act applies to Title VII. *Ariz. Governing Comm. for Tax Deferred Annuity and Deferred Comp. Plans v. Norris*, 463 U.S. 1073, 1099–1103 (1983) (Powell J., joined by Burger, C.J., Blackmun and Rehnquist, JJ., concurring in part and dissenting in part). And the majority of our sister circuits to address the question have determined that the McCarran-Ferguson Act applies to civil rights statutes. * * *

Only the Second Circuit has held that the McCarran-Ferguson Act does not apply to Title VII, and that decision predates *Norris*, *Pilot Life*, and the decisions of the other circuits. *See Spirt v. Teachers Ins. and Annuity Ass'n*, 691 F.2d 1054, 1065 (2d Cir.1982), *vacated on other grounds*, 463 U.S. 1223 (1983). The Second Circuit's decision is also based on the incorrect assumption that interpreting McCarran-Ferguson to apply to Title VII would "prevent" Congress from requiring insurers to comply with civil rights statutes. *See id.* at 1066. Such is not the case. "Congress did not tie its hands; instead it prescribed the consequences of silence and specificity in other acts past and future." *NAACP*, 978 F.2d at 295. The McCarran-Ferguson Act is merely the default; if Congress does not want McCarran-Ferguson to operate on a particular statute, it need only say so directly.

IV.

Having determined that the FHA applies to homeowner's insurance and that the McCarran-Ferguson Act can reverse-preempt the FHA, the remaining dispositive question is whether application of the FHA to Ojo's case might invalidate, impair, or supersede the provisions of the Texas Insurance Code that authorize insurance companies to use credit scoring in setting insurance rates. If Texas law permits insurance companies to use credit scores even if the factors used to compute scores may have a racially disparate impact, then allowing Ojo to sue Defendants under the FHA for this practice would impair Texas law. On the other hand, if Texas law prohibits the use of credit-score factors that would violate the FHA on the basis of a disparate-impact theory, then the FHA would complement—rather than displace and impair—Texas law, and Ojo's FHA disparate-impact suit would not be reverse-preempted by the MFA. *See Humana*, 525 U.S. at 310–14. Because this question of Texas law is unsettled, and because the issue's resolution will have pervasive implications for future claims brought against

Texas insurers, we have concluded that the appropriate course of action is to certify this issue to the Supreme Court of Texas. We stay further proceedings in this case pending resolution of our certified question.

NOTES AND QUESTIONS

1. *Texas Determination on Certified Question.* The Supreme Court of Texas resolved the certified question in favor of Farmers Group, concluding that Ojo's proposed application of the FHA would indeed conflict with Texas insurance regulation. *Ojo v. Farmers Grp., Inc.*, 356 S.W.3d 421 (Tex. 2011). In doing so, the Texas Supreme Court concluded that Texas insurance regulation permits the use of facially neutral risk classifications, even if they may have a disparate impact on protected groups. Most states, however, have not specifically addressed the question of whether their state insurance regulation explicitly permits the use of facially-neutral classification schemes that have a disparate impact on protected groups. As such, the application of the FHA to homeowners insurance will continue to be an important issue in the years to come. Based on what you know from the section on state regulation of unfair discrimination, what do you make of the argument that state insurance regulation permits facially-neutral discrimination that has a disparate impact on protected groups? For an argument that disparate impact theory is never appropriate in insurance, see Matthew Jordan Cochran, Fairness in Disparity: Challenging the Application of Disparate Impact Theory In Fair Housing Claims Against Insurers, 21 Geo. Mason U. C.R. L.J. 159 (2011).

2. *Reverse-Preemption Analysis of Other Federal Statutes.* Courts have concluded that a number of generally-applicable federal statutes apply to insurers because they do not "invalidate, impair, or supersede" state insurance laws. For instance, in *Humana Inc. v. Forsyth*, 525 U.S. 299 (1999), the U.S. Supreme Court held that a suit against an insurance company under the federal Racketeer Influenced and Corrupt Organizations Act (RICO), 18 U.S.C. § 1961 *et seq.*, did not "invalidate, impair, or supersede" Nevada laws regulating insurance. Similarly, courts have found that federal restrictions on class actions contained in the Class Action Fairness Act of 2005, 28 U.S.C. § 1711 *et seq.*, are not reverse-preempted by state insurance regulation. See, e.g., *Valdez v. Metro. Prop. & Cas. Ins. Co.*, 867 F. Supp. 2d 1143 (D.N.M. 2012). At the same time, courts have also found a number of instances in which generally applicable federal statutes can indeed conflict with state insurance law. For instance, a number of courts have concluded that state insurance laws restricting the permissibility of insurance arbitration do indeed reverse-preempt the Federal Arbitration Act, 9 U.S.C. § 1 *et seq.*, which normally limits the ability of state law to prohibit pre-dispute mandatory arbitration provisions. See, e.g., *Am. Bankers Ins. Co. of Fla. v. Inman*, 436 F.3d 490 (5th Cir. 2006). Similiarly, in *United States Department of the Treasury v. Fabe*, 508 U.S. 491 (1993), the Court held that state law providing policyholders with priority over the federal government in claims against an insolvent insurer reverse-preempted inconsistent federal bankruptcy laws.

3. *Who has the Final Say on Reverse Preemption?* The *Ojo* Court certified to the Texas Supreme Court the question of whether the FHA would invalidate, impair, or supersede Texas Law. Is the implication that state courts ultimately have the final say on whether a federal law of

general applicability conflicts with state insurance law? Or should federal courts have the final say on this, given that the issue is ultimately one of interpreting the McCarran-Ferguson Act, which is a federal law? To take a concrete example, could Nevada's Supreme Court reject the U.S. Supreme Court's *Humana* decision, described above, and conclude that RICO does, in fact, conflict with Nevada insurance law? After all, the Nevada Supreme Court, not the U.S. Supreme Court, has ultimate authority on the meaning of Nevada state law.

4. *Federal Antitrust Law and the "Invalidate, Impair, or Supersede" Standard.* Does the federal antitrust exemption apply to the business of insurance even if federal law would not "invalidate, impair, or supersede" state insurance regulation? The classic answer to this question is "yes," because courts have traditionally viewed the antitrust exemption in Section 2(b) of the McCarran-Ferguson Act as independent of the reverse preemption provision. As a result, the antitrust exemption has not been understood to incorporate the exception in the reverse preemption provision for federal law that would not "invalidate, impair, or supersede" state law. See, e.g. *Fed. Trade Comm'n v. Nat'l Cas. Co.*, 357 U.S. 560 (1958). However, Professor Einer Elhauge has convincingly argued that this understanding of the McCarran-Ferguson Act is inconsistent with the Act's text, which is reprinted at the start of this Chapter. Einer Elhauge, United States Antitrust Law and Economics 39–41 (2008). Discussing Section 2(b), Elhauge explains that

> Read literally, the second clause provides no freestanding antitrust exemption, but rather *limits* the first clause's exemption in cases involving antitrust statutes, which means that an antitrust exemption should require a showing that the antitrust statute would "impair" the state regulation in addition to the factors in the second clause.

This interpretation, which has not been adopted by any court, could have a significant impact on the insurance industry. This is because, while federal antitrust law is generally very similar to state antitrust law, federal and state antitrust officials have very different resources and expertise. Thus, allowing federal antitrust personnel to pursue cases involving the business of insurance when doing so would be consistent with state law could result in substantially increased antitrust scrutiny of insurance, particularly in areas such as health insurance, where the federal government already has significant regulatory interests.

5. *Reverse Preemption and Federal Securities Laws.* Many products sold by life insurers have both investment and insurance features. For instance, in a variable annuity, a purchaser's payments are effectively invested in a mutual fund, but the purchaser retains the right to receive his investment via a periodic payment for the remainder of his life, thus insuring against the risk of living longer than expected. Additionally, variable annuities often include a guaranteed death benefit that promises a minimum payment in the event that the purchaser dies before the payout period begins. Variable annuities thus simultaneously operate as investments, insurance against longevity risk, and life insurance. The investment features of variable annuities implicate various federal securities laws. In *Securities & Exchange Commission v. Variable Annuity Life Insurance Co.*, 359 U.S. 65 (1959), the Supreme Court held that the SEC does indeed have the authority to regulate variable annuities under

the federal securities laws and that such efforts are not reverse preempted by the McCarran-Ferguson Act. The Court based this determination on the conclusion that variable annuities are not, in fact, insurance for purposes of the McCarran-Ferguson Act and federal securities laws, because the annuitant, rather than the company, bears the investment risk. At the same time, states continue to categorize variable annuities as insurance under state law, because of their insurance features. The result is that variable annuities and similar insurance-investment hybrid products are subject to both state insurance law and federal securities law. This means, for instance, that individuals who sell these products must be licensed both as insurance intermediaries under state law and as brokers under federal law. For further discussion of these issues, see Stephen J. Williams, Distinguishing "Insurance" from Investment Products under the McCarran-Ferguson Act, 98 Colum. L. Rev. 1996 (1998). The nature of this dual regulation is explored in more depth in Chapter 5.

2. FEDERAL ANTITRUST LAW AND INSURANCE

A core goal of the McCarran-Ferguson Act was to exempt certain insurer practices—particularly the sharing of data on past losses and the preparation of standard form policies—from federal antitrust scrutiny. Due to evolution in U.S. antitrust laws over the last several decades, it is likely that even absent the McCarran-Ferguson Act, these practices would survive federal antitrust scrutiny today. But the scope of the insurance industry's exemption from antitrust scrutiny is nonetheless important, because it creates what amounts to "per se" immunity and minimizes antitrust litigation over the industry's activities.

To understand the scope of the McCarran-Ferguson Act's antitrust exemption, revisit the statutory language of the Act, in particular Sections 2(b) and 3(b), reprinted at the start of this Chapter. This language is generally understood to create a three-part test: 1) the "business of insurance" is exempted from the reach of the federal antitrust laws, 2) except that these antitrust laws are applicable "to the extent that such business is not regulated by State law," and 3) regardless of state regulation, McCarran-Ferguson does not render the Sherman Act inapplicable to "any agreement to boycott, coerce, or intimidate, or act of boycott, coercion, or intimidation." 15 U.S.C. §§ 1012–13. Each of these features of the Act raises its own set of difficult questions, addressed in order below.

a. WHAT CONSTITUTES "THE BUSINESS OF INSURANCE"?

Section 2(b) of the McCarran-Ferguson Act exempts only "the business of insurance" from federal antitrust laws. Insurers, of course, engage in a variety of activities that do not constitute the business of insurance, from paying their employees to renting office space. But defining the precise line between activities that are the business of insurance and those that are not can be difficult.

The Supreme Court faced this precise issue in *United Labor Life Insurance Co. v. Pireno*, 458 U.S. 119 (1982). Pireno was a chiropractor who sued a health insurer, Union Labor Life ("ULL"), after it refused to fully cover its policyholders' receipt of chiropractic treatments from

Pireno. ULL's policy covered only "reasonable" and "necessary" medical care and services, and ULL had concluded that some of Pireno's treatments did not meet these standards. It based this determination substantially on the conclusions of a "peer review" panel of chiropractors that ULL had asked to review Pireno's treatments and charges. Pireno claimed that this peer review practice violated the Sherman Act because it amounted to a conspiracy to fix the prices that chiropractors could charge. ULL argued that such a claim was foreclosed by the McCarran-Ferguson Act's antitrust exemption.

The Supreme Court concluded that the McCarran-Ferguson Act did not preclude Pireno's antitrust claim because the alleged conspiracy did not constitute "the business of insurance" within the meaning of the Act. Drawing on a prior Supreme Court case, *Group Life & Health Insurance Co. v. Royal Drug Co.*, 440 U.S. 205 (1979), the *Pireno* Court laid out a three-part test to define the scope of the business of insurance:

> In sum, *Royal Drug* identified three criteria relevant in determining whether a particular practice is part of the "business of insurance" exempted from the antitrust laws by § 2(b): *first,* whether the practice has the effect of transferring or spreading a policyholder's risk; *second,* whether the practice is an integral part of the policy relationship between the insurer and the insured; and *third,* whether the practice is limited to entities within the insurance industry. None of these criteria is necessarily determinative in itself.

Pireno, 458 U.S. at 129.

The *Pireno* Court then applied this test to ULL's peer-review process. It first concluded that the peer review practice did not have the effect of spreading or transferring risk because it "is logically and temporally unconnected to the transfer of risk accomplished by ULL's insurance policies." Id. at 130. The court thus emphasized that it is the insurance policy that transfers risk in an insurance transaction, and—perhaps more questionably—that this "transfer is complete at the time that the contract is entered." Id. Second, the court concluded that the peer-review practice was not an integral part of the policy relationship, in part because it involved an arrangement between the insurer and third parties not engaged in the business of insurance. In so finding, the Court emphasized that ULL did not outsource benefits determinations to the peer-review committee, but simply used that committee's expertise to assist it in deciding whether or not a particular claim should be covered. In that sense, the court concluded, the peer review practice was merely "an aid in [ULL's] decisionmaking process" and thus "a matter of indifference to the policyholder, whose only concern is *whether* his claim is paid, not *why* it is paid." Id. at 132. Finally, the Court emphasized that the peer-review process was clearly not limited to entities within the insurance industry given that it relied on independent, volunteer chiropractors. Three Justices dissented, concluding that the peer-review process amounted to a mechanism for adjusting claims, which lies "at the heart of the relationship between insurance companies and their policyholders." Id. at 135 (Rehnquist, J., dissenting).

One important criticism of the *Pireno* rule is that it does not provide sufficient predictability as to the scope of the McCarran-Ferguson antitrust exemption. For instance, suppose that an insurer hired outside consultants to provide advice to its policyholders about safety precautions, and offered reductions in future premiums if policyholders' loss rates declined. Would actions taken as part of that process fall within the exemption? Recent disputes about the definition of the "business of insurance" confirm that the issue is often highly fact-intensive. In *Arroyo-Melecio v. Puerto Rican American Insurance Co.*, 398 F.3d 56 (1st Cir. 2005), the court held that alleged price fixing by private insurers and a Joint Underwriting Association constituted the business of insurance. On the other hand, in *In re Insurance Brokerage Antitrust Litigation*, 618 F.3d 300 (3rd Cir. 2010), the court held that alleged bid-rigging and steering by commercial lines insurers and brokers fell outside the business of insurance. If the *Royal Drug* test is not an entirely satisfactory means of predicting these results, can you devise a preferable alternative? Would a test based on whether the activity had a predominant effect in insurance rather than non-insurance markets more clearly isolate the core purpose of the McCarran-Ferguson exemption?

b. WHAT CONSTITUTES "REGULATION" BY THE STATES?

The McCarran-Ferguson Act denies the business of insurance an exemption from the reach of the federal antitrust laws "to the extent the business of insurance is not regulated" by state law. Although there are few decisions interpreting this provision, rough outlines of its meaning have emerged. Generally, the state must have a statute creating authority to regulate the activity in question, and the regulation must be more than mere pretense. See *Fed. Trade Comm'n v. Nat'l Cas. Co.*, 357 U.S. 560 (1958). But the courts seem little concerned with the actual degree of state regulation. See, e.g., *Slagle v. ITT Hartford Ins. Grp.*, 904 F. Supp. 1346 (N.D. Fla. 1995); *Crawford v. Am. Title Ins. Co.*, 518 F.2d 217 (5th Cir. 1975). And state regulation of a general class of activities is apparently sufficient even when the specific activity in question has not been explicitly approved. See, e.g., *Klamath-Lake Pharm. Ass'n v. Klamath Med. Serv. Bureau*, 701 F.2d 1276 (9th Cir. 1983), *cert. denied*, 464 U.S. 822:

> Unless the practice amounts to a boycott, the states are free to regulate it or choose not to regulate. They do not have to expressly authorize a specific activity, or proscribe it, for the exemption to apply. * * * It is enough that a detailed overall scheme of regulation exists.

Id. at 1287.

In general, then, the case law seems to hold that there is state "regulation" within the meaning of the Act if the state has enacted a statute authorizing regulation of insurance and regulatory authorities have not totally ignored the general class of activities into which that activity falls. It is not necessary to point to a state statute that approves or disapproves a particular practice; as long as there is a state regulatory scheme that has jurisdiction over the challenged practice then the regulation requirement is satisfied. See *State of Md. v. Blue Cross & Blue Shield Ass'n*, 620 F. Supp. 907 (D. Md. 1985). On occasion the courts may require a bit more by way of regulatory action or consideration, but only rarely. Does this state of affairs seem consistent with the original intent of the McCarran-Ferguson Act? If not, what test should be used to determine whether a state has sufficiently regulated an activity to trigger the Act's exemption?

c. WHAT CONSTITUTES "BOYCOTT, COERCION, OR INTIMIDATION"?

The McCarran-Ferguson Act's antitrust exemption does not apply to any agreement "to boycott, coerce or intimidate, or act of boycott, coercion, or intimidation," The most important litigation over the application of this provision has arisen as a result of periodic "crises" in the availability and affordability of liability insurance. These crises are part of a recurring cycle in which the cost of insurance is relatively flat for a number of years (i.e. a "soft market"), but then increases sharply during a short period of time (i.e. a "hard market"). One such peak in the cycle occurred in the mid-1970's; another occurred in the mid-1980's; and the most recent occurred in 2002–03.

Some background about these crises is helpful in understanding the *Hartford Fire* case below. Insurers face the most difficulty in setting premiums for "long-tail" forms of coverage such as medical malpractice, products liability, and Commercial General Liability (CGL) insurance. The reason is that such coverage traditionally has been provided by *occurrence policies,* which cover the insured against liability imposed at any time, arising out of bodily injury or property damage occurring during the policy period. Consider the difficulties an insurer faces in insuring against medical malpractice claims brought as a result of injuries not discovered until years after treatment, or products liability actions involving long-latency diseases. To the extent that such liabilities are covered by *occurrence* policies issued during the year when treatment or product-use first occurred, an insurer setting a price for coverage must predict the level of economic and legal inflation that will occur between the time coverage is sold and the time all the claims arising out of injury during the policy period ultimately are brought and paid. Yet this period may extend for ten years or more beyond the date of sale. Thus the term "long tail."

One of the reactions of the insurance industry to the problems it faces in writing occurrence coverage against long-tail liabilities has been to introduce a different form of coverage: claims-made. Both *occurrence* and *claims-made* policies are considered in depth in Chapter Six. For the present, however, it is enough to know that, in contrast to occurrence policies, claims-made policies insure only against liability arising out of claims made during the policy period. Most claims-made policies also include a "retroactive date," further limiting coverage to claims involving injury or damage that occurs after that specified date. Consequently, the insurer selling claims-made coverage must predict only the frequency and severity of losses that it will incur during the policy period in order to set a price for this form of coverage—its task is radically simplified, because under claims-made coverage the insured retains the risk of an uncertain long-term economic and legal future. Because long-tail coverage claims under CGL insurance that began to appear in the 1980s often involved highly complex forms of pollution liability, another reaction of insurers was to add pollution exclusions to their CGL insurance policies and to attempt to limit their exposure even further by providing that their expenditures on defense costs reduced the amount of indemnity provided by their policies, dollar for dollar. All these insurer reactions figure in the following case.

Hartford Fire Insurance Company v. California
Supreme Court of the United States, 1993.
509 U.S. 764.

■ JUSTICE SOUTER announced the judgment of the Court [with respect to what follows].[1]

The Sherman Act makes every contract, combination, or conspiracy in unreasonable restraint of interstate or foreign commerce illegal. 26 Stat. 209, as amended, 15 U.S.C. § 1. These consolidated cases present questions about the application of that Act to the insurance industry, both here and abroad. The plaintiffs (respondents here) allege that both domestic and foreign defendants (petitioners here) violated the Sherman Act by engaging in various conspiracies to affect the American insurance market. A group of domestic defendants argues that the McCarran-Ferguson Act, 59 Stat. 33, as amended, 15 U.S.C. § 1011 *et seq.*, precludes application of the Sherman Act to the conduct alleged * * * We hold that most of the domestic defendants' alleged conduct is not immunized from antitrust liability by the McCarran-Ferguson Act * * *.

I

The two petitions before us stem from consolidated litigation comprising the complaints of 19 States and many private plaintiffs alleging that the defendants, members of the insurance industry, conspired in violation of § 1 of the Sherman Act to restrict the terms of coverage of commercial general liability (CGL) insurance[2] available in the United States. Because the cases come to us on motions to dismiss, we take the allegations of the complaints as true.

A

According to the complaints, the object of the conspiracies was to force certain primary insurers (insurers who sell insurance directly to consumers) to change the terms of their standard CGL insurance policies to conform with the policies the defendant insurers wanted to sell. The defendants wanted four changes.

First, CGL insurance has traditionally been sold in the United States on an "occurrence" basis, through a policy obligating the insurer "to pay or defend claims, whenever made, resulting from an accident or 'injurious exposure to conditions' that occurred during the [specific time] period the policy was in effect." In place of this traditional "occurrence" trigger of coverage, the defendant wanted a "claims-made"

---

[1] [Note from the editor: The opinions of the Court in this case are complicated by the fact that different Justices joined different portions of Justice Souter's and Justice Scalia's opinions, thus composing different majorities for different points, and by the fact that Justice Souter's opinion set out the facts. The excerpts from the opinions printed constitute majority opinions. For simplicity, references to the Record have been omitted without so indicating.]

[2] CGL insurance provides "coverage for third party casualty damage claims against a purchaser of insurance (the 'insured')".

trigger, obligating the insurer to pay or defend only those claims made during the policy period. Such a policy has the distinct advantage for the insurer that when the policy period ends without a claim having been made, the insurer can be certain that the policy will not expose it to any further liability. Second, the defendants wanted the "claims-made" policy to have a "retroactive date" provision, which would further restrict coverage to claims based on incidents that occurred after a certain date. Such a provision eliminates the risk that an insurer, by issuing a claims-made policy, would assume liability arising from incidents that occurred before the policy's effective date, but remained undiscovered or caused no immediate harm. Third, CGL insurance had traditionally covered "sudden and accidental" pollution; the defendants wanted to eliminate that coverage.

Finally, CGL insurance has traditionally provided that the insurer would bear the legal costs of defending covered claims against the insured without regard to the policy's stated limits of coverage; the defendants wanted legal defense costs to be counted against the stated limits (providing a "legal defense cost cap").

To understand how the defendants are alleged to have pressured the targeted primary insurers to make these changes, one must be aware of two important features of the insurance industry. First, most primary insurers rely on certain outside support services for the type of insurance coverage they wish to sell. Defendant Insurance Services Office, Inc. (ISO), an association of approximately 1400 domestic property and casualty insurers (including the primary insurer defendants, Hartford Fire Insurance Company, Allstate Insurance Company, CIGNA Corporation, and Aetna Casualty and Surety Company), is the almost exclusive source of support services in this country for CGL insurance. ISO develops standard policy forms and files or lodges them with each State's insurance regulators; most CGL insurance written in the United States is written on these forms. All of the "traditional" features of CGL insurance relevant to this case were embodied in the ISO standard CGL insurance form that had been in use since 1973 (1973 ISO CGL form). For each of its standard policy forms, ISO also supplies actuarial and rating information: it collects, aggregates, interprets, and distributes data on the premiums charged, claims filed and paid, and defense costs expended with respect to each form, and on the basis of this data it predicts future loss trends and calculates advisory premium rates. Most ISO members cannot afford to continue to use a form if ISO withdraws these support services.

Second, primary insurers themselves usually purchase insurance to cover a portion of the risk they assume from the consumer. This so-called "reinsurance" may serve at least two purposes, protecting the primary insurer from catastrophic loss, and allowing the primary insurer to sell more insurance than its own financial capacity might otherwise permit. Thus, "[t]he availability of reinsurance affects the ability and willingness of primary insurers to provide insurance to their customers." Insurers who sell reinsurance themselves often purchase insurance to cover part of the risk they assume from the primary insurer; such "retrocessional reinsurance" does for reinsurers what reinsurance does for primary insurers. Many of the defendants here are reinsurers or reinsurance brokers, or play some other specialized role in the reinsurance business; defendant Reinsurance Association of America (RAA) is a trade association of domestic reinsurers.

B

The prehistory of events claimed to give rise to liability starts in 1977, when ISO began the process of revising its 1973 CGL form. For the first time, it proposed two CGL forms (1984 ISO CGL forms), one the traditional "occurrence" type, the other "with a new 'claims-made' trigger." The "claims-made" form did not have a retroactive date provision, however, and both 1984 forms covered "'sudden and accidental' pollution" damage and provided for unlimited coverage of legal defense costs by the insurer. Within the ISO, defendant Hartford Fire Insurance Company objected to the proposed 1984 forms; it desired elimination of the "occurrence" form, a retroactive date provision on the "claims-made" form, elimination of sudden and accidental pollution coverage, and a legal defense cost cap. Defendant Allstate Insurance Company also expressed its desire for a retroactive date provision on the "claims-made" form. Majorities in the relevant ISO committees, however, supported the proposed 1984 CGL forms and rejected the changes proposed by Hartford and Allstate. In December 1983, the ISO Board of Directors approved the proposed 1984 forms, and ISO filed or lodged the forms with state regulators in March 1984.

Dissatisfied with this state of affairs, the defendants began to take other steps to force a change in the terms of coverage of CGL insurance generally available, steps that, the plaintiffs allege, implemented a series of conspiracies in violation of § 1 of the Sherman Act. * * *

The first four Claims for Relief of the California Complaint and the Second Claim for Relief of the Connecticut Complaint, charge the four domestic primary insurer defendants and varying groups of domestic and foreign reinsurers, brokers, and associations with conspiracies to manipulate the ISO CGL forms. In March 1984, primary insurer Hartford persuaded General Reinsurance Corporation (General Re), the largest American reinsurer, to take steps either to procure desired changes in the ISO CGL forms, or "failing that, [to] 'derail' the entire ISO CGL forms program." General Re took up the matter with its trade association, RAA, which created a special committee that met and agreed to "boycott" the 1984 ISO CGL forms unless a retroactive-date provision was added to the claims-made form, and a pollution exclusion and defense cost cap were added to both forms. RAA then sent a letter to ISO "announc[ing] that its members would not provide reinsurance for coverages written on the 1984 CGL forms," and Hartford and General Re enlisted a domestic reinsurance broker to give a speech to the ISO Board of Directors, in which he stated that no reinsurers would "break ranks" to reinsure the 1984 ISO CGL forms.

The four primary insurer defendants (Hartford, Aetna, CIGNA, and Allstate) also encouraged key actors in the London reinsurance market, an important provider of reinsurance for North American risks, to withhold reinsurance for coverages written on the 1984 ISO CGL forms. As a consequence, many London-based underwriters, syndicates, brokers, and reinsurance companies informed ISO of their intention to withhold reinsurance on the 1984 forms and at least some of them told ISO that they would withhold reinsurance until ISO incorporated all four desired changes.

For the first time ever, ISO invited representatives of the domestic and foreign reinsurance markets to speak at an ISO Executive Committee meeting. At that meeting, the reinsurers "presented their agreed upon positions that there would be changes in the CGL forms or no reinsurance." The ISO Executive Committee then voted to include a retroactive-date provision in the claims-made form, and to exclude all pollution coverage from both new forms. (But it neither eliminated the occurrence form, nor added a legal defense cost cap.) The 1984 ISO CGL forms were then withdrawn from the marketplace, and replaced with forms (1986 ISO CGL forms) containing the new provisions. After ISO got regulatory approval of the 1986 forms in most States where approval was needed, it eliminated its support services for the 1973 CGL form, thus rendering it impossible for most ISO members to continue to use the form.

The Complaints also charge a conspiracy among a group of London reinsurers and brokers to coerce primary insurers in the United States to offer CGL coverage only on a claims-made basis. The reinsurers collectively refused to write new reinsurance contracts for, or to renew long-standing contracts with, "primary * * * insurers unless they were prepared to switch from the occurrence to the claims-made form," they also amended their reinsurance contracts to cover only claims made before a " 'sunset date,' " thus eliminating reinsurance for claims made on occurrence policies after that date.

The Complaints charge another conspiracy among a somewhat different group of London reinsurers to withhold reinsurance for pollution coverage. The London reinsurers met and agreed that all reinsurance contracts covering North American casualty risks, including CGL risks, would be written with a complete exclusion for pollution liability coverage. In accordance with this agreement, the parties have in fact excluded pollution liability coverage from CGL reinsurance contracts since at least late 1985. * * *

C

Nineteen States and a number of private plaintiffs filed 36 complaints against the insurers involved in this course of events, charging that the conspiracies described above violated § 1 of the Sherman Act, 15 U.S.C. § 1. After the actions had been consolidated for litigation in the Northern District of California, the defendants moved to dismiss for failure to state a cause of action, or, in the alternative, for summary judgment. The District Court granted the motions to dismiss. *In re Insurance Antitrust Litigation*, 723 F.Supp. 464 (1989). It held that the conduct alleged fell within the grant of antitrust immunity contained in § 2(b) of the McCarran-Ferguson Act, 15 U.S.C. § 1012(b), because it amounted to "the business of insurance" and was "regulated by State law" within the meaning of that section; none of the conduct, in the District Court's view, amounted to a "boycott" within the meaning of the § 3(b) exception to that grant of immunity. 15 U.S.C. § 1013(b). * * *

[The Court of Appeals for the 9th Circuit reversed, on the ground (among others) that the behavior alleged constituted a "boycott" under the McCarran-Ferguson Act.]

■ JUSTICE SCALIA delivered the opinion of the Court [with respect to what follows].

I

Determining proper application of § 3(b) of the McCarran-Ferguson Act to the present case requires precise definition of the word "boycott." It is a relatively new word, little more than a century old. It was first used in 1880, to describe the collective action taken against Captain Charles Boycott, an English agent managing various estates in Ireland. The Land League, an Irish organization formed the previous year, had demanded that landlords reduce their rents and had urged tenants to avoid dealing with those who failed to do so. Boycott did not bend to the demand and instead ordered evictions. In retaliation, * * * "The population of the region for miles round resolved not to have anything to do with him, and, as far as they could prevent it, not to allow any one else to have anything to do with him." * * * Thus, the verb made from the unfortunate Captain's name has had from the outset the meaning it continues to carry today. To "boycott" means "[t]o combine in refusing to hold relations of any kind, social or commercial, public or private, with (a neighbor), on account of political or other differences, so as to punish him for the position he has taken up, or coerce him into abandoning it." 2 The Oxford English Dictionary 468 (2nd ed. 1989).

Petitioners have suggested that a boycott ordinarily requires "an absolute refusal to deal on any terms," which was concededly not the case here. We think not. As the definition just recited provides, the refusal may be imposed "to punish [the target] for the position he has taken up, or *coerce him into abandoning it.*" The refusal to deal may, in other words, be *conditional*, offering its target the incentive of renewed dealing if and when he mends his ways. This is often the case—and indeed seems to have been the case with the original Boycott boycott. * * *

It is, however, important—and crucial in the present case—to distinguish between a conditional boycott and a concerted agreement to seek particular terms in particular transactions. A concerted agreement to terms (a "cartelization") is "a way of obtaining and exercising market power by concertedly exacting terms like those which a monopolist might exact." L. Sullivan, Law of Antitrust 257 (1977). The parties to such an agreement (the members of a cartel) are not engaging in a boycott, because:

> "They are not coercing anyone, at least in the usual sense of that word; they are merely (though concertedly) saying *'we will deal with you only on the following trade terms.'* * * * Indeed, if a concerted agreement, say, to include a security deposit in all contracts is a 'boycott' because it excludes all buyers who won't agree to it, then by parity of reasoning every price fixing agreement would be a boycott also. The use of the single concept, boycott, to cover agreements so varied in nature can only add to confusion." *Ibid.* (emphasis added).

Thus, if Captain Boycott's tenants had agreed among themselves that they would refuse to renew their leases unless he reduced his rents, that would have been a concerted agreement on the terms of the leases, but not a boycott. The tenants, of course, did more than that; they refused to engage in other, unrelated transactions with Boycott—e.g., selling him food—unless he agreed to their terms on rents. It is this expansion of the refusal to deal beyond the targeted transaction that gives great coercive force to a commercial boycott: related transactions are used as leverage to achieve the terms desired. * * *

Of course as far as the Sherman Act (outside the exempted insurance field) is concerned, concerted agreements on contract terms are as unlawful as boycotts. * * * These sorts of concerted actions, similar to what is alleged to have occurred here, are not properly characterized as "boycotts," and the word does not appear in the opinions. In fact, in the 65 years between the coining of the word and enactment of the McCarran-Ferguson Act in 1945, "boycott" appears in only seven opinions of this Court involving commercial (nonlabor) antitrust matters, and *not once* is it used as Justice SOUTER uses it—to describe a concerted refusal to engage in particular transactions until the terms of those transactions are agreeable. * * *

The one case in which we have found an activity to constitute a "boycott" within the meaning of the McCarran-Ferguson Act is *St. Paul Fire & Marine Ins. Co. v. Barry*, 438 U.S. 531 (1978). There the plaintiffs were licensed physicians and their patients, and the defendant (St. Paul) was a malpractice insurer that had refused to renew the physicians' policies on an "occurrence" basis, but insisted upon a "claims made" basis. The allegation was that, at the instance of St. Paul, the three other malpractice insurers in the State had collectively refused to write insurance for St. Paul customers, thus forcing them to accept St. Paul's renewal terms. Unsurprisingly, we held the allegation sufficient to state a cause of action. The insisted-upon condition of the boycott (not being a former St. Paul policyholder) was "artificial": it bore no relationship (or an "artificial" relationship) to the proposed contracts of insurance that the physicians wished to conclude with St. Paul's competitors. * * *

Under the test set forth above, there are sufficient allegations of a "boycott" to sustain the relevant counts of complaint against a motion to dismiss. For example, the complaints allege that some of the defendant reinsurers threatened to "withdra[w] entirely from the business of reinsuring primary U.S. insurers who wrote on the occurrence form." Construed most favorably to the respondents, that allegation claims that primary insurers who wrote insurance on disfavored forms would be refused all reinsurance, *even* as to risks written on *other forms*. If that were the case, the reinsurers might have been engaging in a boycott—they would, that is, unless the primary insurers' other business were relevant to the proposed reinsurance contract (for example, if the reinsurer bears greater risk where the primary insurer engages in riskier businesses). Cf. Gonye, Underwriting the Reinsured, in Reinsurance 439, 463–466 (R. Strain ed. 1980); 2 R. Reinarz, J. Schloss, G. Patrik, & P. Kensicki, Reinsurance Practices 21–23 (1990) (same). Other allegations in the complaints could be similarly construed. For example, the complaints also allege that the reinsurers "threatened a boycott of North American CGL risks," not just CGL risks containing dissatisfactory terms; that the "foreign and domestic reinsurer representatives presented their agreed upon positions that there would be changes in the CGL forms or no reinsurance"; that some of the defendant insurers and reinsurers told "groups of insurance brokers and agents * * * that a reinsurance boycott, and thus loss of income to the agents and brokers who would be unable to find available markets for their customers, would ensue if the [revised] ISO forms were not approved."

Many other allegations in the complaints describe conduct that may amount to a boycott if the plaintiffs can prove certain additional facts. For example, General Re, the largest American reinsurer, is alleged to have "agreed to either coerce ISO to adopt [the defendants'] demands or, failing that, 'derail' the entire CGL forms program." If this means that General Re intended to withhold all reinsurance on all CGL forms—even forms having no objectionable terms—that might amount to a "boycott." Also, General Re and several other domestic reinsurers are alleged to have "agreed to boycott the 1984 ISO forms unless a retroactive date was added to the claims made form, and a pollution exclusion and a defense cost cap were added to both [the occurrence and claims made] forms." Liberally construed, this allegation may mean that the defendants had linked their demands so that they would continue to refuse to do business on *either* form until *both* were changed to their liking. Again, that might amount to a boycott. "[A] complaint should not be dismissed unless it appears beyond doubt that the plaintiff can prove no set of facts in support of his claim which would entitled him to relief."

[The Court affirmed the Court of Appeals in part and reversed in part, remanding for further proceedings consistent with its opinions.]

NOTES AND QUESTIONS

1. *Settlement.* On remand, the case was settled before trial. Defendant ISO agreed to change the composition of its Board of Directors to avoid exclusive control by insurers, and the other defendants agreed to a $36 million program to inform business, government, and municipalities about rates, coverage, and risk management programs. See Wall Street Journal, October 7, 1994, page A–2.

2. *"Boycott."* Is it fair to say that according to *Hartford Fire*, every concerted refusal to deal on any terms is a boycott, but that a concerted refusal to deal on specified terms may or may not be a boycott? If this statement is correct, when is the latter a boycott?

3. *The Rationale for the Alleged Conspiracy.* The concern that lies behind Section 3(b) is that boycotts, coercion, or intimidation may have anticompetitive effects. Is there an anticompetitive explanation for the defendants' alleged behavior that goes beyond the need to cooperate in policy preparation that is implicitly permitted by the McCarran-Ferguson Act? How would you evaluate the following arguments?

    a. The defendants were attempting to gain a competitive advantage over their rivals by forcing the adoption of a policy form over which the defendants had a comparative advantage. For example, large insurers such as the defendants can afford the startup costs of marketing a new policy more than the defendants' smaller competitors. See Ian Ayers & Peter Siegelman, The Economics of the Insurance Antitrust Suits: Toward an Exclusionary Theory, 63 Tulane L. Rev. 971, 998–91 (1989). For an opposing view, see George L. Priest, The Antitrust Suits and the Public Understanding of Insurance, 63 Tulane L. Rev. 999 (1989).

    b. The cutthroat competition of the early 1980s kept premiums extremely low—perhaps lower than was economically sensible. This experience caused the defendants concern that there would be continued competition of this sort that would force the defendants to lose their shares of the market unless they priced below their own costs. The cause of this irrational pricing was small companies' underestimation of the threat of long-tail liabilities, such as pollution-related liability, that they faced under the existing occurrence policy. In order to prevent their competitors from engaging in this kind of suicidal price competition in the future, the defendants agreed to the alleged "boycott," which would have limited coverage of long-tail liabilities if the boycott had succeeded.

4. *Fallout.* At about the same time that the state antitrust actions were brewing, several Bills were introduced in Congress proposing repeal or limitation of the McCarran-Ferguson Act exemption of the insurance industry from federal antitrust prohibitions. A major focus of discussion was the role played by the Insurance Services Office in the preparation of advisory premium rates. These rates had been available for use by insurance companies, and ISO had filed them on behalf of participating insurers in certain states. Insurers could then simply inform state regulators that they subscribed to ISO Advisory Rates or indicate the points at which they planned to deviate from these rates. The obvious concern with this practice was its potential for limiting price competition among insurers. Although use of ISO rates was not mandatory, their availability as a focal point for price increases was cause for speculation about the possibility of price fixing by insurers. In addition, the antitrust exemption for the industry's rate preparation process was a public relations disadvantage.

Apparently in reaction to criticism from all these quarters, the Insurance Services Office ceased preparing advisory premium rates in 1990. ISO continued, however, to make available what it called "advisory prospective loss costs"—estimates of future loss payments line-by-line and state-by-state, but without the previously included calculations of insurers' marketing and overhead expenses or underwriting profit and contingencies that were built into rates themselves. See Gregory Krohm, Implications of ISO's Change to Lost Cost Filing for Rate Regulation, 8 J. of Ins. Regulation 316 (1990).

5. *Seeing Both the Forest and the Trees.* Remember that the McCarran-Ferguson exemptions apply only to *federal* antitrust prohibitions that would otherwise apply to the business of insurance. The Act does nothing to limit the application of *state* antitrust law to the business of insurance. Most states have general purpose antitrust laws on their books, meaning that the insurance industry's joint activities are subject to state antitrust scrutiny, except to the extent that the states themselves have enacted their own exemptions from these prohibitions. Several states do indeed have specific authorizations for insurers to participate in rate service organizations such as the ISO. See, e.g., Va. Ann. Code § 38.2–1908. But any state that was unsatisfied with the scope of the McCarran-Ferguson exemptions, or with the interpretations placed on the reach of the boycott exception by the Federal courts, certainly would have the power to prohibit by statute these activities, subject of course to the limitations of geographic jurisdiction.

3. FEDERAL ROLE IN CATASTROPHE INSURANCE

Private insurers often have difficulty providing a reliable source of catastrophe insurance. The reason is that catastrophe insurance, by definition, involves the risk of highly-correlated losses. Recall from Chapter One that such risks cannot be easily smoothed via the ordinary mechanisms of risk pooling. See generally Dwight Jaffee, Catastrophe Insurance, in The Law and Economics of Insurance (Daniel Schwarcz & Peter Siegelman eds., 2015). Additionally, in some catastrophe insurance contexts, it can be very difficult to develop reliable actuarial models of risk because losses are infrequent and risks are changing. As a result, the federal government has come to play a vital role in supporting a variety of catastrophe insurance markets. The two most important such markets involve flood and terrorism insurance.

As we will see in Chapter Four, most property insurance policies exclude losses associated with flooding. In 1968, the federal government responded to the lack of private flood insurance by passing the National Flood Insurance Act (NFIA), 42 U.S.C. § 4001 *et seq.* Under NFIA, the federal government provides flood insurance to individuals in communities that agree to comply with zoning standards and construction limitations designed to limit flood losses. The Federal Emergency Management Agency (FEMA) administers the Act by setting premiums and mapping and updating flood zones. Historically, flood insurance rates have been substantially below actuarial value, particularly for preexisting, high-risk structures. As a result, the program has experienced adverse selection and budgetary problems.

After Hurricane Sandy pushed the federal flood insurance program $18 billion into debt, Congress passed the Biggert-Waters Flood Insurance Reform Act of 2012. The principal goal of Biggert-Waters was to significantly reduce subsidized flood insurance. Under the Act, subsidies for properties that experienced severe repetitive losses would be eliminated with premium increases of up to 25% a year. Newly purchased properties and properties with new or lapsed policies would lose their subsidies completely. In short order, these changes produced massive political backlash. Many homeowners saw their flood insurance premiums skyrocket, and even more saw their property values decrease substantially. In 2014, Congress effectively repealed many elements of Biggert-Waters with The Homeowner Flood Insurance Affordability Act. See Federal Emergency Management Agency, Homeowner Flood Insurance Affordability Act: Overview (2014). The 2014 Act reinstates the subsidies for property that had been sold to a new owner or that had a lapsed flood insurance policy. It also limits the average price increase for any class of properties to 15%, and with limited exceptions it caps increases for any individual property to 18% a year. As of 2014, the federal flood insurance program had accumulated $24 billion in debt, prompting increased efforts to promote private sector involvement in flood insurance markets. U.S. Gov't Accountability Office, GAO–14–127, Flood Insurance: Strategies for Increasing Private Sector Involvement (2014).

A second major federal catastrophe program involves terrorism insurance. Prior to 9/11, few insurance policies specifically excluded losses from terrorist attacks. Insured losses from 9/11 would ultimately amount to almost $40 billion, spanning property, business interruption, aviation, workers' compensation, and life and liability insurance claim costs. Almost immediately after the attacks, private insurers in many coverage lines explicitly excluded from coverage all losses stemming from terrorist attacks. This, in turn, had substantial spill-over effects on the real economy, undermining commercial building projects and impeding the ability of employers to secure workers' compensation coverage. In response, Congress passed the Terrorism Risk Insurance Act of 2002 (TRIA), 15 U.S.C. § 6701.

Unlike flood insurance, the federal government did not attempt to create a program to sell terrorism insurance directly to policyholders. Instead, TRIA requires private insurance companies to offer terrorism insurance, but it provides that the federal government will reinsure this risk. Insurers must offer terrorism insurance on the same terms on which they offer other coverage, which means that standard exclusions for, for instance, nuclear, chemical, and biological weapons still apply to terrorism insurance. See Michelle E. Boardman, Known Unknowns: The Illusion of Terrorism Insurance, 93 Geo. L. J. 783 (2005). TRIA was initially designed as a short-time program, but it has been reauthorized by Congress several times. As designed in 2002, the federal government would cover 90% of losses exceeding a deductible, up to a total of $100 billion. Both the size of the deductible and the percentage of the government's coverage above the deductible have been altered by Congress each time that it has reauthorized the Act. Many credit TRIA with making terrorism insurance broadly available. Others criticize the Act because it provides private insurers with federal reinsurance without charging upfront premiums for this protection. However, TRIA does contain a "recoupment" procedure, whereby federal outlays can be recovered after a loss by taxes on insurers.

NOTES AND QUESTIONS

1. *Reinsurance vs. Direct Sale of Catastrophe Insurance.* TRIA and the federal flood insurance program use very different approaches to facilitate the sale of catastrophe insurance. Many commentators have argued that the reinsurance approach contained within TRIA is favorable to the approach of the federal flood insurance program. See, e.g., Jeffrey Manns, Insuring Against Terror?, 112 Yale L.J. 2509 (2003); J. David Cummins, Should the Government Provide Insurance for Catastrophes?, 88 Fed. Res. Bank of St. Louis Rev. 337 (2006). One of the main benefits of a reinsurance mechanism is that it allows private insurers to price the underlying coverage, rather than relying on the government to set rates. What difficulties do you think the government faces in setting actuarially-fair catastrophe insurance premiums? How does the experience of the federal flood insurance program illustrate these difficulties?

2. *TRIA as Corporate Welfare?* Some critics have alleged that TRIA amounts to "corporate welfare" because it provides federal reinsurance to insurers without charging upfront premiums. See Robert J. Rhee, The Terrorism Risk Insurance Act: Time to End the Corporate Welfare, Cato Institute (2013). What obstacles would the federal government face in setting premiums for terrorism reinsurance? Why might critics of TRIA not be fully satisfied by TRIA's recoupment procedure? How does the fact that no claim has ever been paid under TRIA influence your answers to these questions?

3. *Difficulties in Supplying Catastrophe Insurance.* Why should the fact that losses are highly correlated in catastrophe insurance lines mean that private insurers cannot provide this coverage? After all, the solution to this problem is simply to spread risk across time rather than across policyholders. In other words, highly correlated losses can be made relatively predictable if a long-enough time frame is used to assess these risks. The answer is that insurers face a variety of accounting, tax, regulatory, and corporate governance impediments to holding enough liquid capital to consistently maintain a sufficiently reliable capacity to pay for substantial catastrophe risks. See Dwight M. Jaffe & Thomas Russell, Catastrophe Insurance, Capital Markets, and Uninsurable Risks, 64 J. of Risk & Ins. 205 (1997).

4. *Demand Problems with Catastrophe Insurance.* Another problem facing catastrophe insurance markets is low consumer demand for such coverage. This phenomenon is difficult to explain from an economic perspective, because catastrophe insurance (being a low-probability, but high-consequence, risk) should be particularly desirable within the standard risk-aversion framework. Instead, the most sensible explanation for low demand for catastrophe insurance involves certain behavioral biases and heuristics that cause individuals to make decisions that are not always in their own best interest. For instance, evidence suggests that individuals underestimate the probability that they will experience a catastrophic event and tend to employ a "sequential" approach to insurance, whereby they refuse to even consider insurance once the probability of loss is perceived to be below some threshold level of concern. See generally Howard Kunruether & Mark Pauly, Rules Rather than Discretion: Lessons from Hurricane Katrina, 33 J. of Risk & Uncertainty 101 (2006). How might government programs or insurance regulation respond to such demand-side problems for catastrophe insurance? What do you make of proposals to mandate that homeowners insurance policies include flood insurance? Alternatively, how might selling catastrophe insurance in 5 or 10-year blocks instead of a single year help respond to limited consumer demand for such coverage?

4. FEDERAL REGULATION OF INSURANCE AFTER THE DODD-FRANK ACT

Numerous types of financial institutions and markets played an important role in the 2008 financial crisis. This includes various insurance companies and financial conglomerates predominantly engaged in the business of insurance. Largely as a result, the federal government substantially increased its role in the regulation and oversight of insurance markets in the Dodd-Frank Wall Street Reform and Consumer Protection Act ("Dodd-Frank"), 12 U.S.C. 5311 *et seq.* In order to understand the core insurance provisions of Dodd-Frank, it is first necessary to appreciate the poster-child for insurers' involvement in the 2008 financial crisis, the global financial services conglomerate American International Group (AIG).

a. THE AIG BAILOUT

In the Fall of 2008, arms of the U.S. government injected approximately $180 billion of capital into AIG in order to limit the prospect that the company's failure could substantially exacerbate national and international financial instability. The AIG rescue remains the largest bailout of a private company in history. There were at least two principal causes of AIG's near-failure: its portfolio of Credit Default Swaps ("CDS") and its securities lending operations.

The first, and more widely emphasized, explanation for AIG's financial trouble centers on the CDS operations of one of its many subsidiary companies, AIG Financial Products ("AIGFP"). Unlike many of AIG's subsidiary companies, AIGFP was not itself a regulated insurance company. It was consequently not subject to any of the state regulatory rules described at the start of this Chapter. Yet AIGFP sold to other major financial institutions CDSs that substantially resembled insurance. Under a CDS, a protection purchaser (i.e. policyholder) makes an initial payment (i.e. premium) to the protection seller (i.e. insurer). In exchange, the protection seller promises to pay the purchaser if a specific financial instrument experiences a default or credit event (i.e. if a loss occurs). Most of the CDSs sold by AIGFP insured other major financial institutions against decreases in the value of Residential Mortgage Backed Securities ("RMBSs"), Collateralized Debt Obligations ("CDOs"), and similar financial instruments. The value of all of these insured financial instruments were ultimately tied to mortgage payments from homeowners.

In the years leading up to 2008, AIGFP wrote a tremendous volume of these CDSs, generating massive profits in the process. AIGFP was able to accomplish this because none of the financial instruments it insured via its CDSs had defaulted to that point. Moreover, AIGFP's internal models suggested that it was virtually impossible for the insured financial instruments to default in the future because housing prices could not simultaneously decrease across the entire country. For this reason, AIGFP did not maintain reserves for any expected losses, effectively treating the payments it received for selling CDSs as pure profit. AIGFP's models, of course, proved disastrously wrong: as the financial crisis evolved, most of the financial instruments that it insured via its CDSs defaulted or approached default. Virtually overnight, AIGFP and its parent company, AIG, were forced either to pay claims on almost all of the CDSs or to prove that they could do so by posting collateral.

A second, equally important though often underemphasized, explanation for AIG's near-failure was its securities lending program. In a securities lending transaction, an insurer lends out its securities to other financial firms on a short-term basis. The borrowing firms use these securities for a variety of purposes, such as betting that the price of the security will decrease. These borrowing firms provide the lender-insurer with cash collateral that protects the lender from the prospect that the borrowed securities will not be returned when they are due. In general, securities loans are extremely short term—a single day, typically—though they are routinely "rolled over" each day. Insurer-lenders make money from this arrangement predominantly by reinvesting the cash collateral they receive from the borrower.

Through a series of transactions among its many affiliated companies, AIG consolidated the securities lending operations of its many insurance companies into a single program. In the years leading up to 2008, AIG then adopted an extremely aggressive approach to reinvesting the cash collateral it received from its securities borrowers. In particular, it invested this cash into the very same types of real estate backed financial products that AIGFP had insured through its CDSs. As AIG began experiencing substantial stresses throughout 2007 and 2008, the financial institutions that had borrowed securities from AIG became increasingly concerned that AIG would be unable to return their cash collateral. In September 2008, these borrowers of AIG's securities ended their borrowing en masse and demanded the return of their cash collateral. AIG could not meet these demands because it had invested the cash collateral in the ill-fated mortgage backed securities that were simultaneously triggering its CDS obligations. No one, at that time, was willing to purchase these instruments, meaning that AIG could not sell them to pay back its borrowers' collateral. See Hester Peirce, Securities Lending and the Untold Story in the Collapse of AIG (George Mason Univ. Marcatus Ctr., Working Paper 14–12 (2014)) available at http://mercatus.org/publication/securities-lending-and-untold-story-collapse-aig.

These two explanations for AIG's near-failure in 2008 have very different implications for the blameworthiness of state insurance regulation. On one hand, it is very difficult to blame state insurance regulators for AIGFP's CDS operations or their impact on AIG itself. Neither AIG nor AIGFP were insurance companies and consequently neither one was regulated by state insurance departments. On the other hand, AIG's securities lending problems do seem to reflect issues with state insurance regulation. The securities that AIG had lent out to counterparties were predominantly the assets of its insurance companies. If AIG had not recovered these assets because it could not pay back borrowers' cash collateral, then the solvency of these AIG insurance companies could have been substantially imperiled. Yet, according to a report of the General Accountability Office, "prior to mid-2007, state regulators had not identified losses in the securities lending program and the lead life insurance regulator had reviewed the program without major concerns." U.S. Gov't Accountability Office, GAO–11–616, Financial Crises: Review of Federal Reserve System Financial Assistance to American International Group, Inc. (2011).

NOTES AND QUESTIONS

1. *Group Supervision in Insurance.* All of the state regulatory tools described at the start of this Chapter are applied individually to each individual insurance entity. But most insurance groups operate numerous individual insurance entities, each of which is separately regulated for solvency by its domestic regulator. Since the crisis, improving supervision of insurance groups has been a major topic for regulatory reform, particularly at the international level. State regulators have also moved to enhance group supervision. For instance, they will soon start requiring insurance groups to submit "Own-Risk Solvency Assessments," or ORSAs, that assess an insurer's risk at the group level.

2. *Explanation for AIG's Securities Lending Problems.* To what extent might the fragmented nature of state insurance regulation have been responsible for the failure of state insurance regulators to identify the risks of AIG's securities lending operations? Recall that AIG had

consolidated the securities lending of all its different insurers into a single, immensely complicated, centrally run program. How much incentive would any single state insurance regulator supervising one of dozens of individual AIG companies have had to delve deeply into this program? See Daniel Schwarcz, Consolidated Regulation in Insurance, 5 U. Cal. Irv. L. Rev. (2015).

3. *Other Insurers' Involvement in the 2008 Financial Crisis.* AIG was not the only insurer implicated in the 2008 Financial Crisis. Another set of insurers that played an important role in the crisis were "financial guarantee" insurers. These insurers sold state-regulated insurance against the risk that certain financial products would default. This coverage was typically bought by public entities—such as municipalities and schools—to insure the risk that the securities they issued would default. This helped increase investor interest in these securities, and thus helped fund them. In the years leading up to the crisis, however, financial guarantee insurers also began to insure less traditional financial products, including the very same mortgage-backed securities that were at the heart of AIG's failure. As the crisis wore on, investors came to believe that financial guarantee insurers could not be counted on to pay their claims due to their heavy losses from their portfolio of insurance against the default of mortgage-backed securities. This, in turn, completely undermined the capacity of many public entities to issue securities and secure funding because they could no long offer investors financial guarantee insurance on their obligations. See Fed. Ins. Office, How to Modernize and Improve the System of Insurance Regulation in the United States 19–20 (2013).

Several large life insurers other than AIG also experienced substantial distress during the financial crisis. Two life insurance companies—Lincoln Financial and The Hartford—received federal bailout funds, and many more applied for such funds but later declined them. In part, these problems were the result of the fact that many life insurers other than AIG had also invested in mortgage-backed securities and related instruments. Life insurers that had promised policyholders guaranteed lifetime benefits faced additional stress because regulatory rules forced them to increase their reserves for these promises as a result of declines in stock prices. At the same time, remarkably few insurers actually failed during the financial crisis, and they also rebounded quite quickly from the crisis. See U.S. Gov't Accountability Office, GAO–13–583, Insurance Markets: Impacts of and Regulatory Response to the 2007–2009 Financial Crisis (2013); see also Jeffrey E. Thomas, Insurance Perspectives on Federal Financial Regulatory Reform: Addressing Misunderstandings and Providing a View From a Different Paradigm, 55 Vill. L. Rev. 773 (2010) (arguing that "insurance was not involved in the financial crisis" because "AIG's collapse was not an insurance failure").

b. DODD-FRANK'S INSURANCE REFORMS

Dodd-Frank substantially transformed financial regulation in the United States. See generally Patricia A. McCoy, Systemic Risk Oversight and the Shifting Balance of State and Federal Authority Over Insurance, 5 U. Cal. Irv. L. Rev. (2015). Not surprisingly given AIG's prominence in the crisis, among these sweeping reforms were some important changes in the federal government's role in insurance regulation and oversight. First, the Act subjects certain insurance-focused holding companies to group regulation by the Federal Reserve Bank ("Fed"). These include insurance-focused companies that own a bank or other type of depository institution and insurance-focused companies that are determined to be "systemically risky" by a super-council of financial regulators known as the Financial Stability Oversight Council ("FSOC"). As of 2014, three insurance-focused companies—AIG, Prudential, and Metlife—have been designated by FSOC as Systemically Important Financial Institutions (SIFIs).

Although the Fed will now play a crucial role in the regulation of insurance-focused holding companies, the impact this will have on the insurance industry is still very unclear. As of the summer of 2014, the Fed has not issued regulations explaining exactly how it will conduct its group supervision of insurance-focused entities. Dodd-Frank itself gives the Fed broad discretion in this regard. Many insurance companies have raised substantial concerns that they will be subject to bank-like regulation that does not recognize the fact that insurance is less systemically risky than banking and subject to different types of risks.

The other key insurance-oriented reform in Dodd-Frank was the establishment of the Federal Insurance Office ("FIO") within the U.S. Treasury Department. FIO does not have any regulatory powers. Instead, Dodd-Frank tasks FIO with "[m]onitor[ing] all aspects of the insurance industry, including identifying issues or gaps in the regulation of insurers that could contribute to a systemic crisis in the insurance industry or the United States financial system." It makes the FIO director a non-voting member of FSOC and tasks FIO with representing the U.S. in international fora. In furtherance of these objectives, Dodd-Frank required FIO to produce a report on how to "modernize and improve the system of insurance regulation in the United States." In late 2013, FIO published this report after a lengthy delay.

Federal Insurance Office, How to Modernize and Improve the System of Insurance Regulation in the United States (2013)

* * * For over a century, the debate over reform of insurance regulation in the United States has focused largely on the practical and legal limitations of the state-based insurance regulatory system. The absence of uniformity in the U.S. insurance regulatory system creates inefficiencies and burdens for consumers, insurers, and the international community. For example, per dollar of premium, the costs of the state-based insurance regulatory system are approximately 6.8 times greater for an insurer operating in the United States than for an insurer operating in the United Kingdom, and increase costs for P/C insurers by $7.2 billion annually and for life insurers by $5.7 billion annually.[1] The need for uniformity and the realities of globally active, diversified financial firms compel the conclusion that federal involvement of some kind in insurance regulation is necessary. Regulation at the federal level would improve uniformity, efficiency, and consistency, and it would address concerns with uniform supervision of insurance firms with national and global activities.

---

[1] McKinsey & Company, "Improving Property and Casualty Insurance Regulation In the United States," (April 2009).

The increasingly international dimension of the insurance marketplace, in and of itself, is also an important consideration. U.S. firms are not the only ones with a global reach. Non-U.S. firms have significantly expanded market share around the world, including in the U.S. direct and reinsurance markets, a trend that likely will continue because of the size of the U.S. insurance market. Insurance regulatory issues will increasingly require international attention and cooperation. The federal government's predominant role in foreign affairs is one reason for the necessity of a federal presence in insurance regulation. It would be much less costly, much less prone to arbitrage, and much easier to negotiate internationally for more efficient and effective oversight of the insurance sector if U.S. insurance regulation had greater uniformity and predictability.

The limitations inherent in a state-based system of insurance regulation, however, do not necessarily imply that the ideal solution would be for the federal government to displace state regulation completely. The business of insurance involves offering many products that are tailored for and delivered at a local level. For the most part, effective delivery of the product will require local knowledge and relationships, and local regulation. Moreover, establishing a new federal agency to regulate all or part of the $7.3 trillion insurance sector would be a significant undertaking. The personnel, resources, and institutional expertise needed to execute such an endeavor at a professional and rigorous level would, of necessity, require an unequivocal commitment from the legislative and executive branches of the U.S. government.

In light of these considerations, this Report concludes that the proper formulation of the debate at present is not whether insurance regulation should be state or federal, but whether there are areas in which federal involvement in regulation under the state-based system is warranted. Reframed in this manner, the basic question with respect to reforming any aspect of insurance should be whether federal involvement is warranted at this time and, if so, in what areas. The necessity for federal involvement should depend on assessment of questions such as whether states can take measures to regulate effectively and with uniformity, the degree of the national or federal interest, and the nexus of the issues and the firms with the global marketplace.

If the answer to the first inquiry is that federal involvement is warranted, the inquiry then turns to what kind of federal involvement would best provide for attaining the policy objectives. Federal involvement can take many forms, ranging from direct regulation to standard-setting or operating a program that supports or replaces an otherwise failed insurance market. In all events, federal involvement should be targeted to areas in which that involvement would solve problems resulting from the legal and practical limitations of regulation by states, such as the need for uniformity or the need for a federal voice in U.S. interactions with international authorities.

In light of the foregoing, FIO believes that, in the short term, the U.S. system of insurance regulation can be modernized and improved by a combination of steps by the states and certain actions by the federal government. * * *

Potential Federal Solutions to States' Failure to Modernize and Improve

As detailed further in this Report, many of the areas for which FIO recommends that there be reform of the state regulatory system relate to subject matter areas in which the states already have been working to make changes. For a variety of reasons, however, progress has been uneven despite the absence of any dispute about the need for change. As a result, should the states fail to accomplish necessary modernization reforms in the near term, Congress should strongly consider direct federal involvement.

The precise manner of federal involvement is a matter for Congress to determine. Recent experience suggests that proposals for federal involvement have fallen into two paradigms: (1) the federal government serving as a coordinating body that also adopts national rules and standards that would preempt state law, but that would leave direct enforcement of the rules and standards to the states; and (2) direct federal regulation of selected areas or aspects of the insurance industry, whether it be oversight of one element of the distribution chain (e.g., multi-state producer licensing) or a particular line of insurance.

Federal Standards Implemented by the States

The first paradigm is for the federal government to serve as a coordinating and facilitating body to assist states with developing national standards and rules. One example of this approach occurred in 1990, when Congress mandated the development of standard benefit designs for Medicare supplement policies. This approach imposed uniform product design on so-called "Medi-gap" policies, thereby enabling consumers to comparison shop. Under this approach, Congress permitted the states to develop the product standards promulgated as regulation by the U.S. Department of Health and Human Services Center for Medicare and Medicaid Services.

Another example is the National Association of Registered Agents and Brokers Reform Act of 2013 (NARAB II), which is presently under consideration by Congress. Under NARAB II, a commission would be established and guided by a board comprised of state regulators and producers. The National Association of Registered Agents and Brokers (NARAB) would be responsible for issuing multi-state licenses to producers which would preempt the application of any state law or regulation for purposes of licensing and continuing education. Standards will be established, in part, by state regulators, and producers will benefit from one centralized licensing location and process. * * *

Federal standard-setting schemes can have shortcomings. First, if the legislation delegates a vague standard or objective to the states, it is unlikely to improve uniformity and efficiency as intended. Second, if the legislation contemplates an opt-in by the states, the probability that all states would opt-in may be small.

Thus, while bills to establish federal standards appear to promote incremental improvement on targeted areas, such legislation must specify standards, processes, and a deadline in order to minimize or eliminate the prospect of variance among the states. This experience points to a more general challenge for federal involvement as a standard-setter. Standards themselves may impose a degree of uniformity. However, application of those standards is equally important to imposing uniformity and consistency. Therefore, if federal involvement is to occur through standard-setting, it should be accompanied by mechanisms designed to enhance uniform implementation of the standards through proper, consistent enforcement.

Direct Federal Regulation

One manner of providing for uniform application of rules is to authorize the federal government itself to directly enforce federally-developed and adopted standards and rules. A number of proposals would have subjected much, if not the entirety, of insurance regulation to direct federal oversight. The underlying concept is that the federal government would act not just as standard-setter or rule-maker, but also as regulator and enforcer. Many view this as an essential objective of modernization due to the size and globalization of the insurance sector and its importance to the national economy. Others assert that the federal government need not regulate the entire insurance business, but only certain aspects of it.

For example, one approach would be to adopt federal regulation for those insurance firms that exceed thresholds of size, scale, and complexity, or those that have national or global business operations. Another approach, which has been a focus of prior proposals, is an optional federal charter, whereby those firms that opt for federal charters would be subject to federal regulation. Federal licensing and regulation of insurers, however, could be defined by the terms of eligibility. As proposed in the National Insurance Act of 2007 and the National Insurance Consumer Protection Act of 2009, the optional federal charter approach would leave to insurers the choice to adopt a federal charter and, therefore, to be regulated by the federal government or by the states. Yet another approach would be a combination of the first two, where, in general, firms would have an option to adopt a federal charter, but that federal regulation for certain large, globally active firms would be mandatory.

NOTES AND QUESTIONS

1. *The Future of Federal Involvement in Insurance.* Both of Dodd-Frank's major insurance-oriented reforms leave much to be determined regarding the future role of federal law and regulation in insurance. This is nothing new. Over the course of the last eighty years, the appropriate role for the federal government in insurance regulation has been a topic of perennial debate. As the FIO report suggests, the most prominent of these proposals has been to create an optional federal charter for insurers who do business nationally and might benefit by avoiding state-by-state regulation. For examinations of these issues, see Robert W. Klein, The Insurance Industry and Its Regulation: An Overview, in The Future of Insurance Regulation in the United States 43–48 (Martin F. Grace & Robert W. Klein eds., 2009); Daniel Schwarcz, Regulating Insurance Sales or Selling Insurance Regulation?: Against Regulatory Competition in Insurance, 94 Minn. L. Rev. 1707 (2010); Danielle F. Waterfield, Insurers Jump on Train for Federal Insurance Regulation: Is It Really What They Want or Need?, 9 Conn. Ins. L.J. 283 (2002). What would be the potential costs and benefits of an optional federal charter for insurers?

2. *The Fed as Regulator of Large Insurance Groups.* To what extent does Dodd-Frank's new regulatory regime for insurance-focused financial groups help limit some of the risks that contributed to the 2008 global financial crisis? How confident should we be, for instance, that AIG's CDS and securities lending operations would have been reined in if the Fed had regulated the entire company on a consolidated basis? In thinking about this question, consider the fact that AIG was in fact regulated on a consolidated basis prior to the crisis by a different federal agency, the Office of Thrift Supervision (OTS), because it owned a thrift. See William K. Sjostrom, Jr, The AIG Bailout, 66 Wash. & Lee L. Rev. 943 (2009). On one hand, AIG was able to "select" this consolidated regulator by purchasing a thrift, and the OTS had a reputation for being particularly captured, as recognized by its dissolution in Dodd-Frank. On the other hand, the Fed, along with various other federal agencies, also failed to recognize the regulatory gaps and risks that permeated the financial system prior to 2008.

3. *Subjecting Insurers to Bank-Like Regulatory Rules.* Over the last several years, insurers have repeatedly expressed concern that Dodd-Frank will ultimately subject them to bank-like regulatory rules that fail to recognize some of the key differences between insurers and banks. Insurers have expressed particular consternation that their insurance operations might be subject to bank capital rules. This became a particularly hot political issue in 2014, when the Fed suggested that one provision in Dodd-Frank, known as the Collins Amendment, unintentionally required it to impose the exact same capital rules on insurers that it imposed on banks. Legislation is currently pending before Congress to clarify the Fed's authority to develop tailored capital rules for insurance-focused financial groups. See generally Cheyenne Hopkins, Insurers Urge Lawmakers Not to Impose Bank Capital Requirements on Industry, Insurance Journal (March 11, 2014) http://www.insurancejournal.com/news/national/2014/03/11/322901.htm. How should such rules differ from bank capital rules, in light of the capacity of insurers to match long-term liabilities with long-term assets?

D. INTERNATIONAL REGULATION OF INSURANCE

As the FIO modernization report alluded to, international organizations are playing an increasingly important role in the development of insurance regulation. The most important international organization in insurance is the International Association of Insurance Supervisors ("IAIS"). The following excerpt from the modernization report provides a good overview of the role of the IAIS and its key activities.

Federal Insurance Office, How to Modernize and Improve the System of Insurance Regulation in the United States (2013)

* * * Before the financial crisis, increasing globalization and complexity of the business of insurance had prompted the international regulatory community to reexamine the adequacy of prudential oversight of insurers and the consistency of cross-jurisdictional and cross-sectoral regulatory treatment. The importance of that review has only been underscored by the financial crisis. Currently, domestic and international regulatory discussions around solvency regulation are primarily focused on prudential standards, enterprise risk management, and group (i.e., consolidated) supervision. FIO has authorities that include monitoring all aspects of the industry and the identification of issues or gaps in regulation that could have financial stability consequences, and representing the U.S. government in prudential aspects of international insurance matters. The dual developments of the financial crisis and the unprecedented internationalization of the insurance market have led to increased emphasis on all aspects of solvency oversight, both at the state and federal levels. In addition, international standard-setting activities have grown in importance and focus.

More specifically, the IAIS is the forum through which insurance supervisors and authorities from more than 140 countries, including U.S. state regulators, convene to develop international insurance supervisory standards and best practices. The IAIS does not prescribe a particular approach or structure with which a country must satisfy an international standard. * * *

FIO currently represents the United States on the IAIS Executive and Financial Stability Committees, and is involved with the Macro-Prudential Surveillance Subcommittee, along with other subcommittees. FIO's Director also serves as Chair of the IAIS Technical Committee, which leads the development of substantive, technical standards, including the Common Framework for the Supervision of Internationally Active Insurance Groups (ComFrame).

In its role as representative of the United States, FIO consults with state regulators, relevant federal agencies, consumers, insurers, and other stakeholders and technical experts. FIO's current substantive priorities in this capacity are: (1) developing and field testing ComFrame so that it serves supervisors' interests and reflects the realities of insurance industry practices; (2) refining a methodology and process to identify [Global Systemically Important Insurers, or "G-SIIs;"] (3) establishing enhanced supervisory measures to be applied to a G-SII, including cross-border resolution practices; and (4) enhancing insurance group supervision in light of recent Financial Stability Board (FSB) recommendations. While FIO is not a functional regulator, these international prudential matters fall within the ambit of the authority to develop federal policy on prudential aspects of international insurance matters. In addition, FIO's authority to monitor all aspects of the insurance industry, including its regulation, bring these matters of financial stability and the standards applicable to internationally active insurers directly within FIO's area of focus.

* * * ComFrame is designed to establish a comprehensive framework for supervisors to: (1) address activities and risks at the insurance group level; (2) develop principles for better global supervisory cooperation; and (3) foster global convergence of regulatory and supervisory measures and approaches. The ComFrame concepts, as presently drafted, are likely subject to revision and refinement through the results of the important field testing phase, which is in its early stages and will study the impact of ComFrame's qualitative and quantitative requirements. Through the development of common supervisory approaches, implementation of ComFrame should reduce the compliance and reporting burden on the increasing number of insurers operating in multiple international jurisdictions, and increase

the shared confidence of global supervisors. In addition, ComFrame seeks to further understanding of group structures through risk analysis and transparency. Improved consistency of supervisory approaches to solvency oversight would promote more effective and efficient supervision of groups, build trust among the international supervisory community, and foster markets that allow for the participation of U.S.-based insurers.

In 2010, the FSB instructed the IAIS to develop a methodology to identify G-SIIs and the enhanced prudential measures to which designated firms would be subjected. The IAIS established the Financial Stability Committee (FSC), in which FIO has participated since July 2011 and been actively engaged since April 2012. FIO's FSC priorities have been to work with national and international colleagues to ensure the rigor and quality of the IAIS methodology, as well as to align the IAIS process with the Council's three-stage process for determining whether a nonbank financial company should be designated for supervision by the Federal Reserve.

Insurers, in contrast to banks, are not currently subject to uniform capital requirements at the global level. On July 18, 2013, the FSB issued mandates to change that * * *

On the same day the FSB issued these mandates, it also announced that, in consultation with the IAIS and national authorities, it had identified an initial list of G-SIIs. The population of IAIGs—approximately 50–60 firms from around the world—would include all nine G-SIIs. * * *

Development of international insurance capital standards remains a daunting and unprecedented challenge. Nevertheless, driven by the fast-paced internationalization of insurance markets, IAIS members appear committed to achieving the stated objectives. * * *

Another significant development in solvency oversight has been the EU's 2009 adoption of a regulatory framework known as Solvency II. Solvency II will soon be adopted by the European Parliament as part of an omnibus legislative package, with a scheduled implementation date of 2016. Notably, despite the previous delays with adoption in the EU, components of Solvency II have been adopted in other countries, including China and Mexico.

Broadly structured around the three pillars of capital, supervision, and disclosure, Solvency II would require adherence to RBC requirements at both the individual regulated entity and group levels, whether pursuant to a standardized formula or based on the insurer's own internal models subject to supervisory review. As originally formulated, Solvency II would have been particularly consequential for the U.S. insurance sector because of its requirement for unilateral assessments of insurance regulation in other jurisdictions (including the United States) and because it would impose solvency requirements on insurers doing business in the EU to the extent the home jurisdiction's requirements are deemed to be unsatisfactory in comparison to Solvency II. Through the EU-U.S. Insurance Project, the EU and the United States have committed to a collaborative work plan that will enhance understanding and cooperation and, where appropriate, promote greater consistency between the two jurisdictions.

Thus, the orientation of the discussion has been altered by virtue of the EU-U.S. Insurance Project which will lead, where appropriate, to the increased convergence and compatibility of the two insurance regulatory regimes.

NOTES AND QUESTIONS

1. *The Influence of International Standards.* Standards developed by international bodies such as the IAIS do not have the force of law in the U.S. Instead, they operate as a form of "soft law," not dissimilar to the NAIC's own model laws and rules. Soft law has proven particularly important in international financial regulation generally, because of the importance of coordination and cooperation among different countries with respect to financial regulation. See generally Chris Brummer, Soft Law and the Global Financial System: Rule Making in the 21st Century (2012). If, for instance, U.S. state insurance regulation does not meet international standards, then this will almost certainly have a substantial influence on the debate about the appropriate scope of the federal government's role in insurance regulation. For a draft of the core principles that all insurance supervisory systems should comply with according to the IAIS, see Int'l Ass'n of Ins. Supervisors, Insurance Core Principles, Standards, Guidance and Assessment Methodology (2013).

2. *Who Represents the U.S. in the International Arena?* According to Dodd-Frank, FIO is supposed to represent U.S. interests in international insurance fora. To what extent, however, can FIO accomplish this given that it does not have any regulatory authority within the U.S.? The answer to this question is further complicated by the fact that the NAIC as well as individual states continue to be active participants in the IAIS and other international fora. Moreover, the Fed has also recently become involved in the IAIS, as it too is now a supervisor of companies that predominantly engage in insurance. Given all of these factors, how well can FIO be expected to forcefully represent U.S. interests in the international arena? See Elizabeth F. Brown, Will the Federal Insurance Office Improve Insurance Regulation?, 81 U. Cin. L. Rev. 551, 582 (2012); Fin. Stability Bd., Peer Review of the United States, 10 (2013) ("While the FIO represents the US on international insurance matters and negotiates covered agreements, only the states have the authority (but are under no legal obligation) to implement laws that are consistent with those agreements and international standards agreed within the IAIS.").

CHAPTER FOUR

PROPERTY INSURANCE

This Chapter is the first of five that focus on specific forms of insurance coverage. Although many issues in insurance law arise in connection with several different kinds of insurance, others are peculiar to particular forms of coverage. Even common issues may be raised or resolved in subtly different ways depending on the form of coverage involved. Although studying "general principles" of insurance law often is useful, every lawyer knows that legal decisions normally are made in response to concrete problems rather than general issues. Consequently, this Chapter and those that follow attempt to build insights from the ground up, so to speak, rather than from the top down.

At the outset, the distinction between *first-party* and *third-party* insurance is worth noting. First-party insurance protects the insured against a loss that she (or other insureds such as family members) suffers herself; it is "victim's insurance." Fire, property, life, health, and disability insurance fall into this category. In contrast, third-party insurance protects the insured against legal liability to a third-party resulting from the insured's actions. Third-party, or liability insurance, is "injurer's insurance." This Chapter and Chapter Five are devoted to the different forms of first-party insurance and the issues they raise. Chapters Six and Seven are devoted to third-party insurance, and Chapter Eight covers both, as they are found in automobile insurance.

A. SAMPLE HOMEOWNERS POLICY

There follows a Sample Homeowners Policy insuring against damage to property, ancillary losses, and certain forms of liability. It is a combination of first-party and third-party insurance: Section I of the Policy (pages 3–17) provides property insurance, whereas Section II (pages 17–22) provides liability insurance. (All page references to the Sample Policy are to the internal pagination of the policy itself, rather than to casebook pages). The issues associated with Section II are examined in Chapter Six. However, it is impossible to completely disaggregate these two sections of the Sample Policy, because certain portions of the policy—including the definitions section (pages 1–2) and the final conditions section (pages 23–24)—apply to both Sections I and II. So too does the declarations page immediately before the policy, which lists information about the policyholder and the coverages provided, including deductibles, limits, and applicable endorsements. The policy contains provisions similar to those at issue in many of this Chapter's cases and its organization mirrors that of virtually all property insurance policies. Reading the policy and understanding how it is structured will thus assist your study of property insurance generally.

The Architecture and Scope of Property Insurance Policies

Property insurance policies generally consist of four sections: (1) property coverages, (2) perils insured against, (3) exclusions, and (4) conditions. The "Property Coverages" section of the Sample Policy (pages 3–9) delineates the kinds of property and interests covered, including the dwelling or building that is the principal subject of coverage, any appurtenant structures, certain personal property, and loss of use of certain covered property. The "Perils Insured Against" section (pages 9–12) contains the actual affirmative grant of coverage. It links coverage to the cause of damage to the insured property, with some causes covered and others not covered. It thus contains provisions that limit the scope of coverage, although they are not labeled exclusions. The "Exclusions" section (pages 12–13) further limits coverage. Finally, the "Conditions" section (pages 13–17) contains various provisions that are not conditions in the ordinary sense of conditioning the promises of either the insurer or policyholder on the occurrence of a specific event. For instance, it contains provisions governing dispute resolution (i.e. the appraisal clause on page 15) and specifying the method for calculating insurance recovery (pages 14–15).

The Sample Policy deviates from this structure on pages 5–9, which contain various "additional coverages" that mostly operate as stand-alone mini-insurance policies for a range of losses. Thus, additional coverage 4 (page 6) covers the charge that some property owners must pay when the fire department is called to their premises. Coverage under these provisions may not be subject to the deductible and do not necessarily require the loss to be caused by a peril insured against.

Yet another complication in the structure of many property insurance policies involves the distinction between *all-risk* and *specified-risk* coverage, or as the insurance industry now prefers to call it, between *open-peril* and *named-peril* coverage. An all-risk or open-peril policy covers all risks to the insured property except those that are specifically excluded. In contrast, a specified-risk or named-peril policy covers only damage to insured property caused by specific risks that are named in the policy. The Sample Policy provides all-risk coverage for losses to certain insured property, including the dwelling itself and related structures such as garages (pages 9–10). But it only provides named-peril coverage for personal property (pages 10–12). Which section applies may matter in determining the level of coverage. See, e.g., *Costabile v. Metro. Prop. & Cas. Ins. Co.*, 193 F. Supp. 2d 465 (D. Conn. 2002) (resolving coverage restriction for losses caused by vandalism of vacant premises differently with respect to the named-peril portion of the policy and the open-peril portion of the policy).

The complex and inconsistent structure of property insurance policies is largely attributable to their historical evolution. Property insurance originated as insurance of a single building against fire. As insurers began to insure more than just an individual building, they added a separate section identifying the additional kinds of property covered. Similarly, as insurers decided to cover losses from causes other than fire, they added a separate section identifying additional perils insured against. As insurers added more provisions to the policy, they generally attempted not to disturb the preexisting organizational structure.

HOMEOWNERS POLICY

Declarations applicable to all policy forms

Policy Number

Policy Period: 12:01 a.m. Standard time   From: To:
at the residence premises

Named Insured and mailing address

The residence premises covered by this policy is located at the above address unless otherwise stated:

Coverage is provided where a premium or limit of liability is shown for the coverage.

	Limit of Liability	Premium
SECTION I COVERAGES		
A. Dwelling		
B. Other structures		
C. Personal property		
D. Loss of use		
SECTION II COVERAGES		
E. Personal liability: each occurrence		
F. Medical payments to others: each person		

Total premium for endorsements listed below

Policy Total

Forms and endorsements made part of this policy:

Number	Edition Date	Title	Premium

[Special State Provisions: South Carolina: Valuation Clause (Cov.A) $
Minnesota Insurable Value (Cov.A) $
New York: Coinsurance Clause Applies ___Yes ___No]

DEDUCTIBLE - Section I: $
In case of a loss under Section I, we cover only that part of the loss over the deductible stated.

Section II: Other insured locations:

[Mortgagee/Lienholder (Name and address)]

Countersignature of agent/date   Signature/title - company officer

Ed.4/84

HOMEOWNERS
HO 00 03 05 11

HOMEOWNERS 3 – SPECIAL FORM

AGREEMENT

We will provide the insurance described in this policy in return for the premium and compliance with all applicable provisions of this policy.

DEFINITIONS

A. In this policy, "you" and "your" refer to the "named insured" shown in the Declarations and the spouse if a resident of the same household. "We", "us" and "our" refer to the Company providing this insurance.

B. In addition, certain words and phrases are defined as follows:

1. "Aircraft Liability", "Hovercraft Liability", "Motor Vehicle Liability" and "Watercraft Liability", subject to the provisions in b. below, mean the following:

    a. Liability for "bodily injury" or "property damage" arising out of the:

      (1) Ownership of such vehicle or craft by an "insured";

      (2) Maintenance, occupancy, operation, use, loading or unloading of such vehicle or craft by any person;

      (3) Entrustment of such vehicle or craft by an "insured" to any person;

      (4) Failure to supervise or negligent supervision of any person involving such vehicle or craft by an "insured"; or

      (5) Vicarious liability, whether or not imposed by law, for the actions of a child or minor involving such vehicle or craft.

    b. For the purpose of this definition:

      (1) Aircraft means any contrivance used or designed for flight except model or hobby aircraft not used or designed to carry people or cargo;

      (2) Hovercraft means a self-propelled motorized ground effect vehicle and includes, but is not limited to, flarecraft and air cushion vehicles;

      (3) Watercraft means a craft principally designed to be propelled on or in water by wind, engine power or electric motor; and

      (4) Motor vehicle means a "motor vehicle" as defined in 7. below.

2. "Bodily injury" means bodily harm, sickness or disease, including required care, loss of services and death that results.

3. "Business" means:

    a. A trade, profession or occupation engaged in on a full-time, part-time or occasional basis; or

    b. Any other activity engaged in for money or other compensation, except the following:

      (1) One or more activities, not described in (2) through (4) below, for which no "insured" receives more than $2,000 in total compensation for the 12 months before the beginning of the policy period;

      (2) Volunteer activities for which no money is received other than payment for expenses incurred to perform the activity;

      (3) Providing home day care services for which no compensation is received, other than the mutual exchange of such services; or

      (4) The rendering of home day care services to a relative of an "insured".

4. "Employee" means an employee of an "insured", or an employee leased to an "insured" by a labor leasing firm under an agreement between an "insured" and the labor leasing firm, whose duties are other than those performed by a "residence employee".

5. "Insured" means:

    a. You and residents of your household who are:

      (1) Your relatives; or

      (2) Other persons under the age of 21 and in your care or the care of a resident of your household who is your relative;

    b. A student enrolled in school full-time, as defined by the school, who was a resident of your household before moving out to attend school, provided the student is under the age of:

      (1) 24 and your relative; or

HO 00 03 05 11 © Insurance Services Office, Inc., 2010 Page 1 of 24

(2) 21 and in your care or the care of a resident of your household who is your relative; or

c. Under Section II:

(1) With respect to animals or watercraft to which this policy applies, any person or organization legally responsible for these animals or watercraft which are owned by you or any person described in **5.a.** or **b.** "Insured" does not mean a person or organization using or having custody of these animals or watercraft in the course of any "business" or without consent of the owner; or

(2) With respect to a "motor vehicle" to which this policy applies:

(a) Persons while engaged in your employ or that of any person described in **5.a.** or **b.**; or

(b) Other persons using the vehicle on an "insured location" with your consent.

Under both Sections I and II, when the word an immediately precedes the word "insured", the words an "insured" together mean one or more "insureds".

6. "Insured location" means:

a. The "residence premises";

b. The part of other premises, other structures and grounds used by you as a residence; and

(1) Which is shown in the Declarations; or

(2) Which is acquired by you during the policy period for your use as a residence;

c. Any premises used by you in connection with a premises described in **a.** and **b.** above;

d. Any part of a premises:

(1) Not owned by an "insured"; and

(2) Where an "insured" is temporarily residing;

e. Vacant land, other than farm land, owned by or rented to an "insured";

f. Land owned by or rented to an "insured" on which a one-, two-, three- or four-family dwelling is being built as a residence for an "insured";

g. Individual or family cemetery plots or burial vaults of an "insured"; or

h. Any part of a premises occasionally rented to an "insured" for other than "business" use.

7. "Motor vehicle" means:

a. A self-propelled land or amphibious vehicle; or

b. Any trailer or semitrailer which is being carried on, towed by or hitched for towing by a vehicle described in **a.** above.

8. "Occurrence" means an accident, including continuous or repeated exposure to substantially the same general harmful conditions, which results, during the policy period, in:

a. "Bodily injury"; or

b. "Property damage".

9. "Property damage" means physical injury to, destruction of, or loss of use of tangible property.

10. "Residence employee" means:

a. An employee of an "insured", or an employee leased to an "insured" by a labor leasing firm, under an agreement between an "insured" and the labor leasing firm, whose duties are related to the maintenance or use of the "residence premises", including household or domestic services; or

b. One who performs similar duties elsewhere not related to the "business" of an "insured".

A "residence employee" does not include a temporary employee who is furnished to an "insured" to substitute for a permanent "residence employee" on leave or to meet seasonal or short-term workload conditions.

11. "Residence premises" means:

a. The one-family dwelling where you reside;

b. The two-, three- or four-family dwelling where you reside in at least one of the family units; or

c. That part of any other building where you reside;

and which is shown as the "residence premises" in the Declarations.

"Residence premises" also includes other structures and grounds at that location.

SECTION I – PROPERTY COVERAGES

A. Coverage A – Dwelling

1. We cover:
   a. The dwelling on the "residence premises" shown in the Declarations, including structures attached to the dwelling; and
   b. Materials and supplies located on or next to the "residence premises" used to construct, alter or repair the dwelling or other structures on the "residence premises".
2. We do not cover land, including land on which the dwelling is located.

B. Coverage B – Other Structures

1. We cover other structures on the "residence premises" set apart from the dwelling by clear space. This includes structures connected to the dwelling by only a fence, utility line, or similar connection.
2. We do not cover:
   a. Land, including land on which the other structures are located;
   b. Other structures rented or held for rental to any person not a tenant of the dwelling, unless used solely as a private garage;
   c. Other structures from which any "business" is conducted; or
   d. Other structures used to store "business" property. However, we do cover a structure that contains "business" property solely owned by an "insured" or a tenant of the dwelling, provided that "business" property does not include gaseous or liquid fuel, other than fuel in a permanently installed fuel tank of a vehicle or craft parked or stored in the structure.
3. The limit of liability for this coverage will not be more than 10% of the limit of liability that applies to Coverage **A**. Use of this coverage does not reduce the Coverage **A** limit of liability.

C. Coverage C – Personal Property

1. **Covered Property**

   We cover personal property owned or used by an "insured" while it is anywhere in the world. After a loss and at your request, we will cover personal property owned by:

   a. Others while the property is on the part of the "residence premises" occupied by an "insured"; or
   b. A guest or a "residence employee", while the property is in any residence occupied by an "insured".

2. **Limit For Property At Other Locations**

   a. **Other Residences**

      Our limit of liability for personal property usually located at an "insured's" residence, other than the "residence premises", is 10% of the limit of liability for Coverage **C**, or $1,000, whichever is greater. However, this limitation does not apply to personal property:

      (1) Moved from the "residence premises" because it is:
          (a) Being repaired, renovated or rebuilt; and
          (b) Not fit to live in or store property in; or
      (2) In a newly acquired principal residence for 30 days from the time you begin to move the property there.

   b. **Self-storage Facilities**

      Our limit of liability for personal property owned or used by an "insured" and located in a self-storage facility is 10% of the limit of liability for Coverage **C**, or $1,000, whichever is greater. However, this limitation does not apply to personal property:

      (1) Moved from the "residence premises" because it is:
          (a) Being repaired, renovated or rebuilt; and
          (b) Not fit to live in or store property in; or
      (2) Usually located in an "insured's" residence, other than the "residence premises".

3. **Special Limits Of Liability**

    The special limit for each category shown below is the total limit for each loss for all property in that category. These special limits do not increase the Coverage **C** limit of liability.

    a. $200 on money, bank notes, bullion, gold other than goldware, silver other than silverware, platinum other than platinumware, coins, medals, scrip, stored value cards and smart cards.

    b. $1,500 on securities, accounts, deeds, evidences of debt, letters of credit, notes other than bank notes, manuscripts, personal records, passports, tickets and stamps. This dollar limit applies to these categories regardless of the medium (such as paper or computer software) on which the material exists.

    This limit includes the cost to research, replace or restore the information from the lost or damaged material.

    c. $1,500 on watercraft of all types, including their trailers, furnishings, equipment and outboard engines or motors.

    d. $1,500 on trailers or semitrailers not used with watercraft of all types.

    e. $1,500 for loss by theft of jewelry, watches, furs, precious and semiprecious stones.

    f. $2,500 for loss by theft of firearms and related equipment.

    g. $2,500 for loss by theft of silverware, silver-plated ware, goldware, gold-plated ware, platinumware, platinum-plated ware and pewterware. This includes flatware, hollowware, tea sets, trays and trophies made of or including silver, gold or pewter.

    h. $2,500 on property, on the "residence premises", used primarily for "business" purposes.

    i. $1,500 on property, away from the "residence premises", used primarily for "business" purposes. However, this limit does not apply to antennas, tapes, wires, records, disks or other media that are:

       (1) Used with electronic equipment that reproduces, receives or transmits audio, visual or data signals; and

       (2) In or upon a "motor vehicle".

    j. $1,500 on portable electronic equipment that:

       (1) Reproduces, receives or transmits audio, visual or data signals;

       (2) Is designed to be operated by more than one power source, one of which is a "motor vehicle's" electrical system; and

       (3) Is in or upon a "motor vehicle".

    k. $250 for antennas, tapes, wires, records, disks or other media that are:

       (1) Used with electronic equipment that reproduces, receives or transmits audio, visual or data signals; and

       (2) In or upon a "motor vehicle".

4. **Property Not Covered**

    We do not cover:

    a. Articles separately described and specifically insured, regardless of the limit for which they are insured, in this or other insurance;

    b. Animals, birds or fish;

    c. "Motor vehicles".

    This includes a "motor vehicle's" equipment and parts. However, this Paragraph **4.c.** does not apply to:

       (1) Portable electronic equipment that:

           (a) Reproduces, receives or transmits audio, visual or data signals; and

           (b) Is designed so that it may be operated from a power source other than a "motor vehicle's" electrical system.

       (2) "Motor vehicles" not required to be registered for use on public roads or property which are:

           (a) Used solely to service a residence; or

           (b) Designed to assist the handicapped;

    d. Aircraft, meaning any contrivance used or designed for flight, including any parts whether or not attached to the aircraft.

    We do cover model or hobby aircraft not used or designed to carry people or cargo;

    e. Hovercraft and parts. Hovercraft means a self-propelled motorized ground effect vehicle and includes, but is not limited to, flarecraft and air cushion vehicles;

    f. Property of roomers, boarders and other tenants, except property of roomers and boarders related to an "insured";

g. Property in an apartment regularly rented or held for rental to others by an "insured", except as provided in **E.10.** Landlord's Furnishings under Section **I** – Property Coverages;

h. Property rented or held for rental to others off the "residence premises";

i. "Business" data, including such data stored in:

   (1) Books of account, drawings or other paper records; or

   (2) Computers and related equipment.

   We do cover the cost of blank recording or storage media and of prerecorded computer programs available on the retail market;

j. Credit cards, electronic fund transfer cards or access devices used solely for deposit, withdrawal or transfer of funds except as provided in **E.6.** Credit Card, Electronic Fund Transfer Card Or Access Device, Forgery And Counterfeit Money under Section **I** – Property Coverages; or

k. Water or steam.

D. Coverage D – Loss Of Use

The limit of liability for Coverage **D** is the total limit for the coverages in **1.** Additional Living Expense, **2.** Fair Rental Value and **3.** Civil Authority Prohibits Use below.

1. Additional Living Expense

If a loss covered under Section **I** makes that part of the "residence premises" where you reside not fit to live in, we cover any necessary increase in living expenses incurred by you so that your household can maintain its normal standard of living.

Payment will be for the shortest time required to repair or replace the damage or, if you permanently relocate, the shortest time required for your household to settle elsewhere.

2. Fair Rental Value

If a loss covered under Section **I** makes that part of the "residence premises" rented to others or held for rental by you not fit to live in, we cover the fair rental value of such premises less any expenses that do not continue while it is not fit to live in.

Payment will be for the shortest time required to repair or replace such premises.

3. Civil Authority Prohibits Use

If a civil authority prohibits you from use of the "residence premises" as a result of direct damage to neighboring premises by a Peril Insured Against, we cover the loss as provided in **1.** Additional Living Expense and **2.** Fair Rental Value above for no more than two weeks.

4. Loss Or Expense Not Covered

We do not cover loss or expense due to cancellation of a lease or agreement.

The periods of time under **1.** Additional Living Expense, **2.** Fair Rental Value and **3.** Civil Authority Prohibits Use above are not limited by expiration of this policy.

E. Additional Coverages

1. Debris Removal

a. We will pay your reasonable expense for the removal of:

   (1) Debris of covered property if a Peril Insured Against that applies to the damaged property causes the loss; or

   (2) Ash, dust or particles from a volcanic eruption that has caused direct loss to a building or property contained in a building.

   This expense is included in the limit of liability that applies to the damaged property. If the amount to be paid for the actual damage to the property plus the debris removal expense is more than the limit of liability for the damaged property, an additional 5% of that limit is available for such expense.

b. We will also pay your reasonable expense, up to $1,000, for the removal from the "residence premises" of:

   (1) Your trees felled by the peril of Windstorm or Hail or Weight of Ice, Snow or Sleet; or

   (2) A neighbor's trees felled by a Peril Insured Against under Coverage **C**;

   provided the trees:

   (3) Damage a covered structure; or

   (4) Do not damage a covered structure, but:

      (a) Block a driveway on the "residence premises" which prevents a "motor vehicle", that is registered for use on public roads or property, from entering or leaving the "residence premises"; or

(b) Block a ramp or other fixture designed to assist a handicapped person to enter or leave the dwelling building.

The $1,000 limit is the most we will pay in any one loss, regardless of the number of fallen trees. No more than $500 of this limit will be paid for the removal of any one tree.

This coverage is additional insurance.

2. **Reasonable Repairs**

   a. We will pay the reasonable cost incurred by you for the necessary measures taken solely to protect covered property that is damaged by a Peril Insured Against from further damage.

   b. If the measures taken involve repair to other damaged property, we will only pay if that property is covered under this policy and the damage is caused by a Peril Insured Against. This coverage does not:

   (1) Increase the limit of liability that applies to the covered property; or

   (2) Relieve you of your duties, in case of a loss to covered property, described in **C.4.** under Section I – Conditions.

3. **Trees, Shrubs And Other Plants**

   We cover trees, shrubs, plants or lawns, on the "residence premises", for loss caused by the following Perils Insured Against:

   a. Fire or Lightning;
   b. Explosion;
   c. Riot or Civil Commotion;
   d. Aircraft;
   e. Vehicles not owned or operated by a resident of the "residence premises";
   f. Vandalism or Malicious Mischief; or
   g. Theft.

   We will pay up to 5% of the limit of liability that applies to the dwelling for all trees, shrubs, plants or lawns. No more than $500 of this limit will be paid for any one tree, shrub or plant. We do not cover property grown for "business" purposes.

   This coverage is additional insurance.

4. **Fire Department Service Charge**

   We will pay up to $500 for your liability assumed by contract or agreement for fire department charges incurred when the fire department is called to save or protect covered property from a Peril Insured Against. We do not cover fire department service charges if the property is located within the limits of the city, municipality or protection district furnishing the fire department response.

   This coverage is additional insurance. No deductible applies to this coverage.

5. **Property Removed**

   We insure covered property against direct loss from any cause while being removed from a premises endangered by a Peril Insured Against and for no more than 30 days while removed.

   This coverage does not change the limit of liability that applies to the property being removed.

6. **Credit Card, Electronic Fund Transfer Card Or Access Device, Forgery And Counterfeit Money**

   a. We will pay up to $500 for:

   (1) The legal obligation of an "insured" to pay because of the theft or unauthorized use of credit cards issued to or registered in an "insured's" name;

   (2) Loss resulting from theft or unauthorized use of an electronic fund transfer card or access device used for deposit, withdrawal or transfer of funds, issued to or registered in an "insured's" name;

   (3) Loss to an "insured" caused by forgery or alteration of any check or negotiable instrument; and

   (4) Loss to an "insured" through acceptance in good faith of counterfeit United States or Canadian paper currency.

   All loss resulting from a series of acts committed by any one person or in which any one person is concerned or implicated is considered to be one loss.

This coverage is additional insurance. No deductible applies to this coverage.

b. We do not cover:

(1) Use of a credit card, electronic fund transfer card or access device:

(a) By a resident of your household;

(b) By a person who has been entrusted with either type of card or access device; or

(c) If an "insured" has not complied with all terms and conditions under which the cards are issued or the devices accessed; or

(2) Loss arising out of "business" use or dishonesty of an "insured".

c. If the coverage in a. above applies, the following defense provisions also apply:

(1) We may investigate and settle any claim or suit that we decide is appropriate. Our duty to defend a claim or suit ends when the amount we pay for the loss equals our limit of liability.

(2) If a suit is brought against an "insured" for liability under a.(1) or (2) above, we will provide a defense at our expense by counsel of our choice.

(3) We have the option to defend at our expense an "insured" or an "insured's" bank against any suit for the enforcement of payment under a.(3) above.

7. **Loss Assessment**

a. We will pay up to $1,000 for your share of loss assessment charged during the policy period against you, as owner or tenant of the "residence premises", by a corporation or association of property owners. The assessment must be made as a result of direct loss to property, owned by all members collectively, of the type that would be covered by this policy if owned by you, caused by a Peril Insured Against under Coverage **A**, other than:

(1) Earthquake; or

(2) Land shock waves or tremors before, during or after a volcanic eruption.

The limit of $1,000 is the most we will pay with respect to any one loss, regardless of the number of assessments. We will only apply one deductible, per unit, to the total amount of any one loss to the property described above, regardless of the number of assessments.

b. We do not cover assessments charged against you or a corporation or association of property owners by any governmental body.

c. Paragraph **Q.** Policy Period under Section **I** – Conditions does not apply to this coverage.

This coverage is additional insurance.

8. **Collapse**

a. The coverage provided under this Additional Coverage – Collapse applies only to an abrupt collapse.

b. For the purpose of this Additional Coverage – Collapse, abrupt collapse means an abrupt falling down or caving in of a building or any part of a building with the result that the building or part of the building cannot be occupied for its intended purpose.

c. This Additional Coverage – Collapse does not apply to:

(1) A building or any part of a building that is in danger of falling down or caving in;

(2) A part of a building that is standing, even if it has separated from another part of the building; or

(3) A building or any part of a building that is standing, even if it shows evidence of cracking, bulging, sagging, bending, leaning, settling, shrinkage or expansion.

d. We insure for direct physical loss to covered property involving abrupt collapse of a building or any part of a building if such collapse was caused by one or more of the following:

(1) The Perils Insured Against named under Coverage **C**;

(2) Decay, of a building or any part of a building, that is hidden from view, unless the presence of such decay is known to an "insured" prior to collapse;

(3) Insect or vermin damage, to a building or any part of a building, that is hidden from view, unless the presence of such damage is known to an "insured" prior to collapse;

(4) Weight of contents, equipment, animals or people;

(5) Weight of rain which collects on a roof; or

- **(6)** Use of defective material or methods in construction, remodeling or renovation if the collapse occurs during the course of the construction, remodeling or renovation.

- **e.** Loss to an awning, fence, patio, deck, pavement, swimming pool, underground pipe, flue, drain, cesspool, septic tank, foundation, retaining wall, bulkhead, pier, wharf or dock is not included under **d.(2)** through **(6)** above, unless the loss is a direct result of the collapse of a building or any part of a building.

- **f.** This coverage does not increase the limit of liability that applies to the damaged covered property.

9. Glass Or Safety Glazing Material

- **a.** We cover:
  - **(1)** The breakage of glass or safety glazing material which is part of a covered building, storm door or storm window;
  - **(2)** The breakage of glass or safety glazing material which is part of a covered building, storm door or storm window when caused directly by earth movement; and
  - **(3)** The direct physical loss to covered property caused solely by the pieces, fragments or splinters of broken glass or safety glazing material which is part of a building, storm door or storm window.

- **b.** This coverage does not include loss:
  - **(1)** To covered property which results because the glass or safety glazing material has been broken, except as provided in **a.(3)** above; or
  - **(2)** On the "residence premises" if the dwelling has been vacant for more than 60 consecutive days immediately before the loss, except when the breakage results directly from earth movement as provided in **a.(2)** above. A dwelling being constructed is not considered vacant.

- **c.** This coverage does not increase the limit of liability that applies to the damaged property.

10. Landlord's Furnishings

We will pay up to $2,500 for your appliances, carpeting and other household furnishings, in each apartment on the "residence premises" regularly rented or held for rental to others by an "insured", for loss caused by a Peril Insured Against in Coverage **C**, other than Theft.

This limit is the most we will pay in any one loss regardless of the number of appliances, carpeting or other household furnishings involved in the loss.

This coverage does not increase the limit of liability applying to the damaged property.

11. Ordinance Or Law

- **a.** You may use up to 10% of the limit of liability that applies to Coverage **A** for the increased costs you incur due to the enforcement of any ordinance or law which requires or regulates:
  - **(1)** The construction, demolition, remodeling, renovation or repair of that part of a covered building or other structure damaged by a Peril Insured Against;
  - **(2)** The demolition and reconstruction of the undamaged part of a covered building or other structure, when that building or other structure must be totally demolished because of damage by a Peril Insured Against to another part of that covered building or other structure; or
  - **(3)** The remodeling, removal or replacement of the portion of the undamaged part of a covered building or other structure necessary to complete the remodeling, repair or replacement of that part of the covered building or other structure damaged by a Peril Insured Against.

- **b.** You may use all or part of this ordinance or law coverage to pay for the increased costs you incur to remove debris resulting from the construction, demolition, remodeling, renovation, repair or replacement of property as stated in **a.** above.

- **c.** We do not cover:
  - **(1)** The loss in value to any covered building or other structure due to the requirements of any ordinance or law; or
  - **(2)** The costs to comply with any ordinance or law which requires any "insured" or others to test for, monitor, clean up, remove, contain, treat, detoxify or neutralize, or in any way respond to, or assess the effects of, pollutants in or on any covered building or other structure.

Pollutants means any solid, liquid, gaseous or thermal irritant or contaminant, including smoke, vapor, soot, fumes, acids, alkalis, chemicals and waste. Waste includes materials to be recycled, reconditioned or reclaimed.

This coverage is additional insurance.

12. **Grave Markers**

    We will pay up to $5,000 for grave markers, including mausoleums, on or away from the "residence premises" for loss caused by a Peril Insured Against under Coverage **C**.

    This coverage does not increase the limits of liability that apply to the damaged covered property.

SECTION I – PERILS INSURED AGAINST

A. Coverage A – Dwelling And Coverage B – Other Structures

1. We insure against direct physical loss to property described in Coverages **A** and **B**.

2. We do not insure, however, for loss:

   a. Excluded under Section I – Exclusions;

   b. Involving collapse, including any of the following conditions of property or any part of the property:

      (1) An abrupt falling down or caving in;

      (2) Loss of structural integrity, including separation of parts of the property or property in danger of falling down or caving in; or

      (3) Any cracking, bulging, sagging, bending, leaning, settling, shrinkage or expansion as such condition relates to (1) or (2) above;

      except as provided in **E.8.** Collapse under Section I – Property Coverages; or

   c. Caused by:

      (1) Freezing of a plumbing, heating, air conditioning or automatic fire protective sprinkler system or of a household appliance, or by discharge, leakage or overflow from within the system or appliance caused by freezing. This provision does not apply if you have used reasonable care to:

         (a) Maintain heat in the building; or

         (b) Shut off the water supply and drain all systems and appliances of water.

   However, if the building is protected by an automatic fire protective sprinkler system, you must use reasonable care to continue the water supply and maintain heat in the building for coverage to apply.

   For purposes of this provision, a plumbing system or household appliance does not include a sump, sump pump or related equipment or a roof drain, gutter, downspout or similar fixtures or equipment;

   (2) Freezing, thawing, pressure or weight of water or ice, whether driven by wind or not, to a:

      (a) Fence, pavement, patio or swimming pool;

      (b) Footing, foundation, bulkhead, wall, or any other structure or device that supports all or part of a building, or other structure;

      (c) Retaining wall or bulkhead that does not support all or part of a building or other structure; or

      (d) Pier, wharf or dock;

   (3) Theft in or to a dwelling under construction, or of materials and supplies for use in the construction until the dwelling is finished and occupied;

   (4) Vandalism and malicious mischief, and any ensuing loss caused by any intentional and wrongful act committed in the course of the vandalism or malicious mischief, if the dwelling has been vacant for more than 60 consecutive days immediately before the loss. A dwelling being constructed is not considered vacant;

   (5) Mold, fungus or wet rot. However, we do insure for loss caused by mold, fungus or wet rot that is hidden within the walls or ceilings or beneath the floors or above the ceilings of a structure if such loss results from the accidental discharge or overflow of water or steam from within:

      (a) A plumbing, heating, air conditioning or automatic fire protective sprinkler system, or a household appliance, on the "residence premises"; or

      (b) A storm drain, or water, steam or sewer pipes, off the "residence premises".

For purposes of this provision, a plumbing system or household appliance does not include a sump, sump pump or related equipment or a roof drain, gutter, downspout or similar fixtures or equipment; or

(6) Any of the following:

(a) Wear and tear, marring, deterioration;

(b) Mechanical breakdown, latent defect, inherent vice or any quality in property that causes it to damage or destroy itself;

(c) Smog, rust or other corrosion, or dry rot;

(d) Smoke from agricultural smudging or industrial operations;

(e) Discharge, dispersal, seepage, migration, release or escape of pollutants unless the discharge, dispersal, seepage, migration, release or escape is itself caused by a Peril Insured Against named under Coverage **C**.

Pollutants means any solid, liquid, gaseous or thermal irritant or contaminant, including smoke, vapor, soot, fumes, acids, alkalis, chemicals and waste. Waste includes materials to be recycled, reconditioned or reclaimed;

(f) Settling, shrinking, bulging or expansion, including resultant cracking, of bulkheads, pavements, patios, footings, foundations, walls, floors, roofs or ceilings;

(g) Birds, rodents or insects;

(h) Nesting or infestation, or discharge or release of waste products or secretions, by any animals; or

(i) Animals owned or kept by an "insured".

Exception To c.(6)

Unless the loss is otherwise excluded, we cover loss to property covered under Coverage **A** or **B** resulting from an accidental discharge or overflow of water or steam from within a:

(i) Storm drain, or water, steam or sewer pipe, off the "residence premises"; or

(ii) Plumbing, heating, air conditioning or automatic fire protective sprinkler system or household appliance on the "residence premises". This includes the cost to tear out and replace any part of a building, or other structure, on the "residence premises", but only when necessary to repair the system or appliance. However, such tear out and replacement coverage only applies to other structures if the water or steam causes actual damage to a building on the "residence premises".

We do not cover loss to the system or appliance from which this water or steam escaped.

For purposes of this provision, a plumbing system or household appliance does not include a sump, sump pump or related equipment or a roof drain, gutter, downspout or similar fixtures or equipment.

Section I – Exclusion **A.3.** Water, Paragraphs **a.** and **c.** that apply to surface water and water below the surface of the ground do not apply to loss by water covered under **c.(5)** and **(6)** above.

Under **2.b.** and **c.** above, any ensuing loss to property described in Coverages **A** and **B** not precluded by any other provision in this policy is covered.

B. Coverage C – Personal Property

We insure for direct physical loss to the property described in Coverage **C** caused by any of the following perils unless the loss is excluded in Section I – Exclusions.

1. **Fire Or Lightning**

2. **Windstorm Or Hail**

This peril includes loss to watercraft of all types and their trailers, furnishings, equipment, and outboard engines or motors, only while inside a fully enclosed building.

This peril does not include loss to the property contained in a building caused by rain, snow, sleet, sand or dust unless the direct force of wind or hail damages the building causing an opening in a roof or wall and the rain, snow, sleet, sand or dust enters through this opening.

3. Explosion
4. Riot Or Civil Commotion
5. Aircraft

   This peril includes self-propelled missiles and spacecraft.

6. Vehicles
7. Smoke

   This peril means sudden and accidental damage from smoke, including the emission or puffback of smoke, soot, fumes or vapors from a boiler, furnace or related equipment.

   This peril does not include loss caused by smoke from agricultural smudging or industrial operations.

8. Vandalism Or Malicious Mischief
9. Theft

   a. This peril includes attempted theft and loss of property from a known place when it is likely that the property has been stolen.

   b. This peril does not include loss caused by theft:

   (1) Committed by an "insured";

   (2) In or to a dwelling under construction, or of materials and supplies for use in the construction until the dwelling is finished and occupied;

   (3) From that part of a "residence premises" rented by an "insured" to someone other than another "insured"; or

   (4) That occurs off the "residence premises" of:

   (a) Trailers, semitrailers and campers;

   (b) Watercraft of all types, and their furnishings, equipment and outboard engines or motors; or

   (c) Property while at any other residence owned by, rented to, or occupied by an "insured", except while an "insured" is temporarily living there. Property of an "insured" who is a student is covered while at the residence the student occupies to attend school as long as the student has been there at any time during the 90 days immediately before the loss.

10. Falling Objects

    This peril does not include loss to property contained in a building unless the roof or an outside wall of the building is first damaged by a falling object. Damage to the falling object itself is not included.

11. Weight Of Ice, Snow Or Sleet

    This peril means weight of ice, snow or sleet which causes damage to property contained in a building.

12. Accidental Discharge Or Overflow Of Water Or Steam

    a. This peril means accidental discharge or overflow of water or steam from within a plumbing, heating, air conditioning or automatic fire protective sprinkler system or from within a household appliance.

    b. This peril does not include loss:

    (1) To the system or appliance from which the water or steam escaped;

    (2) Caused by or resulting from freezing except as provided in Peril Insured Against 14. Freezing;

    (3) On the "residence premises" caused by accidental discharge or overflow which occurs off the "residence premises"; or

    (4) Caused by mold, fungus or wet rot unless hidden within the walls or ceilings or beneath the floors or above the ceilings of a structure.

    c. In this peril, a plumbing system or household appliance does not include a sump, sump pump or related equipment or a roof drain, gutter, downspout or similar fixtures or equipment.

    d. Section I – Exclusion A.3. Water, Paragraphs a. and c. that apply to surface water and water below the surface of the ground do not apply to loss by water covered under this peril.

13. Sudden And Accidental Tearing Apart, Cracking, Burning Or Bulging

    This peril means sudden and accidental tearing apart, cracking, burning or bulging of a steam or hot water heating system, an air conditioning or automatic fire protective sprinkler system, or an appliance for heating water.

    We do not cover loss caused by or resulting from freezing under this peril.

14. **Freezing**

    a. This peril means freezing of a plumbing, heating, air conditioning or automatic fire protective sprinkler system or of a household appliance, but only if you have used reasonable care to:

    (1) Maintain heat in the building; or

    (2) Shut off the water supply and drain all systems and appliances of water.

    However, if the building is protected by an automatic fire protective sprinkler system, you must use reasonable care to continue the water supply and maintain heat in the building for coverage to apply.

    b. In this peril, a plumbing system or household appliance does not include a sump, sump pump or related equipment or a roof drain, gutter, downspout or similar fixtures or equipment.

15. **Sudden And Accidental Damage From Artificially Generated Electrical Current**

    This peril does not include loss to tubes, transistors, electronic components or circuitry that is a part of appliances, fixtures, computers, home entertainment units or other types of electronic apparatus.

16. **Volcanic Eruption**

    This peril does not include loss caused by earthquake, land shock waves or tremors.

SECTION I – EXCLUSIONS

A. We do not insure for loss caused directly or indirectly by any of the following. Such loss is excluded regardless of any other cause or event contributing concurrently or in any sequence to the loss. These exclusions apply whether or not the loss event results in widespread damage or affects a substantial area.

1. **Ordinance Or Law**

    Ordinance Or Law means any ordinance or law:

    a. Requiring or regulating the construction, demolition, remodeling, renovation or repair of property, including removal of any resulting debris. This Exclusion **A.1.a.** does not apply to the amount of coverage that may be provided for in **E.11.** Ordinance Or Law under Section I – Property Coverages;

    b. The requirements of which result in a loss in value to property; or

    c. Requiring any "insured" or others to test for, monitor, clean up, remove, contain, treat, detoxify or neutralize, or in any way respond to, or assess the effects of, pollutants.

    Pollutants means any solid, liquid, gaseous or thermal irritant or contaminant, including smoke, vapor, soot, fumes, acids, alkalis, chemicals and waste. Waste includes materials to be recycled, reconditioned or reclaimed.

    This Exclusion **A.1.** applies whether or not the property has been physically damaged.

2. **Earth Movement**

    Earth Movement means:

    a. Earthquake, including land shock waves or tremors before, during or after a volcanic eruption;

    b. Landslide, mudslide or mudflow;

    c. Subsidence or sinkhole; or

    d. Any other earth movement including earth sinking, rising or shifting.

    This Exclusion **A.2.** applies regardless of whether any of the above, in **A.2.a.** through **A.2.d.**, is caused by an act of nature or is otherwise caused.

    However, direct loss by fire, explosion or theft resulting from any of the above, in **A.2.a.** through **A.2.d.**, is covered.

3. **Water**

    This means:

    a. Flood, surface water, waves, including tidal wave and tsunami, tides, tidal water, overflow of any body of water, or spray from any of these, all whether or not driven by wind, including storm surge;

    b. Water which:

    (1) Backs up through sewers or drains; or

    (2) Overflows or is otherwise discharged from a sump, sump pump or related equipment;

    c. Water below the surface of the ground, including water which exerts pressure on, or seeps, leaks or flows through a building, sidewalk, driveway, patio, foundation, swimming pool or other structure; or

    d. Waterborne material carried or otherwise moved by any of the water referred to in **A.3.a.** through **A.3.c.** of this exclusion.

This Exclusion **A.3.** applies regardless of whether any of the above, in **A.3.a.** through **A.3.d.**, is caused by an act of nature or is otherwise caused.

This Exclusion **A.3.** applies to, but is not limited to, escape, overflow or discharge, for any reason, of water or waterborne material from a dam, levee, seawall or any other boundary or containment system.

However, direct loss by fire, explosion or theft resulting from any of the above, in **A.3.a.** through **A.3.d.**, is covered.

4. **Power Failure**

   Power Failure means the failure of power or other utility service if the failure takes place off the "residence premises". But if the failure results in a loss, from a Peril Insured Against on the "residence premises", we will pay for the loss caused by that peril.

5. **Neglect**

   Neglect means neglect of an "insured" to use all reasonable means to save and preserve property at and after the time of a loss.

6. **War**

   War includes the following and any consequence of any of the following:

   a. Undeclared war, civil war, insurrection, rebellion or revolution;

   b. Warlike act by a military force or military personnel; or

   c. Destruction, seizure or use for a military purpose.

   Discharge of a nuclear weapon will be deemed a warlike act even if accidental.

7. **Nuclear Hazard**

   This Exclusion **A.7.** pertains to Nuclear Hazard to the extent set forth in **N.** Nuclear Hazard Clause under Section I – Conditions.

8. **Intentional Loss**

   Intentional Loss means any loss arising out of any act an "insured" commits or conspires to commit with the intent to cause a loss.

   In the event of such loss, no "insured" is entitled to coverage, even "insureds" who did not commit or conspire to commit the act causing the loss.

9. **Governmental Action**

   Governmental Action means the destruction, confiscation or seizure of property described in Coverage **A**, **B** or **C** by order of any governmental or public authority.

This exclusion does not apply to such acts ordered by any governmental or public authority that are taken at the time of a fire to prevent its spread, if the loss caused by fire would be covered under this policy.

B. We do not insure for loss to property described in Coverages **A** and **B** caused by any of the following. However, any ensuing loss to property described in Coverages **A** and **B** not precluded by any other provision in this policy is covered.

1. Weather conditions. However, this exclusion only applies if weather conditions contribute in any way with a cause or event excluded in **A.** above to produce the loss.

2. Acts or decisions, including the failure to act or decide, of any person, group, organization or governmental body.

3. Faulty, inadequate or defective:

   a. Planning, zoning, development, surveying, siting;

   b. Design, specifications, workmanship, repair, construction, renovation, remodeling, grading, compaction;

   c. Materials used in repair, construction, renovation or remodeling; or

   d. Maintenance;

   of part or all of any property whether on or off the "residence premises".

SECTION I – CONDITIONS

A. **Insurable Interest And Limit Of Liability**

   Even if more than one person has an insurable interest in the property covered, we will not be liable in any one loss:

   1. To an "insured" for more than the amount of such "insured's" interest at the time of loss; or

   2. For more than the applicable limit of liability.

B. **Deductible**

   Unless otherwise noted in this policy, the following deductible provision applies:

   With respect to any one loss:

   1. Subject to the applicable limit of liability, we will pay only that part of the total of all loss payable that exceeds the deductible amount shown in the Declarations.

   2. If two or more deductibles under this policy apply to the loss, only the highest deductible amount will apply.

C. Duties After Loss

In case of a loss to covered property, we have no duty to provide coverage under this policy if the failure to comply with the following duties is prejudicial to us. These duties must be performed either by you, an "insured" seeking coverage, or a representative of either:

1. Give prompt notice to us or our agent;
2. Notify the police in case of loss by theft;
3. Notify the credit card or electronic fund transfer card or access device company in case of loss as provided for in **E.6.** Credit Card, Electronic Fund Transfer Card Or Access Device, Forgery And Counterfeit Money under Section I – Property Coverages;
4. Protect the property from further damage. If repairs to the property are required, you must:
   a. Make reasonable and necessary repairs to protect the property; and
   b. Keep an accurate record of repair expenses;
5. Cooperate with us in the investigation of a claim;
6. Prepare an inventory of damaged personal property showing the quantity, description, actual cash value and amount of loss. Attach all bills, receipts and related documents that justify the figures in the inventory;
7. As often as we reasonably require:
   a. Show the damaged property;
   b. Provide us with records and documents we request and permit us to make copies; and
   c. Submit to examination under oath, while not in the presence of another "insured", and sign the same;
8. Send to us, within 60 days after our request, your signed, sworn proof of loss which sets forth, to the best of your knowledge and belief:
   a. The time and cause of loss;
   b. The interests of all "insureds" and all others in the property involved and all liens on the property;
   c. Other insurance which may cover the loss;
   d. Changes in title or occupancy of the property during the term of the policy;
   e. Specifications of damaged buildings and detailed repair estimates;
   f. The inventory of damaged personal property described in **6.** above;
   g. Receipts for additional living expenses incurred and records that support the fair rental value loss; and
   h. Evidence or affidavit that supports a claim under **E.6.** Credit Card, Electronic Fund Transfer Card Or Access Device, Forgery And Counterfeit Money under Section I – Property Coverages, stating the amount and cause of loss.

D. Loss Settlement

In this Condition **D.**, the terms "cost to repair or replace" and "replacement cost" do not include the increased costs incurred to comply with the enforcement of any ordinance or law, except to the extent that coverage for these increased costs is provided in **E.11.** Ordinance Or Law under Section I – Property Coverages. Covered property losses are settled as follows:

1. Property of the following types:
   a. Personal property;
   b. Awnings, carpeting, household appliances, outdoor antennas and outdoor equipment, whether or not attached to buildings;
   c. Structures that are not buildings; and
   d. Grave markers, including mausoleums;

   at actual cash value at the time of loss but not more than the amount required to repair or replace.

2. Buildings covered under Coverage **A** or **B** at replacement cost without deduction for depreciation, subject to the following:
   a. If, at the time of loss, the amount of insurance in this policy on the damaged building is 80% or more of the full replacement cost of the building immediately before the loss, we will pay the cost to repair or replace, without deduction for depreciation, but not more than the least of the following amounts:
      (1) The limit of liability under this policy that applies to the building;
      (2) The replacement cost of that part of the building damaged with material of like kind and quality and for like use; or
      (3) The necessary amount actually spent to repair or replace the damaged building.

      If the building is rebuilt at a new premises, the cost described in **(2)** above is limited to the cost which would have been incurred if the building had been built at the original premises.

b. If, at the time of loss, the amount of insurance in this policy on the damaged building is less than 80% of the full replacement cost of the building immediately before the loss, we will pay the greater of the following amounts, but not more than the limit of liability under this policy that applies to the building:

   (1) The actual cash value of that part of the building damaged; or

   (2) That proportion of the cost to repair or replace, without deduction for depreciation, that part of the building damaged, which the total amount of insurance in this policy on the damaged building bears to 80% of the replacement cost of the building.

c. To determine the amount of insurance required to equal 80% of the full replacement cost of the building immediately before the loss, do not include the value of:

   (1) Excavations, footings, foundations, piers, or any other structures or devices that support all or part of the building, which are below the undersurface of the lowest basement floor;

   (2) Those supports described in (1) above which are below the surface of the ground inside the foundation walls, if there is no basement; and

   (3) Underground flues, pipes, wiring and drains.

d. We will pay no more than the actual cash value of the damage until actual repair or replacement is complete. Once actual repair or replacement is complete, we will settle the loss as noted in **2.a.** and **b.** above.

   However, if the cost to repair or replace the damage is both:

   (1) Less than 5% of the amount of insurance in this policy on the building; and

   (2) Less than $2,500;

   we will settle the loss as noted in **2.a.** and **b.** above whether or not actual repair or replacement is complete.

e. You may disregard the replacement cost loss settlement provisions and make claim under this policy for loss to buildings on an actual cash value basis. You may then make claim for any additional liability according to the provisions of this Condition **D. Loss Settlement**, provided you notify us, within 180 days after the date of loss, of your intent to repair or replace the damaged building.

E. **Loss To A Pair Or Set**

In case of loss to a pair or set we may elect to:

1. Repair or replace any part to restore the pair or set to its value before the loss; or

2. Pay the difference between actual cash value of the property before and after the loss.

F. **Appraisal**

If you and we fail to agree on the amount of loss, either may demand an appraisal of the loss. In this event, each party will choose a competent and impartial appraiser within 20 days after receiving a written request from the other. The two appraisers will choose an umpire. If they cannot agree upon an umpire within 15 days, you or we may request that the choice be made by a judge of a court of record in the state where the "residence premises" is located. The appraisers will separately set the amount of loss. If the appraisers submit a written report of an agreement to us, the amount agreed upon will be the amount of loss. If they fail to agree, they will submit their differences to the umpire. A decision agreed to by any two will set the amount of loss.

Each party will:

1. Pay its own appraiser; and

2. Bear the other expenses of the appraisal and umpire equally.

G. **Other Insurance And Service Agreement**

If a loss covered by this policy is also covered by:

1. Other insurance, we will pay only the proportion of the loss that the limit of liability that applies under this policy bears to the total amount of insurance covering the loss; or

2. A service agreement, this insurance is excess over any amounts payable under any such agreement. Service agreement means a service plan, property restoration plan, home warranty or other similar service warranty agreement, even if it is characterized as insurance.

H. Suit Against Us

No action can be brought against us unless there has been full compliance with all of the terms under Section I of this policy and the action is started within two years after the date of loss.

I. Our Option

If we give you written notice within 30 days after we receive your signed, sworn proof of loss, we may repair or replace any part of the damaged property with material or property of like kind and quality.

J. Loss Payment

We will adjust all losses with you. We will pay you unless some other person is named in the policy or is legally entitled to receive payment. Loss will be payable 60 days after we receive your proof of loss and:

1. Reach an agreement with you;
2. There is an entry of a final judgment; or
3. There is a filing of an appraisal award with us.

K. Abandonment Of Property

We need not accept any property abandoned by an "insured".

L. Mortgage Clause

1. If a mortgagee is named in this policy, any loss payable under Coverage **A** or **B** will be paid to the mortgagee and you, as interests appear. If more than one mortgagee is named, the order of payment will be the same as the order of precedence of the mortgages.
2. If we deny your claim, that denial will not apply to a valid claim of the mortgagee, if the mortgagee:
   a. Notifies us of any change in ownership, occupancy or substantial change in risk of which the mortgagee is aware;
   b. Pays any premium due under this policy on demand if you have neglected to pay the premium; and
   c. Submits a signed, sworn statement of loss within 60 days after receiving notice from us of your failure to do so. Paragraphs F. Appraisal, H. Suit Against Us and J. Loss Payment under Section I – Conditions also apply to the mortgagee.
3. If we decide to cancel or not to renew this policy, the mortgagee will be notified at least 10 days before the date cancellation or nonrenewal takes effect.

4. If we pay the mortgagee for any loss and deny payment to you:
   a. We are subrogated to all the rights of the mortgagee granted under the mortgage on the property; or
   b. At our option, we may pay to the mortgagee the whole principal on the mortgage plus any accrued interest. In this event, we will receive a full assignment and transfer of the mortgage and all securities held as collateral to the mortgage debt.
5. Subrogation will not impair the right of the mortgagee to recover the full amount of the mortgagee's claim.

M. No Benefit To Bailee

We will not recognize any assignment or grant any coverage that benefits a person or organization holding, storing or moving property for a fee regardless of any other provision of this policy.

N. Nuclear Hazard Clause

1. "Nuclear Hazard" means any nuclear reaction, radiation, or radioactive contamination, all whether controlled or uncontrolled or however caused, or any consequence of any of these.
2. Loss caused by the nuclear hazard will not be considered loss caused by fire, explosion, or smoke, whether these perils are specifically named in or otherwise included within the Perils Insured Against.
3. This policy does not apply under Section I to loss caused directly or indirectly by nuclear hazard, except that direct loss by fire resulting from the nuclear hazard is covered.

O. Recovered Property

If you or we recover any property for which we have made payment under this policy, you or we will notify the other of the recovery. At your option, the property will be returned to or retained by you or it will become our property. If the recovered property is returned to or retained by you, the loss payment will be adjusted based on the amount you received for the recovered property.

P. Volcanic Eruption Period

One or more volcanic eruptions that occur within a 72-hour period will be considered as one volcanic eruption.

Q. Policy Period

This policy applies only to loss which occurs during the policy period.

R. Concealment Or Fraud

We provide coverage to no "insureds" under this policy if, whether before or after a loss, an "insured" has:

1. Intentionally concealed or misrepresented any material fact or circumstance;
2. Engaged in fraudulent conduct; or
3. Made false statements;

relating to this insurance.

S. Loss Payable Clause

If the Declarations shows a loss payee for certain listed insured personal property, the definition of "insured" is changed to include that loss payee with respect to that property.

If we decide to cancel or not renew this policy, that loss payee will be notified in writing.

SECTION II – LIABILITY COVERAGES

A. Coverage E – Personal Liability

If a claim is made or a suit is brought against an "insured" for damages because of "bodily injury" or "property damage" caused by an "occurrence" to which this coverage applies, we will:

1. Pay up to our limit of liability for the damages for which an "insured" is legally liable. Damages include prejudgment interest awarded against an "insured"; and
2. Provide a defense at our expense by counsel of our choice, even if the suit is groundless, false or fraudulent. We may investigate and settle any claim or suit that we decide is appropriate. Our duty to settle or defend ends when our limit of liability for the "occurrence" has been exhausted by payment of a judgment or settlement.

B. Coverage F – Medical Payments To Others

We will pay the necessary medical expenses that are incurred or medically ascertained within three years from the date of an accident causing "bodily injury". Medical expenses means reasonable charges for medical, surgical, x-ray, dental, ambulance, hospital, professional nursing, prosthetic devices and funeral services. This coverage does not apply to you or regular residents of your household except "residence employees". As to others, this coverage applies only:

1. To a person on the "insured location" with the permission of an "insured"; or
2. To a person off the "insured location", if the "bodily injury":
   a. Arises out of a condition on the "insured location" or the ways immediately adjoining;
   b. Is caused by the activities of an "insured";
   c. Is caused by a "residence employee" in the course of the "residence employee's" employment by an "insured"; or
   d. Is caused by an animal owned by or in the care of an "insured".

SECTION II – EXCLUSIONS

A. "Motor Vehicle Liability"

1. Coverages E and F do not apply to any "motor vehicle liability" if, at the time and place of an "occurrence", the involved "motor vehicle":
   a. Is registered for use on public roads or property;
   b. Is not registered for use on public roads or property, but such registration is required by a law, or regulation issued by a government agency, for it to be used at the place of the "occurrence"; or
   c. Is being:
      (1) Operated in, or practicing for, any prearranged or organized race, speed contest or other competition;
      (2) Rented to others;
      (3) Used to carry persons or cargo for a charge; or
      (4) Used for any "business" purpose except for a motorized golf cart while on a golfing facility.

2. If Exclusion A.1. does not apply, there is still no coverage for "motor vehicle liability", unless the "motor vehicle" is:
   a. In dead storage on an "insured location";
   b. Used solely to service a residence;
   c. Designed to assist the handicapped and, at the time of an "occurrence", it is:
      (1) Being used to assist a handicapped person; or
      (2) Parked on an "insured location";
   d. Designed for recreational use off public roads and:
      (1) Not owned by an "insured"; or

(2) Owned by an "insured" provided the "occurrence" takes place:

    (a) On an "insured location" as defined in Definition **B.6.a., b., d., e.** or **h.**; or

    (b) Off an "insured location" and the "motor vehicle" is:

       (i) Designed as a toy vehicle for use by children under seven years of age;

       (ii) Powered by one or more batteries; and

       (iii) Not built or modified after manufacture to exceed a speed of five miles per hour on level ground;

e. A motorized golf cart that is owned by an "insured", designed to carry up to four persons, not built or modified after manufacture to exceed a speed of 25 miles per hour on level ground and, at the time of an "occurrence", is within the legal boundaries of:

  (1) A golfing facility and is parked or stored there, or being used by an "insured" to:

    (a) Play the game of golf or for other recreational or leisure activity allowed by the facility;

    (b) Travel to or from an area where "motor vehicles" or golf carts are parked or stored; or

    (c) Cross public roads at designated points to access other parts of the golfing facility; or

  (2) A private residential community, including its public roads upon which a motorized golf cart can legally travel, which is subject to the authority of a property owners association and contains an "insured's" residence.

B. "Watercraft Liability"

1. Coverages **E** and **F** do not apply to any "watercraft liability" if, at the time of an "occurrence", the involved watercraft is being:

  a. Operated in, or practicing for, any prearranged or organized race, speed contest or other competition. This exclusion does not apply to a sailing vessel or a predicted log cruise;

  b. Rented to others;

  c. Used to carry persons or cargo for a charge; or

  d. Used for any "business" purpose.

2. If Exclusion **B.1.** does not apply, there is still no coverage for "watercraft liability" unless, at the time of the "occurrence", the watercraft:

  a. Is stored;

  b. Is a sailing vessel, with or without auxiliary power, that is:

    (1) Less than 26 feet in overall length; or

    (2) 26 feet or more in overall length and not owned by or rented to an "insured"; or

  c. Is not a sailing vessel and is powered by:

    (1) An inboard or inboard-outdrive engine or motor, including those that power a water jet pump, of:

      (a) 50 horsepower or less and not owned by an "insured"; or

      (b) More than 50 horsepower and not owned by or rented to an "insured"; or

    (2) One or more outboard engines or motors with:

      (a) 25 total horsepower or less;

      (b) More than 25 horsepower if the outboard engine or motor is not owned by an "insured";

      (c) More than 25 horsepower if the outboard engine or motor is owned by an "insured" who acquired it during the policy period; or

      (d) More than 25 horsepower if the outboard engine or motor is owned by an "insured" who acquired it before the policy period, but only if:

        (i) You declare them at policy inception; or

        (ii) Your intent to insure them is reported to us in writing within 45 days after you acquire them.

The coverages in **(c)** and **(d)** above apply for the policy period.

Horsepower means the maximum power rating assigned to the engine or motor by the manufacturer.

C. "Aircraft Liability"

This policy does not cover "aircraft liability".

D. "Hovercraft Liability"

This policy does not cover "hovercraft liability".

E. **Coverage E – Personal Liability And Coverage F – Medical Payments To Others**

Coverages **E** and **F** do not apply to the following:

1. **Expected Or Intended Injury**

   "Bodily injury" or "property damage" which is expected or intended by an "insured", even if the resulting "bodily injury" or "property damage":

   a. Is of a different kind, quality or degree than initially expected or intended; or

   b. Is sustained by a different person, entity or property than initially expected or intended.

   However, this Exclusion **E.1.** does not apply to "bodily injury" or "property damage" resulting from the use of reasonable force by an "insured" to protect persons or property;

2. **"Business"**

   a. "Bodily injury" or "property damage" arising out of or in connection with a "business" conducted from an "insured location" or engaged in by an "insured", whether or not the "business" is owned or operated by an "insured" or employs an "insured".

   This Exclusion **E.2.** applies but is not limited to an act or omission, regardless of its nature or circumstance, involving a service or duty rendered, promised, owed, or implied to be provided because of the nature of the "business".

   b. This Exclusion **E.2.** does not apply to:

   (1) The rental or holding for rental of an "insured location";

   (a) On an occasional basis if used only as a residence;

   (b) In part for use only as a residence, unless a single-family unit is intended for use by the occupying family to lodge more than two roomers or boarders; or

   (c) In part, as an office, school, studio or private garage; and

   (2) An "insured" under the age of 21 years involved in a part-time or occasional, self-employed "business" with no employees;

3. **Professional Services**

   "Bodily injury" or "property damage" arising out of the rendering of or failure to render professional services;

4. **"Insured's" Premises Not An "Insured Location"**

   "Bodily injury" or "property damage" arising out of a premises:

   a. Owned by an "insured";

   b. Rented to an "insured"; or

   c. Rented to others by an "insured";

   that is not an "insured location";

5. **War**

   "Bodily injury" or "property damage" caused directly or indirectly by war, including the following and any consequence of any of the following:

   a. Undeclared war, civil war, insurrection, rebellion or revolution;

   b. Warlike act by a military force or military personnel; or

   c. Destruction, seizure or use for a military purpose.

   Discharge of a nuclear weapon will be deemed a warlike act even if accidental;

6. **Communicable Disease**

   "Bodily injury" or "property damage" which arises out of the transmission of a communicable disease by an "insured";

7. **Sexual Molestation, Corporal Punishment Or Physical Or Mental Abuse**

   "Bodily injury" or "property damage" arising out of sexual molestation, corporal punishment or physical or mental abuse; or

8. **Controlled Substance**

   "Bodily injury" or "property damage" arising out of the use, sale, manufacture, delivery, transfer or possession by any person of a Controlled Substance as defined by the Federal Food and Drug Law at 21 U.S.C.A. Sections 811 and 812. Controlled Substances include but are not limited to cocaine, LSD, marijuana and all narcotic drugs. However, this exclusion does not apply to the legitimate use of prescription drugs by a person following the lawful orders of a licensed health care professional.

Exclusions **A.** "Motor Vehicle Liability", **B.** "Watercraft Liability", **C.** "Aircraft Liability", **D.** "Hovercraft Liability" and **E.4.** "Insured's" Premises Not An "Insured Location" do not apply to "bodily injury" to a "residence employee" arising out of and in the course of the "residence employee's" employment by an "insured".

F. **Coverage E – Personal Liability**

Coverage **E** does not apply to:

1. Liability:
   a. For any loss assessment charged against you as a member of an association, corporation or community of property owners, except as provided in **D. Loss Assessment** under Section II – Additional Coverages;
   b. Under any contract or agreement entered into by an "insured". However, this exclusion does not apply to written contracts:
      (1) That directly relate to the ownership, maintenance or use of an "insured location"; or
      (2) Where the liability of others is assumed by you prior to an "occurrence";
      unless excluded in **a.** above or elsewhere in this policy;
2. "Property damage" to property owned by an "insured". This includes costs or expenses incurred by an "insured" or others to repair, replace, enhance, restore or maintain such property to prevent injury to a person or damage to property of others, whether on or away from an "insured location";
3. "Property damage" to property rented to, occupied or used by or in the care of an "insured". This exclusion does not apply to "property damage" caused by fire, smoke or explosion;
4. "Bodily injury" to any person eligible to receive any benefits voluntarily provided or required to be provided by an "insured" under any:
   a. Workers' compensation law;
   b. Non-occupational disability law; or
   c. Occupational disease law;
5. "Bodily injury" or "property damage" for which an "insured" under this policy:
   a. Is also an insured under a nuclear energy liability policy issued by the:
      (1) Nuclear Energy Liability Insurance Association;
      (2) Mutual Atomic Energy Liability Underwriters;
      (3) Nuclear Insurance Association of Canada;
      or any of their successors; or
   b. Would be an insured under such a policy but for the exhaustion of its limit of liability; or
6. "Bodily injury" to you or an "insured" as defined under Definition **5.a.** or **b.**

   This exclusion also applies to any claim made or suit brought against you or an "insured" to:
   a. Repay; or
   b. Share damages with;
   another person who may be obligated to pay damages because of "bodily injury" to an "insured".

G. **Coverage F – Medical Payments To Others**

Coverage F does not apply to "bodily injury":

1. To a "residence employee" if the "bodily injury":
   a. Occurs off the "insured location"; and
   b. Does not arise out of or in the course of the "residence employee's" employment by an "insured";
2. To any person eligible to receive benefits voluntarily provided or required to be provided under any:
   a. Workers' compensation law;
   b. Non-occupational disability law; or
   c. Occupational disease law;
3. From any:
   a. Nuclear reaction;
   b. Nuclear radiation; or
   c. Radioactive contamination;
   all whether controlled or uncontrolled or however caused; or
   d. Any consequence of any of these; or
4. To any person, other than a "residence employee" of an "insured", regularly residing on any part of the "insured location".

SECTION II – ADDITIONAL COVERAGES

We cover the following in addition to the limits of liability:

A. **Claim Expenses**

We pay:

1. Expenses we incur and costs taxed against an "insured" in any suit we defend;
2. Premiums on bonds required in a suit we defend, but not for bond amounts more than the Coverage **E** limit of liability. We need not apply for or furnish any bond;

3. Reasonable expenses incurred by an "insured" at our request, including actual loss of earnings (but not loss of other income) up to $250 per day, for assisting us in the investigation or defense of a claim or suit; and

4. Interest on the entire judgment which accrues after entry of the judgment and before we pay or tender, or deposit in court that part of the judgment which does not exceed the limit of liability that applies.

B. First Aid Expenses

We will pay expenses for first aid to others incurred by an "insured" for "bodily injury" covered under this policy. We will not pay for first aid to an "insured".

C. Damage To Property Of Others

1. We will pay, at replacement cost, up to $1,000 per "occurrence" for "property damage" to property of others caused by an "insured".

2. We will not pay for "property damage":
    a. To the extent of any amount recoverable under Section I;
    b. Caused intentionally by an "insured" who is 13 years of age or older;
    c. To property owned by an "insured";
    d. To property owned by or rented to a tenant of an "insured" or a resident in your household; or
    e. Arising out of:
        (1) A "business" engaged in by an "insured";
        (2) Any act or omission in connection with a premises owned, rented or controlled by an "insured", other than the "insured location"; or
        (3) The ownership, maintenance, occupancy, operation, use, loading or unloading of aircraft, hovercraft, watercraft or "motor vehicles".

        This Exclusion e.(3) does not apply to a "motor vehicle" that:
        (a) Is designed for recreational use off public roads;
        (b) Is not owned by an "insured"; and
        (c) At the time of the "occurrence", is not required by law, or regulation issued by a government agency, to have been registered for it to be used on public roads or property.

D. Loss Assessment

1. We will pay up to $1,000 for your share of loss assessment charged against you, as owner or tenant of the "residence premises", during the policy period by a corporation or association of property owners, when the assessment is made as a result of:
    a. "Bodily injury" or "property damage" not excluded from coverage under Section II – Exclusions; or
    b. Liability for an act of a director, officer or trustee in the capacity as a director, officer or trustee, provided such person:
        (1) Is elected by the members of a corporation or association of property owners; and
        (2) Serves without deriving any income from the exercise of duties which are solely on behalf of a corporation or association of property owners.

2. Paragraph I. Policy Period under Section II – Conditions does not apply to this Loss Assessment Coverage.

3. Regardless of the number of assessments, the limit of $1,000 is the most we will pay for loss arising out of:
    a. One accident, including continuous or repeated exposure to substantially the same general harmful condition; or
    b. A covered act of a director, officer or trustee. An act involving more than one director, officer or trustee is considered to be a single act.

4. We do not cover assessments charged against you or a corporation or association of property owners by any governmental body.

SECTION II – CONDITIONS

A. Limit Of Liability

Our total liability under Coverage E for all damages resulting from any one "occurrence" will not be more than the Coverage E Limit Of Liability shown in the Declarations. This limit is the same regardless of the number of "insureds", claims made or persons injured. All "bodily injury" and "property damage" resulting from any one accident or from continuous or repeated exposure to substantially the same general harmful conditions shall be considered to be the result of one "occurrence".

Our total liability under Coverage **F** for all medical expense payable for "bodily injury" to one person as the result of one accident will not be more than the Coverage **F** Limit Of Liability shown in the Declarations.

B. Severability Of Insurance

This insurance applies separately to each "insured". This condition will not increase our limit of liability for any one "occurrence".

C. Duties After "Occurrence"

In case of an "occurrence", you or another "insured" will perform the following duties that apply. We have no duty to provide coverage under this policy if your failure to comply with the following duties is prejudicial to us. You will help us by seeing that these duties are performed:

1. Give written notice to us or our agent as soon as is practical, which sets forth:
    a. The identity of the policy and the "named insured" shown in the Declarations;
    b. Reasonably available information on the time, place and circumstances of the "occurrence"; and
    c. Names and addresses of any claimants and witnesses;
2. Cooperate with us in the investigation, settlement or defense of any claim or suit;
3. Promptly forward to us every notice, demand, summons or other process relating to the "occurrence";
4. At our request, help us:
    a. To make settlement;
    b. To enforce any right of contribution or indemnity against any person or organization who may be liable to an "insured";
    c. With the conduct of suits and attend hearings and trials; and
    d. To secure and give evidence and obtain the attendance of witnesses;
5. With respect to **C.** Damage To Property Of Others under Section II – Additional Coverages, submit to us within 60 days after the loss a sworn statement of loss and show the damaged property, if in an "insured's" control;
6. No "insured" shall, except at such "insured's" own cost, voluntarily make payment, assume obligation or incur expense other than for first aid to others at the time of the "bodily injury".

D. Duties Of An Injured Person – Coverage F – Medical Payments To Others

1. The injured person or someone acting for the injured person will:
    a. Give us written proof of claim, under oath if required, as soon as is practical; and
    b. Authorize us to obtain copies of medical reports and records.
2. The injured person will submit to a physical exam by a doctor of our choice when and as often as we reasonably require.

E. Payment Of Claim – Coverage F – Medical Payments To Others

Payment under this coverage is not an admission of liability by an "insured" or us.

F. Suit Against Us

1. No action can be brought against us unless there has been full compliance with all of the terms under this Section II.
2. No one will have the right to join us as a party to any action against an "insured".
3. Also, no action with respect to Coverage **E** can be brought against us until the obligation of such "insured" has been determined by final judgment or agreement signed by us.

G. Bankruptcy Of An "Insured"

Bankruptcy or insolvency of an "insured" will not relieve us of our obligations under this policy.

H. Other Insurance

This insurance is excess over other valid and collectible insurance except insurance written specifically to cover as excess over the limits of liability that apply in this policy.

I. Policy Period

This policy applies only to "bodily injury" or "property damage" which occurs during the policy period.

J. Concealment Or Fraud

We do not provide coverage to an "insured" who, whether before or after a loss, has:

1. Intentionally concealed or misrepresented any material fact or circumstance;
2. Engaged in fraudulent conduct; or
3. Made false statements;

relating to this insurance.

SECTIONS I AND II – CONDITIONS

A. Liberalization Clause

If we make a change which broadens coverage under this edition of our policy without additional premium charge, that change will automatically apply to your insurance as of the date we implement the change in your state, provided that this implementation date falls within 60 days prior to or during the policy period stated in the Declarations.

This Liberalization Clause does not apply to changes implemented with a general program revision that includes both broadenings and restrictions in coverage, whether that general program revision is implemented through introduction of:

1. A subsequent edition of this policy; or
2. An amendatory endorsement.

B. Waiver Or Change Of Policy Provisions

A waiver or change of a provision of this policy must be in writing by us to be valid. Our request for an appraisal or examination will not waive any of our rights.

C. Cancellation

1. You may cancel this policy at any time by returning it to us or by letting us know in writing of the date cancellation is to take effect.

2. We may cancel this policy only for the reasons stated below by letting you know in writing of the date cancellation takes effect. This cancellation notice may be delivered to you, or mailed to you at your mailing address shown in the Declarations. Proof of mailing will be sufficient proof of notice.

   a. When you have not paid the premium, we may cancel at any time by letting you know at least 10 days before the date cancellation takes effect.

   b. When this policy has been in effect for less than 60 days and is not a renewal with us, we may cancel for any reason by letting you know at least 10 days before the date cancellation takes effect.

   c. When this policy has been in effect for 60 days or more, or at any time if it is a renewal with us, we may cancel:

      (1) If there has been a material misrepresentation of fact which if known to us would have caused us not to issue the policy; or

      (2) If the risk has changed substantially since the policy was issued.

      This can be done by letting you know at least 30 days before the date cancellation takes effect.

   d. When this policy is written for a period of more than one year, we may cancel for any reason at anniversary by letting you know at least 30 days before the date cancellation takes effect.

3. When this policy is canceled, the premium for the period from the date of cancellation to the expiration date will be refunded pro rata.

4. If the return premium is not refunded with the notice of cancellation or when this policy is returned to us, we will refund it within a reasonable time after the date cancellation takes effect.

D. Nonrenewal

We may elect not to renew this policy. We may do so by delivering to you, or mailing to you at your mailing address shown in the Declarations, written notice at least 30 days before the expiration date of this policy. Proof of mailing will be sufficient proof of notice.

E. Assignment

Assignment of this policy will not be valid unless we give our written consent.

F. Subrogation

An "insured" may waive in writing before a loss all rights of recovery against any person. If not waived, we may require an assignment of rights of recovery for a loss to the extent that payment is made by us.

If an assignment is sought, an "insured" must sign and deliver all related papers and cooperate with us.

Subrogation does not apply to Coverage F or Paragraph C. Damage To Property Of Others under Section II – Additional Coverages.

G. Death

If any person named in the Declarations or the spouse, if a resident of the same household, dies, the following apply:

1. We insure the legal representative of the deceased but only with respect to the premises and property of the deceased covered under the policy at the time of death; and

2. "Insured" includes:
   a. An "insured" who is a member of your household at the time of your death, but only while a resident of the "residence premises"; and
   b. With respect to your property, the person having proper temporary custody of the property until appointment and qualification of a legal representative.

NOTES AND QUESTIONS

1. *Problem: Furnace Explosion.* Suppose that a client comes to you for assistance after her old and poorly-maintained furnace explodes. In addition to the furnace itself being destroyed, the explosion produced extensive smoke damage to the walls of her home and to much of her furniture. Before submitting her claim to the company, she wants to know what coverage she should expect. (a) Should she expect that the damage to her furniture and walls will be covered? How about the damage to her furnace itself? In answering these questions, focus on the following pages/sections of the Sample Policy: (i) page 3 from the "Property Coverages" section, (ii) pages 9–10 and 10–12 from the "Perils Insured Against" section, and (iii) pages 12–13 of the "Exclusions" section. (b) Ten minutes after the explosion, your client called an environmental cleanup company that cleaned the damaged property and walls. Can she recover for the cost of hiring this company? See pages 5–9 of the Sample Policy, in the "Additional Coverages" sub-section of the "Property Coverages" section. (c) Might your client be able to recover if she has to leave her home for several weeks while the smoke damage is permanently remediated? See page 5 in the "Property Coverages" portion of the Sample Policy. (d) Suppose that your client tells you that the smoke also damaged her motorcycle and some expensive equipment she maintained in connection with her business as a professional photographer. Should she expect coverage for these losses? See (i) page 4 in the "Property Coverages" section, and (ii) page 2 in the "Definitions" section. (e) What steps would you recommend your client take? See page 14 of the policy, in the "Conditions" section.

2. *Policy Complexity.* How likely is it that an ordinary consumer could read and understand her homeowners policy? In what ways, if any, does the declaration or policy summary page assist the policyholder in this regard? Do state laws requiring that policies be "readable" in the sense that they meet minimum quantitative measures of word and sentence length—a requirement that the Sample Policy meets—do anything to help improve consumer understanding of insurance policies? Could better rules regarding insurance policy disclosures meaningfully improve matters? See generally Daniel Schwarcz, Transparently Opaque: Understanding the Lack of Transparency in Insurance Consumer Protection, 61 UCLA L. Rev. 394, 441–43 (2014) (advocating for improved disclosure and transparency rules for insurance policies). But cf. Omri Ben-Shahar & Carl E. Schneider, More Than You Wanted to Know: The Failure of Mandated Disclosure (2014) (arguing that mandatory disclosure virtually always fails and creates substantial costs for consumers and firms).

B. THE REQUIREMENT OF AN INSURABLE INTEREST IN PROPERTY INSURANCE

The principle that insurance recovery is limited to policyholders' "insurable interest" is universal in insurance law. It functions as a specific type of public policy restriction in insurance contracts. Both the application and the importance of this idea varies by coverage line. We therefore will revisit the insurable interest requirement when we examine life insurance, in Chapter 5. For now, though, we focus on the principle in the property insurance context.

Richard C. Gossett and Margaret D. Gossett v. Farmers Insurance Company of Washington

Supreme Court of Washington, 1997.
133 Wash.2d 954.

■ MADSEN, J.

In this action for homeowners insurance benefits the parties dispute the nature and extent of the insurable interest which Richard and Margaret Gossett had in an unfinished house destroyed by fire. * * *

In 1990, the Gossetts found an unfinished house in Tacoma which they wished to buy, complete, and sell at a profit. They offered $90,000 and estimated they would need another $60,000 to $70,000 to finish the house. Their offer was accepted by the owner, Mr. Gunns, after two previous offers expired. * * *

In late August, the Gossetts spoke with a Farmers Insurance Company agent about insurance on the home. Mr. Gossett represented to the agent that the Gossetts would be the legal owners of the property. A policy was issued with the Gossetts as the named insureds and Trusty Deed as the mortgagee. According to the agent, the policy would not have been issued in the Gossetts' names had he known that the Gossetts were not legal owners.

On August 30, 1990, the Gossetts assigned all their interest in the purchase and sale agreement to Trusty Deed. They also signed an addendum to the purchase and sale agreement providing "Title to be taken in the name of Trusty Deed...." When the sale closed on September 5, 1990, title was placed in Trusty Deed, and Trusty Deed was listed as the buyer in the closing documents. There is evidence that Trusty Deed did not intend to buy or become record owner of the property. * * *

The record contains no evidence of any written agreement obligating the Gossetts to repay any money loaned for purchase of the property or of any written agreement under which the Gossetts could purchase the property from Trusty Deed.

The Gossetts began to work on the house in early September. Mr. Gossett testified that on November 18, 1990, he was working on the house when he fell and knocked over a kerosene heater, causing a fire that destroyed the house. At the time, the Gossetts were storing some of their belongings in the unfinished house and their sons stayed in the house at least some of the time to watch over things. The Gossetts had been staying at a motel and planned to move into the house the next day.

At the time of the fire, the Gossetts still had not obtained long-term financing. * * *

The Farmers policy provides: "Even if more than one person has an insurable interest in the covered property, we shall not pay more than: (1) an amount equal to the insured's interest, or (b) the applicable limit of insurance." Pursuant to RCW 48.18.040(2), an "insurable interest" is "any lawful and substantial economic interest in the safety or preservation of the subject of the insurance free from loss, destruction, or pecuniary damage." As Farmers concedes, under this definition legal title to property is not dispositive of whether one has an insurable interest in property. Thus, the fact that Trusty Deed held title to the property at the time of the fire does not preclude the Gossetts from having an insurable interest in it. Farmers maintains, however, that the Gossetts had only a speculative, expectation interest in the property at the time of the fire. We agree that on the facts of this case, the Gossetts did not have an insurable interest in the property beyond the improvements they made.

The record shows that the Gossetts intended to purchase the property from Mr. Gunns. However, at the time the fire broke out, they had been unable to carry out that intent because of problems securing long-term financing for the purchase price and construction costs to finish the house. They clearly did not purchase the property.

The Gossetts claim, though, that Trusty Deed merely held the deed to the property as security. Where a party is indebted on property and the property stands as security for the debt, the party has an insurable interest in the property. *See, e.g., Integon Gen. Ins. Corp. v. Gibson,* 485 S.E.2d 576, 578 (1997); *Kilpatrick v. Hartford Fire Ins. Co.,* 701 S.W.2d 755 (Mo.App.1985).

Here, the record does not reveal any obligation on the Gossetts' part to purchase the property. * * * There is no promissory note, no mortgage documentation, and no deed of trust. Nothing prior to the fire documents any security interest given by the Gossetts to either Trusty Deed or Ms. Crennell [who supplied the financing provided by Trusty Deed]. * * *

It is a long-standing rule that when property is conveyed by a deed absolute in form, with nothing in the collateral papers to show any contrary intent, the presumption is that the transaction is what it appears to be on its face and any party who claims that the transaction is other than what it appears to be must prove that claim by clear and convincing evidence. * * *

A fundamental principle of insurance law is that opportunities for net gain to an insured through the receipt of insurance proceeds exceeding a loss should be regarded as inimical to the public interest. In other words, insurance arrangements are structured to provide funds to offset a loss either wholly or partly, and the payments made by an insurer generally are limited to an amount that does not exceed what is required to restore the insured to a condition relatively equivalent to that which existed before the loss occurred. The concept that insurance contracts shall confer a benefit no greater in value than the loss suffered by an insured is usually referred to as the "principle of indemnity." Robert E. Keeton & Alan I. Widiss, *Insurance Law, A Guide to Fundamental Principles, Legal Doctrines, and Commercial Practices, Practitioner's Edition* § 3.1(a), at 135 (1988).

The doctrine of insurable interest is tied to the principle of indemnity and serves a number of purposes, among them the prevention of using insurance contracts as gambling or wagering contracts. *Id.* § 3.1(c), at 136. Additionally, the doctrine is designed to protect against societal waste and to avoid the danger in allowing persons without an insurable interest to purchase insurance, because those persons might then intentionally destroy lives or property. *Id.* at 138. "To destroy life or property in order to receive insurance benefits is, to say the least, unproductive for a society." *Id.*

These purposes of the "insurable interest" doctrine would be ill-served by permitting the Gossetts to recover whatever insurance proceeds would be due based upon the value of the house at the time it was destroyed. They had no documented indebtedness. They would be placed in a far better position than they were before the fire. If we were to accept the-well-after-the-fire execution of quit claim deeds stating for "release of security" as establishing indebtedness for purchase of the property by the Gossetts, under the facts of this case our decision would be an incentive for insurance fraud and arson.

Nor is it an answer that the Gossetts paid insurance premiums. Where the ownership of the property belongs elsewhere, payment of insurance premiums on the property does not give rise to an insurable interest. 3 Lee R. Russ & Thomas F. Segalla, *Couch on Insurance* § 41:11, at 41–26 (3d ed. 1995).

The Gossetts also urge the court to consider their expectation of profit as evidence of an insurable interest. The Court of Appeals found a material issue of fact as to insurable interest in part because the Gossetts expected to buy the house, finish it, and make a profit selling it.

Initially, the policy involved here does not provide coverage for expected profits from a future sale of the insured property. Instead, the policy is a replacement cost policy which provides for coverage for the smaller of "the replacement cost of that part of the building damaged for equivalent construction and use on the same premises[,]" or "the amount actually and necessarily spent to repair or replace the building intended for the same occupancy and use."

Moreover, the Gossetts' expectations do not constitute an insurable interest. This court has previously held that inchoate rights in expectation did not constitute an insurable interest where the expectation never materialized. *Tyree v. General Ins. Co.,* 64 Wash. 2d 748, 751–52. * * *

The Gossetts' hopes and expectations of acquiring the property in the future are insufficient to constitute an insurable interest. At most, any such interest is akin to an option to purchase, and under an ordinary option contract prior to exercise of the option, "the optionee acquires no equitable estate or interest in the optioned land." *Robroy Land Co. v. Prather,* 95 Wash. 2d 66, 71 (1980). Many courts have held that a mere option to purchase is insufficient to constitute an insurable interest. * * * Where an option to purchase is contingent on occurrence of another event, courts have been even less inclined to find an insurable interest. *E.g., Christ Gospel Temple v. Liberty Mut. Ins. Co.,* 273 Pa. Super. 302 (1979); *Bartlett v. Allstate Ins. Co.,* 280 Mont. 63 (1996). Even if the Gossetts had had an option to purchase, it would have been at best an option contingent upon their obtaining long-term financing and thus was insufficient to constitute an insurable interest. The Gossetts, however, do not claim they had even an option to purchase. All they had was an expectation. "The mere possibility of an interest materializing, depending upon the occurrence of an uncertain event, will not give rise to an insurable interest." Russ & Segalla, § 41.11, at 41–26.

The Gossetts also contend that because of their possession of the property, their improvements to the property, their interest in its safety, and their continued efforts to secure long-term financing, they had an insurable interest in the property.

The trial court correctly held that the Gossetts had an interest in preserving the house from damage to the extent of the improvements they made because of their pecuniary loss resulting when those improvements were destroyed along with the rest of the house. See 4 John A. Appleman & Jean Appleman, *Insurance Law and Practice* § 2131, at 49 (1969) (one who has built on the lands of another with the other's permission has an insurable interest in the improvements built). Improvements to property do not, however, entitle the party making the improvements to an insurable interest to the extent of the full replacement value of the property. Under the principle of indemnity discussed above, an insured with a partial interest in the property can generally recover only to the extent of that interest. *See City of Carlsbad v. Northwestern Nat'l Ins. Co.,* 81 N.M. 56 (1970); *see generally* 44 Am. Jur. 2d Insurance, §§ 1515, 1516 (1982). Otherwise, an insurance policy could too readily be used as a device to profit from destruction of property rather than as a contract of indemnification for a loss actually incurred. *See Harrington v. Agricultural Ins. Co.,* 179 Minn. 510 (1930). If improvements to a structure are all that is necessary to obtain an insurable interest in the replacement value of the entire structure, one could, for a small "investment," obtain a huge windfall.

As to possession of the property, the record does not show the Gossetts were purchasers entitled to possession because of a present purchase or an obligation to purchase the property in the future, nor does it show that they were lessees. They had not moved into the house at the time of the fire (though their sons stayed at the house at least some of the time to watch over things). The record is not clear why the Gossetts were allowed to make improvements to the property without any apparent legal obligations arising in connection with the property. However, to the extent they were in possession of the property, their interest in that possession is still insufficient to establish an insurable interest in the entire replacement value of the house. As Farmers points out, so far as the record shows Trusty Deed could have demanded that the Gossetts leave the premises at any time. Under such circumstances, the Gossetts did not have a sufficient pecuniary interest in continued possession of the property. *See, e.g., Boston Ins. Co. v. Beckett,* 91 Idaho 220 (1966) (where right to use a cabin could have been terminated at any time by individual's mother-in-law, the right to use the cabin was not a "substantial economic interest" within meaning of Idaho statute defining "insurable interest," using nearly the same definition as Washington's statute; thus, individual lacked insurable interest in cabin).

We conclude that in this case the trial court correctly granted summary judgment in favor of the Gossetts, while holding that their insurable interest is limited to the improvements they made to the property. The Gossetts have failed to present clear and convincing evidence sufficient to overcome the presumption that the conveyance of the property by a deed absolute in form from Mr. Gunns to Trusty Deed was an outright conveyance of the property. Further, as to other evidence presented, reasonable minds could reach but one conclusion, i.e., that the Gossetts' insurable interest in the property extends only to the improvements they made. Accordingly, the trial court's order on summary judgment is affirmed.

NOTES AND QUESTIONS

1. *The Principle of Indemnity.* The modern function of the requirement of an insurable interest is to serve the principle of indemnity: the notion that the purpose of insurance is to protect the insured against suffering a loss, not to create the opportunity for gain. The requirement of an insurable interest originated in two English statutes enacted in the middle of the 18th century to limit the use of life and marine insurance as methods of gambling. See The Life Assurance Act of 1774, 14 Geo. 3, c. 48; Act of 1746, St. 19 Geo. 2, c. 37. Although state legislatures in the United States eventually enacted statutes governing insurable interest issues, early court decisions first brought the requirement to the U.S. It is now common for property insurance policies themselves to incorporate an insurable interest requirement, as in the policy at issue in *Gosset* as well as the Sample Policy (page 13).

The predominant justification now given for the requirement of an insurable interest is that it combats moral hazard: in the absence of an insurable interest held by the party procuring insurance, the incentive to destroy insured property or persons would be considerably greater. The requirement is intended to test for situations in which the insured party is presumed to be better off if the insured subject matter continues to exist. This policy is so strong that most courts hold that policyholders cannot employ doctrines such as waiver or estoppel to avoid an insurer's claim that they had no insurable interest at all in the damaged property. See *Liverpool & London & Globe Ins. Co., Ltd. v. Bolling,* 176 Va. 182 (1940). But see *Rhead v. Hartford Ins. Co. of the Midwest,* 135 Idaho 446 (2001) (permitting policyholder to claim insurer is estopped from claiming policyholder has no insurable interest when it is aware of facts regarding insurable interest and nonetheless issues or renews the policy).

2. *Four Tests for Insurable Interest.* There are at least four different tests for the existence of an insurable interest. Typically, satisfying one of the tests is enough. A *legal or equitable interest* in property will always suffice, subject sometimes to the condition that the interest have at least some value. In many jurisdictions the *factual expectancy* test that the court in *Gossett* seemed to accept in principle also prevails. See, e.g., *ABB Power T & D Co., Inc. v. Gothaer Versicherungsbank VVAG,* 939 F. Supp. 1568 (S.D. Fla. 1996) (under federal maritime law, any pecuniary interest will support an insurable interest). A *contract right* that depends on the continued existence of property also will support an insurable interest in that property. Secured creditors, for example, fall into this category. Finally, the potential for suffering *legal liability* for the destruction of property will also support an insurable interest in it. See, e.g., *Vill. of Constantine v. Home Ins. Co.,* 427 F.2d 1338 (6th Cir. 1970) (promise to procure insurance on property sold subject to conditional sales contract and later transferred to third party supports insurable interest in seller). To

what extent are the other three tests merely different versions of the factual expectancy test? In a jurisdiction that has adopted all four tests—and many have—counsel would rarely have an excuse for failing to situate a client so that the insurance the client legitimately wished to purchase was supported by an insurable interest in the client.

3. *The Interest Insured.* What would you need to know to determine whether the Gossetts' claim failed because they had no insurable interest, or because the proper documents were not prepared to reflect their interest? Should a distinction be drawn between the existence of an insurable interest in the abstract and the interest that was actually insured, as the court in *Gossett* did? To test your understanding of the rationale of the decision in *Gossett*, consider the following questions: Why did the court think it important that the Gossetts had no obligation to purchase the property? Why did the court apparently consider it irrelevant that the Gossetts could have purchased the property if they had obtained long-term financing? Contrast *Gossett* with *Weber v. Weber*, 142 P.3d 338 (Kan. App. 2006), in which a wife had forfeited all right to her husband's property under an antenuptial agreement. The court nonetheless held that she had an insurable interest in that property while the couple was married. Was her factual expectation greater than the expectation of the Gossetts? Different? Like *Weber*, some courts seem to apply a somewhat looser standard in determining whether the insured had a sufficient factual expectation. See, e.g., *Belton v. Cincinnati Ins. Co.*, 353 S.C. 363 (App. 2003) (expressly rejecting *Gossett*, and holding that a party holding an option to purchase property has an insurable interest in it); *Teague-Strebeck Motors, Inc. v. Chrysler Ins. Co.*, 127 N.M. 603 (App. 1999) (concluding that the insurable interest test should be based on the insured's actual expectations, not the technicalities of a legal interest).

In *Snethen v. Oklahoma State Union of the Farmers Educational & Cooperative Union of America*, 664 P.2d 377 (Okl. 1983), the purchaser of a used car insured it against damage caused by collision and, after a loss, learned that the car had been stolen from its rightful owner and had to be returned. The court in *Snethen* did not question the extent of the insurable interest, although at the time the insured filed his insurance claim he suffered no "loss" from the collision because he did not own the car. Similarly, in *Morgan v. Patrons Mutual Insurance Ass'n*, 813 F. Supp. 1502 (D. Kan. 1993), the court held that a prospective purchaser of a building destroyed by fire had an insurable interest even under an oral contract that was not enforceable under the Statute of Frauds. Are these decisions consistent with *Gossett*? What if a building insured under a fire policy is destroyed ten days prior to the time it was scheduled for demolition? See *New Ponce Shopping Ctr., S.E. v. Integrand Assurance Co.*, 86 F.3d 265 (1st Cir. 1996); *Tublitz v. Glens Falls Ins. Co.*, 179 N.J. Super. 275 (1981) (insurable interest exists, measure of loss unclear). Which provisions in the Definitions and the Conditions sections of the Sample Homeowners Policy address the issues raised in these cases? How clearly do these provisions resolve these issues?

4. *Timing.* Would it make sense to require that there be an insurable interest both at the time the property is first insured and at the time of loss? That is the rule derived from the English case of *The Sadlers Co. v. Badcock*, 26 Eng. Rep. 733 (1743), but most modern courts require that an interest in property exist only at the time of loss. See *United Tech. Corp. v.*

Am. Home Assurance Co., 989 F. Supp. 128 (D. Conn. 1997). If the principal function of the insurable interest requirement in property insurance is to combat moral hazard, does this approach make sense?

C. TRIGGER AND OCCURRENCE ISSUES

Recall the structure of property insurance policies discussed at the beginning of this Chapter. The policies tend to cover "direct physical loss" to specified property caused by any peril not specifically excluded (at least in the case of all-risk, rather than specified-risk, coverage). Although application of this affirmative coverage grant is straightforward in most cases, a number of issues do arise regarding its scope, as in the following case.

Port Authority of New York and New Jersey v. Affiliated FM Insurance Company

United States Court of Appeals, Third Circuit, 2002.
311 F.3d 226.

■ WEIS, CIRCUIT JUDGE.

The District Court held that unless asbestos in a building was of such quantity and condition as to make the structure unusable, the expense of correcting the situation was not within the scope of a first party insurance policy covering "physical loss or damage." We agree and will affirm.

Plaintiffs, the Port Authority of New York and New Jersey and its subsidiary, the Port Authority Trans-Hudson Corporation, own numerous facilities in New York and New Jersey that incorporated asbestos products in their construction. Alleging asbestos contamination, plaintiffs filed suit for damages in the New Jersey state courts against the defendants, a number of insurance companies that had first-party policies on the various structures. The case was removed to the United States District Court for the District of New Jersey.

Plaintiffs seek recovery for expenses incurred in conjunction with the abatement of asbestos-containing materials in their structures such as the World Trade Center complex in New York and Newark International Airport in New Jersey. The plaintiffs contend that physical damage has occurred in these structures as a result of the "presence of asbestos," "threat of release and reintrainment of asbestos fibers," and the "actual release and reintrainment of asbestos fibers."

To support their claims, plaintiffs point to the existence of friable asbestos in some of their buildings. Once an asbestos product reaches the friability stage, it may be crumbled by vibrations or hand pressure and it continues to deteriorate into separate fibers. In this condition, the asbestos becomes more susceptible to dispersion in the air and poses an increased risk to human health. Plaintiffs cite this as a documented problem at Newark Airport, where insulation had to be removed from pipes around the heating and ventilating units. In other locations, asbestos fibers were actually released during the performance of routine building functions, the renovation of existing structures, and demolition projects.

In the mid-1980s, the plaintiffs undertook a renovation program to remove asbestos products from portions of the World Trade Center. Pursuant to OSHA regulations, plaintiffs augmented their abatement policy by conducting regular surveys of asbestos-containing materials and employing air monitoring procedures. During these activities, maintenance and construction workers were subjected to stringent safety requirements, including mandatory protective clothing and equipment. However, air samples taken in each location did not reveal the presence of asbestos fibers exceeding EPA standards.

Even after the World Trade Center was severely damaged by a truck bomb in 1993, extensive air sampling tests indicated that, except for the occasional "spikes of higher levels," the existing conditions were not problematic. Relying on these tests, plaintiffs continually assured their employees, as well as current and prospective tenants, that the buildings were safe and within regulatory limits.

The Port Authority's policy on the asbestos present was to "manage [it] in place and to abate it only when required." The record in the District Court established that none of the plaintiffs' structures violated applicable regulations, and asbestos levels inside the buildings were comparable to background levels on the streets. In the more than 1,000 locations alleged to contain asbestos or an imminent threat of its release, plaintiffs assert claims for 69 abatement projects, which the record shows had been carried out in only 13 instances. During this time, all of plaintiffs' structures continued in normal use.

Plaintiffs made claims against the defendants under their first-party insurance policies which [insured against] "ALL RISKS of physical loss or damage occurring during the period of this policy * * * except as otherwise specifically excluded." * * *

The policies define "loss occurrence" as a "loss or combination of losses caused by all risks of physical loss or damage subject to the perils excluded arising out of one single event . . . or a loss by any peril or combination of perils insured against arising out of a single event." The periods covered in the policies were from 1971 to 1991. Unlike usual contracts of adhesion, the manuscript policies issued by the defendants were drafted by plaintiffs with the aid of counsel and insurance professionals, and, in some respects, negotiated with the underwriters.
* * *

The District Court framed the issue as whether coverage was "triggered in the first instance, without regard to language excluding certain risks of loss." Finding that the language of the policies was unambiguous, the Court determined that the only question that needed to be decided was whether the insured had suffered "physical loss or damage."

The plaintiffs have the burden to establish that their structures were, in fact, physically damaged in order to trigger coverage. *See, Koppers Co. v. Aetna Cas. & Surety Co.*, 98 F.3d 1440, 1446 (3rd Cir.1996); *Cobra Products Inc. v. Federal Ins. Co.*, 722 A.2d 545, 549 (1998). In resolving the issues before it, the Court concluded that "it is important to differentiate between the authorities generated by [first-party and third-party] coverage." Where, in the District Court's opinion, "the central issue is a fundamental one delimiting the scope of coverage under a first party insuring agreement . . . [t]here is more than adequate justification to seek guidance only from first party precedent."

Acknowledging that no controlling case on point existed, the Court reasoned that "physical loss or damage" could be found only if an imminent threat of asbestos release existed, or actual release of asbestos resulted in contamination of the property so as to nearly eliminate or destroy its function, or render it uninhabitable. The mere presence of asbestos, on the other hand, was not enough to trigger coverage.

The Court determined that the plaintiffs had failed to introduce evidence of "physical loss or damage" sufficient to survive summary judgment. Notably, the Court observed that "a significant portion of the [plaintiffs'] claimed losses arise from the presence of asbestos, unaccompanied by even the suggestion of actual release or imminent threat of release of asbestos fibers." Of the plaintiffs' locations where proof of release was shown, the Court noted that the continued and uninterrupted use of the buildings without any indication of elevated airborne asbestos level, coupled with the plaintiffs' own assurances of public safety, "belie the existence of contamination to the extent required to constitute physical loss or damage." Finally, the Court concluded that the plaintiffs cannot create a material issue "based on imminent threat of release of asbestos manifested during the years 1978 to 1991 if it has failed to abate the purported threat to date."

The Port Authority has appealed, asserting that the District Court adopted an incorrect standard for "physical loss" and misconstrued first-party and third-party insurance case law. Moreover, the plaintiffs argue that they produced ample proof that there was physical loss or damage attributable to asbestos in the insured properties. The defendants contend that plaintiffs failed to show physical loss or damage to its buildings and that the District Court correctly relied on first-party insurance law and principles rather than third-party coverage standards. * * * The case before us presents issues of state law. Because the plaintiffs' properties lie in both New York and New Jersey, the law of either state could be applicable to various structures. However, there appears to be no substantive difference in the law of the two states and the parties do not advance conflict of laws issues.

The fundamental differences between liability policies and first-party contracts make the multitude of appellate court opinions in third-party asbestos personal injury suits unhelpful in resolving the issues presented in this case. The primary aim of third-party insurance is to defend and indemnify insureds against liability for claims made against them as a result of their own conduct. First-party coverage, on the other hand, protects against loss caused by injury to the insured's own property. Wholly different interests are protected by the two distinct forms of coverage. * * *

Plaintiffs have cited two first-party appellate decisions referring to asbestos contamination of an apartment building, *Sentinel Mgmt. Co. v. New Hampshire Ins. Co.,* 563 N.W.2d 296 (Minn.Ct.App.1997) and in a later stage of that same litigation, *Sentinel Mgmt. Co. v. Aetna Cas. & Surety Co.,* 615 N.W.2d 819 (Minn.2000). In those cases, plaintiffs sought recovery under their first-party "all risks" policy "not for the mere presence of [asbestos containing materials] in the buildings, but for the release of asbestos fibers and resultant contamination." *Sentinel,* 563 N.W.2d at 300.

The *Sentinel* Courts concluded that asbestos contamination can constitute a direct, physical and fortuitous loss under an "all-risks" first-party insurance policy. In order to meet this standard, plaintiffs had to prove not only the presence of asbestos, but that the contamination presented a health hazard to the building's tenants and as such seriously impaired the building's function. *Sentinel,* 615 N.W.2d at 826. Although the buildings in question remained occupied without significant abatement activity, the proof of actual release of asbestos fibers on carpeting and other surfaces was considered to be enough to trigger the insurance coverage. * * *

Defendants call our attention to *Leafland Group-II v. Insurance Co. of North America,* 118 N.M. 281 (N.M.1994). In that first-party policy dispute, the insured claimed loss of value of an apartment complex caused by the presence of asbestos containing materials. These components, however, were in the buildings when they were purchased by the insured. In denying recovery, the New Mexico Supreme Court noted that no incident or occurrence during the time the policy was in effect caused direct loss or damage to the structures. The Court commented that " 'all risks' first-party insurance coverage . . . does not protect against losses that are certain to happen." *Leafland,* 881 P.2d at 28.

Defendants also cite *Pirie v. Federal Ins. Co.,* 45 Mass.App.Ct. 907 (1998), where plaintiffs sought first-party coverage for lead paint removal. The Court concluded that an internal defect in a building does not amount to an actual physical loss, and, as a result, the costs associated with eliminating lead paint from the house were not covered. In reaching this decision, the Court cited similar results in asbestos cases. *See, e.g., Great Northern Ins. Co. v. Benjamin Franklin Sav. & Loan Ass'n,* 793 F. Supp. 259 (D.Or.1990), *aff'd,* 953 F.2d 1387 (9th Cir.1992).

We thus find ourselves with a diversity case in which applicable state law provides no guidance and the parties rely on appellate decisions from jurisdictions having no relationship with the entities involved in this dispute. Our task is, therefore, one of prediction of what may eventually become the law of the states that are most concerned with the subject matter. * * *

In ordinary parlance and widely accepted definition, physical damage to property means "a distinct, demonstrable, and physical alteration" of its structure. 10 Couch on Insurance § 148:46 (3d ed.1998). Fire, water, smoke and impact from another object are typical examples of physical damage from an outside source that may demonstrably alter the components of a building and trigger coverage. Physical damage to a building as an entity by sources unnoticeable to the naked eye must meet a higher threshold. The Colorado Supreme Court in *Western Fire Ins. Co. v. First Presbyterian Church,* 165 Colo. 34 (Co.1968), concluded that coverage was triggered when authorities ordered a building closed after gasoline fumes seeped into a building's structure and made its use unsafe. Although neither the building nor its elements were demonstrably altered, its function was eliminated.

In the case before us, the policies cover "physical loss," as well as damage. When the presence of large quantities of asbestos in the air of a building is such as to make the structure uninhabitable and unusable, then there has been a distinct loss to its owner. However, if asbestos is present in components of a structure, but is not in such form or quantity as to make the building unusable, the owner has not suffered a loss. The structure continues to function—it has not lost its utility. The fact that the owner may choose to seal the asbestos or replace it with some other substance as part of routine maintenance does not bring the expense within first-party coverage.

The District Court concluded that "physical loss or damage" occurs only if an actual release of asbestos fibers from asbestos containing materials has resulted in contamination of the property such that its function is nearly eliminated or destroyed, or the structure is made useless or uninhabitable, or if there exists an imminent threat of the release of a quantity of asbestos fibers that would cause such loss of utility. The mere presence of asbestos, or the general threat of future damage from that presence, lacks the distinct and demonstrable character necessary for first-party insurance coverage.

We agree with the District Court's articulation of the proper standard for "physical loss or damage" to a structure caused by asbestos contamination. The requirement that the contamination reach such a level in order to come within coverage limitation establishes a reasonable and realistic standard for identifying physical loss or damage. The effect of asbestos fibers in such quantity is comparable to that of fire, water or smoke on a structure's use and function. A less demanding standard would require compensation for repairs caused by the inevitable deterioration of materials used in the construction of the building. This outcome would not comport with the intent of a first-party "all risks" insurance policy, but would transform it into a maintenance contract. *See 80 Broad St. Co. v. U.S. Fire Ins. Co.,* 389 N.Y.S.2d 214 (N.Y.Sup.Ct.1975), *aff'd,* 390 N.Y.S.2d 768 (1st Dep't.1976).

We thus find ourselves in agreement with the District Court's ruling that plaintiffs' inability "to produce evidence concerning the manifestation of an imminent threat of asbestos contamination" forecloses the existence of a viable claim. Although the plaintiffs demonstrated that many of its structures used asbestos-containing substances, those buildings had continuous and uninterrupted usage for many years. The mere presence of asbestos or the general threat of its future release is not enough to survive summary judgment or to show a physical loss or damage to trigger coverage under a first-party "all risks" policy.

Accordingly, the judgment of the District Court will be affirmed.

NOTES AND QUESTIONS

1. *From the Inside or From the Outside?* Although the court held that physical loss or damage had not occurred, it also suggested that there would be coverage if the asbestos had dispersed and made the property uninhabitable. It seems to follow that even if one part of an insured property damages another, there may be coverage. For example, in *Pepsico,*

Inc. v. Winterthur International America Co., 24 A.D.3d 743 (N.Y. App. Div. 2005), the court held that Pepsico's property (soft drinks) had been "physically damaged" when an ingredient that was not harmful nonetheless caused the product to have an "off-taste." Rejecting the insurer's argument that there had to be "distinct demonstrable alteration of physical structure . . . by an external force," the court held that it was "sufficient under the circumstances that the product's function and value have been seriously impaired." See also *Essex Ins. Co. v. BloomSouth Flooring Corp.*, 562 F.3d 399, 406 (1st Cir. 2009) (carpeting that releases a foul odor can cause physical damage to structure). Under this test, would the *Port Authority* case have come out differently?

2. *Internal Defects.* Is the court's suggestion that the policy would cover asbestos damage resulting in the property becoming uninhabitable consistent with the *Leafland Group-II* and *Pirie* cases that the court describes? These two cases suggest that a direct physical loss only occurs when an external force acts upon the insured property. Did this occur in *Port Authority*? We will return to this issue later in the Chapter when we examine exclusions dealing with the issue of intrinsic loss.

3. *How Are Progressively Occurring Losses Treated?* Recall the distinction between occurrence-based and claims-made based liability insurance policies. Suppose there is physical damage to or loss of use of tangible property, but that damage or loss of use occurs during multiple policy periods. Which policy or policies is "triggered," i.e., activated? Is more than one policy potentially responsible for at least part of the loss? These questions implicate what is sometimes termed the "loss in progress" doctrine. The most prominent case addressing the issue is *Prudential-LMI Commercial Insurance v. Superior Court*, 51 Cal.3d 674 (1990). There, cracking in a foundation and floor slab of an apartment building was discovered in 1985 to have been occurring for some time. The court held that only the policy in effect at the time that appreciable property damage was discovered or should have been discovered provided coverage. Most courts agree that only one policy is triggered as a result of a loss in progress, though some depart from *Prudential-LMI* by concluding that the policy that was in effect when the damage first began to occur is triggered, even if the damage was discovered during a later policy period. See, e.g., *Ellis Court Apartments Ltd. P'ship ex rel. Woodside Corp. v. State Farm Fire & Cas. Co.*, 117 Wash. App. 807 (2003).

The argument for denying coverage when a policyholder is aware of a loss prior to purchasing coverage in order to combat adverse selection and moral hazard is straightforward. But when should courts limit coverage if a loss was not in fact known, but arguably *should* have been known prior to coverage? Courts typically set a high bar for excluding coverage on this basis, requiring that the policyholder have actual knowledge of an immediate threat of loss. The doctrine is generally unavailable when insurers are aware of the facts surrounding the known loss at the time they issue the policy. See *Crawfordsville Square, LLC. v. Monroe Guar. Ins. Co.*, 906 N.E.2d 934 (Ind. Ct. App. 2009). What do you think is the rationale for this limitation on the doctrine?

4. *How Many "Occurrences" Caused the Loss?* Property insurance, especially for commercial policyholders, typically is provided on a "per occurrence" basis, but with no annual aggregate limit on the amount of loss that is covered. For each loss that is caused by a separate occurrence, a

"limit of liability," or amount of coverage, is provided. Some policies define an "occurrence" but others do not. For example, the definition in the Sample Homeowners Policy is "an accident, including continuous or repeated exposure to substantially the same general harmful conditions, which results, during the policy period," in bodily injury or property damage (page 2). In effect, an occurrence is a cause of loss. How much coverage is provided when similar causes result in a loss or losses? This was the issue that arose in the *World Trade Center* case described in Chapter Two. Recall that the court in that case found that the destruction of the two WTC towers was caused by only one occurrence under one definition of an "occurrence," but that the issue was a question of fact for the jury with respect to policies that did not define the term "occurrence." See *World Trade Ctr. Props., L.L.C. v. Hartford Fire Ins. Co.*, 345 F.3d 154 (2d Cir. 2003). Does this result argue for defining the term occurrence, placing an annual aggregate limit of liability in commercial property insurance policies, or leaving it to the jury to decide how much coverage is available on a case-by-case basis?

5. *"Physical Loss."* What does it mean for property loss to be "physical," and what types of losses might not meet this test? The issue arises commonly in the context of property damage stemming from mold or similar sources. When mold damage requires the remediation of insured property, courts generally conclude that physical damage has occurred. See *de Laurentis v. United Servs. Autom. Ass'n*, 162 S.W.3d 714 (Tex. Ct. App. 2005). By contrast, economic losses resulting from mold damage, such as moving expenses, decreased value, or lost income, are not generally deemed to constitute physical loss. See *Mastellone v. Lightning Rod Mut. Ins. Co.*, 884 N.E.2d 1130, 1144 (Ohio Ct. App. 2008). Did the *Port Authority* court refuse to find coverage because the damage was not "physical" or because there was no "damage" to the property? Is there an argument that, even if the buildings in *Port Authority* were rendered uninhabitable, there would not have been any "physical" damage to the property?

6. *Varying Formulations of the Coverage Trigger.* In recent years, a variety of homeowners insurers have experimented with changing the coverage trigger in their homeowners policies to "accidental direct physical loss" or "sudden and accidental direct physical loss." See Daniel Schwarcz, Reevaluating Standardized Insurance Policies, 78 U. Chi. L. Rev. 1263, 1281–83 (2011). How significant are these changes?

D. BUSINESS INTERRUPTION COVERAGE

Duane Reade, Inc. v. St. Paul Fire & Marine Insurance Company

United States District Court, Southern District of New York, 2003.
279 F. Supp.2d 235.

■ RAKOFF, DISTRICT JUDGE.

Confirming the Court's telephonic rulings of June 13, 2003 and letter to counsel dated July 8, 2003, defendant's motion for summary judgment is denied in its entirety and plaintiff's motion for summary judgment is granted in part and denied in part, as set forth below.

Additionally, defendant's motion to submit the "number of years" calculation to an appraiser is granted.

By way of background, this case concerns insurance coverage for a drugstore (the "WTC store") that plaintiff Duane Reade, Inc. ("Duane Reade") operated in the retail concourse of the World Trade Center prior to September 11, 2001. After the World Trade Center was destroyed, Duane Reade sought to recover under an insurance policy (the "Policy") issued by defendant St. Paul Fire & Marine Insurance Company ("St. Paul"). When the parties were unable to resolve a dispute concerning the scope of the Policy's coverage for "business interruption losses," Duane Reade brought this action, seeking both declaratory relief as to the scope of coverage and damages for breach of contract. St. Paul responded by moving to dismiss all the claims, but while the Court dismissed the contract claims as premature (because no proof of loss had been filed), it allowed the declaratory judgment claims to proceed. *See Duane Reade, Inc. v. St. Paul Fire & Marine Ins. Co.,* 261 F. Supp.2d 293 (S.D.N.Y.2003).

Following discovery, the parties each moved for summary judgment. Their submissions show that St. Paul does not dispute that the destruction of the WTC store was caused by a covered peril. Indeed, St. Paul has already satisfied Duane Reade's property loss claims. Moreover, although St. Paul now disputes that any monies are due for business interruption losses, previously, in May of 2002, St. Paul paid Duane Reade $9,863,853 to cover what it then perceived to be Duane Reade's business interruption losses.[1]

Nonetheless, genuine disputes remain over the scope of the business interruption coverage, some of them resolvable as a matter of law. The Policy as a whole covers losses at all Duane Reade stores for the period between October 1, 2000 and October 1, 2001 and has a coverage limit of $150 million. The provision dealing with business interruption losses extends coverage to:

> [t]he interest of the Assured in loss of earning (Business Interruption), including ordinary payroll, continuing expenses, loss of royalties and bonus programs as a result of an interruption of the Assured's business (either partial or total) if such interruption is a result of peril, not excluded under this policy, causing direct physical loss or damage to any Real or Personal Property whether insured or not . . . including but not limited to loss or damage to . . . property of the Assured, . . . and property of customers, property of customers of customers.

Declaration of Erik M. Figlio, dated April 11, 2003 ("Figlio Decl."), Ex. A (Policy), at 4. Such coverage, however, does not extend into the indefinite future but is limited by "Restoration Period" clauses, which provide in relevant part as follows:

PERIOD OF RESTORATION AND/OR INDEMNITY

> The measure of recovery or period of indemnity shall not exceed such length of time as would be required with the exercise of due diligence and dispatch to rebuild, repair, or

---

[1] This latter amount was calculated by assuming that a "replacement" for the WTC store could have been opened for business within nine months of the terrorist attacks. *See* Affidavit of James W.B. Benkard, sworn to April 11, 2003, Exhibit Q (Claim History Report).

replace such property that has been destroyed or damaged, and shall commence with the date of such destruction or damage and shall not be limited by the date of expiration of this policy. * * *

Resumption of Operations: As soon as practicable after any loss, the Assured shall resume complete or partial business operations and reduce or dispense with such additional charges and expense as are being incurred. * * *

Extended Recovery Period

This policy is extended to cover the Actual Loss Sustained by the Assured resulting from interruption of business for such additional length of time as would be required with the exercise of due diligence and dispatch to restore the Assured's business to the condition that would have existed had no loss occurred, commencing with the latter [sic] of the following dates:

a) the date on which liability of the Company for loss resulting from interruption of business would terminate if the clause had not been attached to this policy or

b) the date on which repair, replacement, or rebuilding of such part of the property as has been damaged is actually replaced, but in no event for more than twelve months from said later commencement date.

Id. at 17–21. Also, the Policy specifically excludes coverage for "loss or damage caused by . . . loss of market[.]" *Id.* at 9.

The principal coverage issue presented by the instant motions concerns how these clauses should be interpreted in determining the length of the Restoration Period applicable to the WTC store. Specifically, Duane Reade argues that the Policy should be read to provide that

the Restoration Period consists of the actual time period that would, or will, be required to restore Duane Reade's operations to the kind, quality, and level which existed at the WTC Store prior to the terrorist attacks and that such Restoration Period is coterminous with the time necessary to rebuild the complex which will replace the World Trade Center.

Complaint at ¶ 39. St. Paul, by contrast, argues that the Restoration Period terminated when, at a time already past, Duane Reade could have "restored operations" at locations other than the World Trade Center. *See* St. Paul Fire & Marine Ins. Co.'s Memorandum in Support of its Motion for Summary Judgment, dated April 11, 2003, at 11.

The Court concludes, however, that neither side's interpretation accords with the plain language of the Policy, which governs as a matter of law. The "property" referred to is, unambiguously, the specific premises at which Duane Reade operated its WTC store. St. Paul's competing interpretation, *viz,* that the word "property" refers not to a store in any particular location, but to the "business" of the entire Duane Reade chain, finds no support in the text of the Policy and, indeed, is manifestly unreasonable. As St. Paul would have it, either Duane Reade never suffered any business interruption at all because the chain was able to "stay open for business," St. Paul Fire & Marine Ins. Co.'s Memorandum in Opposition to Duane Reade, Inc.'s Motion for Summary Judgment, dated April 25, 2003, at 12, or the period of restoration ended when Duane Reade's chain-wide sales attained pre-peril levels, *see* St. Paul Fire & Marine Ins. Co.'s Memorandum in Support of its Motion for Summary Judgment, dated April 11, 2003, at 12–13. But this would mean that Duane Reade purchased coverage that either (1) only applies when every last one of its stores is destroyed, or (2) unlike all other business interruption insurance, *see* Couch on Insurance, 3d Ed., § 167:9, does not protect against lost profits. Neither alternative makes sense.

Likewise, Duane Reade's contention that the Restoration Period must be coterminous with the time actually required to rebuild the entire complex that will replace the World Trade Center is untenable. On their face, the Restoration Period clauses envision a hypothetical or constructive (as opposed to actual) time frame for rebuilding, as evidenced, for example, by their use of the subjunctive "would." *See* the Court's letter dated July 8, 2003, at 1. Moreover, what is to be hypothesized is the time it would take to rebuild, repair, or replace the WTC store itself, not the entire complex that once surrounded it. *Id.* at 2. Once Duane Reade could resume functionally equivalent operations in the location where its WTC store once stood, the Restoration Period would be at an end. *Id.* Any losses continuing beyond that point would be addressed by the "Extended Recovery Period" provision in the Policy, *see* Policy (Figlio Decl., Ex. A), at 21, not by the Restoration Period clause.

A further limitation to the hypothesized period of reconstruction results from the provision in the Policy mandating that losses be calculated with "due consideration" both to the experience of the WTC store prior to the loss as well as the "probable experience thereafter had no loss occurred." *Id.* at 19; *see Hawkinson Tread Tire Serv. Co. v. Indiana Lumbermens Mut. Ins. Co.*, 245 S.W.2d 24, 28–29 (1951) (construing a similar provision). "Probable experience" includes, *inter alia*, the likelihood *vel non* that Duane Reade's lease for the WTC store would have been renewed. Thus, if Duane Reade is unable to prove at trial that its lease of the WTC store would likely have been renewed absent the events of September 11, 2001, then the period of restoration cannot extend beyond December 31, 2007—the date on which Duane Reade's present lease term ends.

The parties' cross-motions raise two other issues: (1) whether coverage is barred in any event by the "loss of market" exclusion in the Policy; and (2) whether St. Paul's first counterclaim and sixth affirmative defense, both of which allege that Duane Reade misrepresented and/or concealed material facts, can survive summary judgment. Both questions must be answered in the negative.

As to the first issue, St. Paul—relying exclusively on supposed "admissions" by Duane Reade representatives (*e.g.*, "the 9–11 attack deprived us of a marketplace," Figlio Decl., Ex. C (Transcript of Deposition of Anthony Cuti, taken April 3, 2003), at 412)—contends that the loss of market exclusion contained in the Policy bars coverage for Duane Reade's business interruption losses, since the terrorist attack destroyed not just the World Trade Center but the entire downtown market. The argument lacks substance. First, a careful reading of the context of the alleged "admissions" shows that they do not remotely purport to reach the conclusion that St. Paul ascribes to them; nor do they even appear to constitute admissible evidence, since they lack the necessary foundation and, even taken most favorably to St. Paul, suffer from excessive vagueness. Additionally, St. Paul has already foregone the argument it here makes, for it neither disputes that the destruction of the WTC store was caused by a covered peril, *see* St. Paul Fire & Marine Ins. Co.'s Statement in Opposition to Plaintiff Duane Reade Inc.'s Local Rule 56.1 Statement in Support of its Motion for Summary Judgment, dated April 25, 2003 ("St. Paul Opp. 56.1 Stat."), at ¶ 36, nor disputes that the interruption in the business of that store was caused by the same covered peril. In fact, defense counsel represented during oral argument that "there was indeed an interruption as a result of . . . a covered peril." Transcript of Hearing, May 9, 2003, at 23. The loss of market exclusion relates to losses resulting from economic changes occasioned by, *e.g.*, competition, shifts in demand, or the like; it does not bar recovery for loss of ordinary business caused by a physical destruction or other covered peril. *See, e.g., Boyd Motors Inc. v. Employers Ins. of Wausau,* 880 F.2d 270 (10th Cir.1989).

[The court then rejected St. Paul's misrepresentation defense]

In sum, for the foregoing reasons, St. Paul's motion for summary judgment is denied in its entirety, and Duane Reade's motion for summary judgment is granted to the extent of dismissing St. Paul's second counterclaim and fourth and thirteenth affirmative defenses (which assert that coverage is barred by virtue of the loss of market exclusion or other, unidentified exclusions) * * *

NOTES AND QUESTIONS

1. *Business Interruption Coverage.* As the opinion in *Duane Reade* makes clear, Business Interruption (BI) coverage is closely allied with property insurance. Often such coverage is provided as an integral part of a Commercial Property insurance policy, sometimes being referred to as "Time Element" coverage. Conventional BI insurance typically covers economic loss when there has been 1) damage to covered property; 2) caused by a covered peril; 3) resulting in a necessary interruption of business; 4) as a consequence of which there is a covered loss; 5) which occurs during the period of "restoration" of the business. Each of these elements ordinarily must be satisfied to support a claim. As the court indicated, BI coverage does not insure against the risk of economic loss due to changes in the markets that a policyholder serves. See *Harry's Cadillac-Pontiac-GMC Truck Co., Inc. v. Motors Ins. Corp.*, 126 N.C. App. 698 (1997) (upholding coverage denial when evidence suggested that snow, rather than collapse of dealership's roof, caused decrease in business).

Courts have taken a variety of approaches to applying these principles in the context of catastrophes, which often simultaneously impact both the insured property and market conditions. One particularly difficult issue is what weight, if any, courts should give to consideration of local economic conditions in the aftermath of a catastrophe. See generally Christopher C. French, The Aftermath of Catastrophes: Valuing Business Interruption Insurance Losses, 30 Ga. St. U. L. Rev. 461 (2014). How does the *Duane*

Read court suggest that this issue should be resolved? See also *Zurich Am. Ins. Co. v. ABM Indus., Inc.*, 265 F. Supp. 2d 302 (S.D.N.Y. 2003) (holding that a janitorial business located in one of the WTC towers that serviced much of the WTC property could recover for business interruption loss resulting from destruction of its own property, but (to the extent there was a difference) not for loss resulting from the fact that the property of its customers was destroyed and they no longer needed janitorial service). How should these principles be applied in contexts where a catastrophe would have potentially increased a policyholder's income by creating shortages that increased market prices? See *Sher v. Lafayette Ins. Co.*, 973 So. 2d 39, 62 (La. Ct. App. 2007) (holding that policyholder should be able to calculate lost income under business interruption coverage using post-Hurricane Katrina rents, which were higher than pre-Hurricane Katrina rents), rev'd on other grounds, 988 So. 2d 186, 205 (La. 2008).

    2. *Contingent Business Interruption Coverage*. Another form of insurance, Contingent Business Interruption (CBI) insurance, covers the risk of suffering economic loss resulting from damage to others' property, such as that of suppliers or customers. The insuring clause in *Duane Read* provided BI and CBI coverage within the same paragraph, when it referred to "loss or damage to . . . property of the Assured . . . and property of customers." This has been an increasingly important form of coverage for businesses that have reduced their inventories and streamlined their operations with "just in time" systems of supply. If a supplier's property is damaged, these businesses have little accumulated inventory to rely on and are likely to begin suffering loss almost immediately. But even here, often there first must be property damage to the customer's or supplier's property that is caused by a peril that would be covered by the insured's policy if the insured's property had been damaged. One of the principal issues that arises in connection with CBI coverage is which non-owned property must be damaged in order to trigger coverage. The outer reaches of this concept were probably reached in *Archer-Daniels-Midland Co. v. Phoenix Assurance Co. of New York*, 936 F. Supp. 534 (S.D. Ill. 1996), in which the court held that a significant area of midwest farmland damaged by the 1993 Mississippi River flooding could be considered a source of supply for the policyholder, a major processor of food products.

    3. *Calculating Recovery for Business Interruption Claims*. A frequent source of dispute in business interruption claims is how to calculate the appropriate recovery amount. As the decision in *Duane Reade* indicates, the proper period of restoration to use in calculating losses may involve a certain amount of judgment. Why don't insurers simply base recovery on the actual amount of time that it takes policyholders to reopen their business in the wake of a covered loss? Once the restoration period is determined, the insured must show that, but for the suspension of operations, it would have earned a profit during this time. Merely showing lost sales without projection of subsequent expected expenses and net profits is likely to be insufficient. See, e.g., *Fireman's Fund Ins. Co. v. Holland Am. Line-Westours, Inc.*, 25 F. App'x. 602 (9th Cir. 2002). This is necessarily a highly fact-intensive inquiry, often requiring accounting expertise, because certain expenses continue after a business interruption while others do not, and because economic conditions existing immediately prior to loss would not necessarily have continued. It is no surprise that the process of establishing the correct amount of recovery is often referred to as "adjusting" the loss, and that policies sometimes contain an appraisal

clause that submits the issue to a neutral "umpire" rather than a jury. See, e.g., *Jupiter Aluminum Corp. v. Home Ins. Co.*, 225 F.3d 868 (7th Cir. 2000).

4. *Damages in Event of Breach of Business Interruption Coverage.* When an insurer wrongly refuses to pay a business interruption claim, it may expose itself to substantial damages. In any breach of contract claim, consequential damages are available to the non-breaching party if they were reasonably foreseeable to the other party at the time it entered into the contract. One of the main purposes of business interruption coverage, of course, is to allow a business to survive a temporary shut down in its operations due to a covered loss to its property. Therefore, if an insurer wrongly refuses to pay a claim, it is reasonably foreseeable that the business may permanently collapse, resulting in insurer liabillity extending well beyond the contractually specified recovery period. See *Bi-Econ. Mkt., Inc. v. Harleysville Ins. Co. of N.Y.*, 886 N.E.2d 127 (N.Y. 2008).

5. *Loss of Use Coverage.* Closely related to business interruption coverage is loss of use coverage, which is typically included in non-commercial property insurance policies. This coverage is included on page 5 of the Sample Homeowners Policy. Note that the policy language deals with some analogous issues to those discussed above, such as the length of time during which payments will be made. Also note that the homeowners policy includes what amounts to a limited form of business interruption coverage for a homeowner who normally rents out a portion of his home, but is unable to do so as a result of a covered loss.

E. EXCLUSIONS

Because modern property insurance policies tend to provide some or all of their coverage on an all-risk (i.e., open-peril) basis, many coverage issues arise in connection with the limitations and exclusions contained in the policy. The limitations on coverage contained in property insurance policies are many and varied. A few exclusions, such as the "friendly-fire" exception that precludes coverage of damage caused by "friendly" as opposed to "hostile" fires, are implied rather than expressed. Nevertheless, most exclusions in property insurance policies are designed to address one or more of the following four concerns: 1) adverse selection; 2) moral hazard; 3) the problem of catastrophic losses (e.g., "correlated" losses that would be suffered at the same time by many policyholders if they were covered); and 4) market segmentation—avoiding duplication of the coverage provided by different kinds of policies (e.g., homeowners and auto insurance).

The three issues that arise most frequently when these exclusions come into play are addressed below. The first issue involves the problem of *intrinsic loss*. Even when a policy is sold on an all-risk or open-peril basis, typically loss must be caused by some independent force rather than by a characteristic that is inherent in the damaged property itself, or inherent in the portion of the property that is damaged. A number of exclusions attempt to address this notion, some more effectively than others. The second issue involves the problem of *concurrent causation*: when is there coverage of a loss that has more than one cause, if losses resulting from one cause are excluded from coverage but losses resulting from the other cause are not excluded? The third issue involves the problem of *increased risk*: what is the interplay between the effort to combat moral hazard that is at the heart of many of the common property insurance exclusions, and the insured's legitimate expectation that even losses caused by ordinary carelessness or negligence are covered by the standard policy?

1. THE PROBLEM OF INTRINSIC LOSS

Chute v. North River Insurance Company
Supreme Court of Minnesota, 1927.
172 Minn. 13.

■ STONE, J.

Appeal from an order sustaining a general demurrer to the complaint in an action to recover on an insurance policy.

The policy covers "jewelry * * * and/or furs as per schedule attached, against all risks of loss or damage during transportation (including all risks of loss or damage caused by breakage, fire and theft) or otherwise." Claims for "breakage of glass, overwinding, denting and internal damage" to watches and for damage to furs arising "from moth, vermin, wear and tear, or gradual deterioration" are expressly excluded.

Recovery is sought for a fire opal valued at $2,000, because, according to the complaint, while the policy was in force, "the opal * * * became cracked." It "was not cracked at the time said policy of insurance became effective but developed said crack after said policy became effective but during the time it was in force." Then, with commendable candor, the complaint avers "that said crack was due to an inherent vice in said opal and was not the result of outside force." The one question is thus plainly apparent—Can there be recovery for mere cracking arising from an inherent defect or tendency of the insured property and not at all from extraneous and fortuitous cause? According to a work on "Gems and Precious Stones of North America" (George F. Kunz, 293), quoted by counsel for plaintiff, fire opals are as "sensitive" as they are gorgeous. They have a tendency to "fissures" and, with "only a small loss of color, have become entirely flawed, the cracks being such as to render the stones unfit for setting, since they are liable to break."

The diligence of counsel has failed to furnish us any case in point or even of much help except those arising on policies of marine insurance. But they furnish, we think, a fair analogy. The contract is an "all risk" policy, and of a kind which characterizes marine insurance more than any other. The rule of marine insurance is that, under such a policy, the insurer is not liable "for losses resulting from inherent vice, defect, or infirmity in the subject-matter insured." 38 C.J. 1097. In Arnould on Marine Insurance (11th Ed.) § 778, it is put thus:

> * * * The underwriter is not liable for that loss or deterioration which arises solely from a principle of decay or corruption inherent in the subject insured, or, as the phrase is, from its proper vice; as when fruit becomes rotten, or flour heats, or wine turns sour, not from external damage but entirely from internal decomposition.

In applying this rule, we are not unmindful that in marine cases there is on the part of the insured an implied warranty of seaworthiness, and that risks insured against are "perils of the sea." Clarke v. Mannheim Ins. Co. (Tex. Com. App.) 210 S. W. 528. But "the purpose of the policy is to secure an indemnity against accidents which may happen, not against events which must happen." Gulf Transportation Co. v. Fireman's Fund Ins. Co., 121 Miss. 655, 664 (9 A. L. R. 1307) quoting from Lord Herschell in The Xantho, 12 App. Cas. 509. In Providence Washington Ins. Co. v. Adler, 65 Md. 162, 168 (57 Am. Rep. 314) Kent and Parsons are among the authorities quoted for "another rule, that insurers are not liable for property destroyed by the effect of its own inherent deficiencies or tendencies, unless these tendencies are made active and destructive, by a peril insured against. * * * It would, as Emerigon says, be intolerable that the owner should receive pay for goods that destroyed themselves." It is no longer intolerable that the owner should receive pay where goods destroy themselves, but the law remains that he cannot get it under a contract of insurance that does not make it clear that such is the intent and such the indemnity purchased. See, also, Marcy v. Sun Mutual Ins. Co., 11 La. Ann. 748, where recovery was sought for the sinking of a floating dock. A new trial was ordered because, among other things, the jury was not instructed that, if the accident was occasioned "by the inherent defects in the dock," the insured could not recover. * * *

True, literal rendition could lead to a contrary result, and ambiguities in insurance policies are resolved ordinarily against the insurer. But to follow that reasoning to its conclusion here would be to control decision by an interpretation so literal as to ignore the purpose of the contract. Plaintiff purchased and defendant furnished indemnity against loss or damage from fortuitous and extraneous circumstance rather than warranty of the quality and durability of chattels. It takes explicit language indicating that purpose to extend the effect of insurance beyond damage arising from or contributed to by extraneous causes and make it cover loss from automatic deterioration alone. That rule is applied unequivocally in marine insurance. To apply any other here would make the policy cover natural disintegration, something clearly not intended. Because the policy must be considered as one against damage from fortuitous and extraneous risks, it is not permissible to resort to an ultraliteral interpretation which will convert it into a contract of warranty against loss resulting wholly from inherent susceptibility to dissolution.

Order affirmed.

NOTES AND QUESTIONS

1. *An Artifact of All-Risk Coverage.* The intrinsic-loss issue arises largely because all-risk insurance covers all causes of loss that are not specifically excluded. *Chute* is one of the earliest cases to recognize the issue. An even earlier decision is *British & Foreign Marine Insurance Co., Ltd. v. Gaunt*, 2 A.C. 41 (1921). There a quantity of wool transported on the deck of a ship, as was apparently customary, arrived at its destination in damaged condition because of dampness. Denying a claim for coverage, the court explained that:

There are, of course, limits to "all risks." They are risks and risks insured against. Accordingly the expression does not cover inherent vice or mere wear and tear or British capture. It covers a risk, not a certainty; it is something which happens to the subject matter from without, not the natural behavior of the subject matter, being what it is, in the circumstances in which it is carried.

Id. at 57. Why don't property insurance policies cover intrinsic loss? See Kenneth S. Abraham, Peril and Fortuity in Property and Liability Insurance, 36 Tort & Ins. L. J. 777 (2001). Why do manufacturers and retailers provide warranties and optional "insurance" products that cover intrinsic loss? See George L. Priest, A Theory of the Consumer Product Warranty, 90 Yale L.J. 1297 (1981).

2. *Implementation*. It is possible to claim that intrinsic losses do not even amount to "direct physical loss" such that coverage is not triggered at all under an all-risk policy. This approach was hinted at earlier in the Chapter, in connection with the *Port Authority* case involving frayed asbestos fibers. But a much clearer way to exclude coverage for intrinsic losses is through explicit coverage exclusions. Accordingly, modern Homeowners and Commercial Property insurance policies incorporate a variety of coverage limitations implementing the intrinsic-loss principle. Consider subparagraph A(2)(c)(6) in the list of limits on Perils Insured Against in Section I of the Sample Homeowners Policy (page 10). This paragraph excludes "wear and tear, marring, deterioration;" and "[m]echanical breakdown, latent defect, inherent vice or any quality in property that causes it to damage or destroy itself." Note that this subparagraph goes on to provide that "any ensuing loss to property" (i.e., ordinarily to some other part or feature of the covered property) is covered if it is not otherwise excluded. Are these exclusions anything other than an effort to preclude coverage of intrinsic loss? Why are these exclusions applicable only to Coverages A and B (see pages 9–10 of the policy), but not to Coverage C?

Rosen v. State Farm General Insurance Company

Supreme Court of California, 2003.
30 Cal.4th 1070.

■ BROWN, J.

The insurance policy in this case defined "collapse" as "actually fallen down or fallen to pieces." However, sound public policy, the Court of Appeal concluded, requires coverage for imminent, as well as actual, collapse, lest dangerous conditions go uncorrected. By failing to apply the plain, unambiguous language of the policy, the Court of Appeal erred. (Civ.Code, § 1644.) "[W]e do not rewrite any provision of any contract, [including an insurance policy], for any purpose." *Certain Underwriters at Lloyd's of London v. Superior Court,* (2001) 24 Cal.4th 945, 968.

FACTUAL AND PROCEDURAL BACKGROUND

Plaintiff submitted a claim to defendant, his homeowners insurance carrier, for the cost of repairing two decks attached to his home. Plaintiff repaired the decks upon the recommendation of a contractor who had discovered severe deterioration of the framing members supporting the decks. Plaintiff believed his decks were in a state of *imminent* collapse, entitling him to policy benefits.

Defendant denied plaintiff's claim on the ground, among others, that there had been no collapse of his decks within the meaning of the policy, in that its coverage was expressly restricted to *actual* collapse.

The "Losses Not Insured" section of plaintiff's homeowners policy provided that defendant did not insure for any loss to the dwelling caused by "collapse, except as specifically provided in SECTION I—ADDITIONAL COVERAGES, Collapse." That provision stated: "We insure only for direct physical loss to covered property involving the sudden, entire collapse of a building or any part of a building. [¶] Collapse means *actually fallen down or fallen into pieces*. It does not include settling, cracking, shrinking, bulging, expansion, sagging or bowing."

Plaintiff sued defendant for breach of contract and breach of the covenant of good faith and fair dealing. Defendant moved for summary judgment, arguing that plaintiff did not suffer a compensable loss because the decks did not actually collapse. In his opposition to the motion, plaintiff argued there was a material factual issue as to whether his decks were in a state of imminent collapse. Plaintiff also argued that public policy required that the collapse provision of the policy be construed to provide coverage for imminent collapse. The trial court denied defendant's motion for summary judgment, concluding there were triable issues of material fact. The parties agreed to try the case to the court on the narrow issue of whether defendant owed plaintiff policy benefits due to the *imminent* collapse of his decks.

The trial court found for plaintiff. "The public policy of the State of California is . . . that policyholders are entitled to coverage for collapse as long as the collapse is imminent, *irrespective of policy language*." The trial court declined to honor the policy's restriction of coverage because it would, in the court's view, "encourage property owners to place lives in danger in order to allow insurance carriers to delay payment of claims until the structure actually collapses. . . ."

The Court of Appeal affirmed, holding that a homeowner's policy that expressly defines the term *collapse* as *actually fallen down or fallen into pieces* must, nevertheless, for reasons of public policy, be construed as providing coverage for *imminent* collapse.

We reverse.

DISCUSSION * * *

As the Court of Appeal acknowledged, the policy language here was clear and explicit. "The plain language of the collapse provision in Rosen's homeowners policy is unambiguous, in that it is susceptible only of one reasonable interpretation—actual collapse of a building or a portion thereof is a prerequisite to an entitlement to policy benefits. By defining the term 'collapse' to mean 'actually fallen down or fallen into pieces,' State Farm effectively removed any ambiguity in the term collapse. Under no stretch of the imagination does actually mean imminently."

The lack of ambiguity in the collapse provision here distinguishes this case, the Court of Appeal pointed out, from the case upon which the trial court principally relied—*Doheny West Homeowners' Assn. v. American Guarantee & Liability Ins. Co.* (1997) 60 Cal.App.4th 400 (*Doheny West*).

In *Doheny West, supra,* 60 Cal.App.4th at pages 402–403, the homeowners association of a large condominium complex sued its property insurer for breach of contract and bad faith, alleging that the parking structure of the complex, as well as the swimming pool and associated facilities built above the parking structure, had been in a state of imminent collapse, and that the insurer had wrongfully denied a claim for the necessary repairs the association had made to the structure.

Unlike the policy in this case, the *Doheny West* policy did not specify that the reach of the term *collapse* was restricted to *actual* collapse. Instead, the *Doheny West* policy excluded coverage for collapse except " 'for loss or damage caused by or resulting from risks of direct physical loss involving collapse of a building or any part of a building' " resulting from specified causes. (*Doheny West, supra,* 60 Cal.App.4th at p. 402.) While the *Doheny West* trial court held that this language embraced imminent as well as actual collapse, the trial court found for the defendant insurer on the ground the plaintiff homeowners association had not met its burden of proving that any part of the building was in a state of imminent collapse. (*Id.* at p. 403.)

The Court of Appeal affirmed. Noting that its task was not merely to construe the word *collapse* in isolation, but rather to construe the total coverage clause, the Court of Appeal held that the coverage clause before it "cannot be said to be clear, explicit, and unambiguous, and thus must be interpreted to protect the objectively reasonable expectations of the insured. [Citation.]" (*Doheny West, supra,* 60 Cal.App.4th at p. 405.) With these principles in mind, the Court of Appeal stated: "It is undisputed that the clause covers 'collapse of a building,' that is, that there is coverage if a building falls down or caves in. However, the clause does not limit itself to 'collapse of a building,' but covers 'risk of loss,' that is, the threat of loss. Further, on its terms it covers not only loss resulting from an actual collapse, but loss 'involving' collapse. Thus, with the phrases 'risk of loss,' and 'involving collapse,' the policy broadens coverage beyond actual collapse." (*Ibid.,* fn. omitted.)

However, the Court of Appeal rejected the plaintiff's contention that the policy phrases in question "broaden[ed] coverage to the extent that the clause covers 'substantial impairment of structural integrity.' " (*Doheny West, supra,* 60 Cal.App.4th at p. 405.) The Court of Appeal concluded that the trial court had correctly interpreted the policy language before it "by requiring that [the] collapse be actual or imminent." *Id.* at p. 406. "This construction of the policy," the Court of Appeal observed, "avoids both the absurdity of requiring an insured to wait for a seriously damaged building to fall and the improper extension of coverage beyond the terms of the policy, and is consistent with the policy language and the reasonable expectations of the insured." (*Ibid.*)

We agree with the Court of Appeal that *Doheny West* is distinguishable from this case. As the Court of Appeal observed: "It is a well-established rule that an opinion is only authority for those issues actually considered or decided." (*Santisas v. Goodin* (1998) 17 Cal.4th 599, 620.) At no time did the court in *Doheny* [*West*] hold that an unambiguous collapse provision expressly limiting recovery to actual collapse must nevertheless be construed to provide coverage for imminent collapse. The court also did not purport to discern a public policy establishing a contractual entitlement to coverage for imminent collapse in all cases. It simply construed the ambiguous collapse provision before it, as it was required to do. *AIU Ins.*[, *supra,*] 51 Cal.3d 807, 822.) In so doing, it was required to resolve the ambiguity in favor of the insured and in accordance with the reasonable expectations of the insured. (*Kazi v. State Farm Fire & Casualty Co.* (2001) 24 Cal.4th 871, 879.). In construing the collapse provision in *Doheny* [*West*] to provide coverage for both actual and imminent collapse, the court expressly relied on the broad language of that particular policy. Specifically, the court held that the phrases "risk of loss," and "involving collapse" "effectively broaden[ed] coverage beyond actual collapse." The State Farm collapse provision at issue in this case, however, does not contain any comparable language that can be construed to extend coverage beyond actual collapse.

However, "[n]otwithstanding the lack of ambiguity in State Farm's collapse provision," the Court of Appeal held, "as a matter of public policy, that State Farm must provide insurance benefits for imminent collapse of Rosen's two decks."

The Court of Appeal gave the following explanation for its decision not to enforce this unambiguous coverage provision: "The notion that in the absence of coverage for imminent collapse an insured may wait until the full or partial actual collapse of a building simply to ensure coverage is troubling indeed. The actual collapse of a building or any part of a building tragically can result in serious injury or loss of human life, as well as substantial property damage. A requirement that an insurer provide coverage when collapse is imminent clearly is in the best interests not only of the insured and the insured's visitors but also of the insurer. Rectifying the problem prior to an actual collapse may well save lives and money. Moreover, our holding does not unduly burden the insurer because its liability is limited for a loss which is imminent, and, thus, soon to occur anyway. Surely, an insurer's exposure to liability will be far greater in the event of an actual collapse. Any holding to the contrary would encourage property owners to risk serious injury or death or greater property damage simply to ensure that coverage would attach. We cannot and will not sanction such a result. We therefore conclude that notwithstanding the language of the collapse provision, public policy mandates that State Farm afford Rosen coverage for the imminent collapse of his decks."

Applying the same logic, with the same lack of restraint, courts could convert life insurance into health insurance. In rewriting the coverage provision to conform to their notions of sound public policy, the trial court and the Court of Appeal exceeded their authority, disregarding the clear language of the policy and the equally clear holdings of this court. * * *

DISPOSITION

The judgment of the Court of Appeal is reversed and the matter remanded for further proceedings consistent with this opinion.

NOTES AND QUESTIONS

1. *The Function of Collapse Coverage and Collapse Exclusions.* General coverage of damage caused by collapse tends not to be provided as part of all-risk property insurance. Rather, coverage is expressly excluded, but then covered on a named-peril basis, as in the Sample Homeowners Policy (pages 9 and 7–8). Given the scope of what is covered, to what extent is this approach an effort to implement the intrinsic loss principle, and to what extent is it a reflection of concern with increased risk? In this connection, consider the covered causes of collapse in the Sample Policy (pages 7–8), including hidden decay, but not decay that is known to the insured. *Catucci v. Greenwich Ins. Co.*, 37 A.D.3d 513 (N.Y. App. Div. 2007). Some modern homeowners insurance policies now do not cover collapse due to hidden decay. See Daniel Schwarcz, Reevaluating Standardized Insurance Policies, 78 U. Chi. L. Rev. 1263, 1289–90 (2011).

2. *Imminent Collapse or Actual Collapse?* There is a division of authority on the question whether there is coverage when a collapse is merely imminent. As the opinion in *Rosen* suggests, sometimes this division turns on the language of the policy. See, e.g., *Fantis Foods, Inc. v. N. River Ins. Co.*, 753 A.2d 176, 182 (N.J. App. Div. 2000) (holding that the term collapse connotes an imminent threat to the preservation of the building, and that requiring actual collapse would be "unreasonable in light of the insured's duty to mitigate damages and would be economically unsound"); *Residential Mgmt. (N.Y.) Inc. v. Fed. Ins. Co.*, 884 F. Supp. 2d 3 (E.D.N.Y. 2012) (holding that policy language unambiguously requires actual falling down of structure to constitute collapse). The supposition of the cases holding that imminent collapse is covered appears to be that, if it were not, then the insured would have an incentive to let the building collapse in order to secure coverage. Is this supposition realistic, in light of the insured's incentive to protect occupants of the premises (possibly including himself) and the threat of tort liability for failing to protect the premises against collapse? Would it be against public policy to permit coverage in such a situation? In any event, how effective would the "neglect" exclusion (page 13 of the Sample Policy) be in protecting against this eventuality? To the extent that courts do require coverage of imminent collapse, difficult factual issues can arise about whether the condition of a particular structure satisfies this standard. See, e.g., *KAAPA Ethanol, LLC v. Affiliated FM Ins. Co.*, 660 F.3d 299 (8th Cir. 2011) (jury issue whether leaning and sinking of storage tanks in an ethanol plant were in a state of "imminent collapse").

3. *"Sue and Labor" Clauses.* Commercial property insurance policies tend to include a "sue and labor" clause derived from marine insurance that affords the insured coverage of the costs of preventing the occurrence of any imminent loss that would be covered by the policy if the loss were permitted to occur. As the year 2000 approached and businesses across the nation were concerned that their computers would crash because of "Y2K" programming defects, there was debate about whether insurers would be liable for the reprogramming costs of preventing such computer-related losses, under the "sue and labor" clause. Much like Y2K itself, the issue

fizzled because coverage was denied under exclusions for the cost of repairing defective designs or specifications, which is itself a type of "intrinsic loss" exclusion. See *GTE Corp. v. Allendale Mut. Ins. Co*, 372 F.3d 598 (3d Cir. 2004). Sue and labor clauses are broader than the narrow "Reasonable Repairs" coverage provided in the homeowners policy (page 6), which applies only to repairs undertaken after the occurrence of a loss. By analogy, why haven't insurers added coverage for the cost of preventing collapse when it is imminent, or incorporated an equivalent of the "sue and labor" clause in Homeowners policies?

2. THE PROBLEM OF CAUSATION

Property Insurance policies both cover and exclude coverage based on the cause of loss (the "perils" insured against). Consequently, coverage issues often arise when more than one peril can be said to have caused or contributed to the loss and one such peril is covered while the other is excluded. The resulting issue of concurrent or sequential causation produces numerous coverage disputes.

State Farm Fire and Casualty Company v. Bongen

Supreme Court of Alaska, 1996.
925 P.2d 1042.

■ COMPTON, CHIEF JUSTICE.

I. INTRODUCTION

A home owned by Jerome Bongen and Elizabeth Bongen was destroyed by a mudslide. After their insurer denied coverage, the Bongens sued. They alleged that the mudslide was caused by construction activity carried out above their property. On cross-motions for partial summary judgment, the superior court held that a provision in the Bongens' insurance policy excluding from coverage any loss resulting from earth movement, regardless of the cause, was unenforceable. We reverse.

II. FACTS AND PROCEEDINGS

Jerome Bongen and Elizabeth Bongen owned a home on Pillar Mountain in Kodiak. In the late 1980's, Kodiak Electric Association (KEA) clear-cut a right-of-way above the home to install transmission lines on City of Kodiak property. On October 31, 1991, following heavy rains, a mudslide destroyed the Bongen home. According to the Bongens' expert, the KEA transmission line project "contributed to or caused damage" to the Bongen home.

The Bongens filed a claim with their insurer, State Farm Fire and Casualty Company (State Farm). Their policy contained the following exclusion:

> We do not insure under any coverage for any loss which would not have occurred in the absence of one or more of the following excluded events. We do not insure for such loss regardless of: (a) the cause of the excluded event; or (b) other causes of the loss; or (c) whether other causes acted concurrently or in any sequence with the excluded event to produce the loss; or (d) whether the event occurs suddenly or

gradually, involves isolated or widespread damage, arises from natural or external forces, or occurs as a result of any combination of these:

. . . . Earth Movement, meaning the sinking, rising, shifting, expanding or contracting of earth, all whether combined with water or not. Earth movement includes but is not limited to earthquake, landslide, mudflow, sinkhole, subsidence and erosion. Earth movement also includes volcanic explosion or lava flow. . . .

State Farm denied coverage based on this exclusion.

The Bongens thereafter commenced this action against State Farm, KEA, and the City of Kodiak. State Farm moved for partial summary judgment on the ground that the Bongens' policy excluded coverage for mudslides. The Bongens filed a cross-motion for partial summary judgment, which the superior court granted. The superior court held that the "efficient proximate cause" rule applies to multiple causation insurance cases in Alaska, and that public policy prohibits an insurance company from circumventing the rule through contractual language. We granted State Farm's petition for review of this decision. * * *

The Bongens argue that, under the efficient proximate cause rule, the loss of their house is covered under the insurance policy. They claim that "the negligence of [KEA] and the City of Kodiak in undermining the soils above the homes" is a "covered event."

The Bongens' policy excluded from coverage any loss resulting from earth movement, regardless of the cause of the earth movement, and regardless of whether a non-excluded risk acted "concurrently or in any sequence with" earth movement. The superior court found that "both parties apparently agree that the policy terms as written exclude coverage in the present case." In holding that the earth movement exclusion was unenforceable, the superior court relied primarily on *Safeco Insurance Co. v. Hirschmann*, 773 P.2d 413 (1989).

In Hirschmann, the Supreme Court of Washington held that an insurer is obligated to pay for damages resulting from a combination of covered and excluded perils if the efficient proximate cause is a covered peril, regardless of a policy exclusion stating the contrary. *Id.*, 773 P.2d at 416–17. The court criticized the insurer's attempt to circumvent the efficient proximate cause rule, id. at 414, but did not fully explain why such a practice is prohibited. Instead, Hirschmann relied on an earlier Washington case, *Villella v. Public Employees Mutual Insurance Co.*, 725 P.2d 957 (1986), which, in turn, relied on California cases holding that insurers could not circumvent the efficient proximate cause rule. *Villella*, 725 P.2d at 962–64. In California, insurers are statutorily required to provide coverage if the efficient proximate cause is an insured risk. *See* Cal. Ins.Code §§ 530, 532; *Howell v. State Farm Fire & Cas. Co.*, 267 Cal.Rptr. 708, 712 (1990). Neither *Hirschmann* nor *Villella* notes the unique statutory provision behind the California cases.

Most courts addressing the validity of exclusionary language actually or functionally identical to that found in the Bongens' policy have held that the exclusion is enforceable. In *Alf v. State Farm Fire & Casualty Co.*, 850 P.2d 1272 (Utah 1993), for example, the main waterline into the insureds' home ruptured, causing extensive flooding and erosion. *Id.* at 1273. The insureds argued that the earth movement exclusion—identical to the exclusion in the present case—should not apply because the efficient proximate cause of the damage was the burst waterline, a covered risk. The court rejected their argument, holding that under the exclusion, "coverage for damage resulting from earth movement [is excluded], despite the fact that the cause of the earth movement is a covered peril." *Id.* at 1275. The court concluded that "the proper path to follow is to recognize the efficient proximate cause rule only when the parties have not chosen freely to contract out of it." *Id.* at 1277. * * *

We favor the majority rule. It is well established that "[t]he obligations of insurers are generally determined by the terms of their policies." *Bering Strait Sch. Dist. v. RLI Ins. Co.*, 873 P.2d 1292, 1294 (Alaska 1994); *see also State v. Underwriters at Lloyds, London*, 755 P.2d 396, 400 (Alaska 1988) (quoting 6B J. Appleman, *Insurance Law and Practice* § 4254 (Buckley ed. 1979)) ("The intention of the parties as to the coverage of a policy is determined by the words which they have used."). We have held that where an insurer "limits the coverage of a policy issued by it in plain language, this court recognizes the restriction." *Insurance Co. of North America v. State Farm Mut. Auto. Ins. Co.*, 663 P.2d 953, 955 (Alaska 1983). We can discern no sound policy reason for preventing the enforcement of the earth movement exclusion to which the parties in this case agreed. We therefore align ourselves with those courts holding that an insurer may expressly preclude coverage when damage to an insured's property is caused by both a covered and an excluded risk. The earth movement exclusion in the Bongens' policy is enforceable.

[The court then held that the earth movement exclusion was not ambiguous and that it did not violate the reasonable expectations of the insured]. * * *

■ MATTHEWS, JUSTICE, dissenting.

* * * The issue * * * in this case is not whether the efficient proximate cause doctrine is applicable in Alaska. It is whether, given the application of the doctrine and given that a covered peril is the efficient proximate cause of a loss, policy language can negate coverage where an excluded secondary peril also is present in the chain of causation. On this issue the courts are divided. As the majority opinion indicates, decisions in California and Washington deny effect to such an exclusion, whereas authorities in a numerically greater number of jurisdictions give effect to such exclusions. I favor the California and Washington approach because it is consistent with the reasonable expectations of the insured.

The earliest example of the approach taken by the Washington courts is *Graham v. Public Employees Mutual Insurance Co.*, 656 P.2d 1077, 1081 (1983). The policies involved in Graham covered explosions as a peril under certain circumstances but excluded losses resulting "directly or indirectly" from earth movement, including mudflows. *Id.*, 656 P.2d at 1079. The loss in *Graham* resulted from the eruption of Mt. St. Helens. The eruption triggered flooding and mudflows which destroyed houses many miles from the volcano. The court held that it was a jury question whether the eruption was a covered explosion. Id.

The fact that the eruption triggered mudflows would not negate coverage if the jury were to find that the eruption was the efficient or predominant cause of the destruction of the houses and the mudflows were merely "manifestations of the eruption" * * *

Graham was followed by the Supreme Court of Washington in *Villella v. Public Employees Mutual Insurance Co.*, 725 P.2d 957, 962 (1986) ("where an insured risk itself sets into operation a chain of causation in which the last step may have been an excepted risk, the excepted risk will not defeat recovery"), and *Safeco Insurance Co. v. Hirschmann*, 773 P.2d 413, 416 (1989) ("*Graham* . . . suggests that whenever the term 'cause' appears in an exclusionary clause it must be read as 'efficient proximate cause.'"). * * *

[T]he efficient proximate cause rule comports with the reasonable expectations of the insured. If an insured buys a policy seeking protection from a given peril, the insurer issuing the policy should not be able to avoid coverage because an excluded peril is also present in the chain of causation if the covered peril is the dominant cause of the loss.

In sum, I agree with the Washington and California authorities which hold that when an insurer issues a policy protecting against a peril, it cannot avoid coverage where the peril is the dominant cause of the loss merely because an excluded peril is also in the chain of causation operating on a secondary basis. The purpose of insurance is to insure and it is reasonable to expect coverage when an insured peril has, acting as a dominant force, brought about a loss.

In accordance with the foregoing I would remand this case for a determination by the trier of fact as to whether a covered peril was the efficient proximate cause of the loss of the Bongens' home.

NOTES AND QUESTIONS

1. *Division of Authority.* The opinions in *Bongen* parallel the differences among the states in the treatment of concurrent causation. One approach is reflected in the majority opinion in *Bongen*—apply the policy as written. Under this approach, the efficient proximate cause rule is a "default" rule: it is the operative rule if the policy itself does not specify how to deal with a particular causation issue, but it cannot supplant relevant language in the policy itself. A second approach, reflected in the dissent, would permit coverage if a covered peril is the dominant or "efficient proximate cause" of the loss, irrespective of policy terms to the contrary. The efficient proximate cause rule thus amounts to a "mandatory" provision under this line of authority. See generally Joseph Lavitt, The Doctrine of Efficient Proximate Cause, The Katrina Disaster, Prosser's Folly, and the Third Restatement of Torts: Cracking the Conundrum, 54 Loy. L. Rev. 1 (2008); Erik S. Knutsen, Confusion About Causation in Insurance: Solutions for Catastrophic Losses, 61 Ala. L. Rev. 957 (2010). In *Garvey v. State Farm Fire & Casualty Co.*, 48 Cal.3d 395 (1989), the case that put the efficient proximate cause rule on the map, the Supreme Court of California held that for purposes of first-party property insurance there can be only one efficient proximate cause of a loss. Under this rule, losses resulting from one cause that is excluded from coverage (e.g., water damage) as well as from another cause that is not excluded (e.g., the

negligence of a third party in constructing a seawall that collapses and causes the water damage) are not covered if the excluded cause is *the* proximate cause of the loss, but are covered if the non-excluded cause is *the* proximate cause. Some years later, the same court held that insurers could not contract around the efficient proximate cause doctrine through the use of policy language excluding coverage of losses resulting from remote causes. *Julian v. Hartford Underwriters Ins. Co.*, 35 Cal.4th 747 (2005).

    2. *Concurrent Causation, Sequential Causation, and Ensuing Loss.* Homeowners policies typically include two different types of causation provisions, though the scope and language of these two provisions vary by carrier. See Daniel Schwarcz, Reevaluating Standardized Insurance Policies, 78 U. Chi. L. Rev. 1263, 1280–81 (2011) (reporting that some homeowners policies subject a greater number of excluded perils to an anti-concurrent causation provision than the standard ISO policy). The first type, reflected in *Bongen*, attempts to limit coverage whenever an excluded peril contributes in any way to a loss. Under this provision, there is no coverage irrespective of the sequence of covered and excluded perils or whether the excluded peril is merely an "indirect" cause of the loss. This provision, known as an anti-concurrent causation clause, precludes coverage when there is "concurrent" (or "sequential") causation. See the Sample Homeowners Policy, Section I—Exclusions, Subsection A (page 12). Under an all-risk policy, it would seem that there will always be some non-excluded cause of a loss, and there are an infinite number of causes in fact of any event. This tends to explain why the courts that treat the efficient proximate cause rule as a mandatory rule, as well as the minority opinion in *Bongen*, require that the covered cause be "the" sole proximate cause of the loss. Can you see why?

    The second kind of provision creates an exception to the anti-concurrent causation clause for certain "ensuing" losses. Under this type of provision, specified losses are covered if they are caused by an insured peril and not otherwise excluded, even if the ensuing insured peril was itself caused by an uninsured peril. The Sample Homeowners Policy contains two such general provisions, in Section I—Perils Insured Against, Subsection A (last paragraph) (page 10) and Section I—Exclusions, Subsection B (page 13). For instance, even though losses involving wear and tear and faulty design are not themselves covered (e.g., the cost of repairing old electrical wiring), if wear and tear or faulty design resulted in fire damage to the insured property, the loss would be covered because the "ensuing loss" by fire is itself a covered peril.

    3. *Ensuing Loss and Earthquakes.* The earth movement exclusion in the Sample Homeowners Policy (page 12), and in many such policies, contains a specific ensuing loss exception to the exclusion, for direct loss by "fire," "explosion," or "theft." The exclusion itself can be explained as an effort to combat adverse selection and correlated losses. Insurers don't want to provide earthquake coverage as a general matter because earthquakes can produce highly correlated losses among policyholders. In some cases, however, insurers will offer insurance to a subset of policyholders, particularly if their structures are resistant to earthquake damage. Rather than attempting to determine whether every insured lives in an earthquake-prone zone and has a dwelling that is susceptible to major damage as a result of an earthquake, they first require policyholders to affirmatively seek earthquake coverage (typically through an endorsement)

and then decide whether to provide earthquake coverage and, if so, at what premium. But since two important risks associated with earthquakes are fire and explosion resulting from ruptured gas mains and the like, the fire-and-explosion exceptions to the earth movement exclusion would seem to limit a major part of the exclusion, as illustrated in this famous anecdote about the 1906 San Francisco earthquake:

> Shortly after dawn, the geological fissure in California known as the San Andreas fault shifted, causing devastation in San Francisco. Seven hundred people died, a quarter of a million were made homeless, 30,000 houses were ruined—virtually a whole city had been destroyed. Many insurance companies failed, others disputed their liability on the grounds that their policies covered fire but not earthquake damage. Lloyd's took a different course. Cuthbert Heath's famous telegram to his San Francisco agent: "Pay all our policy-holders irrespective of the terms of their policies", became a watchword for fair dealing. It cost Lloyd's underwriters $100 million ($1.5 billion in today's money) but the goodwill it created was worth many times that huge sum.

Adam Raphael, Ultimate Risk: The Inside Story of the Lloyd's Catastrophe 36 (1994). What explanation or explanations can you offer for the ensuing loss exceptions to the earthquake exclusion in contemporary policies?

4. *Causation in Auto Insurance.* Another major area in which causation issues arise involves automobile property insurance. Such insurance is split into *collision* and *comprehensive* coverage. Collision insurance covers losses caused by collision, and comprehensive insurance covers loss other than by collision. Ordinarily an insured is covered by both (or neither) forms of insurance. But when she is covered by only one, causation issues are not uncommon. For example, suppose that an insured has collision but no comprehensive coverage, her vehicle catches fire, and (as a result) collides with a tree. Under the dominant rule, if the fire is the proximate cause of the loss then there is no coverage. However, it may be a question of fact for the jury whether the fire was the proximate cause of the loss. The nature of collision and comprehensive coverage for damage to motor vehicles is addressed in more detail in Chapter Eight.

Liristis v. American Family Mutual Insurance Company

Arizona Appellate Division, 2002.
204 Ariz. 140.

■ GEMMILL, J.

Plaintiffs appeal the summary judgment entered in favor of American Family Mutual Insurance Company ("American Family"). The trial court found there was no coverage under Plaintiffs' homeowners insurance policy for the mold contamination of their home that was allegedly caused by water used to extinguish an accidental fire. We find a question of fact regarding coverage and therefore reverse the judgment in favor of American Family and remand for further proceedings. We affirm the court's denial of American Family's request for attorneys' fees. * * *

Plaintiffs are the owners and residents of a home insured by an American Family homeowners policy. In August 1996, there was a fire in the home resulting in fire damage and also water damage, because of the water used to suppress the fire. A contractor performed repairs, and American Family paid $31,370.99 to the Plaintiffs directly or on their behalf for claims related to that fire. Plaintiffs claim they noticed mold growth in the home within a month or two after the 1996 fire. Upon moving back into the home, Plaintiffs suffered allergic reactions and respiratory and other unexplained illnesses.

Following the repairs after the 1996 fire, the roof leaked each time it rained. Plaintiffs reported the first leak to American Family, and the contractor attempted to repair the roof. However, the roof continued to leak with each rain, which resulted in water soaking the walls, ceiling, carpet and property inside the home. Plaintiffs notified American Family of these additional leaks in July 1997, when Plaintiffs filed a claim for water damage caused by a leaking evaporative cooler on the roof.

In 1998 Plaintiffs retained an expert to perform an environmental assessment of their home. The expert confirmed the presence of mold growth in the home. Specifically, he found *Stachybotrys,* which produces harmful mycotoxins and other molds that produce allergic reactions. American Family also had an environmental assessment done, which confirmed the presence of *Stachybotrys*. American Family's consultant recommended immediate biological remediation to the home.

In July 1998, Plaintiffs made a claim for contamination caused by the mold. American Family denied the claim based on a policy exclusion for mold. Thereafter Plaintiffs filed a complaint alleging breach of contract, bad faith and unfair insurance trade practices. Both parties moved for summary judgment on the issue of coverage. The trial court concluded that there was no coverage for the mold damage, denied Plaintiffs' motion, and granted summary judgment in favor of American Family. The court then entered judgment for American Family on all counts. * * *

The insuring clause of the American Family homeowners policy states in pertinent part:

> **We** cover risks of *accidental direct physical loss* to property * * * unless the loss is excluded in this policy. (Italics added).

The policy then sets forth the following losses-not-covered provisions:

> **We** do not cover *loss* to the property . . . *resulting directly or indirectly from or caused by* one or more of the following. Such loss is excluded regardless of any other cause or event contributing concurrently or in any sequence to the loss. * * *
>
> **6. Other Causes of Loss:**
>
> a. wear and tear, marring, scratching, deterioration;
>
> b. inherent vice, latent or inherent defect, mechanical breakdown;
>
> c. smog, rust, corrosion, frost, condensation, *mold,* wet or dry rot;

d. smoke from agricultural smudging or industrial operations;

e. settling, cracking, shrinking, bulging, or expansion of pavements, patios, foundations, walls, floors, roofs or ceilings;

f. birds, vermin, rodents, insects or domestic animals.

(Italics added).

Plaintiffs argue that the mold damage is an "accidental direct physical loss" to the home, caused by the water used to extinguish the 1996 fire, a covered loss. According to Plaintiffs, the policy does not exclude damages from covered events and mold damage is covered, in contrast to damage caused by mold. * * *

The parties agree that mold could be both a loss and a cause of loss. *See Phillips Home Builders, Inc. v. Travelers Ins. Co.,* 700 A.2d 127, 129–30 (Del.1997) (finding that settling of concrete slab can be both loss and cause of loss). However, the parties disagree about the significance of this distinction. We agree that mold may be either damage or a cause of loss, depending on the circumstances. For the reasons that follow, we hold that mold damage caused by a covered event is covered under the American Family policy in this case. On the other hand, losses caused by mold may be excluded. * * *

Language of the Losses-Not-Covered Provisions

Our analysis begins with the losses-not-covered language. *See* ¶ 7, *supra.* American Family contends that mold damage is excluded under the losses-not-covered provisions because the policy does "not cover loss to the property . . . resulting directly or indirectly from or caused by [mold]." In response, Plaintiffs urge the distinction between mold which is the loss or damage from a covered event compared to loss that is caused by mold. Stated another way, Plaintiffs argue that the loss to the property was not caused by mold; rather, it *was* mold, and thus the losses-not-covered provisions do not apply under these circumstances.

Careful examination of the language used by American Family supports the distinction between mold damage and loss caused by mold. Substituting "mold" for "one or more of the following" yields this language:

> **We** do not cover loss to the property . . . resulting directly or indirectly from or caused by [mold]. Such loss is excluded regardless of any other cause or event contributing concurrently or in any sequence to the loss.

This language does not exclude all mold. Rather, it excludes loss "resulting directly or indirectly from or caused by" mold. If American Family had intended to exclude not only losses caused by mold but also mold itself, it could have easily expressed that intention. *See Indus. Indem. Co. v. Goettl,* 138 Ariz. 315, 322 (App.1983) (an insurance company that wishes to limit coverage must use language that clearly communicates the limitation). For example, the following language from a State Farm policy was quoted in *Millar v. State Farm Fire & Cas. Co.,* 167 Ariz. 93, 95 (App.1990):

> We do not insure for any loss to the property described in Coverage A *either consisting of, or* directly and immediately caused by, one or more of the following:

(Emphasis added). If American Family had added the words "either consisting of, or . . ." to its exclusionary language, then loss "consisting of" mold as well as loss caused by mold would be subject to this restrictive language.

Similarly, the policy lists "mold" in sub-paragraph "6.c" of the losses-not-covered provisions. Paragraph 6 is entitled: "**Other Causes of Loss.**" This language again focuses on "causes" of loss, conveying the intention to exclude mold as a cause of loss. But mold which is the loss is not mentioned. To express the intention to exclude all mold, the company could have chosen "Other Excluded Losses" or "Other Losses Not Covered" as the title of paragraph 6.

American Family responds by arguing that the cost of removing the mold is excluded under the policy as loss caused by mold. We conclude, however, on the basis of the overall policy language and the considerations set forth in this decision, that if Plaintiffs prove the mold resulted from the fire, then the cost of removing the mold is not a "loss" separate from or caused by the mold itself but rather is simply the implementation of the mold damage coverage provided to the homeowners under the policy. Phrased differently, when a covered event causes mold, the mold damage includes the cost of removal.

Purpose of the Transaction as a Whole

* * * Fire insurance "is intended to cover every loss, damage, or injury proximately caused by fire, and every loss necessarily following directly and immediately from such peril or from the surrounding circumstances, the operation and influence of which could not be avoided." 5 John A. Appleman & Jean Appleman, *Insurance Law and Practice* § 3082 (1970). The purpose of the transaction between Plaintiffs and American Family—the purchase of a homeowners policy which includes fire insurance—supports interpreting the policy to cover mold damage caused by fire.

Plaintiffs also contend that American Family covered other losses caused by the fire such as marring, scratching, and deterioration, plus cracking and bulging of walls, floors, and ceiling. These items, like mold, are listed as "other causes of loss" in the policy (quoted in ¶ 7, *supra*). According to Plaintiffs, mold should be either covered or excluded consistent with these other damages, but American Family is attempting to use the losses-not-covered provisions to exclude only mold, while covering these other forms of damage which are also caused by the fire. Plaintiffs argue that American Family's coverage of these other categories of fire and water damage confirms that the policy is intended to provide coverage for all accidental damages caused by a covered event.

American Family contends that Plaintiffs' argument fails to take into account two rules of construction that apply to written instruments: *noscitur a sociis* and *ejusdem generis*. "[*N*]oscitur a sociis [ ] enables one to ascertain the meaning of doubtful words by referring to the meaning of accompanying words." *In re Rubi,* 148 Ariz. 167, 172 (1985). Under *ejusdem generis,* when a general term follows specific terms, "the general term is interpreted as of the same class or type as the specific terms." *In re Julio L.*, 197 Ariz. 1, 4 (2000). We do not find these two rules of construction to be helpful here, and we decline to embrace them in this case.

The overall purpose of the American Family policy was to provide coverage for "risks of accidental direct physical loss to property . . . unless the loss is excluded in this policy." See ¶ 7, *supra*. The policy does not exclude mold damage caused by a covered event. Plaintiffs are entitled to coverage for the mold damage caused by the fire and the water used to extinguish the fire, including the cost of removal or repair of the damage.

Summary Regarding Mold Damage Coverage

Plaintiffs allege that the mold damage in their home was "direct physical loss" from the 1996 fire, a covered event. American Family conceded the causal connection only for purposes of its motion for summary judgment, and argues that the actual mold in the home resulted from one or more excluded causes. A question of fact is presented as to whether some or all of the mold damage was caused by the 1996 fire. *See Schultz v. Erie Ins. Group*, 754 N.E.2d 971, 977 (Ind.App.2001) (remanding to trial court to determine cause of loss). If Plaintiffs can prove the causal connection with the 1996 fire, then the losses-not-covered provisions do not defeat coverage. If Plaintiffs cannot prove the causal connection, then there will be no coverage. Accordingly, we remand for further proceedings consistent with this decision.

Because we have concluded that the policy covers mold damage caused by the fire and because we are remanding for resolution of factual issues, we do not reach or determine the meaning of the "concurrent causation" provision or the "resulting loss" clause. The concurrent causation provision is the second sentence in the losses-not-covered portion of the policy. See ¶ 7, *supra*. The resulting loss clause is the final sentence of the losses-not-covered provisions, and states: "However, we do cover any resulting loss to property . . . from items 2 through 8 above, not excluded or excepted in this policy." If the trier of fact finds the mold in this case to be a cause of loss as opposed to damage from the fire or to be the result of an excluded cause, the applicability and meaning of the concurrent causation provision and the resulting loss clause may need to be determined. * * *

NOTES AND QUESTIONS

1. *The Purpose of the Exclusion.* Why is coverage of mold-related loss excluded at all? If the reason is that naturally-occurring mold is an intrinsic loss, then the result in *Liristis* would seem to be correct. Mold resulting from the addition of "unnatural" water used to fight fire (a covered loss) is not an intrinsic loss at all, but results from an external force. But does the policy really read that way? The court distinguished between mold as a cause of loss and mold as a loss itself. But how would mold ever be a loss "itself?" After all, the policy does not provide health insurance; it covers damage to property. Why wouldn't any damage associated with mold be damage to the part of the property to which the mold adheres, and therefore be the result of mold as a cause of loss?

2. *Alternative Policy Language.* The court notes that insurers other than American Family, such as State Farm, maintain policy language excluding loss "*either consisting of, or* directly and immediately caused by" mold. If this policy language were contained in the American Family policy at issue in *Liristis*, would the outcome have been different? Should it have been different? In recent years, some courts have rejected insurers' attempts to exclude coverage for loss consisting of or involving mold at any point in the chain of causation, at least where this language is invoked to deny coverage that would have "otherwise been covered as a result of the initially covered loss." *Orleans Parish Sch. Bd. v. Lexington Ins. Co.*, 123 So.3d 787, 798 (La. Ct. App. 2013).

3. *A "Growing" Problem.* Claims involving mold and other forms of water damage are among the hottest topics in contemporary property insurance litigation. The claims often turn on the precise language of the policy at issue. Perhaps the most noteworthy decision is *Allison v. Fire Insurance Exchange*, 98 S.W.3d 227 (Tex. App. 2002), reversing a $33 million verdict for the policyholder in a highly publicized case. For a useful summary of the cases, see Robert J. Brennan & James W. MacFarlane, Mold Claims under First-Party Policies: It's a Burgeoning Field of Litigation, 71 Def. Couns. J. 148 (2004). For evidence on the impact of these developments on the price of insurance, see Charles M. North et al, Rainfall or Rainmaking? Lawyers, Courts, and the Price of Mold Insurance in Texas, 79 J. of Risk & Ins. 817 (2012).

Broussard v. State Farm Fire and Casualty Company

United States Court of Appeals for the Fifth Circuit, 2008.
523 F.3d 618.

■ EDITH BROWN CLEMENT, CIRCUIT JUDGE.

Norman and Genevieve Broussard ("the Broussards") lost their home during Hurricane Katrina. State Farm Fire and Casualty Co. ("State Farm") rejected their homeowner's insurance claim, and the Broussards sued to collect benefits under their policy. The case went to trial and, at the close of all the evidence, the district court granted Judgment as a Matter of Law ("JMOL") in favor of the Broussards. * * *

I. FACTS AND PROCEEDINGS

The Broussards' Biloxi home was completely destroyed during Hurricane Katrina, leaving only the foundation slab. The Broussards, who did not have flood insurance, brought a claim under their State Farm homeowners policy. The State Farm claims adjuster who inspected the site concluded that the "[e]vidence suggests [the] home was more damaged by flood than wind," and State Farm denied the Broussards' claim in its entirety.

The Broussards' homeowners policy contained two types of coverage. They had $90,524 in "named peril" coverage for their personal property, which covered losses caused by a list of perils, including windstorms. They had $120,698 in "open peril" coverage for their dwelling, which covered any "accidental direct loss" to their home. Both the personal property and the dwelling coverage excluded losses caused by water damage. Both coverages were also subject to an "Anti-Concurrent Cause" ("ACC") clause, which stated:

We do not insure under any coverage for any loss which would not have occurred in the absence of one or more of the following excluded events. We do not insure for such loss regardless of: (a) the cause of the excluded event; or (b) other causes of the loss; or (c) whether other causes acted concurrently or in any sequence with the excluded event to produce the loss. . . .

It is undisputed that the Broussards' personal property and dwelling were a total loss and that the value of their personal property and dwelling met or exceeded the policy limits.

After State Farm denied their claim, the Broussards filed suit against State Farm in Mississippi state court. The Broussards claimed breach of contract and bad faith on the part of State Farm and sought the policy limits of their coverage, extra-contractual damages, and punitive damages. State Farm removed the case to the Southern District of Mississippi. The case was tried before a jury in two phases, causation and damage. Following the close of the evidence in the causation phase of the trial, both sides made oral motions for JMOL. The district court granted JMOL in favor of the Broussards on both the personal property and dwelling claims. With regard to the personal property claim, the district court found that the parties had stipulated that the Broussards' property was destroyed during Hurricane Katrina, that Hurricane Katrina was a "windstorm," and that State Farm was liable under the "named peril" personal property coverage because "windstorm" was a named peril. With regard to the dwelling claim, the district court held that State Farm bore the burden of proving that the Broussards' loss was caused by the excluded peril of flooding. The district court noted that State Farm's expert admitted that he could not distinguish between the wind and water damage to the Broussards' home with any reasonable degree of probability. In light of this admission, the district court found that "there was no sound evidence upon which the finder of fact could rationally determine that [State Farm] had met its burden of proof" and entered JMOL for the Broussards. * * *

II. DISCUSSION

The Broussards argue that their home was destroyed by "tornadic" winds before the Katrina storm surge arrived, and that they are entitled to recover under their homeowners policy for any losses which State Farm cannot show were caused by water, which is an excluded peril under both the personal property and dwelling coverages. This Court has issued several Katrina-related insurance decisions since this case was tried in early 2007, including *Tuepker v. State Farm Fire & Casualty Co.*, a Mississippi slab case interpreting a State Farm homeowners insurance policy whose provisions were identical to the Broussards' policy in all significant respects.[1] 507 F.3d 346, 350–53 (5th Cir.2007); *see also Leonard v. Nationwide Mut. Ins. Co.*, 499 F.3d

---

[1] The claims in Broussard are different from the claims in Tuepker. The Tuepker plaintiffs challenged the enforceability of the ACC clause and the applicability of the water damage exclusion to a hurricane-created storm surge. 507 F.3d at 348. The main thrust of the Broussards' claim is that their home was destroyed by tornadic winds prior to the arrival of the storm surge.

419, 423 (5th Cir.2007) (holding that Nationwide Mutual homeowners insurance policy, which included an ACC clause, was valid and enforceable under Mississippi law). These and other recent Katrina-related cases inform this decision. Because we hold that the district court erred as a matter of law in entering JMOL for the Broussards, we reverse the district court, vacate the award of punitive damages, and remand for a new trial.

A. *Judgment as a Matter of Law* * * *

(1) Personal Property "Named Peril" Coverage

We reverse the district court's grant of JMOL with regard to the Broussards' "named peril" personal property coverage. The district court erred when it found that the destruction of the Broussards' personal property by Hurricane Katrina was sufficient to establish the separate assertion that the property was destroyed by "windstorm," a "named peril" under the Broussards' personal property coverage.

Lunday v. Lititz Mutual Insurance Co. considered damage sustained by a Mississippi home during Hurricane Camille and held that, under "named peril" coverage, "the burden of proof was on the [insured] to prove that the damages sustained were covered by the peril insured against, that is, by direct action of the wind." 276 So.2d 696, 699 (Miss.1973). Although there was no question that the insured property was destroyed during Hurricane Camille, the *Lunday* court did not find that this automatically established that it was damaged by wind. *Id. British and Foreign Marine Insurance Company, Limited v. Gaunt,* 2 A.C. 41 [1921] Likewise, a stipulation that the Broussards' personal property was destroyed by Hurricane Katrina is insufficient to establish that it was destroyed by a windstorm, since Hurricane Katrina unleashed both wind and water forces. Accordingly, we reverse the grant of JMOL with regard to the Broussards' personal property claim and remand to permit the Broussards to carry their burden of proving that the personal property was destroyed by a peril covered under their policy.

(2) Dwelling "Open Peril" Coverage

We also reverse the district court's grant of JMOL to the Broussards on their dwelling "open peril" coverage. The district court granted JMOL because it found that "there was no sound evidence upon which the finder of fact could rationally determine that [State Farm] had met its burden of proof" to show that the Broussards' home was destroyed by an excluded peril. "This Court reviews ... the determinations that the parties met their burdens [of proof] under the clearly erroneous standard." *Stevens Shipping & Terminal Co. v. JAPAN RAINBOW II MV,* 334 F.3d 439, 443 (5th Cir.2003).

The district court's conclusion that State Farm failed to meet its burden of proof under the dwelling coverage was clear error. State Farm's experts introduced sufficient evidence to permit a reasonable jury to find in its favor. Two of State Farm's experts, Kurt Gurley and Robert Dean, testified that the damage to the actual structure of the Broussards' home came from the storm surge. Gurley stated that it was "75% likely" that wind caused a relatively small amount of damage to the Broussards' roof before the storm surge arrived, but that Hurricane Katrina's winds were not strong enough to cause structural damage to the home. Gurley also opined that, given the data available regarding the Broussards' home, no other wind engineer could state more definitively whether there was wind damage or specify the extent of the damage more precisely.

State Farm's evidence was more than sufficient to withstand a motion for JMOL. A rational jury could conclude, based on the testimony of State Farm's experts, that the Broussards' home and personal property were destroyed by water. *Wall v. Swilley,* 562 So.2d 1252, 1256 (Miss.1990) ("Unless the evidence is so lacking that no reasonable jury could find for plaintiffs, the motion must be denied."). We reverse the district court's entry of JMOL for the Broussards on the dwelling coverage and remand for a new trial.

B. *Burdens of Proof*

State Farm also argues that the district court erred in allocating the burdens of proof. "This Court reviews the allocation of the burden of proof *de novo*...." *Stevens Shipping,* 334 F.3d at 443.

"Under Mississippi law a plaintiff has the burden of proving a right to recover under the insurance policy sued on," and this basic burden never shifts from the plaintiff. *Britt v. Travelers Ins. Co.,* 566 F.2d 1020, 1022 (5th Cir.1978); *see also Home Ins. Co. v. Greene,* 229 So.2d 576, 579 (Miss.1969) ("An insured seeking recovery on a policy insuring against fire has the burden of proving the loss and its extent."). In this case, the parties agreed that the home and its contents were a total loss, and the disputed issue is which peril caused the loss.

The parties bear different burdens of proof under the personal property and dwelling coverages. For

> [personal property] "named peril" coverage ... the plaintiff has the burden of proving that any losses were caused by a peril covered by the policy. Under [dwelling] "open peril" coverage ... the plaintiff still has the basic burden of proving his right to recover. However, under "open peril" coverage the insurer bears the burden of proving that a particular peril falls within a policy exclusion, and must plead and prove the applicability of an exclusion as an affirmative defense.

Tuepker, 507 F.3d at 356–57 (internal quotations and citations omitted). The Broussards' personal property and dwelling coverages are both subject to a water damage exclusion identical to the exclusion in *Tuepker. Id.* at 350–51. The parties do not dispute that this exclusion applies to any damage caused by the Hurricane Katrina storm surge.

State Farm argues that under the dwelling coverage, once it advances evidence to establish its affirmative policy exclusion defenses, the burden shifts back to the Broussards to prove that there is an exception to the defenses or to segregate covered from non-covered damages. In support of its theory, State Farm points to Texas cases such as *Britt v. Cambridge Mutual Fire Insurance Co.*, which hold that "[o]nce an insurer has pled an exception to the insurance policy, the burden is on the insured to prove that the occurrence in question did not come within the exclusion of the policy." 717 S.W.2d 476, 482 (Tex.App.1986). Mississippi courts have not explicitly addressed shifting burdens of proof under "open peril" policies, so we "must make an educated '*Erie* guess' as to how the Mississippi Supreme Court would resolve the issue." *Leonard,* 499 F.3d at 431.

The Mississippi Supreme Court rejected a rule similar to State Farm's "shifting back" theory in a Hurricane Camille slab case construing a "named peril" policy. *Lititz Mut. Ins. Co. v. Boatner,* 254 So.2d 765, 766 (Miss.1971). The factual similarities between *Boatner* and the case at hand are striking. In *Boatner,* nothing was left of the insureds' home and its contents but a concrete slab. *Id.* at 765. The insureds argued that their home was destroyed by wind prior to the arrival of the hurricane-produced tidal wave. *Id.* at 767. The insurer admitted that some wind damage was probable, but withheld full payment under the policy because it argued that the home was actually destroyed by the tidal wave, an excluded peril. *Id.* at 766. The jury found in favor of the insureds and the Mississippi Supreme Court affirmed. *Id.* The court held that the insureds were required to introduce some evidence regarding causation to recover under a "named peril" policy, but rejected the rule "that the burden of proof was upon the homeowners . . . [to] also show that [their home] was in no respect damaged by tidal wave. . . ." *Id.*

In *Grace v. Lititz Mutual Insurance Co.,* another Hurricane Camille case, the Mississippi Supreme Court sustained a jury verdict for the insureds under a windstorm policy which excluded water damage. 257 So.2d 217, 219, 224–25 (Miss.1972). The *Grace* court stated that "[t]he rule is well established in this state that where the question presented to the jury was whether the loss was due to windstorm or to water, the entire question of proximate cause is treated as one of fact independent of the explicit application of any rule of law." *Id.* (citing *Commercial Union Ins. Co. v. Byrne,* 248 So.2d 777, 781 (Miss.1971)). The *Grace* court also reversed the trial court's remittitur of $2500 and awarded damages in the amount of the policy limits because the insurer never contested the fact that the insureds' property was a total loss and did not "offer any evidence at any time during the trial of what value or of what part of the [insureds'] property was destroyed by water prior to its destruction by wind." *Id.* at 225.

Boatner and *Grace* involved "named peril" policies under which the insured was required to prove that his loss was caused by a specified peril as part of his prima facie case. The Mississippi Supreme Court has not explicitly addressed the "shifting back" theory when considering an "open peril" policy. We think it unlikely, however, that the court would reject rules similar to State Farm's "shifting back" theory when considering "named peril" policies and embrace them when considering an "open peril" policy under which the insurer must prove causation by an excluded peril as an affirmative defense.

In support of this view, we note that the rule that causation is a fact question for the jury applies equally to "open peril" and "named peril" policies. In *Byrne,* a Hurricane Camille case involving an "open peril" policy, the Mississippi Supreme Court held that a directed verdict was not proper where the plaintiff introduced some evidence that his house and personal property were damaged by wind prior to the arrival of flood waters from a nearby bayou. 248 So.2d at 781. In language later quoted in *Grace,* the *Byrne* court held that causation was a question of fact "independent of the explicit application of any rule of law" which would take the issue away from the jury. *Id.; see Grace,* 257 So.2d at 224. State Farm's "shifting back" theory seems to be the sort of "rule of law" which would operate in many cases to take the issue of causation away from the jury.

In light of *Boatner, Grace,* and *Byrne,* we hold that State Farm's "shifting back" theory is not the rule in Mississippi. *Grace,* 257 So.2d at 224; *Boatner,* 254 So.2d at 766; *Byrne,* 248 So.2d at 781. On remand, the parties must meet their burdens of proof as outlined in *Tuepker,* 507 F.3d at 356–57, and the ultimate allocation of wind and water damages under the Broussards' dwelling coverage is a question of fact for the jury. *Grace,* 257 So.2d at 224. * * * [The court also vacated and reversed the award of punitive damages, on the ground that such damages are recoverable only if the insurer has no arguable basis for its position in fact or law].

NOTES AND QUESTIONS

1. *Hurricane Katrina Coverage Litigation. Broussard* is just one of many cases involving Hurricane Katrina, which struck the Gulf Coast of the United States in August, 2005. Katrina spawned widespread litigation over the applicability of flood exclusions and anti-concurrent causation clauses in homeowners policies to damage associated with the storm. To avoid these restrictions on coverage policyholders pursued a number of strategies. First, they argued that the flood exclusion was ambiguous because one reasonable interpretation of the term "flood" is that it only applies to natural events, and the breach of levees in New Orleans was attributable to man-made error associated with the negligent construction of the levees. Courts generally rejected this argument, concluding that the term "flood" unambiguously means any overflow of a body of water from its boundaries. *In re Katrina Canal Breaches Litig.,* 495 F.3d 191 (5th Cir. 2007); *Sher v. Lafayette Ins. Co.,* 988 So.2d 186 (La. 2008).

Second, policyholders' attorneys argued that, even if the damage at issue was caused in part by flood (an excluded peril), it was also caused by wind (a covered peril). As illustrated by *Broussard,* this strategy met with mixed success. Compare *Leonard v. Nationwide Mut Ins. Co.,* 499 F.3d 419 (5th Cir. 2007) (holding that under Mississippi law, flood and anti-concurrent causation clauses precluded coverage for damage caused either by storm-surge alone, or by the concurrent or sequential combination of storm-surge and wind, but that coverage was available for damage caused exclusively by wind), with *Corban v. United Servs. Auto. Ass'n,* 20 So.3d 601 (Miss. 2009) (holding that, notwithstanding anti-concurrent causation clause, loss caused by wind is not excluded, even if the loss would soon thereafter have been caused by flood anyway, because coverage effectively vests at the time it occurs). Does it make sense to exclude coverage of loss actually caused by wind if the same damage would have been caused by flood a few minutes later, had the wind damage not occurred? Is this what the lead-in to Nationwide's anti-concurrent causation clause in *Broussard* ("We do not insure under any coverage for any loss which would not have occurred in the absence of one or more of the following excluded events") was getting at?

Policyholders' third effort to deal with restrictions on coverage of Katrina-related losses was to assert that statements by their insurance agents either estopped or otherwise precluded insurers from relying on the language of their policies. For example, in *Leonard*, supra, the policyholder introduced evidence that Nationwide's agent had told the policyholder in 1989 that all hurricane damage was covered by the policy, and had indicated in 1999 that there was no need for the policyholder to buy flood insurance. The court held that, under the law of Mississippi, estoppel cannot expand coverage, but can only prevent the forfeiture of coverage that is otherwise provided, that the agent had no actual or apparent authority to modify the policy, and that the agent's alleged statement that the policyholder did not need flood insurance was not an actionable misrepresentation, in part because the statement was not consistent with the presence of a flood exclusion in the policy. Should the policyholder have a cause of action against the agent under these circumstances?

2. *Burdens of Proof.* As illustrated by *Broussard*, attempting to address concurrent causation issues by separately allocating property damage to different types of perils, such as water and wind, is exceedingly difficult as a factual matter. For that reason, the burdens of proof on policyholders and insurers with respect to what peril caused the underlying loss are particularly important in this context. In general, most states link the allocation of burdens of proof on this issue to whether the underlying coverage is provided on an all-risk or named-peril basis. See generally Eric M. Holmes & Mark S. Rhodes, 1 Holmes' Appleman on Insurance §§ 1.10–11 (Lexis 2d ed. 1996). Does this make sense as a policy matter? Arguably, insurers should always bear the burden of proof to show that a loss was caused by an excluded peril because they have more expertise than policyholders in determining the cause of a loss.

3. *Fragmented Coverage as the Source of Line-Drawing Disputes.* As described in Chapter 3, the federal government offers flood insurance to many Americans through the National Flood Insurance Program (NFIP). As a result, even individuals who have flood insurance can find themselves in the middle of legal disputes between private insurers and FEMA regarding whether the damage to their properties was caused by wind, in which case it is covered by the private insurer, or water, in which case it is covered by NFIP. See generally Donald T, Hornstein, The Balkanization of Cat Property Insurance: Financing and Fragmentation in Storm Risks, 11 Rutgers J.L. & Pub. Pol'y 9 (2013). These difficult line-drawing disputes could be eliminated through the creation of a more unified approach to insuring catastrophic risk to property, such as requiring private carriers to provide flood insurance within the standard homeowners policy. Most recent assessments, however, conclude that such proposals raise a host of complications that are likely to prevent their adoption any time soon in the United States. See generally U.S. Gov't Accountability Office, GAO–14–179, Homeowners Insurance: Multiple Challenges Make Expanding Private Coverage Difficult (2014); Fragmented Risk Symposium, Rutgers 11 J.L. & Pub. Pol'y 1 (2013).

3. THE PROBLEM OF INCREASED RISK

All property insurance policies exclude coverage for harm caused intentionally by the insured. They also exclude coverage for harm that results from the failure of the insured to use reasonable means to protect the property *after* a loss has begun. See, e.g., Sample Homeowners Policy, Section I—Exclusions, paragraphs A(5) & (8) (page 13). However, property insurance policies are generally intended to cover most losses resulting from the insured's own failure to protect the insured property as carefully as might have been possible. The clearest evidence of this intention is the absence of any general exclusion in property insurance policies of coverage for harm caused by the insured's own negligence. From the perspective of policyholders, the absence of such an exclusion makes sense: many losses are arguably the result of negligence, and ordinary risk aversion means that individuals want to be protected against the inevitable lapses in judgment or care that every person experiences on occasion. At the same time, of course, insurers generally must limit the risk of moral hazard if they are to keep premiums in check. There is thus an irreducible minimum of tension between the desire of the insurer to combat moral hazard and the ordinary insured's desire to purchase coverage against certain losses caused by his own insufficient care.

One way some insurance policies address this tension is through an "increase-of-hazard provision," which is derived from the standard New York fire policy. Such provisions provide that insurance is not available "while the hazard is increased by any means within the knowledge or control of the policyholder." To the extent that this exclusion is tied to a knowing increase in the risk of loss, it is arguably narrower than a simple exclusion for negligence. At the same time, the increase-of-hazard exclusion is obviously quite malleable, creating the possibility that insurers could invoke it to deny coverage in response to a broad range of merely negligent actions by policyholders. To limit this risk, courts have restricted the clause's applicability in a variety of ways: by manipulating who is the "insured;" by reading the word "or" in the phrase "by any means within the knowledge or control of the insured" to mean "and;" by requiring that the increase of hazard be substantial in time, magnitude, or both; and by treating these matters as questions of fact to be decided by the jury. Despite these judicial efforts, the malleability and breadth of increase of hazard clauses has limited their use in many modern insurance policies. Indeed, the clause is notably absent from the Sample Homeowners Policy and is included in only a few companies' homeowners policies. See Daniel Schwarcz, Reevaluating Standardized Insurance Policies, 78 U. Chi. L. Rev. 1263, 1283–85 (2011). Such exclusions are more common in commercial property insurance policies.

The predominant modern insurance solution to balancing insurers' desire to combat moral hazard with insureds' desire to insure against their own negligence has been to exclude losses caused by or occurring during certain specifically excluded risk-increasing actions. The following case is one example of such a clause.

Langill v. Vermont Mutual Insurance Company

United States Court of Appeals for the First Circuit, 2001.
268 F.3d 46.

■ COFFIN, SENIOR CIRCUIT JUDGE.

In this Massachusetts diversity case plaintiff-appellant, Grace Langill, the insured owner of a residential property, challenges the invocation by defendant-appellee insurance company, Vermont Mutual Insurance Co., of a statutorily required "vacancy" exclusion in plaintiff's policy, to deny coverage for fire damage to the property. Appellant appeals from a partial summary judgment granted to defendant prior to trial. We affirm.

Factual Background

The insured premises are a rental dwelling at 158 Mansfield Avenue (158) in Norton, Massachusetts, some thirty-five to forty feet away from appellant's own residence at 156 Mansfield Avenue. In February 1999, two tenants who had lived at 158 for twelve years moved out, leaving the property in a condition showing considerable wear and tear. Soon after their departure, appellant's husband undertook to refurbish the house by cleaning, removing debris, filling nail holes, painting walls, repairing several windows, and installing Venetian blinds. During this period, doors were kept locked, utilities were maintained, and heating oil was supplied. In the premises were Mr. Langill's tools, a step ladder, two chairs, a mattress, frame and box spring, a radio and an ash tray.

It was Mr. Langill's practice to spend one to two hours a day working at 158 starting at 11:00 a.m. or noon. A longer time would place undue strain on his arm. He would sometimes visit the premises at night to smoke or meet with friends; he had coffee there with a friend six or seven times. On one night, after an argument with appellant, he had stayed all night.

On May 4, 1999, Mr. Langill was at 158 from 10:30 a.m. until approximately noon. He spent the rest of the day at his house, save a visit to a store to buy a newspaper. At 2:00 a.m. on May 5, he was awakened by appellant and saw "a big orange ball" of fire at 158. By this time the fire was well advanced on one wall. The Norton Fire Investigator concluded that the fire was an arson.

Appellant's "Dwelling Fire Policy" included, as required by Massachusetts General Laws ch. 175, § 99, the following exclusionary clause:

> 27. Vacancy. Unless otherwise provided in writing, we will not be liable for loss caused by fire or lightning occurring while a described building is vacant, whether intended for occupancy by owner or tenant, beyond a period of sixty consecutive days for residential purposes of three units or less, and thirty consecutive days for all other residential purposes.

Discussion

The question presented to us and to the district court is whether under Massachusetts law, the undisputed facts depict a dwelling that had been, at the time of the fire, "vacant" for more than sixty consecutive days. This is a matter of law and our review is de novo. We also are bound by the Massachusetts rule that "[b]ecause the language of the standard policy is prescribed by statute ..., the rule of construction resolving ambiguities in a policy against the insurer is inapplicable.... Instead, we must ascertain the fair meaning of the language used, as applied to the subject matter." *Bilodeau v. Lumbermens Mut. Cas. Co.*, 392 Mass. 537, 541 (1984) (internal citations and quotations omitted).

Two Massachusetts cases have been called to our attention. The earlier is *Will Realty Corp. v. Transportation Ins. Co.*, 22 Mass.App.Ct. 918 (1986). After a tenant was evicted and left a rundown house, the windows were boarded and the only activity occurred on two days when workmen removed from the house doors, windows and sinks. A fire destroyed the building several months later. In reversing a ruling that the property had not been "vacant," the court said, "the policy provision reflects the commonplace observation that the risk of casualty is higher when premises remain unattended.... [P]remises may be vacant despite sporadic entry." 22 Mass.App.Ct. at 919.

A more recent case is helpful, not so much in its precise holding, as in its discussion of policy underlying the "vacancy" exclusion. *See Aguiar v. Generali Assicurazioni Ins. Co.*, 47 Mass.App.Ct. 687 (1999). A restaurant, which had closed for the season on Labor Day, was destroyed by fire approximately two months later. Before the fire, the restaurant had been unoccupied and utilities had been shut off. In affirming the trial court's ruling that the property had been vacant for the required period, the appeals court "illuminated why an insurer would be concerned about an unoccupied building" by explaining that arsonists had attempted to destroy the building several times in the months before they ultimately succeeded. 47 Mass.App.Ct. at 689. Moreover, in discussing the insured's argument that he reasonably expected to be covered under the insurance policy, the court commented:

> [w]hen reasonable expectations analysis comes into play, it is more likely to do so when the task is to interpret an ambiguous provision rather than an unambiguous one whose meaning, as in this case, no one disputes.... They could not reasonably have expected that leaving the building vacant did not alter the underwriting condition.

47 Mass.App.Ct. at 691.

Neither case neatly covers the facts in the case at bar. In both cases no activity was going on in the premises. In *Aguiar*, at least, the premises were not devoid of contents. It is clear, however, that the court was not equating "vacant" with "abandonment," as do some jurisdictions. *See, e.g., Jerry v. Kentucky Cent. Ins. Co.*, 836 S.W.2d 812, 815 (Tex.App.1992) ("entire abandonment"). It is also clear that having the building "attended" and "occupied" is the central theme.

The question remains whether this requirement can be satisfied by regular visits and activities, although of relatively brief nature, by someone other than a resident of the building. We are helped by reflecting on the reasons underlying vacancy exclusions. In considering the vacancy exclusion of a policy insuring a warehouse, the Fourth Circuit explained:

> When a building is not in use, it is more likely that potential fire hazards will remain undiscovered or unremedied. Chances are also greater that a fire in a vacant building will burn for a longer period and cause greater damage before being detected.

Catalina Enter. v. Hartford Fire Ins. Co., 67 F.3d 63, 66 (4th Cir.1995). Surely, these considerations are even more applicable to one insuring a dwelling.

When we review the undisputed facts of this case, in light of these policy concerns, we can readily see their lack of fit. That is, the approximation to an inhabited abode is not measurably advanced by the motley and sparse inventory of chairs, mattress, and step ladder. Nor does the midday hour or so of work activity convey the appearance of residential living. And random evening visits hardly provide the appearance of somebody being at home or effective anti-vandal protection. The fact is that none of the activities of Mr. Langill or others changed the fact that at the critical and likely times for vandalism and arson, there was no one in the house to discourage, see, or hear marauders, or to hear the activation of smoke detectors.

A recent New York case seems both apposite and persuasive. In *Lamoureux v. New York Cent. Mut. Fire Ins. Co.*, 244 A.D.2d 645 (N.Y.App.Div.1997), the insured building was a one-family residence located adjacent to and behind plaintiff's residence. The premises were destroyed by fire three months after the plaintiff's tenant had moved out. The policy excluded coverage for loss if the building were vacant over 60 consecutive days. Plaintiff's principal challenge to a finding of vacancy was that he was personally renovating the house and was inside the building every day for a couple of hours. The court reversed the trial court's denial of the insurer's motion for summary judgment, "[g]iving the word vacant its plain and ordinary meaning...." 244 A.D.2d at 646. It also ruled that because "plaintiff himself was never an inhabitant of the premises, the fact that he frequented the premises for the purpose of renovation is not germane to the issue of vacancy." *Id.*

We think the Massachusetts courts would similarly rule on the record before us. When we consider the nature of the hazard sought to be guarded against, the sustained presence of a resident, particularly in the hours of darkness, appears logically as the critical factor where the premises are a dwelling. Of course, this also assumes the presence of furnishings and amenities "minimally necessary for human habitation." *American Mut. Fire Ins. Co. v. Durrence*, 872 F.2d 378, 379 (11th Cir.1989).

We recognize, as this case illustrates, that there is a wide continuum between residency and absolute absence of human presence from the premises. And we do not intend to foreclose the possibility of a set of facts not involving a resident but so paralleling the conditions of residency as to avoid application of the exclusion clause. But we think that in general the multi-factor approach urged by appellant is inconsistent with Massachusetts law. What seems preeminent in this insurance context, for both insurer and insured, is predictability. To the extent that a multi-factor approach is suggested, such as including the presence or absence of tenants, the habitability or absence thereof, the number, nature, duration, and regularity of activities and visits by non-residents, and the proximity of the insured site to the residence, any predictability is fatally compromised.

Appellant has vigorously invoked dictionary definitions and case law to serve his purpose. As might be suspected, where a host of things can be spoken of as "vacant," from rooms and houses to stores, positions, and expressions, definitions are legion. Appellant has relied on those that stress a space being "devoid of contents." *Webster's New World Dictionary*, 1968 ed., p. 1606. This is a perfectly good definition but it has been impliedly rejected by *Aquiar*. Moreover, reference to absence of contents would be more relevant if one were considering whether a warehouse were vacant. The absence of that for which the premises were intended to be used would seem to be the proper object of inquiry. Appellee's choice of another of Webster's definitions seems more of a fit: "untenanted; not in use, as a room or a house." *Id.* We note as well that the language of the provision, "whether intended for occupancy by owner or tenant," directs us to give no special consideration to purpose of the building as one to rented rather than one to be used by appellant.

Appellant's reliance on cases illustrates the hazard of focusing on text to the exclusion of context. For example, cases are cited for the proposition that efforts to rehabilitate property preclude a finding of vacancy. *See Knight v. United States Fid. & Guar. Co.*, 123 Ga.App. 833 (1971); *Limbaugh v. Columbia Ins. Co. of N.Y.*, 368 S.W.2d 921 (Mo.Ct.App.1963). *Knight* involved installing new equipment, painting, and making ready a service station and restaurant for reopening and Limbaugh similar activities to ready a recreation hall and package liquor store for opening. In both cases there were policy exclusions if the premises were "unoccupied" for sixty days. *Knight* relied on the reasoning of *Limbaugh*, in which the court said:

> The word "occupancy" itself, as used in insurance policies, refers to the presence of persons within the building. This is particularly true as it relates to dwelling houses. They are expected to be places of human habitation where people live and dine and sleep. This cannot be said of a recreation hall and package liquor store, for the nature of the occupancy does not warrant the conclusion.

Limbaugh, 368 S.W.2d at 924. The court accordingly held that cleaning and repainting the interior of the liquor store "would be an activity consistent with its occupation as such." *Id.* at 925.

Not only does the meaning of "vacancy" depend on the type of premises involved, but also the type of insurance policy. Appellant seeks comfort from *Ellmex Constr. Co., Inc. v. Republic Ins. Co.*, 202 N.J.Super. 195 (N.J.Super.Ct.App.Div.1985), which held that the presence in a model home of realtors for four days every week constituted sufficient presence to defeat a thirty day vacancy exclusion clause. But the court noted that the policy involved was a "builder's risk" policy, which should not be interpreted as are policies insuring ordinary homeowners. 202 N.J.Super. at 204. The latter policies, observed the court, "may, and usually do, require the insured dwelling to be occupied as a place of abode." 202 N.J.Super. at 203–04. It consequently felt free to depart from this standard and, resolving ambiguity against the insurer, held that defendant had not required that the premises be "occupied" twenty-four hours per day.

Finally, it is important to distinguish cases according wide elasticity to the word "occupancy," after finding the word ambiguous and construing the term in favor of the insured. *See Smith v. Lumbermen's Mut. Ins. Co.*, 101 Mich.App. 78 (1981); *Drummond v. Hartford Fire Ins. Co.*, 343 S.W.2d 84 (Mo.Ct.App.1960). In *Smith*, the court held that where the insurer knew that a dwelling was under a contract of sale, a temporary vacancy pending arrival of the new resident-owner was "not within the vacancy clause, absent a clear expression of intent in the insurance policy." 101 Mich.App. at 86. Likewise, in *Drummond* the court, relying on early precedent, held that the presence of a caretaker one day and night each week during the specified vacancy period constituted "possessio pedis" and was sufficient. 343 S.W.2d at 87. Suffice it to say that neither case would be considered relevant in interpreting the mandatory vacancy provision under Massachusetts law.

Affirmed.

NOTES AND QUESTIONS

1. *Statutorily Mandated Vacancy Provision.* The vacancy exclusion at issue in *Langill* was mandated by Massachusetts state law, consistent with the practice of some states to use a state-mandated fire policy as a mandatory coverage floor (discussed in Chapter 3). To what extent does the Massachusetts rule limiting the availability of *contra proferentem* in such cases make sense? Do you think the outcome in *Langill* would have been different if the *contra proferentem* were applicable?

2. *Different Versions of the Vacancy Exclusion.* The vacancy exclusion in the Sample Homeowners Policy, Section I—Perils Insured Against (page 9) is both broader and narrower than that at issue in *Langill*. On one hand, the exclusion in the Sample Policy only applies to losses that are the result of "vandalism and malicious mischief." On the other hand, the exclusion in the Sample Policy applies to all causes of property damage, not just fire or lightning. Of course, this can be largely explained by the fact that a homeowners policy covers many more perils than fire and lightning, unlike the policy at issue in *Langill*. How might the outcome in *Langill* have been different if the case were governed by the Sample Policy? What facts might be relevant in making this determination?

3. *Vacancy Provisions in Different Policies and Contexts.* The court rejects a multifactor approach to determining vacancy on the basis that predictability is "paramount" in the insurance context. Does predictability in this context serve policyholder interests, insurer interests, or both? In any event, to what extent is the court's embrace of this policy goal consistent with its later insistence that the meaning of a vacancy clause depends both on the type of policy and the type of property at issue, even if the governing policy language is identical?

4. *Vacancy Provisions in Commercial Property Insurance Policies.* Many commercial property insurance policies do not include exclusions that are tied to vacancy. Part of the explanation may be that such policies contain more general increase of hazard exclusions. But this is not the entire story, as the ISO commercial property insurance policy contains neither of these provisions.

5. *Other Provisions Directed at Increased Risk.* Other policy provisions also address the problem of increased risk. For example, in addition to the general condition suspending coverage while the property is "vacant or unoccupied," many policies contain a provision precluding coverage of loss caused by the freezing of pipes if the premises have been left vacant or unoccupied for a specified period of time. For applications of the clause, see *McCabe v. Allstate Insurance Co.*, 260 A.D.2d 850 (Ark. Ct. App. 1999) and *Smith v. Lumbermen's Mutual Insurance Co.*, 101 Mich.

App. 78 (1980). Similarly, the exclusion for losses resulting from (or consisting of) mold, discussed earlier in the Chapter in connection with *Liristis*, can be justified on the basis that it limits coverage for a type of loss that may be particularly likely to occur as a result of insufficient policyholder care. At the same time, the mold exclusion can be explained on various other grounds, including high investigation costs, high risk of correlated loss, high remediation expenses, and the need for expert witnesses in disputes.

F. THE MEASURE OF RECOVERY

The principle of indemnity, together with the insurer's own interest in combating moral hazard, requires that recovery for a loss to property not produce a net gain for the insured who suffers the loss. A number of limitations on recovery are directed at this goal. All policies contain a limit on the amount insured, set with an eye toward the value of the insured property. In addition, standard policies indicate that coverage is provided only to the extent of an insured's interest, reinforcing the insurable interest requirement. Policies vary, however, in the method to be used in calculating policyholders' recovery for loss within these broad constraints. In some cases, they provide coverage only for the "actual cash value" of the property damaged or destroyed at the time of loss. In other cases, property insurance policies—especially individual homeowners policies—provide coverage for the full cost of replacement, even if that cost exceeds actual cash value. See Johnny Parker, Replacement Cost Coverage: A Legal Primer, 34 Wake Forest L. Rev. 295 (1999). Although the meaning of replacement cost is generally relatively straight forward, the meaning of actual cash value has been the subject of considerable judicial interpretation.

Zochert v. National Farmers Union Property & Casualty Company

Supreme Court of South Dakota, 1998.
576 N.W.2d 531.

■ PER CURIAM.

ACTION

National Farmers Union Property & Casualty Company (Company) appeals the trial court's order granting summary judgment to Ivan and Neil Zochert, d/b/a Zochert Farms, Inc. (Zochert). We reverse and remand for determination of the appropriate depreciation cost.

FACTS

On May 17, 1996, two of Zochert's silos, which were insured by Company under a farmowner's policy and estimated to be approximately twenty years old, sustained wind damage. The policy had a $250 deductible and provided coverage in an amount not to exceed $35,000 for each silo. Company's claim adjuster estimated the total cost of repair (replacement cost) of both silos to be $15,255.76. He calculated depreciation on the silos to be $5,166.96. The depreciation cost and the $250 deductible were subtracted from the replacement cost for a total of $9,838.80. Company issued a check in this amount to Zochert for its loss.

Both parties agreed that under the terms of the policy, "loss . . . will be settled on the basis of the actual cash value of the property damaged, not to exceed the amount of the insurance applicable." They disagreed, however, regarding whether depreciation was to be deducted when calculating the actual cash value. Zochert filed a lawsuit to recover $5,166.96, the amount of depreciation cost deducted by Company. Company asserted depreciation must be deducted to determine actual cash value. Both parties filed motions for summary judgment. The trial court granted summary judgment to Zochert. Company appeals. * * *

In reviewing the loss settlement provisions under Zochert's policy, generally two kinds of settlement are described depending upon the amount of insurance coverage purchased:

> If at the time of loss the amount of insurance in this policy on the damaged dwelling is 80% or more of the full replacement cost of the dwelling immediately prior to the loss, *we will pay the cost of repair or replacement, without deduction for depreciation.* Payment will not exceed the smallest of the following amounts:

> If at the time of loss the amount of insurance in this policy on the damaged dwelling is less than 80% of the full replacement cost of the dwelling immediately prior to the loss, *we will pay the actual cash value of that part of the dwelling damaged.* Payment will not exceed the amount of insurance under this policy applying to the dwelling.

(Emphasis added). If these two kinds of loss settlements carried the same meaning, as Zochert asserts, there would be no need to describe them differently in the policy. Another provision of the policy also notes the distinction between these two types of loss settlements:

> You may elect not to replace some of or all of the destroyed or stolen property. *Settlement for the property not replaced will be on an actual cash value basis.* If you later decide to replace any destroyed or stolen property, you may make an additional claim within 180 days after the loss.

(Emphasis added). Clearly, this provision demonstrates that actual cash value does not equal replacement cost but is determined at some lesser amount. * * *

In *Elberon Bathing Co., Inc. v. Ambassador Ins. Co., Inc.*, 77 N.J. 1 (1978), the court reversed and remanded, holding an appraisal was improper and did not measure "actual cash value" under a fire insurance policy where the appraisal was based upon replacement cost of the property without any consideration of depreciation. The court stated that:

> to the extent that replacement cost is or may be a proper criterion of actual cash value, there must normally be a deduction for depreciation lest the insured receive more than indemnity for his loss. In failing to make such a deduction, the appraisers violated the terms of the policy and committed a mistake of law.

Id. 389 A.2d at 445. The court noted that to allow the insured to recover the original value of real estate that has depreciated would violate the principle of indemnity by providing a windfall to the insured. *Id.* at 442. It further explained the relevant case law reflects three general categories for measuring "actual cash value:" (1) market value; (2) replacement cost less depreciation; and (3) the now most widely accepted test, the "broad evidence rule" *Id.* at 443–44.

In *Lampe Market Co. v. Alliance Ins. Co.*, 22 N.W.2d 427, 428 (1946), we adopted the "broad evidence rule" which permits consideration of all evidence an expert would find relevant to a determination of value. In *Lampe*, the jury had been asked to determine the actual cash value of a building damaged by fire. We held the trial court did not err in instructing the jury that:

> In determining the "actual cash value" of said building the jury should take into consideration *the cost of restoration or replacement of the building less depreciation* thereon since it was erected; any element of obsolescence; the size of the building; the material of which it is composed; its age and state of preservation. You should also take into consideration the amount for which the property would sell for cash at a fair sale in the usual course of business; that is, the amount for which the property would sell at a sale in which the seller was not forced to sell but in which he was ready and willing to sell and the purchaser was not forced to buy but was ready and willing to buy. You should take into consideration the opinions upon value given by qualified witnesses; the gainful uses to which the building might have been put; its value for the purpose of rental; its location in the community, and any other facts disclosed by the evidence which will throw any light upon the actual cash value of the building at the time of the loss.

Id. at 428 (emphasis added). We recognized that replacement cost, less depreciation, is an element to be considered but is not the sole test of actual cash value. *Id.* (Citations omitted).

> Replacement cost, less physical depreciation, establishes the theoretical present cost of reproducing a particular building. It is not the invariable test of value because in a particular case other factors may overcome or qualify its influence upon sound opinion. Value, after all, is a matter of opinion. It cannot be denied that on occasion such considerations as location and obsolescence will reduce value below reproduction cost. "Actual" cash value will not be arrived at by ignoring such realities.

Id. at 429. More recently, in *Heer v. State*, 432 N.W.2d 559 (S.D.1988), we affirmed a verdict wherein a jury instruction effectively equated "actual cash value" with "fair market value," where determination of "fair market value" included the consideration of replacement cost less depreciation. Id. at 565–66 (discussing and reaffirming the *Lampe* analysis). The views expressed in these two cases comport with the majority view. *See* Annotation, *Depreciation as Factor in Determining Actual Cash Value for Partial Loss under Insurance Policy*, 8 A.L.R.4th 533, 537 (1981 & Supp.1997) (noting that, regardless of the valuation method used, it is "generally held" that depreciation is an appropriate or requisite factor in determining cash value); Annotation, *Test or Criterion of "Actual Cash Value" Under Insurance Policy Insurance to Extent of Actual Cash Value at Time of Loss*, 61 A.L.R.2d 711, 715–18 (1958) (general test of the measure of damages for loss is the market value of the property and, in jurisdictions where the replacement cost is the proper criterion of "actual cash value," a deduction for depreciation is made where the value of the replaced property would exceed the value of that destroyed). *See also* Annotation, *Construction and Effect of Property Insurance Provision Permitting Recovery of Replacement Cost of Property*, 1 A.L.R.5th 817, 827 (1992 & Supp.1997) (noting that replacement cost coverage was devised to remedy shortfall in coverage that results under policy compensating for actual cash value alone; standard policy compensating an insured for the actual cash value of damaged or destroyed property makes the insured responsible for bearing the cash difference necessary to replace old property with new property).

In granting summary judgment to Zochert, the trial court held the purpose of this insurance was to allow Zochert to rebuild after a loss. The court stated: "Insureds who faithfully pay their premiums should get the benefit of their bargain. Plaintiffs will be unable to repair their silos if they are not compensated in full for their loss." Affirmance of the trial court in this case would provide Zochert with more coverage than is allowed under its farmowner's policy and would disregard the contractual language. * * *

NOTES AND QUESTIONS

1. *Two Views of Indemnity.* The broad evidence rule adopted by the court in *Zochert* reflects the approach taken by the vast majority of courts in measuring actual cash value. The purpose of this measure of recovery is to assure that the insured's net worth before and after loss remains the same. It thus reflects an *economic conception* of indemnity. By contrast, a replacement cost measure of recovery is more consistent with a *functional conception* of indemnity, which focuses on returning the insured to roughly the same style of life as he or she occupied before loss. The relative merits of these two approaches may depend on whether the underlying policy is for a commercial or individual policyholder. On one hand, deducting depreciation in order to arrive at the actual cash value measure of recovery was clearly correct in *Zochert*, because a replacement cost measure of recovery would have provided an essentially commercial operation with an asset worth more after payment of the fire insurance proceeds than it was worth before the fire. On the other hand, a homeowner whose twenty-year old garage is destroyed by fire needs a new garage. If he recovers only the market value of the old garage, he has the same net-worth before and after loss, but he is worse off nevertheless—because he either has no garage, or must take additional money out of his pocket in order to build a new one. Of course, the homeowner in this example clearly does have a more valuable house if it includes a new garage. To what extent might allowing a business to increase its net worth after a fire be more likely to result in moral hazard than allowing a homeowner to increase his net worth after a fire?

2. *Express Replacement-Cost Coverage.* Many Commercial Property and Homeowners policies, as well as the collision and comprehensive

coverage in many automobile policies, provide insurance for the cost of replacement without deduction for depreciation. For provisions governing these points, see the Sample Homeowners Policy, Section I—Conditions, paragraph D (pages 14–15). Note that under these provisions in the Sample Policy, recovery for personal property is generally calculated on an actual cash value basis, whereas recovery for the dwelling and other structures is generally calculated on a replacement cost basis. Why would the policy provide different measures of recovery for losses to these two different types of property? To counter the moral hazard associated with providing replacement cost coverage, many policies require that unless there is actual replacement, only actual cash value is payable. This provision is generally upheld as valid. See, e.g., *Rhodes v. Farmers Ins. Co.*, 79 Ark. App. 230 (2002); *Higginbotham v. Am. Family Ins. Co.*, 143 Ill. App. 3d 398 (1986).

3. *Appraisal of Valuation Disputes.* Many valuation disputes are resolved though an appraisal process rather than in court. Thus, the Sample Homeowners Policy, Section I—Conditions, paragraph F (page 15), provides that either the policyholder or the insurer may demand that disputes involving "the amount of loss" be resolved by appraisal. Appraisal resembles arbitration, but is much less formal and relies on experts such as contractors or mechanics, rather than legal experts as tends to be the case in arbitration. Timothy P. Law & Jillian L. Starinovich, What Is It Worth? A Critical Analysis of Insurance Appraisal, 13 Conn. Ins. L.J. 291 (2007). Despite the broad evidence rule used to assess actual cash value in courts, it is relatively standard for appraisers to determine actual cash value solely by calculating replacement cost minus depreciation. Because appraisal is generally not available for the resolution of coverage disputes, a variety of issues can arise when disputes involve both coverage and valuation, or claims at the borderline of these categories. See, e.g., *Dike v. Valley Forge Ins. Co.*, 797 F. Supp. 2d 777 (S.D. Tex. 2011) (noting that appraisal should be stayed in cases involving both valuation and coverage disputes, but that litigation should be stayed when a dispute does not involve coverage disputes, but just valuation issues).

4. *Valued Policy Laws.* Some states have attempted to sidestep one aspect of the measure-of-recovery problem by enacting valued policy statutes. These statutes provide that in the case of total loss of the insured property (the kind of property subject to the statutes varies) the measure of recovery is the face amount of the policy, regardless of its actual cash value at the time of loss. See, e.g., Ark. Code. Ann. § 23–88–101. The conventional wisdom has been that these statutes may well be ill-conceived, because they generate unnecessary moral hazard. See, e.g., Robert H Jerry II, & Douglas R. Richmond, Understanding Insurance Law 657–60 (4th ed. 2007); Robert E. Keeton, Insurance Law 140–42 (1971). However, several potential justifications can be offered for valued policy laws. First, they may avoid problems of valuation when there has been a total loss. It is common (though by no means universal) to see insurers pay the insured value of property under such circumstances, whether a statute requires it or not. Second, these statutes might penalize insurers for agents' attempts to earn high commissions by selling policies with face amounts exceeding the actual value of the property insured: both policyholder premiums and agent commissions are determined by the face amount of the policy, not the actual amount that would be recovered in the event of a complete loss. Third, valued policy laws may be justified on the basis that they simply require the insurer to provide the coverage for which the insured has paid

with many years' worth of premiums. Finally, the statutes might encourage insurers to investigate the values insureds place on insured property at the time of an application for coverage, in order to avoid the moral hazard that might stem from over-insuring property. Are these explanations persuasive enough to overcome the moral hazard objection to valued policy laws?

5. *Coinsurance in Property Coverage to Discourage Under-Insurance.* Many property insurance policies, including the Sample Homeowners Policy at Section I—Conditions, Paragraph D(2)(b) (page 15), contain a co-insurance provision that applies when a policyholder has substantially underinsured her property. Under the provision in the Sample Policy, if the policyholder has insured her property for less than 80% of its replacement cost, then she is subject to the co-insurance requirement. As a result, rather than recover the full replacement cost of a loss, she could only recover the amount of that loss multiplied by the coinsurance rate. The coinsurance rate is set by the ratio of (i) the coverage limit to (ii) 80% of the actual replacement cost of her property. For example, if a policyholder had insured her $100,000 home for $60,000 and she experienced a loss that would cost $30,000 to replace, she would receive only 75% (i.e. $60,000 divided by 80% of $100,000) of that loss, or about $22,500.

This requirement is designed to discourage policyholders from under-insuring their homes. Policyholders might have an incentive to do this because property insurance is generally priced per $1000 of property value, but partial loss of property is much more likely than total loss. As a result, policyholders generally would make a "good" gamble, on an expected value basis (ignoring risk aversion), by insuring for much less than the full value of their property. Doing so would provide them with full insurance for partial losses, and coverage up to the face amount of the policy for large losses. To appreciate why this strategy might be appealing, consider an insured who purchases $50,000 of coverage on a $100,000 house. This $50,000 of coverage has a higher expected value for the policyholder than the $50,000 slice of coverage between $50,000 and $100,000 that she would acquire by purchasing full coverage. This is because the second slice of coverage is less likely to be collected than the first slice of coverage. Yet because the insurer prices coverage per $1000 of property value, the partial coverage of $50,000 would cost the same as the (less valuable) $50,000 slice of coverage between $50,000 and $100,000 that she would acquire by purchasing full coverage. Therefore, without a coinsurance requirement, insureds would make a better "investment" on an expected value basis by insuring only the first $50,000 of their home rather than the full $100,000. The coinsurance requirements in property insurance aims to neutralize this incentive to insure against partial losses only. Another way of avoiding this problem would be to vary premiums with the percentage of cash value or absolute dollar value insured. The insured purchasing $100,000 of coverage would then pay a premium less than twice what the insured purchasing $50,000 of coverage would pay. Would the latter approach make more sense?

6. *A Different Perspective on Under-Insurance.* A different set of issues associated with under-insurance arises when policyholders experience total losses and find that their policy limits are insufficient to cover the cost of replacing their property. This is particularly common in the wake of large disasters, when the costs of rebuilding are elevated. Some have argued that such under-insurance is not the result of rational

policyholder gaming of insurance pricing, as contemplated by the coinsurance provision described above, but rather of insurers and agents under-estimating replacement cost in order to secure larger market share by selling cheaper policies. See, e.g., Kenneth S. Klein, When Enough is Not Enough: Correcting Market Inefficiencies in the Purchase and Sale of Residential Property Insurance, 18 Va. J. Soc. Pol'y & L. 345 (2011). These cases can result in litigation against agents and insurers for failing to advise policyholders on the need for higher limits. See, e.g., *Martinonis v. Utica Nat'l Ins. Grp.*, 65 Mass. App. Ct. 418 (2006) (holding that insurance agent only had a duty to advise policyholder to secure a higher limit if he had a special relationship with policyholder, but there was an issue of fact on this point given agent's specific assurances of adequate coverage limit).

G. SUBROGATION

Subrogation is the term used for a kind of legal substitution. One party is said to be "subrogated" to the rights of another when the first party steps into the second party's shoes, as it were, and assumes the second party's rights against a third party. Subrogation is important in a number of fields—suretyship, for example—and figures prominently in property, liability and health insurance. In property insurance, the insurer generally is subrogated to the insured's rights of recovery against any other party for a loss covered by the policy, to the extent of the insurer's payment to the insured. For example, suppose that an insured's home is destroyed by a fire negligently set by her neighbor, and the insured's homeowners insurer pays the insured the amount of the loss. The insurer is then entitled to recover this amount from the neighbor, either directly in a suit against the neighbor (in what might be called "active" subrogation), or as the real party in interest in a suit brought by the insured, through a right to be reimbursed out of the proceeds of such a suit (in what might be called "passive" subrogation).

One rule that follows logically from this arrangement is that any defense that would have been available against the insured is also available against the insurer. A second rule central to subrogation law follows almost tautologically from this description: an insurer cannot have subrogation against its own insured. Such subrogation would simply shift an insured loss back to the policyholder. See, e.g., *Dominion Ins. Co., Ltd. v. State,* 305 A.D.2d 779 (N.Y. App. Div. 2003); *Reich v. Tharp*, 167 Ill. App. 3d 496 (1987).

Types and Functions of Subrogation

There are two types of subrogation, distinguished by the source of the authority to subrogate. *Equitable subrogation* (sometimes called legal subrogation) arises by operation of law, whereas *contractual subrogation* (sometimes called conventional subrogation) results from an agreement of the parties. Most courts hold that a property insurer has rights of subrogation despite the absence of a subrogation provision in the policy, but modern property insurance policies virtually always specify some right of subrogation. See Sample Homeowners Policy at Sections I and II—Conditions, Paragraph F (page 23).

Two main functions of subrogation figure in analyses of the doctrine. First, subrogation is a method of implementing the principle of indemnity that is at the heart of all insurance. Subrogation prevents the insured from recovering more than the amount of his loss, by vesting the insured's rights of recovery against third parties in the insurer, who has already paid the insured for the loss. This reduces the cost of coverage and avoids what might otherwise be perceived as an unjustified windfall for the insured. For example, subrogation prevents the homeowner whose house is set on fire by his neighbor from collecting both the insurance proceeds from his insurer and the tort recovery against his neighbor. Instead, once the insurer pays, it, rather than the homeowner, is the party entitled to collect against the negligent neighbor.

Second, subrogation helps to allocate ultimate financial responsibility for some insured losses to the third parties who cause these losses, without producing the windfalls just noted. In the example above, the negligent neighbor (or his liability insurer) is the party that ultimately pays for the loss, rather than the homeowner insurer. This advances the deterrence and fairness goals of tort law while reducing the cost of property insurance. However, this result only holds if the collateral source rule applies, making evidence of prior payment by plaintiff's insurers to the plaintiff inadmissible in the tort suit. In the absence of the collateral source rule, tortfeasors' liability is reduced by the victim's insurance recovery, thus limiting the extent to which tortfeasors are required to pay for the consequences of their tortious actions. At the same time, the insurer's right of subrogation has no value in the absence of the collateral source rule, and thus it does not reduce premiums in such cases.

Subrogation and Settlement

The general rule is that the insured who interferes with an insurer's rights of subrogation after suffering a loss voids his insurance coverage. Thus, if I release my neighbor from any liability he may have for destroying my house by fire, my insurer is no longer obligated to pay my loss. This rule is of course a trap for the unwary. One important exception to the rule, however, is that the third party is not released from subrogation liability to the insurer if the third party has notice of the insurer's right of subrogation. See, e.g., *Allied Mut. Ins. Co. v. Heiken*, 675 N.W.2d 820 (Iowa 2004); *Markham v. Nationwide Mut. Fire Ins. Co.*, 125 N.C. App. 443 (1997). It follows that an insured signing a release under these circumstances has not interfered with the insurer's subrogation rights and hence has not voided his coverage. This exception strongly suggests that the prudent course of action for an insurer to follow when it receives a claim from its insured is to put any party potentially responsible for the loss on notice of the insurer's subrogation interest.

Another important subrogation issue is whether the insurer or the policyholder should have priority over payments from a third party tortfeasor when the policyholder is not fully compensated for his loss by his first-party insurer. For example, in *Florida Farm Bureau Insurance Co. v. Martin,* 377 So. 2d 827 (Fla. Dist. Ct. App. 1979), the insureds' loss exceeded the total of their recoveries from their insurer and the tortfeasor. The subrogation clause of the policy provided, "This Company may require from the insured an assignment of all right of recovery against any party for loss to the extent that payment therefor is made by the Company." The insurer in *Martin* did not take an assignment as provided by the clause; rather, it brought an action claiming that its right of subrogation entitled it to reimbursement out of the insured's recovery from the tortfeasor. The court acknowledged that the insurer had an equitable right of subrogation independent of the subrogation clause in the policy, but denied the insurer's claim on the ground that the principle underlying equitable subrogation—precluding duplicate recovery by the insured—would not be furthered by allowing subrogation when the amount recovered in tort is less than the insured's loss but is the maximum amount available from the tortfeasor. Should the result be different when the insurer is careful to take an express assignment of the insured's rights against the tortfeasor, as the subrogation clause in *Martin* provided? The problem ought to be avoidable when there is a potential settlement with the tortfeasor, by involving the insurer in advance and specifying the portion of the settlement to be paid to the insurer as reimbursement. But sometimes this does not occur, and the question whether the insured must be "made-whole" before the insurer has a right of subrogation arises. Because the make-whole issue arises most frequently in cases of subrogation by health insurers, it is addressed in more detail in Chapter Five.

Great Northern Oil Company v. St. Paul Fire and Marine Insurance Company

Supreme Court of Minnesota, 1971.
291 Minn. 97.

■ ROGOSHESKE, JUSTICE.

* * * The issue presented is whether plaintiff-insured, who, prior to a business-interruption loss and by an exculpatory clause in a construction contract, released the contractor from liability for negligently causing the loss, is precluded from pursuing recovery upon a policy of "all-risk" insurance in force prior to the release on the ground that exculpation defeated defendant insurance companies' subrogation rights against the contractor. We hold that plaintiff is not thereby precluded from recovering under the policy and affirm the trial court's order.

Plaintiff, Great Northern Oil Company, owns and operates an oil refinery at Pine Bend in Dakota County, Minnesota. On August 12, 1964, plaintiff procured from the several defendants a 3-year policy of "all-risk" insurance covering, among other things, losses due to the interruption of plaintiff's business. The aggregate amount of coverage is $3,000,000. The insurance policy provided:

> "(H) SUBROGATION. In the event of any payment under this policy the Company shall be subrogated to all the Insured's rights of recovery therefor against any person or organization and the Insured shall execute and deliver instruments and papers and do whatever else is necessary to secure such rights. The Insured shall do nothing after loss to prejudice such rights."

On February 7, 1967, during the term of the policy, plaintiff-insured entered into an agreement with the Litwin Corporation, Inc., for the construction of catalytic cracking expansion facilities, designed to materially increase plaintiff's production. So far as pertinent to the question presented, the construction agreement limited Litwin's liability for bodily injury and damage to plaintiff's property during construction and, by an exculpatory clause, provided that "Contractor shall not be responsible or held liable for any damages or liability for loss of use of the Work, loss of profits therefrom, or business interruption thereof however the same may be caused."

On June 16, 1967, a crane accident caused damage to the partially completed construction work. Plaintiff brought this action against defendant-insurers, contending that the accident had caused it to suffer a substantial business-interruption loss for which defendants are responsible under the terms of the all-risk insurance policy. The defendants' joint answer generally denied that plaintiff had sustained any loss covered by the policy and further alleged that the insured could not recover under the policy because the insured, by releasing Litwin from liability before the accident occurred, had defeated the insurers' rights of subrogation under the policy. The parties made cross-motions for summary judgment on this latter claim, and the court granted plaintiff's motion, striking the foregoing specific defense. Defendants appeal. We affirm and hold that plaintiff, in the absence of a prohibition in the insurance contract against entering into any exculpatory agreements, is not precluded from pursuing its action to recover its loss under the insurance policy.

Subrogation is a normal incident of a contract of insurance. Aetna Life Ins. Co. v. Moses, 287 U.S. 530. Its existence does not necessarily depend on the terms of the contract but on the nature of the contract of insurance and on general principles of equity. Bacich v. Homeland Ins. Co., 212 Minn. 375.

Whether or not the insurance policy expressly reserves subrogation rights, it is the universal rule that upon payment of a loss, an insurer is entitled to pursue those rights which the insured party may have against a third party whose negligence or wrongful act caused the loss. See, Board of Trustees of First Congregational Church of Austin v. Cream City Mutual Ins. Co., 255 Minn. 347. However, the insurer, as the subrogee, is entitled to no greater rights than those which the insured-subrogor possesses at the time the subrogee asserts the claim, as the subrogee merely "steps into the shoes" of the subrogor. Employers Liability Assur. Corp. v. Morse, 261 Minn. 259, 263. As an application of this rule, it is thus well established that an insured may defeat the insurance company's rights of subrogation by (1) settling with the wrongdoer after loss but before payment of the insurance (e.g., Bacich v. Homeland Ins. Co. *supra*; Harter v. American Eagle Fire Ins. Co. [6 Cir.] 60 F.2d 245); (2) settling with the wrongdoer after payment under the policy (e.g., National Union Fire Ins. Co. v. Grimes, 278 Minn. 45); or (3) entering into an agreement of release with the wrongdoer before the policy is issued (e.g., Hartford Fire Ins. Co. v. Chicago, M. & St. P. Ry. Co., 175 U.S. 91).

Unlike the foregoing examples, here plaintiff, by the construction contract (executed subsequent to the issuance of the policy but prior to loss), exonerated the contractor from any potential liability for damages resulting by way of business interruption, "however the same may be caused." The parties appear in agreement that this broad language includes damages caused by the contractor's own negligence. Cf. General Mills v. Goldman (8 Cir.) 184 F.2d 359. Such exculpatory agreements releasing a contracting party from liability caused by his own negligence are not uncommon in modern-day construction contracts. They are designed to distribute the burden or risks inherent in the performance of such contracts in such a way as to eliminate foreseeable disputes and to reduce the cost of construction.[1] Such agreements do not contravene public policy, are valid, and are enforceable. Independent School Dist. No. 877 v. Loberg Plumbing & Heating Co., 266 Minn. 426.

Although there appears to be no case specifically so holding, we assume, as do the parties, that an unambiguous and broad exculpatory agreement of the type used in this case defeats the subrogation rights of the insurance company against the contractor even though it was made subsequent to the issuance of the policy and prior to loss. Upon the assumption that subrogation rights are defeated by a release made after issuance of the policy and before loss, the question arises as to whether such impairment of subrogation rights should also preclude plaintiff from pursuing recovery under the all-risk insurance policy.

Treatises contain language which states generally that a release of liability given to a tortfeasor by the insured bars the insured's right of action on the policy because it destroys the insurer's right of subrogation. 6 Appleman, Insurance Law and Practice, § 4093; 44 Am.Jur. (2d) Insurance, § 1839. However, analysis of the cases cited in support of the rule reveals that it was derived from cases in which defeat of the insurer's right of subrogation occurs after loss. E.g., Bacich v. Homeland Ins. Co., *supra*. Some of the cited cases have held that the insured is precluded from recovery on a policy where he has defeated the insurer's right of subrogation by an agreement made before loss. However, in all such cases the insurance policies provided expressly that relinquishment of the insured's rights against a potential wrongdoer rendered the policy void. * * *

Defendants vigorously argue that an insured who, without reservation, releases all claims for damages against a potential wrongdoer either after or prior to loss, thereby defeating the right of subrogation accorded an insurer by the terms of an insurance policy, should be precluded from making recovery upon the policy for damage resulting from the wrongdoer's negligence. They argue that the insurer, prior to loss, has no way of preserving a remedy against the tortfeasor, and that common sense suggests no basis for according any different treatment to an insured who has released a wrongdoer from liability before the loss occurs than to an insured who has released the wrongdoer after the loss occurs since, in either event, the insured has, by his own conduct, deprived the insurer of a valuable right afforded by the insurance contract—the right to recoup its loss from the one

---

[1] Although it would not appear to be legally significant since no misrepresentation or fraud is claimed, the purpose of including the exculpatory clause in the construction contract does not appear in the record. Whether it was merely a part of a standard form of construction contract which the parties signed without careful consideration of its effect upon coverage under defendants' "all-risk" policy, or whether it was deliberately designed to shift liability for the loss which occurred to defendants under the provisions of the policy, as defendants contend, is not revealed by the record.

primarily liable. Defendants argue further that by permitting the contractor to avoid the risk of liability, plaintiff got its new facility at a lower cost, thereby receiving one benefit for relinquishing its claim against the contractor, and that plaintiff now seeks the added benefit of compensation by defendant insurers. They contend that they undertook a defined risk—the indemnification of plaintiff from loss resulting from hazards encountered in the operation of a going refinery—but did not undertake the risk by providing liability insurance to third parties, and that plaintiff's action thereby imposed a new and different kind of risk on the insurer. Defendants insist that if Litwin Corporation and plaintiff intended to place the risk of loss from delay in the commencement of the operation of the new facilities on the defendants, they could have secured the consent of defendants to the relinquishment of their subrogation rights, affording them the opportunity to evaluate the risk, to specifically include it in the insurance policy, and to assess any added premium cost to plaintiff.

These arguments are not without merit. While we are not free from doubt as to the resolution of the question presented, we are persuaded that considerations of public policy and equitable principles do not restrict our upholding the trial court's disposition. Surely, the considerations of public policy have been put to rest in the numerous cases upholding the validity of exculpatory provisions exonerating a party from liability for damages resulting from his own negligence. The important considerations are the equities between the parties. We believe on balance they fall on the side of the plaintiff-insured. The all-risk insurance policy, as its characterization implies, insured all real and personal property of plaintiff against all hazards encountered in the operation of a refinery, expressly including loss directly resulting from necessary business interruptions caused by any damage to the plaintiff's property. It contained a number of exclusions for which coverage was not provided as well as limiting provisions, including the subrogation clause quoted above. While exemplary fair dealing should have prompted plaintiff to notify defendants of the increased hazards occasioned by new construction activities on its premises, there appears no persuasive reason why defendants, at the time the policy was written, could not have expressly prohibited plaintiff from entering into any agreements prospectively releasing third parties, whose presence on plaintiff's premises was surely foreseeable, from liability for damage caused by their negligence. Defendants' argument that the policy was not intended to provide liability insurance coverage to negligent third parties is not persuasive, since the hazard of damage to plaintiff's property and resultant business interruption by either its own or a third party's negligence was surely one which was covered and reflected in the premium charged plaintiff.

Upon this record, the argument that a construction company's presence on plaintiff's premises would have increased the risk covered by the policy is speculative; even more speculative is the argument that a greater premium would have been assessed for such specific coverage. Thus, to allow plaintiff to pursue its recovery under the all-risk policy inflicts no injustice on defendants because the insured has paid for the hazard covered by the policy and has, as defendants acknowledge, the right to negotiate for and enter into construction contracts and to promote its business interests by avoiding overlapping insurance coverage against hazards inherent in the operation as well as the repair and expansion of its facilities. Plaintiff is seeking to recover only what it had a right to assume it paid the defendants a premium to insure against. While the action of plaintiff in releasing the contractor may have been unintentional or unwitting, defendants had the greater opportunity to prohibit such action by exercising their right to vary the coverage under the policy by endorsements as they deemed necessary.[2]

Affirmed.

NOTES AND QUESTIONS

1. *Getting Something for Nothing?* The circumstances under which an insurer should expect to have additional parties benefit from coverage by virtue of their relationship to the named insured are partly determined by the facts on the ground, and partly determined by the applicable legal rules that create these expectations. Was the insurer correct in *Great Northern* when it argued that, in effect, its insured and Litwin entered into an advance agreement to shift the cost of Litwin's negligence to St. Paul, without paying St. Paul the additional premium it deserved? Litwin probably paid Great Northern for this coverage (in the form of a lower contract price than would have been charged in the absence of the exculpatory clause), but then Great Northern kept this sum instead of paying it to St. Paul.

2. *An Alternative.* How would you react to a rule premised on what the court suggested would have been "exemplary fair dealing" by Great Northern—a rule obliging the insured to notify the insurer of a proposed exculpatory clause in any contract relating to the insured subject matter, and permitting the insurer to charge an additional premium if such a clause were executed? Consider the following factors:

    a. The benefits such a rule would afford insureds who do not enter into exculpatory agreements.

    b. The fact that insurers have elected not to include provisions creating such an obligation in the subrogation clauses of their policies.

    c. The leverage such a rule would give the insurer over the insured.

    d. The additional cost of notification.

    e. The difficulty of providing insureds with notice of the judicially-created obligation to notify the insurer or forfeit coverage.

3. *Possible Justifications for the Distinction.* The court's distinction between the treatment of releases of third parties after loss and exculpatory clauses executed prior to loss is generally accepted. See, e.g., *Bakowski v. Mountain States Steel, Inc.*, 52 P.3d 1179 (Utah 2002); *Albany*

---

[2] The action may have been no more deliberate or intentional than that of an owner of an automobile who, as a consideration for renting a garage, exculpates the garage owner from any liability for loss of the automobile, and who, subsequently suffering loss of the vehicle resulting from the garage owner's negligent failure to keep the garage door locked, quite naturally would assume that he would recoup his loss under the insurance policy covering his automobile. Although mindful that the wrongdoer does not escape liability, were we to hold under this hypothetical as defendants urge, we would have to unrealistically assume that exoneration of the garage owner from prospective liability would so increase the risks covered by the policy and the premium therefor as to justify imposing on the automobile owner the burden of informing his insurance carrier of his action or suffer loss of coverage for a risk expressly included in the insurance contract.

Ins. Co. v. United Alarm Servs., Inc., 194 F. Supp. 2d 87 (D. Conn. 2002). Moreover, it is also generally incorporated into policy language, as in the subrogation clause in the Sample Homeowners Policy (page 23). However, does the explanation that because loss has not yet occurred, the insurer has no subrogation right to be interfered with make sense? After all, the exculpatory clause undoubtedly disadvantages the insurer. On the other hand, is it not also clear that as between parties such as Great Northern and Litwin, exculpatory clauses should generally be valid? Exculpatory clauses both permit the parties to apportion the risk of business interruption to the party in the best position to control and/or insure against that risk, and to avoid duplicate insurance against it.

At least two justifications for the distinction between pre-loss exculpation and post-loss settlement seem plausible. First, the lion's share of exculpatory clauses probably are not separately negotiated, but are contained in fine print on standard-form contracts that people bound by them do not read. For example, in *Blume v. Evans Fur Co.*, 126 Ill. App. 3d 52 (1984), the insured stored her fur coat and received a receipt limiting the storage company's liability to $100. Would it be realistic to expect people in Blume's position to identify and appreciate the insurance implications of similar exculpatory or liability-limiting clauses in dry cleaner receipts, storage contracts, garage rental agreements and the like? Does this theory help to explain the difference in the treatment of pre- and post-loss exculpatory clauses, particularly for policies covering individuals?

Second, perhaps property insurers can more precisely risk-classify their insureds than liability insurers can risk-classify their insureds, at least in certain contexts such as construction projects. Property insurers know the value of the property they insure and the potential economic loss if business is interrupted. In contrast, liability insurers in general may have less information about those whom their insureds may injure in the course of their activities, and therefore less information on which to differentiate premium rates from insured to insured. In addition, the cost of paying for loss through property insurance is much lower than the cost of paying through tort suits followed by liability insurance payments. To the extent that these points are correct, a rule that allows property insurance to stand in the face of pre-loss exculpatory clauses would reduce administrative costs by allocating coverage responsibility to the property insurer rather than the liability insurer while allowing risk classification, over the long run, to have more substantial effect. How great would the differences between the refinement of risk classification in property and liability insurance have to be for this rationale to be satisfactory?

H. LIMITED INTERESTS

In most cases, it is fairly obvious who is entitled to the proceeds of insurance when a loss occurs. But in some cases, a party that is not the named insured—such as a lender, tenant, or construction contractor—may be treated as an "additional insured" or "implied co-insured," such that the party is entitled to some of the proceeds of the insurance policy in the event of a loss. This may be a result of a term in the insurance policy itself or a contract between the insured and an otherwise uninsured third party. In other cases, coverage can extend to a party that is not a named insured even in the absence of any clear contractual provision. In this section, we will study examples of such limited interests in the mortgage, lease, and real estate purchase contexts.

1. MORTGAGES

The purchase of most real estate and some personal property is financed by mortgage loans requiring that the lender be granted a security interest in the property, that the property be insured against fire and other physical damage, and that the lender's security interest be protected by that insurance. The means of protection usually is a *standard,* or *union mortgage clause* in the property owner's property insurance policy. For an example of such a clause, see the Sample Homeowners Policy, Section I—Condition L (page 16). The effect of the clause is to render any mortgagee/lender listed on the policy an additional insured party. If the property is destroyed, the insurer pays the mortgagee up to the amount of the outstanding balance of the debt owed by the insured, that debt is extinguished, and the amount of any remaining coverage is paid to the insured. For discussion, see John W. Steinmetz et al., The Standard Mortgage Clause in Property Insurance Policies, 33 Tort & Ins. L.J. 81 (1997).

If the insured breaches his obligations under the policy, however—by making fraudulent misrepresentations or refusing to cooperate with the claims investigation, for example—the standard mortgage clause provides that under specified circumstances the denial of coverage does not apply to the mortgagee. Rather, the insurer pays the mortgagee and is subrogated to the mortgagee's rights against the mortgagor/policyholder. The entire arrangement in this circumstance works as if the only party insured were the mortgagee, whose policy contained a subrogation clause. The standard rule that an insurer cannot have subrogation against its own insured is not violated because the insured, having breached an obligation under the policy, is not an "insured" for this purpose. When the dust settles, the mortgagor/policyholder is held ultimately responsible for his debt, which is as it should be if his insurance does not cover the loss in question.

Northwest Farm Bureau Insurance Company v. Althauser

Court of Appeals of Oregon, 1988.
90 Or. App. 13.

■ JOSEPH, CHIEF JUDGE.

This is a foreclosure action. Northwest Farm Bureau Insurance (plaintiff) issued the Althausers (defendants) a homeowner's insurance contract which included fire insurance coverage and mortgagee protection. After a fire, plaintiff paid the mortgagees. Plaintiff claims that it is subrogated to the mortgagees' rights, because its contract with defendants was made void by defendants' material misrepresentations concerning the fire loss. The trial court entered a summary judgment of foreclosure, and defendants appeal. We affirm.

Defendants owned a house which was subject to two mortgages. Plaintiff's policy provided that any fire loss would be payable to mortgagees named in the policy to the extent of their interests. The policy also provided that the mortgagee's interest was protected even if the mortgagor breached the policy.[1] In 1981, a fire severely damaged the house. In accordance with the policy, plaintiff paid the first mortgagee the full value of its mortgage, and the mortgagee assigned the mortgage to plaintiff. The remainder of the structural damage insurance proceeds was paid to the second mortgagee.

The insurance policy also provided coverage for personal property. Before the present action was filed, defendants sued plaintiff to recover their personal property losses. Plaintiff denied liability on two grounds: arson and material misrepresentation. The jury found that defendants did not commit arson but that they did "breach the insurance contract by knowingly misrepresenting or concealing a material fact relating to [the loss claim]." Judgment was entered for plaintiff.

Plaintiff then filed this action, asserting, *inter alia*, that it is equitably subrogated to both mortgages[2] and seeking to foreclose both, because defendants had not made any mortgage payments since the fire. * * *

Before the fire, defendants were "primarily responsible" for the mortgage debts. The insurance contract required that, after the fire, plaintiff pay the mortgagees, and it did so. If defendants remained primarily responsible for the mortgage debts after the fire, plaintiff is subrogated to the rights of the mortgagees, because it paid debts for which defendants were primarily responsible.

Defendants contend, essentially, that the fire made plaintiff primarily responsible for the debt, because the insurance contract required it to pay in the event of fire. Defendants argue that, if they were still responsible for the debt after the fire, they will have paid for fire insurance but will not have benefitted from it. They are not entitled to the benefits of the insurance, because they made material misrepresentations in connection with the policy. By statute, a fire insurance policy must contain a provision voiding the policy if there have been material misrepresentations by the insureds. ORS 743.612. The jury in the previous case brought by defendants determined that they had made material misrepresentations. The effect of that was to void the entire policy as between plaintiff and defendants. ORS 743.612. The mortgagees' interest was protected, even though defendants' conduct had voided the policy as to themselves. *See* n. 1,

---

[1] The policy provides, in part:

"14. MORTGAGEE. Loss shall be payable to mortgagees named in the coverage summary to the extent of their interest and in the order of precedence.

"We will:

"a. Protect the mortgagee's interest in insured property in the case of breach of warranty, increase in hazard, change of ownership, or foreclosure if the mortgagee has no knowledge of these conditions * * *

"The mortgagee will * * *

"d. Give us the right of recovery against any party liable for loss * * *.

"e. After a loss, permit us to satisfy the mortgage requirements and receive full transfer of the mortgage." *See* ORS 743.639(2).

[2] Plaintiff is not equitably subrogated to the entire second mortgage, but only to the amount that it paid the second mortgagee. *See* n. 3, *supra*.

supra; *see also Scott v. Northwestern Agencies*, 75 Or. App. 187, 192 (1985).

Because the misrepresentations voided the policy, plaintiff's payments to the mortgagees did not, as defendants contend, satisfy defendants' obligation on the mortgages. Rather, the payments satisfied a separate and distinct duty that plaintiff owed the mortgagees under the insurance contract. *See Scott v. Northwestern Agencies, supra,* 75 Or.App. at 192.

> "[W]here one has been compelled to pay a debt which ought to have been paid by another, he is entitled to exercise all of the remedies which the creditor possesses against that other * * *."
> *United States F. & G. Co. v. Bramwell, supra*, 108 Or. at 277.

Defendants "ought to have" paid the mortgage debts, even after the fire, because their insurance was void. Because plaintiff was compelled to pay the debt by its separate duty to the mortgagees, it is entitled to the mortgagees' remedies.

NOTES AND QUESTIONS

1. *The Innocent Co-Insured: Guilt by Association?* The triangular relationship between the insured, the insurer, and the mortgagee is not always so clear as in the principal case. For example, suppose that the property in question is owned jointly and the two owners are co-insureds. Consider the proper result when one of the two owners/insureds takes an action that would void the policy if he were the sole owner. Should the policy be held void or should the innocent co-insured's interest survive? The tendency of the courts is to protect the innocent co-insured, even in the face of policy provisions attempting to preclude his or her coverage. See, e.g., *Allstate Ins. Co. v. LaRandeau*, 261 Neb. 242 (2001); *Williams v. Auto Club Grp. Ins. Co.*, 224 Mich. App. 313 (1997). But see *Deeter v. Ind. Farmers Mut. Ins. Co.*, 999 N.E.2d 82 (Ct. App. Ind. 2013) (enforcing explicit policy language excluding coverage for innocent co-insured). How does the Sample Policy attempt to deal with this issue? See Homeowners Policy, Section I—Exclusion 8 (page 13). A number of states prohibit by statute coverage exclusions for innocent co-insureds when the loss involved domestic violence. See, e.g., KRS 304.12–211(2)(b). What, if any, rationale exists for denying coverage to an innocent co-insured?

2. *Rebuild or Repay?* Suppose that after a building is damaged or destroyed by fire the insured wishes to use the insurance proceeds to repair or rebuild, but the mortgagee wants the mortgage paid off. Does the standard mortgage clause make provision for this contingency? Is the typical lender likely to prosper if it refuses homeowners the right to rebuild? Would your answer differ in circumstances where interest rates have risen sharply since the original loan was made? Some state statutes deal with the problem, as do some mortgage agreements. In the absence of these sources of guidance, the majority of courts have ruled in favor of the mortgagee. See Robert H. Jerry II, Understanding Insurance Law 385 (3d ed. 2002). Under some circumstances, however, courts have given the insured preference. See, e.g., *Schoolcraft v. Ross,* 81 Cal. App. 3d 75 (1978) (residential lender may not refuse to allow rebuilding if security for the loan will not be impaired).

3. *Loss-Payee Issues.* Results quite different from those reached under the standard mortgage clause appear when the mortgagee is listed merely as a loss-payee under what is known as an *open mortgage* clause. The clause omits the standard provision protecting the mortgagee's coverage in the event that the mortgagor voids his own insurance by act or neglect. This kind of clause is rare in real estate mortgages, although it is probably less rare in policies of insurance on personal property such as business inventory. Under such a clause the mortgagee's right to coverage is extinguished whenever the insured commits an act or omission that voids his own coverage.

Conversely, because the mortgagee is not an "insured," the possibility that the insurer may seek subrogation against the *mortgagee* after paying an *insured's* claim may arise. Suppose that Adams builds some apartments for Brown, and Brown names Adams (whom he still owes part of the purchase price) as the loss-payee in a fire insurance policy issued to Brown. After a fire at the apartments, the insurer pays Brown the entire amount of the loss to the property but refuses to pay Adams. Adams sues the insurer. The insurer defends on the ground that the cause of the fire was defective wiring, for which Adams is liable to Brown in tort. The insurer counterclaims against Adams, claiming a right of recovery in the amount of the payment made to Brown by virtue of the insurer's right of subrogation, under Browns' policy, to Browns' rights against Adams. What result? Cf. *Dalrymple v. Royal-Globe Ins. Co.* 280 Ark. 514 (1983). If you were counsel for a fire insurer, under what circumstances would you insist that lenders be listed as loss-payees only, rather than as mortgagees under the standard mortgage clause?

2. LEASEHOLDS

Alaska Insurance Company v. RCA Alaska Communications, Inc.

Supreme Court of Alaska, 1981.
623 P.2d 1216.

■ CONNOR, JUSTICE.

In this appeal the question is whether a commercial tenant is an "implied co-insured" under its landlord's fire insurance policy, when a provision in the lease requires the landlord to obtain and keep in effect an insurance policy on the leased premises covering loss because of fire. Under the facts of this case, we hold that the tenant is, by legal implications, a co-insured of the landlord's policy, thereby precluding the landlord's insurer from exercising subrogation rights against the tenant.

Bachner Rental Co., Inc. [hereinafter Bachner], as landlord and RCA Alaska Communications, Inc. [hereinafter RCA], as tenant, entered into a one-year commercial lease for a warehouse on October 1, 1976, with possession commencing December 1, 1976. In May of the previous year, Bachner had purchased a three-year policy for fire and extended coverage from appellant insurer, Alaska Insurance Company [hereinafter AIC], protecting its interest in four commercial warehouses, including the structure in question. RCA did not procure additional fire insurance covering its leased warehouse, nor was RCA's name added along with Bachner as an additional insured on the pre-existing policy with AIC.

During the second week of January, 1977, a fire occurred in the rented structure, causing extensive smoke and water damage, and the building was subsequently demolished. AIC paid Bachner for the fire loss pursuant to the insurance policy, and then commenced an action as subrogee of Bachner, contending that RCA, acting through its employees, had negligently caused the fire. At trial, RCA moved for a partial summary judgment on the theory that, as lessee of Bachner, RCA was an implied insured of AIC, thereby precluding appellant AIC from exercising its subrogation rights. The superior court granted a partial summary judgment for RCA. We affirm.

It is a well established rule that "an insurer cannot recover by means of subrogation against its own insured." *Graham v. Rockman,* 504 P.2d 1351, 1356 (Alaska 1972). Since subrogation is an equitable doctrine, equity principles apply in determining its availability. * * *

Therefore, if we find that the tenant in this case can be considered a co-insured of the landlord, the insurer cannot exercise a right of subrogation against the tenant. In recent years a number of courts have denied a cause of action to landlords and the right of subrogation to their insurers, when the landlord covenants to carry fire insurance on the leased premises, and the fire damage is allegedly due to the negligence of the tenant. Absent an express provision in the lease establishing the tenant's liability for loss from negligently started fires, the trend has been to find that the insurance obtained was for the mutual benefit of both parties, and that the tenant "stands in the shoes of the insured landlord for the limited purpose of defeating a subrogation claim." *Rizzuto v. Morris,* 592 P.2d 688, 690 (1979), *citing Rock Springs Realty, Inc. v. Waid,* 392 S.W.2d 270, 278 (Mo.1965); *Monterey Corp. v. Hart,* 224 S.E.2d 142, 146 (1976). We think the reasoning of the foregoing cases is sound.

The central issue is whether the lease contains a provision clearly establishing the tenant's liability for negligently caused fire damage. In the case at bar, the lease between the parties contains the following provisions whose significance and construction is in dispute:

4.

"I.   COVENANTS OF THE LESSOR:

    c.   Lessor warrants that all facilities and appurtenances are in good condition, and that all repairs required to maintain the premises and buildings in an adequate and suitable condition for the purpose of this lease shall be at Lessor's sole cost and expense * * * [except] those damages arising from the direct negligence on the part of the Lessee to any portion of said Facility. * * *

II.   COVENANTS OF THE LESSEE:

    b.   Lessee shall use said premises for lawful business purposes and will leave said premises at the expiration of this lease in as good a condition as received, excepting fair wear and tear and/or loss or damage caused by fire, explosion, earthquake or other casualty; provided that such casualty was not caused by the negligent act of the Lessee, its employees or agents. * * *

c. Lessee agrees to indemnify and hold Lessor harmless from and against loss, damage and liability arising from the negligent act of Lessee, its agents, employees, or clients;

III. MUTUAL COVENANTS OF LESSOR AND LESSEE

b. That this lease shall automatically terminate with no penalty to Lessee in event that the leased space becomes unusable due to fire or other cause;

c. Lessor agrees to pay all taxes and assessments made against and levied upon said property. Lessor shall obtain and keep in force during the term of this lease a policy or policies of insurance covering loss or damages to the premises providing protection against all perils and risks including but not limited to the classifications of fire, extended coverage, vandalism and malicious mischief. Lessee agrees that if its usage of leased premises should increase the insurance hazard of the premises in any way during the term of said lease, the Lessee shall bear the additional cost of insurance realized by the Lessor. Lessor agrees to provide Lessee adequate documentation to verify that any additional insurance premium increase is in fact due to Lessee's use of said leased premises."

AIC contends that the absence of an express exemption for negligent liability and the inclusion of paragraphs I. c., II. b., and II. c. of the lease clearly establish RCA's liability for fire damage caused by its own negligence. In the last analysis the question is whether we should give primacy to the redelivery (II. b.) and indemnity (II. c.) covenants of the lessee, or to the insurance clause of III. c., wherein the lessor promises to obtain insurance covering, *inter alia,* damage to the leased premises caused by fire. In our view, the redelivery and indemnity provisions relied on by AIC, when read in conjunction with the insurance clause of III. c., fail to clearly establish RCA's liability for fire damage caused by its own negligence.

We believe that in a situation of this type it would be undesirable as a matter of public policy to permit the risk of loss from a fire negligently caused by a tenant to fall upon the tenant rather than the landlord's insurer.[1] *See* R. Keeton, Insurance Law § 4.4(b), at 210

---

[1] One policy consideration for not permitting a landlord's insurer to subrogate against the landlord's tenant is reduction of litigation. If a landlord's casualty insurer may seek to recoup its payments for fire loss by alleging the negligence of the tenant, many commercial fire losses will result in costly litigation. For similar reasons, we held in *Baugh-Belarde Constr. Co. v. College Utilities Corp.,* 561 P.2d 1211, 1215 (Alaska 1977), that a builder's risk

(1971). Since the ordinary and usual meaning of "loss by fire" includes fires of negligent origin, it would contradict the reasonable expectations of a commercial tenant to allow the landlord's insurer to proceed against it after the landlord had contracted in the lease to provide fire insurance on the leased premises. *Rizzuto v. Morris,* 592 P.2d at 690–91; *Monterey Corp. v. Hart,* 224 S.E.2d at 147. We agree with the court in *Sutton v. Jondahl,* 532 P.2d 478 (Okl.App.1975), which stated:

> "Basic equity and fundamental justice upon which the equitable doctrine of subrogation is established require that when fire insurance is provided for a dwelling it protects the insurable interests of all joint owners including the possessory interests of a tenant absent an express agreement by the latter to the contrary. The company affording such coverage should not be allowed to shift a fire loss to an occupying tenant even if the latter negligently caused it."

532 P.2d at 482.

Therefore, we hold that if the landlord in a commercial lease covenants to maintain fire insurance on the leased premises, and the lease does not otherwise clearly establish the tenant's liability for fire loss caused by its own negligence, by reserving to the landlord's insurer the right to subrogate against the tenant, the tenant is, for the limited purpose of defeating the insurer's subrogation claim, an implied co-insured of its landlord.

Accordingly, the judgment of the superior court is affirmed.

AFFIRMED.

■ RABINOWITZ, CHIEF JUSTICE, dissenting.

I am in agreement with the general principle set out in the majority opinion—*i.e.,* that, "[a]bsent an express provision in the lease establishing the tenant's liability for loss from negligently started fires, the trend has been to find that the insurance obtained was for the mutual benefit of both parties, and that the tenant 'stands in the shoes of the insured landlord for the limited purpose of defeating a subrogation claim.'"

However, here the parties chose to include an express provision establishing the tenant's liability for fires caused by the tenant's own negligence. The majority cites no opinions in which the court has held that the general principle overrules such an express provision, and I would not allow it to do so here. In my opinion, the public policy considerations involved here are not so overwhelming that the parties ought not to be allowed to contract for a different result according to their own preferences; but the majority's treatment of the language here makes this well-nigh impossible.[2]

---

policy prohibited the insurer from subrogating against sub-contractors of the insured general contractor.

[2] * * * I think that there are two clear provisions establishing the tenant's liability for loss from fires started by its own negligence: paragraph II(c), which states "[l]essee agrees to indemnify and hold lessor harmless from and against loss, damage and liability arising from the negligent act of lessee, its agents, employees or clients;" and paragraph II(b), which requires the lessee to "leave said premises at the expiration of this lease in as good a condition as received, excepting fair wear and tear and/or loss or damage caused by fire, explosion,

My view might be different were this lease a product of a disparity of bargaining power, or similar to a contract of adhesion; but no such claim is made here, and properly so, as neither party can be characterized as unsophisticated in such matters.

I do not read the provisions of the lease as being inconsistent. However, even if they were, I agree with the *Rizzuto* court in its statement that "[o]ur review of the cases in this area leads us to conclude that the intent of the parties is the primary factor considered by the courts in construing exemption clauses." *Rizzuto v. Morris,* 592 P.2d 688, 691 (1979). *Rizzuto* was decided after trial *id.* 592 P.2d at 689, based upon "the undisputed testimony of all the parties." *Id.,* 592 P.2d at 691. The instant case is on appeal from a summary judgment, and I think there are still genuine issues of material fact regarding the intent of the parties.

NOTES AND QUESTIONS

1. *A Rose by Any Other Name.* The majority rule now appears to be that, absent a provision in a lease to the contrary, the tenant is an implied co-insured with the landlord. The rationale for this rule is that a tenant would be surprised to find himself a defendant in an action by the landlord's insurer. Relatedly, the rule makes it unnecessary for ordinary tenants to purchase insurance protecting them against liability to the landlord or directly covering the the landlord's property. The seminal case on the issue is *Sutton v. Jondahl,* 532 P.2d 478 (Okla. App. 1975). For more recent confirmations of this view, *SFI Ltd. P'ship 8 v. Carroll,* 288 Neb. 698 (2014). But a number of courts have rejected the *Sutton* doctrine, at least when the lease makes no reference to the landlord's obligation to procure insurance on the premises. See, e.g., *56 Assocs. ex rel. Paolino v. Frieband,* 89 F. Supp. 2d 189 (D.R.I. 2000) (predicting that Rhode Island would reject *Sutton* and citing cases from other states supporting that prediction). How persuasive is the majority rationale in connection with a commercial lease such as the one involving RCA? In any event, what did the court mean when it said that, for the limited purpose of defeating the insurer's subrogation claim, the tenant is an "implied co-insured?" Is this anything other than a holding that the landlord had exculpated the tenant from liability for negligently damaging the premises, in much the same way that the insured in *Great Northern* signed an exculpatory clause releasing Litwin in advance from liability for negligently damaging Great Northern's property? Can this holding be squared with the language of the RCA lease?

2. *Standing the Holding on its Head.* As the dissent indicated, the hornbook rule described in the preceding paragraph is not always applied when the lease contains an express provision establishing the tenant's liability for negligently damaging the premises. If the parties had intended the tenant to be liable for negligently damaging the premises, as suggested by the dissent, then what must they have intended by the lease's requirement that the lessor maintain insurance on the premises? That the tenant was an implied co-insured for all purposes *except* regarding losses

---

earthquake or other casualty; provided that such casualty was not caused by the negligent act of the Lessee, its employees or agents. * * *" In my opinion, the lessee by these provisions clearly and unambiguously covenanted to be responsible for fire damage caused by its own negligence.

caused by the tenant's own negligence? Isn't this at least as plausible an interpretation of the provisions of the lease as the court's interpretation? Should it matter whether paragraph III.c. was individually drafted or merely boiler plate that was already on a printed form that the parties used?

3. *Variations on a Theme.* Suppose that a lease contains an insurance clause similar to paragraph III. c. but no provisions governing the tenant's liability for negligence. In a jurisdiction in which the tenant is liable at common law for damage to the leased premises resulting from his negligence, what should be the result on facts otherwise like those in the *RCA* case? Suppose that the damage exceeds the limits of the landlord's insurance. Should the landlord be able to collect the amount of this excess from the tenant even if the insurer has no subrogation rights against the tenant? See, respectively, *Reliance Insurance Co. v. East-Lind Heat Treat, Inc.*, 175 Mich. App. 452 (1989) and *Agra-By-Products, Inc. v. Agway, Inc.*, 347 N.W.2d 142 (N.D. 1984).

3. REAL ESTATE SALES

In the typical sale of real estate there is a period of time between execution of the contract of sale and the closing at which title to the property is transferred. When the property is damaged or destroyed during this time period, it is not always clear whether the seller or buyer is the party that bears this loss. Many contracts explicitly allocate this risk to the seller as long as it maintains possession, but possession can change before closing. And the default rule that applies when the contract does not explicitly address this issue varies by state. This uncertainty about who bears the risk of loss between contract execution and closing creates the possibility of mismatched insurance, meaning that one party in a real estate sales transaction bears the risk of loss while the other party has insurance against the loss. The most common example of this mismatch is when the purchaser bears the risk of loss to the property but the seller alone is insured. This tends to occur because the inexperienced or legally unrepresented purchaser does not know that she bears the risk of loss immediately upon signing a contract of sale, and (unlike the seller) she does not already have insurance on the property. However, mismatched insurance in real estate sales can also involve the reverse situation, where the seller bears the risk of loss but the purchaser alone is insured.

Courts facing such mismatched insurance cases often hold that the insurance can operate for the benefit of the non-insured party who bears the risk. For instance, when the purchaser bears the risk of loss and the seller alone is insured, courts often hold that the seller is entitled to specific performance of the purchaser's promise to buy, but that the seller holds his insurance in constructive trust for the purchaser. In effect, the purchaser is an implied co-insured under the seller's policy. See, e.g., *King v. Dunlap*, 945 S.W.2d 736 (Tenn. App. 1996); cf. *Hanson v. Hamnes*, 460 N.W.2d 647 (Minn. App. 1990) (purchaser is not entitled to the seller's insurance when the contract requires the purchaser to secure his own insurance). Does this suggest that an insured's intention that another party benefit from his coverage is not a prerequisite to that party's rights under the policy, that real estate transfers are distinguishable from mortgages and leaseholds in this respect, or that something else entirely is going on? If the latter, what is it?

The converse of insurance mismatch problems in real estate transfers is double insurance: both purchaser and seller have insurance against a loss that occurs during the period between contract and transfer of title. In the case that follows the court was faced with precisely this embarrassment of riches.

Paramount Fire Insurance Company v. Aetna Casualty and Surety Company

Supreme Court of Texas, 1962.
163 Tex. 250.

■ GREENHILL, JUSTICE.

This case is an appeal from a summary judgment. The question is one of first impression in Texas and involves the liability of two insurance companies, each issuing a policy covering improvements which were destroyed by fire.

On July 17, 1957, the heirs of Mrs. R.L. Cameron entered into a written agreement labeled "Contract of sale and receipt for earnest money," whereby the seller(s) "sells and agrees to convey" and the purchaser(s), Mr. and Mrs. Sterling D. Holmes and Pauline Reece, "agrees to consummate the sale within fifteen days from date title company approves title" of a tract of land upon which were situated the improvements later destroyed. The contract specified the total purchase price, a down-payment, and terms of $125 monthly until the final closing date one year later, July 17, 1958, when the balance was due. Both seller and purchaser were given the right of specific performance. Purchasers had the right to occupy the premises from the inception of the contract, which they did, and had the right to make all desired improvements on the property.

On October 12, 1957, sellers procured from petitioner, Paramount Fire Insurance Company, an insurance policy for $15,000 covering improvements on the contracted land and payable only to sellers. A clause extending protection to purchasers under this policy was specifically rejected by sellers.

The fire involved occurred on July 7, 1958. By this time, the title company had issued the title insurance policy. The sellers had prepared a warranty deed conveying the property to the purchasers. Some, but not all of the sellers had already signed the deed, and it was being sent to the others for their signatures and acknowledgments. Purchasers had made the monthly payments of $125 and had procured a sufficient loan from Richardson Savings and Loan Association to pay the balance of the purchase price. Purchasers had also procured an $18,000 fire insurance policy from respondent, Aetna Casualty & Surety Company, in their favor with loss payable clause to the mortgagee as its interest might appear. This policy was dated June 25, 1958. All these and related papers, including the Aetna policy, were deposited in escrow with National Title & Abstract Company for final closing of the transaction on July 8, 1958. Because of the July 7 fire, this meeting was postponed until September 3, 1958. At the latter date, purchasers paid the contract price and received the warranty deed. Sellers, at the same time, assigned all their rights and claims under the Paramount policy to the purchasers.

Thereafter, purchasers and their mortgagee filed suit against both insurance companies, claiming property loss of $14,000. This suit was settled as to the plaintiffs by each insurance company's contributing a prorata share of the loss based on the amount of its respective policy, reserving its rights against the other. The suit then proceeded between the two insurance companies to determine liability as against each other. The trial court rendered summary judgment against Aetna, awarding Paramount the amount of money it contributed in the settlement with purchasers. Aetna's motion for summary judgment was consequently denied. On appeal, the judgment was reversed and the loss prorated between both companies in proportion to the face amount of the respective policies. 347 S.W.2d 281.

Both companies filed applications for writ of error to this Court. Paramount, of course, seeks to have the trial court's judgment affirmed. Aetna asks that the full loss be imposed upon Paramount, or, alternatively, that the judgment of the Court of Civil Appeals be affirmed. * * *

Aetna being the insurer of purchasers in possession under a contract of sale, it must bear all the loss unless it has a right to require Paramount to bear a prorata share as held by the Court of Civil Appeals.

Paramount's application attacks this proration holding, arguing that the vendors suffered no actual pecuniary loss from the fire and that, therefore, the vendees' insurance company should incur the total liability. Paramount's position is based on the generally accepted principle that:

> "Since a contract for insurance against fire ordinarily is a contract of indemnity * * * insured is entitled to receive the sum necessary to indemnify him, or to be put, as far as practicable, in the same condition pecuniarily in which he would have been had there been no fire; that is, he may recover to the extent of his loss occasioned by the fire, but no more, and he cannot recover if he sustained no loss." 45 C.J.S. Insurance § 915, p. 1010.

Aetna does not challenge this principle. Instead, the controversy is as to whether or not the insureds of Paramount suffered any "loss" in a legal sense.

The Court of Civil Appeals regarded the date of the fire as controlling and found that the vendors did incur a loss, despite the fact that they received the full contract price from the vendees after the fire. There is a line of cases which supports this viewpoint. * * * The rationale of these cases is that an insurance company contracts to protect an insured against destruction by fire of his property and that liability is fixed if such fire occurs, all other contract terms being met. Any compensation to the insured from third parties, such as payment from the vendees here, is regarded as being unrelated to the insurance contract, of no concern to the insurance company, and in the nature of a windfall to the insured.

On the other hand, there is also a line of cases which supports Paramount's argument that its insureds ultimately suffered no pecuniary loss from the fire and are therefore not entitled to recover on their insurance contract. In Ramsdell v. Insurance Company of North America, 197 Wis. 136, it was said:

> "The court looks to the substance of the whole transaction rather than to seek a metaphysical hypothesis upon which to justify a loss that is no loss. This is not a case where a stranger to the transaction, out of charity, or for other reasons, might make good the loss * * *. The loss has been made good out of a related transaction * * *."

Accord, Tauriello v. Aetna Insurance Co., 14 N.J.Super. 530; Smith v. Jim Dandy Markets, 172 F.2d 616 (9th Cir.). We are inclined toward this latter view.

The complexity of the present problem is heightened, however, by another widely accepted principle upon which the Court of Civil Appeals relied in ordering a proration between Paramount and Aetna. In 64 A.L.R.2d 1406, § 4, it is said:

> "Where the purchaser as equitable owner will bear the loss occasioned by a destruction of the property pending completion of the sale, and the contract is silent as to insurance, the rule quite generally followed is that the proceeds of the vendor's insurance policies, even though the purchaser did not contribute to their maintenance, constitute a trust fund for the benefit of the purchaser to be credited on the purchase price of the destroyed property, the theory being that the vendor is a trustee of the property for the purchaser."

The difficulty is that in some jurisdictions, even where the vendor is regarded as having suffered no loss from a fire, he is allowed to collect on his insurance policy subject to a constructive trust for the vendee's benefit. E.g., Wm. Skinner & Sons Ship-Building and Dry-Dock Co. v. Houghton, 92 Md. 68. Obviously, this result does violence to the indemnity theory of insurance, but as one commentator observed, it represents an attempt by the courts to "accommodate the contract to lay expectation without tarnishing the ideal of freedom of contract." Young, Some "Windfall Coverages" in Property and Liability Insurance, 60 Colum.L.Rev. 1063. The rationale is that if a vendee pays the full contract price for property which has been damaged or destroyed by fire, it is only equitable to allow him the benefit of any insurance proceeds rather than to give the vendor both the insurance proceeds and the proceeds of sale.

Paramount concedes that it is difficult to quarrel with the equity of this rule, but strenuously argues that the rule should have no application when the vendees have secured their own insurance policy. We agree.

Although none of the decisions applying the constructive trust theory purport to base the result on the fact that the vendee had no insurance, yet it appears that such was the situation in all but two cases. The two exceptions are Vogel v. Northern Assurance Co., 219 F.2d 409 (3d Cir.), and Insurance Company of North America v. Alberstadt, 383 Pa. 556. In these cases, the vendee was allowed to benefit from both his and the vendor's policies, even to the extent of being allowed to profit from the fire in the Vogel case. It must be observed, however, that both cases applied Pennsylvania law that an insured's loss is determined as of the date of the fire regardless of any subsequent developments. See Dubin Paper Co. v. Insurance Company of North America and State Mutual Fire Insurance Co. v. Updegraff, supra.

We believe the better result to be that if a vendor is entitled to specific performance under a contract of sale and thereby collects the full purchase price despite fire damage to improvements, he has suffered no legal loss. As it is not before us here, we leave open the question of whether, where the vendee has no insurance, there can be recovery on the vendor's policy subject to a constructive trust for the vendee, who is often ignorant of his legal liability in such a situation. We believe that there is nothing in the present case, however, which would require such an exception to the principle that an insurance policy is basically a personal, indemnity contract.

Here we are not dealing with an unwitting risk bearer, but rather with vendees who are protected by their own insurance. Also, we do not have a situation where the vendors originally intended for their policy to protect the vendees, for they specifically rejected such a provision. Further we note that in the vendors' own policy there is a provision that Paramount's liability should not exceed "the interest of the insured." After the contract of sale, the interest of Paramount's insured became the amount of the unpaid purchase price and, as to that interest, they suffered no loss. Accordingly, there is no liability under the Paramount policy, and Paramount's insureds had no rights to assign to the vendees. * * *

For the reasons stated herein, the judgment of the Court of Civil Appeals is reversed and the judgment of the trial court is affirmed. * * *

■ GRIFFIN, JUSTICE (dissenting).

I do not agree that all of the loss from the destruction of the improvements by fire should fall on Aetna. I believe the law requires that the loss be prorated between Aetna and Paramount as decreed by the Court of Civil Appeals.

The majority opinion recognizes that Paramount's insured had an insurable interest in the property at the time of the issuance of that policy. The majority reasons that the liability of Paramount to the insurer is to be determined by events happening after the loss by fire has occurred. The majority say "we note that in the vendors' own policy there is a provision that Paramount's liability should not exceed 'the interest of the insured.' After the contract of sale, the interest of Paramount's insured became the amount of the unpaid purchase price and, as to that interest, they suffered no loss." This statement is based upon the theory that the vendors' debt was paid by the purchaser after the fire.

Such a holding is in direct violation of and contrary to the language of the policy. The policy provides: "Loss on building items shall be payable to ASSURED address _____ as Mortgagee or Trustee, as their *interest may appear at time of loss,* subject to Mortgage Clause (without contribution) printed elsewhere in this policy." (Emphasis mine.)

Clearly the loss of the building and the time of the fire are contemporary and simultaneous. The mortgage clause referred to above has no application to our cause. Further, the policy also contained a provision that the liability of the company "shall not exceed the actual cash value of the property *at the time of loss.*" (Emphasis mine.) Thus again this clearly fixes the date of the fire as the date on which liability is to be determined.

Let us apply the majority reasoning that Paramount only insured the vendor for the unpaid balance of his purchase price to the fact situation in this cause. Take the date fixed by the policy for determining this interest—which is the "time of loss"—we find that on the date of the loss, which is the date of the fire, the purchaser owed the vendor $12,675.00, plus the contract interest. This figure is computed by subtracting from the total contract price of $15,250.00 the sum of $1,200.00 paid at the time the contract was signed, less eleven monthly payments of $125.00 each totalling $1,375.00. By the terms of the policy contract between the vendor and Paramount, Paramount's liability became fixed to vendor for this sum of $12,675.00. Purchasers hold an assignment from vendor of all his rights against Paramount. Paramount has never paid this liability. Therefore, I maintain that Paramount is still liable on its policy to the assignees of vendor, and its liability is to be prorated in accordance with the terms of the policy.

No public policy is violated; no statute is offended by the parties to the insurance contract making the contract which they did make. Suppose the vendor and purchaser had entered into a contract providing for $5,000.00 cash payment, the balance to be paid in monthly installments of $125.00 each due on the 10th day of each successive succeeding month. This would require 82 months, or approximately seven years, to pay the deferred payments. Vendor could not be forced to take his balance in one lump sum. He could insist on the monthly payments as set out in the contract in order to earn the interest. Under the majority holding Paramount's liability would not be known until the last payment had been made. This example illustrates very clearly the fallacy of the reasoning of the majority opinion.

The interests of the vendors and the purchasers were separate and distinct interests. Appleman, Insurance Law and Practice, Vol. 5, § 3057 at p. 180, et seq. The assignee of a claim under the policy after a loss stands in the same position as the assignor. Id., § 3462 at p. 643; Id., Vol. 4, § 2181 at p. 53. The vendor, under the contract of sale herein, had an insurable interest in the property destroyed. 24B Tex.Jur. 234, § 95. Vendor retained the legal title to the property until the purchase price was paid. 43A Tex.Jur. 290, § 253, and authorities there cited.

There is an exhaustive annotation entitled "Rights of vendor and purchaser, as between themselves, in insurance proceeds" in 64 A.L.R.2d, pp. 1402–1420. Section 4 therein states the general rule to be that "where the purchaser as equitable owner will bear the loss occasioned by a destruction of the property pending completion of the sale, and the contract of sale is silent as to insurance [as our contract here is], * * * the proceeds of the vendor's insurance policies, even though the purchaser did not contribute to their maintenance, constitute a trust fund for the benefit of the purchaser to be credited on the purchase price of the destroyed property, the theory being that the vendor is a trustee of the property for the purchaser." Supporting this rule cases are cited from Alabama, California, Georgia, Iowa, Kentucky, Maryland, Missouri, Nebraska, New Jersey, New York, North Dakota, Ohio, Pennsylvania, South Dakota, Washington and Canada. For this result to be reached, the vendor's policy must be valid as of the date of the fire. We have been cited to no Texas cases in point, nor have we found any in our research.

I would affirm the judgment of the Court of Civil Appeals.

■ WALKER and NORVELL, JJ., join in this dissent.

NOTES AND QUESTIONS

1. *Double Recovery?* The classic case on this issue, cited by the court, is *Vogel v. Northern Assurance Co.*, 219 F.2d 409 (3d Cir.1955). *Vogel* held that the purchaser could recover a sum from both insurers that in total exceeded the amount of his loss. Is there any justification for this result? See generally James M. Fischer, The Presence of Insurance and the Legal Allocation of Risk, 2 Conn. Ins. L. J. 1 (1996); Roger A. Bixby, The Vendor-Vendee Problem: How Do We Slice the Insurance Pie?, 19 Forum 112 (1983).

2. *Prorate?* Even if the seller in a case like *Paramount* has suffered no loss, would it not be appropriate to prorate coverage responsibility in proportion to the value of the interests of the purchaser and seller at the date of the fire, as the dissent suggested? Do the cost and difficulty of valuation in the typical case (in which the seller's interest is minimal) argue against taking the trouble to fine-tune the obligations of the two insurers in this fashion? For other cases reaching divergent results on the main issue, see *State Farm General Insurance Co. v. Stewart*, 288 Ill. App. 3d 678 (1997) (seller's insurer has no right of subrogation against purchaser); *Mutual Benefit Insurance Co. v. Goschenhoppen Mutual Insurance Co.*, 392 Pa. Super. 363 (1990) (proration clauses in respective insurance policies should be applied).

3. *Let the Chips Fall Where They May?* Now that the rules governing mismatched insurance in real estate sales are well established, should there be any concern for the interests of insurers who have not attempted to displace these rules by contract?

4. *Other Limited Interests.* Mortgages, leaseholds, and real estate sales do not exhaust the contexts in which someone other than the named insured may be entitled to insurance proceeds. For instance, in *Home Insurance Co. v. Adler*, 269 Md. 715 (1973) the named insured owned only a life estate in the insured property, and died in the same fire that also damaged the property. Citing the named insured's limited interest in the property, the insurer refused to pay any proceeds to her estate, claiming that her insurable interest in the property terminated at the time of her death. The court first held that a life tenant is entitled to recover the full amount of the insurance that she has purchased. It then concluded that the policyholder's estate was entitled to the full proceeds of her policy because she died approximately 19 minutes after the fire that destroyed the property began.

Limited interest issues can also arise when one party, labeled a "bailee," takes possession of property that is owned by another party, labeled a "bailor." If the property is destroyed while it is in the possession of the bailee, must the bailee's property insurance policy pay the proceeds of the policy to the bailor? In *Folger Coffee Co., Inc. v. Great American Insurance Co.*, 333 F. Supp. 1272 (W.D. Miss. 1971), the court answered this question in the affirmative where the bailee's policy provided that it insured "property of others held by the insured for which the insured is liable." The court held that the term "liable" did not require legal liability on the part of the bailee, but instead only referred to the bailee being "responsible" for the bailor's property.

CHAPTER FIVE

LIFE, HEALTH, AND DISABILITY INSURANCE

A. LIFE INSURANCE

There are two major forms of life insurance: *term* and *permanent* (or *cash value*). Term life insurance provides life insurance alone for a specified period of time, such as 1, 10 or 20 years. Premiums during this period may be flat, or they may increase at a pre-determined rate. Permanent insurance provides lifelong insurance and accumulates cash value on a tax-deferred basis. This cash value is distinct from the amount that is paid to the beneficiary when the policyholder dies (the *face amount*). The policy's cash value is paid to the policyholder if coverage is surrendered (i.e. premiums are not paid). Additionally, policyholders are often permitted to borrow against their policy's cash value without surrendering coverage. There are numerous types of permanent life insurance policies, including traditional whole-life, variable life, and universal life. But because all permanent life insurance policies contain a cash value feature, the insured obtains less pure insurance for a given premium under permanent life than under term insurance. All forms of life insurance are provided both through the individual market (via insurance agents) and through group plans (typically as an employee benefit, governed by ERISA).

About $2.9 trillion in new life insurance (by face amount) was purchased in 2012. At the end of that year, total life insurance coverage in force in the United States amounted to nearly $20 trillion. Approximately 60% of coverage is purchased on the individual market, where permanent insurance policies are more popular than term insurance policies (by about a 2–1 margin). By contrast, most group life insurance policies provide term coverage. For this and additional data, see American Council of Life Insurers, Life Insurers Fact Book (2014).

In addition to life insurance itself (and disability insurance, the subject of a separate section in this chapter), the life insurance industry markets two other associated products. *Annuities* (either fixed or variable, and either deferred or immediate), pay income during either a fixed period of time or the lifetime of the beneficiary. Like pensions, annuities are a method of dealing with the risk of living longer than expected, rather than the risk of dying sooner than expected. Increasingly, policyholders purchase annuities principally as investment products that include certain guarantees and accumulate value on a tax-deferred basis. Payments into annuities amounted to almost $370 billion in 2012, and insurers' reserves for estimated future payments exceeded $3 trillion. *Long-term care insurance* pays the cost of caring for individuals who are unable to care for themselves. Premiums for this form of insurance are comparatively small ($11 billion in 2012) and have been decreasing in recent years due to various disruptions in the market for such coverage.

Lawyers deal with a different set of problems in the context of life insurance than in the property/casualty setting. Most obviously, coverage issues are much less important in the life insurance setting, because whether coverage is owed is typically relatively clear for life and annuity contracts (though less so for long-term care and disability policies). By contrast, litigation involving policyholder misrepresentations, agent misconduct, and insurable interest issues are not uncommon in the context of life insurance. Finally, regulatory issues are often exceedingly important in the life insurance setting, given both the inherently long-term nature of life insurance products and the overlap between these products and the products sold by other financial intermediaries.

1. THE APPLICATION

Gaunt v. John Hancock Mutual Life Insurance Company

United States Court of Appeals, Second Circuit, 1947.
160 F.2d 599, cert. denied, 331 U.S. 849.

■ L. HAND, CIRCUIT JUDGE.

The plaintiff appeals from a judgment, dismissing her complaint after a trial to the judge, in an action, brought as beneficiary, to recover upon a contract of life insurance upon her son's life. There are only two questions: first, whether the defendant insured the son at all; and second, if so, whether he was intentionally shot, in which event a provision for "double indemnity" did not apply. The judge made detailed findings, the substance of which, so far as they are material to this appeal, is as follows. One, Kelman, a solicitor for the defendant authorized to take applications from prospective customers and to give receipts for first premiums, after two preliminary interviews with Gaunt, the insured, on August 3d, procured from him the signed "application," which is the subject of the action. This was a printed document of considerable length and much detail, the only passage in which here relevant we quote in full in the margin.[1] The important words were: "if the Company is satisfied that on the date of the completion of Part B of this application I was insurable * * * and if this application * * * is, prior to my death, approved by the Company at its Home office, the insurance applied for shall be in force as of the date of completion of said Part B." Number 12 of the answers which the insured was to make in the "application" was in the alternative; it read: "Insurance effective: (Check date desired) Date of Part B [ ] Date of issue of Policy [ ]." When Gaunt signed the application he had not checked either of these answers; but after he had delivered it to Kelman, Kelman checked the second, so that, as the "application" read,

---

[1] "If the first premium or installment thereof above stated was paid when this application was signed, and if the Company is satisfied that on the date of the completion of Part B of this application I was insurable in accordance with the Company's rules for the amount and on the plan applied for without modification, and if this application, including said Part B, is, prior to my death, approved by the Company at its Home Office, the insurance applied for shall be in force as of the date of completion of said Part B, but, if this application so provides, such insurance shall be in force as of the date of issue of the policy."

Gaunt was to be insured only from the issuance of the policy. The judge found that "Both Gaunt and Kelman intended that Gaunt should be covered from the date of the completion of the medical examination"; and that Kelman's checking of the wrong answer "was due to a mutual mistake on the part of Gaunt and Kelman."

At the time of signing the "application" Gaunt paid the full first premium and Kelman gave him a receipt containing the words we have just quoted without substantial change: both the "application" and the receipt were upon forms prepared by the defendant for use by solicitors such as Kelman. On the same day Kelman took Gaunt to the defendant's local examining physician who found him insurable under the rules and who recommended him for acceptance. Kelman delivered the "application" and the premium, and the physician delivered the favorable report, to one, Wholey, the defendant's local agent for Waterbury, Connecticut, who prepared a report recommending acceptance, signed by himself and Kelman, which he sent with the "application" and the physician's report to the "home office," where the documents were received on the 9th. Since it appeared from the papers that Gaunt had been classified as "4F" in the draft because of defective eyesight, the "medical department" at the "home office" required another physical examination in Waterbury. This took place on the 17th; on the same day the local physician wrote to the "home office" again passing Gaunt; and on the 19th "a lay medical examiner" for the "medical department" at the "home office" approved the "application." Nevertheless the "home office" on the 20th wrote to Wholey asking further information as to Gaunt's classification in the draft; Wholey answered satisfactorily on the 24th by a letter received on the 25th; and on the 26th one of the "doctors of the medical department * * * approved" the application from a medical standpoint. The "home office" received news on that day of Gaunt's death, and never finally approved the "application," although the judge found that, if Gaunt had lived, it would have done so.

Gaunt left Waterbury on August 19th. He was going to the Pacific Coast or to Alaska in search of work; he arrived at Chicago on the 21st; and on the 24th he had reached Montevideo, Minnesota, where he was seen traveling in an army bus that had been loaded upon a flat car of a west-bound freight train. The only other occupant of this bus was one, Rasch, about whom nothing was learned except that he was later traced to the wheat fields of Wyoming as a casual worker. On the 25th Gaunt's body was found beside the westbound track of the railroad at Milbank, South Dakota, with a hole in his head made by a 38 or 45 calibre bullet, which had entered his right jaw near the ear and had come out at the top of his skull; and although the record contains no evidence on the subject, we may take judicial notice that this must have caused substantially instant death. There was blood inside and outside the bus, and the bullet was found inside which had killed him. On the testimony the judge found that Gaunt had been intentionally killed, which, as we have said, was an exception to the "double indemnity" provision covering "accidental death." The plaintiff asks us to reverse this finding: i.e., to find it "clearly erroneous"; but we should not be warranted in doing so. Neither side contends that Gaunt killed himself; the issue is whether Rasch killed him accidentally or intentionally; and upon that the plaintiff argues that the defendant had the burden of proof. We hold that the evidence justified the finding, even if it did have the burden. It is apparent that Rasch, after he had shot Gaunt, must have dragged him out of the bus and placed him beside the track; and that he then fled, obviously to escape detection. The most reasonable inference is that he did this, hoping that the train would move on and that his presence in the bus with Gaunt would not be remembered, for, although no one saw him in it, one witness had talked with him at Montevideo and had learned that he was travelling in the bus. It is true that the blood stains inside the bus were in any event a tell-tale circumstance of which he must have been aware—although not the presence of the bullet—but they were nothing like as incriminating as the body itself would have been where it was shot. That Rasch should have pulled out his revolver, shot Gaunt while merely examining it, and then have gone so far to escape implication, while possible, seems to us most unlikely. The evidence might not satisfy a jury in a trial for homicide, but there was certainly enough to support the affirmative finding.

The first question is whether Gaunt was covered at all at the time of his death. Curiously, neither party has incorporated in the record "Part B," and we do not know what was the date of its "completion." If it was the approval "from a medical standpoint" as "advised by one of the doctors of the medical department," it was not "completed" before Gaunt's death. On the other hand the judge found that "Gaunt was, at the time of the completion of Part B, insurable in accordance with the rules of the defendant company for the plan and the amount applied for," and that is consistent only with the understanding that "completion" was earlier than the 25th. The defendant has not argued to the contrary and we shall so assume. Thus the question becomes whether the words: "if the application, including Part B, is prior to my death, approved by the Company, at its Home Office," must inescapably be read as a condition precedent upon the immediately following promise: "the insurance * * * shall be in force as of the date of the completion of Part B." It is true that if the clause as a whole be read literally, the insured was not covered if he died after "completion of Part B," but before "approval"; and indeed he could not have been because there must always be an insurable interest when the insurance takes effect. Yet what meaning can be given to the words "as of the date of the completion of Part B" if that be true? The defendant suggests six possible "advantages" to the insured which will satisfy the phrase, "the insurance * * * will be in force," (1) The policy would sooner become incontestable. (2) It would earlier reach maturity, with a corresponding acceleration of dividends and cash surrender. (3) It would cover the period after "approval" and before "issue." (4) If the insured became uninsurable between "completion" and "approval," it would still cover the risk. (5) If the insured's birthday was between "completion" and "approval," the premium would be computed at a lower rate. (6) When the policy covers disability, the coverage dates from "completion." An underwriter might so understand the phrase, when read in its context, but the application was not to be submitted to underwriters; it was to go to persons utterly unacquainted with the niceties of life insurance, who would read it colloquially. It is the understanding of such persons that counts, and not one in a hundred would suppose that he would be covered, not "as of the date of completion of Part B," as the defendant promised, but only as of the date of approval. Had that been what the defendant meant, certainly it was easy to say so; and had it in addition meant to make the policy retroactive for some purposes, certainly it was easy to say that too. To demand that persons wholly unfamiliar with insurance shall spell all this out in the very teeth of the language used, is unpardonable. It does indeed some violence to the words not to make actual "approval" always a condition, and to substitute a prospective approval, however inevitable, when the insured has died before approval. But it does greater violence to make the insurance "in force" only from the date of "approval"; for the ordinary applicant who has paid his first premium and has successfully passed his physical examination, would not by the remotest chance understand the clause as leaving him uncovered until the insurer at its leisure approved the risk; he would assume that he was getting immediate coverage for his money. This is confirmed by the alternatives presented in the twelfth question; the insurance was to be "effective," either when the policy issued, or at the "date of Part B"; there was not an inkling of any other date for the inception of the risk. It is true that in Connecticut as elsewhere the business of writing life insurance is not colored with a public interest; yet in that state, again as elsewhere, the canon contra proferentem is more rigorously applied in insurance than in other contracts, in recognition of the difference between the parties in their acquaintance with the subject matter. A man must indeed read what he signs, and he is charged, if he does not; but insurers who seek to impose upon words of common speech an esoteric significance intelligible only to their craft, must bear the burden of any resulting confusion. We can think of few situations where that canon is more appropriate than in such a case as this.

Situations very close aboard have arisen not infrequently, although the actual words have necessarily varied, so that it is hardly fair to say that any decision is quite on all fours. However, the important question is how far the condition of subsequent approval shall prevail over the promise of immediate coverage as soon as the insured has paid his premium and has passed his physical examination. * * * [The court then discussed a series of cases addressing the issue.] Thus upon a preponderance of the decided cases the answer is in doubt, and we cannot be sure how a Connecticut court would decide for the point has never come up in that state. Unaided as we are, we rest our decision upon the reasons which we have tried to set forth.

Judgment reversed; judgment to be entered for plaintiff for $15,000.

■ CLARK, CIRCUIT JUDGE (concurring).

I agree that the course of negotiations required and controlled by the insurance company was "unpardonable," and am willing to concur in the decision for that reason. But I do not think we can properly or should rest upon the ambiguity of the company's forms of application and receipt. Had this bargaining occurred between parties with equal knowledge of the business and on equal terms, there could be little difficulty in supporting the condition precedent that the "insurance," i.e., the insurance contract or policy, could not "be in force," i.e., take effect, until approved at the home office, and that then it dated back to an earlier time. Moreover, conditions of this general form are unfortunately still too customary for a court to evince too much surprise at them. There have been acute discussions of the legal problems involved; thus, most helpful is the article, Operation of Binding Receipts in Life Insurance, 44 Yale L.J. 1223. There receipts given for the payment of the first premium were held best divisible in two categories, one requiring approval as a condition precedent to the contract, in substance as here, and the other requiring that the company be satisfied that on the date of the medical examination the applicant was an insurable risk, and that the application was otherwise "acceptable" under the company's regulations for the amount and plan of the policy applied for. The first form, it was said, was generally held to prevent the existence of a contract before acceptance, except with a few courts which found the provision too inequitable to support. The second, however, gave no difficulty where its reasonable requirements were afterwards found to have been met. A questionnaire to insurance officials showed an increasing trend towards the second or fairer form— a development warmly supported by the author. There was further the acute observation that use of the former form resulted in continuous litigation in a field of law where certainty was essentially indispensable, since it stimulated judicial interpretation to resolve the "ambiguity" against the company, followed by the latter's renewed attempts to revise and refine the technical words.

Hence a result placed not squarely upon inequity, but upon interpretation, seems sure to produce continuing uncertainty in the law of insurance contracts. Even though for my part I should feel constrained to concede the weight of judicial authority against our view,[2] I think the considerations stated are persuasive to uphold recovery substantially as would occur under the second form of contract stated above. I am somewhat troubled as to the state of local law in view of the stress in *Swentusky v. Prudential Ins. Co. of America,* 116 Conn. 526, upon the absence of unique features to insurance law. But that was actually in another connection, a fact which I think justifies us in not here abdicating our judicial role for that envisioned by Judge Frank in *Richardson v. Commissioner of Internal Revenue,* 2 Cir., 126 F.2d 562, 567, of "ventriloquist's dummy" as to state law.

NOTES AND QUESTIONS

1. *Binders in Life Insurance.* Just as in property/casualty insurance, life insurers may provide applicants with a binder that provides temporary coverage until a final policy is issued. Binders can be particularly important to life insurance applicants because carriers' underwriting processes often take weeks or months. Often, though, life insurers are not willing to provide all applicants with temporary coverage, as there may be enhanced risk of adverse selection and moral hazard (i.e. suicide) in life insurance. For these reasons, life insurers often authorize their agents only to provide policyholders with conditional binders (often described as "conditional receipts"), which provide temporary coverage only if specific

---

[2] Making the distinction between the forms of provision as indicated by my text, I fear I cannot see as much judicial division as my brothers observe; though I do think too far-reaching such statements of annotators with reference to such a conditional receipt: "It is uniformly held that such an instrument is absolutely ineffectual in providing protection to the applicant until the application is approved or accepted." 81 A.L.R. 332, 333; 107 A.L.R. 194, 195.

contingencies are met. These contingencies may include, for instance, explicit approval by an insurer's home office or the policyholder satisfying specific underwriting criteria at the time of application. See generally Peter Nash Swisher, Insurance Binders Revisited, 39 Tort Trial & Ins. Prac. L.J. 1011 (2004). Typically, the provision of temporary coverage through a binder requires the policyholder to pay the first premium. Often the policyholder may be asked to provide a check or credit card information for the provision of temporary coverage, but the insurer will only deposit the check or charge the credit card once it determines that the conditions required for the issuance of temporary coverage are met.

All of this can create confusion for policyholders about the existence of temporary coverage, as illustrated by *Gaunt.* Insurers could avoid this problem by issuing nothing that could be construed to constitute a binder, or by declining to request payment information (such as credit card numbers or checks) with the application, until they have definitively decided to offer temporary coverage. Providing a conditional binder may give the impression that the insured is getting something immediately. Accepting a check or credit card information (even if these are not deposited or charged) both strengthens this impression and makes it less likely that the insured will withdraw his application—for then he must determine whether he has been charged and attempt to secure a refund of the premium if so.

2. *The Rationale of the Decision.* Do you agree with Judge Clark's suggestion that Judge Hand's opinion rested on an interpretation of the binder rather than on the inequity of its provisions? Under the insurer's interpretation of the binder, would an applicant's beneficiary ever be entitled to payment if the applicant died before approval of the application? If not, what did it mean to say that the policy would take effect on the date of completion of Part B? Are insurers in such settings guarding themselves against adverse selection or trying to mislead applicants? Even if the latter, do decisions such as *Gaunt* create unmanageable problems of adverse selection or do they merely require more careful supervision of agents by the home office? For discussion, see Kenneth S. Abraham, Interpretation or Regulation? *Gaunt v. John Hancock Mutual Life Insurance Company*, 2 Nev. L.J. 312 (2002).

3. *Extensions of Hand's Approach.* Many courts have reached the same result as *Gaunt,* sometimes interpreting provisions in applications that purport to make coverage effective "from the date of application" once the conditions specified in the application have been satisfied. The decisions transform the condition precedent stated in the binder or application (insurability of the insured on some specified date, or actual approval by the company) into a condition subsequent. Why is the practical effect of this transformation to create immediate "temporary" life insurance for the applicant? The rationale of some of the cases is that the binder is ambiguous. See, e.g., *Puritan Life Ins. Co. v. Guess,* 598 P.2d 900 (Alaska 1979). Others conclude that the applicant would reasonably expect immediate coverage upon payment of a premium. See, e.g., *Collister v. Nationwide Life Ins. Co.,* 388 A.2d 1346 (Pa. 1978), *cert. denied,* 439 U.S. 1089 (1979). Do you agree? More recent decisions reflect the same views. See, e.g., *Kimmel v. W. Reserve Life Assur. Co. of Ohio,* 678 F. Supp. 2d 783 (N.D. Ind. 2010). Even under these cases, though, a policyholder's misrepresentation on the application can void the coverage that otherwise

would have been provided by the binder if the binder so states. See *Primerica Life Ins. Co. v. Skinner,* 678 N.E.2d 1140, 1142–43 (Ind. Ct. App. 1997).

Some courts hold that denial of immediate coverage is unconscionable. See, e.g., *Smith v. Westland Life Ins. Co.,* 15 Cal.3d 111 (1975). In *Smith,* the insured was informed that his application had been rejected, but he died one day later, before his premium was returned. The Supreme Court of California held that the temporary insurance created upon payment of the first premium does not terminate until the premium is refunded. What makes denial of coverage under such circumstances unconscionable? Some courts have allowed denial of coverage on the ground that a binder does not create a reasonable expectation of immediate coverage. See, e.g., *Altimari v. John Hancock Variable Life Ins. Co.,* 247 F. Supp. 2d 637 (E.D. Pa. 2003). For more detailed discussion of *Smith,* see Kenneth S. Abraham, Distributing Risk: Insurance, Legal Theory, and Public Policy 107–09 (1986).

2. THE REQUIREMENT OF AN INSURABLE INTEREST

We first encountered the insurable interest principle in Chapter Four when examining property insurance. But the requirement has particular importance in the life insurance setting, where it dates back to the enactment of an anti-wagering statute in England in 1774. The Life Assurance Act of 1774, 14 Geo. 3, c. 48. See Timothy Alborn, A License to Bet: Life Insurance and the Gambling Act in the British Courts, 14 Conn. Ins. L.J. 1 (2007). The moral hazard that would be created if a complete stranger could take out insurance on the life of another is too obvious to require discussion; it is also too obvious for insurers to be misled by such strangers in any but highly unusual circumstances. See, e.g., *Liberty Nat. Life Ins. Co. v. Weldon,* 100 So.2d 696 (Ala. 1957), in which an aunt-in-law insured and then murdered her two and one-half year old niece. Most of the cases delineating the scope of the insurable interest requirement, in fact, concern parties with at least a colorable claim to having satisfied the requirement. See, e.g., *First Colony Life Insurance Co. v. Sanford,* 480 F. Supp. 2d 870 (S.D. Miss. 2007), in which the defendant purchased a policy on the life of a minor after he had been declared the minor's guardian, and the minor then died under what the court called "suspicious" circumstances. The court held that the defendant did not have an insurable interest because he had never taken the guardianship oath.

As with property insurance, the insurable interest requirement in life insurance began as a judicially-imposed doctrine, but it is now codified (with some modifications of the common law rules) in many states. The sum and substance of most of these statutes and of decisions in states that have not enacted them is that the insurable interest requirement is satisfied if (to quote the New York statute) the policyholder has a "substantial interest engendered by love and affection" or a "lawful and substantial economic interest" in the continued existence of the person whose life is insured. See New York Ins. Law § 3205. Broad language such as this leaves a good deal of room for judicial backing and filling.

Ryan v. Tickle
Supreme Court of Nebraska, 1982.
316 N.W.2d 580.

■ BRODKEY, J., Retired.

Lois M. Ryan, the plaintiff and appellant herein, is the widow of Eugene Ryan and the executrix of his estate. She commenced this action to recover the proceeds of a life insurance policy which were paid to the decedent's former business partner, appellee Gerald L. Tickle. After a trial in the District Court of Lincoln County, Nebraska, the appellee demurred to the evidence presented by the appellant and moved to dismiss appellant's petition. In its judgment entered on June 4, 1980, the trial court sustained the appellee's motions and dismissed the appellant's petition with prejudice. We affirm.

The facts as revealed in the record disclose that the decedent, Eugene Ryan, was a licensed mortician doing business in North Platte as the manager and president of Ryan Funeral Home, Inc. Tickle was licensed as a mortician doing business in Arnold, Nebraska, as owner of the Quig-Tickle Funeral Home. It appears that the two men had known each other since 1964, and in October 1971 they went into business together. The Ryan Funeral Home, Inc., had 477 outstanding shares of stock distributed among 12 shareholders. Ryan owned 50 shares of the company and Tickle purchased 25 shares. The two men also obtained an option to purchase the remaining outstanding stock in the Ryan Funeral Home from the other shareholders. The 5-year option was to expire on September 2, 1976, and granted Ryan and Tickle, or the survivor of them, the right to exercise the option.

In March 1972 Ryan and Tickle were offered an opportunity to purchase the Mullen Funeral Home located in nearby Mullen, Nebraska. They purchased the funeral home together for $20,000, as equal partners. They borrowed $7,000 for the down-payment and arranged to finance the balance over a period of 5 to 6 years.

Shortly after the purchase of the Mullen Funeral Home, Ryan and Tickle decided to purchase life insurance policies on each other's lives, their ultimate business goal being to acquire ownership of the Ryan and Mullen funeral homes and to provide a fund by which the survivor could purchase the homes upon the death of one of the partners. It was their estimate that if one died, the survivor would need $20,000 to $25,000 to purchase the other's interest in the Mullen Funeral Home and an additional $75,000 to purchase the outstanding stock of the Ryan Funeral Home from the owners thereof under the option agreement.

Ryan and Tickle thereupon purchased decreasing term life insurance policies on their joint lives in the total amount of $100,000. Tickle was designated the owner of one policy which had a face value of $50,000, and Ryan was designated the owner of a second policy, also valued at $50,000. Both policies insured the joint lives of Ryan and Tickle so that the entire proceeds were payable to the survivor of them. The premiums for the insurance were paid by an automatic bank withdrawal arrangement through a partnership bank account maintained for the Mullen Funeral Home.

In early 1973 it was discovered that Ryan had cancer from which he subsequently died on October 25, 1975. Following Ryan's death, Tickle collected a total of $88,000 as the beneficiary of the two life insurance policies. On September 22, 1976, Tickle and the appellant entered into a settlement agreement in which Tickle purchased the decedent's interest in the Mullen Funeral Home for the sum of $15,000. In addition, Tickle agreed to pay an additional $3,000 to the appellant in full and complete distribution of any sum of money claimed to be distributable to the decedent as undistributed earnings from the Mullen partnership. Tickle also agreed to assume and pay the unpaid balance due on the Mullen Funeral Home in the amount of $9,000. He also purchased all the assets of the Ryan Funeral Home from the board of directors and shareholders of the corporation for the sum of $147,000.

On November 7, 1977, the appellant, as executrix of the estate of Eugene Ryan, instituted this action alleging that the estate was entitled to all insurance proceeds paid upon the death of the decedent. In her brief on appeal to this court, appellant makes two principal arguments, to wit: That Tickle did not have an insurable interest in the life of the deceased, Eugene Ryan, and hence was not entitled to receive the proceeds of the insurance policies as the surviving partner of the deceased; and that the proceeds paid under the insurance agreement on decedent's life exceeded by $73,000 the amount of decedent's insurable interest in the Mullen Funeral Home, thus creating a wagering contract which is void as against public policy.

We note at the outset that the evidence in the record clearly indicates that the agreement between the partners had a dual purpose: not only to acquire for the survivor the Mullen Funeral Home but also to acquire the outstanding shares of stock in Ryan Funeral Home, Inc. The trial court found, and we conclude that the record sustains such finding, that the parties made a good faith estimate that the amount of money necessary to accomplish both such purposes would be approximately $100,000. That being so, appellee argues that the insurance contract was not a "wagering" contract but, rather, was a valid and enforceable contract of insurance. Also, with regard to appellant's contention that appellee did not have an insurable interest in the life of the decedent, appellee points out that the term "insurable interest" is defined in Neb.Rev.Stat. § 44–103(13) (Reissue 1978) as follows: "Insurable interest, in the matter of life and health insurance, exists when the beneficiary because of relationship, either pecuniary or from ties of blood or marriage, has reason to expect some benefit from the continuance of the life of the insured." In view of their avowed purpose in obtaining the insurance in question, in addition to the fact that evidence in the record discloses income tax returns showing increased profits from the operation of the funeral homes since the association of the parties as partners, appellee argues that there was clearly an expectation of benefit from the continuance of the life of the insured, and that therefore Tickle had an "insurable interest" in the life of the decedent Ryan.

We conclude, however, that we need not, and indeed may not, decide these issues, for the reason that the appellant herein has no standing or right to bring this lawsuit.

The law is well established throughout the country that only the insurer can raise the objection of want of an insurable interest. "The question of the lack of insurable interest in a life insurance policy may be raised only by the insurance company, and, where the company recognizes the validity of the policy, as by paying the amount thereof to the person named therein or into court, ordinarily adverse claimants to the fund may not raise the objection of lack of insurable interest." 44 C.J.S. *Insurance* § 212 at 915 (1945). See, also, *Poland v. Fisher's Estate,* 329 S.W.2d 768 (Mo.1959); *Ryan v. Andrewski,* 206 Okla. 199 (1952); *Edgington v. Equitable L. Assur. Soc.,* 236 Iowa 903 (1945). "The heirs of the insured have no cause of action against the insurer upon a policy the proceeds of which have been paid by the insurer to a third person who was the beneficiary designated in the policy, on the ground that the insurer could have refused to make the payment for want of an insurable interest on the part of the beneficiary." 3 Couch on Insurance 2d, Insurable Interest, § 24:6 at 76 (1960).

The above-cited authorities make it clear that only an insurer has standing to complain of a lack of insurable interest and that the heirs of the insured may not proceed on such cause of action against the designated beneficiary. This position was recently discussed in an excellent opinion by the Michigan Court of Appeals in *Secor v. Pioneer Foundry,* 20 Mich.App. 30 (1969). In that case Pioneer Foundry obtained a $50,000 life insurance policy on Secor, who was a 9-year employee of the company. Three years later Secor terminated his employment; however, the company paid the 1964 policy premium 8 months after Secor had terminated his employment. Secor died a month later, and the company collected the proceeds of the insurance. Secor's widow filed suit, alleging that Pioneer Foundry had no insurable interest in Secor's life and sought a constructive trust to be imposed in favor of Secor's estate. The trial court dismissed Mrs. Secor's suit.

On appeal, the Michigan court, citing *Hicks v. Cary,* 332 Mich. 606 (1952), held: " 'We hold to the rule that lack in the beneficiary of an insurable interest equal to the full amount of the insurance policy, to the extent that it thereby renders the policy a wagering contract, constitutes a barrier to the beneficiary's right to receive and retain the full amount of the insurance proceeds, but that *it is one which may be raised by and for the benefit of the insurer alone.*' " *Id.* 20 Mich.App. at 33. The court concluded that it was the insurer alone who had standing to complain of a lack of insurable interest and noted that the insurance company had paid the proceeds of the policy to Pioneer Foundry without raising the issue. The court affirmed the dismissal of the plaintiff's action based on a lack of standing to complain.

In *Secor* the court at 33, stated: "The rule that only the insurer can raise the question of lack of insurable interest appears to be well supported in other jurisdictions," and cites in support thereof, 3 Couch on Insurance, *supra;* 2 Appleman, Insurance Law & Practice, § 765 (1966); Vance on Insurance, § 31 at 199 (3d ed. 1951). In the opinion, the court at 34 states: "In recognition of these considerations the almost universal rule of law in this country is that if the insurable interest requirement is satisfied at the time the policy is issued, the proceeds of the policy must be paid upon the death of the life insured without regard to whether the beneficiary has an insurable interest at the time of death." The court in *Secor* also recognized that there are cases that hold that a creditor who acquires insurance on his debtor's life may not recover more than the amount of the debt and the premiums he paid. In this connection, however, the court at 37, stated: "This analysis has been rejected in the better-reasoned cases; it is contrary to the principle that the termination of an insurable interest does not affect the rights of an owner-beneficiary in a life policy." The court also noted at 35: "Life insurance is not meant to assuage grief; its primary function is monetary. It serves fundamentally the same purpose whether the beneficiary is a widow or a business; it seeks to replace with a sum of money the earning capacity of the life insured." The court concluded at 36: "We also decline to limit Pioneer Foundry's recovery to the amount of its investment in the policy and its financial loss (probably nil) upon Secor's death. Pioneer Foundry's investment in the policy was large both quantitatively and relatively."

The holding and reasoning of the Michigan Court of Appeals is persuasive in the instant case, and we conclude that appellant is without standing to object that no insurable interest existed between the decedent and the appellee, or that the parties had entered into an illegal wagering agreement. The judgment of the District Court dismissing appellant's cause of action must be, and hereby is, affirmed.

AFFIRMED.

NOTES AND QUESTIONS

1. *Wager Nonetheless?* Was the court correct in suggesting that because Ryan and Tickle purchased insurance on each other's lives in order to help the survivor finance purchase of the other's interest in their business, they were not wagering? What other factors would have to exist for this not to be a wager? Given the vagueness of the insurable interest concept in situations such as this, is the concept too imperfect a proxy for the existence of moral hazard? For an argument favoring abolution of the insurable interest requirement, both because of its vagueness and because insurers are more likely to issue policies that create moral hazard when they can rely on the insurable interest doctrine as a defense, see Jacob Loshin, Insurance Law's Hapless Busybody: A Case Against the Insurable Interest Requirement, 117 Yale L. J. 475 (2007).

2. *The Creditor's Insurable Interest.* As *Ryan* suggests, the policyholder must not only have an insurable interest in the life of the party insured; he must have an insurable interest at least equal to the amount of the coverage purchased. Where the relationship is between debtor and creditor, the amount of the debt typically is the limit of the creditor's interest. See, e.g., *Hershberger v. Young*, 59 S.W.3d 614 (Mo. App. 2001). There are occasional decisions, however, allowing the creditor to insure for a greater amount. See, e.g., *Cosentino v. William Penn Life Ins. Co. of N.Y.*, 224 A.D.2d 777 (N.Y. 1996); *Am. Cas. Co. v. Rose*, 340 F.2d 469 (10th Cir. 1964). In other kinds of business relationships there must be some flexibility to the requirement, because the business value of individuals is somewhat subjective, and because both the value of a business and an individual's value to it can fluctuate.

In rare cases, it is immediately evident that the amount insured is excessive. One of the most extraordinary cases addressing this issue is

Rubenstein v. Mutual Life Insurance Co. of New York, 584 F. Supp. 272 (E.D. La. 1984). Rubenstein was the owner of a taxi cab when he became interested in starting a "TV Journal." He hired a 23 year old unemployed person, Connor, to sell advertising in the journal. Connor's salary was between $100 and $150 per week. Rubenstein also sold Connor a TV Journal "franchise" for an amount that could not exceed $2000. They then obtained insurance on Connor's life in the amount of $240,000, naming Rubenstein as beneficiary. One month after delivery of the policy, Connor and Rubenstein went deer hunting with a group that included a friend of Rubenstein's, who was a convicted felon on probation. In the course of the hunting expedition, Rubenstein's friend shot Connor in the back from a range of ten feet. Connor died from his wounds, and Rubenstein claimed the $240,000 insurance proceeds. The insurer refused to pay, asserting both fraud on Rubenstein's part and the absence of an insurable interest. The court held that Rubenstein had no insurable interest in Connor's life because the value of the life insurance was grossly disproportionate to the amount actually owed by Connor. Other cases of obvious abuse also occasionally appear in the reports. See, e.g., *Ky. Cent. Life Ins. Co. v. McNabb*, 825 F. Supp. 269 (D. Kan. 1993) (defendant established fraudulent debtor-creditor relationship with severely disabled individual and purchased over $1 million total of life insurance from seven different carriers on his life).

3. *Owner, Beneficiary, and CQV.* The person who owns a life insurance policy has the right to designate the beneficiary of the policy. The party whose life is insured by a life insurance policy is sometimes referred to as the "CQV," an abbreviation of "cestui que vi," Latin for "the one who lives." In the most common case, the CQV is also the owner of the policy. But there are a variety of circumstances in which this is not the case. For example, I may insure my spouse's life, in which case I am the owner and presumably the beneficiary of the policy, but my spouse is the CQV. No modern court has held (and no statute provides) that a beneficiary must have an insurable interest when the owner and CQV are the same individual. But when the owner of a life insurance policy insures the life of another, not only the owner but also any third-party who is a named beneficiary must have an insurable interest in the life of the CQV. Some states go further and also require that the CQV give consent when insurance is procured on her life. For such a statutory requirement (containing exceptions for spouses and minors), see New York Insurance Law § 3205(c).

4. *Standing.* Is there a justification for the common law rule that only the insurer has standing to question the insurable interest of the owner or beneficiary of a life insurance policy? Can this rule be squared with the purpose underlying a different rule we encountered back in Chapter Four: that the insurer's prior conduct cannot estop it to question an insurable interest? The argument for the denial of standing to any other party is that normally the policyholder/primary beneficiary had no hand in bringing about the death of the CQV, in which case the purpose underlying the insurable interest requirement will not have been violated. In the rare cases in which the policyholder is responsible for that death, other rules can be invoked to preclude his recovery. See Robert H. Jerry II & Douglas I. Richmond, Understanding Insurance Law 310–12 (4th ed. 2007). About half of the states have reversed the common law rule with statutes that allow the individual insured, the executor, or the administrator of the

insured's estate to bring suit for the insurance proceeds against the beneficiary or other payee of a policy issued in violation of the insurable interest requirement. See, e.g., 24 Haw. Rev. Stat. § 431:10–204; Okla. Stat. Ann., tit. 36, § 3604.

5. *Time of Interest*. In contrast to property insurance, in life insurance the insurable interest requirement is said to be satisfied if the interest exists at the time a policy is procured, even if the interest has ceased to exist at the time of the CQV's death. This rule seems to adequately limit the risk that insurance will be purchased as a wager or as part of a murder scheme. But does it adequately deal with the prospect that insurance may serve as an inducement to murder those in whose life one once had but no longer has an insurable interest? Alternatively, does this approach adequately deal with situations in which individuals anticipate the eventual disappearance of an insurable interest at the time a policy is procured? For example, in the *Secor* case cited in *Ryan*, the deceased's employer had purchased "key man" insurance on his life, and continued to pay the premiums after he retired. That the employee might retire rather than die during employment was highly predictable. If moral hazard in principle, rather than in fact, is at stake in insurable interest cases, should the rule that only the insurer has standing to question insurable interest be inapplicable in cases like *Secor*? If moral hazard in fact is what is at stake, is there any way to avoid the kind of individualized inquiry that *per se* rules governing insurable interest are designed to avoid? The court in *Secor* also said that the employer "chose to make the premium payment 8 months after Secor's employment terminated to preserve recovery of its prior expenditures." Would this argument seem to be unavailable if the employer had purchased term rather than permanent insurance, or was the court suggesting that Secor's unanticipated ill-health had become an asset of the employer that it had a right to protect even if it had purchased term insurance only? Should decisions on facts resembling those in *Secor* depend on whether the employer's policy is permanent rather than term insurance?

6. *Limitations on Recovery by Beneficiaries*. Independently of the insurable interest requirement, many states provide either by statute or common law that a beneficiary may be denied a life insurance recovery if he or she is convicted of murdering the CQV. Issues sometimes arise under these statutes when a beneficiary is suspected of murdering the CQV, but the evidence is not sufficient to meet the high "beyond a reasonable doubt" standard of criminal law. Most courts to address this situation have concluded that beneficiaries who have murdered the CQV should be denied coverage irrespective of whether they are convicted of the underlying crime. See, e.g., *State Mut. Life Assurance Co. of Am. v. Hampton*, 696 P.2d 1027 (Okla. 1985) (accepting a preponderance of the evidence as sufficient to deny coverage). State law is more variable when the beneficiary causes the death of the CQV without a clear intent to kill. See, e.g., *Bolin v. Bolin*, 99 S.W.3d 102 (Tenn. App. 2002) (conviction of reckless homicide may bar recovery); *Ford v. Ford*, 512 A.2d 389 (Md. App. 1986) (beneficiary who was insane at the time he killed the insured is not necessarily precluded from taking under the insured's will or an insurance policy). To what extent do restrictions of this type limit the need for an insurable interest requirement?

Mayo v. Hartford Life Insurance Company

United States Court of Appeals, 5th Circuit, 2004.
354 F.3d 400.

■ E. GRADY JOLLY, CIRCUIT JUDGE:

Wal-Mart Stores, Inc. ("Wal-Mart") took out life insurance on its employees and made itself the beneficiary. This interlocutory appeal arises from a grant of partial summary judgment involving a dispute over death benefits from one of these company-owned life insurance ("COLI") policies. Douglas Sims' estate sued Wal-Mart on the ground that the COLI policy taken out in Sims' name violated the Texas insurable interest doctrine. We hold that: 1) Texas law, which requires an "insurable interest" for valid life insurance policies, governs the dispute; 2) an employer has no insurable interest in an ordinary employee under Texas law; and 3) Wal-Mart failed to establish its affirmative defense that the estate's claims were barred by limitations. In so holding, we affirm the district court's denial of summary judgment for Wal-Mart and affirm its grant of partial summary judgment for the Sims estate.

I

In 1993, Wal-Mart established a trust to serve as the legal holder of life insurance policies insuring the lives of its employees and naming itself as beneficiary. The instrument establishing the trust provided that Georgia law would govern the trust's construction, validity, and administration, and named Wachovia Bank of Georgia, N.A. ("Wachovia") as trustee. Wal-Mart acted in pursuit of tax benefits related to the deductibility of premium payments, and was only one of many similarly situated companies which took this course of action. After Congress and the IRS eliminated the tax advantages of Wal-Mart's COLI program, Wal-Mart unwound the otherwise unprofitable program, surrendering the last of its policies by 2000.

Wal-Mart's COLI policies insured the lives of all employees (also called "associates") with service time sufficient for enrollment in the Wal-Mart Associates' Health and Welfare Plan, unless those associates elected not to participate in a special death benefit program that Wal-Mart introduced in conjunction with the COLI program. Fewer than one percent of the 350,000 eligible employees opted out of the program, which was discontinued by early 1998. Wal-Mart's COLI program was intended to be "mortality neutral," such that the death benefits paid to Wal-Mart upon its associates' deaths would fund employee benefit plans and death expenses, or otherwise be repaid to the insurer as self-correcting "cost of insurance" adjustments.

Douglas Sims was a Wal-Mart associate from May 1987 until his death on December 1, 1998, and was insured under a COLI policy from December 21, 1993 until his death (though the special death benefit program had been discontinued prior to Sims' death). On June 28, 2001, after his estate discovered the existence of this policy, it sued Wal-Mart, alleging a violation of the Texas insurable interest doctrine. The estate sought, in relevant part, a declaratory judgment of its rights under Sims' COLI policy, the imposition of a constructive trust on the policy benefits, and disgorgement of the money Wal-Mart unjustly received at some point in 1999. * * *

We now apply Texas' insurable interest doctrine. Wal-Mart contends that, even if Texas law applies, the district court erred in determining that its COLI policy violated the Texas insurable interest doctrine. The district court concluded that the policy was void because Wal-Mart lacks a sufficient financial interest in the lives of its rank-and-file employees. * * *

Texas requires a person insuring the life of another to have an insurable interest in the insured person's life. *Empire Life Ins. Co. of America v. Moody,* 584 S.W.2d 855, 859 (Tex.1979); *Drane v. Jefferson Standard Life Ins. Co.,* 161 S.W.2d 1057, 1058–59 (1942). The state's common law insurable interest doctrine deems that "it is against the public policy of the State of Texas to allow anyone who has no insurable interest to be the owner of a policy of insurance upon the life of a human being." *Griffin v. McCoach,* 123 F.2d 550, 551 (5th Cir.1941). Consequently, insurance policies procured by those lacking a sufficient interest in the life of the insured are unenforceable. Going back to 1942, Texas courts have recognized three categories of individuals having an adequate interest: 1) close relatives; 2) creditors; and 3) those having an expectation of financial gain from the insured's continued life. *Drane,* 161 S.W.2d at 1058–59; *Tamez v. Certain Underwriters at Lloyd's, London,* 999 S.W.2d 12, 17–18 (Tex.App.1998); *Stillwagoner v. Travelers Ins. Co.,* 979 S.W.2d 354, 361 (Tex.App.1998).

Wal-Mart argues that it has a reasonable expectation of pecuniary benefit in the continued lives of its employees sufficient to bring it within the last of the three categories described in *Drane.* Texas courts have held, however, that the state of employment alone does not give an employer an insurable interest. *See, e.g., Stillwagoner,* 979 S.W.2d at 361 ("The mere existence of an employer/employee relationship is never sufficient to give the employer an insurable interest in the life of the employee.").

Wal-Mart contends that, in addition to the bare employer/employee relationship, it possesses an expectation of financial gain from the continued lives of its employees by virtue of the costs associated with the death of an employee, such as productivity losses, hiring and training a replacement, and payment of death benefits. These are costs that are associated with the loss of *any* employee, however, and, as Texas precedent clearly indicates, employers lack an insurable interest in ordinary employees. *E.g., id.* at 362. Indeed, Texas courts have recently rejected similar arguments based on the costs flowing from an employee's death.[1] And, as Sims ripostes, Wal-Mart does not claim that Sims was of any special importance to the company, much less that Wal-Mart's "success or failure was dependent upon [the insured employee]." *Stillwagoner,* 979 S.W.2d at 362–63.

Given that courts will uphold the insurable interest doctrine in the absence of contrary legislation, Wal-Mart argues that just such legislative pronouncements have expanded the definition of insurable

---

[1] *See Tamez,* 999 S.W.2d at 18–19 ("[A]n employer does not have a pecuniary interest in the continued life of its employee, unless that employee is crucial to the operation of the business."); *Stillwagoner,* 979 S.W.2d at 361–62 ("Even in the absence of evidence we may assume that [decedent's] death forced some readjustments which normally accompany the death of an employee. But an insurable interest does not result from the cessation of ordinary service.").

interest after *Drane*. A review of this legislation shows, however, that while the Texas Legislature has crafted certain addenda to the insurable interest doctrine, none of these modifications are relevant to the present case.

In 1951, for example, the Texas Legislature re-codified article 5048 of the Texas Civil Statutes as article 3.49 of the Texas Insurance Code. This provision allows a business to be named as beneficiary in a policy insuring the lives of officers, stockholders, and partners—the individuals in whom the business has an insurable interest. Tex. Ins. Code §§ 1103.003–.004 (Vernon 2003). As the district court pointed out, this provision is inapplicable because Sims was not a stockholder, officer, or partner of Wal-Mart.

Next, in 1953, the Legislature enacted article 3.49–1 of the Texas Insurance Code, which was amended in 1999. Originally, insureds of new or existing life insurance policies could grant (in writing) an insurable interest to "any person" or entity by naming him or her as beneficiary or owner of that policy. With the 1999 legislation, adults can, as of January 1, 2000, consent in writing to the "purchase" of, or the "application" for, *new* insurance on their lives, which policies are purchased or applied for by a third party. Tex. Ins. Code §§ 1103.054–056 (Vernon 2003). This provision was not retroactive. Though "this subchapter shall be liberally construed to effectuate [its] purposes," Tex. Ins. Code § 1103.052 (Vernon 2003), Sims never designated Wal-Mart as a beneficiary or owner of an insurance policy on his life. Sims also never provided consent, written or otherwise, for Wal-Mart to take out insurance on—or otherwise acquire an insurable interest in—his life. As such, article 3.49–1 and its re-codified progeny are also inapplicable.

Finally, in 1989, the Legislature enacted a provision that, under certain circumstances, allows an employer to obtain insurance on the lives of its employees to provide funds to offset fringe-benefit-related liabilities. The COLI policy at issue does not meet the requirements of the 1989 statute, however, and Wal-Mart does not contend that it does (Wal-Mart merely cites the statute as an example of the Legislature's action in this area). Thus, to the extent that this provision expanded insurable interests, it did so in a way that does not affect the disposition of this case.

None of these legislative enactments—which were thoroughly briefed by the parties and analyzed by the district court—apply to the facts of this case, and we have found no other ones that do. Indeed, *Tamez* and *Stillwagoner* were both decided in the light of the law as it stood in 1998 (the year of Sims' death), and both clearly rejected employers' claims of having insurable interests in ordinary employees.

Further, as the district court noted, the insurable interest doctrine was last taken up by the Texas Supreme Court in 1979 (not 1942, as Wal-Mart implies). *Empire Life*, 584 S.W.2d 855. *Empire Life* quoted and adopted the *Drane* decision and repeated the longstanding rule that a putative beneficiary or owner only has an insurable interest in the life of another where the beneficiary is "(1) so closely related by blood or affinity that he wants the other to continue to live, irrespective of the monetary considerations; (2) a creditor; [or] (3) one possessing a reasonable expectation of pecuniary benefit or advantage from the continued life of another." 584 S.W.2d at 859; *Drane*, 161 S.W.2d at 1058–59; *Tamez*, 999 S.W.2d at 17; *Stillwagoner*, 979 S.W.2d at 360–61. This Court has also recently acknowledged this Texas line of cases. *DeLeon v. Lloyd's, London*, 259 F.3d 344, 350 (5th Cir.2001) (quoting the *Drane* rule and its enumeration of the three valid insurable interest classes).

It is clear that *Drane* and its progeny have held fast to the common law insurable interest doctrine, and the Texas Legislature's enactments altering that well-established doctrine have been slow and careful. While the statutory provisions analyzed *supra* demonstrate an ever-broadening approach to insurable interests, there is no indication that the Texas Supreme Court would create other exceptions without explicit statutory authorization. And, as the district court concisely put it, it is not the role of federal courts sitting in diversity to ignore longstanding and consistently applied Texas legal authorities. We decline to either contradict state court precedent or expand upon the express language of legislative enactments.

We therefore reject Wal-Mart's challenge to the Texas insurable interest doctrine, and find that its COLI policy on the life of Douglas Sims violated Texas law.[2] The district court's ruling on this issue is AFFIRMED.

NOTES AND QUESTIONS

1. *Explanations for COLI.* There are several reasons why a business entity might purchase COLI. The most familiar explanation is that it may want to protect itself against the risk that one of its essential employees dies. This use of COLI is often referred to as "key man" insurance. COLI may also be useful for a business entity that has entered into in a stock redemption agreement, which can obligate it to purchase the interest of partner, owner, or shareholder upon that individual's death. Similarly, it can be useful to help fund a deferred compensation package for highly compensated corporate officers. COLI also continues to be used by some companies to finance certain employee benefit plans, particularly post-retirement health insurance plans.

2. *Federal Tax Laws and COLI.* As illustrated by *Mayo*, tax considerations play an important role in almost all forms of COLI. For instance, like all forms of permanent life insurance, the cash value of COLI policies is not taxed as it accrues. Similarly, like all forms of life insurance, the death benefits of COLI policies are not taxable. However, under recent changes to the tax code, this latter tax benefit generally requires that the CQV be notified of, and consent to, the existence of the COLI policy prior to the policy being issued. See I.R.C. § 101(j) (2012).

The specific COLI plan at issue in *Mayo* had little purpose other than to operate as a tax shelter. At the time that Walmart devised its COLI scheme, tax laws allowed corporations to obtain a tax deduction for the

---

[2] In such a case, once the named beneficiary (the one lacking an insurable interest) is paid, Texas law applies the equitable remedy of constructive trust to enable recovery by the wronged party. *DeLeon*, 259 F.3d at 350–51; *Cheeves v. Anders*, 28 S.W. 274, 275–76 (1894); *Tamez*, 999 S.W.2d at 15–16 and n. 1; *Stillwagoner*, 979 S.W.2d at 360. In this manner—and if there is no procedural bar such as the statute of limitations discussed *infra*—the lawful beneficiary, Sims, recovers the proceeds unlawfully procured by Wal-Mart.

interest paid on loans made to finance premiums on COLI policies. If a large corporation insured all of its employees, then it was in essence getting an unlimited tax deduction for financing the purchase of insurance against the risk of a set of actuarially certain events. Premiums equal losses plus minor administrative costs, so there was a tax deduction for merely transferring money from one pocket to another. As noted in *Mayo*, the IRS cracked down on this tax shelter by limiting the deduction for COLI to insurance on the lives of "key" employees, in an amount up to $50,000 of indebtedness per employee. See I.R.C. § 264 (2012).

    3. *Moral Hazard?* Should employees object to COLI? Occasionally, there may be real moral hazard associated with COLI. The *Tamez* case discussed in *Mayo* involved COLI purchased on the lives of convenience-store clerks, who are at high risk of being killed during nighttime robberies. Presumably the fact that the corporation employing these clerks would benefit from their death would create at least some disincentive to take precautions that would enhance the safety of their employees. But in most cases, the moral hazard concern from COLI is presumably minimal. If so, then don't employees have at least the potential to share in the tax benefit the corporation obtains from COLI? Or is the benefit more likely to go to shareholders, managers, or customers? For further discussion of COLI issues, see *DeLeon v. Lloyd's London, Certain Underwriters*, 259 F.3d 344 (5th Cir. 2001); Susan L. Martin, Corporate-Owned Life Insurance: Another Financial Scheme that Takes Advantage of Employees and Shareholders, 58 U. Miami L. Rev. 653 (2004); Michael J. Henke, Corporate-Owned Life Insurance Meets the Texas Insurable Interest Requirement: A Train Wreck in Progress, 55 Baylor L. Rev. 51 (2003).

3. ASSIGNMENT OF LIFE INSURANCE POLICIES

    A life insurance policy is an asset that can be sold, or "assigned," as insurance terminology puts it. It is virtually everywhere agreed that an assignment that complies with the notice provisions of a policy automatically makes a valid assignee's rights superior to those of any named beneficiary. The question then becomes whether the rules governing insurable interest not only govern purchase of the policy outright, but the validity of an assignment as well. The closer one comes to death, the more valuable a life insurance policy becomes. Rules restricting assignability therefore also constrain a policyholder's ability to convert the value represented by a policy into capital prior to death.

Grigsby v. Russell
Supreme Court of the United States, 1911.
222 U.S. 149.

■ MR. JUSTICE HOLMES delivered the opinion of the court.

    This is a bill of interpleader brought by an insurance company to determine whether a policy of insurance issued to John C. Burchard, now deceased, upon his life, shall be paid to his administrators or to an assignee, the company having turned the amount into court. The material facts are that after he had paid two premiums and a third was overdue, Burchard, being in want and needing money for a surgical operation, asked Dr. Grigsby to buy the policy and sold it to him in consideration of one hundred dollars and Grigsby's undertaking to pay the premiums due or to become due; and that Grigsby had no interest in the life to be assured. The Circuit Court of Appeals in deference to some intimations of this court held the assignment valid only to the extent of the money actually given for it and the premiums subsequently paid. 168 Fed. 577.

Of course the ground suggested for denying the validity of an assignment to a person having no interest in the life insured is the public policy that refuses to allow insurance to be taken out by such persons in the first place. A contract of insurance upon a life in which the insured has no interest is a pure wager that gives the insured a sinister counter interest in having the life come to an end. And although that counter interest always exists, as early was emphasized for England in the famous case of Wainewright (Janus Weathercock), the chance that in some cases it may prove a sufficient motive for crime is greatly enhanced if the whole world of the unscrupulous are free to bet on what life they choose. The very meaning of an insurable interest is an interest in having the life continue and so one that is opposed to crime. And, what perhaps is more important, the existence of such an interest makes a roughly selected class of persons who by their general relations with the person whose life is insured are less likely than criminals at large to attempt to compass his death.

But when the question arises upon an assignment it is assumed that the objection to the insurance as a wager is out of the case. In the present instance the policy was perfectly good. There was a faint suggestion in argument that it had become void by the failure of Burchard to pay the third premium *ad diem,* and that when Grigsby paid he was making a new contract. But a condition in a policy that it shall be void if premiums are not paid when due, means only that it shall be voidable at the option of the company. Knickerbocker L. Ins. Co. v. Norton, 96 U.S. 234; Oakes v. Manufacturers' F. & M. Ins. Co., 135 Mass. 248. The company waived the breach, if there was one, and the original contract with Burchard remained on foot. No question as to the character of that contract is before us. It has been performed and the money is in court. But this being so, not only does the objection to wagers disappear, but also the principle of public policy referred to, at least in its most convincing form. The danger that might arise from a general license to all to insure whom they like does not exist. Obviously it is a very different thing from granting such a general license, to allow the holder of a valid insurance upon his own life to transfer it to one whom he, the party most concerned, is not afraid to trust. The law has no universal cynical fear of the temptation opened by a pecuniary benefit accruing upon a death. It shows no prejudice against remainders after life estates, even by the rule in Shelley's Case. Indeed, the ground of the objection to life insurance without interest in the earlier English cases was not the temptation to murder but the fact that such wagers came to be regarded as a mischievous kind of gaming. Stat. 14 George III., chap. 48.

On the other hand, life insurance has become in our days one of the best recognized forms of investment and self-compelled saving. So far as reasonable safety permits, it is desirable to give to life policies the ordinary characteristics of property. This is recognized by the

Bankruptcy Law, § 70, which provides that unless the cash surrender value of a policy like the one before us is secured to the trustee within thirty days after it has been stated the policy shall pass to the trustee as assets. Of course the trustee may have no interest in the bankrupt's life. To deny the right to sell except to persons having such an interest is to diminish appreciably the value of the contract in the owner's hands. The collateral difficulty that arose from regarding life insurance as a contract of indemnity only (Godsall v. Boldero, 9 East, 72), long has disappeared. Phoenix Mut. L. Ins. Co. v. Bailey, 13 Wall. 616. And cases in which a person having an interest lends himself to one without any as a cloak to what is in its inception a wager have no similarity to those where an honest contract is sold in good faith.

Coming to the authorities in this court, it is true that there are intimations in favor of the result come to by the Circuit Court of Appeals. But the case in which the strongest of them occur was one of the type just referred to, the policy having been taken out for the purpose of allowing a stranger association to pay the premiums and receive the greater part of the benefit, and having been assigned to it at once. Warnock v. Davis, 104 U.S. 775.

On the other hand it has been decided that a valid policy is not avoided by the cessation of the insurable interest, even as against the insurer, unless so provided by the policy itself. Connecticut Mut. L. Ins. Co. v. Schaefer, 94 U.S. 457. And expressions more or less in favor of the doctrine that we adopt are to be found also in Aetna L. Ins. Co. v. France, 94 U.S. 561; Mut. L. Ins. Co. v. Armstrong, 117 U.S. 591. It is enough to say that while the court below might hesitate to decide against the language of Warnock v. Davis, there has been no decision that precludes us from exercising our own judgment upon this much debated point. It is at least satisfactory to learn from the decision below that in Tennessee, where this assignment was made, although there has been much division of opinion, the Supreme Court of that State came to the conclusion that we adopt, in an unreported case, Lewis v. Edwards, December 14, 1903. The law in England and the preponderance of decisions in our state courts are on the same side.

Some reference was made to a clause in the policy that "any claim against the company arising under any assignment of the policy shall be subject to proof of interest." But it rightly was assumed below that if there was no rule of law to that effect and the company saw fit to pay, the clause did not diminish the rights of Grigsby as against the administrators of Burchard's estate.

Decree reversed.

NOTES AND QUESTIONS

1. *Problems.* The *Grigsby* Court distinguished between policies procured as wagers from the inception, and policies assigned some time after they are procured in good faith. Is the insurance in each of the following situations valid?

a. Burchard is told he needs an operation. A friend gives Burchard the necessary funds; in return, Burchard takes out a policy on his (Burchard's) life, designating the friend as beneficiary.

b. The facts are otherwise the same, except that Burchard assigns the policy to the friend immediately after purchase. In *New England Mutual Life Insurance Co. v. Null,* 605 F.2d 421 (8th Cir. 1979), the court held that a policy purchased with the intent to assign it virtually immediately to a third party (who later murdered the assignor/former owner) was void.

c. The facts are otherwise the same, except the friend gives Burchard money for the operation, in return for which Burchard takes out a policy on his (Burchard's) life, designates his own estate as beneficiary, and executes a contract with the friend to make a will naming the friend as a legatee for an amount equal to the face amount of the life insurance. Contracts to make a will are enforceable in most jurisdictions.

If you were advising a client in Burchard's situation, which of the above alternatives would you prefer? If you represented Burchard's friend, which alternative would you prefer? To what extent do your answers suggest that the rule against wagers in the form of life insurance is merely a trap for the unwary?

2. *The Life Insurance Settlement Industry. Grigsby v. Russell* provides the legal foundation for the life insurance settlement industry. This industry began in the 1980s, when, largely as a result of the spread of HIV and AIDS, "viatical" companies ("viaticum" is the Latin term for provisions carried by a traveler) offered to buy life insurance policies from individuals with a short life expectancy for a percentage of the policy's face value. Viatical companies offered sick policyholders dramatically enhanced options for unlocking the value of their life insurance to pay for medical treatment or other expenses: these companies were often willing to pay much more than the cash surrender value of permanent insurance policies, and term insurance policies do not include any cash surrender value. Although the viatical company would take on responsibility for continuing to make premium payments, it could make a profit if the purchased policy's death benefit was larger than the amount paid for the policy plus anticipated future premiums.

With the success of the viatical industry, a broader life settlement industry emerged that offered to purchase life insurance policies from a larger segment of policyholders, particularly those over 65 years of age who do not necessarily have short life expectancies. In general, this industry consists of a web of intermediaries that facilitate the transfer of ownership in these policies to third-party investors, either by facilitating the direct sale of the policy to the investor or by purchasing the policy directly and then reselling it to the third party. According to industry estimates, in recent years the life settlement industry has purchased over $10 billion a year of life insurance, measured by face value.

The life settlement industry has had a substantial impact on the primary life insurance market. For instance, largely in response to the evolution of the life settlement industry, many life insurers now offer "accelerated" benefits that allow an insured (if he or she is the CQV) to claim a percentage of a policy's face value before death. Both policy lapse and policy surrender have decreased dramatically in recent years, a trend presumably related to the growth of the life settlement industry. See Afonso V. Januario & Narayan Y. Naik, Empirical Investigation of Life Settlements: The Secondary Market for Life Insurance Policies (2013). Meanwhile, one recent estimate suggests that the secondary market generates tremendous benefits for policyholders, allowing them to receive over four times the cash they would have received had they surrendered their policies. Id.

Life settlements and accelerated benefits function in essentially the same way. The company providing the benefits estimates the life expectancy of the CQV based on medical records, discussions with his physician, and statistical tables, and offers a lump-sum payment based on these estimates, usually between 60% and 80% of the policy's face value. The shorter the life expectancy of the CQV, the less uncertainty and risk to the company, and the higher the percentage of payment. For many new diseases, morbidity tables and life expectancy estimates are not particularly accurate and can increase the risk to the company if a CQV lives much longer than expected. In such a case, the CQV's benefits are unaffected, but the settling company is left with the responsibility for premium payments for much longer than expected, as well as a costly postponement of proceeds, both of which lower the value of the settlement for the company. As a result of this increased risk, companies generally pay a lower percentage of the policy's value when they cannot confidently predict life expectancy related to a particular disease. Thus, in the mid-1990s the availability and effectiveness of AIDS treatments increased rapidly, prolonging the lives of many patients and lowering the value of settlements for viatical companies.

3. *Regulation of the Life Insurance Settlement Industry*. Though life insurance settlements may be of great benefit to policyholders, the industry sometimes suffers from an unsavory reputation and has been the subject of increased regulation addressing potential areas of abuse. According to a recent Government Accoutability Office (GAO) report, 38 states as of 2010 had enacted insurance laws and regulations governing the sale of policies to life settlement providers. See generally GAO, Life Insurance Settlements: Regulatory Inconsistencies May Pose a Number of Challenges (2010). These laws are often patterned either on an NAIC model law or on a model law developed by the National Conference of Insurance Legislators. See, e.g., NAIC, Viatical Settlements Model Act, Model Law 697 (2008). In general, they impose licensing, disclosure, and reporting requirements on life settlement brokers and providers. See GAO Report, supra. However, states laws vary. See, e.g. N.Y. Ins. Code §§ 7801-10 (providing for regulation of the settlement process by the state department of insurance, including disclosure of alternatives to viatication and the possible effects and tax consequences of a settlement; a 15-day rescission window for the patient; a prohibition on finder's fees; restrictions on advertising; and confidentiality requirements). These regulations are driven by concerns that policyholders may end up paying excessive fees, receiving non-competitive settlements, or suffering harms from the sale of their policies that they do not fully appreciate.

Investors in life settlements also face potential risks. Policyholders may misrepresent their true health status when applying for a policy in the hope of later selling it, or may mislead the life settlement company about actual life expectancy in an effort to get a larger settlement. See, e.g., *Am. United Life Ins. Co. v. Martinez*, 480 F.3d 1043 (11th Cir. 2007) (life insurers' suit against viatical companies for fraud was barred by incontestability clause). State insurance laws generally do not protect investors in life settlements from these risks. State and federal securities laws, meanwhile, provide varying protections for investors in life settlements. The scope of such protections is complicated by inconsistent court holdings about whether life settlement investments are within the scope of federal securities laws. See *SEC v. Life Partners*, 87 F.3d 536 (D.C. Cir. 1996) (holding that viatical settlements are not securities and not subject to the tight federal regulation governing that industry); *SEC v. Mut. Benefits Corp.*, 408 F.3d 737 (11th Cir. 2005) (concluding that life settlements are indeed securities). Life settlements are generally regulated as securities under most states' laws. For general discussion, see Susan Lorde Martin, Life Settlements: The Death Wish Industry 64 Syr. L. Rev. 91 (2014); Kelly J. Bozanic, An Investment to Die For: From Life Insurance to Death Bonds, The Evolution and Legality of the Life Settlement Industry, 113 Penn. St. L. Rev. 229 (2008). The overlap between insurance and securities regulation is further addressed later in this Chapter.

4. *Stranger-Originated Life Insurance ("STOLI")*. The answer to Problem 1(b) above, and the result in the *Null* case cited therein, is that life insurance purchased from the outset with the intent to assign the policy to a stranger without an insurable interest is invalid. This is stranger-"originated" life insurance. Yet there seems to be a small industry engaged in exactly this practice. Under this form of STOLI, a party purchases insurance on his own life, paying premiums with money loaned to him by a party to whom it is intended that the policy will be assigned after the expiration of a period of a year or two. If the purchaser dies before assignment he gets the proceeds and the loan is repaid. If he assigns the policy, he does so in return for forgiveness of the loan. The practice continues, notwithstanding its apparent unlawfulness, because of the difficulty of proving that the stranger originated the transaction. The NAIC has promulgated model legislation to preclude the practice, and it has been enacted in a few states. But disputes on this issue increasingly find their way into court. See, e.g., *Life Prod. Clearing, LLC v. Angel*, 530 F. Supp. 2d 646 (S.D.N.Y. 2008) (assignment of life insurance policy within weeks of purchase, to a stranger who lent purchaser funds to pay the premium, rendered assignee-lender's interest void).

Life insurers attempt to combat stranger-originated life insurance through a variety of mechanisms, including asking questions on applications regarding whether the applicant has any intent to sell his or her policy or has been contacted by an individual who offered to finance the purchase of the policy. Litigation regarding the truthfulness of policyholder answers to such questions is not uncommon. See, e.g., *Principal Life Ins. Co. v. Lawrence Rucker 2007 Ins. Trust*, 869 F. Supp. 2d 556 (D. Del 2012).

4. DESIGNATING BENEFICIARIES

Recall that the owner of a life insurance policy is entitled to designate the beneficiary of that policy. Designation and change of the beneficiary of a life insurance policy are reasonably straightforward exercises. The applicant indicates on the application whom he designates, and the policy (or a copy of the application attached to the policy) lists the beneficiary. The beneficiary named may be changed by following procedures specified in the policy itself. These procedures may be more or less formal, but always require some form of notification to the insurance company. The former beneficiary normally is not notified of the change by the company.

One much-litigated issue is whether full or only "substantial" compliance with the formalities specified in the policy is required. The obvious differences between courts on this issue in part reflect their greater or lesser emphasis on formality rather than substance. But a reading of a number of the decisions on the issue suggests that the difference in emphasis on compliance with formalities also sometimes masks the courts' concern that the insured have expressed a firm rather than merely tentative intention to make a change of beneficiary. For this reason, expressed intention *plus* the taking of at least some step to make the change seem much more likely to yield a finding that substantial compliance suffices than the former alone. For example, in *Scherer v. Wahlstrom,* 318 S.W.2d 456 (Tex. Civ. App. 1958), the insured designated "Mariam Amelia Tatum, Fiancee" as his beneficiary. While he was in the military she sent him a "Dear John" letter and married someone else, but he did not change the beneficiary designation. Six months later he died, and his father claimed the proceeds, but Mariam prevailed, notwithstanding that she had been identified as "Fiancee" in the policy. On the other hand, in *Connecticut General Life Insurance Co. v. Gulley,* 668 F.2d 325 (7th Cir. 1982), the insured completed a change of beneficiary form and left it with his daughter, indicating that he would return for it. The daughter mailed it after he died. The court held that this constituted substantial compliance with the requirements of the policy.

This general issue has been complicated not only by the courts' understandable sympathy for disappointed (and sometimes quite surprised) relatives of the deceased, but also by the need for rules that provide insurers with a modicum of certainty about the identity of the beneficiaries to whom they are obligated. The less clear the rules, the more incumbent it is upon the insurer to refrain from paying anyone, lest it have to make payment twice: first to a beneficiary named in the policy, and then also to a beneficiary (successful in a suit against the insurer) intended by the insured. Once an insurer becomes aware of a dispute between two putative beneficiaries in any situation of uncertainty, the filing of an interpleader action and the payment of the proceeds into court is the only truly safe action. The clearer the rules governing change of beneficiary, the fewer such interpleader actions there will have to be, and the fewer rightful beneficiaries will have payment delayed and litigation costs imposed on them. But even clear rules will not necessarily suffice, as the case that follows demonstrates.

Engelman v. Connecticut General Life Insurance Company

Supreme Court of Connecticut, 1997.
240 Conn. 287.

■ BERDON, ASSOCIATE JUSTICE.

The dispositive issue in this appeal is whether a change of beneficiary in a life insurance policy can be accomplished by substantial compliance with the policy requirements, as opposed to strict compliance, where the policy requires that the change of beneficiary be requested "on a form satisfactory to the company." The plaintiff, Robert Engelman, is the executor of the estate of the decedent, Ella B. Ryder, who, prior to her death, owned a life insurance policy (policy) issued by the defendant, Connecticut General Life Insurance Company. The trial court, Booth, J., held that Ryder had not effectively changed the beneficiary of the policy and rendered judgment for the defendant. We reverse the judgment of the trial court.

The undisputed facts found by the trial court are as follows. In 1961, the defendant issued a policy insuring the life of Ryder for $100,000. Her husband was listed as the owner and primary beneficiary of the policy, and her nephew, Philip G. Zink, was named as a contingent beneficiary. The policy provided, in pertinent part, as follows: "A new beneficiary may be designated from time to time by filing with the home office a written request therefore *on a form satisfactory to the company* and signed by the owner.... No change of beneficiary shall take effect until such change shall have been recorded in writing by the company." (Emphasis added.) The policy did not define or explain the terms "on a form satisfactory to the company" or "recorded in writing by the company."

Upon her husband's death in 1973, Ryder, as executrix of his estate, became the owner of the policy and, as such, had the right to change the beneficiary. Ryder's relationship with her nephew Zink began to deteriorate and it continued to worsen up to the time of her death. In 1976, through her insurance agent, Ryder unsuccessfully attempted to change the beneficiary on the policy. In 1977, Ryder asked the plaintiff, her attorney, to revise her estate plan. The revised estate plan was predicated, in part, on making Ryder's estate the beneficiary of the policy. On the basis of the plaintiff's advice, Ryder wrote directly to the defendant in February, 1978, asking it to prepare a change of beneficiary form naming as beneficiaries the executors or administrators of her estate and to send the form to the plaintiff for his review. The trial court found that there was no evidence that the defendant sent Ryder the requested form at that time. Consequently, nothing ever came of this request.[1]

In January, 1979, Ryder sent a letter, prepared by the plaintiff, to the defendant purporting to change the beneficiary from Zink to the executor of her estate.[2] The letter referenced the policy by number and

---

[1] This attempt to change beneficiaries was unsuccessful because Ryder had not provided the defendant with a policy number and, therefore, the defendant was unable to locate the policy in its files. The record does indicate that the defendant advised the plaintiff of this problem by letter and requested the necessary information. The record is silent as to whether the plaintiff ever responded to this request.

[2] The letter provided as follows:

"1377 Boston Post Road Milford, Connecticut 06460 January 8, 1979

Connecticut General Life Insurance Co. 950 Cottage Grove Road Bloomfield, Connecticut 06002

Re: Policy No. 1021625

Mrs. Ella B. Ryder

Gentlemen:

I hereby revoke all previous beneficiary designations with respect to the death proceeds on the above policy on my life, and I direct that the death proceeds shall be paid in one sum to the Executor of my estate.

I retain all rights of ownership on the policy and all right[s] to make a future change of beneficiary.

name, was dated January 8, 1979, and was signed by Ryder and witnessed by the plaintiff. The defendant received the letter and placed it in the policy file, however, the defendant did not "record" the change of beneficiary on the policy. Instead, as a result of this letter, the defendant immediately sent the plaintiff a change of beneficiary form, which he forwarded to Ryder at her Florida residence. The change of beneficiary form sent by the defendant was accompanied by a form cover letter which provided, in pertinent part, that "[a]ll forms must be dated, signed, witnessed and returned to us. Until this is done, the changes you have requested cannot be made." The form was neither returned to the defendant nor to the plaintiff, and it is not known whether Ryder ever received the form from the plaintiff. The trial court found that "[t]here was no evidence that [Ryder] did anything after the letter of January, 1979, to show that she had changed her mind about making her estate the beneficiary."

Ryder continued to pay the premiums on the policy until her death on July 2, 1990. When the plaintiff, as executor of Ryder's estate, demanded payment of the policy proceeds from the defendant a few weeks after her death, an appropriate claim form was provided to him. The form was completed and returned to the defendant. The defendant, however, refused to pay the proceeds of the policy, claiming, initially, that Ryder did not have authority to change the beneficiary because she was not the owner of the policy. Subsequently, the defendant changed its position, and, by letter dated June 26, 1992, formally denied the plaintiff's claim for the policy proceeds on the ground that Ryder had not effectively changed the beneficiary because she had failed to submit the change on the defendant's form.[3]

The defendant took this position notwithstanding its admission that Ryder's letter of January 8, 1979, fully complied with the formalities required by the defendant's change of beneficiary form, in that it was a signed, dated and witnessed written request, and that it clearly indicated the new beneficiary. The defendant understood that Ryder's letter expressed her intent to name her estate as the beneficiary on her policy, and it also conceded that Ryder's intent never changed between the time of her 1979 letter to the defendant and the time of her death in 1990. The defendant, however, refused to commence an interpleader action, which had been proposed by the plaintiff, in order to obtain a judicial determination as to who was entitled to the

---

My intention is that this change of beneficiary become effective immediately; however, if you wish confirmation of this beneficiary change on your own form, please supply the form to my attorney, Robert J. Engelman, Esq., Schwartz & Knight, P.O. Box 679, New Haven, Connecticut, 06503.
Very truly yours,
Witnessed:
/s/ Robert Engelman /s/ Ella B. Ryder"

[3] The June, 1992 letter provided in pertinent part as follows: "The policy records contain a letter signed by the Insured, Ella B. Ryder, dated January [8], 1979, revoking all previous beneficiaries and directing that the death proceeds be payable to the Executor of her estate.... It is Company practice to require that a Change of Beneficiary be submitted on a company provided form [in order] to constitute a 'form satisfactory to the Company' [as required by the terms and conditions of the policy]. This condition was not satisfied by the Insured. The Company was under no legal obligation to change the beneficiary pursuant to the letter request and did not, in fact, record a Change of Beneficiary on its records."

insurance proceeds. Instead, the defendant sought out Zink, the beneficiary that Ryder had purportedly replaced, sent him a claim form, and subsequently paid the proceeds of the policy to him.

The plaintiff then brought the present action, alleging breach of the life insurance contract, and violations of the Connecticut Unfair Trade Practices Act (CUTPA), General Statutes § 42–110a et seq., based upon unfair insurance practices as defined in the Connecticut Unfair Insurance Practices Act (CUIPA). General Statutes § 38a–816 et seq.

The trial court rendered judgment in favor of the defendant on all of the plaintiff's claims. The trial court found that the policy's requirement that a written request for a change of beneficiary be on a "form satisfactory to the company" meant that the form had to be on a "company approved form." Although the defendant represented to the plaintiff, in its June, 1992 letter denying the plaintiff's claim for the insurance proceeds, that a "form satisfactory to the company" meant on a "company provided form," the trial court found that in practice the defendant had approved several different forms for use in making beneficiary changes. The trial court also found that although Ryder's intent was clear regarding the change of beneficiary, she never requested the change of beneficiary on a "company approved form" as required by the terms of the policy. Consequently, the trial court held that Ryder had failed to do all in her power to comply with the change of beneficiary provision in the policy, and that her failure to do so was not due to circumstances beyond her control. The plaintiff argues on appeal that the trial court applied the wrong legal standard and improperly concluded that Ryder had not legally changed the beneficiary. We agree with the plaintiff. * * *

Although "the general rule [is] that a change of beneficiary of an insurance policy can be effected by following the procedure prescribed in the policy", *Bigley v. Pacific Standard Life Ins. Co.*, 229 Conn. 459, 464 (1994), the plaintiff in this case relies on the "substantial compliance doctrine," an exception to the general rule.

The substantial compliance doctrine has its genesis in Connecticut as a narrow exception to the requirement that the owner of an insurance policy could change the beneficiary only by strictly complying with the terms of the policy. In *Bachrach v. Herrup*, 128 Conn. 74, 76 (1941), this court stated that "[t]he general rule is that a change of beneficiary can only be effected by following the mode prescribed by the policy, however clear the intention to make the change may be. Insurance companies usually require . . . that the original policy be surrendered for indorsement. To this rule there is a well recognized exception and a change is effective where the insured has done all in his power to comply therewith but has failed because the policy is beyond his control." See also *O'Connell v. Brady*, 136 Conn. 475, 479–80 (1950).

Subsequent to *Bachrach* and *O'Connell*, this court stated, by way of dicta in *Aetna Life Ins. Co. v. Hartford National Bank & Trust Co.*, 146 Conn. 537, 541–42 (1959), that in addition to the exception where the insured has done all in his or her power to comply with the procedure set out in the policy, but has failed because of some circumstance beyond his or her control, "there might exist equitable considerations of a character such that they, rather than technical legal principles, should prevail. . . . Proof of intention alone is not sufficient, but where the intention is manifest and substantial affirmative action has been taken by the insured to effectuate a change of beneficiary the courts generally will make the change effective even though there has not been a strict compliance with the terms of the [insurance] contract.... The number of cases on the matter involved here is legion. They are resolved primarily on issues of fact." (Citations omitted.) Indeed, in *O'Connell*, this court provided a harbinger for the refinement of the substantial compliance doctrine in *Aetna Life Ins. Co.* by stating that "the insured desiring a change of beneficiary must comply with the requirements of the policy *or at least make every reasonable effort to comply with them in order to obtain relief through equitable principles.*" (Emphasis added.) *O'Connell v. Brady*, supra, 136 Conn. at 480.

We believe that this case presents the opportunity to embrace and apply the substantial compliance doctrine as set forth in *Aetna Life Ins. Co.* We conclude that the doctrine applies regardless of whether the issue of a purported change of beneficiary is raised in an equitable or legal action. Other courts, assuming that we would adopt the dicta in *Aetna Life Ins. Co.*, have already applied the substantial compliance doctrine as Connecticut law. See *Kulmacz v. New York Life Ins. Co.*, 39 Conn.Supp. 470, 474 (1983) (quoting dicta from *Aetna Life Ins. Co.* and referring to it as substantial compliance doctrine); see also *Mann v. Metropolitan Life Ins. Co.*, 683 F.Supp. 27, 30 (D.Conn.1988) (applying Connecticut law and citing and applying substantial compliance doctrine from *Kulmacz* and *Aetna Life Ins. Co.*). "The application of a rule which does not require absolute compliance with all formalities specified in a life insurance policy concerning a change of a beneficiary seems appropriate in some situations. This approach is especially justified when the evidence shows that an insured has taken substantial affirmative action in an attempt to effectuate the change. The majority of the decisions [on] point adopt rules embracing this approach. Several courts have observed or concluded, '[a]ll that is required is that every reasonable effort under the circumstances be made to effect the change.' These decisions are sometimes viewed as having adopted a rule of substantial compliance." R. Keeton & A. Widiss, Insurance Law (1988) § 4.11(d)(1), pp. 430–31, quoting *Provident Mutual Life Ins. Co. v. Ehrlich*, 508 F.2d 129, 133 (3d Cir.1975) (applying Pennsylvania law); see also *Lopez v. Massachusetts Mutual Life Ins. Co.*, 170 A.D.2d 583, 584 (1991) ("even in the absence of such a waiver [of the policy provision requiring a written request satisfactory to the insurance company], we would conclude that the signed letter sent to the insurer constituted substantial compliance with the policy requirements ... so as to effect a valid change of beneficiary" [citations omitted]).

We conclude that, under the substantial compliance doctrine, which we affirm as the law of this state, the owner of a life insurance policy will have effectively changed the beneficiary if the following is proven: (1) the owner clearly intended to change the beneficiary and to designate the new beneficiary; and (2) the owner has taken substantial affirmative action to effectuate the change in the beneficiary.

The trial court in this case narrowly formulated the substantial compliance doctrine by limiting it to the contours of *Bachrach*, and rejecting the dicta in *Aetna Life Ins. Co.* Indeed, the trial court held that "[u]nder all the facts and circumstances of the case, the court finds that the insured, [Ryder], failed to do all in her power to comply with the procedures set [out] in the policy and that this failure was not occasioned by circumstances beyond her control." The trial court based its decision on the failure of Ryder to change the beneficiary on a "company approved form."

Nevertheless, the trial court found that Ryder had submitted a dated, signed, witnessed and unequivocal letter to the defendant, by which she sought to change the beneficiary in her policy, which finding none of the parties dispute. It is also undisputed that the letter referenced the policy by number and name. These are the same requirements that the defendant required in its company provided form. The trial court also found, and the parties do not dispute, that the defendant received this letter, understood it to mean exactly what it expressed, and placed the letter in Ryder's policy file but did not record the change in its records. Finally, the trial court found that it was Ryder's intention to change the beneficiary, and that there was no evidence that she had ever abandoned that intention. Counsel for the defendant conceded at oral argument that if we were to embrace what we have today denominated as the substantial compliance doctrine from *Aetna Life Ins. Co.*, then Ryder's letter requesting the beneficiary changes would be in substantial compliance with the policy provisions. On the basis of these undisputed facts found by the trial court, we hold, as a matter of law, that Ryder substantially complied with the change of beneficiary provision in the policy. * * *

NOTES AND QUESTIONS

1. *Avoiding Payment by Mistake.* The most prominent exception to the requirement of at least substantial compliance with the formalities required by the policy involves divorce decrees. In most states, divorce alone does not operate to change the designated beneficiary of a life insurance policy. See, e.g., *Life Ins. Co. of N. Am. v. Ortiz*, 535 F.3d 990 (9th Cir. 2008) (with a stinging dissent by Judge Kozinski); *Maddux v. Philadelphia Life Ins. Co.*, 77 F. Supp. 2d 1123 (S.D. Cal. 1999). However, some states have passed laws voiding an ex-spouse's life insurance benefits after divorce. See e.g. Minn. Stat. § 524.2–804 (2012). Should the law presume that after a divorce an insured no longer wants the proceeds of her life insurance policy to go to her ex-spouse? For more on the effects of divorce on life insurance benefits, see Kristen P. Raymond, Double Trouble—An Ex-Spouse's Life Insurance Beneficiary Status & State Automatic Revocation Upon Divorce Statutes: Who Gets What?, 19 Conn. Ins. L.J. 399 (2013).

Even when divorce decrees do not automatically void an ex-spouse's interests, they will generally have this effect if the decree specifies that the former spouse shall no longer be the beneficiary of a policy. This is true even if the insurer is not notified of a change in the beneficiary. See, e.g., *Estate of Keeton v. Cherry*, 728 S.W.2d 694 (Mo. App. 1987). Some courts require that the decree state specifically the change in the spouse's status as beneficiary; others find a surrender of all interest in the policy sufficient. Similarly, under a separation agreement specifying that the divorced spouse will remain the beneficiary under a life insurance policy that had been in force during the marriage, the divorced spouse is entitled to recover the proceeds notwithstanding that a third-party has subsequently been named as the beneficiary. *Foster v. Hurley*, 826 N.E.2d 719 (Mass. 2005). Suppose the spouse whose rights have been divested by a divorce decree files proof of his or her former spouse's death and claims the proceeds before the successor beneficiary can do so. Is there any way the insurer can protect itself from mistakenly paying the surviving former spouse?

Another problem arises when the owner/CQV complies with all the requisite formalities but dies while the change-of-beneficiary form is in the mail or otherwise in transit. The general rule appears to be that an interest in life insurance benefits vests at the time of the CQV's death, and that a requirement that the form be received by the insurer in order to accomplish a change is not met if the CQV dies first. Suppose, however, that the policy provides that the beneficiary can be changed as of the date of the request, irrespective of the date of death? See, e.g., *Bowers v. Kushnick*, 774 N.E.2d 884 (Ind. 2002) (the change is valid).

2. *The Purpose of Change of Beneficiary Provisions.* Some courts say that the formalities associated with change of beneficiary provisions in life insurance policies are intended to protect insurers from the kind of predicaments described in the preceding paragraph. Nonetheless, the interests and expectations of those who are harmed by strict adherence to formalities sometimes elicit judicial concern. The result is a tension between form and substance that is never definitively resolved, but appears increasingly to be resolved in favor of a substantial compliance rule. See, e.g., *Adams v. Jefferson-Pilot Life Ins. Co.*, 558 S.E.2d 504 (N.C. App. 2002) (filing change of beneficiary form with agent constitutes sufficient compliance); *Davis v. Combes*, 294 F.3d 931 (7th Cir. 2002) (life insurance that is subject to federal law due to ERISA preemption is governed by a federal substantial compliance rule).

3. *The Effect of a Contrary Will.* Suppose that an insured attempts to alter the beneficiary of her policy through a will, but does not also change the named beneficiary on file with the insurer. Should the will govern in such cases if it was executed after the policyholder's designation of a beneficiary? Most courts reject this argument. See, e.g., *Cook v. Equitable Life Assur. Soc. of U.S.*, 428 N.E.2d 110 (Ind. App. 1981) (holding that decedent's attempt to bequeath his life insurance policy to his second wife was ineffective because he did not attempt to change the named beneficiary from his first wife). What public policy interests might the court be trying to protect in rejecting the use of a will to change a beneficiary? Are they sufficient to override what seems to be the clear desire of the insured?

5. INCONTESTABILITY

All life insurance policies issued in this country, and some health and disability insurance policies, contain what is known as an "incontestability clause." Some states require that such clauses conform to specified requirements; others do not. Incontestability clauses create a kind of contractual statute of limitations on certain defenses of the insurer—primarily those involving misstatements by the insured that eventuate in defenses of fraud, misrepresentation, concealment, or breach of warranty.

The purpose of incontestability clauses is twofold. First, they provide the insured with assurance that once the period of contestability (almost always two years) passes, his coverage is firm and his beneficiaries are protected. Second, these clauses adjust the balance of advantage that would strongly favor the insurer if it were permitted to raise misstatement defenses after the insured's death made it impossible for him to respond to them. See generally Robert R. Googins, The Incontestable Clause: A Modest Proposal for Change, 2 Conn. Ins. L.J. 51 (1996); William F. Young, Incontestable—As to What?, 1964 Ill. L. Forum 323.

Of course, life insurance policies do not become incontestable for all purposes after two years. Otherwise the beneficiary of any person who had purchased a policy more than two years before his death would always automatically be entitled to coverage upon that person's death. Rather, the courts distinguish the kinds of defenses to coverage that must be raised prior to the expiration of the contestability period from those which may be raised thereafter as well. A series of labels has been applied to identify the two categories of defenses, the first in each pair being unavailable after the period of contestability has run: *validity* versus *coverage; conditions* of coverage versus *limitations* of the risk covered; defenses that render coverage merely *voidable* versus those that make it *void ab initio; conditions* of coverage versus *exclusions* from coverage; and defenses based on *potential causes* of loss versus defenses based on *actual causes*. These labels, however, are often unhelpful in the absence of a substantive theory of what should and should not be contestable. Unfortunately, no substantive theory that is entirely satisfactory has come upon the scene. The best-known is the discoverability test, exemplified by the following case.

Amex Life Assurance Company v. Superior Court
Supreme Court of California, 1997.
930 P.2d 1264.

■ CHIN, JUSTICE.

In 1991, the Amex Life Assurance Company (Amex) issued a life insurance policy to Jose Morales. The policy contained what is called an "incontestability" clause: "We will not contest coverage under the Certificate [of insurance] after it has been in force during the life of the Covered Person for two years from the Certificate Effective Date, if all premiums have been paid."

As early as 1915, this court described this type of incontestability clause—now required by statute in all group and individual life insurance policies—as " 'in the nature of . . . statutes of limitations and repose. . . .' " (*Dibble v. Reliance Life Ins. Co.* (1915) 170 Cal. 199, 209 (*Dibble*); see Ins.Code, §§ 10113.5, 10206.) After the premiums have been paid and the insured has survived for two years, the insurance company may not contest coverage even if the insured committed fraud in applying for the policy. The incontestability clause, we have explained, " 'is not a stipulation absolutely to waive all defenses and to condone fraud. On the contrary, it recognizes fraud and all other defenses but it provides ample time and opportunity within which they may be, but beyond which they may not be, established.' " (*Dibble*, supra, 170 Cal. at p. 209.)

In this case, Morales knew he was HIV (human immunodeficiency virus) positive when he applied for life insurance. He lied on the application form and sent an impostor to take the mandatory medical examination. With minimal effort, Amex could have discovered the fraud even before it issued the policy, but instead it collected the premiums for more than two years until Morales died. After the beneficiary filed a claim, Amex discovered from information long available that an impostor had taken the examination, and it denied the claim. * * *

I. FACTS AND PROCEDURE BELOW

Jose Morales applied for a life insurance policy from Amex in January 1991. Although he apparently knew he was HIV positive, he lied on the application form and denied having the AIDS (acquired immune deficiency syndrome) virus. As part of the application process, Amex required him to have a medical examination. In March 1991, a paramedic working for Amex met a man claiming to be Morales and took blood and urine samples. It is not disputed in this proceeding that this man was an impostor. On his application, Morales listed his height as five feet six inches, and his weight as one hundred forty-two pounds. The examiner stated the man claiming to be Morales was five feet ten inches tall and weighed one hundred seventy-two pounds. The examiner also noted that the man produced no identification and appeared to be "unhealthy or older than stated age." The blood sample tested HIV negative.

Amex issued Morales a life insurance policy containing the incontestability clause effective May 1, 1991. All premiums have been paid. Morales died of AIDS-related causes on June 11, 1993. * * * Amex denied payment on the basis that "When Mr. Morales applied for life insurance on his own life but substituted another individual for himself in the examination so that the policy would be issued based on the other person's medical condition, he caused Amex to issue a policy on the life of someone other than himself." * * *

"Incontestability clauses have been used by the insurance industry for over one hundred years to encourage persons to purchase life insurance." (Note, *AIDS and the Incontestability Clause* (1990) 66 N.D.L.Rev. 267.) "Insurance companies initially offered the incontestability clause as a policy provision because of public distrust of insurers and their promises to pay benefits in the future." (*Id.* at p. 268.) Today, these clauses are "required by statute in most states because without them, insurers were apt to deny benefits on the grounds of a pre-existing condition years after a policy had been issued. This left beneficiaries, particularly those in life insurance settings, in the untenable position of having to do battle with powerful insurance carriers. *See* 7 *Williston on Contracts* § 912.394 (3d ed.1963) (noting that these clauses came from the 'early greed and ruthlessness of the insurers' who 'too often . . . resisted liability stubbornly on the basis of some misstatement made by the insured at the time of applying for the policy')." (*Wischmeyer v. Paul Revere Life Ins. Co.* (S.D.Ind.1989) 725 F.Supp. 995, 1000.) The "clauses are designed 'to require the insurer to investigate and act with reasonable promptness if it wishes to deny liability on the ground of false representation or warranty by the insured.' G. Couch, 18 *Couch on Insurance* § 72.2 at 283 (1983). 'It prevents an insurer from lulling the insured, by inaction, into fancied security during the time when the facts could best be ascertained and proved, only to litigate them belatedly, possibly after the death of the insured.' *Id.* at 283–84." (*Ibid.*) * * *

A recent decision has reaffirmed the continuing application of incontestability clauses to fraud claims. In *United Fidelity Life Ins. Co. v. Emert* (1996) 49 Cal.App.4th 941, the insurance company issued Emert a life insurance policy with a disability rider. Although knowing he was HIV positive, Emert stated on the application he did not have an "immune deficiency disorder," and, when asked to list all physicians he had seen in the last five years, listed only a general practitioner and not an HIV specialist who had been treating him regularly. (*Id.* at p. 943.) After the two-year contestability period, Emert submitted a disability claim. Relying on many of the cases cited above, the Court of Appeal held that the incontestability clause prevented the insurance company from contesting the claim on the basis of the fraudulent conduct. (*Id.* at pp. 945–947.)

With this backdrop, we now consider the "impostor defense" that Amex seeks to assert. * * *

The basic rationale of the cases recognizing the impostor defense is that when a person applies for the insurance and takes the medical examination, but uses the name of someone else who then dies, no contract ever existed insuring the life of the person who has died and whose name is stated in the insurance policy. No California decision has considered this question, but Amex cites *Crump v. Northwestern Nat. Life Ins. Co.* (1965) 236 Cal.App.2d 149. In *Crump*, the insurance company argued that because the named insured did not personally sign the application, "there was never a meeting of the minds as between the insurer and the insured, and that the purported policy was void ab initio." (*Id.* at p. 151.) Although the *Crump* court found a valid contract under its facts, it stated, as relevant here, "Incontestability does not apply to a policy which is void ab initio. The invocation of an incontestability provision presupposes a basically valid contract." (*Id.* at p. 157.) As stated in *K.C. Working Chemical Co. v. Eureka-Sec. Fire & Marine Ins. Co.* (1947) 82 Cal.App.2d 120, 131, "To constitute a valid contract of insurance the minds of the parties must have met on the identity of the person with whom they are dealing."

Amex argues it insured, if anyone, the person who appeared for the medical examination, not Morales, and that to the extent the policy purported to insure Morales, it was void from the beginning or, to use the term in the cases, *ab initio*. The incontestability clause, it further argues, does not prevent a claim the policy never insured Morales. In this case, however, there was a meeting of the minds on the identity of the person with whom Amex was dealing. Morales, the named insured, personally applied for the insurance. Amex insured his life, not someone else's. Amex did not know that an impostor appeared for the medical examination and, we may assume, would not have insured Morales's life had it known the true facts. But the fraud is similar to other frauds that the incontestability clause clearly covers. If, for example, an applicant falsely claims on the application to be healthy and then appears for the medical examination but somehow substitutes a healthy blood sample for the tainted one, the fraud would be similar in effect to that here, but there could be no question whose life was being insured. * * *

Rejecting the impostor defense under these facts furthers the policy behind incontestability clauses. When the named insured applies for the policy, and the premiums are faithfully paid for over two years, the beneficiaries should be assured they will receive the expected benefits, and not a lawsuit, upon the insured's death. The incontestability clause requires the insurer to investigate fraud before it issues the policy or within two years afterwards. The insurer may not accept the premiums for two years and investigate a possible defense only after the beneficiaries file a claim. Here, with minimal effort, Amex could have discovered the fraud at the outset, as it did finally from information available before it issued the policy. The person who appeared for the examination did not produce identification although Amex could easily have demanded it. The impostor's height and weight differed considerably from Morales's. The signatures of the applicant and the impostor were transparently different. Amex ignored this information and merely accepted the premiums for the entire period of contestability. Then it became too late to claim for the first time that an impostor took the medical examination. Beneficiaries have the right to expect that after the premiums are paid for the specified time, the insurer will promptly pay the policy proceeds upon the insured's death. The incontestability clause protects that right.

In some cases, to be sure, the fraud will be harder to discover than here. But presumably, it would be no easier to discover fraud two years after the events than at the outset. More importantly, if the fraud is harder to discover, defending against a claim of fraud would also be more difficult after years have passed and the named insured—no doubt the key witness—has died. Again, we agree with the Court of Appeal: "[T]he deception could well have been discovered at the start had Amex simply required all applicants to produce photographic identification before conducting a medical exam and issuing a policy. Given the relatively light burden of such a requirement, combined with the burden of diligence which [Insurance Code] section 10113.5 places on the insurer, application of the incontestability clause to bar Amex's challenge is proper. To hold otherwise might lead to no end of mischief as insurance companies who have taken no steps to verify the identity of their applicants or medical examinees then comb their files after the incontestability period expires, looking for some basis to contend that someone other than the named insured took part in the application or examination process. Both the courts and the Legislature have recognized the occasional inequity which the incontestability clause may allow. The inequity here was no different. While Morales's fraud was abhorrent, he did nothing more than adopt another means of supplying false information to further his own application. Amex was deceived by this, but always intended to contract with Morales." * * *

We conclude that, after the contestability period has expired, an insurer may not assert the defense that an impostor took the medical examination if, as here, the named insured personally applied for insurance.

NOTES AND QUESTIONS

1. *Fraud as to What?* Suppose that an individual whose real name is John Smith applies for a life insurance policy using the name of another person—e.g., James Jones. Some courts hold that such a policy is void *ab initio*, and therefore does not become incontestable. See, e.g., *Fioretti v. Mass. Gen. Life Ins. Co.*, 53 F.3d 1228 (11th Cir. 1995); *Maslin v. Columbian Nat'l Life Ins. Co.*, 3 F. Supp. 368 (S.D.N.Y. 1932). Is the distinction between this kind of "imposter" fraud and the kind that occurred in *Amex Life* a tenable one or an empty formalism? After *Amex Life* was decided, the California Legislature decided not to draw such a distinction, and amended the California incontestability statute to overrule the decision. The statute provides that a life insurance policy is void "if an imposter is substituted for the named insured in any part of the application process . . ." Cal. Ins. Code § 10113.5. Many courts, however, still apply the rule reflected in the *Amex Life* decision. See, e.g., *Allstate Life Ins. Co. v. Miller*, 424 F.3d 1113 (11th Cir. 2005).

2. *Discoverability.* The central notion that does the court's work in *Amex* is the discoverability or non-discoverability of a fact at the time the policy is issued. Since the court indicates that that the ease of discovering a fact does not matter, the test seems to rest on the distinction between present facts and future facts. How should the discoverability test deal with an insurer's defense that the purchaser of a life insurance policy lacked the requisite insurable interest in the life of the CQV at the inception of the policy? Compare *PHL Variable Ins. Co. v. Price Dawe 2006 Ins. Trust, ex rel. Christiana Bank & Trust Co.*, 28 A.3d 1059 (Del. 2011) (the lack of an insurable interest is not subject to incontestability because valid contract never came into being), with *New England Mut. Life Ins. Co. v. Caruso*, 535 N.E.2d 270 (N.Y. 1989) (lack of insurable interest defense becomes incontestable). This issue takes on particular importance in the context of stranger-originated life insurance. See *W. Reserve Life Assurance Co. of Ohio v. ADM Assocs., LLC*, 737 F.3d 135 (1st Cir. 2013) (upholding certification to the Rhode Island Supreme Court of question whether insurable interest issue was subject to incontestability clause in the context of a stranger-originated annuity scheme). Can you see why?

3. *Eligibility Status in Group Insurance.* Many group insurance policies provide that only certain individuals are eligible for coverage—for example, those who are employed full rather than part time by the employer providing life insurance as a fringe benefit of employment. Two leading cases take different positions on the question whether such eligibility issues do or do not become incontestable. Compare *Simpson v. Phoenix Mut. Life Ins. Co.*, 247 N.E.2d 655 (N.Y. 1969) (eligibility is a discoverable condition of coverage and therefore is subject to incontestability), with *Simpson, Crawford v. Equitable Life Assurance Soc'y of U.S.*, 305 N.E.2d 144 (Ill. 1973) (eligibility is a limitation on the risk insured and does not become incontestable). No consensus on the issue has emerged, though recent decisions seem to lean towards the view that eligibility is not subject to incontestability provisions. See *PHL Variable Ins. Co. v. Price Dawe 2006 Ins. Trust*, 28 A.3d 1059 (Del. 2011); *Anspach v. United of Omaha Life Ins. Co.*, 2013 WL 842450 (D.S.D. 2013). One policy justification for this approach is that it helps to preserve a major benefit of group insurance—its lower cost because of economies of scale. At the same

time, it threatens to undermine the policies underlying incontestability itself.

4. *Accidental Death Insurance.* One important limitation on coverage that is clearly not subject to incontestability rules involves life insurance policies that provide coverage for death caused by accident. Accident insurance can also provide protection against disability. Accident insurance is less common than it used to be, but it is still sold in a variety of contexts because it requires reduced underwriting on the part of insurers, provides protection against important risks for some who work in high-risk industries, and is substantially cheaper than ordinary life and disability insurance policies due to the comparatively narrow coverage it provides. However, coverage disputes regarding whether a particular CQV's death was truly accidental are not uncommon, particularly when an accident causes death in combination with some preexisting medical condition. The classic case on this issue is *Silverstein v. Metropolitan Life Insurance Co.*, 171 N.E. 914 (N.Y. 1930). There the insured fell and ultimately died, for reasons relating to a preexisting duodenal ulcer that "was unknown to the insured, and, were it not for the blow, would have had no effect upon his health." The underlying policy only provided coverage for bodily injuries "caused directly and independently of all other causes by accidental means." Writing for the court, Justice Cardozo held that the policyholder was entitled to coverage because the ulcer was not itself sufficiently "considerable or significant that it would be characterized as disease or infirmity in the common speech."

Coverage under accidental death policies can also be complicated for other reasons. For instance, a significant body of case law exists addressing whether accident policies are triggered in the event of death occurring while the insured was driving under the influence of alcohol. The majority rule is that such deaths are not accidental. See, e.g., Douglas R. Richmond, Drunk in the Serbonian Bog: Intoxicated Drivers' Deaths as Insurance Accidents, 22 Seattle U. L. Rev. 83 (2008). The seminal modern case on the meaning of "accidental death" under a first-party insurance policy, *Wickman v. Northwestern National Insurance Co.*, 908 F.2d 1077 (1st Cir. 1990), suggests that, in general, these types of disputes should turn on whether the insured expected, intended, or at least appreciated, that there was a high probability that death would result from his conduct. Recent cases emphasize, however, that mere evidence that drunk driving is dangerous is not sufficient under this test, as this logic would effectively create an unwritten intoxication exclusion in the policy. See, e.g., *Kovacs v. Zurich Am. Ins. Co.*, 587 F.3d 323 (6th Cir. 2009).

6. NEGLIGENCE ACTIONS AGAINST THE INSURER

Mauroner v. Massachusetts Indemnity and Life Insurance Company

Court of Appeal of Louisiana, 1988.
520 So.2d 451.

■ CHEHARDY, CHIEF JUDGE.

This appeal arises from a judgment awarding plaintiff, Susan Mauroner, the proceeds of a life insurance policy insuring her deceased husband, Milton Mauroner, Jr., who died by suicide. The policy was issued by defendant Massachusetts Indemnity and Life Insurance Company (MILICO) through its agents, defendants Steve Modica and Associates (Modica), a Division of A.L. Williams Company, and Bill Whittle and Associates, Inc. (Whittle). We affirm.

The facts in this case were stipulated to by the parties and show that Modica sold the Mauroners a life insurance policy in the amount of $100,000 covering Milton Mauroner, Jr., with a rider on Susan Mauroner for $10,000. The application was prepared by Steve Modica with information given to him by the applicants. While a medical examination was not required, a medical history was included with the application, along with an authorization for MILICO to consult the doctors and hospital where the Mauroners had previously received treatment or advice. The application was signed and mailed with a check for one month's premium ($60.90) to MILICO on November 6, 1981. Along with the application Modica completed a "MILICO New Business Transmittal Form" describing the coverage sought. It was further stipulated that the normal processing period for acceptance or rejection of these policies was four to eight weeks.

In return for payment of the initial premium, the Mauroners were given a conditional receipt. Under the terms of the receipt, MILICO agreed to provide insurance against any covered loss as of November 6, 1981, if the information in the application was found to be accurate and complete, if the Mauroners were otherwise found qualified and if the policy was thereafter issued.

After receipt of the modification, MILICO notified Modica, through Whittle's office, that a clarification was needed on the coverage for Mr. Mauroner. That letter was dated November 20, 1981 and clarification was needed because Modica erroneously listed on the transmittal form a request for two "MOD 15" base plans for $50,000 each. The correct listing should have been either one "MOD 15" base plan for $100,000 or a "MOD 15" base plan for $50,000 with a companion rider for an additional $50,000.

No further action was taken until January 4, 1982, when someone in Whittle's office telephoned MILICO underwriting in Atlanta, Georgia, to find out the status of the application. After another telephone call the next day, it was determined that a "RVP" (regional vice president) was needed to telephone the correct coverage to MILICO. Upon receipt of the information, MILICO replied on January 7, 1982 that it was forwarding the information to the underwriting section. However, sometime after January 8, but prior to January 25, MILICO sent a copy of its underwriting memo of November 20, 1981, which originally requested the clarification, to the agents stamped "Final Notice". On January 25, 1982, Leslie Whittle of Bill Whittle's office telephoned MILICO again inquiring about the Mauroners' application. On that same day Mrs. Whittle also sent a written memo to MILICO reiterating the correct coverage. MILICO acknowledged receipt of the information the following day. The policy was thereafter issued ten days later on February 4, 1982. It was delivered to the Mauroners on February 28, 1982 at their home by Steve Modica. At that time he discussed the policy contents including the date of issuance (February 11, 1982) and the two-year suicide incontestability clause. In that respect he explained Mr. Mauroner could not "blow his brains out" for at least two years after the issue date of the policy in order for Mrs. Mauroner to collect the proceeds of the life insurance policy.

At the time Steve Modica sold the policy to the Mauroners he was aware that Mr. Mauroner was insured for $100,000 under a policy with State Farm Insurance Company. The Mauroners paid the last premium on that policy in December, 1981 which continued coverage to January 2, 1982. The State Farm coverage thereafter remained in effect through the application of dividends to the payment of premiums until March 2, 1982. From March until August 17, 1982, coverage was continued through the use of the cash surrender value of the policy.

Mr. Mauroner committed suicide on January 13, 1984. Because the death occurred three weeks prior to the end of the two-year suicide exclusion, MILICO refused to pay Mrs. Mauroner the proceeds of the life insurance policy, but refunded the premiums paid ($1,221.21) pursuant to the policy terms. As a result, Mrs. Mauroner filed suit against the above-named defendants.

The case was fixed for trial on February 7, 1987, and at that time was submitted on the record. Judgment was rendered on May 8, 1987 in plaintiff's favor for the full amount of the policy. In his reasons for judgment the trial judge determined the agents of MILICO were negligent in failing to correct the coverage error timely and that the negligent delay caused Mrs. Mauroner's loss of the policy proceeds. He further concluded because of the negligence the policy's issuance date was November 6, 1981 and Mr. Mauroner's suicide occurred after the two-year suicide limitation period.

On appeal, defendants first contend the trial judge erred in finding the negligent delay between the application and the issuance of the policy justified changing the issue date from the actual date of February 4, 1982 to the application date of November 6. Defendants contend the policy issue date controls the commencement of the running of the two years under the suicide clause and that there is neither law nor a factual basis to support the substitution of the application date so as to place the death outside the two-year preclusion of coverage. Defendants secondly assert plaintiff has no cause of action for negligent delay in the issuance of the policy. Alternatively, defendants argue that the trial judge erred in holding the delay in processing the application was negligence or that it caused the plaintiff's damage.

In their first argument, defendants contend the suicide limitation and the incontestability clauses preclude plaintiff's recovery of the policy proceeds, because Milton Mauroner, Jr. committed suicide prior to the expiration of two years from the date the policy was issued. Defendants argue that the trial judge's substitution of the application date for the issue date was legally incorrect and was contrary to the policy and the stipulation of the parties.

> The pertinent clauses state as follows: "SUICIDE—If the Insured dies by suicide, while sane or insane, within two years of the date of issue, our only liability will be the amount of premiums paid."

and

"INCONTESTABILITY—This policy will be incontestable after it has been in force for two years. The two years will begin as of the date of issue. This provision does not apply: (1) when any premium is unpaid beyond the grace period; and (2) to any rider for disability benefits or additional insurance specifically for death by accident."

Under these two provisions, it is the date of issue that controls the commencement of the two years and we find no cases which would justify a substitution of the application date for the issue date on the basis of the agent's negligence. However, in rebuttal, plaintiff asserts defendants are estopped from denying liability by the language of the insurance application and receipt. Plaintiff argues that language provides retroactive coverage to the date of application once the policy has been approved and issued.

The application and receipt signed by the parties and dated November 6, 1981 states in pertinent part:

"CONDITIONS OF COVERAGE

I understand and agree that, except as set forth below, I will not be covered for any loss occurring prior to the date on which the Company issues the policy for which I have on this date applied.

However, if all the following conditions are met, I understand and agree that if the Company does issue a policy to me, such policy will cover me in accordance with its provisions, limitations and exceptions for losses on or after the date set forth below:

1. All the information given by me in my insurance application must be accurate and complete to the best of my knowledge and belief.

2. The Company must find me qualified for the policy plan and amount applied for in accordance with its normal and customary underwriting standards and practices.

3. At least one monthly premium for the policy plan and amount applied for must be paid with my insurance application."

It is clear that the policy does provide for retroactive coverage once the conditions have been met and the policy issued. However, the coverage provided is "in accordance with its [the policy's] *provisions, limitations and exceptions.*" Since the two-year suicide clause is a provision or a limitation or an exception, it must be given effect. Consequently, we find the trial judge erred in substituting the application date for the date the policy was actually issued, although the finding does not per se negate defendants' liability.

In his reasons for judgment the trial judge found the defendants' actions in delaying correction of the error committed by Steve Modica was negligent and caused plaintiff's loss of the policy proceeds. Defendants contend the trial judge erred in this finding in that plaintiff has no cause of action for negligent delay in the issuance of a policy. Further, defendants assert that if a cause of action exists, the delay was not unreasonable and did not cause the loss.

Defendants argue plaintiff has no cause of action because a review of the jurisprudence which has addressed negligent delay has done so only in the context of rejections or cancellations of policies. Since the policy here was issued, defendants conclude there is no cause of action.

Our review of the cases indicates the particular problem we have before us has not been addressed by the courts of this state. The cases, as defendants point out, involve the agents' or brokers' failure to obtain the insurance, the rejection of the applicant, or the cancellation of a policy. In those instances the critical issue was whether the negligent delay prevented the applicant or insured from obtaining coverage elsewhere which would have prevented their loss of particular policy benefits. * * * However, simply because an issue has not been addressed by the courts does not mean a cause of action does not exist. Persons are liable for acts of commission or omission that cause damage to another if a duty imposed by the relationship of the parties is breached by such act or omission. *Smith v. Travelers Ins. Co.,* 430 So.2d 55 (La.1983); see: LSA-C.C. art. 2315, et seq.; LSA-C.C. art. 2985, et seq.; LSA-C.C. art. 1994, et seq.

In plaintiff's petition she alleges she sustained damage (loss of the insurance proceeds) because of defendants' negligent delay in issuing the policy. Negligence requires a finding that defendants breached a duty to plaintiff and that breach was the legal cause of the damage. In *Davis & Landry v. Guar. Income Life Ins.,* supra, the court stated the insurance company has a duty to act upon an application within a reasonable time and a violation of that duty will subject the company to resultant damages for negligence. Although that case involved the death of the applicant before the policy was approved and issued, we find the holding applicable to these facts as well. Thus, we find plaintiff has stated a cause of action for loss of the insurance proceeds.

The next question presented by defendants' appeal is whether the trial judge erred in finding the defendants' delay in correcting its error constituted negligence. In this regard defendants assert the delay in processing the application was reasonable.

It was stipulated by the parties that MILICO normally processed applications within four to eight weeks, or at the maximum, 56 days. In this case the policy was issued 92 days from the date of application, a delay of 36 days. Such a delay was unreasonable in light of the fact that MILICO sought correction of the error in November 1981, but the error was not corrected until January 1982. Our conclusion that this delay was unreasonable is further supported by the fact that once the mistake was corrected, MILICO issued the policy within ten days. Thus, we find the trial judge did not err in finding the defendants were negligent in their handling of plaintiff's application.

Finally, defendants assert that even if their delay in processing the application was negligent, it was not the cause of plaintiff's loss. In this regard defendants contend the damages sustained by plaintiff were caused solely by the deceased's choice in committing suicide three weeks prior to expiration of the two-year preclusion period.

As to this claim by defendants, the evidence shows that had the error not occurred, or had it been corrected promptly, it was more likely than not the suicide would have occurred after the two year period excluding suicide expired. Consequently, the cause of plaintiff's loss was not the deceased's choice in committing suicide on January 13, 1984, but defendants' breach of its duty to the insureds to correct its mistake timely. Thus, we find the trial judge did not err in finding defendants' negligence was the cause of plaintiff's injury and casting them in damages for the amount of the policy ($100,000).

Accordingly, the judgment of the trial court is hereby affirmed. Costs are to be paid by appellant.

AFFIRMED.

NOTES AND QUESTIONS

1. *Liability for Delay.* It is well established that an agent or broker may be held liable for negligent failure to procure a policy that would have covered the plaintiff's loss. Similarly, some courts hold that the insurer's negligent delay in processing an application subjects it to liability for damages that proximately result. See, e.g., *Huberman v. John Hancock Mut. Life Ins. Co.*, 492 So.2d 416 (Fla. App. 1986). But see *Kimmel v. W. Reserve Life Assurance Co. of Ohio*, 678 F. Supp. 2d 783, 804 (N.D. Ind. 2010). In the latter situation, however, what basis is there for holding that the insurer owes a duty to the applicant? Does the mere furnishing of an application create such a duty? Once such a duty exists, does the holding in *Mauroner* necessarily follow, or might a court properly hold that the delay was not a proximate cause of the loss the plaintiff claimed?

2. *Liability for Negligent Issuance or Misprocessing.* As the opinion in *Mauroner* indicates, there are occasional decisions holding life insurers liable for negligently issuing policies to those without an insurable interest in the life of the CQV. See, e.g., *Bajwa v. Metro. Life Ins. Co.*, 804 N.E.2d 519 (Ill. 2004). The claim in *Bacon v. Federal Kemper Life Assurance Co.*, 512 N.E.2d 941 (Mass. 1987) went further, alleging liability for a death resulting from negligently processing a fraudulent change of beneficiary form. Although rejecting the claim on the ground that there was no evidence that the insurer's conduct fell below the standard of the reasonably prudent insurance company, the court acknowledged that at least in principle the insurer owes the insured a duty to process a change of beneficiary request with due care.

3. *A Duty to Notify Applicants, Beneficiaries, or Assignees?* Should insurers be held liable for failing to notify applicants of the results of blood tests or medical examinations? In *Doe (Jane, John) v. Prudential Insurance Co.*, 860 F. Supp. 243 (D. Md. 1993), the plaintiff sued on a variety of grounds, alleging that the insurer was liable for failing to notify her that she had tested HIV positive. In that case the insurer had notified her, however, that her application had been rejected because of the result of her blood test, and indicated that the details of the test would be made available to her physician. Other courts have held that there is no duty to disclose at all. See, e.g., *McLachlan v. N.Y. Life Ins. Co.*, 488 F.3d 624 (5th Cir. 2007); *Petrosky v. Brasner*, 279 A.D.2d 75 (N.Y. 2001); *Nolan v. First Colony Life Ins. Co.*, 784 A.2d 81 (N.J. App. 2001).

Should insurers be obligated to notify beneficiaries or assignees of changes made in their status? If so, on what legal theory? The courts have proved extremely reluctant to accept any such liability. See, e.g., *Norwest Bank, N.A. v. Fed. Kemper Life Ins. Co.*, 110 F.Supp.2d 774 (N.D. Ind. 2000) (rejecting the claim of the holders of assigned policies that they had a right to be notified of a lapse in payment of premiums); *Wells v. John Hancock Mut. Life Ins. Co.*, 149 Cal. Rptr. 171 (1978) (same). Some courts have held that life insurers owe a duty of care to advise individuals when a policy has been taken out on their life by someone else. See *Bajwa v. Metro. Life Ins. Co.*, 804 N.E.2d 519 (Ill. 2004).

7. LIFE INSURANCE PRODUCTS AND SECURITIES REGULATION

American Equity Investment Life Insurance Company, et al. v. Securities and Exchange Commission

United States Court of Appeals, D.C. Circuit, 2010.
613 F.3d 166.

■ SENTELLE, CHIEF JUDGE.

The Securities Act of 1933, 15 U.S.C. §§ 77a *et seq.* (the Act), exempts from federal regulation annuity contracts issued by a corporation subject to regulation by state insurance laws. Petitioners seek review of a rule promulgated by the Securities and Exchange Commission (SEC or Commission) stating that fixed indexed annuities (FIAs) are not annuity contracts within the meaning of the Act. As a result of this new rule, FIAs are subject to the full panoply of requirements set forth by the Act, instead of being subject solely to state insurance laws. Petitioners argue that the Commission unreasonably interpreted the term "annuity contract" not to include FIAs. Petitioners also assert that the SEC failed to fulfill its statutory responsibility under the Act to consider the effect of the new rule on efficiency, competition, and capital formation. Because we hold that the SEC's interpretation of "annuity contract" is reasonable under Chevron, we deny the petitions with respect to this issue. We grant the petitions, however, with respect to petitioners' alternate ground that the SEC failed to properly consider the effect of the rule upon efficiency, competition, and capital formation. Accordingly, we vacate the rule.

I. BACKGROUND

A.

The Securities Act of 1933 governs the offer or sale of any security through interstate commerce. The Act defines the term "security" as including any "investment contract." 15 U.S.C. § 77b(a)(1); *SEC v. Variable Annuity Life Ins. Co. of Am. (VALIC)*, 359 U.S. 65, 67–68 (1959). Section 3(a)(8) of the Act, however, provides an exemption under the Act for an "annuity contract" or "optional annuity contract" subject to state insurance laws. 15 U.S.C. § 77c(a)(8).

A traditional fixed annuity is a contract issued by a life insurance company, under which the purchaser makes a series of premium payments to the insurer in exchange for a series of periodic payments from the insurer to the purchaser at agreed upon later dates. In a fixed annuity, the insurance company guarantees that the purchaser will earn a minimum rate of interest over time. Fixed annuities are subject to state insurance law regulation, and are exempt from federal securities laws. See id. State insurance laws governing fixed annuity contracts require insurance companies to guarantee a minimum of the contract value after any costs and charges are applied. These state laws generally require the minimum guarantee be at least 87.5 percent of the premiums paid, accumulated at an annual interest rate of 1 to 3 percent. Indexed Annuities and Certain Other Insurance Contracts (*Final FIA Rule*), 74 Fed.Reg. 3138, 3141 (Jan. 16, 2009) (to be codified at 17 C.F.R. Parts 230 and 240). The laws also generally impose disclosure and suitability requirements, which vary from state to state.

A fixed index annuity (FIA) is a hybrid financial product that combines some of the benefits of fixed annuities with the added earning potential of a security. Like traditional fixed annuities, FIAs are subject to state insurance laws, under which insurance companies must guarantee the same 87.5 percent of purchase payments. Unlike traditional fixed annuities, however, the purchaser's rate of return is not based upon a guaranteed interest rate. In FIAs the insurance company credits the purchaser with a return that is based on the performance of a securities index, such as the Dow Jones Industrial Average, Nasdaq 100 Index, or Standard & Poor's 500 Index. Depending on the performance of the securities index to which a particular FIA is tied, the return on an FIA might be much higher or lower than the guaranteed rate of return offered by a traditional fixed annuity. Due to the fact that the purchaser's actual return is linked to the performance of a securities index, however, the purchaser's return cannot be calculated until the end of the crediting period. Insurance companies typically apply an annual crediting period; that is, the index-linked interest of an FIA is typically calculated on an annual basis after each one-year period ends.

B.

While this is the first case in which we have had occasion to address the § 3(a)(8) annuity exemption as it regards FIAs, the Supreme Court has offered guidance on the scope of the exemption in *VALIC*, 359 U.S. 65, and *SEC v. United Benefit Life Ins. Co.*, 387 U.S. 202 (1967). In *VALIC*, the Supreme Court considered whether a variable annuity fell within the § 3(a)(8) exemption. A variable annuity is a financial product under which purchasers pay premiums that are invested in common stocks and other equities to a greater degree than traditional annuities, and the benefit payments vary with the success of the investment management. *See* VALIC, 359 U.S. at 69. The Court explained that a variable annuity did not fall within the § 3(a)(8) exemption because it placed "all the investment risks on the [purchaser], none on the company." *Id*. at 71. As the Court said, "the concept of 'insurance' involves some investment risk-taking on the part of the company." *Id*. " '[I]nsurance' involves a guarantee that at least some fraction of the benefits will be payable in fixed amounts." *Id*. Therefore, an issuer of an annuity "that has no element of a fixed return assumes no true risk in the insurance sense." *Id*. The fact that there exists a risk of declining returns in difficult economic times is not sufficient to show that the insurer has assumed more risk under the contract. *See id*. Accordingly, because the variable annuity at issue did not offer a "true underwriting of risks, the one earmark of insurance," the Court held that it did not fall within the exemption offered to traditional fixed annuities offered by insurers. *Id*. at 73. In a concurring opinion later approved by the full Court in *United Benefit*, Justice Brennan explained that when "a brand-new form of investment arrangement emerges which is labeled 'insurance' or 'annuity' by its promoters, the functional distinction that Congress set up in 1933 . . . must be examined to test whether the contract falls within the sort of investment form that Congress was then willing to leave exclusively to the State Insurance Commissioners." *Id.* at 76 (Brennan, J., concurring); *see United Benefit*, 387 U.S. at 210.

In *United Benefit*, the Court concluded that another product similar to a variable annuity called a "Flexible Fund Annuity" was not exempt under § 3(a)(8) of the Act. A Flexible Fund functioned in much the same way as a variable annuity. Most notably, the purchaser paid premiums into a separate account that was primarily invested in common stocks, with the object of producing capital gains as well as an interest return. *United Benefit*, 387 U.S. at 205. Unlike the variable annuity in *VALIC*, however, the insurer guaranteed that the purchaser would receive a percentage of his premiums back. This percentage gradually increased from 50 percent of net premiums in the first year to 100 percent after 10 years. *Id.* United Benefit argued that, under *VALIC*, the existence *vel non* of substantial investment risk by the insurer ultimately determined whether a product fell within the § 3(a)(8) exemption.

The Court disagreed that *VALIC* should be interpreted so narrowly. *Id.* at 210. Rather, the critical inquiry under § 3(a)(8) was whether the product at issue " 'involve[d] considerations of investment not present in the conventional contract of insurance.' " *Id.* (quoting *Prudential Ins. Co. v. SEC*, 326 F.2d 383, 388 (3d Cir.1964)). In concluding that the Flexible Fund did not fall within § 3(a)(8), the Court relied significantly on the fact that the Flexible Fund "appeal[ed] to the purchaser not on the usual insurance basis of stability and security but on the prospect of 'growth' through sound investment management." *United Benefit*, 387 U.S. at 211. Though the Court acknowledged that the "guarantee of cash value based on net premiums reduces substantially the investment risk of the contract holder," it reasoned further that "the assumption of an investment risk [by the insurer] cannot by itself create an insurance provision under the federal definition." *Id.* (citing *Helvering v. Le Gierse*, 312 U.S. 531, 542 (1941)). The Court recognized that a "basic difference" exists between "a contract which to some degree is insured and a contract of insurance." *United Benefit*, 387 U.S. at 211. In the case of the Flexible Fund, the insurer's assumption of risk was minimal. The insurer was "obligated to produce no more than the guaranteed minimum at maturity, and this amount is substantially less than that guaranteed by the same premiums in a conventional deferred annuity contract." *Id.* at 208.

C.

Since the Court's decisions in *VALIC* and *United Benefit*, the SEC has engaged in rulemaking to address the newer financial products that have entered the market. In the mid-1980s, the SEC promulgated Rule 151 in response to the creation of a new hybrid financial product called a guaranteed investment contract. *See* 17 C.F.R. § 230.151. Guaranteed investment contracts are like traditional fixed annuities, in that they promise a return at a guaranteed rate of return for the life of the contract. In some guaranteed investment contracts, however, the insurer may agree to periodically pay the purchaser an additional discretionary amount above the already guaranteed return amount.

Rule 151 provided that, under certain conditions, a guaranteed investment contract would qualify for the § 3(a)(8) exemption notwithstanding an insurer's ability to pay a discretionary amount to the purchaser. Under Rule 151, a contract falls within the § 3(a)(8) exemption if:

> (1) The annuity or optional annuity contract is issued by a corporation (the insurer) subject to the supervision of the insurance commissioner, bank commissioner, or any agency or officer performing like functions, of any State or Territory of the United States or the District of Columbia;
>
> (2) The insurer assumes the investment risk under the contract as prescribed in paragraph (b) of this section; and
>
> (3) The contract is not marketed primarily as an investment.

17 C.F.R. § 230.151(a). Though the SEC considered excluding from the Rule 151 safe harbor any product in which an issuer calculates the rate of any excess return by reference to an index, it concluded that an issuer may reference an index to set the excess return rate, but only if the rate is set before each crediting period begins and remains in effect for at least one year. *Definition of Annuity Contract or Optional Annuity Contract*, S.E.C. Release No. 6645, 1986 WL 703849, at *11 (May 29, 1986).

In the mid-1990s, insurance companies began marketing FIAs. The SEC did not take any regulatory action with respect to FIAs until 2007. By this time, the sales volume of FIAs had increased to $24.8 billion; indexed annuity assets totaled $123 billion. A total of 322 FIAs were being offered by 58 insurance companies. Having grown increasingly concerned that these FIAs were not being sold through registered broker-dealers and were not registered with the SEC despite their tie-in to a securities market, the SEC proposed Rule 151A. Rule 151A provides that a contract that is regulated as an annuity under state insurance law is not an "annuity contract" under § 3(a)(8) of the Act if:

> (1) The contract specifies that amounts payable by the issuer under the contract are calculated at or after the end of one or more specified crediting periods, in whole or in part, by reference to the performance during the crediting period or periods of a security, including a group or index of securities; and
>
> (2) Amounts payable by the issuer under the contract are more likely than not to exceed the amounts guaranteed under the contract.

17 C.F.R. § 230.151A(a). By redefining an "annuity contract" to exclude FIAs, the Commission sought to ensure that purchasers of FIAs would be entitled to the full protection of the federal securities laws, including disclosure, antifraud, and sales practice protections.

To support this new rule, the SEC first noted that the Securities Act did not define "annuity contract," and that FIAs were not in existence at the time the "annuity contract" exemption in the Securities Act was enacted. *Final FIA Rule*, 74 Fed.Reg. at 3142–43. Without express statutory guidance, the Commission looked to the reasoning set forth in the Supreme Court's decisions in *VALIC* and *United Benefit* to assess whether FIAs were the type of financial product that Congress would have been willing to leave to state insurance regulation. *Id.* at 3143.

The SEC began its analysis by considering the level of risk associated with FIAs. Citing *VALIC*, the Commission reasoned that "Congress intended to include in the insurance exemption only those policies and contracts that include a 'true underwriting of risks' and 'investment risk-taking' by the insurer." *Id.* (citing *VALIC*, 359 U.S. at 71–73). The annuities that were offered at the time of the enactment of the § 3(a)(8) exemption were fixed annuities that generally involved no investment risk to the purchaser. *Final FIA Rule*, 74 Fed.Reg. at 3143. Therefore, the SEC reasoned, Congress was willing to offer a securities law exemption to these types of no risk products because, by their nature, they did not raise the kinds of problems or risks that the federal securities laws were intended to address. *Id.* Additionally, the state insurance laws in existence could adequately deal with any issues that might arise from such low risk insurance products. *Id.* On the other hand, the SEC explained, "[i]ndividuals who purchase [FIAs] are exposed to a significant investment risk—i.e., the volatility of the underlying securities index." *Id.* at 3138. At the time an FIA is purchased, the purchaser "assumes the risk of an uncertain and fluctuating financial instrument, in exchange for participation in future securities-linked returns." *Id.* at 3143. Unlike the guaranteed, fixed return offered by a traditional fixed annuity, the SEC asserted that an FIA's return was neither known nor guaranteed. *Id.* The SEC acknowledged that "indexed annuities contracts provide some protection against the risk of loss," but determined that these provisions did not adequately transfer the investment risk from the purchaser to the insurer. *Id.* Because the value of the purchaser's investment was entirely dependent upon an unknown and fluctuating securities index, the assumption of a guaranteed minimum percentage of the FIA, though giving FIAs an outward aspect of insurance, was a superficial and unsubstantial offset of the purchaser's risk. *Id.* Therefore, the SEC reasoned that an FIA's value is much like that of a security, as the value of each product depends on the performance of the market. This securities-like investment risk, the SEC explained, was the exact type of investment risk that the Securities Act was created to address. *Id.*

The SEC supplemented its analysis of Rule 151A by undertaking a consideration of the rule's promotion of efficiency, competition, and capital formation, as is required by § 2(b) of the Act for certain SEC rulemakings. *See* 15 U.S.C. § 77b(b). The SEC first concluded that Rule 151A would promote efficiency, reasoning that the rule would extend the benefits of the disclosure and sales practice protections of the federal securities laws to FIAs that offered payments to the purchaser that fluctuated with the securities markets. *Id.* at 3169. The imposition of disclosure requirements would enable investors to make more informed investment decisions about purchasing FIAs, and would promote more suitable recommendations by issuers of FIAs to purchasers. *Id.* at 3169–70. Next, the SEC asserted that the improvement in investors' ability to make informed investment decisions would increase competition between issuers of FIAs. The SEC reasoned that the imposition of federal securities laws to regulate FIAs was particularly important because it would "bring about clarity in what has been an uncertain area of law," *id.* at 3171, which would in turn increase competition because registered broker-dealers "who currently may be unwilling to sell unregistered [FIAs] because of their uncertain regulatory status may become willing to sell [FIAs] that are registered." *Id.* at 3170. Finally, the SEC concluded that, based upon the increased efficiency resulting from the enhanced investor protections under federal law, Rule 151A would promote capital formation "by improving the flow of information among insurers that issue [FIAs], the distributors of those annuities, and investors." *Id.* at 3171.

Petitioners seek review of Rule 151A.

II. ANALYSIS

A.

Petitioners first argue that the SEC erred in excluding FIAs from the definition of "annuity contract" under § 3(a)(8) of the Act. Petitioners assert that their argument is supported by the plain language of the provision, as well as by the Supreme Court's decisions in *VALIC* and *United Benefit*. Petitioners argue that Rule 151A is in conflict with the text of § 3(a)(8), the aforementioned decisions of the Court, and the text of the SEC's prior rule, Rule 151. Finally, petitioners argue that the SEC failed to undertake properly its statutory responsibility to consider Rule 151A's effect on efficiency, competition, and capital formation, pursuant to § 2(b) of the Act. We will address each argument in turn.

When an agency is given express authority to execute and enforce its enabling statute and to prescribe such rules and regulations as are or may be necessary to carry out provisions of the statute, courts must apply a two-step analysis in reviewing the agency's interpretation of the statute under *Chevron U.S.A., Inc. v. Natural Res. Def. Council, Inc.*, 467 U.S. 837 (1984). Section 19(a) of the Act bestows upon the SEC the power to define terms and make rules to that effect. 15 U.S.C. § 77s(a). Rule 151A, which interprets the term "annuity contract" in § 3(a)(8) of the Act is clearly such a rule.

Under *Chevron*, we first determine whether the statute being interpreted is ambiguous. If "Congress has directly spoken to the precise question at issue . . . [then] that is the end of the matter; for the court, as well as the agency, must give effect to the unambiguously expressed intent of Congress." *Chevron*, 467 U.S. at 842–43. On the other hand, if the court determines that the statute is either "silent or ambiguous with respect to the specific issue," then *Chevron* Step One is satisfied. *Id.* at 843. Here, *Chevron* Step One is satisfied because the Act is ambiguous, or at the very least silent, on whether the term "annuity contract" encompasses all forms of contracts that may be described as annuities. Indeed, the analyses in the Supreme Court's decisions in *VALIC* and *United Benefit* confirm this ambiguity. *See generally VALIC*, 359 U.S. 65; *United Benefit*, 387 U.S. 202. Had the statute been unambiguous, the Court need not have undertaken such an exhaustive inquiry in determining whether the two products at issue in those cases were annuities under § 3(a)(8) of the Act.

Petitioners nevertheless argue that the Court's decisions in *VALIC* and *United Benefit* establish that an "annuity" falls outside of § 3(a)(8) only if it is subject to the insurer's investment management, and not subject to state insurance laws. Given the absence of these two elements, petitioners assert, § 3(a)(8) clearly governs FIAs because FIAs are not subject to the insurer's investment management and are governed by a panoply of state insurance laws. Petitioners' argument misses the mark because it interprets *VALIC* and *United Benefit* too restrictively.

Nothing in those cases indicated that the Court's determination whether the § 3(a)(8) exemption applies to particular contracts depends on the investment management of the issuer and the applicability of state insurance regulation. Rather, the Court embraced a broader approach in its § 3(a)(8) analysis. The Court clearly indicated in both *VALIC* and *United Benefit* that the § 3(a)(8) exemption applied to products that "'did not present very squarely the sort of problems that the Securities Act . . . [was] devised to deal with, and which were, in many details, subject to a form of state regulation of a sort which made the federal regulation even less relevant.'" *United Benefit*, 387 U.S. at 210 (quoting *VALIC*, 359 U.S. at 75 (Brennan, J., concurring)). The Court therefore focused its § 3(a)(8) analysis on whether the product at issue "involve[d] considerations of investment not present in the conventional contract of insurance." *Id.* (quotation omitted). Though an insurer's investment management actions associated with a product may be relevant to determining whether that product is an annuity, this is not the only relevant characteristic. Petitioners' reliance on the existence of state law regulation governing FIAs is also too limited. The Court recognized in *United Benefit* that it had "conclusively rejected" in VALIC the argument that the existence of adequate state regulation was the basis for the § 3(a)(8) exemption. *Id.* (quotation omitted). Therefore, the fact that FIAs are subject to state insurance regulation does not, without more, place them within the § 3(a)(8) exemption. Accordingly, the language of § 3(a)(8) does not unambiguously include FIAs within the § 3(a)(8) exemption. In light of the fact that the statute is ambiguous with respect to the term "annuity contract," we reiterate that Chevron Step One is satisfied.

We must next determine whether the SEC's rule is a reasonable interpretation of the statute. The SEC's rule will satisfy Step Two of the Chevron analysis so long as it meets this requirement. It is irrelevant that this court might have reached a different—or better—conclusion than the SEC. *See Nat'l Cable & Telecomm. Ass'n v. Brand X Internet Servs.*, 545 U.S. 967, 980 (2005).

In this case, the SEC has adopted an interpretation that is based in reason. By their nature, FIAs "appeal to the purchaser not on the usual insurance basis of stability and security but on the prospect of 'growth' through sound investment management." *United Benefit*, 387 U.S. at 211. An FIA is akin to an annuity contract with respect to its pay-in and guaranteed minimum value of purchase payment features. The interest return rate of an FIA, however, is decidedly more like a security in that the index-based return of an FIA is not known until the end of a crediting cycle, as the rate is based on the actual performance of a specified securities index during that period. Similar to an investor in securities, a purchaser of an FIA knows the level of annual return he will receive once the year is concluded and the index's value is compared with its value at the beginning of the year. In FIAs, as in securities, there is a variability in the potential return that results in a risk to the purchaser. By contrast, an annuity contract falling under Rule 151's exemption avoids this variability by guaranteeing the interest rate ahead of time. As these characteristics show, FIAs "involve considerations of investment not present in the conventional contract of insurance." Id. at 210 (quotation omitted). Accordingly, the SEC's interpretation that an FIA does not constitute an "annuity contract" under § 3(a)(8) of the Act was reasonable. * * *

For these reasons, we hold that the SEC's interpretation of "annuity contract" was reasonable and Chevron Step Two is satisfied.

B.

Even though the SEC's interpretation of "annuity contract" was reasonable, petitioners argue that the SEC contravened § 2(b) of the Act because it failed to consider the efficiency, competition, and capital formation effects of the new Rule 151A. Section 2(b) of the Act states that, for every rulemaking in which the SEC "is required to consider or determine whether an action is necessary or appropriate in the public interest, the Commission shall also consider, in addition to the protection of investors, whether the action will promote efficiency, competition, and capital formation." 15 U.S.C. § 77b(b). Petitioners argue that the costs of implementing Rule 151A are too burdensome and that the imposition of additional regulations would be inefficient. They also contend that the SEC failed to properly assess the existence of abuses of FIAs before applying securities regulations on the issuers of those products. The SEC counters that it properly rejected petitioners' concerns regarding duplicative regulation because the Supreme Court's decisions in *VALIC* and United Benefit made clear that state regulatory approaches to new products are not conclusive in a § 3(a)(8) analysis. * * *

We now turn to the merits of the SEC's § 2(b) analysis. We review the analysis under the statutory standard set by the Administrative Procedure Act. 5 U.S.C. § 706. The APA requires the court to set aside agency action that is "arbitrary, capricious, an abuse of discretion, or otherwise not in accordance with law." *Id.* at § 706(2)(A). We hold that the Commission's consideration of the effect of Rule 151A on efficiency, competition, and capital formation was arbitrary and capricious. The SEC purports to have analyzed the effect of the rule on competition, but does not disclose a reasoned basis for its conclusion that Rule 151A would increase competition. The SEC concluded that enacting the rule would resolve the present uncertainty prevailing over the legal status of FIAs. * * *

This reasoning is flawed. The lack of clarity resulting from the "uncertain legal status" of the financial product is only another way of saying that there was not a regulation in place prior to the adoption of Rule 151A determining the status of those products under the annuity exemption of § 3(a)(8). The SEC cannot justify the adoption of a particular rule based solely on the assertion that the existence of a rule provides greater clarity to an area that remained unclear in the absence of any rule. Whatever rule the SEC chose to adopt could equally be said to make the previously unregulated market clearer than it would be without that adoption. * * *

The SEC's competition analysis also fails because the SEC did not make any finding on the existing level of competition in the marketplace under the state law regime. The SEC asserted competition would increase based upon its expectation that Rule 151A would require fuller public disclosure of the terms of FIAs and thereby increase price transparency. The SEC could not accurately assess any potential increase or decrease in competition, however, because it did not assess the baseline level of price transparency and information disclosure under state law. * * *

The Commission's efficiency analysis is similarly arbitrary and capricious. The SEC concluded that Rule 151A would promote efficiency because the required disclosures under the rule would enable investors to make more informed investment decisions about purchasing indexed annuities. The SEC advanced further that the rule's sales practice protections would enable sellers to promote more suitable recommendations to investors; this, in turn, would lead to investors making even better informed decisions, which would offer greater efficiency. As with its analysis of competition, however, the SEC's analysis is incomplete because it fails to determine whether, under the existing regime, sufficient protections existed to enable investors to make informed investment decisions and sellers to make suitable recommendations to investors. The SEC's failure to analyze the efficiency of the existing state law regime renders arbitrary and capricious the SEC's judgment that applying federal securities law would increase efficiency. * * *

Having determined that the SEC's § 2(b) analysis is lacking, we grant the petitions insofar as they assert the SEC failed properly to consider the effect of the rule upon efficiency, competition, and capital formation. * * * We therefore order that Rule 151A be vacated.

So ordered.

NOTES AND QUESTIONS

1. *The Harkin Amendment.* Although *American Equity* vacated Rule 151A, it also held that the SEC had authority to regulate fixed indexed annuities under the Securities Act of 1933 ('33 Act). Fearful that the SEC would exercise this authority by re-promulgating regulations covering fixed indexed annuities, the life insurance industry lobbied extensively for a provision in Dodd-Frank that would limit this risk. This lobbying helped result in the inclusion in Dodd-Frank of the Harkin Amendment. This provision requires the SEC to treat both annuities and life insurance products as exempt from the '33 Act if three criteria are met: (i) the product complies with state non-forfeiture laws requiring that policyholders cannot lose more than a specific percentage of their premiums, (ii) the product's value cannot be derived by separate accounts, which are the vehicle through which variable annuities link policyholder returns to the performance of a bundle of securities, and (iii) the company's state of domicile or the state in which the product is sold must adopt suitability requirements by June, 2013 that meet or substantially exceed the NAIC's Suitability in Annuities Model Law, Model Law 275 (2010), or the company

must voluntarily adopt standards that meet the requirements of the law. Dodd-Frank § 989J. As noted in Chapter 3, until recently states varied significantly in their suitability laws, both with respect to annuities and other insurance products. As of the June 2013 deadline, only about 2/3 of states had, in fact, adopted the 2010 NAIC model law. See Linda Koco, Harkin Day Has Passed, Now What?, Annuity News (6/25/13).

    2. *Dual Regulation of Certain Life Insurance Products.* Nothing in either *American Equity* or in the Harkin Amendment altered the long-standing rule, originating in *SEC v. Variable Annuity Life Insurance Co. of America (VALIC)*, 359 U.S. 65 (1959), that variable annuities and similar products, including variable life and universal life insurance, are subject to federal securities laws. Recall that this is because these products are not deemed to be "annuities" or "insurance" as those terms are used in the '33 Act. At the same time, these products are universally considered to be subject to state insurance regulation because they fall within the definition of "insurance" or "annuities" under state law. As noted in Chapter Three, the result is that these products are subject to dual regulation by state insurance regulators and federal securities regulators. The most tangible consequence of this dual regulation is that these products can only be sold by individuals who are both licensed to sell insurance under state law and licensed as broker/dealers under federal securities laws. Additionally, these products are subject to both state and federal laws on disclosure and suitability. Although federal and state regulators attempt to coordinate these laws, there is little doubt that dual regulation places a large compliance burden on the insurers and producers who sell these products.

    3. *State Regulation of Fixed-Indexed Annuities.* The impetus for the SEC's promulgation of Rule 151A was the agency's belief that substantial consumer abuses were occurring in connection with the sale of these products and that state insurance regulation was not adequately responding to these abuses. In a statement at an open meeting in 2008, the then-chairman of the SEC described a survey of state securities regulators showing that seniors made a disproportionate number of complaints to state securities regulators and that fixed indexed annuities "are among a handful of products most often involved in senior investment fraud." Chairman Christopher Cox, Statement at Open Meeting on Equity-Indexed Annuities, U.S. Securities and Exchange Commission (June 25, 2008). He went on to explain that:

> [A] variety of fees and charges, limitations on accumulation, calculations of index values, and other detailed features are baked into equity indexed annuities. And although the contract guarantees a minimum value, that's typically less than what the investor gives the insurance company in the first place. * * * [B]ecause there are so many features among various products, investors have a difficult time comparing one equity indexed annuity to another.
>
> Surrender charges are another way that investors can find that they get back less money than they put in. The charges can be as high as 15 to 20 percent of the amounts invested. Although the surrender charges decline to zero over time, that process can take more than 15 years. In the meantime, if an investor who buys an equity indexed annuity needs his or her money sooner—

for medical expenses or rent, for example—he or she can be forced to forfeit a substantial amount of the investment.

Unfortunately, many equity indexed annuities appear to have been marketed to investors who are least able to scrutinize the details.

Id. The SEC was not the only entity to express concerns about consumer protection and the sale of fixed-indexed annuities. For instance, a magazine article that received a substantial amount of attention argued that fixed-indexed annuities generally amount to a "safety trap" because agents receive very high commissions and use aggressive sales tactics to sell the products to consumers who do not appreciate the fees and surrender charges associated with them. See Lisa Gibbs, Index Annuities are a Safety Trap, Money Magazine (Jan. 17, 2011). As emphasized by both the industry and the *American Equity* court, however, rigorous evidence regarding either the comparative prevalence of consumer abuses in this arena or the ability of federal securities regulation to curb such abuses is limited. Are there any good reasons to think that federal regulators are better situated than state regulators to identify and respond to consumer abuses in the domain of annuities sales?

B. HEALTH INSURANCE

The most extensive healthcare reform legislation in United States history became law in the spring of 2010. The Patient Protection and Affordable Care Act ("Affordable Care Act," "ACA," or "Obamacare"), 42 U.S.C. § 18001 et seq., fundamentally altered health insurance law and regulation. This is hardly surprising, as health insurance plays a central role in healthcare. Taken together, private health insurance and publicly-provided insurance programs such as Medicare and Medicaid fund over 75% of total national healthcare expenditures. See Anne B. Martin et al., National Health Spending In 2012: Rate Of Health Spending Growth Remained Low For The Fourth Consecutive Year, 33 Health Aff. 67, 68 (2014). Health insurers are not only the primary payers for medical and hospital costs, but also for related items, such as prescription drugs and physical therapy. Insurers consequently exert a tremendous amount of actual and potential influence over the structure and delivery of American healthcare. At the same time, insurance is the central mechanism for ensuring access to healthcare for most Americans. A basic course in insurance law cannot provide a comprehensive understanding of this vast area, but it can survey the major issues in the field and provide a broad overview of the ACA's impact on health insurance.

1. THE STRUCTURE OF HEALTH INSURANCE MARKETS

Even before the ACA, the law and regulation of health insurance was importantly linked to the structure of health insurance markets. This link is even stronger as a result of the ACA. In most important ways, the ACA left unchanged the basic structure of health insurance markets. As was true before reform, individuals can acquire health insurance through three basic sources: (i) employers, (ii) the individual market, and (iii) government programs.

First, a majority of the population—about 60% when the ACA was passed—secures health insurance through their own employer, a spouse's employer, or a parent's employer. Most employers who offer their employees coverage do so through a group insurance policy that they purchase from a health insurer. Such group policies are sold either in the large-group or small-group market, depending on the employer's size (the cut-off is typically 50 or 100 employees). Alternatively, many large employers (and some small employers) "self-insure" their employees' coverage, effectively providing insurance directly to their employees. Even in these cases, employers almost always hire health insurers or other entities to help administer this benefit.

The prominence of employer-provided health insurance dates back to the Second World War. At that time, wage controls and a labor shortage caused employers to compete for workers by offering group health insurance as a fringe benefit of employment. See Kenneth S. Abraham, The Liability Century: Insurance and Tort Law from the Progressive Era to 9/11 112–15 (2008). From this beginning, employer-based health insurance expanded for several reasons. Most importantly, the federal government established various tax benefits for employer-provided health insurance that persist to this day. For instance, any contribution that an employer makes to an employee's premiums is not treated as income to the employee and is deductible to the employer as a business expense. Just as importantly, so long as employers meet certain Internal Revenue Code criteria, employees can use pre-tax dollars to pay their share of premiums. In addition to these tax benefits, employer-based coverage has historically generated comparatively low administrative costs because of the economies of scale that are associated with purchasing insurance on a group basis. Finally, employer-based coverage provides a natural pooling mechanism because being hired is a pre-condition of obtaining coverage but generally does not correlate with an individual's health status. These latter two benefits are muted in the context of the small group insurance market, which has traditionally fared less well than the large group insurance market as a result.

As we saw in Chapters Two and Three, employer-provided insurance is subject to ERISA because it constitutes an "employee benefit plan." ERISA incorporates provisions of the Health Insurance Portability and Accountability Act ("HIPAA") that prohibit employers from linking premiums, coverage terms, or coverage availability to employees' health status, age, or gender, among other things. Additionally, employers who offer their employees health insurance may owe fiduciary duties to their employees to the extent that they exercise discretion over the administration of those benefits. At the same time, ERISA preempts many state laws governing health insurance in the context of employer-sponsored health insurance. The extent of this preemption depends on whether an employer is self-insured: as we will see later in this Chapter, state law is almost entirely preempted for self-insured employers, but is generally not preempted (outside of the area of remedies for coverage denials) for employers who purchase group insurance policies. Historically, one of the primary motivations for an employer to self-insure its employees' health benefits was to avoid the application of state insurance law generally, and state mandated benefit laws in particular.

A second source of insurance is the individual market. In the individual market, individuals purchase health insurance just as they usually purchase homeowners or automobile insurance: by directly acquiring coverage from a private insurer. Unlike employer-provided health insurance, individuals must pay for insurance on the individual market with after-tax dollars, even after passage of the ACA. Prior to the ACA, competitive pressures caused insurers to individually rate applicants based on their age, medical experience, claims history, and various other factors. Applicants with chronic preexisting conditions might be denied coverage entirely or offered coverage only at very high rates. The principal constraints on insurers' capacity to engage in such medical underwriting were state laws, which varied dramatically. Whereas some states maintained guaranteed issue laws and limited permissible underwriting factors, others gave insurers a virtual free hand in their underwriting practices. Many states that did attempt to limit insurer underwriting or issuance experienced substantial adverse selection in their individual markets. As a result, few people with access to employer-provided insurance opted to purchase coverage in the individual market prior to the ACA. As we will see below, a core goal of the ACA is to dramatically alter the individual market for health insurance.

The Structure of Health Insurance Markets

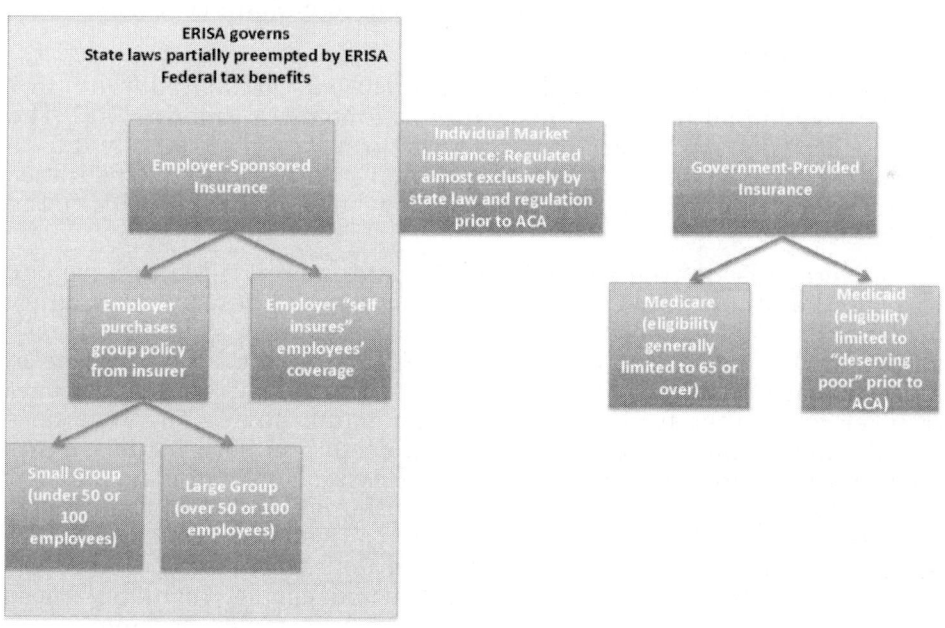

The third and final source of health insurance is government programs, such as Medicare and Medicaid. The common feature of all public health insurance programs is that they are only available to a sub-set of the population that meets specific eligibility criteria. Medicare, for instance, is (with certain limited exceptions) available only to Americans who are 65 years of age or older. Among those who are eligible, about 96% of individuals enroll, though a substantial percentage of this population has private coverage as well. Medicaid eligibility varies by state. Prior to the ACA, Medicaid was only available to a subset of individuals with very low incomes (often described as "the deserving poor") or to certain individuals with disabilities, although eligibility rules were typically loosened for children. As we will see below, the ACA substantially broadened the scope of Medicaid eligibility, though states still vary on this issue. In contrast to Medicare, most people with Medicaid do not have alternative sources of insurance. At the time of the ACA's passage, about one quarter of the population had some form of publicly-provided health insurance.

2. THE NEED FOR REFORM PRIOR TO THE ACA

a. COVERAGE, COST AND QUALITY PRIOR TO THE ACA

The debate over healthcare reform was, and continues to be, politically divisive. Yet this debate has also been remarkable for the common supposition, echoed by commentators on both the left and right, that comprehensive reform of some sort was necessary at the time the ACA was passed. The following report was prepared as the debate began.

Congressional Research Service, Health Care Reform: An Introduction (Bob Lyke, April 14, 2009)

Interest in reform is [ ]driven by three predominant concerns. * * *

Coverage

In August, 2008, the U.S. Census Bureau estimated that 45.7 million people had no health insurance at a point in time in 2007. The number had declined from 47 million the previous year, largely due to increases in Medicaid and CHIP (the State Children's Health Insurance Program) enrollment. The number may now be going back up due to the recession. * * *

Coverage is not the same as access, and it is possible to have one without the other. Some uninsured people can get care in community health clinics or from doctors providing pro bono work, even if they have no money. If people need emergency care, hospitals that participate in Medicare are required to stabilize them or provide an appropriate transfer to another facility. On the other hand, having coverage does not guarantee that one can easily find a doctor, as both Medicare and Medicaid participants sometime report. Having coverage also does not ensure that one can pay for care. People with high deductible insurance, perhaps chosen when they were healthy or because premiums were lower, may have to pay several thousand dollars out of pocket before their plan begins reimbursements. For some people, including those who lose their jobs, paying for health care is a major problem. Even people with comprehensive plans with low deductibles may have difficulty paying the ongoing costs of chronic conditions or the major costs of serious illnesses. * * *

Cost and Spending

Spending on health care in the United States has increased from 7.2% of GDP in 1970 to 12.3% in 1990 and 16.2% in 2007. Barring changes in law, the Congressional Budget Office (CBO) projected in

2008 that it would rise to 25% of GDP in 2025 and much higher levels beyond. CBO has cautioned that "as health care spending consumes a greater and greater share of the nation's economic output in the future, Americans will be faced with increasingly difficult choices between health care and other priorities."

The United States spends considerably more on health care than other industrialized countries: on a per capita basis, its spending is more than two times greater than the spending of the median Organization for Economic Cooperation and Development (OECD) country. It has been argued that some of the higher health care spending has added real value through medical advances. Some of it may be attributable to the higher per capita GDP in the United States, which simply allows Americans to spend more. However, its value has been questioned in light of the mixed performance of the United States on many indicators of health care quality, as described in the next section. * * *

Controlling cost and spending is unlikely to be easy. Many economists argue that the principal factor driving increases in health care spending is technology, both new pharmaceuticals and other products and services and wider use of existing ones. It is not obvious whether some developments can be limited or their application blocked (for example, by limiting diffusion on the basis of clinical evidence) and some would question whether they should. One challenge in controlling costs is that payers may shift burdens to others, sometimes in ways that are not clearly understood or measurable. For example, most economists argue that employer payments for health insurance are actually borne by workers through reduced wages and other forms of compensation. Attempts to limit employer-paid insurance may lead to increases in wages in ways that are difficult to predict.

One particular congressional concern is the cost of federal health insurance programs. In 2007, Medicare and Medicaid, the two largest programs, accounted for about 20% of the federal budget and over 27% of total national health care expenditures. * * *

Quality

Despite spending more on health care than other industrialized countries, the United States scores only average or somewhat worse on many quality of care indicators. It is near the top for some measures, such as survival rates for breast and colorectal cancer, but near the bottom for others, such as mortality and hospitalization rates for asthma. A recent Centers for Disease Control and Prevention (CDC) report found that the United States ranked 29th in the world in infant mortality in 2004. The U.S. position in rankings on this measure has been declining. Notwithstanding difficulties of cross-national comparisons, these indicators show that Americans do not receive the best value for their health care spending and that there is room for improvement.

Concerns about health care quality in the United States go beyond international comparisons, and they cannot be reduced simply to returns on the dollar. Medical errors appear to be one systemic shortcoming. An influential 1999 Institute of Medicine study found that at least 44,000 people, and perhaps as many as 98,000, die from in-patient hospital care every year. The study found that most medical errors do not result from individual recklessness or actions of a particular group; rather, they are attributable to "faulty systems, processes, and conditions that lead people to make mistakes or fail to prevent them." * * *

Not adhering to evidence-based practice or clinical practice guidelines is also a problem. One 2003 study found that Americans receive recommended evidence-based care only about 55% of the time. Recommended care was provided more often for conditions such as breast cancer (75.7%) and hypertension (64.7%) than it was for others such as a trial fibrillation (24.7%) or hip fracture (22.8%).

* * *

b. UNDER-INSURANCE PRIOR TO THE ACA

Approximately one-seventh of the U.S. population was uninsured prior to the passage of the ACA. This statistic may suggest that about 86% of the population possessed reliable insurance prior to reform. In fact, though, even *insured* Americans often enjoyed only tenuous protection from health risks prior to reform. Consider one study finding that about 80% of the families who turned to bankruptcy after a medical problem in 1999 had some form of health insurance. See Melissa Jacoby, Teresa Sullivan, & Elizabeth Warren, Rethinking the Debates over Health Care Financing: Evidence from the Bankruptcy Courts, 76 N.Y.U. L. Rev. 375, 377 (2001). The study also found that approximately 500,000 middle-class families were forced into bankruptcy following an illness or injury in 1999 and that half of all individual bankruptcies involved a medical problem. Id. Bankruptcy, of course, simply represents the worst-case financial scenario for those with medical debt—a tremendous additional number of individuals and families struck by illness presumably saw their savings compromised and their debt soar due to healthcare expenditures, even if they did not enter bankruptcy as a result. See Robert W. Seifert & Mark Rukavina, Bankruptcy Is The Tip Of A Medical-Debt Iceberg, 25 Health Aff. 89 (2006). This Section reviews several of the most important forms of under-insurance prior to reform.

(1) Moral Hazard, Cost-Sharing and Consumer-Driven Health Care

One important explanation for the cost problems in American health care is moral hazard. Some commentators have argued that health insurance coverage can result in *ex ante* moral hazard, in the form of individuals exercising less or consuming less healthy food. See Richard Epstein, Mortal Peril (1997). However, by far the dominant moral hazard concern in the health insurance context is *ex post* moral hazard, or the risk that individuals who become sick will over-consume health care because they do not pay the full cost of such care. The most famous study in health policy empirically documented this phenomenon: the Rand Health Insurance Experiment showed that individuals who were randomly assigned to health insurance policies with higher deductibles and copayments consumed less care than individuals who were randomly assigned to more complete coverage.

Health insurance universally takes various measures to reduce *ex post* moral hazard. The most familiar examples of such efforts are cost-sharing requirements in the form of deductibles (which generally apply over a policy year), coinsurance (coverage for a percentage of healthcare costs), and copayments (fixed amounts that policyholders must pay for specified services). Limits on coverage for specific services may also be designed to reduce *ex post* moral hazard. In recent decades, insurers have also become more directly involved in independently evaluating the necessity of medical interventions, managing policyholders' access to doctors and other providers, and even providing medical care directly to policyholders. We will examine the coverage issues associated with such efforts at "managed care" later in this Chapter.

Various laws and regulations attempt to encourage insurers' efforts to reduce *ex post* moral hazard, with the larger goal of reducing the healthcare cost problem. Such "consumer-driven" health care reforms generally incentivize individuals to purchase health insurance that includes large cost-sharing requirements. For instance, Health Savings Accounts (HSAs) are interest-bearing savings accounts into which individuals can make tax-free contributions in order to pay for medical expenses. These accounts must be paired with a high-deductible health insurance policy. Consistent with the Rand Health Insurance Experiment, the evidence suggests that consumer-driven health care does indeed reduce the amount of care individuals consume.

However, consumer-driven health care can create substantial risks of under-insurance. As with most efforts to limit moral hazard, consumer-driven health care shifts risk on to individuals. In many cases, this reallocation of risk to individuals can be excessive, particularly for those with a low income. See Jacob Hacker, The Great Risk Shift (2006); Timothy Stoltzfus Jost, Is Health Insurance a Bad Idea? The Consumer-Driven Perspective, 14 Conn. Ins. L.J. 377 (2008). Put simply, many individuals cannot afford the deductibles, copayments, and coinsurance that are associated with substantial unexpected health events. As a result, they may be forced to forego necessary care, particularly if they cannot clearly distinguish between care that can reasonably be put off and healthcare that is essential. Melinda Beeuwkes Buntin et al., Consumer-Directed Health Care: Early Evidence About Effects on Cost and Quality, 25 Health Aff. w516 (2006).

(2) Preexisting Condition Exclusions

Prior to the ACA, virtually all insurance policies sold in the individual market contained preexisting condition exclusions. Although the precise language of these exclusions varied, they generally stated that the insurer was not obligated to provide coverage for any sickness or injury that had in any way manifested itself prior to the purchase of coverage. The intent of these clauses was to limit the risk of adverse selection. But insurers could invoke these exclusions in a way that injected substantial uncertainty into the coverage that individuals thought they had purchased. For instance, an individual might be denied coverage for treatment of cancer that was diagnosed while coverage was in force if, before acquiring health insurance, she had received treatment for symptoms that arguably were precursors of the disease. This was true even if the precursors of the disease were seemingly minor, such as a cough, achiness, or fatigue. As a result, even people who believed they were in good health at the time they acquired coverage could find themselves facing coverage denials because of an insurer's argument that the patient had unknowingly received treatment for the condition prior to acquiring coverage. Preexisting condition exclusions have long been a smaller problem in group insurance markets, as they were substantially restricted by ERISA and another federal statute HIPAA prior to the ACA.

(3) Rescissions

As described in Chapter 1, insurers are generally free to rescind coverage on the basis of material misrepresentations made by policyholders at the time they applied for coverage. Prior to the ACA, health insurers in the individual market were no exception. (ERISA and HIPAA prohibited employers from individually underwriting their coverage, so rescissions were not an issue for employer-sponsored coverage). However, many have long claimed that some health insurers engaged in post-claim underwriting, targeting policyholders who became sick with scrutiny of their insurance applications. Leading up to the ACA's passage, an investigation and hearing by the House Committee on Energy and Commerce in 2009 documented such post-claim underwriting. It not only described cases in which insurers targeted patients with breast cancer, lymphoma and other serious conditions for scrutiny, but it also concluded that insurers frequently rescinded coverage based on trivial omissions in policyholders' applications that were innocent and/or unrelated to policyholders' illnesses. See Committee on Energy and Commerce, Case Studies: Examples of Health Insurance Companies Rescinding Individual Policies (7/27/09).

(4) Annual and Lifetime Coverage Limits

Prior to reform, many insurance policies in both group and individual markets contained annual or lifetime limits on coverage. Although systematic information about the prevalence of these coverage caps is limited, one study estimated that about 55% of individuals with employer provided health insurance were subject to lifetime limits, usually of either $1 million or $2 million. See Price Waterhouse Coopers, The Impact of Lifetime Limits (March 2009). It is likely that such limits were even more common in the individual market. In practice, these coverage limits often had the effect of cutting off health insurance coverage for people with chronic illnesses that required consistent and expensive care, such as Hemophilia, Cystic Fibrosis, or Multiple Sclerosis.

(5) Loss of Employer-Sponsored Coverage

Recall that the primary source of coverage for most Americans, both before and after the ACA, is employer-provided coverage. However, this type of coverage is inherently insecure: most employees work "at will," meaning that they can be fired or laid off for any reason. This reality was particularly problematic for those with spotty health records. Insurers on the individual market could often effectively refuse to issue insurance to those who had recently lost employer-provided coverage by charging very large premiums (an especially daunting prospect for someone who just lost a job). And even those able to find new jobs might find that illnesses from preexisting conditions were not covered under a new employer's plan, subject to ERISA and HIPAA's restrictions on preexisting condition exclusions. The loss of one's job is not the only way in which employer-provided coverage was less secure than many imagined: as described below, employers have long been free to change or drop their coverage at any time, meaning that the security employer-sponsored coverage provides is largely dependent on one's employer continuing to choose to offer this coverage.

NOTES AND QUESTIONS

1. *The Interrelations Among Coverage, Cost and Quality.* The problems associated with the American health insurance system are fundamentally interrelated. To take one example, uninsured and under-insured individuals tend to receive insufficient preventive care, meaning that potentially treatable illnesses or conditions can balloon into serious medical conditions. When this happens, they can seek treatment at hospitals' emergency rooms, which are required by the Emergency Medical Treatment and Labor Act, 42 U.S.C. § 1395dd (2005), to treat all comers, irrespective of their capacity to pay. As a result, hospitals often incur substantial losses, which are then passed on to others in the form of higher costs. See Elizabeth Weeks, After the Catastrophe: Disaster Relief for Hospitals, 85 N.C. L. Rev. 223, 230–55 (2006). In some cases, this may also result in overcrowding of emergency rooms. Cf. Manya F. Newton et al., Uninsured Adults Presenting to US Emergency Departments: Assumptions vs Data Available, 300 JAMA 1914 (2008) (although available data suggests that increasing numbers of uninsured patients present to emergency rooms, they do not support the common "assumptions that uninsured patients are a primary cause of [emergency room] overcrowding, present with less acute conditions than insured patients, or seek [emergency room] care primarily for convenience").

2. *Broader Economic Consequences.* America's healthcare problems also have broader impacts on the national economy. For instance, faced with the prospect of uninsurance or under-insurance, many employees (especially those with spotty health records) may have felt in the past that they were effectively "locked" into their jobs because pursuing a new career or small business might jeopardize their health insurance coverage (a phenomenon known as "job lock"). Even more importantly, the persistently high rate of medical care inflation has increased the cost of government healthcare programs such as Medicare and Medicaid. If costs per enrollee continued to accelerate at their pre-reform rate, then government health insurance would constitute 20% of GDP by 2050. See Peter Orszag, Health Costs Are the Real Deficit Threat, Wall St. J. (5/15/09).

3. *A Right to Healthcare?* The healthcare debate has been heavily influenced by the notion that there should be a right to healthcare. From this perspective, health insurance can be understood not simply as a privately purchased commodity but as one of several mechanisms through which that right is provided. To what extent does it make sense to use insurance—particularly privately-provided insurance—to help assure that individuals' rights are protected? More generally, is there any good reason

to use insurance, which is generally designed to protect against low-risk high-cost events, to provide acces to routine health care services?

4. *Moral Hazard in Health Insurance.* As described above, the core goal of "consumer-driven" health care is to limit the risk of moral hazard by forcing policyholders to bear more of the costs of their healthcare decisions. But moral hazard in the context of health insurance raises uniquely complicated issues, because one of the primary values of health insurance is precisely that it allows individuals to acquire medical care that they would otherwise be unable to afford. Technically, this constitutes moral hazard. Yet this effect can hardly be categorically described as socially harmful. See generally John A. Nyman, Moral and Other Hazards of Economic Analysis of Health Insurance, in The Law and Economics of Insurance (Daniel Schwarcz & Peter Siegelman eds., 2015) (distinguishing between "efficient moral hazard" and "inefficient moral hazard" in the context of health insurance). For instance, while individuals assigned to plans with high cost-sharing in the Rand Health Insurance Experiment did indeed cut back on some unnecessary care, they also chose not to consume seemingly necessary health services, such as immunizations and hypertension medications. See Joseph P. Newhouse, Consumer-Directed Health Plans and the RAND Health Insurance Experiment, 23 Health Aff. 107 (2004). To what extent do large cost-sharing requirements make sense in the case of medical interventions that are unambiguously medically necessary? Would cost-sharing requirements be more effective or fair if they were explicitly linked to policyholders' ability to pay?

5. *Coverage Limits in Health Insurance.* Virtually all forms of insurance come along with coverage limits. Such limits seem to be uncontroversial in contexts such as property/casualty and life insurance. Why do coverage limits raise unique issues in the context of health insurance? Is there a good argument for permitting insurers to include annual or lifetime coverage limits in their policies in exchange for lower premiums?

6. *Awareness of Under-Insurance Prior to Reform.* As suggested by the Congressional Research Services report, commentators have long focused on uninsurance, cost, and quality in discussing the need for healthcare reform. By contrast, the under-insurance issues discussed above often received less attention in public debates of healthcare reform. One explanation for this fact is that those who possessed health insurance prior to reform were often not fully aware of the under-insurance risks they faced. For instance, those with employer-sponsored insurance may not have realized the risks they faced if they lost their jobs. Similarly, relatively healthy people with insurance may not have realized the fact that their policies included coverage limits or preexisting condition exclusions or could be rescinded due to innocent mistakes on their insurance applications. To the extent that many insured individuals did not appreciate the health-related risks they bore prior to reform, they may also have failed to appreciate the various ways in which healthcare reform limited these risks and thus afforded them enhanced security. See Allison Hoffman, Health Care Spending and Financial Security after the Affordable Care Act, 92 N.C. L. Rev. 101 (2014) (exploring both the ways in which healthcare reform limits risk and the ways in which it fails to do so).

3. THE ACA'S REFORM OF HEALTH INSURANCE

As of January 1, 2014, almost all of the ACA's core provisions have gone into effect. The principal goals of these provisions are to guarantee the availability of health insurance, close gaps in coverage, and make health insurance affordable for individuals. The extent to which the ACA also addresses the cost and quality issues described above is more debatable. As of publication, it is still too early to assess how well the ACA has achieved its objectives. The following discussion describes three core areas of health insurance reform in the ACA: (a) reforms of private health insurance, (b) mandates, subsidies, and taxes relating to insurance, and (c) public insurance reforms.

a. REFORMS OF PRIVATE HEALTH INSURANCE

The ACA includes a broad range of provisions governing the terms and sale of health insurance. Many of these reforms apply to "all health insurance plans," a category that includes insurance purchased in individual and group markets as well as self-insured employer plans. However, some of the ACA's regulatory reforms apply only to insurance policies sold in the individual market or to small employer groups (employers with under fifty employees), but not to those that are sold to large groups or to self-insured employer plans. And a few ACA provisions apply to all insurance plans, but not to self-insured employer plans. In general, the ACA's regulatory reforms of private health insurance can be subdivided into three categories: (1) reforms governing the pricing, offering, and renewal of coverage, (2) reforms governing the content of coverage, and (3) the creation of insurance exchanges.

(1) The ACA's Regulation of Insurers' Pricing, Offering, and Renewal of Coverage

Extension of Dependent Coverage. The ACA requires that all health insurance plans permit policyholders to claim children up to 26 years old who do not have their own coverage as dependents on their own policies. ACA § 1001 (adding § 2714 to the Public Health Service Act (PHSA)).

Prohibition of Rescissions. Under the ACA, all health insurance plans are prohibited from rescinding or cancelling coverage, except for fraud or an intentional misrepresentation of a material fact. ACA § 1001 (adding § 2712 to the PHSA).

Regulation of Medical Loss Ratios. The ACA requires all insurers (but not employers with self-funded plans) to provide Health and Human Services (HHS) with a report documenting their Medical Loss Ratio (MLR). The MLR is equal to the percentage of total premium revenue that the insurer expends on "on reimbursement for clinical services," "activities that improve health care quality," and certain related expenses. ACA § 1001 (adding § 2718(a) to the PHSA). Because insurer profits and administrative expenses are excluded from this tally, the MLR effectively operates as a cap on the sum of profits and administrative expenses. Insurers must provide rebates to their policyholders when their MLRs drop below 85% in the large group market or 80% in the small group and individual markets (i.e. when the sum of their profits and administrative expenses exceed 15% or 20%, respectively). HHS, in consultation with the NAIC, developed detailed regulations on the calculation of the MLR. See 77 Fed. Reg. 70584–70617 (2012). The issue provoked extensive debate about how to account for expenses such as disease management programs, nurse hotlines, quality assurance oversight, health information technology expenses and fraud prevention. All such programs arguably straddle the line between administrative expenses and expenditures that improve the health of policyholders. See Timothy Stoltzfus Jost, Writing New Rules for Insurers—Progress on the Medical Loss Ratio, 363 N. Eng. J. Med. 1883 (2010).

Rate Regulation. The ACA directs HHS, in conjunction with the states, to establish a process for the annual review of "unreasonable" premium increases. ACA § 1003 (adding § 2794 to the PHSA). HHS issued final rules on this topic in 2013. See 78 Fed. Reg. 13406–13442 (2013). The ACA does not give power to states or HHS to prohibit these rate increases, but it instead requires the public posting of rate increases that are deemed unreasonable. Some states, however, do allow their departments of insurance to deny rate increases, using the same basic process for assessing proposed rate increases that we examined in Chapter 3.

Community Rating and Other Premium Restrictions. The ACA requires health insurers in the individual and group market not to condition premiums on policyholder characteristics other than age, rating areas, individual or family enrollment, and tobacco use. ACA § 1001 (adding § 2701 to the PHSA). Even these factors are limited in the impact they can have on premiums: premiums based on age cannot vary by more than a ratio of 3 to 1, and they cannot vary based on tobacco use by more than a ratio of 1.5 to 1. These rules limit insurer pricing of individual and group insurance policies, but they do not apply to the rates that can be charged to the individual employees within an employer group. As noted above, preexisting law in ERISA and HIPAA requires that, in most cases, all employees must be charged the same premiums for coverage. However, for employer-sponsored plans, the ACA does permit premium discounts of up to 30% to be offered to individual employees if they participate in certain "wellness" programs, as long as these are not a subterfuge for discriminating on the basis of health status. In 2013, HHS and several other federal agencies issued final regulatory roles implementing these provisions. See 78 Fed. Reg. 33158–33192 (2013).

Guaranteed Issue and Renewal: Except in limited cases, insurers in the individual and group markets are required to offer and renew coverage to any individual or employer who applies. ACA § 1001 (adding §§ 2702, 2703 to the PHSA).

(2) The ACA's Regulation of the Content of Coverage

Prohibition on Annual and Lifetime Limits. The ACA prohibits all health insurance plans from imposing lifetime or annual limits. ACA § 1001 (adding § 2711 to the PHSA).

Coverage for Preventive Care with No Cost Sharing. The ACA requires that all health insurance plans must cover without any cost-sharing certain preventive care (e.g., immunizations). ACA § 1001 (adding § 2713 to the PHSA Act). After passage of the ACA, HHS promulgated regulations providing that contraceptives constitute covered preventive care, thereby requiring all insurance plans, including employer sponsored health plans, to provide contraceptive coverage with no cost sharing. 77 Fed. Reg. 8725–8726 (2012). This regulation generated a wave of protests from employers who argued that compliance conflicted with their religious convictions. In *Burwell v. Hobby Lobby Stores, Inc.*, 134 S.Ct. 2751 (2014), the Supreme Court held that the law violated the Religious Freedom Restoration Act (RFRA), at least for closely-held corporate employers. That holding, in turn, generated a wave of (so far unsuccessful) efforts among Democrats to overturn *Hobby Lobby* by statute.

Essential Health Benefits. All health insurance coverage offered in the individual or small group markets must provide "[e]ssential health benefits," or EHBs. ACA § 1302. Importantly, as described more fully below, large and self-insured employers are not required to offer plans containing EHBs. EHBs must include ten broad categories of services specified in the statute—including hospitalization, ambulatory care, maternity care, and prescription drug coverage—and must be comparable to the benefits provided in "a typical employer plan." These parameters are quite broad, and the ACA gives authority to HHS to define them with more specificity. In 2013, HHS released the final regulations defining EHBs, after a prolonged process. See 78 Fed. Reg. 12834–12872 (2013). The regulations did not define a uniform national set of essential health benefits, as most had anticipated and as the language of the ACA seems to contemplate. Instead, it required each state to establish an individualized EHB that would be based on a "benchmark" plan to be chosen by the state. One important implication of this approach is that states have not been forced to modify their own state mandated benefit laws in order to avoid owing funds to the federal government. A provision in the ACA created this risk by providing that states must reimburse the federal government for state-specific coverage mandates that exceed EHBs. HHS's approach eliminates the prospect of such a charge by allowing states to define EHBs using a benchmark plan that includes all state insurance mandates.

Cost-Sharing Restrictions. The ACA limits out of pocket expenses—including all copayments, coinsurance, and deductibles—to an amount set by the rules governing Health Savings Accounts (HSA). ACA § 1302. In 2014, the maximum out of pocket limits for HSA plans were $6,350 for self-only coverage and $12,700 for families. Other than these restrictions, though, the ACA does not broadly limit the ability of plans to utilize consumer-driven health insurance strategies.

Prohibition of Preexisting Condition Exclusions. Since January 2014, all health insurance plans have been prohibited from including preexisting condition exclusions in their policies. ACA § 1201 (adding § 2704 to the PHSA).

Grandfathered Plans. Insurance plans in existence at the time of the ACA's enactment are generally not required by the ACA to alter their coverage, despite the above requirements. ACA § 1251. There are a few exceptions: grandfathered plans are subject to the rules governing rescissions, lifetime limits, and the extension of coverage to dependents.

Grandfathered plans that are also group plans are subject to the provisions governing annual limits.

(3) The ACA's Creation of Health Insurance Exchanges

Since January 2014, an insurance exchange has been available in every state to facilitate the purchase of health insurance by individuals and small groups (employers with fewer than 50 employees). ACA §§ 1311–12. Insurance exchanges operate primarily to facilitate effective consumer shopping among different private health insurance plans on an apples-to-apples basis. Within an insurance exchange, only "Qualified Health Plans" may be offered by insurers, and such plans must not only include essential health benefits, but also meet several other requirements, such as maintaining an adequate network of providers. Premium support and cost-sharing subsidies (described below) are only available to individuals who purchase their coverage on an insurance exchange. However, the ACA does not prohibit insurance policies from being sold outside of an insurance exchange.

The ACA permits each state to establish its own insurance exchange. If a state does not choose to do so, then the Act authorizes the federal government to do so in its place. As of publication, approximately half of the states operate part or all of their own insurance exchange, with the remainder refusing to operate their own exchange and thus relying on a federally-facilitated exchange (www.healthcare.gov).

b. HEALTH INSURANCE MANDATES, SUBSIDIES, AND TAXES UNDER THE ACA

In addition to extensive reforms of the rules governing private insurance, the ACA includes a substantial number of tax and spending provisions.

(1) The Individual Mandate/Tax

Since January 2014, most individuals must either have "minimum essential coverage" or make a "shared responsibility payment" in the form of a tax penalty. ACA § 1501. This is the "individual mandate" that has received so much public attention and that is the subject of the U.S. Supreme Court decision set out below. One potentially important exception to this requirement is that individuals are not required to acquire minimum essential coverage if they cannot afford such coverage. The statute defines a person as being unable to afford coverage if that person's health insurance premium would exceed 8% of household income. Individuals who receive subsidies to purchase coverage (described below) may find that they can indeed "afford" coverage under this provision. But it is entirely possible that individuals and families who just miss receiving subsidies, or who receive only small subsidies, will be unable to acquire coverage for less than 8% of their income.

The ACA defines "minimum essential coverage" very broadly. It includes both any employer-sponsored plan and any health plan offered in the individual market in a state. The shared responsibility payment—the tax paid for not purchasing coverage—will eventually be the greater of $695 per adult (and a lesser sum for each child) or 2.5% of the excess of household income over the threshold that requires filing a federal income tax return.

(2) Individual Subsidies

For eligible individuals, the ACA makes available a sliding-scale tax credit for premium reductions. ACA §§ 1401, 1402. Individuals with incomes of up to 400% of the federal poverty line are eligible for these subsidies, with the subsidy level increasing as income decreases. In 2014, the federal poverty line for a family of four was approximately $24,000 a year in income, meaning that a family of four earning up to $96,000 would be eligible for subsidies. For individuals with incomes of up to 250% of the federal poverty line, the ACA also includes subsidies designed to reduce cost-sharing by limiting out-of-pocket expenses. Both subsidies are only available to individuals who purchase individual insurance through an exchange.

(3) Employer Mandate/Tax

The ACA provides that, starting in 2014, employers with at least 50 employees are subject to a shared responsibility payment if any of their employees purchase insurance through an exchange and receive individual subsidies. ACA § 1315. HHS postponed operation of this "employer mandate" to 2015. The policy behind this provision is to encourage large employers to offer satisfactory coverage to their employees. The employer mandate is also intended to prevent employers from attempting to induce their employees to take advantage of the individual subsidies that are available through the insurance exchanges. This is a particularly salient risk for employers of low-income employees, both because low-income employees can receive comparatively large subsidies on the insurance exchanges and because the tax subsidies associated with any employer-sponsored coverage they receive are relatively small.

If employers do not offer "minimum essential coverage" through an employer-sponsored plan and have employees receiving individual subsidies, they must make a payment determined by the lesser of (i) $3000 for each employee receiving a premium credit or (ii) $2000 for each full-time employee excluding the first thirty employees. For employers who do offer "minimum essential coverage," the amount of their shared responsibility payment is determined by multiplying the number of employees who receive individual subsidies on an exchange by $3000 per year. This shared responsibility payment cannot exceed the amount that would have been due if the employer did not offer its employees minimum essential coverage.

(4) Cadillac Tax

Starting in 2018, a 40% tax will be imposed on employer-sponsored health plans to the extent that their aggregate value exceeds a threshold level. ACA § 9001. The threshold limits are $10,200 for an individual plan and $27,500 for a family plan. Both thresholds are multiplied by a health cost adjustment measure, and additional adjustments are included to ensure that employers with a comparatively old or sick workforce are not disadvantaged by this provision.

(5) Small Employer Subsidies

Starting shortly after the ACA's passage, eligible small employers who offered their employees coverage and paid at least 50% of the cost of premiums were permitted to claim a sliding scale tax credit. ACA § 1421. Employers are eligible for the credit only if they have 25 or fewer full time employees and the average annual compensation of these employees is less than $50,000. Since the insurance exchanges were established in 2014, small employers must participate in the exchange in order to receive this credit. Employers are only eligible to receive this credit in two tax years. According to a 2012 Government Accountability Report, 170,300 employers claimed this credit in 2010, far short of initial estimates.

c. PUBLIC INSURANCE REFORMS UNDER THE ACA

In addition to substantially altering the rules governing private insurance markets and establishing various subsidies and taxes, the ACA radically changes various features of the two core public insurance programs, Medicare and Medicaid.

(1) Medicaid Eligibility

As described above, Medicaid eligibility historically varied substantially by state, and was typically available only to certain segments of the very poor or disabled populations. The reason for this variability is that Medicaid is a cooperative federalism program: the federal government establishes broad rules about how Medicaid must operate and makes funds available to states, which then establish programs satisfying these rules. The ACA attempted to substantially reform Medicaid by expanding eligibility so that, starting in 2014, the program would extend to everyone in the population below 133% of the federal poverty line. ACA §§ 2001–2007. The federal government funds the vast majority of the costs of this expansion of Medicaid coverage. However, as described more fully below, the Supreme Court's decision in *National Federation of Independent Business et al. v. Sebelius*, 132 S. Ct. 2566 (2012), held that Constitutional principles require that states must be free to reject this Medicaid expansion without jeopardizing federal funding for their preexisting Medicaid programs.

(2) Medicare and Medicaid Payment Reforms

The ACA contains numerous provisions impacting Medicare and Medicaid's payment of providers. Although quite technical, these reforms represent one of the central cost-control measures in the ACA. See Peter R. Orszag & Ezekiel J. Emanuel, Health Care Reform and Cost Control, 363 New England J. of Med. 601 (2010). In combination with several other ACA provisions described above—including rate regulation, MLR rules, the Cadillac tax, and insurance exchanges—the goal of these reforms is to reduce the rate of health care inflation so that private insurance becomes more affordable and Medicare and Medicaid become less of a fiscal burden.

To accomplish this, the ACA's payment reforms for Medicare and Medicaid are intended to promote a shift away from "fee for service" payment of health care providers. Many commentators identify fee for service payment methods as a core driver of the healthcare cost problem. Simply put, paying doctors and other healthcare providers for each service they provide incentivizes them to provide too much care, because they are paid more when they provide more medical services. The payment reforms in Medicare and Medicaid seek to instead pay providers on the basis of the outcomes they produce for patients rather than on the quantity of care they provide. To the extent that these reforms prove successful in Medicare and Medicaid, the hope is that private insurers will mimic them. There is substantial precedent for payment reforms in Medicare migrating into the private insurance sector. See Stuart Gutterman et al., Innovation In Medicare and Medicaid Will Be Central To Health Reform's Success, 29 Health Aff. 1188 (2010).

Perhaps the most important payment reform in the ACA establishes a program through which providers can organize as Accountable Care Organizations (ACOs). ACA § 3022 (adding § 1829 to the Social Security Act). To the extent that ACOs meet specific quality thresholds and generate savings in the cost of caring for Medicare enrollees, then they can share in these savings. As with virtually all of the ACA's provisions, federal agencies have promulgated extensive regulations governing the details of how these programs will operate. See 76 Fed. Reg. 67802–67990 (2012). Another payment reform provision reduces Medicare and Medicaid reimbursements for preventable hospital readmissions. ACA § 3025. In addition to these specific payment reform plans, the ACA establishes the Center for Medicare and Medicaid Innovation to test additional payment and service delivery models that may reduce costs while preserving quality.

NOTES AND QUESTIONS

1. *The ACA's Response to Uninsurance and Underinsurance.* How well does the ACA address the uninsurance and under-insurance problems described above? Which provisions of the ACA are most important in limiting uninsurance and under-insurance? How substantially does the ACA reduce health-related risk for the American population, including both the risk of being unable to access needed medical care and the risk of experiencing a substantial monetary loss due to large medical needs?

2. *Prohibiting Health Insurers from Assessing Policyholder Risk.* Many of the ACA's core regulatory reforms effectively prohibit health insurers from using standard insurance tools that link coverage terms, premiums and policyholder eligibility to insurers' assessments of policyholder risk. By comparison, the restrictions imposed on life and property/casualty insurers' underwriting, rating and coverage are negligible. What accounts for the ACA's fundamentally different treatment of health insurance? Why shouldn't insurers be able to charge higher premiums or offer more limited coverage to those who present higher health-related risks? Why does healthcare reform allow older individuals and those who smoke to be charged higher premiums, but not permit charging higher premiums to individuals who are obese or who injure themselves in extreme sporting events, for instance? For insightful analysis

of these questions, see Tom Baker, Health Insurance, Risk and Responsibility After the Affordable Care Act, 159 Penn. L. Rev. 1577, 1578–1606 (2011); Wendy K. Mariner, The Affordable Care Act and Health Promotion: The Role of Insurance in Defining Responsibility for Health Risks and Costs, 50 Duquesne L. Rev. 271 (2012); Allison Hoffman, Oil and Water: Mixing Individual Mandates, Fragmented Markets, and Health Reform, 36 Am. J. of Law & Med. 7 (2010).

The ACA's efforts to limit health insurers' use of standard insurance tools faces a fundamental difficulty: for-profit insurers inevitably face strong competitive pressures to employ these tools, as we learned at the very start of Chapter One. It is easy enough for the ACA to prohibit the most obvious approaches to classifying risks, such as charging more to those with spotty health records or denying coverage for preexisting conditions. But it may be much harder for the ACA to limit more subtle attempts by insurers to attract less risky policyholders. For instance, insurers might devise marketing strategies, benefit packages, or provider networks that disproportionately appeal to young and/or healthy policyholders. Anticipating this, the ACA employs various risk-sharing and reinsurance regimes that are intended to limit the benefits and costs to insurers of having a relatively healthy or unhealthy set of policyholders. See generally Mark A. Hall, The Three Types of Reinsurance Created by Federal Health Care Reform, 29 Health Aff. 1168 (2010). The effectiveness of these regimes remains to be seen.

3. *Preventing Adverse Selection.* Because the ACA largely eliminates the capacity of insurers to link coverage and premiums to risk, it obviously creates a substantial risk of adverse selection. In its most extreme form, this would manifest itself in individuals waiting to purchase coverage until they became very ill. But adverse selection also might take more subtle forms, such as relatively young and/or healthy individuals purchasing less comprehensive coverage. The ACA employs various techniques to combat these threats. Perhaps the most important, and certainly the most controversial, is the "individual mandate," which we will examine in greater detail later in this Chapter when we focus on the Supreme Court case on the topic. But other elements of the ACA are also central to stemming the risk of adverse selection. First, the individual subsidies available through the insurance exchanges reduce the effective cost of coverage for many relatively low-risk policyholders. Second, the ACA allows individuals to be charged premiums on the basis of their age and smoking history (within specified limits). Third, individuals under thirty or who can establish a hardship exemption can purchase limited, and cheaper, catastrophic coverage. Fourth, insurance is generally only available through an insurance exchange during designated open enrollment periods or in the case of a qualifying event, such as the loss of one's job. How do each of these design features limit the risk of adverse selection against insurance exchanges? How effective do you think they will be in limiting adverse selection? If you did not (or do not) currently have health insurance, would you purchase coverage through an insurance exchange for an amount that exceeded what you expected your total healthcare costs would be in the next year?

4. *Implementing Healthcare Reform.* The ACA left an extraordinary amount of work to be done by HHS in implementing healthcare reform. This role has proven to be even more significant than anticipated by the

ACA, given the refusal of many states to operate their own insurance exchanges or otherwise cooperate in the Act's implementation. HHS has clearly experienced mixed success in these ongoing implementation efforts. The most publicly-visible implementation failure was the technical "glitches" that initially plagued the federal insurance exchange in late 2013. Shortly after open-enrollment first began in the federal insurance exchange, the website healthcare.gov—the primary entry-point to the federal insurance exchange—repeatedly crashed. In response, President Obama ordered a "technology surge" that ultimately proved relatively successful in remedying most of the major technical problems of the insurance exchange. For critics of healthcare reform, this embarrassing rollout of the federal insurance exchange was yet further proof of the fact that the ACA relies too heavily on inherently-limited federal bureaucracies to accomplish what should be left to the private market. For supporters of the law, the bumpy rollout of the insurance exchanges was a one-time problem caused both by poor leadership at HHS and by the active resistance to reform by Republican-led states and federal Republican lawmakers.

5. *"If You Like Your Coverage You Can Keep It."* During the lengthy debate preceding the Affordable Care Act, President Obama repeatedly stated that, under the act, "if you like your coverage, you can keep it." This commitment was intended to limit the force of political attacks warning that people could lose their insurance coverage as a result of healthcare reform; such attacks had proven extremely successful in undermining the Clinton Administration's "HillaryCare" healthcare reform proposal in the early 1990s. However, towards the end of 2013, many individuals were informed by their carriers that their coverage was being cancelled because it did not comply with the ACA's restrictions that came into effect in 2014. These cancellation notices caused a storm of protest and claims that President Obama lied in selling healthcare reform to the American public. The core explanation for the discrepancy lies in the fact that the plans that were non-renewed were not eligible for grandfathered status, either because they were established after the ACA was passed or because they made significant changes in their design or cost structure since that time. See generally Elizabeth Weeks Leonard, Can You Really Keep Your Health Plan? The Limits of Grandfathering Under the Affordable Care Act, 36 J. Corp. L. 753 (2011). Did the ACA go as far as President Obama's public assurances suggested it would in protecting policyholders against the risk that their coverage would be altered as a result of the law? Independent of any public confusion on the issue, to what extent is it a bad thing that policies failing to meet the ACA's requirements were non-renewed and are no longer being sold?

6. *The Fiscal Cost of HealthCare Reform.* A core concern about the ACA is that it creates a massive new source of government spending that may negatively influence the country's long-term fiscal health. The primary sources of this spending are the Act's subsidies for coverage purchased on insurance exchanges and its expansion of Medicaid. However, a very influential report from the Congressional Budget Office, produced shortly before the ACA was finally enacted, concluded that the ACA was fully paid for by its revenue-raising provisions (particularly certain payment reforms to Medicare), and will ultimately reduce the size of the federal deficit. However, critics have raised legitimate concerns about the CBO report. See Douglas Holtz-Eakin, The Real Arithmetic of Health Care Reform, N.Y.

Times (3/20/10). In particular, the CBO projections were based on crucial assumptions that everyone agrees are unrealistic—for example, it assumed that employers will not change the healthcare options they offer in response to the implementation of the Cadillac Tax. In fact, some of the criteria that the CBO was required to use to project costs were explicitly gamed by the ACA's designers. For instance, the CBO's projections were based on a ten-year time horizon. Knowing this, the drafters reduced the ten-year fiscal impact of some provisions by delaying their implementation. At the same time, the rate of healthcare inflation since the ACA's passage has declined dramatically as of mid-2014. As a result, so too has the government's spending on Medicare and Medicaid. If this effect persists—as the CBO has recently projected it will—then it will more than offset the ACA's direct costs.

4. Constitutional Challenges to the ACA

Almost immediately after the ACA's passage, various state Attorneys General instituted lawsuits claiming that portions of the Act violated the federal Constitution. Two of these challenges resulted in the most high-profile decision of the Supreme Court since *Bush v. Gore*. The first challenged the constitutionality of the individual mandate, and the second challenged the expansion of Medicaid. In the following case, the Supreme Court upheld the constitutionality of the individual mandate and determined that the Medicaid expansion was also permissible so long as states that refused to expand coverage as contemplated by the ACA would not thereby lose the Medicaid funding they had received prior to the ACA's expansion of the program.

National Federation of Independent Business et al. v. Sebelius

Supreme Court of the United States, 2012.
132 S.Ct. 2566.

■ CHIEF JUSTICE ROBERTS announced the judgment of the Court and delivered the opinion of the Court with respect to Parts I, II, and III–C, an opinion with respect to Part IV, in which JUSTICE BREYER and JUSTICE KAGAN join, and an opinion with respect to Parts III–A, III–B, and III–D.

Today we resolve constitutional challenges to two provisions of the Patient Protection and Affordable Care Act of 2010: the individual mandate, which requires individuals to purchase a health insurance policy providing a minimum level of coverage; and the Medicaid expansion, which gives funds to the States on the condition that they provide specified health care to all citizens whose income falls below a certain threshold. We do not consider whether the Act embodies sound policies. That judgment is entrusted to the Nation's elected leaders. We ask only whether Congress has the power under the Constitution to enact the challenged provisions. * * *

I

In 2010, Congress enacted the Patient Protection and Affordable Care Act, 124 Stat. 119. The Act aims to increase the number of Americans covered by health insurance and decrease the cost of health care. The Act's 10 titles stretch over 900 pages and contain hundreds of provisions. This case concerns constitutional challenges to two key provisions, commonly referred to as the individual mandate and the Medicaid expansion.

The individual mandate requires most Americans to maintain "minimum essential" health insurance coverage. 26 U.S.C. § 5000A. The mandate does not apply to some individuals, such as prisoners and undocumented aliens. § 5000A(d). Many individuals will receive the required coverage through their employer, or from a government program such as Medicaid or Medicare. See § 5000A(f). But for individuals who are not exempt and do not receive health insurance through a third party, the means of satisfying the requirement is to purchase insurance from a private company.

Beginning in 2014, those who do not comply with the mandate must make a "[s]hared responsibility payment" to the Federal Government. § 5000A(b)(1). That payment, which the Act describes as a "penalty," is calculated as a percentage of household income, subject to a floor based on a specified dollar amount and a ceiling based on the average annual premium the individual would have to pay for qualifying private health insurance. § 5000A(c). In 2016, for example, the penalty will be 2.5 percent of an individual's household income, but no less than $695 and no more than the average yearly premium for insurance that covers 60 percent of the cost of 10 specified services (*e.g.*, prescription drugs and hospitalization). *Ibid.*; 42 U.S.C. § 18022. The Act provides that the penalty will be paid to the Internal Revenue Service with an individual's taxes, and "shall be assessed and collected in the same manner" as tax penalties, such as the penalty for claiming too large an income tax refund. 26 U.S.C. § 5000A(g)(1). The Act, however, bars the IRS from using several of its normal enforcement tools, such as criminal prosecutions and levies. § 5000A(g)(2). And some individuals who are subject to the mandate are nonetheless exempt from the penalty—for example, those with income below a certain threshold and members of Indian tribes. § 5000A(e).

On the day the President signed the Act into law, Florida and 12 other States filed a complaint in the Federal District Court for the Northern District of Florida. Those plaintiffs—who are both respondents and petitioners here, depending on the issue—were subsequently joined by 13 more States, several individuals, and the National Federation of Independent Business. The plaintiffs alleged, among other things, that the individual mandate provisions of the Act exceeded Congress's powers under Article I of the Constitution. * * *

III

The Government advances two theories for the proposition that Congress had constitutional authority to enact the individual mandate. First, the Government argues that Congress had the power to enact the mandate under the Commerce Clause. Under that theory, Congress may order individuals to buy health insurance because the failure to do so affects interstate commerce, and could undercut the Affordable Care Act's other reforms. Second, the Government argues that if the commerce power does not support the mandate, we should nonetheless uphold it as an exercise of Congress's power to tax. According to the Government, even if Congress lacks the power to direct individuals to buy insurance, the only effect of the individual mandate is to raise taxes on those who do not do so, and thus the law may be upheld as a tax.

A

The Government's first argument is that the individual mandate is a valid exercise of Congress's power under the Commerce Clause and the Necessary and Proper Clause. According to the Government, the health care market is characterized by a significant cost-shifting problem. Everyone will eventually need health care at a time and to an extent they cannot predict, but if they do not have insurance, they often will not be able to pay for it. Because state and federal laws nonetheless require hospitals to provide a certain degree of care to individuals without regard to their ability to pay, see, *e.g.*, 42 U.S.C. § 1395dd; Fla. Stat. Ann. § 395.1041, hospitals end up receiving compensation for only a portion of the services they provide. To recoup the losses, hospitals pass on the cost to insurers through higher rates, and insurers, in turn, pass on the cost to policy holders in the form of higher premiums. Congress estimated that the cost of uncompensated care raises family health insurance premiums, on average, by over $1,000 per year. 42 U.S.C. § 18091(2)(F).

In the Affordable Care Act, Congress addressed the problem of those who cannot obtain insurance coverage because of preexisting conditions or other health issues. It did so through the Act's "guaranteed-issue" and "community-rating" provisions. These provisions together prohibit insurance companies from denying coverage to those with such conditions or charging unhealthy individuals higher premiums than healthy individuals. See §§ 300gg, 300gg–1, 300gg–3,300gg–4.

The guaranteed-issue and community-rating reforms do not, however, address the issue of healthy individuals who choose not to purchase insurance to cover potential health care needs. In fact, the reforms sharply exacerbate that problem, by providing an incentive for individuals to delay purchasing health insurance until they become sick, relying on the promise of guaranteed and affordable coverage. The reforms also threaten to impose massive new costs on insurers, who are required to accept unhealthy individuals but prohibited from charging them rates necessary to pay for their coverage. This will lead insurers to significantly increase premiums on everyone. See Brief for America's Health Insurance Plans et al. as *Amici Curiae* in No. 11–393 etc. 8–9.

The individual mandate was Congress's solution to these problems. By requiring that individuals purchase health insurance, the mandate prevents cost-shifting by those who would otherwise go without it. In addition, the mandate forces into the insurance risk pool more healthy individuals, whose premiums on average will be higher than their health care expenses. This allows insurers to subsidize the costs of covering the unhealthy individuals the reforms require them to accept. The Government claims that Congress has power under the Commerce and Necessary and Proper Clauses to enact this solution. * * *

The Government contends that the individual mandate is within Congress's power because the failure to purchase insurance "has a substantial and deleterious effect on interstate commerce" by creating the cost-shifting problem. Brief for United States 34. The path of our

Commerce Clause decisions has not always run smooth, see *United States v. Lopez*, 514 U.S. 549, 552–559 (1995), but it is now well established that Congress has broad authority under the Clause. We have recognized, for example, that "[t]he power of Congress over interstate commerce is not confined to the regulation of commerce among the states," but extends to activities that "have a substantial effect on interstate commerce." *United States v. Darby*, 312 U.S. 100, 118–119 (1941). Congress's power, moreover, is not limited to regulation of an activity that by itself substantially affects interstate commerce, but also extends to activities that do so only when aggregated with similar activities of others. See *Wickard*, 317 U.S., at 127–128.

Given its expansive scope, it is no surprise that Congress has employed the commerce power in a wide variety of ways to address the pressing needs of the time. But Congress has never attempted to rely on that power to compel individuals not engaged in commerce to purchase an unwanted product.[1] Legislative novelty is not necessarily fatal; there is a first time for everything. But sometimes "the most telling indication of [a] severe constitutional problem . . . is the lack of historical precedent" for Congress's action. *Free Enterprise Fund v. Public Company Accounting Oversight Bd.*, 561 U.S. ___ (2010) (internal quotation marks omitted). At the very least, we should "pause to consider the implications of the Government's arguments" when confronted with such new conceptions of federal power. *Lopez, supra*, at 564. * * *

The individual mandate [ ] does not regulate existing commercial activity. It instead compels individuals to become active in commerce by purchasing a product, on the ground that their failure to do so affects interstate commerce. Construing the Commerce Clause to permit Congress to regulate individuals precisely because they are doing nothing would open a new and potentially vast domain to congressional authority. Every day individuals do not do an infinite number of things. In some cases they decide not to do something; in others they simply fail to do it. Allowing Congress to justify federal regulation by pointing to the effect of inaction on commerce would bring countless decisions an individual could potentially make within the scope of federal regulation, and—under the Government's theory—empower Congress to make those decisions for him. * * *

The individual mandate's regulation of the uninsured as a class is, in fact, particularly divorced from any link to existing commercial activity. The mandate primarily affects healthy, often young adults who are less likely to need significant health care and have other priorities for spending their money. It is precisely because these individuals, as an actuarial class, incur relatively low health care costs that the mandate helps counter the effect of forcing insurance companies to

---

[1] The other examples of congressional mandates cited by Justice GINSBURG, *post*, at ___, n. 10 (opinion concurring in part, concurring in judgment in part, and dissenting in part), are not to the contrary. Each of those mandates—to report for jury duty, to register for the draft, to purchase firearms in anticipation of militia service, to exchange gold currency for paper currency, and to file a tax return—are based on constitutional provisions other than the Commerce Clause. See Art. I, § 8, cl. 9 (to "constitute Tribunals inferior to the supreme Court"); id., cl. 12 (to "raise and support Armies"); id., cl. 16 (to "provide for organizing, arming, and disciplining, the Militia"); id., cl. 5 (to "coin" Money); id., cl. 1 (to "lay and collect Taxes").

cover others who impose greater costs than their premiums are allowed to reflect. See 42 U.S.C. § 18091(2)(I) (recognizing that the mandate would "broaden the health insurance risk pool to include healthy individuals, which will lower health insurance premiums"). If the individual mandate is targeted at a class, it is a class whose commercial inactivity rather than activity is its defining feature. * * *

The individual mandate forces individuals into commerce precisely because they elected to refrain from commercial activity. Such a law cannot be sustained under a clause authorizing Congress to "regulate Commerce." * * *

B

That is not the end of the matter. Because the Commerce Clause does not support the individual mandate, it is necessary to turn to the Government's second argument: that the mandate may be upheld as within Congress's enumerated power to "lay and collect Taxes." Art. I, § 8, cl. 1.

The Government's tax power argument asks us to view the statute differently than we did in considering its commerce power theory. In making its Commerce Clause argument, the Government defended the mandate as a regulation requiring individuals to purchase health insurance. The Government does not claim that the taxing power allows Congress to issue such a command. Instead, the Government asks us to read the mandate not as ordering individuals to buy insurance, but rather as imposing a tax on those who do not buy that product.

The text of a statute can sometimes have more than one possible meaning. To take a familiar example, a law that reads "no vehicles in the park" might, or might not, ban bicycles in the park. And it is well established that if a statute has two possible meanings, one of which violates the Constitution, courts should adopt the meaning that does not do so. Justice Story said that 180 years ago: "No court ought, unless the terms of an act rendered it unavoidable, to give a construction to it which should involve a violation, however unintentional, of the constitution." *Parsons v. Bedford*, 3 Pet. 433, 448–449 (1830). Justice Holmes made the same point a century later: "[T]he rule is settled that as between two possible interpretations of a statute, by one of which it would be unconstitutional and by the other valid, our plain duty is to adopt that which will save the Act." *Blodgett v. Holden*, 275 U.S. 142, 148 (concurring opinion).

The most straightforward reading of the mandate is that it commands individuals to purchase insurance. After all, it states that individuals "shall" maintain health insurance. 26 U.S.C. § 5000A(a). Congress thought it could enact such a command under the Commerce Clause, and the Government primarily defended the law on that basis. But, for the reasons explained above, the Commerce Clause does not give Congress that power. Under our precedent, it is therefore necessary to ask whether the Government's alternative reading of the statute—that it only imposes a tax on those without insurance—is a reasonable one.

Under the mandate, if an individual does not maintain health insurance, the only consequence is that he must make an additional payment to the IRS when he pays his taxes. See § 5000A(b). That, according to the Government, means the mandate can be regarded as establishing a condition—not owning health insurance—that triggers a tax—the required payment to the IRS. Under that theory, the mandate is not a legal command to buy insurance. Rather, it makes going without insurance just another thing the Government taxes, like buying gasoline or earning income. And if the mandate is in effect just a tax hike on certain taxpayers who do not have health insurance, it may be within Congress's constitutional power to tax.

The question is not whether that is the most natural interpretation of the mandate, but only whether it is a "fairly possible" one. *Crowell v. Benson*, 285 U.S. 22, 62 (1932). As we have explained, "every reasonable construction must be resorted to, in order to save a statute from unconstitutionality. *Hooper v. California*, 155 U.S. 648, 657 (1895). The Government asks us to interpret the mandate as imposing a tax, if it would otherwise violate the Constitution. Granting the Act the full measure of deference owed to federal statutes, it can be so read, for the reasons set forth below.

C

The exaction the Affordable Care Act imposes on those without health insurance looks like a tax in many respects. The "[s]hared responsibility payment," as the statute entitles it, is paid into the Treasury by "taxpayer[s]" when they file their tax returns. 26 U.S.C. § 5000A(b). It does not apply to individuals who do not pay federal income taxes because their household income is less than the filing threshold in the Internal Revenue Code § 5000A(e)(2). For taxpayers who do owe the payment, its amount is determined by such familiar factors as taxable income, number of dependents, and joint filing status. § 5000A(b)(3), (c)(2), (c)(4). The requirement to pay is found in the Internal Revenue Code and enforced by the IRS, which—as we previously explained—must assess and collect it "in the same manner as taxes." Supra. This process yields the essential feature of any tax: it produces at least some revenue for the Government. *United States v. Kahriger*, 345 U.S. 22, 28, n. 4 (1953). Indeed, the payment is expected to raise about $4 billion per year by 2017. Congressional Budget Office, Payments of Penalties for Being Uninsured Under the Patient Protection and Affordable Care Act (Apr. 30, 2010), in Selected CBO Publications Related to Health Care Legislation, 2009–2010, p. 71 (rev. 2010). * * *

The same analysis here suggests that the shared responsibility payment may for constitutional purposes be considered a tax, not a penalty: First, for most Americans the amount due will be far less than the price of insurance, and, by statute, it can never be more.[2] It may often be a reasonable financial decision to make the payment rather than purchase insurance, unlike the "prohibitory" financial punishment in *Drexel Furniture*. 259 U.S. at 37. Second, the individual mandate

---

[2] In 2016, for example, individuals making $35,000 a year are expected to owe the IRS about $60 for any month in which they do not have health insurance. Someone with an annual income of $100,000 a year would likely owe about $200. The price of a qualifying insurance policy is projected to be around $400 per month. See D. Newman, CRS Report for Congress, Individual Mandate and Related Information Requirements Under ACA 7, and n. 25 (2011).

contains no scienter requirement. Third, the payment is collected solely by the IRS through the normal means of taxation except that the Service is not allowed to use those means most suggestive of a punitive sanction, such as criminal prosecution. See § 5000A(g)(2). The reasons the Court in *Drexel Furniture* held that what was called a "tax" there was a penalty support the conclusion that what is called a "penalty" here may be viewed as a tax.

None of this is to say that the payment is not intended to affect individual conduct. Although the payment will raise considerable revenue, it is plainly designed to expand health insurance coverage. But taxes that seek to influence conduct are nothing new. Some of our earliest federal taxes sought to deter the purchase of imported manufactured goods in order to foster the growth of domestic industry. See W. Brownlee, Federal Taxation in America 22 (2d ed. 2004); cf. 2 J. Story, Commentaries on the Constitution of the United States § 962, p. 434 (1833) ("the taxing power is often, very often, applied for other purposes, than revenue"). Today, federal and state taxes can compose more than half the retail price of cigarettes, not just to raise more money, but to encourage people to quit smoking. And we have upheld such obviously regulatory measures as taxes on selling marijuana and sawed-off shotguns. See *United States v. Sanchez*, 340 U.S. 42, 44–45 (1950); *Sonzinsky v. United States*, 300 U.S. 506, 513 (1937). Indeed, "[e]very tax is in some measure regulatory. To some extent it interposes an economic impediment to the activity taxed as compared with others not taxed." *Sonzinsky, supra,* at 513. That § 5000A seeks to shape decisions about whether to buy health insurance does not mean that it cannot be a valid exercise of the taxing power.

In distinguishing penalties from taxes, this Court has explained that "if the concept of penalty means anything, it means punishment for an unlawful act or omission." *United States v. Reorganized CF & I Fabricators of Utah, Inc.*, 518 U.S. 213, 224 (1996); see also *United States v. La Franca*, 282 U.S. 568, 572 (1931) ("[A] penalty, as the word is here used, is an exaction imposed by statute as punishment for an unlawful act"). While the individual mandate clearly aims to induce the purchase of health insurance, it need not be read to declare that failing to do so is unlawful. Neither the Act nor any other law attaches negative legal consequences to not buying health insurance, beyond requiring a payment to the IRS. The Government agrees with that reading, confirming that if someone chooses to pay rather than obtain health insurance, they have fully complied with the law. Brief for United States 60–61; Tr. of Oral Arg. 49–50 (Mar. 26, 2012).

Indeed, it is estimated that four million people each year will choose to pay the IRS rather than buy insurance. See Congressional Budget Office, *supra,* at 71. We would expect Congress to be troubled by that prospect if such conduct were unlawful. That Congress apparently regards such extensive failure to comply with the mandate as tolerable suggests that Congress did not think it was creating four million outlaws. It suggests instead that the shared responsibility payment merely imposes a tax citizens may lawfully choose to pay in lieu of buying health insurance. * * *

Our precedent demonstrates that Congress had the power to impose the exaction in § 5000A under the taxing power, and that

§ 5000A need not be read to do more than impose a tax. That is sufficient to sustain it. The "question of the constitutionality of action taken by Congress does not depend on recitals of the power which it undertakes to exercise." *Woods v. Cloyd W. Miller Co.*, 333 U.S. 138, 144. * * *

IV

A

The States also contend that the Medicaid expansion exceeds Congress's authority under the Spending Clause. They claim that Congress is coercing the States to adopt the changes it wants by threatening to withhold all of a State's Medicaid grants, unless the State accepts the new expanded funding and complies with the conditions that come with it. This, they argue, violates the basic principle that the "Federal Government may not compel the States to enact or administer a federal regulatory program." *New York*, 505 U.S., at 188.

There is no doubt that the Act dramatically increases state obligations under Medicaid. The current Medicaid program requires States to cover only certain discrete categories of needy individuals—pregnant women, children, needy families, the blind, the elderly, and the disabled. 42 U.S.C. § 1396a(a)(10). There is no mandatory coverage for most childless adults, and the States typically do not offer any such coverage. The States also enjoy considerable flexibility with respect to the coverage levels for parents of needy families. § 1396a(a)(10)(A)(ii). On average States cover only those unemployed parents who make less than 37 percent of the federal poverty level, and only those employed parents who make less than 63 percent of the poverty line. Kaiser Comm'n on Medicaid and the Uninsured, Performing Under Pressure 11, and fig. 11 (2012).

The Medicaid provisions of the Affordable Care Act, in contrast, require States to expand their Medicaid programs by 2014 to cover all individuals under the age of 65 with incomes below 133 percent of the federal poverty line. § 1396a(a)(10)(A)(i)(VIII). The Act also establishes a new "[e]ssential health benefits" package, which States must provide to all new Medicaid recipients—a level sufficient to satisfy a recipient's obligations under the individual mandate. §§ 1396a(k)(1), 1396u–7(b)(5), 18022(b). The Affordable Care Act provides that the Federal Government will pay 100 percent of the costs of covering these newly eligible individuals through 2016. § 1396d(y)(1). In the following years, the federal payment level gradually decreases, to a minimum of 90 percent. *Ibid.* In light of the expansion in coverage mandated by the Act, the Federal Government estimates that its Medicaid spending will increase by approximately $100 billion per year, nearly 40 percent above current levels. Statement of Douglas W. Elmendorf, CBO's Analysis of the Major Health Care Legislation Enacted in March 2010, p. 14, Table 2 (Mar. 30, 2011). * * *

The States, however, argue that the Medicaid expansion is far from the typical case. They object that Congress has "crossed the line distinguishing encouragement from coercion," *New York, supra*, at 175, in the way it has structured the funding: Instead of simply refusing to grant the new funds to States that will not accept the new conditions,

Congress has also threatened to withhold those States' existing Medicaid funds. The States claim that this threat serves no purpose other than to force unwilling States to sign up for the dramatic expansion in health care coverage effected by the Act.

Given the nature of the threat and the programs at issue here, we must agree. We have upheld Congress's authority to condition the receipt of funds on the States' complying with restrictions on the use of those funds, because that is the means by which Congress ensures that the funds are spent according to its view of the "general Welfare." Conditions that do not here govern the use of the funds, however, cannot be justified on that basis. When, for example, such conditions take the form of threats to terminate other significant independent grants, the conditions are properly viewed as a means of pressuring the States to accept policy changes. * * *

B

Nothing in our opinion precludes Congress from offering funds under the Affordable Care Act to expand the availability of health care, and requiring that States accepting such funds comply with the conditions on their use. What Congress is not free to do is to penalize States that choose not to participate in that new program by taking away their existing Medicaid funding. Section 1396c gives the Secretary of Health and Human Services the authority to do just that. It allows her to withhold all "further [Medicaid] payments . . . to the State" if she determines that the State is out of compliance with any Medicaid requirement, including those contained in the expansion. 42 U.S.C. § 1396c. In light of the Court's holding, the Secretary cannot apply § 1396c to withdraw existing Medicaid funds for failure to comply with the requirements set out in the expansion. * * *

The Affordable Care Act is constitutional in part and unconstitutional in part. The individual mandate cannot be upheld as an exercise of Congress's power under the Commerce Clause. That Clause authorizes Congress to regulate interstate commerce, not to order individuals to engage in it. In this case, however, it is reasonable to construe what Congress has done as increasing taxes on those who have a certain amount of income, but choose to go without health insurance. Such legislation is within Congress's power to tax.

As for the Medicaid expansion, that portion of the Affordable Care Act violates the Constitution by threatening existing Medicaid funding. Congress has no authority to order the States to regulate according to its instructions. Congress may offer the States grants and require the States to comply with accompanying conditions, but the States must have a genuine choice whether to accept the offer. The States are given no such choice in this case: They must either accept a basic change in the nature of Medicaid, or risk losing all Medicaid funding. The remedy for that constitutional violation is to preclude the Federal Government from imposing such a sanction. That remedy does not require striking down other portions of the Affordable Care Act.

The Framers created a Federal Government of limited powers, and assigned to this Court the duty of enforcing those limits. The Court does so today. But the Court does not express any opinion on the wisdom of the Affordable Care Act. Under the Constitution, that judgment is reserved to the people.

The judgment of the Court of Appeals for the Eleventh Circuit is affirmed in part and reversed in part.

It is so ordered.

NOTES AND QUESTIONS

1. *Fate of the Medicaid Expansion.* Although *Sebelius* concludes that the Medicaid expansion as written in the ACA is unconstitutional, it also concludes that this constitutional infirmity can be entirely remedied if states who choose to reject the Medicaid expansion in the ACA do not lose preexisting Medicaid funding for making this choice. As of September 2014, 28 states have opted to expand their Medicaid programs, with the remainder refusing to do so. Many believe that more states will embrace the Medicaid expansion in time, because it comes along with massive federal subsidies and requires individual states only to contribute a small percentage of the cost of the expansion. See, e.g., Elizabeth Weeks Leonard, Crafting a Narrative for the Red State Option, 102 Ky. L.J. 381 (2014). The case for an individual state expanding Medicaid under the ACA may be even stronger than this suggests: expanding Medicaid may actually save states more money than it requires them to spend by (i) reducing the amount currently spent to reimburse hospitals for the cost of uncompensated care, and (ii) limiting state expenditures for mental health services.

2. *Severability and the Centrality of the Individual Mandate.* The Supreme Court's precedents suggest that congressional intent is the key consideration in assessing the consequences of a finding that a specific provision within a larger statute is unconstitutional. Applying this principle, all of the dissenting Justices in *Sebelius* wrote that invalidating the individual mandate required invalidating the entire statute. The ACA, they reasoned, could not function as Congress intended if just the individual mandate had been struck down. By contrast, the Solicitor General argued that even if the Supreme Court struck down the individual mandate, it could preserve the remainder of the ACA's provisions aside from those governing guaranteed issue and premium rating. Yet a third view was that even the guaranteed issue provision and premium rating restrictions could be maintained if the individual mandate were struck down because the mandate was not absolutely essential for these provisions to operate as intended by Congress.

How central is the "individual mandate" to the ACA? Does *Sebelius* go too far in describing the mandate as "Congress's solution" to the risk of adverse selection? As noted above, it is hardly the only element of the Act that aims to prevent adverse selection. In fact, as a presidential candidate, President Obama argued that a mandate was not necessary for healthcare reform to work because people would want to buy health insurance if it were affordable. Moreover, even as designed in the ACA, the individual mandate seems only partially effective as a tool to limit the risk of adverse selection: it does not apply to individuals who do not have access to "affordable" coverage, and the penalty for not complying is much less than the after-subsidy cost of health insurance will be for most individuals. See generally Amy Monahan, On Subsidies and Mandates: A Regulatory Critique of ACA, 36 J. Corp. Law 781 (2011).

3. *New Legal Challenges to the ACA.* Critics of the ACA have not relented in their attempts to challenge the Act's legality. The latest serious threat to the Act relates to the availability of subsidies on federal insurance exchanges. Recall that approximately half of the states rely on a federal insurance exchange because they refused to set up their own state-run exchange. Unfortunately, the text of the ACA provides that individual subsidies can be provided on an "[e]xchange established by the State." ACA § 1401 (adding § 36B to the Internal Revenue Code). Virtually everyone agrees that this was a drafting error in the statute, as individual subsidies are vital to making coverage in insurance exchanges affordable for much of the population. Likely, this provision was simply drafted on the assumption—which was widely shared during the ACA's drafting—that every state would choose to establish its own insurance exchange. Consistent with this view, the IRS has issued regulations providing that federal subsidies are indeed available through federally-operated insurance exchanges.

However, serious legal challenges have argued that the IRS exceeded its statutory authority in authorizing subsidies on federal exchanges because such subsidies contradict the ACA's express terms. See *Halbig v. Burwell*, 758 F.3d 390 (D.C. Cir. 2014), *vacated and rehearing en banc granted on September 4, 2014* (concluding that the IRS exceeded its statutory authority in concluding that subsidies could be administered through a federally-operated insurance exchange); *King v. Burwell*, 759 F.3d 358 (4th Cir. 2014) (concluding that the IRS acted within the permissible scope of its discretion in resolving conflicting provisions of the ACA). In late 2014, the Supreme Court granted certiorari to hear this issue in *King v. Burwell*, setting up yet another high-stakes Supreme Court case on a key component of the ACA. How should the Supreme Court resolve the issue? How much leeway should agencies such as HHS and the IRS have in implementing a law as sprawling and massively complex as the ACA? To what extent should the political gridlock that has characterized Congress for the last several years impact the answer to this question? If the Supreme Court does conclude that the ACA does not authorize subsidies on federal insurance exchanges, what will be the impact?

5. EMPLOYER-SPONSORED COVERAGE AFTER THE ACA

Prior to the ACA, employer-sponsored insurance ("ESI")—particularly that provided by large employers—had long served as the backbone of the American health insurance system. As described above, the key drivers of this fact were generous tax breaks for ESI and the natural risk-pooling mechanism provided by large employer groups. Nothing about the ACA altered either of these important advantages of ESI in general, and of large group ESI in particular. Much to the contrary, the ACA explicitly attempted to minimally impact large group and self-insured ESI (historically, self-insured employers were quite large) by only slightly altering the rules governing these segments of the marketplace, while radically remaking the individual and (to a lesser extent) small group markets.

The ACA's relatively minimal intrusion on the large group and self-insured markets is easiest to see with respect to its provisions that explicitly do not apply to these markets. This includes some of the most important provisions in the ACA, including the establishment of individual subsidies and insurance exchanges and the requirement that insurance policies provide essential health benefits. But many other core elements of reform—such as restrictions on rescissions, health-based underwriting, and preexisting condition exclusions—nominally apply to all health plans, including large group and self-insured employer plans, but represent only a minimal change in the regulatory landscape for these plans. In large part, this is because ERISA and HIPAA had long prohibited all employer health plans from discriminating on the basis of health factors with respect to eligibility, benefits, or premiums. Meanwhile, even before reform, insurers did not underwrite large groups (whose medical expenses matched broader population trends) and self-insured employers (who do not purchase group insurance policies in the first place). Similarly, ERISA and HIPAA had long substantially limited the capacity of ESI to include preexisting condition exclusions, meaning that the ACA's complete ban on such provisions had only a minimal impact on ESI.

To be sure, large group and self-insured plans did not wholly avoid the ACA's reforms. Perhaps most notably, the "employer mandate" requires large employers to pay a tax when their employees receive subsidized coverage on an insurance exchange. But even this provision—if and when it is implemented (recall that HHS delayed the implementation of this provision)—is unlikely to affect most large employers, who were already offering generous coverage prior to the ACA. Simply by maintaining this coverage, most large employers could ensure that their employees would not be eligible for subsidies through an insurance exchange, and thus that they would not face a penalty via the employer mandate.

In sum, the ACA directly changed the legal and regulatory landscape in only a few important ways with respect to large group and self-insured employer plans. In fact, for these segments of the marketplace, ERISA, rather than the ACA, continues to be the most important federal statute. As the following case illustrates, although ERISA substantially restricts employers' ability to discriminate among employees on the basis of health-related factors or to impose preexisting condition exclusions, it actually imposes remarkably few restrictions on the content of employer-sponsored insurance plans.

McGann v. H & H Music Company

United States Court of Appeals, Fifth Circuit, 1991.
946 F.2d 401.

■ GARWOOD, CIRCUIT JUDGE:

* * * McGann, an employee of H & H Music, discovered that he was afflicted with AIDS in December 1987. Soon thereafter, McGann submitted his first claims for reimbursement under H & H Music's group medical plan, provided through Brook Mays, the plan administrator, and issued by General American, the plan insurer, and informed his employer that he had AIDS. McGann met with officials of H & H Music in March 1988, at which time they discussed McGann's illness. Before the change in the terms of the plan, it provided for lifetime medical benefits of up to $1,000,000 to all employees.

In July 1988, H & H Music informed its employees that, effective August 1, 1988, changes would be made in their medical coverage. These changes included, but were not limited to, limitation of benefits payable for AIDS-related claims to a lifetime maximum of $5,000.[1] No limitation was placed on any other catastrophic illness. H & H Music became self-insured under the new plan and General American became the plan's administrator. By January 1990, McGann had exhausted the $5,000 limit on coverage for his illness.

In August 1989, McGann sued H & H Music, Brook Mays and General American under section 510 of ERISA, which provides, in part, as follows:

"It shall be unlawful for any person to discharge, fine, suspend, expel, discipline, or discriminate against a participant or beneficiary for exercising any right to which he is entitled under the provisions of an employee benefit plan, * * * or for the purpose of interfering with the attainment of any right to which such participant may become entitled under the plan." 29 U.S.C. § 1140.

McGann claimed that defendants discriminated against him in violation of both prohibitions of section 510. He claimed that the provision limiting coverage for AIDS-related expenses was directed specifically at him in retaliation for exercising his rights under the medical plan and for the purpose of interfering with his attainment of a right to which he may become entitled under the plan.

Defendants, conceding the factual allegations of McGann's complaint, moved for summary judgment. These factual allegations include no assertion that the reduction of AIDS benefits was intended to deny benefits to McGann for any reason which would not be applicable to other beneficiaries who might then or thereafter have AIDS, but rather that the reduction was prompted by the knowledge of McGann's illness, and that McGann was the only beneficiary then known to have AIDS.[2] On June 26, 1990, the district court granted defendants' motion on the ground that they had an absolute right to alter the terms of the plan, regardless of their intent in making the alterations. The district court also held that even if the issue of discriminatory motive were relevant, summary judgment would still be proper because the defendants' motive was to ensure the future existence of the plan and not specifically to retaliate against McGann or to interfere with his exercise of future rights under the plan.

DISCUSSION

McGann contends that defendants violated both clauses of section 510 by discriminating against him for two purposes: (1) "for exercising any right to which [the beneficiary] is entitled," and (2) "for the purpose

---

[1] Other changes included increased individual and family deductibles, elimination of coverage for chemical dependency treatment, adoption of a preferred provider plan and increased contribution requirements.

[2] We assume, for purposes of this appeal, that the defendants' knowledge of McGann's illness was a motivating factor in their decision to reduce coverage for AIDS-related expenses, that this knowledge was obtained either through McGann's filing of claims or his meetings with defendants and that McGann was the only plan beneficiary then known to have AIDS.

of interfering with the attainment of any right to which such participant may become entitled." * * *

Thus, in order to survive summary judgment McGann must make a showing sufficient to establish that a genuine issue exists as to defendants' specific intent to retaliate against McGann for filing claims for AIDS-related treatment or to interfere with McGann's attainment of any right to which he may have become entitled.

Although we assume there was a connection between the benefits reduction and either McGann's filing of claims or his revelations about his illness, there is nothing in the record to suggest that defendants' motivation was other than as they asserted, namely to avoid the expense of paying for AIDS treatment (if not, indeed, also for other treatment), no more for McGann than for any other present or future plan beneficiary who might suffer from AIDS. McGann concedes that the reduction in AIDS benefits will apply equally to all employees filing AIDS-related claims and that the effect of the reduction will not necessarily be felt only by him. He fails to allege that the coverage reduction was otherwise specifically intended to deny him in particular medical coverage except "in effect." He does not challenge defendants' assertion that their purpose in reducing AIDS benefits was to reduce costs.

Furthermore, McGann has failed to adduce evidence of the existence of "any right to which [he] may become entitled under the plan." The right referred to in the second clause of section 510 is not simply any right to which an employee may conceivably become entitled, but rather any right to which an employee may become entitled pursuant to an existing, enforceable obligation assumed by the employer. "Congress viewed [section 510] as a crucial part of ERISA because without it, employers would be able to circumvent the provision of *promised benefits*." *Ingersoll-Rand Co. v. McClendon*, 498 U.S. 133 (1990) (emphasis added).

McGann's allegations show no *promised* benefit, for there is nothing to indicate that defendants ever promised that the $1,000,000 coverage limit was permanent. The H & H Music plan expressly provides: "Termination or Amendment of Plan: The Plan Sponsor may terminate or amend the Plan at any time or terminate any benefit under the Plan at any time." There is no allegation or evidence that any oral or written representations were made to McGann that the $1,000,000 coverage limit would never be lowered. Defendants broke no promise to McGann. The continued availability of the $1,000,000 limit was not a right to which McGann may have become entitled for the purposes of section 510.[3] To adopt McGann's contrary construction of this portion of section 510 would mean that an employer could not effectively reserve the right to amend a medical plan to reduce benefits respecting subsequently incurred medical expenses, as H & H Music did here, because such an amendment would obviously have as a purpose preventing participants from attaining the right to such future benefits as they otherwise might do under the existing plan absent the

---

[3] McGann does not claim that he was not fully reimbursed for all claimed medical expenses incurred on or prior to August 1, 1988; or that the full $5,000 has not been made available to him in respect to AIDS related medical expenses incurred by him on or after July 1, 1988.

amendment. But this is plainly not the law, and ERISA does not require such "vesting" of the right to a continued level of the same medical benefits once those are ever included in a welfare plan. *See Moore v. Metropolitan Life Insurance Co.*, 856 F.2d 488, 492 (2d Cir.1988).

McGann appears to contend that the reduction in AIDS benefits alone supports an inference of specific intent to retaliate against him or to interfere with his future exercise of rights under the plan. McGann characterizes as evidence of an individualized intent to discriminate the fact that AIDS was the only catastrophic illness to which the $5,000 limit was applied and the fact that McGann was the only employee known to have AIDS. He contends that if defendants reduced AIDS coverage because they learned of McGann's illness through his exercising of his rights under the plan by filing claims, the coverage reduction therefore could be "retaliation" for McGann's filing of the claims. Under McGann's theory, any reduction in employee benefits would be impermissibly discriminatory if motivated by a desire to avoid the anticipated costs of continuing to provide coverage for a particular beneficiary. McGann would find an implied promise not to discriminate for this purpose; it is the breaking of this promise that McGann appears to contend constitutes interference with a future entitlement.

McGann cites only one case in which a court has ruled that a change in the terms and conditions of an employee-benefits plan could constitute illegal discrimination under section 510.[4] *Vogel v. Independence Federal Sav. Bank*, 728 F.Supp. 1210 (D.Md.1990). In *Vogel*, however, the plan change at issue resulted in the plaintiff and only the plaintiff being excluded from coverage. McGann asserts that the *Vogel* court rejected the defendant's contention that mere termination of benefits could not constitute unlawful discrimination under section 510, but in fact the court rejected this claim not because it found that mere termination of coverage could constitute discrimination under section 510, but rather because the termination at issue affected only the beneficiary. *Id.* at 1225. Nothing in *Vogel* suggests that the change there had the potential to then or thereafter exclude any present or possible future plan beneficiary other than the plaintiff. *Vogel* therefore provides no support for the proposition that the alteration or termination of a medical plan could alone sustain a section 510 claim. Without necessarily approving of the holding in *Vogel*, we note that it is inapplicable to the instant case. The post-August 1, 1988 $5,000 AIDS coverage limit applies to any and all employees.

McGann effectively contends that section 510 was intended to prohibit any discrimination in the alteration of an employee benefits plan that results in an identifiable employee or group of employees being treated differently from other employees. The First Circuit rejected a somewhat similar contention in *Aronson v. Servus Rubber, Div. of Chromalloy*, 730 F.2d 12 (1st Cir.1984), *cert. denied*, 469 U.S. 1017 (1984). In *Aronson*, an employer eliminated a profit sharing plan with respect to employees at only one of two plants. The

---

[4] We assume that discovery of McGann's condition—and realization of the attendant, long-term costs of caring for McGann—did in fact prompt defendants to reconsider the $1,000,000 limit with respect to AIDS-related expenses and to reduce the limit for future such expenses to $5,000.

disenfranchised employees sued their employer under section 510, claiming that partial termination of the plan with respect to employees at one plant and not at the other constituted illegal discrimination. The court rejected the employees' discrimination claim, stating in part:

> "[Section 510] relates to discriminatory conduct directed against individuals, not to actions involving the plan in general. The problem is with the word 'discriminated.' An overly literal interpretation of this section would make illegal any partial termination, since such terminations obviously interfere with the attainment of benefits by the terminated group, and, indeed, are expressly intended so to interfere * * * This is not to say that a plan could not be discriminatorily modified, intentionally benefitting, or injuring, certain identified employees or a certain group of employees, but a partial termination cannot constitute discrimination per se. A termination that cost alone independently established lines—here separate divisions—and that has a readily apparent business justification, demonstrates no invidious intent." *Id.*, at 16 (citation omitted).

The Supreme Court has observed in dictum: "ERISA does not mandate that employers provide any particular benefits, and does not itself proscribe discrimination in the provision of employee benefits." *Shaw v. Delta Air Lines, Inc.*, 463 U.S. 85 (1983). * * *

To interpret "discrimination" broadly to include defendants' conduct would clearly conflict with Congress's intent that employers remain free to create, modify and terminate the terms and conditions of employee benefits plans without governmental interference.

The Sixth Circuit, in rejecting a challenge to an employer's freedom to choose the terms of its employee pension plan, stated that

> "[i]n enacting ERISA, Congress continued its reliance on *voluntary* action by employers by granting substantial tax advantages for the creation of qualified retirement programs. Neither Congress nor the courts are involved in either the decision to establish a plan or in the decision concerning which benefits a plan should provide. In particular, courts have no authority to decide which benefits employers must confer upon their employees; these are decisions which are more appropriately influenced by forces in the marketplace and, when appropriate, by federal legislation. Absent a violation of federal or state law, a federal court may not modify a substantive provision of a pension plan." *Id.* (citation omitted) (emphasis in original).

As persuasively explained by the Second Circuit, the policy of allowing employers freedom to amend or eliminate employee benefits is particularly compelling with respect to medical plans:

> "With regard to an employer's right to change medical plans, Congress evidenced its recognition of the need for flexibility in rejecting the automatic vesting of welfare plans. Automatic vesting was rejected because the costs of such plans are subject to fluctuating and unpredictable variables. Actuarial decisions concerning fixed annuities are based on fairly stable data, and

vesting is appropriate. In contrast, medical insurance must take account of inflation, changes in medical practice and technology, and increases in the costs of treatment independent of inflation. These unstable variables prevent accurate predictions of future needs and costs." *Moore v. Metropolitan Life Ins. Co.*, 856 F.2d 488, 492 (2d Cir.1988) (*Metropolitan Life*).

In *Metropolitan Life,* the court rejected an ERISA claim by retirees that their employer could not change the level of their medical benefits without their consent. The court stated that limiting an employer's right to change medical plans increased the risk of "decreas[ing] protection for future employees and retirees." *Id.* at 492; *see also Reynolds Metals*, 740 F.2d at 457 ("judicial interference into the establishment of pension plan provisions * * * would serve only to discourage employers from creating voluntarily pension plans") (footnote omitted).

McGann's claim cannot be reconciled with the well-settled principle that Congress did not intend that ERISA circumscribe employers' control over the content of benefits plans they offered to their employees. McGann interprets section 510 to prevent an employer from reducing or eliminating coverage for a particular illness in response to the escalating costs of covering an employee suffering from that illness. Such an interpretation would, in effect, change the terms of H & H Music's plan. Instead of making the $1,000,000 limit available for medical expenses on an as-incurred basis only as long as the limit remained in effect, the policy would make the limit *permanently* available for all medical expenses as they might thereafter be incurred because of a single event, such as the contracting of AIDS. Under McGann's theory, defendants would be effectively proscribed from reducing coverage for AIDS once McGann had contracted that illness and filed claims for AIDS-related expenses. If a federal court could prevent an employer from reducing an employee's coverage limits for AIDS treatment once that employee contracted AIDS, the boundaries of judicial involvement in the creation, alteration or termination of ERISA plans would be sorely tested.

As noted, McGann has failed to adduce any evidence of defendants' specific intent to engage in conduct proscribed by section 510. A party against whom summary judgment is ordered cannot raise a fact issue simply by stating a cause of action where defendants' state of mind is a material element. *Clark*, 854 F.2d at 771. " 'There must be some indication that he can produce the requisite quantum of evidence to enable him to reach the jury with his claim.' " *Id.* at 771 (quoting *Hahn v. Sargent*, 523 F.2d 461, 468 (1st Cir.1975), *cert. denied*, 425 U.S. 904 (1976)).

Proof of defendants' specific intent to discriminate among plan beneficiaries on grounds proscribed by section 510 does not enable McGann to avoid summary judgment. ERISA does not broadly prevent an employer from "discriminating" in the creation, alteration or termination of employee benefits plans; thus, evidence of such intentional discrimination cannot alone sustain a claim under section 510. That section does not prohibit welfare plan discrimination between or among categories of diseases. Section 510 does not mandate that if some, or most, or virtually all catastrophic illnesses are covered, AIDS (or any other particular catastrophic illness) must be among them. It does not prohibit an employer from electing not to cover or continue to cover AIDS, while covering or continuing to cover other catastrophic illnesses, even though the employer's decision in this respect may stem from some "prejudice" against AIDS or its victims generally. The same, of course, is true of any other disease and its victims. That sort of "discrimination" is simply not addressed by section 510. Under section 510, the asserted discrimination is illegal only if it is motivated by a desire to retaliate against an employee or to deprive an employee of an existing right to which he may become entitled. The district court's decision to grant summary judgment to defendants therefore was proper. Its judgment is accordingly

AFFIRMED.

NOTES AND QUESTIONS

1. McGann *After the ACA*. *McGann's* primary holding—that employers have almost complete freedom to change the terms of their group plan due to cost concerns—generally remains good law even after the ACA, at least with respect to large group and self-insured employers. This is because large group policies and self-insured employers are not required by the ACA to provide essential health benefits (small group policies are so required). Although the ACA does restrict annual or lifetime limits even for large group and self-insured plans in a way that might have applied to H & H Music's AIDS-related lifetime limit of $5,000, the employer would presumably be free under the ACA to completely exclude AIDS-related coverage. As noted above, the explanation for the ACA's limited incursions on the freedom of large (and self-insured) employers to design and alter the content of their group health plans is that large employers have historically played a vital role in providing health insurance. The ACA sought to maintain this state of affairs by avoiding dramatic new changes in the rules governing these marketplaces.

2. *The ACA's Impact on Large Group Employer-Sponsored Insurance.* Despite the ACA's general strategy of imposing only limited new rules on large group and self-insured employer plans, many commentators have expressed concern that the ACA may, in fact, substantially disrupt these marketplaces. Perhaps the primary concern is that the ACA's radical reworking of the individual insurance market will reduce large employers' incentives to continue offering generous employer-sponsored coverage. By dropping coverage, employers could redirect funds into employees' salaries, while their employees could receive government subsidies towards the purchase of community-rated coverage on the insurance exchanges. See generally David A. Hyman, Employment-Based Health Insurance: Is Health Reform a "Game Changer?", 1 N.Y.U. Rev. Emp. Benefits & Exec. Comp. 1A–1 (2010); Thomas Buchmueller, Colleen Carey & Helen G. Levy, Will Employers Drop Health Insurance Coverage Because Of The Affordable Care Act?, 32 Health Aff. 1522 (2013). On the other hand, even after reform, all of the tax advantages associated with employer-provided coverage still remain. And, at least once the employer mandate is implemented, employers who do not provide coverage and have employees who receive subsidized coverage are subject to fines, though many question whether these fines are sufficiently large. The effectiveness of the employer

mandate in discouraging large employers from dropping coverage has only grown more difficult to assess due to its postponement until 2015.

Others have suggested that large employers' incentives to offer comprehensive coverage in the future may be altered in different ways. For instance, some have suggested that employers may have an incentive to decrease the desirability of their coverage in much the same way that H & H Music did in order to encourage employees with high health care costs, such as McGann, to secure their coverage through the individual market. Unlike in *McGann,* as a result of the ACA the sick employee would be able to purchase coverage in the individual market without any preexisting conditions at community-average rates. Yet the employer would still enjoy the benefit of substantially reducing its health plan expenses, particularly if it were self-insured. See Amy Monahan & Daniel Schwarcz, Will Employers Undermine Healthcare Reform By Dumping Sick Employees, 97 Va. L. Rev. 125 (2011).

3. *The ACA's Impact on Small Group Employer-Sponsored Insurance.* The ACA is virtually certain to have a dramatic impact on the small group market, though the long-term character of that impact remains cloudy. On one hand, the ACA's alteration of the rules governing this marketplace is quite substantial, with small group policies required to offer essential health benefits, new subsidies available for small employers, and small group coverage being sold via insurance exchanges. Moreover, because small groups were medically underwritten prior to the ACA, the Act's prohibition on medical underwriting has much more bite in this context than it does for large employers. All of this suggests the ACA's intention to revitalize the small group market.

On the other hand, many commentators have expressed substantial concerns about the future of small group insurance markets. One of the main concerns is that small groups that are relatively low risk will choose to self-insure rather than purchase plans at community rates. Although historically only large employers opted to self-insure their health plans, small groups are increasingly exploring this option because it effectively allows them to avoid many of the ACA's rules. For low-risk small employers, this avoidance of the ACA is particularly valuable, because it effectively allows the small employer to enjoy the cost-savings associated with its relatively healthy and/or young workforce. Meanwhile, insurers have increasingly been willing to provide small employers with "stop loss" insurance, which protects them against the risk that their employees will experience much greater health costs than expected. In effect, such stop loss insurance operates as reinsurance for self-insured employers.

Self-insurance is such a threat to the small group market place because it could result in adverse selection, with healthier small groups opting to self-insure, and only less healthy small groups seeking to purchase small group coverage. This, in turn, could lead small employers with less healthy employees to drop coverage completely and encourage their employees to purchase coverage on the individual market. Unlike large employers, small employers are not subject to the employer mandate if their employees receive subsidized insurance coverage on an insurance exchange. See generally Amy Monahan & Daniel Schwarcz, Saving Small Employer Health Insurance, 98 Iowa L. Rev. 1935 (2013); Timothy Stoltzfus Jost & Mark A. Hall, Self-Insurance for Small Employers Under the Affordable Care Act: Federal and State Regulatory Options, 68 N.Y.U. Ann. Survey Am. L. 539 (2013).

4. *ERISA's Procedural Protections.* Despite the dearth of affirmative coverage requirements in ERISA, the statute does provide beneficiaries of employee benefit plans with important procedural protections. The Supreme Court has explained that:

> The federal statute does not go about protecting plan participants and their beneficiaries by requiring employers to provide any given set of minimum benefits, but instead controls the administration of benefit plans, as by imposing reporting and disclosure mandates, funding standards, and fiduciary standards for plan administrators. It envisions administrative oversight, imposes criminal sanctions, and establishes a comprehensive civil enforcement scheme. It also pre-empts some state law.

N.Y. State Conference of Blue Cross & Blue Shield Plans v. Travelers Ins. Co., 514 U.S. 645, 651–57 (1995).

5. *Other Federal Protections for Sick Employees?* The federal circuits are divided on the question whether the Americans with Disabilities Act (ADA), 42 U.S.C. § 12101 et seq., prohibits discrimination against the disabled as to the terms of health insurance, though most have held that it does not. Compare *Kolling v. Blue Cross & Blue Shield of Mich.*, 318 F.3d 715 (6th Cir. 2003) (ADA only applies to public accommodations and not to employee benefit plans) with *Pallozzi v. Allstate Life Ins. Co.*, 198 F.3d 28 (2d Cir. 1999) (Title III of ADA does apply to the underwriting practices of insurers, but classifications based on actuarial data do not violate the Act).

The Mental Health Parity and Addiction Equity Act of 2008, 29 U.S.C. §1185a, limits the capacity of employer-provided plans to impose certain limits on mental health benefits. In particular, it requires that all cost-sharing provisions and treatment limitations for mental health benefits be no more restrictive than the predominant provisions applicable to other medical benefits. However, the Act does not mandate that employer plans provide benefits. Instead, it merely requires that any provision of mental health benefits be provided on the same terms and conditions as other health benefits.

6. *State Protections and ERISA Express Preemption.* Although ERISA did not provide McGann protection against the reduction in benefits at issue, and (as the preceding note indicates) other federal protections are uncertain, individual states are still free to enact such protections, at least to the extent that they are not preempted by ERISA. As we have seen before, ERISA expressly preempts state laws that "relate to" employee benefit plans. 29 U.S.C. § 1144(b)(2)(A). The basic purpose of such "express preemption" is to "avoid a multiplicity of regulation in order to permit the nationally uniform administration of employee-benefit plans." *N.Y. State Conference of Blue Cross & Blue Shield Plans v. Travelers Ins. Co.*, 514 U.S. 645, 651–57 (1995) (citations omitted).

ERISA does not, however, preempt all state laws that relate to an employee benefit plan. Even state laws that "relate to" an employee benefit plan are "saved" from preemption if they "regulate . . . insurance." As noted in Chapter Three, states acting under this so-called "savings clause" have mandated that a wide variety of benefits be included in any policy of health insurance. See generally Amy Monahan, Federalism, Federal Regulation, or Free Market? An Examination of Mandated Health Benefit Reform, 2007 U. Ill. L. Rev. 1361. In *Metropolitan Life Insurance Co. v. Massachusetts*, 471 U.S. 724 (1985), the Supreme Court confirmed that such laws do indeed regulate insurance, and are therefore saved from ERISA express preemption. Whether or not a law regulates insurance, and therefore falls within ERSA's savings clause, depends on whether the law is "specifically directed toward entities engaged in insurance" and "substantially affect[s] the risk pooling arrangement between the insurer and the insured." *Kentucky Ass'n of Health Plans v. Miller*, 538 U.S. 329 (2003). *Miller* specifically rejected earlier cases' reliance on the McCarran-Ferguson "business of insurance" definition in determining the scope of ERISA's exemption for "law[s] . . . which regulate insurance." The court explained that the "use of the McCarran-Ferguson case law in the ERISA context has misdirected attention, failed to provide clear guidance to lower federal courts, and . . . added little to the relevant analysis." Id. at 339–40.

Irrespective of the scope of the savings clause, states are not free to regulate health plans provided by self-insured employers. Recall that many large employers, and some small employers, self-insure their employees' health plans by directly bearing the financial risk that their employees will incur greater than expected healthcare costs. Historically, the primary reason that employers do this is because ERISA's savings clause has been interpreted so that it does not save from preemption state laws and regulations that purport to apply to self-insured plans. Self-insuring is thus a mechanism for employers to avoid the costs of state insurance regulation generally, and the costs of complying with state mandated benefit laws in particular. Does this fact help to explain why McGann's employer became self-insured immediately after it changed the scope of the insurance coverage that it provided to employees?

7. *Coverage for Same-Sex Partners*. Employment-based health plans often provide coverage to family members of the employee. Under recent regulations promulgated under the ACA, group insurance policies that provide coverage to opposite-sex couples must also offer coverage to same-sex couples who are legally married. See 45 C.F.R. § 147.104(e). These rules, however, do not apply to self-insured employer plans. Additionally, a number of suits have been brought against state or municipal governments regarding the validity of the governmental provision of benefits to same sex domestic partners, on both equal protection and statutory grounds. See, e.g., *Nat'l Pride at Work, Inc. v. Governor of Mich.*, 732 N.W.2d 139 (Mich. 2007) (providing health insurance benefits to same-sex domestic partners of public employees violates Michigan's marriage amendment which states that "the union of one man and one woman in marriage shall be the only agreement recognized as a marriage or similar union for any purpose"); *Lewis v. N.Y. State Dep't of Civil Servs.*, 872 N.Y.S.2d 578 (N.Y. App. Div. 2009) (permitting state to extend health insurance benefits to spouses of public employees following such couples' out-of-state same-sex marriage). On the other hand, suits challenging the denial of such benefits have thus far met with mixed success. See, e.g., *Alaska Civil Liberties Union v. State of Alaska & Municipality of Anchorage*, 122 P.3d 781 (Alaska 2005) (denial of health insurance and death benefits to the same-sex domestic partners of public employees violates the equal protection clause of the Alaska Constitution); *Rutgers Council of AAUP Chapters v. Rutgers, The State Univ.*, 689 A.2d 828 (N.J. 1997) (denial of health insurance coverage under

state plan to same-sex domestic partners of employees did not violate state or federal law).

6. MANAGED CARE AND THE DEFINITION OF "MEDICALLY NECESSARY"

Historically, health insurance was provided almost exclusively on a "fee-for-service" or "indemnity" basis. Insured individuals sought treatment from the health care provider of their choice, and were covered for services provided, subject to deductibles, coinsurance and standard exclusions from coverage. This fee-for-service approach kept separate the *financing function* provided by insurance from the *health care delivery function* provided by physicians and hospitals.

As described above, however, increases in the cost of health care have long outpaced inflation. And the fee-for-service approach of traditional health insurance has long been identified as a central culprit in America's health care cost problem. Physicians, hospitals, and other health care providers who were paid by a fee-for-service insurance system had strong incentives to increase the amount of care they provided, even when doing so produced minimal health benefits. Meanwhile, insured patients had only minimal reason to resist such efforts, given the fact that most of the costs of such intervention were paid for by insurers (this, of course, is simply ex post moral hazard).

Beginning in the mid-1980's, insurers experimented with transitioning from fee-for-service coverage to "managed care" in order to control the cost of health care. Managed care is a cluster of devices that integrate, in whole or in part, the financing and delivery of health care. For instance, Health Maintenance Organizations (HMO's) are arrangements under which insured individuals must generally receive all of their care from the specified physicians and hospitals employed by or under contract with the HMO. Through its employed or affiliated health care providers, the HMO can use various techniques to "manage" health care utilization and control health care costs. Preferred Provider Organizations (PPO's), in contrast, permit insured individuals to receive services from any provider they choose, but impose more limited cost-sharing if the services of physicians and hospitals within the PPO "network" are used. These "preferred providers" typically have contracted with the PPO to accept lower fees and to follow the PPO's health care utilization guidelines in return for their preferred status.

Managed Care Organizations' efforts to combat excessive utilization can often result in coverage disputes between insurers and policyholders. In many, if not most, cases, these disputes turn on whether medical services are "medically necessary," as is required by virtually all health insurance policies.

Fuja v. Benefit Trust Life Insurance Company
United States Court of Appeals, Seventh Circuit, 1994.
18 F.3d 1405.

■ COFFEY, CIRCUIT JUDGE.

Grace Rodela Fuja, a thirty-seven year-old woman suffering from breast cancer, sued her insurer, the defendant, Benefit Trust Life Insurance Company ("Benefit Trust"), for its refusal to pay for a "high-dose chemotherapy treatment with autologous bone marrow transplantation" ("HDC/ABMT"). Fuja sought injunctive and declaratory relief to prevent the defendant from denying coverage for the treatment under the Employee Retirement Income Security Act ("ERISA"), 29 U.S.C. § 1132(a)(1)(B) and (a)(3). The court entered judgment for Fuja enjoining the defendant from denying coverage. The defendant Benefit Trust Life Insurance Company, subsequently paid for the treatment but now appeals the judgment. We reverse.

FACTS

In August, 1989, Fuja was diagnosed with breast cancer and underwent a lumpectomy and a modified radical mastectomy. Immediately thereafter, beginning in September 1989, she received six months of standard-dose chemotherapy treatment and seemed to remain in remission until February of 1992 when her oncologist observed that the cancer had spread to both her lungs. From February through December of 1992, Fuja responded to standard-dose chemotherapy but during this period her physician came to the conclusion that continued treatment with such standard dose chemotherapy offered her but a negligible chance of survival. Thus she prescribed a regimen of HDC/ABMT.

HDC/ABMT is a two-step procedure. Physicians first extract ("harvest") the bone marrow cells from the patient's body and place them temporarily in frozen storage. At this time, the patient undergoes a cycle of high-dose chemotherapy in hopes of killing the cancer cells. Because the high-dose chemotherapy also attacks the bone marrow cells, it is necessary to withdraw some of the bone marrow prior to undergoing the high-dose chemotherapy. Without initially removing a portion of the bone marrow cells, the high-dose chemotherapy would be lethal to the patient because of its myeloblative effect (it destroys bone marrow cells which produce blood cells (red and white) as well as platelets) rendering the patient highly susceptible to infection. After completing the administration of the high-dose chemotherapy, the patient's own ("autologous") stored marrow is reinfused intravenously into the blood-stream to relieve the patient from the toxic effects of the chemotherapy. HDC/ABMT in the past has proven effective in treating certain cancerous blood diseases such as leukemia and Hodgkin's disease but is not as yet universally accepted treatment for solid-type tumors including breast cancer.

Benefit Trust refused to cover the treatment because it did not fall within the parameters of procedures that are "medically necessary" as defined in the insurance contract. Fuja brought this suit in federal district court seeking to enjoin Benefit Trust from denying coverage. Following a hearing on December 17, 1992, the court issued a decision ordering the insurer to pay for the treatment. Fuja underwent the treatment in January of 1993. Unfortunately, the treatment was unsuccessful and she expired in April of 1993.

ISSUES

The defendant, Benefit Trust, maintains that the district court erred in ruling that the insurer was liable for coverage of the treatment arguing: (1) that the treatment was provided in connection with medical research, and (2) the treatment is not authorized for reimbursement by the Health Care Financing Administration ("HCFA").

DISCUSSION

We note at the outset that cases of this nature pose most difficult policy questions of who should bear the burden of paying for expensive medical treatments that are at the time of treatment of unknown efficacy. Although we fully realize the heartache Mrs. Fuja's family has endured, as judges we are called upon to resolve the legal question presented in this appeal, i.e., interpreting the Benefit Trust insurance contract. * * *

The Contract

To satisfy the plaintiff-appellee's burden and obtain coverage for the HDC/ABMT treatment, Fuja must demonstrate that the treatment is "medically necessary" under all five criteria enumerated in the insurance contract entered into between Benefit Trust and Fuja's employer, Emsco Management Services, on behalf of their employees. The contract itself defines medically necessary as: "required and appropriate for care of the Sickness or the Injury; and that are given in accordance with generally accepted principles of medical practice in the U.S. at the time furnished; and *that are approved for reimbursement by the Health Care Financing Administration*; and that are not deemed to be experimental, educational or investigational in nature by any appropriate technological assessment body established by any state or federal government; and *that are not furnished in connection with medical or other research*." (Emphasis added).

In this appeal, Benefit Trust is challenging the trial court's ruling on only two of the provisions: (1) whether the treatment is in connection with medical or other research and (2) whether it is approved for reimbursement by HCFA. If Benefit Trust establishes that the treatment is provided in connection with medical research or that it is not approved for reimbursement by HCFA we must reverse the trial court because Fuja has failed to carry her burden of establishing that the treatment is medically necessary under all five criteria. * * *

Analysis

The threshold question we are called upon to interpret is whether the phrase "in connection with medical or other research" is ambiguous. As stated above, because contract interpretation is a question of law, we review the issue of whether the phrase is ambiguous *de novo*. *Central States Pension Fund v. Hartlage Truck Serv.*, 991 F.2d 1357, 1361 (7th Cir.1993). The district court found the phrase ambiguous and hypothesized that Benefit Trust might try to use this phrase to deny coverage for any medical procedure that was merely being reported in a study. First of all, we reject the trial court's unfavorable assessment of Benefit Trust's intentions in this case as the court has not delineated nor have we been able to find any evidence in this record that Benefit Trust exploited or expanded the use of the "in connection with medical or other research" contract term. In fact, the evidence is to the contrary as Benefit Trust had paid for all of Mrs. Fuja's standard cancer treatments prior to the HDC/ABMT. Moreover, we are of the opinion that to adopt the district court's construction of the term "in connection with medical or other research" would contravene the explicit language of the contract by requiring the insurer to pay for a treatment whose medical efficacy is questioned and thus still under investigation in medically recognized and accepted research studies. *See Awbrey v. Pennzoil Co.*, 961 F.2d 928, 930–31 (10th Cir.1992) ("[a] court is without authority to alter or amend contract terms and provisions absent an ambiguity in the contract * * * [w]e will not read into the [contract] a requirement that, by its clear and unambiguous language, is absent"); *Senn v. United Dominion Indust, Inc.*, 951 F.2d 806, 818 (7th Cir.1992) ("we are not permitted to allow our sympathies and desires to vitiate clear principles of contract and labor law, and in particular, we refuse to amend the clear terms of the health and welfare benefits contained in the [agreement]"), *rehearing en banc denied*, 962 F.2d 655 (7th Cir.1992), *cert. denied*, 509 U.S. 903 (1993); *Heller v. Equitable Life Assur. Soc.*, 833 F.2d 1253, 1257 (7th Cir.1987) ("In the absence of a clear, unequivocal and specific contractual requirement [placing a duty on a party,] we refuse to order the same. To hold otherwise and to impose such a requirement would, in effect, enlarge the terms of the policy beyond those clearly defined in the policy agreed to by the parties"). Like the Eighth Circuit in *Farley*, which construed the very same Benefit Trust contract language, we are convinced that the phrase "in connection with medical research" is unambiguous, *see Farley*, 979 F.2d at 661 ("[n]or do we consider the language of any of the criteria so vague as to be ambiguous or unenforceable"), and we refuse to "artificially create ambiguity where non exists." *Hammond*, 965 F.2d at 430 (citation omitted). This clause in the contract clearly excludes coverage for treatment that is of uncertain medical efficacy and subject to ongoing, recognized and accepted medical research procedures. Certainly it is conceivable that an insurer might attempt to exploit this phrase and deny coverage for a treatment whose results were merely being tabulated (as opposed to being collected to assess the very efficacy of the treatment itself) but there is no evidence in this record that Benefit Trust is guilty of exploiting the contract term "in connection with medical research." The uncontradicted expert testimony and documentary evidence presented to the trial court establishes that HDC/ABMT is still of uncertain medical value and is presently being researched at a number of leading medical colleges and oncology research centers throughout the country.

The evidence presented in the trial court convinces us that the treatment in question was provided "in connection with medical or other research." The most significant evidence is the testimony of the plaintiff's own expert, Dr. Stephanie Williams, who performed the procedure on Mrs. Fuja. In her deposition, Dr. Williams testified that a research protocol is the written document defining the objectives and methodology of the proposed study and must be approved by an Institutional Review Board. Dr. Williams further testified that the treatment would be provided under a protocol approved by the

Institutional Review Board at the University of Chicago Medical Center. She testified that Mrs. Fuja was informed that "her treatment [would] be furnished in connection with medical research," and explained that the treatment was part of a "clinical trial" that involved human subject research and that such clinical trials are investigative. All clinical cancer trials occur in four phases (Phase I, Phase II, Phase III, and Phase IV), that are classified by the research objective and methodology. In Phase I, the researchers attempt to determine the patients' maximum tolerated dose of an agent (drug). In Phase II trials, the researcher is trying to assess the efficacy of a certain agent or combination of agents by analyzing the response of a statistically reliable number of subjects. Phase III involves randomized clinical trials in which some patients receive the experimental treatment (HDC/ABMT in this case) and others receive the conventional, nonexperimental treatment (standard chemotherapy). The responses of the two groups of subjects are documented, analyzed and compared to assess the efficacy of the experimental treatment. Phase IV occurs after the drug is approved by the Food and Drug Administration ("FDA") and seeks to determine if the drug is effective in other settings.

The FDA and the Department of Health and Human Services have promulgated, as well they should, strict requirements dealing with human subject research. Before such research may be performed the protocol must be approved by an Institutional Review Board and must be clearly explained to the plaintiff who is required to sign an informed consent. The informed consent includes advising the patient of the possible risks, any alternative treatments available and above all that the treatment is part of a research study. *See* 21 C.F.R. Parts 50 and 56; 45 C.F.R. Part 46.

The research protocol in which Mrs. Fuja participated was entitled "A Phase II Study Mitoxantrone, Vincristine, 5-Fluorouracil with Leucovorin (MVF) Chemotherapy Followed by Cyclophosphamide and Thiotepa High Dose Intensification Therapy in Breast Cancer." The Introduction to the protocol stated "Our studies have been one of the first in this area of investigation * * *." The protocol made clear that because of the "excessive" treatment related mortality rate under the previous protocol,[1] the present protocol was being undertaken. As part of the protocol, the subjects signed an informed consent form labeled "Consent by Subject for Participation in Research Protocol." The form repeatedly stated that the subject was part of a "research project", "research study" or "research protocol" and that the "safety and efficacy of this two-step approach in the treatment of breast cancer will be evaluated." The informed consent also set forth that "all experimental procedures have been identified and no guarantee has been given about the possible results." Finally, each subject attested, "I, the undersigned, hereby consent to participate as a subject in the above described research project conducted at the University of Chicago Medical Center."

As is evident from the documents referred to above and the testimony of plaintiff's expert, Dr. Williams, the treatment Mrs. Fuja received was part of a Phase II clinical research study. In order to

---

[1] Twenty-seven percent of the patients in the original protocol expired directly from the effects of receiving the high-dose chemotherapy and/or from the bone marrow transplant.

receive the treatment the patient had to sign an informed consent that clearly identified the treatment as "research" and "experimental." Moreover, the research protocol under which the treatment was provided stated that the University of Chicago Medical Center "studies have been one of the first in this area of investigation * * *". Finally, Dr. Williams testified that Mrs. Fuja was informed that "her treatment [would] be furnished in connection with medical research." We are of the opinion that the contract term we are called upon to interpret is clear, definite and unambiguous and that the evidence is overwhelming and uncontradicted that Mrs. Fuja's HDC/ABMT was to be provided "in connection with medical or other research." Thus we hold that the district court committed error in ordering Benefit Trust Life Insurance Company to cover a procedure that the contract clearly exempts.

Having concluded that Fuja has failed to satisfy her burden of proof concerning the "in connection with medical or other research" we need not address whether the treatment has been "approved for reimbursement by HCFA."

CONCLUSION

* * * In order to resolve the question of whether health insurance providers should cover treatments like HDC/ABMT, the prudent course of action might be to establish some sort of regional cooperative committees comprised of oncologists, internists, surgeons, experts in medical ethics, medical school administrators, economists, representatives of the insurance industry, patient advocates and politicians. Through such a collective task force perhaps some consensus might be reached concerning the definition of experimental procedures, as well as agreement on the procedures, which are so cost prohibitive that requiring insurers to cover them might result in the collapse of the healthcare industry. While such a committee would in no way be a panacea for our skyrocketing health care costs, it may help to reduce the incidence of suits in which one "expert" testifies that a procedure is experimental and another equally qualified "expert" testifies to the opposite effect. This so called battle of the experts occurs all too frequently in federal court.

Under the present state of the law, we are bound to interpret the language of the specific contract before us and cannot amend or expand the coverage contained therein. *See supra* at 1409 (citing *Awbrey*, 961 F.2d at 930–31; *Senn*, 951 F.2d at 818; *Heller*, 833 F.2d at 1257). The Benefit Trust Insurance contract is unambiguous in that it denies coverage for treatment provided "in connection with medical or to other research." Accordingly, the judgment of the district court is

REVERSED.

NOTES AND QUESTIONS

1. *Drawing the Line.* At what point does a treatment cease to be experimental? Should an insurer whose policy fails to specify this point with precision be at a disadvantage in a close case? Did the insurer in *Fuja* do so or not? A number of courts addressing claims for coverage of the same therapy that the patient in *Fuja* sought at the time of her treatment found that it was not experimental or that it was otherwise covered. See, e.g., *Bailey v. Blue Cross & Blue Shield of Va.*, 67 F.3d 53 (4th Cir. 1995).

Perhaps ironically, however, studies later failed to find any clinical benefit from this therapy. See William M. Sage, Managed Care's Crimea: Medical Necessity, Therapeutic Benefit, and the Goals of Administrative Process in Health Insurance, 53 Duke L. J. 593, 612 (2004), citing Michelle M. Mello & Troyen A. Brennan, The Controversy over High-Dose Chemotherapy with Autologous Bone Marrow Transplantation for Breast Cancer, Health Aff. Sept.-Oct. 2001, at 101–02.

The case law on the meaning of the phrase "medically necessary" and of exclusions for experimental treatment is mixed. For example, in *Mario v. P & C Food Markets, Inc.*, 313 F.3d 758 (2d Cir. 2002), the court held that gender reassignment surgery was not "medically necessary" for the particular patient seeking coverage. But where the coverage question turns on an experimental-treatment exclusion, a similarly vague phrase may be interpreted in favor of coverage. Thus, in *Steil v. Humana Kansas City, Inc.*, 124 F.Supp.2d 660 (D. Kan. 2000), the policy excluded coverage for "experimental and investigational" treatment. Based on the policy language, the court held that the proposed treatment was investigational but not experimental. On the other hand, in *Coram Healthcare Corp. v. Wal-Mart Stores, Inc.*, 238 F.Supp.2d 586 (S.D.N.Y. 2002), the court held that off-label use of drugs can be considered "experimental" and upheld a denial of coverage.

2. *Why the Exclusion?* Is an exclusion of coverage for treatment that is, in effect, "experimental" (however the exclusion is phrased) necessarily a sensible approach? Evaluate the following arguments: a) policyholders would be willing to pay extra to be entitled to coverage of "experimental" treatment that preliminary tests show has a chance of being cost-effective; b) coverage of experimental treatment will yield cost-effective new treatments that will save money in the long run; c) a bias in favor of covering experimental treatment of diseases (such as breast cancer) that women suffer is necessary to counteract the historic bias in favor of research regarding characteristically-male afflictions (such as cardio-vascular disease).

3. *The Role of Preadmission Review.* Many health insurers now require preadmission review if non-emergency services provided during a hospital stay are to be covered. This review can provide the insured some assurance that costs incurred will be covered. But given the complicated schedule of coverages, deductibles, and coinsurance included in most health insurance, such review at most indicates that the services provided during the hospitalization will be eligible for coverage, but not that all costs incurred actually will be covered. On the other hand, there may not be any real alternative method of controlling excessive utilization in a system in which health care costs are so heavily financed by private insurance.

4. *Clinical Trials Under the ACA.* Although the ACA contains few provisions implicating the meaning of "medically necessary" or "experimental care," it does provide that an insurer must cover "routine patient costs" that are incurred in the context of an approved clinical trial. ACA § 1201 (adding § 2709 to the PHSA). In general, this provision requires insurers to cover any costs that would be paid for if the subjects were not in the clinical trial. This does not include "items and services that are provided solely to satisfy data collection and analysis needs and that are not used in the direct clinical management of the patient" or "a service that is clearly inconsistent with widely accepted and established standards

of care for a particular diagnosis." Id. The purpose of the provision is to prevent policyholders from forfeiting coverage to which they would otherwise be entitled simply because they are participating in a clinical trial.

7. CHALLENGING COVERAGE DENIALS UNDER ERISA

The typical disputed coverage claim is a simple breach of contract action that is ultimately resolved by a court. But when insurance is acquired through an employer, as most private health insurance still is even after the ACA, then the nature of both the underlying cause of action and the parties who adjudicate that claim changes substantially. This is because employer-sponsored insurance is subject to ERISA. We have previously encountered one form of ERISA preemption—express preemption. The primary effect of express preemption to limit the application of state insurance law and regulation to self-insured employer benefit plans. But as the following case (which concerns disability insurance, but is equally applicable to health insurance) describes, a second form of ERISA preemption—often termed "complete preemption"—has the effect of preempting virtually all state contract law that is relevant to resolving coverage disputes, irrespective of whether the employer's plan is self-insured. Suits for what amounts to breach of contract for denying coverage still may be brought, but they are governed by ERISA. It is for this reason that *Fuja*, above, is styled exclusively as an ERISA case rather than as a state contract law case.

Pilot Life Insurance Company v. Dedeaux
Supreme Court of the United States, 1987.
481 U.S. 41.

■ JUSTICE O'CONNOR delivered the opinion of the Court.

This case presents the question whether the Employee Retirement Income Security Act of 1974 (ERISA), 88 Stat. 829, as amended, 29 U.S.C. § 1001 *et seq.,* pre-empts state common law tort and contract actions asserting improper processing of a claim for benefits under an insured employee benefit plan.

I

In March 1975, in Gulf Port, Mississippi, respondent Everate W. Dedeaux injured his back in an accident related to his employment for Entex, Inc. (Entex). Entex had at this time a long term disability employee benefit plan established by purchasing a group insurance policy from petitioner, Pilot Life Insurance Co. (Pilot Life). Entex collected and matched its employees' contributions to the plan and forwarded those funds to Pilot Life; the employer also provided forms to its employees for processing disability claims, and forwarded completed forms to Pilot Life. Pilot Life bore the responsibility of determining who would receive disability benefits. Although Dedeaux sought permanent disability benefits following the 1975 accident, Pilot Life terminated his benefits after two years. During the following three years Dedeaux's benefits were reinstated and terminated by Pilot Life several times.

In 1980, Dedeaux instituted a diversity action against Pilot Life in the United States District Court for the Southern District of

Mississippi. Dedeaux's complaint contained three counts: "Tortious Breach of Contract"; "Breach of Fiduciary Duties"; and "Fraud in the Inducement." Dedeaux sought "[d]amages for failure to provide benefits under the insurance policy in a sum to be determined at the time of trial," "[g]eneral damages for mental and emotional distress and other incidental damages in the sum of $250,000.00," and "[p]unitive and exemplary damages in the sum of $500,000.00." Dedeaux did not assert any of the several causes of action available to him under ERISA.

At the close of discovery, Pilot Life moved for summary judgment, arguing that ERISA pre-empted Dedeaux's common law claim for failure to pay benefits on the group insurance policy. The District Court granted Pilot Life summary judgment, finding all Dedeaux's claims pre-empted. App. to Pet.Cert. 16a.

The Court of Appeals for the Fifth Circuit reversed, primarily on the basis of this Court's decision in *Metropolitan Life Ins. Co. v. Massachusetts,* 471 U.S. 724 (1985). We granted certiorari, 478 U.S. 1004 (1986), and now reverse.

II

In ERISA, Congress set out to

"protect * * * participants in employee benefit plans and their beneficiaries, by requiring the disclosure and reporting to participants and beneficiaries of financial and other information with respect thereto, by establishing standards of conduct, responsibility, and obligation for fiduciaries of employee benefit plans, and by providing for appropriate remedies, sanctions, and ready access to the Federal courts." § 2, as set forth in 29 U.S.C. § 1001(b).

ERISA comprehensively regulates, among other things, employee welfare benefit plans that, "through the purchase of insurance or otherwise," provide medical, surgical, or hospital care, or benefits in the event of sickness, accident, disability or death. § 3(1), 29 U.S.C. § 1002(1).

Congress capped off the massive undertaking of ERISA with three provisions relating to the pre-emptive effect of the federal legislation:

"Except as provided in subsection (b) of this section [the saving clause], the provisions of this subchapter and subchapter III of this chapter shall supersede any and all State laws insofar as they may now or hereafter relate to any employee benefit plan. * * *" § 514(a), as set forth in 29 U.S.C. § 1144(a) (pre-emption clause).

"Except as provided in subparagraph (B) [the deemer clause], nothing in this subchapter shall be construed to exempt or relieve any person from any law of any State which regulates insurance, banking, or securities." § 514(b)(2)(A), as set forth in 29 U.S.C. § 1144(b)(2)(A) (saving clause).

"Neither an employee benefit plan * * * nor any trust established under such a plan, shall be deemed to be an insurance company or other insurer, bank, trust company, or investment company or to be engaged in the business of insurance or banking for purposes of any law of any State purporting to regulate insurance companies, insurance contracts, banks, trust companies, or investment companies." Section 514(b)(2)(B), 29 U.S.C. § 1144(b)(2)(B) (deemer clause).

To summarize the pure mechanics of the provisions quoted above: If a state law "relate[s] to * * * employee benefit plan[s]," it is pre-empted. § 514(a). The saving clause excepts from the pre-emption clause laws that "regulat[e] insurance." § 514(b)(2)(A). The deemer clause makes clear that a state law that "purport[s] to regulate insurance" cannot deem an employee benefit plan to be an insurance company. § 514(b)(2)(B).

"[T]he question whether a certain state action is pre-empted by federal law is one of congressional intent. The purpose of Congress is the ultimate touchstone." *Allis-Chalmers Corp. v. Lueck,* 471 U.S. 202, 208 (1985), quoting *Malone v. White Motor Corp.,* 435 U.S. 497, 504 (1978), quoting *Retail Clerks v. Schermerhorn,* 375 U.S. 96, 103 (1963). We have observed in the past that the express pre-emption provisions of ERISA are deliberately expansive, and designed to "establish pension plan regulation as exclusively a federal concern." *Alessi v. Raybestos-Manhattan, Inc.,* 451 U.S. 504, 523 (1981). As we explained in *Shaw v. Delta Air Lines, Inc.,* 463 U.S. 85, 98 (1983):

> "The bill that became ERISA originally contained a limited pre-emption clause, applicable only to state laws relating to the specific subjects covered by ERISA. The Conference Committee rejected those provisions in favor of the present language, and indicated that section's pre-emptive scope was as broad as its language. See H.R.Conf.Rep. No. 93–1280, p. 383 (1974); S.Conf.Rep. No. 93–1090, p. 383 (1974)." * * *

III

There is no dispute that the common law causes of action asserted in Dedeaux's complaint "relate to" an employee benefit plan and therefore fall under ERISA's express pre-emption clause, § 514(a). In both *Metropolitan Life, supra,* and *Shaw v. Delta Air Lines, Inc., supra,* 463 U.S., at 96–100, we noted the expansive sweep of the pre-emption clause. In both cases "[t]he phrase 'relate to' was given its broad common-sense meaning, such that a state law 'relate[s] to' a benefit plan 'in the normal sense of the phrase, if it has a connection with or reference to such a plan.'" *Metropolitan Life,* 471 U.S., at 739, quoting *Shaw v. Delta Air Lines, supra,* 463 U.S., at 97. In particular we have emphasized that the pre-emption clause is not limited to "state laws specifically designed to affect employee benefit plans." *Shaw v. Delta Air Lines, supra,* at 98. The common law causes of action raised in Dedeaux's complaint, each based on alleged improper processing of a claim for benefits under an employee benefit plan, undoubtedly meet the criteria for pre-emption under § 514(a).

Unless these common law causes of action fall under an exception to § 514(a), therefore, they are expressly pre-empted. Although Dedeaux's complaint pled several state common law causes of action, before this Court Dedeaux has described only one of the three counts—called "tortious breach of contract" in the complaint, and "the Mississippi law of bad faith" in respondent's brief—as protected from the pre-emptive effect of § 514(a). The Mississippi law of bad faith, Dedeaux argues, is a law "which regulates insurance," and thus is saved from pre-emption by § 514(b)(2)(A).¹

In *Metropolitan Life,* we were guided by several considerations in determining whether a state law falls under the saving clause. First, we took what guidance was available from a "common-sense view" of the language of the saving clause itself. 471 U.S., at 740. Second, we made use of the case law interpreting the phrase "business of insurance" under the McCarran-Ferguson Act, 15 U.S.C. § 1011 *et seq.,* in interpreting the saving clause. Three criteria have been used to determine whether a practice falls under the "business of insurance" for purposes of the McCarran-Ferguson Act:

> "*[F]irst,* whether the practice has the effect of transferring or spreading a policyholder's risk; *second,* whether the practice is an integral part of the policy relationship between the insurer and the insured; and *third,* whether the practice is limited to entities within the insurance industry." *Union Labor Life Ins. Co. v. Pireno,* 458 U.S. 119, 129 (1982) (emphasis in original).

In the present case, the considerations weighed in *Metropolitan Life* argue against the assertion that the Mississippi law of bad faith is a state law that "regulates insurance." * * *

Certainly a common-sense understanding of the phrase "regulates insurance" does not support the argument that the Mississippi law of bad faith falls under the saving clause. A common-sense view of the word "regulates" would lead to the conclusion that in order to regulate insurance, a law must not just have an impact on the insurance industry, but be specifically directed toward that industry. Even though the Mississippi Supreme Court has identified its law of bad faith with the insurance industry, the roots of this law are firmly planted in the general principles of Mississippi tort and contract law. Any breach of contract, and not merely breach of an insurance contract, may lead to liability for punitive damages under Mississippi law.

Neither do the McCarran-Ferguson Act factors support the assertion that the Mississippi law of bad faith "regulates insurance." Unlike the mandated-benefits law at issue in *Metropolitan Life,* the Mississippi common law of bad faith does not effect a spreading of policyholder risk. The state common law of bad faith may be said to concern "the policy relationship between the insurer and the insured." The connection to the insurer-insured relationship is attenuated at best, however. In contrast to the mandated-benefits law in *Metropolitan Life,* the common law of bad faith does not define the terms of the relationship between the insurer and the insured; it declares only that, whatever terms have been agreed upon in the insurance contract, a breach of that contract may in certain circumstances allow the policyholder to obtain punitive damages. The state common law of bad faith is therefore no more "integral" to the insurer-insured relationship

---

¹ Decisional law that "regulates insurance" may fall under the saving clause. The saving clause, § 514(b)(2)(A), covers "any law of any State." For purposes of § 514, "[t]he term 'State law' includes all laws, decisions, rules, regulations, or other State action having the effect of law, of any State." 29 U.S.C. § 1144(c)(1) and (2).

than any state's general contract law is integral to a contract made in that state. Finally, as we have just noted, Mississippi's law of bad faith, even if associated with the insurance industry, has developed from general principles of tort and contract law available in any Mississippi breach of contract case. Cf. *Hart v. Orion Ins. Co.*, 453 F.2d 1358 (C.A.10 1971) (general state arbitration statutes do not regulate the business of insurance under the McCarran-Ferguson Act); *Hamilton Life Ins. Co. v. Republic National Life Ins. Co.*, 408 F.2d 606 (C.A.2 1969) (same). Accordingly, the Mississippi common law of bad faith at most meets one of the three criteria used to identify the "business of insurance" under the McCarran-Ferguson Act, and used in *Metropolitan Life* to identify laws that "regulat[e] insurance" under the saving clause.

In the present case, moreover, we are obliged in interpreting the saving clause to consider not only the factors by which we were guided in *Metropolitan Life,* but also the role of the saving clause in ERISA as a whole. On numerous occasions we have noted that " '[i]n expounding a statute, we must not be guided by a single sentence or member of a sentence, but look to the provisions of the whole law, and to its object and policy.' " *Kelly v. Robinson,* 479 U.S. 36, 43 (1986), quoting *Offshore Logistics, Inc. v. Tallentire,* 477 U.S. 207, 221 (1986) (quoting *Mastro Plastics Corp. v. NLRB,* 350 U.S. 270, 285 (1956) (in turn quoting *United States v. Heirs of Boisdoré,* 8 How. 113 (1849))). Because in this case, the state cause of action seeks remedies for the improper processing of a claim for benefits under an ERISA-regulated plan, our understanding of the saving clause must be informed by the legislative intent concerning the civil enforcement provisions provided by ERISA, § 502(a), 29 U.S.C. § 1132(a).

The Solicitor General, for the United States as *amicus curiae,* argues that Congress clearly expressed an intent that the civil enforcement provisions of ERISA § 502(a) be the exclusive vehicle for actions by ERISA-plan participants and beneficiaries asserting improper processing of a claim for benefits, and that varying state causes of action for claims within the scope of § 502(a) would pose an obstacle to the purposes and objectives of Congress. Brief for United States as *Amicus Curiae* 18–19. We agree. The conclusion that § 502(a) was intended to be exclusive is supported, first, by the language and structure of the civil enforcement provisions, and second, by legislative history in which Congress declared that the pre-emptive force of § 502(a) was modeled on the exclusive remedy provided by § 301 of the Labor-Management Relations Act (LMRA), 61 Stat. 156, 29 U.S.C. § 185.

The civil enforcement scheme of § 502(a) is one of the essential tools for accomplishing the stated purposes of ERISA.[2] The civil

---

[2] Section 502(a), as set forth in 29 U.S.C. § 1132(a) provides:

"A civil action may be brought—

"(1) by a participant or beneficiary—

"(2) by the Secretary, or by a participant, beneficiary or fiduciary for appropriate relief under section 1109 of this title [breach of fiduciary duty];

"(3) by a participant, beneficiary, or fiduciary (A) to enjoin any act or practice which violates any provision of this subchapter or the terms of the plan, or (B) to obtain other

enforcement scheme is sandwiched between two other ERISA provisions relevant to enforcement of ERISA and to the processing of a claim for benefits under an employee benefit plan. Section 501, 29 U.S.C. § 1131, authorizes criminal penalties for violations of the reporting and disclosure provisions of ERISA. Section 503, 29 U.S.C. § 1133, requires every employee benefit plan to comply with Department of Labor regulations on giving notice to any participant or beneficiary whose claim for benefits has been denied, and affording a reasonable opportunity for review of the decision denying the claim. Under the civil enforcement provisions of § 502(a), a plan participant or beneficiary may sue to recover benefits due under the plan, to enforce the participant's rights under the plan, or to clarify rights to future benefits. Relief may take the form of accrued benefits due, a declaratory judgment on entitlement to benefits, or an injunction against a plan administrator's improper refusal to pay benefits. A participant or beneficiary may also bring a cause of action for breach of fiduciary duty, and under this cause of action may seek removal of the fiduciary. § 502(a)(2), 409. In an action under these civil enforcement provisions, the court in its discretion may allow an award of attorney's fees to either party. § 502(g). See *Massachusetts Mutual Life Ins. Co. v. Russell,* 473 U.S. 134, 147 (1985). In *Russell,* we concluded that ERISA's breach of fiduciary duty provision, § 409(a), 29 U.S.C. § 1109(a), provided no express authority for an award of punitive damages to a beneficiary. Moreover, we declined to find an implied cause of action for punitive damages in that section, noting that " '[t]he presumption that a remedy was deliberately omitted from a statute is strongest when Congress has enacted a comprehensive legislative scheme including an integrated system of procedures for enforcement.' " *Russell, supra,* at 147, quoting *Northwest Airlines, Inc. v. Transport Workers,* 451 U.S. 77, 97 (1981). Our examination of these provisions made us "reluctant to tamper with an enforcement scheme crafted with such evident care as the one in ERISA." *Russell, supra,* 473 U.S., at 147.

In sum, the detailed provisions of § 502(a) set forth a comprehensive civil enforcement scheme that represents a careful balancing of the need for prompt and fair claims settlement procedures against the public interest in encouraging the formation of employee benefit plans. The policy choices reflected in the inclusion of certain remedies and the exclusion of others under the federal scheme would be completely undermined if ERISA-plan participants and beneficiaries were free to obtain remedies under state law that Congress rejected in ERISA. "The six carefully integrated civil enforcement provisions found in § 502(a) of the statute as finally enacted * * * provide strong evidence

---

appropriate equitable relief (i) to redress such violations or (ii) to enforce any provisions of this subchapter or the terms of the plan;

"(4) by the Secretary, or by a participant, or beneficiary for appropriate relief in the case of a violation of 1025(c) of this title [information to be furnished to participants];

"(5) except as otherwise provided in subsection (b) of this subsection, by the Secretary (A) to enjoin any act or practice which violates any provision of this subchapter, or (B) to obtain other appropriate equitable relief (i) to redress such violation or (ii) to enforce any provision of this subchapter;

"(6) by the Secretary to collect any civil penalty under subsection (i) of this section."

that Congress did *not* intend to authorize other remedies that it simply forgot to incorporate expressly." *Russell, supra,* at 146 (emphasis in original).

The deliberate care with which ERISA's civil enforcement remedies were drafted and the balancing of policies embodied in its choice of remedies argue strongly for the conclusion that ERISA's civil enforcement remedies were intended to be exclusive. * * *

Considering the common-sense understanding of the saving clause, the McCarran-Ferguson Act factors defining the business of insurance, and, most importantly, the clear expression of congressional intent that ERISA's civil enforcement scheme be exclusive, we conclude that Dedeaux's state law suit asserting improper processing of a claim for benefits under an ERISA-regulated plan is not saved by § 514(b)(2)(A), and therefore is pre-empted by § 514(a). Accordingly, the judgment of the Court of Appeals is

Reversed.

NOTES AND QUESTIONS

1. *Different Damages Rules for Group and Individual Policies.* As a result of *Pilot Life*, the options available to policyholders seeking to challenge coverage denials are much more limited for those who acquire insurance through their employer than for those who acquire insurance via the individual market. As we saw in Chapter Two, under ordinary state law, aggrieved policyholders can typically recover reasonably foreseeable consequential damages, and can often recover attorneys' fees, emotional distress damages, and even punitive damages depending on the extent to which an insurer's wrongful coverage denial is deemed to constitute bad faith. *Pilot Life* holds that ERISA's remedial scheme preempts these expansive state remedies for those who acquire coverage through an ERISA-governed plan. Under ERISA's remedial scheme, punitive damages, emotional distress damages, and consequential damages are not available, even for coverage denials that might be deemed to have constituted "bad faith." Attorneys' fees may be available, but that is within the court's discretion. See generally John H. Langbein, Trust Law as Regulatory Law: The Unum/Provident Scandal and Judicial Review of Benefit Denials under ERISA, 101 Nw. U. L. Rev. 1315 (2007). The ACA did not alter the limited availability of remedies for wrongful coverage denials under ERISA.

2. *Different Procedural Rules for Group and Individual Policies.* ERISA's procedural rules for adjudicating coverage denials are also radically different from, and narrower than, the state rules that govern policyholder challenges to insurers' coverage denials. Most importantly, while ERISA itself does not establish the standard of review applicable to such challenges, in *Firestone Tire & Rubber Co. v. Bruch*, 489 U.S. 101, 115 (1989), the U.S. Supreme Court held that "a denial of benefits . . . is to be reviewed under a de novo standard unless the benefit plan gives the administrator or fiduciary [the employer or insurer] discretionary authority to determine eligibility for benefits or to construe the terms of the plan." Where such discretion is in fact reserved, review takes place under an abuse of discretion standard. Application of this abuse of discretion standard effectively reverses the normal *contra proferentem* rule when it comes to judicial review of coverage claims, creating a presumption against

coverage when the relevant policy language is ambiguous and coverage under a group policy has been denied.

An important limit on *Firestone* is that a reviewing court may take into account as a factor in determining whether there was an abuse of discretion the fact that the administrator may have a conflict of interest. Such a conflict of interest may exist when the administrator of the plan is the insurer that will have to pay a claim if it finds that the claim is covered. *Metropolitan Life Ins. Co. v. Glenn*, 554 U.S. 105 (2008). Although lower courts apply the deferential standard of review when they feel compelled to do so, see *Mario v. P & C Food Markets, Inc.*, 313 F.3d 758 (2d Cir. 2002), the case law reflects a decided judicial tendency to distinguish *Firestone* and review benefit denials *de novo*, where possible. See, e.g., *Jebian v. Hewlett-Packard*, 349 F.3d 1098 (9th Cir. 2003) (plan reserved discretion, but the court found that because the claim was denied before discretion was exercised, it would review the denial *de novo*); *Waupaca Foundry, Inc. v. Gehlhausen*, 104 F.Supp.2d 1052 (S.D. Ind. 2000) (plan reserved discretion but because plaintiff sought injunctive relief the *Firestone* standard did not apply).

Challenges to coverage denials under ERISA are also subject to a host of additional procedural restrictions that do not ordinarily exist in state law. First, before a beneficiary can seek judicial review of a coverage denial, she must generally exhaust all internal processes that the plan provides for contesting a coverage decision unless she can show that such efforts would have been futile. See, e.g., *Schorsch v. Reliance Standard Life Ins. Co.*, 693 F.3d 734, 739 (7th Cir. 2012); *Davenport v. Harry N. Abrams, Inc.*, 249 F.3d 130, 133 (2d Cir. 2001); Cf. *Stephens v. Pension Ben. Guar. Corp.*, 755 F.3d 959 (D.C. Cir. 2014) (exhaustion requirement does not apply to suits against plan fiduciaries alleging that they have violated their statutory duties). Second, jury trials are generally not available to those seeking remedies under ERISA. *Muller v. First Unum Life Ins. Co.*, 341 F.3d 119, 124 (2d Cir. 2003); *Koehler v. Aetna Health Inc.*, 683 F.3d 182 (5th Cir. 2012). Third, defendants in ERISA coverage cases may generally seek removal of the case from state to federal court even when the normal "well pleaded complaint" test for removal—which asks whether a federal question is presented on the face of the plaintiff's properly pleaded complaint—is not met. Thus, any case "within the scope of the civil enforcement provisions of § 502(a)" is removable to federal court. *Metropolitan Life Ins. Co. v. Taylor*, 481 U.S. 58, 66 (1987).

3. *Criticisms of* Pilot Life *and Its Progeny*. Numerous commentators have criticized the court's ERISA jurisprudence as it applies to the ability of beneficiaries to challenge coverage denials. See, e.g., Peter J. Wiedenbeck, ERISA's Curious Coverage, 76 Wash. U. L.Q. 311 (1998); John H. Langbein, What ERISA Means by "Equitable": The Supreme Court's Trail of Error in *Russell*, *Mertens*, and *Great-West*, 103 Colum. L. Rev. 1317 (2003); Brendan Maher & Peter Stris, ERISA & Uncertainty, 88 Wash. U. L. Rev. 433 (2010). See also Peter D. Jacobson et al., The Role of the Courts in Shaping Health Policy: An Empirical Assessment, 29 J. Law Med. & Ethics 278, 285 (finding that the federal courts take cost-consideration arguments seriously and that it is difficult for a claimant to succeed in a challenge to a benefit denial under ERISA).

It is ironic that a statute that Congress believed would expand employees' benefit rights has, in fact, sharply contracted them with respect to their ability to challenge coverage denials. Is there any justification for a regime that grants more expansive remedial rights to holders of individual policies than holders of group policies provided by employers? Are the ERISA remedies satisfactory substitutes for state regimes? If the concern of Congress in preempting state law with ERISA was to assure that there is a uniform body of law governing the *lawfulness* of employer actions regarding employment benefits, would that purpose be undermined by varying state rights regarding *remedies* for unlawful denial of benefits by insurers? To what extent do policyholders appreciate that they have such different rights when it comes to challenging coverage disputes depending on whether or not they acquire their coverage through their employer? See, e.g., Brendan Maher, The Benefits of Opt-in Federalism, 52 B.C. L. Rev. 1733 (2011) (arguing that one benefit of the different remedial regimes available under state and federal law is that it allows people with the option of employer-sponsored coverage to opt for coverage in the individual market, which comes along with broader remedial rights).

Aetna Health Inc. v. Davilla

Supreme Court of the United States, 2004.
542 U.S. 200.

■ JUSTICE THOMAS delivered the opinion of the Court.

In these consolidated cases, two individuals sued their respective health maintenance organizations (HMOs) for alleged failures to exercise ordinary care in the handling of coverage decisions, in violation of a duty imposed by the Texas Health Care Liability Act (THCLA), Tex. Civ. Prac. & Rem.Code Ann. §§ 88.001–88.003 (2004 Supp. Pamphlet). We granted certiorari to decide whether the individuals' causes of action are completely pre-empted by the "interlocking, interrelated, and interdependent remedial scheme," *Massachusetts Mut. Life Ins. Co. v. Russell,* 473 U.S. 134, 146 (1985), found at § 502(a) of the Employee Retirement Income Security Act of 1974 (ERISA), 88 Stat. 891, as amended, 29 U.S.C. § 1132(a) *et seq.* 540 U.S. 981 (2003). We hold that the causes of action are completely pre-empted and hence removable from state to federal court. The Court of Appeals, having reached a contrary conclusion, is reversed.

I

A

Respondent Juan Davila is a participant, and respondent Ruby Calad is a beneficiary, in ERISA-regulated employee benefit plans. Their respective plan sponsors had entered into agreements with petitioners, Aetna Health Inc. and CIGNA Healthcare of Texas, Inc., to administer the plans. Under Davila's plan, for instance, Aetna reviews requests for coverage and pays providers, such as doctors, hospitals, and nursing homes, which perform covered services for members; under Calad's plan sponsor's agreement, CIGNA is responsible for plan benefits and coverage decisions.

Respondents both suffered injuries allegedly arising from Aetna's and CIGNA's decisions not to provide coverage for certain treatment and services recommended by respondents' treating physicians. Davila's treating physician prescribed Vioxx to remedy Davila's arthritis pain, but Aetna refused to pay for it. Davila did not appeal or contest this decision, nor did he purchase Vioxx with his own resources and seek reimbursement. Instead, Davila began taking Naprosyn, from which he allegedly suffered a severe reaction that required extensive treatment and hospitalization. Calad underwent surgery, and although her treating physician recommended an extended hospital stay, a CIGNA discharge nurse determined that Calad did not meet the plan's criteria for a continued hospital stay. CIGNA consequently denied coverage for the extended hospital stay. Calad experienced postsurgery complications forcing her to return to the hospital. She alleges that these complications would not have occurred had CIGNA approved coverage for a longer hospital stay.

Respondents brought separate suits in Texas state court against petitioners. Invoking THCLA § 88.002(a), respondents argued that petitioners' refusal to cover the requested services violated their "duty to exercise ordinary care when making health care treatment decisions," and that these refusals "proximately caused" their injuries. *Ibid.* Petitioners removed the cases to Federal District Courts, arguing that respondents' causes of action fit within the scope of, and were therefore completely pre-empted by, ERISA § 502(a). The respective District Courts agreed, and declined to remand the cases to state court. Because respondents refused to amend their complaints to bring explicit ERISA claims, the District Courts dismissed the complaints with prejudice.

B

Both Davila and Calad appealed the refusals to remand to state court. The United States Court of Appeals for the Fifth Circuit consolidated their cases with several others raising similar issues. The Court of Appeals recognized that state causes of action that "duplicat[e] or fal[l] within the scope of an ERISA § 502(a) remedy" are completely pre-empted and hence removable to federal court. *Roark v. Humana, Inc.,* 307 F.3d 298, 305 (2002) (internal quotation marks and citations omitted). After examining the causes of action available under § 502(a), the Court of Appeals determined that respondents' claims could possibly fall under only two: § 502(a)(1)(B), which provides a cause of action for the recovery of wrongfully denied benefits, and § 502(a)(2), which allows suit against a plan fiduciary for breaches of fiduciary duty to the plan. * * *

Congress enacted ERISA to "protect . . . the interests of participants in employee benefit plans and their beneficiaries" by setting out substantive regulatory requirements for employee benefit plans and to "provid[e] for appropriate remedies, sanctions, and ready access to the Federal courts." 29 U.S.C. § 1001(b). The purpose of ERISA is to provide a uniform regulatory regime over employee benefit plans. To this end, ERISA includes expansive pre-emption provisions, see ERISA § 514, 29 U.S.C. § 1144, which are intended to ensure that employee benefit plan regulation would be "exclusively a federal concern." *Alessi v. Raybestos-Manhattan, Inc.,* 451 U.S. 504, 523 (1981).

ERISA's "comprehensive legislative scheme" includes "an integrated system of procedures for enforcement." *Russell,* 473 U.S., at 147 (internal quotation marks and citation omitted). This integrated enforcement mechanism, ERISA § 502(a), 29 U.S.C. § 1132(a), is a distinctive feature of ERISA, and essential to accomplish Congress' purpose of creating a comprehensive statute for the regulation of employee benefit plans. As the Court said in *Pilot Life Ins. Co. v. Dedeaux,* 481 U.S. 41 (1987):

> "[T]he detailed provisions of § 502(a) set forth a comprehensive civil enforcement scheme that represents a careful balancing of the need for prompt and fair claims settlement procedures against the public interest in encouraging the formation of employee benefit plans. The policy choices reflected in the inclusion of certain remedies and the exclusion of others under the federal scheme would be completely undermined if ERISA-plan participants and beneficiaries were free to obtain remedies under state law that Congress rejected in ERISA. 'The six carefully integrated civil enforcement provisions found in § 502(a) of the statute as finally enacted * * * provide strong evidence that Congress did *not* intend to authorize other remedies that it simply forgot to incorporate expressly.'" *Id.,* at 54 (quoting *Russell, supra,* at 146).

Therefore, any state-law cause of action that duplicates, supplements, or supplants the ERISA civil enforcement remedy conflicts with the clear congressional intent to make the ERISA remedy exclusive and is therefore pre-empted. See 481 U.S., at 54–56; see also *Ingersoll-Rand Co. v. McClendon,* 498 U.S. 133, 143–145 (1990).

The pre-emptive force of ERISA § 502(a) is still stronger. In *Metropolitan Life Ins. Co. v. Taylor,* 481 U.S. 58, 65–66 (1987), the Court determined that the similarity of the language used in the Labor Management Relations Act, 1947 (LMRA), and ERISA, combined with the "clear intention" of Congress "to make § 502(a)(1)(B) suits brought by participants or beneficiaries federal questions for the purposes of federal court jurisdiction in like manner as § 301 of the LMRA," established that ERISA § 502(a)(1)(B)'s pre-emptive force mirrored the pre-emptive force of LMRA § 301. Since LMRA § 301 converts state causes of action into federal ones for purposes of determining the propriety of removal, see *Avco Corp. v. Machinists,* 390 U.S. 557 (1968), so too does ERISA § 502(a)(1)(B). Thus, the ERISA civil enforcement mechanism is one of those provisions with such "extraordinary pre-emptive power" that it "converts an ordinary state common law complaint into one stating a federal claim for purposes of the well-pleaded complaint rule." *Metropolitan Life,* 481 U.S., at 65–66. Hence, "causes of action within the scope of the civil enforcement provisions of § 502(a) [are] removable to federal court." *Id.,* at 66.

III

A

ERISA § 502(a)(1)(B) provides:

"A civil action may be brought—(1) by a participant or beneficiary—... (B) to recover benefits due to him under the terms of his plan, to enforce his rights under the terms of the plan, or to clarify his rights to future benefits under the terms of the plan." 29 U.S.C. § 1132(a)(1)(B).

This provision is relatively straightforward. If a participant or beneficiary believes that benefits promised to him under the terms of the plan are not provided, he can bring suit seeking provision of those benefits. A participant or beneficiary can also bring suit generically to "enforce his rights" under the plan, or to clarify any of his rights to future benefits. Any dispute over the precise terms of the plan is resolved by a court under a *de novo* review standard, unless the terms of the plan "giv[e] the administrator or fiduciary discretionary authority to determine eligibility for benefits or to construe the terms of the plan." *Firestone Tire & Rubber Co. v. Bruch,* 489 U.S. 101, 115 (1989).

It follows that if an individual brings suit complaining of a denial of coverage for medical care, where the individual is entitled to such coverage only because of the terms of an ERISA-regulated employee benefit plan, and where no legal duty (state or federal) independent of ERISA or the plan terms is violated, then the suit falls "within the scope of" ERISA § 502(a)(1)(B). *Metropolitan Life, supra,* at 66. In other words, if an individual, at some point in time, could have brought his claim under ERISA § 502(a)(1)(B), and where there is no other independent legal duty that is implicated by a defendant's actions, then the individual's cause of action is completely pre-empted by ERISA § 502(a)(1)(B).

To determine whether respondents' causes of action fall "within the scope" of ERISA § 502(a)(1)(B), we must examine respondents' complaints, the statute on which their claims are based (the THCLA), and the various plan documents. Davila alleges that Aetna provides health coverage under his employer's health benefits plan. Davila also alleges that after his primary care physician prescribed Vioxx, Aetna refused to pay for it. The only action complained of was Aetna's refusal to approve payment for Davila's Vioxx prescription. Further, the only relationship Aetna had with Davila was its partial administration of Davila's employer's benefit plan.

Similarly, Calad alleges that she receives, as her husband's beneficiary under an ERISA-regulated benefit plan, health coverage from CIGNA. She alleges that she was informed by CIGNA, upon admittance into a hospital for major surgery, that she would be authorized to stay for only one day. She also alleges that CIGNA, acting through a discharge nurse, refused to authorize more than a single day despite the advice and recommendation of her treating physician. Calad contests only CIGNA's decision to refuse coverage for her hospital stay. And, as in Davila's case, the only connection between Calad and CIGNA is CIGNA's administration of portions of Calad's ERISA-regulated benefit plan.

It is clear, then, that respondents complain only about denials of coverage promised under the terms of ERISA-regulated employee benefit plans. Upon the denial of benefits, respondents could have paid for the treatment themselves and then sought reimbursement through a § 502(a)(1)(B) action, or sought a preliminary injunction, see *Pryzbowski v. U.S. Healthcare, Inc.,* 245 F.3d 266, 274 (C.A.3 2001) (giving examples where federal courts have issued such preliminary injunctions).

Respondents contend, however, that the complained-of actions violate legal duties that arise independently of ERISA or the terms of the employee benefit plans at issue in these cases. Both respondents brought suit specifically under the THCLA, alleging that petitioners "controlled, influenced, participated in and made decisions which affected the quality of the diagnosis, care, and treatment provided" in a manner that violated "the duty of ordinary care set forth in §§ 88.001 and 88.002." Respondents contend that this duty of ordinary care is an independent legal duty. They analogize to this Court's decisions interpreting LMRA § 301, 29 U.S.C. § 1081, with particular focus on *Caterpillar Inc. v. Williams,* 482 U.S. 386 (1987) (suit for breach of individual employment contract, even if defendant's action also constituted a breach of an entirely separate collective bargaining agreement, not pre-empted by LMRA § 301). Because this duty of ordinary care arises independently of any duty imposed by ERISA or the plan terms, the argument goes, any civil action to enforce this duty is not within the scope of the ERISA civil enforcement mechanism.

The duties imposed by the THCLA in the context of these cases, however, do not arise independently of ERISA or the plan terms. The THCLA does impose a duty on managed care entities to "exercise ordinary care when making health care treatment decisions," and makes them liable for damages proximately caused by failures to abide by that duty. § 88.002(a). However, if a managed care entity correctly concluded that, under the terms of the relevant plan, a particular treatment was not covered, the managed care entity's denial of coverage would not be a proximate cause of any injuries arising from the denial. Rather, the failure of the plan itself to cover the requested treatment would be the proximate cause.[1] More significantly, the THCLA clearly states that "[t]he standards in Subsections (a) and (b) create no obligation on the part of the health insurance carrier, health maintenance organization, or other managed care entity to provide to an insured or enrollee treatment which is not covered by the health care plan of the entity." § 88.002(d). Hence, a managed care entity could not be subject to liability under the THCLA if it denied coverage for any treatment not covered by the health care plan that it was administering.

Thus, interpretation of the terms of respondents' benefit plans forms an essential part of their THCLA claim, and THCLA liability would exist here only because of petitioners' administration of ERISA-regulated benefit plans. Petitioners' potential liability under the THCLA in these cases, then, derives entirely from the particular rights and obligations established by the benefit plans. So, unlike the state-law claims in *Caterpillar, supra,* respondents' THCLA causes of action are not entirely independent of the federally regulated contract itself. Cf. *Allis-Chalmers Corp. v. Lueck,* 471 U.S. 202, 217 (1985) (state-law tort of bad faith handling of insurance claim pre-empted by LMRA § 301, since the "duties imposed and rights established through the state tort . . . derive[d] from the rights and obligations established by the contract"); *Steelworkers v. Rawson,* 495 U.S. 362, 371 (1990) (state-law tort action brought due to alleged negligence in the inspection of a

---

[1] To take a clear example, if the terms of the health care plan specifically exclude from coverage the cost of an appendectomy, then any injuries caused by the refusal to cover the appendectomy are properly attributed to the terms of the plan itself, not the managed care entity that applied those terms.

mine was pre-empted, as the duty to inspect the mine arose solely out of the collective-bargaining agreement).

Hence, respondents bring suit only to rectify a wrongful denial of benefits promised under ERISA-regulated plans, and do not attempt to remedy any violation of a legal duty independent of ERISA. We hold that respondents' state causes of action fall "within the scope of" ERISA § 502(a)(1)(B), *Metropolitan Life,* 481 U.S., at 66, and are therefore completely pre-empted by ERISA § 502 and removable to federal district court.[2] * * *

Respondents also argue—for the first time in their brief to this Court—that the THCLA is a law that regulates insurance, and hence that ERISA § 514(b)(2)(A) saves their causes of action from pre-emption (and thereby from complete pre-emption).[3] This argument is unavailing. The existence of a comprehensive remedial scheme can demonstrate an "overpowering federal policy" that determines the interpretation of a statutory provision designed to save state law from being pre-empted. *Rush Prudential,* 536 U.S., at 375. ERISA's civil enforcement provision is one such example. See *ibid.* * * *

As this Court stated in *Pilot Life,* "our understanding of [§ 514(b)(2)(A)] must be informed by the legislative intent concerning the civil enforcement provisions provided by ERISA § 502(a), 29 U.S.C. § 1132(a)." 481 U.S., at 52. The Court concluded that "[t]he policy choices reflected in the inclusion of certain remedies and the exclusion of others under the federal scheme would be completely undermined if ERISA-plan participants and beneficiaries were free to obtain remedies under state law that Congress rejected in ERISA." *Id.,* at 54. The Court then held, based on

> "the common-sense understanding of the saving clause, the McCarran-Ferguson Act factors defining the business of insurance, and, *most importantly,* the clear expression of congressional intent that ERISA's civil enforcement scheme be exclusive, . . . that [the plaintiff's] state law suit asserting improper processing of a claim for benefits under an ERISA-regulated plan is not saved by § 514(b)(2)(A)." *Id.,* at 57 (emphasis added).

Pilot Life's reasoning applies here with full force. Allowing respondents to proceed with their state-law suits would "pose an obstacle to the purposes and objectives of Congress." *Id.,* at 52. As this Court has recognized in both *Rush Prudential* and *Pilot Life,* ERISA § 514(b)(2)(A) must be interpreted in light of the congressional intent to create an exclusive federal remedy in ERISA § 502(a). Under ordinary principles of conflict pre-emption, then, even a state law that can

---

[2] Respondents also argue that ERISA § 502(a) completely pre-empts a state cause of action only if the cause of action would be pre-empted under ERISA § 514(a); respondents then argue that their causes of action do not fall under the terms of § 514(a). But a state cause of action that provides an alternative remedy to those provided by the ERISA civil enforcement mechanism conflicts with Congress' clear intent to make the ERISA mechanism exclusive. See *Ingersoll-Rand Co. v. McClendon,* 498 U.S. 133, 142 (1990) (holding that "[e]ven if there were no express pre-emption [under ERISA § 514(a)]" of the cause of action in that case, it "would be pre-empted because it conflict[ed] directly with an ERISA cause of action").

[3] ERISA § 514(b)(2)(A), 29 U.S.C. § 1144(b)(2)(A), reads, as relevant: "[N]othing in this subchapter shall be construed to exempt or relieve any person from any law of any State which regulates insurance, banking, or securities."

arguably be characterized as "regulating insurance" will be pre-empted if it provides a separate vehicle to assert a claim for benefits outside of, or in addition to, ERISA's remedial scheme. * * *

We hold that respondents' causes of action, brought to remedy only the denial of benefits under ERISA-regulated benefit plans, fall within the scope of, and are completely pre-empted by, ERISA § 502(a)(1)(B), and thus removable to federal district court. The judgment of the Court of Appeals is reversed, and the cases are remanded for further proceedings consistent with this opinion.

It is so ordered.

■ JUSTICE GINSBURG, with whom JUSTICE BREYER joins, concurring.

The Court today holds that the claims respondents asserted under Texas law are totally preempted by § 502(a) of the Employee Retirement Income Security Act of 1974 (ERISA or Act), 29 U.S.C. § 1132(a). That decision is consistent with our governing case law on ERISA's preemptive scope. I therefore join the Court's opinion. But, with greater enthusiasm, as indicated by my dissenting opinion in *Great-West Life & Annuity Ins. Co. v. Knudson,* 534 U.S. 204 (2002), I also join "the rising judicial chorus urging that Congress and [this] Court revisit what is an unjust and increasingly tangled ERISA regime." *DiFelice v. Aetna U.S. Healthcare,* 346 F.3d 442, 453 (C.A.3 2003) (Becker, J., concurring).

Because the Court has coupled an encompassing interpretation of ERISA's preemptive force with a cramped construction of the "equitable relief" allowable under § 502(a)(3), a "regulatory vacuum" exists: "[V]irtually all state law remedies are preempted but very few federal substitutes are provided." *Id.,* at 456 (internal quotation marks omitted).

A series of the Court's decisions has yielded a host of situations in which persons adversely affected by ERISA-proscribed wrongdoing cannot gain make-whole relief. First, in *Massachusetts Mut. Life Ins. Co. v. Russell,* 473 U.S. 134 (1985), the Court stated, in dicta: "[T]here is a stark absence—in [ERISA] itself and in its legislative history—of any reference to an intention to authorize the recovery of extracontractual damages" for consequential injuries. *Id.,* at 148. Then, in *Mertens v. Hewitt Associates,* 508 U.S. 248 (1993), the Court held that § 502(a)(3)'s term "'equitable relief' ... refer [s] to those categories of relief that were *typically* available in equity (such as injunction, mandamus, and restitution, but not compensatory damages)." *Id.,* at 256 (emphasis in original). Most recently, in *Great-West,* the Court ruled that, as "§ 502(a)(3), by its terms, only allows for *equitable* relief," the provision excludes "the imposition of personal liability ... for a contractual obligation to pay money." 534 U.S., at 221 (emphasis in original).

As the array of lower court cases and opinions documents, see, *e.g., DiFelice; Cicio v. Does,* 321 F.3d 83 (C.A.2 2003), cert. pending *sub nom. Vytra Healthcare v. Cicio,* No. 03–69, 72 USLW 3093 (2003), fresh consideration of the availability of consequential damages under § 502(a)(3) is plainly in order. See 321 F.3d, at 106, 107 (Calabresi, J., dissenting in part) ("gaping wound" caused by the breadth of preemption and limited remedies under ERISA, as interpreted by this Court, will not be healed until the Court "start[s] over" or Congress "wipe[s] the slate clean"); *DiFelice,* 346 F.3d, at 467 ("The vital thing . . . is that either Congress or the Court act quickly, because the current situation is plainly untenable."); Langbein, What ERISA Means by "Equitable": The Supreme Court's Trail of Error in *Russell, Mertens,* and *Great-West,* 103 Colum. L.Rev. 1317, 1365 (2003) (hereinafter Langbein) ("The Supreme Court needs to . . . realign ERISA remedy law with the trust remedial tradition that Congress intended [when it provided in § 502(a)(3) for] 'appropriate equitable relief.' "). * * *

NOTES AND QUESTIONS

1. *The Relationship Between Express Preemption and Complete Preemption.* Pilot Life ultimately rested its holding on both § 502 (complete preemption) and § 514 (express preemption). By contrast, *Aetna* makes clear that express preemption analysis is subservient to complete preemption. In other words, any "state-law cause of action that duplicates, supplements, or supplants the ERISA civil enforcement remedy" is preempted under § 502 irrespective of how that provision would be analyzed under § 514. A crucial implication of this holding is that ERISA's complete preemption of state remedies applies to all employer-sponsored insurance, irrespective of whether or not the employer plan is self-insured. This is because self-insurance is only relevant under § 514's deemer clause. It does not vary the scope of § 502 complete preemption.

2. *Complete Preemption and External Review.* Although *Aetna* makes clear that § 502 is broad, it is not unlimited. For instance, many states have passed "external review" statutes that offer those who have been denied coverage for services deemed not to be medically necessary with an opportunity to have those determinations reviewed by an independent panel of doctors. In *Rush Prudential HMO, Inc. v. Moran,* 536 U.S. 355 (2002), the Court held that an Illinois statute providing for such external review was not preempted by § 502(a) because it did not provide the policyholder with any new benefits. The court's holding did not, however, require self-insured employer plans to provide their beneficiaries with external review pursuant to state laws so requiring, as external review statutes are subject to § 514 conflict preemption. The ACA extended the scope and importance of state external review statutes, requiring all health plans—including self-insured plans—to provide policyholders with an internal appeals process as well as external review that includes the consumer protections contained in the NAIC's Uniform External Review Model Act, Model Law 76 (2010). ACA § 1001 (adding § 2719 to PHSA). HHS, along with the Departments of Labor and Treasury, have issued almost a dozen rules, amendments, and guidance documents describing the scope of the external review processes that must be provided by self-insured plans and carriers in states that have not passed the NAIC model law.

3. *Inadequate Options Under ERISA?* To what extent did the ERISA remedial scheme provide adequate options to the plaintiffs in *Aetna v. Davila*? Anticipating this type of concern, the majority opinion notes that "[u]pon the denial of benefits, respondents could have paid for the treatment themselves and then sought reimbursement through a § 502(a)(1)(B) action, or sought a preliminary injunction. . . ." What downsides would this type of strategy posed for the respondents in *Davila*?

Is it clear that they even could have afforded to pay for the disputed treatment on their own?

4. *ERISA's Regulatory Vacuum and the ACA*. As Justice Ginsburg's concurrence indicates, many commentators have concluded that ERISA creates a "regulatory vacuum" for employer-sponsored insurance. How exactly does ERISA do this? And what are the potential adverse consequences of this regulatory vacuum? See John H. Langbein, Trust Law as Regulatory Law: The Unum/Provident Scandal and Judicial Review of Benefit Denials Under ERISA, 101 Nw. U. L. Rev. 1315 (2007) (linking a major disability carrier's systematic bad faith in handling claims to the fact that it prinicipally provided its policies through employers, and hence fell within ERISA's regulatory vacuum). From a purely descriptive matter, many have linked the absence of strong health insurance provisions in ERISA to the fact that the statute was understood at the time of its passage principally to govern pensions and other retirement plans. See generally James A. Wooten, The Employee Retirement Income Security Act of 1974: A Political History (2005). Of course neither its express preemption provisions nor its remedial provisions—which are the source of complete preemption—are restricted to health-related benefits.

To what extent do the ACA's provisions regarding external review (described in the previous note) have the potential to close this regulatory vacuum? Note that these provisions do not in any way alter the damages that are available to aggrieved policyholders. How they interact with the procedural limitations associated with ERISA is less clear. For instance, the ACA is unclear how, if at all, its external review provisions impact the preexisting *Firestone* rule that judges must defer to plan administrators or fiduciaries. Should, judges defer to internal reviews, but not external reviews? Or defer to neither? See Brendan Maher, The Affordable Care Act, Remedy, and Litigation Reform, 63 Am. U. L. Rev. 649 (2014) (arguing that courts should either review cases de novo or defer to external review, because otherwise they would undermine the ACA's mandate of external review).

8. COORDINATION OF COVERAGE

One common legal problem encountered in the health insurance field involves the "coordination" of coverage. Because of the patchwork system of health insurance in this country, there not only are gaps in coverage; in some cases insurance provided by more than one source is available to cover a single loss. In addition, sometimes the insured is entitled not only to health insurance benefits, but later recovers a judgment in tort from a party responsible for causing his losses. The method by which overlaps of this sort are coordinated is partly a matter of contract, partly of statute, and partly of judicial decision. Given these different sources of authority, it may not be possible to develop a theory of coordination; the accommodation among different sources of coverage may instead have to remain partly ad hoc. For discussion of issues associated with developing a theory of coordinated coverage, see Kenneth S. Abraham, Distributing Risk: Insurance, Legal Theory, and Public Policy 133–72 (1986). Notwithstanding the absence of a fully developed theory of coordination, the system confronts certain recurring issues: how to set priorities as between overlapping sources of coverage; how far coordination rules should be allowed to reduce the coverage that would otherwise be available to the insured; and how to mesh rules governing subrogation in tort actions with health insurance coordination procedures.

In practice, the courts often must confront the failure of insurers to provide a consistent method of coordination. Occasionally the courts' frustration at this failure escapes normal judicial restraints, as seems to have occurred in *South Carolina Insurance Co. v. Fidelity & Guaranty Insurance Underwriters, Inc.*, 489 S.E.2d 200, 201 (S.C. 1997):

> When judges first set about the task of interpreting insurance policies, we looked confidently to tried and true principles of contract law. After all, lawyers are taught in their earliest classes that the common law rules of contract are the bedrock of Anglo-American jurisprudence, thus judges clearly had at hand the perfect tools for crafting fair and lucid interpretations of insurance agreements. We failed utterly to anticipate the linguistic excesses to which the insurance industry would resort in order to avoid paying claims when "other insurance" may be available. This is an area in which hair splitting and nit picking has been elevated to an art form.

Harris Corporation v. Humana Health Insurance Company of Florida, Inc.

United States Court of Appeals, 11th Circuit, 2001.
253 F.3d 598.

■ PER CURIAM:

Two health insurance plans provided coverage for the same individual. The district court held that the plan of the Harris Corporation ("Harris") was primary, and not entitled to recover its expenditures on behalf of that individual from the plan of Humana Health Insurance Company of Florida, Inc. ("Humana"). After review, we affirm.

I. BACKGROUND

Margaret Shallenberger, a Harris employee, enrolled in the Harris plan on November 4, 1991. At that time, she was already enrolled in the Humana plan as the wife of an employee of the City of Ft. Lauderdale, whose coverage under Humana had commenced in 1990. On May 23, 1992, Shallenberger became ill and qualified for and elected to purchase long-term disability benefits in connection with her Harris employment. On July 1, 1994, she became entitled to Medicare A and B coverage based upon her disability and illness. She died on December 4, 1995.

From the time Shallenberger became eligible for Medicare coverage in July 1994 through her death in December 1995, Harris paid approximately $780,267.88 in benefits on her behalf and recovered approximately $13,643.99 from various providers.[1] Harris first submitted a claim for reimbursement of these expenditures to

---

[1] Although it appears that Harris also paid all benefits on behalf of Shallenberger after she became ill in February 1992 and before her Medicare eligibility in July 1994, Harris does not seek reimbursement from Humana of any amounts paid prior to Shallenberger's Medicare eligibility in July 1994.

Medicare, which declined to pay and noted Shallenberger's dependent coverage through Humana. Thereafter, Harris submitted a claim for reimbursement to Humana, which Humana declined to pay, and this litigation commenced.

Harris and Humana each had specific language in their respective health plans intended to define the priority of benefits when benefits appeared to be available under two or more plans. The Harris plan did not contain an "internal coordination of benefits" paragraph, but contained an explanation of "nonduplication." The nonduplication provision did not deal with the situation of a Harris covered employee who was also entitled to benefits under a plan in which her spouse was an employee beneficiary.

The Humana plan, however, contained a "Coordination of Benefits Provision," which included: "1. A plan which does not contain a coordination of benefits provision is considered to determine its benefits before a plan which does contain a coordination of benefits provision." Thus, under this language, the Humana plan would have the advantage if a dispute arises with another plan not having a "COB" provision.

In interpreting the relevant plan language, the district court noted that, "as regards Harris employees, there is nothing in the Harris plan that states that other plans (such as Humana's) are primary under any circumstances." After concluding that the Harris plan contained no "coordination of benefits provision," and that the Humana plan did contain such a provision, the court held that the Harris plan is primary. Accordingly, the district court granted summary judgment in favor of Humana and entered a take nothing final judgment against Harris.

On appeal, Harris does not challenge the district court's findings with respect to the plain language of the above provisions in the two insurance plans and the priority of payment established by those provisions. Instead, Harris contends that the Medicare Secondary Payer statute, 42 U.S.C. § 1395y(b), operates to reverse the priority of payment created by those provisions. As such, Harris contends that the district court erred in dismissing count one of its amended complaint for double damages against Humana under the Medicare Secondary Payer statute, and in granting summary judgment in favor of Humana based upon the priority created by the plan language without regard to the Medicare Secondary Payer statute. * * *

II. DISCUSSION

On appeal, Harris claims that the Medicare Secondary Payer statute makes Humana primarily liable for the costs of Shallenberger's health care and entitles Harris to double damages from Humana arising out of its expenditures on Shallenberger's behalf. Thus, Harris contends that the district court erred with regard to the Medicare Secondary Payer statute in: (1) dismissing count one of its amended complaint and (2) finding Humana secondary to Harris and granting summary judgment in favor of Humana.

A. *The Medicare Secondary Payer Statute*

Prior to 1981, Medicare coverage was generally primary to coverage under an employee health benefit plan. *Baptist Memorial Hosp. v. Pan American Life Ins. Co.*, 45 F.3d 992, 996 (6th Cir.1995). "As a cost-cutting measure, however, Congress eventually enacted a series of amendments designed to make Medicare a 'secondary' payer with respect to such plans. These amendments have been codified as 42 U.S.C. § 1395y(b), which is referred to as the 'Medicare as Secondary Payer' ('MSP') statute." *Id.* (quoting *Health Ins. Ass'n of America v. Shalala*, 23 F.3d 412, 414 (D.C.Cir.1994)); *see also Perry v. United Food and Commerical Workers District Unions*, 64 F.3d 238, 243 (6th Cir.1995) ("In the MSP statute Congress made Medicare coverage secondary to any coverage provided by private insurance programs. It did so in order to lower Medicare costs.").

In order to make Medicare secondary to such private insurance plans, the MSP statute provides that a group health plan may not "take into account" the fact that an individual or that individual's spouse, who is covered by the plan by virtue of the individual's current employment status, is entitled to benefits under Medicare in covering claims. 42 U.S.C. § 1395y(b)(1)(A)(i)(I). Specifically, 42 U.S.C. § 1395y(b)(1)(A)(i)(I) provides:

A group health plan—

(I) may not take into account that an individual (or the individual's spouse) who is covered under the plan by virtue of the individual's current employment status with an employer is entitled to benefits under this subchapter under section 426(a) of this title, * * *

42 U.S.C. § 1395y(b)(1)(A)(i)(I). Thus, the MSP statute prohibits private insurers providing coverage as a result of an individual's *current* employment status from making Medicare primary to its coverage for that individual or that individual's spouse. Instead, Medicare is the "secondary payer" with respect to claims by an individual who is entitled to benefits under Medicare and also covered by private insurance as a result of the current employment status of that individual or that individual's spouse. The MSP statute contains no similar provision with respect to private insurance plans covering such individuals for reasons *other* than current employment status. Thus, private plans covering such individuals for reasons other than current employment status of that individual or that individual's spouse *may* make their coverage secondary to Medicare when those individuals are simultaneously eligible for Medicare.

The MSP statute provides a private cause of action for double damages against insurance carriers covering individuals by virtue of such current employment status that fail to provide for payment primary to Medicare consistent with the statute's mandate. 42 U.S.C. § 1395y(b)(3)(A). Specifically, the statute provides:

(A) Private cause of action

There is established a private cause of action for damages (which shall be in an amount double the amount otherwise provided) in the case of a primary plan which fails to provide for primary payment (or appropriate reimbursement) in accordance with such paragraphs (1) and (2)(A).

42 U.S.C. § 1395y(b)(3)(A); *See also Baptist Memorial Hosp.*, 45 F.3d at 998 ("Where a hospitalization plan that is primary to Medicare under the MSP statute fails to provide for primary payment in accordance

with the statute, a private cause of action exists for damages 'in an amount double the amount otherwise provided.' ").

B. Private Insurers Vis-a-Vis Medicare

We first apply the MSP statute to each private insurer vis-a-vis Medicare. Because Shallenberger's coverage through Humana after July 1, 1994, when she became eligible for Medicare, was the result of her husband's then *current employment status* with the City of Ft. Lauderdale, the MSP statute makes Humana's coverage primary to Medicare. Humana does not dispute its primary status vis-a-vis Medicare.

In contrast, because Harris covered Shallenberger during the same time period as an inactive former employee and not as a result of her current employment status (or that of her spouse), the MSP statute did not prevent Harris from making its coverage secondary to Medicare or, in other words, in making Medicare the primary as opposed to secondary payer of her benefits vis-a-vis Harris. The parties do not appear to dispute Harris's claims that its plan contains a provision to this effect. Thus, after Shallenberger became eligible for Medicare, Harris became secondary vis-a-vis Medicare.

These priorities of each insurer vis-a-vis Medicare appear clear under the MSP statute.

C. Parties' Contentions

The issue in this case, however, addresses what effect, if any, the MSP statute has on reordering the priorities of Harris vis-a-vis Humana under the factual circumstances of this case. Harris contends the MSP statute not only reorders the priorities between private insurers and Medicare, but also between private plans once a covered individual becomes eligible for Medicare. Specifically, Harris argues that Humana became the primary payer *as between the two private insurance carriers* by virtue of the MSP statute because the statute requires Humana to pay in advance of Medicare, but allows Harris to pay after Medicare. Thus, Harris argues that it may maintain a private cause of action for double damages against Humana for its failure to reimburse Harris according to its primary status under the MSP statute.

Humana responds that the MSP statute was designed to save money for the Medicare program by establishing the priority of payment as between Medicare and private insurance carriers under certain circumstances. Humana claims that the MSP statute simply does not apply to determine the relative payment priority as between private insurance plans only and that the coordination of benefits terms of the plan documents control the priority of liability as between private carriers. Where Humana has refused to pay because of the terms of Harris's and Humana's private plans and has not refused to pay Shallenberger's medical expenses as a result of her Medicare eligibility, Humana argues that the statute does not affect its priority with respect to Harris and that Harris may not bring a private cause of action against it under the MSP statute.

D. The Sixth Circuit Decisions

In accepting Humana's argument in this regard, the district court relied on two Sixth Circuit cases directly on point. In *Baptist Memorial Hosp. v. Pan American Life Ins. Co.*, 45 F.3d 992 (6th Cir.1995), Horace Thomas, a retired postal worker, was simultaneously covered for hospitalization by three separate entities. Blue Cross/Blue Shield provided coverage in connection with Thomas's former federal employment. Thomas was also covered by Pan-American as a dependent of his wife by virtue of her current employment. *Id.* at 993. Finally, Thomas was enrolled in Medicare. *Id.*

After an automobile accident, Thomas was hospitalized for several months, incurring a hospital bill of almost $600,000. Blue Cross/Blue Shield refused to pay the bill, claiming that Pan-American's dependent coverage was primary. Pan-American likewise refused to pay the bill, claiming that Blue Cross/Blue Shield was the primary payer as Thomas's former employer.

The hospital brought suit against both Blue Cross/Blue Shield and Pan-American, seeking a determination as to which insurer was primary. *Id.* Medicare was not joined as a party and the hospital apparently never demanded payment from Medicare. *Id.* Although the coordination of benefits provisions of both plans demonstrated that the Blue Cross/Blue Shield coverage was primary to the Pan-American coverage, the district court entered summary judgment against Pan-American. The district court found that Pan-American became primary to Blue Cross/Blue Shield by virtue of the MSP statute. While Pan-American was not permitted to make Medicare primary to its coverage for Thomas because his coverage was based upon his wife's current employment status, Blue Cross/Blue Shield was permitted to do so and had done so. Based upon this priority under the MSP statute, the district court found Pan-American primarily responsible for Thomas's hospital bill.

On appeal, the Sixth Circuit reversed, finding that the MSP statute had no impact on the priority as between solely private insurers and did not trump the plan language adopted by the private insurers as to priority:

> What difference does the MSP statute make as far as priority of payment obligations between Blue Cross and Pan-Am is concerned? None at all, in our view, on the facts presented here. In precluding Pan-Am from making its coverage secondary to the coverage provided by *Medicare*, Congress did not purport to preclude either Pan-Am or Blue Cross from making the Pan-Am coverage secondary to the coverage provided by *Blue Cross.* * * *

Medicare has no dog in this particular fight. Medicare has never been asked to pay anything, as far as we know, and has not been made a party to the lawsuit. Congress manifested no interest whatever in who would pay first as between private insurance carriers such as Pan-Am and Blue Cross. The sole interest of Congress, as far as the statute discloses, was to provide that Medicare would not have to pay ahead of private carriers in certain situations. Where that interest is not affected—and it does not seem to be here—we see no reason why the pertinent contractual provisions should not be enforced in accordance with their terms. Baptist Memorial, 45 F.3d at 996 & 998 (emphasis in original). * * *

E. *Analysis*

We find the thorough analysis of the Sixth Circuit regarding the intent and limited operation of the Medicare Secondary Payer statute persuasive, and adopt the reasoning set forth in *Baptist Memorial Hosp. v. Pan American Life Ins. Co.,* 45 F.3d 992 (6th Cir.1995) and *Perry v. United Food and Commercial Workers District Unions,* 64 F.3d 238 (6th Cir.1995) with respect to the applicability of the MSP statute to coverage disputes solely between private insurers.

Both Sixth Circuit cases are directly on point with respect to the facts of this case. As of July 1, 1994, Shallenberger was eligible to receive Medicare benefits as a result of her disability. Shallenberger was also covered by Harris between July 1, 1994 and her death in December 1995 based on her status as a former employee of Harris. Thus, Harris was entitled to make its benefits secondary to Medicare under the MSP statute. During the same time period, Shallenberger was covered as a dependent by Humana based on her husband's current employment status with the City of Ft. Lauderdale. Thus, Humana was primary to Medicare under the MSP statute. Harris has sued Humana claiming that Humana is responsible for Shallenberger's medical expenses as a result of its primary status vis-a-vis Medicare.

As in *Baptist Memorial,* Medicare is not a party to this case and the fiscal integrity of the Medicare program is not at risk. The instant suit is between solely private insurance plans and involves their priority vis-a-vis one another in connection with the payment of Shallenberger's medical expenses. As in *Perry,* Humana has never claimed that Medicare is the primary payer of Shallenberger's medical expenses in contravention of the priority created between it and Medicare under the MSP statute. Indeed, Humana has denied coverage based upon legal and equitable defenses to Harris's claim for reimbursement unrelated to Shallenberger's Medicare eligibility. Because it is only the priority as between these two private insurance plans that is at issue in this case, the respective priority of the two insurers is not affected by the MSP statute. While Harris was free to alter the coordination of benefits of its plan to align the priority of its liability vis-a-vis Medicare with the priority of its liability vis-a-vis other private insurance plans, the MSP statute was not enacted to address such private priorities and does not operate to reprioritize the obligations of private insurance plans where the liability of Medicare is not at issue.

Contrary to Harris's argument that the Sixth Circuit cases are wrongly decided, the reasoning of both cases appears thorough and persuasive. Harris does not dispute that the MSP statute was designed only to lower Medicare costs. Where Medicare's liability to pay health care expenses is not at issue, it follows that the statute would not operate to rearrange the priority of payment as between purely private insurance plans.

Furthermore, this conclusion does not render the private cause of action in the MSP statute superfluous. Indeed, both *Baptist Memorial* and *Perry* acknowledged the existence of such a private right of action in cases involving the failure of an insurance plan to make its coverage primary to Medicare as required by the statute. *See Baptist Memorial Hosp.,* 45 F.3d at 998 ("Where a hospitalization plan that is primary to Medicare under the MSP statute fails to provide for primary payment in accordance with the statute, a private cause of action exists for damages 'in an amount double the amount otherwise provided.'"); *Perry,* 64 F.3d at 244 ("Although § 1395y(b)(3)(A) provides for 'a private cause of action' for double damages when a primary payer does not pay benefits in accordance with the MSP statute's provisions, this language is irrelevant outside the scope of the MSP statute."). For example, if Humana had been Shallenberger's only private insurer and had denied a timely claim for benefits based solely on her eligibility for Medicare, it appears that the MSP statute would afford Shallenberger a private cause of action for double damages against Humana. Further, it appears that Harris could assert a private cause of action for double damages against Humana acting on behalf of Shallenberger *if* Humana was primary to Harris under the private coordination of benefits provisions, Humana asserted no coverage defenses to Shallenberger's claims, and Humana refused to pay Shallenberger's medical expenses solely based on her eligibility for Medicare. A private cause of action for double damages in these contexts serves Congress' interest in the fiscal integrity of the Medicare program by deterring private insurers primary to Medicare under the statute from attempting to lay medical costs at the government's doorstep.

Under the particular facts of this case, however, the MSP statute does not appear to allow Harris to assert a private cause of action against Humana for its failure to reimburse it for Shallenberger's medical expenses. Humana has never claimed that it was not required to pay Shallenberger's claims because *Medicare* was responsible for them. Indeed, Humana appears to concede that it is primary to *Medicare* under the MSP statute with respect to Shallenberger's expenses. Instead, Humana has refused to reimburse Harris for the medical costs relying on Harris's status as the primary carrier under the plain language of the two insurance plans and asserting other legal and equitable defenses to coverage. Thus, the plain language of the insurance plans governs the priority of payment as between the two insurance companies in this case.

III. CONCLUSION

In sum, it appears that the district court correctly: (1) dismissed Harris's claim against Humana under the MSP statute and (2) relied on the plain language of the two insurance plans and disregarded the MSP statute in determining the priority of obligations as between Harris and Humana in granting summary judgment with respect to Harris's remaining claim.

AFFIRMED.

NOTES AND QUESTIONS

1. *Proliferation of Coverage.* Was the court's decision a principled resolution of the dispute, or an effort to untangle a circular relationship among three sources of coverage that cannot be untangled in a principled way? For a decision that appears to reject the 6th and 11th Circuit

approach, see *Cooperative Health Insurance Fund v. Blue Cross & Blue Shield*, 237 A.D.2d 963 (N.Y. 1997). There are an array of combinations of coverage that may be available to cover any given health care cost, depending on the situation: sources of private health insurance that are not governed by ERISA; private sources, only one of which is governed by ERISA; private and public sources, such as Medicare, Medicaid, or Veteran's benefits; private sources of health insurance and private sources of other coverage, such as uninsured motorists benefits, etc. For illustrative combinations, see *Blue Cross & Blue Shield of Kansas v. Riverside Hospital*, 703 P.2d 1384 (Kan. 1985) (private health insurance and self-insurance health plan subject to ERISA); *Primax Recoveries v. State Farm Mutual*, 147 F.Supp.2d 775 (E.D. Mich. 2001) (auto no-fault and a health plan subject to ERISA).

2. *Hierarchies of Authority*. The starting point for understanding coordination is the notion that it takes two to coordinate. Unless the two or more policies that cover the same loss provide for a consistent method of coordination, the fact that both policies contain coordination-of-benefit provisions is of no use; the policies' directives conflict. Thus, the primary authority for coordination is contract—the insurance policies themselves. If contract fails to coordinate, either because policy provisions conflict or (as in the case of Medicare, for example) there is no relevant policy provision, then a regulatory source of law—a statute or administrative regulation, for example—may resolve the issue. That is what the MSP statute at issue in *Harris* did. Similarly, some state insurance departments have adopted regulations governing coordination that indicate how coordination conflicts should be resolved. Often these regulations are based on the NAIC model. See NAIC Coordination of Benefits Model Regulation, Model Law 120 (2013). Under that model, factors such as whether the insured is covered as an employee or dependent, or as an active employee or retired employee, are used to determine which plan is primary and which is secondary. ERISA may also be relevant to coordination of benefit disputes to the extent that it is held to preempt such state laws governing coordination. Finally, in the absence of consistent contractual coordination or regulatory resolution, the courts may be called upon to resolve the issue.

3. *Clarity in Coordination of Benefits Rules*. One principle that seems unassailable is that coordination rules should be sufficiently clear and easily applied that resort to litigation should be rare. How did the *Harris* court fare in this regard? To what extent would an arbitrary but extremely clear rule for resolving conflicts when neither the policies themselves, administrative regulation, nor an applicable statute does so be preferable to a case-by-case approach that attempts to get it right in each instance? One such approach is the "birthday rule," which places primary coverage responsibility on the policy of the party whose birthday comes first in the year. See, e.g., *PM Group Life Ins. Co. v. W. Growers Assurance Trust*, 953 F.2d 543 (9th Cir.1992).

4. *Pro-Rata Allocation?* In health insurance the courts and state laws have tended to treat one source of coverage as primary—i.e., pays first—and the other source as secondary, meaning that it pays only when the coverage provided by the primary source is exhausted. But it would also be at least theoretically possible to provide for some sort of sharing, or pro-rata rule. This is a common approach in connection with other forms of insurance (as addressed later in Chapter Eight). But pro-ration in these

fields is usually based on the policy limits of the respective policies, whereas in health insurance the ACA now prohibits annual or lifetime limits in health insurance, and many policies did not contain such limits even before healthcare reform.

Associated Hospital Service of Philadelphia v. Pustilnik

Superior Court of Pennsylvania, 1979.
396 A.2d 1332.

■ SPAETH, JUDGE:

This case arises on cross appeals in an equity action. The issues raised involve the right of subrogation.

On May 27, 1968, Alan Pustilnik was injured when he was struck by a SEPTA subway car in Philadelphia. As a result of the accident, Pustilnik was hospitalized on three separate occasions. Medical bills accruing from these hospitalizations [totaled] $30,200.87, but Pustilnik was given a credit of $18,960.18 against this amount under the terms of his subscription agreement with Associated Hospital Service of Philadelphia (Blue Cross).

Soon after the accident, Pustilnik instituted suit against SEPTA. During pendency of this suit, Blue Cross notified Pustilnik and his attorney, Malcolm Waldron, of its subrogation interest in any recovery ultimately obtained from SEPTA. Blue Cross also invited Waldron to represent its interest in the suit in return for 25% of any recovery as an attorney's fee, or 33% if the case went to trial. Waldron rejected this offer, demanding 50% of any recovery as a prerequisite for his representation of Blue Cross' interests. Blue Cross did not agree to pay this fee, but nevertheless continued to advise Waldron of its increasing subrogation interest as a result of Pustilnik's second and third hospitalizations.

Pustilnik's suit against SEPTA went to trial in May 1971. After the fifth day of trial, but before a verdict was returned, the parties settled the suit. Pustilnik agreed to take $235,000 in return for his release relieving SEPTA from additional liability. Upon learning of the settlement, Blue Cross, which did not participate in the trial, immediately alerted SEPTA and the trial judge of its subrogation claim. Eventually, when Pustilnik and Blue Cross were unable to agree on the size of Blue Cross' interest, the trial judge placed $30,000 of the settlement monies into an escrow fund. Thereafter, Blue Cross brought the present action in equity to obtain an adjudication governing the disbursement of the escrowed monies.

Trial was held in November 1975. At the close of the evidence, the court ruled that Blue Cross was entitled to subrogation for the amounts it spent on Pustilnik's behalf, but that it had not proved that it had paid $18,960.18, the amount credited against Pustilnik's hospital bills. The court found that although Blue Cross might have paid this sum, its proof failed to show with reasonable certainty that it had expended more than $16,721.64. The court therefore ruled that Blue Cross' subrogation recovery should be limited to this amount. The court further ruled that this amount was subject to the following additional deductions. First, finding that Pustilnik's $235,000 settlement was less than the full value of his personal injury claim, the court reduced Blue Cross' recovery by 50%. Next, the court reduced Blue Cross' recovery by another 40% to reflect its proportionate share of Waldron's attorney's fee. Finally, the court imposed a reduction of $120 to cover Blue Cross' share of the litigation expenses incurred by Waldron in the suit against SEPTA. Judgment was accordingly entered for Blue Cross in the amount of $4,889.49. Both parties filed exceptions to the court's adjudication, which were dismissed by an opinion and order dated February 15, 1977. Pustilnik and Blue Cross cross-appealed (in Nos. 1136 and 1223 October Term, 1977) to this court. * * *

Blue Cross' Appeal

Blue Cross argues that it was entitled to $18,960.18, less a one third attorney's fee for Waldron, leaving a total recovery of $12,640.12. Blue Cross admits that it failed to prove at trial that it paid $18,960.18 on Pustilnik's behalf, but it justified this failure on the ground that its manner of providing medical coverage makes such an exact calculation impossible.

Unlike profit-making insurance carriers, Blue Cross contracts directly with hospitals to provide services to its subscribers.[1] When a hospital under contract with Blue Cross provides services to a subscriber, it credits the subscriber's bill to the extent that it is covered by the subscriber's agreement with Blue Cross. Blue Cross then makes a partial, interim payment to the hospital on the basis of the hospital's bill to the subscriber. Final payment, however, is postponed until Blue Cross conducts its annual audit of the hospital's operations. At that time, all the hospital's costs are [totaled], as well as all its charges to Blue Cross. If Blue Cross determines that some of the hospital's costs were unnecessary or resulted from waste, it deducts an appropriate amount from its yearly bill, and pays only the reduced amount. Because of this reimbursement system, which is based on generalized auditing procedures, Blue Cross was unable to isolate the exact amount it paid on account of Pustilnik's hospitalizations.

The trial court reasoned that "no subrogation can rise any higher than what the person paid out," and since Blue Cross did not show that it actually paid out the total amount credited on Pustilnik's bills, it was entitled only to a lesser sum. To illustrate the equity of its holding, the trial court used the following hypothetical example:

> Let us suppose an insurance carrier under its collision policy estimated the damage to a policyholder's car as $500.00 but only paid out $400.00 to a friendly repair shop to fix the car. Should such carrier be able to recover $500.00 because that was the value of the benefits rather than the $400.00 it actually paid out? We think not.

Slip opinion at 11.

The trial court's example does not accurately reflect the facts of the present case; it assumes that it was *Blue Cross* that initially "estimated

---

[1] Not all hospitals, of course, have contracts with Blue Cross; but since Pustilnik was hospitalized only at hospitals that were under contract, we need not describe the reimbursement procedures used by Blue Cross for services provided hospitals not under contract.

the damage." However, it was Pustilnik, in his suit against SEPTA, who alleged that the face amount of his hospital bills stated the amount of special damages he had suffered as a result of the accident. Therefore, we do not have, as the trial court supposed, a situation where a subrogee sues a tortfeasor for the fair value of the services it provided the subrogor, even though it procured those services at less than fair value. Instead, we have a situation where the subrogor, after recovering from a tortfeasor an amount alleged by the subrogor to be the fair value of services provided by a subrogee, then refuses to hand over that amount to subrogee, assigning as the reason for the refusal the subrogee's inability to determine whether it actually paid that amount for the services. Equity will not allow such a result. The Restatement of Restitution § 162 states:

> Where property of one person is used in discharging an obligation owed by another * * *, under such circumstances that the other would be unjustly enriched by the retention of the benefit thus conferred, the former is entitled to be subrogated to the position of the obligee. * * *

Cited with approval in Employers Mutual Liability Insurance Co. of Wisconsin v. Melcher, 378 Pa. 598, 601 (1954). To allow Pustilnik to gain a windfall by taking inconsistent positions in the two lawsuits would result in his unjust enrichment. Once he represented to SEPTA that the $18,960.18 represented the fair value of a part of his special damage, he could not then turn to Blue Cross and claim that the amount was inflated and his special damages were limited to a lesser sum.

The trial court also erred in reducing Blue Cross' recovery by 50% on the ground that Pustilnik had settled with SEPTA for less than the full value of his claim. In *Illinois Automobile Insurance Exchange v. Braun,* 280 Pa. 550, 557–58 (1924), the Supreme Court held that when a subrogor settles instead of pressing his suit against an alleged tortfeasor to verdict, he cannot defeat a subrogee's claim by asserting that his loss exceeded the settlement recovery. Sound policy requires this result. It is of course possible that in some cases a subrogor will be well advised to settle for substantially less than his claim because of the tenuous proof establishing the alleged tortfeasor's liability. This possibility, however, does not imply that the subrogor should be permitted to assert against the subrogee that after all, his claim against the tortfeasor really was worth more than he had settled for—which is what the trial court permitted to happen here. Such a procedure would encourage unethical practice, if not perjured testimony: a representation in the court where the suit against the tortfeasor was tried that the case for liability was strong, to obtain a high settlement, followed by a representation in the court where the subrogation claim was tried that the case for liability was weak. Liability should be determined, whenever possible in one proceeding. When a subrogor settles, he waives his right to a judicial determination of his losses, and conclusively establishes the settlement amount as full compensation for his damages.

The final issue concerns the propriety of the trial court's reduction of Blue Cross' recovery to reflect its proportionate share of the attorney's fee and litigation expenses involved in Pustilnik's suit against SEPTA. Pustilnik argues that the reductions were too small, Blue Cross, that they were too large.

In *Furia v. Philadelphia,* 180 Pa.Super. 50 (1955), we held that when a subrogor's attorney creates a common fund for the benefit of the subrogor and subrogee, the attorney is entitled to reimbursement from the subrogee for its proportionate share of reasonable attorney's fees and litigation expenses. Here, therefore, Waldron is entitled to reimbursement from Blue Cross for a reasonable fee; since the parties failed to agree to a fee themselves, the court must determine what fee is reasonable. [The court then upheld the trial court's reduction of Blue Cross' award by 40 percent to reflect Waldron's counsel fee.] * * *

The judgment is set aside and the case remanded for further disposition in accordance with this opinion.

NOTES AND QUESTIONS

1. *Equitable Versus Contractual Subrogation.* Recall that sources of authority to subrogate fall into two categories: judicially-created authority—known as equitable, or legal subrogation; and authority created by the insurance policy itself, known as conventional, or contractual subrogation. In decades past there was some question whether health insurers were entitled to equitable subrogation. See Spencer L. Kimball & Don A. Davis, The Extension of Insurance Subrogation, 60 Mich. L. Rev. 841 (1962). An interesting case discussing the issue is *Cunningham v. Metropolitan Life Insurance Co.,* 360 N.W.2d 33 (Wis. 1985), which focused on whether a health insurance policy was designed for indemnity or investment. The court held that if it was the former, then equitable subrogation was to be allowed in order to further the principle of indemnity. If the latter, however, then subrogation was not to be allowed absent a provision for it in the policy. Does this distinction explain why there has never been equitable subrogation in life insurance? Why have life insurers never included express subrogation provisions in their policies?

Today, virtually all health insurance policies contain subrogation provisions, and most courts permit the contractual subrogation for which they provide. There have been statutory modifications of the collateral source rule in tort cases by a number of states, however, that are likely to shrink the scope of health insurers' subrogation rights. These statutes provide that evidence of payment to the tort plaintiff by collateral sources of insurance is admissible and should be offset against any recovery. Obviously, an insurer cannot be reimbursed for a tort recovery that did not exist at all. And some states have enacted express "anti-subrogation" statutes that prohibit specified insurers from exercising subrogation rights against third parties or seeking reimbursement out of their policyholders' tort recoveries. See, e.g., 75 Pa. Const. Stat. § 720 (relating to tort recoveries associated with auto accidents); Va. Code Ann. § 38.2–3405 (precluding health insurers from exercising any subrogation rights or seeking any reimbursement from policyholders).

2. *Priority over Judgments. Pustilnik* involved the insurer's subrogation rights in the event of a settlement. But should the insured be heard to complain if the insurer is reimbursed off the top of any recovery awarded at trial? In theory such a judgment constitutes an award of all the insured's damages; reimbursing the insurer in full out of the recovery

therefore does not deny the insured full indemnity. Suppose, however, that in a comparative negligence jurisdiction the award has been reduced in proportion to the amount of negligence attributed to the insured. Should the insurer's reimbursement be reduced in that proportion as well? What role should the insured's counsel fees play in the allocation?

3. *Three Approaches to Subrogation and Settlement.* As in property insurance, a health insured who settles with a tortfeasor after suffering injury may have interfered with her insurer's subrogation rights and thereby voided her coverage, unless the tortfeasor had notice of the insurer's interest. The kind of problems addressed in *Pustilnik* arise, however, when settlement of the insured's tort claim occurs after her receipt of health insurance benefits, as it almost always does. Settlements that operate against the insurer's interest cannot be prevented by a rule that settlement voids coverage, because coverage has already been provided. In this situation the insurer's interest can be protected, if at all, only by rules governing apportionment of the insured's tort recovery between insurer and insured.

Analytically, there are at least three potential approaches to defining an insurer's subrogation rights in the event of a settlement. The first, adopted in *Pustilnik*, is to adopt a conclusive presumption that the sum for which an insured settles always constitutes full compensation for all his losses. Is this an empirical conclusion or a rule designed to force the insured to consider the insurer's interests in reaching settlements? More realistically, suppose that settlements do not constitute full compensation (after taking into account the insured's uninsured out-of-pocket losses and pain and suffering, for example). Then this method of apportionment prevents the insured from settling for a sum that will heavily compensate him while reimbursing the insurer nothing, or only a small portion of the benefits it has already paid the insured. In effect, it tells the insured that her health insurer needs to be given a seat at the table when the settlement is negotiated. See Tom Baker, Blood Money, New Money, and the Moral Economy of Tort Law in Action, 35 Law & Soc. Rev. 275, 304–08 (2001) (reporting results of a survey suggesting that in practice there is a three-way split among plaintiff, her attorney, and the health insurer).

A second method of apportionment is a *pro-rata* rule that would pay the insurer a portion of the settlement equal to the proportion its payment to the insured bears to the insured's total losses. For example, if the insured's losses were $100,000, of which the insurer had paid $20,000, and the insured settled with the tortfeasor for $45,000, then the insurer would be reimbursed for 20% of the settlement, or $9000. Obviously this approach protects the insurer's interest less strongly than the *Pustilnik* approach, because it focuses more on assuring full (or more nearly full) indemnity for the insured.

A third method of apportionment—the *make-whole* approach noted above—would attempt to provide more nearly full indemnity for the insured by reimbursing her first for her uninsured losses. The insurer would then be reimbursed out of any sums remaining, and if a portion of the settlement still remained after such reimbursement, the insured would retain it. See Katherine Polak, ERISA: Subrogation, Sereboff, and the "Make Whole" Doctrine: The D.C. Circuit Defines Ambiguity in ERISA Subrogation Clauses, 34 J. L. Med. & Ethics 828 (2006) Johnny C. Parker, The Made-Whole Doctrine: Unraveling the Enigma Wrapped in the

Mystery of Insurance Subrogation, 670 Mo. L. Rev. 723 (2005); Roger M. Baron, Public Policy Considerations Warranting Denial of Reimbursement to ERISA Plans: It's Time to Recognize the Elephant in the Courtroom, 55 Mercer L. Rev. 595 (2004).

The first approach has the advantage of administrative simplicity, but the disadvantage of depriving the insured of the opportunity to obtain more nearly full compensation. The second and third approaches have the advantage of providing the insured with more nearly full compensation, but the disadvantage of administrative complexity. Can you see why? Even apart from administrative considerations, as a matter of policy does it make sense to emphasize tort as a source of compensation through a make-whole or pro-rata rule, or to emphasize more efficient methods of compensation such as health insurance through a *Pustilnik* approach. Alan O. Sykes, Subrogation and Insolvency, 30 J. Legal Stud. 383 (2001) (arguing that granting greater subrogation rights to insurers will reduce the cost of first-party insurance, which is the more desirable form of coverage).

4. *Conflicting State Approaches to Subrogation and Settlements*. The decision in *Pustilnik* itself was overruled on other grounds. *Assoc. Hosp. Serv. of Philadelphia v. Pustilnik*, 439 A.2d 1149 (Pa. 1981). And a number of states—probably a majority—have rejected the *Pustilnik* approach, holding instead that the insured must have been "made whole" before the insurer can exercise a subrogation right to reimbursement. See, e.g., *Steinke v. Safeco Ins. Co. of Am.*, 270 F.Supp.2d 1196 (D. Mont. 2003); *Health Cost Controls, Inc. v. Gifford*, 108 S.W.3d 227 (Tenn. 2003); *Franklin v. Healthsource of Ark.*, 942 S.W.2d 837 (Ark. 1997); *Rimes v. State Farm Mut. Auto. Ins. Co.*, 316 N.W.2d 348 (Wis. 1982); *Powell v. Blue Cross & Blue Shield of Ala.*, 581 So.2d 772 (Ala. 1990). Others subscribe to the *Pustilnik* approach. But this kind of binary breakdown is a bit oversimplified, since in many states certain sources of coverage are given statutory rights of subrogation—workers' compensation insurers, for example. Conversely, in many states, anti-subrogation statutes apply a make-whole rule to certain categories of sources. See, e.g., Ann. Code of Md. § 19–109 (2002) (prohibiting subrogation by insurers providing medical payments coverage under auto insurance policies); Minn. Stat. § 62A.095 (prohibiting subrogation by health insurers where insured has not been made whole and even then subject to pro rata subtraction of attorneys' fees and disbursements).

5. *ERISA Preemption and Subrogation*. Insurers' subrogation rights are further complicated when the health plan is subject to ERISA—as the vast majority of health plans are—for then the state-created rule governing the insurer's subrogation right may be preempted. Recent decisions have held that state anti-subrogation statutes are saved from preemption under ERISA and escape complete preemption because they implicate a duty independent of a health plan's provision of benefits. See, e.g, *Wurtz v. Rawlings Co., LLC*, 761 F.3d 232 (2d Cir. 2014); *Marin Gen. Hosp. v. Modesto & Empire Traction Co.*, 581 F.3d 941 (9th Cir. 2009). But this result is different to the extent that these statutes purport to apply to self-insured plans. See, e.g., *FMC Corp. v. Holliday*, 498 U.S. 52 (1990) (holding that ERISA preempted application of a Pennsylvania anti-subrogation statute to a self-funded benefits plan). Can you see why?

If state law on subrogation is preempted, then parties must look to ERISA itself to determine the health plan's subrogation rights. But ERISA's approach to subrogation is cloudy, because it derives from an ERISA provision permitting the insurer or health plan to bring a civil action "to obtain other appropriate equitable relief." ERISA § 502(a)(3)(B). In *Great-West Life & Annuity Insurance Co. v. Knudson*, 534 U.S. 204 (2002), the U.S. Supreme Court denied the insurer the right to seek reimbursement after a tort recovery by the insured out of the insured's general assets, even before the insured had been made whole, on the ground that the action was not "equitable" and therefore was not permitted under ERISA. On the other hand, in *Sereboff v. Mid Atlantic Medical Services, Inc.*, 547 U.S. 356 (2006), the court permitted an action seeking reimbursement out of specifically identifiable funds of the insureds, because the action qualified as "equitable relief." The court left open the question whether, under ERISA, such action was "appropriate" equitable relief when the insured has not been made whole by a tort recovery. Circuit Courts of Appeal have taken conflicting positions on whether the make-whole prerequisite to the insurer's right of subrogation is the default rule under ERISA. See, e.g., *Copeland Oaks v. Haupt*, 209 F.3d 811 (6th Cir. 2000) (make-whole rule is default); *Harris v. Harvard Pilgrim Health Care, Inc.*, 208 F.3d 274 (1st Cir. 2000) (make-whole rule should not be default). Irrespective of the default, courts have expressed a willingness to defer to language in the ERISA plan explicitly rejecting the make-whole rule. See *Moore v. CapitalCare, Inc.*, 461 F.3d 1 (D.C. Cir. 2006). Although state law may preclude an insurer from drafting such a contract provision, such laws would be preempted to the extent that they applied to self-insured plans. For discussion, see Brendan S. Maher & Radha A. Pathak, Understanding and Problematizing Contractual Tort Subrogation, 40 Loy. Chi. L. J. 49 (2008); Roger M. Baron, Public Policy Considerations Warranting Denial of Reimbursement to ERISA Plans: It's Time to Recognize the Elephant in the Courtroom, 55 Mercer L. Rev. 596 (2004); Lisa M. Bleed, Enforcing Subrogation Provisions as "Appropriate Equitable Relief" under ERISA Section 502(a)(3), 35 U.S.F.L. Rev. 727 (2001); Elaine M. Rinaldi, Apportionment of Recovery Between Insured and Insurer in a Subrogation Case, 29 Tort & Ins. L.J. 803 (1994). Medicare presents a parallel set of issues, dependent not on ERISA (which is inapplicable) but on the particular terms of the Medicare statute. See Rick Swedloff, Can't Settle, Can't Sue: How Congress Stole Tort Remedies from Medicare Beneficiaries, 41 Akron L. Rev. 557 (2008).

C. Disability Insurance

The principal forms of disability insurance—insurance against loss of wages or other income resulting from the inability to work—come not from private first-party insurance, but from two other sources. First, Social Security Disability Insurance (SSDI) covers those who have paid into federal social security against "permanent, total disability." Benefits top out at a comparatively low maximum. Second, workers compensation is a no-fault substitute for employers' tort liability and is mandated in every state except Texas, where employers may opt-out, and about one-third of employers do so. Workers compensation makes employers responsible to employees for medical costs and lost wages resulting from work-related injury and disease, up to a maximum ranging from approximately $30,000 per year to $75,000 per year in lost wages, depending on the state. Many employers buy workers compensation insurance to cover them against these responsibilities. SSDI pays benefits of roughly $144 billion per year, and workers compensation pays disability-related benefits of roughly $30 billion per year.

In contrast, private disability insurance coverage against wage loss resulting from illness or injury has less economic significance. Disability insurance is provided principally as an employee benefit, though it is also sold through the individual market. Approximately 38% of American private workers receive short-term disability insurance through their employer. Such coverage typically protects against disability lasting for a short period of time, ranging from 3 to 6 months. About 31% of American private workers receive long-term disability insurance as an employee benefit. Such coverage typically picks up where short-term disability leaves off, and can provide benefits for a set period of years or until retirement age. See Bureau of Labor Statistics, Employee Benefits Survey (2014). According to one survey, the percentage of American workers with disability insurance increases to approximately 49% for short-term disability and 44% for long-term disability when policies purchased on the individual market are included in the count. See NAIC, Survey on Disability Insurance (2007).

Part of the reason for the thin market for private disability insurance, particularly in the individual market, is the threat of adverse selection and moral hazard. Both the attractiveness of subsidized unemployment and the difficulty of assessing someone's ability to work or to return to work make these serious threats for disability insurers. Disability insurers typically offer coverage for no more than roughly 60% of the insured's after tax income, in order to preserve the insured's incentive to recover from his disability and return to work. Interestingly—and perhaps unsurprisingly—insurers report that disability insurance claims tend to rise during periods of high unemployment and to fall during periods when unemployment is low. See Charles E. Soule, Disability Insurance: The Unique Risk 67–76 (4th ed. 1998).

Another major reason for the thin market in private disability insurance, however, is that SSDI and workers compensation already cover large numbers of people for at least subsistence levels of protection. One of the advantages of these disability insurance programs is that because coverage under these programs is automatic, adverse selection problems are eliminated. But whether a disability insurance program is mandatory or elective, moral hazard issues remain.

Mossa v. Provident Life and Casualty Insurance Company

United States District Court, Eastern District of New York, 1999.
36 F.Supp.2d 524.

■ DEARIE, DISTRICT JUDGE.

Plaintiff Patrick Mossa ("plaintiff" or the "insured") brought this action against Provident Life and Casualty Insurance Company ("defendant" or the "insurer") to recover total disability benefits under a disability policy (the "Policy") purchased from defendant. Defendant moves for summary judgment, arguing that plaintiff is able to engage in any number of gainful occupations and is therefore not "totally disabled" within the meaning of the Policy. For the reasons set forth below, defendant's motion is denied.

FACTS

In January 1973, plaintiff earned a degree in economics from Queens College. From 1976 to 1982, plaintiff co-owned and operated a retail store that sold fruits and vegetables. Beginning in March, 1983, plaintiff was employed by MarBev Mechanical, Inc. ("MarBev"), a plumbing, heating and air conditioning contractor. MarBev is co-owned by plaintiff's wife, Beverly Petrosino, and Marilyn DeGasperis, the wife of another employee of MarBev.

On or about January 9, 1989, plaintiff applied to defendant for disability insurance. On March 9, 1989, defendant issued to plaintiff Disability Income Policy No. 36–295–6002235, which provided for the payment of $5,000 in monthly benefits upon submission of proof that plaintiff is disabled within the meaning of the Policy.

The Policy initially provides benefits in the event that due to sickness or injury "you [the Insured] are not able to perform the substantial and material duties of your occupation (hereinafter 'own occupation' provision).[1] After benefits have been paid for two years, the Policy provides that plaintiff is entitled to continued benefits of $5000 per month until age 65 if due to sickness or injury 'you are not able to engage in any gainful occupation in which you might reasonably be expected to engage because of education, training or experience (hereinafter "other occupation" provision).'"

From March 1989 through July 1993, plaintiff paid premiums to defendant. On March 19, 1993, while working as a steamfitter on a construction site for MarBev, plaintiff fell from the height of one story and fractured both knee caps. On or about March 29, 1993, plaintiff properly submitted a claim for benefits under the Policy. On July 17, 1993, defendant commenced the payment of monthly disability benefits and continued to pay plaintiff a total of $125,000 in disability benefits for two years and one month, ending in September, 1995. * * * In a November 6, 1995 letter to plaintiff, defendant informed plaintiff that based upon its records, plaintiff was able to return to "gainful occupation." * * *

DISCUSSION

The parties agree that New York law governs this diversity action. * * *

A. The Construction of the Policy

The Policy provides, in pertinent part:

After benefits have been paid for two years for a period of disability, Total Disability or totally disabled means that due to Injuries or Sickness:

---

[1] Occupation is defined in the Policy as "the occupation (or occupations, if more than one) in which you are regularly engaged at the time you become disabled."

1) you are not able to engage in any gainful occupation in which you might reasonably be expected to engage because of education, training, or experience (emphasis added); and

2) you are receiving care by a Physician which is appropriate for the condition causing the disability. * * *

While no published New York case has interpreted a disability policy containing this precise provision, a number of long-established New York cases have confronted similar disability policies. * * * The hallmark of these cases is that they address "more restrictive policies [lacking any 'education, training or experience' proviso] which covered only disability from any occupation." *Hoffert v. Commercial Ins. Co. of Newark*, 739 F.Supp. 201, 204 n. 5 (noting that policies with an "education, training or experience" proviso "came into use because the courts of many states were engrafting such interpretations into the more restrictive policies . . .").

The parties rely on two somewhat more recent cases to support their construction of the "other occupation" provision. Defendant asserts that the case of *Tschida v. Continental Cas. Co.*, 264 N.Y.S.2d 72 (Sup.Ct. New York Co.1965), modified on other grounds, otherwise aff'd, 293 N.Y.S.2d 948 (1st Dep't 1968) is controlling, and that it stands for the proposition that salary comparisons are not proper considerations in construing "other occupation" provisions. The Court disagrees.

The policy in *Tschida* initially provided for benefits in the event the plaintiff was unable to engage in her own occupation. Id. at 73–74. After a period of 52 weeks, the policy provided for the payment of benefits in the event plaintiff was "prevented by reason of said injury from engaging in each and every occupation or employment for wage or profit for which he is reasonably qualified by training, education or experience." Id. At the time of the onset of her injury, Ms. Tschida was a professional dancer. Despite her various employments during and after the initial 52 week period of disability (as either a full or part-time model, receptionist, salesperson, and teacher), plaintiff claimed to be "reasonably qualified by training, education or experience" for only one occupation, dancing. Id. at 74.

After a plenary trial, the court concluded that plaintiff was "at least qualified to engage in any of the common forms of employment available to girls of a similar age and background. Furthermore, her injury was not of a type which would, because of undue strain, disable her from such employment." Id. at 76. Defendant urges that the *Tschida* court's construction of the "other occupation clause" controls this Court's construction of the Policy. The court stated:

> The Court is not unmindful that such employment opportunities are not as rewarding financially as professional dancing . . . Unfortunately, the clause under consideration was not intended to indemnify such a contingency. It is sufficient to bar a recovery thereunder that the assured can qualify for other employment which, in a fair sense, is remunerative.

Id.

For a number of reasons, the *Tschida* court's construction of the *Tschida* policy does not bind this Court to adopt defendant's proposed construction of the Mossa policy. First, the policy language confronted by the Tschida court is facially more restrictive than the Policy in the instant case. Compare *Tschida*, at 74 (insured must be prevented "from engaging in each and every occupation for wage or profit for which he is reasonably qualified") with Policy (insured must be "[un]able to engage in any gainful occupation in which he might reasonably be expected to engage").

Second, the *Tschida* court cited as primary authority for its construction of the clause two early New York cases, *Waldman v. Mutual Life Ins. Co. of New York*, 299 N.Y.S. 490 (2d Dep't 1937) and *Shabotzky v. Equitable Life Assur. Soc.*, 12 N.Y.S.2d 848 (1st Dep't 1939), both of which addressed far more restrictive policy language than in the instant case, see *Waldman*, at 493 (policy provides benefits only in event that the insured is prevented "from performing any work for compensation, gain, or profit, and from following any gainful occupation") and neither of which confronted any "training, education or experience" language.

Finally, despite its ostensibly unequivocal holding that "other occupation" clauses preclude a salary comparison, the *Tschida* court proceeded to temporize its statement by actually making a salary comparison. The court stated:

> "Furthermore, any comparison between plaintiff's capacity to earn money before the accident and her salary potential in other forms of employment after the accident which uses her salary at the time of the accident as a standard of the former, is unfair. Until her engagement in 'My Fair Lady', a show of extraordinary box office appeal, plaintiff had been earning approximately $85 weekly, an amount comparable to what she might reasonably expect to earn in other forms of employment. In addition . . . plaintiff at the time of her accident was still subject to the vicissitudes of show business (emphasis added)."

Tschida, at 76. This Court is not bound to construe the "other occupation" provision of the Mossa Policy, which in any event is facially dissimilar to the provision in *Tschida*, to preclude a comparative salary analysis.

Plaintiff relies on the more recent case of *Hoffert v. Commercial Ins. Co. of Newark, NJ*, 739 F.Supp. 201 (S.D.N.Y.1990) for the proposition that an examination of plaintiff's salary history and a comparable wage analysis is appropriate. In *Hoffert*, the court interpreted a disability policy that had been issued to a general and vascular surgeon. The policy provided that "if disability . . . shall prevent the Insured from engaging in any occupation or employment for which he is fitted by reason of education, training and experience . . . such disability shall be deemed Permanent Total Disability." Id. at 202. When the plaintiff injured his shoulder, the insurance company conceded that he was no longer able to perform surgery. However, the insurance company claimed that plaintiff suffered no Permanent Total Disability preventing him from engaging in a variety of occupations proposed by the insurance company's vocational specialist, including a job as a surgical consultant to patients seeking a second opinion and teaching at a medical school. Id. at 205–06.

The *Hoffert* court disagreed. The court began its analysis by noting that:

> while one old New York case did equate the word "fitted" with "qualified" . . . in light of the total phraseology used here, we view the requirement as requiring far more than qualifications. As a licensed physician and surgeon, even with his substantial physical impairment, he is "qualified" to do a number of medical jobs. The issue is whether he is "fitted by reason of education, training and experience" to them.

Id. at 205. Rather than finding the "other occupation" provision ambiguous, the *Hoffert* court interpreted the plain meaning of the provision to include an analysis of the plaintiff's salary history and the availability of the proposed occupations. Id. at 206. Specifically, the court concluded that consulting work was not suitable, because "it is clear that the availability of such work is not great." *Hoffert*, at 206. Finally, the Court agreed with the plaintiff that "the suitability of other employment must be measured financially." Id.

While *Hoffert* and *Tschida* appear to be the only published New York cases construing a disability policy similar to plaintiff's Policy, other jurisdictions have analyzed similar disability policies at great length. The overwhelming majority of other jurisdictions hold that "other occupation" provisions, "although [they are] framed in terms of disability to perform or engage in any occupation for wages or profit, [are] generally construed to relate to an occupation in which the insured has been trained and has worked during his working life; or it may relate to an occupation that, as a practical matter, the insured could follow considering his age, training, experience, reputation, station in life, and other relevant circumstances." Earl L. Kellett, LL.B., Annotation, What constitutes permanent or total disability within coverage of insurance policy issued to physical laborer or workman, 32 ALR3dFED 922 (1971–1997). * * *

This Court adopts the reasoning of the majority of jurisdictions and finds that an ordinary person deciding whether to purchase such a disability insurance policy would reasonably expect that he was insuring against the inability to engage in a living wage, not merely a job paying any wage. See *Mason v. Loyal Protective Life Ins. Co.*, 91 N.W.2d 389, 392 (Iowa 1958); *Kooker v. Benefit Ass'n of Ry. Employees*, 246 N.W.2d 743, 745 (N.D.1976). To hold otherwise would be to ignore the purposes for which individuals purchase disability insurance policies. Like the *Hoffert* court, therefore, this Court construes the plain meaning of the entire "other occupation" provision of the Policy to permit the factfinder to consider plaintiff's salary history, as well as a wage analysis of other available occupations, to determine in what other "gainful occupation" . . . [plaintiff] might reasonably be expected to engage because of [his] education, training or experience.

B. Disputed Issues of Material Fact Preclude Summary Judgment

* * * The severity of plaintiff's disability and the extent of his prior "education, training and experience" are factual issues central to the determination in what occupations plaintiff might reasonably be expected to engage. However, the parties' differing interpretations of

the available evidence, as evidenced by their Rule 56.1 statements, demonstrate that numerous questions of fact exist which require a trial of this action.

Conclusion

The Court construes the plain meaning of the entire "other occupation" provision to permit the factfinder to consider plaintiff's salary history, as well as a wage analysis of other available occupations, in order to determine in what other "gainful occupation . . . [plaintiff] might reasonably be expected to engage because of [his] education, training or experience." In addition, the Court denies defendant's motion for summary judgment because there remain questions of fact regarding the severity of plaintiff's injury and the extent of his "education, training and experience".

SO ORDERED.

NOTES AND QUESTIONS

1. *Partial Disability.* Virtually all disability policies provide all or nothing coverage; the insured is either totally disabled, in which case he receives the full amount of coverage afforded by the policy, or he is not disabled, in which case he is not covered. Coverage is structured in this manner in order to avoid the problems associated with assessing partial disability. For an example of a rare policy that provided lower benefits for partial disability, see *Giustra v. Unum Life Insurance Co. of America*, 815 A.2d 811 (Me. 2003). One method of coping indirectly with the partial disability problem is the occupational-disability clause, which treats the partially disabled insured as though he is totally disabled, though sometimes only for a specified period. In *Mossa* that period was two years; in many policies it is five years. Some insurers offer occupational disability coverage for an unlimited period for an additional premium. In the absence of such coverage, there is frequent litigation over the extent of the insured's disability after the expiration of the occupational disability period. See, e.g., *Lopes v. Metropolitan Life Ins. Co.*, 332 F.3d 1 (1st Cir. 2003) (concluding that insured who could engage in sedentary work was not totally disabled). See generally Charles E. Soule, Disability Income Insurance: The Unique Risk 79–80 (4th ed. 1998).

2. *Subjective Disability and Objective Medical Evidence.* One particularly difficult form of disability to verify involves conditions such as pain, stress, and chronic fatigue. The case law is increasingly populated with disputes over such "subjective" conditions. Some courts uphold coverage denials when there is no "objective" medical evidence of such conditions, sometimes even in the absence of a policy provision requiring such evidence. Other courts weigh all the evidence, medical or otherwise. For representative decisions, see *Salomaa v. Honda Long Term Disability Plan*, 542 F.Supp.2d 1068 (C.D. Cal. 2008) (objective evidence that claimant had chronic fatigue syndrome not required, but objective evidence of the physical limitations it caused can be required); *Rodriguez v. McGraw-Hill Cos.*, 297 F.Supp.2d 676 (S.D.N.Y. 2004) (objective medical evidence not required when there is no accepted test for diagnosing condition); *Pokol v. E.I. du Pont de Nemours & Co.*, 963 F.Supp. 1361 (D.N.J. 1997) (objective medical evidence required); *Clausen v. Standard*

Insurance Co., 961 F.Supp. 1446 (D.Colo. 1997) (objective medical evidence not required).

In the ERISA context—which controls in most disability insurance disputes given the predominance of employer-provided coverage—there is an analogous division of authority. However, as a result of *Firestone's* rule that courts must defer to plan administrators when the plan so requires (discussed above, in the health insurance section), the issue is typically whether or not the plan administrator abused her discretion in denying benefits. See *Torgeson v. Unum Life Ins. Co. of Am.*, 466 F.Supp.2d 1096 (N.D. Iowa 2006) (plan administrator abused his discretion in denying benefits because there was no objective medical evidence of disability, as the plan did not require such evidence). When the underlying plan requires objective medical evidence of a disability, courts almost universally conclude that it is appropriate for a plan administrator to enforce this provision. See *Judge v. Metropolitan Life Ins. Co.*, 710 F.3d 651, 660 (6th Cir. 2013) ("Requiring a claimant to provide objective medical evidence of disability is not irrational or unreasonable."); *Hobson v. Metropolitan Life Ins. Co.*, 574 F.3d 75, 88 (2nd Cir. 2009).

3. *Social or Legal Disability*. Cases occasionally arise in which the insured is physically capable of continuing to work, but is precluded or prohibited from doing so for social or legal reasons. For example, the insured may be completely or partially quarantined because he has contracted a communicable disease. See, e.g., *Doe v. Great-West Life & Annuity Ins. Co.*, 208 F.3d 213 (6th Cir. 2000) (physician infected with Hepatitis virus was disabled within the meaning of insurer's policy); *Dang v. Northwestern Mut. Life Ins. Co.*, 960 F.Supp. 215 (D.Neb. 1997) (*contra*). Should a distinction be drawn between cases where the insured's inability to work is wholly involuntary (as in *Doe*) and those in which the cause is at least partly the insured's responsibility? See, e.g., *Walker v. UnumProvident Corp.*, 2002 WL 31474521 (D. Minn. 2002) (it was a question of fact whether a physician's inability to refrain from exposing himself to female patients, or the consequent subsequent revocation of his medical license, was the reason for his inability to work); *Ohio Nat'l Life Assurance Corp. v. Crampton*, 822 F.Supp. 1230 (E.D.Va.1993), aff'd, 53 F.3d 328 (4th Cir.1995) (because insured's incarceration for aggravated sexual battery and exposing himself to a minor was the result of a mental illness, he was disabled within the meaning of the policy).

4. *Differences in Policy Language*. As the court in *Mossa* indicated, many decisions turn on nuances in the policy language defining a disability. It is also true, however, that different courts exhibit different attitudes toward the general disability issue, some reading policy language strictly and others applying what amounts to a reasonableness test even apart from the particular language at issue. For example, in *Johnson v. Trustmark Insurance Co.*, 771 So.2d 307 (La. App. 2000), a surgeon covered by a total disability policy was capable of performing non-surgical work within the hospital, but the court held that he was disabled nonetheless. Similarly, in *Moots v. Bankers Life Co.*, 707 P.2d 1083 (Kan. 1985), the court held that the insured's work as a bus driver after the insurer discontinued paying benefits did not preclude coverage, notwithstanding policy language requiring that the insured "does not engage in any occupation, work or employment for wage or profit during any such disability." In light of this judicial tendency to treat the notion of total

disability as flexible, does the quoted clause not at least imply, "and we really mean *complete inability* to work?" If the clause does add this meaning, how should the courts make it operational without requiring that the insured be paralyzed from head to toe in order to be totally disabled?

5. *Selective Denial and the Rule of Contract "Law."* One argument for active judicial limitation on insurers' attempts to employ provisions like the one at issue in *Moots* is that insurers can invoke such clauses selectively in a manner that is difficult for the courts to supervise except by what amounts to wholesale reinterpretation. For example, suppose that insurers tend not to enforce such a clause literally so long as they believe that the insured is in fact functionally disabled. Suppose further that when insurers believe the insured is malingering, they invoke the clause and deny all benefits, instead of proving directly that the insured is not disabled. Selective enforcement of the clause in this manner may constitute a kind of lawlessness. In effect, everyone is entitled to engage in minimal work without becoming ineligible for benefits, except those the insurer suspects but does not want to take the trouble to prove are not functionally disabled. Is the inequity entailed in this stance sufficient justification for a judicial interpretation that transfers this decision to the jury? Will the treatment of all insureds who engage in minimal work be any more equitable or desirable under the latter approach?

Heller v. Equitable Life Assurance Society of the United States

United States Court of Appeals, Seventh Circuit, 1987.
833 F.2d 1253.

■ COFFEY, CIRCUIT JUDGE.

The Equitable Life Assurance Society, defendant-appellant, appeals from the order of the district court entering a declaratory judgment in favor of Dr. Stanley Heller, plaintiff-appellee, for the defendant's alleged breach of a disability income insurance contract. The district court found that Dr. Heller was entitled to receive $5,880 per month from Equitable on the insurance contract from March 21, 1984, through February 5, 1986, and thereafter for the time period Dr. Heller was totally disabled. Dr. Heller cross-appeals from the district court's order reducing the total amount of disability benefits payable from Equitable, as well as from the district court's refusal to award taxable costs, including attorneys' fees, under Illinois law. We affirm in part, reverse in part, and remand for further proceedings consistent with this opinion.

I

Dr. Stanley Heller, a physician, is licensed to practice medicine in the state of Illinois. Dr. Heller is a board-certified physician in the field of Cardiovascular Diseases and specializes in invasive cardiology. He was also the Director of the Cardiovascular Catheterization Laboratory at St. Joseph's Hospital, Chicago.

In early 1983 Dr. Heller met with Paul Berlin, an agent for the Equitable Life Assurance Society (Equitable) to discuss simplifying his existing professional disability insurance coverage, for at the time he was insured under six or seven different policies issued by at least two different companies. After evaluating Dr. Heller's existing policies, Mr. Berlin informed Dr. Heller that if he decided to purchase the Equitable disability income policy as offered ($7,000 monthly), he would be required to cancel his other disability policies. At the time Dr. Heller applied for disability coverage in March of 1983, he represented on the application that he had no other disability coverage as he intended to cancel his other disability policy at the time Equitable's coverage took effect. Equitable's policy, issued the following month in April of 1983, provided that Dr. Heller would be paid the sum of $7,000 per month, after a 90-day elimination period incorporated therein. Dr. Heller testified that he directed his office manager to cancel all his other disability policies when the Equitable policy became effective, and "to the best of [his] knowledge," she canceled the policies. He further testified that it was not until November of 1984, some eight months after his withdrawal from practice, that he was informed by an office employee that he still had an American Motorist Insurance Co. (American Motorists) disability policy in full force and effect.

During the latter quarter of 1983 Dr. Heller developed a painful and crippling condition in his left wrist and hand diagnosed as carpal tunnel syndrome. Dr. Heller testified that as he experienced the debilitating symptoms of the condition in his left wrist and into his hand, he was prevented from practicing in his specialty as an invasive cardiologist after March 20, 1984. Dr. Heller applied for benefit payments on his Equitable disability income policy in late March 1984. The policy issued to Dr. Heller defined "total disability" as follows:

> "Total disability means the complete inability of the Insured, because of injury or sickness, to engage in the Insured's regular occupation, * * * provided, however, the total disability will not be considered to exist for any period during which the Insured is not under the regular care and attendance of a physician. * * * "

Dr. Heller claimed that because he was unable to engage in his profession as an invasive cardiologist as a result of the carpal tunnel syndrome condition, and because he was under the regular care of a physician and had made timely premium payments, he was entitled to disability benefits under the policy. Initially, Equitable made payments pursuant to the disability income provisions, but terminated these payments after May 5, 1985, because he (Dr. Heller) refused to undergo carpal tunnel surgery upon Equitable's insistence. As a result of Equitable's refusal to continue payments under the contract, Dr. Heller initiated the present action. * * *

II

Illinois law controls this case as Equitable issued the policy to Dr. Heller in Illinois, the state where Dr. Heller resided and practiced medicine. Our research reveals, and both parties agree, that the Illinois courts have not directly addressed the question of whether a disability income policy providing that the claimant must be "under the regular care and attendance of a physician" requires an insured to submit to surgical treatment for the condition causing the total disability in order to receive benefits. Thus, we rely on the traditional principles of insurance and contract law, long recognized by the Illinois courts as an appropriate basis for resolving whether the clause conditions coverage on the insured's undergoing surgery. Initially, Illinois courts apply the rule that any ambiguities in the provisions of an insurance policy will be construed against the drafter of the instrument, the insurer, and in favor of the insured, *see, e.g., Burton v. Government Employees Insurance Company,* 135 Ill.App.3d 723 (1985); *Dora Twp. v. Indiana Insurance Company,* 78 Ill.2d 376 (1980); however, "where * * * there is no ambiguity, [the courts] will not ignore the *very plain language of the policy.*" *Rock Island Bank v. Time Ins. Co.,* 14 Ill.Dec. 719, 720 (1978) (emphasis added). Secondly, insurance policy "[e]xceptions to liability must be expressed in unequivocal language so that it is reasonable to assume the insured understood and accepted these limitations." *Garman v. New York Life Insurance Company,* 501 F.Supp. 51, 52 (N.D.Ill.1980) (citing *Michigan Mutual Liability Company v. Hoover Brothers Inc.,* 96 Ill.App.2d 238 (1968)).

A reading of the Equitable disability policy discloses that it fails to set forth any limitation of coverage requiring an insured to submit to surgery for treatment of the condition causing the total disability. The policy provides coverage where (1) the insured is prevented from engaging in his or her regular occupation because of sickness or injury and is totally disabled; and (2) that the insured be under "the regular care and attendance of a physician." Equitable does not dispute that Dr. Heller is presently unable to practice as an invasive cardiologist but argues that his failure to submit to surgery for his disabling condition as recommended[1] requires a finding by the Court that he is no longer "under the regular care and attendance of a physician." Therefore, Equitable asserts that Dr. Heller is no longer entitled to disability income benefits.

We reject Equitable's arguments because the language in the policy stating that the claimant must be "under the regular care and attendance of a physician" clearly does not include surgical procedures. Although the policy does not define the parameters of the clause "under the regular care and attendance of a physician," we refuse to add to and construe the policy beyond its clear and obvious language, to require the insured to submit to surgery, if and when surgery is recommended by the physician "rendering regular care and [in] attendance." The language is clear on its face to the average citizen and even more so to a member of the medical profession. We are convinced that under Illinois law the clause "under the regular care and attendance" means just what it says, namely, that the insured is obligated to periodically consult and be examined by his or her treating physician at intervals to be determined by the physician. Clearly the language does not condition disability payments on the insured's undergoing surgery if recommended by the physician rendering "regular care and [in] attendance." We refuse to indulge in judicial activism and condition coverage under the contract on the insured's undergoing surgery, when the insurer failed to provide such a conditional clause in the policy.

The clause, "under the regular care and attendance of a physician," was not intended to allow the insurer to scrutinize, determine, and direct the method of treatment the claimant receives. We are convinced that the purpose of the clause requiring the insured to be "under the

---

[1] Dr. Heller was examined by and consulted with a number of doctors, and at least two recommended surgery.

regular care and attendance of a physician" is to determine that the claimant is actually disabled, *see, e.g., Russell v. Prudential Insurance Company of America,* 437 F.2d 602, 607 (5th Cir.1971), is not malingering, and to prevent fraudulent claims.

The insurance industry by its very nature offers insurance coverage on a non-negotiable basis, and consumers are unable to participate in the drafting of the language or the terms of the policy. Case law and fairness require that ambiguities in insurance policies be construed against the drafter of the policy, the insurance company.

In the absence of a clear, unequivocal and specific contractual requirement that the insured is obligated to undergo surgery to attempt to minimize his disability, we refuse to order the same. To hold otherwise and to impose such a requirement would, in effect, enlarge the terms of the policy beyond those clearly defined in the policy agreed to by the parties. *See, e.g., John Hancock Mutual Life Insurance Company v. Spurgeon,* 175 Tenn. 319 (1939). Thus, under the terms of this disability policy, Dr. Heller is not required to undergo surgery for treatment of his carpal tunnel syndrome condition before he receives disability income payments. * * *

Lastly, Equitable argues that the "principle of fairness and good faith, a policy of motivating persons to correct rather than accept physical disabilities," necessitates that an insured suffering from causes that disabled him, avail himself of all reasonable means and remedies to relieve his disability, including surgery. Once again, we reject Equitable's argument. The record clearly establishes that Dr. Heller acted in good faith. Initially, Dr. Heller properly reported his disability to Equitable and consulted with and remained under the regular care of his physician as required under the policy. Further, at Equitable's request, Dr. Heller acquiesced to an examination performed by two specialists selected by Equitable, one a hand surgeon and the other a neurologist, at the Mayo Clinic in Rochester, Minnesota. Additionally, there is nothing in the record to establish that Dr. Heller failed to provide Equitable with any and/or all supplemental information required. The record further demonstrates that after Dr. Heller's condition was diagnosed and before he filed a claim for disability payments, Dr. Heller was forced to reduce his case load beginning in December 1983 to March 1984, and thereafter was forced to withdraw from practice.[2] The trial court found that Dr. Heller fulfilled his obligations under the policy; we agree and hold that Dr. Heller did all that was required of him under the terms of the Equitable disability policy.

However, Equitable insists that the insured, as a party to an insurance contract, has a good faith "duty to cure his disability if he can do so without reasonable risk and pain to himself." Equitable ignores the fact that many insureds like the plaintiff-appellee, choose not to undergo surgery because of the accompanying risks of infection, transfusion (hepatitis), bleeding, motor enervation of the median nerve, adhesions, scar tissue, possible anesthetic shock, trauma, anxiety, and

---

[2] It is significant to point out that Dr. Heller received treatment for his carpal tunnel syndrome condition. Dr. Loughran, an orthopedic surgeon at St. Joseph Hospital, injected a steroid into Dr. Heller's wrist, attempting to minimize the disability and allow him to return to practice.

even reoccurrence of the carpal tunnel syndrome condition. We are convinced that under Illinois law an insured is not required to undergo these risks in the absence of a specific contractual requirement. Furthermore, it seems very evident that because of these risks and other risks in the majority of surgical procedures, courts have wisely adopted the doctrine of informed consent.

Although we might not choose to follow the same course of conduct and path of reasoning as Dr. Heller,[3] there is no moral, much less legal obligation or compelling reason, to second guess an insured's, and in this case Dr. Heller's, decision to forego surgery. The insurance company seeking to condition coverage on its insureds' acquiescence to undergo surgery to minimize the extent of their disabilities, as well as the financial loss to the insurer, need only incorporate a specific requirement to that effect in the policy, and we would not hesitate to enforce the same. On the other hand, insurers who fail to include this express surgical contractual requirement, and who refuse to cover an insured after entering into a binding and enforceable agreement after accepting substantial premiums, in circumstances such as those before us, cause problems not only for the insured, but for the insurance industry as well. Insurance companies, members of a service industry, must recognize that, like their insureds, they have corresponding duties and obligations under the policy and must conduct themselves accordingly instead of attempting to rely on the courts to correct their own deficiencies in underwriting and/or careless policy drafting. * * *

The judgment of the district court is affirmed in part and reversed in part, and the case is remanded to the district court for further proceedings consistent with this opinion.

NOTES AND QUESTIONS

1. *An Implied Duty to Mitigate?* Would it have been inappropriate for the court to hold that the insured had an implied duty to mitigate his losses? Did the court imply that there might be such a duty when it distinguished the availability of medical treatment for an ailment from the availability of surgical treatment? Many courts are willing to require the insured to submit to medical care or treatment, but cases requiring the insured to undergo surgery are extremely rare. Are the problems entailed in deciding when it would be reasonable to seek surgical treatment too great an obstacle, or would they closely resemble tort defendants' frequently raised defense of plaintiffs' failure to mitigate?

2. *Under the Regular Care and Attendance of a Physician.* Under what circumstances should the requirement that an insured be under the regular care of a physician be read as an exclusive evidentiary condition of coverage? Might this clause create undue moral hazard—but for health insurers, rather than the disability insurers who include it in their policies?

---

[3] We note that Dr. Heller has apparently abandoned his profession as a surgeon to pursue a new career in law.

CHAPTER SIX

LIABILITY INSURANCE: INDEMNITY

This Chapter is about the protection that liability insurance provides against amounts owed due to legal judgments and settlements, otherwise known as indemnity. The next Chapter is about defense and the settlement process under liability insurance policies. There are many different kinds of liability insurance. One of the most significant is Commercial General Liability (CGL) insurance. As its name suggests, this form of coverage provides "general" insurance against the kinds of liability that any business may face, principally for bodily injury and property damage. In addition, the liability insurance portion of Homeowners Insurance (Section II of the Sample Policy set out at the beginning of Chapter Four) provides "general" insurance against the principal kinds of liability that any homeowner may face. These general forms of liability insurance are the subject of Section A of this Chapter. Section B considers issues arising under two other forms of liability insurance: Directors & Officers and Professional Liability, or Malpractice, insurance. Auto Liability insurance is considered in Chapter Eight, which considers auto insurance of various sorts.

A. GENERAL LIABILITY INSURANCE

The Commercial General Liability (CGL) Policy set out below is the successor to the Comprehensive General Liability (CGL) Policy that was in use (in successive revisions) from 1941 to 1985. Insurers began marketing the CGL policy under the new name in 1986. Some of the cases in this Chapter involve interpretations of older CGL policy provisions that closely resemble those in newer CGL policies. For reasons that will become clearer as you study the "trigger" of coverage under the occurrence version of this policy, the provisions of the older policies will remain relevant for years to come, but the new policies have come to dominate legal disputes. As you compare the provisions of the Sample Policy with those at issue in the cases set out below, consider the following questions: Which provisions suggest that the drafters were attempting to reverse the effect of previous judicial decisions? To what extent are these efforts successful? Which provisions have failed to make a difference in the probable outcome of the same dispute under the new policy?

Billions of dollars have been spent litigating the meaning of several phrases in Coverage A of the standard Insuring Agreement in CGL policies (pages 1–6 of the Sample Policy, below). This section surveys the highlights of this litigation, by addressing the meaning of the key terms and phrases in the Insuring Agreement that, in language identical to or highly similar to the following, promises to pay "*those sums* the insured becomes *legally obligated* to pay *as damages,* because of *bodily injury or property damage,* caused by an *occurrence* * * * This insurance applies only to bodily injury or property damage which occurs *during the policy period.*" (italics added).

Prior to 1966, the standard CGL policy provided coverage of liability for damage caused by "accident" rather than by an "occurrence." Some courts held that the term had a temporal element, and that gradually accumulating damage or damage resulting from long-term hazardous exposure therefore was not covered; others interpreted the term more broadly. See, e.g., *Beryllium Corp. v. American Mutual Liability Ins. Co.*, 223 F.2d 71 (3d Cir. 1955). The 1966 revisions made "occurrence" the touchstone of coverage. The term "occurrence" was defined in roughly the following language: "An accident, including continuous or repeated exposure to conditions, which results during the policy period in bodily injury or property damage neither expected nor intended from the standpoint of the insured." This definition made it clear that damage need not occur at a single point in time in order to be covered, so long as that damage is neither expected nor intended. Because the "neither expected nor intended" limitation was shifted from the definition of an "occurrence" to the Exclusions in the 1986 revision, the meaning of that phrase is addressed below in connection with the CGL exclusions. However, because the term "accident" is still included in the definition of "occurrence," there is sometimes a question whether there has been an occurrence at all, depending on what "accident" means. See, e.g., *AES v. Steadfast Ins. Co.*, 725 S.E. 2d 532 (Va. 2012), holding that environmental property damage caused by a power company's emissions of greenhouse gases did not constitute an "occurrence" under the power company's CGL insurance policy because the emissions were not an "accident."

In contrast to Coverage A, which pertains to bodily injury and property damage, Coverage B of the Sample CGL Policy, and of most CGL policies, provides coverage of what it terms "Personal and Advertising Injury" liability (pages 6–7). Although the term "personal injury" is often used interchangeably with "bodily injury," that is not its meaning in Coverage B. Rather, "Personal and Advertising Injury" are defined to include a variety of "intentional torts" that do not result in bodily injury—among others, false arrest, malicious prosecution, and defamation. Advertising injury means "the use of another's advertising idea" in an advertisement, and "infringing upon another's copyright, trade dress, or slogan" in an "advertisement." There has been comparatively little litigation about coverage of these forms of liability, in part because the exclusions that apply to this coverage often substantially limit its scope. One common issue in the litigation that has taken place, however, has concerned the meaning of an "advertising injury." The message of the decisions is that there must be a causal nexus between an advertisement and the resulting injury for the injury to be covered. See, e.g. *Rose Acre Farms, Inc. v. Columbia Cas. Co.*, 662 F. 3d 765 (7th Cir. 2011).

SECTION A GENERAL LIABILITY INSURANCE 437

1. **SAMPLE CGL POLICY**

POLICY NUMBER: _____   COMMERCIAL GENERAL LIABILITY
CG DS 01 10 01

COMMERCIAL GENERAL LIABILITY DECLARATIONS

COMPANY NAME AREA	PRODUCER NAME AREA

NAMED INSURED: _____
MAILING ADDRESS: _____

POLICY PERIOD: FROM _____ TO _____ AT 12:01 A.M. TIME AT YOUR MAILING ADDRESS SHOWN ABOVE

IN RETURN FOR THE PAYMENT OF THE PREMIUM, AND SUBJECT TO ALL THE TERMS OF THIS POLICY, WE AGREE WITH YOU TO PROVIDE THE INSURANCE AS STATED IN THIS POLICY.

LIMITS OF INSURANCE		
EACH OCCURRENCE LIMIT	$ _____	
DAMAGE TO PREMISES RENTED TO YOU LIMIT	$ _____	Any one premises
MEDICAL EXPENSE LIMIT	$ _____	Any one person
PERSONAL & ADVERTISING INJURY LIMIT	$ _____	Any one person or organization
GENERAL AGGREGATE LIMIT	$ _____	
PRODUCTS/COMPLETED OPERATIONS AGGREGATE LIMIT	$ _____	

RETROACTIVE DATE (CG 00 02 ONLY)

THIS INSURANCE DOES NOT APPLY TO "BODILY INJURY", "PROPERTY DAMAGE" OR "PERSONAL AND ADVERTISING INJURY" WHICH OCCURS BEFORE THE RETROACTIVE DATE, IF ANY, SHOWN BELOW.
RETROACTIVE DATE: _____
(ENTER DATE OR "NONE" IF NO RETROACTIVE DATE APPLIES)

DESCRIPTION OF BUSINESS

FORM OF BUSINESS:

☐ INDIVIDUAL   ☐ PARTNERSHIP   ☐ JOINT VENTURE   ☐ TRUST

☐ LIMITED LIABILITY COMPANY   ☐ ORGANIZATION, INCLUDING A CORPORATION (BUT NOT IN-
CLUDING A PARTNERSHIP, JOINT VENTURE OR LIMITED LIABILITY
COMPANY)

BUSINESS DESCRIPTION: _____

ALL PREMISES YOU OWN, RENT OR OCCUPY	
LOCATION NUMBER	ADDRESS OF ALL PREMISES YOU OWN, RENT OR OCCUPY

CLASSIFICATION AND PREMIUM							
LOCATION NUMBER	CLASSIFICATION	CODE NO.	PREMIUM BASE	RATE		ADVANCE PREMIUM	
				Prem/ Ops	Prod/Comp Ops	Prem/ Ops	Prod/Comp Ops
			$	$	$	$	$

PREMIUM SHOWN IS PAYABLE:	STATE TAX OR OTHER (if applicable)	$	
	TOTAL PREMIUM (SUBJECT TO AUDIT)	$	
	AT INCEPTION	$	
	AT EACH ANNIVERSARY	$	
	(IF POLICY PERIOD IS MORE THAN ONE YEAR AND PREMIUM IS PAID IN ANNUAL INSTALLMENTS)		
AUDIT PERIOD (IF APPLICABLE)	☐ ANNUALLY ☐ SEMI-ANNUALLY	☐ QUARTERLY	☐ MONTHLY

ENDORSEMENTS
ENDORSEMENTS ATTACHED TO THIS POLICY:

THESE DECLARATIONS, TOGETHER WITH THE COMMON POLICY CONDITIONS AND COVERAGE FORM(S) AND ANY ENDORSEMENT(S), COMPLETE THE ABOVE NUMBERED POLICY.

Countersigned:	By:
(Date)	(Authorized Representative)

NOTE

OFFICERS' FACSIMILE SIGNATURES MAY BE INSERTED HERE, ON THE POLICY COVER OR ELSEWHERE AT THE COMPANY'S OPTION.

COMMERCIAL GENERAL LIABILITY
CG 00 01 04 13

COMMERCIAL GENERAL LIABILITY COVERAGE FORM

Various provisions in this policy restrict coverage. Read the entire policy carefully to determine rights, duties and what is and is not covered.

Throughout this policy the words "you" and "your" refer to the Named Insured shown in the Declarations, and any other person or organization qualifying as a Named Insured under this policy. The words "we", "us" and "our" refer to the company providing this insurance.

The word "insured" means any person or organization qualifying as such under Section II – Who Is An Insured.

Other words and phrases that appear in quotation marks have special meaning. Refer to Section V – Definitions.

SECTION I – COVERAGES

COVERAGE A – BODILY INJURY AND PROPERTY DAMAGE LIABILITY

1. Insuring Agreement

a. We will pay those sums that the insured becomes legally obligated to pay as damages because of "bodily injury" or "property damage" to which this insurance applies. We will have the right and duty to defend the insured against any "suit" seeking those damages. However, we will have no duty to defend the insured against any "suit" seeking damages for "bodily injury" or "property damage" to which this insurance does not apply. We may, at our discretion, investigate any "occurrence" and settle any claim or "suit" that may result. But:

   (1) The amount we will pay for damages is limited as described in Section III – Limits Of Insurance; and

   (2) Our right and duty to defend ends when we have used up the applicable limit of insurance in the payment of judgments or settlements under Coverages **A** or **B** or medical expenses under Coverage **C**.

   No other obligation or liability to pay sums or perform acts or services is covered unless explicitly provided for under Supplementary Payments – Coverages **A** and **B**.

b. This insurance applies to "bodily injury" and "property damage" only if:

   (1) The "bodily injury" or "property damage" is caused by an "occurrence" that takes place in the "coverage territory";

   (2) The "bodily injury" or "property damage" occurs during the policy period; and

   (3) Prior to the policy period, no insured listed under Paragraph **1.** of Section II – Who Is An Insured and no "employee" authorized by you to give or receive notice of an "occurrence" or claim, knew that the "bodily injury" or "property damage" had occurred, in whole or in part. If such a listed insured or authorized "employee" knew, prior to the policy period, that the "bodily injury" or "property damage" occurred, then any continuation, change or resumption of such "bodily injury" or "property damage" during or after the policy period will be deemed to have been known prior to the policy period.

c. "Bodily injury" or "property damage" which occurs during the policy period and was not, prior to the policy period, known to have occurred by any insured listed under Paragraph **1.** of Section II – Who Is An Insured or any "employee" authorized by you to give or receive notice of an "occurrence" or claim, includes any continuation, change or resumption of that "bodily injury" or "property damage" after the end of the policy period.

d. "Bodily injury" or "property damage" will be deemed to have been known to have occurred at the earliest time when any insured listed under Paragraph **1.** of Section II – Who Is An Insured or any "employee" authorized by you to give or receive notice of an "occurrence" or claim:

   (1) Reports all, or any part, of the "bodily injury" or "property damage" to us or any other insurer;

   (2) Receives a written or verbal demand or claim for damages because of the "bodily injury" or "property damage"; or

   (3) Becomes aware by any other means that "bodily injury" or "property damage" has occurred or has begun to occur.

e. Damages because of "bodily injury" include damages claimed by any person or organization for care, loss of services or death resulting at any time from the "bodily injury".

CG 00 01 04 13 © Insurance Services Office, Inc., 2012 Page 1 of 16

2. Exclusions

This insurance does not apply to:

a. Expected Or Intended Injury

"Bodily injury" or "property damage" expected or intended from the standpoint of the insured. This exclusion does not apply to "bodily injury" resulting from the use of reasonable force to protect persons or property.

b. Contractual Liability

"Bodily injury" or "property damage" for which the insured is obligated to pay damages by reason of the assumption of liability in a contract or agreement. This exclusion does not apply to liability for damages:

(1) That the insured would have in the absence of the contract or agreement; or

(2) Assumed in a contract or agreement that is an "insured contract", provided the "bodily injury" or "property damage" occurs subsequent to the execution of the contract or agreement. Solely for the purposes of liability assumed in an "insured contract", reasonable attorneys' fees and necessary litigation expenses incurred by or for a party other than an insured are deemed to be damages because of "bodily injury" or "property damage", provided:

   (a) Liability to such party for, or for the cost of, that party's defense has also been assumed in the same "insured contract"; and

   (b) Such attorneys' fees and litigation expenses are for defense of that party against a civil or alternative dispute resolution proceeding in which damages to which this insurance applies are alleged.

c. Liquor Liability

"Bodily injury" or "property damage" for which any insured may be held liable by reason of:

(1) Causing or contributing to the intoxication of any person;

(2) The furnishing of alcoholic beverages to a person under the legal drinking age or under the influence of alcohol; or

(3) Any statute, ordinance or regulation relating to the sale, gift, distribution or use of alcoholic beverages.

This exclusion applies even if the claims against any insured allege negligence or other wrongdoing in:

   (a) The supervision, hiring, employment, training or monitoring of others by that insured; or

   (b) Providing or failing to provide transportation with respect to any person that may be under the influence of alcohol;

if the "occurrence" which caused the "bodily injury" or "property damage", involved that which is described in Paragraph (1), (2) or (3) above.

However, this exclusion applies only if you are in the business of manufacturing, distributing, selling, serving or furnishing alcoholic beverages. For the purposes of this exclusion, permitting a person to bring alcoholic beverages on your premises, for consumption on your premises, whether or not a fee is charged or a license is required for such activity, is not by itself considered the business of selling, serving or furnishing alcoholic beverages.

d. Workers' Compensation And Similar Laws

Any obligation of the insured under a workers' compensation, disability benefits or unemployment compensation law or any similar law.

e. Employer's Liability

"Bodily injury" to:

(1) An "employee" of the insured arising out of and in the course of:

   (a) Employment by the insured; or

   (b) Performing duties related to the conduct of the insured's business; or

(2) The spouse, child, parent, brother or sister of that "employee" as a consequence of Paragraph (1) above.

This exclusion applies whether the insured may be liable as an employer or in any other capacity and to any obligation to share damages with or repay someone else who must pay damages because of the injury.

This exclusion does not apply to liability assumed by the insured under an "insured contract".

f. Pollution

(1) "Bodily injury" or "property damage" arising out of the actual, alleged or threatened discharge, dispersal, seepage, migration, release or escape of "pollutants":

  (a) At or from any premises, site or location which is or was at any time owned or occupied by, or rented or loaned to, any insured. However, this subparagraph does not apply to:

    (i) "Bodily injury" if sustained within a building and caused by smoke, fumes, vapor or soot produced by or originating from equipment that is used to heat, cool or dehumidify the building, or equipment that is used to heat water for personal use, by the building's occupants or their guests;

    (ii) "Bodily injury" or "property damage" for which you may be held liable, if you are a contractor and the owner or lessee of such premises, site or location has been added to your policy as an additional insured with respect to your ongoing operations performed for that additional insured at that premises, site or location and such premises, site or location is not and never was owned or occupied by, or rented or loaned to, any insured, other than that additional insured; or

    (iii) "Bodily injury" or "property damage" arising out of heat, smoke or fumes from a "hostile fire";

  (b) At or from any premises, site or location which is or was at any time used by or for any insured or others for the handling, storage, disposal, processing or treatment of waste;

  (c) Which are or were at any time transported, handled, stored, treated, disposed of, or processed as waste by or for:

    (i) Any insured; or

    (ii) Any person or organization for whom you may be legally responsible; or

  (d) At or from any premises, site or location on which any insured or any contractors or subcontractors working directly or indirectly on any insured's behalf are performing operations if the "pollutants" are brought on or to the premises, site or location in connection with such operations by such insured, contractor or subcontractor. However, this subparagraph does not apply to:

    (i) "Bodily injury" or "property damage" arising out of the escape of fuels, lubricants or other operating fluids which are needed to perform the normal electrical, hydraulic or mechanical functions necessary for the operation of "mobile equipment" or its parts, if such fuels, lubricants or other operating fluids escape from a vehicle part designed to hold, store or receive them. This exception does not apply if the "bodily injury" or "property damage" arises out of the intentional discharge, dispersal or release of the fuels, lubricants or other operating fluids, or if such fuels, lubricants or other operating fluids are brought on or to the premises, site or location with the intent that they be discharged, dispersed or released as part of the operations being performed by such insured, contractor or subcontractor;

    (ii) "Bodily injury" or "property damage" sustained within a building and caused by the release of gases, fumes or vapors from materials brought into that building in connection with operations being performed by you or on your behalf by a contractor or subcontractor; or

    (iii) "Bodily injury" or "property damage" arising out of heat, smoke or fumes from a "hostile fire".

  (e) At or from any premises, site or location on which any insured or any contractors or subcontractors working directly or indirectly on any insured's behalf are performing operations if the operations are to test for, monitor, clean up, remove, contain, treat, detoxify or neutralize, or in any way respond to, or assess the effects of, "pollutants".

(2) Any loss, cost or expense arising out of any:

   (a) Request, demand, order or statutory or regulatory requirement that any insured or others test for, monitor, clean up, remove, contain, treat, detoxify or neutralize, or in any way respond to, or assess the effects of, "pollutants"; or

   (b) Claim or suit by or on behalf of a governmental authority for damages because of testing for, monitoring, cleaning up, removing, containing, treating, detoxifying or neutralizing, or in any way responding to, or assessing the effects of, "pollutants".

However, this paragraph does not apply to liability for damages because of "property damage" that the insured would have in the absence of such request, demand, order or statutory or regulatory requirement, or such claim or "suit" by or on behalf of a governmental authority.

g. Aircraft, Auto Or Watercraft

"Bodily injury" or "property damage" arising out of the ownership, maintenance, use or entrustment to others of any aircraft, "auto" or watercraft owned or operated by or rented or loaned to any insured. Use includes operation and "loading or unloading".

This exclusion applies even if the claims against any insured allege negligence or other wrongdoing in the supervision, hiring, employment, training or monitoring of others by that insured, if the "occurrence" which caused the "bodily injury" or "property damage" involved the ownership, maintenance, use or entrustment to others of any aircraft, "auto" or watercraft that is owned or operated by or rented or loaned to any insured.

This exclusion does not apply to:

(1) A watercraft while ashore on premises you own or rent;

(2) A watercraft you do not own that is:

   (a) Less than 26 feet long; and

   (b) Not being used to carry persons or property for a charge;

(3) Parking an "auto" on, or on the ways next to, premises you own or rent, provided the "auto" is not owned by or rented or loaned to you or the insured;

(4) Liability assumed under any "insured contract" for the ownership, maintenance or use of aircraft or watercraft; or

(5) "Bodily injury" or "property damage" arising out of:

   (a) The operation of machinery or equipment that is attached to, or part of, a land vehicle that would qualify under the definition of "mobile equipment" if it were not subject to a compulsory or financial responsibility law or other motor vehicle insurance law where it is licensed or principally garaged; or

   (b) The operation of any of the machinery or equipment listed in Paragraph **f.(2)** or **f.(3)** of the definition of "mobile equipment".

h. Mobile Equipment

"Bodily injury" or "property damage" arising out of:

(1) The transportation of "mobile equipment" by an "auto" owned or operated by or rented or loaned to any insured; or

(2) The use of "mobile equipment" in, or while in practice for, or while being prepared for, any prearranged racing, speed, demolition, or stunting activity.

i. War

"Bodily injury" or "property damage", however caused, arising, directly or indirectly, out of:

(1) War, including undeclared or civil war;

(2) Warlike action by a military force, including action in hindering or defending against an actual or expected attack, by any government, sovereign or other authority using military personnel or other agents; or

(3) Insurrection, rebellion, revolution, usurped power, or action taken by governmental authority in hindering or defending against any of these.

j. Damage To Property

"Property damage" to:

(1) Property you own, rent, or occupy, including any costs or expenses incurred by you, or any other person, organization or entity, for repair, replacement, enhancement, restoration or maintenance of such property for any reason, including prevention of injury to a person or damage to another's property;

(2) Premises you sell, give away or abandon, if the "property damage" arises out of any part of those premises;

(3) Property loaned to you;

- **(4)** Personal property in the care, custody or control of the insured;
- **(5)** That particular part of real property on which you or any contractors or subcontractors working directly or indirectly on your behalf are performing operations, if the "property damage" arises out of those operations; or
- **(6)** That particular part of any property that must be restored, repaired or replaced because "your work" was incorrectly performed on it.

Paragraphs **(1)**, **(3)** and **(4)** of this exclusion do not apply to "property damage" (other than damage by fire) to premises, including the contents of such premises, rented to you for a period of seven or fewer consecutive days. A separate limit of insurance applies to Damage To Premises Rented To You as described in Section III – Limits Of Insurance.

Paragraph **(2)** of this exclusion does not apply if the premises are "your work" and were never occupied, rented or held for rental by you.

Paragraphs **(3)**, **(4)**, **(5)** and **(6)** of this exclusion do not apply to liability assumed under a sidetrack agreement.

Paragraph **(6)** of this exclusion does not apply to "property damage" included in the "products-completed operations hazard".

k. Damage To Your Product

"Property damage" to "your product" arising out of it or any part of it.

l. Damage To Your Work

"Property damage" to "your work" arising out of it or any part of it and included in the "products-completed operations hazard".

This exclusion does not apply if the damaged work or the work out of which the damage arises was performed on your behalf by a subcontractor.

m. Damage To Impaired Property Or Property Not Physically Injured

"Property damage" to "impaired property" or property that has not been physically injured, arising out of:

- **(1)** A defect, deficiency, inadequacy or dangerous condition in "your product" or "your work"; or
- **(2)** A delay or failure by you or anyone acting on your behalf to perform a contract or agreement in accordance with its terms.

This exclusion does not apply to the loss of use of other property arising out of sudden and accidental physical injury to "your product" or "your work" after it has been put to its intended use.

n. Recall Of Products, Work Or Impaired Property

Damages claimed for any loss, cost or expense incurred by you or others for the loss of use, withdrawal, recall, inspection, repair, replacement, adjustment, removal or disposal of:

- **(1)** "Your product";
- **(2)** "Your work"; or
- **(3)** "Impaired property";

if such product, work, or property is withdrawn or recalled from the market or from use by any person or organization because of a known or suspected defect, deficiency, inadequacy or dangerous condition in it.

o. Personal And Advertising Injury

"Bodily injury" arising out of "personal and advertising injury".

p. Electronic Data

Damages arising out of the loss of, loss of use of, damage to, corruption of, inability to access, or inability to manipulate electronic data.

However, this exclusion does not apply to liability for damages because of "bodily injury".

As used in this exclusion, electronic data means information, facts or programs stored as or on, created or used on, or transmitted to or from computer software, including systems and applications software, hard or floppy disks, CD-ROMs, tapes, drives, cells, data processing devices or any other media which are used with electronically controlled equipment.

q. Recording And Distribution Of Material Or Information In Violation Of Law

"Bodily injury" or "property damage" arising directly or indirectly out of any action or omission that violates or is alleged to violate:

- **(1)** The Telephone Consumer Protection Act (TCPA), including any amendment of or addition to such law;
- **(2)** The CAN-SPAM Act of 2003, including any amendment of or addition to such law;
- **(3)** The Fair Credit Reporting Act (FCRA), and any amendment of or addition to such law, including the Fair and Accurate Credit Transactions Act (FACTA); or

(4) Any federal, state or local statute, ordinance or regulation, other than the TCPA, CAN-SPAM Act of 2003 or FCRA and their amendments and additions, that addresses, prohibits, or limits the printing, dissemination, disposal, collecting, recording, sending, transmitting, communicating or distribution of material or information.

Exclusions **c.** through **n.** do not apply to damage by fire to premises while rented to you or temporarily occupied by you with permission of the owner. A separate limit of insurance applies to this coverage as described in Section III – Limits Of Insurance.

COVERAGE B – PERSONAL AND ADVERTISING INJURY LIABILITY

1. Insuring Agreement

a. We will pay those sums that the insured becomes legally obligated to pay as damages because of "personal and advertising injury" to which this insurance applies. We will have the right and duty to defend the insured against any "suit" seeking those damages. However, we will have no duty to defend the insured against any "suit" seeking damages for "personal and advertising injury" to which this insurance does not apply. We may, at our discretion, investigate any offense and settle any claim or "suit" that may result. But:

(1) The amount we will pay for damages is limited as described in Section III – Limits Of Insurance; and

(2) Our right and duty to defend end when we have used up the applicable limit of insurance in the payment of judgments or settlements under Coverages **A** or **B** or medical expenses under Coverage **C**.

No other obligation or liability to pay sums or perform acts or services is covered unless explicitly provided for under Supplementary Payments – Coverages **A** and **B**.

b. This insurance applies to "personal and advertising injury" caused by an offense arising out of your business but only if the offense was committed in the "coverage territory" during the policy period.

2. Exclusions

This insurance does not apply to:

a. **Knowing Violation Of Rights Of Another**

"Personal and advertising injury" caused by or at the direction of the insured with the knowledge that the act would violate the rights of another and would inflict "personal and advertising injury".

b. **Material Published With Knowledge Of Falsity**

"Personal and advertising injury" arising out of oral or written publication, in any manner, of material, if done by or at the direction of the insured with knowledge of its falsity.

c. **Material Published Prior To Policy Period**

"Personal and advertising injury" arising out of oral or written publication, in any manner, of material whose first publication took place before the beginning of the policy period.

d. **Criminal Acts**

"Personal and advertising injury" arising out of a criminal act committed by or at the direction of the insured.

e. **Contractual Liability**

"Personal and advertising injury" for which the insured has assumed liability in a contract or agreement. This exclusion does not apply to liability for damages that the insured would have in the absence of the contract or agreement.

f. **Breach Of Contract**

"Personal and advertising injury" arising out of a breach of contract, except an implied contract to use another's advertising idea in your "advertisement".

g. **Quality Or Performance Of Goods – Failure To Conform To Statements**

"Personal and advertising injury" arising out of the failure of goods, products or services to conform with any statement of quality or performance made in your "advertisement".

h. **Wrong Description Of Prices**

"Personal and advertising injury" arising out of the wrong description of the price of goods, products or services stated in your "advertisement".

i. **Infringement Of Copyright, Patent, Trademark Or Trade Secret**

"Personal and advertising injury" arising out of the infringement of copyright, patent, trademark, trade secret or other intellectual property rights. Under this exclusion, such other intellectual property rights do not include the use of another's advertising idea in your "advertisement".

However, this exclusion does not apply to infringement, in your "advertisement", of copyright, trade dress or slogan.

j. **Insureds In Media And Internet Type Businesses**

"Personal and advertising injury" committed by an insured whose business is:

(1) Advertising, broadcasting, publishing or telecasting;

(2) Designing or determining content of web sites for others; or

(3) An Internet search, access, content or service provider.

However, this exclusion does not apply to Paragraphs **14.a.**, **b.** and **c.** of "personal and advertising injury" under the Definitions section.

For the purposes of this exclusion, the placing of frames, borders or links, or advertising, for you or others anywhere on the Internet, is not by itself, considered the business of advertising, broadcasting, publishing or telecasting.

k. **Electronic Chatrooms Or Bulletin Boards**

"Personal and advertising injury" arising out of an electronic chatroom or bulletin board the insured hosts, owns, or over which the insured exercises control.

l. **Unauthorized Use Of Another's Name Or Product**

"Personal and advertising injury" arising out of the unauthorized use of another's name or product in your e-mail address, domain name or metatag, or any other similar tactics to mislead another's potential customers.

m. **Pollution**

"Personal and advertising injury" arising out of the actual, alleged or threatened discharge, dispersal, seepage, migration, release or escape of "pollutants" at any time.

n. **Pollution-related**

Any loss, cost or expense arising out of any:

(1) Request, demand, order or statutory or regulatory requirement that any insured or others test for, monitor, clean up, remove, contain, treat, detoxify or neutralize, or in any way respond to, or assess the effects of, "pollutants"; or

(2) Claim or suit by or on behalf of a governmental authority for damages because of testing for, monitoring, cleaning up, removing, containing, treating, detoxifying or neutralizing, or in any way responding to, or assessing the effects of, "pollutants".

o. **War**

"Personal and advertising injury", however caused, arising, directly or indirectly, out of:

(1) War, including undeclared or civil war;

(2) Warlike action by a military force, including action in hindering or defending against an actual or expected attack, by any government, sovereign or other authority using military personnel or other agents; or

(3) Insurrection, rebellion, revolution, usurped power, or action taken by governmental authority in hindering or defending against any of these.

p. **Recording And Distribution Of Material Or Information In Violation Of Law**

"Personal and advertising injury" arising directly or indirectly out of any action or omission that violates or is alleged to violate:

(1) The Telephone Consumer Protection Act (TCPA), including any amendment of or addition to such law;

(2) The CAN-SPAM Act of 2003, including any amendment of or addition to such law;

(3) The Fair Credit Reporting Act (FCRA), and any amendment of or addition to such law, including the Fair and Accurate Credit Transactions Act (FACTA); or

(4) Any federal, state or local statute, ordinance or regulation, other than the TCPA, CAN-SPAM Act of 2003 or FCRA and their amendments and additions, that addresses, prohibits, or limits the printing, dissemination, disposal, collecting, recording, sending, transmitting, communicating or distribution of material or information.

COVERAGE C – MEDICAL PAYMENTS

1. Insuring Agreement

a. We will pay medical expenses as described below for "bodily injury" caused by an accident:

(1) On premises you own or rent;

(2) On ways next to premises you own or rent; or

(3) Because of your operations;

provided that:

(a) The accident takes place in the "coverage territory" and during the policy period;

(b) The expenses are incurred and reported to us within one year of the date of the accident; and

(c) The injured person submits to examination, at our expense, by physicians of our choice as often as we reasonably require.

b. We will make these payments regardless of fault. These payments will not exceed the applicable limit of insurance. We will pay reasonable expenses for:

(1) First aid administered at the time of an accident;

(2) Necessary medical, surgical, X-ray and dental services, including prosthetic devices; and

(3) Necessary ambulance, hospital, professional nursing and funeral services.

2. Exclusions

We will not pay expenses for "bodily injury":

a. **Any Insured**

To any insured, except "volunteer workers".

b. **Hired Person**

To a person hired to do work for or on behalf of any insured or a tenant of any insured.

c. **Injury On Normally Occupied Premises**

To a person injured on that part of premises you own or rent that the person normally occupies.

d. **Workers' Compensation And Similar Laws**

To a person, whether or not an "employee" of any insured, if benefits for the "bodily injury" are payable or must be provided under a workers' compensation or disability benefits law or a similar law.

e. **Athletics Activities**

To a person injured while practicing, instructing or participating in any physical exercises or games, sports, or athletic contests.

f. **Products-Completed Operations Hazard**

Included within the "products-completed operations hazard".

g. **Coverage A Exclusions**

Excluded under Coverage A.

SUPPLEMENTARY PAYMENTS – COVERAGES A AND B

1. We will pay, with respect to any claim we investigate or settle, or any "suit" against an insured we defend:

a. All expenses we incur.

b. Up to $250 for cost of bail bonds required because of accidents or traffic law violations arising out of the use of any vehicle to which the Bodily Injury Liability Coverage applies. We do not have to furnish these bonds.

c. The cost of bonds to release attachments, but only for bond amounts within the applicable limit of insurance. We do not have to furnish these bonds.

d. All reasonable expenses incurred by the insured at our request to assist us in the investigation or defense of the claim or "suit", including actual loss of earnings up to $250 a day because of time off from work.

e. All court costs taxed against the insured in the "suit". However, these payments do not include attorneys' fees or attorneys' expenses taxed against the insured.

f. Prejudgment interest awarded against the insured on that part of the judgment we pay. If we make an offer to pay the applicable limit of insurance, we will not pay any prejudgment interest based on that period of time after the offer.

g. All interest on the full amount of any judgment that accrues after entry of the judgment and before we have paid, offered to pay, or deposited in court the part of the judgment that is within the applicable limit of insurance.

These payments will not reduce the limits of insurance.

2. If we defend an insured against a "suit" and an indemnitee of the insured is also named as a party to the "suit", we will defend that indemnitee if all of the following conditions are met:

a. The "suit" against the indemnitee seeks damages for which the insured has assumed the liability of the indemnitee in a contract or agreement that is an "insured contract";

b. This insurance applies to such liability assumed by the insured;

c. The obligation to defend, or the cost of the defense of, that indemnitee, has also been assumed by the insured in the same "insured contract";

d. The allegations in the "suit" and the information we know about the "occurrence" are such that no conflict appears to exist between the interests of the insured and the interests of the indemnitee;

e. The indemnitee and the insured ask us to conduct and control the defense of that indemnitee against such "suit" and agree that we can assign the same counsel to defend the insured and the indemnitee; and

f. The indemnitee:

(1) Agrees in writing to:

(a) Cooperate with us in the investigation, settlement or defense of the "suit";

(b) Immediately send us copies of any demands, notices, summonses or legal papers received in connection with the "suit";

(c) Notify any other insurer whose coverage is available to the indemnitee; and

(d) Cooperate with us with respect to coordinating other applicable insurance available to the indemnitee; and

(2) Provides us with written authorization to:

(a) Obtain records and other information related to the "suit"; and

(b) Conduct and control the defense of the indemnitee in such "suit".

So long as the above conditions are met, attorneys' fees incurred by us in the defense of that indemnitee, necessary litigation expenses incurred by us and necessary litigation expenses incurred by the indemnitee at our request will be paid as Supplementary Payments. Notwithstanding the provisions of Paragraph 2.b.(2) of Section I – Coverage A – Bodily Injury And Property Damage Liability, such payments will not be deemed to be damages for "bodily injury" and "property damage" and will not reduce the limits of insurance.

Our obligation to defend an insured's indemnitee and to pay for attorneys' fees and necessary litigation expenses as Supplementary Payments ends when we have used up the applicable limit of insurance in the payment of judgments or settlements or the conditions set forth above, or the terms of the agreement described in Paragraph f. above, are no longer met.

SECTION II – WHO IS AN INSURED

1. If you are designated in the Declarations as:

a. An individual, you and your spouse are insureds, but only with respect to the conduct of a business of which you are the sole owner.

b. A partnership or joint venture, you are an insured. Your members, your partners, and their spouses are also insureds, but only with respect to the conduct of your business.

c. A limited liability company, you are an insured. Your members are also insureds, but only with respect to the conduct of your business. Your managers are insureds, but only with respect to their duties as your managers.

d. An organization other than a partnership, joint venture or limited liability company, you are an insured. Your "executive officers" and directors are insureds, but only with respect to their duties as your officers or directors. Your stockholders are also insureds, but only with respect to their liability as stockholders.

e. A trust, you are an insured. Your trustees are also insureds, but only with respect to their duties as trustees.

2. Each of the following is also an insured:

   a. Your "volunteer workers" only while performing duties related to the conduct of your business, or your "employees", other than either your "executive officers" (if you are an organization other than a partnership, joint venture or limited liability company) or your managers (if you are a limited liability company), but only for acts within the scope of their employment by you or while performing duties related to the conduct of your business. However, none of these "employees" or "volunteer workers" are insureds for:

      (1) "Bodily injury" or "personal and advertising injury":

         (a) To you, to your partners or members (if you are a partnership or joint venture), to your members (if you are a limited liability company), to a co-"employee" while in the course of his or her employment or performing duties related to the conduct of your business, or to your other "volunteer workers" while performing duties related to the conduct of your business;

         (b) To the spouse, child, parent, brother or sister of that co-"employee" or "volunteer worker" as a consequence of Paragraph (1)(a) above;

         (c) For which there is any obligation to share damages with or repay someone else who must pay damages because of the injury described in Paragraph (1)(a) or (b) above; or

         (d) Arising out of his or her providing or failing to provide professional health care services.

      (2) "Property damage" to property:

         (a) Owned, occupied or used by;

         (b) Rented to, in the care, custody or control of, or over which physical control is being exercised for any purpose by;

         you, any of your "employees", "volunteer workers", any partner or member (if you are a partnership or joint venture), or any member (if you are a limited liability company).

   b. Any person (other than your "employee" or "volunteer worker"), or any organization while acting as your real estate manager.

   c. Any person or organization having proper temporary custody of your property if you die, but only:

      (1) With respect to liability arising out of the maintenance or use of that property; and

      (2) Until your legal representative has been appointed.

   d. Your legal representative if you die, but only with respect to duties as such. That representative will have all your rights and duties under this Coverage Part.

3. Any organization you newly acquire or form, other than a partnership, joint venture or limited liability company, and over which you maintain ownership or majority interest, will qualify as a Named Insured if there is no other similar insurance available to that organization. However:

   a. Coverage under this provision is afforded only until the 90th day after you acquire or form the organization or the end of the policy period, whichever is earlier;

   b. Coverage **A** does not apply to "bodily injury" or "property damage" that occurred before you acquired or formed the organization; and

   c. Coverage **B** does not apply to "personal and advertising injury" arising out of an offense committed before you acquired or formed the organization.

No person or organization is an insured with respect to the conduct of any current or past partnership, joint venture or limited liability company that is not shown as a Named Insured in the Declarations.

SECTION III – LIMITS OF INSURANCE

1. The Limits of Insurance shown in the Declarations and the rules below fix the most we will pay regardless of the number of:

   a. Insureds;

   b. Claims made or "suits" brought; or

   c. Persons or organizations making claims or bringing "suits".

2. The General Aggregate Limit is the most we will pay for the sum of:

   a. Medical expenses under Coverage **C**;

   b. Damages under Coverage **A**, except damages because of "bodily injury" or "property damage" included in the "products-completed operations hazard"; and

   c. Damages under Coverage **B**.

3. The Products-Completed Operations Aggregate Limit is the most we will pay under Coverage **A** for damages because of "bodily injury" and "property damage" included in the "products-completed operations hazard".

4. Subject to Paragraph **2.** above, the Personal And Advertising Injury Limit is the most we will pay under Coverage **B** for the sum of all damages because of all "personal and advertising injury" sustained by any one person or organization.

5. Subject to Paragraph **2.** or **3.** above, whichever applies, the Each Occurrence Limit is the most we will pay for the sum of:

   a. Damages under Coverage **A**; and
   b. Medical expenses under Coverage **C**

   because of all "bodily injury" and "property damage" arising out of any one "occurrence".

6. Subject to Paragraph **5.** above, the Damage To Premises Rented To You Limit is the most we will pay under Coverage **A** for damages because of "property damage" to any one premises, while rented to you, or in the case of damage by fire, while rented to you or temporarily occupied by you with permission of the owner.

7. Subject to Paragraph **5.** above, the Medical Expense Limit is the most we will pay under Coverage **C** for all medical expenses because of "bodily injury" sustained by any one person.

The Limits of Insurance of this Coverage Part apply separately to each consecutive annual period and to any remaining period of less than 12 months, starting with the beginning of the policy period shown in the Declarations, unless the policy period is extended after issuance for an additional period of less than 12 months. In that case, the additional period will be deemed part of the last preceding period for purposes of determining the Limits of Insurance.

SECTION IV – COMMERCIAL GENERAL LIABILITY CONDITIONS

1. **Bankruptcy**

   Bankruptcy or insolvency of the insured or of the insured's estate will not relieve us of our obligations under this Coverage Part.

2. **Duties In The Event Of Occurrence, Offense, Claim Or Suit**

   a. You must see to it that we are notified as soon as practicable of an "occurrence" or an offense which may result in a claim. To the extent possible, notice should include:

      (1) How, when and where the "occurrence" or offense took place;
      (2) The names and addresses of any injured persons and witnesses; and
      (3) The nature and location of any injury or damage arising out of the "occurrence" or offense.

   b. If a claim is made or "suit" is brought against any insured, you must:

      (1) Immediately record the specifics of the claim or "suit" and the date received; and
      (2) Notify us as soon as practicable.

      You must see to it that we receive written notice of the claim or "suit" as soon as practicable.

   c. You and any other involved insured must:

      (1) Immediately send us copies of any demands, notices, summonses or legal papers received in connection with the claim or "suit";
      (2) Authorize us to obtain records and other information;
      (3) Cooperate with us in the investigation or settlement of the claim or defense against the "suit"; and
      (4) Assist us, upon our request, in the enforcement of any right against any person or organization which may be liable to the insured because of injury or damage to which this insurance may also apply.

   d. No insured will, except at that insured's own cost, voluntarily make a payment, assume any obligation, or incur any expense, other than for first aid, without our consent.

3. **Legal Action Against Us**

   No person or organization has a right under this Coverage Part:

   a. To join us as a party or otherwise bring us into a "suit" asking for damages from an insured; or
   b. To sue us on this Coverage Part unless all of its terms have been fully complied with.

   A person or organization may sue us to recover on an agreed settlement or on a final judgment against an insured; but we will not be liable for damages that are not payable under the terms of this Coverage Part or that are in excess of the applicable limit of insurance. An agreed settlement means a settlement and release of liability signed by us, the insured and the claimant or the claimant's legal representative.

4. Other Insurance

If other valid and collectible insurance is available to the insured for a loss we cover under Coverages **A** or **B** of this Coverage Part, our obligations are limited as follows:

a. Primary Insurance

This insurance is primary except when Paragraph **b.** below applies. If this insurance is primary, our obligations are not affected unless any of the other insurance is also primary. Then, we will share with all that other insurance by the method described in Paragraph **c.** below.

b. Excess Insurance

(1) This insurance is excess over:

(a) Any of the other insurance, whether primary, excess, contingent or on any other basis:

(i) That is Fire, Extended Coverage, Builder's Risk, Installation Risk or similar coverage for "your work";

(ii) That is Fire insurance for premises rented to you or temporarily occupied by you with permission of the owner;

(iii) That is insurance purchased by you to cover your liability as a tenant for "property damage" to premises rented to you or temporarily occupied by you with permission of the owner; or

(iv) If the loss arises out of the maintenance or use of aircraft, "autos" or watercraft to the extent not subject to Exclusion **g.** of Section **I** – Coverage **A** – Bodily Injury And Property Damage Liability.

(b) Any other primary insurance available to you covering liability for damages arising out of the premises or operations, or the products and completed operations, for which you have been added as an additional insured.

(2) When this insurance is excess, we will have no duty under Coverages **A** or **B** to defend the insured against any "suit" if any other insurer has a duty to defend the insured against that "suit". If no other insurer defends, we will undertake to do so, but we will be entitled to the insured's rights against all those other insurers.

(3) When this insurance is excess over other insurance, we will pay only our share of the amount of the loss, if any, that exceeds the sum of:

(a) The total amount that all such other insurance would pay for the loss in the absence of this insurance; and

(b) The total of all deductible and self-insured amounts under all that other insurance.

(4) We will share the remaining loss, if any, with any other insurance that is not described in this Excess Insurance provision and was not bought specifically to apply in excess of the Limits of Insurance shown in the Declarations of this Coverage Part.

c. Method Of Sharing

If all of the other insurance permits contribution by equal shares, we will follow this method also. Under this approach each insurer contributes equal amounts until it has paid its applicable limit of insurance or none of the loss remains, whichever comes first.

If any of the other insurance does not permit contribution by equal shares, we will contribute by limits. Under this method, each insurer's share is based on the ratio of its applicable limit of insurance to the total applicable limits of insurance of all insurers.

5. Premium Audit

a. We will compute all premiums for this Coverage Part in accordance with our rules and rates.

b. Premium shown in this Coverage Part as advance premium is a deposit premium only. At the close of each audit period we will compute the earned premium for that period and send notice to the first Named Insured. The due date for audit and retrospective premiums is the date shown as the due date on the bill. If the sum of the advance and audit premiums paid for the policy period is greater than the earned premium, we will return the excess to the first Named Insured.

c. The first Named Insured must keep records of the information we need for premium computation, and send us copies at such times as we may request.

6. Representations

By accepting this policy, you agree:

a. The statements in the Declarations are accurate and complete;

b. Those statements are based upon representations you made to us; and

   c. We have issued this policy in reliance upon your representations.

7. Separation Of Insureds

   Except with respect to the Limits of Insurance, and any rights or duties specifically assigned in this Coverage Part to the first Named Insured, this insurance applies:

   a. As if each Named Insured were the only Named Insured; and

   b. Separately to each insured against whom claim is made or "suit" is brought.

8. Transfer Of Rights Of Recovery Against Others To Us

   If the insured has rights to recover all or part of any payment we have made under this Coverage Part, those rights are transferred to us. The insured must do nothing after loss to impair them. At our request, the insured will bring "suit" or transfer those rights to us and help us enforce them.

9. When We Do Not Renew

   If we decide not to renew this Coverage Part, we will mail or deliver to the first Named Insured shown in the Declarations written notice of the nonrenewal not less than 30 days before the expiration date.

   If notice is mailed, proof of mailing will be sufficient proof of notice.

SECTION V – DEFINITIONS

1. "Advertisement" means a notice that is broadcast or published to the general public or specific market segments about your goods, products or services for the purpose of attracting customers or supporters. For the purposes of this definition:

   a. Notices that are published include material placed on the Internet or on similar electronic means of communication; and

   b. Regarding web sites, only that part of a web site that is about your goods, products or services for the purposes of attracting customers or supporters is considered an advertisement.

2. "Auto" means:

   a. A land motor vehicle, trailer or semitrailer designed for travel on public roads, including any attached machinery or equipment; or

   b. Any other land vehicle that is subject to a compulsory or financial responsibility law or other motor vehicle insurance law where it is licensed or principally garaged.

   However, "auto" does not include "mobile equipment".

3. "Bodily injury" means bodily injury, sickness or disease sustained by a person, including death resulting from any of these at any time.

4. "Coverage territory" means:

   a. The United States of America (including its territories and possessions), Puerto Rico and Canada;

   b. International waters or airspace, but only if the injury or damage occurs in the course of travel or transportation between any places included in Paragraph **a.** above; or

   c. All other parts of the world if the injury or damage arises out of:

   (1) Goods or products made or sold by you in the territory described in Paragraph **a.** above;

   (2) The activities of a person whose home is in the territory described in Paragraph **a.** above, but is away for a short time on your business; or

   (3) "Personal and advertising injury" offenses that take place through the Internet or similar electronic means of communication;

   provided the insured's responsibility to pay damages is determined in a "suit" on the merits, in the territory described in Paragraph **a.** above or in a settlement we agree to.

5. "Employee" includes a "leased worker". "Employee" does not include a "temporary worker".

6. "Executive officer" means a person holding any of the officer positions created by your charter, constitution, bylaws or any other similar governing document.

7. "Hostile fire" means one which becomes uncontrollable or breaks out from where it was intended to be.

8. "Impaired property" means tangible property, other than "your product" or "your work", that cannot be used or is less useful because:

   a. It incorporates "your product" or "your work" that is known or thought to be defective, deficient, inadequate or dangerous; or

   b. You have failed to fulfill the terms of a contract or agreement;

   if such property can be restored to use by the repair, replacement, adjustment or removal of "your product" or "your work" or your fulfilling the terms of the contract or agreement.

9. "Insured contract" means:
   a. A contract for a lease of premises. However, that portion of the contract for a lease of premises that indemnifies any person or organization for damage by fire to premises while rented to you or temporarily occupied by you with permission of the owner is not an "insured contract";
   b. A sidetrack agreement;
   c. Any easement or license agreement, except in connection with construction or demolition operations on or within 50 feet of a railroad;
   d. An obligation, as required by ordinance, to indemnify a municipality, except in connection with work for a municipality;
   e. An elevator maintenance agreement;
   f. That part of any other contract or agreement pertaining to your business (including an indemnification of a municipality in connection with work performed for a municipality) under which you assume the tort liability of another party to pay for "bodily injury" or "property damage" to a third person or organization. Tort liability means a liability that would be imposed by law in the absence of any contract or agreement.

   Paragraph **f.** does not include that part of any contract or agreement:
   (1) That indemnifies a railroad for "bodily injury" or "property damage" arising out of construction or demolition operations, within 50 feet of any railroad property and affecting any railroad bridge or trestle, tracks, road-beds, tunnel, underpass or crossing;
   (2) That indemnifies an architect, engineer or surveyor for injury or damage arising out of:
      (a) Preparing, approving, or failing to prepare or approve, maps, shop drawings, opinions, reports, surveys, field orders, change orders or drawings and specifications; or
      (b) Giving directions or instructions, or failing to give them, if that is the primary cause of the injury or damage; or
   (3) Under which the insured, if an architect, engineer or surveyor, assumes liability for an injury or damage arising out of the insured's rendering or failure to render professional services, including those listed in (2) above and supervisory, inspection, architectural or engineering activities.

10. "Leased worker" means a person leased to you by a labor leasing firm under an agreement between you and the labor leasing firm, to perform duties related to the conduct of your business. "Leased worker" does not include a "temporary worker".

11. "Loading or unloading" means the handling of property:
    a. After it is moved from the place where it is accepted for movement into or onto an aircraft, watercraft or "auto";
    b. While it is in or on an aircraft, watercraft or "auto"; or
    c. While it is being moved from an aircraft, watercraft or "auto" to the place where it is finally delivered;

    but "loading or unloading" does not include the movement of property by means of a mechanical device, other than a hand truck, that is not attached to the aircraft, watercraft or "auto".

12. "Mobile equipment" means any of the following types of land vehicles, including any attached machinery or equipment:
    a. Bulldozers, farm machinery, forklifts and other vehicles designed for use principally off public roads;
    b. Vehicles maintained for use solely on or next to premises you own or rent;
    c. Vehicles that travel on crawler treads;
    d. Vehicles, whether self-propelled or not, maintained primarily to provide mobility to permanently mounted:
       (1) Power cranes, shovels, loaders, diggers or drills; or
       (2) Road construction or resurfacing equipment such as graders, scrapers or rollers;
    e. Vehicles not described in Paragraph **a.**, **b.**, **c.** or **d.** above that are not self-propelled and are maintained primarily to provide mobility to permanently attached equipment of the following types:
       (1) Air compressors, pumps and generators, including spraying, welding, building cleaning, geophysical exploration, lighting and well servicing equipment; or
       (2) Cherry pickers and similar devices used to raise or lower workers;
    f. Vehicles not described in Paragraph **a.**, **b.**, **c.** or **d.** above maintained primarily for purposes other than the transportation of persons or cargo.

However, self-propelled vehicles with the following types of permanently attached equipment are not "mobile equipment" but will be considered "autos":

(1) Equipment designed primarily for:

    (a) Snow removal;

    (b) Road maintenance, but not construction or resurfacing; or

    (c) Street cleaning;

(2) Cherry pickers and similar devices mounted on automobile or truck chassis and used to raise or lower workers; and

(3) Air compressors, pumps and generators, including spraying, welding, building cleaning, geophysical exploration, lighting and well servicing equipment.

However, "mobile equipment" does not include any land vehicles that are subject to a compulsory or financial responsibility law or other motor vehicle insurance law where it is licensed or principally garaged. Land vehicles subject to a compulsory or financial responsibility law or other motor vehicle insurance law are considered "autos".

13. "Occurrence" means an accident, including continuous or repeated exposure to substantially the same general harmful conditions.

14. "Personal and advertising injury" means injury, including consequential "bodily injury", arising out of one or more of the following offenses:

    a. False arrest, detention or imprisonment;

    b. Malicious prosecution;

    c. The wrongful eviction from, wrongful entry into, or invasion of the right of private occupancy of a room, dwelling or premises that a person occupies, committed by or on behalf of its owner, landlord or lessor;

    d. Oral or written publication, in any manner, of material that slanders or libels a person or organization or disparages a person's or organization's goods, products or services;

    e. Oral or written publication, in any manner, of material that violates a person's right of privacy;

    f. The use of another's advertising idea in your "advertisement"; or

    g. Infringing upon another's copyright, trade dress or slogan in your "advertisement".

15. "Pollutants" mean any solid, liquid, gaseous or thermal irritant or contaminant, including smoke, vapor, soot, fumes, acids, alkalis, chemicals and waste. Waste includes materials to be recycled, reconditioned or reclaimed.

16. "Products-completed operations hazard":

    a. Includes all "bodily injury" and "property damage" occurring away from premises you own or rent and arising out of "your product" or "your work" except:

    (1) Products that are still in your physical possession; or

    (2) Work that has not yet been completed or abandoned. However, "your work" will be deemed completed at the earliest of the following times:

        (a) When all of the work called for in your contract has been completed.

        (b) When all of the work to be done at the job site has been completed if your contract calls for work at more than one job site.

        (c) When that part of the work done at a job site has been put to its intended use by any person or organization other than another contractor or subcontractor working on the same project.

Work that may need service, maintenance, correction, repair or replacement, but which is otherwise complete, will be treated as completed.

    b. Does not include "bodily injury" or "property damage" arising out of:

    (1) The transportation of property, unless the injury or damage arises out of a condition in or on a vehicle not owned or operated by you, and that condition was created by the "loading or unloading" of that vehicle by any insured;

    (2) The existence of tools, uninstalled equipment or abandoned or unused materials; or

    (3) Products or operations for which the classification, listed in the Declarations or in a policy Schedule, states that products-completed operations are subject to the General Aggregate Limit.

17. "Property damage" means:

    a. Physical injury to tangible property, including all resulting loss of use of that property. All such loss of use shall be deemed to occur at the time of the physical injury that caused it; or

    b. Loss of use of tangible property that is not physically injured. All such loss of use shall be deemed to occur at the time of the "occurrence" that caused it.

For the purposes of this insurance, electronic data is not tangible property.

As used in this definition, electronic data means information, facts or programs stored as or on, created or used on, or transmitted to or from computer software, including systems and applications software, hard or floppy disks, CD-ROMs, tapes, drives, cells, data processing devices or any other media which are used with electronically controlled equipment.

18. "Suit" means a civil proceeding in which damages because of "bodily injury", "property damage" or "personal and advertising injury" to which this insurance applies are alleged. "Suit" includes:

   a. An arbitration proceeding in which such damages are claimed and to which the insured must submit or does submit with our consent; or

   b. Any other alternative dispute resolution proceeding in which such damages are claimed and to which the insured submits with our consent.

19. "Temporary worker" means a person who is furnished to you to substitute for a permanent "employee" on leave or to meet seasonal or short-term workload conditions.

20. "Volunteer worker" means a person who is not your "employee", and who donates his or her work and acts at the direction of and within the scope of duties determined by you, and is not paid a fee, salary or other compensation by you or anyone else for their work performed for you.

21. "Your product":

   a. Means:

   (1) Any goods or products, other than real property, manufactured, sold, handled, distributed or disposed of by:

   (a) You;

   (b) Others trading under your name; or

   (c) A person or organization whose business or assets you have acquired; and

   (2) Containers (other than vehicles), materials, parts or equipment furnished in connection with such goods or products.

   b. Includes:

   (1) Warranties or representations made at any time with respect to the fitness, quality, durability, performance or use of "your product"; and

   (2) The providing of or failure to provide warnings or instructions.

   c. Does not include vending machines or other property rented to or located for the use of others but not sold.

22. "Your work":

   a. Means:

   (1) Work or operations performed by you or on your behalf; and

   (2) Materials, parts or equipment furnished in connection with such work or operations.

   b. Includes:

   (1) Warranties or representations made at any time with respect to the fitness, quality, durability, performance or use of "your work"; and

   (2) The providing of or failure to provide warnings or instructions.

2. THE INSURING AGREEMENT

a. THE MEANING OF "DAMAGES," "PROPERTY DAMAGE," AND "BODILY INJURY"

The following case concerns the liability of a CGL insurer for the costs incurred by its insured in connection with the cleanup of a hazardous waste deposit site. The opinion describes a small part of a national cleanup program that began in the 1980's under both state cleanup regimes and at the federal level under the Comprehensive Environmental Response, Compensation, and Liability Act of 1980, abbreviated "CERCLA" and often nicknamed the "Superfund" Act. See 42 U.S.C. § 9601 et seq., as amended by the Superfund Amendments and Reauthorization Act of 1986. Decades later, that cleanup program, and the insurance litigation that it spawned, still continue. CERCLA also applies to new spills and pollution incidents, some of which involve substantial damage or injury. Consequently, CERCLA remains highly relevant to insurance and insurance law. CERCLA has been interpreted to provide that the generators of hazardous waste, those who transport it, and those who own or operate sites where waste is disposed of, are retroactively, strictly, and jointly and severally liable for the costs of cleaning up sites where there is a release or a substantial threat of a release of hazardous substances into the environment. See CERCLA § 107, 42 U.S.C. § 9607.

Thus, whether and to what extent the cost of such remedial action is insured under pre-existing CGL policies has been a matter of extraordinary importance to the insurance industry and to CGL policyholders. Even more importantly, beginning in the 1980s, litigation over coverage of CERCLA and analogous toxic tort liabilities brought major law firms into the field of insurance litigation, and they have never left. The precedents that have been set in connection with these issues have been focal points for decisions involving similar issues arising in other important insurance coverage contexts.

A.Y. McDonald Industries, Inc. v. Insurance Company of North America

Supreme Court of Iowa, 1991.
475 N.W.2d 607.

■ LAVORATO, JUSTICE.

This case presents certified questions from the federal district court for the northern district of Iowa. *See* Iowa Code § 684A (1991); Iowa R.App.P. 451–61. The underlying action arises out of environmental contamination claims asserted by a federal governmental agency against the plaintiff A.Y. McDonald Industries, Inc. (A.Y. McDonald). A.Y. McDonald contends that because of these claims it was forced to incur, and will incur in the future, certain costs. A.Y. McDonald sought from the defendants a recovery of these costs as well as a civil penalty assessed against it. The defendants are various insurance companies that had insured A.Y. McDonald with comprehensive general liability (CGL) policies over a period of years.

* * *

I. The Facts.

In its certification order the federal district court made the following findings of fact, which are essentially undisputed. From about 1949 to October 31, 1983, A.Y. McDonald manufactured brass valves in its brass foundry in Dubuque, Iowa. Any sand remaining after the completion of the process was dumped on the foundry site. Mixed in with the sand was a residue of brass. Lead is a component of brass residue. * * *

On August 19, 1987, A.Y. McDonald, the Iowa department of transportation (IDOT), and the EPA entered into a consent order pursuant to section 106 of the Comprehensive Environmental Response, Compensation, and Liability Act 1980 (CERCLA). *See* 42 U.S.C. § 9601, *et seq.*, as amended by the Superfund Amendments and Reauthorization Act of 1986. The consent order required A.Y. McDonald to (1) design and construct a clay cap over a specified portion of the property; (2) expand its groundwater monitoring system; and (3) develop and implement a postclosure plan for a period of thirty years.

II. The Certified Questions.

In its certification order the federal district court certified the following three questions to us:

1. Does the language "all sums which the insured shall become legally obligated to pay as damages because of * * * property damage" or similar language as used in the policies issued to plaintiff by defendants The Aetna Casualty and Surety Company, American Insurance Company and National Surety Corporation (collectively "FFIC") and Insurance Company of North America include coverage for amounts expended or paid by plaintiff in order to comply with the terms of the * * * consent order entered into on August 19, 1987, by plaintiff, the EPA and IDOT pursuant to CERCLA? If so, do these words encompass all or only part of such amounts expended or paid? * * *

As one writer describes it, CERCLA was designed "to bring order to the array of partly redundant, partly inadequate federal hazardous substances cleanup and compensation laws." F. Anderson, D. Mandelker & A. Tarlock, *Environmental Protection: Law and Policy* 568, 568 (1984).

CERCLA's objectives include the following:

> to encourage maximum care and responsibility in the handling of hazardous waste; to provide for rapid response to environmental emergencies; to encourage voluntary clean-up of hazardous waste spills; to encourage early reporting of violations of the statute; and to ensure that parties responsible for release of hazardous substances bear the costs of response and costs of damage to natural resources.

Chemical Waste Management, Inc. v. Armstrong World Indus., Inc., 669 F.Supp.1285, 1290 n. 6 (E.D.Pa.1987).

CERCLA gives the federal government broad authority to combat contamination of the environment and to protect the health and welfare of the public. The Act imposes liability on parties responsible for the "incurrence of response costs" resulting from "a release, or a threatened release," of a "hazardous substance." 42 U.S.C. § 9607(a). The responsible parties include (1) current owners and operators of hazardous waste facilities; (2) any person who formerly owned or operated a facility at the time of the disposal of any hazardous substance; and (3) waste generators, disposers, and transporters. * * *

Here the design and construction of the clay cap, the expansion of the groundwater monitoring system, and the development and implementation of a postclosure plan for a period of thirty years constituted a remedial action response covered by 42 U.S.C. § 9601(24).

In responding to a hazardous waste problem, CERCLA gives the EPA three alternatives. Using Superfund money,[1] the EPA may clean up the site and seek reimbursement from the responsible parties for the costs incurred. *See* 42 U.S.C. §§ 9604(a)(1), 9607. Or the EPA may seek injunctive relief to require the responsible parties to clean up the site. *See* 42 U.S.C. § 9606(a).

In addition section 9606(a) provides a third alternative. The EPA may issue an administrative order requiring the responsible parties to clean up the site. A violation of, or a failure or refusal to comply with, this order carries a fine of not more than $25,000 "for each day in which such violation occurs or such failure to comply continues." 42 U.S.C. § 9606(b)(1). In addition, the responsible parties may be liable to the United States for punitive damages if they fail to comply with the order. 42 U.S.C. § 9607(c)(3).

The EPA may enter into an agreement with the responsible parties to perform any necessary response action. *See* 42 U.S.C. § 9622(a). The agreement must be "entered in the appropriate United States district court as a consent decree." 42 U.S.C. § 9622(d)(1)(A). Apparently this is the route the EPA took with A.Y. McDonald.

IV. *A.Y. McDonald's Suit.*

In its petition for declaratory relief A.Y. McDonald claims it has incurred and will continue to incur substantial response costs as a result of the EPA proceedings. These costs include engineering fees, personnel costs, construction costs, postclosure monitoring costs, and other costs necessary to comply with the consent order. The company has also incurred a civil penalty. A.Y. McDonald seeks a declaration that these response costs and the penalty are damages within the insuring provision of the CGL policies and therefore covered by the policies. * * *

V. *The Coverage Question.*

That leads us to the first certified question: whether the response costs and the penalty are covered by the CGL policies here.

There are persuasive arguments for and against permitting insurance against the costs of abating pollution. But we think these

---

[1] Section 9611 authorized a federal fund from which the popular "Superfund" pseudonym of CERCLA came. In the initial Act Congress allocated $1.6 billion for this trust fund. *See* 42 U.S.C. § 9611 (1982). Amended in 1986, section 9611 now authorizes $8.5 billion for use over a five-year period. *See* 42 U.S.C. § 9611(a) (1988). The funds for the Superfund come from taxes collected on petroleum products and certain inorganic chemicals as well as from federal revenue. *See* 26 U.S.C.A. § 9507(b) (West 1989).

arguments are not relevant on the question of coverage. CERCLA expressly permits responsible parties to insure against the costs of relief under this legislation. *See* 42 U.S.C. § 9607(e). From this we conclude that Congress has already made the relevant public policy determinations. So our task is not to determine whether the policies may provide the coverage A.Y. McDonald seeks, but whether they do provide it according to their terms. The answer lies solely in the language of the policies, not in public policy considerations.

The coverage question centers on the following language in the CGL policies: "all sums which the insured shall become legally obligated to pay as damages because of * * * property damage." Our task is to determine whether this language covers the response costs that A.Y. McDonald has incurred and will incur and the penalty assessed against it. Numerous state appellate courts have considered the response cost coverage issue. Nearly all have concluded that response or cleanup costs incurred under environmental protection statutes are indeed covered by policy language identical to the language under consideration. The highest courts in Massachusetts, Minnesota, North Carolina, Washington, and Wyoming are included in the majority; the highest courts in Maine and New Hampshire are included in the minority.

Some of these decisions deal with costs of reimbursing the government or third parties for their costs in remedying and mitigating environmental damage. In finding coverage for these costs, courts in these cases have relied on either one of two theories. Such costs are plainly "damages" that the insured is "legally obligated" to pay as compensatory damages because of "property damage." * * * Or these terms—damages and legally obligated—are ambiguous and therefore must be resolved in favor of coverage. * * *

A more troublesome question concerns costs incurred in compliance with environmental injunctions. But even here, most state appellate courts have held that these costs are likewise covered. Some of these courts view such costs as fitting the ordinary meaning of "damages." *See, e.g., AIU Ins. Co.*, 51 Cal.3d at 825; *Specialty Coatings Co.*, 180 Ill.App.3d at 390–93; *Boeing Co.*, 113 Wash.2d at 877. And some are convinced that a contrary holding would unreasonably make coverage depend on the "mere fortuity" of which alternatives—injunction, reimbursement, or damages to natural resources—the EPA chooses in enforcing CERCLA. *See, e.g., AIU Ins. Co.*, 51 Cal.3d at 840; *C.D. Spangler Constr. Co.*, 326 N.C. at 150; *United States Aviex Co. v. Travelers Ins. Co.*, 125 Mich.App. 579, 5903 (1983). Other courts reason that such costs are damages according to the reasonable expectations of the parties. *See, e.g., AIU Ins. Co.*, 51 Cal.3d at 840; *C.D. Spangler Constr. Co.*, 326 N.C. at 152; *Broadwell Realty Servs. Inc.*, 218 N.J.Super. at 524.

In contrast, federal courts are sharply divided on the question whether environmental response or cleanup costs are covered by the CGL policies. In their decisions, these courts purport to apply state law in resolving the issue. Like the majority of state courts, some federal courts see both forms of relief—recovery of cleanup costs and costs of compliance with environmental injunctions—as constituting "damages" under the CGL policies.

For various reasons other federal courts have reached the opposite result regarding these two forms of relief. One reason centers on the separate provisions in CERCLA. One provision allows the EPA to recover for damages to natural resources, while another provision allows the EPA to recover response costs. See 42 U.S.C. §§ 9607(a)(4)(C), 9607(a)(4)(A). Because the statute makes such a distinction, several federal courts have reasoned that only "damages to natural resources," and not response costs, can be considered as damages under the CGL policies. * * *

Some federal courts have noted that under CERCLA the EPA can recover response costs without a showing that the agency has suffered harm to property or resources in which it has a proprietary interest. These courts reason that such a recovery is not for "damages" as that term has been traditionally defined in the law, and so have denied coverage. *See, e.g. Aetna Cas. & Sur. Co.*, 709 F.Supp. at 961; *Mraz*, 804 F.2d at 1329.

Several federal courts have concluded that the term "damages" under CGL policies has a legal, technical meaning that is unambiguous in the insurance context. Under this meaning these courts have found that the term "damages" does not include costs of complying with injunctive relief available under CERCLA and similar statutes. These courts note that the policies there—as here—obligate the insurer to pay "all sums which the insurer shall become legally obligated to pay as damages because of * * * property damage." They point out that if the term "damages" were given its ordinary meaning then the term "would become mere surplusage, because any obligation to pay would be covered. The limitation implied by employment of the phrase 'to pay as damages' would be obliterated." * * *

In reaching this conclusion, *Armco* and *NEPACCO* rely on several decisions involving injunctive relief. *See NEPACCO*, 842 F.2d at 986; *Armco*, 822 F.2d at 1353. All were decided before CERCLA, and all hold that an insured's costs of complying with mandatory injunctions are not "damages" under a liability insurance policy. *See, e.g., Aetna Cas. & Sur. Co. v. Hanna*, 224 F.2d 499, 503 (5th Cir.1955); *Garden Sanctuary, Inc. v. Insurance Co. of N.Am.*, 292 So.2d 75, 77 (Fla.App.1974); *Desrochers v. New York Cas. Co.*, 99 N.H. 129, 131 (1954).

Another reason given for denying such coverage lies in the distinction between equitable and legal relief. The two federal circuits that have given the term "damages" a legal, technical meaning look to whether the form of relief sought is legal or equitable. Both reason that legal damages—payments to third persons when those persons have a legal claim for damages—are substantially different from injunction, restitution, or other equitable remedies. They conclude, therefore, that the term "damages" in the legal sense does not include these equitable remedies. And they conclude that a reasonably prudent insurance purchaser would expect that an insurance policy limited to "damages" would not cover restitution or injunctive costs. * * *

The eighth and the fourth circuits look upon response costs under CERCLA as either restitutionary (where the government seeks reimbursement) or injunctive (where the responsible party is ordered to clean up the site). Because of the way they view response costs, these courts would deny coverage for them under the CGL policies. *NEPACCO*, 842 F.2d at 986–87; *Armco*, 822 F.2d at 1352–54.

To resolve the coverage question, we need to address two issues. First, are government mandated response costs under CERCLA "damages" within the meaning of the CGL policies? Second, are such costs the measure of "property damage," that is, "damages because of property damage"? Before we can say there is coverage, we must answer both questions affirmatively.

A. "Damages" within the meaning of CGL policies.

The CGL policies obligate the defendants to pay "all sums which the insured shall become legally obligated to pay as damages because of * * * property damage." The defendants say this provision does not obligate them to pay "*all sums*" which the insured shall become legally obligated to pay. To the contrary, the defendants say they have agreed to indemnify the insured for all sums the insured is legally obligated to pay "as damages." They argue that the term "damages" therefore limits the "all sums" provision in the policy. In the defendants' view, the term "damages" provides the key to their obligation to pay all sums imposed upon the insured by law due to property damage.

The defendants want us to give the term "damages" the narrow, technical definition given to it by *NEPACCO* and *Armco*. * * *

We agree with those courts that have viewed the term "damages" in CGL policies as ambiguous because it is susceptible to more than one reasonable interpretation. As one court put it, the ordinary meaning of "damages" as defined by the dictionary supports this conclusion:

> This policy language, "all sums which the insured shall become legally obligated to pay as damages because of property damage," can reasonably be interpreted to cover any claim asserted against the insured arising out of property damage, which requires the expenditure of money, regardless of whether the claim can be characterized as legal or equitable in nature. This interpretation is supported by the dictionary definition of "damages" which makes no distinction between damages at law and actions in equity. *See* Webster's Third New International Dictionary 571 (P. Gove ed. 1961) ("damages" are "the estimated reparation in money for detriment or injury sustained: compensation or satisfaction imposed by law for a wrong or injury caused by [a] violation of a legal right").

Minnesota Mining, 457 N.W.2d at 179–80; *according AIU Ins. Co.*, 51 Cal.3d at 825–26; *C.D. Spangler Constr. Co.*, 326 N.C. at 152; *Boeing Co.*, 113 Wash.2d at 877.

Even insurance dictionaries define "damages" in the same broad manner. *See, e.g.,* Merit, *Glossary of Insurance Terms* 47 (1980) (damages defined as "the amount required to pay for a loss"); Rubin, *Barons Dictionary of Insurance Terms* 71 (1987) (damages defined as "the sum the insurance company is legally obligated to pay an insured for losses incurred"); Davids, *Dictionary of Insurance* 72 (1977) (damages defined as "the estimated reparation in money for injury sustained").

Interestingly enough, *NEPACCO* and *Armco* concede that the ordinary meaning of the term "damages" is broad and all inclusive:

> The dictionary definition does not distinguish between legal damages and equitable monetary relief. Thus, from the viewpoint of the lay insured, the term "damages" could reasonably include all monetary claims, whether such claims are described as damages, expenses, costs, or losses.

NEPACCO, 842 F.2d at 985 (citations omitted); *Armco*, 822 F.2d at 1352 (citations omitted).

This is not the first time our court has been asked to interpret the term "damages" in a CGL policy. We have interpreted the term "damages" broadly to include "punitive" as well as "compensatory" damages. *City of Cedar Rapids v. Northwestern Nat'l Ins. Co.*, 304 N.W.2d 228, 231 (Iowa 1981), *overruled on other grounds*, 440 N.W.2d 377 (1989). We adopted the following language from a case decided by the Missouri Court of Appeals:

> Clearly the language of the policy before us does not limit recovery to actual or compensatory damages but *undertakes to pay for all losses*.

Id. (citing *Colson v. Lloyd's of London*), 435 S.W.2d 42, 43–44, 47 (Mo.App.1968) (emphasis added). * * *

Our inquiry on the coverage question does not end with our conclusion that government mandated response costs under CERCLA are damages within the meaning of the CGL policies. We must next determine whether such costs are the proper measure of property damage. In other words, are these "damages because of property damage" within the meaning of the policies? [the court then went on to hold that the "damages" were imposed "because of property damage."] * * *

NOTES AND QUESTIONS

1. *An Early Division of Authority Recedes.* The issue addressed in *A.Y. McDonald* is one of the many insurance coverage questions associated with the massive federal and state programs for cleaning up hazardous waste disposal sites. Case law on the "damages" issue was at first divided. For example, compare *Maryland Casualty Co. v. Armco*, 822 F.2d 1348 (4th Cir. 1987), holding that cleanup costs are not "damages," with *United States Aviex Company v. Travelers Insurance Co.*, 336 N.W.2d 838 (1983), holding that they are. As the court noted, however, in recent years all but three of more than a dozen state supreme courts to rule on the issue have taken positions similar to the decision in *A.Y. McDonald*. See, e.g., *Aetna Cas. & Surety Co. v. Commonwealth*, 179 S.W.3d 830 (Ky. 2005); *Patrons Oxford Mutual Ins. Co. v. Marois*, 573 A.2d 16 (Me. 1990). And Wisconsin, which originally ruled with the minority in *City of Edgerton v. General Casualty Co. of Wisconsin*, 517 N.W.2d 463 (Wis.1994), later reversed itself in *Johnson Controls, Inc. v. Employers Insurance of Wassau*, 665 N.W.2d 257 (Wis. 2003).

2. *Forms of CERCLA Liability.* There are three separate situations under CERCLA in which the "damages" issue may arise: potentially responsible parties (PRPs, in the argot of the trade) may decide to clean up

a site in anticipation of government action; the government may order PRPs to take action; or the government may cleanup and sue PRPs for recovery of cleanup costs.

a. Is an insured who undertakes voluntary cleanup in anticipation of governmental investigation or action "legally obligated" to incur cleanup costs within the meaning of the CGL insuring agreement? See *Weyerhaeuser v. Aetna Cas. & Sur. Co.*, 874 P.2d 142 (1994) (holding in the affirmative). See also *Cent. Illinois Light Co. v. Home Ins. Co.*, 821 N.E.2d 206 (Ill. Ct. App. 2004) (although the mere existence of an obligation may not suffice, if insured acted in response to a claim the requirement is satisfied). Outside the CERCLA context the courts have split on the question whether a policyholder-initiated undertaking where there is in fact a legal obligation to act is sufficient to trigger coverage. See, e.g., *Detroit Water Team Joint Venture v. Agricultural Ins. Co.*, 371 F.3d 336 (6th Cir. 2004) (no coverage when insured contractor made expensive repairs after construction mistake by a subcontractor because the contractor was never "legally obligated" to make the repairs); *Desert Mountain Ltd. P'ship v. Liberty Mut. Fire Ins. Co.*, 236 P.3d 421 (Ariz. Ct. Ap. 2010) (contractual obligation to make repairs is sufficient to render the developer "legally obligated" even without a lawsuit). Should the correct answer in the CERCLA context depend on whether the insured would be committing an unlawful act by failing to correct conditions at the site? Note that CERCLA itself does not make it unlawful to create or maintain hazardous conditions requiring remedial action; it merely permits the government to undertake cleanup itself or to order cleanup under specified circumstances, and creates a set of liabilities for the costs of cleanup.

b. Sometimes the state or federal government issues an administrative order or seeks a mandatory injunction directing the insured to remedy a threat to the environment posed by conditions at a site. See CERCLA § 106, 42 U.S.C. § 9606. The obvious question here is whether the insured has incurred "damages" when an injunction (or administrative order) does not order the payment of any money to a third party, but simply requires the insured to take remedial action or to assure that it is taken. The "traditional" rule is that the costs of complying with an injunctive order are not insured by a general liability policy. But in fact the rule is derived mainly from two cases. See *Aetna Cas. & Sur. Co. v. Hanna*, 224 F.2d 499 (5th Cir.1955); *Desrochers v. New York Cas. Co.*, 106 A.2d 196 (N.H. 1954). Since both these decisions pre-date the enactment of CERCLA, it is unclear how much bearing they have on the unique liability regime CERCLA employs. Most of the courts that have addressed the issue suggest that the difference between an injunctive remedy under CERCLA or an analogous state statute and governmental cleanup followed by a cost recovery action is inconsequential for insurance purposes. See, e.g., *Boeing Co. v. Aetna Cas. & Sur. Co.*, 784 P.2d 507 (Wash. 1990). The Supreme Court of California has been one of the few to take a partially bifurcated approach, holding that cost recovery liability is payable "as damages," but that the cost of complying with an administratively-issued injunctive order is not. See *Certain Underwriters at Lloyds v. Superior Court*, 16 P.3d 94 (Cal. 2001). In a later phase of the case against certain excess insurers, however, the court held that these insurers could be held liable for the policyholder's cost of compliance with injunctive and similar orders, because their policies did not contain the "as damages" limitation. *Powerine Oil Co. v. Superior Court*, 118 P.3d 589 (Cal. 2005).

c. The third remedy available under CERCLA involves cleanup by one or more agencies of government (and in some cases, by third parties) followed by an action to recover the costs of cleanup under CERCLA § 107, 42 U.S.C. § 9607. This is the approach that most resembles an action for traditional civil damages: it involves a loss incurred by another party, followed by an action to recover for the loss. In the most general sense, therefore, it is an action for damages. If the costs for which the government seeks reimbursement in a § 107 action constitute damages within the meaning of the CGL insuring agreement, would a holding that costs incurred by the insured under either of the first two approaches are not "damages" create excessive moral hazard? How?

3. *Because of Property Damage.* Most courts have held that liability for cleanup costs incurred under CERCLA is payable as damages incurred "because of property damage" under CGL policies. See, e.g., *United States Fid. & Guar. Co v. Thomas Solvent Co.*, 683 F.Supp. 1139 (W.D. Mich. 1988). A comparatively recent (and unusual) decision to the contrary is *Industrial Enterprises, Inc. v. Penn American Insurance Co.*, 637 F. 3d 481 (4th Cir. 2011). Suppose that there has not yet been property damage, and the insured is ordered to take measures to prevent property damage from occurring? See *Cinergy Corp. v. Associated Elec. & Gas Ins. Services, Ltd.*, 865 N.E.2d 571 (Ind. 2007) (no coverage for the cost of measures that might reduce power companies' contribution to global warming). A separate question is whether, assuming there was "property damage," damages were imposed "because of" that damage. Ordinarily, consequential damages resulting from property damage, such as lost profits, are imposed "because of" that damage and therefore are covered.

Eyeblaster, Inc. v. Federal Insurance Company

United States Court of Appeals, Eighth Circuit, 2010.
613 F.3d 797.

■ JOHN R. GIBSON, CIRCUIT JUDGE.

Eyeblaster, Inc. ("Eyeblaster") appeals from an adverse entry of summary judgment in its action against Federal Insurance Company ("Federal") arising out of Federal's denial of coverage under two insurance policies. A computer user sued Eyeblaster, alleging that Eyeblaster injured his computer, software, and data after he visited an Eyeblaster website. Eyeblaster tendered the defense of the lawsuit to Federal, seeking coverage under a General Liability policy and an Information and Network Technology Errors or Omissions Liability policy. Federal denied that it had a duty to defend Eyeblaster, and Eyeblaster brought this action seeking a declaration that Federal owed such a duty. The district court entered summary judgment in favor of Federal, and Eyeblaster appeals. We reverse.

Eyeblaster is a worldwide online marketing campaign management company that advertisers, advertising agencies, and publishers use to run campaigns across the Internet and other digital channels. Its primary product assists in the creation, delivery, and management of online interactive advertising. The company was established in 1999 and has fourteen offices worldwide, with six employees located in North America. In 2007, Eyeblaster delivered online marketing campaigns for nearly 7000 brand advertisers and served ads across more than 2700 global web publishers.

The industry in which Eyeblaster provides services is known as rich media advertising. Rich media allows customers to create interactive ads in a wide range of formats, and to track and manage the performance of the advertising campaigns. Eyeblaster has the capacity to deliver ads simultaneously to billions of users globally and to constantly monitor its systems with network and system technicians and engineers. Its service uses cookies, which are typically used in the advertising industry to measure and enhance the effectiveness of an advertising campaign. It also uses JavaScript and Flash technology, which enliven web pages and increase the Internet's utility. Eyeblaster does not use spyware or introduce malicious contact such as spam, viruses, or malware.

Eyeblaster purchased General Liability and Information and Network Technology Errors or Omissions insurance policies from Federal for the period from December 5, 2005 to December 5, 2007. Subject to the policies' terms, Federal had a duty to defend Eyeblaster against lawsuits, even if such suits were false, fraudulent, or groundless.

David Sefton filed a lawsuit against Eyeblaster in Harris County, Texas in October 2006. Eyeblaster removed the action to federal court, where Sefton filed his First Amended Complaint the following month. Eyeblaster provided notice of and tendered defense of the First Amended Complaint to Federal in December 2006. On March 12, 2007, Federal sent Eyeblaster a letter denying all coverage. When Sefton amended his complaint a second time, Eyeblaster once again tendered defense of the suit to Federal, and again Federal denied coverage. Federal's position was that it owed no coverage under the General Liability policy because Sefton did not assert claims for bodily injury caused by an occurrence, as defined by the policy. In addition, to the extent that Sefton alleged property damage, he did not allege that the property damage was caused by an accident or occurrence as the policy required. Federal also noted three exclusions but offered no explanation as to why they would apply. [the court's discussion of the Information and Network Technology Errors and Omissions policy is omitted] * * *

In his Second Amended Complaint, Sefton alleges that his computer was infected with a spyware program from Eyeblaster on July 14, 2006, which caused his computer to immediately freeze up. He further alleges that he lost all data on a tax return on which he was working and that he incurred many thousands of dollars of loss. Sefton hired a computer technician to repair the damage. Although he alleges that no repair was possible, he stated that his computer became operational again. Sefton asserted that he has experienced the following: numerous pop-up ads; a hijacked browser that communicates with websites other than those directed by the operator; random error messages; slowed computer performance that sometimes results in crashes; and ads oriented toward his past web viewing habits. * * *

Eyeblaster disclosed to Federal that its core business activity is the technology used for interactive advertising content delivery and management, and any allegation that Eyeblaster intentionally served an ad would have been in the ordinary course of its business. Eyeblaster points out that it reasonably expected to be covered by Federal's policies at issue, and to suggest otherwise would reduce Federal's coverage to the point where it had no commercial justification. * * *

The General Liability policy Eyeblaster purchased from Federal obligates the insurer to provide coverage for property damage caused by a covered occurrence. Property damage means "physical injury to tangible property, including resulting loss of use of that property . . . ; or loss of use of tangible property that is not physically injured." The definition of "tangible property" excludes "any software, data or other information that is in electronic form."

The district court concluded that the Sefton complaint does not allege damage to tangible property because it only claims damage to software, which is by definition excluded. The district court relied on *America Online, Incorporated v. St. Paul Mercury Insurance Company*, 347 F.3d 89 (4th Cir. 2003), in which America Online, Inc. ("AOL") attempted to require its insurer to defend against claims that AOL's proprietary software package had "altered the customers' existing software, disrupted their network connections, caused them loss of stored data, and caused their operating systems to crash." 347 F.3d at 93. The Fourth Circuit rejected AOL's argument because its insurance policy covered liability for "physical damage to tangible property," and the court identified the configuration instructions, data, and information as intangible and abstract. *Id.* at 96. Eyeblaster attempts to distinguish this portion of the AOL case without success. The Sefton complaint alleges direct injury to the operation of his computer, but it alleges no damage to the hardware itself. The complaint would have had to make a claim for physical injury to the hardware in order for Eyeblaster to have coverage for "physical injury to tangible property."

Eyeblaster argues that the district court erred in failing to consider Federal's duty under the second part of the definition of "property damage," which obligates the company to provide coverage if Eyeblaster is alleged to have caused the "loss of use of tangible property that is not physically injured." The tangible property is Sefton's computer, and Eyeblaster points to language from the Sefton complaint in which he alleges his computer was "taken over and could not operate," "froze up," and would "stop running or operate so slowly that it will inessence become inoperable." Sefton also alleges that he experienced "a hijacked browser—a browser program that communicates with websites other than those directed by the operator," and "slowed computer performance, sometimes resulting in crashes." Sefton asserts that his computer has three years of client tax returns that he cannot transfer because he believes the spyware files would also be transferred, and he therefore must reconstruct those records on a new computer. He thus argues that his computer is no longer usable, as he claims among his losses "the cost of his existing computer."

Federal did not include a definition of "tangible property" in its General Liability policy, except to exclude "software, data or other information that is in electronic form." The plain meaning of tangible property includes computers, and the Sefton complaint alleges repeatedly the "loss of use" of his computer. We conclude that the allegations are within the scope of the General Liability policy. *See Am. Online, Inc. v. St. Paul Mercury Ins. Co.*, 207 F.Supp. 2d 459, 470

(E.D.Va.2002) (district court found loss of use of tangible property when complaint alleged that AOL caused loss of use of computers and computer functionality, but concluded no coverage existed because allegations were otherwise excluded), aff'd, 347 F.3d 89 (4th Cir.2003); *State Auto Prop. & Cas. Ins. Co. v. Midwest Computers & More*, 147 F.Supp.2d 1113, 1116 (W.D. Okla. 2001) (in case with "property damage" language identical to language of Eyeblaster policy, court holds that "[b]ecause a computer clearly is tangible property, an alleged loss of use of computers constitutes 'property damage' within the meaning of plaintiff's policy"). * * *

NOTES AND QUESTIONS

1. *Cyber-Liability Insurance.* Much cyber-damage is likely not to involve hardware, and therefore to fall outside the holding in *Eyeblaster*. CGL policies typically exclude "electronic data" from the definition of "property damage." But ISO has developed an Electronic Data Liability Endorsement that insurers may offer as an add-on the CGL policy, and special-purpose cyber-liability policies also are available.

2. *Coverage of Liability for Cyber-Bullying.* Suppose that cyber-bullying results in liability imposed on a teenager. Under the liability insurance provisions of the Sample Homeowners policy set out in Chapter Four, under what circumstances would such liability be covered?

3. *Loss of Use.* Note that there are two ways in which the definition of "property damage" covers loss of use. Both loss of use resulting from physical injury to tangible property and loss of use of tangible property that is not physically injured fall within the definition. Sometimes, however, there is something physical that is neither physical injury nor loss of use. For example, in *F&H Construction v. ITT Hartford Insurance Co. of the Midwest*, 118 Cal. App. 4th 364 (Cal. Ct. App. 2004), the insured supplied defective pile caps that had to be modified in place after installation. The modification did not cause physical injury, and was accomplished without delaying the project. The court held, therefore, that the insured's liability was not because of "property damage" because there had been neither physical injury nor loss of use of the piles. On the other hand, in *Shade Foods, Inc. v. Innovative Products Sales & Marketing, Inc.*, 93 Cal. Rptr. 2d 364 (Cal. Ct. App. 2000), there were splinters in nut clusters used in cereal, making the cereal unfit to eat, and the court held that there was property damage.

Heacker v. Safeco Insurance Company of America

United States Court of Appeals, Eighth Circuit, 2012.
676 F.3d 724.

■ BENTON, CIRCUIT JUDGE.

Lewis Heacker sued Jessica Wright in the Circuit Court of Jackson County, Missouri, for hacking into his voicemail and Facebook services, sending disparaging letters and emails about him, and making anonymous phone calls and texts to harass or defame him, among other things. This conduct began around 2005, continuing for nearly five years. Heacker alleged emotional distress, which manifested itself physically and through post-traumatic stress disorder and alcoholism. * * *

The district court also held that the Homeowner's Policy's bodily injury coverage would not apply to Heacker's mental illnesses and alcohol addiction, relying on *Rockgate Management Co. v. CGU Insurance, Inc.*, 88 P.3d 798, 804 (2004). The Policy here defines bodily injury as "bodily harm, sickness or disease." Heacker argues that his physical symptoms of distress, PTSD, and alcoholism are "bodily injury" under this definition. The court in *Rockgate* pointed out that the interpretation of the contract—not any state law—governs the definition of bodily injury. In that case, the contract—similar to the one here—defined bodily injury as "bodily injury, sickness or disease." *Id.* The *Rockgate* court stated: "Where the policy defines bodily injury as bodily injury, it seems to imply that actual physical injury must occur for policy coverage." *Id.* Based on this, the district court here correctly concluded: "Physical manifestations of emotional distress or other related emotional harm may offer insight into the severity or extent of the emotional trauma suffered, but, absent some physical, bodily harm, such physical manifestations arise out of and are directly caused by purely emotional injury, which is clearly excluded from coverage." Heacker argues that PTSD and alcoholism are sicknesses or diseases. The *Rockgate* case indicates that Kansas is one of many jurisdictions where the word "bodily" in the bodily injury definition modifies injury, sickness, and disease. *See id.* (declining to adopt New York's definition of "bodily injury," which includes mental sickness, because of a "disconnect" between that definition and the specific language of the policy); *Citizens Ins. Co. of Am. v. Leiendecker,* 962 S.W.2d 446, 452 (Mo. Ct. App.1998) (compiling cases); *see also Lapeka, Inc. v. Security Nat'l Ins. Co.*, 814 F.Supp. 1540, 1548 (D.Kan.1993) (concluding Kansas would not find bodily injury in a case of emotional distress "severe enough to manifest itself in the form of physical injury"). PTSD and alcoholism are not bodily sicknesses or diseases and are excluded from coverage. * * *

The Umbrella Policy covers personal injury arising from defamation or privacy violations. It excludes, however, coverage for personal injury arising from mental abuse. The term "mental abuse" is not defined in the Policy. Heacker says this renders the term ambiguous. "The failure of an insurance policy to specifically define a word does not necessarily create ambiguity." *First Fin. Ins. Co. v. Bugg,* 962 P.2d 515, 525 (1998) (citation omitted). "The test to determine whether an insurance contract is ambiguous is not what the insurer intends the language to mean, but what a reasonably prudent insured would understand the language to mean." *Id.* at 519. The possibility of slight deviations in the insured's perceived meanings does not create ambiguity. *Id.* at 525 ("Although assault and battery have varying definitions, these definitions only slightly deviate and regardless of the definition used, they all convey the same general meaning. In the case at hand, the definitions of assault and battery do not present various and distinct definitions."). A reasonably prudent insured would discern that mental abuse is mental maltreatment, often resulting in mental or emotional injury. *See* **Black's Law Dictionary 10** (8th ed. 2004) (defining abuse as "[p]hysical or mental maltreatment, often resulting in mental, emotional, sexual, or physical injury."); *cf. Bugg,* 962 P.2d at

524 (interpreting insurance policy exclusion using Black's Law definitions of "assault and battery"). According to the Policy, the mental abuse exclusion includes both intentional and unintentional acts. Thus, the acts in the case—whether or not they were the result of Wright's negligence—were mental abuse. Heacker cites Kansas criminal cases and statutes defining mental abuse. These cases and statutes are irrelevant because according to the Policy, the mental abuse exclusion applies whether or not the acts violate a criminal code or accompany physical or sexual abuse. Heacker finally argues that even if some of the defamatory acts and invasions of privacy were mental abuse, not all of them were. All of the acts, however, were maltreatment meeting the reasonable definition of mental abuse.

The judgment of the district court is affirmed.

NOTES AND QUESTIONS

1. *Division of Authority.* The courts are divided on the question whether "bodily injury" includes mental or emotional distress when the term is defined as it was in *Heacker*. See, e.g., *Am. Economy Ins. Co. v. Fort Deposit Bank*, 890 F.Supp. 1011 (M.D. Ala. 1995) (claim of mental anguish alleges "bodily injury"); *Trinity Universal Ins. Co. v. Cowan*, 945 S.W. 2d 819 (Tex. 1997) ("bodily injury" does not include purely emotional injuries). A number of courts have held that the term is ambiguous and construed it in favor of coverage. See, e.g., *Lavanant v. Gen. Accident Ins. Co. of Am.*, 595 N.E.2d 819 (N.Y. 1992). And still other courts have held that whether bodily injury resulting from mental distress is *bodily injury*, as in *Heacker,* poses a question of fact for the jury. See, e.g., *Pekin Ins. Co. v. Hugh*, 501 N.W.2d 508 (Iowa 1993).

2. *A Tenable Distinction?* Given that it is increasingly understood that mental states involve physical (electrical, biochemical, or sub-cellular) changes to the body, is the distinction between physical injury and emotional distress valid? Should these developments in our understanding result in abolition of the distinction, case-by-case adjudication, or legally maintaining the distinction as long as insurance policy language does not directly address it? Note that the Umbrella policy in *Heacker* did address the issue in part, with a "mental abuse" exclusion. The standard-form Homeowners' policy contains a similar exclusion.

3. *"Because of" Bodily Injury.* For a holding that cellular damage constitutes "bodily injury," see *Associated Aviation Underwriters v. Wood*, 98 P.3d 572 (Ariz. Ct. App. 2004). Note that, whatever "bodily injury" means, liability insurance policies insure not only for bodily injury itself, but also for damages "because of" bodily injury. Damages imposed as a consequence of bodily injury therefore are covered. See, e.g., *Motorola, Inc. v. Associated Indem. Corp.*, 878 So. 2d 874 (La. Ct. App. 2004) (cost of purchasing headsets to protect against alleged risk of brain damage caused by exposure to radiation from cellphones is "because of" bodily injury).

4. *Why No Redrafting?* The basic question addressed in *Heacker* has arisen repeatedly, yet standard-form liability insurance policies continue not to address it, by either more clearly including or excluding mental distress from the definition of "bodily injury." What are the possible explanations for this failure?

b. THE TRIGGER AND ALLOCATION OF COVERAGE

American Home Products Corporation v. Liberty Mutual Insurance Company

United States District Court, Southern District of New York, 1983.
565 F.Supp. 1485.

■ SOFAER, DISTRICT JUDGE.

Plaintiff American Home Products Corporation ("AHP"), a diversified company manufacturing drugs, foods, and household products, is the defendant in fifty-four products-liability suits arising from AHP's manufacture and sale of six pharmaceuticals: Ovral and L/Ovral (oral contraceptives), DES (Diethylstilbestrol), Mysoline, Atromid–S, Premarin, and Anacin. Defendant Liberty Mutual Insurance Company ("Liberty"), which provided AHP with insurance from 1944 until 1976, has refused to assume AHP's burden of defense or to indemnify AHP in those lawsuits, because in each case physical harm did not become manifest until after termination of the insurance policies. In this action AHP seeks a judgment declaring that Liberty is obliged to defend and to indemnify AHP in the underlying lawsuits because, regardless of when physical harm became manifest, exposure to the alleged agents of harm occurred during the policy periods, thereby triggering coverage.

Jurisdiction is based on diversity of citizenship, 28 U.S.C. § 1332 (1976), and New York law controls. AHP contends there are no disputed issues of material fact, and has moved for summary judgment awarding the declaration it seeks. * * *

Several courts have recently ruled on the scope of insurance policies covering liability for insidious diseases, which are illnesses that become manifest long after initial exposure to the substances believed to cause them. The policy provisions at issue in these cases were all variants of the Comprehensive General Liability Policy ("CGL"), a standard-form policy for liability coverage drafted during the 1960's by representatives of the insurance industry to deal with the problem of liability for injuries caused over a period of time. Instead of covering only "accidents", a word that connotes an event causing immediate or contemporaneous injury, the CGL was written to cover "occurrences", defined to include "an accident, including injurious exposure to conditions, which results, during the policy period, in bodily injury * * * neither expected nor intended from the standpoint of the insured." CGL, Pl.Ex. 22 at 12. This change in terminology made clear the intent of insurers to provide coverage for insidious diseases. But the new language provided no definition of "bodily injury" other than the words themselves, thereby creating a basis for disputes as to the trigger of coverage.

AHP's insurance policies with Liberty were "manuscript" policies written specifically for AHP. Like the 1966 version of the CGL, however, AHP's policies throughout the period relevant to this litigation provided liability coverage for "occurrences" that result in "personal injury, sickness or disease including death resulting therefrom * * * sustained by any person." An occurrence is defined by inference from

Article IV: "This policy applies only to (1) personal injury, sickness or disease including death resulting therefrom * * * which occurs during the policy period." The ultimate question under both the CGL language and the AHP policies at issue here is therefore the same: when does "injury, sickness or disease" occur? Under both policies, coverage exists only for injuries occurring during the policy period. Moreover, both the CGL and AHP's policies require the insurer to defend any suit against the insured that seeks damages for an injury alleged to have occurred under the policy, even if the suit is groundless or fraudulent. * * *

For the reasons that follow the policies in this case are construed as they are written—to require a showing of actual injury, sickness or disease occurring during the policy period, based upon the facts proved in each particular case. Thus, an occurrence of "personal injury, sickness, or disease" is read to mean any point in time at which a finder of fact determines that the effects of exposure to a drug actually resulted in a diagnosable and compensable injury. Depending upon the facts of each case, the drug involved, the period and intensity of exposure, and the person affected, an injury may occur in this sense upon exposure, at some point in time after exposure but before manifestation of the injury, and at manifestation. This construction is supported by the policy's language and background, the intentions and expectations of the parties, and considerations of practicability and fairness. It provides liberal protection to the insured, without doing violence to the principle—long a part of the law of New York—that insurance policies are contracts under which insureds obtain all the protection for which they may reasonably be said to have paid, but not more. * * *

A. *Governing Legal Principles*

AHP correctly argues that insurance contracts must be liberally construed, with ambiguities in the policy language resolved in favor of the insured. *See Pan American World Airways, Inc. v. Aetna Casualty & Surety Co.,* 505 F.2d 989, 999 (2d Cir.1974); *Breed v. Insurance Co. of North America,* 46 N.Y.2d 351, 353 (1978). This rule of construction, in fact, appears to be the single factor that unifies the discordant opinions applying the CGL and its derivatives to insidious diseases. Whether or not explicitly finding ambiguities, and irrespective of the construction adopted, every court construing these provisions has reached the result that extended coverage to the insured. *See, e.g., Eagle-Picher Industries,* 682 F.2d at 17 (manifestation); *Keene,* 667 F.2d at 1041 (manifestation and exposure); *Forty-Eight Insulations,* 663 F.2d at 1223 (exposure). * * *

B. *Proposed Constructions of the Parties*

Neither construction proffered by the parties is supported by the plain meaning of the terms employed.

1. *The Exposure Theory.* An exposure theory is inconsistent with the policies' plain meaning, and AHP has offered no evidence or explanation to demonstrate how an "occurrence" could logically include every exposure to the substances it manufactures. The policies require that the resulting injury and not the exposure occur "during the policy period." Moreover, the policies were designed to protect against liability from law suits brought because of compensable injuries. To that end

they cover "occurrences" wherein both exposure and an injury take place.

The only New York case on point also rejected the exposure theory as unsupported by the language of a policy that covered "[a]n accident or injurious exposure to conditions which results, during the policy period, in bodily injury. * * * " The injured plaintiffs, who had sued the insured, were the daughters of women who had ingested DES while pregnant with the plaintiffs in 1952, 1953, and 1961 respectively; the plaintiffs thereafter developed cervical cancers that were discovered in 1970, 1971, and 1975. Justice Greenfield concentrated on the policy language:

> A reading of the policy language would appear to indicate that coverage is predicated not on the act which might give rise to ultimate liability, but upon the result. It would be a strained interpretation to construe the occurrence clause as though it covered "exposure during the policy period which results in bodily injury." It is the *result* which is keyed to the policy period, and not the accident or exposure.

American Motorists Ins. v. E.R. Squibb & Sons, 406 N.Y.S.2d 658, 659–60 (N.Y.Sup.Ct.1978) (emphasis in original).

A limited version of the exposure theory, adopted in some litigations, is at least linguistically respectable. Some courts, relying on medical evidence, have found that, on exposure, asbestos particles enter the body and cause discrete injuries to lung and other tissue, and that these injuries are sufficient to establish coverage under the CGL language, even though they must aggregate over time to cause diseases and sicknesses such as asbestosis, carcinoma, and mesothelioma. *Keene,* 667 F.2d at 1044; *Insurance Co. of North America v. Forty-Eight Insulations, Inc.,* 451 F.Supp. 1230, 1239 (E.D.Mich.1978), *modified,* 633 F.2d 1212, 1222–23 (6th Cir.1980), *cert. denied,* 454 U.S. 1109 (1981). *But see, e.g., Eagle-Picher,* 523 F.Supp. at 115 & 682 F.2d at 17 (medical evidence establishes that (1) not every exposure to asbestos results in injury of any sort, since body's natural mechanisms often remove fibers before they become embedded; and (2) even when discrete injuries are caused, they frequently fail to lead to any compensable injury).

AHP cannot rely on the rationale of cases that have found immediate injury from the ingestion of asbestos fibers, because the drugs at issue in this case differ markedly from asbestos in the manner in which they are alleged to injure humans. AHP has failed to submit any proof with respect to the effects of any of the drugs involved, and has not claimed that any of them injures upon every exposure. The record establishes without material dispute, moreover, that at least two of the drugs at issue (Ovral and DES) do not injure upon every exposure. Flessa Aff'd, Def.Ex. 35 (Feb. 14, 1982) (Ovral); Mattingly Aff't, Def.Ex. 36 (Feb. 10, 1982) (DES). As discussed below, a particular plaintiff might be able to establish, despite this evidence, that a particular exposure to one of the drugs at issue constituted an actual and compensable injury. No evidence has been presented, however, that could support a general declaration that every exposure to any of the drugs at issue in this case causes injury, and therefore triggers coverage, under the AHP policies. * * *

2. *The Manifestation Theory.* Liberty contends that the policy words "injury", and "disease" or "sickness" are ordinary words which the average person would understand respectively to mean "damage" and an "abnormal condition," and that the average person would think of these consequences as having occurred when they take place or are discovered. The First Circuit accepted this view in extending coverage to the claims at issue in *Eagle-Picher:*

> [W]e agree with the district court that the common, ordinary meaning of the policy language supports the manifestation theory. An individual with tiny subclinical insults to her lungs would not say that she had any injury or disease, given one expert's testimony that "over 90% of all urban city dwellers have asbestos-related scarring." Rather, she would say that a disease resulted when she had symptoms which impaired her sense of well-being, or when a doctor was able to detect sufficient scarring to make a prognosis that the onset of manifested disease was inevitable. "Injury" is defined by Webster as "hurt, damage, or loss sustained"; it is a broad term which covers the "result of inflicting on a person or thing something that causes loss, pain, distress, or impairment." As sweeping as this definition is, it is difficult to consider subclinical insults to the lung to constitute an "injury" when these insults do not cause "loss, pain, distress, or impairment" until, if ever, they accumulate to become clinically evident or manifest.

682 F.2d at 19 (footnote omitted).

The "manifestation" theory adopted in *Eagle-Picher,* and now advanced by Liberty, is in part a departure from what has conventionally been understood as the manifestation approach. The meaning of manifestation proposed in prior cases is that an injury, sickness, or disease becomes manifest only when symptoms become noticeable or a diagnosis is made. "The manifestation theorists contend that the date of manifestation is 'the date on which the condition became known or should have become known to plaintiff or the date on which plaintiff's condition was medically diagnosed, whichever comes first.'" Wrubel, *supra,* 48 Fordham L.Rev. at 668 n. 58 (quoting *Forty-Eight Insulations,* 451 F.Supp. at 1238). Thus stated, the manifestation theory refuses to recognize that any bodily injury may have existed prior to the appearance of symptoms or an actual diagnosis. Under this construction, the manifestation theory would be convenient to apply, but it is inconsistent with the policy language.

The ordinary person may construe an "occurrence" of injury to mean manifestation in the sense of discovery. Discovery of an injury or disease is a truly significant event which makes the victim aware of what had theretofore been only a latent, medical problem without conscious significance. The plain meaning of the policy language is not measured, however, by the understanding of a lay person, but by the understanding of a person engaged in the insured's course of business. *See Champion International Corp. v. Continental Casualty Co.,* 546 F.2d 502, 505–06 (2d Cir.1976); *McGrail v. Equitable Life Assurance Society,* 292 N.Y. 419, 424–25 (1944); *Loblaw, Inc. v. Employers' Liability Assurance Corp.,* 446 N.Y.S.2d 743, 745 (4th Dep't 1981). From the point of view of a drug manufacturer, familiar with the potential development of insidious diseases from its products, and seeking to insure against liability for harm, an injury, sickness, or disease would include any compensable, medical condition that is fully developed, even though dormant.

For example, a particular drug may cause a heart attack in some women long after they ingest it. Under the manifestation theory, liability for the heart attack would be covered by a CGL-type policy in effect when the injury occurs. But the manufacturer would also expect that a latent, undiscovered disease caused by the same drug prior to the heart attack would be covered by a policy in effect at the time it arose, regardless of when the disease was discovered or the heart attack or some other manifestation occurred. The CGL policy language covers *all* injuries, sicknesses, or diseases that occur during coverage, not merely those that become manifest.

The restriction imposed on the policy language by the manifestation approach is, moreover, inconsistent with insurance law principles. If the policy language were deemed ambiguous enough to permit reading in a manifestation requirement, the process of doing so would be unacceptable in New York because that reading is not "the only construction which may fairly be placed on" the policy's words, *Filor, Bullard & Smyth v. Insurance Co. of North America,* 605 F.2d 598, 602 (2d Cir.1978), *cert. denied,* 440 U.S. 962 (1979) (emphasis omitted) (citing *Lachs v. Fidelity & Casualty Co.,* 306 N.Y. 357, 365–66 (1954)), and because the construction proposed would be more restrictive than one that treated as "occurrences" all injuries, diseases, and sicknesses, whether manifest or merely discoverable, *see Thomas J. Lipton, Inc. v. Liberty Mutual Insurance Co.,* 34 N.Y.2d 356, 361 (1974); *National Screen Service Corp. v. United States Fidelity & Guaranty Co.,* 364 F.2d 275, 277 (2d Cir.1966); *Vargas v. Insurance Co. of North America,* 651 F.2d 838, 839–40 (2d Cir.1981). Significantly, courts that have accepted the manifestation theory have invariably done so in extending, rather than restricting, the coverage of an ambiguous policy.
* * *

C. *Plain Meaning of the Policy Provisions*

1. *The Occurrence Clause.* The plain meaning of the "occurrence" clause is no secret to the parties. Courts and writers have recognized that "occurrence" is most logically construed to include only those injuries, sicknesses, or diseases that are proved to have existed during coverage. For example, in *Forty-Eight Insulations* the Sixth Circuit stated:

> In each case where a plaintiff sues an asbestos manufacturer, a hearing could be held to determine at what point the build-up of asbestos in the plaintiff's lungs resulted in the body's defenses being overwhelmed. At that point, asbestosis could truly be said to "occur". From then on, all companies which insured the manufacturer would be treated as being "on the risk".

633 F.2d at 1217 (footnote omitted); *see also Schering Corp. v. Home Insurance Co.,* 544 F.Supp. 613, 616 (E.D.N.Y.1982). *See generally* Wrubel, *supra.* Indeed, while Liberty has advanced its position as based

on a manifestation theory requiring knowledge or actual diagnosis, Liberty at times defines "manifestation" to include the unknown presence of diagnosable and compensable disease. *See, e.g.,* Portmann Dep., Pl.Ex. 3 at 136, 138; Stevens Dep., Pl.Ex. 8 at 113–17.

This straight-forward interpretation has been rejected, however, as impractical and unfair. According to critics, to require the courts and the parties to CGL-type contracts to determine coverage in the many thousands of pending and anticipated latent-injury claims on a case-by-case basis would be impossible, *e.g., Forty-Eight Insulations,* 633 F.2d at 1218, and also inconsistent with the reasonable expectations of the insured, and with developing tort-law doctrine in the latent-disease area, *e.g., Keene,* 667 F.2d at 1044 n. 20; *Forty-Eight Insulations,* 633 F.2d at 1219. These practical and ethical concerns are shown below to be unpersuasive. Before addressing them, however, a full appraisal of the policy's plain meaning is in order to demonstrate why, linguistically at least, the injury-in-fact approach is plainly the proper construction.

The most basic demand of the policy language is that to establish Liberty's liability the insured must prove that an "occurrence"—injury, sickness, or disease—arose during the policy period. The plain language demands that the insured prove the cause of the occurrence (accident or exposure), and that the result occurred during the policy period. An exposure that does not result in injury during coverage would not satisfy the policy's terms. On the other hand, a real but undiscovered injury, proved in retrospect to have existed at the relevant time, would establish coverage, irrespective of the time the injury became manifest.

This approach is faithful to the policy language because it gives separate meaning to the three concepts of exposure, injury, and discovery. The policy expressly gives separate significance to the first two concepts, and its provisions strongly suggest that an occurrence means something different—and more expansive—than manifestation or discovery. On the other hand, nothing in the policy language precludes a finding that a single exposure, or a single period of exposures, immediately injured a person to a compensable extent; similarly the policy language also permits courts or juries to find that injury, sickness, or disease, occurred in a particular case at the time it became manifest. So long as the insured is held liable for an identifiable and compensable injury, sickness, or disease that is shown to have existed during coverage, that liability will be insured against whether or not the injury coincides with exposure or manifestation. * * *

IV. Conclusion

The policies at issue in this case explicitly cover liability for injuries, sicknesses, or diseases that occur during each period of coverage. They were intended to cover no more and no less. Coverage is triggered by neither exposure nor manifestation, except when those events constitute in themselves an injury, sickness, or disease for which an injured may be held liable. The policies also expressly require Liberty to bear the costs of defending AHP in all suits, however meritless, that can be read to permit proof that an injury, sickness, or disease occurred during a period of coverage. No considerations of practicability or fairness justify ignoring the plain meaning and purposes of these policies.

The parties will submit within twenty days a declaratory order encompassing these rulings.

SO ORDERED.

NOTES AND QUESTIONS

1. *Semantics.* The majority of courts considering the trigger issue have adopted some form of multi-year trigger when there has been proof of multi-year injury or damage, although the names they have given to this approach vary. See, e.g., *Allstate Ins. Co. v. Dana Corp.*, 759 N.E.2d 1049 (Ind. 2001) (adopting the injury-in-fact trigger). The consequence is that, sometimes unintentionally, different terminology may sometimes have substantive effects. As the Supreme Court of New Hampshire explained in adopting the injury-in-fact trigger in a case involving damage caused by hazardous waste,

> In some situations there is little practical difference between the theories utilized. For instance, "there is little practical difference between 'exposure' and 'injury in fact' in instances where contamination occurs almost immediately upon release." * * * Likewise, "[w]here the release or discharge of hazardous waste into the environment is identifiable, or even obvious, 'manifestation' occurs simultaneously with 'exposure' and 'injury.'" Under the continuous trigger theory, however, it is assumed "without substantiation, that once property damage begins it always continues and that property damage results when property is first exposed to hazardous materials."

EnergyNorth Natural Gas, Inc. v. Underwriters at Lloyd's, 848 A.2d 715 (N.H. 2004).

2. *The Causative-Event Trigger.* Sometimes variations in policy language result in a different trigger of coverage. The most prominent examples involve certain Lloyds and London-market CGL policies issued in the 1950's and 1960's. For instance, a number of the policies at issue in *Energy North* provided that they applied only to "accidents occurring during the policy" period or to "occurrences happening during the currency hereof" and said nothing about whether bodily injury or property damage were required to occur during the policy period. The court held that these policies were triggered by a causative event (i.e., an accident or an occurrence, respectively) that occurred during the policy period, even if the resulting effects (bodily injury or property damage) occurred after expiration of the policy period.

3. *Practical Problems of Proof.* On appeal in *American Home Products*, the court's adoption of the injury-in-fact trigger was affirmed, but the holding that the injury occurs when it is "diagnosable and compensable" was reversed. *American Home Products Corp. v. Liberty Mutual Ins. Co.*, 748 F.2d 760 (2d Cir. 1984). Does this sort of injury-in-fact trigger of coverage turn out to be an ideal that cannot be implemented in practice? The Sixth Circuit Court of Appeals thought so, at least in asbestos cases:

> The only problem with this Solomonian interpretation is that no one wants it. The principal reason is cost. If medical testimony as to asbestosis' origin would have to be taken in each of the

thousands of asbestosis cases, the cost of litigation would be prohibitive. This appears to be especially true since many of the asbestosis cases are settled before trial. In addition, it is almost impossible for a doctor to look back and testify with any precision as to when the development of asbestosis "crossed the line" and became a disease. The only thing on which all parties agree is that there is a need for us to arrive at an administratively manageable interpretation of the insurance policies—one that can be applied with minimal need for litigation. Reaching such a beneficial result is certainly desirable, but it greatly complicates our task. In the real world, there are few Solomonian possibilities. And, as we have just seen, those that do exist are often impractical.

Ins. Co. of North America v. Forty-Eight Insulations, Inc., 633 F.2d 1212, 1218 (6th Cir. 1980), cert. denied, 454 U.S. 1109 (1981). Was the *American Home Products* court overlooking the practical problems posed by the exposure test that it adopted? For example, could it be argued that in cases in which the exposure occurred several decades before suit was brought, pinpointing the year or years of exposure will often be just as difficult as pinpointing the year of injury? Similarly, in hazardous waste cleanup coverage cases in which the damage does not occur until 55 gallon steel drums rust, leak, and eventually contaminate groundwater, it may require Herculean expert testimony from groundwater hydrologists to identify the year when such contamination first began to occur, regardless of what name is given to the trigger employed.

4. *Manifestation.* Few courts have adopted manifestation as the exclusive trigger of coverage. In one of the leading cases that did adopt the single-year, manifestation trigger, the result was to enable the insured to call upon the only coverage potentially available to it. See *Eagle-Picher Indus., Inc. v. Liberty Mutual Ins. Co.*, 523 F.Supp. 110 (D.Mass. 1981), modified, 682 F.2d 12 (1st Cir. 1982). If you had been counsel for a liability insurer in 1975, when cascades of asbestos suits first began to be filed, and the manifestation trigger already had been widely adopted in other long-latency disease cases, what would you have advised your client to do about renewing liability insurance policies that would expire shortly? Does your answer help to explain the unpopularity of the manifestation trigger?

In contrast, the disadvantage to a policyholder of a trigger that focuses on the earliest possible years when damage occurred is that the limits of liability afforded by the older policies that are triggered tend to be unduly low in light of the magnitude of modern damages. Liability policies purchased even in the 1950's, for example, often provided only $50,000 or $100,000 of coverage. Of course, a continuous trigger, adopted in cases such as *Keene Corp. v. Insurance Co. of North America*, 667 F.2d 1034 (D.C.Cir. 1981), cert. denied, 455 U.S. 1007 (1982), avoids at least some of the problems associated with triggers based exclusively on manifestation or exposure. But as the court in *Energy North* noted, the plausibility of a continuous trigger depends on proof that there was a "continuing" injury from exposure through manifestation—proof that may be available in some kinds of long-latency disease or property damage cases, but not in others.

5. *Coverage of Liability as a Successor Corporation.* Suppose that Corporation B is liable in tort for bodily injury or property damage that was caused by and occurred while Corporation A was doing business, on the ground that Corporation B now owns Corporation A's business? Is

Corporation B covered under Corporation A's CGL insurance policy? In *Henkel Corp. v. Hartford Accident & Indemnity Corp.*, 62 P.3d 69 (Cal. 2003), the Supreme Court of California held that such coverage is available in the case of a merger, because the successor corporation assumes the liabilities and becomes owner of the assets of the predecessor corporation (including its insurance policies) by operation of law. However, when the successor corporation merely purchases the assets and liabilities of the predecessor and by contract takes an assignment of the predecessor's liability insurance policies, if the assignment violates a "no assignment" clause of the policies the assignment is invalid. This rule continues to be applied. See, e.g., *Bondox Int'l, Inc. v. Hartford Accident & Indem. Co.*, 667 F. 3d 699 (6th Cir. 2011) (corporation that has "absorbed another" is entitled to its insurance*); Axis Reinsurance Co. v. Telekenex, Inc.*, 913 F. Supp. 2d 793 (D. Ca. 2012) (corporation that has merely purchased the assets of another corporation is not entitled to its insurance). Suppose that Company B then turns to its own insurers for coverage. Would the Insuring Agreement of Company B's own past policies be triggered to cover its liability for injuries caused by Company A? See generally Patrick F. Hofer, Corporate Succession and Insurance Rights After *Henkel*: A Return to Common Sense, 42 Tort Trial & Ins. Prac. J. 763 (2007).

In re Silicone Implant Insurance Coverage Litigation

Supreme Court of Minnesota, 2003.
667 N.W.2d 405.

■ ANDERSON, PAUL H., JUSTICE.

This appeal stems from a declaratory judgment action brought by several of 3M's high-level, excess-layer, occurrence-based policy insurers. These insurers sought to clarify their coverage obligations in 3M's ongoing silicone gel breast implant mass tort litigation. The insurance policies at issue were in place from 1977 to 1985 and covered claims arising from injuries occurring during that time period. The implant claims for which 3M sought reimbursement were brought in the early 1990s, but were based largely on implantations that occurred during the policy periods, which implants allegedly caused various systemic autoimmune diseases. * * *

Between 1977 and 1985, 3M purchased significant amounts of occurrence-based insurance for product liability exposure. 3M purchased primary policies and ascending layers of excess coverage. The petitioner-insurers each provided high-level excess policy coverage, which means that their payment obligations arise only after judgments or settlements have exhausted the substantial primary and lower-level excess policies. Under these occurrence-based policies, coverage is determined by when the alleged bodily injury or property damage took place: all sums related to any such injury or damage that occurred during the policy period are covered by the policy, even if the claim is not asserted until after the end of the policy period. * * *

We begin our analysis with the policy language. The insurers provided 3M with occurrence-based excess liability coverage. The policies at issue indemnify 3M "for all sums which the insured shall become legally obligated to pay as damages because of injury or damage to which this policy applies." The policies apply to "injury or damage arising out of: bodily injury or property damage caused by an occurrence."[1]

Both sides agree that the actual-injury trigger rule is the proper method of determining which policies are activated by an occurrence. We adopted the "actual-injury" or "injury-in-fact" trigger in *NSP*. Under such a rule, "the time of the occurrence is not the time the wrongful act was committed but the time the complaining party was actually damaged." *Singsaas v. Diederich*, 307 Minn. 153, 156 (1976). Thus, under the actual-injury trigger rule, only those policies in effect when the bodily injury or property damage occurred are triggered. *NSP*, 523 N.W.2d at 662; *see also Jenoff, Inc. v. N.H. Ins. Co.*, 558 N.W.2d 260, 261 (Minn.1997); *Fairview Hosp. and Health Care Serv. v. St. Paul Fire & Marine Ins. Co.*, 535 N.W.2d 337, 341 (Minn.1995); *Singsaas*, 307 Minn. at 155.

To trigger a policy, "the insured must show that *some damage* occurred during the policy period." *NSP*, 523 N.W.2d at 663. For purposes of the actual-injury trigger theory, an injury can occur even though the injury is not "diagnosable," "compensable," or manifest during the policy period as long as it can be determined, even retroactively, that some injury did occur during the policy period. *Am. Home Prods. Corp. v. Liberty Mut. Ins. Co.*, 748 F.2d 760, 765–66 (2d Cir.1984).

3M argues that the district court's conclusion that the policies were triggered "at or about the time of implant" was based on substantial evidence in the form of expert testimony and, therefore, is not clearly erroneous. In response, the insurers argue that the court erred as a matter of law because it found that nonexistent cellular injuries triggered the policies in question. The insurers reason that the cellular injuries the court found are "fictional" and therefore those injuries cannot trigger the policies because no injury actually took place during the policy period. They contend that in using a nonexistent cellular injury to calculate when the policies were triggered, the court dispensed with the actual-injury trigger theory and erred as a matter of law. Thus, the insurers urge us to conclude that, here, the only policy coverage triggers are the demonstrable manifestations of the plaintiffs' autoimmune disease.

The insurers' argument that a "fictional" cellular injury cannot trigger coverage is unpersuasive. We acknowledge that conceptually the plaintiffs' injuries are fictional because medical "science has failed to establish a causal connection between silicone gel breast implants and systemic autoimmune disease." Nevertheless, we conclude for purposes of this insurance coverage litigation, which arises from a settlement that is premised on the notion that silicone gel breast implants caused plaintiffs' injuries, that the district court properly assumed the plaintiffs' injuries are authentic and were caused by the silicone gel breast implants. This assumption, on which the district court's finding of cellular injury is based, was necessary to determine when the policies were triggered. The experts agreed that if silicone caused autoimmune

---

[1] Occurrence is defined as "an accident, event or happening, including injurious exposure to conditions, which results, during the policy period, in bodily injury or property damage neither expected nor intended from the standpoint of the insured."

disease, then cellular injuries would occur sometime before the symptoms appeared. By arguing that the cellular injury is "fictional" or "nonexistent," the insurers, in effect, are arguing that the plaintiffs were not injured. But, as the insurers concede, they cannot at this post-settlement stage of the proceedings deny coverage for the losses 3M incurred in its settlement on the theory that the silicone did not injure the plaintiffs.

Having dismissed the insurers' argument that "fictional" cellular injury cannot trigger coverage, we now must determine whether the district court's finding that the injuries occurred on or about the time of implant is clearly erroneous. The district court accurately concluded that Minnesota follows an "actual injury" trigger rule. The court then heard expert medical testimony to determine the timing of the plaintiffs' bodily injuries. Experts for 3M testified that injury occurs at or about the time of implant, while the insurers' experts urged the court to find that injury occurs shortly before manifestation of symptoms. When there is conflicting medical testimony, we give deference to the fact finder. *See Raze v. Mueller,* 587 N.W.2d 645, 648 (Minn.1999) (stating that we give deference to the jury's verdict when there is conflicting medical testimony); *Gaspers v. Minneapolis Elec. Steel Castings Co.,* 290 N.W.2d 743, 745 (Minn.1980) (stating that when the opinions of medical experts conflict, the function of the trier of fact is to resolve the conflict). Here, the court weighed the conflicting expert medical testimony and after doing so determined that "bodily injury" occurs at the time of implant. Based upon our review of the record, we conclude that the district court's determination of when bodily injury occurred is not clearly erroneous.

We turn next to the insurers' argument that the district court dispensed with the actual-injury trigger rule when it determined that the policies were triggered at or about the time of implantation. After reviewing conflicting medical testimony, the court found that the damage done to the plaintiffs occurred on a cellular level, "at or about the time of implant," years before the plaintiffs began experiencing symptoms of systemic disease. This finding is consistent with the actual-injury trigger rule, which requires that bodily injury occur during the policy period, but does not require that the injury be diagnosable or even evident during the policy period. *Am. Home Prods.,* 748 F.2d at 765–66. In *American Home Products,* the court stated:

> For example, a person may suffer an injury or illness that does not become diagnosable until after some period of gestation; it may be possible after diagnosis to infer that the harm must have begun some time prior to diagnosability because of the stage of the illness at the time it is diagnosed and the fact that the type of illness that is diagnosed does not occur without a gestation period. *Id.* at 765.

We conclude that the district court did not dispense with the actual-injury trigger rule and that the court's finding that the plaintiffs' injuries occurred at or about the time of implantation is not clearly erroneous. Accordingly, because damage occurred at or about the time of implantation, we conclude that the policies were triggered at or about the time of implantation.

II.

Having concluded that the insurance policies were triggered at or about the time of implantation, the next issue we must decide is whether the district court erred in deciding to allocate 3M's losses from those injuries among the insurers. 3M asserts that the decision to apply allocation is purely legal and therefore reviewable de novo. We have stated, however, that damages are very fact-dependent, so "trial courts must be given the flexibility to apportion them in a manner befitting each case." *NSP,* 523 N.W.2d at 663. Such language indicates that allocation decisions should be reviewed under an abuse of discretion standard and that is the standard we apply here.

The district court found that from the time of implantation, the damages were continuous and the "actual injury" continued to occur as silicone came in contact with new cells. The court therefore determined that 3M's losses should be allocated pro rata by time on the risk among all triggered policies. The court of appeals affirmed the allocation ruling, concluding that the district court had made specific findings that "the injury causing event was the continuous leakage of silicone that comes into contact with the body's cells." Based on this continuous injury finding, the court of appeals affirmed the need for allocation.

All parties and both lower courts recognized that the most apposite case law for the allocation issue consists of three of our earlier cases addressing environmental damage liability: *NSP,* 523 N.W.2d 657; *SCSC Corp. v. Allied Mut. Ins. Co.,* 536 N.W.2d 305 (Minn.1995); and *Domtar,* 563 N.W.2d 724. In these three cases, we discussed the pro rata by time on the risk allocation method and how it applies to continuous injuries arising from environmental contamination.

In *NSP,* the insured, NSP, was required by the Minnesota Pollution Control Agency (MPCA) to clean up two adjacent property sites that were contaminated by NSP's use of the properties as coal-tar gasification sites. *NSP,* 523 N.W.2d at 658. The MPCA discovered that as a result of NSP's operations on those sites between 1910 and 1933, the groundwater at both sites was contaminated with coal tars and spent oxide waste. The MPCA required NSP to pay clean-up and monitoring costs for the sites. *Id.* at 659. NSP then sought coverage for its costs from its comprehensive general liability insurers.

We discussed in *NSP* the special problems associated with environmental liability insurance cases, where damages are continuous and where "for all practical purposes the bodily injury or property damage suffered during different policy periods is indivisible." *Id.* at 663 (quoting Kenneth S. Abraham, *Environmental Liability Insurance Law: An Analysis of Toxic Tort and Hazardous Waste Insurance Coverage Issues,* 120 (1991)). We noted that determining how to allocate damages in such cases "may require a more flexible approach. As with all insurance contract-related issues, courts must consider many factors when deciding this issue, including the policy language, parties' intent or reasonable expectations, canons of construction and public policy." *Id.* at 661. We went on to state that a pro rata by limits approach to allocation, as advocated by NSP, is inconsistent with the actual-injury trigger theory that we adopted. *Id.* at 662. In so doing, we stated that the goal of the actual-injury trigger theory is to ensure that insurers are not made liable for injuries occurring outside of their policy periods. We said:

> Where the policy periods do not overlap, therefore, the insurers are *consecutively,* not *concurrently* liable. A "pro rata by limits" allocation method effectively makes those insurers with higher limits liable for damages incurred outside their policy periods and is therefore inconsistent with the actual injury trigger theory.

Id.

In *NSP,* we chose the time on the risk allocation method because it has the advantage of being a "more or less per se rule." *Id.* at 663. "This method assumes that the damages in a contamination case are evenly distributed (or continuous) through each policy period from the first point at which damages occurred to the time of discovery, cleanup or whenever the last triggered policy period ended." *Id.* Because the contamination in *NSP* was "regarded as a continuous process in which the property damage is evenly distributed over the period of time from the first contamination to the end of the last triggered policy (or self-insured) period," there was no period during which more or less damage occurred, so allocation according to time on the risk was appropriate. *Id.* at 664.

One year later, in *SCSC,* we revisited the issue of allocation in the environmental liability context. *SCSC,* 536 N.W.2d at 305. In *SCSC,* a dry cleaning and laundry supply distribution facility purchased, stored, repackaged, and distributed perchloroethylene (PCE), which the MPCA had identified as a volatile organic compound. *Id.* at 308. SCSC stored the PCE in two above-ground tanks from which the PCE was dispensed through an outgoing fill pipe to the trucks that delivered the chemical to retailers. *Id.* at 309. The MPCA discovered PCE contamination in the groundwater near the SCSC plant and SCSC was required to pay clean-up costs, for which it sought reimbursement from its general liability insurers. *Id.* at 309–10. At trial, SCSC alleged that the contamination was not the result of consistent dripping of PCE from the fill pipe during the normal course of operations, as was asserted by the insurers, but was instead the result of a significant spill that occurred in August 1977. The jury found that "property damage arose in August 1977, as the result of an unintended, unexpected, sudden and accidental event, and that the damage was neither divisible nor attributable to an overriding cause." *Id.* at 310. The district court adopted a "vertical triggering" approach by which the primary policies for 1977 were first in line for coverage and paid out in full, then the excess policies for 1977, then the primary policies for the next year, and so on until the insurers' full liabilities were paid. *Id.* at 317.

On appeal, we reversed the district court's vertical triggering scheme and also refused to allocate pro rata by time on the risk as we did in *NSP*. We did so because "*NSP* was an equitable decision based upon the complexity of proving in which policy periods covered property damage arose," and in *SCSC* no such complexity existed as a result of the jury having determined the damage arose from a single event in 1977. *Id.* at 318. We noted that the jury found the damage was not divisible: "the only covered 'occurrence' was the 1977 spill. The continual leaching of the chemicals from the soil into the groundwater did result in damages to SCSC because of property damage," but that damage is not covered by insurers that were not on the risk in 1977, the year during which the only covered "occurrence" occurred. *Id.* at 318. We refused to allocate any damages to insurers that were not on the risk in 1977. All the damages from continued leaching potentially could have been covered if there were enough insurance coverage in the 1977 policies, but SCSC could not look to insurers from later years to help cover that liability.

Finally, in *Domtar,* the insured sought reimbursement for clean-up costs it incurred in association with its tar refining plant. *Domtar,* 563 N.W.2d at 728. The plant was operated from 1924 to 1929 and from 1934 to 1948, and it was dismantled in 1954 or 1955. *Id.* Pollution was first detected in 1979. The property where the plant was located was subsequently declared a Superfund site and the MPCA named Domtar as one of the responsible parties. *Id.* at 729. Domtar sought declaratory judgment of liability for reimbursement for clean-up costs against its 1956–1970 insurers. It limited its claim to insurers from this time period because earlier policies had been lost and later insurers were dismissed from the action. *Id.* The record indicated two general causes for Domtar's share of damages: (1) damage was caused by leaks during routine waste-handling and accidental spillage during plant operation; and (2) the bulk of the damage arose from residual sludge discharges from the storage tanks during dismantling of the plant before the property was sold. *Id.* All pollutants were discharged before Domtar sold the property and before the 1956–1970 insurers sold policies to Domtar. Experts for both sides agreed that the contamination could not be apportioned among causes because leakage to the groundwater had become commingled with and inseparable from other migrating contaminants. *Id.* at 730. Domtar asserted that the damage continued after the plant was dismantled because "contaminants were migrating deeper into the soil and through the groundwater during the ensuing years, including the present time * * * [and] 'property damage at the site was indivisible * * * [and] it continued and expanded' over the years." *Id.*

In contrast to Domtar's assertions, experts for the insurance companies testified that contamination occurred in the years following the initial spills and leakage, and "the contamination has been ameliorated by biodegradation in the ensuing years," during which time period the 1956–1970 insurers provided coverage. *Id.* The jury determined that the property damage commenced in 1933 and that "some" property damage took place during each of the insurers' policy periods, rejecting insurers' argument that no "appreciable" damage occurred during their policy periods. *Id.* The district court determined that liability costs would be allocated evenly from 1933 to the year in which clean-up efforts began and that Domtar would be responsible for the costs outside of the insurers' policy periods, i.e., before 1956 and after 1970. *Id.* Domtar appealed the allocation ruling and the court of appeals affirmed. *Id.* at 730–31.

In *Domtar,* we summarized *NSP* as establishing that in "*continuous and indivisible* environmental contamination cases" (1) general liability policies are triggered when property damage occurred during the policy period; (2) insurer liability is consecutive, limited to property damage occurring during the insurer's policy period; and (3) one way to allocate loss among consecutively liable insurers, in the absence of applicable policy language, is pro rata by time on the risk. *Id.* at 732 (emphasis added). We then discussed the shifting of burdens in cases like these.

> [T]he insured bears the burden of proving that a policy has been triggered, but if the insured proves when the contamination began and when it ended or was discovered, then the trial court should presume that property damage was continuous from its initiation until the time of clean up or discovery. The burden of proof then shifts to any party seeking to demonstrate that no appreciable damage occurred during a particular time period. All policies in effect when damages occurred are triggered, and liability is allocated to each policy according to the proportion of time each was on the risk.

Id. Accordingly, in *Domtar,* we affirmed the use of allocation pro rata by time on the risk, specifically rejecting Domtar's argument that this allocation method unfairly allocated losses to Domtar by allocating losses to periods during which Domtar was uninsured, self-insured, or underinsured. *Id.* at 732–33. We also emphasized the limits of our holding, however, and attempted to remedy some of the confusion created by our discussion of allocation in *NSP* and *SCSC:*

> The proper scope of coverage also will depend on the facts of the case. When environmental contamination arises from discrete and identifiable events, then the actual-injury trigger theory allows those policies on the risk at the point of initial contamination to pay for all property damage that follows. [citing *SCSC*] * * * It is only in those difficult cases in which property damage is both continuous and so intermingled as to be practically indivisible that *NSP* properly applies. *NSP* provides a judicially manageable way for trial courts to adjudicate certain pollution-coverage disputes when it is difficult to determine when an "event" or "occurrence" or "damage" giving rise to legal liability has occurred. *NSP* does not establish hard-and-fast rules; it offers a practical solution in the face of uncertainty.

Id. at 733–34.

Domtar established guidelines for allocating losses from a continuing injury, like the immune diseases at issue here, using an injury-in-fact approach. The first, and most obvious, is that only insurance policies that are appropriately "triggered" are on the risk. Therefore, before an allocation discussion can occur, the district court needs to identify the triggered policies among which to allocate. The second, and most helpful guideline in this case, is that when there is a continuing injury that "arises from discrete and identifiable events, then the actual-injury trigger theory allows those policies on the risk at the point of initial contamination to pay for all property damage that follows." *Id.* at 733. In other words, the issue of allocation should be raised only if the triggering injury does not "arise [ ] from discrete and identifiable events."

In determining whether the district court erred in choosing to allocate 3M's losses, we follow the analytical progression provided in *Domtar.* First, we determine whether the plaintiffs' injuries are continuous. If they are not, under the actual-injury trigger theory, the policies on the risk at the time of the injury would pay all losses arising from that injury. Here, the court found that the injuries are continuous, so we move to the next determination: whether the continuous injury arose from some discrete and identifiable event. If it does, the policies on the risk at the time of that event are liable for all sums arising from the event. If not, allocation may be appropriate.

It is at this point in the dispute that the two sides diverge in their allocation analysis. Relying on the analytical framework from *Domtar,* 3M asserts that the time of implantation of the silicone gel breast implant is the discrete and identifiable event that the district court labeled as the onset of the continuing injury, so allocation among the triggered policies is not appropriate. Instead, 3M asserts that any policy in place at the time of implant is liable up to the limits of the policy for all sums paid in settlement of injuries allegedly arising from that implantation. This is an application of the classic actual-injury trigger rule applied to a continuing injury whose origin can be clearly established. Unlike in *Domtar,* where there was "agreement that the contamination could not be apportioned among causes," *Domtar,* 563 N.W.2d at 730, 3M asserts that here the cause is clear and it is akin to *SCSC,* in which no allocation was applied because the continuous leaching of chemicals was attributable to a discrete and identifiable 1977 chemical spill. *SCSC,* 536 N.W.2d at 318. This result, 3M argues, will advance the general principle underlying the actual-injury trigger rule, which is to allow policies on the risk at the point of initial contamination to pay for the resulting property damage. *See Domtar,* 563 N.W.2d at 733; *SCSC,* 536 N.W.2d at 318.

In contrast, the insurers argue that the continuing injuries at issue here are equally as difficult to define and assign to specific time periods as are the damages involved in environmental contamination cases. The insurers cite the court of appeals' observation that "[t]he district court specifically found that putting an implant in the body was not the injury or the injury-causing event. Instead, the court found that the injury-causing event was the continuous leakage of silicone that comes into contact with the body's cells, causing incremental cellular damage and eventually producing disease." *In re Silicone Implant Ins. Coverage Lit.,* 652 N.W.2d at 60. Unlike in *SCSC* where there was "a single event of" spillage of a contaminant that for some time afterward leached into and damaged the soil, *SCSC,* 536 N.W.2d at 318, the insurers argue that with silicone breast implants, "[a]s cells later come into contact with the silicone and provoke an autoimmune response, new cell distortions, and hence new injuries, occur." The insurers assert that the underlying rationale for apportioning loss that we have used in environmental cases applies here. Policies are designed to cover injuries from a certain time period, and the insurers claim the pro rata by time on the risk method achieves this result without forcing insureds to specifically prove how much damage took place during a specific policy period.

We find 3M's arguments to be more consistent with our analysis in *Domtar* and the district court's findings. In our actual-injury trigger framework, allocation is meant to be the exception and not the rule because "[i]t is only in those difficult cases" that allocation is appropriate. *Domtar,* 563 N.W.2d at 733. If we can identify a discrete originating event that allows us to avoid allocation, we should do so. Here, the district court labeled the time of implant as the beginning of the continuing injury process. The implantation, therefore, is a readily identifiable discrete event from which all of the plaintiffs' alleged injuries arose. Such implantation is more akin to the single spill that led to continuing soil damage in *SCSC* than it is to the situation in *NSP* or *Domtar* where "contamination could not be apportioned among causes." *Id.* at 730.

Accordingly, we conclude that this case is not one of the "difficult cases" in which allocation is appropriate and, therefore, we hold that the lower courts erred in allocating the damages among the insurers in this case. *Id.* at 733. Consistent with our actual-injury trigger theory, we hold that those insurers on the risk at the time of implantation are liable up to the limits of their respective policies for 3M's losses arising from that implantation.

NOTES AND QUESTIONS

1. *Counterfactual Trigger.* Did it make sense for the court to hold that, even if silicone implants do not cause immune system damage, the policies on the risk when such injury would have occurred, if it had occurred, were triggered? What was the basis for this ruling?

2. *Self-Serving Arguments.* 3M argued that only one year of coverage was triggered for each injured party whose claim was settled; the insurers apparently argued that each year from the date of implantation to the date that injury was manifested was triggered. On the theory that litigants don't make arguments that are against their own interests, can you explain why these arguments must have served the interests of 3M and the insurers, respectively?

3. *Alternative Approaches to Allocation.* To what extent does Paragraph 1 c. of the Sample CGL Policy (page 1) adopt the approach the court says should be taken in discrete and identifiable occurrence cases? Only a few courts have interpreted this provision, although it has been included in the standard policy for more than ten years. See, e.g., *Grange Mut. Cas. Co. v. W. Bend Mut. Ins. Co.,* 946 N.E. 2d 593 (Ind. Ct. App. 2011).

Note that the allocation problem only arises when there is multi-year damage and that damage is indivisible by year. For example, if a company deposits waste at a site during different years, the waste mixes together, and then migrates from the site, the damage caused by each year's deposits cannot be divided by year. In such situations, Pro-rata allocation based on the insurer's time-on-the-risk is the approach that appears to be preferred by the majority of courts that have addressed the allocation issue. See, e.g., *Boston Gas Co. v. Century Indem. Co.,* 910 N.E.2d 290 (Mass. 2009); *Towns v. N. Security Ins. Co.,* 964 A.2d 1150 (Vt. 2008); *Consolidated Edison Co. of New York, Inc. v. Allstate Ins. Co.,* 774 N.E.2d 687 (N.Y. 2002); *Mayor & City Council of Baltimore v. Utica Mut. Ins. Co.,* 802 A.2d 1070 (Md. Ct.

Spec. App. 2002). But the courts are deeply divided. The major alternative is to impose what resembles joint and several liability on all triggered policies. This approach permits the insured to collect in full from any policy (up to its dollar limit of liability) and leave the insurers to work out contribution rights among themselves. One of the bases for this approach is the provision in pre-1986 CGL policies obligating the insurer to pay "all sums" which the insured becomes legally obligated to pay as damages because of property damage. Leading cases adopting this approach include *State v. Continental Insurance Co.*, 281 P.3d 1000 (Cal. 2012); *Plastics Engineering Co. v. Liberty Mutual Insurance Co.*, 759 N.W.2d 613 (Wis. 2009); *Goodyear Tire & Rubber Co. v. Aetna Casualty & Surety Co.*, 769 N.E.2d 835 (Oh. 2002); *Allstate Insurance Co. v. Dana Corp.*, 759 N.E.2d 1049 (Ind. 2001); and *J.H. France Refractories Co. v. Allstate Insurance Co.*, 626 A.2d 502 (Pa. 1993). A third approach, adopted only in New Jersey, but nonetheless important because of the sheer number of hazardous waste sites in that state, is that of *Owens-Illinois, Inc. v. United Insurance Cp.*, 650 A.2d 974 (N.J. 1994). Under *Owens-Illinois*, coverage responsibility is allocated by year, but the amount of each year's responsibility is proportional to the total amount of insurance in force for that year. Thus, a year in which $50 million of primary and excess insurance was in force is allocated twice as much coverage responsibility as a year in which $25 million of insurance was in force. As to the impact of a policyholder's settlement with some but fewer than all insurers on the remaining insurers' liability, see *Dresser Industries, Inc. v. Underwriters at Lloyd's, London*, 106 S.W.3d 767 (Tex. App. 2003); *Koppers Co., Inc. v. Aetna Casualty & Surety Co.*, 98 F.3d 1440 (3d Cir. 1996); Kenneth S. Abraham, Allocation of Settlements in Multi-Insurer Coverage Disputes, 48 FICC Quart. 427 (1998).

4. *Layers of Coverage.* One of the issues that the choice among these approaches resolves is the proper relation between "layers" of primary and excess coverage in different years. Businesses with large liability exposures tend to purchase coverage in layers. The first layer, often subject to a deductible or self-insured retention (SIR), is termed the primary layer. Other layers are said to be "excess" over the primary or retained layers. Large businesses may have a number of layers of coverage provided by different insurers, which taken together constitute an "excess program." When multiple years are triggered, the time-on-the-risk approach requires the insured to exhaust its coverage "horizontally"—i.e., allocate coverage responsibility to the lower dollar levels of coverage in each triggered year before next accessing higher dollar levels of coverage. In effect, this approach allocates an equal amount of coverage responsibility to each triggered policy year. In contrast, the joint-and-several-liability approach adopted in *J.H. France* and other cases allows the insured to pick any of the triggered years to provide coverage, before seeking coverage from the policies covering any other triggered year. In effect, this approach allows the insured to allocate "vertically," accessing higher levels of coverage in a single year before seeking coverage from lower levels covering other years.

5. *Relation to Exclusions.* Note, however, that merely because a policy is triggered does not mean that it covers the liability in question. For example, an exclusion in the policy may preclude coverage. Therefore, the great advantage to the insured of joint and several liability, and the great disadvantage to insurers, is that by using joint and several liability the insured may be able to avoid the application of exclusions in triggered

policies that would reduce the amount of recovery under a time-on-the-risk approach. For example, if ten years are triggered and an exclusion precludes coverage under policies covering five of those years, under joint and several liability the insured may still recover the entire amount of its covered liability from the other five years. In contrast, under a time-on-the-risk allocation, the insured may recover only the amount allocated to the five years that actually cover the loss.

6. *The Problem of Uninsured Years.* Another way in which this allocation issue manifests itself is in the problem of uninsured years. Sometimes the insured cannot prove that it had any coverage during certain years when a policy would be triggered if it existed. The cause of the gap in coverage varies. The gap may result from the insured's decision not to purchase coverage for a given year; often the explanation is that the insured's thirty or forty-year old records have disappeared and it simply does not know which company, if any, provided coverage for years long past; a policy may have been in force but a court may find that it provides no coverage for that year because of the insured's breach of a condition of coverage; or liability may arise out of very old occurrences that antedate the first year when the insured purchased liability insurance of any sort. Some courts adopting joint and several liability have declined to allocate any coverage responsibility to uninsured years. See, e.g., *Keene v. Ins. Co. of North America,* 667 F.2d 1034 (D.C. Cir. 1981), *cert. denied,* 455 U.S. 1007 (1982). On the other hand, under *Owens-Illinois,* "coverage responsibility" is allocated to uninsured years, by estimating the amount of coverage that the insured could have but did not purchase and plugging that figure into the allocation calculation.

Consultants specializing in tracking down old coverage (insurance "archeologists") now offer their services to putative policyholders searching for old policies. For discussion of methods of proving the existence of coverage without introducing lost policies into evidence, see *Emons Industries, Inc. v. Liberty Mutual Fire Insurance Co.,* 545 F.Supp. 185 (S.D.N.Y.1982).

7. *Solutions Under the Newer CGL Policy.* The Sample CGL Policy set out at the beginning of this Chapter was drafted after the insurance industry became aware of the problems associated with trigger and allocation of coverage in long-tail, multi-year liability claims. How satisfactorily does the new CGL resolve the issues that the old policy seems to have left open?

c. THE NUMBER OF OCCURRENCES

We have already seen in Chapter Two that the number-of-occurrences issue sometimes arises under property insurance policies. That same issue arises more frequently under liability insurance policies and, as in property insurance, is important because of its implication for both per occurrence deductibles and per occurrence limits of liability.

Metropolitan Life Insurance Company v. Aetna Casualty & Surety Company

Supreme Court of Connecticut, 2001.
255 Conn. 295.

■ KATZ, J.

This appeal requires us to determine the scope and meaning of the "per occurrence" limit of liability under certain excess insurance policies issued by the defendant insurers to the plaintiff, Metropolitan Life Insurance Company (Metropolitan). In particular, we must determine whether, under the circumstances of this case, there was one occurrence under the policies, namely, Metropolitan's alleged failure to warn of the dangers of asbestos exposure, which resulted in bodily injury to the underlying claimants, or whether each claimant's exposure was a separate occurrence. The trial court rendered summary judgment in favor of all of the defendants, concluding that each claimant's exposure to asbestos was a separate occurrence. Because we agree that there are multiple occurrences in this case, we affirm the judgment of the trial court.

The trial court found the following facts. "Metropolitan ... is a large mutual insurance company that insured employee health care plans of various manufacturers and distributors of asbestos and products containing asbestos. * * * Beginning in the 1970s and continuing to the present time, [Metropolitan] has been named as a defendant in thousands of lawsuits filed throughout the United States seeking recovery for asbestos-related bodily injuries resulting from [Metropolitan's] alleged failure to publicize adequately the health risks of asbestos exposure. These underlying claims refer to a period of time beginning in the 1930s when [Metropolitan] engaged in medical research activities. Certain reports and articles were generated either by or under the direction of Dr. Anthony Lanza, [Metropolitan's] assistant medical director.

"To date, approximately 200,000 claims against [Metropolitan] have been filed; half of them have been settled, at a 'nuisance value' averaging about $2500 per claim. The underlying claims themselves basically allege that Dr. Lanza, and therefore [Metropolitan], knew or should have known of the hazards of asbestos exposure through the research activities and failed to warn the public by publication of the results of those studies. There are also claims that [Metropolitan] distorted or misstated the results in various articles and reports. Many of the underlying claimants are industrial, shipyard and construction workers who are not [Metropolitan] policyholders or persons who worked in asbestos plants where [Metropolitan] performed studies. Rather, liability is predicated on the claim that [Metropolitan] assumed a duty to disclose to the general public when it undertook its research on asbestos.

"The underlying claimants allegedly suffered bodily injuries resulting from exposure to asbestos over a period of several years. In paying the settlement sums in addition to its defense costs, [Metropolitan] has expended hundreds of millions of dollars in connection with this litigation and anticipates substantial expenditures in the future." * * *

"From 1976 to 1986, the [defendant Travelers] sold primary, umbrella and first-layer excess comprehensive general liability insurance policies to [Metropolitan]. During the same period, Travelers and the remaining defendants sold excess liability insurance policies to [Metropolitan]. None of the excess liability policies provide coverage for underlying claims unless and until an amount equal to the total annual coverage provided by the underlying Travelers policies ($25 million) is exhausted." * * *

The following undisputed facts and procedural history are also relevant to this appeal. The defendants' insurance policies "all provide a stated dollar amount of insurance on a 'per occurrence' basis, and are in excess of [the] Travelers coverage of $25 million per occurrence." * * * Thus, the defendants' policies are not implicated until Metropolitan exhausts the underlying coverage of $25 million *per occurrence.* In addition, the defendants' policies contain, or incorporate by reference, the following batch clause (hereinafter referred to as the continuous exposure clause) contained in the Travelers' umbrella insurance policies: " 'The total liability of the company for all damages, including damages for care and loss of services, as the result of any one occurrence shall not exceed the limit of liability stated in the declarations as applicable to 'each occurrence.' For purposes of determining the limit of the company's liability and the retained limit, all bodily injury and property damage arising out of continuous or repeated exposure to substantially the same general conditions shall be considered as arising out of one occurrence.' " * * *

We conclude that the occurrence in this case is each claimant's initial exposure to asbestos, rather than Metropolitan's alleged failure to warn. We therefore agree with the trial court that there are multiple occurrences in this case. In addition, we also conclude that the continuous exposure clause in the defendants' policies serves to combine claims arising from exposure to asbestos at the same place at roughly the same time into one occurrence, not to combine hundreds of thousands of exposures at different times and locations into one occurrence. Thus, despite the continuous exposure clause, there are still several occurrences in this case. Our conclusion is based on both the wording of the policies, and the interpretation of the word "occurrence" under New York and Connecticut law.

I
THE LANGUAGE OF THE POLICIES

* * * In the present case, the defendants' insurance policies are not ambiguous. Although the term occurrence is not defined in the policies, the Second Circuit Court of Appeals, applying New York law consistently has held that it is unambiguous.[1] * * *

Metropolitan's argument regarding the continuous exposure clause is essentially that all related claims emanating from substantially the same *conduct,* that is, Metropolitan's alleged failure to warn, should be aggregated into a single occurrence. The policy, however, provides that

---

[1] Even if the term occurrence were ambiguous, Metropolitan cannot rely on the contra proferentem rule, which is applicable only where there *is* an ambiguity, because "the contra-insurer rule does not apply in actions by one insurer against another. . . ." (Citations omitted.) *In re Prudential Lines Inc.,* supra, 158 F.3d at 77.

"bodily injury and property damage arising out of continuous or repeated exposure to substantially the same general *conditions* shall be considered as arising out of one occurrence." (Emphasis added.) The policy is silent as to aggregation of claims based solely on similar conduct. Indeed, several courts have rejected the theory that a continuous exposure clause permits aggregation of claims based on similar conduct. * * *

Finally, it is important to note that the purpose of a continuous exposure clause is to combine claims that occur "when people or property are physically exposed to some injurious phenomenon such as heat, moisture, or radiation . . . [at] *one location*." (Emphasis in original.) *Champion International Corp. v. Continental Casualty Co.*, 546 F.2d 502, 507–508 (2d Cir.1976) (Newman, J., dissenting), cert. denied, 434 U.S. 819 (1977). "The clause simply broadens . . . 'occurrence' beyond the word 'accident' to include a situation where damage occurs (continuously or repeatedly) over a period of time, rather than instantly, as the word 'accident' usually connotes." *Id*. The continuous exposure clause has doubtful application in a situation such as the present case, wherein Metropolitan claims that the occurrence was its alleged failure to warn, rather than the claimants' exposure to asbestos, and where it is attempting to combine hundreds of thousands of claims for bodily injury that have occurred in several locations, spanning six decades. As noted previously, an application of the continuous exposure clause to an allegation of negligent failure to warn places "considerable strain on the words 'exposure' and 'conditions.' " *Id.*, at 508. Such an interpretation is inconsistent with the purpose of the clause.

We conclude that the language of the defendants' insurance policies is not ambiguous. A plain reading of the policies indicates that the occurrence in this case was the exposure of the claimants to asbestos, not Metropolitan's alleged failure to warn. Moreover, the proper interpretation of the continuous exposure clause is that it combines exposures to asbestos that occurred at the same place, at approximately the same time, resulting *still,* in multiple occurrences under the policy. The clause cannot be read plausibly, as Metropolitan contends, to combine hundreds of thousands of exposures that occurred under different circumstances throughout the country over a period of sixty years, into one occurrence. As we have explained, such an interpretation is inconsistent with the plain language of the policy and the purpose of a continuous exposure clause.

II
CASE LAW

The number of occurrences issue is of critical importance to the parties in this case because the defendants' excess policies are not implicated until Metropolitan exhausts the underlying coverage limits provided in the various Travelers policies; the Travelers policies insured layers of coverage up to $25 million for *each occurrence*. Metropolitan requests a finding that there was but one occurrence, namely, its negligent failure to warn, for which it was liable in the claimants' underlying suits. Under this view, the defendants' excess policies would be triggered. The defendants request a finding that each claimant's initial exposure to asbestos was a separate occurrence. Under this theory, the defendants' excess policies would not be implicated. As stated previously, the plain language of the defendants' policies clearly supports their position. In addition, we are persuaded that, even if the policies were ambiguous on this issue, New York law mandates that the defendants' multiple occurrence position is the correct interpretation of the policies.

In identifying the occurrence or occurrences for insurance purposes, courts have applied three tests. See generally annot., 64 A.L.R.4th 668 (1988). Some courts have concluded that an occurrence is determined by reference to the underlying cause or causes of the damage. * * *

Metropolitan's claim that this court, in determining the number of occurrences, should ignore the immediate event that caused the claimants' injuries, and instead, look to an earlier event in the causal chain, has been rejected repeatedly by courts applying the event test. The two leading cases involving asbestos exposure that interpret the term occurrence in an insurance policy are *In re Prudential Lines, Inc.*, supra, 158 F.3d 65, and *Stonewall Ins. Co. v. Asbestos Claims Management Corp.*, supra, 73 F.3d 1178. See also *Babcock & Wilcox Co. v. Arkwright-Boston Mfg. Mutual Ins. Co.*, supra, 53 F.3d at 767–68 (concluding that relevant event was exposure to asbestos, not a more remote cause, such as plaintiff's failure to warn customers about dangers of asbestos). * * *

Applying the reasoning set forth in *Stonewall Ins. Co.* and *In re Prudential Lines, Inc.*, it becomes clear in this case that exposure to asbestos was the immediate event that caused the claimants' injuries. Indeed, the "last link in the causal chain" leading to Metropolitan's liability was the claimants' exposure to asbestos. *Id.*, at 81. Metropolitan's alleged failure to warn, while possibly a cause of the claimants' injuries, occurred earlier in the "causal chain," creating merely a "potential for future injury...." (Internal quotation marks omitted.) *Id.*, at 82. Thus, if the claimants had never been exposed to the asbestos, there would have been no occurrence at all for which Metropolitan could have been held liable. But once the claimants were exposed, there was liability for any resulting damages. * * *

Metropolitan attempts to distinguish *Stonewall Ins. Co.* and *In re Prudential Lines, Inc.*, from the present case by arguing that, because those cases did not contain a continuous exposure clause, they are not the proper authority on which to rely. In addition, Metropolitan contends in its brief that, "[t]he trial court's holding, if allowed to stand, would eliminate insurance under excess policies for virtually all mass tort claims, which typically involve multiple injuries arising out of a common cause and result in small payments per claim." Both contentions are without merit.

As the defendants correctly observed and noted in their brief, "in a case such as [*In re Prudential Lines, Inc.*], the addition of a 'continuous exposure' clause might have been significant, because it might have combined claims arising from exposure to asbestos on the same ship at roughly the same time." See *In re Prudential Lines, Inc.*, supra, 158 F.3d at 82 n. 9. In the present case, the appropriate analogy would be to combine claims originating at the same plant at approximately the same time. See *Endicott Johnson Corp. v. Liberty Mutual Ins. Co.*, 928 F.Supp. 176, 181 (N.D.N.Y.1996) (holding that continuous exposure clause combined many instances of property damage *at each site* into one occurrence; viewing *Stonewall Ins. Co.* as "place-specific" decision). Thus, under the trial court's ruling, many mass tort claims may be treated as a single occurrence.[2] * * *

As the defendants correctly note in their brief, many of the other authorities relied upon by Metropolitan are also of no precedential value because they are from jurisdictions that use the "cause test" in determining the number of occurrences, which both New York and Connecticut have rejected. * * * Even the cause test, however, as applied to the facts of this case, would not dictate a finding of a single occurrence.[3] * * *

Norfolk & Western Ry. Co. is analogous to the present case because both involve negligence as a possible "occurrence" under the subject insurance policies. As in *Norfolk & Western Ry. Co.*, while Metropolitan's negligence here may indeed have been a cause of the injuries, it would be nonsensical to conclude that, as a matter of law, that negligence constitutes the single occurrence out of which the 200,000 claims arose. Claimants were exposed to asbestos in several different places, in varying amounts, over the course of many years, making this case "one in which multiple occurrences created multiple injuries." *Id.* Under the cause test, each exposure was a separate occurrence that caused the claimants' injuries. Metropolitan's attempt to convert the cause test into a "rubber stamp" in order to maximize its coverage would "[remove] any limit from the category of things which might be found to be a cause" and would mandate coverage in every case. *Id.* Thus, even under the cause test, we are not persuaded that thousands of exposures to asbestos, occurring at different times and places, constitute one occurrence.

Finally, it is important to note that the holdings of many of the cases cited by Metropolitan were based on a finding that, absent a single occurrence construction, the insured would have been deprived of the coverage for which it had bargained and the insurance policies at issue would have been meaningless. * * *. This reasoning is inapplicable

---

[2] The defendants correctly have provided the following examples of mass tort claims that would be treated as a single occurrence under the trial court's decision: "[1] [I]f there is an airplane crash where there are likely to be multiple claims and injuries, there [would] be a single occurrence because the 'event of unfortunate character' is the accident or crash itself; [2] if co-workers at a plant are minimally exposed to radiation during a period of time, the 'continuous exposure' clause likely [would] combine the claims into a single occurrence; and [3] if hundreds of people are exposed to toxic chemicals from a single batch of bad soda cans, and there is a true 'batch' clause in the policy at issue, there [would] be a single occurrence." See *Norfolk & Western Ry. Co. v. Accident & Casualty Ins. Co. of Winterthur*, 796 F.Supp. 929, 937 (W.D.Va.1992) (noting that, "[t]he typical single occurrence giving rise to multiple claims is the automobile accident which gives rise to a chain of events which results in injury to several parties"), aff'd in part, dismissed in part as moot, 41 F.3d 928 (4th Cir.1994); *id.*, at 938 (analogizing automobile accident chain of events scenario to train wreck, where train was carrying toxic chemicals that spilled in heavily populated area).

[3] "The general rule [under the cause test] is that an occurrence is determined by the cause or causes of the resulting injury. . . . Using this analysis, the court asks if [t]here was but one proximate, uninterrupted, and continuing cause which resulted in all of the injuries and damages." (Internal quotation marks omitted.) *Appalachian Ins. Co. v. Liberty Mutual Ins. Co.*, supra, 676 F.2d at 61. Applying this test, the defendants would still prevail because Metropolitan's alleged failure to warn, while possibly a cause of the claimants' injuries, was not one proximate, uninterrupted cause of the injuries, as evidenced by the fact that the injuries occurred at several different places over a period of sixty years.

in the present case. First, such a "result-oriented approach" should be entertained only when the "per occurrence" language in the defendants' policies is ambiguous. *American Red Cross v. Travelers Indemnity Co. of Rhode Island*, supra, 816 F. Supp. at 761 n. 8. As we stated previously herein, the term occurrence is not ambiguous. Second, even if that term were ambiguous, the contra proferentum rule, which directs a court to interpret a policy against the insurer when ambiguous language cannot be resolved in favor of either party, is not appropriate in this case because both parties are insurance companies. *In re Prudential Lines, Inc.*, supra, 158 F.3d at 77. Finally, the concern that a finding of multiple occurrences would render the defendants' insurance policies meaningless, simply is not present in this case. *Norfolk & Western Ry. Co. v. Accident & Casualty Ins. Co. of Winterthur*, supra, 796 F.Supp. at 938. As we have explained, the continuous exposure clause acts to combine claims originating at the same plant at approximately the same time into one occurrence, thus covering most mass tort claims. "Absent a holding of [a] single occurrence, the policies at issue remain vital, meaningful agreements." *Id*.

The judgment is affirmed.

NOTES AND QUESTIONS

1. *Ulimate Cause, Immediate Cause, or Effect?* Issues of both definition and application must be resolved in determining the number of insured occurrences under a liability policy. In most single-injury cases, of course, there is only one occurrence almost by definition. In continuous exposure or multiple injury cases, however, definition and application can be critically important. As *Metropolitan Life* indicates, there are three possible tests. Some version of the *cause test* is dominant, however, although New York and some other states refer to their cause tests as the "unfortunate event" or "triggering event" test. The principal rationale for the cause test is that the number of occurrences should be determined from the standpoint of the insured, not its victims. An *effects test*, adopted by a few courts, vastly expands coverage in most, but not all, multiple injury cases. The variable interaction among the size of any per occurrence deductibles, the amount of available coverage, and the amount of the insured's liability, however, make it impossible to say in the abstract which approach will benefit an insured or an insurer in any given case. How should deductibles and self-insured retentions (SIR's) be handled when a single, multi-year occurrence is held to trigger multiple years' policies, each containing such deductibles or SIR's? Should it make a difference if the amount of these deductibles or SIR's varies from year to year? It seems possible that Metropolitan Life's primary policies were subject to SIR's that were greater in magnitude than the average amount for which Metropolitan Life was settling individual claims; thus its need to argue that there had been only one occurrence, so as to gain access to its policies rather than paying its deductible for each claim. In recent years, the majority of the courts addressing the issue have tended to hold that claims for coverage of asbestos-related injury involve multiple occurrences, though, as in *Metropolitan Life*, not necessarily one occurrence per plaintiff. See, e.g., *Plastics Eng'g Co. v. Liberty Mut. Ins. Co.*, 759 N.W.2d 613 (Wis. 2009); *Appalachian Ins. Co. v. Gen. Electric Co.*, 863 N.E.2d 994 (N.Y. 2007); *London Market Ins. v. Superior Court*, 146 Cal. App. 4th 648 (2007).

But see *Liberty Mut. Ins. Co. v. Treesdale, Inc.*, 418 F.3d 330 (3d Cir. 2005) (the cause of loss resulting from multiple exposures is the manufacture and sale of asbestos-containing products, constituting a single occurrence).

Even apart from these issues, the manner in which courts count causes varies. See, e.g., *Roman Catholic Diocese of Brooklyn v. National Union Fire Ins. Co.*, 991 N.E. 2d 666 (N.Y. 2013) (sexual abuse that took place over a seven year period was at least one occurrence per year); *Addison Ins. Co. v. Fay,* 905 N.E.2d 747 (Ill. 2009) (if cause and result are so closely linked in time and space as to be considered one event, then the injuries will be deemed to result from one occurrence); *U.S. Gypsum v. Admiral Ins. Co.*, 643 N.E.2d 1226 (Ill. App. 1994) (if the continuous production and sale of an intrinsically harmful product results in similar kinds of injury or property damage, then all such injury or property damage results from a common occurrence); *Michigan Chemical Corp. v. Am. Home Assurance Co.*, 728 F.2d 374 (6th Cir. 1984) (the number occurrences is determined by the number of shipments of contaminated animal feed); *H.E. Butt Grocery Co. v. National Union Fire Ins. Co. of Pittsburgh, Pa.*, 150 F.3d 526 (5th Cir.1998) (independent acts of sexual abuse of two separate children by insured's employee constituted two separate occurrences); *Transport Ins. Co. v. Lee Way Motor Freight, Inc.*, 487 F.Supp. 1325 (N.D. Tx. 1980) (liability for engaging in a pattern and practice of discrimination constituted one occurrence); *Koikos v. Travelers Ins. Co.*, 849 So. 2d 263 (Fla. 2003) (separate acts of shooting two different people in the same room constituted two occurrences); *Washoe County v. Transcontinental Ins. Co.*, 878 P.2d 306 (Nev. 1994) (county's alleged negligence in monitoring day-care center, which resulted in multiple acts of child molestation by day-care center employee, was a single occurrence).

2. *Dual Limits of Liability.* Many older policies contain only a per occurrence limit of liability; usually newer policies, including the Sample Policy in Section A, also contain an aggregate limit. The latter places a ceiling on the total coverage provided during the policy period, regardless of how many occurrences have taken place. In certain situations the inclusion of an aggregate limit renders debate about how many occurrences there have been irrelevant; in others the issue remains despite the aggregate limit.

3. *The Continuous Exposure Clause.* This general kind of clause has also been referred to as a "batch" clause, as an "aggregation" clause, and as a "unifying directive." The court noted that the purpose of a "continuous exposure" clause is to combine claims that occur "when people or property are physically exposed to some injurious phenomenon such as heat, moisture, or radiation * * * [at] *one location.*" Does it make sense that the clause would be concerned exclusively with location, as opposed to, or in addition to, other considerations? Reconsider the transition of CGL policies from an accident to an occurrence basis, defining an occurrence to include "continuous or repeated exposure" to injurious conditions. In light of this transition, might the purpose of the continuous exposure clause be to confirm that, whether coverage is triggered by a short-term accident or event or by long-term "continuous or repeated exposure," the number-of-occurrences issue should be resolved in the same manner. If liability results from multiple different causes then there are still multiple occurrences. So the clause makes it clear that the question still is whether there has been essentially only one cause, whether short-term (an "accident" or "event") or

long-term ("continuous or repeated exposure"), or there have instead been multiple different causes.

4. *Contra Proferentem.* Why shouldn't an insurer suing in its capacity as a policyholder be permitted to take advantage of *contra proferentem*? Is the answer that the insurer should be able to recognize ambiguity, or something else?

3. EXCLUSIONS AND CONDITIONS

Standard personal and CGL insurance policies contain a series of exclusions and conditions. A review of the Sample CGL Policy set out in Section A will yield an overall idea of their nature. A key to understanding the different purposes of these provisions is to recognize that there is a tension between the desire of ordinary individuals and businesses to purchase general-purpose liability protection in a single policy, and the need for insurers to segregate from the pool of such insureds those whose activities pose special risks. One method of achieving this aim is simply to price general liability insurance in accordance with the different levels of risk posed by different insureds. In addition, however, insurers also exclude coverage of certain special risks from general liability policies, leaving those who pose special risks to purchase separate coverage targeted at and priced in accordance with these risks. The material that follows addresses some of the exclusions and conditions that figure most prominently in general liability insurance

a. EXPECTED OR INTENDED HARM

CGL policies and the liability portion of Homeowners policies incorporate exclusions from, or limitations on, coverage of liability for harm that is "expected or intended." The following two cases address the meaning and application of this provision in these two forms of coverage. In reading them, keep in mind that, especially in cases involving individual policyholders whose principal means of satisfying a judgment is their liability insurance, plaintiffs may engage in "strategic" pleading. For example, if the plaintiff pleads an intentional tort, the "expected or intended" exclusion may apply, and the insurer may not be available to indemnify the defendant, resulting in the defendant being unable to pay the plaintiff. In such cases, plaintiffs will have strong incentives to plead in a manner that preserves the defendant's access to liability insurance. By contrast, where the policyholder has ample assets, pleading an intentional tort may create extra pressure on the defendant/policyholder because of the prospect that it may not be insured against liability. For discussion of these and other issues related to strategic pleading, see Ellen S. Pryor, The Stories We Tell: Intentional Harm and the Quest for Insurance Funding, 75 Texas L. Rev. 1722 (1997).

Stonewall Insurance Company v. Asbestos Claims Management Corporation

United States Court of Appeals, Second Circuit, 1995.
73 F.3d 1178.

■ JON O. NEWMAN, CHIEF JUDGE:

These consolidated appeals and cross-appeals present numerous issues concerning liability insurance coverage in the context of claims for personal injury and property damage arising from exposure to asbestos. * * *

National Gypsum Company ("NGC") * * * and a number of its liability insurers (collectively referred to as "the Insurers") sought declaratory relief clarifying the extent to which NGC is entitled to indemnification for claims arising from NGC's manufacture of asbestos products. * * *

NGC was founded in Buffalo, New York, in 1925 and became a leading manufacturer of gypsum wallboard and other building materials. From 1930 until 1981, NGC manufactured construction products that contained asbestos, including acoustical plasters, joint compounds, textures, ceiling tiles, asbestos-cement siding, and asbestos-cement corrugated and flat-sheet products. NGC discontinued the sale of asbestos-containing products over the period from 1970–81.

Since 1972, NGC has been sued by approximately 100,000 claimants seeking damages for bodily injury allegedly resulting from exposure to and inhalation of asbestos fibers contained in products manufactured, sold, installed, or distributed by NGC at some time in the past. These claimants typically allege that they did not become aware of their injuries until shortly before they filed suit. They contend that they have suffered from a wide range of injuries and diseases, including mesothelioma and asbestosis.

In addition, since 1980, the owners of several thousand buildings have asserted asbestos-related claims against NGC. These suits are founded upon allegations that the incorporation and continued presence of asbestos-containing materials ("ACMs") in buildings has caused physical damage to the buildings and tangible property therein as a result of contamination by asbestos fibers. Such contamination results from the continued breakdown of the ACMs, which releases fibers into the air, and the re-entrainment of these fibers, which creates an unreasonable health hazard. Typically, the complainants seek monetary damages measured by the cost of testing and evaluating ACMs in buildings; the cost of repairing, removing, enclosing, encapsulating, or abating the ACMs; the cost of operations and maintenance programs; consequential damages for loss of use of the properties; and diminution of value.

B. NGC's Insurance Program

This action involves all the liability insurance policies, both primary and excess, issued through 1985 to provide coverage to NGC for asbestos-induced bodily injury and property damage claims, except policies issued by those insurers with whom NGC has settled its coverage disputes. The amounts of NGC's excess insurance typically increased with most insurers over time until 1985, when NGC's insurers placed asbestos exclusions into NGC's policies. * * *

C. "Expected or Intended" Injury Defense

Through various formulations, NGC's policies exclude coverage for bodily injuries that are expected or intended by NGC. For example, the 1974–77 CU policy provides coverage for NGC's liability arising out of "personal injuries" caused by an "occurrence." An occurrence, in turn, is defined as "an accident or a continuous or repeated exposure to conditions which results during the policy period in personal injury, property damage or advertising liability neither expected nor intended from the standpoint of the insured." In both the jury and bench trials, the Insurers contended that coverage of the underlying asbestos-related bodily injury claims should be precluded because NGC "expected" or "intended" the injuries within the meaning of the "occurrence" definition. Both fact-finders rejected this contention, finding that NGC did not "expect" or "intend" the bodily injuries.

On appeal, Continental Casualty Company ("CCC"), joined by various other insurers, points to four purported errors of law on this issue that it contends require reversal of the Jury Trial BI Judgment and the Bench Trial BI Judgment. First, these insurers argue that the trial court should not have placed on them the burden of proving that NGC expected or intended the underlying injuries. Allocation of the burden of proof is determined pursuant to New York law, even with respect to those policies whose substantive interpretation is governed by Texas law. See *Woodling v. Garrett Corp.*, 813 F.2d 543, 552 (2d Cir.1987) ("The question of burden of proof . . . is regarded by New York law as a question of procedure to which the law of the forum applies.").

Because the exclusionary language of NGC's policies is located in a section of the policy denominated "definitions" or "insuring agreement" rather than "exclusions," the Insurers contend that NGC must bear the burden of proving that it did not expect or intend the injuries for which it seeks coverage. However, under New York law, the exclusionary effect of policy language, not its placement, controls allocation of the burden of proof. See *Utica Mutual Insurance Co. v. Prudential Property and Casualty Insurance Co.*, 103 A.D.2d 60, 64 (2d Dep't 1984) ("[I]t is the insurer which has the burden of proof to establish that a claim is encompassed by an exclusion in a policy . . . and any limitation in coverage must be described in clear and explicit language."), aff'd, 64 N.Y.2d 1049 (1985). Several decisions treat the "expected" or "intended" policy language as an exclusion. See, e.g., *City of Johnstown v. Bankers Standard Insurance Co.*, 877 F.2d 1146 (2d Cir.1989); *Town of Moreau v. Orkin Exterminating Co.*, 165 A.D.2d 415 (3d Dep't 1991).

Second, the Insurers argue that the trial court should not have applied a subjective standard with respect to whether NGC expected or intended injury. They contend that even if NGC did not actually expect or intend the underlying harm, NGC should be deprived of coverage if the evidence established that NGC "should have" expected such harm. However, the policies on their face preclude coverage only if NGC expected or intended the injuries, and not if NGC merely should have expected injury. See *City of Johnstown*, 877 F.2d at 1151 n. 1 (adopting subjective standard). Moreover, as we noted in *City of Johnstown*, ordinary negligence does not constitute an intention to cause damage, and a calculated risk does not amount to an expectation of damage. Id. at 1150. A number of courts applying the "expected" or "intended" policy language under Texas law have similarly inquired into the insured's actual expectations or intent without consideration of whether the insured "should have" expected or intended the underlying harm. See, e.g., *American Home Assurance Co. v. Safway Steel Products Co.*, 743 S.W.2d 693, 701 (Tex.Ct.App.1987) ("punitive damages arising out of the insured's gross negligence are not . . . excluded from coverage" by "expected or intended" clause).

Third, the Insurers argue that the form of the jury verdict concerning the "expected or intended" issue injected a prejudicial requirement that they prove on a product-by-product basis NGC's expectations or intentions. This argument is meritless. On the jury verdict form, the jury was requested to evaluate NGC's expectations or intentions with respect to persons exposed to asbestos (1) as a result of working in the NGC mine, (2) as a result of working in the NGC plant, (3) contained in non-spray plasterers and textures, (4) contained in asbestos cement board products, and (5) contained in joint compounds. The District Court's instructions and the jury verdict form simply acknowledged that the product and workplace exposures to asbestos at issue in the underlying cases were different. Some products were more hazardous than others, and a finding that NGC knew that one product sold for only a few years was hazardous would not necessarily be sufficient to show that NGC "expected" or "intended" injuries to persons using different products at different times.

Thus, the jury could have determined that NGC's expectations and intentions were sufficiently proved to justify a finding in favor of the Insurers regarding injuries of NGC's own employees exposed in the course of manufacturing asbestos products, but not regarding injuries suffered by third parties' employees as a result of exposure in the course of using NGC's joint compound products. The Insurers were free, however, to argue that NGC's knowledge of the hazards of asbestos in connection with one set of products and exposures should be deemed sufficient to support an inference of knowledge or expectation with respect to all sets of exposures or products.

Finally, CCC argues that the trial court erred in admitting the testimony of Russell L. Ward in the bench trial, and asserts that in the absence of Ward's testimony, the only competent evidence proved beyond question that NGC expected or intended the underlying injuries. Ward was an NGC employee for 36 years. During that period of time, he was employed by NGC in various facets of NGC's operations from credit and sales to production and distribution. In 1985, he began to serve as NGC's records custodian, and reviewed most of the documents in NGC's collection of asbestos-related documents. He also conversed with hundreds of NGC employees over the years. His testimony was introduced by NGC as evidence that NGC did not expect or intend to cause injury.

Though CCC raises various objections to this testimony, we conclude that the trier of fact reasonably could have found from the evidence that Ward possessed sufficient personal knowledge regarding NGC's historical documents and regarding the lack of any showing therein of an expectation or intention that injuries would occur to persons who used NGC's products. Consequently, the District Court did not abuse its discretion in determining that Ward could testify. We further conclude that even apart from Ward's testimony, NGC presented sufficient evidence to support the trial court's finding that NGC did not expect or intend the asbestos-related injuries. * * *

"Known Loss" Defense

Several insurers contend that they are exempted from indemnity obligations because of the "known loss" defense—the insurance law principle that an insured may not obtain insurance to cover a loss that is known before the policy takes effect. See, e.g., *Bartholomew v. Appalachian Insurance Co.*, 655 F.2d 27, 28–29 (1st Cir.1981). The issue is presented by CSIC, which issued 1983 and 1984 policies to NGC for $15 million of excess coverage. * * *

In the District Court, the "known loss" defense was raised by CSIC in a motion for summary judgment considered by Magistrate Judge Bernikow. Discussing the issue in the context of property damage, he recommended rejecting the defense except for cases filed, or for which NGC received a pre-suit demand letter, before the policies incepted. Judge Martin accepted this recommendation, observing that, despite the extent of awareness about potential asbestos claims, "all that can fairly be said is that there was a known risk that there would be losses extending into the policy period and, therefore, obtaining insurance was a sensible business judgment." * * *

NGC broadly contends, citing *City of Johnstown v. Bankers Standard Insurance Co.*, 877 F.2d 1146 (2d Cir.1989), that the "known loss" defense exists only with respect to first-party insurance and does not even apply to third-party liability insurance. It also contends that this defense is merely another way of arguing that the losses were "expected or intended" and therefore not within the definition of "occurrence," an argument we have already rejected. * * *

City of Johnstown, however, does not purport to rule that the "known loss" defense is unavailable in third-party insurance. Though the classic statement of the defense is the observation that first-party insurance cannot be validly purchased for a home that has already burned down, it is not readily apparent why the defense should not also apply in the third-party context. *City of Johnstown* did not hold that insurance can be validly purchased to indemnify against a third party's specific loss that the insurance buyer knows has already occurred. What *City of Johnstown* decided is that an insured's knowledge of a risk of losses does not bar indemnity coverage. Id. at 1152–53; see *Gulf Chemical & Metallurgical Corp. v. Associated Metals & Minerals Corp.*, 1 F.3d 365, 369–70 (5th Cir.1993) (following *City of Johnstown*).

Nor do we agree with NGC's contention that the "known loss" defense is merely another way of claiming that the injury was "expected or intended" within the meaning of the "occurrence" definition. The "expected or intended" claim requires consideration of whether, at the time of the acts causing the injury, the insured expected or intended the injury, an inquiry that generally asks merely whether the injury was accidental. See *City of Johnstown*, 877 F.2d at 1150. The "known loss" defense requires consideration of whether, at the time the insured bought the policy (or the policy incepted), the loss was known. The contentions may overlap, but they are distinct, as the separate discussions in *City of Johnstown* recognized.

Though NGC was aware, prior to the inception of many of the policies, that its products risked asbestosis and cancer diseases and had received a large number of claims, it was highly uncertain, as Judge Martin found, as to the prospective number of injuries, the number of claims, the likelihood of successful claims, and the amount of ultimate losses it would be called upon to pay. NGC was fully entitled to replace the uncertainty of its exposure with the precision of insurance premiums and leave it to the insurers' underwriters to determine the appropriate premiums. See *Gulf Chemical*, 1 F.3d at 369–70 (applying Texas law); *Montrose Chemical*, 10 Cal.4th at 663.

The cases relied on by CSIC are inapposite. *Bartholomew v. Appalachian Insurance Co.*, 655 F.2d 27 (1st Cir.1981), involved an attempt to obtain coverage for a loss for which suit had been filed before the policy took effect. Id. at 29. *Appalachian Insurance Co. v. Liberty Mutual Insurance Co.*, 676 F.2d 56 (3d Cir.1982), involved what the court considered to be a single occurrence that had injured women who had filed an EEOC complaint prior to the policy period. *Carpenter Plastering Co. v. Puritan Insurance Co.*, CIV.A. No. 3–87–2435–R, 1988 WL 156829 (N.D.Tex. Aug.23, 1988), involved a claim for damages resulting from a specific sale of defective wall panels, which the insured knew had begun to crack before the policy periods began.

The District Court's findings concerning the extent of unknown liabilities support rejection of the "known loss" defense. * * *

NOTES AND QUESTIONS

1. *The Nature of the Test.* Some courts hold that the terms "expected" and "intended" in homeowners and CGL policies are synonymous. See, e.g., *Maine Mut. Fire Ins. Co. v. Gervais*, 745 A.2d 360 (Me. 1999). This interpretation conflicts with the principle that each word or phrase in a legal document should be interpreted so that it has a separate meaning. Other courts hold that actions taken where the insured knows that there is a very high probability of damage, even when there is no intention to cause damage, fall within the exclusion.

Most courts continue to follow the *Stonewall* approach in holding that whether harm is expected or intended is assessed by a subjective test. See, e.g., *Westfield Ins. Co. v. Tech Dry, Inc.*, 336 F.3d 503 (6th Cir. 2003) (coverage of employer for murder committed by employee not excluded because from the employer's standpoint "the injury was not actually and subjectively intended."). Sometimes, however, subjective intent or expectation can be inferred from the circumstances, perhaps even as a matter of law. See, e.g., *Am. Bumper & Mfg. Co. v. Nat. Union Fire Ins. Co.*, 683 N.W.2d 161 (Mich. App. 2004) (employer showed such disregard for worker safety in maintaining dangerous machinery that intent to injure is implied as a matter of law). Whether an event is "expected" is sometimes a question of the degree of the insured's knowledge, but mere negligence in failing to foresee an event does not constitute expectation. The idea is to combat clear cases of moral hazard while preserving coverage for the kind of carelessness that most tort actions allege. The problem posed by this language, however, is that it is not entirely congruent with the categories employed by tort law; yet mainly it is tort liability against which the policy insures. It is possible, therefore, that there is coverage under the CGL policy against liability for certain intentional torts, and, conversely, no coverage against certain forms of liability that would not be described by tort law as intentional. Notice that this difference in terminology means that the question whether there is coverage will often have to be litigated separately from the question whether the insured is liable in tort. For discussion of this issue, see Chapter Seven.

2. *The Burden of Proof and the Availability of Evidence.* The Sample CGL Policy provides roughly the same coverage as the Insuring Agreement at issue in the *Stonewall* policy, but transfers the "neither expected nor intended" limitation from the Insuring Agreement to the list of exclusions (page 2). As noted in Chapter Four, the insured bears the burden of proving that a loss falls within the terms of the Insuring Agreement, but the insurer bears the burden of proving that an exclusion applies. The *Stonewall* court followed the approach taken by many courts, elevating substance over form. The court's *Erie* prediction of New York law on the issue, however, turned out to be inaccurate. See *Consol. Edison Co. of New York, Inc. v. Allstate Ins. Co.*, 774 N.E.2d 687 (N.Y. 2002) (holding that the policyholder has the burden of proving that there has been an "accident" when that term is used in the definition of an "occurrence").

In any event, neither court addressed two potentially important factors in reaching their decisions. First, in long-tail liability cases evidence of the insured's intent and expectation many decades ago may simply be unavailable. Witnesses may die or forget and over long periods of time former employees may disappear. In the absence of any evidence on the "expected or intended" issue, the party bearing the burden of proof will lose. Does that fact help to explain why the insurers in *Stonewall* argued for an objective standard, notwithstanding what appeared to be clear policy language employing a subjective standard? A second factor worth considering is differential access to evidence. Other things being equal, the party with easiest access to evidence should bear the burden of producing it, and perhaps also the burden of persuasion regarding the issue to which the evidence is relevant. Which way does this factor cut in cases involving long-tail claims?

3. *Whose Expectation?* Suppose a very low-ranking employee of a large company is the only individual who expected or intended harm. For example, suppose that, contrary to orders, a janitor dumped toxic waste into a lake instead of transporting it to a licensed disposal facility. Should the exclusion for harm that is "expected or intended" apply in such a case? In answering this question, is the language "from the standpoint of the insured" in the exclusion helpful? See, e.g., *RJC Realty Holding Corp. v. Republic Franklin Insurance Co.*, 808 N.E.2d 1263 (N.Y. 2004), in which the employer of a masseuse who sexually assaulted a client was sued under the doctrine of *respondeat superior*, and the court held that the employee's actions were not expected or intended by RJC and that the exclusion therefore did not apply. That kind of distinction, however, will not necessarily be routinely accepted by other courts.

4. *Known Losses.* How would the known-loss issue posed in *Stonewall* be resolved under Insuring Agreement Paragraph 1.(b)(3) of the Sample CGL policy (page 1)? As the *Stonewall* court noted, even in the absence of a policy provision directly addressing known losses, a number of

courts have adopted the "known loss doctrine," based on the principle that insurance is only appropriate to cover fortuitous losses. The courts that have recognized the doctrine are divided as to its scope. Some have construed it narrowly, barring coverage only when the insured knew with certainty both that it had caused harm and would be held liable for that harm. See, e.g., *Westchester Fire Ins. Co. v. Gulf Coast Rod, Reel & Gun Club*, 64 S.W.3d 609 (Tex. App. 2001) (no bar to coverage if insured was not aware of potential liability); *Montrose Chem. Corp. v. Admiral Ins. Co.*, 913 P.2d 878 (Cal. 1995); *City of Johnstown v. Bankers Standard Ins. Co.*, 877 F.2d 1146 (2d Cir. 1989). And see *Estate of Patout v. City of New Iberia*, 849 So.2d 535 (La. Ct. App. 2002), rejecting the known-loss doctrine entirely. Other courts have invoked the doctrine when the insured was aware that there was a high probability that a loss would occur or had already occurred. See, e.g., *Rohm & Haas Co. v. Continental Cas. Co.*, 781 A.2d 1172 (Pa. 2001); *Outboard Marine Corp. v. Liberty Mutual Ins. Co.*, 607 N.E.2d 1204 (Ill. 1992). The *Stonewall* court said somewhat cryptically that an independent known-loss defense overlaps with but is not identical to the expected or intended defense. When one also considers the insurer's other independent right to deny coverage based on concealment or misrepresentation in the application for coverage, however, does the known loss doctrine still have independent scope?

Unigard Mutual Insurance Company v. Argonaut Insurance Company

Court of Appeals of Washington, 1978.
20 Wash.App. 261.

■ MCINTURFF, ASSOCIATE JUSTICE.

The insurers of School District No. 81 appeal from a declaratory judgment that Unigard Mutual Insurance Co. (Unigard) is not obligated to defend or indemnify its insureds, William Winkler and Mr. and Mrs. Charles Hensley, in an action by the school district against them for $250,000 in fire damage to Wilson Elementary School in Spokane.

This action arises from a suit brought by the school district in August 1974 alleging that William Winkler carelessly and negligently caused the fire and that his parents, the Hensleys, having knowledge of his propensities, negligently failed to supervise and control him. Unigard filed this action for declaratory judgment in November 1974 seeking to avoid any liability to any of the parties covered by its policy.

The policy in question was issued by Unigard to Ruth Winkler Hensley as the named insured in December 1972. It establishes the duty to defend and indemnify in the following manner:

> This Company agrees to pay on behalf of *the Insured* all sums which *the Insured* shall become legally obligated to pay as damages because of bodily injury or property damage, to which this insurance applies, caused by an occurrence. This Company shall have the right and duty, at its own expense, to defend any suit against the Insured seeking damages on account of such bodily injury or property damage, even if any of the allegations of the suit are groundless, false or fraudulent, but

may make such investigation and settlement of any claim or suit as it deems expedient.

(Italics ours.)

The policy defined "occurrence" as "an accident, including injurious exposure to conditions, which results, during the endorsement term, in bodily injury or property damage." And, the following exclusionary provision was included, "This policy does not apply * * * to bodily injury or property damage which is either expected or intended from the standpoint of *the insured*." (Italics ours.) There is no dispute that both William Winkler and the parents are "insureds" within the meaning of the policy.[1]

The record reveals the following facts. On July 8, 1973, William Winkler, who was then 11 years old, broke into the school building and set fire to the contents of a trash can. He watched the fire burn for a short while, then ran to a nearby drinking fountain for water with which to douse the blaze. It was not working though, so he returned to the fire, became frightened and ran out of the building. He did not notify anyone of the blaze. The fire spread, causing extensive damage to the building and its contents.

He testified he did not intend or expect to cause damage to the school building but that he did intend to light the fire. At the time of the blaze he knew that fire could spread, and he had previously been involved in a fire-starting venture between two neighborhood garages.

The court concluded the school building fire was not an insurable "occurrence" under the policy because it was not an "accident." Instead, the court found the fire damage resulted from the deliberate acts of the boy. The court reasoned that since there was not an insurable "occurrence," Unigard did not have a duty to defend or indemnify either the boy or his parents.

Error is first assigned to the court's conclusion that the fire damage did not result from an insurable "occurrence." The school district's insurers offer two arguments: (1) the term "accident" within the policy is ambiguous in that it is not clear whether the insured's act or the results of his act must be accidental so as to provide coverage; and (2) since the boy neither expected nor intended the fire damage to the school, the exclusionary clause is inapplicable.

The argument that the term "accident" is ambiguous is not well taken. In a long line of cases our courts have said that an accident is never present when a deliberate act is performed unless some additional unexpected, independent and unforeseen happening occurs which produces or brings about the result of injury or death. The means as well as the result must be unforeseen, involuntary, unexpected and unusual. The intentional and deliberate act of William Winkler in starting the fire which caused the school building blaze cannot be said to be involuntary. Therefore, as to William Winkler, the damage to the school was not caused by accidental means nor can it be considered, under the policy definitions, an insurable "occurrence."

---

[1] The policy provides: "1. 'Insured' means a. the Named Insured stated in the Declarations of this endorsement; b. if residents of the Named Insured's household, his spouse, the relatives of either, and any other person under the age of twenty-one in the care of any insured; * * *"

Nonetheless, the school district insurers argue that the policy is applicable because in order to exclude the intentional acts of the insured from coverage, the damage must be expected or intended from the standpoint of the insured. There is a definite split of authority as to whether the intentional injury exclusion clause which exempts expected or intended damage requires specific intent on the part of the insured to cause the resultant damage.[2] Here, though, there is substantial evidence from which the court could have found that the damage to the school building was expected or intended on the part of the boy despite his in-court declarations to the contrary. Thus, as to William Winkler, the fire damage to the building was the expected or intended result of a clearly intentional act. Therefore, Unigard has no duty to defend the youth or indemnify him for any sums he may become legally obligated to pay as a result of the school district action against him.

Error is next assigned to the court's conclusion that since the fire damage was not caused by an "accident" within the terms of the policy, Unigard does not have a duty to defend or indemnify the boy's parents in the action brought against them by the school district. Essentially, the school district's insurers argue that the intentional act of one insured cannot be imputed to other insureds so as to exclude insurance coverage for all; that the liability of the Hensleys, if any, is grounded in their negligent failure to supervise the boy which is not an excluded intentional act. Unigard maintains there was no evidence of negligence on the part of the Hensleys and that the policy of excluding intentional acts from liability insurance coverage would be seriously undermined if coverage was provided to the parents of minors who have committed intentional acts.

We agree with Unigard that public policy prevents an insured from benefitting from his wrongful acts; but here, as in other cases which have considered the question, it is not the intentional act of the parents which has caused the damage. Precedent and the language of the Unigard insurance policy require coverage for Mr. and Mrs. Hensley.

The policy extends defense and indemnification to "the Insured," and it excludes from coverage intentional acts resulting in injury or damage "expected or intended from the standpoint of the insured." The parties concede the boy and the Hensleys are all "insureds" under the policy. In such instances, where coverage and exclusion is defined in terms of "the insured," the courts have uniformly considered the contract between the insurer and several insureds to be separable, rather than joint, i.e., there are separate contracts with each of the insureds. The result is that an excluded act of one insured does not bar coverage for additional insureds who have not engaged in the excluded conduct.

---

[2] See cases collected in Annot., *Liability Insurance: Specific Exclusion of Liability for Injury Intentionally Caused by Insured*, 2 A.L.R.3d 1238, 1241 (1965). There the author states: "The courts have generally held that injury or damage is 'caused intentionally' within the meaning of an 'intentional injury exclusion clause' if the insured has acted with the specific intent to cause harm to a third party, with the result that the insurer will not be relieved of its obligations under a liability policy containing such an exclusion unless the insured has acted with such specific intent."

The judgment of the Superior Court is affirmed insofar as it denies coverage to William Winkler and reversed insofar as it denies coverage to the Hensleys.

NOTES AND QUESTIONS

1. *The Scope of Homeowners Coverage.* Like the liability portion of most Homeowners policies, the *Unigard* insuring agreement contained no provision limiting coverage to liability arising out of the use of the property insured under the first-party portion of the policy. Instead, the liability insurance portions of the policy are structured to provide general liability coverage, subject to a long list of exclusions—liability for business operations, liability arising out of the ownership, maintenance or use of automobiles, watercraft, and aircraft, and liability for defamation, among others. When these exclusions are combined with the exclusion of coverage against liability for harm expected or intended, the apparently unlimited liability insurance provided by a Homeowners policy turns out to be (roughly) against liability for non-motor vehicle related negligence in one's personal life that causes bodily injury or property damage.

2. *Type of Harm Expected.* For the exclusion to apply, should the harm that is expected or intended be precisely the harm for which liability is imposed, or need it only be harm of the same general sort? The cases are divided. In *State Farm Fire & Casualty Co. v. Muth,* 207 N.W.2d 364 (Neb. 1973), the insured was a minor who shot a B–B gun out of a moving automobile and injured a friend. The insured testified that he intended "to scare somebody," and, on redirect examination, that he did not think he was taking a chance of hitting the friend. The court upheld a finding by the trial judge that the exclusion was inapplicable. Suppose that the insured had shot the friend in the eye, and testified that he intended only to cause temporary discomfort with a grazing shot to the leg, but that his aim was disturbed when the car hit a bump in the road? The Sample Homeowners Policy addresses this issue in Section II, Exclusion E (1) (page 19), cutting back on *Muth*. But the Sample CGL insurance policy contains no similar provision. Suppose that a manufacturer of asbestos knows that exposure to asbestos doses higher than those to which insulation workers normally are exposed causes lung disease, and conspires with other manufacturers to suppress evidence of this effect. Is the exclusion of liability for harm expected or intended applicable when it turns out that exposure at doses lower than expected also causes lung disease? For other cases addressing the type-of-harm-expected issue and preserving the possibility of coverage even when there was expectation of some harm, see *SL Industries, Inc. v. American Motorists Insurance Co.*, 607 A.2d 1266 (N.J. 1992); *United Services Automobile Association v. Elitzky*, 517 A.2d 982 (Pa. Super. 1986). Cases holding that once there is intent to harm, the type of harm that occurs is not relevant, include *American Family Insurance Co. v. Walser*, 628 N.W.2d 605 (Minn. 2001) and *Farmers Mutual Insurance Co. v. Kment*, 658 N.W.2d 662 (Neb. 2003).

3. *"Accident."* The court in *Unigard* implied that both the act committed by the insured and the harmful result must be unintentional. Does this make sense? Suppose a restaurant negligently serves food that it should know is contaminated. Is coverage precluded because the restaurant intentionally served the food? Would there be much left of liability insurance if not only the harmful result, but also the act causing the result,

had to be "accidental?" At this point the courts appear to be divided about whether the term "accident" in the Insuring Agreement of CGL and homeowners policies has a significance that is independent of the "expected or intended" exclusion. See, e.g., *Colorado Pool Systems, Inc. v. Scottsdale Ins. Co.*, 317 P.3d 1262 (Colo. App. 2012) (independent significance); *State Farm Gen. Ins. Co. v. Frake*, 197 Cal. App. 4th 568 (Cal. Ct. of App. 2011) (there is an accident if any aspect of the causal series of events leading to the harm was unintended). In any event, was it consistent to hold in *Unigard* that the child insured was precluded from coverage because the damage his act produced was not "caused by an occurrence" (i.e., an "accident") but that the parents' coverage was not precluded on the same ground?

4. *Shootings.* When an individual discharges a firearm intending to cause harm, that is not an "accident" and therefore is not an "occurrence." Moreover, the harm is expected or intended and therefore excluded. In some cases, however, the facts and issues are a bit more clouded. For example, in *Donovan v. Commercial Union Insurance Co.*, 493 N.W. 2d 581 (Minn. Ct. App. 1992), the insured fired a gun intending to frighten his wife and the plaintiff into leaving his house. The court ruled that harm was expected or intended. On the other hand, in *Scott v. Underhill*, 734 N.E. 2d 717 (Ind. Ct. App. 2000), the insured shot a trespasser three times but alleged that he intended only to hit the ground in front of him. The court held that the injury was not expected. Finally, as in *Unigard*, parents may be sued for negligent supervision after a shooting spree by their child. Coverage is sometimes available based on the *Unigard* theory. See, e.g., *Donegal Mut. Ins. Co. v. Baumhammers*, 938 A.2d 286 (Pa. 2007).

5. *Suits for Sexual Abuse.* Child victims of sexual molestation have very little chance of securing payment of damage awards from their attacker's insurer. In almost every jurisdiction in which an attacker has sought coverage for damages awarded to his victim, courts have defined sexual abuse as an act intended to cause harm as a matter of law. As such, the act falls within the "expected or intended" exclusion and coverage is denied. See, e.g., *Cotton States Mut. Ins. Co. v. Daniel*, 2008 WL 4999097 (M.D. Ala. 2008); *J.C. Penney Cas. Ins. Co. v. M.K.*, 804 P.2d 689 (Cal. 1991) (following "the rule that a child molester's subjective intent is irrelevant to the question of insurance coverage"); *CNA Ins. Co. v. McGinnis*, 666 S.W.2d 689 (Ark. 1984) (finding that psychiatric testimony to the effect that no harm was intended by a child molester flies "in the face of all reason, common sense, and experience"). Because so many of the cases involve clear and egregious examples of sexual abuse, little case law has developed regarding the right to indemnity or defense against claims of "merely" negligent abuse, although plaintiffs may find it in their interest to frame molestation claims as negligent in order to increase the likelihood that liability insurance will be available to fund any judgment. Thus, occasionally a defense may be available. For example, in *Horace Mann Insurance Co. v. Barbara B.*, 846 P.2d 792 (Cal. 1993), the plaintiff's complaint against a school teacher not only alleged intentional molestation but also such behavior as kissing the plaintiff on the forehead and putting his arm around her, both in front of other students. Because this type of behavior could be found to constitute negligence covered by the policy, the California Supreme Court held that summary judgment should not have been granted to the insurer as to the duty to defend.

The chances of recovering from someone other than the attacker for negligent supervision or under a respondeat superior theory, however, are greater. See, e.g., *Doe v. Shaffer*, 738 N.E.2d 1243 (Ohio 2000), in which the Supreme Court of Ohio overruled prior precedent and held that public policy permits a party to obtain liability insurance coverage for negligence related to sexual molestation when that party has not committed the molestation. In that case a mentally retarded alleged victim of molestation and his parents had sued the Catholic Diocese of Columbus for damages resulting from molestation, including death resulting from AIDS. For discussion of the nature of the underlying claims and liabilities in these cases, see Ellen M. Bublick, Tort Suits Filed by Rape and Sexual Assault Victims in Civil Courts: Lessons for Courts, Classrooms and Constituencies, 59 SMU L. Rev. 55 (2006); Marc L. Gouthro, Abusive Priests and the Catholic Church's Potential Liability, 37 Suffolk U. L. Rev. 479 (2004); Mark E. Chopko, Stating Claims Against Religious Institutions, 44 B.C. L. Rev. 1089 (2003).

6. *Construction Defect Suits.* An entire jurisprudence regarding suits alleging defects in or faulty workmanship involving the construction of buildings or equipment is developing, much of it concerned with the question whether the property damage alleged in such suits results from an "occurrence." Insurers typically argue that defective construction is not an "accident." Policyholders argue that if the defect is not intended, then there has been an "accident" within the meaning of the definition of an "occurrence." A representative decision holding that defective construction does constitute an occurrence *is American Empire Surplus Lines Insurance Co. v. Hathaway*, 707 S.E. 2d 369 (Ga. 2011). A representative decision to the contrary is *Nautilus Insurance Co. v. 1735 W. Diversey, LLC*, 2011 WL 3176675 (N.D. Ill. 2011). Some state legislatures also have addressed the issue, both pro and con. Additional issues in such litigation involve the question whether, even if faulty workmanship constitutes an occurrence, there has been "property damage," and whether, in any event, the business-risk exclusions (addressed next) preclude coverage when there has only been damage to the property that has been faultily constructed.

b.   THE BUSINESS RISK EXCLUSIONS

Weedo v. Stone-E-Brick, Inc.
Supreme Court of New Jersey, 1979.
81 N.J. 233.

■ CLIFFORD, J. We granted certification, 75 N.J. 615 (1978), to review the Appellate Division's determination that the appellant insurance carrier was obliged to defend two claims brought against its assureds. *Weedo v. Stone-E-Brick, Inc.,* 155 N.J.Super. 474 (1977). Resolution of both cases, argued here together, calls for construction of the same comprehensive general liability provisions of a policy issued to a masonry contracting concern. Specifically, the question is whether that policy indemnifies the insured against damages in an action for breach of contract and faulty workmanship on a project, where the damages claimed are the cost of correcting the work itself. The Appellate Division held that certain exclusions of the policy, when read together, were ambiguous and hence had to be resolved against the insurer. We reverse.

I

Pennsylvania National Mutual Insurance Company (hereinafter Pennsylvania National) issued a general automobile liability policy to Stone-E-Brick, Inc., a corporation engaged in masonry contracting. As part of the policy there was included Comprehensive General Liability Coverage (hereinafter CGL). During the term of the policy Calvin and Janice Weedo contracted with Stone-E-Brick to pour a concrete flooring on a veranda and to apply stucco masonry to the exterior of their home. The completed job revealed cracks in the stucco and other signs of faulty workmanship, such that the Weedos had to remove the stucco and replace it with a proper material. Thereupon the Weedos instituted suit against Stone-E-Brick and its principal, defendant Romano, alleging in pertinent part that

> [a]s a result of the defective and unworkmanlike manner in which the defendants applied the said stucco, plaintiffs were compelled to and did cause the defects existing therein to be remedied, where possible, and the omissions to be supplied, and, in general, were *compelled to and did furnish all the work, labor, services and materials necessary to complete the application of the said stucco in accordance with the contract and were compelled to and did expend large sums of money for that purpose in excess of the price which plaintiffs agreed to pay defendants for the application of said stucco, all of which was to plaintiffs' damage.* [Emphasis supplied.]

While the same CGL policy was in effect, Stone-E-Brick performed roofing and gutter work on a house being constructed for plaintiff Gellas, under a sub-contract agreement with the general contractor, defendant Vivino. After completion of the home the Gellases brought suit against Vivino based on breach of contract due to defects in workmanship and seeking recovery of costs "in connection with the repair and/or replacement of material necessary to correct the * * * defects in construction." Vivino in turn sought indemnification from Stone-E-Brick by way of third-party complaint, contending that plaintiffs' damages were the result of Stone-E-Brick's "faulty workmanship, materials or construction * * *."

II

Under the CGL provisions of the policy in question Pennsylvania National agreed to pay "on behalf of the insured all sums which the insured shall become legally obligated to pay as damages because of * * * bodily injury * * * or *property damage to which this insurance applies,* caused by an occurrence * * *." (Emphasis supplied). This is the standard language found in the great majority of CGLs written in this country. These provisions, developed by casualty rating bureaus over a period of nearly fifty years, have become an established norm of underwriting policy. Tinker, "Comprehensive General Liability Insurance—Perspective and Overview," 25 *Feder.Ins.Coun.Q.* 217, 218–21 (1975); Henderson, "Insurance Protection for Products Liability and

Completed Operations—What Every Lawyer Should Know," 50 *Neb.L.Rev.* 415, 418 (1971).[1]

These agreements set forth, in fundamental terms, the general outlines of coverage, e.g., "for property damage to which this insurance applies." The qualifying phrase, "to which this insurance applies" underscores the basic notion that the premium paid by the insured does not buy coverage for all property damage but only for that type of damage provided for in the policy. The limitations on coverage are set forth in the exclusion clauses of the policy, whose function it is to restrict and shape the coverage otherwise afforded.[2] *Capece v. Allstate Ins. Co.,* 88 N.J.Super. 535, 541 (Law Div.1965); Tinker, *op. cit., supra,* 25 *Feder.Ins.Coun.Q.* at 264. For example, a tavern-owners' liability coverage under the CGL is limited by force of the "dram shop" exclusion, where personal injury or property damage results from service of intoxicants to an incapacitated patron. See generally *Mt. Hope Inn v. Travelers Indemnity Company,* 157 N.J.Super. 431, 436–38 (Law Div.1978).

We set forth these basic principles simply to emphasize that, semantical rules of construction aside, contracts of insurance do contain relevant language (frequently developed, as here, see *n. 1, supra,* over the years after experience with different terms of expression) which serves to define the risks underwritten. In the present instance Pennsylvania National's policy undertook to furnish certain coverage to Stone-E-Brick as a concern engaged in masonry contracting. In order to determine whether the claims of plaintiffs fall within the coverage provided, we start with an examination of the insured's business relationships with its customers.

In the usual course of its business Stone-E-Brick negotiates with homeowners to provide masonry work. As part of the bargaining process the insured may extend an express warranty that its stone, concrete and stucco products and services will be provided in a reasonably workmanlike fashion. See, e.g., *Henningsen v. Bloomfield Motors, Inc.,* 32 N.J. 358, 370 (1960). Regardless of the existence of express warranties, the insured's provision of stucco and stone "generally carries with it an implied warranty of merchantability and often an implied warranty of fitness for a particular purpose." *McDonald v. Mianecki,* 79 N.J. 275, 284 (1979); see also *Hodgson v. Chin,* 168 N.J.Super. 549 (App.Div.1979). These warranties arise by operation of law and recognize that, under common circumstances, the insured-contractor holds himself out as having the capacity to apply the stonework in a workmanlike manner, and further, that the homeowner relies upon the representation and anticipates suitable goods and services. *McDonald v. Mianecki, supra,* 79 N.J. at 289–90.

---

[1] The standard provisions of the CGL have undergone four principal revisions—in 1943, 1955, 1966 and 1973—since their initial promulgation in 1940. Tinker, op. cit., supra, 25 Feder.Ins.Coun.Q. at 221. The terms pertinent to the present case have not been altered in a manner relevant to the issues before the Court since the 1966 revision.

[2] Pennsylvania National conceded at oral argument before us, as apparently it did before the Appellate Division, see 155 N.J.Super. at 479, that but for the exclusions in the policy, coverage would obtain. Hence we need not address the validity of one of the carrier's initially-offered grounds of non-coverage, namely, that the policy did not extend coverage for the claims made even absent the exclusions.

Where the work performed by the insured-contractor is faulty, either express or implied warranties, or both, are breached. As a matter of contract law the customer did not obtain that for which he bargained. The dissatisfied customer can, upon repair or replacement of the faulty work, recover the cost thereof from the insured-contractor as the standard measure of damages for breach of warranties. *Id.* at 282 n. 1; *525 Main Street Corp. v. Eagle Roofing Co. Inc.*, 34 N.J. 251, 255 (1961).

As explained in *McDonald v. Mianecki, supra,* a principal justification for imposing warranties by operation of law on contractors is that these parties are often "in a better position to prevent the occurrence of major problems" in the course of constructing a home than is the homeowner. 79 N.J. at 288–89. The insured-contractor can take pains to control the quality of the goods and services supplied. At the same time he undertakes the risk that he may fail in this endeavor and thereby incur contractual liability whether express or implied. The consequence of not performing well is part of every business venture; the replacement or repair of faulty goods and works is a business expense, to be borne by the insured-contractor in order to satisfy customers. See Tinker, *op. cit. supra,* 25 *Feder.Ins.Coun.Q.* at 224; Henderson, *op. cit., supra,* 50 *Neb.L.Rev.* at 441.

There exists another form of risk in the insured-contractor's line of work, that is, injury to people and damage to property caused by faulty workmanship. Unlike business risks of the sort described above, where the tradesman commonly absorbs the cost attendant upon the repair of his faulty work, the accidental injury to property or persons substantially caused by his unworkmanlike performance exposes the contractor to almost limitless liabilities. While it may be true that the same neglectful craftsmanship can be the cause of both a business expense of repair and a loss represented by damage to persons and property, the two consequences are vastly different in relation to sharing the cost of such risks as a matter of insurance underwriting.

In this regard Dean Henderson has remarked:

> The risk intended to be insured is the possibility that the goods, products or work of the insured, once relinquished or completed, will cause bodily injury or damage to property other than to the product or completed work itself, and for which the insured may be found liable. The insured, as a source of goods or services, may be liable as a matter of contract law to make good on products or work which is defective or otherwise unsuitable because it is lacking in some capacity. This may even extend to an obligation to completely replace or rebuild the deficient product or work. This liability, however, is not what the coverages in question are designed to protect against. The coverage is for tort liability for physical damages to others and not for contractual liability of the insured for economic loss because the product or completed work is not that for which the damaged person bargained. [Henderson, *op. cit., supra,* 50 *Neb.L.Rev.* at 441.]

An illustration of this fundamental point may serve to mark the boundaries between "business risks" and occurrences giving rise to insurable liability. When a craftsman applies stucco to an exterior wall of a home in a faulty manner and discoloration, peeling and chipping result, the poorly-performed work will perforce have to be replaced or repaired by the tradesman or by a surety. On the other hand, should the stucco peel and fall from the wall, and thereby cause injury to the homeowner or his neighbor standing below or to a passing automobile, an occurrence of harm arises which is the proper subject of risk-sharing as provided by the type of policy before us in this case. The happenstance and extent of the latter liability is entirely unpredictable—the neighbor could suffer a scratched arm or a fatal blow to the skull from the peeling stonework. Whether the liability of the businessman is predicated upon warranty theory or, preferably and more accurately, upon tort concepts, injury to persons and damage to other property constitute the risks intended to be covered under the CGL.

The standardized provisions in the CGL intended to convey this concept include, *inter alia,* the very exclusion clauses at issue herein. Tinker, *op, cit., supra,* 25 *Feder.Ins.Coun.Q.* at 244–45. These exclusions—"insured products" (exclusion "(n)") and "work performed" (exclusion "(o)")—are as follows:

> * * * This insurance does not apply (n) to property damage to the named insured's products arising out of such products or any part of such products;
>
> (o) to property damage to work performed by or on behalf of the named insured arising out of the work or any portion thereof, or out of materials, parts or equipment furnished in connection therewith.

We agree with Pennsylvania National that, given the precise and limited form of damages which form the basis of the claims against the insured, either exclusion is, or both are, applicable to exclude coverage. In short, the indemnity sought is not for "property damage to which this insurance applies." Tinker, *op. cit., supra,* 25 *Feder.Ins.Coun.Q.* at 233; see also, *Adams Tree Service Inc. v. Hawaiian Insurance & Guaranty Co. Ltd.,* 117 Ariz. 385 (Ct.App.1977).

Our view is consistent with the treatment of the "insured's products" and "work performed" exclusions in the great majority of courts elsewhere. Because of the factual similarity and the uniform wording of the exclusionary clauses, the reasoning in these decisions is thoroughly persuasive.[3] *Biebel Bros., Inc. v. United States Fidelity & Guar. Co.,* 522 F.2d 1207 (8th Cir.1975), is illustrative. In *Biebel,* a roofing contractor instituted an action against its liability insurer to recover the costs of removing defective roofing and the additional expense of supplying adequate roofing thereafter—work which was called for by the contract with the dissatisfied customer. Not unlike the instant case, the insured's faulty work was not alleged to have caused any property damage to property other than the work product of or materials supplied by the insured. *Id.,* at 1209. * * *

---

[3] The "insured's products" and the "work performed" exclusions, denominated "(n)" and "(o)" in the present standard CGL, appeared as exclusions "(l)" and "(m)" in policies written before the last decade. The literal wording of the exclusions, however denominated, has remained constant for some fifteen years.

III

Our review of twenty years' worth of judicial treatment of the "business risk" exclusion demonstrates that, if nothing else, the underwriting policy sought to be articulated by clauses "n" and "o" has been widely recognized as a valid limitation upon standard, readily-available liability insurance coverage. Indeed, several courts have remarked in ruling upon the impact of these clauses that the terms used to convey the "business risk" exclusions are straightforward and without ambiguity. * * *

The clarity and effect of the "business risk" exclusion clauses is called into question only under a curious reading of the standard CGL. The court below indulged this reading of the policy when it accepted Stone-E-Brick's argument that an ambiguity existed in the policy when the exclusions for "business risk" were read correlatively with another exclusion clause. This latter clause, denominated exclusion "(a)" in the policy, reads:

This insurance does not apply:

(a) to liability assumed by the insured under any contract or agreement except an incidental contract; but this exclusion does not apply to a warranty of fitness or quality of the named insured's products or a warranty that work performed by or on behalf of the named insured will be done in a workmanlike manner; * * *

On the basis of three decisions which considered the proposed ambiguity between "(a)" and the "business risk" clauses discussed earlier, the Appellate Division found that the "co-existence" of the provisions "creates, at the very least, an ambiguity which must be resolved in favor of the insured so as to provide coverage." 155 N.J.Super. at 486. The import of the "business risk" exclusions is thereby rendered nugatory.

Because we are of the view that exclusion "(a)" cannot serve to becloud the clear import of the "business risk" exclusions, we necessarily disagree that an ambiguity exists in the policy before us. We have only recently reaffirmed the view that only genuine ambiguities engage the so-called "doctrine of ambiguity," see *DiOrio v. New Jersey Manufacturers Insurance Co.,* 79 N.J. 257, 269 (1979); and without intending in any wise to undercut the salutary effects of this "doctrine," we observe that it is, and indeed always has been, one of construction, simply an aid to the proper interpretation of terms devised by the professional underwriter. As Chief Justice Weintraub suggested in another context, such an aid "usually serves to describe a result rather than to assist in reaching it." *Reilly v. Ozzard,* 33 N.J. 529, 539 (1960).

We conceive a genuine ambiguity to arise where the phrasing of the policy is so confusing that the average policyholder cannot make out the boundaries of coverage. In that instance, application of the test of the objectively reasonable expectation of the insured often will result in benefits of coverage never intended from the insurer's point of view. The benefits granted, however, will pertain to the same landscape of risk as contemplated by the policy in issue, that is, the "doctrine of ambiguity" works to effectuate the consumer's expectation that the policy purchased extended greater coverage in the particular underwriting area. The rule of construction embraces ambiguities which are artificial, however, when the reading of coverage urged by the insured affords indemnity in an area of insurance completely distinct from that to which the policy applies in the first instance. To use an extreme example, no amount of semantical ingenuity can be brought to bear on a fire insurance policy so as to afford coverage for an intersection collision. Such an interpretation of a fire policy would hardly be based on any "objectively reasonable" expectation. See *DiOrio, supra,* 79 N.J. at 269.

In this case Stone-E-Brick's interpretation of the policy would result in coverage for repair and replacement of its own faulty workmanship. This interpretation relies on the supposition that the exception to exclusion "(a)"—"but this exclusion does not apply to a warranty that work performed by or on behalf of the named insured will be done in a workmanlike manner"—*grants* coverage for claims based on the warranty described. Not so. The contention runs directly counter to the basic principle that exclusion clauses *subtract* from coverage rather than grant it. Precisely this point was made by the Supreme Court of South Dakota, in construing the very clauses we have before us:

> * * * Exclusion (a) does not extend or grant coverage. To the contrary it is a limitation or restriction on the insuring clause. The exception to exclusion (a) merely removes breach of implied warranty of fitness, quality or workmanship from the specific exclusion relating to contractual liability. The exception [to clause (a)] remains subject to and limited by all other related exclusions contained in the policy. When considered with exclusion (m) [(o) in the instant case] it clearly appears that property damage claims of third persons resulting from the insured's breach of an implied warranty are covered unless the claimed loss is confined to the insured's work or work product. [*Haugan v. Home Indem. Co., supra,* 197 N.W.2d at 22.]

To the same effect, see *St. Paul Fire & Marine Insurance Co. v. Coss, supra,* 145 Cal.Rptr. at 841.

As a variant of its argument that exclusion "(a)" grants the coverage it seeks, Stone-E-Brick contends that this exception, when read in conjunction with the "business risk" exceptions, is confusing in that coverage "granted" by the former clause is taken away by the latter two. 155 N.J.Super. at 486. But this argument too ignores the principle that

> [e]ach exclusion is meant to be read with the insuring agreement, independently of every other exclusion. The exclusions should be read seriatim, not cumulatively. If any one exclusion applies there should be no coverage, regardless of inferences that might be argued on the basis of exceptions or qualifications contained in other exclusions. There is no instance in which an exclusion can properly be regarded as inconsistent with another exclusion, since they bear no relationship with one another. [Tinker, *op. cit., supra.,* 25 Feder.Ins.Couns.Q. at 223.]

When presented with an identical claim of ambiguity as arising out of comparison of exclusions (a) and the "business risk" clauses, the court in *Biebel Bros., Inc. v. United States F. & G. Co.,* supra, stated flatly that the language of the exception in "(a) * * * has no application whatsoever to exclusions (*l*) [n] or (m) [o] * * *." 522 F.2d at 1212. We agree, and accordingly do not perceive any ambiguity in the instant policy. * * *

But what does exclusion "(a)" mean and what is its function? As we have endeavored to make clear, the policy in question does not cover an accident of faulty workmanship but rather faulty workmanship which causes an accident. See *Hamilton Die Cast, Inc. v. United States F. & G. Co.,* 508 F.2d 417, 420 (7th Cir.1975); *Dreis & Krump Mfg. Co. v. Phoenix Insurance Co.,* 548 F.2d 681, 689 (7th Cir.1977). Within this structure, contractual liability is excluded under the terms of exclusion "(a)". The exception to this exclusion insures, however, that claims premised upon quasi-contract or contract by implication, such as warranty actions, will be covered. Such claims must nevertheless be otherwise cognizable under the general grant of coverage in the first instance in order to constitute a claim "to which this insurance applies." This analysis of the import of the "(a)" exclusion accords with the generally-held view of other courts, see *e.g., Carboline Co. v. Home Indem. Co.,* 522 F.2d 363, 366 (7th Cir.1975) (same construction given to similar clause in contractual liability policy); *Biebel Bros., Inc. v. United States F. & G. Co., supra,* 522 F.2d at 1212; *Haugan v. Home Indem. Co., supra,* 197 N.W.2d at 22; *Aetna Insurance Co. v. Pete Wilson Roofing & Heating Co., Inc.,* 272 So.2d 232, 234–35 (1972) (contractual liability policy construed), and at the same time saves the clear import of the exclusions for "business risks."

IV

The judgments under review are reversed and the matters remanded to the respective trial courts for entry there of judgments in favor of Pennsylvania National. No costs.

NOTES AND QUESTIONS

1. *The Rationale of the Decision.* What was the rationale for the court's decision: that the exclusions mean what they say, that the parties did not intend to cover the kind of liability at issue, or that because it would not make sense to insure against that kind of liability, the exclusions preclude such coverage? Were you comfortable with the court's conclusions about the absence of any relationship between exclusion (a) and the business risk exclusions? Is the rule that ambiguities are construed against the insurer consistent with the rule that the exclusions in a liability insurance policy are to be read as having no relation to each other?

2. *Faulty Product or Work Distinguished from Consequential Injury or Damage.* Recent decisions confirm the continued vitality of the distinction drawn by *Weedo.* See, e.g., *Essex Ins. Co. v. BloomSouth Flooring Corp.,* 562 F.3d 399 (1st Cir. 2009); *Hathaway Dev. Co. v. Illinois Union Ins. Co.,* 274 Fed. Appx. 787 (11th Cir. 2008). But distinguishing damage to the insured's work or product from damage to other property is not always a simple exercise. For example, suppose that a manufacturer of building materials containing asbestos is sued by a Board of Education for

the cost of removing and replacing the materials in the schools under the Board's jurisdiction. Do the business risk exclusions insulate the manufacturer's CGL insurer from liability? See *United States Fidelity & Guaranty Co. v. Wilkin Insulation Co.*, 78 N.E.2d 926 (Ill. 1991); *Dayton Independent School District v. National Gypsum Co.*, 682 F.Supp. 1403 (E.D. Tex.1988), both holding that the exclusions do not bar coverage. In any event, was the court's argument that it would not make sense to insure against liability for the cost of repairing faulty work persuasive? One strand in this argument is that a party purchasing such work does not get what she bargained for. Is that not also true of faulty work that causes bodily injury or damages other property, liability for which is covered? In addition, because the same faulty work causes the harm at issue, whether the claim is for the cost of repair or for damage to other property or personal injury, an argument based on moral hazard cannot explain why coverage against liability for faulty work is excluded, but coverage for injury or damage caused by the faulty work is not.

3. *An Alternative Explanation.* Consider an alternative way of explaining the function of the business risk exclusions: The CGL policy contains these exclusions because faulty work appears with enough frequency and involves average losses that are low enough that even small businesses can safely self-insure against them. Consequently, it would not be worth paying the cost of transferring these risks to an insurance company, given the moral hazard and adverse selection that would raise the cost of market insurance against liability for faulty work far above its expected value for any individual business. In contrast, liability for bodily injury or damage to other property is sufficiently infrequent and the average cost of such liability sufficiently high that self-insuring against this kind of liability would be too risky for most small and medium-sized businesses. The business risk exclusions therefore do not pertain to this kind of liability.

4. *The Impaired Property and Subcontractor Exceptions.* Note that there is a separate exclusion for Impaired Property, defined as a property that has not been physically injured and into which the insured's product or work has been incorporated. This exclusion does not preclude coverage, however, when such product or work has caused physical injury to the property into which it has been incorporated and that property therefore cannot be restored to use merely by removing the defective component. *Netherlands Ins. Co. v. Main Street Ingredients, LLC*, 745 F. 3d 309 (8th Cir. 2014). Thus, the maker of a component part may be covered against liability for physical damage to the larger product of which it is a part. But the maker of the larger product into which a component part is incorporated appears to be precluded from coverage by the Your Product exclusion. Does this distinction make sense in light of any of the explanations for the business risk exclusions?

Conversely, however, there is an exception to the Your Work exclusion for damage that arises from the work of a subcontractor. Is the availability of this coverage consistent with the unavailability of coverage for damage to Your Product resulting from a faulty component part? For application of the subcontractor exception, see *Wanzek Construction, Inc. v. Employers Insurance of Wassau*, 679 N.W.2d 322 (Minn.2004), in which the court held that the Your Work exclusion did not apply to the liability of a contractor who built a municipal swimming pool whose coping stones caused bodily injury, because the stones were provided and installed by a subcontractor. Does this exception threaten to swallow up the exclusion?

5. *The Sistership Exclusion.* An exclusion not referred to in *Weedo*, lettered (n) in the Sample CGL policy (page 5), is worth separate explanation. Traditionally termed the "sistership" exclusion, it excludes coverage of the cost of recalling certain products or work. The exclusion apparently takes its name from a leading case applying it, in which the issue was whether the exclusion precluded coverage of the cost of recalling from service one airplane (the "sistership") after another was discovered to be defective. *Arcos Corp. v. Am. Mut. Liab. Ins. Co.*, 350 F.Supp. 380, 384 n. 2 (E.D.Pa. 1972).

c. THE POLLUTION EXCLUSION

American States Insurance Co. v. Koloms
Supreme Court of Illinois, 1997.
177 Ill.2d 473.

■ JUSTICE MCMORROW delivered the opinion of the court:

We granted leave to appeal in this case (155 Ill.2d R. 315) in order to examine the scope of the absolute pollution exclusion provision contained in a commercial general liability (CGL) policy. The dispositive issue for our review is whether that exclusion bars coverage for claims of carbon monoxide poisoning caused by an allegedly defective furnace. For the reasons that follow, we hold it does not.

Background

The facts of this case, as taken from the pleadings, are relatively straightforward. On September 17, 1990, a furnace in a two-story commercial building located in Lincolnshire, Illinois, began to emit carbon monoxide and other noxious fumes. Several employees of one of the building's tenants, Sales Consultants, Inc., inhaled the fumes and became ill. Six of those employees eventually filed suit against the beneficial owners of the property, Harvey and Nina Koloms (hereinafter referred to as Koloms). In the complaints, the employees alleged that Koloms had negligently maintained the furnace and had failed to keep it in good working condition. They also claimed that Koloms had not properly inspected some repair work which had been performed on the furnace. Each employee sought damages as compensation for his or her injuries.

Koloms, in turn, tendered the complaints to American States Insurance Company (ASI), which had insured the building under a standard-form CGL policy. After reviewing the complaints, ASI agreed to defend Koloms subject to a reservation of rights. Specifically, ASI reserved the right to contest coverage on the basis of the absolute pollution exclusion contained in the policy. That exclusion provided in pertinent part:

"This insurance does not apply to: * * *

f.(1) 'Bodily injury' or 'property damage' arising out of actual, alleged or threatened discharge, dispersal, release or escape of pollutants:

(a) At or from premises you own, rent or occupy * * *."

The exclusion further defined "pollutants" as "any solid, liquid, gaseous or thermal irritant or contaminant, including smoke, vapor, soot, fumes, acids, alkalis, chemicals and waste."

Shortly thereafter, ASI instituted the present action in the circuit court of Cook County, seeking a declaration that it did not have a duty to defend or indemnify Koloms. The gravamen of ASI's complaint centered upon the meaning of the term "pollutants." ASI alleged that the term was unambiguous and that, in accordance with its plain meaning, the emission of carbon monoxide fumes constituted the "release" of a gaseous "irritant or contaminant." ASI insisted, therefore, that any bodily injuries resulting from such emissions were excluded from coverage.

In response, Koloms denied the material allegations of the complaint and filed two separate affirmative defenses. In one of the affirmative defenses, Koloms alleged that the pollution exclusion did not apply to injuries caused by a leaking furnace, but rather was limited to injuries resulting from industrial, commercial or large scale pollution. They claimed that the CGL policy exclusion was ambiguous to that extent, and that an insured person in their position would not reasonably expect carbon monoxide, a commonly occurring chemical compound, to be considered a pollutant.

Analysis

* * * [O]ur determination of whether the pollution exclusion applies to the types of injuries at issue in this case turns primarily upon the language of the exclusion itself. ASI contends, as it did in the lower courts, that the language is unambiguous and must be given its plain and ordinary meaning. In support of this contention, ASI points out that the exclusion specifically applies to injuries arising out of the "release or escape of pollutants." ASI further notes that the exclusion defines "pollutants" as any "gaseous * * * irritant or contaminant, including * * * fumes." According to ASI, all of these words have commonly understood meanings and usages which render the provision free of doubt. ASI adds that, given the absence of any ambiguity, it "strains all credibility" to suggest that carbon monoxide fumes emitted from an allegedly defective furnace fall outside the scope of the exclusion. This is particularly true, ASI stresses, since carbon monoxide is not only defined in common dictionaries as a "colorless odorless very toxic gas" (Webster's Third New International Dictionary 336 (1981)), but it is also regulated by the federal government as a "pollutant." See 40 C.F.R. Part 50 (1996) (establishing carbon monoxide as a "criteria air pollutant" endangering public health under the Clean Air Act (42 U.S.C. § 7408(a)(1) (1994))).

In addition to the above arguments, ASI also relies upon several cases from other jurisdictions which have, under similar circumstances, enforced the policy exclusion as written. For example, in *Bernhardt v. Hartford Fire Insurance Co.*, 102 Md.App. 45 (1994), cert. allowed, 337 Md. 641 (1995), a chimney flue in a residential apartment complex became obstructed with debris, which then resulted in an excessive accumulation of carbon monoxide gas. As in the instant case, several of the building's tenants became ill. One of the tenants brought suit against the owner of the property, claiming that the furnace had been improperly maintained. The building's owner, like Koloms, tendered the complaint to his insurer, but was denied coverage on the basis of the pollution exclusion. A trial court in a subsequent declaratory action found that the exclusion was clear and unambiguous, and held that the exclusion applied. *Bernhardt*, 102 Md.App. at 48. The insured appealed.

In affirming the decision of the trial court, the Maryland Court of Special Appeals observed that an insurance policy can be viewed as ambiguous in one of two ways. First, the language itself " 'may be intrinsically unclear, in the sense that a person reading it without the benefit of some extrinsic knowledge simply [could] not determine what it means.' " *Bernhardt*, 102 Md.App. at 54, quoting *Town & Country Management Corp. v. Comcast Cablevision*, 70 Md.App. 272, 280 (1987). Second, the language, although clear on its face, may become uncertain when applied to a particular object or circumstance. *Bernhardt*, 102 Md.App. at 55. As to this latter type of ambiguity, the court noted that it is well settled " '[t]hat a term may be free from ambiguity when used in one context but of doubtful application in another context.' " *Bernhardt*, 102 Md.App. at 55, quoting *Tucker v. Fireman's Fund Insurance Co.*, 308 Md. 69, 74 (1986). After reviewing the language of the exclusion, the court of appeals determined that neither type of ambiguity was present. The court explained that, although the title "pollution exclusion" could, standing alone, be viewed as ambiguous, the actual language contained in the exclusion was "quite specific." *Bernhardt*, 102 Md.App. at 54. The court also found that "a person of ordinary intelligence reading the language" would conclude that the exclusion applied to carbon monoxide poisoning. *Bernhardt*, 102 Md.App. at 54.

Equally important, the *Bernhardt* court also rejected the insured's contention that, "notwithstanding the literal language of the exclusion, the parties intended that [the exclusion] apply only to persistent industrial pollution of the environment, and not to an accident of the kind generally covered by a comprehensive business liability policy." *Bernhardt*, 102 Md.App. at 48–49. As ASI notes, this argument is virtually identical to the argument relied upon by our appellate court when it determined that the exclusion did not apply. See 281 Ill.App.3d at 731 ("we too find that the clause is ambiguous, as it can reasonably be interpreted as applying only to environmental pollution"). ASI argues that our appellate court erred in this regard, and instead should have adopted the reasoning of the *Bernhardt* court. The court there stated in pertinent part:

> "Quite apart from the problems inherent in determining what may or may not be 'industry-related,' we are required to state the obvious—nowhere in this exclusion does the word 'industry' or 'industrial' appear. There is simply no such limitation. Moreover, we would be hard pressed to conclude that the insurance industry intended such a limitation in an exclusion it intentionally included as an endorsement in policies covering non-industrial business, and indeed, even in homeowner's policies." *Bernhardt*, 102 Md.App. at 55.

The *Bernhardt* court then rejected the insured's related argument that the pollution exclusion be limited only to active polluters, i.e., those individuals who knowingly emit pollutants over an extended period of time. The court explained that the exclusion neither draws a distinction between an intentional and nonintentional discharge of pollutants nor suggests that "only chronic emission of the defined pollutants is excluded from coverage." *Bernhardt*, 102 Md.App. at 55. As such, the exclusion could be applied to the owner of a residential apartment complex, notwithstanding the fact that the owner may not have been an active polluter of the environment. *Bernhardt*, 102 Md.App. at 56. For these reasons, the *Bernhardt* court upheld the lower court's finding of no coverage. *Bernhardt*, 102 Md.App. at 56. See also *Essex Insurance Co. v. Tri–Town Corp.*, 863 F.Supp. 38 (D.Mass.1994) (finding that carbon monoxide emissions from an ice resurfacing machine at a hockey game fell within the scope of the exclusion); *League of Minnesota Cities Insurance Trust v. City of Coon Rapids*, 446 N.W.2d 419 (Minn.App.1989) (same).

Based upon the above analysis, ASI urges this court to follow *Bernhardt* and other similar cases and hold that the pollution exclusion is neither ambiguous nor limited to incidents of industrial pollution.

Koloms, on the other hand, do not dispute that the drafters of the policy employed commonly understood words when they sought to remove pollution related injuries from the scope of coverage. Rather, they maintain that, regardless of its facial clarity, the exclusion does not apply to "damages due to routine commercial hazards such as a faulty heating and ventilation system." Koloms base their conclusion, in part, upon their view of the historical purpose of the exclusion, which they believe supports limiting the clause to large scale, environmental contamination. Specifically, Koloms assert that both the original pollution exclusion, first instituted in the early part of the 1970s, and the current pollution exclusion, drafted in 1985, were intended solely to protect insurers from having to defend and indemnify insureds in connection with governmental clean-up costs. Koloms insist, therefore, that because this case involves personal injuries caused by exposure to materials which do not constitute "pollution" in the traditional sense of the word, the exclusion does not apply.

Koloms further add that, if this court were to adopt ASI's interpretation, we would not only be extending the exclusion far beyond its historical purpose, but we would also be nullifying most of the coverage currently afforded under the standard-form CGL policy. Koloms direct our attention to several recent opinions in which courts have criticized the insurance industry's broad definition of the terms "irritant" and "contaminant." For example, in *Westchester Fire Insurance Co. v. City of Pittsburg*, 768 F.Supp. 1463, 1470 (D.Kan.1991), aff'd, 987 F.2d 1516 (10th Cir.1993), a federal district court objected to the exclusion's potentially limitless reach, noting that "there is virtually no substance or chemical in existence that would not irritate or damage some person or property." In a similar vein, the Seventh Circuit Court of Appeals observed:

> "Without some limiting principle, the pollution exclusion clause would extend far beyond its intended scope and lead to some absurd results. To take but two simple examples, reading the clause broadly would bar coverage for bodily injuries suffered by one who slips and falls on the spilled contents of a

bottle of Drano, and for bodily injury caused by an allergic reaction to chlorine in a public pool. Although Drano and chlorine are both irritants or contaminants that cause, under certain conditions, bodily injury or property damage, one would not ordinarily characterize these events as pollution." *Pipefitters Welfare Educational Fund v. Westchester Fire Insurance Co.*, 976 F.2d 1037, 1043 (7th Cir.1992).

Koloms submit that, in the absence of some judicially imposed parameters, the terms "irritants" and "contaminants" could even be applied to such everyday elements as water or air. For this reason, they urge that the exclusion must be limited, in accordance with its historical purpose, to incidents of environmental pollution.

As is evident from the foregoing discussion, the parties have presented this court with compelling reasons which support their respective positions. Indeed, the strength of their arguments is perhaps best reflected in the vast divergence of the jurisprudence from courts across the country which have already struggled with the question now facing this court. Unfortunately, despite the abundance of opinions construing the exclusion, courts have not reached a clear consensus as to its proper interpretation. This is true even within the fairly rare context of carbon monoxide poisoning. Some courts have construed the provision in favor of the insured, holding that the exclusion is vague and ambiguous. See, e.g., *Motorists Mutual Insurance Co. v. RSJ, Inc.*, 926 S.W.2d 679 (Ky.App.1996); *Gamble Farm Inn v. Selective Insurance Co.*, 440 Pa.Super. 501 (1995); *Kenyon v. Security Insurance Co.*, 163 Misc.2d 991 (1993). Other courts, however, have denied coverage on the grounds that the exclusion is plain and unambiguous. See, e.g., *Reliance Insurance Co. v. Moessner*, 121 F.3d 895, (3d Cir.1997); *Bernhardt v. Hartford Fire Insurance Co.*, 102 Md.App. 45 (1994), cert. allowed, 337 Md. 641 (1995); *League of Minnesota Cities Insurance Trust v. City of Coon Rapids*, 446 N.W.2d 419 (Minn.App.1989). Still other courts have largely ignored the language of the exclusion and have found coverage on the basis of the reasonable expectations of the insured. See, e.g., *Regional Bank v. St. Paul Fire & Marine Insurance Co.*, 35 F.3d 494 (10th Cir.1994). Meanwhile, courts have also considered the exclusion in the context of other types of "pollutants." They too, have failed to achieve a consistent interpretation of the clause.

The source of the disagreement within the jurisprudence seems to lie in the fact that the language of the clause is, as the *Bernhardt* court observed, "quite specific" on its face, and yet a literal interpretation of that language results in an application of the clause which is "quite broad." We note that when the definition of the term "pollutant" is inserted into the body of the exclusion, the clause eliminates coverage for " '[b]odily injury' or 'property damage' arising out of actual, alleged or threatened discharge, dispersal, release or escape of * * * any solid, liquid, gaseous or thermal irritant or contaminant, including smoke, vapor, soot, fumes, acids, alkalis, chemicals and waste." A close examination of this language reveals that the exclusion (i) identifies the types of injury-producing materials which constitute a pollutant, i.e., smoke, vapor, soot, etc., (ii) sets forth the physical or elemental states in which the materials may be said to exist, i.e., solid, liquid, gaseous or thermal, and (iii) specifies the various means by which the materials can be disseminated, i.e., discharge, dispersal, release or escape. To that extent, therefore, the exclusion is indeed "quite specific," and those courts wishing to focus exclusively on the bare language of the exclusion will have no difficulty in concluding that it is also unambiguous. See, e.g., *Reliance Insurance Co. v. Moessner*, 121 F.3d 895 (3d Cir.1997).

Not all courts, however, find the bare language of the exclusion dispositive. A number of courts, while acknowledging the lack of any facial ambiguity, have nevertheless questioned whether the breadth of the language renders application of the exclusion uncertain, if not absurd. For instance, in addition to the cases discussed above, the Ohio Court of Appeals has observed that "the extremely broad language of the 1987 exclusion, in conjunction with the definition of a pollutant, raises an issue as to whether the exclusion is so general as to be meaningless." *Ekleberry, Inc. v. Motorists Mutual Insurance Co.*, No. 3–91–39, 1992 WL 168835 (1992); see also *American States Insurance Co. v. Kiger*, 662 N.E.2d 945, 948 (Ind.1996) ("Clearly, this clause cannot be read literally as is would negate virtually all coverage"); *Sullins v. Allstate Insurance Co.*, 340 Md. 503 (1995) (same); *Motorists Mutual Insurance Co. v. RSJ, Inc.*, 926 S.W.2d 679 (Ky.App.1996) (same). These courts, troubled by the results which obtain when the terms of the clause are applied in the context of an actual claim, often decline to apply the pollution exclusion to injuries other than those caused by traditional environmental contamination. See, e.g., *Weaver v. Royal Insurance Co. of America*, 140 N.H. 780, 783 (1996) ("While courts freely apply the pollution exclusion to environmental contamination, they are generally unwilling to hold that its scope reaches other pollution-related injuries").

We have carefully reviewed all of the foregoing decisions as well as each of the contentions raised by the parties. Notwithstanding ASI's arguments to the contrary, we believe that a purely literal interpretation of the disputed language, without regard to the facts alleged in the underlying complaints, fails to adequately resolve the issue presented to this court. Like many courts, we are troubled by what we perceive to be an overbreadth in the language of the exclusion as well as the manifestation of an ambiguity which results when the exclusion is applied to cases which have nothing to do with "pollution" in the conventional, or ordinary, sense of the word. See, e.g., *Minerva Enterprises, Inc. v. Bituminous Casualty Corp.*, 312 Ark. 128 (1993). Accordingly, we agree with those courts which have restricted the exclusion's otherwise potentially limitless application to only those hazards traditionally associated with environmental pollution. We find support for our decision in the drafting history of the exclusion, which reveals an intent on the part of the insurance industry to so limit the clause.

The events leading up to the insurance industry's adoption of the pollution exclusion are "well-documented and relatively uncontroverted." *Morton International, Inc. v. General Accident Insurance Co.*, 134 N.J. 1, 31 (1993). Prior to 1966, the standard-form CGL policy provided coverage for bodily injury or property damage caused by an "accident." *Center for Creative Studies v. Aetna Life & Casualty Co.*, 871 F.Supp. 941, 943 n. 3 (E.D.Mich.1994), quoting J. Stempel, Interpretation of Insurance Contracts: Law and Strategy for

Insurers and Policyholders 825 (1994). The term "accident," however, was not defined in the policy. As a result, courts throughout the country were called upon to define the term, which they often interpreted in a way as to encompass pollution-related injuries. In response, the insurance industry revised the CGL policy in 1966 and changed the former "accident"-based policy to an "occurrence"-based policy. The new policy specifically defined an "occurrence" as "an accident, including injurious exposure to conditions, which results, during the policy period, in bodily injury and property damage that was neither expected nor intended from the standpoint of the insured." *Morton International, Inc.*, 134 N.J. at 32 (and cases cited therein). Despite these changes, courts continued to construe the policy to cover damages resulting from long-term, gradual exposure to environmental pollution. As one court observed, "[s]o long as the ultimate loss was neither expected nor intended, courts generally extended coverage to all pollution-related damage, even if it arose from the intentional discharge of pollutants." *New Castle County v. Hartford Accident & Indemnity Co.*, 933 F.2d 1162, 1196–97 (3d Cir.1991).

Meanwhile, at about the same time, the United States Congress substantially amended the Clean Air Act in an effort to protect and enhance the quality of the nation's air resources. Pub.L. No. 91–604, 84 Stat. 1676 (1970) (now codified at 42 U.S.C. §§ 7401 through 7642 (1983), as amended). The passage of these amendments, which included provisions for cleaning up the environment, imposed greater economic burdens on insurance underwriters, particularly those drafting standard-form CGL policies. *Westchester Fire Insurance Co. v. City of Pittsburg*, 768 F.Supp. 1463, 1469 n. 8 (D.Kan.1991), aff'd, 987 F.2d 1516 (10th Cir.1993). The insurer's burdens further increased with the relatively recent, and now well-publicized, environmental disasters of Times Beach, Love Canal and Torrey Canyon. See *Center for Creative Studies*, 871 F.Supp. at 944; see also *Morton International, Inc.*, 134 N.J. at 33–34.

In the wake of these events, the insurance industry became increasingly concerned that the 1966 occurrence-based policies were "tailor-made" to cover most pollution-related injuries. *Morton International, Inc.*, 134 N.J. at 33, quoting Note, The Pollution Exclusion Clause Through the Looking Glass, 74 Geo. L.J. 1237, 1251 (1986). To that end, changes were suggested, and the industry proceeded to draft what was to eventually become the pollution exclusion. The Supreme Court of New Jersey explained, "[f]oreseeing an impending increase in claims for environmentally-related losses, and cognizant of the broadened coverage for pollution damage provided by the occurrence-based, CGL policy, the insurance industry drafting organizations began in 1970 the process of drafting and securing regulatory approval for the standard pollution-exclusion clause." *Morton International, Inc.*, 134 N.J. at 32. Consequently, the General Liability Governing Committee of the Insurance Rating Board instructed its drafting committee "to consider the question and determine the propriety of an exclusion, having in mind that pollutant-caused injuries were envisioned to some extent in the adoption of the current [policies]." *Morton International, Inc.*, 134 N.J. at 34, quoting T. Reiter, D. Strasser & W. Pohlman, The Pollution Exclusion Under Ohio Law: Staying the Course, 59 U. Cin. L.Rev. 1165, 1197 (1991).

The result of these efforts was the addition of an endorsement to the standard-form CGL policy in 1970. The endorsement provided in pertinent part:

> "[This policy shall not apply to bodily injury or property damage] arising out of the discharge, dispersal, release or escape of smoke, vapors, soot, fumes, acids, alkalis, toxic chemicals, liquids or gases, waste materials or other irritants, contaminants or pollutants into or upon land, the atmosphere or any watercourse or body of water; but this exclusion does not apply if such discharge, dispersal, release or escape is sudden and accidental."

Three years later, in 1973, the insurance industry incorporated the above endorsement directly into the body of the policy as exclusion "f."[1]

During the next 13 years, various courts labored over the exact meaning of the words "sudden and accidental." Much of the litigation focused on whether the word "sudden" was intended to be given a strictly temporal meaning such that, in order for the exception to apply, the discharge of pollution had to have been "abrupt." See *Outboard Marine Corp. v. Liberty Mutual Insurance Co.*, 154 Ill.2d 90 (1992). This controversy generated an enormous amount of litigation, leading one commentator to describe the dispute as one of "the most hotly litigated insurance coverage questions of the late 1980's." J. Stempel, Interpretation of Insurance Contracts: Law and Strategy for Insurers and Policyholders 825 (1994), quoted in *Center for Creative Studies*, 871 F.Supp. at 943. Not surprisingly, insurance companies responded by drafting a new version of the exclusion, which, first appearing in 1985, is now commonly known as the "absolute pollution exclusion." We note that it is this version, the pertinent terms of which have been set forth at the outset of this opinion, that is the subject of the dispute between ASI and Koloms. The two most notable features of this latest version are (i) the lack of any exception for the "sudden and accidental" release of pollution, and (ii) the elimination of the requirement that the pollution be discharged "into or upon land, the atmosphere or any watercourse or body of water." See *Weaver v. Royal Insurance Co. of America*, 140 N.H. 780 (1996). Significantly, the purpose of the current exclusion, like its predecessor, is "to exclude governmental clean up costs from [the scope of] coverage." *West American Insurance Co. v. Tufco Flooring East, Inc.*, 104 N.C.App. 312, 324 (1991).

Our review of the history of the pollution exclusion amply demonstrates that the predominate motivation in drafting an exclusion for pollution-related injuries was the avoidance of the "enormous expense and exposure resulting from the 'explosion' of environmental litigation." (Emphasis added.) *Weaver*, 140 N.H. at 783, quoting *Vantage Development Corp. v. American Environment Technologies Corp.*, 251 N.J.Super. 516, 525 (1991). Similarly, the 1986 amendment to the exclusion was wrought, not to broaden the provision's scope beyond its original purpose of excluding coverage for environmental pollution, but rather to remove the "sudden and accidental" exception to

---

[1] We note, parenthetically, that the definition of the term "occurrence" was also modified in that same year, and is now defined as "an accident, including continuous and repeated exposures to conditions, which results in bodily injury or property damage neither expected nor intended from the standpoint of the insured."

coverage which, as noted above, resulted in a costly onslaught of litigation. We would be remiss, therefore, if we were to simply look to the bare words of the exclusion, ignore its raison d' etre, and apply it to situations which do not remotely resemble traditional environmental contamination. The pollution exclusion has been, and should continue to be, the appropriate means of avoiding "'the yawning extent of potential liability arising from the gradual or repeated discharge of hazardous substances into the environment.'" (Emphasis in original.) *Tufco*, 104 N.C.App. at 323, quoting *Waste Management of Carolinas, Inc. v. Peerless Insurance Co.*, 315 N.C. 688, 698 (1986). We think it improper to extend the exclusion beyond that arena.

Notwithstanding the above, ASI submits that the deletion of the requirement that the pollution be "[discharged] into or upon land, the atmosphere, or any watercourse or body of water" should be viewed by this court as a clear signal of the industry's intent to broaden the exclusion beyond traditional environmental contamination. We disagree. This same argument was rejected in *West American Insurance Co. v. Tufco Flooring East, Inc.*, 104 N.C.App. 312 (1991), a case which involved the application of the pollution exclusion to damages caused by the release of fumes from a flooring sealant. In *Tufco*, the court noted that, even after its amendment in 1986, the absolute pollution exclusion continued to employ terms of art which bespeak of environmental contamination. The court reasoned:

> "Because the operative policy terms 'discharge,' 'dispersal,' 'release,' and 'escape' are environmental terms of art, the omission of the language 'into or upon land, the atmosphere or any watercourse or body of water' in the new pollution exclusion is insignificant. The omission of the phrase only removes a redundancy in the language of the exclusion that was present in the earlier pollution exclusion clause. Consequently, we find that any 'discharge, dispersal, release, or escape' of a pollutant must be into the environment in order to trigger the pollution exclusion clause and deny coverage to the insured." *Tufco*, 104 N.C.App. at 325.

See also *Center for Creative Studies*, 871 F.Supp. at 946 ("the fact that the [former version] contained language relating to discharge 'into or upon land, the atmosphere . . .' is not significant"). We agree with this analysis. In our view, the deletion of the aforementioned language does not portend an expansion of the pollution exclusion beyond the context of traditional environmental contamination.

Conclusion

Given the historical background of the absolute pollution exclusion and the drafters' continued use of environmental terms of art, we hold that the exclusion applies only to those injuries caused by traditional environmental pollution. The accidental release of carbon monoxide in this case, due to a broken furnace, does not constitute the type of environmental pollution contemplated by the clause. Accordingly, the judgment of the appellate court is affirmed.

NOTES AND QUESTIONS

1. *The Scope of the Exclusion.* As the opinion in *Koloms* indicates, the courts are divided as to the scope of the absolute pollution exclusion, of which there are a number of variations. Compare the version at issue in *Koloms* with Exclusion (F)(1)(a)(1) (page 3). Positions vary: a) Some courts apply the exclusion to any discharge of a pollutant, whereas others require that the discharge be into the environment. b) Some courts require that the substance be waste or a byproduct rather than a useful product, whereas others apply the exclusion to any substance that is a contaminant or irritant. c) And some courts apply the exclusion in a manner they describe as being "as it is written," whereas others do not apply the exclusion where it would preclude coverage of the main risk posed by the policyholder's activities. For a sample of cases, see *Bituminous Casualty Corp. v. Sand Livestock Systems, Inc.*, 728 N.W.2d 216 (Iowa 2007) (carbon monoxide is a pollutant); *Allen v. Scottsdale Insurance Co.*, 307 F.Supp. 2d 1170 (D. Haw. 2004) ("fugitive dust" emitted by concrete factory that caused allergic reaction can be considered a pollutant even though it is chemically inert); *Belt Painting Corp. v. TIG Insurance Co.*, 795 N.E.2d 15 (N.Y.2003) (damage caused by exposure to paint and paint solvent fumes not excluded because it is not "environmental"); *Westview Associates v. Guaranty National Insurance Co.*, 740 N.E.2d 220 (N.Y .2000) (damage caused by lead paint exposure not excluded); *Stoney Run Co. v. Prudential–LMI Commercial Insurance Co.*, 47 F.3d 34 (2d Cir. 1995) (damage caused by emission of carbon monoxide from defective heating system not excluded); *Shalimar Contractors, Inc. v. American States Insurance Co.*, 975 F.Supp. 1450 (N.D. Ala. 1997) (lead paint claims are excluded because lead paint is a "contaminant" or "irritant"); *West American Insurance Co. v. Tufco Flooring East, Inc.*, 104 N.C.App (N.C. App. 1991) (food contamination resulting from vapors emitted during floor resurfacing is not excluded). Notwithstanding these distinctions, presumably no court would always apply the exclusion "literally." For example, suppose that the insured negligently left an open bottle of Tabasco sauce on a shelf, and was sued for damages resulting when a third party bumped into the shelf and the sauce dripped into his eye. The sauce was "discharged" and clearly is an "irritant," but it seems unlikely that the exclusion would preclude coverage in any jurisdiction. For analyses of the exclusion, see J. Wylie Donald & Craig W. Davis, Carbon Dioxide: Harmless, Ubiquitous, and Certainly Not a "Pollutant" Under a Liability Policy's Absolute Pollution Exclusion, 39 Seton Hall L. Rev. 107 (2009); Jeffrey W. Stempel, Reason and Pollution: Correctly Construing the "Absolute" Exclusion in Context and in Accord with its Purpose and Party Expectations, 34 Tort & Ins. L.J. 1 (1998).

2. *The "Sudden and Accidental" Exclusion.* The court in *Koloms* recounted the story leading up to the promulgation of the "absolute" exclusion. Litigation over the meaning of the prior exclusion, which precluded coverage unless the discharge of a pollutant was "sudden and accidental," continues to this day. The reason, of course, is that older policies covering liability for property damage occurring before the absolute exclusion was introduced may still be the subject of claims, because of their trigger of coverage.

The courts have divided as to the meaning of this exclusion. Some courts have held that the term "sudden and accidental" means abrupt and accidental, and that the exclusion therefore precludes coverage of liability for either gradual or intentional pollution. A roughly equal number of courts, however, have ruled that the term "sudden" does not necessarily have a temporal component and that the exclusion therefore does not preclude coverage of liability for unintentional, gradual pollution. Some of these latter courts have so ruled on the ground that the term "sudden" is ambiguous, because it may mean either "abrupt" or "unexpected." See, e.g., *Textron, Inc. v. Aetna Cas. & Sur. Co.*, 754 A.2d 742 (R.I. 2000); *Claussen v. Aetna Cas. & Sur. Co.*, 380 S.E.2d 686 (Ga. 1989). Other courts have so ruled on the ground that, at the time the insurance industry sought regulatory approval of the exclusion, it represented that the "impact of the [exclusion] on the vast majority of risks would be no change" in the coverage provided by CGL policies. These courts have in effect created a doctrine of "regulatory estoppel" to bar literal application of the exclusion. See, e.g., *Sunbeam Corp. v. Liberty Mutual Ins. Co.*, 781 A.2d 1189 (Pa. 2001); *Morton Int'l, Inc. v. Gen. Accident Ins. Co. of Am.*, 629 A.2d 831 (N.J. 1993). For analysis, see Kenneth S. Abraham, Environmental Liability Insurance Law 145–60 (1991).

3. *Time-Based Pollution Buybacks.* Some specialized policies and endorsements to CGL policies now provide pollution liability buybacks, under which liability for damage caused by pollution is available if the insured becomes aware of discharge within a specified number of days following the commencement of discharge, and provides notice of commencement to the insurer within another specified number of days. The obvious aim of such buybacks is to capture some of the benefits afforded by the old "sudden and accidental" exception to the pollution exclusion without running the risk that was entailed in subjecting the provision to judicial interpretation, as described in the preceding note.

4. *Mold.* One of the hottest pollution-related topics of the 21st century has been mold, especially in residential property. A series of issues arises under pollution exclusions in connection with claims for coverage of liability for damage caused by mold. See *McKnight v. USAA Cas. Ins. Co.*, 871 A.2d 446 (Del. Super. Ct. 2005) (recovery is limited by the "mold or fungus" provision); *Droegkamp v. Langdon*, 668 N.W.2d 563 (Wis. App. 2003) (mold is not a "pollutant" or "contaminant"); *Lexington Ins. Co. v. Unity/Waterford–Fair Oaks, Ltd.*, 2002 WL 356756 (N.D. Tex. 2002) (mold was "released" or "discharged"). For discussion, see Kellie MacCready, The Mold Rush, 15 Vill. Envtl. L. J. 89 (2004). In addition, although the standard-form policy contains no express reference to mold as a pollutant, some policies have added a specific mold or fungus exclusion. See, e.g., *Clarendon Am. Ins. Co. v. S. States Plumbing, Inc.*, 803 F. Supp. 2d 544 (D. La. 2011).

5. *Climate Change.* Lawsuits alleging legal responsibility for contributing to climate change are a new feature of the landscape that may increase in the coming years. For one such example, *American Electric Power Co. v. Connecticut*, 131 S. Ct. 2527 (2011) (holding that some plaintiffs had standing to challenge refusal of EPA to regulate greenhouse gas emissions). Claims for coverage of the costs of defending and indemnifying suits seeking to impose such responsibility also may increase. See, e.g., *AES Corp. v. Steadfast Ins. Co.*, 725 S.E.2d 532 (Va. 2012) (emissions are not caused by "accident"); *Cinergy Corp. v. Associated Electric & Gas Ins. Servs., Ltd.*, 865 N.E.2d 571 (Ind. 2007) (no coverage for the cost of measures that might reduce power companies' contribution to

global warming). See also James S. Malloy & John M. Sylvester, Insurance coverage for Global Warming Liability Claims, 45 Tort & Ins. Practice L.J. 811 (2010). The extent to which the various pollution exclusions that have been incorporated in CGL policies over the years might preclude such coverage is unclear, but insurers certainly can be expected to rely on these exclusions when and if more coverage claims are made.

6. *The Owned-Property Exclusion.* Another exclusion that figures in pollution cases is Exclusion J in the Sample Policy (pages 4–5), which applies among other things to "Property Damage to: (1) Property you own." Suppose that pollution occurs on the insured's own property but there is a risk that it may migrate offsite. It is useful to recognize the variety of situations to which the owned-property exclusion may then be applicable. These include the following: (i) only owned property has been damaged and damage to non-owned property is not imminent; (ii) only owned property has been damaged but damage to non-owned property is imminent; (iii) non-owned property has been damaged and further damage is imminent. Virtually all courts apply the owned-property exclusion to the first case. Most courts apply the owned-property exclusion to the second case as well. See, e.g., *Aggio v. Estate of Aggio*, 2008 WL 2491697 (N.D. Cal. 2008); *State v. Signo Trading Int'l, Inc.*, 612 A.2d 932 (N.J. 1992). The vast majority of courts, however, do not apply the owned-property exclusion to the third case, in which non-owned property has been damaged and remedying harm to owned property will prevent further damage to non-owned property. However, these courts still typically require some form of allocation of the costs expended as between those that are and are not excluded. See, e.g, *Hakim v. Massachusetts Ins. Insolvency Fund*, 675 N.E. 2d 1161 (Mass. 1997).

The high cost of cleanup of hazardous waste under CERCLA is due largely to the cost of remedying contamination of "groundwater"—that is, underground water. Interestingly, many courts have held not only that the owned-property exclusion does not preclude coverage of the cost of remedying contamination that has spread to groundwater outside the policyholder's property, but also that the exclusion does not preclude coverage of the cost of decontaminating groundwater under the policyholder's own property. These rulings are based on state common law rules and statutes providing that groundwater is not owned, or at least not owned exclusively, by the owner of the property above it. Rather, groundwater is owned by the state as *parens patriae* or as trustee for the people. See, e.g., *United Co-op. v. Frontier FS Co-op.*, 738 N.W.2d 578 (Wis. App. 2007); *Schnitzer Inv. Corp. v. Certain Underwriters at Lloyd's of London*, 137 P.3d 1282 (Or. 2006); *Norfolk S. Corp. v. California Union Ins. Co.*, 859 So.2d 167 (La. App. 2003). As a consequence, in many states the vast majority of the cost of cleanup on a policyholder's property may not be subject to the exclusion.

Occasionally the owned-property exclusion figures in non-pollution disputes as well. See, e.g., *Aetna Ins. Co. v. Aaron*, 685 A.2d 858 (Md. App. 1996) (owned-property exclusion does not preclude coverage of the cost of altering a glass enclosure in a condominium unit that caused water damage to neighboring property).

d. NOTICE CONDITIONS

Most courts hold that even policy provisions requiring immediate notice are complied with when notice is given within a reasonable time. But the amount of a delay that is reasonable varies. See, e.g., *Mighty Midgets, Inc. v. Centennial Ins. Co.*, 389 N.E. 2d 180 (N.Y. 1979) (question of fact whether seven month delay in providing notice was reasonable); *Pile Foundation Constr. Co. v. Investors Ins. Co. of Am.*, 769 N.Y.S.2d 290 (N.Y. App. Div. 2003) (five month delay is unreasonable as a matter of law). However, the following case reflects an additional, majority rule: even an unreasonable delay does not breach the policy so long as the insurer suffers no prejudice as a result of the delay. See, e.g., *Johnson v. Westhoff Sand Co., Inc.*, 62 P.3d 685 (Kan. App. 2003). Some courts also require that the delay be in "good faith." See, e.g., *Erie Ins. Exch. v. Szamatowicz*, 597 S.E.2d 136 (N.C. App. 2004).

West Bay Exploration v. AIG Specialty Agencies
United States Court of Appeals, Sixth Circuit, 1990.
915 F.2d 1030.

■ RALPH B. GUY, JR., CIRCUIT JUDGE.

The plaintiff, West Bay Exploration Company (West Bay), appeals entry of summary judgment in this diversity of citizenship contract action against three of its insurers: International Surplus Lines Insurance Company (International), Great Southwest Fire Insurance Company (Great Southwest), and Zurich American Insurance Company of Illinois (Zurich). West Bay argues that the district court erred in its interpretation of Michigan law and improperly resolved disputed issues of fact in holding that West Bay had failed to satisfy notice conditions contained in insurance policies written by the defendants. Upon *de novo* review of the record, we agree with the district court that the plaintiff has failed to raise a genuine issue of fact with regard to satisfaction of the notice requirements and, accordingly, affirm.

I.

West Bay is an independent oil and gas producer operating approximately 24 wells in northern lower Michigan. The defendants each issued general liability insurance policies covering the plaintiff's operations for the years 1982 through 1985. This case arose from the defendants' denial of coverage for cleanup costs that the plaintiff incurred as a result of the discharge of toxic chemicals at seven of its natural gas wells during the covered period.

The discharges were the product of a procedure West Bay employs to remove water vapor from natural gas so that the gas can be conveyed through pipelines without freezing. West Bay processes the gas from its wells through a device known as a glycol dehydrator. In the dehydrator, the gas is mixed with glycol, a desicant or drying agent, which absorbs the water vapor. The dry gas is then sent out through a pipeline and the glycol is reclaimed. The reclamation process involves heating the glycol to a temperature below its boiling point but above the boiling point of water, thus causing the water to escape in the form of steam. The glycol is then returned to the gas stream to absorb more water vapor, while the steam is sent through a "downpipe" where it condenses and is collected in a "drum" or "drip barrel." The water is discharged into a drip barrel rather than into the air because of the danger that it will carry trace amounts of the potentially carcinogenic aromatic hydrocarbons benzene, ethylbenzene, toluene, and xylene (BTEX). These toxins may appear naturally in water vapor from the wells.

In August 1984, the Michigan Department of Natural Resources (MDNR) prepared a report which revealed the presence of BTEX in "oil field associated water (brines) from all Michigan oil producing formations." The MDNR found that acceptable benzene levels had been exceeded by a factor of 3500, making the aquifer that was tested "totally unsafe for human consumption" or even bathing.

Acting upon the information discovered in the August report, the MDNR obtained a warrant to search seven of West Bay's gas wells. The warrant was posted on October 31, 1985, and on that same date the MDNR sent West Bay a "Letter of Noncompliance" stating that the department had reason to believe that West Bay had improperly disposed of glycol condensate and thereby unlawfully "committed waste in the development of oil," in violation of Michigan's Supervisor of Wells Act, 1939 P.A. 61, Mich.Comp.Laws § 319.4. The MDNR ordered West Bay to either replace a leaking drip barrel by November 11 or shut down the wells, and to take samples of the groundwater beneath the unsound barrel. The MDNR report indicates that at least one of West Bay's drip barrels had been intentionally perforated so as to allow collected water to seep into the ground.

On February 19, 1986, the MDNR wrote West Bay to inform the company that, due to the amount of BTEX that had seeped into the ground, corrective action would be required. The MDNR ordered West Bay to "remove contaminated soils in the vicinity of the dehydrator discharge point" and place them in a licensed landfill, replace the soils with clean backfill, install groundwater monitor wells, submit groundwater samples to an EPA approved laboratory, and regularly inspect the dehydrator collection vessel. The letter specified that these actions were to be coordinated with the MDNR and performed within 40 days. * * *

On October 27, 1987, approximately two years after receiving the letter of noncompliance from the MDNR, West Bay commenced this action in the United States District Court for the Western District of Michigan seeking a declaratory judgment of liability against International and various other insurance companies no longer parties to this action. West Bay sought to have the defendants declared jointly and severally liable for costs West Bay had incurred as a result of the BTEX discharge. On July 7, 1988, West Bay amended its complaint to add Southwest and Zurich as defendants. In addition to the claims for declaratory judgment, the plaintiff's amended complaint requested damages alleging breach of contract by each defendant and negligence for failure to provide an insurance contract free from ambiguity.

In June 1989, the three defendants each filed motions for summary judgment, arguing that the plaintiff had failed to satisfy a condition precedent to their duty under the insurance contracts by not notifying them of the facts underlying the claim "as soon as practicable," and that, in any event, various provisions within the policies excluded coverage for costs associated with the clean up.

Our inquiry begins with an examination of the terms of the policies. See *Jones v. Farm Bureau Mutual Ins. Co.,* 172 Mich. App. 24, 27 (1988). The notice provisions contained in the three policies are substantially identical, each providing in relevant part as follows:

> In the event of an occurrence, written notice containing particulars sufficient to identify the insured and also reasonably obtainable information with respect to the time, place and circumstances thereof, and the names and addresses of the injured and of available witnesses, shall be given by or for the insured to the company or any of its authorized agents as soon as practicable. * * *
>
> No action shall lie against the company unless, as a condition precedent thereto, there shall have been full compliance with all of the terms of this policy. * * *

The terms of the policies require that notice be provided to an "authorized agent[ ]" of the defendant, and that the notice be provided "as soon as practicable." Our review of the record convinces us that the plaintiff satisfied neither of these requirements as they are construed under Michigan law. * * *

B. Prejudice Due to Untimely Notice

Under Michigan law, late notice to an insurance company will not eliminate an insurer's obligations under a policy unless the insurer can demonstrate that it has been prejudiced by the delay.[1] *Wendel v. Swanberg,* 384 Mich. 468, 478 (1971); *Wehner v. Foster,* 331 Mich. 113, 117 (1951); *Weller v. Cummins,* 330 Mich. 286, 292–93 (1951); *Kennedy v. Dashner,* 319 Mich. 491 (1947); *Wood v. Duckworth,* 156 Mich.App. 160 (1986); *Burgess v. American Fidelity Fire Ins. Co.,* 107 Mich.App. 625 (1981).

The burden of showing prejudice rests upon the insurer. *Wendel,* 384 Mich. at 478; *Wehner,* 331 Mich. at 117; *Burgess,* 107 Mich.App. at 628; *Steelcase, Inc. v. American Motorists Ins. Co.,* No. 89–1344, slip op. at 5 (6th Cir. July 3, 1990) [907 F.2d 151 (Table)] (unpublished per curiam). Prejudice will be found where the delay "materially" impairs an insurer's ability to contest its liability to an insured or the liability of the insured to a third party. *Wendel,* 384 Mich. at 479; *Burgess,* 107 Mich.App. at 630; *Anderson v. Kemper Ins. Co.,* 128 Mich.App. 249, 254 (1983) (defendants must show "they have been materially injured in their ability to contest the merits of the case. . . ."). Michigan law does *not* require an insurer to prove that but for the delay it would have avoided liability. *Steelcase,* 907 F.2d 151 (explaining that this circuit misstated Michigan law when we announced the "but for" test in *Stonewall Ins. Co. v. Webb,* 746 F.2d 1479 (6th Cir.1984) (unpublished per curiam)).

---

[1] The Michigan courts have developed this rule through an inquiry into the purpose of notice provisions. As the Michigan Supreme Court wrote in *Wendel v. Swanberg,* 384 Mich. 468, 477 (1971), these provisions "allow the insurer to make a timely investigation of the accident in order to evaluate claims and to defend against fraudulent, invalid, or excessive claims." (Citation omitted.) *See also Wehner v. Foster,* 331 Mich. 113, 119 (1951) (stating that the purpose of the provision is "to give the insurer an opportunity to investigate the facts and circumstances affecting the question of liability and the extent of such liability.").

While the question of prejudice is generally to be left to the trier of fact, *Wendel*, 384 Mich. at 478 n. 8, where the facts are so clear that "one conclusion only is reasonably possible," the question is one of law. *Wehner*, 331 Mich. at 120 (citation omitted) (trial court erred in submitting the question to the jury); *Wendel*, 384 Mich. at 479; *Wood*, 156 Mich.App. 160. Under the circumstances of this case, we believe that the district court reached the only reasonable conclusion in finding prejudice as a matter of law.

The defendants have been most obviously prejudiced by West Bay's failure to notify them before disposing of the drip barrels from which the BTEX escaped. Each of the three policies includes an identical "pollution exclusion" which excludes from coverage:

> bodily injury or property damage arising out of the discharge, dispersal, release or escape of smoke, vapors, soot, fumes, acids, alkalis, toxic chemicals, liquids or gases, waste materials or other irritants, contaminants or pollutant into or upon land, the atmosphere or any water course or body of water; *but this exclusion does not apply if such discharge, dispersal, release or escape is sudden and accidental.*

(Emphasis added). If this action were to proceed to trial, the defendants could escape liability under this provision only by showing that the discharge of BTEX occurred either gradually or intentionally. *See FL Aerospace v. Aetna Casualty Sur. Co.*, 897 F.2d 214, 219–20 (6th Cir.1990) (Michigan law); *Grant-Southern Iron & Metal Co. v. CNA Ins. Co.*, 905 F.2d 954, 955 (6th Cir.1990) (Michigan law) ("the phrase 'sudden and accidental' has a temporal component and does not describe continuous or ongoing polluting events.") Both showings could best be made by presenting evidence of the condition of the discharge barrels at the time the discharge was discovered. If the MDNR report is accurate, and at least one of the barrels was perforated, the defendants would make out a powerful case that the discharge was both intentional and gradual. By destroying the drip barrels in its cleanup effort, West Bay has materially compromised the defendants' ability to present their most powerful defense to liability under the policy.

In addition, we agree with the district court that, through its lengthy delay, West Bay left the defendants "without the option of suggesting, or even mandating, the use of less costly, more efficient procedure[s] in responding to [M]DNR's request for cleanup." While it is true that the insurers have not presented evidence that they would have developed a less costly method of responding to the MDNR's orders, we feel that this is a case in which " 'the lapse of time which removes the opportunity for prompt investigation, also destroys the possibility of showing prejudice arising from delayed inquiry.' " *Wehner*, 331 Mich. at 120 (quoting *Purefoy v. Pacific Automobile Indem. Exchange*, 5 Cal.2d 81 (1935)). To require the defendants to make an accounting of the money they might have saved had these two and three-year delays not taken place would be to allow the plaintiff to profit from the length of the delay. The Michigan courts have recognized that where enough time has passed, "it virtually becomes impossible to learn what facts, favorable to defendant, could have been ascertained through prompt inquiry." In such situations, the Michigan courts have been "impelled to the conclusion that prejudice must be presumed * * *." *Id.*

The plaintiff has accurately noted a general reluctance on the part of the Michigan courts to allow insurers to escape liability due to notice provisions. The cases cited, however, all involve attempts by injured parties to recover in garnishment proceedings against an insurer of a principal defendant. Under these circumstances, the Michigan courts have proceeded with sensitivity to the equities of the cases before them. As the court of appeals state in *Burgess*:

> In most instances, the practical effect of a ruling in favor of the insurance carrier in a garnishment action leaves the injured plaintiff with an uncollectible judgment, while fairness also dictates that the insurance carrier must not be deprived of an opportunity to protect its interests where it has no notice. Erosion of rights of the insurance carrier adds to the costs of doing business. There exists a delicate balancing of these respective social interests.
>
> Insurance companies are professionals in the arena of litigation. Hence, evolution of the concept that the insurance carrier must show prejudice from the lack of notice of accident or suit before it will not be required to respond.

107 Mich.App. at 629–30; *see also Wood*, 156 Mich.App. at 164. The need for delicate balancing of the equities to avoid injury to an innocent third party is absent from this case. Here, the plaintiff delayed making a claim on its policies with the expressed intention of avoiding an increase in its insurance premiums. Having acted in its own financial interest, it cannot now complain because it has been injured thereby.

We find that the delays of two and three years materially prejudiced the defendants and therefore operate to relieve them of any liability on their policies of insurance. Summary judgment for the defendants is AFFIRMED.

NOTES AND QUESTIONS

1. *The Burden of Proof on Prejudice.* In the majority of jurisdictions prejudice to the insurer is required in order for the insurer to deny coverage on the basis of late notice. For many decades, however, New York had rejected the prejudice rule. See, e.g., *Security Mutual Insurance Co. v. Acker-Fitzsimons Corp.*, 293 N.E.2d 76 (1972), holding that the insurer need not show prejudice before it can assert a defense of non-compliance with the notice requirement. That rule has been largely reversed by statute. See N.Y. Ins. Law § 3420 (McKinney 2008). In the past, and in connection with suits arising out of policies issued prior to the new New York rule, the lurking potential application of New York law, or the law of another state that still rejects the prejudice rule, sometimes has prompted and still will prompt the insured to sue at the same time it gives notice, for the following reason. Insureds who give notice that could be characterized as late are concerned that if they merely give notice without simultaneously bringing suit, their insurer(s) will institute a declaratory judgment action in a state whose law (or choice of law) on notice is less favorable on the prejudice issue (or on issues unrelated to notice) than the state where the insured sues. Since many states' choice of law rule is that the law of the state where a contract was delivered governs, and so many major corporations have or had (at the time an earlier policy was delivered)

corporate headquarters in New York City or Westchester County, New York law was a real threat. So insureds made sure to sue rather than be sued, and to do so in a state whose choice of law rules might not dictate the application of New York law to the notice issue.

In the other, "notice-prejudice" states, the burden of proof is critically important, for often it is impossible to pinpoint any prejudice that has occurred. For example, sometimes it will simply be unclear whether potentially beneficial evidence disappeared, or whether the case is substantially more difficult to defend for other reasons as a result of the delay in providing notice. The courts are split on the question of who bears the burden of proof, though the majority seem to place it on the insurer. Compare *Weaver Brothers, Inc. v. Chappel*, 684 P.2d 123 (Alaska 1984) (burden on insurer to show that a six-year delay caused prejudice); *Fireman's Fund Ins. Co. of Wisconsin v. Bradley Corp.*, 660 N.W.2d 666 (Wis. 2003) (prejudice is presumed if notice is one year late and burden is on insured to prove its absence).

2. *What Kind of Prejudice?* There are at least four ways in which the policyholder might have combatted the insurer's contention that it had been prejudiced. Can you identify them? Until the advent of the mega-coverage suits of the 1980's, the prejudice inquiry focused heavily on the possible prejudice resulting from late notice to the insurer's capacity to defend the insured effectively. In such suits this kind of prejudice was likely to be absent, since the typical insured was a major industrial corporation that had retained a prominent law firm to defend it against the underlying lawsuits in question. *West Bay* and similar cases introduce a different kind of prejudice—the difficulty of proving a coverage defense resulting from late notice. Should the difficulty of making out this defense be treated under the same rule as the more traditional prejudice claim? In any event, not all cases are as clear as *West Bay* in finding prejudice to the insurer's coverage defense. For example, in *Canron, Inc. v. Federal Insurance Co.*, 918 P.2d 937 (Wash. App. 1996), the insurer identified a number of possible ways in which it was prejudiced by late notice, but "presented no evidence of specifics." It failed to isolate any changes at the site during the period of delay, identify lost records or name specific witnesses whose testimony had become unavailable. Further, "once notified, the [insurer] conducted no investigation." The court held that the evidence was insufficient to support a jury verdict that the insurer suffered actual prejudice—in effect, that there was no prejudice as a matter of law. On the significance of the insurer's failure to conduct an investigation once it does receive notice, see *Darcy v. Hartford Insurance Co.*, 554 N.E.2d 28 (Mass. 1990). In addition, consider whether there ought to be a difference in the timeliness standard for notice provided to excess, as distinguished from primary insurers. Excess insurers typically have no duty to defend (though often they have a right to participate in a defense should they elect to do so) and their dollar limits may not be reached by claims falling within the primary limits. See *Am. Home Assurance Co. v. Int'l Ins. Co.*, 684 N.E.2d 14 (N.Y. 1997).

3. *What Is a "Claim" or "Suit"?* The typical CGL policy requires the insured to provide the insurer with notice of a "claim" or "suit." Ordinarily there is no problem determining whether there has been a "claim" or "suit." CERCLA and similar state statutes, however, tend to operate extra-judicially until very late in the process. For example, CERCLA cleanup

investigations typically begin with notice to the potentially responsible party—a "PRP Letter"—that it has been identified as a party with possible legal responsibility. The wording of these letters varies, some being far more demanding or conclusive than others. In effect a PRP letter commences an administrative process, but no judgment can result without recourse to court, although the failure to comply with certain administrative orders issued under CERCLA can result in severe monetary sanctions. See CERCLA § 106, 42 U.S.C. § 9606. Given the mismatch between the CERCLA process and the typical CGL policy language, it is no surprise that there has been litigation over the meaning of the phrases "claim" or "suit," and no surprise that there is a division of authority, some cases holding that a PRP Letter falls within those terms, some holding that it does not, and some holding that the issue depends on the particular facts. Cases holding that a PRP letter or similar administrative actions constitutes a "suit" include *R.T. Vanderbilt Co., Inc. v. Continental Casualty Co.*, 870 A.2d 1048 (Conn. 2005) and *Pacific Employers Insurance Co. v. Servco Pacific, Inc.*, 273 F.Supp.2d 1149 (D. Haw. 2003). Cases holding to the contrary include *Powerine Oil Co., Inc. v. Superior Court*, 118 P.3d 589 (Cal. 2005) and *Simon Wrecking Co., Inc. v. AIU Insurance Co.*, 350 F.Supp. 2d 624 (E.D. Pa. 2004). Interestingly, since the typical CGL policy not only requires the *insured* to provide notice of a "claim" or "suit," but requires the *insurer* to defend any "suit" against the insured, any decision on this issue has the potential to be double-edged.

4. *Notice of Claim Versus Notice of Occurrence*. The issue in some cases is not the timeliness of a notice of claim, but the timeliness of a notice of "occurrence." The insured is also obligated to provide timely notice of any "claim or suit." The insured almost always knows that a claim has been made, because he has received written notice or has been served with a complaint. Suppose that there have been injuries caused by the insured's product, but it does not learn of these until three years after the injuries began to occur. Would the provision of notice three years after what in retrospect was the first occurrence be sufficient?

5. *Late Notice by the Insurer*. Should the insurer be under a corresponding duty to notify the insured within a reasonable time that it is denying coverage? Based on a statutory duty to this effect, the New York Court of Appeals held that a 48-day delay by an insurer in providing such notice was unreasonable as a matter of law under the circumstances. See *First Fin. Ins. Co. v. Jetco Contracting Corp.*, 769 N.Y.S.2d 459 (N.Y. 2003).

B. CLAIMS-MADE POLICIES

In addition to CGL occurrence-based coverage, there are many other forms of liability insurance, much of which is sold on a claims-made basis. We first encountered claims-made coverage in Chapter Three, in connection with the *Hartford Fire* case. In contrast to occurrence coverage, which insures against liability for injury or damage that occurs during the policy period even if suit is brought later, claims-made coverage insures against claims made (and usually, also reported) during the policy period. Thus, the principal difference between occurrence and claims-made policies is what triggers coverage: a harm during the policy period or a claim made during the policy period.

The difference between occurrence and claims-made coverage may be easier to understand visually. In the following diagrams an "O" indicates the year in which harm or loss must first occur under the two kinds of policies, and a "C" indicates the year or years in which a claim arising out of that occurrence may or must be made in order to be covered. Note further that most claims-made policies contain a retroactive date, limiting coverage to injury or loss that occurs after that date, thus replacing "Beginning of time" in the Claims-Made chart with that date.

A 2015 Occurrence Policy

	OOO	
	CCC	CCCCCCCCCCCCCCCCC
Beginning of time	2015	End of Time

A 2015 Claims-Made Policy

OOOOOOOO	OOO	
	CCC	
Beginning of time	2015	End of Time

Consider an example. Suppose that Surgeon Sally operates on Patient Patty in May, 2013. In December, 2013, Patient Patty begins to experience adverse symptoms, and discovers that they are attributable to the fact that certain surgical equipment was left inside her body by Surgeon Sally. Patty immediately has surgery to correct the error. In February of 2014, she then sues Surgeon Sally for medical malpractice, and Surgeon Sally immediately notifies her carrier. If Surgeon Sally maintained occurrence liability coverage for both 2013 and 2014, her 2013 policy would be triggered. If she maintained claims-made policies during these years, then her 2014 policy would be triggered. If Sally maintained occurrence coverage in 2013 but switched to claims-made coverage in 2014, both policies would be triggered. And if Sally maintained claims-made coverage in 2013, but occurrence coverage in 2014, then neither policy would be triggered.

This Section considers selected issues under two of the most prominent forms of claims-made coverage: Directors & Officers and Professional Liability insurance. Directors & Officers, or "D&O" liability insurance, is a specialized insurance product that has come to prominence as corporate and securities litigation has increased in recent decades. D&O insurance covers corporate and other organizational directors and officers against liability for "wrongful acts" committed in their insured capacity, when the corporation cannot indemnify them. The primary example of such liability involves liability imposed by judgment in shareholder derivative suits. Corporate law prohibits corporations from indemnifying officers and directors in derivative suits if liability is adjudicated (though in many states settlements of such suits are indemnifiable). This is often called "Side A" coverage (Insuring Clause A on page 1 of the Sample Policy set out below). D&O insurance also covers corporations and organizations themselves for the costs they incur when they can and do indemnify their officers and directors against liability. This corporate reimbursement coverage is often called "Side B" coverage (Insuring Clause B on page 1 of the Sample Policy). These two forms of coverage are the core of D&O insurance; note that under Side A and Side B coverage, the corporation is not covered against liability to third parties that it incurs in its own right. An additional form of coverage has grown up to cover the corporate entity against such liability—typically in securities suits—and has come to be called "entity" or "Side C" coverage (Insuring Clause C on page 1 of the Sample Policy). In addition to Side C coverage, corporate policyholders may also be given the option to purchase coverage of the cost of certain investigations ("Inquiry Coverage" under the Sample Policy). Additional options that may be available include coverage of liability incurred by their officers while serving on other corporate boards (Outside Director Liability, or "ODL"); Employment Practices Liability or "EPL" coverage; coverage for spousal liability; and coverage for the liability of non-officer corporate counsel. The language of most policies already covers liability incurred by the corporate General Counsel if he or she is an officer of the corporation. Note also that D&O policies typically do not impose a duty to defend on the insurer. Rather, the insured controls its own defense and defense costs are covered as part of the insurer's indemnity obligation. To limit moral hazard (among other things), payments for defense costs erode the amount of indemnity coverage.

A number of distinctive coverage issues tend to arise under D&O policies. One is whether the insurer has a right to rescind the policy on the ground that there has been a misstatement on the application (note how the issue is handled by Paragraph XXI (D) of the Sample Policy (page 9)). Many securities suits involve allegations that the corporation's financial condition has been misrepresented to the public; it is not uncommon for the insurer to allege that similar misrepresentations have been included in the application for coverage. The law of misrepresentation that applies in these cases is the same law that was surveyed in Chapter One; there is no need to repeat it here. But it is worth noting that, with the corporate scandals that have occurred during the 21st century, much of the litigation in the field of misrepresentation involves D&O insurance policies. See, e.g., *In re Adelphia Commc'n Corp.*, 307 B.R. 404 (Bankr. S.D. N.Y. 2004); *Cutter & Buck, Inc. v. Genesis Ins. Co.*, 306 F.Supp.2d 988 (W.D. Wash. 2004). Related to misrepresentation is the question of severability. Does a misrepresentation by one insured (normally, the corporation) make the coverage afforded to the other insureds void or voidable (again, note the various ways in which the issue is handled under Paragraph XXI of the Sample Policy). In the absence of a provision preserving coverage for innocent insureds, their coverage is at risk. See, e.g., *TIG Ins. Co. of Michigan v. Homestore, Inc.*, 137 Cal.App. 4th 749 (2006) (permitting rescission as to innocent insureds). To avoid this issue, many recently-issued policies contain a provision expressly preserving coverage for non-misrepresentors.

Another issue involves the status of the policy when the corporation is in bankruptcy. Note that the main value of a D&O policy to individual directors and officers arises if the corporation is unable or unwilling to indemnify them. Aside from derivative suits, in which indemnificiation is prohibited, this often occurs because the corporation's assets are exhausted first by the prior claims of other creditors. Thus, it is in bankruptcy where a D&O policy may prove to be most valuable. But suppose that the corporation has purchased Side C coverage, then enters bankruptcy proceedings, and the creditors claiming that the corporation is liable to them for securities law violations argue that they should have prior claims to the coverage (under Side C) provided by the D&O policy? The courts have divided on the question whether the D&O policy proceeds are an asset of the bankrupt estate or of the individual directors and officers in this situation. See, e.g., *In re Laminate Kingdom, LLC*, 2008 WL 1766637 (Bankr. S.D. Fla. 2008) (proceeds of D&O policy do not qualify as assets of the bankrupt estate); *In re Metro. Mortg. & Sec. Co.*, 325 B.R. 851 (Bankr. E.D. Wash. 2005) (proceeds are assets of the bankrupt estate); *Nat'l Century Fin. Enters. v. Gulf Ins. Co.*, 2005 WL 6242169 (Bankr. S.D. Ohio 2005) (purpose of the policy is to protect the individual insureds). A frequently used method of dealing with this issue is for the corporation to purchase, in addition to its basic D&O insurance, freestanding or separate Side A coverage, which is accessible only by the insured individual directors and officers.

Some of the most important recent scholarship on D&O insurance is a series of articles by Tom Baker and Sean Griffith, detailing findings about the market, and about insurer and policyholder behavior in this field, based among other things on a series of confidential interviews with individuals working in the field. See Tom Baker & Sean J. Griffith, How the Merits Matter: Directors' and Officers' Insurance and Securities Settlements, 157 U. Pa. L. Rev. 755 (2009); The Missing Monitor in Corporate Governance: The Directors' and Officers' Liability Insurer, 95 Geo. L. J. 1795 (2007); Predicting Corporate Governance Risk: Evidence from the Directors and Officers' Insurance Market, 74 U. Chi. L. Rev. 487 (2007).

Beginning on the following pages is a Sample D&O Liability Insurance Policy, reprinted with the permission of the Chubb Insurance Company, a major writer of D&O insurance. Chubb requests us to say that "This specimen policy is provided for illustrative purposes only. The precise coverage afforded by any policy is subject to the terms and conditions of the policy as issued."

1. SAMPLE DIRECTORS AND OFFICERS POLICY

 Chubb Group of Insurance Companies
15 Mountain View Road
Warren, New Jersey 07059

The Chubb Primary
Directors & Officers and Entity
Securities Liability Insurance

DECLARATIONS

FEDERAL INSURANCE COMPANY
A stock insurance company, incorporated under the laws of Indiana, herein called the Company

Capital Center, 251 North Illinois, Suite 1100
Indianapolis, IN 46204-1927

Policy Number: [Formatted Policy Number]

NOTICE: THIS IS A CLAIMS MADE POLICY, WHICH APPLIES ONLY TO "CLAIMS" FIRST MADE DURING THE "POLICY PERIOD", INCLUDING ANY APPLICABLE EXTENDED REPORTING PERIOD. THE LIMIT OF LIABILITY TO PAY "LOSS" WILL BE REDUCED, AND MAY BE EXHAUSTED, BY "DEFENSE COSTS", AND "DEFENSE COSTS" SHALL BE APPLIED AGAINST THE RETENTION AMOUNT. THE COMPANY SHALL NOT BE LIABLE FOR "DEFENSE COSTS" OR THE AMOUNT OF ANY JUDGMENT OR SETTLEMENT UPON EXHAUSTION OF THE APPLICABLE LIMIT OF LIABILITY. READ THE ENTIRE POLICY CAREFULLY.

Item 1. **Parent Organization:**
[Account Name]
[Account Address including address1 and address2]
[Account City Name] , [Account Domicile State] [Account Zip Code]

Item 2. **Policy Period:** From: [Effective Date]
To: [Expiration Date of the Policy]
At 12:01 A.M local time at the address shown in Item 1.

Item 3. **Limit of Liability:**

Each **Policy Period:**   <BD&OABCAGGLMT>

Item 4. **Retentions:**

(A) Insuring Clause (A):   None

(B) Insuring Clause (B) (**Claims** other than **Securities Claims**):   <BD&OABCDED>

(C) Insuring Clauses (B) and (C) (**Securities Claims** only):   <BD&OABCDED2>

(D) Inquiry Coverage (A):   None

(E) Inquiry Coverage (B)(1):   None

(F) Inquiry Coverage (B)(2):   <BD&OINQDED>

item 5. **Extended Reporting Period:**

(A) Additional Period: [Discovery]

(B) Additional Premium: [Discovery]%

Item 6. **Pending or Prior**   <BNDTPPDPELP>
Proceedings Date:

14-02-18480D (03/2012)   Page 1 of 2
<NYFTZFOOTER><NYFTZNOTICE>

Chubb Group of Insurance Companies
15 Mountain View Road
Warren, New Jersey 07059

The Chubb Primary
*Directors & Officers and Entity
Securities Liability Insurance*

In witness whereof, the Company issuing this policy has caused this policy to be signed by its authorized officers, but it shall not be valid unless also signed by a duly authorized representative of the Company.

FEDERAL INSURANCE COMPANY

_____
Secretary

_____
President

04/09/2014
_____
Date

_____
Authorized Representative

SPECIMEN

14-02-18480D (03/2012)

Chubb Group of Insurance Companies
15 Mountain View Road
Warren, New Jersey 07059

The Chubb Primary
Directors & Officers and Entity Securities Liability Insurance

In consideration of payment of the premium and subject to the Declarations and the limitations, conditions, provisions and other terms of this Policy, the Company and the Insureds agree as follows:

I. INSURING CLAUSES

(A) Individual Non-Indemnified Liability Coverage

The Company shall pay, on behalf of an **Insured Person**, **Loss** on account of a **Claim** first made against the **Insured Person** during the **Policy Period**, except to the extent that such **Loss** has been paid or indemnified.

(B) Individual Indemnified Liability Coverage

The Company shall pay, on behalf of an **Organization**, **Loss** on account of a **Claim** first made against an **Insured Person** during the **Policy Period**, to the extent the **Organization** pays or indemnifies such **Loss**.

(C) Entity Securities Coverage

The Company shall pay, on behalf of an **Organization**, **Loss** on account of a **Securities Claim** first made against the **Organization** during the **Policy Period**.

II. INQUIRY COVERAGES

(A) Securityholder Derivative Demand Investigation Coverage

The Company shall pay, on behalf of an **Organization**, **Defense Costs** in an amount not to exceed $500,000 per **Policy Period** on account of all **Securityholder Derivative Demand Investigations** first made during the **Policy Period**, which amount is part of, and not in addition to, the Limit of Liability set forth in Item 3 of the Declarations.

(B) Interview Coverage

(1) The Company shall pay, on behalf of an **Insured Person**, **Defense Costs** incurred solely by such **Insured Person** on account of an **Interview** first made during the **Policy Period**, except to the extent that such **Defense Costs** have been paid or indemnified.

(2) The Company shall pay, on behalf of an **Organization**, **Defense Costs** incurred solely by an **Insured Person** on account of an **Interview** first made during the **Policy Period**, to the extent the **Organization** pays or indemnifies such **Defense Costs**.

III. EXCLUSIONS

The Company shall not be liable for **Loss** on account of any **Claim**:

(A) Prior Notice
based upon, arising from or in consequence of any fact, circumstance or **Wrongful Act** that was the subject of any notice accepted under any policy of which this Policy is a direct or indirect renewal or replacement;

Chubb Group of Insurance Companies
15 Mountain View Road
Warren, New Jersey 07059

The Chubb Primary
Directors & Officers and Entity Securities
Liability Insurance

(B) <u>Pending or Prior Proceedings</u>
based upon, arising from or in consequence of any written demand first received by, or action, proceeding, **Claim** or **Related Claim** commenced against, any **Insured** on or prior to the Pending or Prior Proceedings Date set forth in Item 6 of the Declarations;

(C) <u>Entity v. Insured</u>

(1) brought by, or on behalf of, an **Organization** against another **Organization**; or

(2) brought by, or on behalf of:

(a) an **Organization** against an **Insured Person**; or

(b) an **Outside Entity** against an **Insured Person** serving in his capacity as such for such **Outside Entity**,

provided that Paragraph (C)(2) above shall not apply to a **Claim** brought:

(i) outside the United States of America or Canada;

(ii) while the **Parent Organization** is in **Financial Impairment**;

(iii) against an **Insured Person** serving in his capacity as such for an **Outside Entity** while such **Outside Entity** is in **Financial Impairment**;

(iv) as a securityholder derivative action; or

(v) while such **Insured Person** is no longer serving in his capacity as such;

(D) <u>Bodily Injury/Violation of Right of Privacy/Property Damage</u>
for bodily injury, violation of any right of privacy, mental anguish, humiliation, emotional distress, sickness, disease or death of any person or damage to or destruction of any tangible property, including loss of use thereof, whether or not it is damaged or destroyed; provided that this Exclusion (D) shall not apply to any invasion of privacy, mental anguish, humiliation or emotional distress for which a claimant seeks compensation in an employment-related claim;

(E) <u>ERISA</u>
for any violation of the responsibilities, obligations or duties imposed by **ERISA**; or

(F) <u>Conduct</u>
based upon, arising from or in consequence of:

(1) any deliberate fraud, any criminal act, or any knowing and willful violation of any statute or regulation, by an **Insured**; or

(2) an **Insured** having gained any profit, remuneration or other advantage to which such **Insured** was not legally entitled,

established by a final, non-appealable adjudication in any underlying action or proceeding (other than a declaratory action or proceeding brought by or against the Company), provided that:

(a) no conduct pertaining to any **Insured Person** shall be imputed to any other **Insured Person**; and

(b) conduct pertaining to any past, present, or future chief financial officer, chief executive officer or chief operating officer (or an equivalent position to any of the foregoing worldwide) of an **Organization** shall be imputed to such **Organization** and its **Subsidiaries**.

Chubb Group of Insurance Companies
15 Mountain View Road
Warren, New Jersey 07059

The Chubb Primary
Directors & Officers and Entity Securities
Liability Insurance

IV. LIMIT OF LIABILITY

(A) The Company's maximum aggregate liability for all **Loss** shall be the Limit of Liability set forth in Item 3 of the Declarations, subject to any sublimits in this Policy.

(B) **Defense Costs** are part of, and not in addition to, the Limit of Liability set forth in Item 3 of the Declarations.

(C) The limit of liability available during the Extended Reporting Period, if applicable, shall be part of, and not in addition to, the Limit of Liability set forth in Item 3 of the Declarations.

V. RETENTION

(A) The Retentions shall apply as set forth in Item 4 of the Declarations and shall only apply to covered **Loss**.

(B) If different parts of a single **Claim** are subject to different Retentions, then the total amount of **Loss** applied to the applicable Retentions shall not exceed the largest applicable Retention.

(C) Any payment by an **Organization** of a Retention on account of an **Interview** shall reduce any Retention due from the **Organization** on account of a **Claim** subsequently afforded coverage under Insuring Clause (B), Individual Indemnified Liability Coverage, that is based upon, arising from or in consequence of any fact or circumstance that was the subject of such **Interview**.

VI. REPORTING

(A) The **Insureds** shall, as a condition precedent to exercising any right to coverage under this Policy, give to the Company written notice of any **Claim** no later than:

(1) one hundred and eighty (180) days after this Policy expires and is renewed with the Company; provided, however, if the **Parent Organization** can prove to the Company's satisfaction that it was not reasonably possible for the **Insureds** to give such notice within the one hundred and eighty (180) day time period and that subsequent notice was given as soon as reasonably possible thereafter, the Company shall waive the foregoing time period; or

(2) sixty (60) days after: (a) this Policy expires or terminates and is not renewed with the Company; or (b) the expiration date of the Extended Reporting Period, if applicable.

(B) If during the **Policy Period** an **Insured** gives written notice to the Company of:

(1) circumstances which could give rise to a **Claim**;

(2) receipt of a written request to toll or waive a statute of limitations applicable to a **Wrongful Act**; or

(3) an **Interview** or a **Securityholder Derivative Demand Investigation**,

then any **Claim** subsequently arising from the circumstances, **Wrongful Act**, **Interview** or **Securityholder Derivative Demand Investigation** described in Paragraph (B)(1) or (B)(2) or (B)(3) above shall be deemed to have been first made during the **Policy Period** in which such written notice was first given by an **Insured** to the Company; provided any such subsequent **Claim** is reported to the Company as soon as practicable after the in-house general counsel or risk manager of the **Parent Organization** becomes aware of such **Claim**.

14-02-18480 (06/2012)   Page 3 of 15

Chubb Group of Insurance Companies
15 Mountain View Road
Warren, New Jersey 07059

The Chubb Primary
Directors & Officers and Entity Securities
Liability Insurance

(C) The **Insured** shall give to the Company in any written notice described in Subsection (A) or (B) above a description of the **Claim**, circumstances, request to toll or waive a statute of limitations, **Interview** or **Securityholder Derivative Demand Investigation**, the nature of any alleged **Wrongful Acts**, the nature of the alleged or potential damage and the names of all actual or potential defendants.

VII. ADVANCEMENT OF DEFENSE COSTS

(A) The Company shall advance covered **Defense Costs** on account of a **Claim** reported pursuant to Section VI, Reporting, on a current basis after receipt by the Company of bills detailing such **Defense Costs** and all other information requested by the Company with respect to such bills until the applicable Limit of Liability set forth in Item 3 of the Declarations has been satisfied.

Furthermore, if an **Organization** refuses in writing, or fails within sixty (60) days of an **Insured Person's** written request for indemnification, to advance, pay or indemnify an **Insured Person** for **Loss** on account of a **Claim**, then, upon the reporting of the **Claim** pursuant to Section VI, Reporting, the Company shall advance covered **Defense Costs** until such time that the **Organization** accepts the **Insured Person's** request for indemnification or the applicable Limit of Liability set forth in Item 3 of the Declarations has been exhausted, whichever first occurs.

(B) Any advancement of **Defense Costs** shall be repaid to the Company by the **Insureds**, severally according to their respective interests, if and to the extent it is determined that such **Defense Costs** are not insured under this Policy. However, the Company shall not seek repayment from an **Insured** of advanced **Defense Costs** that are uninsured pursuant to Exclusion III(F), Conduct, unless a final, non-appealable adjudication has occurred.

(C) Any advancement of **Defense Costs** by the Company shall reduce the Limit of Liability set forth in Item 3 of the Declarations. If the Company recovers any such **Defense Costs** paid, the amount of such **Defense Costs** less all costs incurred by the Company to obtain such recovery shall be reinstated to the Limit of Liability set forth in Item 3 of the Declarations.

VIII. DEFENSE AND SETTLEMENT

(A) The **Insured**:

  (1) shall have the sole duty to defend **Claims** made against the **Insured**;

  (2) agrees not to settle or offer to settle any **Claim**, incur any **Defense Costs** or otherwise assume any contractual obligation or admit any liability with respect to any **Claim** without the Company's prior written consent, subject to Paragraph (A)(3) below;

  (3) may settle a **Claim** without the Company's prior consent if the **Claim** is reported pursuant to Section VI, Reporting, and the amount of such settlement and **Defense Costs** does not exceed the amount of the applicable Retention; and

  (4) agrees to provide the Company with all information, assistance and cooperation which the Company may reasonably require and agrees that, in the event of a **Claim**, the **Insured** shall not do anything that could prejudice the Company's position or its potential or actual rights of recovery; provided that the failure of any **Insured Person** to give the Company such information, assistance or cooperation shall not impair the rights of any other **Insured Person** under this Policy.

Chubb Group of Insurance Companies
15 Mountain View Road
Warren, New Jersey 07059

The Chubb Primary
Directors & Officers and Entity Securities
Liability Insurance

(B) The Company:

(1) shall have the right and shall be given the opportunity to effectively associate with the **Insured** and shall be consulted in advance by the **Insured**, regarding the investigation, defense and settlement of any **Claim** that appears reasonably likely to be covered in whole or in part under this Policy, including selecting appropriate defense counsel and negotiating any settlement;

(2) shall not be liable for any element of **Loss** incurred in excess of the amount of the applicable Retention, for any obligation assumed, or for any admission made, by any **Insured** without the Company's prior written consent, which the Company shall not unreasonably withhold; and

(3) may, in its sole discretion, waive the consent requirement in Paragraph (B)(2) above with respect to **Defense Costs** incurred within ninety (90) days prior to the reporting of a **Claim** pursuant to Section VI, Reporting.

IX. RELATED CLAIMS

All **Related Claims** shall be deemed a single **Claim** made in the **Policy Period** in which the earliest of such **Related Claims** was either first made or deemed to have been made in accordance with Section VI(B), Reporting.

X. ALLOCATION

The **Insureds** and the Company shall use their best efforts to determine an allocation between **Loss** that is covered and **Loss**, or any other amount, that is not covered based on the relative legal and financial exposures of the covered parties to the covered matters.

XI. PRIORITY OF PAYMENTS

(A) It is understood and agreed that any coverage provided under this Policy is principally intended to protect and benefit the **Insured Persons**. Accordingly, in the event that: (1) **Loss** for which an **Insured Person** has not been paid or indemnified; and (2) any other **Loss**, are concurrently due under this Policy, then the **Loss** described in (1) above shall be paid first.

(B) Except as otherwise provided in Subsection (A) above, the Company may pay covered **Loss** as it becomes due under this Policy without regard to the potential for other future payment obligations under this Policy.

XII. OTHER INSURANCE AND INDEMNITY

(A) If any **Loss** covered under this Policy is insured under any other valid and collectible insurance policy (other than an insurance policy that is issued specifically as excess over the Limits of Liability provided by this Policy or a personal umbrella policy or personal directorship liability policy purchased by an **Insured Person**), then this Policy shall cover such **Loss**, subject to its terms and conditions, only to the extent that the amount of such **Loss** is in excess of the applicable retention or deductible and limit of liability under such other insurance, whether such other insurance is stated to be primary, contributory, excess, contingent or otherwise.

14-02-18480 (06/2012)

Chubb Group of Insurance Companies
15 Mountain View Road
Warren, New Jersey 07059

The Chubb Primary
*Directors & Officers and Entity Securities
Liability Insurance*

(B) This Policy shall be specifically excess of, and shall not contribute with, any insurance policy for: third party liability coverage for environmental exposures, employment practices liability or professional liability.

(C) Any payment by an **Insured** of a retention or deductible under any other insurance policy described in Subsection (A) or (B) above shall reduce the applicable Retention under this Policy by the amount of such payment which would otherwise have been covered **Loss** under this Policy.

(D) Any coverage afforded under this Policy for a **Claim** in connection with an **Insured Person** serving in his capacity as such for an **Outside Entity** shall be specifically excess of any indemnity and insurance available to such **Insured Person** by, or on behalf of, such **Outside Entity**. Notwithstanding the foregoing, if the Company or any subsidiary or affiliate of The Chubb Corporation makes payment under another policy on account of such **Claim**, the Limit of Liability for this Policy with respect to such **Claim** shall be reduced by the amount of such payment.

XIII. INDEMNIFICATION AND SUBROGATION

(A) This Policy has been issued to the **Parent Organization** with the understanding and agreement that each **Organization** agrees to fulfill its indemnification obligations to each **Insured Person** to the fullest extent permitted by: (1) any United States law; and (2) any contract or agreement providing an indemnification obligation exceeding any such law. If the Company pays as **Loss** any indemnification owed to any **Insured Person** by any **Organization**, the Company does not waive or compromise any of its rights to recover such **Loss** from such **Organization**.

(B) In the event of any payment of **Loss** under this Policy, the Company shall be subrogated to the extent of such payment of **Loss** to all of the **Insureds**' rights of recovery, including any such right to indemnification from any **Organization**, **Outside Entity**, other insurer or other source. The **Insureds** shall take all reasonable actions to secure and preserve the Company's rights, including any action against any **Organization** for indemnification.

XIV. EXTENDED REPORTING PERIOD

(A) If this Policy does not renew or otherwise terminates for a reason other than for non-payment of premium (each a "Termination of Coverage"), then an **Insured** shall have the right to purchase the Extended Reporting Period for the Additional Period and Additional Premium set forth in Item 5 of the Declarations and the Extended Reporting Period shall become part of the **Policy Period**.

(B) The right to purchase the Extended Reporting Period shall lapse unless written notice of election to purchase the Extended Reporting Period, together with payment of the Additional Premium, is received by the Company within sixty (60) days after the effective date of a Termination of Coverage.

(C) If the Extended Reporting Period is purchased, then coverage otherwise afforded by this Policy shall be extended to apply to **Claims** that are:

(1) first made during the Extended Reporting Period;

(2) reported to the Company in accordance with Section VI, Reporting; and

(3) for **Wrongful Acts** before the effective date of a Termination of Coverage or the date of any conversion of coverage described in Section XVI, Acquisition of the Parent Organization, whichever first occurs.

Chubb Group of Insurance Companies
15 Mountain View Road
Warren, New Jersey 07059

The Chubb Primary
Directors & Officers and Entity Securities
Liability Insurance

(D) The Additional Premium for the Extended Reporting Period shall be deemed fully earned at the inception of the Extended Reporting Period.

(E) No coverage shall be available under this Section XIV for that portion of any **Claim**, **Securityholder Derivative Demand Investigation** or **Interview** covered under insurance purchased subsequent to the effective date of a Termination of Coverage.

XV. ACQUISITION OR CESSATION OF SUBSIDIARIES

(A) Acquisition of a Subsidiary

(1) If before or during the **Policy Period** an **Organization** acquires voting rights in another entity, such that the acquired entity becomes a **Subsidiary**, then such **Subsidiary** and the **Insured Persons** thereof, shall be **Insureds** only with respect to **Wrongful Acts** after such acquisition.

(2) If a **Subsidiary** is acquired during the **Policy Period** pursuant to Paragraph (1) above and the total assets of such **Subsidiary** exceed fifteen percent (15%) of the total assets of the **Parent Organization** (as reflected in the most recent audited consolidated financial statements of such **Subsidiary** and the **Parent Organization**, respectively, as of the date of such acquisition), the **Parent Organization** shall, no later than sixty (60) days after the date of such acquisition, give written notice of such acquisition to the Company together with all information the Company may require. Coverage for any such acquired **Subsidiary** and its **Insured Persons** shall be subject to additional or different terms and conditions and payment of additional premium.

If the **Parent Organization** fails to give such notice and information in accordance with the foregoing, coverage for such acquired **Subsidiary** and its **Insured Persons** shall terminate with respect to **Claims** first made more than sixty (60) days after such acquisition.

(B) Cessation of a Subsidiary

If before or during the **Policy Period** an **Organization** ceases to be a **Subsidiary**, then with respect to such **Subsidiary** and its **Insured Persons** coverage shall continue for **Claims** for **Wrongful Acts** while such **Organization** was a **Subsidiary** in accordance with either Section XVI, Acquisition of the Parent Organization, or Section XIX, Termination of Policy, whichever first occurs.

XVI. ACQUISITION OF THE PARENT ORGANIZATION

(A) If during the **Policy Period** the **Parent Organization** is acquired such that another entity, person or group of entities or persons acting in concert, acquires more than fifty percent (50%) of the outstanding securities representing the present right to vote for the election of directors or **LLC Managers** of the surviving entity, then:

(1) coverage under this Policy shall continue until the expiration of the current **Policy Period**, solely for **Claims** for **Wrongful Acts** prior to such acquisition; and

(2) the entire premium for this Policy shall be deemed fully earned as of the effective date of such acquisition.

(B) If the **Parent Organization** gives the Company written notice of an acquisition described in Subsection (A) above at least thirty (30) days prior to the date of such acquisition together with all information that the Company may require, the Company shall provide the **Parent Organization** with

Chubb Group of Insurance Companies
15 Mountain View Road
Warren, New Jersey 07059

The Chubb Primary
Directors & Officers and Entity Securities Liability Insurance

---

a quote for up to a six (6) year extension of coverage solely for **Claims** for **Wrongful Acts** prior to such acquisition (the "Run-Off Quote"). Coverage offered pursuant to the Run-Off Quote shall be subject to additional or different terms and conditions and payment of additional premium. If the **Parent Organization** accepts the Run-Off Quote, the extension of coverage provided pursuant to the Run-Off Quote shall replace any extension of coverage that would otherwise be available to the **Insureds** pursuant to Section XIV, Extended Reporting Period.

XVII. SPOUSES, DOMESTIC PARTNERS, ESTATES AND LEGAL REPRESENTATIVES

Coverage under this Policy shall extend to **Claims** for **Wrongful Acts** of an **Insured Person** made against:

(A) the estate, heirs, legal representatives or assigns of such **Insured Person** if such **Insured Person** is deceased or the legal representatives or the assigns of such **Insured Person** if such **Insured Person** is legally incompetent, insolvent or bankrupt; or

(B) the lawful spouse or domestic partner of such **Insured Person** solely by reason of such spouse's or domestic partner's: (1) status as a spouse or domestic partner; or (2) ownership interest in property which the claimant seeks as recovery for an alleged **Wrongful Act** of such **Insured Person**,

provided that, no coverage provided by this Section XVII shall apply with respect to loss arising from an act, error or omission by an **Insured Person's** estate, heirs, legal representatives, assigns, spouse or domestic partner.

XVIII. NOTICE

(A) All notices to the Company under this Policy of a **Claim**, circumstances which could give rise to a **Claim**, a written request to toll or waive a statute of limitations, a **Securityholder Derivative Demand Investigation** or an **Interview** shall be given in writing to one of the following addresses:

  (1) specialtyclaims@chubb.com;

  (2) Attn: Claims Department
  Chubb Group of Insurance Companies
  82 Hopmeadow St.- P.O. Box 2002
  Simsbury, CT 06070-7683; or

  (3) Attn: Claims Department
  Chubb Group of Insurance Companies
  82 Hopmeadow St.
  Simsbury, CT 06089.

(B) All other notices to the Company under this Policy shall be given in writing addressed to:

  Attn: Chubb Specialty Insurance Underwriting Department
  Chubb Group of Insurance Companies
  15 Mountain View Road
  Warren, New Jersey 07059.

(C) Any notice described in Subsection (A) or (B) above shall be effective on the date of receipt by the Company.

14-02-18480 (06/2012)

Chubb Group of Insurance Companies
15 Mountain View Road
Warren, New Jersey 07059

The Chubb Primary
Directors & Officers and Entity Securities
Liability Insurance

XIX. TERMINATION OF POLICY

This Policy shall terminate at the earliest of the following times:

(A) ten (10) days after receipt by the **Parent Organization** of written notice of termination from the Company for non-payment of premium;

(B) upon expiration of the **Policy Period**; or

(C) at such other time as may be agreed upon by the Company and the **Parent Organization**, in which case any returned premium shall be computed on a pro rata basis.

XX. BANKRUPTCY

(A) Bankruptcy or insolvency of any **Insured** shall not relieve the Company of its obligations nor deprive the Company of its rights or defenses under this Policy.

(B) In the event a liquidation or reorganization proceeding is commenced by or against an **Organization** under United States bankruptcy law, the **Organization** and the **Insured Persons** hereby agree not to oppose or object to any efforts by the Company, the **Organization** or an **Insured Person** to obtain relief from any stay or injunction.

XXI. REPRESENTATIONS AND SEVERABILITY

(A) The Company, in issuing this Policy, has relied upon the statements, representations and information in the **Application** as being true and accurate. The **Application** is the basis for, and considered incorporated into, this Policy and shall be construed as a separate request for coverage by each **Insured**.

(B) With respect to any statements, representations and information contained in the **Application**, no knowledge possessed by any **Insured Person** shall be imputed to any other **Insured Person**.

(C) If the **Application** contains any misrepresentations which were made with the actual intent to deceive or which materially affect the Company's acceptance of the risk or the hazard assumed, the Company shall not be liable for **Loss** on account of any **Claim** based upon, arising from, or in consequence of, any such misrepresentations under:

(1) Insuring Clause (A), Individual Non-Indemnified Liability Coverage, with respect to any **Insured Person** who had actual knowledge of the matters misrepresented;

(2) Insuring Clause (B), Individual Indemnified Liability Coverage, with respect to any **Organization** to the extent such **Organization** indemnifies any **Insured Person** who had actual knowledge of the matters misrepresented; or

(3) Insuring Clause (C), Entity Securities Coverage, with respect to any **Organization** if a past or present chief executive officer or chief financial officer of the **Parent Organization** had actual knowledge of the matters misrepresented.

(D) The Company shall not be entitled under any circumstances to void or rescind this Policy with respect to any **Insured**.

Chubb Group of Insurance Companies
15 Mountain View Road
Warren, New Jersey 07059

The Chubb Primary
Directors & Officers and Entity Securities
Liability Insurance

XXII. VALUATION AND FOREIGN CURRENCY

All premiums, limits, retentions, **Loss** and other amounts under this Policy are expressed and payable in the currency of the United States of America. Except as otherwise provided in this Policy, if a judgment is rendered, a settlement is denominated or any element of **Loss** under this Policy is stated in a currency other than United States of America dollars, payment under this Policy shall be made in United States of America dollars at the rate of exchange published in The Wall Street Journal on the date the judgment becomes final, the amount of the settlement is agreed upon or any element of **Loss** is due, respectively.

XXIII. ACTION AGAINST THE COMPANY

No action may be taken against the Company unless, as a condition precedent thereto, there shall have been full compliance with all the terms of this Policy. No person or entity shall have any right under this Policy to join the Company as a party to any action against any **Insured** to determine such **Insured's** liability nor shall the Company be impleaded by such **Insured** or legal representatives of such **Insured**.

XXIV. ROLE OF PARENT ORGANIZATION

By acceptance of this Policy, the **Parent Organization** agrees that it shall be considered the sole agent of, and shall act on behalf of, each **Insured** with respect to: (A) the payment of premiums and the receiving of return premiums that may become due under this Policy; (B) the negotiation, agreement to and acceptance of endorsements; and (C) the giving or receiving of any notice provided for in this Policy (except the giving of notice of a **Claim**, circumstances which could give rise to a **Claim**, a written request to toll or waive a statute of limitations, a **Securityholder Derivative Demand Investigation** or an **Interview** as provided in Section VI, Reporting, or the giving of notice to apply for an Extended Reporting Period as provided in Section XIV, Extended Reporting Period). Each **Insured** agrees that the **Parent Organization** shall act on its behalf with respect to all such matters.

XXV. ALTERATION AND ASSIGNMENT

No change in, modification of, or assignment of interest under, this Policy shall be effective except when made by written endorsement to this Policy which is signed by an authorized representative of the Company.

XXVI. WORLDWIDE TERRITORY AND APPLICATION OF LAW

(A) This Policy shall apply anywhere in the world.

(B) Any reference to United States law shall include:

   (1) United States federal, state and local statutory law and any rule or regulation promulgated thereunder;

   (2) United States common law; and

   (3) with respect to Paragraphs (B)(1) and (B)(2) above, any equivalent body of law anywhere in the world.

Chubb Group of Insurance Companies
15 Mountain View Road
Warren, New Jersey 07059

The Chubb Primary
Directors & Officers and Entity Securities Liability Insurance

(C) If the **Parent Organization** requests directors and officers liability policies for issuance to its foreign **Subsidiaries** in their own countries, the Company or a subsidiary or affiliate of The Chubb Corporation shall provide a quote to the **Parent Organization** for such policies; provided that the Company or a subsidiary or affiliate of The Chubb Corporation can support or facilitate the issuance of the policies to such foreign **Subsidiaries** in their applicable foreign countries. Any coordination of coverage under such policies with coverage under this Policy shall be set forth in an endorsement attached to this Policy.

XXVII. HEADINGS

The descriptions in the headings and sub-headings of this Policy are solely for convenience and form no part of the terms and conditions of coverage.

XXVIII. COMPLIANCE WITH APPLICABLE TRADE SANCTION LAWS

This insurance does not apply to the extent that any United States trade or economic sanctions law or any other similar United States law prohibits the Company from providing insurance.

XXIX. DEFINITIONS

When used in this Policy:

Application means:

(A) any application, including attachments, or any written information or representations, provided to the Company by, or on behalf of, an **Insured** during the negotiation of this Policy or for the purposes of the Company's underwriting of this Policy;

(B) all publicly available documents filed by an **Organization** with the Securities and Exchange Commission during the twelve (12) months preceding this Policy's inception date; and

(C) if applicable, any warranty provided to the Company within the past three (3) years in connection with any policy of which this Policy is a renewal or replacement.

Claim means any:

(A) written demand (other than a securityholder derivative demand) for:

(1) monetary or non-monetary (including injunctive) relief; or

(2) arbitration or mediation,

against an **Insured** for a **Wrongful Act**, commenced by the first receipt of such demand by an **Insured**;

(B) proceeding, including any appeal therefrom, against an **Insured** for a **Wrongful Act**, commenced by:

(1) the service of a civil complaint or similar pleading;

Chubb Group of Insurance Companies
15 Mountain View Road
Warren, New Jersey 07059

**The Chubb Primary
Directors & Officers and Entity Securities
Liability Insurance**

    (2) the filing of a notice of charges or the entry of a formal order of investigation in connection with a formal civil administrative or formal civil regulatory proceeding; provided that such proceeding is pending against at least one named **Insured Person**; or

    (3) solely with respect to a criminal proceeding: (a) an arrest; (b) the return of an indictment, information or similar document; or (c) the receipt of an official request for **Extradition**;

(C) investigation of an **Insured Person** for a **Wrongful Act**, commenced by the **Insured Person's** receipt of a written document from an **Enforcement Unit** identifying such **Insured Person** as the target of an investigation, including a Wells Notice, target letter or search warrant; or

(D) written request upon an **Insured Person** for witness testimony or document production, commenced by the service of a subpoena or other similar document compelling such testimony or production of documents in connection with any matter described in Subsections (A) through (C) above; provided that in such event the Company shall pay, on behalf of such **Insured Person**, **Defense Costs** incurred solely by such **Insured Person** in responding to such request.

Defense Costs means that part of **Loss** consisting of reasonable costs, charges, fees (including, attorneys' fees and experts' fees) and expenses (other than regular or overtime wages, salaries, fees or benefits of any **Insured Person**) incurred with the Company's prior written consent: (A) in investigating, defending, opposing or appealing any **Claim** and the premium for appeal, attachment or similar bonds; (B) in a **Securityholder Derivative Demand Investigation**; or (C) as a result of an **Interview**.

Enforcement Unit means any federal, state, local or provincial law enforcement or governmental regulatory authority worldwide (including the U.S. Department of Justice, the U.S. Securities and Exchange Commission and any attorney general) or the enforcement unit of any securities exchange or similar self-regulatory organization.

ERISA means the Employee Retirement Income Security Act of 1974 (including amendments relating to the Consolidated Omnibus Budget Reconciliation Act of 1985 and the Health Insurance Portability and Accountability Act of 1996), all as amended, or any similar United States law.

Extradition means any formal process by which an **Insured Person** located in any country is surrendered to any other country for trial or otherwise to answer any criminal accusation, including the execution of an arrest warrant where such execution is an element of such process.

Financial Impairment means the status of an **Organization** resulting from:

(A) the appointment by a state or federal official, agency or court of any receiver, conservator, liquidator, trustee, rehabilitator or similar official to take control of, supervise, manage or liquidate such **Organization**; or

(B) such **Organization** becoming a debtor in possession under United States bankruptcy law.

Insured means any **Organization** and any **Insured Person**.

Insured Person means any natural person who was, now is or shall become:

(A) a duly elected or appointed director, officer, **LLC Manager**, trustee, regent, governor, risk manager or the in-house general counsel of any **Organization** organized in the United States of America;

(B) a holder of an equivalent position to those described in Subsection (A) above in an **Organization** that is organized in a jurisdiction other than the United States of America;

14-02-18480 (06/2012)

Chubb Group of Insurance Companies
15 Mountain View Road
Warren, New Jersey 07059

The Chubb Primary
Directors & Officers and Entity Securities Liability Insurance

---

(C) a holder of an equivalent position to those described in Subsection (A) or (B) above in an **Outside Entity**, but solely while serving at the specific request or direction of the **Organization**; or

(D) solely with respect to **Securities Claims**, any other employee of an **Organization**.

Interview means a request for an interview or meeting with, or a sworn statement from, an **Insured Person** by:

(A) an **Enforcement Unit** in connection with: (1) such **Insured Person** acting in his capacity as such; or (2) an **Organization's** business activities; or

(B) an **Organization** in connection with: (1) an inquiry or investigation of the **Organization** by an **Enforcement Unit**; or (2) a securityholder derivative demand, commenced by the first receipt of such request by such **Insured Person**,

provided that **Interview** does not include: (a) any request for document production or discovery; (b) any request by an **Enforcement Unit** that is part of any routine or regularly scheduled **Enforcement Unit** oversight, compliance, audit, inspection or examination; or (c) any request by an **Enforcement Unit** that is part of an employment-related investigation or claim.

LLC Manager means any natural person who was, now is or shall become a manager, member of the Board of Managers or equivalent executive of an **Organization** that is a limited liability company.

Loss means the amount which any **Insured** becomes legally obligated to pay as a result of any **Claim**, **Securityholder Derivative Demand Investigation** or **Interview**, including:

(A) compensatory damages;

(B) punitive, exemplary or multiplied damages, if and to the extent that such damages are insurable under the law of the jurisdiction most favorable to the insurability of such damages; provided such jurisdiction has a substantial relationship to the relevant **Insureds**, to the Company, or to the **Claim** giving rise to such damages;

(C) civil fines or penalties assessed against an **Insured Person** for a violation of any United States law, including civil fines or penalties assessed pursuant to 15 U.S.C. §78dd-2(g)(2)(B) (the Foreign Corrupt Practices Act); provided that such violation is neither intentional nor willful and such fines or penalties are insurable under the law pursuant to which this Policy is construed;

(D) judgments, including pre-judgment and post-judgment interest;

(E) settlements; and

(F) **Defense Costs**;

Loss does not include any portion of such amount that constitutes any:

(1) cost incurred by the **Organization** to comply with any order for non-monetary (including injunctive) relief, or to comply with an agreement to provide such relief;

(2) amount not insurable under the law pursuant to which this Policy is construed; provided that the Company shall not assert that any amount attributable to violations of Sections 11, 12 or 15 of the Securities Act of 1933, as amended, is subject to this Paragraph (2), unless such amount is determined to be uninsurable in a final, non-appealable adjudication in any action or proceeding (other than a declaratory or equivalent action or proceeding brought by or against the Company);

14-02-18480 (06/2012)   Page 13 of 15

Chubb Group of Insurance Companies
15 Mountain View Road
Warren, New Jersey 07059

The Chubb Primary
Directors & Officers and Entity Securities
Liability Insurance

---

(3) amount that represents or is substantially equivalent to an increase in the consideration paid (or proposed to be paid) by an **Organization** in connection with its purchase of any securities or assets;

(4) tax; except, solely for the purposes of Insuring Clause (A), Individual Non-Indemnified Liability Coverage, any tax imposed upon an **Insured Person** in his capacity as such in connection with any bankruptcy, receivership, conservatorship, or liquidation of an **Organization**, to the extent that such tax is insurable under the law pursuant to which this Policy is construed;

(5) fine or penalty, except as provided in Subsection (B) or (C) above; or

(6) cost incurred in cleaning-up, removing, containing, treating, detoxifying, neutralizing, assessing the effects of, testing for or monitoring **Pollutants**.

Organization means the **Parent Organization** and any **Subsidiary**. **Organization** shall also mean any such entity as a debtor in possession under United States bankruptcy law.

Outside Entity means:

(A) any non-profit corporation, community chest, fund or foundation that is exempt from federal income tax as an entity described in Section 501(c)(3) of the United States Internal Revenue Code, as amended; or

(B) any other entity specifically added as an **Outside Entity** by written endorsement attached to this Policy,

that is not an **Organization**.

Parent Organization means the entity named in Item 1 of the Declarations.

Policy Period means the period of time set forth in Item 2 of the Declarations (subject to any termination in accordance with Section XIX, Termination of Policy) and the Extended Reporting Period, if applicable.

Pollutants means any solid, liquid, gaseous or thermal irritants or contaminants, including smoke, vapor, soot, fumes, acids, alkalis, chemicals, asbestos, asbestos products or waste. Waste includes materials to be recycled, reconditioned or reclaimed.

Related Claims means all **Claims** based upon, arising from or in consequence of the same or related facts, circumstances or **Wrongful Acts**.

Securities Claim means a **Claim**:

(A) against an **Insured** for a violation of any United States securities law, but solely in connection with the securities of an **Organization**;

(B) against an **Insured** for a common law cause of action, pled in tandem with, or in lieu of, any securities law violation described in Subsection (A) above and brought by:

(1) a securityholder of an **Organization** with respect to his interest in the securities of such **Organization**; or

(2) any person or entity in connection with the purchase, sale or offer to purchase or sell securities of an **Organization**; or

Chubb Group of Insurance Companies
15 Mountain View Road
Warren, New Jersey 07059

The Chubb Primary
Directors & Officers and Entity Securities
Liability Insurance

(C) brought as a derivative action, on behalf of an **Organization** against an **Insured Person**, including an action brought by or on behalf of the **Organization** seeking to dismiss a derivative action that a committee of such **Organization's** Board of Directors has concluded is not in the best interest of the **Organization**.

Securityholder Derivative Demand Investigation means an investigation by an **Organization** to determine whether it is in the best interest of such **Organization** to prosecute the claims alleged in a securityholder derivative demand or action, commenced upon:

(A) receipt of such demand; or

(B) service of a civil complaint or similar proceeding with respect to such action.

Subsidiary means:

(A) any entity while more than fifty percent (50%) of the outstanding securities or other equity ownership, representing the present right to vote for election of, or to appoint, directors, **LLC Managers**, or the foreign equivalent of any such directors or **LLC Managers** of such entity, are owned or controlled by the **Parent Organization** directly or indirectly through one or more **Subsidiaries**; or

(B) any entity while the **Parent Organization** has the right, pursuant to either written contract or the by-laws, charter, operating agreement or similar documents of an **Organization**, to elect or appoint a majority of the Board of Directors of a corporation or **LLC Managers**.

Wrongful Act means:

(A) any error, misstatement, misleading statement, act, omission, neglect, or breach of duty committed, attempted, or allegedly committed or attempted by: (1) an **Insured Person** in his capacity as such; or (2) for purposes of any coverage afforded under Insuring Clause (C), Entity Securities Coverage, by the **Organization**; or

(B) any other matter claimed against an **Insured Person** solely by reason of serving in his capacity as such.

14-02-18480 (06/2012)

2. SELECTED CLAIMS-MADE EXCLUSIONS AND CONDITIONS

The important subjects of litigation regarding claims-made policies typically involve the scope and application of the exclusions and conditions in these policies. A number of these are addressed in the following cases.

Alstrin v. St. Paul Mercury Insurance Company
United States District Court, Delaware, 2002.
179 F.Supp.2d 376.

■ MCKELVIE, DISTRICT JUDGE.

This is a dispute over directors and officers insurance coverage for liabilities in connection with a securities class action lawsuit and related bankruptcy adversary proceedings. The plaintiffs in this insurance coverage dispute, J. Christopher Alstrin, Melvin Pearl, Jeffrey Taylor, Bruce Taylor, and Sidney Taylor (collectively, "the D&O plaintiffs") are former officers and directors of the Cole Taylor Financial Group, Inc. . . . They are also among the defendants in a securities class action and in related adversary proceedings brought by the Estate Representative of the company, which is now a Chapter 11 Debtor. * * *

The D&O plaintiffs seek coverage from National Union under the D&O insurance policy for two groups of claims. First, they seek coverage for liabilities arising from the consolidated shareholder class actions brought before this court that principally assert violations of the federal securities laws. Second, plaintiffs seek coverage for the liabilities arising from the claims filed by the Estate Representative in the two adversary proceedings that have also been consolidated before this court. These lawsuits assert claims for fraudulent conveyance and breach of fiduciary duty. * * *

The court will next address the portions of the D&O plaintiffs' motion relating to the policy form exclusions 4(a), (c), (d), and (i). These exclusions are contained in section 4 of the pre-printed insurance policy form that is part of the National Union policy. * * * Plaintiffs argue that each of the exclusions does not apply to the claims at issue as a matter of law and contend that National Union attempts to interpret its exclusions so as to swallow up the very coverage the policy purports to offer. * * *

2. Does the Plain Language of the Section 4 Exclusions Preclude National Union from Denying Coverage?

Plaintiffs next contend that the plain language of each of the four exclusions indicates that it does not apply to the claims for which plaintiffs seek coverage. National Union contends that summary judgment is improper because there remain disputed issues of material fact with respect to each exclusion.

a. *Exclusion 4(c): crime or deliberate fraud*

Exclusion 4(c) excludes claims "arising out of, based upon or attributable to the committing in fact of any criminal or deliberate fraud." Plaintiffs contend that this provision cannot be read so broadly as to cover securities fraud, because the policy purports to cover "Securities Claims" and exclusions should not be read to override an explicit grant of coverage.

National Union asserts in its opposing brief that there is an issue of fact in the Reliance Securities Litigation as to whether various CTFG directors, including some of the D&O plaintiffs, acted with the requisite scienter for the purpose of section 10(b) liability. National Union also takes issue with the plaintiffs' contention that this exclusion renders its coverage for securities claims illusory and sets forth two reasons why it believes the exclusion can be consistent with its coverage for securities claims. First, there can be a violation of the federal securities laws without a finding of criminal or deliberate fraudulent intent. * * * Therefore, a policy can cover a number of securities fraud claims while still providing an exclusion for claims that arise out of "deliberate fraudulent intent." Second, there must be a judicial determination of deliberate fraudulent conduct before 4(c) is available to bar coverage under the policy. Thus, National Union explains, exclusion 4(c) may not be used to deny coverage for legal fees and expenses associated with defending a claim otherwise covered by the policy. *See National Union Fire Ins. Co. v. Continental Ill. Corp.,* 666 F.Supp. 1180, 1197–98 (N.D.Ill.1987).

In order to evaluate the parties' positions, the court must first review the relevant portions of the National Union policy coverage grant. The coverage grant in the insuring agreement purports to cover all loss "arising from a Claim." The term "claim" is defined within to include "a civil, criminal, or administrative proceeding for monetary or on monetary relief." The definition of "claim" then adds that:

> the term "Claim" shall include a "Securities Claim"; provided, however, that with respect to Coverage B(i) [entity coverage] only, Claim or Securities Claim shall not mean a criminal or administrative proceeding against the Company.

A "Securities Claim" is defined as:

> a Claim made against the insured that alleges a violation of the Securities Act of 1933 or the Securities Exchange Act of 1934 . . . which alleges a Wrongful Act in connection with the claimant's purchase or sale of, or the offer to purchase or sell to the claimant, any securities of the Company, whether on the open market or arising from a public or private offering of securities by the Company.

"Wrongful Act" is defined as "any breach of duty, neglect, error, misstatement, misleading statement, omission, or act by the Directors and Officers of the Company in their respective capacities as such. . . ." Thus, according to the definitions set forth in the policy, the National Union policy provides an explicit and broad grant of coverage for securities fraud claims. With respect to individual officers and directors, the securities fraud coverage includes even criminal proceedings commenced by indictment.

Given that the National Union policy explicitly covers securities fraud claims, the issue before the court is whether exclusion 4(c), which excludes claims "arising out of, based upon or attributable to the committing in fact of any criminal or deliberate fraud," can be properly

construed to exclude coverage for securities fraud claims. The D&O plaintiffs argue that it cannot and submit that if exclusion 4(c) it is so interpreted it will directly conflict with the coverage grant of the policy. The D&O plaintiffs reason that when one provision of an insurance policy appears to cancel coverage provided for in another provision, this creates an ambiguity that must be construed in favor of the insured.
* * *

In response, National Union argues that securities fraud coverage would not be eliminated by the deliberate fraud exclusion because certain securities fraud claims can be sustained based on recklessness or negligence, and exclusion 4(c) only applies to "deliberate fraud." In the face of the National Union policy's broad coverage for securities claims under both the '33 Act and '34 Act, the court finds National Union's argument unconvincing. In essence, National Union is suggesting that where the policy states that it provides coverage for securities claims under the '33 and '34 Acts, it actually only provides coverage for those claims that are based on reckless or negligent behavior. The fact that some limited amount of coverage might survive the intentional act exclusion is not sufficient grounds to apply an exclusion that is irreconcilable with the coverage grant itself, because no one purchasing a policy that provides coverage for securities claims under the '33 and '34 Acts would intend to purchase such restricted coverage. *See Imperial Cas. and Indem.,* 714 A.2d at 1238 (rejecting interpretation that would only cover non-intentional torts); *Davidson v. Cincinnati Ins. Co.,* 572 N.E.2d 502, 508 (Ind.App.1991) (holding that intentional act exclusion did not apply to slander and malicious prosecution coverage, even though such claims might be based on reckless behavior, because "most cases involving malicious prosecution and slander are a result of an intentional wrongdoing"). Even though certain securities claims do not require intentional misconduct, applying the intentional fraud exclusion to the securities coverage at issue would eviscerate coverage for the majority of securities claims.

If the deliberate fraud exclusion applied to securities claims, there would be little or nothing left to that coverage. Particularly, in a D&O insurance policy, where securities fraud claims are among the most common claims filed against directors and officers, the effect of such an exclusion would be particularly devastating. No insured would expect such limited coverage from a policy that purports to cover all types of securities fraud claims. *See Steigler,* 384 A.2d at 401 (holding that insurance contract should be read "to accord with the reasonable expectations of the purchaser"). Accordingly, the court finds that exclusion 4(c) may not be relied upon by National Union to defeat coverage for the claims asserted by the D&O plaintiffs and will grant summary judgment in favor of the D&O plaintiffs on National Union's Separate Defense 7.

b. *Exclusion 4(a): illegal profit or advantage*

Exclusion 4(a) excludes claims "arising out of, based upon or attributable to the gaining in fact of any profit or advantage to which an insured was not legally entitled." To invoke this exclusion, plaintiffs assert that National Union must first show that there are allegations of an insured gaining illegal profit or advantage and then National Union must prove that such illegal profit or gain actually occurred. *See*

National Union Fire Ins. Co. of Pittsburgh, 666 F.Supp. at 1199 (noting that claims are "not 'based on or attributable to' certain conduct unless they *allege* such conduct"). Furthermore, National Union must prove this separately for each insured because the policy provides that "the Wrongful Act of a Director or Officer shall not be imputed to any other Director or Officer."

With respect to the class action securities claim and Estate Representative's breach of fiduciary duty claims, plaintiffs contend that there are no allegations that their profit or gain itself was illegal. Rather, the "illegal" conduct that is alleged is the dissemination of false or misleading disclosures in violation of federal securities laws. With respect to the Estate Representative's fraudulent transfer claims, while conceding that these claims fall within the scope of the illegal profit or gain exclusion, the plaintiffs contend that National Union must prove these claims on the merits. Plaintiffs also argue, as they did above in opposing exclusion 4(c), that if the exclusion is given the broad construction sought by National Union, then the exclusion eviscerates the very coverage that the policy was purchased to provide, because plaintiffs allege in virtually all securities fraud claims that the offending directors and officers secured some gain from their unlawful conduct. * * *

The court's analysis necessarily begins with the language of the exclusion at issue. Exclusion 4(a) excludes claims "arising out of, based upon or attributable to the gaining in fact of any profit or advantage to which an insured was not legally entitled." As plaintiffs correctly note, the successful invocation of this exclusion requires National Union to identify allegations in the complaints that allege that the D&O plaintiffs gained "any profit or advantage to which [they] were not entitled." *See id.* While National Union characterizes the allegations in the Graham complaint as alleging that "the Taylor family defendants obtained the Cole Taylor Bank by issuing false and misleading statements regarding the financial condition of CTFG . . . ," without identifying a specific allegation, the exclusion at issue requires the court to more carefully examine the allegations in the complaint to determine if they contained any allegation that the D&O plaintiffs obtained an illegal profit or gain.

Paragraphs 128 and 129 of the securities class action complaint state that the false or misleading representations regarding the financial condition of RAG,

> inflated the price of Reliance's common stock and the value of the defendant's personal holdings, and permitted defendants to protect and enhance their executive positions and substantially increase their compensation. These falsehoods permitted the Taylor family defendants and their allies Tinsberg, Pearl, Dougherty, and Alstrin to convince the majority of shareholders to vote to approve the transaction in which the Taylor's took the valuable bank subsidiary while the other shareholders received ownership of the subprime subsidiary, which was virtually worthless.

Similarly, the Estate Representative's adversary proceeding complaint alleges that the Taylor defendants "looted the Company of its only valuable assets and [ ] managed and operated the Company principally for their own benefit," detailing that:

> Once the Taylors understood the severity of the problems that their own program of unrestrained growth had engendered, they began to develop an alternative, whereby, in hope of extricating themselves from RAC's financial morass, they would buy CT Bank and CT Mortgage with their own RAG common stock and leave existing shareholders with a greater percentage ownership interests in the resultant worthless enterprise. This alternative came to be known as the Split-Off [Transaction].

As previously noted, the underlying causes of action alleged in the securities case were violations of §§ 10(b), 14(a), and 20(a) of the Exchange Act of 1934 and breach of fiduciary duty. The Estate Representative's complaint also alleged a breach of fiduciary duty. The court finds that while the allegations detailed above state that as a result of the D&O plaintiffs fraudulent conduct the Taylor family benefitted from the split-off transaction, they fail to allege that the D&O plaintiffs' profit or gain was itself illegal and do not seek disgorgement of illegal profit or gain. This is what is required for exclusion 4(a), which excludes claims "arising out of, based upon or attributable to" the gaining of profit to which the D & O is not legally entitled. Exclusion 4(a), by its terms, requires a profit or gain that is illegal; not an illegal act that produces a profit or gain to the insured as a by-product. This exclusion, therefore, would be applicable in cases of theft, such as insider trading, but is inapplicable to illegalities such as securities misrepresentation to which a private gain might be incidental. While the securities complaint arguably alleges that the financial benefit to the Taylor defendants was a reason for their conduct, the only illegalities alleged are false and misleading disclosures in violation of the federal securities law. The "illegal" conduct is the alleged dissemination of false information. Similarly, the breach of fiduciary duty claim alleges that the Taylor's breached their duty of loyalty to the company in the manner in which they ran the company and in various actions concerning the split-off transaction. The alleged "illegal" conduct is the breach of this duty; not the incidental gains therefrom.

Almost all securities fraud complaints will allege that the defendants did what they did in order to benefit themselves in some way. If such an allegation were sufficient to invoke the protections of 4(a), the broad coverage for "Securities Claims" provided by the National Union policy would be rendered valueless by this exclusion. The proper inquiry, therefore, must focus not only on the factual allegations, but on the elements of the causes of action that are alleged. If an element of the cause of action that must be proved requires that the insured gained a profit or advantage to which he was not legally entitled, then, if proved, this exclusion would be applicable. That is not the case here. * * *

Accordingly, the court finds that exclusion 4(a) may not be relied upon by National Union to defeat coverage for the claims asserted by the D&O plaintiffs for coverage for securities claims and breach of fiduciary duty and will grant partial summary judgment in favor of the

D&O plaintiffs on National Union's Separate Defense 6. However, with respect to the fraudulent transfer claims, the court finds that the D&O plaintiffs have failed to meet their burden on summary judgment. National Union, should it be able to use the facts developed during discovery to prove that the allegations of fraudulent transfer are true, could rely on exclusion 4(a) to deny coverage. The court will deny the D&O plaintiffs motion for partial summary judgment on this portion of National Union's Separate Defense 6. * * *

d. *Exclusion 4(i): insured v. insured*

Exclusion 4(i), the insured v. insured exclusion, excludes from coverage any claim made against an Insured "which is brought by any Insured or by the Company...." With respect to exclusion 4(i), the plaintiffs rely on the briefing in prior summary judgment motions submitted by the Estate Representative. In those briefs, the Estate Representative argues that exclusion 4(i) does not apply to bar coverage with respect to claims that the Estate Representative has asserted against the plaintiffs because the RAG Estate Representative is not the "Insured" within the meaning of exclusion 4(i). While RAG was the debtor-in-possession at the time the plaintiffs originally filed this action on May 28, 1998, under Bankruptcy Rule 2012(a), once the Estate Representative was appointed, "the debtor-in-possession" ceases to exist and the Estate Representative is deemed automatically substituted for the debtor-in-possession "as a party in any pending action, proceeding, or matter." *In re TS Indus., Inc.,* 125 B.R. 638, 641 (Bankr.D.Utah 1991).

National Union also relies on its earlier briefing and that of the other insurance companies with respect to this exclusion and asserts that this exclusion is applicable to the claims that have been interposed by the Estate Representative against the former directors and officers of RAG because the RAG Estate shares identity with RAG, the Insured.

The court agrees with the D&O plaintiffs and the Estate Representative that the "insured v. insured" exclusion should not apply to claims brought by a bankruptcy Estate Representative against the former directors and officers of the Debtor where the Debtor is the insured entity, because the Debtor's Estate Representative (the RAG Estate) and the Debtor (RAG) are separate entities. *See In re Buckeye Countrymark, Inc.,* 251 B.R. 835 (Bkrtcy.S.D.Ohio 2000); *Pintlar Corp. v. Fidelity and Cas. Co. of N.Y. (In re Pintlar Corp.),* 205 B.R. 945 (Bankr.D.Idaho 1997); *but see Reliance Co. of Illinois v. Weis,* 148 B.R. 575, 581–82 (E.D.Mo.1992) (finding identity between estate and Debtor in evaluating applicability of an insured v. insured provision because claims could have been brought by the company).

In *In re Buckeye,* the court rejected an argument that claims for breach of fiduciary duties brought by a bankruptcy trustee against the debtor's former officers and directors were barred by an insured v. insured provision that excluded claims brought "by" or "on behalf of" the Debtor against its directors, officers, and managers. The court finds the reasoning of *Buckeye* particularly applicable to its explain why it now determines that the claims made by the Estate Representative against the D&O plaintiffs in this case do not fall within the National Union policy's insured v. insured exclusion. Simply put, the court finds that claims brought "by" the Estate Representative are not the same as claims brought "by" the Debtor under the exclusionary provision. As the *Buckeye* court explained:

> the very purpose of the an "insured v. insured" exclusion does not apply to adversarial claims brought by the Trustee against the Debtor's directors and officers and managers. The intent behind the "insured v. insured" exclusion in a [D&O] Policy is to protect the insurance companies against collusive suits between the insured corporation and its insured officers and directors. [citation omitted] When the plaintiff is not the corporation but a bankruptcy trustee acting as a genuinely adverse party to the defendant officers and directors, there is no threat of collusion. 251 B.R. at 840–41.

Here, there is no collusion between the Estate Representative and the D&O plaintiffs. While it is true that the company itself could have brought such claims against its directors and officers, the Estate's claims are asserted on behalf of the Debtor's creditors and not on behalf of the Debtor itself. Thus, the Estate Representative is acting as a genuinely adverse party to the Debtor's former directors and officers.

National Union argues that reliance on cases such as *Buckeye*, which examine the intent behind insured v. insured provisions, is misplaced because the intent behind a provision should not be examined unless an ambiguity is found. Courts, however, are required to interpret the language of a contract in such a way as to give effect to the intention of the parties at the time the agreement was entered into. The court, here, has not varied the plain language of the agreement, but rather, in determining that the Estate is not the Debtor, has resolved the insured v. insured dispute by determining that due to the status of the Debtor Estate, the adversary proceeding claims do not fall within the plain language of the exclusion. Accordingly, the court finds that exclusion 4(i) may not be relied upon by National Union to defeat coverage for the claims asserted by the D&O plaintiffs and will grant summary judgment in favor of the D&O plaintiffs on National Union's Separate Defense 11.

NOTES AND QUESTIONS

1. *Illusory Coverage?* Would coverage of securities liability have been as illusory as the court suggested if it were limited in the way that National Union argued? Do insureds reasonably expect coverage of liability for the consequences of criminal or deliberately fraudulent conduct? A number of policies have attempted to resolve this dilemma by excluding coverage of liability for "adjudicated" fraud. See, e.g., Paragraph III (F)(1) of the Sample Policy (page 2); *AT&T v. Clarendon Am. Ins. Co.*, 2008 WL 2583007 (Del. Super. Ct. 2008) (holding that the policy required adjudication); *PMI Mortg. Ins. Co. v. Am. Int'l Specialty Lines Ins. Co.*, 2006 WL 825266 (N.D. Cal. 2006) (in the absence of an express provision requiring adjudicated fraud, requiring only proof of "evidentiary facts supporting a criminal or fraudulent act"). In doing so, they afford coverage for the cost of settling what policyholders may regard as groundless claims for fraud—coverage that they probably do reasonably expect. On the other hand, such coverage creates incentives to settle suits that might otherwise be litigated, precisely in order to preserve coverage, and may thus act as a magnet for securities suits.

2. *Illegal Profit or Advantage.* As the court noted, certain securities claims (as well as certain common law actions against directors and officers) seek what amounts to restitution, through disgorgement of ill-gotten gains or profits. The dominant rule appears to be that this form of liability is not covered. The seminal case on the issue is *Level 3 Commcns. v. Fed. Ins. Co.*, 272 F.3d 908 (7th Cir. 2001). Can you articulate the argument for such a rule? How does the Sample Policy handle this issue in Paragraph III (F)(2) (page 2)?

3. *The Insured v. Insured Exclusion.* As the court indicated, the underlying purpose behind this exclusion is to preclude collusive suits, in which the corporation (an insured) sues directors or officers alleging that they made a negligent or reckless decision that resulted in the loss of corporate profits. The exclusion arose in the 1980's after a number of cases in which insurers felt victimized by what they thought were unjustified but apparently-covered claims. Note that the exclusion typically makes an exception (among other thing) for shareholder derivative suits, which are brought in the name of the corporation and would therefore otherwise be subject to the exclusion. Sometimes the particular role that the former officer or director played in bringing the suit makes a difference. For example, in *Sphinx International, Inc. v. National Union Fire Insurance Co. of Pittsburgh, Pennsylvania*, 412 F.3d 1224 (11th Cir. 2005), the exclusion was applied to preclude coverage of a suit brought by a group of shareholders who had been solicited to bring suit along with a former director. But in *Federal Insurance Co. v. Infoglide Corp.*, 2006 WL 2050694 (W.D. Tex. 2006), the exclusion was held to be inapplicable to a suit brought by former officers and several additional parties. The court distinguished *Sphinx* on the ground that the suit in that case had been brought "at the behest" of the former director.

There are dozens of decisions holding that the insured v. insured exclusion is to be applied as it is written, without inquiry into whether the suit in question is or is not collusive. See, e.g., *Am. Med. Int'l, Inc. v. Nat'l Union Fire Ins. Co.*, 244 F.3d 715 (9th Cir. 2001); *Finci v. Am. Cas. Co.*, 593 A.2d 1069 (Md. 1991). However, there are also a number of decisions that look behind the language to the purpose of the exclusion, as the court did in *Alstrin*. See, e.g., *Fidelity & Deposit Co. of Maryland v. Zandstra*, 756 F.Supp. 429 (N.D. Cal. 1990). Depending on the breadth of the exclusion, in some situations its literal application can prove to be contrary to policyholders' reasonable expectations and/or to the underlying purpose of the exclusion. Paragraph III (C) of the Sample Policy (page 2) is more favorable to policyholders than many of the provisions that are at issue in the reported cases. For example, most policies define a "director" or "officer" to include any past director or officer (so as to ensure that former directors and officers are covered under claims-made policies issued after they leave office). Further, some policies exclude coverage not only of suits by one insured against another, but also of suits brought with the participation or assistance of an insured. The result is that derivative suits brought by plaintiffs who are aided by a disgruntled former director or officer and that are obviously not collusive may nonetheless threaten to deprive current directors and officers of coverage that they can reasonably expect. See, e.g., *Harris v. Gulf Ins. Co.*, 297 F.Supp.2d 1220 (N.D. Cal. 2003) (declining to apply the exclusion literally under these circumstances). If you were negotiating on behalf of a corporation purchasing D&O coverage, how would you propose to modify the insured v. insured exclusion in order to take into account the concerns of both the insurer and the individual directors and officers?

A recurring issue is whether the insured v. insured exclusion applies to suits brought by bankruptcy trustees or receivers. For relatively recent cases holding that the exclusion does not apply to such parties, *Unified Western Grocers v. Twin City Fire Insurance Co.*, 457 F.3d 1106 (9th Cir. 2006); *Rigby v. Underwriters at Lloyds, London*, 907 So. 2d 1187 (Fla. Dist. Ct. App. 2005).

Federal Insurance Company v. Raytheon Company

United States Court of Appeals, First Circuit, 2005.
426 F.3d 491.

■ DYK, CIRCUIT JUDGE.

This is an insurance coverage dispute. On May 19, 2003, a class action was filed against Raytheon Company ("Raytheon") under the Employee Retirement Income Security Act of 1974 ("the ERISA action"). At that time, Raytheon was insured under a liability insurance policy issued by Federal Insurance Company ("Federal") and an excess policy issued by Axis Surplus Insurance Company ("Axis"). Raytheon requested coverage from the insurers. In response, the insurers filed suits for declaratory judgment of non-coverage, invoking the district court's diversity jurisdiction. The insurers contended that the ERISA action was excluded from coverage under the pending and prior litigation exclusions of the policies because there were overlapping allegations between the ERISA action and an earlier securities lawsuit brought against Raytheon in 1999, before the effective dates of the policies. The district court held that coverage was excluded under the prior and pending litigation exclusion clauses of both policies. We hold that coverage for both insurers is excluded under the Federal policy. We accordingly affirm the judgment of the district court. * * *

Raytheon provides products and services in the areas of defense and commercial electronics. It is a public company listed on the New York Stock Exchange. On October 12, 1999, the Wall Street Journal published an article reporting that Raytheon, unbeknownst to investors, experienced cost overruns and was behind schedule on many defense-related contracts. Later that day, Raytheon reported one-off charges totaling $638 million and reduced earnings expectations. The charges and reduced earnings forecast caused a sharp decline in Raytheon's stock price.

On October 19, 1999, a class action invoking section 10 the Securities Exchange Act of 1934, 15 U.S.C. § 78j (2000), and Rule 10b–5, 17 C.F.R. § 240.10b–5 (2005), was filed in the District of Massachusetts against Raytheon and several of its senior officers ("the Securities action"). *In re Raytheon Co. Sec. Litig.*, No. 99–CV–12142 (D. Mass. June 12, 2000) (amended complaint). The lead plaintiff was the New York State Common Retirement Fund, which sought to represent a class of persons who purchased Raytheon stock from October 7, 1998, to October 12, 1999 (the date of the Wall Street Journal article). The complaint in the Securities action alleged that during the class period, Raytheon issued materially false and misleading statements regarding its financial performance. Briefly, the Securities complaint alleged that

(1) Raytheon's Engineering & Constructors division ("RE & C") failed to disclose losses on major contracts; (2) RE & C misleadingly reported revenues on existing and anticipated contracts; (3) Raytheon failed to disclose that projects relating to the P–3 Orion aircraft and other defense equipment were over budget and behind schedule; and (4) Raytheon failed to disclose that the Joint Primary Aircraft Training System was over budget and behind schedule. The Securities action apparently settled in December 2004.

In May 2003 a second class action was filed against Raytheon and several of its officers and employees in the District of Massachusetts, this time based on the Employee Retirement Income Security Act of 1974, 29 U.S.C. § 1001 *et seq. In re Raytheon ERISA Litig.*, No. 03–CV–10940 (D.Mass. Apr. 20, 2004) (amended complaint). The lead plaintiffs were Benjamin Wall and Joseph Duggan III, former Raytheon employees who sought to represent a class of persons who were participants in or beneficiaries of Raytheon's Savings and Investment Plan (the "Plan") at any time between October 7, 1998, and date of the complaint. In contrast to the Securities complaint, the ERISA complaint alleged that the defendants were ERISA fiduciaries of the Plan; that the defendants regularly communicated to Plan participants during the all relevant times; and that the defendants had financial interests tied to the Raytheon stock price at all relevant times. It then charged the defendants with four counts of breach of fiduciary duty, specifically (1) imprudent investment; (2) failure to monitor other fiduciaries; (3) misrepresentation and failure to disclose information to beneficiaries; and (4) failure to avoid conflicts of interest. The ERISA litigation is ongoing.

Apart from differences in parties and legal theories, the factual allegations of the ERISA complaint were in many respects nearly identical to the Securities complaint, but in other respects were different from the Securities complaint. With respect to alleged misdeeds by Raytheon occurring prior to October 12, 1999 (the cut-off date for the Securities class action), the factual allegations of the ERISA complaint mirrored those of the Securities complaint; including (1) RE & C failed to disclose and improperly accounted for losses on major contracts; (2) RE & C misleadingly recognized revenues on existing and anticipated contracts; and (3) Raytheon failed to disclose material cost overruns and delays affecting projects related to the P–3 Orion aircraft. With the exception of allegations concerning several Raytheon Systems Corporation projects and the Joint Primary Aircraft Training System, it is fair to say that all the allegations of Raytheon misdeeds made in the Securities complaint were also included in the ERISA complaint.

However, in two major respects the ERISA complaint included allegations not found in the Securities complaint. First, there were substantial allegations of misdeeds pertaining to the post-October 12, 1999, period in the ERISA complaint that were not alleged in the Securities complaint. For example, the ERISA complaint alleged the existence of "recurring indications of accounting and control irregularities...." J.A. at 194. It alleged that "Defendants' misleading, inaccurate, and incomplete statements regarding the Company's fiscal health extended from 1998 through 1999, and beyond." *Id.* at 195.

Other post-October 12, 1999, events alleged included (1) the SEC commenced an investigation into Raytheon's accounting practices in 2003; (2) Raytheon made material misrepresentations in selling the RE & C division to Washington Group International ("WGI"), leading to litigation by WGI and its shareholders; and (3) the SEC commenced proceedings against Raytheon and its former CFO relating to violations of SEC regulations.

Second, to support the different legal theories asserted under ERISA in contrast to the Securities Exchange Act, relevant facts not contained in the Securities complaint were alleged in the ERISA complaint. The complaint alleged that the defendants were ERISA plan fiduciaries. To support the imprudent investment charge, the ERISA complaint alleged that at "[a]ll relevant times, Defendants knew or should have known that Raytheon was engaged in the questionable business practices detailed above which made Raytheon stock an imprudent Plan investment." *Id.* at 215. To support the failure to disclose and misrepresentation charge, the complaint alleged that "Raytheon regularly communicated with employees, including Plan participants, about Raytheon's performance" and failed to disclose and misrepresented material information to Plan beneficiaries. *Id.* at 217. To support the conflict of interest charge, the complaint alleged that the defendants' "compensation was [ ] closely tied to the price of Raytheon Stock" and that the defendants had failed to avoid improper conflicts of interest. *Id.* at 218.

After the ERISA action was filed, Raytheon sought coverage from the insurers. The insurers denied coverage and filed suit in the District of Massachusetts, seeking a declaratory judgment of non-coverage. The insurers contended that coverage was excluded under the prior and pending litigation clause in the Federal Insurance policy, which states

> The Company [Federal] shall not be liable for Loss on account of any Claim made against any Insured . . . based upon, arising from, or in consequence of any demand, suit or other proceeding pending, or order, decree or judgment entered against any Insured, on or prior to [September 15, 2000], or the same or any substantially similar fact, circumstance or situation underlying or alleged therein. * * *

The Federal policy is a "claims-made" policy, where liability for coverage is triggered by the filing of a claim during the policy period instead of the occurrence of an underlying event in the policy period. The policy defines a "claim" as including "a civil proceeding commenced by the service of a complaint or similar pleading . . . against any Insured for a Wrongful Act." J.A. at 37. Thus a claim for present purposes is equivalent to a complaint.

The language of the policy cannot reasonably be given the broadest possible construction, under which any overlapping fact between the two proceedings—for example, the identity of Raytheon as the defendant in the context of otherwise unrelated facts—would trigger the exclusion. We do not understand any party to contend otherwise. At the same time, complete identity between the lawsuits is plainly not required. Indeed, all parties agree that the two complaints need not be identical, and that differences in theories of recovery or the identity of the parties in the proceedings do not in and of themselves preclude exclusion. Beyond that, they disagree. The district court here construed "based upon . . . any substantially similar fact, circumstance or situation underlying or alleged" to exclude coverage when there are "any overlapping claims." The district court, however, did not make clear the degree of overlap required for the allegations in the complaint, instead finding only that Raytheon cannot "credibly argue that the core allegations of the prior litigation complaint and the ERISA complaint do not overlap" and that "a comparison of the complaints reveals numerous allegations of substantially similar facts, circumstances or situations." * * *

We think that the policy thus requires the allegations in the second complaint find substantial support in the first complaint, i.e. that the allegations of the second complaint substantially overlap those of the first. Only with a substantial overlap can the first complaint be said to be a "foundation or logical basis" for the second. "Based" also suggests that the appropriate inquiry is whether the second complaint substantially overlaps the first with respect to relevant facts, without regard to whether the first complaint substantially overlaps the second.

Requiring a substantial but not complete overlap with the prior complaint also serves the policy behind such prior and pending litigation exclusion clauses. Most directly, prior and pending litigation exclusions "promote the giving of prompt notice and [ ] avoid stacking the limits of successive policies to cover essentially the same or very closely related claims." Kenneth S. Abraham, *Insurance Law and Regulation: Cases and Materials* 587 (4th ed. 2005). Prior and pending litigation exclusions thus combat the problem of adverse selection or "insuring the building already on fire"; that is, an insured who has previously been sued faces a greater risk of related litigation and has a corresponding incentive to seek insurance. John H. Mathias, Jr., et al., *Directors and Officers Liability: Prevention, Insurance and Indemnification* § 8.09 (2003) (internal quotations omitted); *see* George L. Priest, *The Current Insurance Crisis and Modern Tort Law,* 96 Yale L.J. 1521, 1574 (1987). The insurance company's legitimate interest in combating the adverse selection problem is properly implicated when there is a real and substantial overlap with the complaint in the prior lawsuit, as opposed to an incidental or fortuitous relationship to the prior complaint.

Accordingly, we hold that the Federal exclusion, excluding any subsequent claim "based upon . . . the same or any substantially similar fact, circumstance or situation underlying or alleged" in a prior claim, applies when there is substantial overlap in the second complaint with the facts underlying or alleged in the first complaint. * * *

Applying the policy as we have interpreted it to the allegations of the complaints, there is little doubt that there is substantial overlap in the allegations of the two complaints. Raytheon's counsel readily conceded at oral argument that "there is no question that the ERISA plaintiffs cut and pasted a lot of the factual allegations from the securities lawsuit." * * *

To be sure, not all of the facts alleged in the ERISA complaint are contained in the Securities complaint. In particular, most of the activities occurring after the Securities class cut-off date of October 12, 1999, do not appear in the Securities complaint. * * * So too, some allegations pertaining exclusively to the elements of an ERISA lawsuit, such as communication with Plan beneficiaries by the fiduciary defendant, do not appear in the Securities complaint. Some of these non-overlapping facts are critical to the ERISA action—for example, the defendants' ERISA fiduciary status is a *sine qua non* of the ERISA action. But acknowledging that there are substantial areas of non-overlap does not defeat the fact here that there is substantial overlap between the two complaints. * * *

We conclude that the Federal prior and pending litigation exclusion, excluding "any Claim made against any Insured . . . based upon, arising from, or in consequence of any demand, suit or other proceeding pending, or order, decree or judgment entered against any Insured . . . , or the same or any substantially similar fact, circumstance or situation underlying or alleged therein," is properly construed to exclude coverage if there is substantial overlap between allegations in the complaint of the claimed proceeding and allegations in the complaint of the prior proceeding. While we recognize that our interpretation will not cleanly resolve every case involving exclusionary policy language similar to that involved here, it easily resolves this case. There is clearly substantial overlap between the allegations in the ERISA complaint and the allegations in the Securities complaint. Coverage is therefore excluded. Accordingly, the judgment of the district court is affirmed.

It is so ordered.

NOTES AND QUESTIONS

1. *Know It When You See It?* The test the court adopted reflects, in substance, the test that most courts apply to the issue. Some courts describe it as a "sufficient nexus" test. See, e.g., *Cont'l Cas. Co. v. Howard Hoffman Assocs.*, 955 N.E. 2d 151 (Ill. Ct. of App. 2011) (multiple claims arising out of single embezzlement scheme are "related"); *Checkrite Ltd., Inc. v. Illinois Nat'l Ins. Co.*, 95 F. Supp.2d 180 (S.D.N.Y. 2000). Given the two alternatives to this test—requiring complete overlap or requiring only minimal overlap—the sufficient nexus test is a middle ground. But does the apparent fairness of the test require so much fact-dependent judicial judgment that it renders outcomes hard to predict, and therefore settlement in anticipation of outcomes less likely to occur?

2. *The Function of Such Provisions.* The provision at issue in *Raytheon* is one of a number of similar provisions contained in claims-made policies. These include, among others, exclusions and provisions addressed to prior related claims, prior or pending proceedings, and related claims. See, e.g., Paragraphs III (A) and (B) (pages 1–2) and IX of the Sample Policy (page 5). Each in one way or another involves the "relation" back of one claim or set of facts to an earlier claim or set of facts. Such provisions attempt to serve a number of functions: they coordinate coverage by indicating whether an earlier policy or a later policy covers a claim; they attempt to preclude coverage of certain claims that might otherwise be covered by a policy that was procured in the face of adverse selection; they encourage the insured to give early notice, if necessary using the "notice of circumstances" provision contained in most policies (see Paragraph VI (B)(1) of the Sample Policy (page 3)); and they attempt to limit the stacking

of coverage provided by policies issued in multiple years. Can you see how and why?

* * *

As noted above, another important type of liability insurance policy that is sometimes provided on a claims-made basis is professional liability, or malpractice, insurance. The following case addresses one important issue that arises not infrequently in this context.

Thoracic Cardiovascular Associates, Ltd. v. St. Paul Fire and Marine Insurance Company

Court of Appeals of Arizona, 1994.
181 Ariz. 449.

■ TOCI, JUDGE.

Thoracic Cardiovascular Associates, Ltd. and Thomas J. Trahan (collectively, "Thoracic") sued St. Paul Fire and Marine Insurance Company ("St. Paul") seeking a declaratory judgment requiring St. Paul to provide coverage on a claims made professional liability insurance policy. St. Paul appeals from the trial court's grant of summary judgment in favor of Thoracic.

We must decide whether coverage exists under a claims made professional liability insurance policy when a claim is not reported to the insurer within the policy period. In order to resolve this question, we must also decide whether the doctrine of impossibility excuses untimely reporting of a claim under a claims made policy.

We conclude that the trial court erred in granting summary judgment against St. Paul. We hold that because notice of a claim within the policy period is a material part of the consideration for a claims made policy, to invoke coverage a claim must be made and reported to the insurer during the policy period. We further hold that the doctrine of impossibility does not excuse late reporting of claims under claims made policies. Accordingly, we reverse the trial court's grant of summary judgment against St. Paul and remand with directions to enter judgment for St. Paul.

I. FACTS AND PROCEDURAL HISTORY

St. Paul issued a claims made professional liability insurance policy to Thoracic for the period from November 1, 1987 through May 1, 1988. The policy stated two requirements for coverage: (1) "the professional service must have been performed (or should have been performed) after [the] retroactive date that applies,"[1] and (2) "[t]he claim must also first be made while this agreement is in effect." Under the policy, a "claim is made on the date [the insured] first report[s] an incident or injury to" St. Paul or its agent.

The policy also contained a provision allowing Thoracic to purchase an optional extension of coverage, referred to as a "reporting endorsement." This endorsement would have allowed Thoracic to report claims to St. Paul after the policy term and before the end of the term of

---

[1] According to the policy in this case, the retroactive date is September 1, 1979.

the reporting endorsement. The policy provided that St. Paul would sell the reporting endorsement to Thoracic for a premium based on the rules and rating plans being used on the day coverage would begin. According to the policy, the reporting endorsement must be requested in writing within thirty days after the end of the policy term.

On February 16, 1988, before the end of the policy term, Thoracic canceled the liability policy issued by St. Paul. On March 4, 1988, sixteen days after the policy was canceled, St. Paul's underwriting department sent a certified letter to Thoracic advising Thoracic that its policy covered only claims made within the policy term. The letter warned that unless Thoracic purchased the optional reporting endorsement coverage within the time stated in the policy or obtained coverage under a replacement policy, it would not be covered for claims arising out of acts performed prior to the termination date that were not reported until after the termination date. Specifically, the letter stated:

> This is a "claims made" form of coverage. This means you do not have coverage for claims arising out of acts performed prior to the termination for which a claim may be made after the termination date, unless you purchase reporting endorsement coverage.
>
> Reporting endorsement coverage extends the time in which a claim may be made for acts which occurred before the termination date. . . .
>
> You may not need this endorsement extension if you have obtained a replacement policy providing coverage for prior acts.
>
> IF YOU DO NOT PURCHASE THE OPTIONAL REPORTING ENDORSEMENT WITHIN THE TIME PERIOD STATED IN YOUR POLICY, OR IF YOU DO NOT OBTAIN COVERAGE UNDER A REPLACEMENT POLICY, THEN YOU DO NOT HAVE COVERAGE FOR CLAIMS ARISING OUT OF ACTS PERFORMED PRIOR TO THE TERMINATION DATE FOR WHICH A CLAIM MAY BE MADE AFTER THE TERMINATION DATE.

This letter clearly indicated that St. Paul would not provide coverage for claims reported after termination of the policy unless the reporting endorsement was purchased. Despite this warning, Thoracic neither purchased the endorsement nor obtained a replacement policy.

To further ensure that Thoracic understood the effect of its decision to cancel the policy and decline the reporting endorsement coverage, on March 21, 1988, Jacque Cumbie, an authorized insurance broker for St. Paul, sent another letter to Thoracic. The letter again addressed the effect of the cancellation:

> You had advised our office that you did not want to buy the Extended Reporting Period Endorsement from St. Paul. The policy was on a "claims made" form of coverage. This means that you will note [sic] have coverage from claims arising out of acts performed prior to the termination date for which a claim may be made after termination date, unless you purchase Reporting Period Endorsement coverage.

Please sign the paper attached stating you understand "Claims Made" form of coverage and did not wish to purchase endorsement, and return to our office.

As requested, Thoracic signed and returned the form. By signing the form, Thoracic acknowledged that it understood "the 'Claims Made' form of coverage and did not wish to purchase endorsement."

On October 15, 1987, Alfonso and Linda Grimaldi filed a medical malpractice suit against Thoracic. The Grimaldi complaint alleged that Thoracic negligently provided professional health care services in 1985. When the Grimaldi lawsuit was filed, Thoracic was covered by the claims made professional liability insurance policy issued by St. Paul. Thoracic was not served with the summons and complaint in the Grimaldi suit, however, until July 12, 1988, approximately five months after it canceled its policy with St. Paul. Prior to that date, Thoracic was not aware of the existence of the Grimaldi claim.

On August 30, 1988, more than six months after terminating coverage, Thoracic notified St. Paul of the Grimaldi lawsuit. Thoracic requested that St. Paul confirm coverage and provide legal representation to defend against the Grimaldi claim. St. Paul denied coverage and refused to provide legal representation because the claim had not been reported to St. Paul during the policy period as required under the claims made policy. * * *

II. DISCUSSION

A. Background

We initially consider the difference between an "occurrence" policy and a "claims-made" policy. An "occurrence" policy of professional liability insurance covers an act or omission that occurs within the policy period, regardless of the date of discovery or the date the claim is made or asserted. *Gulf Ins. Co. v. Dolan, Fertig & Curtis*, 433 So.2d 512, 514 (Fla.1983) citing *Samuel N. Zarpas, Inc. v. Morrow*, 215 F.Supp. 887, 888 (D.N.J.1963); *Bill Binko Chrysler-Plymouth, Inc. v. Compass Ins. Co.*, 385 So.2d 692, 693 (Fla.Dist.Ct.App.1980); *Ranger Ins. Co. v. United States Fire Ins. Co.*, 350 So.2d 570, 572 (Fla.Dist.Ct.App.1977). This type of policy requires that notice be given to the insurer "within a specified time after the insured event." *Stine v. Continental Casualty Co.*, 349 N.W.2d 127, 134 (1984). Because injuries from professional malpractice claims may not manifest themselves for years after the occurrence policy has expired, however, an exposure time, or a "tail," is created. A tail is the time lapse between the date of the negligent act or omission and the time when a claim is made. *Gulf*, 433 So.2d at 515.

Thus, occurrence policies with a "tail" that extends beyond the policy period are historically associated with certain difficulties. One problem with occurrence policies is that the insurer cannot calculate the premium for the risk with any certainty. The insurer must compute premiums for occurrence professional liability policies at current rates while claims must be resolved at market rates, sometimes long after the premiums have been paid. Gerald Kroll, Comment, The "Claims Made" Dilemma in Professional Liability Insurance, 22 UCLA L.Rev. 925, 928 (1975). Another difficulty with occurrence policies is that when professional negligence continues over a period of time, and an insured changes from one occurrence carrier to another, uncertainty exists about which insurer will provide coverage. Id. at 930.

Consequently, to reduce exposure to an unpredictable and lengthy "tail" of lawsuits filed years after the occurrence they agreed to protect against, underwriters shifted to the "claims made" policy. *Pacific Employers Ins. Co. v. Superior Court*, 270 Cal.Rptr. 779, 784 (1990). An insurer who knows that claims will not arise under the policy after its expiration can underwrite a risk and calculate premiums with greater certainty. Id. 270 Cal.Rptr. at 785. The insurer can establish its reserves "without having to consider the possibilities of inflation beyond the policy period, upward-spiralling jury awards, or later changes in the definition and application of negligence." Id.

The "claims made" policy differs from an "occurrence" policy in several important aspects. Because it triggers coverage, transmittal of the notice of the claim to the insurer is the most important aspect of the claims made policy. A claims made policy extends coverage if " 'the negligent or omitted act is discovered and brought to the attention of the insurer within the policy term.' " Id. (quoting 7A John Alan Appleman, Insurance law and Practice § 4504.01, at 312 (Berdal ed. 1979)). "The timing of the making of the claim in such policies stands in equal importance with the error or omission as the insured event." *Stine*, 349 N.W.2d at 134. Notice to the insurer of a claim made against the insured is generally required to be given during the policy period or within a specified amount of time after the policy period. "The essence, then, of a claims-made policy is notice to the carrier within the policy period." *Gulf*, 433 So.2d at 514 (emphasis added).

B. Analysis

Against this backdrop, we turn to the insurance policy in this case. It is clearly a claims made policy. The coverage summary that is attached to the policy provides: "This Coverage Summary shows the limits and extent of coverage under your Physicians' Professional Liability Protection—Claims Made." Further, the reporting language in the policy provides:

> When you're covered
>
> To be covered the professional service must have been performed (or should have been performed) after your retroactive date that applies. The claim must also first be made while this agreement is in effect.
>
> When is a claim made?
>
> A claim is made on the date you first report an incident or injury to us or our agent. You must include the following information:
>
> - Date, time and place of the incident.
> - What happened and what professional service you performed.
> - Type of claim you anticipate.
> - Name and address of injured party.
> - Name and address of any witness.

(Emphasis added.) We find that this plain and unambiguous language requires that the insured report a claim to the insurer while the policy is in effect. See *Sletten*, 161 Ariz. at 596–97 (claims made professional liability policy unambiguously required claims to be reported to insurer during policy period); *Slater v. Lawyers' Mut. Ins. Co.*, 278 Cal.Rptr. 479, 482 (1991) (same). Such a report to the insurer within the policy period is an express condition precedent to coverage. See *Gulf*, 433 So.2d at 515 (coverage depends on claim being made and reported to the insurer during policy period); *Zuckerman v. National Union Fire Ins. Co.*, 495 A.2d 395, 406 (1985) ("event that invokes coverage under a 'claims made' policy is transmittal of notice of the claim to the insurance carrier").

Here, the negligence upon which the Grimaldis' medical malpractice lawsuit is based occurred in 1985, during the term of Thoracic's policy with St. Paul. And, when the Grimaldis filed their lawsuit in superior court on October 15, 1987, the policy was still in effect. Thoracic, however, did not report the claim to St. Paul until August 30, 1988, approximately six months after cancellation of the policy. Thus, the report was too late to trigger coverage. * * *

Because the essence of a claims made policy is notice to the insurer within the policy period, *Gulf*, 433 So.2d at 514, the reasoning of *Sletten* and *Gulf* applies equally where an insured has no knowledge of the claim and, therefore, cannot report the claim to the insurer. To hold that the reporting requirement should be excused any time that the claim was not discovered during the policy period is to essentially convert claims made policies into occurrence policies in those cases. This we will not do. See*Sletten*, 161 Ariz. at 597.

Rather, we agree with the rationale of the New Jersey Supreme Court in *Zuckerman*, 495 A.2d at 406, "that an extension of the notice period in a 'claims made' policy constitutes an unbargained-for expansion of coverage, gratis, resulting in the insurance company's exposure to a risk substantially broader than that expressly insured against in the policy." Such a change in the coverage provided by claims made policies would significantly affect both the basis upon which premiums have been calculated and the cost of claims made insurance. Id. "So material a modification in the terms of this form of insurance widely used to provide professional liability coverage both in this State and throughout the country would be inequitable and unjustified." Id.

Our decision is buttressed by the California Court of Appeals decision in *Slater*. There, a lawsuit was filed against an insured during the period his claims made insurance policy was in effect. The insured, however, did not become aware of the claim until after his policy had expired; thus, he did not notify his insurer until after the policy period had expired. The insurer denied coverage, due to late reporting. 278 Cal.Rptr. at 480.

As in this case, in *Slater*, the insured had been "offered the opportunity to protect himself against unknown claims by purchasing an extended reporting period endorsement, which he declined." Id. at 484. The *Slater* court concluded that the provisions of the policy requiring that a claim be made and reported to the insurer during the policy period were plain and unambiguous. *Slater*, 278 Cal.Rptr. at 482. Further, the court concluded that the late notice/prejudice rule was not applicable. Id. at 482–83. The court held that because the insured failed to report the claim within the policy period, the insurer was not required to provide coverage under the policy. Id. at 484.

Notwithstanding, Thoracic argues that the doctrine of impossibility or impracticability should excuse its failure to comply with the notice requirement as a condition precedent to coverage. Thoracic contends that had the insured in *Slater* raised the defense of impossibility, the outcome of the case may have been different. Thoracic believes that the defense of impossibility should be available where it is impossible for the insured to give the required notice because he had no knowledge of the claim. We disagree. * * *

St. Paul was entitled to limit its coverage by clear and unambiguous language. "[I]n the absence of conflict with statute or public policy, insurers may be unambiguous and clearly noticeable provisions limit their liability and impose such reasonable conditions as they wish upon the obligations they assume by their contract." *Livingston Parish Sch. Bd. v. Fireman's Fund Am. Ins. Co.*, 282 So.2d 478, 481 (La.1973); see also *Slater*, 278 Cal.Rptr. at 483–84 (insurance company has right to limit coverage of policy issued by it and when it does so, the plain language of the limitation must be respected). "[T]he insured received what [it] paid for by the present policy, with premiums presumably reduced to reflect the limited coverage." *Livingston Parish*, 282 So.2d at 483; see also *Gulf*, 433 So.2d at 516 (same). Here, St. Paul has limited its risk by clearly stating that no coverage exists unless the insured complies with the requirement of discovering and reporting the claim within the policy period.

A word about the dissent. According to the dissent, the policy is ambiguous because it blurs the distinction between the different usages of "claim." The dissent also asserts that the St. Paul letter to Thoracic did not plainly and unambiguously state that if the reporting endorsement was rejected, the policy would not apply to claims that were made against Thoracic but not reported during the policy period. We are not persuaded by those arguments.

Reading the policy as a whole, as we must, there is no blurring of the different meanings of "claim." Thoracic is protected against a professional liability claim that might be brought against it so long as the medical incident or accident that might give rise to such claim is reported within the policy term. If such incident or accident is reported, Thoracic is covered, even if the patient has not made any demand or filed any "claim." Conversely, where there has been a "claim" filed by a patient, but no report by the insured, no coverage exists. The policy thus makes it crystal clear that coverage is not dependent on the timing of the "claim" made by the patient but instead on the timing of the "claim" made by Thoracic. That is precisely why Thoracic was offered an optional reporting endorsement.

III. CONCLUSION

For the foregoing reasons, we reverse the judgment of the trial court and remand for entry of judgment in favor of St. Paul, determining that there is no coverage for the Grimaldi claim.

NOTES AND QUESTIONS

1. *Ambiguity?* At one point the policy defined a claim as a demand made upon the insured. But at another point it stated "A claim is made on the date you first report an incident or injury to us or our agent." The dissent argued that the two uses of the term "claim" contradicted each other and rendered it ambiguous. Even if this were so, the statement quoted by the dissent implies that the claim at issue was not even "made" until after expiration of the policy period. Does that leave the insured any better off? For the same reason, should the argument that the claim was not "made" against the insured until the summons was served be unavailing, because then the claim would have been both "made" and "reported" outside the policy period?

2. *Claims-Made and Reported.* Most courts follow the rule reflected in *Thoracic*: the requirement that a claim not only be made but also be reported during the policy period is not merely a notice requirement, but an element of the trigger of coverage under claims-made policies. See, e.g., *Sigma Fin. Co. v. Am. Int'l Speciality Lines Ins. Co.*, 200 F.Supp. 2d 710 (E.D. Mich. 2002). As a consequence, prejudice to the insurer as a result of late notice is not required in order to deny coverage. See, e.g., *Fed. Ins. Co. v. CompUSA, Inc.*, 319 F.3d 746 (5th Cir. 2003). Recently, however, a number of courts have applied a prejudice requirement under their states' notice statutes to late reporting under claims-made policies. See, e.g., *Anderson v. Aul*, 844 N.W. 2d 636 (Wis. Ct. App. 2014); *Sherwood Brands, Inc. v. Great Am. Ins. Co.*, 13 A.3d 1268 (Md. 2011). And some courts apply the prejudice rule to claims that are not reported "promptly," or "as soon as practicable" as required by a policy with claims-made trigger but no reporting-during-the-policy-period trigger. See *Fin. Indus. Corp. v. XL Specialty Ins. Co.*, 285 S.W.3d 877 (Tex. 2009).

The availability of an Extended Reporting Endorsement tends to plug the gap in coverage that could otherwise be created when an insured terminates coverage or switches insurers. In effect, the court in *Thoracic* held that, rather than merely reporting a claim late, the insured had in fact failed to purchase coverage of the claim. Of course, claims-made insurers could omit the requirement that claims be reported during the policy period, thus relaxing the trigger requirement. This would provide every insured with what would amount to an Extended Reporting Endorsement, regardless of which insureds would want or need that protection.

3. *Covering the Tail.* Claims-made policies were introduced in professional liability lines in the mid-1970's, when concern over the difficulty of predicting the scope of long-tail liabilities became pronounced. In the mid-1980's there was also an effort to shift from occurrence to claims-made commercial general liability insurance. These were the same efforts that figured in the *Hartford Fire* case decided by the U.S. Supreme Court and excerpted in Chapter Three. In contrast to claims-made professional liability insurance, however, claims-made CGL policies have met with very little success, both because many commercial purchasers have not been attracted to claims-made coverage and because some state regulators have refused to approve the policies providing it.

The advantage of claims-made coverage, of course, is that premiums for this form of coverage can be set much more reliably than for occurrence coverage. This advantage is to a large extent achieved on the backs of insureds, however, who bear a much greater portion of the risk of an uncertain liability future under claims-made than under occurrence policies. In addition, for insureds who are retiring, some method of protecting against liability for claims that will be made in the future (but arising out of past activities) must be obtained. As was the case in *Thoracic*, typically claims-made insurers address this need by giving their insureds an option to purchase an *Extended Reporting Endorsement* which, for a multiple of the premium paid for the last claims-made policy the insured had purchased, provides coverage against liability for the "tail" of claims that may be made against the insured in the future.

4. *Covering the Front End: The Retroactive Date Issue.* Most claims-made policies are subject to retroactive dates: no coverage is provided for claims arising out of services provided before the retroactive date, which is typically the first day of the policy period of the first claims-made policy the insured has purchased from a particular insurer. When would an insured need coverage against claims resulting from actions taken prior to the date her first claims-made policy took effect—what the court in *Thoracic* called "prior acts" coverage? Consider the following situations. First, if the insured were just starting to do business or entering professional practice she would have no need for such coverage. Second, if she were shifting from occurrence to claims-made coverage and the trigger of coverage under the former was harm occurring during the policy period, then her earlier occurrence policies would cover liability for such harm occurring prior to the retroactive date (presumably the date her first claims-made policy took effect), and her claims-made policies would cover her against claims arising out of harm occurring after the retroactive date. In these situations, the presence of a retroactive date is harmless.

In a third situation, however, a retroactive date might be harmful: the insured might be disadvantaged upon shifting from one claims-made insurer to another. If the new insurer were unwilling to write coverage with the same retroactive date as the former insurer's policies contained, then the insured would be left with a gap in coverage for claims arising out of services provided prior to the new retroactive date. Purchasing an Extended Reporting Endorsement from the old insurer is a means of protecting against this risk.

5. *"Professional Services."* Professional Liability policies require that liability arise out of the provision of professional services. Other policies—for example, some CGL policies, and the liability insurance part of Homeowners policies—contain professional services exclusions. The meaning of the term therefore figures in a considerable body of case law. One of the seminal decisions on the issue is *Marx v. Hartford Accident & Indem. Co.*, 157 N.W. 2d 870 (Neb. 1968). The court there stated that something more than an act "flowing from mere employment or vocation is essential. The act or service must be such as exacts the use or application of special learning or attainments of some kind." Representative contemporary cases include *BCS v. Big Thyme Enterprises*, 2013 WL 594858 (D. S.C. 2013) (unsolicited fax blasting by insurance agents is not a professional service); *Saint Consulting Group v. Endurance American Specialty Insurance Co.*, 669 F.3d 544 (1st Cir. 2012) (discarding of documentary evidence is not a professional service); and *National Fire Insurance Co. of Hartford v. Lewis,* 898 F.Supp. 2d 1142 (D. Ariz. 2012) (inappropriate touching of patients' breasts by an oncologist constituted the

provision of professional services and therefore was excluded by a general liability insurance policy).

CHAPTER SEVEN

LIABILITY INSURANCE: DEFENSE, SETTLEMENT, AND EXCESS COVERAGE

A. THE DUTY TO DEFEND AND THE CONSEQUENCES OF BREACH

Most primary liability insurance policies not only provide indemnity to the insured; they also provide the right to a defense of all claims alleging liability that would be covered by the policy if the allegations were true. This coverage provides important "litigation insurance," since the costs of defending against even unsuccessful lawsuits can be substantial. Older policies indicated that this duty to defend existed even if the allegations are "groundless, false, or fraudulent." Most recent policies have dropped this clarification, although it seems likely that the courts will continue to interpret policies as though they contained this clarification. In any event, it is clear that, as the courts say repeatedly, in general the duty to defend is broader than the duty to indemnify. The question, however—one of a number that this Chapter attempts to answer—is exactly what this means.

In recent years there has been an explosion of litigation over the duty to defend, for two major reasons. First, insurance policies state the duty in only general terms; insurers have not taken the opportunity to specify the scope and limits of the duty. The courts have therefore stepped into this vacuum and created a body of common law rules governing the duty. Apparently insurers can live with these rules and have not revised their policies to alter them. Second, the duty to defend arises in a great variety of different circumstances and contexts, resulting in substantial uncertainty about its scope. This Section divides these circumstances into two general categories. The first category involves the conventional situation in which the insurer's duty is at issue, without any complicating conflict of interest in defending the insured. The second arises when the insurer has an actual or potential conflict of interest in defending the insured.

1. The Scope of the Duty

Beckwith Machinery Company v. Travelers Indemnity Company

United States District Court, Western District of Pennsylvania, 1986.
638 F.Supp. 1179.

■ COHILL, CHIEF JUDGE.

Presently before us are the Plaintiff's and Defendant's Motions for Summary Judgment. Beckwith Machinery Company ("Beckwith") filed the instant action against Travelers Indemnity Company ("Travelers") alleging a breach of contract when Travelers withdrew its defense of Beckwith in an underlying lawsuit brought by Trumbull Corporation ("Trumbull") against Beckwith and Caterpillar Tractor Company ("Caterpillar"). The issues presented by the cross-motions are * * * whether Travelers, as insurer, had a duty to defend Beckwith, as insured, in the prior Trumbull litigation. For the reasons which follow, we will grant summary judgment in favor of Beckwith.

FACTS

Travelers contracted with Beckwith to provide Beckwith with comprehensive general liability insurance pursuant to manuscript insurance policy number TR–NSL–103T891–6–74, which is the controlling policy in this dispute. Travelers agreed to pay all sums which Beckwith became obligated to pay by reason of liability imposed by law, or assumed by Beckwith under any contract, "for damages because of bodily injury, personal injury or property damage to which the policy applied." Further, the policy provided that Travelers "agreed to defend any suit brought against Plaintiff within the United States, even if any of the allegations of the suit were groundless, if said suit alleged bodily injury, personal injury or property damage."

In 1973, Beckwith recommended, and eventually sold, various Caterpillar tractor scrapers and earthmoving equipment to Trumbull, which utilized some of this equipment at a construction job site in the southern part of Florida. This project, which began on or around March 1, 1974, required Trumbull to excavate a reservoir and build a "soil cement" (a mixture of sand and cement) dike to hold water to be used for cooling a power plant, and other related construction. * * *

However, as early as April, 1975, the tractor scrapers supplied by Beckwith broke down from time to time due to engine and transmission problems; thus, hampering the progress of Trumbull's Florida construction project. Consequently, warranty, maintenance and other repairs were performed on the tractor scrapers by a local Caterpillar dealer as well as by representatives of Caterpillar and Beckwith. Counsel for Trumbull formally notified Beckwith by a letter dated September 27, 1976, of its claim that the Caterpillar tractor scrapers were defective and that their failure to perform caused Trumbull to suffer damages in excess of three million dollars ($3,000,000). * * *

On March 17, 1976, prior to Trumbull's written notification to Beckwith that it intended to file a claim, Beckwith had informed

Johnson & Higgins, its insurance broker, which then informed Travelers, of the possibility of a claim by Trumbull.

On or about April 15, 1977, Trumbull initiated a lawsuit against Beckwith and Caterpillar in the Court of Common Pleas of Allegheny County, GD 76–22608 (hereinafter the "Trumbull" case). The Trumbull case included claims against Beckwith for breach of warranties and misrepresentation of quality (i.e., failure to inform Trumbull of design defects) in thirteen (13) earth moving tractor scrapers that were manufactured by Caterpillar and sold or rented to Trumbull by Beckwith.

In its complaint, Trumbull alleged *inter alia* that it incurred substantial damages caused by the allegedly defective Caterpillar 651 and 657 tractor scrapers, which included excessive down time, a decrease in their market value and substantial damages in the performance of certain contractual obligations of Trumbull, including, but not limited to, increased project costs for labor, increased machinery down time, impact costs and overall job extension and costs.

Travelers, through the law firm of Stein & Winters, assumed the defense of the Trumbull case from the initiation of the lawsuit with respect to all claims except those pertaining to punitive damages. Based on Stein & Winters' advice that punitive damages might not be covered under the insurance policy, Travelers notified Beckwith in a letter dated June 9, 1977, that it would not provide coverage for the punitive damages claimed by Trumbull and suggested that Beckwith engage counsel to pursue that aspect of its case. At the time, Travelers did not advise Beckwith that any other claims made by Trumbull might not be covered or defended. Thereafter, in response to Travelers' refusal to provide a defense for the claim for punitive damages, Beckwith retained the law firm of Thorp, Reed and Armstrong, which notified Travelers that Beckwith was holding Travelers responsible for coverage and defense of Trumbull's punitive damages claim.

The parties have stipulated that the Trumbull Complaint stated claims of property damage which were potentially within the coverage afforded by the policy. In fact, in its "Claim Experience Review Form" dated September 20, 1977, Travelers stated that the Trumbull Complaint included:

> Multiple allegations against our insured re sale of equipment to contractor for Florida project. Complaint contains many areas of covered and noncovered counts. We will have to get into discovery before we will be in a position to make a final determination.

Moreover, in an internal memorandum authored by Associate Manager Charles E. Michaux, and dated April 10, 1978, Travelers noted the possibility that Beckwith, as a joint tortfeasor, could be liable for as much as 50% of the Trumbull claims. Referring to an opinion from outside counsel, Mr. Michaux stated his belief that Travelers was estopped from withdrawing its defense and coverage at this point. Several other internal memoranda and/or letters were circulated among Travelers' personnel, which reflected the insurer's vacillation and confusion over potential coverage of the Trumbull claims.

Despite the existing differences among Travelers' employees over what course of action to take regarding the Trumbull claims, by letter dated May 19, 1978, thirteen months after the initiation of the Trumbull lawsuit and Travelers' defense of Beckwith for all compensatory damage claims, Travelers suddenly denied coverage and withdrew its defense of Beckwith. In its letter to Beckwith, Travelers stated that it "can no longer afford you defense for any of the causes of action sued upon."

Subsequent to its denial of a defense on the Trumbull claims, Travelers pondered drafting a reservation of rights letter or filing a declaratory action to resolve the coverage issue. In a memorandum dated July 14, 1978 Travelers' Regional Assistant, James R. Murphy, acknowledged that the "initial investigation was lacking and we must now pick up the ball and put this file in a good defense posture." At one point, Travelers proposed to resume the defense of the Trumbull case without providing coverage, if Beckwith, in turn, would waive its claim of "prejudice" against Travelers. Beckwith rejected this offer, believing it was owed both defense and coverage.

On July 24, 1978, Thorp, Reed and Armstrong notified Travelers that Beckwith had instructed them to take over the entire defense of the Trumbull case. Subsequently, in October of 1978, Stein & Winters petitioned and received leave of this Court to withdraw as Beckwith's counsel. Moreover, Travelers was put on notice that Beckwith intended to proceed against Travelers for all costs and expenses it incurred in the defense of the Trumbull lawsuit.

The record discloses that after continued discovery and defense by Beckwith's counsel, the Trumbull case was eventually settled on November 12, 1982, with Beckwith's portion of the settlement payment to Trumbull being $100,000.00. The instant lawsuit followed. * * *

Duty to Defend

The law of Pennsylvania is well settled regarding an insurer's duty to defend its insured. In consideration for the insured's payment of premiums, the insurer becomes contractually obliged to defend its insured. *American Contract Bridge v. Nationwide Mutual Fire Insurance Co.,* 752 F.2d 71, 75 (3d Cir.1985). This obligation arises whenever allegations against the insured state a claim which is *potentially* within the scope of the policy's coverage, even if such allegations are "groundless, false or fraudulent." *Gedeon v. State Farm Mutual Automobile Insurance Co.,* 410 Pa. 55, 58 (1963); *Zeitz v. Zurich General Accident Liability Insurance Co.,* 165 Pa.Super. 295 (1949). There were two obligations undertaken by Travelers: the obligation to indemnify Beckwith against Trumbull's damages and the separate duty to defend a lawsuit covered by the policies. It is well settled that an insurer's obligation to defend is separate and distinct from its duty to indemnify; the insurer's duty to defend is broader than its obligation to indemnify the insured. *Liberty Mutual Insurance Co. v. Pacific Indemnity Co.,* 557 F.Supp. 986, 989 (W.D.Pa.1983); *Gedeon,* 410 Pa. at 58–59; 7C J. Appleman, Insurance Law and Practice, § 4682 (Berdal ed. 1979) (hereinafter "Appleman").

However, once a third party has raised allegations against an insured which potentially fall within the coverage period, the insurer is obligated to defend its insured fully until it can confine the possibility of recovery to claims outside the coverage of the policy. *Lee v. Aetna Casualty & Surety Co.*, 178 F.2d 750, 753 (2d Cir.1949); *Cadwallader v. New Amsterdam Casualty Co.*, 396 Pa. 582 (1959). *See also Commercial Union Insurance Co. v. Pittsburgh Corning Corp.*, 789 F.2d at 218; *Bituminous Insurance Cos. v. Pennsylvania Manufacturers' Association Insurance Co.*, 427 F.Supp. 539, 555 (E.D.Pa.1976). Therefore, it is clear that where a claim potentially may become one which is within the scope of the policy the insurer's refusal to defend at the outset of the dispute is a decision it makes at its own peril. *American Contract Bridge League*, 752 F.2d at 76; *Pittsburgh Plate Glass Co.*, 752 F.2d at 76; *Pittsburgh Plate Glass Co.*, 281 F.2d at 540; *Cadwallader*, 396 Pa. at 589.

Conversely, "[t]here is no principle of Pennsylvania law that the duty to defend automatically attaches at the outset of the litigation and cannot afterwards terminate." *Commercial Union Insurance Co.*, 789 F.2d at 218. Pennsylvania courts have held that an insurance company is under no obligation to defend when the suit against its insured is based on a cause of action excluded from the policy's coverage. *See Wilson v. Maryland Casualty Co.*, 377 Pa. 588, 594 (1954); *Seaboard Industries, Inc. v. Monaco*, 258 Pa.Super. 170, 179 (1978). "However, if coverage (indemnification) depends upon the existence or nonexistence of facts outside of the complaint that have yet to be determined, the insurer must provide a defense until such time as the facts are determined, and the claim is narrowed to one patently outside of coverage." *C. Raymond Davis & Sons, Inc. v. Liberty Mutual Insurance Co.*, 467 F.Supp. 17, 19 (E.D.Pa.1979).

In *Aetna Life and Casualty Co. v. McCabe*, 556 F.Supp. 1342, 1354 (E.D.Pa.1983), the court stated "that 'a liability insurer, by assuming the defense of an action against the insured, is thereafter estopped to claim that the loss resulting to the insured from an adverse judgment [or settlement] in such action is not within the coverage of the policy, or to assert against the insured some other defense existing at the time of the accident.'" *Id.* (quoting Annot., 38 A.L.R.2d 1148, 1150 (1954)). *See Jones v. Robbins*, 258 F.Supp. 585, 588 (E.D.Pa.1966), *aff'd*, 374 F.2d 1002 (3d Cir.1967); *Perkoski v. Wilson*, 371 Pa. 553 (1952).

When the insurance company believes a claim is not covered, it may protect itself by a timely reservation of rights under the policy which fairly informs the insured of its position. *Aetna Life and Casualty Co. v. McCabe*, 556 F.Supp. at 1354–55. Insurers who contemplate refusing to indemnify a claim must inform their insureds so as to allow them to protect their interests and avoid detrimental reliance on indemnity. *Nichols v. American Casualty Co.*, 423 Pa. 480 (1966). If an insurer undertakes to defend a claim under a reservation of rights it is not precluded from denying coverage. *Brugnoli v. United National Insurance Co.*, 284 Pa.Super. 511 (1981). Under Pennsylvania law, "reservation of rights" letters do not require the assent of the insured and are given the same effect as a nonwaiver agreement. *See Draft Systems, Inc. v. Alspach*, 756 F.2d 293, 296 (3d Cir.1985) for a cogent review of the feasibility and utilization of non-waiver agreements and reservation of rights letters.

It is hornbook law that if an insurer assumes the insured's defense without sending the insured a reservation of rights letter or bringing a declaratory relief action, the insurer will later be precluded from denying coverage. *See generally,* 7C Appleman, at §§ 4689, 4694. Moreover, in *Alspach,* the court stated that if the insurer affords representation without some understanding with its insured, the carrier may later be estopped from asserting an otherwise valid coverage defense. *Id.* at 296.

We now apply the above principles of law to the facts before us.

The Trumbull complaint, while not as specific in its allegations of damages as it might have been, contained sufficient information to put Travelers on notice that a claim of property damage, potentially covered by its policy, was being raised against Beckwith, its insured. As noted previously, the parties stipulated that the Trumbull complaint stated claims that were potentially within the scope of coverage, and this is buttressed by the internal memoranda of Travelers' personnel plus the Hill Report. Obviously, Travelers had a duty to defend any potential claims that were within the scope of the policy's coverage. *Gedeon, supra; Cadwallader, supra; Zeitz, supra.*

Alternatively, even if Travelers had a legitimate coverage defense regarding the Trumbull claims of property damage, it assumed the defense of the *Trumbull* case without reserving its rights as to indemnification. The record reveals that Travelers' denial letter of May 19, 1978, only informed Plaintiff that Trumbull's claim for punitive damages was not covered. In no way can this be construed as a denial of coverage as to the compensatory damages claims at issue here.

While some of Travelers' personnel considered filing a reservation of rights letter and/or a declaratory relief action to protect the carrier from having to indemnify Plaintiff, the record discloses that neither course of action was taken by Travelers, Beckwith's Appendix PXZ 3, 5, 6, 9, 11. Without any subsequent revelations excluding coverage and without conducting a proper investigation into the facts supporting the Trumbull claims, Travelers abruptly denied coverage on May 19, 1978, after Beckwith had relied on it for coverage for thirteen months. Based on this obdurate and contumacious conduct on the part of Travelers, we hold that it has waived and is estopped from raising any valid coverage defenses. *Aetna Life and Casualty Co. v. McCabe,* 556 F.Supp. at 1354. *See also Jones v. Robbins,* 258 F.Supp. 585 (E.D.Pa.1966), *aff'd,* 374 F.2d 1002 (3d Cir.1967) (disclaimer of coverage more than two years after notice of claim); *New Amsterdam Casualty Co. v. Kelly,* 57 F.Supp. 209 (E.D.Pa.1944) (disclaimer of coverage nine months after notice of claim).

Here, Travelers had virtual carte blanche over the defense of the Trumbull case for a period of over two years, and Beckwith justifiably relied on Travelers for indemnification of all claims except the claim for punitive damages.

While Travelers denied coverage of the punitive damages claim, it still had a duty to defend that ancillary claim because, as we stated earlier, the duty to defend is broader than the duty to indemnify, and some of the claims for compensatory damages were potentially covered by the policy. *Gedeon, supra.* However, since the payment of punitive damages by the insurer is invalid and against public policy in Pennsylvania, *see D'Ambrosio v. Pennsylvania National Mutual Casualty Insurance Co.,* 494 Pa. 501 (1981), we need not address that issue further.

Because of its reliance on Travelers to defend the compensatory damages claims, Beckwith was deprived of the opportunity to itself investigate and defend the Trumbull claims. The record in the case before us reveals that Travelers failed to conduct a proper investigation or a thorough discovery, and at one point, fearful of losing Plaintiff as a "valued account," offered to reassume the defense of the Trumbull claims if Plaintiff would drop its claim that it was prejudiced by Defendant's mishandling of the Trumbull case. Beckwith's Appendix PX 10, 14.

Travelers asserted in the policy the right and duty to "defend any suit against the insured * * * and make such investigation, negotiation and settlement * * * as it deems expedient." An insurer who asserts such a right stands in a fiduciary relationship toward the insured and is obligated to act in good faith and with due care in representing the insured's interests. *Gray v. Nationwide Mutual Insurance Co.,* 422 Pa. 500 (1966). In the instant case, Travelers failed to refrain from exhibiting a greater concern for its own interests than for those of its insured.

In conclusion, we find that: 1) the Trumbull complaint stated claims that were potentially covered by the insurance policy issued by Travelers to Beckwith; 2) Travelers breached its duty to defend Beckwith in the underlying Trumbull case; 3) Travelers failed to reserve its rights to contest indemnity regarding the compensatory damage claims raised in the Trumbull case; and 4) Travelers is estopped from denying coverage because Beckwith detrimentally relied on Travelers' policy for indemnification.

Accordingly, because there are not genuine issues of material fact, we will grant Plaintiff's motion for summary judgment on Counts One, Two and Three. * * *

Damages

The law of Pennsylvania clearly recognizes that when an insurer breaches its duty to defend, the appropriate measure of damages is the cost of hiring substitute counsel and other defense costs. *American Contract Bridge League,* 752 F.2d at 76; *Gedeon,* 410 Pa. at 60. Consequently, Beckwith is entitled to recover its attorneys' fees and defense costs in the Trumbull case.

In addition, we find that Beckwith is also entitled to recover the $100,000.00 it paid to settle the Trumbull claims on the theory that Travelers, by its defense of these claims for some thirteen months without any reservation of rights, was estopped to claim that the loss resulting to Beckwith (i.e., the $100,000.00 settlement payment) was not within the policy's coverage. *Aetna Life and Casualty v. McCabe,* 556 F.Supp. at 1354. By asserting in its policy the right to handle all claims against the insured, including the right to "settlement of any such suit defended by the company as it deems expedient," Travelers, by its failure to act in good faith and with due care in representing the interests of Beckwith, is liable for the $100,000.00 suit. *Gray,* 422 Pa. at

504; *Gedeon,* 410 Pa. at 59–60. *See also Oliver B. Cannon & Son v. Fidelity and Casualty Co. of New York,* 484 F. Supp. 1375, 1385–87 (D.Del.1980) (applying Pennsylvania law); Keeton, *Liability Insurance and Responsibility for Settlement,* 67 Harv. L. Rev. 1136 (1954).

Moreover, in *Pacific Indemnity Co. v. Linn,* the United States Court of Appeals for the Third Circuit affirmed the district court's rationale that where settlement renders it impossible to determine factually and with exactitude what claims were actually covered, the duty to indemnify must follow the duty to defend. *Id.* at 766. Thus, Plaintiff is entitled to recover the $100,000.00 it paid to settle the Trumbull case.
* * *

NOTES AND QUESTIONS

1. *The "Scope of the Pleadings" Rule and the Insurer's Choices.* It is very well established, both as a matter of insurance policy interpretation and legal doctrine, that the insurer must defend any suit whose allegations would fall within coverage if the allegations were proved to be true. See RLLI, § 15. This rule is often called the "scope of the pleadings," "four corners of the complaint," or "potentiality" rule. Occasionally it is called the "eight corners" rule, referring to the comparison between what is contained within the four corners of the complaint and what is contained within the four corners of the policy. It is almost equally clear that the insurer must defend even when the complaint does not allege facts within coverage, if the insurer possesses extrinsic information that the claim does fall within coverage. Whenever the insurer receives notice of a suit against the insured, four choices are possible: refuse to defend, defend unconditionally, defend subject to a reservation of the right to contest coverage if the suit is not defeated, or bring a declaratory judgment action seeking a ruling that it has no duty to defend or indemnify. Different choices have different consequences, depending on the facts.

2. *Refuse to Defend: Legal Uncertainty Versus Factual Uncertainty.* In some cases, it is legally uncertain whether a suit against an insured would be covered if the allegations were true. For example, the complaint may allege liability for the cost of pollution cleanup at a time when the jurisdiction has not yet ruled on the question (addressed in Chapter Six in *A.Y. MacDonald*) whether cleanup liability constitutes "damages" under the defendant's CGL insurance policy. In this situation, the duty to defend and the duty to indemnify are co-extensive. If a court later rules that cleanup costs are "damages," then there was a duty to defend, because the allegations would be covered if they were proved to be true. On the other hand, if the court later rules that cleanup costs are not "damages," then there was neither a duty to indemnify nor a duty to defend, because the allegations would not have been covered even if they were proved to be true. When there is only legal uncertainty, therefore, most courts hold that the duty to defend is not broader than the duty to indemnify, and the insurer can take its chances about whether to defend, based on how it thinks the legal uncertainty will be resolved—for or against coverage.

In other cases, it is factually uncertain whether the allegations in the complaint would fall within coverage if they were true because it is unclear what the facts are. For example, the complaint may allege liability for damage resulting from a defect in the insured's product, without specifying whether that damage was to the insured's product alone, or also involved damage to other property. If the former, then the claim would be excluded under a business-risk exclusion, but if the latter, it would be (at least partially) covered. Such a claim is factually uncertain. Under the scope-of-the-pleadings rule there is a duty to defend, because the allegations have the potential to be covered, depending on the facts. In this situation the duty to defend is broader than the duty to indemnify because, after the insurer has complied with its duty to defend, a coverage suit still may determine that the claim was not covered and that the insurer owes no indemnity. An insurer that refuses to defend when there is only factual uncertainty has therefore breached the duty to defend.

3. *Defend Unconditionally.* The insurer that defends unconditionally (without issuing the "Reservation of Rights" described below in Note 4) waives its right to later contest coverage. This is because the insurer is only required to defend a suit whose allegations would fall within coverage if proved to be true. Having defended unconditionally, the insurer has impliedly agreed that this is the case. When and if the allegations are proved to be true, and the insured is held liable, the insurer may not then contradict itself and assert that the proved allegations are not covered. Many courts reach the same result by saying (as in *Beckwith*) that the insurer in this situation is "estopped" to deny coverage, but without requiring proof of the detrimental reliance that estoppel ordinarily requires. Apparently the insurer's first error in *Beckwith* was defending unconditionally (except with respect to punitive damages); it therefore waived its right or was estopped to contest coverage regarding the other allegations.

4. *Defend Subject to a Reservation of Rights.* The accepted method of assuring that, by providing a defense, the insurer has not waived or is not later estopped to deny coverage, is by presenting the insured with a "Reservation of the Right to Contest Coverage," also sometimes known as a "Reservation of Rights" or just a "Reservation." This document, often a letter, informs the insured that the insurer's provision of a defense does not constitute waiver of the right to deny coverage later. In most jurisdictions the presentation of a unilateral Reservation of Rights is sufficient to avoid waiver or estoppel; in a few others, the insurer must obtain the insured's consent to continued representation, through a "Non-Waiver Agreement," in order to achieve this protection. If the insurer defends under a reservation, then it has preserved the right to contest coverage regarding the potential coverage defenses that it has identified in the reservation. But the price the insurer has paid for preserving its right to contest is the cost of defending.

5. *Bring a Declaratory Judgment Action.* An insurer that does not defend, brings a declaratory judgment action on the indemnity and defense issues, and wins, obviously owes nothing. Many, though not all states permit such actions, though sometimes they are stayed even in states that permit them in principle, while the underlying suit proceeds. An insurer that does not defend and loses the declaratory judgment action has breached the duty to defend. And an insurer that brings a declaratory judgment action while defending subject to a reservation has the potential to be relieved of its duty to defend if it wins the declaratory judgment action while the underlying suit against the insured is still pending.

The advantage of a declaratory judgment action, obviously, is that it yields certainty. A court rules either that there is, or is not, a duty to defend. From the standpoint of overall policy, however, there are also disadvantages to this approach. First, it is possible that facts which are at issue in the underlying tort suit against the policyholder may be discovered or even adjudicated in the declaratory judgment action, thus putting the policyholder in a weaker position in that underlying tort suit. For example, suppose the insurer wishes to show in the declaratory judgment action that it has no duty to defend because, as a matter of law, the policyholder expected or intended harm. If the insurer succeeds, then the policyholder may be collaterally estopped to deny in the tort suit that it expected or intended harm. And even if this problem is handled by a rule that no finding in the declaratory judgment action can have collateral estoppel effect in the tort suit, fact development by the policyholder's own insurer may aid the plaintiff in the tort suit to prove the same thing independently. This problem can conceivably be handled by making discovery and other matters in the declaratory judgment action subject to a confidentiality order. But at this point the whole process has become more complex. Moreover, whenever there is a declaratory judgment action, the insurer has forced the policyholder to fight two wars instead of one—the first against the plaintiff in the underlying tort suit, and the second against its own liability insurer, and to incur the costs associated with doing so.

6. *The Consequences of Breach.* As indicated in Note 2, if the insurer breaches the duty to defend when there is legal but not factual uncertainty as to the duty, then the insurer owes both indemnity and the insured's costs of defense, because the claim was covered. On the other hand, if the insurer breaches the duty to defend when there is factual uncertainty, there is a division of authority regarding the consequences. Some courts hold, as the court in *Beckwith* apparently held (regarding the insurer's breach through withdrawal), that a breaching insurer waives the right or is estopped to deny coverage. This view is adopted by the RLLI, § 21, *Beckwith*, the *Gray* case set out next, and a number of other courts. Under this view, an insurer that refuses to defend "rolls the dice": if it should have defended, it loses the right to contest coverage and owes both indemnity and defense costs. But there is a contrary approach that rejects automatic waiver and estoppel, which can result in the insurer owing indemnity for claims that were not in fact covered by the policy. This contrary approach (followed by the majority of courts, according to some commentators) is to hold that the insurer that breaches in this situation may still contest coverage—i.e., has not waived the right and is not estopped to deny coverage—unless the insured has detrimentally relied (which often will not be the case). Thus, there are two quite opposed approaches to the consequences of breach. See, e.g., *K2 Inv. Grp., LLC v. Am. Guar. & Liab. Ins. Co.*, 6 N.E. 3d 1117 (N.Y. 2014) (holding that the insurer that breaches is not estopped to contest coverage).

A natural reaction to the latter, no-waiver/no-estoppel-for-breaching rule would be to wonder why an insurer not subject to waiver or estoppel for breaching the duty to defend would ever defend. There would always be a possibility of saving defense costs, and there would never be any more liability than the insurer would have incurred if it had complied with its duty to defend. But insurers certainly have reasons to defend even in jurisdictions that reject waiver or estoppel: among other reasons, doing so may preserve their reputations, and may allow the insurer to keep control of a defense so as to defeat the claim against the insured, and thereby avoid the coverage question entirely. Nonetheless, the courts that invoke waiver or estoppel when an insurer has breached the duty to defend undoubtedly do so at least in part in order to give insurers an added incentive to defend in cases where there is doubt about the duty.

7. *Terminating the Duty to Defend.* Suppose that the insurer defends a suit that appears to fall within coverage, but learns in the course of the defense that the claim, even if proved, would not fall within coverage. Or suppose that the insurer has doubts about its duty to defend, but does not want to risk the consequences of breaching the duty if it later is determined that there was a duty to defend. How is the duty to defend terminated? It is said to have been settled at least since Judge Learned Hand's decision in *Lee v. Aetna Casualty & Surety Co.,* 178 F.2d 750 (2d Cir.1949), that the insurer may withdraw once it is clear there is no duty, or there no longer is a duty, to defend. In *Lee,* Hand wrote as follows: "[I]f the plaintiff's complaint against the insured alleged facts which would have supported a recovery covered by the policy, it was the duty of the defendant to undertake the defence, until it could confine the claim to a recovery that the policy did not cover." Id. at 753.

But how does the insurer (in Hand's words) "confine the claim to a recovery that the policy did not cover"? One way would be to get the potentially covered count or counts in a complaint against the insured dismissed, leaving only the not-even-potentially-covered counts, as to which there would be no duty to defend. The other way would be to resolve any legal uncertainty about coverage in the insurer's favor through a declaratory judgment or in the insured's simultaneous coverage suit. In *Montrose Chemical Corp. of California v. Superior Court,* 861 P.2d 1153 (Cal. 1993), the California Supreme Court held that, in order to terminate its duty to defend, the insurer must show as a matter of law that there would be no coverage of the claim under the policy if the claim succeeded. This appears to be the emerging rule See RLLI, § 20; *Erie Ins. Exch. v. Lansberry,* 2008 WL 852453 (Ohio Ct. App. 2008); *Cotter Corp. v. Am. Empire Surplus Lines Ins. Co.,* 90 P.3d 814 (Colo. 2004). In other words, the insured need only show that the underlying claim could fall within coverage to maintain the insurer's duty to defend, while the insurer must show that it could not possibly do so to terminate the defense. Whether the insurer can simply cease defending once the claim is "confined" in the way that Hand meant, or must first demonstrate in court that the remaining counts are not even potentially covered, is unclear.

2. "MIXED" CLAIMS AND CONFLICTS OF INTEREST

Many cases involve a series of allegations, some of which satisfy the scope-of-the-pleadings rule and some of which do not. The insurer's duty to defend these "mixed" claims has been the subject of continuing debate and development. Most liability insurance policies provide that the insurer must defend any "suit" alleging liability for damages covered by the policy. Based at least in part on this policy language, the dominant rule is that the insurer must defend an entire "suit" if any of the allegations satisfy the scope-of-the-pleadings rule.

Gray v. Zurich Insurance Company
Supreme Court of California, 1966.
65 Cal.2d 263.

■ TOBRINER, JUSTICE.

This is an action by an insured against his insurer for failure to defend an action filed against him which stemmed from a complaint alleging that he had committed an assault. The main issue turns on the argument of the insurer that an exclusionary clause of the policy excuses its defense of an action in which a plaintiff alleges that the insured intentionally caused the bodily injury. Yet the language of the policy does not clearly define the application of the exclusionary clause to the duty to defend. Since in that event we test the meaning of the policy according to the insured's reasonable expectation of coverage and since the language of the policy would lead the insured here to expect defense of the third party suit, we cannot exonerate the carrier from the rendition of such protection.

Plaintiff, Dr. Vernon D. Gray, is the named insured under an insurance policy issued by defendant. A "Comprehensive Personal Liability Endorsement" in the policy states, under a paragraph designated "Coverage L" that the insurer agrees "(T)o pay on behalf of the insured all sums which the insured shall become legally obligated to pay as damages because of bodily injury or property damage, and the company shall defend any suit against the insured alleging such bodily injury or property damage and seeking damages which are payable under the terms of this endorsement, even if any of the allegations are groundless, false or fraudulent; but the company may make such investigation and settlement of any claim or suit as it deems expedient." The policy contains a provision that "(T)his endorsement does not apply" to a series of specified exclusions set forth under separate headings, including a paragraph (c) which reads, "under coverages L and M, to bodily injury or property damages caused intentionally by or at the direction of the insured."

The suit which Dr. Gray contends Zurich should have defended arose out of an altercation between him and a Mr. John R. Jones.[1] Jones filed a complaint in Missouri alleging that Dr. Gray "wilfully, maliciously, brutally and intentionally assaulted" him; he prayed for actual damages of $50,000 and punitive damages of $50,000. Dr. Gray notified defendant of the suit, stating that he had acted in self-defense, and requested that the company defend. Defendant refused on the ground that the complaint alleged an intentional tort which fell outside the coverage of the policy. Dr. Gray thereafter unsuccessfully defended on the theory of self-defense; he suffered a judgment of $6,000 actual damages although the jury refused to award punitive damages.

Dr. Gray then filed the instant action charging defendant with breach of its duty to defend. Defendant answered, admitting the execution of the policy but denying any such obligation. The record on

---

[1] Immediately preceding the altercation Dr. Gray had been driving an automobile on a residential street when another automobile narrowly missed colliding with his car. Jones, the driver of the other car, left his vehicle, approached Dr. Gray's car in a menacing manner and jerked open the door. At that point Dr. Gray, fearing physical harm to himself and his passengers, rose from his seat and struck Jones.

appeal has been augmented to include an offer of proof, presented by plaintiff and rejected by the trial court, which detailed the circumstances surrounding the altercation. The augmented record also includes exhibits introduced at the trial, consisting of copies of the pleadings and verdict in the Missouri suit and a copy of the subject insurance policy. The parties waived written findings of fact and conclusions of law; the court rendered judgment in favor of defendant. We must decide whether or not defendant bore the obligation to defend plaintiff in the Missouri action.

Defendant argues that it need not defend an action in which the complaint reveals on its face that the claimed bodily injury does not fall within the indemnification coverage; that here the Jones complaint alleged that the insured committed an assault, which fell outside such coverage. Defendant urges, as a second answer to plaintiff's contention, that the contract, if construed to require defense of the insured, would violate the public policy of the state and that, indeed, the judgment in the third party suit upholding the claim of an intentional bodily injury operates to estop the insured from recovery. Defendant thirdly contends that any requirement that it defend the Jones suit would embroil it in a hopeless conflict of interest. Finally it submits that, even if it should have defended the third party suit, the damages against it should encompass only the insured's expenses of defense and not the judgment against him.

We shall explain our reasons for concluding that defendant was obligated to defend the Jones suit, and our grounds for rejecting defendant's remaining propositions. Since the policy sets forth the duty to defend as a primary one and since the insurer attempts to avoid it only by an unclear exclusionary clause, the insured would reasonably expect, and is legally entitled to, such protection. As an alternative but secondary ground for our ruling we accept, for purposes of argument, defendant's contention that the duty to defend arises only if the third party suit involves a liability for which the insurer would be required to indemnify the insured, and, even upon this basis, we find a duty to defend. * * *

Our holding that the insurer bore the obligation to defend because the policy led plaintiff reasonably to expect such defense, and because the insurer's exclusionary clause did not exonerate it, cuts across defendant's answering contention that the duty arises only if the pleadings disclose a cause of action for which the insurer must indemnify the insured. Defendant would equate the duty to defend with the complaint that pleaded a liability for which the insurer was bound to indemnify the insured. Yet even if we accept defendant's premises, and define the duty to defend by measuring the allegations in the Jones case against the carrier's liability to indemnify, defendant's position still fails. We proceed to discuss this alternative ground of liability of the insurer, accepting for such purpose the insurer's argument that we must test the third party suit against the indemnification coverage of the policy. We point out that the carrier must defend a suit which potentially seeks damages within the coverage of the policy; the Jones action was such a suit.

Defendant cannot construct a formal fortress of the third party's pleadings and retreat behind its walls. The pleadings are malleable, changeable and amendable. Although an earlier decision reads: "In determining whether or not the appellant was bound to defend * * * the language of its contract must first be looked to, and next the allegations of the complaints * * *" (*Lamb v. Belt Casualty Co.*, supra, 3 Cal.App.2d 624, 630), courts do not examine only the pleaded word but the potential liability created by the suit. Since the instant action presented the potentiality of a judgment based upon nonintentional conduct, and since liability for such conduct would fall within the indemnification coverage, the duty to defend became manifest at the outset.

To restrict the defense obligation of the insurer to the precise language of the pleading would not only ignore the thrust of the cases but would create an anomaly for the insured. Obviously, as *Ritchie v. Anchor Casualty Co.*, supra, 135 Cal.App.2d 245, points out, the complainant in the third party action drafts his complaint in the broadest terms; he may very well stretch the action which lies in only nonintentional conduct to the dramatic complaint that alleges intentional misconduct. In light of the likely overstatement of the complaint and of the plasticity of modern pleading, we should hardly designate the third party as the arbiter of the policy's coverage.

Since modern procedural rules focus on the facts of a case rather than the theory of recovery in the complaint, the duty to defend should be fixed by the facts which the insurer learns from the complaint, the insured, or other sources. An insurer, therefore, bears a duty to defend its insured whenever it ascertains facts which give rise to the potential of liability under the policy. In the instant case the complaint itself, as well as the facts known to the insurer, sufficiently apprised the insurer of these possibilities; hence we need not set out when and upon what other occasions the duty of the insurer to ascertain such possibilities otherwise arises.

Jones' complaint clearly presented the possibility that he might obtain damages that were covered by the indemnity provisions of the policy. Even conduct that is traditionally classified as "intentional" or "wilful" has been held to fall within indemnification coverage. Moreover, despite Jones' pleading of intentional and wilful conduct, he could have amended his complaint to allege merely negligent conduct. Further, plaintiff might have been able to show that in physically defending himself, even if he exceeded the reasonable bounds of self-defense, he did not commit wilful and intended injury, but engaged only in nonintentional tortious conduct. Thus, even accepting the insurer's premise that it had no obligation to defend actions seeking damages not within the indemnification coverage, we find, upon proper measurement of the third party action against the insurer's liability to indemnify, it should have defended because the loss could have fallen within that liability. * * *

Nor can we accept defendant's argument that the duty to defend dissolves simply because the insured is unsuccessful in his defense and because the injured party recovers on the basis of a finding of the assured's wilful conduct. Citing *Abbott v. Western Nat. Indem. Co.* (1958) 165 Cal.App.2d 302, the insurer urges that if the judgment in a third party suit goes against the insured it operates as "res judicata or collateral estoppel in the insured's action or proceeding against the insurer."

We have explained that the insured would reasonably expect a defense by the insurer in all personal injury actions against him. If he is to be required to finance his own defense and then, only if successful, hold the insurer to its promise by means of a second suit for reimbursement, we defeat the basic reason for the purchase of the insurance. In purchasing his insurance the insured would reasonably expect that he would stand a better chance of vindication if supported by the resources and expertise of his insurer than if compelled to handle and finance the presentation of his case. He would, moreover, expect to be able to avoid the time, uncertainty and capital outlay in finding and retaining an attorney of his own. "The courts will not sanction a construction of the insurer's language that will defeat the very purpose or object of the insurance." (*Ritchie v. Anchor Casualty Co.*, supra, 135 Cal.App.2d 245, 257.)

Similarly, we find no merit in the insurer's third contention that our holding will embroil it in a conflict of interests. According to the insurer our ruling will require defense of an action in which the interests of insurer and insured are so opposed as to nullify the insurer's fulfillment of its duty of defense and of the protection of its own interests. For example, the argument goes, if defendant had defended against the Jones suit it would have sought to establish either that the insured was free from any liability or that such liability rested on intentional conduct. The insured, of course, would also seek a verdict holding him not liable but, if found liable, would attempt to obtain a ruling that such liability emanated from the nonintentional conduct within his insurance coverage. Thus, defendant contends, an insurer, if obligated to defend in this situation, faces an insoluble ethical problem.

Since, however, the court in the third party suit does not adjudicate the issue of coverage, the insurer's argument collapses. The only question there litigated is the insured's liability. The alleged victim does not concern himself with the theory of liability; he desires only the largest possible judgment. Similarly, the insured and insurer seek only to avoid, or at least to minimize, the judgment. As we have noted, modern procedural rules focus on whether, on a given set of facts, the plaintiff, regardless of the theory, may recover. Thus the question of whether or not the insured engaged in intentional conduct does not normally formulate an issue which is resolved in that litigation.[2]

In any event, if the insurer adequately reserves its right to assert the noncoverage defense later, it will not be bound by the judgment. If the injured party prevails, that party or the insured will assert his claim against the insurer. At this time the insurer can raise the noncoverage defense previously reserved. In this manner the interests of insured and insurer in defending against the injured party's primary suit will be identical; the insurer will not face the suggested dilemma.

Finally, defendant urges that our holding should require only the reimbursement of the insured's expenses in defending the third party action but not the payment of the judgment. Defendant acknowledges the general rule that an insurer that wrongfully refuses to defend is

---

[2] In rare cases the issue of punitive damages or a special verdict might present a potential conflict of interests, but such a possibility does not outweigh the advantages of the general rule. Even in such cases, however, the insurer will still be bound, ethically and legally, to litigate in the interests of the insured.

liable on the judgment against the insured. (*Arenson v. Nat. Automobile & Cas. Ins. Co.* (1955) 45 Cal.2d 81, 84; Civ.Code, § 2778.) Defendant argues, however, that the instant situation should be distinguished from that case because here the judgment has not necessarily been rendered on a theory within the policy coverage. Thus defendant would limit the insured's recovery to the expenses of the third party suit.

We rejected a similar proposal in *Tomerlin v. Canadian Indemnity Co.*, supra, 61 Cal.2d 638, 649–650. In that case, as we have noted, the insurer's obligation to defend arose out of estoppel. The insurer contended that we should apply a "tort" theory of damages to its wrongful refusal to defend. Such a theory, we explained, would impose upon the insured "the impossible burden" of proving the extent of the loss caused by the insurer's breach. As this court said in an analogous situation in *Arenson v. National Auto. & Cas. Ins. Co.* (1957) 48 Cal.2d 528, 539: "Having defaulted such agreement the company is manifestly bound to reimburse its insured for the full amount of any obligation reasonably incurred by him. It will not be allowed to defeat or whittle down its obligation on the theory that plaintiff himself was of such limited financial ability that he could not afford to employ able counsel, or to present every reasonable defense, or to carry his cause to the highest court having jurisdiction, * * *. Sustaining such a theory * * * would tend * * * to encourage insurance companies to similar disavowals of responsibility with everything to gain and nothing to lose."

In summary, the individual consumer in the highly organized and integrated society of today must necessarily rely upon institutions devoted to the public service to perform the basic functions which they undertake. At the same time the consumer does not occupy a sufficiently strong economic position to bargain with such institutions as to specific clauses of their contracts of performance, and, in any event, piecemeal negotiation would sacrifice the advantage of uniformity. Hence the courts in the field of insurance contracts have tended to require that the insurer render the basic insurance protection which it has held out to the insured. This obligation becomes especially manifest in the case in which the insurer has attempted to limit the principal coverage by an unclear exclusionary clause. We test the alleged limitation in the light of the insured's reasonable expectation of coverage; that test compels the indicated outcome of the present litigation.

The judgment is reversed and the trial court instructed to take evidence solely on the issue of damages alleged in plaintiff's complaint including the amount of the judgment in the Jones suit, and the costs, expenses and attorney's fees incurred in defending such suit.

NOTES AND QUESTIONS

1. *Strategic Pleading?* Does *Gray* imply that plaintiffs suing defendants who are otherwise judgment-proof should make every effort to include in their complaints allegations that will trigger a duty to defend, and thereby create potential coverage? See Ellen S. Pryor, The Stories We Tell: Intentional Harm and the Quest for Insurance Funding, 75 Texas L. Rev. 1721 (1997). Professor Pryor suggests that this is precisely what has happened, not only in order to create potential coverage, but to bring the

insurer into the defense and thereby to enhance the chances of settlement. On the implications of *Gray* more generally, see James M. Fischer, Broadening the Insurer's Duty to Defend: How *Gray v. Zurich Insurance Company* Transformed Liability Insurance into Litigation Insurance, 25 U.C. Davis L. Rev. 141 (1991).

2. *An Alternative to* Gray. The *Gray* test for the duty to defend mixed claims now predominates throughout the United States. As noted in Note 6 after *Beckwith*, however, the courts are divided as to the consequences that follow from the insurer's breach of this duty. The principal, though distinctly minority, alternative to the *Gray* approach is exemplified by *Burd v. Sussex Mutual Insurance Co.*, 267 A.2d 7 (N.J.1970), and a series of later cases following it. Under *Burd*, the insurer is not required to defend in two situations. First, if there is a conflict between the interests of the insurer and insured because the case may be defended by the insurer in a manner that would prejudice the insured's later coverage claim against the insurer, then the insurer may not defend. Second, if the trial of the liability claim against the insured will leave the question of coverage unresolved, the insurer need not defend. In both these two cases, the question whether there is a duty to defend is resolved in the later coverage suit, and the insurer pays defense costs only if it turns out that there was coverage of the liability action. In these cases, the insurer's duty to defend is transformed into a duty to pay defense costs if the later coverage suit against the insurer is successful. For ordinary individuals, who may not have the resources to hire expensive defense counsel, this approach may result in the provision of a less vigorous defense than would have been provided by the insurer.

The *Burd* approach obviously provides much less defense insurance than *Gray*, since defense costs are paid only after trial, and only if there is proof of coverage. In contrast, under *Gray*, the insured gets an insured defense from the start, and presumably even if it later turns out (in the coverage suit) that the claim was not in fact covered. This latter presumption has recently been challenged, however, by the growing number of cases, referenced in the next principal case, holding that the insured may sometimes be required to reimburse the insurer for the cost of defending the uncovered portion of a suit.

3. *Coverage Conflicts Versus Strategic Conflicts*. *Gray* purports to eliminate any conflict between the interests of the insurer and the insured by holding that the insurer is free to contest coverage later, without any collateral estoppel effect arising from facts or issues adjudicated in the liability suit against the insured. Under *Burd*, facts and issues determined in the underlying liability action may determine coverage, presumably through collateral estoppel effect. Therefore, under the *Burd* approach there is a potential conflict between the interests of the insurer defending the suit and the insured.

Even under *Gray*, however, less obvious conflicts are possible, wholly apart from collateral estoppel effects. For example, suppose that during the course of trial preparation, the insured admitted to counsel supplied by the insurer that he had intended to injure the plaintiff. Could this admission be used directly against the insured in the later suit to determine whether he was covered? If not, could knowledge of this admission nonetheless lead an insurer considering whether to deny coverage to investigate its possible defenses against a claim of coverage more carefully than it might in the absence of such knowledge? Would an insured being defended by counsel selected by the insurer be more reluctant to be candid under such circumstances than with counsel independently obtained? Similarly, would an insurer defending under circumstances where it doubted its ultimate duty to indemnify be inclined to defend less vigorously, and therefore to risk incurring a larger judgment—for all of which the insured might later turn out to be liable?

4. *Independent Counsel.* Recognizing these possibilities, a number of courts have held that the *Gray* rule does not afford the insured sufficient protection when there are potential conflicts of interest between the insurer and the insured. These courts have therefore held that unless the insured in a situation of potential conflict gives his informed consent to being represented by counsel selected by the insurer, he has a right to select independent counsel himself, to be paid by the insurer. The leading case is *San Diego Navy Federal Credit Union v. Cumis Insurance Society, Inc.*, 162 Cal.App.3d 358 (Cal. App. 1984). In 1987, the California legislature responded with a limitation on but substantial acceptance of *Cumis.* California Civil Code § 2860 (West 1994). Nonetheless, the independent-counsel rule is often referred to as the "*Cumis*" rule. The rule may not extend to all conflicts, however, but only to those in which the insurer's control of the defense would create the potential for abuse. RLLI, § 18, provides that independent counsel should be available "when the claim could be defended in a manner that would advantage the insurer at the expense of the insured." A demand for damages in excess of the policy limits ordinarily would not seem to be such a case. For further discussion, see Leo P. Martinez, Coverage Advice: The Missing Piece of the *Cumis* Puzzle, 43–4/44–1 Tort Trial & Ins. Prac. L.J. 63 (2008); William T. Barker, Insurer Control of the Defense: Reservations of Rights and Right to Independent Counsel, 71 Def. Counsel J. 16 (2004).

5. *When Should the Coverage Issue Be Resolved?* The conflict of interest in cases involving potentially non-covered claims would disappear if the coverage issue were resolved first. Either there would be coverage pursuant to the potentiality rule, in which case there would no conflict, or there would be no coverage, in which case there would be no defense. Under the approach in *Gray,* however, the insurer must always defend if there is a chance that there might be coverage, or it loses the right to deny coverage later. The insured thus sometimes obtains a defense even when it turns out (later) that the claim against him did not fall within the potentiality test.

To deal with this dilemma, should there be a firm rule about when to resolve the underlying coverage dispute, or should the sequencing be left to the parties? A declaratory judgment action, at the outset (as described above in Note 5 to the *Beckwith* case) would resolve the coverage issue, and thereby also determine whether the insurer has a duty to defend. The courts have under some circumstances seemed to encourage such actions. See, e.g., *Mowry v. Badger State Mutual Casualty Company,* 385 N.W.2d 171 (Wis. 1986); *Miller v. Shugart,* 316 N.W.2d 729 (Minn. 1982). But such an action would be unnecessary if the insured or the insurer later defeated the tort action against the insured, and the insured (in the meantime) would have incurred the cost of litigating the declaratory judgment action. Should the rule that the insurer is not liable for the costs incurred by the insured (including counsel fees) in proving that there is coverage be reversed in order to encourage resolution of the coverage question?

Conversely, determination of the underlying coverage question could await resolution of the tort action against the insured. Such an approach would avoid unnecessary expenditures in declaratory judgment actions preceding tort suits, but would preserve the conflict of interest problems addressed by the rules in *Burd* and *Gray*. Is there reason to think that one approach will be systematically preferable to the other?

Shoshone First Bank v. Pacific Employers Insurance Company

Supreme Court of Wyoming, 2000.
2 P.3d 510.

■ THOMAS, JUSTICE.

The only question presented in this case relates to the allocation to, and recovery from, an insured by an insurance carrier of part of the costs and expenses of litigation. Pacific Employers Insurance Company (Pacific) seeks to allocate and recover for both the costs attributable to non-covered claims under the policy and the costs attributable to a counterclaim. Shoshone First Bank and United Bancorporation of Wyoming, Inc. (collectively Shoshone) vigorously assert that the allocation and recovery of the costs of litigation should not be permitted. This case comes to us as a question certified from the United States District Court for the District of Wyoming. In answering the certified question, we hold that the allocation and recovery of the costs attributable to the defense of claims that were not covered by the policy of insurance is not permitted under Wyoming law so long as one or more of the claims alleged is covered by the insurance policy. We further hold that the allocation and recovery of costs attributable to the prosecution of a counterclaim belonging to the insured is permitted, without regard to any tactical or strategic justification for asserting the counterclaim. * * *

Pacific issued a policy of commercial general liability insurance (Policy) to Shoshone for a policy period from December 5, 1990 through December 5, 1991. The Policy contains a standard commercial general liability coverage form issued by the Insurance Service Office. The duty to defend clause states:

> We will pay those sums that the insured becomes legally obligated to pay as damages because of "bodily injury" or "property damage" to which this insurance applies. * * * We will have the right and duty to defend any "suit" seeking those damages * * *.

Coverage under the Policy for "bodily injury" and "property damage" applies only if the injury or damage is caused by an "occurrence" during the policy period, as those terms are defined therein:

> 3. "Bodily injury" means bodily injury, sickness or disease sustain by a person, including death resulting from any of these at any time. * * *
>
> 9. "Occurrence" means an accident, including continuous or repeated exposure to substantially the same general harmful conditions.

The Policy also contains "Coverage B" for personal and advertising injury liability:

> We will pay those sums that the insured becomes legally obligated to pay as damages because of "personal injury" or "advertising injury" to which this insurance applies.

The Policy contains the following exclusion:

> This insurance does not apply to: "Bodily injury" or "property damage" expected or intended from the standpoint of the insured.

The action out of which the current dispute arose was filed on November 7, 1995, by a disgruntled former director, alleging that his termination on November 15, 1991 constituted a breach of contract, breach of the covenant of good faith and fair dealing, invasion of privacy, infliction of severe emotional distress, and abuse of process. On November 8, 1995, the chairman of Shoshone mailed copies of the complaint to Shoshone's insurance agent, seeking defense of the claims, and also to Shoshone's retained attorneys. Pacific did not respond prior to the date an answer was due. Therefore, Shoshone's retained attorneys filed an answer and a counterclaim. Following that filing, Shoshone received, a December 4, 1995, letter from a liability specialist at Pacific reserving the insurer's rights pending further investigation of its rights and obligations concerning the complaint. In March of 1996, Pacific agreed to defend Shoshone under a continuing reservation of rights. Pacific undertook the defense because, according to the liability specialist, Count IV of the complaint, alleging invasion of privacy, was potentially covered by Shoshone's policy. Pacific, however, asserted that it was entitled to allocate to Shoshone the costs of the defense related to uncovered claims. The director's action later was settled by court-ordered mediation. The total settlement, the exact amount of which is confidential, was a fraction of the more than $215,000.00 paid by Pacific to defend the suit and the additional $40,000.00 in fees and costs that Pacific declined to pay and Shoshone did pay. On December 4, 1997, Pacific sued Shoshone seeking recovery of the portion of the defense costs paid to defend the uncovered claims and to assert the counterclaim. * * *

Pacific acknowledged that the coverage of its policy extended to the claim for invasion of privacy because, at least potentially, that claim would qualify under the "personal injury" coverage. The plain language of the Policy issued to Shoshone by Pacific in the general liability policy Coverage B, states:

> We will pay those sums that the insured becomes legally obligated to pay as damages because of "personal injury" or "advertising injury" to which this insurance applies. * * * We will have the right and duty to defend any "suit" seeking those damages.

"Suit," as defined by the Policy, "means a civil proceeding in which damages because of 'bodily injury,' 'property damage,' 'personal injury,' or 'advertising injury' to which this insurance applies are alleged." The claim asserting an invasion of privacy specifically qualifies under the "personal injury" coverage of Shoshone's policy.

The problem presented by Pacific and Shoshone relates to the assumption by Pacific for the total cost of defending all the claims presented in the director's complaint. Pacific contends that it is responsible for those defense costs attributable to the claim for invasion of privacy only. It contends that it is entitled to allocate the defense costs between the claim for invasion of privacy and all the other claims involved and seek compensation from Shoshone for the costs of defending the other claims. Shoshone contends that the allocation of and claim for reimbursement of the other defense costs is inappropriate and should be denied. In *Alm,* 369 P.2d at 219, we adopted, with approval, this language from *Ritchie v. Anchor Cas. Co.,* 286 P.2d 1000, 1006 (1955): "If the complaint filed against the insured alleges several causes of action, some of which are not covered by the policy but one or more is within its terms, the insurer is bound to defend the action * * *." We went on to point out that even if doubt exists with respect to the duty to defend, it should be resolved in favor of the insured. The duty to defend, therefore, extends to the entire suit brought against the insured. Even though the duty to defend is present, it does not require payment of a judgment based on claims other than those covered by the policy.

The question of allocation of the costs of defense is an issue of first impression in Wyoming. Pacific urges upon us the majority position which permits allocation of litigation expenses when the action against the insured involves both covered and uncovered claims. Recognizing that in other jurisdictions allocation is allowed between the insurer and the insured, we eschew this theory, and hold that unless an agreement to the contrary is found in the policy, the insurer is liable for all of the costs of defending the action. *See Timberline Equipment Co., Inc. v. St. Paul Fire & Marine Ins. Co.,* 576 P.2d 1244, 1247 (1978).

Pacific contends that under the authorities it favors it is only required to pay those defense costs in the action by the director that relate to the covered claim for invasion of privacy, and Shoshone is responsible for the costs of defending the other five non-covered claims set forth in the complaint. No definition of the "duty to defend" nor of "claims" is set forth in the Policy. Under our articulated principles of contract interpretation relating to insurance policies, an ambiguity arises because of the undefined terms, and the policy will be strictly construed against the insurer, requiring Pacific to defend Shoshone on all claims. *Albany County School Dist. No. 1,* 763 P.2d at 1258. Any doubt with respect to that coverage must be resolved in favor of the insured. *Alm,* 369 P.2d at 219. Pacific's failure to treat with the allocation of defense costs in the policy results in an assumption by the insured that Pacific will pay the full cost of the defense. We construe the policy in favor of Shoshone to that end.

Pacific urges the adoption of the reasoning of the Supreme Court of California in *Buss v. Superior Court,* 16 Cal.4th 35 (1997), which allowed the allocation of the costs of defense. We have opted to follow a different policy with respect to the duty to defend, but we think the court in *Buss* very eloquently articulated the pragmatic difficulty of mounting only a partial defense of the insured:

> [W]e can, and do, justify the insurer's duty to defend the entire "mixed" action prophylactically, as an obligation imposed by

law in support of the policy. To defend meaningfully, the insurer must defend immediately. (*Montrose Chemical Corp. v. Superior Court, supra,* [6 Cal.4th 287, 295].) To defend immediately, it must defend entirely. It cannot parse the claims, dividing those that are at least potentially covered from those that are not. To do so would be time consuming. It might also be futile: The "plasticity of modern pleading" (*Gray v. Zurich Insurance Co., supra,* [65 Cal.2d 263, 276 (1966)]) allows the transformation of claims that are at least potentially covered into claims that are not, and vice versa.

Buss, 939 P.2d at 775. This language illustrates the problems that can be anticipated if the insurer is permitted to pick and choose which claims it will defend. Added to those difficulties would be the predicament of the insured in having to obtain separate counsel to defend non-covered claims and potential disagreements between members of the defense team. Such a policy necessarily would lead to inefficiency and perhaps inconsistency in the resolution of disputes.

Because of our prior recognition that the insurer is charged with the duty of defending the entire suit, and in light of the problems discussed in *Buss,* we opt to follow the minority rule, and we will not permit allocation. Illinois and Louisiana do not allow allocation of defense costs. In *Riley Stoker Corp. v. Fidelity and Guar. Ins. Underwriters, Inc.,* 26 F.3d 581, 589 (5th Cir.1994), the United States Court of Appeals for the Fifth Circuit looked to the law of Louisiana to determine whether apportionment between covered and uncovered claims could be made. The court cited *Yount v. Maisano,* 627 So.2d 148, 153 (La.1993) in which the Louisiana Supreme Court held "that the insurer, who had a duty to defend, was obligated to pay defense costs even though it was ultimately determined in the coverage suit that none of the claims were covered." *Riley Stoker Corp.,* 26 F.3d at 589–90. The United States Court of Appeals for the Fifth Circuit rejected the insurance company's effort to apportion the costs of defense. The Appellate Court of Illinois considered the policy requiring defense on the entire suit, and it also refused to allow allocation of defense costs. *Bedoya v. Illinois Founders Ins. Co.,* 688 N.E.2d 757, 762 (1997).

It is obvious that no right of allocation should exist if the costs incurred for the defense of a non-covered claim were necessarily incurred or would have had to be incurred because of the defense of a covered claim. *See* 1 Allan D. Windt, *Insurance Claims & Disputes,* § 4.13 at 201–03 & n. 162 (3d ed. Shepard's/McGraw-Hill 1995). This indeed was the case so far as Shoshone and Pacific were concerned. The Policy required Pacific to defend Shoshone in any suit and not simply for specific claims. There is no indication in the Policy of any distinction to be made between covered and non-covered claims so far as the defense of those claims is concerned, and we will not permit the Policy to be modified by subsequent letters from the insurer to the insured. Pacific attempts to modify the Policy despite the deficiencies of the Policy.

Pacific claims the right to allocate the defense costs for the uncovered claims through a reservation of rights letter. In the reservation of rights letter, written January 8, 1997, from Pacific to Shoshone, Pacific specifically reserved the right to make an allocation of the fees, expenses and indemnity payments when the case was resolved, and it addressed both covered and uncovered claims. The insurer is not permitted to unilaterally modify and change policy coverage. We agree with the Supreme Court of Hawaii that a reservation of rights letter "does not relieve the insurer of the costs incurred in defending its insured where the insurer was obligated, in the first instance, to provide such a defense." *First Ins. Co. of Hawaii, Inc. v. State, by Minami,* 665 P.2d 648, 654 (1983). Pacific could have included allocation language in the Policy, but it failed to do so. We look only to the four corners of the policy to determine coverage, and where the policy is unambiguous, extrinsic evidence is not considered. *Doctors' Co.*, 864 P.2d at 1024. The Policy issued to Shoshone by Pacific states a duty to defend, and allocation is not mentioned. In light of the failure of the policy language to provide for allocation, we will not permit the contract to be amended or altered by a reservation of rights letter.

Usually we do not cite to judicial decisions that have not been published. We have been advised, however, of a very clear and incisive articulation of the problem that confronts us in a recent order of the United States District Court for the District of Wyoming granting a summary judgment. In that order, the United States District Court Judge captured the public policy with respect to why insurers should not be entitled to recoup defense costs from their insureds under a reservation of rights. The court said:

15. A reservation of rights letter does not create a contract allowing an insurer to recoup defense costs from its insureds.

16. The question as to whether there is a duty to defend an insured is a difficult one, but because that is the business of an insurance carrier, it is the insurance carrier's duty to make that decision.

If an insurance carrier believes that no coverage exists, then it should deny its insured a defense at the beginning instead of defending and later attempting to recoup from its insured the costs of defending the underlying action. Where the insurance carrier is uncertain over insurance coverage for the underlying claim, the proper course is for the insurance carrier to tender a defense and seek a declaratory judgment as to coverage under the policy. However, to allow the insurer to force the insured into choosing between seeking a defense under the policy, and run the potential risk of having to pay for this defense if it is subsequently determined that no duty to defend existed, or giving up all meritorious claims that a duty to defend exists, places the insured in the position of making a Hobson's choice. Furthermore, endorsing such conduct is tantamount to allowing the insurer to extract a unilateral amendment to the insurance contract. If this became common practice, the insurance industry might extract coercive arrangements from their insureds, destroying the concept of liability and litigation insurance. Order on Plaintiff's Motion for Summary Judgment, *America States Ins. Co. v. Ridco, Inc., Riddles Jewelry, Inc., and Ken B. Berger,* Civ. No. 95CV158D (D.Wyo.1999).

We turn then to the other question presented by the certification order of the United States District Court for the District of Wyoming which addresses the allocation of costs in connection with Shoshone's counterclaim. We invoke our rule that if an insurance policy fails to specify coverage for prosecuting counterclaims, the policy language will not be "tortured" to create an ambiguity. *Sinclair Oil Corp. v. Republic Ins. Co.,* 929 P.2d 535, 539 (Wyo.1996); *Doctors' Co.,* 864 P.2d at 1024. The policy issued to Shoshone by Pacific did not obligate the insurer to prosecute any claims. For that reason, we will not require Pacific to assume any of the costs incurred with respect to Shoshone's counterclaims for indemnity and breach of duty of loyalty against the director. * * *

NOTES AND QUESTIONS

1. *Majority Rule?* The court indicated that it would not follow what it regarded as the "majority" rule that the insured may be required to reimburse the insurer for the cost of defending uncovered claims. But at present the majority of jurisdictions still have not ruled authoritatively, and the decisions continue to go both ways. See, e.g., *Am & Foreign Ins. Co. v. Jerry's Sport Ctr., Inc.*, 2 A.3d 526 (Pa. 2010) (no right to recoup defense costs in the absence of a policy provision providing for it*); Nobel Ins. Co. v. Austin Power Co.*, 256 F.Supp. 2d 937 (W.D. Ark. 2003) (recoupment permitted if provided for in Reservation of Rights). RLLI, § 24 takes the position that no recoupment is the proper default rule, subject to displacement in the policy itself but not by a mere reservation of rights.

2. *Recoupment of Defense Costs in Two Situations.* The decisions address two situations in which insurers seek to recoup some costs they incurred in providing a defense. The first category is the "mixed" claim that the insurer defends because one or more counts are potentially covered. *Shoshone* falls into this category, as does *Buss v. Superior Court*, 939 P.2d 766 (Cal. 1997), the leading case supporting a right of reimbursement. In *Buss,* the Supreme Court of California addressed cases in which a portion of the complaint contained an allegation that was never potentially within coverage, and the insurer specifically proved the cost of defending the uncovered portion. The court held that the insurer could recoup the portion of its defense costs that it could prove were expended for defending the uncovered claims. For analysis, see Angela R. Elbert & Stanley C. Nardoni, Buss Stop: A Policy Language Based Analysis, 13 Conn. Ins. L. J. 61 (2006).

The second category is the claim as to which there was never any duty to defend at all, because no part of the suit is potentially covered. Subsequent to its decision in *Buss,* the Supreme Court of California ruled that there was a right to recoupment in this situation as well. *Scottsdale Ins. Co. v. MV Transp. Co.*, 115 P.3d 460 (Cal. 2005). See also *Cincinnati Ins. Co. v. Grand Pointe, LLC*, 501 F.Supp. 2d 1145 (E.D. Tenn. 2007) (upholding a right of recoupment in this situation); *Gen. Agents Ins. Co. of Am., Inc. v. Midwest Sporting Goods Co.*, 828 N.E.2d 1092 (Ill. 2005) (denying such a right). Thus, in *Grinnell Mutual Reinsurance Co. v. Shierk*, 996 F.Supp. 836 (S.D. Ill. 1998), the insured had been convicted of criminal assault before the insurer defended the civil action against him. The insurer was entitled to recoupment because there was never any potential for coverage and thus never any duty to defend. And in *Colony Insurance Co. v. G & E Tires & Service, Inc.*, 777 So. 2d 1034 (Fla. App. 2000), the court indicated that the insurer was seeking costs "expended in defending claims which do not, as alleged, give rise even to a potential duty to defend." Some decisions address the first category, and some the second. Yet the courts that refer to a "majority" rule seem to be combining the two categories and then doing their counting. Is there a better argument for a right to recoup defense costs for defending mixed claims than for defending claims in which there was never any potential for coverage at all? Consider the suggestions in the next paragraph.

3. *"Unjust" Enrichment?* Some of the courts holding that the insurer has a right to recoup defense costs do so under circumstances that they suggest reveal that the insurers' provision of a defense has "unjustly" enriched the insured. This suggestion implies that, where the insurer was not required to defend because the claim was not a "mixed" one, the provision of a defense was wholly without benefit to the insurer. Consider whether the following constitute benefits that accrue to the insurer when it defends these suits: a) the insurer can defer its determination of coverage issues, thus avoiding being estopped to deny its indemnity obligation if it later turns out that it did have a duty to defend; b) the insurer can control defense expenditures; c) the insurer can ensure that the claim is effectively defended, thus minimizing its potential indemnity exposure; d) the insurer can participate in, and perhaps control, settlement negotiations; and e) the insurer can gain access to otherwise-privileged communications. To what extent do the existence of these benefits to the insurer of providing what may later prove to have been a defense that the insurer was not obligated to provide undercut the argument that the insured has been unjustly enriched when the insurer defends?

4. *What's Left of the Duty to Defend?* Where there is a right to recoup defense costs is the duty to defend still broader than the duty to indemnify? Would the insurer in *Gray* have been entitled to reimbursement for the cost of defending the battery claim against the insured? If so, is the duty to defend anything more than the duty to loan the insured the cost of defense, subject to a repayment obligation respecting the defense of uncovered claims? That is, will the conventional provision of a defense subject to a reservation of the right to contest coverage be transformed into the provision of a defense subject to a reservation of the right to seek reimbursement for the cost of defending uncovered claims?

5. *Between a Rock and a Hard Place.* Some commentators have argued for the right to reimbursement of defense costs on the ground that policyholders do not want to subsidize the defense of claims that fall outside the scope of coverage. See, e.g., Robert H. Jerry II, The Insurer's Right to Reimbursement of Defense Costs, 42 Ariz. L. Rev. 13 (2000). Yet the issue has been the subject of litigation for over twenty years, and standard-form policies have not been revised to provide for an express right to recoup defense costs. Does this suggest a flaw in the market, or that in fact policyholders would not find such a provision attractive, even in return for lower premiums? To what extent does the risk that through strategic pleading the plaintiff in the underlying case can put the insured in a position of jeopardy regarding defense costs complicate the issue?

Parsons v. Continental National American Group

Supreme Court of Arizona, En Banc, 1976.
113 Ariz. 223.

■ GORDON, JUSTICE:

Appellants Ruth, Dawn and Gail Parsons obtained a judgment against appellant Michael Smithey, and then had issued and served a writ of garnishment on appellee, Continental National American Group (hereinafter referred to as CNA). The Superior Court of Pima County entered judgment in favor of the garnishee, CNA and from this judgment appellants appealed. The Court of Appeals, Division Two, reversed the judgment of the Superior Court, 23 Ariz.App. 597, 535 P.2d 17 (1975). Opinion of the Court of Appeals vacated and judgment of the Superior Court of Pima County reversed, and it is ordered that the judgment be entered in favor of appellants in the sum of $50,000.

We accepted this petition for review because of the importance of the question presented. We are asked to determine whether an insurance carrier in a garnishment action is estopped from denying coverage under its policy when its defense in that action is based upon confidential information obtained by the carrier's attorney from an insured as a result of representing him in the original tort action.

Appellant, Michael Smithey, age 14, brutally assaulted his neighbors, appellants Ruth, Dawn and Gail Parsons, on the night of March 26, 1967.

During April, 1967, Frank Candelaria, CNA claims representative, began an investigation of the incident. On June 6, 1967, he wrote to Howard Watt, the private counsel retained by the Smitheys, advising him that CNA was "now in the final stages of our investigation," and to contact the Parsons' attorney to ascertain what type of settlement they would accept. Watt did contact the Parsons' attorney and requested that a formal demand settlement be tendered and the medical bills be forwarded to Candelaria. On August 11, 1967, Candelaria wrote a detailed letter to his company on his investigation of Michael's background in regards to his school experiences. He concluded the letter with the following:

> "In view of this information gathered and in discussion with the boy's father's attorney, Mr. Howard Watts, and with the boy's parents, I am reasonably convinced that the boy was not in control of his senses at the time of this incident.
>
> "It is, therefore, my suggestion that, and unless instructed otherwise, I will proceed to commence settlement negotiations with the claimant's attorney so that this matter may be disposed of as soon as possible."

Prior to the following dates: August 15, 1967, August 28, 1967, and October 23, 1967, Candelaria tried to settle with the Parsons for the medical expenses and was unsuccessful.

On October 13, 1967, the Parsons filed a complaint alleging that Michael Smithey assaulted the Parsons and that Michael's parents were negligent in their failure to restrain Michael and obtain the necessary medical and psychological attention for him. At the time that the Parsons filed suit they tendered a demand settlement offer of $22,500 which was refused by CNA as "completely unrealistic."

CNA's retained counsel undertook the Smithey's defense and also continued to communicate with CNA and advised him on November 10, 1967:

> "I have secured a rather complete and confidential file on the minor insured who is now in the Paso Robles School for Boys, a

maximum-security institution with facilities for psychiatric treatment, and he will be kept there indefinitely and certainly for at least six months * * *.

"The above referred-to confidential file shows that the boy is fully aware of his acts and that he knew what he was doing was wrong. It follows, therefore, that the assaults he committed on claimants can only be a deliberate act on his part."

After CNA had been so advised they sent a reservation of rights letter to the Smitheys stating that the insurance company, as a courtesy to the insureds, would investigate and defend the Parsons' claim, but would do so without waiving any of the rights under the policy. The letter further stated that it was possible the act involved might be found to be an intentional act, and that the policy specifically excludes liability for bodily injury caused by an intentional act. This letter was addressed only to the parents and not to Michael.

In preparing for trial the CNA attorney retained to undertake the defense of the Smitheys interviewed Michael and received a narrative statement from him in regards to the events of March 26, 1967, and then wrote to CNA: "His own story makes it obvious that his acts were willful and criminal."

CNA also requested an evaluation of the tort case and the same attorney advised CNA: "Assuming liability and coverage, the injury is worth the full amount of the policy or $25,000.00."

On the issue of liability the trial court directed a verdict for Michael's parents on the grounds that there was no evidence of the parents being negligent. This Court affirmed, *Parsons v. Smithey,* 109 Ariz. 49, 504 P.2d 1272 (1973). On the question of Michael's liability the trial court granted plaintiff's motion for a directed verdict after the defense presented no evidence and there was no opposition to the motion. Judgment was entered against Michael in the amount of $50,000.

The Parsons then garnished CNA, and moved for a guardian ad litem to be appointed for Michael which was granted by the trial court. On November 23, 1970, appellee Parsons offered to settle with CNA in the amount of its policy limits, $25,000. This offer was not accepted.

CNA successfully defended the garnishment action by claiming that the intentional act exclusion applied. The same law firm and attorney that had previously represented Michael represented the carrier in the garnishment action.

Appellants contend that CNA should be estopped to deny coverage and have waived the intentional act exclusion because the company took advantage of the fiduciary relationship between its agent (the attorney) and Michael Smithey. We agree.

The attorneys, retained by CNA, represented Michael Smithey at the personal liability trial and, as a result, obtained privileged and confidential information from Michael's confidential file at the Paso Robles School for Boys, during the discovery process and, more importantly, from the attorney-client relationship. Both the A.B.A. Committee on Ethics and Professional Responsibility and the State Bar of Arizona, Committee on Rules of Professional Conduct have held that an attorney that represented the insured at the request of the insurer owes undivided fidelity to the insured, and, therefore, may not reveal any information or conclusions derived therefrom to the insurer that may be detrimental to the insured in any subsequent action. The A.B.A. Committee on Ethics and Professional Responsibility in Informal Opinion Number 949 stated:

> "If the firm does represent the insured in the personal injury action, to subsequently reveal to the insurer any information received from the insured for possible use by the insurer in defense of a garnishment proceeding by the injured person, would be a clear violation of both Canon 6 and Canon 37 regarding confidences of a client. A successful defense of the garnishment proceeding by the insurer would be contrary to the interests of the insured, because if the insurer is not obligated to pay the judgment, execution against the insured can be expected. The result would not be different in practical effect from a suit directly against the insured to escape liability under the policy.
>
> "If the firm does not defend the insured in the personal injury action, the firm cannot reasonably expect the attorney who does represent the insured to furnish either to the firm or to the insurer, for use in a garnishment action by the injured person against the insurer, information that attorney learns during the course of defending the insured, since that attorney should not be expected to breach his professional obligations by furnishing information Canons 6 and 37 prohibit him from furnishing." August 8, 1966.

The Arizona Ethics Opinion No. 261 adopted November 15, 1968 stated:

> "A.B.A. Informal Opinion C728 makes it very clear that the inquiring attorney is the attorney for the insured, B, even though the attorney would be paid by G Insurance Company. The undivided fidelity owed by the attorney, then, is to B and not to G Insurance Company.
>
> "* * * it was unethical for the inquiring attorney to represent the insurance company in an action against the insured, after judgment against the insured, to declare that the policy did not provide coverage. A full reading of that opinion and in particular the last paragraph thereof, lead us to this conclusion. That opinion ended as follows:
>
>> "Is it now ethical for you to represent the company in an action against the insured to declare that the policy does not cover? We believe that to do so without full disclosure and full consent on the part of the insured would be a violation of Canon 6. Your connection with the case on behalf of the insured no doubt has resulted in the development of confidences of a nature that should in good conscience require you to decline representation of the company in a case so intimately tied to your original litigation. This is particularly true when one of the ideas involved is not only to be fair but to give all appearances of fairness * * *."

The State Bar Committee in its Arizona Ethics Opinion No. 282 adopted May 21, 1969 stated:

> "No better statement of the basis for our position on this question occurs to us than the following quotation from the Blakslee article cited above (55 A.B.A.Jour. at p. 263):
>
>> "Although the opinions of the Committee state that the lawyer represents both the insurer and insured, *it is clear that his highest duty is to the insured and that the lawyer cannot be used as an agent of the company to supply information detrimental to the insured.* The lawyer is a professional retained pursuant to the terms of a contract between the insurer and insured. The company has a right to expect that the issue of liability for injury and damages will be effectively and forcefully presented by the lawyer it has chosen. It has agreed, by its contract, to pay damages once they are determined.
>>
>> "The client, on the other hand, in order to obtain an insurance policy, has given up the right to direct the incidents of the trial by agreeing that the company shall have the right to choose the attorney. This also is fair since it is the company that will ultimately pay the judgment. *But counsel should not be expected to communicate information received in confidence or to betray confidences lodged in them by trusting clients.* To do so would not only destroy public confidence in the legal profession, but also would make defense attorneys investigators for carriers. That the company has not satisfied itself concerning coverage by its other, independent methods, is no compelling reason why defense counsel should be asked to betray the trust reposed in him by the insured. The fact that the company may be required to pay a monetary judgment does not alter the situation, since the company voluntarily has assumed this contractual obligation by virtue of its existence as an insurer. Its contractual obligation, voluntarily assumed, should not be permitted to be used as the basis for converting the defense counsel into something beyond a lawyer defending a client." (Emphasis supplied.)

The attorney who represents an insured owed him "undeviating and single allegiance" whether the attorney is compensated by the insurer or the insured. *Newcomb v. Meiss,* 263 Minn. 315 (1962).

The attorney in the instant case should have notified CNA that he could no longer represent them when he obtained any information (as a result of his attorney-client relationship with Michael) that could possibly be detrimental to Michael's interests under the coverage of the policy.

The attorney representing Michael Smithey in the personal injury suit instituted by the Parsons had to be sure at all times that the fact that he was compensated by the insurance company did not "adversely affect his judgment on behalf of or dilute his loyalty to [his] client, [Michael Smithey]." Ethical consideration 5–14. Where an attorney is representing the insured in a personal injury suit, and, at the same time advising the insurer on the question of liability under the policy it is difficult to see how that attorney could give individual loyalty to the insured-clients. "The standards of the legal profession require undeviating fidelity of the lawyer to his client. No exceptions can be tolerated." *Van Dyke v. White,* 55 Wash.2d 601 (1960). This standard is in accord with Ethical Consideration 5–1.

> "EC 5–1. The professional judgment of a lawyer should be exercised, within the bounds of the law, solely for the benefit of his client and free of compromising influences and loyalties. Neither his personal interests, the interests of other clients, nor the desires of third persons should be permitted to dilute his loyalty to his client."

The attorney in the present case continued to act as Michael's attorney while he was actively working against Michael's interests. When an attorney who is an insurance company's agent uses the confidential relationship between an attorney and a client to gather information so as to deny the insured coverage under the policy in the garnishment proceeding we hold that such conduct constitutes a waiver of any policy defense, and is so contrary to public policy that the insurance company is estopped as a matter of law from disclaiming liability under an exclusionary clause in the policy. *Employers Casualty Company v. Tilley,* 496 S.W.2d 552 (Tex.1973). In the *Tilley* case the Texas Supreme Court also noted that such conduct on the part of an attorney and insurance carrier has been the subject of litigation in other jurisdictions especially in regards to the situation where an attorney representing the carrier does not fully and completely disclose to the insured the specific conflict of interest involved.

> "Conduct in violation of the above principles by the insurer through the attorney selected by it to represent the insured has been condemned by the highest courts of several other jurisdictions. In *Perkoski v. Wilson,* 371 Pa. 553 (1952); *Tiedtke v. Fidelity & Casualty Company of New York,* 222 So.2d 206 (Fla.1969); *Bogle v. Conway,* 199 Kan. 707 (1967); *Crum v. Anchor Casualty Company,* 264 Minn. 378, 119 N.W.2d 703 (1963); *Merchants Indemnity Corp. v. Eggleston,* 37 N.J. 114 (1962); and *Van Dyke v. White,* 55 Wash.2d 601 (1960), analogous conduct in violation of such principles was held to preclude or estop the insurer from denying coverage or liability. See also general criticisms and consequences of such conduct discussed in *Meirthew v. Last,* 376 Mich. 33 (1965); and *Newcomb v. Meiss,* 263 Minn. 315 (1962)." *Employers Casualty Company v. Tilley,* 496 S.W.2d at 559.

Appellee urges that the personal liability matter was defended under a reservation of rights agreement and this agreement had the effect of allowing the insurance company to investigate and defend the claim and still not waive any defenses. We hold that the reservation of rights agreement is not material to this case because the same attorney was representing conflicting clients. Appellee further urges that the procedure followed in the instant case is provided for by statute in Arizona. A.R.S. § 20–1130 states inter alia:

> "Without limitation of any right of defense of an insurer otherwise, none of the following acts by or on behalf of an

insurer shall be deemed to constitute a waiver of any provision of a policy or of any defense of the insurer thereunder: * * *

"3. Investigating any loss or claim under any policy or engaging in negotiations looking toward a possible settlement of any such loss or claim."

Appellee misconstrues the protection offered to the carrier under A.R.S. § 20–1130. This statute does not grant to a carrier the right to engage an attorney to act on behalf of the insured to defend a claim against the insured while at the same time build a defense against the insured on behalf of the insurer. This conflict of interest constitutes a source of prejudice upon which the insured may invoke the doctrine of estoppel. See *Pacific Indemnity Co. v. Acel Delivery Service, Inc.*, 485 F.2d 1169 (1973), *cert. den.*, 415 U.S. 921 (1974). * * *

NOTES AND QUESTIONS

1. *Whose Lawyer?* The problem dramatized in *Parsons* is present even in much more conventional situations. There is a tripartite relationship between the insurer, the insured and defense counsel; yet that relationship may create a conflict between the interests of insurer and insured. In that situation, whom does the attorney represent—the insured, the insurer, or both? Some state courts have taken the view that defense counsel represents the insured alone, from the outset. See, e.g., *In re Rules of Prof'l Conduct*, 2 P.3d 806 (Mont. 2000); *Brohawn v. Transamerica Ins. Co.*, 347 A.2d 842 (Md. 1975). Others hold that defense counsel can and does represent both the insured and the insurer, at least until conflicts arise. See, e.g., *Paradigm Ins. Co. v. Langerman Law Offices*, 2 P.3d 663 (Ariz. Ct. App. 1999); *Cincinnati Ins. Co. v. Wills*, 717 N.E.2d 151 (Ind. 1999). At this point counsel owes its primary duty to the insured. For a listing of the states that subscribe to the one-client and two-client views, see William T. Barker, Insurer Control of Defense: Reservations of Rights and Right to Independent Counsel, 71 Def. Counsel J. 16 (2004).

In theory it is relatively easy for an attorney to avoid deliberately entering into a situation in which there is a conflict between her interests and those of her client. When the attorney has multiple clients, however, or a single client whose interests conflict with those of others with whom the attorney also has relations—such as the insurance company that pays her fees—practical problems are not so easy to avoid. Should the attorney who consents to represent an insured and be paid by the insurer recognize that she is automatically in a position of potential conflict? Is there not always a possibility in an ordinary negligence action that the attorney's factual investigation will reveal information relevant to the insurer's possible coverage defense, as it did in *Parsons?*

2. *An Exclusive Duty to the Insured?* One solution would be to permit the insured to hire his own attorney, to be reimbursed by the insurer, in all cases. This is the "*Cumis*" approach described above in Note 4 after *Gray*. This would assure that the attorney's loyalty is to the insured alone. That solution is massive and expensive overkill, however, since actual conflicts probably arise in only a small percentage of claims. Another is to hold, as in *Parsons,* that the insurer retains the right to select the defense attorney, but that the attorney owes an exclusive duty of loyalty to the insured. Another is to permit "dual" representation. Rule 1.7(b) of the Model Rules

of Professional Conduct (1999) permits an attorney to represent the interests of multiple clients "if the lawyer reasonably believes that the lawyer will be able to provide competent and diligent representation to each affected client." On the other hand, Rule 1.6 states that "a lawyer shall not reveal information relating to the representation of a client unless the client gives informed consent, the disclosure is impliedly authorized in order to carry out the representation or the disclosure is permitted by paragraph (b)." Paragraph (b) provides:

> b) A lawyer may reveal information relating to the representation of a client to the extent the lawyer reasonably believes necessary:
>
> (1) to prevent reasonably certain death or substantial bodily harm;
>
> (2) to prevent the client from committing a crime or fraud that is reasonably certain to result in substantial injury to the financial interests or property of another and in furtherance of which the client has used or is using the lawyer's services;
>
> (3) to prevent, mitigate or rectify substantial injury to the financial interests or property of another that is reasonably certain to result or has resulted from the client's commission of a crime or fraud in furtherance of which the client has used the lawyer's services;
>
> (4) to secure legal advice about the lawyer's compliance with these Rules;
>
> (5) to establish a claim or defense on behalf of the lawyer in a controversy between the lawyer and the client, to establish a defense to a criminal charge or civil claim against the lawyer based upon conduct in which the client was involved, or to respond to allegations in any proceeding concerning the lawyer's representation of the client; or
>
> (6) to comply with other law or a court order.

In one of its opinions, the ABA Committee on Ethics and Professional Responsibility held that an attorney who comes into possession of information relevant to the insurer's coverage defense in the course of defending the insured may not reveal that information to the insurer without the insured's consent. See Informal Opinion Number 1476 (1981). The Committee considered information gained from a third-party to fall within this rule. One exception to the rule would seem to be information that fraud is being committed by the client. Rule 3.3 of the Model Rules of Professional Conduct (1999) requires the attorney to reveal such fraud to the party or tribunal affected.

Suppose the attorney discovers from information provided by a third-party that his client is lying about facts which, if known, would provide the insurer with a coverage defense. Must the attorney reveal these facts to the insurer or only to the court? See *Montanez v. Irizarry-Rodriguez*, 641 A.2d 1079 (N.J. Super. 1994). For analysis of a range of issues associated with insurer-provided defenses, see James M. Fischer, Insurer-Policyholder Interests, Defense Counsel's Professional Duties, and the Allocation of Power to Control the Defense, 14 Conn. Ins. L. J. 21 (2007); Susan Randall, Managed Litigation and the Professional Obligations of Insurance Defense

Lawyers, 51 Syracuse L. Rev. 1 (2001); Ellen S. Pryor & Charles Silver, Defense Lawyers' Profession Responsibilities: Part I—Excess Exposure Cases, 78 Tex. L. Rev. 599 (2000); Ellen S. Pryor & Charles Silver, Defense Lawyers' Profession Responsibilities: Part II—Contested Coverage Cases, 15 Geo. J. Legal Ethics 29 (2001); Symposium, Liability Insurance Conflicts and Professional Responsibility, 4 Conn. Ins. L.J. 1 (1997–98); Thomas D. Morgan, Whose Lawyer Are You Anyway?, 23 Wm. Mitchell L. Rev. 11 (1997); Charles Silver & Kent D. Syverud, The Professional Responsibilities of Insurance Defense Lawyers, 45 Duke L.J. 255 (1995). See also Restatement (Third) of the Law Governing Lawyers, §§ 121–22 (specifying circumstances under which a client's informed consent to a conflict of interest is required when legal fees are being paid by a third party).

3. *Withdraw From the Case?* One reason conflicts problems in this field are so troubling is that the attorney's standard response to a conflict—withdrawal from the case—is often an unrealistic solution. For example, what kind of message would the attorney's withdrawal and subsequent silence in a case like *Parsons* have sent to the insurer about how vigorously to investigate possible coverage defenses? In such situations, a quiet withdrawal may have nearly the same impact as a noisy withdrawal. For discussion of this kind of problem in an only slightly different context, see James M. Fischer, The Professional Obligations of *Cumis* Counsel Retained for the Policyholder But Not Subject to Insurer Control, 43 Tort Trial & Ins. Prac. L.J. 173 (2008). Does the ABA Committee approach—say nothing to the insurer, continue to represent the client, and feel free in the future to be retained by the insurer on other matters—deal satisfactorily with the attorney's fear that if the insurer independently discovers the information the attorney did not reveal, that the insurer will never again hire the attorney? For discussion, see Karon O. Bowdre, Conflicts of Interest Between Insurer and Insured: Ethical Traps for the Unsuspecting Defense Counsel, 17 Amer. J. of Trial Advocacy 101 (1993).

4. *Damages.* Notice that the court in *Parsons* awarded not only the policy limits of $25,000, but the full amount of the $50,000 judgment against the insured. What theory explains this excess-of-policy-limits award?

B. SETTLEMENT

Although standard liability insurance policies create a *duty of defense,* they purport to give the insurer a *privilege to settle* or not as it desires, without any obligation even to consult with the policyholder in deciding whether to settle. See, for example, the Sample CGL Policy in Chapter Six, Section I—Coverages (page 1): "We may, at our discretion, investigate any 'occurrence' and settle any claim or 'suit' that may result." Such provisions impliedly deny the insured the right to refuse to have a case settled; they also seems to deny the insured the corresponding right to require that a case be settled. The judicial treatment of the privilege to settle, however, has drained some of the insurer's discretion from these provisions.

Crisci v. Security Insurance Company of New Haven, Connecticut

Supreme Court of California, 1967.
66 Cal.2d 425

■ PETERS, JUSTICE.

In an action against The Security Insurance Company of New Haven, Connecticut, the trial court awarded Rosina Crisci $91,000 (plus interest) because she suffered a judgment in a personal injury action after Security, her insurer, refused to settle the claim. Mrs. Crisci was also awarded $25,000 for mental suffering. Security has appealed.

June DiMare and her husband were tenants in an apartment building owned by Rosina Crisci. Mrs. DiMare was descending the apartment's outside wooden staircase when a tread gave way. She fell through the resulting opening up to her waist and was left hanging 15 feet above the ground. Mrs. DiMare suffered physical injuries and developed a very severe psychosis. In a suit brought against Mrs. Crisci the DiMares alleged that the step broke because Mrs. Crisci was negligent in inspecting and maintaining the stairs. They contended that Mrs. DiMare's mental condition was caused by the accident, and they asked for $400,000 as compensation for physical and mental injuries and medical expenses.

Mrs. Crisci had $10,000 of insurance coverage under a general liability policy issued by Security. The policy obligated Security to defend the suit against Mrs. Crisci and authorized the company to make any settlement it deemed expedient. Security hired an experienced lawyer, Mr. Healy, to handle the case. Both he and defendant's claims manager believed that unless evidence was discovered showing that Mrs. DiMare had a prior mental illness, a jury would probably find that the accident precipitated Mrs. DiMare's psychosis. And both men believed that if the jury felt that the fall triggered the psychosis, a verdict of not less than $100,000 would be returned.

An extensive search turned up no evidence that Mrs. DiMare had any prior mental abnormality. As a teenager Mrs. DiMare had been in a Washington mental hospital, but only to have an abortion. Both Mrs. DiMare and Mrs. Crisci found psychiatrists who would testify that the accident caused Mrs. DiMare's illness, and the insurance company knew of this testimony. Among those who felt the psychosis was not related to the accident were the doctors at the state mental hospital where Mrs. DiMare had been committed following the accident. All the psychiatrists agreed, however, that a psychosis could be triggered by a sudden fear of falling to one's death.

The exact chronology of settlement offers is not established by the record. However, by the time the DiMares' attorney reduced his settlement demands to $10,000, Security had doctors prepared to support its position and was only willing to pay $3,000 for Mrs. DiMare's physical injuries. Security was unwilling to pay one cent for the possibility of a plaintiff's verdict on the mental illness issue. This conclusion was based on the assumption that the jury would believe all of the defendant's psychiatric evidence and none of the plaintiff's.

Security also rejected a $9,000 settlement demand at a time when Mrs. Crisci offered to pay $2,500 of the settlement.

A jury awarded Mrs. DiMare $100,000 and her husband $1,000. After an appeal (*DiMare v. Cresci*, 58 Cal.2d 292) the insurance company paid $10,000 of this amount, the amount of its policy. The DiMares then sought to collect the balance from Mrs. Crisci. A settlement was arranged by which the DiMares received $22,000, a 40 percent interest in Mrs. Crisci's claim to a particular piece of property, and an assignment of Mrs. Crisci's cause of action against Security. Mrs. Crisci, an immigrant widow of 70, became indigent. She worked as a babysitter, and her grandchildren paid her rent. The change in her financial condition was accompanied by a decline in physical health, hysteria, and suicide attempts. Mrs. Crisci then brought this action.

The liability of an insurer in excess of its policy limits for failure to accept a settlement offer within those limits was considered by this court in *Comunale v. Traders & General Ins. Co.,* 50 Cal.2d 654. It was there reasoned that in every contract, including policies of insurance, there is an implied covenant of good faith and fair dealing that neither party will do anything which will injure the right of the other to receive the benefits of the agreement; that it is common knowledge that one of the usual methods by which an insured receives protection under a liability insurance policy is by settlement of claims without litigation; that the implied obligation of good faith and fair dealing requires the insurer to settle in an appropriate case although the express terms of the policy do not impose the duty; that in determining whether to settle the insurer must give the interests of the insured at least as much consideration as it gives to its own interests; and that when "there is great risk of a recovery beyond the policy limits so that the most reasonable manner of disposing of the claim is a settlement which can be made within those limits, a consideration in good faith of the insured's interest requires the insurer to settle the claim." (50 Cal.2d at p. 659).

In determining whether an insurer has given consideration to the interests of the insured, the test is whether a prudent insurer without policy limits would have accepted the settlement offer.

Several cases, in considering the liability of the insurer, contain language to the effect that bad faith is the equivalent of dishonesty, fraud, and concealment. (See *Critz v. Farmers Ins. Group,* supra, 230 Cal.App.2d 788, 796; *Palmer v. Financial Indem. Co.,* 215 Cal.App.2d 419, 429; *Davy v. Public National Ins. Co.,* supra, 181 Cal.App.2d 387, 396). Obviously a showing that the insurer has been guilty of actual dishonesty, fraud, or concealment is relevant to the determination whether it has given consideration to the insured's interest in considering a settlement offer within the policy limits. The language used in the cases, however, should not be understood as meaning that in the absence of evidence establishing actual dishonesty, fraud, or concealment no recovery may be had for a judgment in excess of the policy limits. *Comunale v. Traders & General Ins. Co.,* supra, 50 Cal.2d 654, 658–659, makes it clear that liability based on an implied covenant exists whenever the insurer refuses to settle in an appropriate case and that liability may exist when the insurer unwarrantedly refuses an offered settlement where the most reasonable manner of disposing of the claim is by accepting the settlement. Liability is imposed not for a bad faith breach of the contract but for failure to meet the duty to accept reasonable settlements, a duty included within the implied covenant of good faith and fair dealing. Moreover, examination of the balance of the *Palmer, Critz,* and *Davy* opinions makes it abundantly clear that recovery may be based on unwarranted rejection of a reasonable settlement offer and that the absence of evidence, circumstantial or direct, showing actual dishonesty, fraud, or concealment is not fatal to the cause of action.

Amicus curiae argues that, whenever an insurer receives an offer to settle within the policy limits and rejects it, the insurer should be liable in every case for the amount of any final judgment whether or not within the policy limits. As we have seen, the duty of the insurer to consider the insured's interest in settlement offers within the policy limits arises from an implied covenant in the contract, and ordinarily contract duties are strictly enforced and not subject to a standard of reasonableness. Obviously, it will always be in the insured's interest to settle within the policy limits when there is any danger, however slight, of a judgment in excess of those limits. Accordingly the rejection of a settlement within the limits where there is any danger of a judgment in excess of the limits can be justified, if at all, only on the basis of interests of the insurer, and, in light of the common knowledge that settlement is one of the usual methods by which an insured receives protection under a liability policy, it may not be unreasonable for an insured who purchases a policy with limits to believe that a sum of money equal to the limits is available and will be used so as to avoid liability on his part with regard to any covered accident. In view of such expectation an insurer should not be permitted to further its own interests by rejecting opportunities to settle within the policy limits unless it is also willing to absorb losses which may result from its failure to settle.

The proposed rule is a simple one to apply and avoids the burdens of a determination whether a settlement offer within the policy limits was reasonable. The proposed rule would also eliminate the danger that an insurer, faced with a settlement offer at or near the policy limits, will reject it and gamble with the insured's money to further its own interests. Moreover, it is not entirely clear that the proposed rule would place a burden on insurers substantially greater than that which is present under existing law. The size of the judgment recovered in the personal injury action when it exceeds the policy limits, although not conclusive, furnishes an inference that the value of the claim is the equivalent of the amount of the judgment and that acceptance of an offer within those limits was the most reasonable method of dealing with the claim.

Finally, and most importantly, there is more than a small amount of elementary justice in a rule that would require that, in this situation where the insurer's and insured's interests necessarily conflict, the insurer, which may reap the benefits of its determination not to settle, should also suffer the detriments of its decision. On the basis of these and other considerations, a number of commentators have urged that the insurer should be liable for any resulting judgment where it refuses to settle within the policy limits. (Note (1966) 18 Stan.L.Rev. 475, 482–

485; Note (1951) 60 Yale L.J. 1037, 1041–1042; Comment (1949) 48 Mich.L.Rev. 95, 102; Note (1945) 13 U.Chi.L.Rev. 105, 109.)

We need not, however, here determine whether there might be some countervailing considerations precluding adoption of the proposed rule because, under *Comunale v. Traders & General Ins. Co.,* supra, 50 Cal.2d 654, and the cases following it, the evidence is clearly sufficient to support the determination that Security breached its duty to consider the interests of Mrs. Crisci in proposed settlements. Both Security's attorney and its claim manager agreed that if Mrs. DiMare won an award for her psychosis, that award would be at least $100,000. Security attempts to justify its rejection of a settlement by contending that it believed Mrs. DiMare had no chance of winning on the mental suffering issue. That belief in the circumstances present could be found to be unreasonable. Security was putting blind faith in the power of its psychiatrists to convince the jury when it knew that the accident could have caused the psychosis, that its agents had told it that without evidence of prior mental defects a jury was likely to believe the fall precipitated the psychosis, and that Mrs. DiMare had reputable psychiatrists on her side. Further, the company had been told by a psychiatrist that in a group of 24 psychiatrists, 12 could be found to support each side.

The trial court found that defendant "knew that there was a considerable risk of substantial recovery beyond said policy limits" and that "the defendant did not give as much consideration to the financial interests of its said insured as it gave to its own interests." That is all that was required. The award of $91,000 must therefore be affirmed.

We must next determine the propriety of the award to Mrs. Crisci of $25,000 for her mental suffering. In *Comunale v. Traders & General Ins. Co.,* supra, 50 Cal.2d 654, 663, it was held that an action of the type involved here sounds in both contract and tort and that "where a case sounds both in contract and tort the plaintiff will ordinarily have freedom of election between an action of tort and one of contract. *Eads v. Marks,* 39 Cal.2d 807, 811. An exception to this rule is made in suits for personal injury caused by negligence, where the tort character of the action is considered to prevail [citations], but no such exception is applied in cases, like the present one, which relate to financial damage [citations]." Although this rule was applied in *Comunale* with regard to a statute of limitations, the rule is also applicable in determining liability. * * * Insofar as language in *Critz v. Farmers Ins. Group,* supra, 230 Cal.App.2d 788, 799, might be interpreted as providing that the action for wrongful refusal to settle sounds solely in contract, it is disapproved.

Fundamental in our jurisprudence is the principle that for every wrong there is a remedy and that an injured party should be compensated for all damage proximately caused by the wrongdoer. Although we recognize exceptions from these fundamental principles, no departure should be sanctioned unless there is a strong necessity therefor.

The general rule of damages in tort is that the injured party may recover for all detriment caused whether it could have been anticipated or not. (Civ.Code, § 3333; see *Hunt Bros. Co. v. San Lorenzo etc. Co.,* 150 Cal. 51, 56.) In accordance with the general rule, it is settled in this state that mental suffering constitutes an aggravation of damages when it naturally ensues from the act complained of, and in this connection mental suffering includes nervousness, grief, anxiety, worry, shock, humiliation and indignity as well as physical pain. The commonest example of the award of damages for mental suffering in addition to other damages is probably where the plaintiff suffers personal injuries in addition to mental distress as a result of either negligent or intentional misconduct by the defendant. (*DiMare v. Cresci,* supra, 58 Cal.2d 292, 300–301; *Deevy v. Tassi,* 21 Cal.2d 109, 120; *Dryden v. Continental Baking Co.,* 11 Cal.2d 33, 39–40.) Such awards are not confined to cases where the mental suffering award was in addition to an award for personal injuries; damages for mental distress have also been awarded in cases where the tortious conduct was an interference with property rights without any personal injuries apart from the mental distress. * * *

We are satisfied that a plaintiff who as a result of a defendant's tortious conduct loses his property and suffers mental distress may recover not only for the pecuniary loss but also for his mental distress. No substantial reason exists to distinguish the cases which have permitted recovery for mental distress in actions for invasion of property rights. The principal reason for limiting recovery of damages for mental distress is that to permit recovery of such damages would open the door to fictitious claims, to recovery for mere bad manners, and to litigation in the field of trivialities. (Prosser, Torts (3d ed. 1964) § 11, p. 43.) Obviously, where, as here, the claim is actionable and has resulted in substantial damages apart from those due to mental distress, the danger of fictitious claims is reduced, and we are not here concerned with mere bad manners or trivialities but tortious conduct resulting in substantial invasions of clearly protected interests.

Recovery of damages for mental suffering in the instant case does not mean that in every case of breach of contract the injured party may recover such damages. Here the breach also constitutes a tort. Moreover, plaintiff did not seek by the contract involved here to obtain a commercial advantage but to protect herself against the risks of accidental losses, including the mental distress which might follow from the losses. Among the considerations in purchasing liability insurance, as insurers are well aware, is the peace of mind and security it will provide in the event of an accidental loss, and recovery of damages for mental suffering has been permitted for breach of contracts which directly concern the comfort, happiness or personal esteem of one of the parties. (*Chelini v. Nieri,* 32 Cal.2d 480, 482.)

It is not claimed that plaintiff's mental distress was not caused by defendant's refusal to settle or that the damages awarded were excessive in the light of plaintiff's substantial suffering.

The judgment is affirmed.

NOTES AND QUESTIONS

1. *The Reasonable-Offer Test.* The *Crisci* rule is standard law now in most jurisdictions, although a number of states follow an approach that requires something more than negligence or even actual "bad-faith" on the part of the insurer in order for the policyholder to challenge the insurer's

refusal to settle. See Kent D. Syverud, The Duty to Settle, 76 Va. L.Rev. 1113 (1990). Under the reasonable-offer test, the question is whether an insurer under a policy without limits would have accepted the offer. For this reason, the RLLI, § 27 calls it the "disregard the limits" rule. That same section also makes clear that reasonableness is "a range, not a point." Testimony by experts (almost always lawyers) after the fact about whether an offer was reasonable is bound to be based on judgment and experience, rather than objective fact. Some courts also hold that a liability insurer has a "duty to contribute" to a reasonable offer that is above its limits, by making those limits available to the insured or an excess insurer. See RLLI, § 2, comment j; Richard Squire, How Collective Settlements Camouflage the Cost of Shareholder Lawsuits, 62 Duke L. J. 1 (2012).

Some courts hold that a liability insurer has a duty to attempt to make reasonable settlements even when there has not been an offer to settle by the plaintiff. See, e.g., *State Farm Auto Ins. Co. v. Rowland*, 427 S.W.2d 35 (Tenn. 1968). But most courts appear to require that the plaintiff make an offer to settle within the policy limits. See, e.g., *Am. Physicians Ins. Exch. v. Garcia*, 876 S.W. 2d 842 (Tex. 1994). If the plaintiff has not made an offer, what questions of causation would arise if there nevertheless were a duty of the insurer to attempt to effectuate a reasonable settlement?

2. *The Insurer's Strict Liability for Excess Judgments?* No court has squarely adopted the strict liability test described in *Crisci*. The closest any court has come to embracing strict liability is the Supreme Court of Appeals of West Virginia decision in *Shamblin v. Nationwide Mutual Insurance Co.*, 396 S.E.2d 766 (W.Va. 1990), in which the court adopted what might be called *prima facie strict liability*. Under that approach, the insurer is strictly liable for the failure to settle a claim within policy limits unless it proves by clear and convincing evidence that the failure to settle was based on "reasonable and substantial" grounds. For a time there was discussion of adopting strict liability in New Jersey, but the move to this standard never took place. See *Rova Farms Resort, Inc. v. Investors Ins. Co. of Am.*, 323 A.2d 495 (N.J. 1974). And there is a Rhode Island decision that might be interpreted to contemplate strict liability. See *Asermely v. Allstate Ins. Co.*, 728 A.2d 461 (R.I. 1999). In theory, a strict liability test should create precisely the same incentives as the *Crisci* test; the only difference would be that insurers also would bear liability for excess judgments even when it was reasonable for them to reject earlier settlement demands. In practice, however, proving that offers close to the line of reasonableness should have been accepted might be difficult and expensive—consider what would be involved in such proof. A strict liability test might therefore solve this under-enforcement problem, by causing insurers to accept offers they would reject under a reasonable offer test, because of the difficulties of proof that insureds would encounter in attempting to show that an offer that the insurer rejected was in fact reasonable. See Kenneth S. Abraham, Distributing Risk: Insurance, Legal Theory, and Public Policy 193–95 (1986).

3. *The Measure of Damages*. *Crisci* is in a minority in allowing recovery of noneconomic damages for the failure to settle. From a deterrence standpoint, is there any need to award such damages if the reasonable offer rule works properly? See *The Birth Center v. St. Paul Cos., Inc.*, 787 A.2d 376 (Pa. 2001), holding that the insurer can be held liable for extra-contractual compensatory damages even if it has eventually paid the

excess verdict. Should the availability of noneconomic damages be used to counterbalance the under-enforcement problems described in the preceding paragraph? On the question whether the insurer can be held liable for otherwise-uninsured punitive damages resulting from its failure to settle, see *PPG Industries, Inc. v. Transamerica Insurance Co.*, 975 P.2d 652 (Cal. 1999) (denying recovery).

4. *Doubts About Coverage and the Recoupment of Indemnity.* Suppose the insurer recognizes that an offer is reasonable, but has doubts about its coverage responsibility. Some courts have held that the insurer may take these doubts into account. In effect, these courts have adopted a subjective bad-faith rule. See, e.g., *Guebara v. Allstate Ins. Co.*, 237 F.3d 987 (9th Cir. 2001); *Snodgrass v. State Farm Mut. Auto. Ins. Co.*, 804 P.2d 1012 (Kan. 1991); Michael F. Aylward, Other People's Money: Insurer Liability for Failing to Settle Within Policy Limits, 54 FDCC Quart. 267 (2004). What advantages would flow from a rule requiring the insurer to weigh settlement offers in cases where coverage is in doubt as though the insurer would be liable without limit if there were coverage? The Supreme Court of California adopted this requirement in *Johansen v. California State Automobile Association Inter-Insurance Bureau*, 538 P.2d 744 (Cal. 1975). Under the *Johansen* rule presumably insurers do not always accept such offers merely because they are liable for the consequences of rejecting them. Rather, insurers take into account the probability that an ensuing judgment will not exceed the policy limit if the offer is rejected, and the probability that a later resolution of the coverage dispute will determine that the policy does not cover the loss in question.

The argument for the *Johansen* approach is that it requires insurers to internalize not only the benefits of rejecting offers, but the costs of doing so as well. This avoids unnecessary litigation, at least in cases where the insured simply cannot produce the funds necessary to accept the claimant's offer of settlement. The court in *Johansen* suggested that the insurer that settled a case despite its doubts about coverage could later seek recoupment from the insured for the amount of the settlement that turned out not to be covered. And in *Blue Ridge Insurance Co. v. Jacobsen*, 22 P.3d 313 (Cal. 2001), it finally permitted precisely such a recovery. Under these circumstances, should the insurer or the insured control the decision about whether to settle? In contrast, the Supreme Court of Texas at first held that an excess insurer could recoup settlement costs if it later proved that its policy did not provide coverage, but then on rehearing held that there could be no such recoupment in the absence of the insured's prior consent to the insurer's right to seek recoupment after paying the settlement. *Excess Underwriters at Lloyd's, London v. Frank's Casing Crew & Rental Tools, Inc.*, 246 S.W.3d 42 (Tex. 2008). Most courts have not addressed the issue, however, probably because until recently few observers would have thought that there could be any right to recoup indemnity payments. More of the few courts that have addressed the issue, however, seem to be following *Frank's Casing* and precluding reimbursement in the absence of the insured's consent. RLLI, § 28, comment c takes the position that the default rule should be no recoupment.

5. *The Duty to Defend, the Duty to Settle, and Covenants Not to Execute.* The conventional duty to settle rule has been developed in cases in which the insurer was defending the insured. Somewhat different rules may be required, however, when the insurer is not defending, either

because it has wrongfully refused to defend or because it has agreed to permit the insured to defend and to reimburse the insured's defense costs. Suppose, for example, that the insured receives an offer to settle when the insurer is not defending. Should the insurer have a duty to settle under these circumstances? This duty can then be translated into a duty to reimburse the insured for any settlement that is reasonable. See, e.g., *Miller v. Shugart*, 316 N.W.2d 729 (Minn. 1982), set out in Chapter Eight. Some courts hold further that, in this situation, the insured need only prove that the claim was *prima facie* covered. See, e.g., *Luria Bros. & Co. v. Alliance Assurance Co.*, 780 F. 2d 1091 (2d Cir. 1986). For discussion of these and a cluster of other complications that arise in different settings, see James M. Fischer, Insurer or Policyholder Control of the Defense and the Duty to Fund Settlements, 2 Nev. L.J. 1 (2002).

Suppose, however, that the insurer does not defend and the insured settles with the plaintiff, but the settlement agreement provides that the plaintiff will not seek to recover payment from the insured, in return for which the insured transfers his right to recover from the insurer to the plaintiff. A version of this arrangement seems to have been reached in *Crisci*, though after verdict. Many courts hold that transfers of the right to recover in return for a covenant not to sue or execute are valid, although some require that the insured not be formally released from liability. See *Red Giant Oil Co. v. Lawlor*, 528 N.W.2d 524 (Iowa 1995). Take a look at the Condition labeled "Legal Action Against Us", sometimes called the "No Action" clause, in the Sample CGL policy in Chapter Six (page 11). Does this clause preclude this form of settlement? Should public policy permit it to do so?

6. *Order of Payment.* Suppose that there is more than one insured under a policy, and both are sued. May the insurer settle the claim against one insured and thereby reduce or exhaust the limits available to the remaining insured? The majority rule appears to be that the insurer may do so: first in time, first in right. See, e.g., *Scott v. Gallacher*, 939 N.E. 2d 803 (Mass. App. Ct. 2011). But California takes the opposite position. See, e.g., *Atlantic Mut. Ins. Co. v. Equinox Ins. Co.*, 2010 WL 5175465 (Cal. Ct. App. 2010).

C. THE RIGHTS AND OBLIGATIONS OF EXCESS INSURERS

Businesses with large liability exposures tend to purchase coverage in layers. The first layer—often subject to a retained deductible, or "self-insured retention"—is termed the primary layer. Other layers are said to be "excess" over the primary or retained layers. Large businesses may have a number of layers of coverage provided by different insurers, which taken together constitute an "excess program." Excess liability insurance falls into two major categories: *follow-form* and *umbrella* coverage. The former provides insurance above the primary limits according to the same terms as the primary policy. The latter not only provides excess liability insurance, but also provides some primary insurance that fills gaps in the coverage provided by the primary policy. Three of the most important issues that may arise in connection with excess coverage involve the nature and scope of "exhaustion" requirements in excess policies; the duty to settle (if any) owed to an excess insurer; and the possibility that an excess insurer will "drop down" when coverage is unavailable from a lower-layer insurer.

1. EXHAUSTION

Comerica, Inc. v. Zurich American Insurance Company

United States District Court, Eastern District of Michigan, 2007.
498 F. Supp. 2d 1019.

■ LAWSON, DISTRICT JUDGE.

Plaintiff Comerica, Inc., a financial services corporation (i.e., bank), entered into a settlement of five securities fraud class action lawsuits (which had been consolidated into two actions) for $21 million. Comerica's primary insurance carrier, Federal Insurance Company-which disputed coverage on at least some of the claims on various grounds and whose policy carried a $20-million limit of liability-ultimately agreed to pay $14 million toward the settlement, leaving Comerica to pay the other $7 million, which it did. Defendant Zurich American Insurance Company wrote a following form excess insurance policy that was triggered "after all such 'Underlying Insurance' has been reduced or exhausted by payments for losses." Comerica sought $1 million plus costs of defense ($2.6 million) from defendant Zurich under the excess policy in connection with the class action settlements. Zurich refused to pay on the grounds that the primary coverage had not been exhausted. * * * The Court heard the parties' arguments in open court on January 8, 2007 and now finds that the plain language of the excess policy issued by Zurich requires exhaustion of the primary insurance's liability limits by actual payment of losses by the primary insurer before the excess policy is triggered. Since Federal's $20 million liability limit was not exhausted by payment of $14 million on the claim by Federal, Zurich has no obligation to Comerica under the excess policy. Therefore, the defendant's motion for summary judgment will be granted and the plaintiff's motions for partial summary judgment will be denied. * * *

Defendant Zurich was Comerica's excess insurance carrier under a following form policy with a policy period of January 1, 2002 through January 1, 2003 and a liability limit of $20 million. As a following form policy, coverage under the Zurich policy was no broader than the Federal policy, except of course for the liability limits. It contained the following provisions: * * *

V. DEPLETION OF UNDERLYING LIMIT(S)

In the event of the depletion of the limit(s) of liability of the "Underlying Insurance" solely as a result of actual payment of loss thereunder by the applicable insurers, this Policy shall . . . continue to apply to loss as excess over the amount of insurance remaining. . . . In the event of the exhaustion of the limit(s) of liability of such "Underlying Insurance" solely as a result of payment of loss thereunder, the remaining limits available under this Policy shall . . . continue for subsequent loss as primary insurance. . . .

This Policy only provides coverage excess of the "Underlying Insurance." This policy does not provide coverage for any loss not covered by the "Underlying Insurance" except and to the extent that such loss is not paid under the "Underlying Insurance" solely by reason of the reduction or exhaustion of the available "Underlying Insurance" through payments of loss thereunder. . . . * * *

As mentioned, the defendant believes that its summary judgment motion proves that the clear and unambiguous terms of the insurance policy do not require it to pay the plaintiff. The plaintiff * * * argues that Zurich is obligated to pay for the amount of the settlement above the $20 million limit of the Federal policy because the failure to do so violates public policy by causing delay and encouraging litigation. The plaintiff cites *Zeig v. Massachusetts Bonding & Ins. Co.*, 23 F.2d 665 (2d Cir. 1928), and several other cases that follow *Zeig* in support of that proposition. * * *

Comerica insists that its own payment of $6 million toward the settlement filled the gap between Federal's payment and the balance of the policy limit, and that should serve as the functional equivalent of exhausting the primary policy limit because it exposes Zurich to no greater liability than if Federal had made the payment. The foundation of its argument is *Zeig v. Massachusetts Bonding & Ins. Co.*, 23 F.2d 665 (2d Cir. 1928), and cases based on that decision.

In *Zeig,* an excess insurance contract required that the underlying policy be exhausted but was silent about whether the full amount of the underlying policy needed to be collected or actually paid out before the excess policy was triggered. The opinion is not clear about why the underlying policy was not collected, but presumably it was due to a settlement. The Second Circuit held that the underlying policy was exhausted by discharge under the settlement, and therefore the excess policy was implicated. The court concluded that the insurance company had not been prejudiced and public policy encouraged settlement:

> The defendant argues that it was necessary for the plaintiff actually to collect the full amount of the policies for $15,000, in order to 'exhaust' that insurance. Such a construction of the policy sued on seems unnecessarily stringent. It is doubtless true that the parties could impose such a condition precedent to liability upon the policy, if they chose to do so. But the defendant had no rational interest in whether the insured collected the full amount of the primary policies, so long as it was only called upon to pay such portion of the loss as was in excess of the limits of those policies. To require an absolute collection of the primary insurance to its full limit would in many, if not most, cases involve delay, promote litigation, and prevent an adjustment of disputes which is both convenient and commendable. A result harmful to the insured, and of no rational advantage to the insurer, ought only to be reached when the terms of the contract demand it.

> We can see no reason for a construction so burdensome to the insured. Nothing is said about the 'collection' of the full amount of the primary insurance. The clause provides only that it be 'exhausted in the payment of claims to the full

amount of the expressed limits.' The claims are paid to the full amount of the policies, if they are settled and discharged, and the primary insurance is thereby exhausted. There is no need of interpreting the word 'payment' as only relating to payment in cash. It often is used as meaning the satisfaction of a claim by compromise, or in other ways. To render the policy in suit applicable, claims had to be and were satisfied and paid to the full limit of the primary policies. Only such portion of the loss as exceeded, not the cash settlement, but the limits of these policies, is covered by the excess policy.

Zeig, 23 F.2d at 666.

The cases that follow *Zeig* generally rely on an ambiguity in the definition of "exhaustion" or lack of specificity in the excess contract as to how the primary insurance is to be discharged. *See, e.g., Stargatt v. Fid. and Cas. Co. of New York,* 67 F.R.D. 689 (D. Del. 1975) (construing excess policy that took effect "only when the Primary Policy in the amount of $250,000 . . . has been exhausted" to mean that "[t]he settlement under a primary policy of claims equaling the amount of the policy permits recovery on a secondary policy made applicable only where the primary insurance is exhausted in payment of claims"); *Gasquet v. Commercial Union Ins. Co.,* 391 So. 2d 466 (La. Ct. App.1980) (holding that an excess policy that did not become effective "unless and until the insured, or the insured's underlying insurer, shall have paid the amount of the underlying limits on account of such occurrence" was triggered by a settlement that gave the excess carrier "a 'credit' for the policy limits of the primary insurer"). * * *

A different result occurs when the policy language is more specific. For instance, in *Danbeck v. Am. Family Mut. Ins. Co.,* 245 Wis. 2d 186 (2001), the plaintiff was riding a bicycle when he was struck by a vehicle whose driver had $50,000 worth of liability insurance through Country Mutual. The plaintiff had $100,000 of uninsured motorist insurance through American Family Mutual under a policy that attached "only after the limits of liability under any bodily injury liability bonds or policies have been exhausted by payment of judgements or settlements." *Id.* at 190. The plaintiff settled with the driver and Country Mutual for $48,000 and agreed to give American Family credit for the whole $50,000. American Family then refused to pay the uninsured motorist claim because the plaintiff had not exhausted the full $50,000 limit against Country Mutual. The plaintiff sued American Family. The Wisconsin Supreme Court held that the Country Mutual policy had not been exhausted and American Family was therefore not required to pay under the unambiguous terms of the insurance policy:

> We agree with American Family and the court of appeals that while the "settlement plus credit" approach to exhaustion has the same practical effect as payment of full policy limits, it is not consistent with the plain language of the policy, which unambiguously requires exhaustion *"by payment of judgements or settlements,"* not "settlement plus credit."

Id. at 194. The court noted the public policy favoring settlement, but stated that this policy, "as important as it is, cannot supersede unambiguous policy language or impose obligations under the contract which otherwise do not exist. The generalized public policy favoring settlements is insufficient to justify voiding or refusing to enforce the clear language of the policy in this case." *Id.* at 197–98. * * *

The Court believes that the excess policy in this case likewise requires that the primary insurance be exhausted or depleted by the actual payment of losses by the underlying insurer. Payments by the insured to fill the gap, settlements that extinguish liability up to the primary insurer's limits, and agreements to give the excess insurer "credit" against a judgment or settlement up to the primary insurer's liability limit are not the same as actual payment. Zurich's policy requires "actual payment of losses" by the underlying insurer and states that its "policy does not provide coverage for any loss not covered by the 'Underlying Insurance' except and to the extent that such loss is not paid under the 'Underlying Insurance' solely by reason of the reduction or exhaustion of the available 'Underlying Insurance' through payments of loss thereunder." That never happened in this case.

It is clear that the amount Comerica agreed to pay to the securities litigation plaintiffs potentially implicated Zurich's excess policy because the settlement amount exceeded the primary insurance coverage. But Comerica had a fundamental disagreement with its primary insurer as to whether Federal was liable for *any* amount of the settlement. That dispute did not directly involve Zurich, and Comerica did not have the right to tie Zurich to any aspect of its settlement with Federal without Zurich's consent. Comerica could have litigated its dispute with Federal, which of course would have involved the risk of losing all coverage for the securities liability; but it also could have resulted in a finding that Federal was liable for the entire $20 million, it which case Zurich's coverage would have been triggered. Comerica seeks the certainty that its settlement brought and the benefit of coverage from its excess carrier as if it had won its dispute with the primary insurer, despite language in the excess policy to the contrary. No public policy argument says that Comerica may have its cake and eat it too.

The *Zeig* court noted that requiring actual payment by the primary insurer by itself does not contravene public policy. Requiring such a condition may guard against collusive settlements with underlying insurers or claimants, and "[i]t is doubtless true that the parties could impose such a condition precedent to liability upon the policy, if they chose to do so." *Zeig,* 23 F.2d at 666. The contract language here states that is exactly what the parties did, and Comerica's argument to the contrary would require a contract rewrite, which this Court is not inclined to do. * * *

Comerica's argument that the excess policy contains no instruction on whether the primary insurer must itself pay losses to exhaust the underlying insurance, thereby creating an ambiguity, does not withstand a comparison to the insurance document itself. The Zurich policy plainly requires the Federal policy to be exhausted by payment of losses by Federal. Zurich's coverage "shall attach only after all such 'Underlying Insurance' has been reduced or exhausted by payments for losses." * * *

"An insurance contract is ambiguous when its provisions are capable of conflicting interpretations." *Klapp v. United Ins. Group Agency,* 468 Mich. 459 (2003). There is no reasonable way to read this policy to require Zurich to pay unless the Federal policy was exhausted "solely . . . through payments of loss thereunder." The parties could not have been clearer about their intentions. Zurich agreed to cover losses by the plaintiff exceeding $20 million only if Federal first paid $20 million. "[A]n insurance policy must be enforced in accordance with its terms," *Michigan Millers,* 445 Mich. at 558, and the "court may not read ambiguity into a policy where none exists." *Ibid.*

The plaintiff states that other language in the policy makes clear Zurich's intention that actual payment of losses by the primary insurer is not required to trigger coverage, referring to provisions that allow Comerica to fill the gap with its own payment up to the primary policy limit when (1) the underlying insurance lapses for some reason, (2) the underlying insurer becomes insolvent, or (3) the underlying insurance is exhausted by a claim made before the effective date of the excess policy, when the primary and excess policy dates are not aligned. Of course, none of these provisions applies in this case, and they undermine Comerica's argument that it should be able to fill the gap by its own payment, since the possibility of such an instance apparently occurred to the parties and they chose not to include the present scenario among the circumstances where gap payments by the insured would be acceptable.

To find the Zurich policy ambiguous would essentially require a holding that parties simply cannot contract for an excess policy to be triggered only upon full, actual payment by the underlying insurer. Comerica could have bargained for a contract under which Zurich agreed to pay for any liabilities over $20 million, even if the underlying insurer did not actually pay the entire $20 million, or when the insured filled the gap, or a settlement extinguished liability up to the primary insurer's limits, or there was an agreement to give the excess insurer "credit" up to the amount of the underlying insurance. However, the present agreement does not say that, and it cannot be rewritten now.
* * *

The Court finds that the unambiguous language of the excess policy issued by defendant Zurich required that Comerica's primary insurer in this case, Federal Insurance Company, exhaust its limit of liability by actual payment of claims before Zurich would be obliged to contribute to indemnity or defense costs. That did not occur. Zurich's coverage was never implicated, and it is not liable to Comerica in this case.

NOTES AND QUESTIONS

1. *Follow Gus? Comerica* rejects (or at least distinguishes) the 1928 First Circuit decision in *Zeig*, which until around 2010 was the leading decision on the exhaustion issue. The author of *Zeig* was Judge Augustus Hand, the cousin of his colleague on the First Circuit, Learned Hand. A lawyers' adage at the time was, "cite Learned but follow Gus," which evidently meant that Learned Hand's opinions were memorable but that Augustus ("Gus") Hand's decisions were more reliable. In the last decade, the pendulum has begun to swing against Gus, with an increasing number of decisions adopting the *Comerica* approach. See, e.g., *Intel Corp. v. Am. Guar. & Liab. Ins. Co.*, 51 A.3d 442 (Del. 2012); *Qualcomm, Inc. v. Certain Underwriters at Lloyd's, London*, 161 Cal. App. 4th 184 (Cal. Ct. App.

2008). A number of courts, however, continue to reject the *Comerica* approach. See, e.g., *Trinity Homes LLC v. Ohio Cas. Ins. Co.*, 629 F.3d 653 (7th Cir. 2010). Policyholders make the following three basic arguments in exhaustion cases.

2. *Ambiguity.* The first argument is that the policy language purporting to require exhaustion is ambiguous. Since there is no single, widely-used, standard-form exhaustion clause, the success of this argument depends on both the particular language used and on the interpretive inclinations of the particular court addressing the issue. A provision in an excess policy requiring that underlying insurance be "exhausted by payment" is more likely to be held ambiguous than the *Comerica* policy's requirement of "depletion of the limit(s) of liability of the 'Underlying Insurance' solely as a result of actual payment of loss thereunder by the applicable insurers." The former clause could reasonably be understood to require only a total payment equal to the underlying limits, whether by the policyholder or the underlying insurers, whereas the *Comerica* clause requires payment "by the applicable insurers." Moreover, in some cases the excess policy at issue contained an exhaustion clause that was arguably unambiguous on its face, but also contained another clause (addressing, drop-down, insolvency, or some other issue) that seemed to contradict the exhaustion clause and thereby created "structural" ambiguity. The policyholder's argument that this was the case in *Comerica* was unsuccessful. But depending on the wording of other policy provisions, the structural ambiguity argument can sometimes succeed. For these reasons, the apparent division of authority in the case law regarding the exhaustion requirement can be partly explained by differences in the language of the exhaustion clauses and other policy provisions whose meaning is at issue in the cases.

3. *The Functional Equivalent of Exhaustion?* Policyholders' second argument, going all the way back to *Zeig*, is that when they have paid more than the limits of liability of their underlying insurance, this is the functional equivalent of exhausting all underlying insurance. For example, if the inception point of an excess policy is $20 million, the policyholder is held liable in or settles a lawsuit against it for $25 million, and then settles with its underlying insurers for $15 million, more than $20 million has been paid to the plaintiff, and that is all the excess insurer should care about. In effect, by paying the difference between its settlement with the underlying insurers and their total limits of liability, the policyholder has for practical purposes exhausted its insurance limits by payment. The assumption behind this argument, of course, is that the principal influence on the excess insurer's premium was the probability that the policyholder would be held be liable for more than $20 million, and that this probability is unaffected by whether the underlying insurers alone pay $20 million in full, or the policyholder and the underlying insurers together make that payment. Therefore, it should make no difference to the excess insurer which party or parties pay the plaintiff, as long as the total paid is enough to reach the inception point of the excess policy.

Excess insurers respond that this functional-equivalence argument is wrong. They say that a second factor that influences excess premiums is their expectation that, because of the exhaustion requirement, they receive protections that the functional-equivalence argument ignores. Excess insurers rely on underlying insurers to "vet" both the strength of the suit against the policyholder, and the policyholder's coverage claim against the underlying insurer or insurers. If excess insurance is available even when underlying insurance has not been exhausted through full payment of their limits by the underlying insurers, this vetting function will be undermined. Excess insurers will have to do more vetting, more often, at greater cost to the excess insurers. Excess insurers argue that their premiums have been premised on the protection against this vetting-risk provided by the exhaustion requirement.

However, in practice many excess insurers have been willing, when the issue is raised in negotiations, to remove or modify their exhaustion clauses, with little apparent effect on their premiums. The result has been that policyholders and brokers who are aware of the *Comerica* line of decisions are able to negotiate around the holdings of these decisions, that only unsophisticated policyholders and brokers still have strong exhaustion requirements in their excess policies, and that they discover these clauses only after they are sued and want to settle with their underlying insurers

4. *Settlement Incentives.* That brings us to the effect of an exhaustion requirement on settlement of coverage disputes. Policyholders' third argument, sometimes couched in terms of public policy and often based on *Zeig*, is that an exhaustion requirement severely impedes settlement. Settlement with an underlying insurer for anything less than its full limits of liability would completely deny a policyholder access to excess insurance if exhaustion requirements apply in the manner that excess insurers assert that they should. Indeed, it is reasonable to wonder how often the policyholders in the reported exhaustion cases were aware of the exhaustion clauses in their policies when they settled with their underlying insurers, thus placing their excess insurance at risk. Probably some such policyholders settled with their underlying insurers in the *pre-Comerica* period, supposing that they were permitted to do so under *Zeig*, but then found themselves litigating their coverage claims post-*Comerica*. In any event, in the post-*Comerica* era, policyholders whose excess policies contain conventional exhaustion clauses will have to rethink whether, when, and under what circumstances they should settle with their underlying insurers, unless the public policy favoring settlement causes the courts to reject the *Comerica* line of decisions.

2. PRIMARY INSURERS' DUTY TO EXCESS INSURERS TO SETTLE

Commercial Union Assurance Companies v. Safeway Stores, Inc.

Supreme Court of California, 1980.
26 Cal.3d 912.

■ BY THE COURT:

We granted a hearing herein in order to resolve a conflict between Court of Appeal opinions in this case and the earlier case of *Transit Casualty Co. v. Spink Corp.* (1979) 94 Cal.App.3d 124. After an independent study of the issue, we have concluded that the thoughtful opinion of Justice Sabraw (assigned) for the Court of Appeal, First Appellate District, 158 Cal.Rptr. 97, in this case correctly treats the issues, and that we should adopt it as our own opinion. That opinion, with appropriate deletions and additions,[1] is as follows:

> This case presents the question of whether an insured owes a duty [ ] to its excess liability insurance carrier which would require it to accept a settlement offer below the threshold figure of the excess carrier's exposure where there is a substantial probability of liability in excess of that figure.
>
> ### *Facts:*
>
> At all times relevant herein Safeway Stores, Incorporated (hereafter Safeway) had liability insurance coverage as follows:
>
> > (a) Travelers Insurance Company and Travelers Indemnity Company (hereafter Travelers) insured Safeway for the first $50,000 of liability.
> >
> > (b) Safeway insured itself for liability between the sums of $50,000 and $100,000.
> >
> > (c) Commercial Union Assurance Companies and Mission Insurance Company (hereafter conjunctively referred to as Commercial) provided insurance coverage for Safeway's liability in excess of $100,000 to $20 million.
>
> One Hazel Callies brought an action against Safeway in San Francisco Superior Court and recovered judgment for the sum of $125,000. Thereafter, Commercial was required to pay $25,000 of said judgment in order to discharge its liability under the excess insurance policy.
>
> Commercial, as excess liability carrier, brought the instant action against its insured Safeway and Safeway's primary insurance carrier, Travelers, to recover the $25,000 which it had expended. Commercial alleged that Safeway and Travelers had an opportunity to settle the case for $60,000, or possibly even $50,000, and knew or should have known that there was a possible and probable liability in excess of $100,000. It was further alleged that said defendants had a duty to settle the claim for a sum less than $100,000 when they had an opportunity to do so. Commercial's complaint attempts to state two causes of action against Safeway and Travelers, one in negligence and another for breach of the duty of good faith and fair dealing.
>
> Safeway demurred to the complaint on the grounds of failure to state a cause of action. The court sustained the demurrer with 20 days' leave to amend. When Commercial failed to amend its complaint, the complaint was dismissed as to Safeway. Commercial now appeals from the judgment of dismissal. [ ]
>
> The present case is unusual in that the policyholder, Safeway, was self-insured for liability in an amount below Commercial's initial exposure. While this status may explain Safeway's reluctance to settle, it remains to be determined if the insured owes an independent duty to his excess carrier to accept a reasonable settlement offer so as to avoid exposing the latter to pecuniary harm. [Both of Commercial's theories of

---

[1] Brackets together, in this manner [ ], are used to indicate deletions from the opinion of the Court of Appeal; brackets enclosing material (other than the editor's parallel citations) are, unless otherwise indicated, used to denote insertions or additions by this court. (*Estate of McDill* (1975) 14 Cal.3d 831, 834.)

recovery, negligence and breach of good faith, depend upon the existence of such a duty.]

It is now well established that an insurer may be held liable for a judgment against the insured in excess of its policy limits where it has breached its implied covenant of good faith and fair dealing by unreasonably refusing to accept a settlement offer within the policy limits (*Crisci v. Security Ins. Co of New Haven, Conn.* 66 Cal.2d 425, 429; *Comunale v. Traders & General Ins. Co.* (1958) 50 Cal.2d 654, 661). The insurer's duty of good faith requires it to "settle within policy limits when there is substantial likelihood of recovery in excess of those limits." (*Murphy v. Allstate Ins. Co.* (1976) 17 Cal.3d 937, 941.)

Although an insurance policy normally only carries an express statement of a duty to defend, an insurer's duty to settle is derived from the implied covenant of good faith and fair dealing which is part of any contract (see 4 Witkin, Summary of Cal.Law (8th ed., 1974) § 754, p. 3050, and cases collected therein). This duty was first recognized in *Comunale v. Traders & General Ins. Co.*, supra, 50 Cal.2d 654. The rationale for the "*Comunale* duty" was articulated by [us] at page 659, 328 P.2d at page 201: "It is common knowledge that a large percentage of the claims covered by insurance are settled without litigation and that this is one of the usual methods by which the insured receives protection." (See *Douglas v. United States Fidelity & Guaranty Co.*, 81 N.H. 371; *Hilker v. Western Automobile Ins. Co.* [204 Wis. 1, 231 N.W. 257] supra.) * * *

"The insurer, in deciding whether a claim should be compromised, must take into account the interest of the insured and give it at least as much consideration as it does to its own interest. (See *Ivy v. Pacific Automobile Ins. Co.*, 156 Cal.App.2d 652, 659.) When there is great risk of a recovery beyond the policy limits so that the most reasonable manner of disposing of the claim is a settlement which can be made within those limits, a consideration in good faith of the insured's interest requires the insurer to settle the claim. Its unwarranted refusal to do so constitutes a breach of the implied covenant of good faith and fair dealing."

It has been held in California and other jurisdictions that the excess carrier may maintain an action against the primary carrier for [ ] [wrongful] refusal to settle within the latter's policy limits (*Northwestern Mut. Ins. Co. v. Farmers' Ins. Group* (1978) 76 Cal.App.3d 1031; *Valentine v. Aetna Ins. Co.*, 564 F.2d 292; *Estate of Penn v. Amalgamated General Agencies* (1977) 148 N.J.Super. 419). This rule, however, is based on the theory of equitable subrogation: Since the insured would have been able to recover from the primary carrier for a judgment in excess of policy limits caused by the carrier's wrongful refusal to settle, the excess carrier, who discharged the insured's liability as a result of this tort, stands in the shoes of the insured and should be permitted to assert all claims against the primary carrier which the insured himself could have asserted (see *Northwestern Mut. Ins. Co. v. Farmers' Ins. Group*, supra, 76 Cal.App.3d at pp. 1040, 1049–1050). Hence, the rule does not rest upon the finding of any separate duty owed to an excess insurance carrier.

Commercial argues that the implied covenant of good faith and fair dealing is reciprocal, binding the policyholder as well as the carrier (see

Liberty Mut. Ins. Co. v. Altfillisch Constr. Co. (1977) 70 Cal.App.3d 789, 797). It is further contended, in effect, that turnabout is fair play: that the implied covenant of good faith and fair dealing applies to the insured as well as the insurer, and thus the policyholder owes a duty to his excess carrier not to unreasonably refuse an offer of settlement below the amount of excess coverage where a judgment of liability above that amount is substantially likely to occur.

This theory, while possessing superficial plausibility and exquisite simplicity, cannot withstand closer analysis. We have no quarrel with the proposition that a duty of good faith and fair dealing in an insurance policy is a two-way street, running from the insured to his insurer as well as vice versa (*Liberty Mut. Ins. Co. v. Altfillisch Constr. Co.*, supra, 70 Cal.App.3d at p. 797; *Crisci v. Security Ins. Co.*, supra, 66 Cal.2d at p. 429). However, what that duty embraces is dependent upon the nature of the bargain struck between the insurer and the insured and the legitimate expectations of the parties which arise from the contract.

The essence of the implied covenant of good faith in insurance policies is that " 'neither party will do anything which injures the right of the other to receive the benefits of the agreement' " (*Murphy v. Allstate Ins. Co.*, supra, 17 Cal.3d at p. 940, quoting from *Brown v. Superior Court* (1949) 34 Cal.2d 559, 564). One of the most important benefits of a maximum limit insurance policy is the assurance that the company will provide the insured with defense and indemnification for the purpose of protecting him from liability. Accordingly, the insured has the legitimate right to expect that the method of settlement within policy limits will be employed in order to give him such protection.

No such expectations can be said to reasonably flow from an excess insurer to its insured. The object of the excess insurance policy is to provide additional resources should the insured's liability surpass a specified sum. The insured owes no duty to defend or indemnify the excess carrier; hence, the carrier can possess no reasonable expectation that the insured will accept a settlement offer as a means of "protecting" the carrier from exposure. The protection of the insurer's pecuniary interests is simply not the object of the bargain.

As [ ] [we have] stated: "The duty to settle is implied in law to protect the insured from exposure to liability in excess of coverage as a result of the insurer's gamble—on which only the insured might lose." (*Murphy v. Allstate Ins. Co.*, supra, 17 Cal.3d at p. 941.) Similar considerations do not apply where the situation is reversed: where the insured is fully covered by primary insurance, the primary insurer is entitled to take control of the settlement negotiations and the insured is precluded from interfering therewith (see *Shapero v. Allstate Ins. Co.* (1971) 14 Cal.App.3d 433, 437–438, quoting from *Ivy v. Pacific Automobile Ins. Co.* (1958) 156 Cal.App.2d 652, 659–660). Where, as here, the policyholder is self-insured for an amount below the beginning of the excess insurance coverage, he is gambling as much with his own money as with that of the carrier. The crucial point is that the excess carrier has no legitimate expectation that the insured will " 'give at least as much consideration to the financial well-being' " of the insurance company as he does to his " 'own interests' " (*Shapero*, supra, 14 Cal.App.3d at p. 438), in considering whether to settle for an amount below the excess policy coverage. In fact, the primary reason excess insurance is purchased is to provide an available pool of money in the event that the decision is made to take the gamble of litigating.

With these principles in mind, it becomes clear that the case of *Liberty Mut. Ins. Co. v. Altfillisch Constr. Co.,* supra, 70 Cal.App.3d 789, upon which Commercial bases its argument, is easily distinguishable.

In *Liberty,* the insurance policy contained the standard clauses giving the company the right of subrogation against third parties, plus a provision which expressly prohibited the insured from doing anything which would prejudice such right (*id.,* at p. 796). The insured leased the equipment covered in the policy to a third party under a contract which effectively released that party from liability for damage, thus cutting off the company's right of subrogation. The court held that the reciprocal covenant of good faith and fair dealing in the insurance policy was breached by the insured, since its act had destroyed "Liberty's expectation of opportunities to subrogate in the event of payment of a loss caused by the negligence of a third party." (p. 797.)

In the instant case, whether Commercial could harbor any legitimate expectation that its insured would settle a claim for less than the threshold amount of the policy coverage must be determined in the light of what the parties bargained for. The complaint makes no reference to any language in the policy which would give rise to such expectation. We must therefore ask the question: Did Safeway, when it purchased excess coverage, impliedly promise that it would take all reasonable steps to settle a claim below the limits of Commercial's coverage so as to protect Commercial from possible exposure? Further, did Commercial extend excess coverage with the understanding and expectation that it would receive such favorable treatment from Safeway under the policy? We think not.

At this point, two recent appellate decisions which bear upon this issue, deserve mention.

First, in the case of *Kaiser Foundation Hospitals v. North Star Reinsurance Corp.* (1979) 90 Cal.App.3d 786 (the Court of Appeal for the Second District, Division Five, concluded that the relationship between an insured and primary carrier vis-a-vis the excess carrier was governed by an implied covenant of good faith and fair dealing p. 792). That decision, however, dealt with a situation where the insured and its primary carrier acted in collusion to wrongfully allocate certain dates of loss so as to maximize the liability of the excess carrier. It appears that the aggravated conduct on the part of the insured and the primary carrier in taking advantage of the excess carrier prompted the Court of Appeal to invoke the basic principles of good faith and fair dealing in order to give proper redress to the excess carrier. It is to be noted that the opinion takes careful pains to emphasize that in speaking of a good faith and fair dealing duty owed by the insured to the excess carrier under these circumstances, it was expressly not amplifying on the nature of such duty: "[W]e make no attempt to define precisely what rights and duties that entails in a case such as this. Such questions are best decided in the light of concrete facts * * *" (p. 794).

We acknowledge that equity requires fair dealing between the parties to an insurance contract. We view the *Kaiser* and *Liberty* cases as pointing up a recognition in the law that the insured status as such is not a license for the insured to engage in unconscionable acts which would subvert the legitimate rights and expectations of the excess insurance carrier.

However, we are unable to derive from this sound principle, the precipitous conclusion that the covenant of good faith and fair dealing should be extended to include a "*Comunale duty*"—that is, a duty which would require an insured contemplating settlement to put the excess carrier's financial interests on at least an equal footing with his own. Such a duty cannot reasonably be found from the mere existence of the contractual relationship between insured and excess carrier in the absence of express language in the contract so providing.

We observe that an apparently contrary conclusion has been reached by the Third District in the recent case of *Transit Casualty Co. v. Spink Corp.* [supra] 94 Cal.App.3d 124. [We disapprove that case] insofar as it holds that an insured's duty of good faith and fair dealing to his excess carrier compels him to accept a settlement offer or proceed at his peril where there is a substantial likelihood that an adverse judgment will bring excess insurance coverage into play.

In conclusion, we hold that a policy providing for excess insurance coverage imposes no implied duty upon the insured to accept a settlement offer which would avoid exposing the insurer to liability. Moreover such a duty cannot be predicated upon an insured's implied covenant of good faith and fair dealing. If an excess carrier wishes to insulate itself from liability for an insured's failure to accept what it deems to be a reasonable settlement offer, it may do so by appropriate language in the policy. We hesitate, however, to read into the policy obligations which are neither sought after nor contemplated by the parties.

The judgment is affirmed.

NOTES AND QUESTIONS

1. *The Source of the Duty.* It is generally accepted that the primary insurer's duty to the insured to accept reasonable offers of settlement may be enforced through a subrogation action by an excess insurer. RLLI § 32. See, e.g., *RSUI Indem. Co. v. Discover P&C Ins. Co.*, 2014 WL 1513973 (D. Cal. 2014). Similarly, a lower-layer excess insurer may be held liable to a higher-layer excess insurer on the same basis. *Cent. Illinois Pub. Serv. Co. v. Agric. Ins. Co.*, 880 N.E.2d 1172 (Ill. 2008). The *Safeway* court's explanation of the duty that runs from the primary to the excess insurer as arising from equitable subrogation virtually decided the case for it. If the source of that duty is the insured's right against the primary insurer, then the duty obviously cannot create rights in an excess insurer against the insured. Thus, if the insured and the primary jointly agree to reject a settlement offer, the excess insurer has no ground for avoiding liability for a judgment in excess of the primary limits of liability, even if the settlement offer would be considered "reasonable" (and therefore improper to reject) in the primary insurer/insured setting. See *Puritan Ins. Co. v. Canadian Universal Ins. Co., Ltd.*, 775 F.2d 76 (3d Cir. 1985).

Adhering literally to this notion that equitable subrogation is the source of the primary's duty to the excess insurer, the Alabama Supreme

Court has held that, if an excess insurer pays for a settlement because the primary has earlier refused to settle for a sum within its limits, the excess has no cause of action against the primary for failure to settle, because the insured was never subject to personal loss from a final judgment. Therefore, there was no loss to the insured to which the excess insurer could be subrogated. See *Fed. Ins. Co. v. Travelers Cas. & Sur. Co.*, 843 So. 2d 140 (Ala. 2002). Does this make sense as a matter of policy, in view of the effect such a rule will have on the excess insurer's willingness to settle? For a decision considering the possibility that there is a direct duty between primary and excess insurers, see *Russo v. Rochford,* 472 N.Y.S. 2d 954 (N.Y. S.Ct., Trial Term 1984). For further discussion, see Thomas M. Hamilton & Troy A. Stark, Excess-Primary Insurer Obligations and the Rights of the Insured, 69 Def. Counsel J. 315 (2002).

2. *Allocation of Defense Costs.* While the traditional rule appears to be that the primary insurer alone bears the costs of the defense, some courts hold that the excess insurer is liable for a pro-rata share of the costs of defense. See, e.g., *Gen. Accident Ins. Co. v. Safety Nat'l Cas. Corp.*, 825 F.Supp. 705 (E.D.Pa. 1993); *Jostens, Inc. v. Mission Ins. Co.*, 387 N.W.2d 161 (Minn. 1986); *Aetna Cas. & Sur. Co. v. Certain Underwriters at Lloyds of London,* 56 Cal.App.3d 791 (Cal. 1976). Can this liability be explained in terms of subrogation, or must its source be some sort of equitable right that runs directly from the primary to the excess insurer?

3. *Does the Following-Form Excess Insurer Have Independent Rights?* Suppose that the policyholder secures a judgment that the primary policy provides coverage, but the excess insurer is not a party to that suit. Does the follow-form excess insurer have the right to contest coverage, or is the meaning of its policy already determined? The answer would seem to be that the excess insurer may still contest coverage. In effect, since the follow-form excess insurer was not a party to the suit, it cannot be collaterally estopped by a judgment. A following-form excess policy has merely saved the cost of printing the terms of the primary policy, but its fortunes do not rise or fall with the fortunes of the primary policy. See, e.g., *Allmerica Fin. Cor. v. Certain Underwriters at Lloyd's, London,* 871 N.E.2d 418 (Mass. 2007); *Allstate Ins. Co. v. Dana Co.,* 759 N.E.2d 1049 (Ind. 2001). Similarly, if the excess policy generally follows-form to a primary (or lower-layer excess) policy, but also contains a specific provision that precludes coverage where the primary policy would provide it, the specific provision governs. *Rick Franklin Cor. v. State ex rel. Dep't of Transp.*, 140 P.3d 1136 (Or. 2006).

3. DROP-DOWN LIABILITY

Mission National Insurance Company v. Duke Transportation Company

United States Court of Appeals, Fifth Circuit, 1986.
792 F.2d 550.

■ ROBERT MADDEN HILL, CIRCUIT JUDGE:

In this Louisiana diversity case, Duke Transportation Company (Duke) appeals from the district court's grant of a motion for summary judgment in favor of Mission National Insurance Company (Mission).

The district court held that Mission, an excess insurance carrier, was not required to provide primary coverage to or to defend its insured, Duke, after the primary insurance carrier, Northwest Insurance Company (Northwest), became insolvent. Finding the district court's ruling entirely correct, we affirm.

I.

Neither party contests the facts of this case. Duke purchased primary insurance coverage from Northwest for general liability, automobile, and worker's compensation claims. The Northwest policy provided for general liability coverage up to a maximum amount of $300,000 for an injury to one person. Duke also purchased umbrella or excess insurance coverage from Mission. The Mission policy provided for individual occurrence and aggregate annual maximum liability coverage in the amount of $5,000,000, subject to the following limitations:

> The Company shall only be liable for ultimate net loss the excess of either:
>
> (a) the limits of the underlying insurance as set out in the attached schedule [$300,000] in respect of each occurrence *covered* by said underlying insurance, or
>
> (b) the amount as set out in item 2(c) of the Declarations [$10,000] ultimate net loss in respect of each occurrence *not covered* by said underlying insurance, (hereinafter called the "underlying limits"),
>
> and then only up to a further sum as stated in item 2(a) of the Declarations [$5,000,000] in all in respect of each occurrence—subject to a limit as stated in item 2(b) of the Declarations [$5,000,000] in the aggregate for each annual period during the currency of this Policy separately in respect of Products Liability and in respect of Personal Injury (fatal or non-fatal) by Occupational Disease sustained by any employees of the Insured.
>
> In the event of reduction or exhaustion of the aggregate limits of liability under said underlying insurance by reason of losses paid thereunder, this policy subject to all the terms, conditions and definitions hereof shall
>
> (1) in the event of reduction pay the excess of the reduced underlying limit
>
> (2) in the event of exhaustion continue in force as underlying insurance.

(emphasis added). The Mission policy also contained the following limited obligation to defend:

> As respects occurrences *covered* under this policy, but *not covered* under the underlying insurances as set out in the attached schedule or under any other collectible insurance, the Company shall
>
> (a) defend in his name and behalf any suit against the Insured alleging liability insured under the provisions of this policy and seeking damages on account thereof, even if such

suit is groundless, false or fraudulent, but the Company shall have the right to make such investigation, negotiation and settlement of any claim or suit as may be deemed expedient by the company.

(b) pay all premiums on bonds to release attachments for an amount not in excess of the limit of liability of this policy, all premiums on appeal bonds required in any such defended suit but without any obligations to apply for or furnish such bonds, all costs taxed against the insured in any such suit, all expenses incurred by the Company and all interest accruing after the entry of judgment until the company has paid, tendered or deposited in court that part of such judgment as does not exceed the limit of the Company's liability thereon.

(c) reimburse the Insured for all reasonable expenses, other than loss of earnings incurred at the Company's request

(emphasis added).

When it became apparent that due to insolvency Northwest would be unable to fulfill its obligations of primary coverage and defense and would be placed in liquidation, Duke requested that Mission provide Duke with primary coverage and defense for suits arising during the period covered by the Northwest policy. After Mission refused the request to provide primary coverage and to defend the pending suits, Duke brought a declaratory judgment action in Louisiana state court, requesting that the court require Mission to provide primary coverage and to defend Duke. Mission removed the case to federal district court and also filed a declaratory judgment action asking the district court to declare that Mission owed no primary insurance coverage or duty to defend to Duke; the district court consolidated the two cases. On cross-motions for summary judgment the district court granted Mission's motion. The district court stated that:

> Under the plain language of Mission's policy there is no obligation to pay for any loss which is within the limits of the Northwest policy, that is, until the loss exceeds $300,000. The occurrences involved in these cases were *covered* by the underlying insurance. Further reduction or exhaustion of the limits of the underlying insurance can only be accomplished under the terms of umbrella policy *by payment of losses under the underlying insurance and not by the insolvency of Northwest.* See, Molina v. U.S. Fire Ins. Co., 574 F.2d 1176, 1178 (4th Cir.1978).
>
> The provision of the insurance agreement containing Mission's obligation to defend provides that Mission shall defend every case not covered by the underlying coverage *or,* by other collectible insurance. Since it is undisputed that the claims involved herein were covered under the Northwest policy, there is no duty to defend by Mission.

(emphasis in original). This appeal followed.

II.

A.

Duke argues that the district court erred in its interpretation of the insurance contract. Duke reads the limitation of liability section as limiting Mission's liability to amounts over the primary coverage only when the primary coverage remains collectible. In the case where the primary insurer collapses, Duke reads the policy as providing "drop down" coverage, i.e., the excess insurer drops down and assumes the primary insurer's responsibilities.

Duke bases its argument on its interpretation of the words "covered" and "not covered" in subsections (a) and (b) of the limitation of liability section of the Mission policy. Duke interprets "covered" to mean covered by the coverage terms of an underlying policy on which the insured can collect. Mission, and the district court, interpret "covered" to mean covered by an underlying policy without regard to whether the insured can collect from the primary insurer.

While our research has not uncovered, nor have the parties cited to us, any Louisiana cases or any other state's cases interpreting the words "covered" and "not covered," we are confident in predicting that a Louisiana court would hold that the use of the words "covered" and "not covered" in the Mission policy does not result in drop down coverage in favor of Duke. Recently, in a case arising out of the collapse of the same primary insurance carrier, we held that the following policy provision did not provide drop down coverage:

> The company shall be liable only for ultimate net loss resulting from any one occurrence in excess of * * * if the insurance afforded by such underlying insurance is inapplicable to the occurrence, the amount stated in the declarations as the retained limit.

Continental Marble & Granite v. Canal Insurance Co., 785 F.2d 1258, 1259 (5th Cir.1986) (construing Louisiana law). In *Continental Marble* the insured argued that the primary insurer's insolvency rendered the underlying insurance "inapplicable" and that, therefore, the excess liability policy dropped down to become the primary policy. We rejected the insured's contention. *Id.*

We believe the term "covered" provides at least as narrow, if not narrower, excess coverage than does the term "inapplicable." Just as the primary insurance coverage in *Continental Marble* remained applicable to the insured so too does the primary insurance coverage in the instant case cover the occurrences Duke claims that Mission should provide primary coverage for and defend Duke against. The terms of the Northwest policy specifically provide coverage for all of the claims that Duke asserts Mission should provide primary coverage for and defend Duke against.

The cases from outside Louisiana also support this interpretation. The only cases where the courts have found that the excess insurer drops down involve policies where the excess insurer used the terms "inapplicable," "collectible," or "recoverable." *E.g. Reserve Insurance Co. v. Pisciotta*, 640 P.2d 764, 772 (1982) ("recoverable"); *Gros v. Houston Fire & Casualty Insurance Co.*, 195 So.2d 674, 676 (La.Ct.App.1967) ("collectible"); *Macalco, Inc. v. Gulf Insurance Co.*, 550 S.W.2d 883, 896

(Mo.Ct.App.1977) ("inapplicable"). Of course, our ruling in *Continental Marble* establishes, at least until the Louisiana courts advise us otherwise, the interpretation to be given to the term "inapplicable." And the terms "collectible" and "recoverable" are clearly distinguishable from the term "covered." When an excess insurer uses the term "collectible" or "recoverable" it is agreeing to drop down in the event the primary coverage becomes uncollectible or unrecoverable; on the other hand, when an excess insurer uses the term "covered" or "not covered," it is agreeing to drop down only in the event that the terms of the underlying policy do not provide coverage for the occurrence or occurrences in question.

B.

Duke also proffers as a reason for its contention that Mission should have to assume Northwest's obligation to provide primary coverage to and defend Duke that the limits of the underlying policy have been exhausted and that, therefore, under the terms of the Mission policy, Mission's policy continues in force as the underlying insurance. We disagree. The policy provides that: "In the event of reduction or exhaustion of the aggregate limits of liability under said underlying insurance by reason of losses paid thereunder, this policy * * * shall * * * in the event of exhaustion continue in force as underlying insurance." Duke's argument ignores the phrase "by reason of losses paid thereunder." Duke argues that the underlying policy is exhausted because Northwest is unable to pay any claim under the policy; however, the policy specifically provides that it functions as the underlying insurance only when the exhaustion occurs by reason of losses paid under the policy. Since Duke is not claiming exhaustion due to losses paid under the policy, its argument must fail. *See Molina v. United States Fire Insurance Co.,* 574 F.2d 1176, 1178 (4th Cir.1978); *St. Vincent's Hospital & Medical Center v. Insurance Co. of North America,* 457 N.Y.S.2d 670, 672 (N.Y.Sup.Ct.1982).

C.

Duke's last argument for its contention that Mission should have to assume Northwest's obligation to provide primary coverage to and defend Duke is based on the language of the policy in the section defining "ultimate net loss:"

> Except as provided in insuring Agreement II, the term "Ultimate Net Loss" shall mean the total sum which the insured, or his *Underlying Insurers as scheduled,* or both, become obligated to pay by reason of personal injuries, property damage or advertising liability claims, either through adjudication or compromise, and shall also include hospital, medical and funeral charges and all sums paid as salaries, wages, compensation, fees, charges and law costs, premiums on attachment or appeal bonds, interest, expenses for doctors, lawyers, nurses and investigators and other persons, and for litigation, settlement, adjustment and investigation of claims and suits which are paid as a consequence of any occurrence covered hereunder.

> The Company shall not be liable for expenses as aforesaid when such expenses are included in *other valid and collectible insurance.*

(emphasis added). Duke contends that, because the policy refers to "other valid and collectible insurance," there is an implication that any insurance which might apply to limit Mission's liability must be collectible. Again, we must disagree. When the entire section is read in context, it is clear that the phrase "other valid and collectible insurance" refers to any insurance Duke carried in addition to the underlying insurance listed in the schedule contained in the Mission policy, i.e., the Northwest policy. The Mission policy clearly provides that Mission's liability is excess both to occurrences covered by the Northwest policy and to expenses included in any other valid and collectible insurance. Thus, the use of the term "collectible" in no way refers to the Northwest policy, and Duke's last argument is therefore without merit.

None of the arguments offered by Duke support its contention that Mission's excess liability policy drops down to become the primary policy. We therefore affirm the judgment of the district court.

AFFIRMED.

NOTES AND QUESTIONS

1. *"Covered" Versus "Recoverable."* The issue in *Duke Transportation* has been widely litigated. The answer tends to turn, as did *Duke Transportation,* on the language the excess policy employs in obligating the insured to maintain primary coverage under the excess layer. Subtle differences produce divergent results, but the decided majority of cases interpret policy language as did the court in *Duke.* See, e.g., *Scottsdale Ins. Co. v. Knox Park Constr., Inc.*, 488 F.3d 680 (5th Cir. 2007); *Caldwell Freight Lines, Inc. v. Lumbermen's Mut. Cas. Co., Inc.*, 947 So. 2d 948 (Miss. 2007). For example, in *Reserve Insurance Co. v. Pisciotta,* 628, 640 P.2d 764 (Cal. 1982), the excess liability policy required the insured to maintain a specified layer of primary coverage. But it also indicated that the excess insurer would be liable for the insured's "ultimate net loss in excess of * * * the amount *recoverable* under the underlying insurance" [emphasis added]. The Supreme Court of California held the provision ambiguous, construed it in favor of the insured, and imposed a drop-down obligation on the excess insurer. Was this provision really ambiguous, or did it instead suggest unambiguously that there was a drop-down obligation in the event of the primary insurer's insolvency?

2. *Allocating the Incentive to Monitor Solvency.* The policy language in *Duke* created an incentive for the insured to monitor the primary insurer's solvency, whereas the policy language in *Pisciotta* created a similar incentive for the excess insurer. Is there reason to prefer one approach to the other? If you were an Insurance Commissioner, would you consider requiring that all excess policies contain the same language?

CHAPTER EIGHT

AUTOMOBILE INSURANCE

This Chapter examines a range of issues associated with automobile insurance coverage. Automobile accidents are an important social problem in this country. Approximately 40,000 people a year are killed in motor vehicle accidents, and over 3 million people are injured. We spend over $190 billion a year on various forms of auto insurance to address these deaths and injuries and the property damage that results from auto accidents.

A reading of the Sample Policy in the next Section will reveal that many of its provisions run parallel to those in other standard property and liability insurance policies. This Chapter focuses on the issues that are characteristic of automobile insurance alone, for two reasons. First, and most obviously, they are issues with which any student of insurance law should be familiar. In addition, however, it is important to recognize that the law governing other forms of insurance—especially liability insurance—should not be uncritically used as a model for automobile insurance law. Automobile insurance coverage issues have so predominant an impact on ordinary individuals and account for so large a portion of the personal injury lawsuits brought in the United States that the field is necessarily special. The result is that consumer-protection and victim-protection concerns often operate more strongly in this area of insurance than others.

We begin, as before, with a Sample Policy, and follow the policy with cases and materials on the four kinds of coverage provided by automobile insurance policies: liability, property damage, uninsured motorists, and medical payments or broader personal injury protection.

A. SAMPLE PERSONAL AUTOMOBILE INSURANCE POLICY

PERSONAL AUTO
PP 00 01 01 05

PERSONAL AUTO POLICY

AGREEMENT

In return for payment of the premium and subject to all the terms of this policy, we agree with you as follows:

DEFINITIONS

A. Throughout this policy, "you" and "your" refer to:
1. The "named insured" shown in the Declarations; and
2. The spouse if a resident of the same household.

If the spouse ceases to be a resident of the same household during the policy period or prior to the inception of this policy, the spouse will be considered "you" and "your" under this policy but only until the earlier of:
1. The end of 90 days following the spouse's change of residency;
2. The effective date of another policy listing the spouse as a named insured; or
3. The end of the policy period.

B. "We", "us" and "our" refer to the Company providing this insurance.

C. For purposes of this policy, a private passenger type auto, pickup or van shall be deemed to be owned by a person if leased:
1. Under a written agreement to that person; and
2. For a continuous period of at least 6 months.

Other words and phrases are defined. They are in quotation marks when used.

D. "Bodily injury" means bodily harm, sickness or disease, including death that results.

E. "Business" includes trade, profession or occupation.

F. "Family member" means a person related to you by blood, marriage or adoption who is a resident of your household. This includes a ward or foster child.

G. "Occupying" means:
1. In;
2. Upon; or
3. Getting in, on, out or off.

H. "Property damage" means physical injury to, destruction of or loss of use of tangible property.

I. "Trailer" means a vehicle designed to be pulled by a:
1. Private passenger auto; or

2. Pickup or van.

It also means a farm wagon or farm implement while towed by a vehicle listed in **1.** or **2.** above.

J. "Your covered auto" means:
1. Any vehicle shown in the Declarations.
2. A "newly acquired auto".
3. Any "trailer" you own.
4. Any auto or "trailer" you do not own while used as a temporary substitute for any other vehicle described in this definition which is out of normal use because of its:
   a. Breakdown;
   b. Repair;
   c. Servicing;
   d. Loss; or
   e. Destruction.

   This Provision (**J.4.**) does not apply to Coverage For Damage To Your Auto.

K. "Newly acquired auto":
1. "Newly acquired auto" means any of the following types of vehicles you become the owner of during the policy period:
   a. A private passenger auto; or
   b. A pickup or van, for which no other insurance policy provides coverage, that:
      (1) Has a Gross Vehicle Weight Rating of 10,000 lbs. or less; and
      (2) Is not used for the delivery or transportation of goods and materials unless such use is:
         (a) Incidental to your "business" of installing, maintaining or repairing furnishings or equipment; or
         (b) For farming or ranching.
2. Coverage for a "newly acquired auto" is provided as described below. If you ask us to insure a "newly acquired auto" after a specified time period described below has elapsed, any coverage we provide for a "newly acquired auto" will begin at the time you request the coverage.

a. For any coverage provided in this policy except Coverage For Damage To Your Auto, a "newly acquired auto" will have the broadest coverage we now provide for any vehicle shown in the Declarations. Coverage begins on the date you become the owner. However, for this coverage to apply to a "newly acquired auto" which is in addition to any vehicle shown in the Declarations, you must ask us to insure it within 14 days after you become the owner.

   If a "newly acquired auto" replaces a vehicle shown in the Declarations, coverage is provided for this vehicle without your having to ask us to insure it.

b. Collision Coverage for a "newly acquired auto" begins on the date you become the owner. However, for this coverage to apply, you must ask us to insure it within:

   (1) 14 days after you become the owner if the Declarations indicate that Collision Coverage applies to at least one auto. In this case, the "newly acquired auto" will have the broadest coverage we now provide for any auto shown in the Declarations.

   (2) Four days after you become the owner if the Declarations do not indicate that Collision Coverage applies to at least one auto. If you comply with the 4 day requirement and a loss occurred before you asked us to insure the "newly acquired auto", a Collision deductible of $500 will apply.

c. Other Than Collision Coverage for a "newly acquired auto" begins on the date you become the owner. However, for this coverage to apply, you must ask us to insure it within:

   (1) 14 days after you become the owner if the Declarations indicate that Other Than Collision Coverage applies to at least one auto. In this case, the "newly acquired auto" will have the broadest coverage we now provide for any auto shown in the Declarations.

   (2) Four days after you become the owner if the Declarations do not indicate that Other Than Collision Coverage applies to at least one auto. If you comply with the 4 day requirement and a loss occurred before you asked us to insure the "newly acquired auto", an Other Than Collision deductible of $500 will apply.

PART A – LIABILITY COVERAGE

INSURING AGREEMENT

A. We will pay damages for "bodily injury" or "property damage" for which any "insured" becomes legally responsible because of an auto accident. Damages include prejudgment interest awarded against the "insured". We will settle or defend, as we consider appropriate, any claim or suit asking for these damages. In addition to our limit of liability, we will pay all defense costs we incur. Our duty to settle or defend ends when our limit of liability for this coverage has been exhausted by payment of judgments or settlements. We have no duty to defend any suit or settle any claim for "bodily injury" or "property damage" not covered under this policy.

B. "Insured" as used in this Part means:

  1. You or any "family member" for the ownership, maintenance or use of any auto or "trailer".

  2. Any person using "your covered auto".

  3. For "your covered auto", any person or organization but only with respect to legal responsibility for acts or omissions of a person for whom coverage is afforded under this Part.

  4. For any auto or "trailer", other than "your covered auto", any other person or organization but only with respect to legal responsibility for acts or omissions of you or any "family member" for whom coverage is afforded under this Part. This Provision (B.4.) applies only if the person or organization does not own or hire the auto or "trailer".

SUPPLEMENTARY PAYMENTS

We will pay on behalf of an "insured":

1. Up to $250 for the cost of bail bonds required because of an accident, including related traffic law violations. The accident must result in "bodily injury" or "property damage" covered under this policy.

2. Premiums on appeal bonds and bonds to release attachments in any suit we defend.

3. Interest accruing after a judgment is entered in any suit we defend. Our duty to pay interest ends when we offer to pay that part of the judgment which does not exceed our limit of liability for this coverage.

4. Up to $200 a day for loss of earnings, but not other income, because of attendance at hearings or trials at our request.
5. Other reasonable expenses incurred at our request.

These payments will not reduce the limit of liability.

EXCLUSIONS

A. We do not provide Liability Coverage for any "insured":

1. Who intentionally causes "bodily injury" or "property damage".
2. For "property damage" to property owned or being transported by that "insured".
3. For "property damage" to property:
    a. Rented to;
    b. Used by; or
    c. In the care of;
    that "insured".
    This Exclusion (**A.3.**) does not apply to "property damage" to a residence or private garage.
4. For "bodily injury" to an employee of that "insured" during the course of employment. This Exclusion (**A.4.**) does not apply to "bodily injury" to a domestic employee unless workers' compensation benefits are required or available for that domestic employee.
5. For that "insured's" liability arising out of the ownership or operation of a vehicle while it is being used as a public or livery conveyance. This Exclusion (**A.5.**) does not apply to a share-the-expense car pool.
6. While employed or otherwise engaged in the "business" of:
    a. Selling;
    b. Repairing;
    c. Servicing;
    d. Storing; or
    e. Parking;
    vehicles designed for use mainly on public highways. This includes road testing and delivery. This Exclusion (**A.6.**) does not apply to the ownership, maintenance or use of "your covered auto" by:
    a. You;
    b. Any "family member"; or
    c. Any partner, agent or employee of you or any "family member".

7. Maintaining or using any vehicle while that "insured" is employed or otherwise engaged in any "business" (other than farming or ranching) not described in Exclusion **A.6.**
    This Exclusion (**A.7.**) does not apply to the maintenance or use of a:
    a. Private passenger auto;
    b. Pickup or van; or
    c. "Trailer" used with a vehicle described in **a.** or **b.** above.
8. Using a vehicle without a reasonable belief that that "insured" is entitled to do so. This Exclusion (**A.8.**) does not apply to a "family member" using "your covered auto" which is owned by you.
9. For "bodily injury" or "property damage" for which that "insured":
    a. Is an insured under a nuclear energy liability policy; or
    b. Would be an insured under a nuclear energy liability policy but for its termination upon exhaustion of its limit of liability.
    A nuclear energy liability policy is a policy issued by any of the following or their successors:
    a. Nuclear Energy Liability Insurance Association;
    b. Mutual Atomic Energy Liability Underwriters; or
    c. Nuclear Insurance Association of Canada.

B. We do not provide Liability Coverage for the ownership, maintenance or use of:

1. Any vehicle which:
    a. Has fewer than four wheels; or
    b. Is designed mainly for use off public roads.
    This Exclusion (**B.1.**) does not apply:
    a. While such vehicle is being used by an "insured" in a medical emergency;
    b. To any "trailer"; or
    c. To any non-owned golf cart.
2. Any vehicle, other than "your covered auto", which is:
    a. Owned by you; or
    b. Furnished or available for your regular use.
3. Any vehicle, other than "your covered auto", which is:
    a. Owned by any "family member"; or
    b. Furnished or available for the regular use of any "family member".

SECTION A — SAMPLE PERSONAL AUTOMOBILE INSURANCE POLICY

However, this Exclusion (**B.3.**) does not apply to you while you are maintaining or "occupying" any vehicle which is:

a. Owned by a "family member"; or

b. Furnished or available for the regular use of a "family member".

4. Any vehicle, located inside a facility designed for racing, for the purpose of:

a. Competing in; or

b. Practicing or preparing for;

any prearranged or organized racing or speed contest.

LIMIT OF LIABILITY

A. The limit of liability shown in the Declarations for each person for Bodily Injury Liability is our maximum limit of liability for all damages, including damages for care, loss of services or death, arising out of "bodily injury" sustained by any one person in any one auto accident. Subject to this limit for each person, the limit of liability shown in the Declarations for each accident for Bodily Injury Liability is our maximum limit of liability for all damages for "bodily injury" resulting from any one auto accident.

The limit of liability shown in the Declarations for each accident for Property Damage Liability is our maximum limit of liability for all "property damage" resulting from any one auto accident.

This is the most we will pay regardless of the number of:

1. "Insureds";

2. Claims made;

3. Vehicles or premiums shown in the Declarations; or

4. Vehicles involved in the auto accident.

B. No one will be entitled to receive duplicate payments for the same elements of loss under this coverage and:

1. Part **B** or Part **C** of this policy; or

2. Any Underinsured Motorists Coverage provided by this policy.

OUT OF STATE COVERAGE

If an auto accident to which this policy applies occurs in any state or province other than the one in which "your covered auto" is principally garaged, we will interpret your policy for that accident as follows:

A. If the state or province has:

1. A financial responsibility or similar law specifying limits of liability for "bodily injury" or "property damage" higher than the limit shown in the Declarations, your policy will provide the higher specified limit.

2. A compulsory insurance or similar law requiring a nonresident to maintain insurance whenever the nonresident uses a vehicle in that state or province, your policy will provide at least the required minimum amounts and types of coverage.

B. No one will be entitled to duplicate payments for the same elements of loss.

FINANCIAL RESPONSIBILITY

When this policy is certified as future proof of financial responsibility, this policy shall comply with the law to the extent required.

OTHER INSURANCE

If there is other applicable liability insurance we will pay only our share of the loss. Our share is the proportion that our limit of liability bears to the total of all applicable limits. However, any insurance we provide for a vehicle you do not own, including any vehicle while used as a temporary substitute for "your covered auto", shall be excess over any other collectible insurance.

PART B – MEDICAL PAYMENTS COVERAGE

INSURING AGREEMENT

A. We will pay reasonable expenses incurred for necessary medical and funeral services because of "bodily injury":

1. Caused by accident; and

2. Sustained by an "insured".

We will pay only those expenses incurred for services rendered within 3 years from the date of the accident.

B. "Insured" as used in this Part means:

1. You or any "family member":

a. While "occupying"; or

b. As a pedestrian when struck by;

a motor vehicle designed for use mainly on public roads or a trailer of any type.

2. Any other person while "occupying" "your covered auto".

EXCLUSIONS

We do not provide Medical Payments Coverage for any "insured" for "bodily injury":

1. Sustained while "occupying" any motorized vehicle having fewer than four wheels.
2. Sustained while "occupying" "your covered auto" when it is being used as a public or livery conveyance. This Exclusion (2.) does not apply to a share-the-expense car pool.
3. Sustained while "occupying" any vehicle located for use as a residence or premises.
4. Occurring during the course of employment if workers' compensation benefits are required or available for the "bodily injury".
5. Sustained while "occupying", or when struck by, any vehicle (other than "your covered auto") which is:
    a. Owned by you; or
    b. Furnished or available for your regular use.
6. Sustained while "occupying", or when struck by, any vehicle (other than "your covered auto") which is:
    a. Owned by any "family member"; or
    b. Furnished or available for the regular use of any "family member".

   However, this Exclusion (6.) does not apply to you.
7. Sustained while "occupying" a vehicle without a reasonable belief that that "insured" is entitled to do so. This Exclusion (7.) does not apply to a "family member" using "your covered auto" which is owned by you.
8. Sustained while "occupying" a vehicle when it is being used in the "business" of an "insured". This Exclusion (8.) does not apply to "bodily injury" sustained while "occupying" a:
    a. Private passenger auto;
    b. Pickup or van; or
    c. "Trailer" used with a vehicle described in a. or b. above.
9. Caused by or as a consequence of:
    a. Discharge of a nuclear weapon (even if accidental);
    b. War (declared or undeclared);
    c. Civil war;
    d. Insurrection; or
    e. Rebellion or revolution.
10. From or as a consequence of the following, whether controlled or uncontrolled or however caused:
    a. Nuclear reaction;
    b. Radiation; or
    c. Radioactive contamination.
11. Sustained while "occupying" any vehicle located inside a facility designed for racing, for the purpose of:
    a. Competing in; or
    b. Practicing or preparing for;

    any prearranged or organized racing or speed contest.

LIMIT OF LIABILITY

A. The limit of liability shown in the Declarations for this coverage is our maximum limit of liability for each person injured in any one accident. This is the most we will pay regardless of the number of:
   1. "Insureds";
   2. Claims made;
   3. Vehicles or premiums shown in the Declarations; or
   4. Vehicles involved in the accident.

B. No one will be entitled to receive duplicate payments for the same elements of loss under this coverage and:
   1. Part A or Part C of this policy; or
   2. Any Underinsured Motorists Coverage provided by this policy.

OTHER INSURANCE

If there is other applicable auto medical payments insurance we will pay only our share of the loss. Our share is the proportion that our limit of liability bears to the total of all applicable limits. However, any insurance we provide with respect to a vehicle you do not own, including any vehicle while used as a temporary substitute for "your covered auto", shall be excess over any other collectible auto insurance providing payments for medical or funeral expenses.

PART C – UNINSURED MOTORISTS COVERAGE

INSURING AGREEMENT

A. We will pay compensatory damages which an "insured" is legally entitled to recover from the owner or operator of an "uninsured motor vehicle" because of "bodily injury":

1. Sustained by an "insured"; and
2. Caused by an accident.

The owner's or operator's liability for these damages must arise out of the ownership, maintenance or use of the "uninsured motor vehicle".

Any judgment for damages arising out of a suit brought without our written consent is not binding on us.

B. "Insured" as used in this Part means:

1. You or any "family member".
2. Any other person "occupying" "your covered auto".
3. Any person for damages that person is entitled to recover because of "bodily injury" to which this coverage applies sustained by a person described in **1.** or **2.** above.

C. "Uninsured motor vehicle" means a land motor vehicle or trailer of any type:

1. To which no bodily injury liability bond or policy applies at the time of the accident.
2. To which a bodily injury liability bond or policy applies at the time of the accident. In this case its limit for bodily injury liability must be less than the minimum limit for bodily injury liability specified by the financial responsibility law of the state in which "your covered auto" is principally garaged.
3. Which is a hit-and-run vehicle whose operator or owner cannot be identified and which hits:
   a. You or any "family member";
   b. A vehicle which you or any "family member" are "occupying"; or
   c. "Your covered auto".
4. To which a bodily injury liability bond or policy applies at the time of the accident but the bonding or insuring company:
   a. Denies coverage; or
   b. Is or becomes insolvent.

However, "uninsured motor vehicle" does not include any vehicle or equipment:

1. Owned by or furnished or available for the regular use of you or any "family member".
2. Owned or operated by a self-insurer under any applicable motor vehicle law, except a self-insurer which is or becomes insolvent.
3. Owned by any governmental unit or agency.
4. Operated on rails or crawler treads.
5. Designed mainly for use off public roads while not on public roads.
6. While located for use as a residence or premises.

EXCLUSIONS

A. We do not provide Uninsured Motorists Coverage for "bodily injury" sustained:

1. By an "insured" while "occupying", or when struck by, any motor vehicle owned by that "insured" which is not insured for this coverage under this policy. This includes a trailer of any type used with that vehicle.
2. By any "family member" while "occupying", or when struck by, any motor vehicle you own which is insured for this coverage on a primary basis under any other policy.

B. We do not provide Uninsured Motorists Coverage for "bodily injury" sustained by any "insured":

1. If that "insured" or the legal representative settles the "bodily injury" claim and such settlement prejudices our right to recover payment.
2. While "occupying" "your covered auto" when it is being used as a public or livery conveyance. This Exclusion (**B.2.**) does not apply to a share-the-expense car pool.
3. Using a vehicle without a reasonable belief that that "insured" is entitled to do so. This Exclusion (**B.3.**) does not apply to a "family member" using "your covered auto" which is owned by you.

C. This coverage shall not apply directly or indirectly to benefit any insurer or self-insurer under any of the following or similar law:

1. Workers' compensation law; or
2. Disability benefits law.

D. We do not provide Uninsured Motorists Coverage for punitive or exemplary damages.

LIMIT OF LIABILITY

A. The limit of liability shown in the Declarations for each person for Uninsured Motorists Coverage is our maximum limit of liability for all damages, including damages for care, loss of services or death, arising out of "bodily injury" sustained by any one person in any one accident. Subject to this limit for each person, the limit of liability shown in the Declarations for each accident for Uninsured Motorists Coverage is our maximum limit of liability for all damages for "bodily injury" resulting from any one accident.

This is the most we will pay regardless of the number of:

1. "Insureds";
2. Claims made;
3. Vehicles or premiums shown in the Declarations; or
4. Vehicles involved in the accident.

B. No one will be entitled to receive duplicate payments for the same elements of loss under this coverage and:

1. Part **A** or Part **B** of this policy; or
2. Any Underinsured Motorists Coverage provided by this policy.

C. We will not make a duplicate payment under this coverage for any element of loss for which payment has been made by or on behalf of persons or organizations who may be legally responsible.

D. We will not pay for any element of loss if a person is entitled to receive payment for the same element of loss under any of the following or similar law:

1. Workers' compensation law; or
2. Disability benefits law.

OTHER INSURANCE

If there is other applicable insurance available under one or more policies or provisions of coverage that is similar to the insurance provided under this Part of the policy:

1. Any recovery for damages under all such policies or provisions of coverage may equal but not exceed the highest applicable limit for any one vehicle under any insurance providing coverage on either a primary or excess basis.
2. Any insurance we provide with respect to a vehicle you do not own, including any vehicle while used as a temporary substitute for "your covered auto", shall be excess over any collectible insurance providing such coverage on a primary basis.
3. If the coverage under this policy is provided:

   a. On a primary basis, we will pay only our share of the loss that must be paid under insurance providing coverage on a primary basis. Our share is the proportion that our limit of liability bears to the total of all applicable limits of liability for coverage provided on a primary basis.

   b. On an excess basis, we will pay only our share of the loss that must be paid under insurance providing coverage on an excess basis. Our share is the proportion that our limit of liability bears to the total of all applicable limits of liability for coverage provided on an excess basis.

ARBITRATION

A. If we and an "insured" do not agree:

1. Whether that "insured" is legally entitled to recover damages; or
2. As to the amount of damages which are recoverable by that "insured";

from the owner or operator of an "uninsured motor vehicle", then the matter may be arbitrated. However, disputes concerning coverage under this Part may not be arbitrated.

Both parties must agree to arbitration. If so agreed, each party will select an arbitrator. The two arbitrators will select a third. If they cannot agree within 30 days, either may request that selection be made by a judge of a court having jurisdiction.

B. Each party will:

1. Pay the expenses it incurs; and
2. Bear the expenses of the third arbitrator equally.

C. Unless both parties agree otherwise, arbitration will take place in the county in which the "insured" lives. Local rules of law as to procedure and evidence will apply. A decision agreed to by at least two of the arbitrators will be binding as to:

1. Whether the "insured" is legally entitled to recover damages; and
2. The amount of damages. This applies only if the amount does not exceed the minimum limit for bodily injury liability specified by the financial responsibility law of the state in which "your covered auto" is principally garaged. If the amount exceeds that limit, either party may demand the right to a trial. This demand must be made within 60 days of the arbitrators' decision. If this demand is not made, the amount of damages agreed to by the arbitrators will be binding.

PART D – COVERAGE FOR DAMAGE TO YOUR AUTO

INSURING AGREEMENT

A. We will pay for direct and accidental loss to "your covered auto" or any "non-owned auto", including their equipment, minus any applicable deductible shown in the Declarations. If loss to more than one "your covered auto" or "non-owned auto" results from the same "collision", only the highest applicable deductible will apply. We will pay for loss to "your covered auto" caused by:

1. Other than "collision" only if the Declarations indicate that Other Than Collision Coverage is provided for that auto.
2. "Collision" only if the Declarations indicate that Collision Coverage is provided for that auto.

If there is a loss to a "non-owned auto", we will provide the broadest coverage applicable to any "your covered auto" shown in the Declarations.

B. "Collision" means the upset of "your covered auto" or a "non-owned auto" or their impact with another vehicle or object.

Loss caused by the following is considered other than "collision":

1. Missiles or falling objects;
2. Fire;
3. Theft or larceny;
4. Explosion or earthquake;
5. Windstorm;
6. Hail, water or flood;
7. Malicious mischief or vandalism;
8. Riot or civil commotion;
9. Contact with bird or animal; or
10. Breakage of glass.

If breakage of glass is caused by a "collision", you may elect to have it considered a loss caused by "collision".

C. "Non-owned auto" means:

1. Any private passenger auto, pickup, van or "trailer" not owned by or furnished or available for the regular use of you or any "family member" while in the custody of or being operated by you or any "family member"; or
2. Any auto or "trailer" you do not own while used as a temporary substitute for "your covered auto" which is out of normal use because of its:
   a. Breakdown;
   b. Repair;
   c. Servicing;
   d. Loss; or
   e. Destruction.

TRANSPORTATION EXPENSES

A. In addition, we will pay, without application of a deductible, up to a maximum of $600 for:

1. Temporary transportation expenses not exceeding $20 per day incurred by you in the event of a loss to "your covered auto". We will pay for such expenses if the loss is caused by:
   a. Other than "collision" only if the Declarations indicate that Other Than Collision Coverage is provided for that auto.
   b. "Collision" only if the Declarations indicate that Collision Coverage is provided for that auto.
2. Expenses for which you become legally responsible in the event of loss to a "non-owned auto". We will pay for such expenses if the loss is caused by:
   a. Other than "collision" only if the Declarations indicate that Other Than Collision Coverage is provided for any "your covered auto".
   b. "Collision" only if the Declarations indicate that Collision Coverage is provided for any "your covered auto".

However, the most we will pay for any expenses for loss of use is $20 per day.

B. Subject to the provisions of Paragraph **A.**, if the loss is caused by:

1. A total theft of "your covered auto" or a "non-owned auto", we will pay only expenses incurred during the period:
   a. Beginning 48 hours after the theft; and
   b. Ending when "your covered auto" or the "non-owned auto" is returned to use or we pay for its loss.
2. Other than theft of a "your covered auto" or a "non-owned auto", we will pay only expenses beginning when the auto is withdrawn from use for more than 24 hours.

Our payment will be limited to that period of time reasonably required to repair or replace the "your covered auto" or the "non-owned auto".

EXCLUSIONS

We will not pay for:

1. Loss to "your covered auto" or any "non-owned auto" which occurs while it is being used as a public or livery conveyance. This Exclusion (**1.**) does not apply to a share-the-expense car pool.

2. Damage due and confined to:
   a. Wear and tear;
   b. Freezing;
   c. Mechanical or electrical breakdown or failure; or
   d. Road damage to tires.

   This Exclusion (**2.**) does not apply if the damage results from the total theft of "your covered auto" or any "non-owned auto".

3. Loss due to or as a consequence of:
   a. Radioactive contamination;
   b. Discharge of any nuclear weapon (even if accidental);
   c. War (declared or undeclared);
   d. Civil war;
   e. Insurrection; or
   f. Rebellion or revolution.

4. Loss to any electronic equipment that reproduces, receives or transmits audio, visual or data signals. This includes but is not limited to:
   a. Radios and stereos;
   b. Tape decks;
   c. Compact disk systems;
   d. Navigation systems;
   e. Internet access systems;
   f. Personal computers;
   g. Video entertainment systems;
   h. Telephones;
   i. Televisions;
   j. Two-way mobile radios;
   k. Scanners; or
   l. Citizens band radios.

   This Exclusion (**4.**) does not apply to electronic equipment that is permanently installed in "your covered auto" or any "non-owned auto".

5. Loss to tapes, records, disks or other media used with equipment described in Exclusion **4.**

6. A total loss to "your covered auto" or any "non-owned auto" due to destruction or confiscation by governmental or civil authorities.

   This Exclusion (**6.**) does not apply to the interests of Loss Payees in "your covered auto".

7. Loss to:
   a. A "trailer", camper body, or motor home, which is not shown in the Declarations; or
   b. Facilities or equipment used with such "trailer", camper body or motor home. Facilities or equipment include but are not limited to:
      (1) Cooking, dining, plumbing or refrigeration facilities;
      (2) Awnings or cabanas; or
      (3) Any other facilities or equipment used with a "trailer", camper body, or motor home.

   This Exclusion (**7.**) does not apply to a:
   a. "Trailer", and its facilities or equipment, which you do not own; or
   b. "Trailer", camper body, or the facilities or equipment in or attached to the "trailer" or camper body, which you:
      (1) Acquire during the policy period; and
      (2) Ask us to insure within 14 days after you become the owner.

8. Loss to any "non-owned auto" when used by you or any "family member" without a reasonable belief that you or that "family member" are entitled to do so.

9. Loss to equipment designed or used for the detection or location of radar or laser.

10. Loss to any custom furnishings or equipment in or upon any pickup or van. Custom furnishings or equipment include but are not limited to:
    a. Special carpeting or insulation;
    b. Furniture or bars;
    c. Height-extending roofs; or
    d. Custom murals, paintings or other decals or graphics.

    This Exclusion (**10.**) does not apply to a cap, cover or bedliner in or upon any "your covered auto" which is a pickup.

11. Loss to any "non-owned auto" being maintained or used by any person while employed or otherwise engaged in the "business" of:
    a. Selling;
    b. Repairing;

c. Servicing;
d. Storing; or
e. Parking;

vehicles designed for use on public highways. This includes road testing and delivery.

12. Loss to "your covered auto" or any "non-owned auto", located inside a facility designed for racing, for the purpose of:
   a. Competing in; or
   b. Practicing or preparing for;

   any prearranged or organized racing or speed contest.

13. Loss to, or loss of use of, a "non-owned auto" rented by:
   a. You; or
   b. Any "family member";

   if a rental vehicle company is precluded from recovering such loss or loss of use, from you or that "family member", pursuant to the provisions of any applicable rental agreement or state law.

LIMIT OF LIABILITY

A. Our limit of liability for loss will be the lesser of the:
   1. Actual cash value of the stolen or damaged property; or
   2. Amount necessary to repair or replace the property with other property of like kind and quality.

   However, the most we will pay for loss to:
   1. Any "non-owned auto" which is a trailer is $1500.
   2. Electronic equipment that reproduces, receives or transmits audio, visual or data signals, which is permanently installed in the auto in locations not used by the auto manufacturer for installation of such equipment, is $1,000.

B. An adjustment for depreciation and physical condition will be made in determining actual cash value in the event of a total loss.

C. If a repair or replacement results in better than like kind or quality, we will not pay for the amount of the betterment.

PAYMENT OF LOSS

We may pay for loss in money or repair or replace the damaged or stolen property. We may, at our expense, return any stolen property to:
1. You; or
2. The address shown in this policy.

If we return stolen property we will pay for any damage resulting from the theft. We may keep all or part of the property at an agreed or appraised value.

If we pay for loss in money, our payment will include the applicable sales tax for the damaged or stolen property.

NO BENEFIT TO BAILEE

This insurance shall not directly or indirectly benefit any carrier or other bailee for hire.

OTHER SOURCES OF RECOVERY

If other sources of recovery also cover the loss, we will pay only our share of the loss. Our share is the proportion that our limit of liability bears to the total of all applicable limits. However, any insurance we provide with respect to a "non-owned auto" shall be excess over any other collectible source of recovery including, but not limited to:

1. Any coverage provided by the owner of the "non-owned auto";
2. Any other applicable physical damage insurance;
3. Any other source of recovery applicable to the loss.

APPRAISAL

A. If we and you do not agree on the amount of loss, either may demand an appraisal of the loss. In this event, each party will select a competent and impartial appraiser. The two appraisers will select an umpire. The appraisers will state separately the actual cash value and the amount of loss. If they fail to agree, they will submit their differences to the umpire. A decision agreed to by any two will be binding. Each party will:
   1. Pay its chosen appraiser; and
   2. Bear the expenses of the appraisal and umpire equally.

B. We do not waive any of our rights under this policy by agreeing to an appraisal.

PART E – DUTIES AFTER AN ACCIDENT OR LOSS	

We have no duty to provide coverage under this policy if the failure to comply with the following duties is prejudicial to us:

A. We must be notified promptly of how, when and where the accident or loss happened. Notice should also include the names and addresses of any injured persons and of any witnesses.

B. A person seeking any coverage must:

1. Cooperate with us in the investigation, settlement or defense of any claim or suit.
2. Promptly send us copies of any notices or legal papers received in connection with the accident or loss.
3. Submit, as often as we reasonably require:
   a. To physical exams by physicians we select. We will pay for these exams.
   b. To examination under oath and subscribe the same.
4. Authorize us to obtain:
   a. Medical reports; and
   b. Other pertinent records.
5. Submit a proof of loss when required by us.

C. A person seeking Uninsured Motorists Coverage must also:

1. Promptly notify the police if a hit-and-run driver is involved.
2. Promptly send us copies of the legal papers if a suit is brought.

D. A person seeking Coverage For Damage To Your Auto must also:

1. Take reasonable steps after loss to protect "your covered auto" or any "non-owned auto" and their equipment from further loss. We will pay reasonable expenses incurred to do this.
2. Promptly notify the police if "your covered auto" or any "non-owned auto" is stolen.
3. Permit us to inspect and appraise the damaged property before its repair or disposal.

PART F – GENERAL PROVISIONS	

BANKRUPTCY

Bankruptcy or insolvency of the "insured" shall not relieve us of any obligations under this policy.

CHANGES

A. This policy contains all the agreements between you and us. Its terms may not be changed or waived except by endorsement issued by us.

B. If there is a change to the information used to develop the policy premium, we may adjust your premium. Changes during the policy term that may result in a premium increase or decrease include, but are not limited to, changes in:

1. The number, type or use classification of insured vehicles;
2. Operators using insured vehicles;
3. The place of principal garaging of insured vehicles;
4. Coverage, deductible or limits.

If a change resulting from **A.** or **B.** requires a premium adjustment, we will make the premium adjustment in accordance with our manual rules.

C. If we make a change which broadens coverage under this edition of your policy without additional premium charge, that change will automatically apply to your policy as of the date we implement the change in your state. This Paragraph (**C.**) does not apply to changes implemented with a general program revision that includes both broadenings and restrictions in coverage, whether that general program revision is implemented through introduction of:

1. A subsequent edition of your policy; or
2. An Amendatory Endorsement.

FRAUD

We do not provide coverage for any "insured" who has made fraudulent statements or engaged in fraudulent conduct in connection with any accident or loss for which coverage is sought under this policy.

LEGAL ACTION AGAINST US

A. No legal action may be brought against us until there has been full compliance with all the terms of this policy. In addition, under Part **A**, no legal action may be brought against us until:

1. We agree in writing that the "insured" has an obligation to pay; or
2. The amount of that obligation has been finally determined by judgment after trial.

B. No person or organization has any right under this policy to bring us into any action to determine the liability of an "insured".

OUR RIGHT TO RECOVER PAYMENT

A. If we make a payment under this policy and the person to or for whom payment was made has a right to recover damages from another we shall be subrogated to that right. That person shall do:
   1. Whatever is necessary to enable us to exercise our rights; and
   2. Nothing after loss to prejudice them.

   However, our rights in this Paragraph (A.) do not apply under Part D, against any person using "your covered auto" with a reasonable belief that that person is entitled to do so.

B. If we make a payment under this policy and the person to or for whom payment is made recovers damages from another, that person shall:
   1. Hold in trust for us the proceeds of the recovery; and
   2. Reimburse us to the extent of our payment.

POLICY PERIOD AND TERRITORY

A. This policy applies only to accidents and losses which occur:
   1. During the policy period as shown in the Declarations; and
   2. Within the policy territory.

B. The policy territory is:
   1. The United States of America, its territories or possessions;
   2. Puerto Rico; or
   3. Canada.

   This policy also applies to loss to, or accidents involving, "your covered auto" while being transported between their ports.

TERMINATION

A. Cancellation

   This policy may be cancelled during the policy period as follows:
   1. The named insured shown in the Declarations may cancel by:
      a. Returning this policy to us; or
      b. Giving us advance written notice of the date cancellation is to take effect.
   2. We may cancel by mailing to the named insured shown in the Declarations at the address shown in this policy:
      a. At least 10 days notice:
         (1) If cancellation is for nonpayment of premium; or

      (2) If notice is mailed during the first 60 days this policy is in effect and this is not a renewal or continuation policy; or
      b. At least 20 days notice in all other cases.
   3. After this policy is in effect for 60 days, or if this is a renewal or continuation policy, we will cancel only:
      a. For nonpayment of premium; or
      b. If your driver's license or that of:
         (1) Any driver who lives with you; or
         (2) Any driver who customarily uses "your covered auto";

         has been suspended or revoked. This must have occurred:
         (1) During the policy period; or
         (2) Since the last anniversary of the original effective date if the policy period is other than 1 year; or
      c. If the policy was obtained through material misrepresentation.

B. Nonrenewal

   If we decide not to renew or continue this policy, we will mail notice to the named insured shown in the Declarations at the address shown in this policy. Notice will be mailed at least 20 days before the end of the policy period. Subject to this notice requirement, if the policy period is:
   1. Less than 6 months, we will have the right not to renew or continue this policy every 6 months, beginning 6 months after its original effective date.
   2. 6 months or longer, but less than one year, we will have the right not to renew or continue this policy at the end of the policy period.
   3. 1 year or longer, we will have the right not to renew or continue this policy at each anniversary of its original effective date.

C. Automatic Termination

   If we offer to renew or continue and you or your representative do not accept, this policy will automatically terminate at the end of the current policy period. Failure to pay the required renewal or continuation premium when due shall mean that you have not accepted our offer.

   If you obtain other insurance on "your covered auto", any similar insurance provided by this policy will terminate as to that auto on the effective date of the other insurance.

D. Other Termination Provisions

1. We may deliver any notice instead of mailing it. Proof of mailing of any notice shall be sufficient proof of notice.
2. If this policy is cancelled, you may be entitled to a premium refund. If so, we will send you the refund. The premium refund, if any, will be computed according to our manuals. However, making or offering to make the refund is not a condition of cancellation.
3. The effective date of cancellation stated in the notice shall become the end of the policy period.

TRANSFER OF YOUR INTEREST IN THIS POLICY

A. Your rights and duties under this policy may not be assigned without our written consent. However, if a named insured shown in the Declarations dies, coverage will be provided for:

1. The surviving spouse if resident in the same household at the time of death. Coverage applies to the spouse as if a named insured shown in the Declarations; and
2. The legal representative of the deceased person as if a named insured shown in the Declarations. This applies only with respect to the representative's legal responsibility to maintain or use "your covered auto".

B. Coverage will only be provided until the end of the policy period.

TWO OR MORE AUTO POLICIES

If this policy and any other auto insurance policy issued to you by us apply to the same accident, the maximum limit of our liability under all the policies shall not exceed the highest applicable limit of liability under any one policy.

B. Auto Liability Insurance

1. The Scope of Compulsory Insurance Requirements

St. Paul Fire & Marine Insurance Company v. Smith

Appellate Court of Illinois, 2003.
337 Ill.App.3d 1054.

■ Presiding Justice Theis delivered the opinion of the court:

Plaintiff St. Paul Fire & Marine Insurance Company (St. Paul) appeals an order of the trial court granting the motion of defendants Allen Smith, Marjorie Ocasek, as special administrator of the estate of William Smith, deceased, Elizabeth Ing, as special administrator of the estate of Audrey Hardwidge, deceased, and independent administrator of the estate of William Hardwidge, deceased (collectively, defendants), for summary judgment declaring that the named driver exclusion contained in St. Paul's automobile liability insurance policy was void as against public policy. On appeal, St. Paul contends that the named driver exclusion does not violate the mandatory insurance laws of the Illinois Vehicle Code (the Code) (625 ILCS 5/1–100 *et seq.* (West 1996)). St. Paul also argues that the named driver exclusion applies to bar coverage for the underlying wrongful death lawsuit because the exclusion was part of the St. Paul policy and was not ambiguous, and contends that the negligent entrustment claim against Allen Smith falls within the scope of the exclusion.

The main issue before this court is one of first impression in Illinois, whether a named driver exclusion in an automobile liability insurance policy violates Illinois public policy. We find that it does not and reverse and remand for further proceedings.

On June 3, 1996, William Smith (William), while driving a vehicle owned by his father, Allen, collided with an automobile carrying William and Audrey Hardwidge. All three individuals died as a result of their injuries. At the time of the accident, William had an automobile liability insurance policy issued by Valor Insurance Company (Valor). The car was insured by St. Paul, under a personal insurance package policy including homeowners and automobile liability insurance procured by William's parents, Allen and June Smith. The St. Paul policy initially listed Allen and June as insureds and drivers covered under the policy. On January 2, 1996, William was added as a covered driver to Allen and June's policy. St. Paul then received William's driving record, which revealed that his license had previously been suspended and revoked because he had been convicted of driving under the influence of alcohol twice and driving with a revoked license. St. Paul removed William as a covered driver from Allen and June's policy on January 22, 1996, and required Allen and June to sign a named driver exclusion, which excluded liability for any accidents or losses incurred while the car was driven by William.

In July 1997, the administrators of the estates of William and Audrey Hardwidge filed a lawsuit against the estate of William Smith and Allen (the underlying suit). The complaint included several wrongful death counts against William's estate and a negligent entrustment count against Allen, alleging that Allen allowed William to use his car even though he knew that William had been abusing alcohol for a substantial period of time, William had previously been convicted of driving under the influence of alcohol and William was not covered by Allen's automobile insurance policy. Both Allen and William's estate tendered their defenses to Valor, which provided their defenses. Neither Allen nor William's estate tendered their defenses to St. Paul. In January 2000, a verdict of $5 million was entered against Allen and William's estate. Valor then paid its policy limits of $20,000 to each of the Hardwidge estates.

In April 1998, St. Paul filed a complaint for declaratory judgment, seeking a declaration that it did not owe a duty to defend and/or indemnify Allen or William's estate in the underlying suit because the named driver exclusion in Allen's insurance policy barred coverage for any accident involving a vehicle driven by William. Several months after paying its policy limits in the underlying suit, Valor was granted leave to intervene in St. Paul's declaratory judgment action and filed a counterclaim for declaratory judgment. St. Paul filed a motion for summary judgment, arguing that the named driver exclusion operated to bar any coverage obligation to Allen and William's estate. Valor and defendants filed cross-motions for summary judgment, contending that the named driver exclusion violated Illinois public policy as contained in the mandatory insurance requirements of the Code. Defendants also argued that the exclusion was ambiguous, was not attached to the insurance policy and did not apply to bar claims of negligent entrustment.

The trial court granted Valor's and defendants' summary judgment motions and denied St. Paul's motion on July 27, 2001. On December 12, 2001, the trial court clarified that order and held that the sole basis of its ruling was that the named driver exclusion was void because it violated public policy. * * *

Courts apply terms in an insurance policy as written unless those terms contravene public policy. *State Farm Mutual Automobile Insurance Co. v. Smith,* 197 Ill.2d 369, 372 (2001). Statutes are an expression of public policy. *Smith,* 197 Ill.2d at 372. "Statutes in force at the time an insurance policy was issued are controlling, and a statute's underlying purpose cannot be circumvented by a restriction or exclusion written into an insurance policy. [Citation.] Accordingly, insurance policy provisions that conflict with a statute are void." *Smith,* 197 Ill.2d at 372.

In this case, the named driver exclusion in Allen's St. Paul automobile liability insurance policy provided:

"Driver Exclusion Policy Number: PK01200772

Named Insured: Smith, Allen & June

This endorsement changes the policy.

Please read it carefully.

We will not be liable for any accidents or losses while any auto or motorhome is driven by: William R. Smith[.]"

The exclusion was signed by Allen, June and William in January 1996.

Section 7–601(a) of the mandatory insurance provision in the Code requires that all vehicles be insured through a liability insurance policy. 625 ILCS 5/7–601(a) (West 1996); *Smith,* 197 Ill.2d at 373. Section 7–317(b)(2) of the Code's safety responsibility law requires that a motor vehicle liability policy "insure the person named therein and any other person using or responsible for the use of such motor vehicle or vehicles with the express or implied permission of the insured." 625 ILCS 5/7–317(b)(2) (West 1996). Construing these provisions together, our supreme court interpreted these statutes to mandate that " 'a liability insurance policy issued to the owner of a vehicle must cover the named insured and any other person using the vehicle with the named insured's permission.' " *Smith,* 197 Ill.2d at 373, quoting *State Farm Mutual Automobile Insurance Co. v. Universal Underwriters Group,* 182 Ill.2d 240, 244 (1998). In affirming the appellate court, our supreme court in *Smith* noted that " '[t]he purpose of mandatory automobile liability insurance is not only to protect the owner against liability or some other insurance company; rather, its principal purpose is to protect the public by securing payment of their damages.' " *Smith,* 197 Ill.2d at 376, quoting *State Farm Mutual Automobile Insurance Co. v. Fisher,* 315 Ill.App.3d 1159, 1163.

Defendants maintain that the trial court was correct in holding that the named driver exclusion in St. Paul's liability insurance policy violates Illinois public policy because it conflicts with the language of the Code. The Code requires that every insurance policy cover the named insured and "any other person" using the vehicle with the insured's express or implied permission. 625 ILCS 5/7–317(b)(2) (West 1996). However, the named driver exclusion allows the insurer to exclude certain individuals from coverage. Defendants contend that the definition of the term "any other person" necessarily includes the driver who was purportedly excluded from coverage by the named driver exclusion, assuming he had the insured's permission to operate the vehicle. Thus, defendants argue, the exclusion conflicts with the statute and is void.

In response, St. Paul argues that the named driver exclusion does not violate public policy. Citing section 7–602 of the Code, St. Paul contends that this section clearly creates a limited exception for named driver exclusions to the mandatory insurance laws. 625 ILCS 5/7–602 (West 1996). We agree.

Section 7–602 of the Code discusses the requirements for insurance cards and provides in relevant part:

"If the insurance policy represented by the insurance card does not cover any driver operating the motor vehicle with the owner's permission, or the owner when operating a motor vehicle other than the vehicle for which the policy is issued, the insurance card shall contain a warning of such limitations in the coverage provided by the policy." 625 ILCS 5/7–602 (West 1996).

The plain language of this statute appears to recognize that insurance policies may exclude named drivers from coverage and conflicts with the mandatory insurance requirements of sections 7–601 and 7–317(b)(2).

When there is an alleged conflict between two statutes, a court interprets those statutes to avoid inconsistency and give effect to both statutes where such an interpretation is reasonably possible. *Ferguson,* 202 Ill.2d at 311–12. Sections of the same statute should be considered *in pari materia* and each section should be construed with every other part or section of the statute to produce a harmonious whole. *Land,* 202 Ill.2d at 422. We presume that when enacting the statute, the legislature did not intend absurdity, inconvenience or injustice. *Land,* 202 Ill.2d at 422.

In interpreting section 7–602, we note that this section is located in Article VI, entitled "Mandatory Insurance," of the Illinois Safety and Family Financial Responsibility Law of the Code. Further, section 7–602 is situated directly after section 7–601, which requires vehicles to be covered by a liability insurance policy. Section 7–602 was added to the Code by the same public act that created section 7–601, and the mandatory insurance article and both sections share the same effective date. Although section 7–602 has been amended several times since its enactment in 1989, the legislature has never removed or changed this language concerning policy limitations. Thus, after construing section 7–602 with section 7–601, we hold that by enacting section 7–602, the legislature intended to create a limited exception for named driver exclusions to the mandatory insurance laws.

We find additional support for our holding from the administrative regulations promulgated by the Secretary of State. Section 7–602 specifically authorizes the Secretary of State to prescribe rules and regulations concerning the form, content and manner of issuance of insurance cards. 625 ILCS 5/7–602 (West 1996). Properly promulgated administrative regulations have the force and effect of law. *Chandler v. Illinois Central R.R. Co.,* 333 Ill.App.3d 463, 472 (2002). The regulation concerning insurance card requirements provides that: "d) The insurance card shall contain the following insurance information: * * * 7) a warning of excluded drivers or vehicles, when applicable." 50 Ill. Adm.Code § 8010.20(d)(7) (1996). Therefore, this administrative regulation is further evidence that the legislature intended to carve out a narrow exception for the named driver exclusion. Accordingly, we find that the named driver exclusion in St. Paul's insurance policy is valid and does not violate public policy.

Although defendants rely on *Smith* to support their argument that named driver exclusions violate public policy, we find that case distinguishable. In *Smith,* State Farm invoked its automobile business exclusion to bar coverage for an accident occurring while the insured vehicle was operated by a valet driver. That exclusion purported to deny liability coverage while any insured vehicle was being repaired, serviced or used by any person employed in a car business. *Smith,* 197 Ill.2d at 373. In explaining Illinois's public policy, our supreme court reiterated that a motor vehicle liability policy must cover the named insured and any other person using the vehicle with the insured's permission. Because when a vehicle owner gives his vehicle to a person engaged in an automobile business, he is also giving that person permission to operate the vehicle, the court found that the automobile business exclusion violated section 7–317(b)(2). *Smith,* 197 Ill.2d at 374. However, unlike the present case, there was no additional statutory language in *Smith* implying that the legislature intended to create such an exception. Further, *Smith* concerned a broad exclusion that barred liability for accidents caused by an entire class of people, those involved in any automobile business. In contrast, the present case involves a more limited exclusion, only precluding coverage for certain individuals. Additionally, *Smith* specifically limited its decision to the validity of the automobile business exclusion only, stating that "[t]he permissibility of other possible policy exclusions is not before us today, and we express no opinion as to any other exclusion." *Smith,* 197 Ill.2d at 379. Thus, we find *Smith* distinguishable.

Additionally, we note that other states upholding the validity of named driver exclusions have delineated several public policy reasons supporting the exclusions. A Texas appeals court found that named driver exclusions furthered Texas's public policy of protecting all potential claimants from damages resulting from automobile accidents by enabling drivers with family members having poor driving records to procure affordable insurance, rather than obtaining coverage from an assigned risk pool at a greater cost or not securing insurance at all. Further, these exclusions deterred insured drivers from entrusting their vehicles to unsafe excluded drivers which kept those unfit drivers off the road. *Zamora v. Dairyland County Mutual Insurance Co.,* 930 S.W.2d 739, 741 (Tex.Ct.App.1996). See also *Pierce v. Oklahoma Property & Casualty Insurance Co.,* 901 P.2d 819, 823 (Okla.1995) ("[o]ur legislature realized that premiums might be too costly in some circumstances, and chose to allow the contracting parties to exclude specifically named individuals," allowing families to obtain affordable insurance); *State Farm Mutual Automobile Insurance Co. v. Washington,* 641 A.2d 449, 451–52 (Del.1994) (named driver exclusions "ensure continued coverage of an automobile where the driving record of a household member warrants non-issuance or cancellation"); *Dairyland Insurance Co. v. State Farm Mutual Automobile Insurance Co.,* 882 P.2d 1143, 1146 (Utah 1994) (the rationale of the exclusion "is to enable households that include a family member who has a poor driving record to obtain insurance at a reasonable cost by excluding the poor driver"). We agree that these policy reasons are sound and further support our holding.

Therefore, we hold that the named driver exclusion in St. Paul's automobile insurance liability policy does not contravene Illinois public policy because the legislature created a limited exception to the mandatory insurance laws for this exclusion. We note that our decision in this case concerns only the named driver exclusion and we express no opinion as to any other exclusions. Accordingly, we reverse the trial court's grant of summary judgment to defendants. While the parties raise several other factual issues concerning the application of this named driver exclusion to the underlying suit, we note that the trial court never considered these issues and we decline to address them. Rather, we remand this cause to the trial court for further proceedings.

For the foregoing reasons, the judgment of the circuit court of Cook County is reversed and the cause remanded for further proceedings.

Reversed and remanded.

NOTES AND QUESTIONS

1. *Liability Insurance Requirements.* Every state has enacted some form of statutory requirement regarding automobile insurance. In most states this is a straightforward requirement that a specified minimum amount of liability insurance be purchased by every person registering a motor vehicle in the state. Typically these requirements are stated as a specified minimum amount of bodily injury liability coverage per person injured and per accident no matter how many persons are injured, plus a specified minimum for property damage liability. The typical amounts are something like $20,000, $40,000, and $5000, respectively. Thus the occasional shorthand reference to coverage that is 20/40/5. The comparatively low amount of insurance that William was required to buy from what ultimately became his insurance company (Valor) is of course the explanation for the effort by the plaintiffs to gain access to other sources of liability insurance, such as the St. Paul policy.

2. *Victim Protection or Driver Insurance?* As the court in *Smith* noted, the function of compulsory insurance requirement is not only to protect negligent drivers against the risk of financially disastrous liability, but also—perhaps even predominantly—to protect victims against the cost of suffering otherwise uncompensated injury. That policy was not strong enough to overcome the Named Driver exclusion in *Smith*, but it was strong enough to overcome what would otherwise have been a perfectly acceptable Valet Exclusion that was referred to in the opinion. It was also strong enough (under peculiar facts) for the Illinois Supreme Court to hold that the owner of an insured vehicle could not be the subject of a Named Driver exclusion. *Am. Access Cas. Co. v. Reyes,* 1 N.E. 3d 524 (Ill. 2013). Any number of other exclusions have been declared against the public policy expressed in compulsory insurance statutes.

There is a tension, however, between declaring exclusions invalid and promoting insurance in the long run. Consider the possible reaction of insurers if their Named Driver exclusions will not be enforced in situations such as *Smith*. Fewer insurers will then be willing to sell coverage to drivers who are otherwise perfectly acceptable risks, such as William's parents, on the ground that the insurers will be unable to avoid covering William if he gets his hands on the insured vehicle. The State may find it necessary to develop a government-sponsored mechanism to ensure that these acceptable risks can find insurance. That is not a happy prospect for a political jurisdiction in which most relatively safe drivers are also probable voters.

A related issue that has sometimes troubled the courts is the role to be played by intentional-injury and similar exclusions and limits on coverage. For example, in *State Farm Fire & Casualty Co. v. Tringali,* 686 F.2d 821 (9th Cir. 1982), the court held that an insurance policy covering liability caused by "accident" did not preclude coverage where the insured deliberately drove his car into the plaintiff's stationary motor cycle, injuring the plaintiff, because of the policy underlying the state of Hawaii's compulsory insurance requirement. There is serious question whether

Tringali is still good law. See, e.g., *AIG Hawai'i Ins. Co. v. Caraang*, 851 P.2d 321 (Haw. 1993). But the fact that the U.S. Court of Appeals had plausible support for its decision in the law of Hawaii at the time it decided *Tringali* illustrates the strength of the public policy underlying compulsory insurance legislation: an important purpose of such legislation has been to assure compensation of victims. Many other courts have held that this policy is not strong enough to require coverage against liability for intentionally causing harm. See, e.g., *State Farm Mut. Auto. Ins. Co. v. Wertz*, 540 N.W.2d 636 (S.D.1995). Nevertheless, the moral hazard created by decisions such as *Tringali* is sometimes tolerated in order to help ensure victim compensation. For example, in *Mendoza v. Rivera-Chavez*, 999 P.2d 29 (Wash. 2000), the court interpreted Washington public policy to preclude application of a policy provision that excluded coverage of liability for injury caused by use of the vehicle "in the commission of any felony."

3. *Reimbursement of the Insurer.* Some states have resolved this dilemma by requiring or permitting insurers to make provision in their policies for paying the victim, but seeking reimbursement from the policyholder in situations where he committed intentional injury or is otherwise denied coverage because of a policy exclusion. Thus, in relation to the victim, the policyholder is insured; in relation to his insurer, however, the policyholder is merely a debtor whose obligation has been paid by a guarantor. See, e.g., *Odum v. Nationwide Mut. Ins. Co.*, 401 S.E.2d 87 (N.C. App. 1991). Does this approach violate the rule that an insurer cannot have subrogation against its own insured? Does it matter?

4. *The Household Exclusion.* Another issue whose resolution is influenced by the purposes underlying compulsory automobile liability insurance legislation is the validity of policy provisions excluding coverage of liability to persons residing in the insured's own home. There is more likelihood of collusion (e.g., admitting negligence) in suits between family members than between strangers, since any insurance payment will stay within the family. The *household exclusion* (sometimes termed the *family exclusion*) is designed to eliminate the possibility of fraudulent suits within the family that arises once intra-family tort immunity is abolished, as it has been in many states. A typical compulsory liability insurance statute requires the purchase of insurance in specified amounts against liability for bodily injury or property damage "to any person." Most courts interpreting such statutory provisions have held the household exclusion to be inconsistent with the requirement and invalidated it. See, e.g., *Gov't Emps. Ins. Co. v. Welch*, 90 P.3d 471 (N.M. 2004). But see *State Farm Mut. Auto Ins. Co. v. Daprato*, 840 A.2d 595 (Del. 2003) (exclusion in a personal umbrella policy is valid). On the other hand *Purkey v. American Home Assurance Co.*, 173 S.W.3d 703 (Tenn. 2005), refused to declare such an exclusion in an umbrella policy invalid.

Some courts explain their refusal to enforce household exclusions by saying that the exclusion is against public policy. This is little more than a tautology if what they mean is that insurance policy provisions that violate statutes violate public policy. If this is not all that these courts mean—that is, if there is more to their reasoning than mere application of a statutory prohibition—what is going on in such decisions? For example, suppose that a son sues his father (who is a member of the same household) for negligence in the operation of the insured auto, and the jury awards the son $100,000. The father has auto liability insurance covering him against liability to any single person in the amount of $100,000, and the state has a compulsory liability insurance statute requiring the purchase of at least $20,000 of such insurance. The father's policy contains the following provision:

> We do not provide Liability Coverage for any person for bodily injury to you or any family member to the extent that the limits of liability for this coverage exceed the limits of liability required by the state Compulsory Insurance Act.

Is the father entitled to $100,000 or $20,000 of coverage? See *Hartline v. Hartline*, 39 P.3d 765 (Okla. 2001) (family exclusion void as to minimum amount of coverage required, valid as applied to coverage above the minimum). *A fortiori* it would seem to follow that if no statutory requirement applies to a policy, a family or household exclusion in the policy is valid. See, e.g., *Page v. Mountain W. Farm Bureau Mut. Ins. Co.*, 2 P.3d 506 (Wyo. 2000).

2. THE OMNIBUS CLAUSE

Curtis v. State Farm Mutual Automobile Insurance Company

United States Court of Appeals, Tenth Circuit, 1979.
591 F.2d 572.

■ HOLLOWAY, CIRCUIT JUDGE.

Defendant State Farm Mutual Automobile Insurance Company appeals from a declaratory judgment, entered on a jury verdict, declaring that a liability insurance policy issued by State Farm to Robert E. Ahrens and JoAnn Ahrens extended coverage to one Joseph Wallace, the driver of the Ahrens vehicle at the time of the accident involved herein. Jurisdiction is founded upon diversity. The primary question before us is whether Wallace comes within the definition of "insured" contained in the policy's omnibus clause as "any * * * *person* while using the *owned motor vehicle*, PROVIDED THE OPERATION AND THE ACTUAL USE OF SUCH VEHICLE ARE WITH THE PERMISSION OF THE NAMED INSURED * * * AND ARE WITHIN THE SCOPE OF SUCH PERMISSION * * *."[1]

---

[1] The omnibus clause constitutes only one part of the five-part definition of "insured" contained in the policy. The definition as a whole states that the unqualified word "insured" includes:

(1) the named insured, and

(2) if the named insured is a *person or persons,* also includes his or their spouse(s), if a *resident* of the same household, and

(3) if *residents* of the same household, the relatives of the first *person* named in the declarations, or of his spouse, and

(4) any other *person* while using the *owned motor vehicle,* PROVIDED THE OPERATION AND THE ACTUAL USE OF SUCH VEHICLE ARE WITH THE PERMISSION OF THE NAMED INSURED OR SUCH SPOUSE AND ARE WITHIN THE SCOPE OF SUCH PERMISSION, and

(5) under coverages A and B any other *person* or organization, but only with respect to his or its liability for the use of such *owned motor vehicle* by an *insured* as defined in the four subsections above.

The Ahrens family had three cars—an Oldsmobile, a Volkswagen owned by Mr. and Mrs. Ahrens, and a pickup. The older Ahrens girls, Beth and Shawnna, mainly used the Oldsmobile and Volkswagen, and Mr. Ahrens used the pickup to drive to work.

The accident in question occurred in the early morning of July 5, 1973, outside of Cheyenne, Wyoming. During the previous afternoon, Deborah Ahrens, the 14-year-old daughter of Robert and JoAnn Ahrens, had made arrangements with her friend Helen Curtis and with Brian Tottenhoff and Joseph Wallace to meet at the local ballpark between 1:00 and 2:00 a.m. to shoot off some fireworks. (II R. 40). Helen was spending the night of July 4 with Deborah at her home. Sometime between 1:30 and 2:00 a.m., Deborah and Helen left the Ahrens home—after Deborah's parents had gone to bed—and proceeded to drive the family Volkswagen to the chosen meeting place.

Deborah was not licensed to drive. She had taken the car keys from their customary location on top of the television set without her parents' knowledge. (Id. 33, 45–46, 141). On their way out of the Ahrens' neighborhood, the girls encountered Deborah's older sister, Beth, driving home in the family Oldsmobile. The two sisters stopped and talked for five or ten minutes, but Deborah's use of the Volkswagen was never discussed. (Id. 47). Before she left home, Deborah had also told Shawnna what they were going to do that night; Shawnna knew the girls were going out and made no comment either to forbid or consent to their going. However, Deborah did not tell Beth or Shawnna that she and Helen were going to pick up the boys. (Id. 48–49, 52–53, 54).

Deborah and Helen picked up the boys and went to shoot off the fireworks. The four then started home around 3:30 a.m. Deborah had been driving all along, but at this point Joe Wallace asked if he could drive, and she agreed. (Id. 49). Wallace, like Deborah, was unlicensed. According to Deborah, the accident occurred about five minutes after Wallace took the wheel: "He was going too fast, and he went airbound with the car, and it went over on to the embankment." (Id. 51).

Helen Curtis suffered extensive injuries in the accident, and her father incurred about $15,000 in medical expenses for her treatment. When State Farm disclaimed coverage as to Wallace, Helen's father brought this suit on her behalf for a determination that the defendant State Farm was obligated to defend and indemnify Wallace under the company's policy issued to Mr. and Mrs. Ahrens. As noted, a verdict and declaratory judgment adverse to the company resulted. This appeal followed.

I

The company's primary contention on appeal is that the evidence is clear that Wallace did not have permission to drive the vehicle under the terms of the omnibus clause of the policy, so that coverage did not extend to him. The company says that the district court therefore erred in its denial of a motion for a directed verdict made at the conclusion of

---

(Plaintiff's Ex. No. 1). It is evident that Wallace can fit—if at all—only within the omnibus clause (4), since he is unrelated to the named insureds, Robert E. Ahrens and JoAnn Ahrens. (II R. 166).

plaintiff's case and again at the end of defendant's case, as well as in its denial of a motion for judgment n.o.v.

Wallace was not covered by the policy unless his operation and actual use of the Volkswagen were with the permission of a named insured. The district court instructed the jury that Robert Ahrens and his wife JoAnn were the named insureds under the policy and that neither named insured gave Wallace actual permission to drive the car. (II R. 166). Thus, the controlling question is whether Wallace had implied permission for use of the car so as to bring him within the coverage of the policy.

In *United Services Automobile Association v. Preferred Accident Insurance Co.,* 190 F.2d 404, 406 (10th Cir.), we stated that:

> The necessary permission may be in the form of implied affirmative consent. It may result by implication from the relationship of the parties and their course of conduct in which they mutually acquiesced. And it may arise from a course of conduct pursued with knowledge of the facts for such time and in such manner as to signify clearly and convincingly an understanding consent which amounts in law to a grant of the privilege involved.

The question of implied permission is thus one of fact. *Phoenix Assurance Co. v. Latta,* 373 P.2d 146, 149 (Wyo.). Plaintiff points to much in the record which, it is said, supports the jury's implicit finding of implied permission. In view of such evidence, plaintiff argues that it would have been improper for the trial court to direct a verdict or grant judgment n.o.v. for defendant, because the evidence did not point "all one way" in favor of the moving party. *Bertot v. School District No. 1,* 522 F.2d 1171, 1178 (10th Cir.).

The foundation for a finding of implied permission, plaintiff argues, is the fact that JoAnn Ahrens, Deborah's mother and one of the named insureds, has been blind due to the effects of diabetes since before 1973. Because of this tragic fact, Mrs. Ahrens has had to rely on her three daughters to "take care of everything" around the house. (II R. 14). In July 1973, the two older daughters, Beth (then age 17) and Shawnna (age 16), were licensed drivers and had free use of the family cars, both for carrying out family-related responsibilities such as grocery shopping and for going to and from their part-time jobs. (Id. 16, 26). As noted, the family custom was to keep the car keys on top of the television set; anyone who had used the car would lay the keys down on the set and anyone who wanted to use the car would take the keys off the set. (Id. 19).

Around that time Beth also often took one of the cars out of town on recreational trips to Steamboat Springs and similar places, staying two or three days. Mrs. Ahrens knew that on such trips friends of Beth's went with her and drove the car. There was testimony that Beth's friends McCue and Fleming would sometimes drive the car on such trips and that, while neither JoAnn nor Robert Ahrens gave express permission to them to drive, both parents knew about such driving and neither objected to it. (Id. 20, 29, 143, 145). Also, Shawnna was allowed to take the family cars around town frequently and drove one of the cars to work sometimes. (Id. 18).

Thus, Beth and Shawnna were allowed to drive the cars "as they needed or liked" (Id. 26)—except when their father was using them. They bought gas "when they had money and they were out and they needed it"—though customarily their father would maintain the automobiles in working condition. (Id. 35–36). And with Beth at least, there was precedent for allowing other persons to drive the family automobiles without express permission from either parent.

With respect to Deborah, there was testimony that Mr. Ahrens had signed a statement that he had never given Deborah any restrictions as to her use of the car and that there had been no express prohibition to its use. The statement also said, however, that "Debbie was not supposed to drive this vehicle." (Id. 80–82). Mr. Ahrens testified that he thought his wife had been asked during the taking of earlier statements whether the parents had ever specifically told Deborah she could not take the car, that he had said they never specified she could not take it, but that it was "understood on down the line, that I think it probably started with Beth and then Shawnna and then Debbie." (Id. 146). Both Mr. and Mrs. Ahrens testified that they had not given Deborah permission to use the car on the night of the accident and did not know that she had taken the car until they were notified about the accident. (Id. 26–27, 34, 140, 142).

Deborah testified that one time she had driven a family car with her father to a friends' house. She also said that once about a month before the accident she had driven the car without her father. (Id. 38–39). However, her parents both testified they had not known that Deborah had taken the Volkswagen out on any occasion before the accident. (Id. 23, 140).

Plaintiff argues that because of the unusual circumstances relating to the blindness of Mrs. Ahrens, the mother and father had permitted the two older daughters to operate the family vehicles as if they had actually been owners, and that when the older daughters were aware of Deborah's going for the ride in the Volkswagen on the night of July 4, they had unqualified permission to allow Deborah to operate the car. (Brief of Appellee, 4). From Beth and Shawnna's implied consent that Deborah drive the car, and from Deborah's actual consent for Wallace to drive, plaintiff says there was implied consent by Mr. and Mrs. Ahrens that Wallace drive the Volkswagen at the time of the accident.[2]

We must hold that, on this record, the judgment in favor of coverage cannot stand. Plaintiff had the burden of proof to establish coverage. See *Chronister v. State Farm Mutual Automobile Insurance Co.*, 381 P.2d 673, 675; 46 C.J.S. Insurance § 1641. Under the terms of the omnibus clause, permission of the named insureds, Mr. and Mrs. Ahrens, to the operation and actual use of the Volkswagen was required for coverage to apply. The only plausible theory in this case is that permission flowed from the parents to Beth and Shawnna, from them to Deborah, and from Deborah then to Wallace, the driver at the time of

---

[2] There is no evidence which would support an inference that Deborah had direct permission to drive the Volkswagen from her parents. For this reason it cannot be said that Wallace had implied permission from Mr. and Mrs. Ahrens as the named insureds merely because he had Deborah's actual permission to drive. See *Travelers Insurance Co. v. Weatherford*, 520 S.W.2d 726 (Tenn.); *State Farm Mutual Automobile Insurance Co. v. Strang*, 27 Utah 2d 362; *Bilsten v. Porter*, 547 P.2d 255 (Colo.Ct.App.).

the accident. As noted, however, Beth and Shawnna were not told by Deborah that Wallace would even be accompanying Deborah and Helen the night of the accident and, of course, the parents did not even know that Deborah was going to use the car.

In view of the broad permission given by the parents to Beth and Shawnna for use of the family cars, an inference might be drawn that the older daughters as first permittees could permit Deborah to use the Volkswagen. See *Gillen v. Globe Indemnity Co.,* 377 F.2d 328, 331 (8th Cir.); *Krebsbach v. Miller,* 125 N.W.2d 408, 411; *Baesler v. Globe Indemnity Co.,* 162 A.2d 854, 857; *Government Employees Insurance Co. v. Lammert,* 483 S.W.2d 652 (Mo.Ct.App.). The trial judge apparently accepted such a view as valid under Wyoming law since he charged the jury that "the named insured's permission to a second permittee need not be express, *but may be implied from the broad nature of scope of the initial permission,* or from the conduct of the parties and from the attendant facts and circumstances." (II R. 167) (emphasis added).

The difficulty, however, is that here it is not the driving of Deborah as a second permittee which is in question, but that of Wallace as a *third* permittee. We note again that neither of the first permittees, Beth and Shawnna, were told by Deborah that Wallace was to be in the car with Deborah and Helen. We are convinced that implied permission cannot be stretched so far as to include the driving of Wallace on the night of the accident. See *West v. McNamara,* 159 Ohio St. 187; *Bailey v. General Insurance Co.,* 265 N.C. 675; *Novo v. Employers' Liability Assurance Corp.,* 295 Mass. 232, denying coverage as to third permittees. A scintilla of evidence, such as the remote permission of the parents given to Beth and Shawnna to drive the family cars, was not enough to raise a jury question of implied permission for Wallace to drive the Volkswagen. We are convinced that the evidence points only one way and is not susceptible of a reasonable inference that Wallace had any implied permission of the parents to drive their car. *Bertot v. School District No. 1, supra,* 522 F.2d 1171, 1175–76.

We find two Wyoming cases dealing with omnibus clauses, *Wyoming Farm Bureau Mutual Insurance Co. v. May,* 434 P.2d 507 (Wyo.), and *Phoenix Assurance Co. v. Latta,* 373 P.2d 146 (Wyo.). These cases do not support the plaintiff's theory for extending implied permission as far as Deborah's friend Wallace, and we feel they indicate that the Wyoming courts would not go that far. We are mindful that the views of a resident district judge on the unsettled law of his state are persuasive and ordinarily accepted. *Sade v. Northern Natural Gas Co.,* 483 F.2d 230, 234 (10th Cir.). However, regardless of whether some such expression of views on state law was made here by the trial court's rulings and charge,[3] or whether the court merely treated the issue as one for the jury, we feel it was clearly error on this record to enter

---

[3] As noted, the trial judge referred in the charge to implied permission to a *second* permittee only, and he apparently found some basis for treating Wallace as a second permittee. On this record we do not, however, find any basis for so treating Wallace. There was no proof that Deborah was a *first* permittee of the parents; her permission to use the car can only be premised on implied permission coming to her through her sisters. Thus Deborah was at best a *second* permittee and Wallace a *third* permittee—too remote to have implied permission of the parents to use the car.

judgment affording coverage to Wallace.[4] The evidence simply does not stretch far enough to support any reasonable inference that Wallace had implied permission from the named insureds, Mr. and Mrs. Ahrens, for coverage under the omnibus clause as written.

II

As another basis for sustaining the judgment, plaintiff argues that the facts did not even involve a primary-secondary permission situation, that this was rather a situation where the two older daughters became the named insureds because of the mother's blindness, and that since there was no way in which JoAnn Ahrens could have operated the vehicle herself, her designation as a "named insured" was only a technicality. (Brief of Appellee, 4). Thus, the argument seems to be that Deborah was a *first* permitted authorized to drive by Beth and Shawnna as named insureds, that Wallace was admittedly authorized by Deborah to drive, and that the reasoning of cases rejecting coverage of third permittees as too remote is therefore not applicable.

We cannot agree with the position that Beth and Shawnna should be treated as named insureds. It is clear that by the terms of the policy the "named insureds" were defined as Robert and JoAnn Ahrens. That term carries special meaning in such policies affecting the rights and obligations of the parties. We cannot "rewrite the policy," *American Casualty Co. v. Myrick,* 304 F.2d 179, 184 (5th Cir.), because of the unusual circumstances in the family. See *Alm v. Hartford Fire Insurance Co.,* 369 P.2d 216, 217 (Wyo.). The family circumstances are relevant, as we have recognized, in connection with the factual issue relating to implied permission for use of the family cars. However, nothing in the facts here demonstrates a change in the agreement of the policyholders with the company, as was the case in *Unigard Insurance Co. v. Studer,* 536 F.2d 1337 (10th Cir.), where an endorsement to the policy effected a change naming an additional insured. The insurer has a right to assume that the risk undertaken will not be enlarged beyond the agreement. See *Travelers Insurance Co. v. Weatherford,* 520 S.W.2d 726, 728 (Tenn.). We therefore feel there is no warrant for varying from the terms of the policy definition of the "named insured."

Plaintiff Curtis further contends that if the company were to prevail here, then an undesirable situation would result, contrary to the public's understanding about insurance coverage. The argument is that if any children were riding in a vehicle driven and operated by a child of the owner, and that child were to permit another child to drive, then according to the company there would be no coverage, contrary to the public's expectation. This policy argument does not persuade us. We cannot impose liability contrary to the terms of the agreement and without justification in the facts of record. As the Supreme Court of Wyoming stated in *Wyoming Farm Bureau Mutual Insurance Co. v.*

---

[4] Plaintiff relies, *inter alia,* on *State Farm Mutual Automobile Insurance Co. v. Cook,* 186 Va. 658 and *Baesler v. Globe Indemnity Co.,* 33 N.J. 148. The holding in *Cook* and the dictum in *Baesler* would merely uphold coverage as to a *second* permittee given permission to drive by a first permittee having general use of the vehicle. The cases in no way support extension of coverage as far as a third permittee like Wallace, whose use of the vehicle had not been disclosed by Deborah to the named insureds or to the first permittees, Beth and Shawnna.

May, supra, 434 P.2d at 511–12, in rejecting a similar public policy argument:

> Granting that the need for better regulation of use of highways is a meritorious and even a necessary objective, to argue that liability coverage of one person should be extended to cover another simply because it is desirable that all drivers of motor vehicles should be covered, is whimsical and unsupported either in reason or by law. This contention is without merit.

For these reasons we conclude that the verdict and judgment cannot stand and that the defendant was entitled to judgment notwithstanding the verdict. Accordingly, the judgment is reversed and the cause is remanded for entry of judgment in accordance with this opinion.

NOTES AND QUESTIONS

1. *The Relation Between the Omnibus and DOC Clauses.* The omnibus clause—usually made operative as a definition of the term "insured"—is universally included in auto liability policies. In addition, most policies contain "drive other cars," or "DOC" coverage, providing insurance for the named insured against liability arising out of the permitted use of a non-owned vehicle. Many plain-language policies have omitted some or all of the language in the omnibus and DOC clauses, apparently relying on precedent to fill in the gaps. Once the DOC clause became common, the need for an omnibus clause in every policy declined, although it did not disappear. But the two clauses must still be coordinated by the "other insurance" provisions in the two policies (the driver's and the owner's) that potentially provide coverage when a permittee is sued. For more discussion of coordination under "other insurance" see the *Carriers* case later in this Chapter.

2. *The Meaning of "Permission."* Most state statutes contain language suggesting that an omnibus clause must be included in auto liability policies. The purpose of such statutes often figures in the interpretation of omnibus clauses, sometimes prompting rulings that "public policy" requires that the term "permission" in the clause be given an expansive interpretation. But even absent a statutory requirement, concern for the compensation of victims—and for not bankrupting drivers who are not thieves—seems to influence some courts' interpretations. The threefold breakdown of judicial approaches to interpretation of the permission provisions in omnibus and DOC clauses generally distinguishes among the liberal, minor-deviation, and conservative approaches. Note that this breakdown not only involves the question whether there was permission at all, but also the scope of permission. On this latter issue, see *Old American County Mutual Fire Insurance Co. v. Renfrow,* 130 S.W.3d 70 (Tex. 2004) (deviation from permitted scope does not satisfy the requirements of the clause); *Hartford Fire Insurance Co. v. Davis,* 436 S.E.2d 429 (Va. 1993) (permission to drive the vehicle for purposes of repair does not include permission to drive for pleasure).

   a. Under the *liberal rule,* once the named insured gives permission to another to drive the insured vehicle, that driver and all others in the chain of permission have full authority to grant further permission, and full authority to make use of the vehicle, regardless of any restrictions on the scope of use contained in the original permission. As a consequence there is coverage, so to speak, all the way down. See, e.g., *Mitchell v. Allstate Ins. Co.*, 244 S.W.3d 59 (Ky. 2008); *Odolecki v. Hartford Accident & Indem. Co.*, 264 A.2d 38 (N.J. 1970). This statement of the liberal rule may well employ a bit more caricature than characterization, for all courts would probably draw the line short of this pure approach. Nonetheless, some courts would hold that whether there was permission on the facts in cases like *Curtis* is a question for the jury.

  b. The *minor deviation* approach is by far the most predominant. The issue for most courts is the degree of the deviation from the owner's permission, and the question—as it was in *Curtis* at the trial court level—becomes one of fact and degree. See, e.g. *Minter v. Great Am. Ins. Co.*, 423 F.3d 460 (5th Cir. 2005) (holding that it was a question of fact whether driving while intoxicated constituted more than a minor deviation from the scope of permission); *O'Neill v. Long*, 54 P.3d 109 (Okl. 2002); *Shelter Mut. Ins. Co. v. See*, 46 S.W.3d 65 (Mo. App. 2001). Probably *Curtis* itself should be placed in this category. If the minor deviation rule relies on juries for its application, are insurers likely to be much comforted when it rather than the liberal rule prevails?

  c. The *conservative rule* simply goes one step further, holding that deviations from the scope of the original grant of permission take the use of the vehicle outside the scope of coverage. Since the question under this rule is the precise scope of the permission given, the issue is usually fact-sensitive and therefore leaves the jury itself considerable discretion. Would the issue be as critical as the division between these rules suggests if DOC coverage were available regardless of actual permission, so long as the driver in question reasonably believed he had permission? Would such an approach have been helpful in *Curtis*?

  3. *A "Reasonable Belief."* The Sample Policy handles this problem in Part A, Exclusion (8) (page 3), providing that there is no coverage for a driver who lacks a "reasonable belief" that he has permission to drive. If this provision had governed the issue in *Curtis*, would the result have been different? In *Patrons Oxford Insurance Co. v. Harris*, 905 A.2d 819 (Me. 2006), an unlicensed, intoxicated individual was a passenger in a friend's vehicle. They arrived at a party and got out of the car, but were threatened with immediate bodily harm. The former passenger then jumped into the driver's seat and started the car, with his friend in the passenger seat. While attempting to drive away, he struck a pedestrian at the party. The court held that he had a "reasonable belief" that he had permission to drive, despite his intoxication and lack of a valid license.

3. "USE" OF THE VEHICLE

Farm Bureau Mutual Insurance Company v. Evans
Court of Appeals of Kansas, 1981.
7 Kan.App.2d 60.

■ ABBOTT, JUDGE:

  This is an appeal by two automobile liability insurance carriers from an order granting summary judgment against them holding that the respective policies issued by them provided coverage for the accident in question.

The determinative issue in this case is whether liability for bodily injury caused by the throwing of a lighted firecracker (M–80) from the rear of a parked station wagon "arose out of the use of an automobile" so as to be covered under the automobile liability insurance policies in issue.

On April 28, 1979, a going-away party was being held for David and Karen Evans. The party was held in a large, open field. Several bonfires were going; keg beer was available. It started to rain and turn cold. Damon Rose (not a party to this action), at his wife's request, parked the Roses' station wagon so that the back seat was facing a bonfire. The Rose station wagon has three seats, the back one of which faces the rear of the station wagon. The tailgate was open. Mike Ehinger was sitting in the middle of the back seat facing the fire. Kathy Rose and Danny Ireland were beside him. It is alleged that Ehinger, with the aid of Rose and Ireland, lit an explosive device known as an M–80 and threw it out of the rear of the station wagon. It landed in a glass of beer held by Karen Evans. When it exploded, Karen Evans received extensive damage to her hand and a number of puncture wounds to her body from the shattered glass.

The Evanses are plaintiffs in a personal injury action brought against Kathy Rose, Mike Ehinger and Danny Ireland for Karen's personal injuries sustained as a result of the explosion. Farm Bureau Mutual Insurance Company, Inc., insures the Rose automobile and Farmers Insurance Company, Inc., insures an automobile owned by Mike Ehinger. Both policies provide coverage for bodily injury "arising out of the ownership, maintenance or use" of the insured vehicle.

The question before the trial court was whether the two policies provided coverage for Mike Ehinger, Danny Ireland and Kathy Rose, or any of them, with regard to claims made against them by the Evanses. The trial court determined that there was coverage because the automobile was being used as shelter, a reasonable incident of its use and one reasonably contemplated by the parties to the insurance contract.

The policy provision in question is mandated by the legislature. K.S.A.1980 Supp. 40–3107(b). As an automobile liability coverage clause, it is to be interpreted broadly to afford the greatest possible protection to the insured. United States Fidelity & Guar. Co. v. Farm Bureau Mut. Ins. Co., 2 Kan.App.2d 580 (1978). In the case before us, the trial court found the vehicle was being "used" within the meaning of the coverage clause because of its use as a shelter. But mere use of a vehicle, standing alone, is not sufficient to trigger coverage. Thus, even though the vehicle was being used within the meaning of the automobile liability policies, the question remains whether that use is so remote from the negligent act that it can be said there was no causal relationship between the use of the car and the injuries sustained.

Kansas has construed the word "use" in connection with automobile liability policies on three occasions: Alliance Mutual Casualty Co. v. Boston Insurance Co., 196 Kan. 323; Esfeld Trucking, Inc. v. Metropolitan Insurance Co., 193 Kan. 7 (1964); United States Fidelity

& Guar. Co. v. Farm Bureau Mut. Ins. Co., 2 Kan.App.2d 580. None of these cases is exactly in point, but language found in Esfeld indicates Kansas follows the majority rule that there must be some causal connection between the use of the insured vehicle and the injury. In Esfeld, the court stated:

> "In determining the coverage of a policy such as our present one a court must consider whether the injury sustained was a natural and reasonable incident or consequence of the use of the vehicle involved for the purposes shown by the declarations of the policy though not foreseen or expected." 193 Kan. at 11.

The general rule in other jurisdictions is that "arising out of the use" of a vehicle requires the finding of some causal connection or relation between the use of the vehicle and the injury. E.g., Richland Knox Mutual Insurance Company v. Kallen, 376 F.2d 360 (6th Cir. 1967); Government Employees Insurance Company v. Melton, 357 F.Supp. 416 (D.S.C.1972), aff'd in unpublished opinion, 473 F.2d 909 (1973); Mazon v. Farmers Insurance Exchange, 107 Ariz. 601 (1971); Speziale v. Kohnke, 194 So.2d 485 (La.App.1967); National Family Ins. Co. v. Boyer, 269 N.W.2d 10 (Minn.1978); 7 Am.Jur.2d, Automobile Insurance s 194, p. 703; Annot., 89 A.L.R.2d 150, 153; 8 Blashfield, Automobile Law & Practice s 317.1, p. 5; 12 Couch on Insurance 2d s 45:56. Stated another way, an injury does not arise out of the "use" of a vehicle within the meaning of the coverage clause of an automobile liability policy if it is caused by some intervening cause not identifiable with normal ownership, maintenance and use of the insured vehicle and the injury complained of. Kangas v. Aetna Casualty Co., 64 Mich.App. 1, 235 N.W.2d 42 (1975); Norgaard v. Nodak Mutual Insurance Company, 201 N.W.2d 871 (N.D.1972); Plaxco v. U. S. Fidelity & Guaranty Co., 252 S.C. 437 (1969); State Farm Ins. v. Centennial Ins., 14 Wash.App. 541 (1975). The provision, however, imparts a more liberal concept of a causation than "proximate cause" in its traditional, legal sense. Watson v. Watson, 326 So.2d 48 (Fla.App.1976); Dairyland Insurance Co. v. Concrete Products Co., 203 N.W.2d 558 (Iowa 1973); Shinabarger v. Citizens Mutual Ins. Co., 90 Mich.App. 307 (1979); Cameron Mut. Ins. Co. v. Ward, 599 S.W.2d 13 (Mo.App.1980); State Farm Mut. Auto. Ins. v. Centennial Ins., 14 Wash.App. 541; 7 Am.Jur.2d, Automobile Insurance s 194, p. 703; 8 Blashfield, Automobile Law & Practice s 317.1, pp. 5–6; 12 Couch on Insurance 2d s 45:56, p. 147.

We need not decide whether a different result might be reached if the vehicle had been in motion at the time. Some courts have held that if a vehicle is moving and the speed of the car contributed to the impact of a thrown missile, such would be a sufficient causal connection. Likewise, the mere throwing of the contents of an ashtray or other trash normally found in a vehicle could constitute a use. The throwing of an explosive device from a car, however, has generally been held to be so remotely connected with the use of the vehicle that it is not causally related to the injury. Kraus v. Allstate Insurance Company, 379 F.2d 443 (3rd Cir. 1967); Wirth v. Maryland Casualty Company, 368 F.Supp. 789 (W.D.Ky.1973), aff'd in unpublished opinion, 497 F.2d 925 (1974); McDonald v. Great American Insurance Company, 224 F.Supp. 369 (D.R.I.1963); Speziale v. Kohnke, 194 So.2d 485.

The use of the Roses' vehicle did not causally contribute to Karen's injuries anymore than it would have if one of the occupants under the facts present in this case had shot her with a firearm. The fact that the M–80 was lit inside the vehicle and the defendants might have had difficulty lighting it if no shelter had been available is so remote that it does not furnish the necessary causal relationship between the use of the car and her injuries. We see no more difference in the use of the vehicle here under the facts present than if the owner of the vehicle had been outside the car and in order to avoid the rain had held the device under the car or stood on the leeward side of it to light the device.

Having concluded the trial court erred in determining that the insurance policies in question provided coverage, we deem the remaining issues moot.

Reversed with directions to enter judgment for the insurance carriers on their motions for summary judgment.

NOTES AND QUESTIONS

1. *Plain-Language Terminology.* The Farm Bureau policy contained detailed language, referring to "ownership, maintenance or use, loading or unloading" of the insured vehicle. Should plain-language policies that simply refer to liability for "automobile accidents" or "use" of the vehicle be interpreted any differently?

2. *I Know It When I See It?* Can the kind of problem addressed in *Evans* be resolved on a principled basis without depriving victims of compensation in sympathetic situations? What "rule," if any, can you derive from the proper resolution of the following situations? Would use of a proximate cause test advance the inquiry?

   a. Suppose that a policyholder involved in a road rage incident threatened another driver while he was parked, reached into the other driver's car, and that driver shot him. Was either of these drivers involved in the "use" their vehicles? *Cole v. U.S. Auto. Assoc.*, 68 P.3d 513 (Colo. App. 2002); *Allstate Ins. Co. v. Gillespie*, 455 So.2d 617 (Fla. App. 1984).

   b. The insured injures a bicyclist by throwing a bottle out of a moving vehicle. *Nationwide Mut. Ins. Co. v. Webb*, 512 S.E.2d 764 (N.C. App. 1999).

   c. The insured's dog bites a passenger while the passenger is opening the car door to exit the vehicle. *Hartford Accident & Indem. Co. v. Civil Serv. Emp. Ins. Co.*, 33 Cal. App. 3d 26 (1973). The insured's dog bites a pedestrian while the dog is in the cargo area of a parked pickup truck. *Diehl v. Cumberland Mut. Fire Ins. Co.*, 686 A.2d 785 (N.J. Super. 1997).

3. *The Problem Under Other Auto Coverages.* Would the result reached in *Evans* be the same under the medical payment provisions of an auto policy? See *White v. Am. Cas. Ins. Co.*, 756 N.E.2d 1208 (Mass. App. 2001). Under the uninsured motorist provisions? See *Race v. Nationwide Mut. Fire Ins. Co.*, 542 So. 2d 347 (Fla.1989). See also *Niglio v. Omaha Prop. & Cas. Ins. Co.*, 679 So. 2d 323 (Fla. Ct. App. 1996).

4. *Dovetailing With Homeowners Coverage.* Should there be any doubt that if the loss in *Evans* did not arise out of the use of a vehicle, then it would be covered under the liability insurance provisions of a Homeowners or Tenants policy? If not, is the only question from the victim

protection standpoint whether such coverage is as likely to be available as auto liability insurance?

4. NOTICE AND COOPERATION CONDITIONS

All automobile insurance policies provide that the insured must provide the insurer with notice of any claim or suit, and cooperate in the investigation or defense of such claims or suits. The issues surrounding the obligation to provide notice parallel those already surveyed in connection with general liability insurance. The scope of the insured's duty to cooperate and the effect of any breach of that duty, however, are common issues in auto liability insurance litigation.

State Farm Mutual Automobile Insurance Company v. Davies
Supreme Court of Virginia, 1983.
226 Va. 310.

■ CARRICO, CHIEF JUSTICE.

This appeal in a declaratory judgment proceeding involves the conceded breach of the cooperation clause of an automobile liability insurance policy and presents the question whether the breach prejudiced the insurance carrier in its defense of an action for damages. The question is presented against the following background:

On August 2, 1974, Dixie K. Davies was injured when the vehicle she was driving collided with an automobile operated by Patricia Ann Turner. At the time, Turner was an insured under a policy issued by State Farm Mutual Automobile Insurance Company (State Farm), containing the usual cooperation clause, and Davies was an insured under a policy issued by Government Employees Insurance Company (GEICO), with standard provisions for uninsured motorist coverage.

Davies filed a personal injury action against Turner, who delivered the suit papers to State Farm. When the case came on for trial, Turner failed to appear, and State Farm defended the action under a reservation of rights.

The trial resulted in a verdict and judgment in favor of Davies for $10,725.00. Thereafter, the judgment remaining unpaid, Davies brought this declaratory judgment proceeding to determine which of the two insurance companies was liable to her. State Farm disclaimed liability on the ground that Turner's failure to appear at trial constituted a material and prejudicial breach of the cooperation clause of the State Farm policy. GEICO defended on the basis that State Farm's disclaimer of liability was ineffective and, hence, that Turner was not an uninsured motorist.

After a hearing, the trial court ruled that State Farm had not been prejudiced by Turner's failure to appear at trial. Accordingly, the court entered judgment in favor of Davies against State Farm and dismissed GEICO. Because we believe these actions were erroneous, we will reverse.

Under the terms of State Farm's policy, Turner was required to "cooperate with the company and to * * * attend hearings and trials and assist in securing and giving evidence and obtaining the attendance of witnesses." Pursuant to Code § 38.1–381(a1), however, an insurance carrier cannot escape liability on the ground of noncooperation unless the failure to cooperate "prejudices the insurer in the defense of an action for damages."

The parties stipulated below that Turner failed to cooperate as required and that State Farm had not waived its right to rely upon the defense of noncooperation. The only issue for determination, therefore, the parties agreed, was whether Turner's failure to cooperate prejudiced State Farm in the defense of Davies' personal injury action.

On this issue, the trial court properly held that State Farm had the burden of proving prejudice. *See Shipp v. Connecticut Indem. Co.,* 194 Va. 249, 258 (1952). The court found, however, that the "evidence of liability [in the personal injury action] was rather overwhelming and it would stretch the imagination to believe that a different result would have been obtained."

GEICO argues that the importance of this finding of fact "cannot be overemphasized" and that the finding may not be set aside since it is supported by credible evidence. The difficulty with GEICO's argument is that the so-called "finding of fact" contains a built-in rule of law imposing upon State Farm the burden of proving that Turner's appearance and testimony at trial *would* have produced a different result. We believe this was an improper burden, and we think one of our prior decisions demonstrates the error in the trial court's holding. For this reason, we need not consider the several out-of-state decisions cited by GEICO.

In *Cooper v. Insurance Company,* 199 Va. 908 (1958), Traynham, an insured under a policy issued by Employers Mutual Automobile Insurance Company, was involved in an accident with Cooper. Traynham notified the insurance company of the accident and gave it a signed statement concerning the details of the incident. Thereafter, Traynham disappeared and failed to cooperate further with the company. Cooper obtained a judgment against Traynham in a personal injury action which the company defended under a reservation of rights. When Cooper brought an action on the policy, the company defended on the ground of Traynham's noncooperation. Affirming the trial court's finding in favor of the company, we said:

> [Traynham] did not assist in any manner in the preparation for trial nor did he appear at the trial. These facts and circumstances constituted a wilful lack of cooperation with the company and such lack of cooperation was substantial and material and was prejudicial to [the company]. His failure to assist in the preparation for trial and to attend the trial unquestionably prejudiced his case, especially in view of the fact that his report of the accident * * * indicated a defense to the action.

Id. at 915. * * *

Admittedly, *Cooper* does not discuss the nature of the evidence that is required to establish prejudice. It is clear from the opinion, however, that where the insured's willful absence from trial deprives the insurer of evidence sufficient to establish a defense to the original claim, then prejudice results. And we believe it is implicit that evidence necessary to establish a defense means evidence of sufficient quality and weight to take the issue of the insured's conduct to the jury and to support a verdict in his or her favor.

It follows that we favor neither a *per se* rule that would permit an insurer to show merely that its insured failed to appear at trial nor a rule that would require an insurer to show that, had its insured appeared, the result would have been in his or her favor. Instead, we believe that the proper rule lies midway between these two extremes and emanates from the rationale of *Cooper*: in an action on the policy, when the insurer shows that the insured's willful failure to appear at the original trial deprived the insurer of evidence which would have made a jury issue of the insured's liability and supported a verdict in his or her favor, the insurer has established a reasonable likelihood the result would have been favorable to the insured and has carried its burden of proving prejudice under Code § 38.1–381(a).

To determine whether State Farm carried its burden of proving prejudice, we turn now to the evidence adduced in the present proceeding. This evidence, most of which was stipulated, shows that the accident in question occurred on a rainy afternoon in early August, 1974, at the intersection of City Park Avenue and Park Manor Road in the City of Portsmouth. A traffic island is located on Park Manor Road at the intersection, and traffic turning left from City Park Avenue onto Park Manor Road passes to the left of the island. Davies, who had been proceeding northward on City Park Avenue, was in the process of turning left onto Park Manor Road. Turner was travelling eastward on Park Manor Road intending to turn right onto City Park Avenue. The two vehicles collided left side to left side.

Turner reported the accident to State Farm and signed an "Automobile Claim Report" setting forth her version of the incident, which indicated she had a defense. State Farm made a prompt and full investigation. As part of the investigation, a State Farm claims representative interviewed Turner some four months after the accident. Repeating her version of the accident, Turner stated in the interview that she was approaching the intersection about five miles per hour when Davies, travelling around fifteen miles per hour, "turned too short" onto Park Manor Road and proceeded toward Turner on Davies' wrong side of the road. Turner pulled to her right "in the dirt off of the road" but was hit on her left front fender by Davies, and the impact "spun [Turner's] car around." When police officers arrived, they did not issue any summons or indicate who was at fault in the accident.

Jimmy Smith, Turner's brother, was a passenger in her car at the time of the accident. He was also interviewed by the State Farm claims representative, and he corroborated Turner's version of the accident.

Following the filing of Davies' personal injury action on August 2, 1976, Turner was served with process, and she turned the suit papers over to State Farm. George Gray, an attorney, was designated by State Farm to defend the action and he filed defensive pleadings on Turner's behalf.

Trial of the personal injury action was set for February 22, 1977. Gray notified Turner of the trial date and requested that she contact him to arrange a pretrial interview. She telephoned his office to make an appointment but, following this call, she moved from her local address and never again contacted Gray or anyone else connected with State Farm. Because of her absence, the case was continued several times during a period of more than two years. Despite "every reasonable effort" made by State Farm, she could not be found.

Jimmy Smith did cooperate with State Farm in the early stages of the case, and he indicated to Gray he would give testimony favorable to Turner. In late 1978, however, after Smith had joined the Army and left the state, Gray attempted to take his deposition, but Smith did not appear at the scheduled time. Gray talked with him on the phone later, and he was "an entirely different person." He told Gray that he remembered "little, if anything, about the accident" and that he did not wish to be deposed. Gray made no further attempt to depose Smith.

The personal injury action was finally heard on August 3, 1979, in the absence of both Turner and her brother. The testimony presented at trial was stipulated into the present record. According to Davies' version of the accident, as she was making her left turn from City Park Avenue onto Park Manor Road, she saw Turner approaching in the middle of Park Manor Road at a speed of thirty-five miles per hour in a twenty-five mile zone. Davies moved to her right and had come to a stop partially on the traffic island when the left side of her vehicle was struck by the left side of Turner's automobile.

Park Ranger Caviness was the first police officer to arrive on the scene. He observed both vehicles on Davies' side of the road, with a portion of Davies' vehicle on the traffic island. Davies' husband, who was also a police officer, and Officer Burke later arrived on the scene. They corroborated Caviness' statements concerning the positions of the vehicles. All three police officers and Mrs. Davies heard Turner admit fault for the accident.

There was no evidence presented in the personal injury trial supporting Turner's version of the accident. Specifically, there was no testimony that Davies "cut the corner short," that Turner turned to her right in an attempt to avoid the accident, or that the impact occurred on Turner's side of the road.

Testifying in the present proceeding as a witness for State Farm, Gray said Turner and her brother were the "only [possible] witnesses * * * who [could] provide a defense in the case." Gray said further that the statements Turner and her brother made in their interviews with State Farm's claims representative "indicated, to [Gray], that [he] did have a defense * * * which [he] could classify as substantial"; by "substantial defense," he meant "evidence which can be presented to a jury which, if believed, would result in a verdict for [the defendant]."

Gray testified further that when Turner and her brother failed to appear at the personal injury trial, he "lost every chance of any defense on the issue of liability"; he was unable through cross-examination or otherwise to develop any "evidence or testimony [he] could put on to defend." Gray conceded he had advised State Farm some time prior to the personal injury trial that there was "apparent liability" in the case. Gray insisted, however, that this advice to State Farm did not "mean that [he had] backed off from what [he thought was] a substantial defense."

We believe the evidence in this case compels the conclusion that had Turner appeared at the personal injury trial and testified as State Farm had the right to assume she would testify, that is, by reciting the same version of the accident she gave in her interview with State Farm's claims representative, then a jury issue of her liability would have been established. A jury issue exists " '[i]f there is conflict of the testimony on a material point, or if reasonably fair-minded [persons] may differ as to the conclusions of fact to be drawn from the evidence, or if the conclusion is dependent on the weight to be given the testimony.' " *Hoover v. Neff & Son,* 183 Va. 56, 62 (1944) (quoting M. Burkes, *Pleading and Practice* 543 (3d ed. 1934)).

While these are alternative criteria and all three exist in the present case, we need only point out that, had Turner repeated at the personal injury trial her version of the accident, her testimony would have been in direct conflict with Davies' evidence. Turner's version was not inherently incredible, and the question then would have become one of credibility for the jury. Had the jury accepted Turner's version and returned a verdict in her favor, the verdict would have been supported by evidence. Yet, by willfully failing to attend and testify at the personal injury trial and by failing to assist in securing her brother's testimony, Turner deprived State Farm of the very evidence necessary to make a jury issue of her liability. These failures, concededly in breach of the cooperation clause, clearly prejudiced State Farm in its defense of the personal injury action.

Accordingly, the judgment of the trial court will be reversed. The parties have stipulated that if it is determined Turner's breach of the cooperation clause prejudiced State Farm in the defense of the personal injury action, "then [GEICO] owes [Davies] the amount of the said previous judgment, plus interest and the Court costs of this [declaratory judgment] action." Pursuant to this stipulation, we will dismiss State Farm and enter final judgment in favor of Davies against GEICO in the amounts indicated.

Reversed and final judgment.

NOTES AND QUESTIONS

1. *Forms of Non-Cooperation.* The behavior that constitutes breach of the insured's duty to cooperate often involves the failure to appear at trial, or the repeated failure to appear for depositions or interviews. On this issue, in addition to *Davies,* see *United Auto Insurance Co. v. Buckley,* 962 N.E. 2d 548 (Ill. App. Ct. 2011). To the extent that the insurer has made special efforts to assist or assure cooperation, its case is strengthened. Conversely, an insurer that does nothing to encourage cooperation has a much weaker—indeed, in some instances empty—claim to be relieved of its obligations. For example, suppose the insurer persists in sending communications in English to a Spanish-speaking insured or in scheduling depositions during working hours without taking affirmative steps to facilitate the insured's appearance. When the insured does not reply to communications or appear as requested, and the insurer claims non-cooperation, who prevails? See, e.g., *State Farm Mut. Auto. Ins. Co. v.*

Secrist, 33 P.3d 1272 (Colo. App. 2001); *Allstate Ins. Co. v. Loester*, 675 N.Y.S.2d 832 (N.Y. App. Div. 1998). A number of other forms of non-cooperation also appear in the cases; the most common are collusion with the plaintiff and lying or giving false testimony. See, e.g., *Charter Oak Fire Ins. Co. v. Interstate Mech., Inc.*, 958 F.Supp. 2d 1188 (D. Or. 2013); *Emprs. Mut. Cas. Co. v. Nelson*, 241 A.2d 207 (N.H. 1968). Finally, however, some courts hold that an insurer cannot invoke the cooperation requirement to avoid coverage under policies that satisfy the state's compulsory insurance requirement. See, e.g., *U.S. Auto. Assoc. v. Markosky*, 530 S.E.2d 660 (S.C. App. 2000); *Harris v. Prudential Prop. & Cas. Ins. Co.*, 632 A.2d 1380 (Del. Sup. Ct.1993).

2. *Forms of Prejudice.* Determining what kind of behavior constitutes non-cooperation is only the first step in applying the cooperation clause. Prejudice to the insurer, or at least materiality of breach, is almost always required before breach of the notice and cooperation clause voids coverage. The court in *Davies* staked out a middle ground between a requirement that there be proof that but for the insured's failure to cooperate the claim would have failed, and the requirement that the insured's failure to cooperate merely have some effect on the insurer's prospect of defeating the claim. Most courts seem to adopt a *substantial impact test* in fact, if not in name, that makes predicting results difficult. In many cases there can be no real evidence—short of trying a hypothetical case in which cooperation *is* provided—regarding the effect of non-cooperation. The court can either estimate based on its own experience and judgment what impact cooperation by the insured might have had on the outcome of the case, or throw up its hands in despair of estimating that impact based on the meager evidence available. The *Davies* test avoids at least gives the court a metric by which to make a judgment.

The key question in many cases, therefore, is not so much the character of the test to be applied, but the party bearing the burden of proof. If the insurer bears the burden of proving prejudice, it is likely to lose all but the clearest cases of prejudice. If the insured bears that burden, he is likely to prevail only occasionally. Most jurisdictions place the burden of proof on the insurer.

3. *Shortsighted Strategy?* Why was GEICO, a high-volume auto insurer, pressing so hard for a rule that would make it more difficult for auto insurers to avoid liability when the insured has breached the cooperation condition of an auto policy? If you were general counsel for GEICO, would you have advised GEICO to try to settle the case before appeal?

Miller v. Shugart

Supreme Court of Minnesota, 1982.
316 N.W.2d 729.

■ SIMONETT, JUSTICE.

While Milbank Mutual Insurance Company was litigating whether it had coverage for both the insured car owner and the driver, the insured owner and the driver settled with the injured plaintiff and confessed judgment for a stipulated sum. After the coverage question was decided adversely to Milbank, plaintiff commenced a garnishment action against Milbank to collect on the judgment. Milbank appeals from an order in the garnishment proceeding granting plaintiff summary judgment to collect from Milbank on defendants' confessed judgment to the extent of the policy limits plus interest. Finding that Milbank must indemnify, we affirm plaintiff's recovery of the policy limits but reverse the ruling on interest.

Plaintiff Lynette Miller was injured in an automobile accident on June 19, 1976, when a car owned by defendant Barbara Locoshonas and driven by defendant Mark Shugart, in which Lynette was a passenger, struck a tree. Locoshonas had an auto liability policy with Milbank. Milbank, however, contended Shugart, the driver of the car, was not an agent of the owner and thus not covered under the policy. To determine this coverage question, Milbank, shortly after the accident, commenced a declaratory judgment action. Milbank provided separate counsel at its expense to represent the insured and the driver.

On January 8, 1979, judgment was entered in the declaratory judgment action adjudging that Milbank's policy afforded coverage to both Locoshonas and Shugart. On January 31, 1979, plaintiff Lynette Miller commenced her personal injury action against Locoshonas and Shugart. In April 1979 Milbank appealed the declaratory judgment decision to this court, and in April 1980 we summarily affirmed.

Twice while the appeal was pending, counsel for Locoshonas and Shugart advised Milbank they were negotiating a settlement with plaintiff's attorney and invited Milbank to participate in the negotiations. Milbank refused, pointing out it could not do so while the coverage question was unresolved.

In September 1979, plaintiff and the two defendants signed a stipulation for settlement of plaintiff's claims in which defendants confessed judgment in the amount of $100,000, which was twice the limit of Milbank's policy. The stipulated judgment further provided that it could be collected only from proceeds of any applicable insurance with no personal liability to defendants. Milbank was advised of the stipulation. Judgment on the stipulation was entered on November 15, 1979.

In May 1980, following this court's summary affirmance on the coverage issue, plaintiff Miller served a garnishment summons on Milbank. Milbank interposed an answer to the supplemental complaint setting out the history of the litigation and alleging that the confession of judgment was in violation of its policy and that Milbank was thus not bound by the judgment. Plaintiff then moved for summary judgment in her favor for $50,000, the policy limits, plus interest and costs. Milbank countered with its own motion for summary judgment, claiming defendants had breached the cooperation clause of the policy, that garnishment did not lie, and that the confessed judgment was invalid. The trial court granted plaintiff's motion, adjudging plaintiff was entitled to recover the $50,000 limits plus interest on $100,000.

Three main issues present themselves: (1) Does garnishment lie, (2) may Milbank avoid responsibility for the confessed judgment, and (3) if Milbank is bound by the judgment, must it also pay interest on the entire $100,000? * * *

The next question is whether the judgment stipulated to by the plaintiff and the defendant insureds is the kind of liability the insurer has agreed under its policy to pay. This involves an inquiry into whether the judgment is the product of fraud or collusion perpetrated on the insurer and whether the judgment reflects a reasonable and prudent settlement.

A. We first must deal with a threshold issue. Milbank argues the indemnity agreement of its policy has been voided because the insureds breached their duty under the policy to cooperate.[1] We disagree.

Under the auto liability policy, Milbank has a duty to defend and indemnify its insureds, and the insureds have a reciprocal duty to cooperate with their insurer in the management of the claim. Plaintiff contends that defendants were relieved from their duty to cooperate because Milbank breached its duty to defend. We would put the issue differently. Milbank has never abandoned its insureds nor, by seeking a determination of its coverage, has it repudiated its policy obligations. Milbank had a right to determine if its policy afforded coverage for the accident claim, and here Milbank did exactly as we suggested in *Prahm v. Rupp Construction Co.*, 277 N.W.2d 389, 391 (1979), where we said a conflict of interest might be avoided by bringing a declaratory judgment action on the coverage issue prior to trial. This is the route Milbank followed, appropriately providing another set of attorneys to defend the insureds in the declaratory judgment action.

On the other hand, while Milbank did not abandon its insureds neither did it accept responsibility for the insureds' liability exposure. What we have, then, is a question of how should the respective rights and duties of the parties to an insurance contract be enforced during the time period that application of the insurance contract itself is being questioned. Viewed in this context, Milbank's position, really, is that it has a superior right to have the coverage question resolved *before* the plaintiff's personal injury action is disposed of either by trial or settlement. It is unlikely plaintiff could have forced defendants to trial before the coverage issue was decided. Put this way, the question becomes: Did the insureds breach their duty to cooperate by not waiting to settle until after the policy coverage had been decided? In our view, the insureds did not have to wait and, therefore, did not breach their duty to cooperate.

While the defendant insureds have a duty to cooperate with the insurer, they also have a right to protect themselves against plaintiff's claim. The attorneys hired by Milbank to represent them owe their allegiance to their clients, the insureds, to best represent their interests. If, as here, the insureds are offered a settlement that effectively relieves them of any personal liability, at a time when their insurance coverage is in doubt, surely it cannot be said that it is not in their best interest to accept the offer. Nor, do we think, can the insurer who is disputing coverage compel the insureds to forego a settlement which is in their best interests.

---

[1] The insurance policy provides in pertinent part: "The insured shall cooperate with the company and, upon the company's request, assist in making settlements * * *. The insured shall not, except at his own cost, voluntarily make any payment, assume any obligation or incur any expense other than for first aid for others at the time of the accident."

A breach of the cooperation clause must be a substantial and material breach which prejudices the insurer. *Juvland v. Plaisance*, 255 Minn. 262 (1959).

On the facts of this case we hold, therefore, that the insureds did not breach their duty to cooperate with the insurer, which was then contesting coverage, by settling directly with the plaintiff.

B. The next issue is whether Milbank may avoid the stipulated judgment on the grounds of fraud or collusion. We hold as a matter of law that the judgment was not obtained by fraud or collusion.

We start with the general proposition that a money judgment confessed to by an insured is not binding on the insurer if obtained through fraud or collusion. *Coblentz v. American Security Co. of New York*, 416 F.2d 1059 (5th Cir. 1969); *cf. Spencer v. Hawkeye Security Ins. Co.*, 216 N.W.2d 406 (Iowa 1974). In this case, however, Milbank has not made any showing of fraud or collusion. In its answer to the supplemental complaint, Milbank has neither pleaded fraud or collusion nor pleaded facts for such a defense. *See* Rules of Civil Procedure, Rule 9.02 ("In all averments of fraud or mistake, the circumstances constituting fraud or mistake shall be stated with particularity.") Neither, in opposing plaintiff's motion for summary judgment, has Milbank submitted affidavits or other evidence to make out any fact issue of fraud or collusion. Rules of Civil Procedure, Rule 56.05.

As we understand Milbank's argument, it is that the fraud and collusion consist of the defendant insureds settling the claims over Milbank's objections and contrary to the insurer's best interests, and in confessing judgment for a sum twice the amount of the policy limits. This conduct, however, need be neither fraudulent nor collusive. As we have just held, the defendant insureds had a right to make a settlement relieving them of liability. They also advised Milbank of what they were doing. Moreover, they waited to settle until after the district court had found coverage to exist. We see nothing improper in defendants' conduct. Nor is there anything wrong with the insureds' confessing judgment in an amount double the policy limits, since plaintiff, in her motion for summary judgment, has recognized Milbank's coverage is only $50,000 and seeks to recover no more than that sum from Milbank. The interest question will be addressed separately.

This is not to say that Milbank's position is enviable. As the trial court observed, it had "serious doubts about the propriety of the procedure whereby the insurer is placed in a 'no-win' situation as was done here." If the insurer ignores the "invitation" to participate in the settlement negotiations, it may run the risk of being required to pay, even within its policy limits, an inflated judgment. On the other hand, if the insurer decides to participate in the settlement discussions, ordinarily it can hardly do so meaningfully without abandoning its policy defense. Nevertheless, it seems to us, if a risk is to be borne, it is better to have the insurer who makes the decision to contest coverage bear the risk. Of course, the insurer escapes the risk if it should be successful on the coverage issue, and, in that event, it is plaintiff who loses.

We hold, as a matter of law, on the showing made on plaintiff's motion for summary judgment, that the stipulated judgment against the defendant insureds was not obtained by fraud or collusion.

C. Although having found that the stipulated judgment is untainted by fraud or collusion, our inquiry is not at an end. It seems to us there must also be a showing that the settlement on which the stipulated judgment is based was reasonable and prudent.

The settlement stipulation recites that defendants confess judgment in favor of plaintiff in the amount of $100,000 "upon the condition that plaintiff agree that her judgment may be satisfied only from liability insurance policies in force at the time * * * and that this judgment is not satisfiable nor may it be a lien upon any other assets of defendants * * *." Defendants agreed judgment could be entered *ex parte* adjudging the driver Shugart negligent although the parties further agreed, somewhat inconsistently, that the stipulation "does not constitute an admission by either defendant of his or her negligence," and it was also agreed the stipulation and judgment could not be used as an admission by the defendants in any other lawsuit.

Plainly, the "judgment" does not purport to be an adjudication on the merits; it only reflects the settlement agreement. It is also evident that, in arriving at the settlement terms, the defendants would have been quite willing to agree to anything as long as plaintiff promised them full immunity. The effect of the settlement was to substitute the claimant for the insureds in a claim against the insurer. Thus on this appeal we see only the plaintiff claimant and the defendants' insurer in dispute, with the insureds taking a passive, disinterested role. Moreover, it is a misnomer for the parties to call plaintiff's judgment a "confessed" judgment. If this were truly a confessed judgment or even a default judgment, it is doubtful that it could stand. It seems more accurate to refer to the judgment as a judgment on a stipulation.

In these circumstances, while the judgment is binding and valid as between the stipulating parties, it is not conclusive on the insurer. The burden of proof is on the claimant, the plaintiff judgment creditor, to show that the settlement is reasonable and prudent. The test as to whether the settlement is reasonable and prudent is what a reasonably prudent person in the position of the defendant would have settled for on the merits of plaintiff's claim. This involves a consideration of the facts bearing on the liability and damage aspects of plaintiff's claim, as well as the risks of going to trial. This can be compared with the somewhat analogous situation in which a joint tortfeasor seeking consideration from a co-tort-feasor must prove the settlement made was reasonable. *See, e.g., Samuelson v. Chicago, Rock Island & Pacific R. Co.*, 287 Minn. 264 (1970).

It may be instructive to point out how this case differs from *Butler Brothers v. American Fidelity Co.*, 120 Minn. 157 (1913). In *Butler* we held that a stipulated judgment, while not conclusive on the insurer, was presumptively so, and that the burden was on the insurer to show the settlement was unreasonable. In *Butler*, however, the insured entered into a settlement with the plaintiff in the course of a "real trial" while defending itself after being abandoned by its insurer. Thus the *Butler* settlement had quite different *bona fides* than the settlement made here. Here we think it appropriate, and so hold, that the burden of proving reasonableness is on the plaintiff claimant.

This leaves us with the question of what to do in this case. The trial court granted plaintiff summary judgment against Milbank for its policy limits of $50,000. The question is whether the record shows, as a matter of law, that the stipulated judgment, to the extent of $50,000, was reasonable and prudent. Not much proof was submitted to the trial court on this issue at the hearing on the motions for summary judgment. Nonetheless, it does appear, without dispute, that this was a one-car accident, with the plaintiff as passenger, in which the car left the road and hit a tree. As to damages, the settlement stipulation recites, and it is undisputed by Milbank, that plaintiff suffered "severe and disfiguring personal injuries," that no-fault benefits in excess of $20,000 were paid and that the no-fault benefits were likely to total $35,000 or more. The trial court states in its memo that Mr. Forsythe, retained by Milbank to represent the insureds, had reviewed the liability and damage aspects of the claim and had concluded "there was a substantial likelihood that ultimately judgment would be entered against his clients * * * for more than any possible insurance coverage * * *." On this showing, not disputed, we conclude the trial court did not err in granting summary judgment in favor of plaintiff and against Milbank to the extent of $50,000.

NOTES AND QUESTIONS

1. *Public Policy and No-Settlement-Without-Consent Clauses.* Note that the No-Action clause quoted in footnote 2 of the court's opinion purports to preclude coverage of the settlements to which the insurer denies consent. Would a better way of describing the result in cases like *Miller v. Shugart* be to say that when the insurer does not defend, or defends subject to a reservation of rights, the insured is entitled not to cooperate in deciding whether to settle? The case law seems to be developing in support this result. See, e.g., *Patrons Oxford Ins. Co. v. Harris*, 905 A.2d 819 (Me. 2006)

2. *Lose-Lose for the Insurer?* In situations like the one in *Miller*, are insurers in a lose-lose situation in the sense that, if they defend subject to a reservation of rights, they not only must pay defense costs but may lose control of settlement, but that if they do not defend they may be subject to coverage by estoppel for breaching the duty to defend? Is insurers' proper response simply to raise premiums in order to cover the cost of this additional coverage for policyholders? Is there any reason to think that policyholders would not want such coverage, as long as they were required to prove that the settlements they reached on their own were reasonable?

5. OTHER INSURANCE CLAUSES

Carriers Insurance Company v. American Policyholders' Insurance Company

Supreme Judicial Court of Maine, 1979.
404 A.2d 216.

■ DELAHANTY, JUSTICE.

This action was brought in the Superior Court, Kennebec County, by the plaintiff, Carriers Insurance Company (Carriers), seeking contribution from the defendant, American Policyholders' Insurance Co. (American). The parties joined issue upon whether and to what extent

American was required to contribute to a settlement made by the plaintiff. Upon an agreed statement of facts, the presiding Justice found for Carriers, and American has appealed. We deny the appeal.

During April of 1963, Cummings Bros. (Cummings) entered into a contractual agreement with Merrill's Rental Service, Inc. (Merrill's) whereby it leased certain motor vehicles from Merrill's. Pursuant to the lease and for Cummings' benefit, Merrill's agreed to provide insurance coverage—both personal injury and property damage—for its vehicles while they were being operated by Cummings' employees. In 1971, this personal injury liability coverage which Merrill's obtained through Carriers stood at approximately $3,000,000 with $500,000 of property damage coverage. In the meantime, Cummings independently procured $250,000 of liability insurance through the defendant, American.

In March of 1972, one of Cummings' employees, while negligently driving a vehicle leased from Merrill's, collided with a Lincoln Continental killing the driver and extensively damaging his automobile. Carriers, acting in good faith and in the best interests of its insured, settled a wrongful death claim for $200,000 and a property damage claim for approximately $8,000. Both prior and subsequent to the settlement, American refused Carriers' demand for contribution. Thereafter, Carriers instituted the present action and received a judgment against the defendant for approximately $104,000. Both Carriers and American had "other insurance" clauses in their insurance policies. Carriers' contract stated:

OTHER INSURANCE

> If there is other insurance against an occurrence covered by this policy the insurance afforded by this policy shall be deemed *excess insurance* over and above the applicable limits of all such other insurance. (emphasis supplied.)

American's policy contained an endorsement specifically covering "hired automobiles" which provided:

OTHER INSURANCE

> This insurance shall be *excess insurance* over any other valid and collectible insurance for Bodily Injury Liability for Property Damage Liability and for Automobile Medical Payments. (emphasis supplied.)

Faced with these competing clauses, the presiding Justice disregarded them as "mutually repugnant." American assigns this as error and insists that its clause should be given preference over Carriers.

I

We begin our discussion by acknowledging the utter confusion that pervades the entire realm of "other insurance" clauses. *See Insurance Company of Texas v. Employers Liability Assurance Corp.,* 163 F.Supp. 143, 145 (S.D.Cal.1958). Originating in the property insurance field, these clauses were designed to prevent fraudulent claims induced by overinsuring. With automobiles, however, the fear of death or injury was in itself sufficient to deter specious accidents. The original purpose of other insurance clauses has little relevance, therefore, to automobile liability insurance other than to limit, reduce, or even avoid an insurer's loss in those cases where there is multiple coverage. *See* Comment, *"Other Insurance" Clauses: The Lamb-Weston Doctrine,* 47 Or.L.Rev. 430 (1968); Note, *Concurrent Coverage in Automobile Liability Insurance,* 65 Colum.L.Rev. 319 (1965). However, these clauses violate no public policy and in the absence of a statute to the contrary they will be given effect, even if the insured is unaware of the existence of the other insurance. 8 D. Blashfield, Automobile Law and Practice § 345.10 (3rd ed. 1966).

There are three basic types of other insurance clauses which regulate how liability is to be divided when multiple coverage exists. The first, a "pro-rata" clause, limits the liability of an insurer to a proportion of the total loss. The second, an "escape" clause, seeks to avoid all liability. The third, an "excess" clause, the provision used in the present case, provides that the insurance will only be excess. *See* 8 J. Appleman, Insurance Law and Practice § 4911 (Cum.Supp.1973); 7 Am.Jur.2d *Automobile Insurance* §§ 200–202 (2d ed. 1963).

No problems arise as long as only one policy contains an other insurance clause since the particular provision can be given effect as written. Complications and conflicts occur where more than one applicable policy contains an other insurance clause. In that situation, the court is faced with a battle of the clauses.

In the case at bar, each policy, in virtually identical language, states that it will be excess over any other valid and collectible insurance. Any attempt at a literal reconciliation of the clauses involves hopeless circular reasoning. One clause cannot be given effect as "excess" unless the other is considered "primary." Since both claim to be excess, neither could operate as primary and hence neither could take effect as excess. Taken to its *reductio ad absurdum* conclusion, even though each insurer concedes that its policy would have covered the loss in the absence of the other, where there is double coverage both would escape liability, a result which neither party advocates. As well stated in *State Farm Mutual Insurance Co. v. Travelers Insurance Co.,* 184 So.2d 750, 753–54 (La.App.1966) (Tate, J., concurring),

> [i]ndeed, there is actually no way by logic or word-sense to reconcile two such clauses, where each policy by itself can apply as a primary insurer, but where the clause in each policy nevertheless attempts to make its own liability secondary to that of any other policy issued by a similar primary insurer: For then the primary and (attempted) secondary liability of each policy chase the other through infinity, something like trying to answer the question: Which came first, the chicken or the egg?

Faced with this logical logjam, a number of different and conflicting methods have at various times been used to determine which policy is primary and hence which should bear the brunt of the loss. Thus, it has been stated that the primary policy is the one: covering the tortfeasor, *Employers Mutual Liability Insurance Company of Wisconsin v. Pacific Indemnity Company,* 167 Cal.App.2d 369 (1959); issued prior in time, *Automobile Insurance Company of Hartford v. Springfield Dyeing Company,* 109 F.2d 533 (3d Cir.1940); insuring the vehicle's owner, *Farm Bureau Mut. Automobile Ins. Co. v. Preferred Acc. Ins. Co.,* 78 F.Supp. 561 (W.D.Va.1948); whose policy covered the particular loss more specifically, *Trinity Universal Insurance Co. v. General Accident, Fire & Life Assurance Corp.,* 138 Ohio St. 488 (1941); or whose other insurance clause is written in more general terms, *Zurich General Accident & Liability Insurance Co. v. Clamor,* 124 F.2d 717 (7th Cir.1941).

Seizing on one of these approaches, American argues that Carriers' policy should be construed as primary based upon minute differences in the language of the excess insurance clauses. We prefer not to engage in such semantic microscopy. "It [merely] encourages the continuing draftsmanship battle by which insurers seek still more specific policy terms, and the end is not in sight." Note, *Concurrent Coverage in Automobile Liability Insurance, supra* at 322. Fairly read, each insurer, through its excess clause, seeks to place the initial loss on any other applicable insurance, saving for itself a role as secondary insurer.

As an alternative argument, American asserts that the intent of the underlying parties should be given effect. Merrill's, for valuable consideration, contractually agreed to insure Cummings.[1] Merrill's insurance should therefore be considered primary.

We disagree.

American's argument would be well taken were this suit simply one for breach of contract between Cummings and Merrill's. We fail, however, to see the relevance in this case of the lease agreement to which the insurers were neither parties nor beneficiaries. The only appropriate considerations are the two insurance policies through which the respective insurers and insureds manifested their contractual intent. *See Farm Bureau Mutual Insurance Co. v. Waugh,* 159 Me. 115 (1963). An examination of the policies issued is the single criteria [sic] for analyzing an insurer's obligations which can neither be enlarged nor diminished beyond the terms employed. *Limberis v. Aetna Casualty & Surety Co., Me.,* 263 A.2d 83 (1970). A determination of the primary insurer must turn, therefore, upon a construction of the insurance contracts and not upon a collateral agreement between an insured and a third party. * * *

We perceive no methodology which is neither arbitrary nor utterly mechanical by which we could rationally resolve the enigma of which policy should be given effect over the other. Both clauses attempt to occupy the same legal status. Any construction this Court renders

---

[1] In pertinent part, the lease provided:

F. INSURANCE COVERAGE AND LIABILITY

Subject to the following conditions, MERRILL shall provide, at its expense, insurance coverage for its benefit and the benefit of CUMMINGS and the drivers and/or operator of CUMMINGS.

1. All rental units described in Schedule A including any emergency spares or other vehicles or trailers of MERRILL's used by CUMMINGS under the terms hereof will be covered, for the benefit of CUMMINGS and its operating and driving personnel:

(a) Personal injury, [$2,990,000.00].

(b) Property damage, $500,000.00.

2. CUMMINGS shall not be liable to MERRILL for any damages or injuries sustained to the rental units described in Schedule A while being used by CUMMINGS under the terms hereof if occasioned by:

(a) The negligent operation of CUMMINGS' drivers or operators while operating or driving said rental units in the scope of their employment with CUMMINGS.

should attempt to maintain this status quo. This goal can be achieved only by abandoning the search for the mythical "primary" insurer and insisting instead that both insurers share in the loss. Such an approach best carries out the intent of the insurers which was to reduce or limit their liability.

There are additional benefits to adopting this rule. It would introduce certainty and uniformity into the insurance industry, discourage litigation between insurers, and enable underwriters to predict the losses of the insurers more accurately. Note, *Conflicts Between "Other Insurance" Clauses in Automobile Liability Insurance Policies,* 20 Hastings L.J. 1292, 1304 (1969). We hold that where there are conflicting excess insurance clause provisions they are to be disregarded as mutually repugnant thus rendering applicable the general coverage of each policy. This, we note, is the clear majority rule.[2]

[t]here is a growing tendency in the entire picture to reject the circular reasoning, more prevalent in an earlier day, whereby the restrictive clause of one policy will be given prior effect, or one of two policies affording coverage upon different hypotheses will be deemed "specific," and, therefore, to constitute the "primary" insurance. This rejection has been strongest in cases where the conflict has been between like "other insurance" clauses. * * *

II

Having found that both policies are to be considered "primary," we are brought to the question of how should the liability be prorated where the total loss does not exceed the limits of either policy. American argues that the loss should be prorated according to the policy limits. Because Carriers provided $2,990,000 of coverage compared to only $250,000 for American, appellant contends that Carriers should bear close to ninety percent of the settlement cost. Carriers, on the other hand, argues that the loss should be shared equally between the insurers, the approach adopted by the presiding Justice.

There are three basic methods of proration. The majority rule, the one urged upon by appellant, prorates liability according to the limits contained in each policy.[3] The next, which is seldom followed, prorates on the basis of the premiums paid to each insurer.[4] Finally, there is a minority but growing number of courts which prorate the loss equally up to the limits of the lower policy,[5] the approach adopted by the court below.

Each method is grounded on the premises, often unarticulated, that on equitable principles the loss should be shared among the insurers either on the basis of the risk that they have undertaken or the benefit

---

[2] As stated in 69 A.L.R.2d, *supra* note 1 at 1123–24.

[3] *See, e.g., State Farm Mut. Auto. Ins. Co. v. General Mut. Ins. Co.,* 282 Ala. 212 (1968); *Buckeye Union Ins. Co. v. State Auto. Mut. Ins. Co., supra* note 2; *Lamb-Weston, Inc. v. Oregon Auto. Ins. Co.,* 219 Or. 130 (1959); *Pacific Indem. Co. v. Federated Am. Ins. Co.,* 82 Wash.2d 412 (1973).

[4] *Insurance Co. of Tex. v. Employers Liab. Assur. Corp., supra.*

[5] *See, e.g., Ruan Transport Corp. v. Truck Rentals, Inc.,* 278 F.Supp. 692 (D.Colo.1968); *Ryder Truck Rental, Inc. v. Schapiro & Whitehouse, Inc.,* 259 Md. 354 (1970): *Cosmopolitan Mut. Ins. Co. v. Continental Cas. Co., supra* note 2.

they have received. In its clearest expression, the majority rule has been justified on the theory that

> the burden imposed on each insurer is generally proportional to the benefit which he received, since the size of the premium is most always directly related to the size of the policy. *Lamb-Weston, Inc. v. Oregon Automobile Insurance Company, supra* note 3 at 137.

On precisely these grounds, the majority rule has been criticized since "[it] is commonly known that the cost of liability insurance does not increase proportionately with the policy limits." *Cosmopolitan Mutual Insurance Company v. Continental Casualty Co., supra* note 4 at 564. Once minimum coverage has been obtained, significant supplemental coverage can be provided at only a modest increase in cost.

On the other hand, if the majority rule is less equitable than that minority approach which apportions on the basis of premiums received, it has the advantage of facile application. Unless the multiple policies cover the identical risks, there would be too many variables affecting the premiums to permit them to serve as a benchmark for an equitable adjustment. *Nationwide Mutual Insurance Company v. State Farm Mutual Automobile Insurance Company,* 209 F.Supp. 83 (N.D.W.Va.1962).

The minority rule adopted by the presiding Justice utilizes the best aspects of both approaches without the limitations. Like the majority rule, it is easy to administer. It would simply require each company to contribute equally until the limits of the smaller policy were exhausted, with any remaining portion of the loss then being paid from the larger policy up to its limits. *Nationwide Mutual Insurance Company v. State Farm Mutual Automobile Insurance Company, supra; Dairyland Insurance Company v. Drum,* 568 P.2d 459, 464 (Colo.1977) (Carrigan, J., dissenting in part).

Unlike the majority rule, this Solomon-like approach comports with a most basic sense of justice. *See* Exodus, ch. 21, par. 35 ("When one man's ox hurts another's ox so badly that it dies, they shall sell the live ox and divide this money as well as the dead animal they shall divide equally between them.") Moreover, the majority rule unfairly discriminates against the larger policy by apportioning the loss in proportion to the respective policy limits, utterly forgetting that both insurers, by their contracts, have in fact agreed to cover a loss up to the limits of the lesser policy. Until that point is reached, the majority rule amounts to no more than an unacceptable subsidy from the high-coverage to the low-coverage carrier. We are in complete accord with the presiding Justice when he adopted the persuasive opinion of Judge Doyle in *Ruan Transport Corp. v. Truck Rentals, Inc., supra* note 5 at 696.

The majority method of prorating operates inequitably in its differentiating treatment of the high-loss and low-loss insurer. In return for a greater premium the insurer providing higher coverage has undertaken to protect the insured against accidents involving high losses. Yet because of this undertaking to protect against high loss the larger insurer is in an unfavorable position vis-a-vis the other insurer even in cases of low loss, since under the majority method of prorating the insurer affording the greater maximum coverage pays the greater segment of any loss incurred, regardless of the amount of the loss. This seems inequitable since both insurers have equally undertaken to insure against the low-loss accident.

The majority rule would hardly encourage an insurer from increasing its coverage where it is aware that there is a lesser policy. It would increase the insurer's potential liability not only in the high-risk situation which the additional premiums are presumably meant to recompense, but it would have the untoward effect of increasing liability in the more likely to occur low-risk situation. Carried to its extreme, it would further increase the cost of additional insurance thereby reducing the likelihood that an insured would choose such coverage. *See Dairyland Insurance Company v. Drum, supra,* (Carrigan, J., dissenting in part). The Court would be reluctant to adopt a rule which would seemingly have little social utility.

For all of the aforesaid reasons, the presiding Justice correctly prorated the loss between Carriers and American.

Accordingly, the entry shall be:

Appeal denied.

Judgment affirmed.

NOTES AND QUESTIONS

1. *Predictability of Result.* Some courts hold that whether an excess and a pro-rata clause are consistent depends on the precise language of the policies. See, e.g, *Yates v. Estate of Ferguson,* 2010 WL 877536 (Ohio. Ct. App. 2010); *Cincinnati Ins. Co. v. Am. Alternative Ins. Corp.,* 866 N.E.2d 326 (Ind.App. 2007). The issue arises not only in auto insurance, but in other situations where more than one liability insurance policy is applicable to the claim against the insured. See, e.g., *Wright-Ryan Constr., Inc. v. AIG Ins. Co. of Canada,* 647 F.3d 411 (1st Cir. 2011); *Jones v. Medox, Inc.,* 430 A.2d 488 (D.C. App. 1981). Would it make sense to adopt a per se rule that such policies conflict, or to interpret the particular language of each clause when disputes arise in order to determine the appropriate result? For surveys of the field, see Rory A. Goode, Self-Insurance as Insurance in Liability Policy "Other Insurance" Provisions, 56 Wash. & Lee L. Rev. 1245 (1999); Douglas R. Richmond, Issues and Problems in "Other Insurance," Multiple Insurance, and Self-Insurance, 22 Pepp. L. Rev. 1373 (1995).

2. *Methods of Coordination.* What should be the preferred method of avoiding conflicts between other insurance clauses: statutory or regulatory prescriptions regarding their terms, intra-industry cooperation to assure that clauses in different policies are consistent, or judicial interpretation of the clauses on a case-by-case basis? Note that at least in the auto insurance field, the problem has been largely solved by the adoption of standard policies containing identical "other insurance" clauses. See the Sample Personal Auto Policy, which provides (in each of its Parts) (e.g., page 4) that the coverage it provides is pro-rata with respect to the owned vehicle, and excess with respect to non-owned vehicles. Consequently, whenever a permittee is driving another party's car, the owner's policy is primary and the driver's policy is excess. This allocation yields perfect clarity, but should the priorities it adopts be reversed?

3. *Other Insurance Clauses and Rate Regulation.* In a line of insurance subject to extensive rate regulation in some states, in theory an insurer would want to argue in advance that its policies contain other insurance clauses that render them primary, but argue in subsequent coverage disputes that the clauses render the policies secondary. What, if anything, prevents insurers from doing this? How difficult would it be for an Insurance Commissioner to estimate the incidence and outcome of "other insurance" conflicts in a given line or subclass of insurance in order to evaluate insurers' arguments on this issue?

4. *Methods of Pro-Rating.* Was the court in *Carriers* correct in suggesting that pro-rating equally up to policy limits is the approach most consistent with the coverage expectations of the insurers that had issued conflicting policies? Can an estimate of these expectations be anything but circular before a rule governing the method by which coverage will be pro-rated when other insurance clauses conflict is adopted? The courts continue to split on the question whether to pro-rate up to the limits of the policy with the lower limits or to pro-rate by limits.

5. *Toward a System of Coordination.* With the proliferation of different forms and sources of insurance coverage, the possibility that there will be overlapping coverage for a single loss has increased exponentially. Although insurers issuing the policies in cases such as *Carriers* have no contract relations with or rights against each other, does it make sense to continue to treat separate insurance policies as the product of atomistic contracts? For an argument that there has developed a private insurance *system,* requiring legal intervention that creates legal relations among insurers through rules governing coordination, see Kenneth S. Abraham, Distributing Risk: Insurance, Legal Theory, and Public Policy 133–72 (1986).

C. COLLISION AND COMPREHENSIVE COVERAGE

Most purchasers of auto liability insurance elect to purchase coverage against damage to their own vehicles as well. This is first-party property insurance, much like the fire and homeowners coverage discussed in Chapter Four, but limited to the insured vehicle and other vehicles driven by the insured with the permission of the owner. The insurance is payable in the event that damage to the insured vehicle resulting from specified causes occurs, regardless of whether the cause is negligence by any third-party and regardless of any negligence by the insured or other operator of the vehicle.

Automobile property insurance comes in two forms. *Collision coverage* insures against damage to the insured vehicle caused by the upset of the vehicle or by its impact with another vehicle or object. The term "collision" also tends to be defined by reference to a set of causes which the policy specifies do not constitute collision—including fire, theft, and windstorm. The principal legal issue that arises in connection with collision coverage is whether this definition, which has the effect of excluding coverage of damage caused by certain kinds of collisions, creates a conclusive or a merely inconclusive exclusion for purposes of determining the cause of damage. For example, suppose that a windstorm upsets the vehicle, or a fire burns out the brakes while the vehicle is moving, and it collides with a tree: is collision coverage excluded?

By contrast, *comprehensive* coverage insures against loss resulting from many of the causes excluded from the definition of collision: fire, windstorm, theft, breakage of glass, vandalism, and flood, among others. For the full list, see the Sample Personal Auto Policy, Part D (page 8), where comprehensive coverage is denominated "other than collision." The obvious intent of this approach is that collision and comprehensive coverage should dovetail, but not overlap.

Two major issues have arisen in recent years governing the valuation of automobile damage losses. The first is whether, in recovering for damage to a vehicle, the diminished value of the vehicle that results from the mere fact that it has been involved in a collision should be taken into account, even if the vehicle has been completely repaired. The courts have tended to hold that diminished value is not covered, though the differences between these decisions and a number finding in favor of coverage have sometimes tended to turn on differences in policy language. See, e.g., *Culhane v. W. Nat'l Mut. Ins. Co.*, 704 N.W.2d 287 (S.D. 2005) (diminished value not covered); *Given v. Commerce Ins. Co.*, 796 N.E.2d 1275 (Mass. 2003) (same); *State Farm Mut. Auto. Ins. Co. v. Mabry*, 556 S.E.2d 114 (Ga. 2001) (diminished value is covered). It is not entirely clear whether this issue will persist, since it is a matter that could quickly be taken care of by policy revisions. A second set of issues associated with automobile physical damage involves the availability of coverage when a policyholder has purchased either Collision or Comprehensive coverage, but not both, and the loss falls on the borderline between the two. When a driver is covered by one form of coverage but not the other, some courts interpret provisions in the driver's policy to cover certain losses that the other form of coverage also would have covered. Perhaps the principal reason that policyholders purchase only comprehensive and not collision coverage (when they do) is to insure older vehicles against theft even when it would not be worth repairing them and therefore not sensible to insure them against collision.

Allison v. Iowa Mutual Insurance Company

Court of Appeals of North Carolina, 1979.
43 N.C.App. 200.

This is a civil action wherein plaintiff seeks to recover $8,500.00 under a "general automobile liability" insurance policy for damages resulting to his dump truck when the bridge upon which the truck was traveling collapsed. Defendant answered, admitting that the policy was in effect on the date of the accident, but denying that it provided coverage for the type of accident that occurred. A stipulation entered into between the parties, except where quoted, is summarized as follows:

Defendant issued an insurance policy, numbered G2075509, to plaintiff on 10 February 1975, which provided comprehensive insurance coverage on certain personal property owned by plaintiff, but did not extend collision coverage. On 31 October 1975 the plaintiff was the owner of a 1970 white, two-ton dump truck, Serial No. 735485, which was included in the personal property covered by the policy, and which was "being operated across the South Mills River Bridge No. 185 on Highlander Camp Road * * * transporting a load of gravel." As the truck was being driven across the bridge, "said bridge collapsed and the plaintiff's truck slid into the river or creek running under said bridge and turned on its right side, therein damaging said vehicle." The truck was subsequently repaired at a cost of $8,500.00. Plaintiff in due time submitted a claim to defendant for the total repair of the truck, but, except for paying $111.00 to repair the windshield, defendant "has refused to pay said claim taking the position that said damage was caused by collision and was not covered under * * * the aforesaid policy. * * *"

After considering the above stipulation, the trial judge made findings of fact in accordance therewith, drew separate conclusions of law, and entered judgment for plaintiff in the amount of $8,500.00. Defendant appealed. * * *

■ HEDRICK, JUDGE.

Defendant's exceptions to each of the trial judge's conclusions of law present for review the single question of whether the court erred in entering judgment for plaintiff. The question is not whether plaintiff's truck was covered under the policy. It was. Rather, the question is whether the event which gave rise to the damage is excluded from the kind of loss for which the policy provides protection.

Defendant argues that the collapse of the bridge resulting in damage to plaintiff's truck was an accident by collision and that the occurrence was therefore excluded from coverage since the plaintiff had not insured this vehicle against loss by collision. Plaintiff, on the other hand, contends that the collapse of the bridge did not constitute a collision and asserts that the policy includes such an occurrence under its provisions for comprehensive coverage. The relevant inquiry for this Court is thus refined into determining whether the trial judge erred in concluding that the accident occasioned by the collapse of the bridge was not a "collision" within the meaning of the policy which provides in pertinent part as follows:

> 1. The company will pay for loss to covered automobiles: COVERAGE O—COMPREHENSIVE—*from any cause except collisions;* but, for the purpose of this coverage, breakage of glass and loss caused by missiles, falling objects, fire, theft or larceny, windstorm, hail, earthquake, explosion, riot or civil commotion, malicious mischief or vandalism, water, flood, or (as to a covered automobile of the private passenger type) colliding with a bird or animal, shall not be deemed loss caused by collisions. * * * [Emphasis added.]

Elsewhere the policy defines "collision" to mean "(i) collision of a covered automobile with another object or with a vehicle to which it is attached, or (ii) upset of such covered automobile. * * *"

The principles of law with respect to the interpretation and construction of insurance policies are firmly established. As with any contract, the ultimate goal is to divine the parties' intentions at the time the policy was issued. *Woods v. Nationwide Mutual Insurance Co.,* 295 N.C. 500 (1978). Where the policy defines a term, that definition must be used. Conversely, nontechnical words which are not defined "are to be given the same meaning they usually receive in ordinary speech, unless the context requires otherwise." *Grant v. Emmco Insurance Co.*, 295 N.C. 39, 42 (1978) [citing *Wachovia Bank & Trust Co. v. Westchester Fire Insurance Co.*, 276 N.C. 348, 354 (1970); *State Farm Insurance Co. v. Shaffer,* 250 N.C. 45 (1959); *Powers v. Travelers' Insurance Co.*, 186 N.C. 336 (1923)]. Moreover, if the meaning of language "or *the effect of provisions* is uncertain or capable of several reasonable interpretations," *Woods v. Nationwide Mutual Insurance Co.*, 295 N.C. at 506 [emphasis added], such ambiguity will be resolved in favor of the insured and against the insurance company since, as it is said, the company chose the language. *Grant v. Emmco Insurance Co., supra.*

In the instant case, although the policy sets out three types of occurrences that are deemed to constitute a collision, the term itself is not defined. The word is popularly understood, however, to mean a striking together of two objects. "The term denotes the act of colliding; striking together; violent contact. * * * [It] implies an impact or sudden contact of a moving body with an obstruction in its line of motion, whether both bodies are in motion or one stationary. * * * " Black's Law Dictionary 330 (4th ed. 1968). *See also Morton v. Blue Ridge Insurance Co.*, 255 N.C. 360 (1961).

In 7 Am.Jur.2d, *Automobile Insurance* § 65 (1963), it is said:

> While the ground of a highway is considered an "object" within the meaning of a collision insurance policy, it is generally held that contact of an automobile with the roadbed itself does not constitute a "collision" with an object within the meaning of the term as used in a collision insurance policy.

Furthermore, in a case which presents strikingly similar facts to the case at bar, the Florida Supreme Court held that the giving way of the roadbed over which the plaintiff's car was traveling, resulting in the car's sliding down into the soft sand under the road and getting stuck, was not a collision within the popular and usual meaning of the term. *Aetna Casualty & Surety Co. v. Cartmel,* 87 Fla. 495 (1924).

With reference to defendant's contention that the event giving rise to the damage in this case was a "collision", we have carefully considered each case upon which defendant purports to rely and find only one of them to be worthy of comment. Our Supreme Court held, in *Morton v. Blue Ridge Insurance Co., supra,* that a collision, within the meaning of that term as used in the policy being construed there, resulted when the plaintiff's automobile suddenly rolled backwards into a canal. The car had been backed down a launching ramp to launch a boat from a trailer hooked to the rear of the car. While the driver and passengers were lowering the boat into the water, the unattended and previously stationary car suddenly rolled into the water. When the insurance company refused to honor his claim, plaintiff brought suit, and the Court held that the car's striking of the water in the canal and of the bottom of the canal was a collision, entitling plaintiff to recover under the collision provisions of the policy.

We find this case to be readily distinguishable on its facts. The impetus of the accident in *Morton* was obviously occasioned by the manner in which the vehicle was being used. Although there was no evidence regarding what caused the car to suddenly roll backwards, the driver had driven it onto and parked it on the ramp, thereby initiating the chain of events that culminated in the collision of his car with the bottom of the canal. Conversely, in the present case, there is plainly no element of driver control. Nothing the operator of the truck did can be said to have set in force the succeeding events. The collapse of the bridge, and that occurrence only, engendered the consequent accident and damage. We think the cases are clearly distinguishable and find the *Morton* case to be inapposite.

In the case at bar, we hold that the collapse of the bridge upon which plaintiff's truck was being operated, resulting in the truck's sliding down into the river or creek underneath the bridge and thereby being damaged, was not a "collision" either within the usual meaning of the term or as contemplated by the policy and the parties. Since it is not disputed that the policy provides coverage for losses arising from all causes except collision, it follows that the losses suffered under the circumstances here are covered, and the company is liable on plaintiff's claim. Thus, in the conclusions and judgment of the trial judge, we find no error.

Affirmed.

Rodemich v. State Farm Mutual Automobile Insurance Company

Court of Appeals of Arizona, 1981.
130 Ariz. 538.

■ EUBANK, JUDGE.

The main issue to be decided on this appeal is whether the trial court erred in directing a verdict in favor of the appellees on the issue of comprehensive insurance coverage.

The appellees, Mr. and Mrs. Rodemich, were owners of a 1973 Winnebago motor home. On May 7, 1975, Mr. Rodemich was driving the motor home at approximately 15–20 m.p.h. on a paved two-lane road in Alamo State Park, Arizona. According to Mr. Rodemich, a gray four-legged animal, approximately four feet high, suddenly appeared in the roadway. Mr. Rodemich swerved to avoid hitting the animal, causing the motor home to go off the road where it rolled over and was severely damaged. Neither the animal nor any of its hair or blood were found on or near the motor home.

At the time of the accident, the appellees had allowed their collision policy to lapse and retained only comprehensive coverage on the Winnebago. That coverage afforded the appellees the following protection:

COVERAGE D—COMPREHENSIVE

(1) The Owned Motor Vehicle. To pay for *loss* to the *owned motor vehicle* EXCEPT *LOSS* CAUSED BY *COLLISION* but only for the amount of each such *loss* in excess of the deductible amount, if any, stated in the declarations as applicable thereto. The deductible amount

shall not apply to *loss* caused by a fire or by a theft of the entire vehicle. Breakage of glass, or *loss* caused by missiles, falling objects, fire, theft, larceny, explosion, earthquake, windstorm, hail, water, flood, malicious mischief or vandalism, riot or civil commotion or colliding with birds or animals shall not be deemed to be *loss* caused by collision.

(underlined in the policy—indicating defined terms).

Appellees filed a claim under this provision eight months after the rollover incident occurred. Appellant insurance carrier repudiated any liability under the policy except for glass breakage. Appellees then commenced this action on July 29, 1976, asserting coverage under the comprehensive provision (Coverage D, *supra*) and seeking damages for the damaged Winnebago.

The matter was tried to a jury. After the plaintiffs-appellees rested their case, appellant moved for a directed verdict on the grounds that there existed no competent evidence of any actual contact between the Winnebago and an animal, and that since no contact occurred, no comprehensive coverage under the policy could exist. The trial court denied this motion. The trial continued and at the close of all the evidence, appellees moved for a directed verdict on the coverage issue and the court granted this motion. In granting it the trial judge stated that a "swerving to miss an animal was covered by the policy." He further stated that whether or not an animal was present at the time to cause the accident was a fact question for the jury. Thus the issue of the presence or nonpresence of an animal went to the jury. The jury found in favor of the appellees and assessed damages against the defendant in the amount of $10,000. Judgment was entered pursuant to the verdict. Appellant then filed a motion for new trial and/or judgment notwithstanding the verdict, which was denied. This appeal followed.

Appellant first contends that the trial court erred in directing a verdict in appellees' favor because the court equated a "near miss" with a "collision" thereby withdrawing the coverage issue from the jury's consideration. Appellees, on the other hand, take the position that "as a matter of law, in interpreting an insurance contract, there is no difference between an actual collision with an animal and a near collision with an animal which the insured successfully avoids when in both situations the collision or avoidance results in a subsequent collision or upset." * * *

In the case *sub judice,* the comprehensive provision protected appellees against loss to the motor home except loss caused by collision. The term "collision" is defined in Section II of the policy as follows:

Collision—means collision of a motor vehicle covered by this policy *with another object* or with a vehicle to which it is attached or *upset of such motor vehicle.* (Emphasis added).

However, a "loss caused by * * * *colliding* with birds or animals shall not be deemed to be loss caused by collision." (Emphasis added). Hence, Coverage D. provides that a loss caused by *colliding* with an animal would be within the comprehensive coverage. We believe that the policy's use of the term "colliding," rather than the term "collision" which was specifically defined in the policy, indicates that, "collision" and "colliding" are not the same thing under the policy. "Collision" is defined to include "upsets" of the covered vehicle, regardless of the cause, and therefore does not require any contact between the vehicle and any other object. Because the policy used the different term "colliding" in excluding from the definition of "collision" any "loss caused by * * * colliding with birds or animals," we believe that the terms of the policy indicate that the parties intended "colliding with * * * animals" to be read in its ordinary dictionary sense and thus to require an actual striking, clashing, or coming together of the motor home and an animal. Therefore, unless the motor home actually struck the animal, there was no "loss caused by * * * colliding with * * * animals." Instead, the motor home suffered an upset, within the definition of "collision" excluded from the comprehensive coverage.

Appellees, however, contend that coverage exists in this fact situation "where imminent collision with an animal precipitates evasive action all of which directly and proximately results in a collision or upset." Appellees acknowledge that there are no cases directly on point relating to this fact situation, but cite a number of cases and authorities holding and stating that where a risk insured against operates to subject the insured property to a risk not insured against, the loss is covered. *Rust Tractor Co. v. Consolidated Constructors, Inc.,* 86 N.M. 658 (1974); Annot. 160 A.L.R. 946 (1946); 5 Appleman, *Insurance Law and Practice,* § 3803 (1970). The simple answer to this contention is that the policy *sub judice* did not insure appellees against the risk of collision and therefore the cited authorities are not particularly helpful. We find that the language of the policy governs the coverage here, and that unless the motor home actually struck the animal, the loss caused by the upset of the motor home was within the policy's exclusion for loss caused by "collision." Therefore we find as a matter of law that appellees' loss is not covered under the comprehensive coverage of the policy unless in fact the motor home struck an animal, as appellees allege.

A directed verdict is justified only where the evidence is insufficient to support a contrary verdict or so weak that the court would feel constrained to set aside the verdict. *Pruett v. Precision Plumbing,* 27 Ariz.App. 288 (1976). At the trial, appellee stated that he heard a "thump," presumably caused by his motor home striking the animal, directly before the wheels of the motor home went off the pavement. On the other hand, no blood or hair was found on the motor home or on the highway. We believe that reasonable minds could differ as to whether this evidence showed that appellees' motor home actually struck an animal. Because coverage in this case depends on whether the motor home actually struck an animal, we hold that the trial court erred in granting a directed verdict to appellees on the issue of coverage where that proper fact issue was not presented and determined by the jury.

The remaining issues raised in the brief were waived at oral argument by appellant and will not be discussed.

Since the trial court erred in determining the coverage under the policy, and in instructing the jury, the matter is reversed and remanded for a new trial.

NOTES AND QUESTIONS

1. *The Boundary Between Collision and Comprehensive.* Several methods of distinguishing collision from comprehensive coverage are available. One is simply to construe the term "collision" according to ordinary usage. Another is to apply collision coverage to operational risks and comprehensive to non-operational risks. A third is to distinguish between the application of force to the vehicle independently of the vehicle's momentum and the application of force in which the vehicle's momentum is also a substantial contributing cause. How satisfactory are these tests? Sometimes the differences promote extreme legal creativity. See, e.g., *McKay v. State Farm Mutual Auto. Insurance Co.*, 933 F.Supp. 635 (S.D. Tex. 1995), in which the court rejected the insured's argument that damage caused by a drunk pedestrian was the result of a collision with an animal.

2. *Colliding With an Animal.* Does *Rodemich* hold that under comprehensive coverage, colliding with an animal does not constitute a collision, but that the results of avoiding a collision with an animal can constitute a collision? Is this a sensible way to structure the two forms of coverage?

3. *The Purpose of the Coverage.* Collision coverage is generally sold subject to a deductible; often comprehensive coverage is not—it is "first-dollar" coverage. Does this difference imply anything about the kinds of losses the two forms of insurance are intended to cover? For example, could it be argued that because drivers normally do not want to repair small dents, they purchase collision coverage subject to a deductible, but that the kinds of losses covered by comprehensive coverage—broken windshields, flooded radiators, stolen radios—always need repair or replacement? Is this distinction powerful enough to resolve disputes that are not clearly resolved by the language in policies affording collision and comprehensive coverage?

D. UNINSURED MOTORISTS COVERAGE

Allstate Insurance Co. v. Boynton
Supreme Court of Florida, 1986.
486 So.2d 552.

■ EHRLICH, JUSTICE.

In this uninsured motorist case, Allstate Insurance Company seeks review of the decision of the District Court of Appeal, Fifth District, in *Boynton v. Allstate Insurance Co.*, 443 So.2d 427 (Fla. 5th DCA 1984). Acknowledging conflict with *Centennial Insurance Co. v. Wallace*, 330 So.2d 815 (Fla. 3d DCA), *cert. denied,* 341 So.2d 1087 (Fla.1976), the district court reversed a summary judgment that had been entered in favor of the uninsured motorist insurance carrier. * * *

We quash the district court's decision. We agree with the district court that a vehicle may be an "uninsured motor vehicle" under section 627.727(1), Florida Statutes (Supp.1978),[1] even when it is covered by a

---

[1] Section 627.727(1) provides in pertinent part:

(1) No automobile liability insurance covering liability arising out of the ownership, maintenance, or use of any motor vehicle shall be delivered or issued for delivery in this state with respect to any motor vehicle registered or principally garaged in this state unless

liability insurance policy, if that policy does not provide coverage for the particular occurrence that caused plaintiff's damages. However, we also hold that the phrase "legally entitled to recover" in the context of section 627.727(1) does not encompass claims where the uninsured tortfeasor is immune from liability because of the Workers' Compensation Law, chapter 440; Florida Statutes.

In this case, the plaintiff, Richard Boynton, was employed by Sears, Roebuck & Company as an auto mechanic. While on the job, Boynton was struck and injured by a car on which his co-employee, James Luke, was working. The car was leased to Xerox Corporation and was left at the Sears Auto Center for repairs. Boynton first brought suit against Sears, Xerox, and their insurance carriers. He voluntarily dismissed his suit against Sears and its insurer because Sears was immune from tort suit under section 440.11, Florida Statutes.[2] The trial court granted summary judgment in favor of Xerox and its insurer based on *Castillo v. Bickley,* 363 So.2d 792 (Fla.1978). That case held that an automobile owner, absent his own negligence, is not liable for the negligent operation of a vehicle left at a repair shop. Boynton then sought to recover damages from Luke's automobile liability insurance carrier, but that carrier denied coverage because of a provision in Luke's policy excluding injuries occurring during the pursuit of a business.

Boynton then amended his complaint to allege that Luke was an uninsured motorist and sought to recover under his own uninsured motorist policy with Allstate.[3] The trial court entered summary

---

coverage is provided therein or supplemental thereto for the protection of persons insured thereunder who are *legally entitled to recover damages from owners or operators of uninsured motor vehicles* because of bodily injury, sickness, or disease, including death, resulting therefrom. However, the coverage required under this section shall not be applicable when, or to the extent that, any insured named in the policy shall reject the coverage. (Emphasis added.)

[2] (1) The liability of an employer prescribed in s. 440.10 shall be exclusive and in place of all other liability of such employer to any third-party tortfeasor and to the employee, the legal representative thereof, husband or wife, parents, dependents, next of kin, and anyone otherwise entitled to recover damages from such employer at law or in admiralty on account of such injury or death, except that if an employer fails to secure payment of compensation as required by this chapter, an injured employee, or the legal representative thereof in case death results from the injury, may elect to claim compensation under this chapter or to maintain an action at law or in admiralty for damages on account of such injury or death. In such action the defendant may not plead as a defense that the injury was caused by negligence of a fellow servant, that the employee assumed the risk of the employment, or that the injury was due to the contributory negligence or comparative negligence of the employee. The same immunities from liability enjoyed by an employer shall extend as well to each employee of the employer when such employee is acting in furtherance of the employer's business and the injured employee is entitled to receive benefits under this chapter. Such fellow-employee immunities shall not be applicable to an employee who acts, with respect to a fellow employee, with willful and wanton disregard or unprovoked physical aggression or with gross negligence when such acts result in injury or death or such acts proximately cause such injury or death, nor shall such immunities be applicable to employees of the same employer when each is operating in the furtherance of the employer's business but they are assigned primarily to unrelated works within private or public employment.

[3] In Boynton's uninsured motorist policy, Allstate agreed that:

We will pay damages for bodily injury, sickness, death or disease which you are *legally entitled to recover from the owner or operator of an uninsured auto.* Injury must be caused by accident and arise out of the ownership, maintenance or use of an uninsured or underinsured auto. (Emphasis added.)

judgment in favor of Allstate. On appeal from this judgment, Boynton raised two issues:

> (1) Is a vehicle an uninsured vehicle when a policy of liability insurance covers it, but the policy does not provide coverage for the particular occurrence?
>
> (2) Is the insured "legally entitled to recover" from the operator of an insured motor vehicle when there is a statutory bar to an action against the operator, but for which bar, recovery would lie?

The Fifth District reversed. It held that in the context of the Florida uninsured motorist statute, a vehicle is an "uninsured vehicle" when a policy of liability insurance covers it, but the policy does not provide coverage for the particular occurrence and that an insured is "legally entitled to recover" from the operator of an insured motor vehicle when there is a statutory bar to an action against the operator, but for which bar, recovery would lie.

First Issue

Allstate asserts that the vehicle in question was not "uninsured" because Xerox had a liability insurance policy that would have provided coverage if Boynton had a cause of action against Xerox. We reject this argument. The fact that an owner or operator of a motor vehicle has a liability insurance policy does not always mean that the vehicle is insured in the context of section 627.727(1). A vehicle is insured in this context only when the insurance in question is available to the injured plaintiff. It is undisputed that Xerox was without fault as a matter of law and that it could not be held responsible for Luke's negligence. That being the case, Xerox's liability insurance was not available to Boynton. In the context of Boynton's uninsured motorist claim, it cannot be said that this was an insured motor vehicle just because Xerox had liability insurance coverage.

Allstate next asserts that the vehicle in question was not "uninsured" because Luke also had a liability insurance policy. We likewise reject this contention. Luke's policy specifically excluded injuries occurring in the pursuit of a business. This exclusion is applicable to the facts of this case. Luke's policy, therefore, did not provide coverage for this particular occurrence.

An analogous situation is found in *American Fire & Casualty Co. v. Boyd*, 357 So.2d 768 (Fla. 1st DCA 1978). In that case, Boyd was injured in an automobile accident caused by the negligence of Hansen. Hansen had a liability policy which excluded coverage while traveling on military orders, which is what he was doing at the time of the accident. The district court correctly found that Hansen's automobile was "uninsured" in the context of Boyd's uninsured motorist policy and permitted him to recover motorist benefits. The district court reasoned:

> Although Hansen had procured a policy of insurance, that policy afforded no coverage because of the exclusionary clause; and the mere fact that Hansen was in such a position as to cause to be invoked by his negligence the provisions of the Federal Tort Claims Act does not mean that he is thereby "insured" within the meaning of the statute.

Id. at 769. The availability of a collateral remedy, the Federal Tort Claims Act in *Hansen,* workers' compensation in this case, likewise does not render a vehicle "insured."

In the present case, we hold that in the context of Boynton's uninsured motorist policy, the motor vehicle which injured him was "uninsured." Xerox's policy afforded no coverage because Xerox was without fault as a matter of law. Luke's liability policy afforded no coverage because of the policy exclusion.[4]

Second Issue

Although the vehicle was technically uninsured as to respondents, section 627.727(1) and the policy endorsement still require the policyholder be "legally entitled to recover" from the owner or operator of the uninsured vehicle. The plain meaning of the requirement would appear to be that the insured must have a claim against the tortfeasor which could be reduced to judgment in a court of law. The district court, however, construes the phrase in more limited fashion:

> The majority of courts which have construed the words "legally entitled to recover" have construed them to mean simply that the insured must be able to establish fault on the part of the uninsured motorist which gives rise to the damages and to prove the extent of the damages. See, *e.g., Winner v. Ratzlaff,* 211 Kan. 59 (1973), and cases cited in Anno., 73 A.L.R.3d 632, 649. Recovery may be had under this coverage when the claimant shows conduct on the part of the tortfeasor which would entitle the claimant to recover damages, even though a defense available to the tortfeasor would defeat actual recovery.

Boynton v. Allstate, 443 So.2d 427, 430 (Fla. 5th DCA 1984). However, none of the cases cited in support of this interpretation were decided in the context of a statutory bar by a workers' compensation law.

For instance, in *Winner v. Ratzlaff* the issue was not even whether some statutory bar to recovery against the tortfeasor prevented recovery from the insurer, but rather whether the insured could sustain a direct action against his insurer. The insured had originally sued only the tortfeasor, but after discovery revealed the defendant was uninsured, the insured added his UM carrier as a defendant. He then sought to dismiss the tortfeasor from the suit. The Kansas Supreme Court held it was error for the trial judge to refuse to dismiss the tortfeasor. The court reasoned that the Kansas uninsured motorist law had been enacted, in part, to avoid any requirement that a judgment be had against the tortfeasor before liability would arise against the UM carrier. In reaching this conclusion, the court discussed the phrase at issue here.

---

[4] Allstate, citing *Reid v. State Farm Fire & Casualty Co.,* 352 So.2d 1172 (Fla.1977), asserts in its brief that a valid exclusion in a liability policy does not make a vehicle uninsured for uninsured motorist purpose. In *Reid* we held that a vehicle cannot be both an insured and uninsured vehicle under the *same* policy. The present case is distinguishable because it involves separate policies. *Reid* is inapplicable.

Also, denial of coverage of Luke's carrier renders the vehicle uninsured within the express terms of Boynton's Allstate policy, which provides: "An uninsured auto is * * * [a] motor vehicle for which the insurer denies coverage. * * *."

> We construe the words "legally entitled to recover as damages" to mean simply that the insured must be able to establish fault on the part of the uninsured motorist which gives rise to the damages and to prove the extent of those damages. This would mean in a direct action against the insurer the insured has the burden of proving that the other motorist was uninsured, that the other motorist is legally liable for damage to the insured, and the amount of this liability. *In resisting the claim the insurer would have available to it, in addition to policy defenses compatible with the statute, the substantive defenses that would have been available to the uninsured motorist such as contributory negligence, etc.*

211 Kan. at 64 (citation omitted, emphasis added). The district court was correct in noting that the insured need only show fault and damages, but neglected to note the qualification that the insurer has available all substantive defenses the tortfeasor could have raised.

The *Winner* court looked to the cogent observations of a commentator on UM law in reaching its conclusion. His explanation of the origins of UM coverage sheds light on the problem before us.

> The antecedent of the uninsured motorist endorsement * * * can be found in the unsatisfied judgment insurance first offered in about 1925 by the Utilities Indemnity Exchange. This insurance provided indemnification when the insured showed both (1) that he had reduced a claim to judgment and (2) that he was unable to collect the judgment from the negligent party. Such insurance was available from several companies during the years from 1925 and 1956. When the uninsured motorist coverage became generally available, the unsatisfied judgment insurance was abandoned. *It should be noted that the uninsured motorist endorsement—as proposed and subsequently issued—differed significantly from its predecessor in that it eliminated the requirement that the insured obtain a judgment against the uninsured motorist prior to recovering under his policy.* A. Widiss, *A Guide to Uninsured Motorist Coverage* § 1.9 (1969) (emphasis added) (hereinafter cited as *Widiss*).

Uninsured motorist coverage therefore arose in the context of providing a less cumbersome method for an insured to receive payment from the party with the ultimate financial responsibility, the insurer. UM coverage, with its normal procedure of settling disputes through arbitration, would save both the insured and insurer the time and expense of a trial against the uninsured motorist, and would also help the insurer avoid the complications inherent in a trial where the interests of the tortfeasor and the insurer may not necessarily coincide.

None of this suggests that UM coverage was developed to expand the coverage previously provided by unsatisfied judgment insurance. Indeed, *Widiss* notes that "[t]he insurance industry conceived and developed the uninsured motorist endorsement in an attempt to forestall the enactment of state legislation directed at either creating compulsory insurance requirements or otherwise altering the character of the then-existing insurance market in order to deal with the hazard created by [financially irresponsible] uninsured motorists." *Widiss* at § 1.12. It seems unlikely that the companies would deliberately relinquish valid substantive defenses when it was wholly unnecessary to do so to achieve the goal of protecting against financially irresponsible motorists. Widiss also observes that in most states where UM coverage has been made mandatory subsequent to its development, the legislation has merely required a UM endorsement. While Florida's section 627.727 does go into some detail regarding UM coverage, the first sentence of the statute, containing the language at issue here, merely defines UM coverage in terms sufficient to identify it as such. This does not suggest any legislative intent to expand UM coverage beyond that contemplated by the insurance-industry-developed endorsement.

The legislature wisely enacted a scheme whereby a motorist may obtain a limited form of insurance coverage for the uninsured motorist, by requiring that every insurer doing business in this state offer and make available to its automobile liability policyholders UM coverage in an amount equal to the policyholder's automobile liability insurance. The policyholder pays an additional premium for such coverage. The uninsured motorist statute provides that coverage is "for the protection of persons insured thereunder who are legally entitled to recover damages from owners or operators of uninsured motor vehicles because of bodily injury." § 627.727(1). The UM coverage, in purpose and effect, provides a limited form of insurance coverage up to the applicable policy limits for the uninsured motorist. The carrier effectually stands in the uninsured motorist's shoes and can raise and assert any defense that the uninsured motorist could urge. In other words, UM coverage is a limited form of third party coverage inuring to the limited benefit of the tortfeasor to provide a source of financial responsibility if the policyholder is entitled under the law to recover from the tortfeasor. It is not first party coverage even though the policyholder pays for it. In first party coverage, such as medical, collision or theft insurance, fault is not an element. The insurance carrier pays even though the policyholder is totally at fault. With UM coverage, the carrier pays only if the tortfeasor would have to pay, if the claim were made directly against the tortfeasor.

One involved in an accident with an uninsured motorist can bring a common law action against the uninsured motorist, if he so desires. The uninsured motorist can of course defend and interpose any defense available to him at law including contributory negligence and the exclusiveness of worker's compensation. If the injured party recovers a judgment, he may endeavor to satisfy his judgment from the tortfeasor's assets. However, the insured motorist may opt to make claim against his UM carrier instead of suing the tortfeasor. In so doing he has a policy prerequisite, namely, proof that the tortfeasor is uninsured. The tortfeasor may be financially responsible, but if he is without insurance or has not complied with the self-insurance provisions of the statutes, the injured party may make claim against his UM carrier. The insurer is subrogated to any sum that it pays the policyholder under the UM coverage and may bring suit against the uninsured motorist to recover all sums it has paid its insured under the UM policy. The subrogation right would be frustrated if the insurer were forced to pay claims when it would be barred by a substantive defense from winning a judgment against a tortfeasor.

The district court and respondent dispute the argument that the case is controlled by the proposition that the insurer stands in the shoes of the tortfeasor. The court relied in part on *Sahloff v. Western Casualty & Surety Co.,* 45 Wis.2d 60 (1969), which held that the expiration of the statute of limitations which would bar an action against the tortfeasor did not bar an action against the insurer when the suit was brought before expiration of the statute of limitations for contract actions. From the portion of *Sahloff* quoted by the district court, it is clear the Wisconsin court relied heavily on the notion that the relationship between insurer and insured arises in contract, not tort. *See also Mendlein v. United States Fidelity & Guaranty Co.,* 277 So.2d 538 (Fla. 3d DCA 1973) (the district court did not dispute the assumption of all parties that the contract statute of limitations controlled the UM claim at issue). Also, while substantive defenses are available to the insurer, *Winner,* a procedural defense such as a statute of limitations is not necessarily also available. However, the statute of limitations issue is not before us, and we reserve a decision on this for a later day. It is enough that we here find that the insurer has the tortfeasor's substantive defenses available, and we need not decide whether this is to the exclusion of some or all procedural defenses.

There is another reason for our decision here. Widiss writes, in the context of whether the insurer should be able to claim the protection of the tortfeasor's tort immunities:

> The issue raised by such immunities is whether, for purposes of the uninsured motorist coverage, the claimant is "legally entitled to recover" as contemplated in the endorsement. * * *
>
> Professor Prosser states that "such immunity does not mean that conduct which would amount to a tort on the part of other defendants is not equally tortious in character, but merely that for protection of the particular defendant or interests which he represents, he is given absolution from liability." [W. Prosser, *Law of Torts* 996 (3d ed. 1964).] Professor Prosser's language seems to suggest that the insured party *is* legally entitled to recover, but that the immunity involved absolves the defendant from liability. * * *
>
> Attempting to resolve this issue as a problem in semantics—that is, over whether the claimant is "legally entitled"—is not especially productive. * * * To the extent that there is a strong interest in protecting the insurance company's right of subrogation following the payment of a claim, there is a persuasive reason why the existence of an immunity from liability should mean that the insurer will not be liable under the policy. On the other hand, to the extent that the objective of providing indemnification is a stronger policy in this context, the technicality of whether the tortfeasor is immune from litigation assumes a much smaller degree of importance. It seems probable that in those states where the trend is to assure that a source of indemnification is available, the courts are likely to reject an argument as to the

applicability of such tort immunities. However, it may not be appropriate to attempt to speak of all these immunities as an undivided group. For example, in a jurisdiction which affirms the importance of the interspousal immunity, the court might well be inclined to distinguish this type of case on the basis that the policy and goals underlying the establishment of this type of immunity are sufficiently important to warrant separate consideration and treatment.

Widiss at § 2.27 (footnotes deleted, emphasis in original). In Florida a source of indemnification for a worker injured by a co-worker driving an uninsured vehicle is already available, i.e. the benefits of the Workers' Compensation Law. Society's goal of protecting the worker under this circumstance has been achieved. We do not need to torture the meaning of a statute aimed at curing another ill entirely to provide a remedy where one has already been provided.

In addition, the immunity offered through workers' compensation exists not only to protect the employer in exchange for his provision of immediate, guaranteed benefits, but also to protect society by limiting the impact of a work-related injury to the remedy offered. Expanding UM coverage to cover the circumstance before us here would, as Judge Upchurch noted in his dissent in the district court, 443 So.2d at 433, create a large class of uninsured vehicles. The ensuing litigation would roil the waters in an area where the legislature has attempted to calm the seas. Absent a clear statement of intent from the legislature that it considers the benefits of broader UM coverage to outweigh the detriment, we will not disturb its clear and unambiguous statement that coverage exists only when the insured is legally entitled to recover from the tortfeasor.

Accordingly, the decision of the district court is quashed and remanded for further proceedings in accord herewith.

It is so ordered.

NOTES AND QUESTIONS

1. *Forms of UM Coverage.* In some states the purchase of UM coverage is mandatory; in certain others, purchase is not mandatory, but insurers are required to offer such coverage to any purchaser of liability insurance. A supplement to UM coverage, "underinsured motorist coverage," has developed to fill the gap between the amount of liability insurance covering the defendant and the amount of UM coverage the insured has purchased. See generally Alan Widiss, Uninsured and Underinsured Motorist Insurance (2d ed. 1985). Since the insured in *Boynton* was already covered by workers compensation and would not be entitled to duplicate recovery of his medical expenses or lost wages, why did he care whether he was also covered by his uninsured motorists insurance? The obvious answer is that, because a UM recovery replicates what is available in tort, he wanted pain and suffering damages. The availability of this form of payment under UM coverage sometimes results in farfetched efforts at recovery. See, e.g., *Mayor v. Wedding*, 2003 WL 22931354 (Ohio App. 2003), in which the claimant argued (unsuccessfully, in a victory for the credibility of our judicial system) that a cow was an uninsured motor vehicle.

2. *Subrogation as a Test.* To what extent did the district court's decision in *Boynton* in effect convert UM coverage into no-fault insurance? How much point would there be in purchasing UM coverage if its availability depended on whether the UM insurer could vindicate its subrogation rights after making payment to its insured?

3. *Arbitration of UM Disputes.* Suppose that the insured and insurer agree that the party who injured the insured was driving an uninsured vehicle, but disagree about whether the insured is "legally entitled to recover" from that driver. For example, there may be a dispute about whether that driver was negligent. Standard UM policies provide that such disputes may be arbitrated if both parties agree, which would almost certainly be the case anyway. See Sample Personal Auto Policy, Part C (page 7). What advantages are there to this approach for each party? If you were an attorney for the insured, would you prefer arbitration or trial? Some states have prohibited or invalidated policy provisions requiring arbitration of UM disputes. See, e.g., Ga.Code Ann. § 33–7–11(g); Md. Code Ann. § 19–509(j).

4. *Plain-Language UM Coverage.* How would the first issue the court in *Boynton* addressed be resolved under the definition of an uninsured motor vehicle contained in Part C of the Sample Personal Auto Policy in Section A of this Chapter (page 6): "a land motor vehicle or trailer of any type * * * to which no bodily injury liability bond or policy applies at the time of the accident."? Is the term "applies" in this definition ambiguous?

Simpson v. Farmers Insurance Company, Inc.

Supreme Court of Kansas, 1979.
225 Kan. 508.

■ PRAGER, JUSTICE.

This is an action brought by the plaintiff-appellant Yvonne Joanne Simpson, against the defendant-appellee, Farmers Insurance Company, Inc., seeking a declaratory judgment concerning the coverage and rights of the plaintiff under the uninsured motorist endorsement to an automobile insurance policy issued by the defendant to the plaintiff. The basic issue presented for determination is one of law and, simply stated, is as follows: Is the "physical contact" requirement in the "hit and run" clause in the uninsured motorist provision of an automobile insurance policy void and unenforceable as contrary to the public policy and legislative intent of the Kansas Uninsured Motorist Statute (K.S.A. 40–284)? The district court answered this question in the negative. We have concluded that it should be answered in the affirmative and, accordingly, we reverse.

For the purposes of this appeal, the facts in the case are assumed to be as follows: On December 12, 1976, the plaintiff, Simpson, was forced to drive her automobile into a ditch in order to avoid a collision with another vehicle at 34th and Steele Road in Kansas City, Kansas. After it left the highway, the automobile struck a utility pole, causing plaintiff to suffer personal injuries. The unidentified vehicle immediately fled from the scene and the identity of the driver or owner of that vehicle remains unknown. There was no actual physical contact between the unidentified vehicle and the vehicle driven by Mrs. Simpson.

Following the accident, plaintiff sought to recover under the uninsured motorist provision of her automobile insurance policy. The defendant, Farmers Insurance Company, refused to pay the claim on the basis that the insurance policy required that a recovery under that section be limited to those instances where the unidentified vehicle came into physical contact with the insured vehicle. Mrs. Simpson then brought this action for a declaratory judgment to determine whether her injuries fell within the uninsured motorist coverage of her Farmers policy. The insurance company filed a motion for summary judgment, contending that the plaintiff was not entitled to recover under the terms of the policy, because, admittedly, there was no physical contact between the unknown vehicle and the insured's vehicle. The trial court sustained the motion and granted summary judgment to the defendant. The plaintiff appealed to this court.

We should first examine the pertinent sections of the insurance policy. The policy contains the standard policy provisions relating to uninsured motorist coverage:

> "Coverage J—Uninsured Motorists (Damages for Bodily Injury) to pay all sums which the insured or his legal representatives shall be legally entitled to recover as damages *from the owner or operator of an uninsured automobile because of bodily injury,* * * * *caused by accident and arising out of the ownership, maintenance or use of such uninsured automobile* * * *" (Emphasis supplied.)

Under the definition section, an uninsured automobile is defined to include a "hit and run" automobile. A "hit and run" automobile is then defined as follows:

> "Hit and run motor vehicle means a motor vehicle which causes bodily injury *arising out of physical contact* of such motor vehicle with the insured or with the automobile which the insured is occupying at the time of the accident, provided (a) there cannot be ascertained the identity of either the operator or the owner of such 'hit and run motor vehicle,' * * *." (Emphasis supplied.)

Since, admittedly, there was no physical contact between the insured's vehicle and the "hit and run" vehicle, there would be no coverage afforded by the policy if the "physical contact" requirement is a valid and enforceable provision.

We should now consider the Kansas Uninsured Motorist Statute (K.S.A. 40–284) which provides as follows:

> "40–284. Coverage relating to injury or death caused by uninsured motorist; rejection; renewal policies; effect of prior policies. No automobile liability insurance policy covering liability arising out of the ownership, maintenance, or use of any motor vehicle shall be delivered or issued for delivery in this state with respect to any motor vehicle registered or principally garaged in this state, unless the policy contains or has endorsed thereon, a provision with coverage limits not less than the limits for bodily injury or death set forth in K.S.A.1967 Supp. 8–729, providing for payment of part or all sums which the insured or his legal representative shall be

legally entitled to recover as damages from the uninsured owner or operator of the motor vehicle because of bodily injury, sickness or disease, including death, resulting therefrom sustained by the insured, caused by accident and arising out of ownership, maintenance or use of such motor vehicle, or providing for such payment irrespective of legal liability of the insured or any other person or organization. *Provided,* That the coverage required under this section shall not be applicable where any insured named in the policy shall reject the coverage in writing: *Provided further,* That unless the insured named in the policy requests such coverage in writing, such coverage need not be provided in or supplemental to a renewal policy where the named insured had rejected the coverage in connection with a policy previously issued him by the same insurer. Provisions affording such insurance protection against uninsured motorists issued in this state prior to the effective date of this act shall, when afforded by any authorized insurer, be deemed, subject to the limits prescribed in this section, to satisfy the requirements of this section."

The primary question is whether the legislature, by the enactment of the uninsured motorist statute (K.S.A. 40–284), intended to include within the term "uninsured motorist" all hit and run drivers. In order to answer this question, we must consider the uninsured motorist statute from a historical perspective.

K.S.A. 40–284 was enacted in 1968 and has not been amended. In *Winner v. Ratzlaff,* 211 Kan. 59 (1973), this court determined the legislative purpose in enacting the statute to be as follows:

> "The purpose of legislation mandating the offer of uninsured motorist coverage is to fill the gap inherent in motor vehicle financial responsibility and compulsory insurance legislation and this coverage is intended to provide recompense to innocent persons who are damaged through the wrongful conduct of motorists who, because they are uninsured and not financially responsible, cannot be made to respond in damages." (Syl. ¶ 1.)

In *Winner,* the court also stated that, as remedial legislation, the statute should be liberally construed to provide the intended protection. The legislative purpose was again recognized in *Forrester v. State Farm Mutual Automobile Ins. Co.,* 213 Kan. 442 (1973). In *Forrester,* this court further stated in regard to the legislative intent:

> "The intent of the legislature in requiring the mandatory offering of uninsured motorist coverage was to insure that those insured under the contract of insurance would be protected generally against injuries caused by motorists who are uninsured and that such protection would complement the liability coverage." (Syl. ¶ 3.)

The court, in addition, stated that K.S.A. 40–284 becomes a part of the policy of insurance to which it is applicable to the same effect as if the provisions thereof were written out in full in the policy itself.

After the uninsured motorist statute was enacted, some insurance companies attempted to dilute the broad coverage contemplated by

K.S.A. 40–284. In *Clayton v. Alliance Mutual Casualty Co.,* 212 Kan. 640 (1973), the insurance policy contained clauses described as the "consent to sue" clause, the "arbitration" clause, the "other insurance" clause, the "proof of loss" clause, the "medical authorization" clause, and the "furnishing of medical reports" clause. All of them placed certain restrictions on the right of the insured to bring an action against the insurance company under the uninsured motorist coverage. This court held that all of the clauses were an attempt to place requirements on the insured which constituted a condition precedent to the commencement of an action to recover damages under an uninsured motorist endorsement and were void and of no effect as an attempt to condition, limit, or dilute the statutory mandate of uninsured motorist coverage under K.S.A. 40–284.

A similar problem was before the court in *Van Hoozer v. Farmers Insurance Exchange,* 219 Kan. 595 (1976). The policy involved in that case contained a provision that, in substance, stated that any loss payable under the uninsured motorist coverage should be reduced by any amount paid or payable to the insured under any workmen's compensation law, disability benefits law, or any similar law. It was held that the trial court was correct in striking down that provision since it was void and of no effect as an attempt to limit or dilute the statutory mandate of uninsured motorist coverage. The policy also contained a provision which prohibited the stacking of policies owned by the insured. This provision was also held to be invalid as being contrary to the provisions of the statute. The policy in *Van Hoozer* contained another provision which sought to define the word "insured" under the uninsured motorist coverage in such a way as to eliminate some of the coverage contemplated by the statute. This was likewise held to be invalid. *Van Hoozer,* like *Clayton,* is important to the resolution of the case now before us because it supports the rule that insurance policy provisions which purport to condition, limit, or dilute the broad, unqualified uninsured motorist coverage mandated by K.S.A. 40–284, are void and unenforceable.

In all of the cases just discussed, this court has made it crystal clear that the uninsured motorist statute is remedial in nature and should be liberally construed to provide a broad protection to the insured against all damages resulting from bodily injuries sustained by the insured, caused by an automobile accident, and arising out of the ownership, maintenance, or use of the insured motor vehicle, where those damages are caused by the acts of an uninsured motorist. A provision placed in the policy by an insurance company which denies protection to an insured for damages and injuries caused by a "hit and run" vehicle unless there is actual physical contact between the vehicles, like the various policy restrictions discussed in *Clayton* and *Van Hoozer,* is an attempt to limit or dilute the unqualified uninsured motorist coverage mandated by K.S.A. 40–284 and is therefore void and unenforceable. The rationale of *Clayton* and *Van Hoozer* is clearly applicable to such a restrictive provision.

Although, as noted above, the question is one of first impression in Kansas, the issue of the validity of the "physical contact" requirement in an insurance policy has been faced by courts of other states for quite a long period of time. See the annotation at 25 A.L.R.3d 1299 and the supplement. In most states there is a general statute requiring insurance companies to offer uninsured or unknown motorist coverage. There is, however, usually no specific statutory requirement to include coverage for "hit and run" drivers, nor a requirement that physical contact must have occurred before an insured can recover for damages due to a "hit and run" vehicle. The courts of those states have been almost unanimous in holding that the operator of a "hit and run" vehicle is an uninsured or unknown motorist. As to the physical contact issue, there is definitely a split of authority among the various states.

A number of jurisdictions hold that it is reasonable to require physical contact between a "hit and run" vehicle and the insured vehicle before coverage is allowed under the uninsured or unknown motorist provisions. * * * The rationale of those cases is based on the premise that requiring physical contact will prevent fraud upon the insurance company and will prevent recovery of damages in those cases where the insured's injuries are actually the result of his own negligence, without the intervention of any other vehicle, but the insured falsely claims that the accident was caused by an unidentified vehicle which subsequently left the scene of the accident.

The other line of authority, which now appears to be the majority rule, holds that the physical contact requirement is an impermissible limitation on the uninsured or unknown motorist statute, is contrary to public and legislative policy, and is, thus, invalid. * * *

It should be noted that in a few states the uninsured motorist statute specifically provides that, where recovery is sought for injuries caused by a hit and run vehicle, the claimant must show that there was physical contact with the unidentified vehicle. * * *

Those cases which hold the physical contact requirement to be invalid have stated a variety of reasons for its invalidity. However, the common theme of all the cases is that the uninsured or unknown motorist statute was adopted, and the clear legislative intent was, to expand insurance protection to the public who use the streets and highways. The public was to be protected from damage or injury caused by other motorists who were not insured and who could not make the injured party whole. The public was no longer to be faced with the financial calamity often caused by negligent and insolvent drivers. These cases have recognized the possibility of fraud by an insured who claims injury due to an unidentified "hit and run" driver, when, in fact, there was no such driver. A criticism of the "physical contact" requirement as an anti-fraud measure has been expressed by A. Widiss, *A Guide to Uninsured Motorist Coverage* (1969), which is quoted in *Montoya v. Dairyland Insurance Company,* 394 F.Supp. at 1340. It states:

> " 'It seems unreasonable to establish a rule under which recovery is possible if there is a minute scratch on the insured's car, but no impartial witnesses—and to deny all rights where there was no contact, even though there are many witnesses and there is no reason to suspect collusion or fraud. Some standard assuring adequate evidence in support of a claim that the injuries (for which indemnification is sought) are the result of an evasive action executed to avoid a collision with an unidentified negligent driver is certainly warranted. It

is suggested that the claimant should bear the burden of persuasion, leaving to the judge, jury or arbitrator the determination of whether the claimant has sustained the requisite burden of proof, and providing an opportunity for the insurance company to raise fraud or collusion as a defense to such a claim.'" * * *

We agree with the rationale of those cases which hold that the physical contact requirement violates the public policy of those uninsured or unknown motorist statutes which provide a broad and unrestricted protection for damage and injury caused by an uninsured motorist. We hold, therefore, that the "physical contact" requirement in the "hit and run" provisions of the automobile liability policy under consideration in this case is in derogation of the Kansas Uninsured Motorist Statute, and is therefore, void as against public policy.

The judgment of the district court sustaining the defendant's motion for summary judgment is reversed. The case is remanded to the district court with instructions to proceed to ascertain any issues remaining in the case and to determine the rights of the parties under the facts and the law.

NOTES AND QUESTIONS

1. *The Statutory Policy.* Was the policy of the Kansas legislature favoring the provision of UM coverage sufficiently precise to yield the *Simpson* decision? Did this legislative policy, as described, prohibit every limitation on recovery in a UM policy?

2. *Phantom Headlights.* The physical contact requirement is very common in UM policies. Among other purposes, it is designed to avoid the "phantom headlight" problem—possibly fraudulent claims by the insured that an oncoming vehicle came into his lane at night and that the insured swerved off the road (and into a tree or ditch) to avoid a collision. Did the Kansas statute mandate that UM policies cover accidents involving unidentifiable drivers at all? If not, then why was the failure of the Simpson policy to cover losses caused by all such drivers held to be a violation of the statute? *Simpson* is not alone in declaring the physical contact requirement against public policy. For a similar decision, see *Lowing v. Allstate Insurance Co.*, 859 P.2d 724 (Ariz. 1993). On the other hand, courts in many other states addressing the issue have upheld the physical contact requirement against public policy challenges.

Taft v. Cerwonka
Supreme Court of Rhode Island, 1981.
433 A.2d 215.

■ MURRAY, JUSTICE.

The plaintiffs, Earl W. Taft and his wife, Marian F. Taft, brought this civil action to recover for the alleged wrongful death of their daughter, Beverly A. Taft (Beverly), alleging that the negligence of the defendant Eric A. Cerwonka (Cerwonka) in operating a motor vehicle was the proximate cause of their daughter's death. Because the defendant Cerwonka, and the defendant Richard A. Miller (Miller), the owner of the vehicle, were uninsured at the time of the fatal mishap, the plaintiffs also filed a complaint against their insurer, Allstate Insurance Company (Allstate) under the uninsured-motorist provisions of their policy. Prior to trial, the two suits were consolidated. * * *

Prior to trial, plaintiffs moved for partial summary judgment on the issue of whether they would be able to "stack" the uninsured-motorist coverage provided for each automobile on the one policy underwritten by defendant Allstate. Such motion was granted by a justice of the Superior Court. The matter then proceeded to trial in the Superior Court. After all parties had rested, defendant Allstate moved for a directed verdict, stating "that if there is a verdict for the plaintiff, and I see no reason why at this juncture that the verdict for the plaintiff should not be entered, that the jury be instructed and directed that the verdict should be the minimum verdict of five thousand dollars * * *." The trial justice denied this motion and then gave his instructions to the jury, which returned a verdict in favor of plaintiffs in the sum of $33,000. Subsequently, Allstate moved for a new trial on the issue of damages, and it also moved the court to enter judgment against it in the amount of $10,000, the amount it contended was the limit of its liability under the policy issued to plaintiffs. The trial justice's denial of these motions and his entry of judgment in the amount of $20,000 (the aggregate limits of Allstate's liability) against defendant Allstate forms the basis of its present appeal.

I

In passing upon defendant's contention, we are called upon to determine an issue of first impression in this jurisdiction. That issue is whether plaintiffs should be permitted to "stack" the uninsured-motorist coverage provided for each of the two automobiles insured by Allstate.

Because the fact situations in "stacking" cases tend to be similar and because the Rhode Island uninsured-motorist statute is typical of those in other jurisdictions, decisions of other courts that have confronted this issue merit analysis here. In those jurisdictions where intra-policy stacking has been allowed,[1] courts have advanced one or more of three general theories in support of their decisions. *See* Comment, *Intra-Policy Stacking of Uninsured Motorist and Medical Payments Coverage: To Be or Not to Be,* 22 S.D.L.Rev. 349 (1977). One theory advanced is the theory that the applicable provisions of the insurance contract are ambiguous and that such ambiguities are to be resolved against the insurer. For example, in *Jeffries v. Stewart,* 159 Ind.App. 701 (1974), the Supreme Court of Indiana found an ambiguity in that the separability clause and the limits-of-liability clause conflicted with each other. The court resolved the ambiguity in favor of the insured and allowed him to stack the limits of liability. *See Id.* at 709.

Another theory cited in support of stacking is that the particular jurisdiction's uninsured-motorist statute requires such a result. Representative of this class of cases is *Tucker v. Government Employees Insurance Co.,* 288 So.2d 238 (Fla.1973). In that case, the Supreme

---

[1] Intra-policy stacking is the aggregation of the limits of liability for uninsured-motorist coverage of each car covered in one policy, whereas inter-policy stacking involves the aggregation of coverage under more than one policy.

Court of Florida held that their uninsured-motorist statute, Fla.Stat.Ann. § 627.727 (West 1977) "does not disclose any statutory basis for a 'stacking' exclusion in a policy combining auto liability coverage for two or more automobiles of the named insured with uninsured motorist coverage included." *Id.* at 241.[2] Another court in *Holloway v. Nationwide Mutual Insurance Co.,* 376 So.2d 690 (Ala.1979), held that the jurisdiction's uninsured-motorist statute *mandated* stacking for the primary insured.

A final theory is the double-premiums theory, under which courts have held that the payment of separate premiums for uninsured-motorist coverage for each vehicle covered by the policy entitles the insured to stack the limits of liability for each insured vehicle of the policy. A recent case espousing this view is *Kemp v. Allstate Insurance Co.,* Mont., 601 P.2d 20 (1979).

In the jurisdictions where intra-policy stacking has not been allowed, courts have attempted to discredit each of the above theories. In *Grimes v. Concord General Mutual Insurance Co.,* N.H., 422 A.2d 1312 (1980) the Supreme Court of New Hampshire discarded the double-premium theory, stating:

> "Neither can we agree, with confidence that the plaintiff is paying an extra premium without receiving something in return. When an insured owns two vehicles that are constantly available for use, not only by him, but by members of his family and others, the risk that someone operating one of those vehicles will be involved in an accident with an uninsured motorist is obviously greater than if only one vehicle were available for use. Consequently, an insurance carrier's exposure to that risk may be enhanced. Other courts have recognized that the second premium paid on the second car does afford some extra protection that otherwise would not exist." [Citations omitted.] *Id.* 422 A.2d at 1315.

The court went on to hold that their uninsured-motorist statute did not require intra-policy stacking.[3] * * *

It is not disputed that plaintiffs paid two separate premiums for uninsured-motorist coverage; nevertheless, Allstate contends that to allow stacking is to render a "tortured" construction of the policy and of our uninsured-motorist statute. To give credence to Allstate's contentions, however, would defeat the reasonable expectations of a policyholder.

> "It is reasonable to expect the same coverage where comparable premium dollars are paid to insure the same two cars, for convenience, under a single policy. A combination coverage should not be the predicate for an exclusion of coverage. Such a result would allow a simple change in form to defeat the insured's reasonable expectation, as well as the substance of law." [Citation omitted.] *Allstate Insurance Co. v. Maglish,* 94 Nev. 699, 703 (1978).

---

[2] We note here that the legislature in the State of Florida has since passed antistacking legislation. *See* Fla.Stat.Ann. § 627.4132 (West 1977).

[3] See N.H.Rev.Stat.Ann. § 268:15–a.

Indeed if plaintiffs had insured their automobiles under two separate policies and had paid uninsured-motorist premiums for each car, they would be entitled to $20,000 in uninsured-motorist coverage from Allstate. Under these circumstances we find persuasive the statement of dissenting Justice Douglas of the Supreme Court of New Hampshire in *Grimes v. Concord General Mutual Insurance Co.*, N.H., 422 A.2d at 1317, that

> "[i]t is an anomaly that if the same two premiums were paid to two *different* companies, we would permit *inter*-policy stacking of 'as many uninsured motorist policies as are applicable to him, up to his total damages,' *Courtemanche v. Lumbermens Mut. Cas. Co.*, 118 N.H. 168, 173 (1978), but because the two different coverages were both purchased from the same insurer, we do not." (Emphasis in original.)

Other cases have reflected the same view, *e.g., Travelers Insurance Co. v. Pac*, 337 So.2d 397 (Fla.App.1976); *Breaux v. Government Employees Insurance Co.*, 373 So.2d 1335 (La.App.1979); *Allstate Insurance Co. v. Maglish*, 94 Nev. 699 (1978).

We hold therefore that under the circumstances of this case where plaintiffs have paid two separate premiums providing each vehicle with uninsured-motorist coverage, they are entitled to recover under the uninsured-motorist provisions of the policy sums found legally recoverable up to the aggregate sum of the motor vehicles so insured. *Accord, Kemp v. Allstate Insurance Co.*, Mont., 601 P.2d 20, 24 (1979). We are careful to limit our holding on this issue to cases factually similar to the one at bar, for we foresee and rue the day when our reasoning may be twisted to achieve an absurd result. For example, what is the result to be if a plaintiff was injured while riding in an automobile which was insured as only one of a fleet of cars? We defer decision on this and related issues until a case with the appropriate factual setting presents itself for review.[4] * * *

Accordingly, the defendant's appeal is denied and dismissed. The judgment appealed from is affirmed, and the case is remanded to the Superior Court.

NOTES AND QUESTIONS

1. *Sources of Authority.* Whether inter-policy stacking is permitted should (presumably) be resolved by the "other insurance" clauses in the two potentially applicable policies. Whether intra-policy stacking is allowed, however, must be resolved by other sources of authority, within or outside the policy. What are these other sources? See, e.g., *Joslin v. Mitchell*, 584 S.E.2d 913 (W. Va. 2003) (premium discount on additional cars indicates that stacking should not be permitted); *Carrington v. St. Paul Fire & Marine Ins. Co.*, 485 N.W.2d 267 (Wis. 1992) (reasonable expectations of the insured).

---

[4] In these circumstances even in those jurisdictions where intra-policy stacking for two or three vehicles is allowed, courts have uniformly denied such an extension of the stacking theory. *See, e.g. Holloway v. Nationwide Mutual Insurance Co.*, 376 So. 2d 690 (Ala. 1979); *Ohio Casualty Insurance Co. v. Stanfield*, 581 S.W.2d 555 (Ky. 1979); *Linderer v. Royal Globe Insurance Co.*, 597 S.W.2d 656 (Mo. App. 1980); *Continental Casualty Co. v. Darch*, 27 Wash. App. 726 (1980).

2. *A Mixed Picture.* What source of law or contract did the court in *Taft* draw upon to answer the question posed? Should the language of a statute specifying the required scope of UM coverage be consulted? See, e.g., *Upshaw v. Trinity Cos.*, 842 S.W.2d 631 (Tex. 1992) (public policy reflected in the statute does not mandate stacking even where additional premiums were charged for each vehicle). If the fact that two premiums have been paid is relevant, should the language in the policy for which the premiums have been paid also be consulted? Consider the following language from Part C of the Sample Personal Auto Policy (page 7):

> The Limit of Liability shown in the Declarations for this coverage is our maximum limit of liability for all damages resulting from any one accident. This is the most we will pay regardless of the number of: * * * Vehicles or premiums shown in the Declarations.
> * * *

Does this provision definitively preclude intra-policy stacking? For a decision holding that a state statute precluding intra-policy stacking was a unconstitutional because it "violates separation of powers, infringes on fundamental rights, denies equal protection of the law, and, on its face, violates the right of substantive due process," see *Hardy v. Progressive Specialty Insurance Co.*, 67 P.3d 892, 898 (2003). See also *Phen v. Progressive N. Ins. Co.*, 672 N.W.2d 52 (S.D. 2003), holding that a policy provision limiting inter-policy stacking violated public policy.

E. AUTO NO-FAULT

Notwithstanding the effort of state legislatures and the courts to close the automobile injury compensation gap, that gap cannot be closed completely by liability or uninsured motorists insurance. Some drivers (in violation of the law) do not purchase coverage, and some cause injuries under circumstances where the stretching and pulling of coverage still will not close the gap. In addition, injury and damage caused by certain kinds of auto accidents simply cannot be compensated by liability insurance, because no one is liable for it. Automobile tort law, after all, is predicated on an act of negligence by one party that injures another party. Some accidents result even when no one has been negligent, and some are single-party accidents involving only the party injured.

Concern for the uncompensated victim during the 1950's prompted the development of medical payments coverage in the standard personal auto policy. Essentially insurance against health care costs resulting from injuries incurred in auto accidents by family members and passengers in the insured vehicle, medical payments coverage is first-party no-fault insurance: proof of negligence by another party is not required and negligence by the injured party does not preclude recovery. Although the dollar limit of this coverage typically is relatively low ($2000 is a representative limit) it was and still is a simple method of assuring victims a ready source of coverage for medical expenses without having to resort to a tort action. In many states liability insurers are required to offer such coverage to all purchasers of liability insurance. Part B of the Sample Personal Auto Policy (pages 4–5) provides such coverage.

1. MANDATORY NO-FAULT

No-fault automobile insurance systems build on the medical payments coverage model. The central idea of no-fault is that, instead of recovering from another driver under negligence law, an automobile-accident victim recovers out-of-pocket losses from his or her own insurance policy. Thus, auto no-fault consists of two-prongs: the partial abolition of tort liability and the mandatory purchase of insurance directly protecting victims for out-of-pocket damages, but not for pain and suffering. No-fault auto insurance was first proposed in full-blown form by Robert Keeton and Jeffrey O'Connell in Basic Protection for the Traffic Victim (1965), and the no-fault idea caught hold. Proponents of the no-fault system argued that it would reduce the overall cost of the system, increase the amount of money that goes to insureds, speed compensation, and distribute compensation more equitably among the parties.

A form of no-fault was first enacted in Massachusetts in 1970. By 1980, sixteen states had adopted mandatory no-fault systems. However, political backlash against auto no-fault grew, halting the trend and ultimately causing some states to repeal their no-fault laws. Currently, 12 states and Puerto Rico have mandatory no-fault auto insurance laws. For extended discussions of the underlying political, social, and legal reasons for the decline in no-fault's popularity, see Kenneth S. Abraham, The Liability Century 97–100 (2008); Nora Freeman Engstrom, An Alternative Explanation for No-Fault's "Demise, 61 DePaul L. Rev. 303 (2012).

Actual no-fault is a compromise between pure fault and pure no-fault concepts. Under the first prong of actual no-fault, tort liability is abolished for the least serious injuries, but preserved for serious injuries. This partial abolition/partial-immunity approach preserves the legal responsibility of drivers who cause substantial injury and permits the recovery of damages for pain and suffering in these cases. In effect, the smaller cases are removed from the liability system, but the larger cases remain. The distinction between injuries that are compensable only on a no-fault basis and injuries for which a cause of action in tort is preserved is drawn through the use of a "threshold." Claimants whose injuries surpass the threshold may bring tort actions; claimants whose injuries do not surpass the threshold have no cause of action in tort.

There are two types of thresholds. Most states have both and provide that satisfying either one is sufficient. A monetary threshold specifies the dollar amount of medical expenses that a claimant must incur to preserve her cause of action in tort. A verbal threshold lists the various "serious" injuries that qualify for recovery in tort regardless of the medical expenses incurred to treat them. Other than soft tissue injuries and simple fractures, most injuries of any seriousness typically qualify. But since the vast majority of auto-related injuries are not "serious" in this sense, the size of the monetary threshold is critically important. There is considerable variation. These thresholds are as low as a few hundred dollars in some states and as high as several thousand dollars in others.

The result is that in low-threshold states only the most modest tort claims are precluded, while in other states only the most serious are permitted. The effect of this difference, however, depends in part on how the second, mandatory-insurance prong of no fault is handled. If the minimal level of insurance—often referred to as Personal Injury Protection or "PIP"—is high (e.g. $50,000) then most victims are automatically entitled to recover most of their out-of-pocket losses from their own insurance company and typically do so. Since no-fault statutes normally offset tort recoveries by the amount of prior insurance payments (i.e. reverse the collateral source rule with respect to no-fault benefits), for these victims the major effect of preserving their cause of action is that they may recover damages in tort for pain and suffering. In contrast, in states with low minimum levels of mandatory no-fault insurance (e.g. $2,000), many victims do not have enough of their own insurance to cover their out-of-pocket losses. The preservation of a cause of action permits full recovery of out-of-pocket losses (net of PIP benefits already paid) by these victims.

The main criticisms of no-fault at the time it was being enacted, and to this day, have been that it is not fair to eliminate recovery of damages for pain and suffering and that accident rates will rise because no-fault reduces the threat of tort liability. In addition, experience with the actual operation of no-fault has shown that its basic promise of lowering insurance costs has not been fulfilled.

Proponents of no-fault have always argued that swift and certain compensation of out-of-pocket losses is what most drivers would prefer *ex ante*, even at the cost of giving up the right to sue for pain and suffering damages. Further, proponents argue, most auto accidents are the result of momentary lapses of attention that the threat of liability cannot influence very much. Typical drivers commonly commit acts of negligence every few miles; whether their negligence causes serious injury or none at all depends more on luck than on the degree of blame that can be ascribed to them. Because both victims and injurers pay into the same liability insurance pool and premiums are only very roughly calibrated to the individual driver's accident record, the sense of corrective justice resulting from negligence liability is largely symbolic. And because of the administrative cost savings it would achieve and the reduced need for attorneys, no-fault would put more money into the pockets of accident victims and less into the pockets of attorneys and insurance companies. Finally, proponents of no-fault argue that any driver who is not already sufficiently concerned for his own safety to drive carefully will not drive any less carefully once the threat of tort liability is eliminated.

By 2004, premiums in no-fault states were 50 percent higher than those in tort states. In addition, when states repealed no-fault, premiums decreased significantly. In Georgia, which repealed its no-fault legislation in 1991, insurance premiums declined 20 percent. Colorado repealed its no-fault legislation in 2003 and average auto insurance premiums dropped 35 percent from July 2003 to December 2007. Rand Institute for Civil Justice, U. S. Experience with No-Fault Insurance 59 (2010) ("Rand Report").

The Rand Report ascribes the higher cost of no-fault to two factors. First, in no-fault states, auto insurers pay for more medical services for a larger number of victims than in tort states. The Report attributes the difference to victims' knowledge that compensation is guaranteed in no fault states and to the efforts of some victims to incur sufficient medical costs to satisfy the monetary thresholds that will permit them to bring tort suits. It is unclear, however, whether victims in no-fault states are consuming "too much" health care, or whether victims in tort states are consuming "too little" because their compensation is uncertain. In addition, because no-fault limited compensation for pain and suffering, no-fault originally was seen as a way of minimizing fraud. However, it has been argued more recently that the amount of fraud under no-fault is significant, perhaps because there is no legal adversary to contest damages. Rand Report at 111.

Second, according to the Rand Report, not only are auto no-fault insurers paying for more medical services; they are paying more for the same medical services than is paid in tort states, and this difference has increased over time. In 1987 medical costs paid by auto insurers were roughly comparable between no-fault and tort states. But within ten years these costs had more than doubled in no-fault states. The reasons for the difference are not entirely clear, but some explanations are plausible. In most no-fault states medical providers bill auto insurers before billing the victim's health insurer, effectively shifting costs from the health insurance system to the auto insurance system. With multiple possible sources of recovery (health insurance, auto insurance, and workers' compensation if the injury is job related) the priority-of-recovery rules in each state determine the order of payment. In no-fault states, the prevalent order is workers' compensation, followed by no-fault auto, and then other sources such as health insurance. In no-fault states, auto insurance therefore pays for a larger proportion of auto-accident related medical costs than in tort states, where first-party health insurance pays for a higher proportion.

A third reason medical costs are higher in no-fault states may be that health insurers are better able to minimize medical costs than are auto insurers. As discussed in Chapter Five, health insurers engage in various forms of managed care. Auto insurers, by contrast, are neither as adept at managing health care costs nor permitted to employ such devices as co-payment and deductible requirements.

Fourth, although no-fault was initially successful at containing litigation, this advantage has eroded over time. No-fault states boasted a lower volume of automobile cases filed until 1990, when the number of new claims in tort states dropped dramatically. By 1993, the three largest no-fault states surpassed the tort states in the amount of automobile litigation filed. Rand Report at 95–96. In addition to failing to lower the incidence of litigation, over time more victims of accidents in no-fault states have retained lawyers to resolve claims, which has also contributed to litigation costs.

On the other hand, no-fault has succeeded in its goal of providing more certain compensation to the victims of auto accidents. Accident victims in no-fault states reported receiving reimbursements five to eight percent higher than those in tort states. Rand Report at 87. Over time reimbursement rates have remained stable, which indicates that rising premiums probably are more directly related to rising health care costs than higher reimbursement rates. In addition, no-fault processes claims more quickly than tort. First-party claims in no-fault states are approximately 23 percent more likely to be settled within three months than third-party claims in tort states. Id. at 90. Increased access to medical care, higher reimbursement rates, and faster claims processing also have translated into slightly higher customer satisfaction. Respondents in no-fault states were four percent more satisfied with their automobile insurance than those in tort states. Id. at 91.

2. "Add-on" No-Fault

A second approach that is sometimes called "add-on" no-fault is more prevalent but less significant. In fact, it is a bit misleading even to call this no-fault. It is essentially an expansion of the coverage provided under the medical payments coverage provided by auto insurance policies. See the Sample Policy in this Chapter, p. 4. Under this version, no-fault insurance is an "add-on" to the tort system. Tort liability remains untouched, but there is mandatory purchase of first-party insurance for victims. Although formally this add-on form of no-fault is merely auto-insurance reform without any tort reform whatsoever, informally add-on no-fault may have some impact on the incidence of tort liability. By providing an automatic source of recovery for at least a portion of every victim's out-of-pocket losses, add-on no-fault eliminates the need to sue to recover for these losses. Some victims may still wish to bring suit, especially in cases of severe pain and suffering. But for victims with comparatively small claims and modest injuries, suit is not necessary, and some may decline to sue because their out-of-pocket losses have been paid.

3. "Choice" No-Fault

"Choice" or optional no-fault is a last possibility. Kentucky, New Jersey, and Pennsylvania have adopted this approach. Under this approach drivers choose either a less-expensive no-fault option or a more expensive full tort approach that preserves the right to recover in tort. No-fault insureds recover from their own insurers. Tort insureds must bring traditional negligence suits in order to recover. When insureds who have made different choices are involved in an accident, a no-fault insured who is negligently injured by a tort insured is limited to recovery of his own no-fault benefits, unless his injuries surpass the requisite threshold. On the other hand, when a tort insured is negligently injured by a no-fault insured, his cause of action is preserved, and any recovery will be paid by the liability insurance (sometimes referred to as "bodily injury insurance") that still must be maintained by no-fault insureds for this purpose, as well as to protect no-fault insureds against liability to other no-fault insureds in excess of the threshold. See, e.g., Pa. C.S.A. § 1705.

The choice approach blunts the argument that no-fault deprives victims of their right to vindicate their rights through tort suits. In addition, some of the problems that have plagued no-fault states, such as higher premiums, may be minimized in choice states. In Pennsylvania, for example, although more drivers have chosen the no-fault option over time, insurers have been able to offer no-fault rates at or below the regulatory guidelines. Under a choice model, drivers with few or no accidents on their records may tend to choose the full tort option, while drivers with poor records may tend to choose no-fault, because of the partial tort immunity and potentially lower premiums that it provides these drivers. Some critics have argued that choice therefore penalizes good drivers with good records with higher premiums and rewards bad drivers by allowing to them to choose limited liability and lower premiums. The extent to which this occurs, however, has not yet been rigorously studied.

CHAPTER NINE

REINSURANCE

Reinsurance is an agreement between two or more insurers, whereby all or part of the risk of loss under an insurance policy or policies sold by one is transferred to the other. The insurer selling the initial policy is termed the *ceding insurer;* the insurer to whom the ceding insurer transfers some or all of the risk assumed under the initial policy is termed the *reinsurer*. Some reinsurers specialize, sometimes exclusively, in reinsurance; these companies are known as *professional reinsurers*. Other reinsurers are primary insurers who sell reinsurance as a more or less minor part of their business.

A. NATURE AND FUNCTIONS

Reinsurance is a device by which insurance companies diversify their risk. By diversifying risk through the purchase of reinsurance, an insurer can limit its exposure to unexpectedly frequent or severe losses. It can also increase its underwriting capacity and capital levels, since state regulation generally does not require insurers to maintain reserves to cover potential losses associated with business that is ceded to a reinsurer. The proportion of a company's book of business that it reinsures is likely to vary from line to line, depending on the volume of business it does in a given line and the volatility of losses in the line. For example, commercial liability and medical malpractice insurance tend to be more heavily reinsured, other things being equal, than auto property damage insurance. See Patrick L. Brockett, et al., An Overview of Reinsurance and the Reinsurance Markets, 9 J. Ins. Reg. 432 (1991). Reinsurers themselves sometimes need to diversify their own risks; the process by which they reinsure is known as *retrocession*. Reinsurance and sometimes several subsequent retrocessions are a means by which the risk undertaken by primary insurers is diversified widely throughout the global financial markets.

Reinsurance tends to be custom-made; there are no industry-wide form policies or rates. The varieties of reinsurance therefore are manifold. There are, however, general categories into which different types of reinsurance tend to fall. When coverage is specifically arranged to reinsure a particular risk or policy, it is known as *facultative* reinsurance. When coverage applies to a specified type or portion of a primary insurer's business in advance, it is *treaty* reinsurance. In the latter case (and sometimes the former) the document memorializing the parties' agreement is called a treaty rather than a policy. In both facultative and treaty reinsurance, the risks reinsured may be transferred in a variety of ways: in some specified proportion between the ceding insurer and the reinsurer (*proportional* reinsurance), or above a specified retained limit (*excess-of-loss* reinsurance). For more detailed discussion, see Barry R. Ostrager & Mary Kay Viscosil, Modern Reinsurance Law and Practice (3d ed. 2014); R. L. Carter, Reinsurance (3d ed. 1995).

Insurance Information Institute, Reinsurance (2009).*

* * *

Reinsurance is a way for primary insurance companies to transfer risk to another insurance entity. As an industry, reinsurance is less highly regulated than insurance for individual consumers because the purchasers of reinsurance, mostly primary insurance companies that sell car, home and commercial insurance, are considered sophisticated buyers. However, in the early 1980s, state insurance officials became increasingly concerned about the reliability of reinsurance contracts and a primary company's use of them. Following the June 1982 annual meeting of the National Association of Insurance Commissioners (NAIC) in Philadelphia, an advisory committee was formed to review the regulation of reinsurance transactions and parties to those transactions. A model Credit for Reinsurance Act was adopted in 1984.

All insurers submit financial statements to regulators who monitor their financial health. Financial health includes not assuming more risk or liability for future claims than is prudent, given the amount of capital available to support it. The principal value of reinsurance to a ceding company (the purchaser of reinsurance) for regulatory purposes is the recognition on the ceding company's financial statement of a reduction in its liabilities in terms of two accounts: its unearned premium reserve and its loss reserve. The unearned premium reserve is the amount of premiums equal to the unexpired portion of insurance policies, i.e., insurance protection that is still "owed" the policyholder and for which funds would have to be returned to the policyholder should the policyholder cancel the policy before it expired. The loss reserve is made up of funds set aside to pay future claims. The transfer of part of the insurance company's business to the reinsurer reduces its liability for future claims and for return of the unexpired portion of the policy. The reduction in these two accounts is commensurate with the payments that can be recovered from reinsurers, known as recoverables. The insurer's financial statement recognizes as assets on the balance sheet any payments which are due from the reinsurer for coverage paid for by the ceding company.

By statute or administrative practice, all states (but with considerable variation) recognize and grant financial statement credit for reinsurance transactions with reinsurers licensed in the same state, or reinsurers licensed in another state where the company meets the capital and surplus or solvency requirements of the state where the credit is taken. This is known as "authorized" reinsurance. In all other reinsurance transactions, for the ceding company to get credit, reinsurers not licensed in the United States, known as "alien" or offshore companies, must post collateral (such as trust funds, letters of credit, funds withheld) to secure the transaction. An alien company can also participate in the U.S. marketplace by becoming licensed in the states in that it wishes to do business.

For many years, few people outside the insurance industry were aware that such a mechanism as reinsurance existed. The public was first introduced to reinsurance in the mid-1980s during what has now become known as the liability crisis. A shortage of reinsurance was

---

* Copyright 2009, Insurance Information Institute.

widely reported to be one of the factors contributing to the availability problems and high price of various kinds of liability insurance. A few years later, in 1989, the reinsurance business once again became a topic of interest outside the insurance industry as Congress investigated the insolvencies of several large property/casualty insurers.

These investigations culminated in a widely read report, "Failed Promises: Insurance Company Insolvencies," published in February 1990. The publicity surrounding the investigations and the poor financial condition of several major life insurance companies prompted proposals for some federal oversight of the insurance industry, particularly insurers and reinsurers based outside the United States. However, no federal law was enacted. While a large portion of the insurance industry opposes federal regulatory oversight, many U.S. reinsurers and large commercial insurers view compliance with a single federal law as preferable to compliance with the laws of 51 state jurisdictions.

A critical tool for evaluating solvency is the annual "convention" statement, the detailed financial statement submitted by all insurance companies to the NAIC. In 1984, for the first time, the annual statement required insurers ceding liability to unauthorized reinsurers (those not licensed or approved in a designated jurisdiction) to include the amount of incurred but not reported (IBNR) losses in addition to known and reported losses. (IBNR losses are losses associated with events that have already occurred where the full cost will not be known and reported to the insurer until some later date.) This requirement reflects regulators' concern that all liabilities are identified and determined actuarially, including IBNR losses, and that IBNR losses are secured by the reinsurer with additional funds or a larger letter of credit than otherwise would have been required.

Related to solvency is the issue of reinsurance "recoverables, payments due from the reinsurer." In the mid-1980s, some reinsurance companies that had entered the reinsurance business during the period of high interest rates in the early 1980s left the market, due to insolvency or other problems. (When interest rates are high, some insurance/reinsurance companies seek to increase market share in order to have more premiums to invest. Those that fail to pay attention to the riskiness of the business they are underwriting may end up undercharging for coverage and going bankrupt as a result.) Consequently, some of the insurers that reinsured their business with these now-defunct companies were unable to recover monies due to them on their reinsurance contracts.

To enable regulators, policyholders and investors to assess a company's financial condition more accurately, the NAIC now requires insurance companies to deduct 20 percent of anticipated reinsurance recoverables from their policyholders' surplus on their financial statements—surplus is roughly equivalent to capital—when amounts are overdue by more than 90 days. The rule helps regulators identify problem reinsurers for regulatory actions and encourages insurers to purchase reinsurance from companies that are willing and able to pay reinsured losses promptly.

Concern about reinsurance recoverables led to other changes in the annual financial statement filed with state regulators, including changes that improve the quality and quantity of reinsurance data available to enhance regulatory oversight of the reinsurance business.

After Hurricane Andrew hit Southern Florida in 1992, causing $15.5 billion in insured losses at the time, it became clear that U.S. insurers had seriously underestimated the extent of their liability for property losses in a megadisaster. Until Hurricane Andrew, the industry had thought $8 billion was the largest possible catastrophe loss. Reinsurers subsequently reassessed their position, which in turn caused primary companies to reconsider their catastrophe reinsurance needs.

Where reinsurance prices were high and capacity scarce because of the high risk of natural disasters, some primary companies turned to the capital markets for innovative financing arrangements.

The shortage and high cost of traditional catastrophe reinsurance precipitated by Hurricane Andrew and declining interest rates, which sent investors looking for higher yields, prompted interest in securitization of insurance risk. Among the precursors to so-called true securitization were contingency financing bonds such as those issued for the Florida Windstorm Association in 1996, which provided cash in the event of a catastrophe but had to be repaid after a loss, and contingent surplus notes—an agreement with a bank or other lender that in the event of a megadisaster that would significantly reduce policyholders' surplus, funds would be made available at a predetermined price. Funds to pay for the transaction should money be needed, are held in U.S. Treasuries. Surplus notes are not considered debt, therefore do not hamper an insurer's ability to write additional insurance. In addition, there were equity puts, through which an insurer would receive a sum of money in the event of a catastrophic loss in exchange for stock or other options.

A catastrophe bond is a specialized security that increases insurers' ability to provide insurance protection by transferring the risk to bond investors. Commercial banks and other lenders have been securitizing mortgages for years, freeing up capital to expand their mortgage business. Insurers and reinsurers issue catastrophe bonds to the securities market through an issuer known as a special purpose reinsurance vehicle (SPRV) set up specifically for this purpose. These bonds have complicated structures and are typically created offshore where tax and regulatory treatment may be more favorable. SPRVs collect the premium from the insurance or reinsurance company and the principal from investors and hold them in a trust in the form of U.S. Treasuries or other highly rated assets, using the investment income to pay interest on the principal. Catastrophe bonds pay high interest rates but if the trigger event occurs, investors lose the interest and sometimes the principal, depending on the structure of the bond, both of which may be used to cover the insurer's disaster losses. Bonds may be issued for a one-year term or multiple years, often three. * * *

In many ways the rules that govern reinsurance are more lore than law. There are few statutes or judicial decisions governing reinsurance, in part because the duty of *utmost good faith* that is said to run between the parties discourages litigation, and also because any disputes that do occur traditionally have been resolved in binding arbitration. That situation changed has changed in recent decades, however, in part as a result of the entry of non-traditional companies into the reinsurance market a decade earlier. In addition, the huge sums that are at stake once primary layers of coverage for mass toxic tort liability are pierced and excess-of-loss reinsurance comes into play prompted reinsurers to litigate issues that would have been settled or arbitrated in the past. The cases that follow address some of the more salient issues in reinsurance law.

Credit for Reinsurance

In 2012, the NAIC adopted revisions to the Credit for Reinsurance Model Law. Approximately twenty states have adopted this model as of mid-2014. Additionally, in 2012 the federal government passed the Nonadmitted and Reinsurance Reform Act, which preempts the capacity of states to apply their credit for reinsurance laws on an extra-territorial basis.

Under the new regime, an "unauthorized" reinsurer may be considered a "certified reinsurer" if it comes from a "qualified jurisdiction" and meets certain capital and financial strength requirements. "Qualified jurisdictions" must have an appropriate and effective system of reinsurance supervision, recognize reciprocal rights for U.S. reinsurers, and cooperate with the commissioner as requested. Bermuda, Germany, Switzerland, and the United Kingdom have currently been granted priority review for becoming qualified jurisdictions, effective Jan. 1, 2014.

Once a jurisdiction has been qualified, individual reinsurance companies regulated by that regime may be certified by states in which they wish to do business. To be certified, the company must maintain a minimum capital surplus of $250 million, maintain ratings of at least two approved ratings agencies, submit to that state's jurisdiction, meet filing requirements, and meet other requirements as the commissioner proscribes. The commissioner is required to assign a rating for each certified reinsurer and publish those ratings. The amount of collateral that must be posted by a certified reinsurer depends on their rating levels, but very highly rated certified reinsurers need not post any collateral.

B. THE DUTY OF UTMOST GOOD FAITH

Allendale Mutual Insurance Company v. Excess Insurance Co. Limited

United States District Court, Southern District of New York, 1998.
992 F.Supp. 278.

■ SCHEINDLIN, DISTRICT JUDGE.

* * * Allendale is an insurance company incorporated under the laws of Rhode Island. The defendants are reinsurers organized under the laws of the United Kingdom. Effective January 1, 1991, Factory Mutual International ("FMI"), an Allendale subsidiary, issued an insurance policy to Zenith Data Systems France and Zenith Data System Europe ("Zenith") covering physical losses at Zenith's Seclin, France warehouse up to 248,301,000 French francs (approximately $48 million). This policy was 100% reinsured by Allendale, who in turn sought reinsurance for all but $2.5 million of the risk.

Pursuant to this effort, a $7 million layer of the risk was offered to defendants through a series of intermediaries. Defendants indicated a desire to accept for the period between January 1, 1991 and January 1, 1992 by initialing a broker's slip (the "first contract") which briefly described the Seclin warehouse and the terms of the contract. Among these terms was one that provided: "Service of Suit Clause (U.S.A.)." The parties agree that this notation incorporates by reference a clause taken from an industry handbook which provides, in pertinent part: "It is agreed that in the event of the failure of the [defendants] . . . to pay any amount claimed to be due hereunder, the [defendants], at the request of [Allendale], will submit to the jurisdiction of a court of competent jurisdiction within the United States of America." The slip also disclosed that the warehouse was "non sprinklered."

Before initialing the slip, defendants added a handwritten inscription which stated: "sub all recs complied with within 60 days of receipt of survey by reassured." The parties agree that "sub," in this context, is shorthand for "subject to" and that "recs" is short for "recommendations." Shortly after execution of the contract, the parties agreed to change its expiration date to June 1, 1991.

On January 28, 1991, the Seclin warehouse was surveyed by an FMI engineer. The report drafted as a result of this inspection (the "survey report") included a section titled "Recommendations." This section included the following six entries:

[1] A cutting and welding permit procedure should be implemented whenever cutting or welding operations have to take place . . .

[2] Fire hoses fed by the public main should be installed according to Factory Mutual standards throughout the warehouse building . . .

[3] Automatic sprinkler protection should be provided throughout the warehouse according to Factory Mutual standards . . .

[4] The above sprinkler protection should be fed by an adequately sized water supply consisting of a pump and a tank . . .

[5] Given the total value of the goods stored, a second water supply should be provided for reliability . . .

[6] A burglar alarm system should be installed to supplement the present watch service and further protect the goods of the warehouse from theft. . . .

Each recommendation was followed by a "comment;" the comments for recommendations two through five indicated that Zenith did not plan to make the suggested changes. Neither Zenith nor Allendale took any action with regard to any of the recommendations. Defendants did not request, nor did Allendale provide, a copy of the survey report.

Effective June 1, 1991, the parties executed a new agreement (the "second contract") to cover the warehouse risk until June 1, 1992. This contract included terms similar, but not identical, to those of its predecessor. The "Service of Suit Clause (U.S.A.)" and the "non sprinklered" disclosure, for example, were repeated; the "sub all recs" clause, however, was not. The premium rose from $5,000 to $5,500 per annum. Allendale did not inform defendants of the survey report's recommendations or of the fact that no action had been taken with regard to those recommendations.

On June 15, 1991, the Seclin warehouse was completely destroyed by fire. On January 29, 1992, defendants wrote Allendale purporting to rescind the second contract in light of, inter alia, Allendale's alleged failure to disclose the outstanding survey report recommendations. * * *

Defendants contend that their performance under the second contract is excused by Allendale's failure to inform them of the recommendations made in the survey report and Zenith's failure to implement these recommendations. Under New York law, a reassured owes to its reinsurer a duty of "uberrimae fidei," a phrase generally translated as "the utmost good faith." *In re Liquidation of Union Indemnity Ins. Co.*, 89 N.Y.2d 94, 106 (1996). The core of this duty "is a basic obligation of a reinsured to disclose to potential reinsurers all 'material facts' regarding the original risk of loss, and failure to do so renders a reinsurance agreement voidable or rescindable." Id.; See also *Christiania Gen. Ins. Corp. v. Great Am. Ins. Co.*, 979 F.2d 268, 278 (2d Cir.1992) ("The relationship between a reinsurer and a reinsured is one of utmost good faith, requiring the reinsured to disclose to the reinsurer all facts that materially affect the risk...."). This doctrine imposes no duty of inquiry upon a reinsurer; rather, the burden is on the reassured to volunteer all material facts. See *In re Liquidation of Union Indemnity Ins. Co.*, 89 N.Y.2d at 107; *Knight v. U.S. Fire Ins. Co.*, 804 F.2d 9, 13 (2d Cir.1986) ("Since the [reinsured] is in the best position to know of any circumstances material to the risk, [it] must reveal those facts to the underwriter, rather than wait for the underwriter to inquire."); *Reliance Ins. Co. v. Certain Member Companies*, 886 F.Supp. 1147, 1154 (S.D.N.Y.), aff'd, 99 F.3d 402 (2d Cir.1995). Moreover, a reinsured "need not possess a specific intent to conceal information from a reinsurer to make a contract voidable ... an innocent failure to disclose a material fact is sufficient." *In re Liquidation of Union Indemnity Ins. Co.*, 89 N.Y.2d at 107 (internal quotation marks omitted).

A fact is "material" for purposes of the uberrimae fidei doctrine if it "would have either prevented a reinsurer from issuing a policy or prompted a reinsurer to issue it at a higher premium" had it been disclosed before the contract was executed. Id. at 106. Materiality is generally a question of fact, and is determined by consideration of what a reasonable reinsured would have believed to be material to the reinsurer at the time of contracting. See *Christiania*, 979 F.2d at 278–79.

The non-disclosure at issue here meets this standard. Whatever the effect of the "sub all recs" clause on the validity of the parties' contracts, it surely put Allendale on notice that defendants considered the survey report's recommendations—and their implementation—important. See *Christiania*, 979 F.2d at 280 ("Where the insurer specifically inquires as to a fact, the insured is thereby on notice that the insurer considers it material...."). Even plaintiff's expert witness agreed at trial that this was the case.

It is true that the clause was written into the first contract only, and was not included by the defendants six months later. The doctrine of uberrimae fidei, however, would count for very little if a reinsurer not only had to inform its reinsured that it considered desired information material, but had to renew this notice every six months. Such a result would effectively impose on reinsurers a duty of inquiry, despite well-settled precedent to the contrary. See *In re Liquidation of Union Indemnity Ins. Co.*, 89 N.Y.2d at 107; *Knight*, 804 F.2d at 13; *Reliance Ins. Co.*, 886 F.Supp. at 1154; see also *Unigard Security Ins. Co. v. North River Ins. Co.*, 4 F.3d 1049, 1066 (2d Cir.1993) ("Courts should . . . adopt information-forcing default rules based on the good faith the reinsurance market demands.")

Nor could uberrimae fidei retain significance if a reinsurer's notice of materiality was held to lapse every time a new contract is executed. Were that the case, "materiality" would often be limited to those matters required to be disclosed by specific terms of the contract. This result would clearly frustrate the information-forcing purpose of the doctrine.

Given a sufficient passage of time or a sufficient number of new contracts, of course, a reinsurer's notice that it considers certain information material may become "stale." For instance, if the parties here had for years agreed to renewal contracts on the Seclin warehouse risk and defendants had never again demonstrated an interest in the survey report recommendations, Allendale may have reasonably concluded that defendants no longer considered the subject important. However, it cannot be seriously maintained that this conclusion could be reached a mere six months after defendants had expressed unwillingness to enter the contract without the assurance that all recommendations would be complied with within sixty days of Allendale's receipt of the survey. Given the defendants' insistence on the "sub all recs" clause, the fact that the survey contained recommendations that were never implemented was "material" within the meaning of the uberrimae fidei doctrine.

Attempting to resist this conclusion, Allendale points to the testimony of Stanley Chard, lead underwriter on the Seclin warehouse risk for defendant Excess Insurance Company, who testified at trial as follows:

Q. So, your problem is [that Allendale] never advised you [of the outstanding recommendations]; is that correct?

A. One of the problems.

Q. You don't know what you would have done had they advised you?

A. I can't say what we would have done. It is a difficult question.

Unlike Allendale, I do not find this testimony especially probative on the issue of materiality. Mr. Chard's lack of certainty may simply reflect the fact that he does not know whether defendants would have refused to enter into the second contract on any terms, would have done so only upon payment of a larger premium, or would have insisted on further disclosures before deciding. This interpretation is supported by his earlier testimony that he, like every other witness queried on the subject, found the non-disclosure of the outstanding recommendations to be material. Thus, Mr. Chard's "admission" does not alter my conclusion that the existence of outstanding recommendations in the survey report was material.

Allendale also contends that its non-disclosure was immaterial in that the "recommendations" referred to in the "sub all recs" clause were something other than the recommendations made in the survey report. According to Allendale, the "sub all recs" clause referred only to those recommendations required to bring the warehouse to a basic standard of insurability. By contrast, it argues, the recommendations contained in the survey report were meant to raise the warehouse from mere insurability to an exacting "Highly Protected Risk" standard. Because no changes to the warehouse were required to make it merely insurable, Allendale concludes, there were no recommendations—within the meaning of the "sub all recs" clause—to disclose.

This argument has only its creativity to commend it. As noted earlier, a non-disclosure is "material" if, at the time of contract formation, a reasonable reinsured would have believed that the reinsurer would refuse to cover the risk or would charge a higher premium if the disclosure were made. See *Christiania*, 979 F.2d at 278–79. When the second contract was being negotiated prior to June 1, 1991, a reasonable reinsured in Allendale's position would look to clauses required by defendants in the previous contract in identifying information defendants would believe to be material, including the "sub all recs" clause. See id. at 280. Applying the well-established principle that unambiguous contractual terms are understood in their ordinary sense, see *Western World Ins. Co. v. Stack Oil, Inc.*, 922 F.2d 118, 121 (2d Cir.1990), the reinsured would then arrive at the unsurprising conclusion that "all recommendations," as used in the contract, includes, at minimum, all entries in the survey report under the heading "Recommendations." What a reasonable reinsured could not do—as Allendale apparently did—is read the clause to mean "subject to all recommendations necessary to make the warehouse insurable." While this reading may accurately reflect Allendale's definition of the term "recommendations," there is no basis to conclude that defendants shared this highly subjective interpretation.

Of course, the contractual language standing alone is not necessarily dispositive on the issue of materiality: If Allendale had good reason to believe that defendants did not really consider "all" recommendations material, despite the language of the clause, selective disclosure on the subject might have been sufficient. Allendale, however, can point to no such reason. It cites the testimony of Christian Milton, its expert witness, for the proposition that the term "recommendations," as used in the clause and as understood in the insurance industry, refers only to those recommendations relating to housekeeping, maintenance, watch service, and the insured building's physical construction. Mr. Milton, however, did not actually say this: He expressly declined to offer an opinion as to what was meant by the term "recommendations" as used in the clause; moreover, he listed housekeeping, security, maintenance, and construction merely as examples of important areas of concern for surveyors. There is no basis to conclude from this testimony that defendants would not have considered the recommendations in the survey report to be material.

As its last line of defense, Allendale argues that information regarding the survey recommendations could not have been material because, for a variety of reasons, each individual recommendation was immaterial. For instance, Allendale points out that recommendations three, four and five involve the proposed addition of automatic sprinkler protection. Because both contracts disclosed that the warehouse was non-sprinklered, it argues, defendants cannot have considered these recommendations material. It is certainly true that defendants consented to cover the warehouse in an unsprinklered state. However, this is not the same thing as consenting to coverage of an unsprinklered warehouse when a professional surveyor has recommended that sprinklers be added. While defendants agreed that sprinkler protection was not necessarily required for reinsurance to be bound, the "sub all recs" clause suggests that they did not agree to coverage without the unqualified approval of a surveyor. Thus, the "non-sprinklered" contractual disclosure does not significantly detract from the materiality of Allendale's failure to disclose the sprinkler-related recommendations.

As to recommendations one, two and six, Allendale argues that these were not material in that the warehouse already had sufficient protection in these areas. This argument is meritless: Materiality is determined with reference to what the reinsurer considers important, not the reinsured. See *Christiania*, 979 F.2d at 278–79. Having provided Allendale with clear notice that they considered compliance with the survey report recommendations material, defendants were entitled to assume that they would be informed of any non-compliance, even if alternate safeguards had been put in place. Allendale's unilateral decision that the recommendations were overcautious does not ameliorate its failure to disclose those recommendations and Zenith's non-compliance. * * *

For the foregoing reasons, I find that Allendale's failure to disclose the existence of outstanding recommendations made as part of the survey report constituted a violation of its duty of utmost good faith. Because defendants were thereby entitled to recision of the parties' contract, no breach of that contract occurred when defendants refused to pay Allendale's claim for payment on the Seclin warehouse loss, and defendants are not liable now for Allendale's $7 million claim. * * *

NOTES AND QUESTIONS

1. *The Context of the Transaction*. It is common practice for a reinsurer to accept a "line" on a treaty, or even a facultative reinsurance agreement—i.e., to agree to reinsure a portion of the total package of risks the insurer wishes reinsured. This process, especially when reinsurance is being placed overseas, often necessitates use of a reinsurance broker or brokers, as in *Allendale*. The duty of the parties to exercise the "utmost good faith" in dealing with each other is partly a residue of the practices that grew out of Lloyds Coffee House in earlier centuries. One of the key elements of that duty is the obligation to make full disclosure of the character of the risks being transferred. The duty of utmost good faith in reinsurance thus resonates with the strict enforcement of insurance warranties that also prevailed during the period when the duty was evolving.

The duty probably would not have survived into modern times, however, if it had not continued to be useful. With the growth of international reinsurance and the geographical separation of the parties to a reinsurance treaty that accompanied this growth in the twentieth century, the duty was an effective method of avoiding the production of cumbersome, detailed documentation at long distances. Moreover, since reinsurance is virtually pointless unless its expected costs are less than the premiums charged for coverage by the ceding insurer, reinsurers must save on underwriting costs, including the costs of investigating the nature of the risks being transferred by the ceding insurer. The duty of utmost good faith puts the burden on the ceding insurer to disclose what is necessary, without putting the reinsurer to the expense of full inquiry and investigation.

2. *Aspects of the Duty.* A number of different aspects of the duty of good faith have been litigated. For example, there are duties on both sides to communicate with each other when claims discrepancies are discovered. *Munich Reinsurance Am., Inc. v. Am. Nat'l Ins. Co.*, 2014 WL 793129 (D. N.J. 2014). It is a breach of the duty of utmost good faith for an insurer to fail to disclose that it is insolvent. See *Nichols v. Am. Risk Mgm't, Inc.*, 2002 WL 31556384 (S.D.N.Y. 2002). Similarly, the ceding insurer's eleven-year delay in providing notice of a claim to its reinsurer is a breach. *Certain Underwriters at Lloyd's London v. Home Ins. Co.*, 783 A.2d 238 (N.H. 2001).

3. *Decline of the Duty?* As more and more insurers and reinsurers enter the field, a customary duty of utmost good faith that can cement relations among a relatively small group of continuously interacting enterprises may lose strength. The increased possibility of nearly instantaneous electronic transfer of lengthy documents across the globe also may tend to obviate the need for such a duty, since document production by the ceding insurer at the reinsurer's request is not as burdensome, time consuming, and expensive as it once was. One might therefore expect that, over time, courts dealing with reinsurance issues at distances and in jurisdictions far removed from the continents where reinsurers do business might hasten the decline of the duty to exercise the utmost good faith, by applying standard misrepresentation law to disputes over customary reinsurance obligations. A bit of this kind of erosion of the duty may have taken place. See, e.g., *Old Reliable Fire Ins. Co. v. Castle Reinsurance Co., Ltd.*, 665 F.2d 239 (8th Cir. 1981) (disclosure duty judged by misrepresentation standard). Most courts, however, seem to be holding the line, by shaping the duty of utmost good faith so that it lies somewhere in between a fiduciary duty and the ordinary duty of one contracting party dealing at arms length with another. See, e.g., *Travelers Cas. & Sur. Co. v. Ins. Co. of N. Am.*, 609 F.3d 143 (3d Cir. 2010); *Fireman's Fund Ins. Co. v. Gen. Reinsurance Corp.*, 2005 WL 1865424 (N.D. Cal. 2005); For further discussion, see Barry R. Ostrager & Mary Kay Viscosil, Modern Reinsurance Law and Practice §§ 3.01–.03 (1996); Deborah R. Cohen, Timothy E. De Masi, & Aaron Kraus, Uberrima Fides and Reinsurance Recission: Does a Gentlemen's Agreement Have a Place in Today's Market?, 29 Tort & Ins. L.J. 602 (1994); Steven W. Thomas, Utmost Good Faith in Reinsurance: A Tradition in Need of Adjustment, 41 Duke. L.J. 1548 (1993).

4. *The Consequences of Breach.* Just as American courts may pay less attention to the duty of utmost good faith than traditional reinsurance

practice might require, they may also invoke less stringent remedies when they do find the duty to have been breached. For example, in *Security Mutual Casualty Co. v. Century Casualty Co.*, 531 F.2d 974 (10th Cir. 1976), the court found that the ceding insurer had breached an obligation under a reinsurance treaty to provide the reinsurer with notice of all claims reserved in excess of the ceding insurer's retained liability. But the court went on to hold that because the obligation to provide notice was a mere "covenant" in the reinsurance agreement rather than a condition precedent to coverage, the reinsurer was not entitled to void the treaty, but only to recover any damages it suffered as a result of the breach. To what extent does this holding import what amounts to the contribute-to-loss standard found in some state warranty statutes into reinsurance transactions?

C. "Follow-the-Fortunes" Clauses

Travelers Casualty & Surety Company v. Certain Underwriters at Lloyd's of London

Court of Appeals of New York, 2001.
96 N.Y.2d 583.

■ Graffeo, J.

These appeals present a common issue of contract interpretation: whether losses from environmental injury claims involving decades of commercial activities at numerous industrial and waste disposal sites may properly be aggregated as a single "disaster and/or casualty" under certain reinsurance treaties. We conclude, under the facts and reinsurance contracts at issue, that the aggregation of these losses is beyond the scope of the applicable treaties.

We begin with a general explanation of the purpose and structure of reinsurance. As we described in *Matter of Union Indem. Ins. Co.*, "[r]einsurance is 'the insurance of one insurer (the "reinsured") by another insurer (the "reinsurer") by means of which the reinsured is indemnified for loss under insurance policies issued by the reinsured to the public'" (89 N.Y.2d 94, 105–106 [quoting Kramer, *The Nature of Reinsurance*, reprinted in Reinsurance, at 5 (Strain ed. 1980)]; *see also, Matter of Midland Ins. Co.*, 79 N.Y.2d 253, 258; *Sumitomo Mar. & Fire Ins. Co. v. Cologne Reins. Co.*, 75 N.Y.2d 295, 301; Staring, Reinsurance §§ 2:1–2:3, at 1–4 [1993]). When entering into a reinsurance contract, an insurance company agrees to pay a particular premium to a reinsurer in return for reimbursement of a portion of its potential financial exposure under certain direct insurance policies it has issued to its customers. Through this indemnity relationship, the reinsured seeks to "cede" or spread its risk of loss among one or more reinsurers. Reinsurance differs from direct insurance, such as excess insurance, in that the reinsurer is not, in most cases, directly obligated to the original insured; in fact, reinsurance indemnity does not arise until the reinsured has paid a claim.

Reinsurance comes primarily in two forms: facultative and treaty reinsurance. Facultative reinsurance is policy-specific, meaning that all or a portion of a reinsured's risk under a specific contract of direct coverage will be indemnified by the reinsurer in the event of loss. In contrast, a carrier seeking to reduce potential financial losses from policies issued to a class of customers or an industry may purchase treaty reinsurance (*see,* Staring, *supra,* § 2:3). "In a treaty reinsurance relationship, there is '1) no individual risk scrutiny by the reinsurer, 2) obligatory acceptance by the reinsurer of covered business, and 3) a long-term relationship in which the reinsurer's profitability is expected, but measured and adjusted over an extended period of time'" (*Union Indem.,* 89 N.Y.2d, at 106 [quoting Clark, *Facultative Reinsurance: Reinsuring Individual Policies,* reprinted in Reinsurance, at 121 (Strain ed. 1980)]).

Reinsurance can be structured to provide coverage in a number of ways. Two of the more common variations are quota share and excess of loss reinsurance (*see,* Staring, *supra,* §§ 2:4–2:5). "The characteristics of the quota share [reinsurance or proportional reinsurance] are that a reinsurer takes a given percentage of the risk of each underlying policy and also receives a certain percentage of the premiums charged, all within stated upper limits of liability" (*id.,* § 2:4). In excess of loss reinsurance, also called non-proportional reinsurance, the reinsurer indemnifies "all or a percentage, usually high, of the excess of loss on the reinsured risks, above a stated amount, after the collection of any proportional reinsurance and up to a stated limit" (*id.,* § 2:5). The "stated amount" or deductible is referred to as the "retention," above which the reinsurer is obligated to pay the reinsured's loss to the extent set forth in the contract (*see, id.*). Generally, the premiums for excess of loss reinsurance are lower than those for quota share reinsurance as the risks are not shared proportionately by the reinsured and reinsurer (*see,* Webb, *The Pro Rata Property Treaty,* reprinted in Reinsurance, at 72 [Strain ed. 1997]). Here, it is undisputed that the various reinsurance contracts at issue are nonproportional, or excess of loss, reinsurance treaties.

Against this backdrop, we turn to the particular facts before us.

The Koppers Litigation

From 1960 to 1981, plaintiff Travelers Casualty and Surety Company provided primary, excess and umbrella general liability insurance policies to the Koppers Company, a chemical manufacturer that has operated in locations throughout the United States since the early 1900s. The primary policies issued from 1960 to 1972 established varying property damage liability limits per occurrence while the excess policies for the years 1966 to 1972 limited coverage to $10 million per occurrence. Beginning in 1971, the primary policies contained "sudden and accidental" pollution exclusion clauses; a similar clause first appeared in the excess policies the following year.

During the period relevant to this appeal, Travelers purchased various types of reinsurance in connection with its policies issued to Koppers. In particular, Travelers purchased facultative reinsurance for 50% of the limits of its excess liability policies issued to Koppers from January 1, 1966 to March 1, 1972. In addition, it secured catastrophic excess of loss reinsurance from defendants, a number of foreign reinsurance companies, for the years 1960 to 1970. These reinsurance treaties obligate the Reinsurers to pay Travelers for "each and every loss" incurred by Travelers that exceeds the retentions established under the treaties. The treaties define "each and every loss" as

> "*all loss arising out of any one disaster and/or casualty under coverage of any or all insureds of the Companies,* or all loss under the products liability coverage of any one insured, or all loss arising out of the occupational disease hazard under Workmen's Compensation and Employers' Liability coverage of any one insured" (emphasis added).

In turn, the definition of "disaster and/or casualty" is described as

> "each and every accident, occurrence and/or causative incident, it being further understood that all loss resulting from a series of accidents, occurrences and/or causative incidents having a common origin and/or being traceable to the same act, omission, error and/or mistake shall be considered as having resulted from a single accident, occurrence and/or causative incident."

The treaties also contain a so-called "follow the fortunes" clause which reads:

> "Any and all payments made by [Travelers] in settlement of loss or losses under [its] policies, whether in satisfaction of a judgment in any Court against the Insured or [Travelers] or made voluntarily by [Travelers] before judgment, in full settlement or as a compromise, shall be unconditionally binding upon the [Reinsurers] and amounts falling to the share of the [Reinsurers] shall be immediately payable to [Travelers] by [the Reinsurers] upon reasonable evidence of the amount paid by [Travelers] being presented. * * *

> "The [Reinsurers] agree to abide by the loss settlements of [Travelers], such settlements to be considered as satisfactory proofs of loss."

The underlying environmental claims at issue arose in the early 1980s when federal, state and local governments, as well as a number of private parties, commenced environmental actions directed at more than 150 of Koppers' plant and disposal sites throughout the country, many of which had been in operation for over 60 years.

In 1985, Koppers commenced an action in Federal District Court against Travelers and other insurers, including some of the defendants in this action in their capacity as direct insurers, seeking damages and a declaration that the insurers were obligated to defend and indemnify Koppers for its potential liabilities at these sites. Following a decade of litigation, Travelers eventually settled with Koppers for approximately $140 million. According to the parties' stipulation, the "settlement with Koppers resolved Travelers['] alleged liability to provide insurance coverage for pollution liability claims arising at more than 160 separate known sites throughout the United States, as well as at an undetermined number of unknown sites."[1]

Travelers then apportioned its $140 million settlement payment among the underlying direct insurance policies, treating each Koppers site as a separate occurrence. Subsequently, Travelers ceded

---

[1] The action proceeded to trial against the remaining direct insurers, and the jury awarded Koppers $70 million. That verdict was affirmed on appeal (*see, Koppers Co. v. Aetna Cas. & Sur. Co.*, 98 F.3d 1440 [3d Cir.]).

approximately $61.5 million of this settlement to its facultative reinsurance policies. In determining how much of the settlement to allocate to the Reinsurers under the applicable reinsurance treaties, Travelers treated the entire settlement as a single "disaster and/or casualty" and appropriated the settlement monies correspondingly among the implicated treaties. Travelers' rationale was that the Koppers loss resulted from a "common origin" and/or was "traceable to the same act, omission, error and/or mistake," namely, "Koppers' company-wide waste disposal practice." Based on this approach, the total amount Travelers ceded to the Reinsurers is approximately $13 million of the primary insured's claims, or about 9% of the total settlement. After presenting its reinsurance claim to the Reinsurers, Travelers commenced the action underlying this appeal seeking money damages and declaratory relief. Following extensive motion practice, the Reinsurers moved for summary judgment dismissing the claims in their entirety.

The DuPont Litigation

From 1967 to 1985, Travelers provided excess and umbrella liability insurance policies to E.I. DuPont de Nemours & Company, the largest chemical company in the world. Travelers then purchased reinsurance from various entities, including defendant Reinsurers. In particular, Travelers secured three catastrophic excess of loss treaties from the Reinsurers for the year 1967 to cover a "disaster and/or casualty" in excess of a $10 million retention. The relevant provisions in those treaties—including the definitions of "each and every loss," "disaster and/or casualty" and the "follow the fortunes" clause—are identical to the Koppers treaties.

In 1989, DuPont commenced litigation in Delaware against Travelers and other insurers seeking a declaration of insurance coverage for pollution-related claims arising from multiple hazardous waste sites. Travelers eventually paid DuPont $72.5 million in 1995 to settle insurance claims arising from pollution liabilities at those sites and then apportioned this settlement between two direct insurance policies with DuPont. Relevant to this appeal, $69 million was attributed to a 1967–1970 umbrella policy, with 25 different sites identified as separate occurrences for allocation purposes.

Travelers thereafter sought reimbursement from its reinsurers, ceding over $34 million of the settlement to certain facultative reinsurance policies it had secured. After deducting this amount and its retention under the 1967 excess of loss reinsurance treaties, Travelers billed the Reinsurers approximately $7.4 million, or about 9% of the total settlement. As it did with the Koppers allocation, Travelers calculated this amount by treating the environmental contamination at the DuPont sites as a single loss. Specifically, Travelers averred that the polluted sites shared a "common origin," namely, a managerial failure by DuPont in the implementation and enforcement of its company-wide environmental policy.

Similar to the Koppers scenario, Travelers then sued the Reinsurers seeking monetary damages and declaratory relief. The Reinsurers answered and asserted a counterclaim for declaratory relief. The Reinsurers moved for summary judgment dismissing the complaint and for a declaration that they had no further obligation to Travelers with respect to the settlement of insurance claims with DuPont. Both parties asserted substantially the same arguments raised in the Koppers litigation.

Supreme Court granted the Reinsurers' motion dismissing the action against them and granted declaratory relief on their counterclaim. Noting that the language employed in the applicable reinsurance treaties was identical to that in the Koppers action, Supreme Court reiterated its reasons for rejecting the "single loss" aggregation theory as outside the terms of the reinsurance treaties. On appeal, the Appellate Division unanimously affirmed (*see*, 724 N.Y.S.2d 1), relying on its holding in the Koppers appeal decided the same day. We granted Travelers' motion for leave to appeal (*see*, 96 N.Y.2d 706).

We now affirm the orders of the Appellate Division in both actions.

Analysis

The parties' dispute centers on whether Travelers' single allocations of its losses are encompassed by the term "disaster and/or casualty," which includes "all loss resulting from a series of accidents, occurrences and/or causative incidents having a common origin and/or being traceable to the same act, omission, error and/or mistake."

The allocations made by Travelers in the Koppers and DuPont settlements for reinsurance purposes were premised on the theory that pollution at the various sites had a "common origin" or was "traceable to the same act, omission, error and/or mistake," namely Koppers' deficient corporate environmental policy and DuPont's failure to implement and enforce its environmental policy. In support of this argument, Travelers presents the common definition of "origin" as the "beginning, or derivation from a source" (Webster's Third New International Dictionary 1591 [1993]) and "traceable" as "capable of being traced * * * suitable or of a kind to be attributed" (*id.*, at 2420). Thus, Travelers contends that the plain language of the treaties requires the "widest possible search for a unifying factor among the underlying claims."

In support of its proposition, Travelers relies primarily on *Axa Reins. (UK) Plc v. Field* ([1996] 2 Lloyd's Rep. 233 [UK HL, June 20, 1996]), a decision of the British House of Lords. In *Axa*, a reinsurer sought a declaration disallowing the aggregation of losses under a reinsurance policy. Although the reinsurer prevailed, Lord Mustill, writing for the House of Lords, observed a distinction between the use of the phrases "arising out of one event" and "arising from one originating cause" in the context of certain reinsurance agreements. He found the word "originating" implied a broader scope of application, requiring "the widest possible search for a unifying factor in the history of the losses which it is sought to aggregate" (*id.*, at 239). Travelers urges that we adopt a similar view of the meaning of "common origin." We note, however, that the loss provisions discussed in *Axa* differ from those found in the treaties in this appeal.

In the Koppers and DuPont treaties, the terms "common origin" and "traceable to" are modified by the phrase "series of" in the definition of "disaster and/or casualty." The word "series" is commonly defined as "a group of [usually] three or more things or events standing or succeeding in order and having a *like relationship to each other: a spatial or temporal succession of persons or things*" (Webster's Third New International Dictionary 2073 [1993] [emphasis added]). Our established precedent requires that in interpreting reinsurance policies, we give meaning to every sentence, clause and word of a contract of reinsurance (*see, Northville Indus. Corp. v. National Union Fire Ins. Co.*, 89 N.Y.2d 621, 632–633). Simply reading the term "disaster and/or casualty" as Travelers urges—conducting the "widest possible search for a unifying factor among the underlying claims"—would operate to excise the words "series of" from the language of the treaty in derogation of a basic principle of contract interpretation. We avoid this result by incorporating the inherent spatial or temporal boundaries of the phrase "series of" in interpreting the treaties.

Travelers responds that this construction renders the phrase "having a common origin and/or being traceable to the same act, omission, error and/or mistake" superfluous. To the contrary, the words may be read in harmony with the result that under the "disaster and/or casualty" provision, a reinsured could properly aggregate claims if those "accidents, occurrences and/or causative incidents" have a spatial or temporal relationship to one another and a "common origin." Where such a relationship is lacking, however, a reinsured cannot simply ignore the words "series of" and point to any event, however remote in place or time, that could possibly be considered of "common origin."

This construction further comports with the broad definition of "each and every loss," which sets forth the overall parameters of the reinsurer's liability. While coverage is extended to "*all loss* under the products liability coverage" and "*all loss* arising out of the occupational disease hazard under Workmen's Compensation and Employers' Liability coverage," the definition of loss limits the third category to "*any one* disaster and/or casualty" (emphasis added). This limitation, coupled with the above discussion of "disaster and/or casualty," demonstrates that the parties did not intend for the reinsured to simply group together all other losses as a single "disaster and/or casualty," but sought to allow aggregation only where the losses are linked spatially or temporally and share a "common origin." Nonetheless, Travelers seeks to attribute events and losses separated spatially by thousands of miles and temporally by decades to a single "disaster and/or casualty."

A review of the pleadings, affidavits and exhibits submitted on the motions for summary judgment in these actions confirms that Supreme Court and the Appellate Division correctly held that there is no issue of material fact as to whether Travelers' single allocations of the Koppers and DuPont settlements are covered under the definition of loss in the reinsurance treaties. Neither complaint contains an allegation that the contaminated sites bear a spatial or temporal relationship to each other. In fact, the evidence demonstrates the opposite. In the Koppers litigation, the stipulation of facts reveals that the acts of pollution occurred over decades beginning in the 1920s at geographically diverse locations ranging from New Jersey to Oregon and involved dozens of different manufacturing processes and pollutants. The individual site summaries for each of the 160 locations, many prepared for Travelers during the underlying Koppers coverage litigation, are consistent with this conclusion as well. Similarly, the evidence in the DuPont litigation, including like site studies, reveals that the 25 sites where the losses were apportioned were also dispersed across the country and covered a multitude of commercial processes and contaminations spanning 100 years.

Under the allegations of the complaints and the records in these actions, we conclude as a matter of law that Travelers' single allocations of its settlements with Koppers and DuPont do not fall within the ambit of "disaster and/or casualty" in the reinsurance treaties. In light of the fact that, as Travelers concedes, the treatment of each site as a separate "disaster and/or casualty" fails to pierce any of the retention levels of the reinsurance treaties, summary judgment was properly granted in favor of the Reinsurers in both actions.

Travelers makes an additional argument that deserves discussion. Briefly stated, Travelers posits that the "follow the fortunes" clauses found in the reinsurance treaties mandate that the Reinsurers reimburse it for losses it allocates to them reasonably and in good faith.

The "follow the fortunes" doctrine provides that "a reinsurer is required to indemnify for payments reasonably within the terms of the original policy, even if technically not covered by it. A reinsurer cannot second guess the good faith liability determinations made by its reinsured, or the reinsured's good faith decision to waive defenses to which it may be entitled" *Christiania Gen. Ins. Corp. v. Great Am. Ins. Co.*, 979 F.2d 268, 280 [2d Cir.] [internal citation omitted]. The rationale behind this doctrine is two-fold: first, it meets the goal of maximizing coverage and settlement and second, it streamlines the reimbursement process and reduces litigation by preventing a reinsurer from continually challenging the propriety of a reinsured's settlement decision (*see generally, International Surplus Lines Inc. Co. v. Certain Underwriters & Underwriting Syndicates at Lloyd's of London*, 868 F.Supp. 917, 921 [S.D. Ohio]).

While a "follow the fortunes" clause "in most reinsurance agreements leaves reinsurers little room to dispute the reinsured's conduct of the case" (*Unigard Sec. Ins. Co. v. North Riv. Ins. Co.*, 79 N.Y.2d 576, 583), we agree with the rationale of the United States Court of Appeals for the Second Circuit that such a clause does not alter the terms or override the language of reinsurance policies. In *Bellefonte Reins. Co. v. Aetna Cas. & Sur. Co.*, 903 F.2d 910 [2d Cir.], the Second Circuit considered whether reinsurers were obligated to the Aetna Casualty and Surety Company for an amount greater than the sums stated in the reinsurance certificates under the "follow the fortunes" doctrine. In holding that the reinsurers were not liable beyond the liability cap, the court held that "allowing the 'follow the fortunes' clause to override the limitation on liability [ ] would strip the limitation clause and other conditions of all meaning; the reinsurer would be obliged merely to reimburse the insurer for any and all funds paid. Such a reading would be contrary to the parties' express agreement and to the settled law of contract interpretation" (*id.*, at 913; *see also, Christiania*, 979 F.2d at 280 [holding that a reinsurer is not obligated to indemnify for payments "in excess of its agreed-to exposure"]).[2]

---

[2] Commentators concur that a "follow the fortunes" clause does not supersede specific language in a reinsurance contract (*see, e.g.,* Staring, *supra*, § 18:1 ["Simply stated, the

This analysis applies with equal force here. To hold that these "follow the fortunes" clauses supplant the definition of "disaster and/or casualty" in the reinsurance treaties and allow Travelers to recover under its single allocation theory would effectively negate the phrase. The practical result of such an application would be that a reinsurance contract interpreted under New York law that contains a "follow the fortunes" clause would bind a reinsurer to indemnify a reinsured whenever it paid a claim, regardless of the contractual language defining loss.

In support of its position, Travelers relies on *American Bankers Ins. Co. v. Northwestern Natl. Ins. Co.*, 198 F.3d 1332 [11th Cir.] and *International Surplus Lines Ins. Co. v. Certain Underwriters & Underwriting Syndicates at Lloyd's of London*, 868 F.Supp. 917 [S.D.Ohio]. Both cases deal with challenges by reinsurers to the reinsureds' decision to settle claims based on the terms of the underlying policies. The courts held that the reinsurers were bound by "follow the fortunes" clauses in their reinsurance agreements and, as a result, the reinsurers had to indemnify their reinsureds as long as the payments were made reasonably and in good faith. Here, by contrast, the Reinsurers are not contesting Travelers' settlement decisions based on the underlying policies; rather, the challenge is to Travelers' allocation of those settlements based on the contractual language in the reinsurance treaties. Thus, the holdings in *American Bankers* and *International Surplus* are inapposite.

Accordingly, in each case the order of the Appellate Division should be affirmed, with costs.

Travelers Casualty & Surety Company v. Gerling Global Reinsurance Corporation of America

United States Court of Appeals, Second Circuit, 2005.
419 F.3d 181.

■ JOHN M. WALKER, JR., CHIEF JUDGE.

Appellant Travelers Casualty & Surety Company ("Travelers") appeals from an order of the United States District Court for the District of Connecticut (Janet Bond Arterton, *Judge*), granting summary judgment to appellee Gerling Global Reinsurance Corporation ("Gerling") upon Travelers' claim against Gerling for a reinsurance payment. *Travelers Cas. & Sur. Co. v. Gerling Global Reinsurance Corp.*, 285 F.Supp.2d 200 (D.Conn.2003) ("*Travelers*"). After Travelers settled its insurance dispute with its underlying insured, Owens-

---

reinsurer follows the insurer's fortunes under the latter's insurance policies, *subject to the stated exclusions and limitations in the reinsurance agreement*"] [emphasis added]; *Reinsurance: Indemnifying Insurers for Insurance Losses,* reprinted in Reinsurance, at 25 [Strain ed. 1997] ["Following the fortunes means that, so long as the reinsured acts in good faith, its losses from underwriting that looks improvident in retrospect or was simply unlucky will be indemnified *within the terms of the reinsurance contract.*"] [emphasis added]; 1 Russ and Segalla, Couch on Insurance § 9:22, at 9–30 [3d ed. 1995] ["The extent of the liability of the reinsurer is determined by the language of the reinsurance contract, and *the reinsurer cannot be held liable beyond the terms of its contract* merely because the original insurer has sustained a loss."] [emphasis added]).

Corning Fiberglas Corporation ("OCF"), it allocated the settlement amount among the OCF policies in a way that implicated its own reinsurance policies with Gerling, a reinsurer. The district court concluded that because Travelers' settlement with OCF suggested that Travelers had accepted—at the time of settlement—a different allocation position from the position it asserted for reinsurance purposes, Gerling was not required to honor that allocation under the "follow-the-fortunes" doctrine. *Id.* at 211–12. On appeal, Travelers argues that summary judgment in favor of Gerling contravened our recent holding in *North River Insurance Co. v. ACE American Reinsurance Co.*, 361 F.3d 134, 139 (2d Cir.2004) ("*North River II*"), which upheld the district court's grant of summary judgment to North River, the cedent, in *North River Insurance Co. v. ACE American Reinsurance Co.*, No. 00 Civ. 7993, 2002 WL 506682 (S.D.N.Y. Mar. 29, 2002) ("*North River I*"). In addition, even though Travelers did not cross-move for summary judgment below, it now asks us not only to vacate the district court's order granting Gerling summary judgment, but also—in line with *North River I* and *II*—to grant summary judgment in its favor. We agree with the position advanced by Travelers, reverse the district court, and remand for entry of an order granting summary judgment to Travelers.

BACKGROUND

I. The OCF-Travelers and Travelers-Gerling Policies

Between 1953 and 1972, OCF, the world's second-largest manufacturer of asbestos-containing products, manufactured and distributed Kaylo, an insulation product containing asbestos. OCF also installed Kaylo at numerous building sites around the country.

From 1952 through 1979, Travelers insured OCF for bodily injury and property damage through a series of annual primary policies. With respect to claims for bodily injury, the primary policies distinguished between "products" and "non-products" claims. Products coverage protected OCF from claims for asbestos-related injuries that occurred either after asbestos products were placed into the stream of commerce or after an asbestos-related operation was completed. Non-products coverage protected OCF from claims for asbestos-related injuries resulting from asbestos exposure on OCF's premises or during its business operations, for example, injuries occurring during the installation or removal of asbestos products. Each primary policy had a $1 million "per occurrence" limit of liability, regardless of whether the claims arising from that occurrence fell within the products or non-products category. Thus, for any single occurrence, Travelers was not required to pay more than $1 million under any single primary policy.

Each primary policy also had a $1 million "aggregate" limit of liability—but for products coverage only. Thus, if claims arising from multiple occurrences triggered products coverage, the most that Travelers had to pay under any single policy was $1 million. Once the aggregate limit was reached, the policy was exhausted, regardless of any additional occurrences. However, if claims arising from multiple occurrences triggered non-products coverage, then Travelers was exposed to unlimited liability; each occurrence was subject to a $1 million limit on liability, but there was no cap on total liability. Regardless of how much Travelers had paid for previous non-products occurrences under a single policy, each additional non-products occurrence under that policy subjected Travelers to liability anew.

During the same period, Travelers also issued to OCF a number of excess policies that provided the layer of coverage directly above the primary policies. Each excess policy included a $25 million "per occurrence" limit on liability. The combined "per occurrence" limit of all of the OCF-Travelers' policies—both primary and excess—was $273.5 million.

Although the parties disagree as to whether or not Travelers obtained reinsurance on the primary OCF policies, it is undisputed that Travelers obtained reinsurance on its excess policies from a number of reinsurers. Relevant to this litigation are five facultative reinsurance certificates[1] that Travelers purchased from Gerling covering specified portions of the excess policies Travelers had issued to OCF for the period 1975 to 1977. As is customary, those certificates contained provisions under which Gerling agreed to be bound by any loss settlements entered into by Travelers with the underlying insured, so long as they fell within the terms and conditions of the original policy and of the certificate.

II. The OCF-Travelers Dispute

Beginning in the 1970s, asbestos manufacturers faced a crush of lawsuits for asbestos-related injuries, and OCF was no exception. Until the early 1990s, OCF categorized its asbestos-related claims as falling within the products category, and as arising from a single occurrence, when submitting claims to Travelers. But by the early 1990s, Travelers had paid OCF more than $400 million, which included indemnification for one set of occurrence limits as well as defense costs, and OCF's products coverage had been exhausted. OCF then began to submit its asbestos claims as non-products claims. Travelers, however, disputed any additional coverage for these claims. In March 1993, OCF and Travelers entered into arbitration. OCF argued that (1) the claims arising from OCF's contracting operations fell under non-products coverage, and (2) each of the claims, or at least each set of claims arising from a particular job site, was a separate occurrence. Travelers responded that (1) OCF had not adequately documented its assertion that these were non-products claims, and (2) all of OCF's claims, whether products or non-products, arose from a single occurrence. Were Travelers correct as to either assertion, it would not owe OCF any additional amount, since (1) under the terms of the policies, OCF had already reached the aggregate limit on liability for products claims, and (2) Travelers had already paid one set of occurrence limits.

Prior to any final, arbitral determination, OCF and Travelers settled. Travelers agreed to pay roughly $273.5 million, which was approximately one additional occurrence limit. *Travelers,* 285 F.Supp.2d at 205. OCF and Travelers "explicitly disclaimed any particular theory of coverage," and they never reached agreement as to

---

[1] In facultative reinsurance, the reinsurer agrees to cover specific insurance policies. In treaty reinsurance, by contrast, the reinsurer agrees to cover all policies falling within a specified class of policies. *(Unigard Sec. Ins. Co. v. North River Ins. Co.,* 4 F.3d 1049, 1054 (2d Cir.1993) *"Unigard").*

whether the claims arose from a single occurrence or multiple occurrences.

III. The Travelers-Gerling Dispute

Although the settlement did not resolve the occurrence issue, Travelers had to choose an occurrence position in order to allocate the settlement among its primary and excess OCF policies. It decided to allocate most of the settlement amount as a single, additional occurrence of non-products claims, which it represented as best reflecting the OCF-Travelers compromise. Using what is commonly known in the industry as the "rising bathtub" methodology, *North River II*, 361 F.3d at 138 n. 6, Travelers allocated the settlement amount evenly among policy years. Because each year's primary policy had a $1 million per occurrence limit, the primary polices were quickly exhausted. The remaining amount was then spread among the excess policies, including those reinsured by Gerling.

In May 2001, after Gerling had refused to pay the roughly $4.4 million that Travelers billed as Gerling's share of the OCF settlement, Travelers filed the breach-of-contract suit giving rise to this appeal. Gerling's refusal to pay stemmed from its disagreement with Travelers over the allocation method; specifically, Gerling insisted that the allocation be made on a multiple-occurrence, rather than a single-occurrence, basis. *Travelers*, 285 F.Supp.2d at 206. Its reasons for doing so were obvious: given the lack of an aggregate limit on liability for non-products coverage, allocation on a multiple-occurrence basis would necessarily assign a larger portion of the settlement amount to the primary policies, and a much smaller portion to the excess policies that Gerling had reinsured. *Id.* at 207 n. 8. In October 2002, Gerling moved for summary judgment, asking the district court to find that Gerling was not required to follow Travelers' post-settlement, single-occurrence allocation. The district court granted Gerling's motion in September 2003, finding that the follow-the-fortunes doctrine did not apply. *Id.* at 210–13.

The district court's decision was based upon its understanding of the purpose of the follow-the-fortunes doctrine:[2]

> The purpose of the follow the settlements doctrine is to prevent the reinsurer from "second-guessing" the settlement decisions of the ceding company. Absent such a rule, an insurance company would be obliged to litigate coverage disputes with its insured before paying any claims, lest it first settle and pay a claim, only to risk losing the benefit of reinsurance coverage when the reinsurer raises in court the same policy defenses that the original insurer might have raised against its insured.

Id. at 210.

While the district court acknowledged the importance of the follow-the-fortunes doctrine, *id.*, it found it inapplicable to the Travelers-Gerling dispute in light of the positions taken by the parties as to the occurrence issue:

---

[2] The district court refers to the "follow the settlements doctrine," which is the follow-the-fortunes doctrine in the settlement context. *See North River II*, 361 F. 3d at 136 n.2.

Gerling[ ] ... does not challenge Travelers' allocation by advancing a coverage position which Travelers did not press when deciding to settle ... with OCF. Instead, Gerling's position mirrors OCF's arbitration position. [Gerling's] position ... even if known by Travelers at the time ... would thus not have disincentivized that settlement because it was not the position Travelers was advancing against OCF.

Id.

Thus, the district court construed the follow-the-fortunes doctrine as protecting the cedent, where the cedent relinquishes position A in its dispute with the original insured, who advocates position B. In such situations, the reinsurer is precluded from denying coverage on the ground that the cedent should have insisted on position A. Although the settlement between OCF and Travelers followed this formulation in that Travelers, in order to settle, did not insist upon its initial, single-occurrence position, Travelers nevertheless allocated the claims according to the very single-occurrence position it had, according to Gerling, given up. Gerling objected to Travelers' allocating the settlement on the basis of a position that Travelers, in Gerling's view, had necessarily relinquished in the process of settling. Instead, Gerling argued, Travelers should have allocated the settlement according to the multiple-occurrence position that Gerling believed Travelers had implicitly accepted in order to settle with OCF, even though the settlement itself expressly disclaimed resolution of the occurrence issue. In denying reinsurance coverage, Gerling thus argued it was not challenging the terms of the settlement, but was rather seeking to enforce them. The district court agreed and held, in substance, that because there was no "second-guessing" by Gerling, the follow-the-fortunes doctrine was inapplicable.

DISCUSSION

On appeal, Travelers argues that the district court erred by not applying follow-the-fortunes to its post-settlement allocation. Specifically, Travelers argues that under this court's holding in *North River II*, a reinsurer is required to follow the cedent's post-settlement allocation, whether or not the allocation reflects a position initially taken by the cedent as to a particular coverage issue (here, number of occurrences) in the underlying insurance dispute. Travelers argues in addition that it is entitled not just to have summary judgment against it vacated, but to an award of summary judgment in its favor because Gerling cannot establish any other basis upon which to deny application of follow-the-fortunes. We review a grant of summary judgment *de novo*, "examining the evidence in the light most favorable to the non-movant and drawing all inferences in favor of it." *Id.* at 139.

I. The Applicability of *North River*

* * * The *North River* litigation also involved OCF non-products asbestos claims. *North River II*, 361 F.3d at 137–38. North River had provided OCF with several layers of excess insurance, ranging from $26 million to $76 million (i.e., the layers of insurance directly above the excess Travelers policies at issue in the instant litigation). Defendant ACE provided facultative reinsurance to North River, primarily for the lowest layer of coverage, $26 to $30 million. *North River I,* 2002 WL

506682, at *1. Like Travelers, North River ultimately settled with OCF-on the same underlying non-products claims as those at issue here—for approximately $335 million. And like Travelers, North River used the "rising bathtub" methodology to allocate the settlement amount and assumed a single occurrence for each year of coverage. *North River II*, 361 F.3d at 138. As a result, the settlement was allocated almost entirely to the layer of coverage reinsured by ACE. Like Gerling, ACE, upon receiving its bill for $49 million, disputed North River's allocation methodology. *Id.*

Specifically, ACE disputed the post-settlement allocation because it differed from the pre-settlement analysis North River had conducted, which had considered various litigation outcomes, and had identified the potential for greater risk of loss to higher policy levels not reinsured by ACE. *Id.* ACE argued "that the follow-the-fortunes doctrine *either* does not apply at all to the issue of how an insurer chooses to allocate its settlement payment among various policies *or* must at least be consistent with the theory of allocation (if discernible) that the insurer used in negotiating the settlement with its insured. . . ." *North River I*, 2002 WL 506682, at *2.

The district court rejected ACE's argument, noting that

> the attempt to distinguish settlement from allocation would undermine the entire "follow the settlements" doctrine. . . . [T]he determination of which among several policies covers which particular loss . . . is not much different from the more general decision that the losses are covered by the policies. . . . Review of either type of decision has an equal likelihood of undermining settlement and fostering litigation.

Id. at *3 (quoting *Commercial Union Ins. Co. v. Seven Provinces Ins. Co.*, 9 F.Supp.2d 49, 67–68 (D.Mass.1998) ("*Seven Provinces*"), *aff'd* 217 F.3d 33 (1st Cir.2000)) (alteration in original omitted).

On appeal, this court affirmed. Of particular relevance to the present case is the "mutuality of interest" argument raised by ACE: "ACE argues that North River's interests in allocating the loss to it are in conflict with those of ACE and thus a fundamental premise of the follow-the-settlements doctrine, *mutuality of interest*, is missing." *North River II*, 361 F.3d at 140 (emphasis added). We squarely rejected ACE's argument:

> [T]he existence of a mutuality of interest is not the only factor underlying the follow-the-settlements doctrine. In fact, the main rationale for the doctrine is to foster the goals of maximum coverage and settlement and to prevent courts, through de novo review of the cedent's decision-making process, from undermining the foundation of the cedent-reinsurer relationship.

Id. at 140–41 (internal quotation marks and brackets omitted). We held that

> the follow-the-[fortunes] doctrine extends to a cedent's post-settlement allocation decisions, regardless of whether an inquiry would reveal an inconsistency between that allocation and the cedent's pre-settlement assessments of risk, as long as the allocation meets the typical follow-the-[fortunes]

requirements, *i.e.,* is in good faith, reasonable, and within the applicable policies.

Id. at 141.

The similarities between this case and *North River* are striking and ultimately decisive. Both cases involve OCF non-products asbestos claims. In both cases, post-settlement allocations were made using a single-occurrence, rising-bathtub methodology. In both cases, the reinsurer challenged that allocation methodology, which resulted in higher liability for the reinsurer than would have resulted from an alternative methodology. And in both cases, the reinsurer's challenge was based upon the fact that the ultimate allocation differed from an earlier position allegedly taken by the cedent.

The one factual distinction between the cases does not alter *North River's* relevance. In *North River I* and *II*, ACE's challenge was based on the pre-settlement risk analysis conducted by North River, which differed from its post-settlement allocation position. *Id.* at 139. In this case, Gerling's challenge is based on the difference between the concession Travelers presumably made by settling with OCF (i.e., its acceptance of a multiple-occurrence position) and its post-settlement, single-occurrence allocation, which—according to Gerling—was the position it had abandoned in its settlement negotiations. *See Travelers,* 285 F.Supp.2d at 211–12. But this factual distinction does not affect the applicability of the rationale of *North River,* which is that a cedent's post-settlement allocation is subject to follow-the-fortunes, regardless of any pre-settlement position taken by the cedent, whether that position is articulated in a pre-settlement risk analysis, or implicit in the settlement with the underlying insured.

Indeed, the differences between *North River* and this case suggest, if anything, that Gerling's position is even weaker than ACE's. In *North River,* the cedent had clearly considered an alternative allocation position, as evidenced by its documented, pre-settlement analysis. *North River II,* 361 F.3d at 139. ACE thus stood on somewhat firmer ground when it claimed an inconsistency between North River's pre-settlement and post-settlement positions. Here, by contrast, it is not clear that Travelers ever accepted—as a legal matter—OCF's multiple-occurrence position. The settlement explicitly declined to resolve the occurrence issue. *Travelers,* 285 F.Supp.2d at 205. To the extent the settlement indicated any position at all as to the occurrence issue, it arguably suggested a single, additional occurrence. As the district court found, the settlement was for "roughly" one occurrence limit. *Id.* In such a case, where the cedent's earlier position as to a particular coverage issue is unclear, it is even less appropriate than it was in *North River* for the reinsurer to claim an inconsistency between that earlier position and the cedent's subsequent allocation. *Cf. Am. Employers' Ins. Co. v. Swiss Reinsurance Am. Corp.,* 413 F.3d 129, 135–36 (1st Cir.2005) (where (1) settlement between cedent and underlying insured expressly did not resolve annualization issue, (2) cedent adopted annualized approach for post-settlement allocation purposes, and (3) reinsurer argued that settlement should have been allocated on non-annualized basis, district court erred when it agreed with reinsurer).

More important than whether or not the settlement reflected a one-occurrence position, however, is the fact that a number of occurrence positions were on the table. In the OCF-Travelers dispute, OCF had advocated at least two different occurrence positions (i.e., each claimant as a separate occurrence, or, alternatively, each job site as a separate occurrence), while Travelers had advanced the alternatives of either no new occurrence or a single non-products occurrence. That all of these possibilities as to the occurrence issue were subsumed by the settlement only serves to underscore the relevance of *North River*. As the district court in *North River I* noted,

> [w]henever settlements are made in cases involving multiple policies and multiple insurers and reinsurers, numerous good faith methods of allocation will be available and under consideration, but only one will ultimately be chosen. . . . To allow reinsurers to second-guess that allocation would be to make settlement impossible and reinsurance itself problematic.

North River I, 2002 WL 506682, at *3.

In short, we decline to authorize an inquiry into the propriety of a cedent's method of allocating a settlement if the settlement itself was in good faith, reasonable, and within the terms of the policies. *See North River II*, 361 F.3d at 141. *See also Am. Employers' Ins. Co.*, 413 F.3d at 136 (where settlement between cedent and underlying insured was unclear as to annualization issue, and where cedent's post-settlement approach was "ground [ed] in the settlement process itself," the reinsurer was required—"absent a clear limitation in the [reinsurance] certificate"—to "follow the gloss (assuming it is reasonable and made in good faith) given to the underlying policies" by the cedent). Given that Travelers and OCF expressly declined to resolve the occurrence issue, there is no cause for us to do so now. Indeed, were we to undertake such an analysis, we would be engaging in precisely the kind of "intrusive factual inquiry" that the follow-the-fortunes doctrine is meant to avoid. *North River II*, 361 F.3d at 141. Judicial review of either the settlement decision or the allocation decision "has an equal likelihood of undermining settlement and fostering litigation." *Seven Provinces*, 9 F.Supp.2d at 68. * * *

II. Travelers' Summary Judgment Request * * *

A. *Gerling's Bad Faith Argument*

Follow-the-fortunes applies only to claims submitted in good faith. *See, e.g., North River II*, 361 F.3d at 141. A reinsurer who seeks to avoid application of follow-the-fortunes by claiming bad faith, however, must make an "*extraordinary* showing of a disingenuous or dishonest failure. . . ." *CIGNA*, 52 F.3d at 1216 (emphasis added). Gerling relies primarily on two arguments in support of its contention that Travelers submitted its reinsurance claims in bad faith. First, Gerling contends that the allocation of all non-products claims to a single occurrence was inconsistent with the definition of "occurrence" in the underlying policies and rested on a construction of that term that is so legally baseless that it has never been adopted by any court in any jurisdiction. Second, Gerling contends that because Travelers had not reinsured its primary policies (a contention that Travelers disputes), it sought to shift its settlement loss from the primary to the excess policies, so as to maximize its reinsurance recovery.

The former argument may be rejected insofar as allocation on a legally novel theory does not itself constitute evidence of dishonesty or disingenuousness. But we note that this argument of Gerling's is really a challenge under the exception to follow-the-fortunes that allows a reinsurer to challenge a cedent's construction of underlying policy terms as unreasonable, and is therefore addressed in the discussion of this exception, *infra*. Regarding the latter argument, Gerling maintains that Travelers' allocation of the settlement in a manner aimed at maximizing reinsurance recovery constituted bad faith. As a result, Gerling asserts, the excess policies that it reinsured, which otherwise would have faced "virtually no exposure," Appellee's Br., at 42, were allocated the bulk of the settlement amount.

Our review of the record, however, reveals that bad faith cannot provide an alternative basis upon which to sustain the district court's grant of summary judgment to Gerling. Indeed, because Travelers now seeks summary judgment in *its* favor, we ask whether Gerling has raised any genuine issue of material fact as to Travelers' good faith that might prevent us from applying follow-the-fortunes at this stage. We conclude that it has not.

Specifically, Gerling cannot substantiate its claim that had a multiple-occurrence allocation method been used, it would have faced "virtually no exposure" because only the primary policies would have been implicated. As the district court recognized, "the record provides no basis for determining if the adoption of OCF's position would have led to an allocation of greater than one million dollars to any one occurrence." [the court then held that the loss fell within the terms of the Travelers policies] * * *

C. *Reasonableness*

Finally, in order to trigger the deference due under follow-the-fortunes, a settlement must be reasonable, *see Am. Employers' Ins. Co.*, 413 F.3d at 136–37, a standard that we applied to post-settlement allocations in *North River II, see* 361 F.3d at 139. Travelers asserts that its post-settlement allocation was unquestionably reasonable, and we agree.

First, it is undisputed that until the early 1990s, when this controversy arose, OCF had consistently submitted its asbestos claims to Travelers—and Travelers had paid them—on a single-occurrence basis. Only when OCF's products liability coverage was exhausted did OCF argue that its claims actually arose out of multiple occurrences falling under its non-products coverage. In light of this history, it was reasonable for Travelers to adopt a single-occurrence position, both in its negotiations with OCF and, ultimately, in its allocation of the settlement.

Second, Travelers' allocation method was reasonable when viewed in the context of then-prevailing case law. The settlement was concluded in 1995, and Travelers had allocated the settlement by January of 1996, although it did not notify its reinsurers of the allocation until November of 1996. The relevant period was therefore late 1995. At that time, numerous courts—including courts applying Ohio law, which governed OCF's policies, and construing OCF policies—had treated asbestos-related bodily injury claims as arising out a single "occurrence." *See, e.g., Int'l Surplus Lines Ins. Co. v. Certain Underwriters & Underwriting Syndicates at Lloyd's of London*, 868 F.Supp. 917, 919 (S.D.Ohio 1994) (observing that OCF "took the position that the [approximately 85,000 personal injury] asbestos claims against it arose from one occurrence," in context of OCF policy with ISLIC, which contained definition of "occurrence" virtually identical to the definition contained in OCF's Travelers' policies); *Unigard Sec. Ins. Co. v. North River Ins. Co.*, 762 F.Supp. 566, 595 (S.D.N.Y.1991), *aff'd in part and rev'd in part on other grounds*, 4 F.3d 1049 (2d Cir.1993) (observing that under Ohio law, all asbestos claims would be treated as single occurrence). The only pre–1996 case cited by Gerling in support of its multiple-occurrence position was decided by this court on December 13, 1995. *See Stonewall Ins. Co. v. Asbestos Claims Mgmt. Corp.*, 73 F.3d 1178, 1212–14 (2d Cir.1995). We are unwilling to find, based on a single decision issued one month before Travelers completed its allocation, that Travelers' one-occurrence methodology, which was otherwise fully consistent with existing case law and with OCF and Travelers' past dealings, was unreasonable.

Because Travelers' post-settlement allocation was made in good faith and was reasonable, and because we discern no other material factual dispute that might preclude application of follow-the-fortunes to Travelers' reinsurance claim, we conclude that the doctrine applies. Under follow-the-fortunes, we ask only "whether there is any reasonable basis" supporting the cedent's claims. *CIGNA*, 52 F.3d at 1206. Having already concluded that Travelers' post-settlement allocation was reasonable, we find that it easily meets this deferential standard of review. We therefore hold that Gerling is required to indemnify Travelers for that portion of the OCF settlement—as allocated by Travelers—covered by Gerling's reinsurance certificates.

CONCLUSION

For the foregoing reasons, we hold that Travelers is entitled to summary judgment as a matter of law. The judgment of the district court is REVERSED and REMANDED for entry of an order granting summary judgment in favor of appellant.

NOTES AND QUESTIONS

1. *Follow Some Fortunes?* The two *Travelers* decisions represent the two ends of a continuum. In *Travelers v. Lloyds* the reinsurance agreement governed because it contained a provision that was different from the corresponding provision in the reinsured policies. In *Travelers v. Gerling* there was no such difference in provisions. The reinsurer therefore was obliged to follow the fortunes of the ceding insurer as long as that insurer's allocation was in good faith, did not contradict its own policy language, and was reasonable. What happens, however, when the facts fall somewhere in between these two scenarios? For example, in *Allstate Insurance Company v. American Home Assurance Company*, 837 N.Y.S.2d 138 (2007), the trial court in the underlying coverage case had ruled that there were multiple occurrences at certain cites, and the ceding insurer had formally taken the position as to other sites that there were multiple occurrences. The parties subsequently settled. The ceding insurer then allocated its liabilities on a one-occurrence per site basis for purposes of its reinsurance claim. The court held this to be unreasonable, noting that the follow-the-fortunes

doctrine "was intended to foster consistency in losses at both levels, insured and reinsured, not to allow an insurer to use a different set of rules at each level." Suppose that the underlying coverage case had never gone to trial, but that before settlement, the ceding insurer had strongly maintained a position that was different from the position it later took in making its reinsurance claim? Recent decisions suggest that an "objective reasonableness" test governs the ceding insurer's allocations. See, e.g., *U.S. Fid. & Guar. Co. v. Am. Re-Insurance Co.*, 985 N.E. 2d 876 (N.Y. 2013).

2. *The Relation Between Duties.* Given the requirement in *Travelers v. Gerling,* is there a sense in which the follow-the-fortunes doctrine is an application of the duty of utmost good faith? The case law seems to be heading toward a rule that obligates the reinsurer to follow the fortunes of a ceding insurer's settlement if the claim "arguably" falls within the terms of the ceding insurer's policy, but subject to the good faith requirement. See, e.g., *One Beacon Ins. Co. v. Aviva Ins. Ltd.*, 2013 WL 2147958 (E.D. Pa. 2013). Presumably the duty would depend not only on whether coverage was arguable, but also whether the settlement was reasonable in light of the probability that there was in fact coverage and the amount of the ceding insurer's potential liability. But there is also developing case law suggesting that the duty to follow the fortunes is contract-based and that in the absence of an express provision requiring the reinsurer to follow the fortunes, the duty may not exist. See, e.g., *Emp'rs Reinsurance Corp. v. Massachusetts Mut. Life Ins. Co.*, 2008 WL 3890358 (W.D. Mo. 2008); *N. River Ins. Co. v. Emp'rs Reinsurance Corp.*, 197 F.Supp.2d 972 (S.D. Ohio 2002). But see *ReliaStar Life Ins. Co. v. IOA Re, Inc.*, 303 F.3d 874 (8th Cir. 2002) (holding that there was a duty to follow the fortunes even absent an express obligation to do so). This line of cases seems inconsistent with the notion that the follow-the-fortunes doctrine is a corollary of the duty of utmost good faith, as the latter it itself an implied contract term.

3. *Avoiding the Problem.* If you were counsel to ceding insurer in a case like *Travelers v. Gerling* would you advise that there be consultation with your reinsurers before settlement of claims covered in whole or in part by a reinsurance treaty, regardless of whether the treaty expressly required such consultation? If you were counsel for the reinsurers, would you advise your client to enter into any binding agreement prior to settlement of the underlying coverage claim? With regard to the requirement of notice by the ceding insurer to the reinsurer generally, see *Unigard Security Insurance Co. v. North River Insurance Co.*, 594 N.E.2d 571 (N.Y. 1992), holding that in cases of late notice the reinsurer must prove prejudice to avoid coverage.

D. INSOLVENCY CLAUSES

Ainsworth v. General Reinsurance Corporation

United States Court of Appeals, Eighth Circuit, 1985.
751 F.2d 962.

■ FAIRCHILD, SENIOR CIRCUIT JUDGE.

This is an appeal from a judgment holding a reinsurer (General Reinsurance Corporation) liable to the receiver of an insolvent insurance company (Medallion) for the reinsured amount of insured liability, under a so-called insolvency clause of a reinsurance agreement. Federal court jurisdiction is based on diversity, and the parties agree that the law of Missouri governs substantive questions.

I

On January 1, 1971, General Reinsurance entered into Agreement of Reinsurance No. 4191 with Medallion and its subsidiaries, among them Consolidated Underwriters. In late 1972, Medallion assumed all assets and liabilities of Consolidated Underwriters.

Medallion subsequently experienced financial difficulties. On September 12, 1975, the companies were formally declared insolvent and ordered liquidated by the Circuit Court of Jackson County, Missouri. In the present action Medallion's court appointed Receiver recovered for liability incurred by two companies insured by Consolidated Underwriters: Pittsburgh and New England Trucking Company ("P & NE") and B-K Cattle Company ("B-K"). The liabilities arose out of accidents involving company trucks. The parties agree that these accidents constitute "loss occurrences" covered under Agreement of Reinsurance No. 4191 and the insured liabilities remained unpaid at the time Medallion was declared insolvent.

Article IX of the Agreement of Reinsurance, the insolvency clause, provided as follows:

> In the event of the insolvency of the Company the reinsurance afforded by this Agreement shall be payable by the Reinsurer on the basis of the liability of the Company under the policy or policies reinsured, without diminution because of such insolvency, directly to the Company or its liquidator, receiver or statutory successor. The Reinsurer shall be given written notice of the pendency of each claim or loss which may involve the reinsurance afforded by this Agreement within a reasonable time after such claim or loss is filed in the insolvency proceedings. The Reinsurer shall have the right to investigate each such claim or loss and interpose, at its own expense, in the proceeding where the claim or loss is to be adjudicated, any defense which it may deem available to the Company or its liquidator, receiver or statutory successor. The expense thus incurred by the Reinsurer shall be chargeable subject to Court approval against the insolvent Company as part of the expense of liquidation to the extent of a proportionate share of the benefit which may accrue to the Company solely as a result of the defense undertaken by the Reinsurer.

It is clear that this clause was inserted in response to a Missouri statute, § 375.246 RSMo, requiring, similarly to law in many states, that reinsurance must not be treated as an asset or deduction from liability of an insurance company unless the reinsurance is payable "without diminution because of the insolvency of the ceding company."

A. P & NE Loss

On December 9, 1974, plaintiffs Ernest and Alice Nemeth won a jury verdict and money judgment against P & NE in the amount of $485,000 for personal injuries and damages suffered in an accident in West Virginia. Following notice of the insolvency, P & NE sought payment of the judgment from Medallion's Receiver and General Reinsurance. Attorneys for General Reinsurance responded in a March 12, 1976 letter that:

> The commissioner of claims and the attorney for Medallion Insurance Company has taken the position that the reinsurance assets belong to the receiver for the benefit of general creditors and that my client, General Reinsurance Corporation, cannot legally make payments to any claimant or insurer.
>
> Because of the position taken by the attorney for the receiver and the commissioner of claims and the agreement of the reinsurance treaty, we are certainly not in a position to make any payment to the plaintiff or to your client in this suit.

The attorneys again wrote P & NE in April 1976 that:

> [I]t appears to General Reinsurance that the agreement does not provide any means, method, nor language which would warrant payment to you and your client of any sums claimed by your client by reason of judgment or otherwise. The language of the reinsurance agreement seems clear. It would appear that our obligation is solely to the representatives of Medallion Insurance Company, now in receivership.

The position taken in these letters is clearly consistent with Article IX, the insolvency clause, and the underlying statutory requirement. Changing its position, however, General Reinsurance later negotiated and paid the Nemeths and P & NE $25,000 for a release discharging Medallion and its Receiver from all liability arising out of the accident. The Receiver did not participate in the negotiations or settlement of the P & NE case.

The district court concluded that the liability of P & NE to the Nemeths, insured up to policy limits by Consolidated (and Medallion), gave rise to a right of Medallion to proceeds of reinsurance and that such right vested in the Receiver when Medallion was declared insolvent. General Reinsurance was without authority to negotiate a settlement altering that right. In accordance with this holding, the court awarded the Receiver $89,557.53, plus interest from the date of insolvency.[1]

B. B-K Loss

The other loss occurrence concerned a 1972 accident in Texas involving a B-K truck. Plaintiffs in that suit agreed to a court-approved settlement of $85,000 on December 28, 1976. The Texas ancillary receiver of Medallion paid $50,000; B-K contributed $10,000; and B-K's excess insurance carrier contributed $25,000.

General Reinsurance made a payment to the Receiver, apparently on the theory that the settlement determined $50,000 as the amount of insured liability, General's payment represented $50,000, less the amount of retention, and other adjustments not relevant to the issue in

---

[1] Medallion's policy limit on liability to P & NE was $100,000 plus interest. The retention under the reinsurance agreement was $25,000. The award above represents General's $75,000 exposure plus interest and expenses, and the amount was to be disputed before the district court or on appeal.

this case. Although the Receiver originally contended that the appropriate amount of insured liability was $100,000, the policy limit, he ultimately conceded that the settlement determined liability at $85,000, and claimed that amount less the amount of retention. The district court entered judgment reflecting the latter theory.

II

The insolvency clause appears to require that when the insurer becomes insolvent the reinsurer's obligation with respect to an outstanding liability insured by the insurer becomes an asset of the insolvency estate. The amount of the obligation is not to be diminished because of the insolvency. The central issue in this case is whether the reinsurer may reduce or eliminate its obligation by making a settlement directly with the insured and those to whom the insured is liable. General Reinsurance would contend that because the direct settlement discharges the liability of the insurer, fully in a case like P & NE or partially in a case like B-K, and obviates any determination of a claim of liability in the insolvency proceeding, General's obligation is similarly discharged. We think the result contended for is inconsistent with the insolvency clause. It seems very clear that the payment has not been made directly to the Receiver, that the reinsurance has been diminished because of the insolvency, and the obligation of the reinsurer has ceased to be an asset of the insolvent estate.

Clearly the reinsurer has a right to defend against a claim on its merits, but is not given a right to reduce its obligation by taking advantage of the willingness of the insured and the insured's obligee to take less because of the insolvency.

We begin with the general principle that the beneficiary of the reinsurance agreement is usually the insurer (the reinsured) and not the insured under Missouri law. "An ordinary contract of reinsurance, in the absence of provisions to the contrary, operates solely as between the reinsurer and the reinsured. It creates no privity between the original insured and the reinsurer." *First National Bank of Kansas City v. Higgins,* 357 S.W.2d 139, 142 (Mo.1962) (quoting *O'Hare v. Pursell,* 329 S.W.2d 614, 620 (Mo.1959)). "[T]he liability of the reinsuring company is solely to the reinsured company, or to its receiver in the event of its insolvency." *Higgins,* 357 S.W.2d at 143. The only exception to this general rule occurs when the reinsurance contract is "drawn in such form and with such provisions so as to create a liability on the part of the reinsurer directly to the original insured." *Higgins,* 357 S.W.2d at 143. Contrary to General Reliance's assertions, this exception is inapplicable to the Agreement of Reinsurance No. 4191. The same agreement of reinsurance has been considered by Chief Judge Oliver of the same district court, and by this court on appeal. In *General Reinsurance Corp. v. Missouri Gen. Ins.,* 458 F.Supp. 1 (W.D.Mo.1977), there was a claim to reinsurance proceeds upon a theory that a claimant is a third-party beneficiary of the reinsurance agreement. Agreements in some forms have been held in Missouri to create such a right. In rejecting the theory, Judge Oliver emphasized the clarity of the requirement of this agreement that the proceeds are to be paid to the receiver of the insolvent company. 458 F.Supp. at 4. This court affirmed on the basis of the district court opinion, adding our own emphasis on another provision as compelling rejection of a third-party beneficiary theory. *General Reinsurance Corp. v. Mo. General Ins. Co.,* 596 F.2d 330 (8th Cir.1979).

The Missouri Supreme Court held in *Homan v. Employers Reinsurance Corp.,* 136 S.W.2d 289 (1939), that "upon the insolvency of the insurer, the proceeds of the reinsurance are assets to be distributed generally amongst its creditors." 136 S.W.2d at 296.

The principal argument of General Reinsurance on appeal is that the Receiver has no right to reinsurance proceeds under Agreement No. 4191 until the claim is allowed by the commissioner of claims pursuant to Mo.Ann.Stat. § 375.670 (Vernon's 1968). The P & NE claim was withdrawn after settlement, and apparently no claim was filed with respect to the B-K loss.

We do not think that the portion of the insolvency clause making reference to claims supports General's position. Nor does § 375.670 address the liability of a reinsurer to an insolvent insurer. Further, General's interpretation runs counter to the holding of the Missouri Supreme Court in *Clay v. Independence Mutual Insurance Co.,* 359 S.W.2d 679 (Mo.1962), that the appointment of the Superintendent of Insurance as receiver of an insolvent insurance company was, in effect, "an adjudication of insolvency by which the rights of the receiver became fixed." 359 S.W.2d at 683–84. In *Clay,* the court considered an action by the Superintendent to recover premiums held by an agent of an insolvent insurance company at the time the company was placed in receivership. The agent used the premiums to purchase alternative coverage for the policyholders. The court concluded that to permit the agent to use the premiums "to purchase other insurance for these policyholders would result in refunds in full to the policyholders, thus creating a preference over other insureds and creditors." 359 S.W.2d at 684.

The same concerns that prompted the *Clay* court to fix assets due an insolvent corporation in the hands of agents dictate a limit on General's right to settle claims without the participation of Medallion's Receiver. Indeed, without such a limit the potential exists for reinsurers not only to deny general creditors their acknowledged interest in reinsurance proceeds but also, at the same time, a reinsurer would be able to make cheap settlements with insureds facing the prospect of low dividends on their allowed claims.

Admittedly, where the reinsurer settles directly and obviates the determination of liability and its amount through claims procedure, there will arise questions as to proper valuation of outstanding tort claims. But it is the reinsurer's attempt to take advantage of the insolvency which causes the difficulty. The judgment in the P & NE case pretty solidly determined the liability of Medallion for $100,000. Although the settlement in the B-K case, including the payment by the excess carrier, may not be an exact valuation of Medallion's liability for the B-K loss, it provides the best approximation available.

Accordingly, the judgment of the district court is AFFIRMED.

NOTES AND QUESTIONS

1. *Reinsurance "Afforded."* Two propositions are implicit in *Ainsworth.* One is the generally accepted rule that the reinsurer owes no

duty to the policyholders of a ceding company. A fundamental principle of reinsurance is that it is a contract of indemnity and that, absent a provision to the contrary, the reinsurer is not in privity of contract with the insured. In addition to *Ainsworth,* for discussion of this point see *Arrow Trucking Co. v. Continental Insurance Co.,* 465 So.2d 691 (La. 1985); *Fontenot v. Marquette Casualty Co.,* 247 So.2d 572 (La. 1971). The other proposition is that the insolvency of a ceding insurer does not terminate the reinsurer's obligations under its agreement with the insurer. Beyond that, however, did the *Ainsworth* court properly interpret the insolvency clause in the reinsurance agreement, which referred to "reinsurance afforded by this Agreement"? At least in the B-K case, was there any reinsurance "afforded" if the case was settled without final judgment? Would recourse to the reinsurer's duty of utmost good faith assist in resolving this question?

2. *Cut-Through Clauses.* Most state statutes resemble the Missouri statute in requiring the inclusion of insolvency clauses in reinsurance agreements as a condition of the ceding insurer receiving credit for reinsurance (as described earlier in this Chapter under "Credit for Reinsurance), such that it need not maintain reserves for the ceded business. Some state statutes, however, allow an exception to the insolvency clause known as the "cut-through" clause, under which the reinsurer obligates itself directly to the insured under a specified policy, or to all the ceding company's insureds. See, e.g., N.Y. Ins. Law § 1308(2)(B). A policyholder's suit may then be brought directly against the reinsurer, and payment may be made to the insured notwithstanding the ceding insurer's insolvency.

In the absence of a cut-through clause, insureds must seek imaginative methods of reaching the reinsurer's assets, or suffer the consequences of failing to do so. Consider the inventiveness of counsel in *Ott v. All-Star Insurance Corp.,* 299 N.W.2d 839 (Wis. 1981). All-Star, the ceding insurer, was held liable to its liability insured for an excess-over-policy limits judgment entered after the insurer rejected a reasonable offer of settlement. The insurer then became insolvent. Counsel for the insured then argued successfully that a clause in All-Star's reinsurance agreement with North Star Reinsurance Corporation, affording reinsurance of a portion of judgments entered against All-Star in excess of policy limits, was in fact insurance of the insurer rather than reinsurance. Under the Wisconsin Direct Action statute, which applies to insurance but not reinsurance, this permitted the insured to sue North Star directly, in its capacity as insurer of All-Star's liability for bad-faith rejection of reasonable settlement offers.

3. *In Support of the Insolvency Clause.* The message of *Ainsworth* is of course that an insolvency clause makes reinsurance proceeds an asset of an insolvent insurer's creditors generally, not an asset of any single insured. One argument in favor of this approach is that it provides *ex ante* reassurance to prospective creditors, including policyholders, by precluding the creation of preferences for individual creditors. Another argument is that, even absent the clause, it would not always be clear *which insured* would be entitled to the proceeds of recoverable reinsurance. For example, suppose that a treaty provides that the reinsurer will cover 25 percent of all judgments in medical malpractice cases between $100,000 and $500,000, once the insurer has paid $5,000,000 in judgments in any given year. Which insured would be entitled to recover directly from the reinsurer in

the absence of an insolvency clause, once the reinsurer's obligation had been triggered?

4. *Estimating Future Claims.* One of the problems associated with determining the extent of a reinsurer's liability to an insolvent ceding insurer involves long-tail liabilities that are Incurred But Not Reported ("IBNR")—i.e., those for which the ceding insurer would ultimately be liable but which have not yet resulted in claims. Some courts have interpreted the relevant state statute governing the issue to permit estimation of IBNR, whereas others have not. Compare *In re Delta Holdings, Inc.*, 2004 WL 1752857 (Del. Ch. 2004) (dissolution plan must increase funding of an account devoted to combating future IBNR claims) with *In re Liquidation of Integrity Insurance Co.*, 2006 WL 2795343 (N.J. Super. App. Div. 2006) (because IBNR are merely actuarial estimates of future claims, they are barred from sharing in proceeds of bankrupt estate).

E. SET-OFFS IN INSOLVENCY

O'Connor v. Insurance Company of North America

United States District Court, Northern District of Illinois, 1985.
622 F.Supp. 611.

■ PLUNKETT, DISTRICT JUDGE.

Plaintiff, Philip R. O'Connor (the "Liquidator"), brings this diversity action on behalf of Reserve Insurance Company ("Reserve"). Reserve has been found insolvent, pursuant to the provisions of the Illinois Insurance Code ("Insurance Code") and the Final Order of Liquidation entered by the Circuit Court of Cook County in *People ex rel. Mathias v. Reserve Insurance Co.*, 79 Ch. 2828. Defendants include twenty-six insurance companies which acted as reinsurers of Reserve's liability under various reinsurance contracts (sometimes referred to as the "Reinsurers"); American Reserve Insurance Brokers International, Inc. ("ARIB"), which served as the manager under the contracts prior to Reserve's liquidation and shortly thereafter; Montgomery and Collins, Inc. of Texas ("Montgomery"), which purchased ARIB's rights as manager of the contracts after entry of Reserve's order of liquidation; and Petroleum Insurance, Inc. ("Petroleum"), an affiliate of Montgomery, which obtained from Montgomery the right to serve as manager under the contracts. * * *

For the reasons stated below, Defendants' motions for partial summary judgment are granted, and, accordingly, the Liquidator's cross-motion is denied.

Factual Background

The relevant facts as we understand them, although complex, do not appear to be in dispute. On May 29, 1979, an order of liquidation was entered by the Circuit Court of Cook County, naming the Director of Insurance of the State of Illinois the Liquidator of Reserve. The Liquidator has title to Reserve's property and is authorized to deal with the property and business of the company.

For several years prior to the entry of the liquidation order, Reserve was a party to several reinsurance contracts which shared insured property risks in the petroleum and petrochemical industries. In June 1975, Reserve entered into a "Quota Share Contract of Reinsurance" (the "3100 Treaty") with certain reinsurers whereby a portion of the risk on petroleum and petrochemical insurance policies written by Reserve would be carried by the reinsurers. In July 1976, Reserve entered into a "First Surplus Reinsurance Agreement" (the "P3200 Treaty") which established a reinsurance arrangement for risks written above a certain dollar amount under the 3100 Treaty. ARIB acted as the manager under both the 3100 and the 3200 treaties.

Effective January 1, 1979, the 3100 and 3200 reinsurance contracts were replaced by a new contract of reinsurance between various reinsurers, with ARIB as the manager (the "3400 pool"). Reserve was a party to the 3400 pool both as a reinsurer of risks undertaken by other insurance companies and as a reinsured on its own risks. By an agreement dated June 25, 1979, Montgomery purchased ARIB's interest as manager under the reinsurance contracts, and thereafter Petroleum became the new manager under the agreements. (The Liquidator refers to the three companies collectively as the "Manager").

While a participant in the reinsurance pool, Reserve wrote many insurance policies covering property risks in the petroleum and petrochemical industries and ceded to the reinsurers under the 3100, 3200, and 3400 treaties their share of the risk insured by such policies. Reserve also accepted reinsurance risks on policies written by other insurance companies which were members of the pool. The reinsurance pool was governed by a written contract and operated as follows. ARIB collected the insurance premium from the policyholder. ARIB then used approximately 30% of the premium to pay commissions to the producing agent or broker and the ceding company. ARIB retained the remaining 70% which was credited to the ceding company and the reinsurers in proportion to their assumption of the risk. As losses were incurred, ARIB paid the loss payments to claimants out of those retained funds.

Each quarter ARIB provided the reinsurers with an accounting of net written premiums, losses, loss adjustment expense, salvage, etc. If the net written premiums plus salvage recovered exceeded losses and expenses, ARIB paid out the net amount to the pool participants. If losses and expenses exceeded the net written premiums and salvage recoveries, the participants paid the difference to ARIB as manager. Defendants claim, and the Liquidator does not dispute, that from January 1, 1979 to the date of Reserve's insolvency the losses exceeded the net premiums in the pool and Reserve failed to make the necessary payments during that period.

Sometime after January 1, 1979, ARIB ceased issuing Reserve policies. The Liquidator contends that in April and May 1979, ARIB cancelled a large number of Reserve's policies because ARIB was concerned about Reserve's failing financial condition. During that time, ARIB issued new policies in the name of one of the other ceding companies. The Liquidator asserts that this cancellation and rewriting of policies, prior to Reserve's insolvency, was unauthorized and unlawful.

On the basis of the foregoing facts, the Liquidator alleges that he is entitled to recover, among other things, (1) certain reinsurance proceeds for losses incurred by Reserve's policyholders prior to liquidation but not paid as of the date of the liquidation order (Count I); (2) certain monies which the reinsurers and the manager owe Reserve for claims of policyholders which ARIB paid with Reserve's funds prior to liquidation (Count II); (3) Reserve's proportionate share of premiums written (less losses and other expenses) which Reserve earned under the 3400 reinsurance agreement (Count III); (4) the unearned premiums which the Manager or the reinsurers are holding and which relate to Reserve policies which were cancelled on May 30, 1979 as a result of Reserve's insolvency (Count IV); (5) the unearned premiums on Reserve policies to which the Liquidator would have been entitled had the Manager not cancelled such policies during the months prior to the liquidation order (Count V); and (6) the unearned commissions on policies cancelled by the liquidation order and cancelled by ARIB, allegedly without authority, during the months prior to the liquidation order (Count VI).

Defendants' motions for partial summary judgment request, pursuant to Fed.R.Civ.P.Rules 12(b)(6) and 56: (1) a declaration that the amounts, if any, that the Liquidator may ultimately be entitled to receive under Counts I–IV are to be reduced by the debts of Reserve to the Reinsurers and other Defendants, to the extent the amount of those debts may ultimately be proven. * * *

The Liquidator's cross-motion moves the court, pursuant to Fed.R.Civ.P.Rule 56, for partial summary judgment: (1) adjudging and declaring that the amounts the Liquidator is entitled to recover from Defendants may not be reduced by Reserve's debts, or, in the alternative, adjudging and declaring that the amounts the Liquidator is entitled to recover under Counts, I, IV, V, VI, and VII of the complaint may not be reduced by Reserve's debts. * * *

I. *Set-Offs*

Defendants contend that they are entitled to reduce the amount of any debt they may owe the Liquidator by debts Reserve owes to Defendants under the reinsurance agreements.[1] The Liquidator opposes Defendant's motions, arguing (1) that Defendants may not assert their set-off claim in this forum, but only in the liquidation court pursuant to provisions of the Insurance Code and the liquidation order, and (2) that even if Defendants' set-off claims may be considered by this court, certain of those claims do not meet the requirements set out in the statute. *See* Ill.Rev.Stat. ch. 73, § 818 (1983).

1. *The jurisdiction issue*

The heart of the Liquidator's argument is that the Insurance Code provides an exclusive procedure for the filing and determination of claims against an insolvent insurer, and that this procedure

---

[1] Defendants contend that this court should allow a reduction of their amounts owed under the common law doctrine of recoupment. However, the Illinois Insurance Code provides a comprehensive scheme by which insurance companies are to be liquidated, and no provision in the Insurance Code permits a reduction in debt under the recoupment doctrine. Indeed, the careful limitations set forth in the statute would be completely subsumed by the more expansive reach of the recoupment doctrine. While the concept of recoupment makes sense in the context of ordinary contract disputes, it is not applicable in the context of an insolvency, where we must consider the concerns of persons who are not necessarily parties to a contract, but who nonetheless also have claims against assets of the insolvent's estate. We therefore decline Defendants' invitation to base our decision on common law principle and instead rely on the statutory set-off provision of the Insurance Code, Ill.Rev.Stat. ch. 73, § 818 (1983).

encompasses the assertion of set-offs. Furthermore, it is the Liquidator's position that the injunctions contained in the liquidation order pursuant to Ill.Rev.Stat. ch. 73, § 801 (1983) present a bar to Defendants' set-offs in this forum.[2] Thus, the Liquidator argues, Defendants' set-offs must be brought in the liquidation proceedings. Defendants argue that the Insurance Code's provision regarding set-offs mandates that they be entitled to assert set-offs in this proceeding.

To resolve the issue we must examine Ill.Rev.Stat. ch. 73, § 818 (1983) which provides, in relevant part:

> In all cases of mutual debts or mutual credits between the company and another person, such credits and debts shall be set off or counterclaimed and the balance only shall be allowed or paid. * * *

Although the statutory language appears to be mandatory, it has been held that the right of set-off is permissive, not mandatory, and that its application lies within the discretion of the trial court, which exercises such discretion under the general principles of equity. *See* 4 *Collier On Bankruptcy* ¶ 68.02[1] (14th ed. 1978).[3] Even if the statute is not mandatory, however, there can be little question that Defendants are entitled to assert their set-off claims in this proceeding. It is true, as the Liquidator urges, that the liquidation order in sweeping terms bars the assertion of "claims" against the Liquidator or Reserve, except in the liquidation proceedings; however, the Liquidator's argument that the term "claim" in that order is broad enough to encompass set-offs is unavailing. Such an interpretation of the liquidation court's order would mean that the set-off provision under Illinois law had been effectively overridden by the liquidation order. * * *

Defendants do not seek affirmative relief in this proceeding against assets held by the liquidation court, even though they claim that the set-offs asserted in this proceeding may exceed the amounts owed to the Liquidator, and even though the language of the Illinois statute

---

[2] The applicable provisions of the liquidation order provide as follows:

G. That * * * persons be and are hereby enjoined and restrained from bringing or further prosecuting any action at law or in equity or other proceeding against said RESERVE INSURANCE COMPANY or the Director of Insurance of the State of Illinois, or from interfering in any way with the Director's conduct of the business of RESERVE INSURANCE COMPANY, or from obtaining preferences, judgments, attachments, or liens in the making of any levy against said Company or its property and assets while in possession and control of the Director, or from in any way interfering with the Director of Insurance in his possession or control of or in his title, right and interest to the property, books, records and all other assets of the said RESERVE INSURANCE COMPANY.

H. That all persons be and are hereby enjoined and restrained from asserting any claim against the Liquidator or RESERVE INSURANCE COMPANY except insofar as such claims arise in the liquidation proceedings of RESERVE INSURANCE COMPANY and all persons asserting claims against such policyholders, be and are hereby enjoined from instituting or pursuing any action or proceeding in any court * * * which seeks in any way, directly or indirectly to contest or interfere with the Liquidator's exclusive right, title and interest to funds, recoverable under treaties and agreements of reinsurance heretofore entered into by RESERVE INSURANCE COMPANY as the ceding insurer, or otherwise.

[3] The scope of the liquidation court's jurisdiction under the Insurance Code is similar to that granted the bankruptcy courts under the former Bankruptcy Act. *See People ex rel. Gerber v. Central Casualty Co.*, 37 Ill.2d 392, 397 (1967). Accordingly, we refer to bankruptcy cases interpreting the former Act. Similarly, we refer to Collier's 14th edition, which analyzes the former Act, rather than the more recent 15th edition, which analyzes the new Bankruptcy Code.

expressly permitting "counterclaims" might be construed to permit the assertion of claims for affirmative relief. Defendants concede that they must file with the liquidation court their affirmative claims for amounts exceeding that which the Liquidator seeks in this action. All Defendants attempt to do in this action is to show that the Liquidator has no claim or a lesser claim against them. The plain language of the statute gives Defendants that right. * * *

2. *The set-off requirements*

The Insurance Code states that "mutual debts * * * shall be set off or counterclaimed and the balance only shall be allowed or paid." Ill.Rev.Stat. ch. 73, § 818 (1983). The concept of "mutuality" refers to the idea that:

> claims owed by or to the bankrupt prior to bankruptcy cannot be set off against claims owed by or to the bankrupt's estate (as represented by the receiver of trustee) and arising after bankruptcy. This is because the element of mutuality of obligation is lacking.

4 *Collier On Bankruptcy* ¶ 68.10[1] (14th ed. 1978) (analyzing the Bankruptcy Act's similar set-off provision). Essentially this means that "pre-liquidation" debts owed by Reserve can only be set-off against "pre-liquidation" debts owed to Reserve, and similarly that "post-liquidation" debts owed by Reserve can only be set-off against "post-liquidation" debts owed to Reserve. The parties do not dispute that mutuality must exist before a set-off can be asserted; however, they disagree as to what constitutes a "pre-liquidation" rather than a "post-liquidation" debt.[4]

The Liquidator contends that even if Defendants' set-offs may be heard by this court, the debts owed to the Liquidator under Counts I, IV, V, VI and VIII, involving reinsurance proceeds and unearned premiums as a result of the cancellation of the policies upon insolvency, may not be set off because those debts are *post*-liquidation debts while the debts owed by Reserve to Defendants are *pre*-liquidation debts. The Liquidator's position is that since the reinsurance proceeds will not be due until the policyholders' loss claims are allowed or liquidated by the liquidation court, this claim is a post-liquidation claim. Similarly, since unearned premiums do not become due until the cancellation of the policies, there was no obligation to refund those amounts before Reserve's insolvency, and these, too, are post-liquidation debts. Therefore, the Liquidator argues, mutuality does not exist as between these debts and Reserve's pre-liquidation debts, and no set-off may be permitted. Defendants argue that the debts described in Counts I, IV, V, VI, and VIII arise because of provisions in the reinsurance contracts, and that since the contracts had been executed and performed prior to the time of insolvency, the debts in question are all pre-liquidation debts. Mutuality thus exists and set-offs are permitted under the statute.

We agree with defendants. Even if the Liquidator is correct in his assertion that the debts for reinsurance proceeds and unearned premiums were not due at the time of liquidation, that fact has no bearing on whether Defendants may use these debts for set-off

---

[4] All parties agree that the debts owed by Reserve under the contracts are pre-liquidation debts.

purposes. "The right of set-off may be asserted in the bankruptcy proceedings even though at the time the petition is filed one of the debts involved is absolutely owing but not presently due, or where a definite liability has accrued but is as yet unliquidated." 4 *Collier On Bankruptcy* ¶ 68.10[2] (14th ed. 1978). Defendants and Reserve entered into a reinsurance contract which defined all of the parties' rights and obligations. Any liability Defendants may incur to pay reinsurance proceeds or return unearned premiums or ceding commissions arises as a result of provisions in the previously executed reinsurance agreement that require them to make these payments. In *Cunningham v. Commissioner of Banks*, 144 N.E. 447, 459 (1924), the court stated, "[p]rovable debts under the Bankruptcy Act include all liabilities of the bankrupt founded on contract express or implied which existed at the time of the bankruptcy and either were fixed in amount or susceptible of liquidation." In this case, the reinsurance contract was in existence at the time of Reserve's insolvency. With respect to these insurance proceeds, all the claims giving rise to Defendants' liability were filed prior to Reserve's insolvency. Therefore, although the claims were not paid prior to Reserve's insolvency, they were susceptible of liquidation. The unearned premiums on policies still in existence on the date of insolvency became payable on that date, and the amounts were fixed. Accordingly, we find that Defendants' debts are pre-liquidation debts; therefore, mutuality of obligation exists and a set-off is permitted.

The Liquidator directs our attention to *Melco System v. Receivers of Trans-America Ins. Co.*, 105 So.2d 43, 53 (1958), in which the Supreme Court of Alabama held that the reinsurer incurred no debt to the reinsured until the reinsured had actually paid the losses. The court noted that it felt to allow the offset would give a preference to the reinsurer over other creditors because the reinsurer would be receiving full payment on its claim while other creditors would receive only fractional payment. 105 So.2d at 53. It is true that the reinsurer would be paid in full if a set-off is permitted, but of course, that is the case *anytime* a set-off is permitted. The whole point of the statutory set-off section is to make clear that such actions are permissible, even though one creditor may be getting paid more than other creditors. Professor Collier explains:

> The object of the statute is to permit a statement of the account between the bankrupt and its creditors with a view to the application of the doctrine of set-off between mutual debts and credits. And it has been pointed out that while the operation of this privilege of set-off has the effect to pay one creditor more than another, it is a provision based upon the generally recognized right of mutual debtors, which has been enacted as part of the Bankruptcy Act. Without such enactment, it would be argued that any attempt to offset mutual debts or credits between the estate and a creditor would amount to a preference * * * and would, therefore, be invalid. But the Act, instead, has recognized the possible injustice which would thus result and which would, for example, compel a creditor to prove his claim in full and accept possible dividends thereon and at the same time pay in full his indebtedness to the estate.

4 *Collier on Bankruptcy* ¶ 68.02[1] (14th ed. 1978). Thus, we respectfully decline to follow the *Melco* court's reasoning in that it seems to ignore the established policy in an area of bankruptcy law quite analogous to the situation with which we are faced. Defendants' debts are pre-liquidation debts, mutuality exists, and a set-off is permissible. * * *

Conclusion

For all the reasons stated above, Defendants' motions for partial summary judgment are granted. The Liquidator's cross-motion for partial summary judgment is denied.

NOTES AND QUESTIONS

1. *The Impact of Set-Off.* A reinsurer's right of set-off effectively gives priority to the reinsurer's claims over the claims of general creditors. Moreover, creditors usually have no direct notice of potential set off claims by reinsurers and limited practical means of obtaining information about such claims prior to the insurer's receivership. On the other hand, as a practical matter, insurers and reinsurers may have hundreds of monthly debits and credits between them. The denial of a right to set-off would make the clearing of these transactions much more cumbersome. The result in *O'Connor* reflects the current trend. See, e.g., *Commissioner of Ins. v. Munich Am. Reinsurance Co.*, 706 N.E.2d 694 (Mass. 1999).

2. *Contractual Set-Off.* Many reinsurance treaties explicitly provide for right of set-off. See *Transit Cas. Co. v. Selective Ins. Co. of the Southeast*, 137 F.3d 540 (8th Cir.1998); T. Darrington Semple, Jr. & Robert M. Hall, The Reinsurer's Liability in the Event of the Insolvency of A Ceding Property and Casualty Insurer, 21 TIPS J. 407, 419 (1986).

INDEX

References are to Pages

ACCIDENTAL-DEATH INSURANCE
Accidental means, 327
Suicide, 327–332

ADDITIONAL (OMNIBUS) INSUREDS
Generally, 658–665

ADMITTED MARKET
Generally, 151

ADVERSE SELECTION
    Generally, 26–27
Defined, 6–7
Discriminatory rates structures, 133–142
Duty to disclose, 27–31
Health and disability insurance exclusions, 350–351
Liability insurance, 495–502

AFFORDABLE CARE ACT (ACA)
    Generally, 343
Constitutional Challenges to, 362–372
Employer–Sponsored Coverage after, 372–373, 379–380
Reform of Health Insurance, 353–362

AGENTS (INTERMEDIARIES)
    Generally, 64–81
Authority
    Employers as agents, 79–81
    Group insurance, 79–81
    Scope of authority generally, 64–74
Contingent commissions, 73
Direct writers and independent agents, 63–64
Estoppel, 74–78
Indemnity, 72
Reasonable expectations (estoppel), 58–59
Waiver and estoppel, 74–78

AIDS
Changes in Coverage, 373–383
Domestic Partners, ERISA, 382–383
Life Insurance
    Accelerated Benefits, 312–313
    Viatical Settlements, 312–313
Misrepresentation law, 26–27

AIG BAILOUT
Generally, 171–174

ALL-RISK INSURANCE
Property insurance, 184

ANTITRUST LAWS
Federal, 107–111, 157–159
State, 168

ASSIGNED RISK PLANS
Generally, 149–151

AUTOMOBILE INSURANCE
Generally, 637–715
Additional insureds, 658–665
Assigned risk plans, 149–151
Automobile insurance plan, 149–151
Causation examined, 242
Collision coverage, 686–693
Comprehensive coverage, 686–693
Compulsory insurance requirements, 651–658
Cooperation conditions, 669–679
Coordination of multiple coverages, 685–686
Drive other cars (DOC) coverage, 664
Family exclusion, 657–658
"First Dollar" coverage, 693
Household exclusion, 657–658
Liability insurance
    Generally, 651–686
    Compulsory insurance requirements, 651–658
    Financial responsibility statutes, 656
    Moral hazard, 656–657
No-Fault automobile insurance, 710–714
Notice and cooperation conditions
    Generally, 669–679
    Prejudice to insurer, 674
    Settlement without consent, 674–679
Omnibus clause
    Generally, 658–665
    "Permission" examined, 664–665
Reinsurance facility, 149
Residual market mechanisms, 149–151
Sample policy, 638–650
Settlement by insured, 674–679
Underinsured motorists insurance, 700–701
Uninsured motorists insurance, 693–710
"Use" of the vehicle construed, 665–669

AUTOMOBILE INSURANCE PLANS
Generally, 149–151

BAD-FAITH BREACH LIABILITY OF INSURER
Generally, 81–94
Compensatory damages, 81–94
ERISA and agents employers, 390–398
Nature of the cause of action, 91
Punitive damages discussed, 93, 94

BAILEE'S INSURANCE
Generally, 289

BENEFICIARY (LIFE INSURANCE)
Change of beneficiary or assignment of policies, 314–321
Insurable interests required, 215, 298–309

Limitations on recovery
    Generally, 304
    Murder and manslaughter verdicts, 304

BINDING RECEIPTS
Generally, 292–298

BLUE CROSS/BLUE SHIELD
Coordination of coverage, 415–421

BOYCOTT, COERCION, OR INTIMIDATION
Generally, 160–168

BROKERS
See Agents

BUSINESS INTERRUPTION INSURANCE
Generally, 223–229

BUSINESS OF INSURANCE
Antitrust regulation (McCarran-Ferguson Act), 157–159
ERISA's insurance regulation exception, 391–394, 396–398

CAUSATION
Auto insurance
    Causation generally, 242
    Collision coverage, 242, 686–693
    Comprehensive coverage, 242, 686–693
Property insurance, 237–254
Proximate causation, 237–254

CERCLA
See also Hazardous Waste (Liability Insurance); Liability Insurance
"Damages" and "property damage" covered under liability insurance, 435–463

CESTUI QUE VIE
Generally, 303

CLAIMS-MADE COVERAGE
Coverage in the 1980's, 161–168
Medical malpractice insurance, 160–161, 568–576
Related claims, 563–568

COINSURANCE
Generally, 265

COLLAPSE
Generally, 232–237

COLLISION INSURANCE (AUTOMOBILE)
Generally, 686–693

COMPLETED-OPERATIONS EXCLUSION
Generally, 61–62

COMPREHENSIVE INSURANCE (AUTOMOBILE)
Generally, 686–693

COMPULSORY INSURANCE
Automobile insurance, 637–714
Financial responsibility statutes, 656

CONDITIONAL RECEIPTS AND TEMPORARY INSURANCE
Generally, 292–298

CONTINGENT COMMISSIONS
Generally, 73

CONTRA PROFERENTEM
Analyzed, 40–53
Health insurance ("Medically Necessary"), 383–390
Plain language-tension, 47
Reasonable expectations, 42–43, 52–62
Two conceptions, 46–47

CONTRACT TO INSURE FOR ANOTHER
Open-mortgage clauses, 277
Standard (or union) mortgage clauses, 274

COORDINATION OF MULTIPLE COVERAGES
Disability insurance, 406–407
Health insurance, 406–415
Liability and automobile insurance
    Methods of coordination of multiple coverages, 685
    "Other Insurance" clauses, 679–686
    Proration of multiple coverages, 679–686
    Rate regulation, 686
"Stacking" uninsured motorist insurance, 706–710

CORPORATE OWNED LIFE INSURANCE
Generally, 303, 305–309

CQV
Generally, 303

CREDIT DEFAULT SWAPS
Generally, 171–173

CUT-THROUGH CLAUSES
Generally, 750

DIRECTORS & OFFICERS LIABILITY INSURANCE
Generally, 534–568

DISABILITY INSURANCE
Generally, 421–433
Coordination of coverage, 406–407
"Disability" defined, 421–429
Exclusion due to preexisting conditions, 349–350
Market for disability insurance, 421–422
Mitigation (insured's implied duty to mitigate), 433
Moral hazard (conduct clauses), 427–428
Partial disability problem, 427
Preexisting conditions exclusions, 349–350

Public policy, 422–427
Total disability, 422–433

DISPROPORTIONATE FORFEITURE
Generally, 18–19

DIVORCE (AND SEPARATION AGREEMENTS)
Beneficiary change, 315–320

DRAFTING INSURANCE POLICIES
Insurance Services Office, 36–37
Standardized forms, 33–40
Uniformity in drafting
    Generally, 33–40
    Antitrust challenges, 159–182

DRIVE OTHER CARS (DOC) COVERAGE
Generally, 664

DROP-DOWN LIABILITY
Generally, 624–635

DUTY OF CARE (INSURER'S DUTY OF CARE)
Life insurance, 327–333

DUTY OF UTMOST GOOD FAITH
Generally, 721–728

DUTY TO DEFEND
    Generally, 577–609
Conflicts of interest, 587–609
Non-Waiver agreement, 585
Recoupment, 595–601
Reservation of rights notice, 581–585
Scope of the duty to defend, 578–587
Settlement of claims, 609–624
Terminating the duty to defend, 587

DUTY TO DISCLOSE
Generally, 27–31

EMPLOYERS AS AGENTS (GROUP HEALTH)
Generally, 78–81

EMPLOYEE RETIREMENT INCOME SECURITY ACT (ERISA)
Scope of the act
    Bad-Faith actions against insurer agents/insurers, 390–398
    Health insurance, 373–383, 384–388, 398–406
    McCarran-Ferguson Act ("Business of Insurance") test applied, 390–398
    Medically necessary services, 384–390

ESTOPPEL AGAINST INSURER
Agent's actions, 74–78
Reasonable expectations, 53–54, 61–62

EVIDENTIARY CONDITIONS
    Generally, 60–61
Forcible entry requirement, 54–58

EXCESS LIABILITY INSURANCE
    Generally, 624–635
Follow-Form coverage, 617
Relationship of primary and excess insurers
    Generally, 624–635
    Drop-Down liability, 630–635
    Duty to settle, 624–630
Umbrella coverage, 617

EXCLUSIONS AND CONDITIONS (TO COVERAGE)
Automobile Insurance
    Cooperation conditions, 669–679
    Family exclusion, 657–658
    Household exclusion, 657–658
    Notice and cooperation conditions, 669–679
    Prejudice to insurer, 674
    Settlement without consent, 674–679
Directors & Officers Liability Insurance, 555–563
Disability Insurance, Preexisting conditions exclusion, 349–350
Health Insurance, Preexisting conditions exclusion, 349–350
Liability Insurance
    Business risk exclusion, 507–516
    Completed-Operations exclusion, 61–62
    Expected or intended harm, 495–507
    Notice condition, 528–534
    Owned-Property exclusion, 527
    Pollution exclusion, 516–527
Life Insurance
    Approval of the insurer, 292–296
    Conditional receipts and temporary coverage, 296–297
    Incontestability, 321–327
    Insurable interest of beneficiary, 298–308
Property Insurance
    Generally, 229–260
    Causation, 237–253
    Forcible entry requirement, 54–58
    Increased risk exclusions, 253–260
    Knowledge or control of risk, 253–259
    Vacancy exclusions, 259

EXEMPLARY DAMAGES
Bad-Faith breach by the insurer, 81–94

FAMILY EXCLUSION TO AUTO LIABILITY INSURANCE
Generally, 657–658

FINANCIAL RESPONSIBILITY LAWS
Generally, 656

FIRST-DOLLAR COVERAGE
Generally, 693

FOLLOW-FORM COVERAGE
Generally, 617

"FOLLOW-THE-FORTUNES" CLAUSES
Generally, 728–745

FORCIBLE ENTRY REQUIREMENT
Generally, 54–58

FRATERNAL BENEFIT SOCIETIES
Generally, 2

FUNCTIONS OF INSURANCE
Generally, 3–5

GENETIC DISCRIMINATION
Generally, 141–142

GREAT FIRE OF LONDON
Generally, 1

GROUP INSURANCE
Employers as agents, 78–81
ERISA, 78–81

HAZARDOUS WASTE (LIABILITY INSURANCE)
Coverage for cleanup costs, 455–463
Owned-Property exclusion, 527

HEALTH AND DISABILITY INSURANCE
Generally, 3
Disability insurance
    Coordination of coverage, 406–421
    "Disability" defined, 421–429
    Market for disability insurance, 421–422
    Mitigation (insured's implied duty to mitigate), 433
    Moral hazard (conduct clauses), 427–428
    Preexisting conditions exclusions, 349–350
    Public policy, 422–427
    Total disability, 422–433
Health insurance
    Access to care, 373–383, 398–406
    Affordable Care Act, 343, 353–373, 379–380
    Coordination of coverage, 406–421
    Cost containment, 383–421
    Employment-based coverage, 344, 349–350, 372–373
    ERISA, 344, 384–388, 390–406
    Forms of coverage, 343–346, 383
    Health insurance in the U.S. (nature and scope), 343–346
    Health Insurance Portability & Accountability Act (HIPAA), 344
    Health maintenance organizations (HMOs), 383
    HIPPA, 344
    Managed care, 349, 383
    "Medically necessary" services, 384–390
    Moral hazard, 348–349, 384–388
    National health insurance, 345–346, 358–359
    Preadmission review, 389
    Preexisting conditions exclusions, 349–350
    Preferred provider organizations (PPOs), 383
    Reform, 346–352
    Settlement, 420
    Time Limitations on claims, 99–105
    Tort recovery by subrogation, 415–421
HIPPA, 344

HEALTH MAINTENANCE ORGANIZATIONS
Coverage denials, 398–406

HIPPA
Generally, 344

HISTORY OF INSURANCE
Generally, 1–2

HOUSEHOLD EXCLUSION TO AUTO LIABILITY COVERAGE
Generally, 657–658

INCONTESTABILITY
Generally, 321–327
Impostor Defense, 322–327
Limitations of risk, 327

INCREASED RISK EXCLUSIONS
Generally, 253–260

INDEMNITY
Economic conception v. functional conception, 263
Indemnity principle explained, 215
Insurable interest, 215–216
Subrogation, 266–268

INSOLVENCY OF INSURERS
Cut-through clauses, 750
Guaranty funds, 113–126
Insolvency clauses, 745–751
Reinsurer's right of set-off, 751–757

INSURABLE INTEREST
Generally, 210–217, 298–309
Cestui que vie (CQV) insured, 303
Creditor's insurable interest, 302–303
Indemnity principle, 215
Life insurance, 298–309
Property insurance, 210–217

INSURANCE MARKET
Reinsurance, 717–757
Residual market mechanisms, 149–151
Secondary markets
    Generally, 149–151, 717–757
    Automobile insurance, 149–150
    Liability insurance, 150
    Malpractice insurance, 150
    Property insurance, 150
    Reinsurance, 717–757
    Workers' Compensation insurance, 127
Surplus and excess lines, 151

INSURANCE SERVICES OFFICE (ISO)
Generally, 36–37

INSURING AGREEMENT
Damages covered, 455–468
Number of occurrences, 487–495
"Occurrence" defined, 503

INTENTIONAL ACTS
Coverage generally denied, 97–98
Liability insurance
    Intended harms exclusion, 495–507
    "Occurrences" (Not expected), 495–500

JOINT UNDERWRITING ASSOCIATIONS
Generally, 149–150

LEASES AND INSURANCE
Lessees as implied co-insureds, 277–282

LIABILITY INSURANCE
    Generally, 435–576, 651–686
Allocation, 477–487
Asbestos, 488–495, 514–515
Automobile liability insurance, 651–686
Bodily injury, 466–468
CERCLA, 455–463
Claims-made, 534–576
Construction defects, 507
"Damages" covered, 455–468
Directors & Officers liability insurance
    Generally, 534–568
    Exclusions and conditions, 555–563
Drop-down liability, 630–635
Duty to defend
    Generally, 577–609
    Conflicts of interest, 587–609
    Recoupment, 595–601
    Scope of the duty to defend, 578–587
    Settlement of claims, 609–630
    Terminating the duty to defend, 587
Emotional distress, 466–468
Excess insurance
    Generally, 487–495, 624–635
    Follow-form coverage, 617
    Relationship of primary and excess insurers, 624–635
    Umbrella coverage, 617
Exclusions and conditions of coverage
    Generally, 495–534
    Business risk exclusions, 507–516
    Completed–operations exclusion, 61–62
    Expected or intended harm, 495–527
    Notice conditions to coverage
        Generally, 528–534
        Prejudice to insurer, 528–534
    Owned-property exclusion, 527
    Pollution exclusion, 516–527
Exhaustion, 618–624
Hazardous waste, 455–463
Insuring agreement (coverage provided)
    Generally, 455–495

Damages covered, 455–468
Number of occurrences, 487–495
"Occurrence" defined, 503
Known Losses, 501–502
Malpractice, 568–576
No action clause, 674–679
Number of occurrences, 487–495
Other insurance, 679–686
Products liability, 487–495
Professional liability insurance, 534–576
Property damage, 463–466
Related claims, 565–568
Sample CGL policy
    Generally, 538–554
    Bad-faith in settlement, 614–615
    Duty of settlement, 624–630
    Settlement of claims, 624–630
Sex abuse, 506–507
Successor Liability, 476–477
Trigger of coverage
    Generally, 469–487
    Exposure theory, 470–471, 475–476
    Manifestation theory, 472–473, 476
    "Occurrence" clauses construed, 473–474
Uninsured Years, 487

LIFE INSURANCE
    Generally, 3, 291–343
Accelerated benefits, 313
AIDS, 312–313
Application (temporary coverage), 292–298
Armstrong Investigation, 108–109
Assignment of policies, 309–321
Binder or binding receipts, 296–297
Change of beneficiary or assignment of policies
    Generally, 314–321
    Insurable interest required, 298–308
    Limitations on recovery, 304
    Murder or manslaughter, 304
Company owned (COLI), 305–308
Conditional receipts, 296–297
Conversion to present cash value, 309–314
Corporate owned life insurance, 303, 305–308
Incontestability
    Generally, 321–327
    Conditions of coverage (become incontestable), 321–327
Insurable interest requirement
    Generally, 298–309
    Cestui Que Vie (CQV) insured, 303
    Corporate owned life insurance, 303, 305–309
    Creditor's insurable interest, 302–303
    Standing to question in court, 304–305
    Stranger Originated (STOLI), 314
    Time of interest, 304
Insuring the life of another (owner not the insured), 303

Limitations of risk (never incontestable), 327
Negligence actions against the insurer, 327–333
Retroactive coverage upon approval, 292–296
Temporary coverage upon application, 296–297
Term v. Whole Life insurance, 291
Viatical Settlements, 312–314

LIMITED INTERESTS
Generally, 273–289
Bailees, 289
Leaseholds (Lessee as co-insured), 277–282
Life estates (and immediate death of the insured), 288–289
Mortgagees
Generally, 273–277
Open-mortgage clauses, 277
Standard (or union) mortgage clauses, 274
Real estate sales (mismatched or double insurance), 282–289

LLOYDS OF LONDON
Generally, 1

LORD MANSFIELD'S RULE
Generally, 13–14

MALPRACTICE INSURANCE
Generally, 166, 568–576

MANIFESTATION THEORY
Generally, 472–473, 476

McCARRAN-FERGUSON ACT
"Boycott, Coercion, or Intimidation"
Generally, 160–168
Medical malpractice insurance crises, 166
"Business of Insurance," 393
ERISA's insurance regulation exception, 391–394, 396–397
"Regulation" defined, 159–160
State regulation
Generally, 111–149, 175–179
State antitrust provisions, 168
Text of the statute, 109

MEASURE OF RECOVERY
Actual cash value, 260–266
CERCLA (hazardous waste clean-up), 455–463
Coinsurance, 265
Liability insurance for punitive damages, 94–99
Replacement-Cost coverage, 260–266
Valued policies, 264–265

MEDICAL MALPRACTICE INSURANCE
Crisis in the 1970's, 166
Crisis in the 1980's (Claims-made coverage), 161–168
Joint underwriting associations, 150

MISREPRESENTATION
Affirmative misrepresentation, 15–22
Agents-as intermediaries, 22–24
AIDS, 26–27
Concealment, 20
Duty to disclose, 27–31

MOLD
See Property Insurance

MORAL HAZARD
Automobile insurance
Generally, 656–657
Liability insurance, 656–657
Uninsured motorists insurance, 706
Disability insurance conduct clauses, 427–428
Evidentiary conditions, 60–61
Health insurance, 384–388
Liability insurance
Business risk exclusions, 507–516
Expected or intended harms not covered, 495–507
Pollution exclusion, 516–527
Moral hazard defined, 7

MORTGAGEE'S INSURANCE
Generally, 274–277
Open-mortgage clauses, 277
Standard (or union) mortgage clauses, 274

MURDER OR MANSLAUGHTER (LIFE INSURANCE)
Generally, 304

MUTUAL INSURANCE COMPANIES
Generally, 2–3, 117

NATIONAL ASSOCIATION OF INSURANCE COMMISSIONERS (NAIC)
Generally, 111–113

NATIONAL CONFERENCE OF INSURANCE GUARANTY FUNDS
Generally, 123

NATIONAL HEALTH INSURANCE
Generally, 345–346, 384–390

NEGLIGENCE ACTIONS AGAINST INSURERS
Life insurers, 327–333

NEGLIGENT SUPERVISION OF CHILDREN
Generally, 502–505

NO-FAULT INSURANCE
Generally, 710–714
Benefit levels, 712
Relative Cost, 712
Thresholds and benefit levels, 711–712

NON-ADMITTED MARKET
Generally, 151

NON-WAIVER AGREEMENTS
Generally, 585

NOTICE TO INSURER
Notice conditions in automobile insurance, 669–679
Notice conditions in liability insurance
    Generally, 528–534
    Prejudice to insurer, 528–534

OCCURRENCE COVERAGE
Generally, 160–161

OCCURRENCES
Number of occurrences, 487–495
"Occurrence" defined, 503
Trigger of coverage, 469–487

OMNIBUS CLAUSE
Generally, 658–665

OPEN-MORTGAGE CLAUSES
    Generally, 277
    "Other Insurance" clauses, 679–686

PATIENT PROTECTION AND AFFORDABLE CARE ACT
See Affordable Care Act

PERSONAL INJURY PROTECTION (PIP)
Generally, 711–714

PLAIN LANGUAGE POLICIES
Automobile insurance, 668
Uninsured motorist coverage, 701

POLLUTION LIABILITY
Pollution exclusion from liability coverage, 516–527

PREJUDICE TO INSURER (NOTICE)
Automobile insurance, 674
Liability insurance, 528–534

PRODUCTS LIABILITY
Coordination of multiple coverages, 469–487
Number of occurrences insured, 487–495

PROPERTY INSURANCE
    Generally, 3
All-risk coverage vs. specified risk coverage, 184
Binders, 40
Business interruption insurance, 223–229
Causation, 237–253
Collapse, 232–237
Exclusions
    Generally, 229–260
    Causation, 237–253
    Collapse, 232–237
    Flood, 247–253
    Hurricane Katrina claims, 247–253
    Increased risk exclusions, 253–260
    Intrinsic losses, 230–237
    Progressive losses, 222
    Vacancy exclusions, 259
Increase of hazard, 253–260
Insurable interest requirement, 210–217
Intrinsic losses, 230–237
Limited interests insured
    Bailees, 289
    Leaseholds (lessee as co-insured), 277–282
    Life estates (and immediate death of the insured), 288
    Mortgagees, 274–277
    National Flood Insurance Program, 253
    Real estate sales (mismatched or double insurance), 282–289
Measure of recovery
    Generally, 260–265
    Actual cash value, 260–265
    Coinsurance, 265
    Replacement-cost coverage, 260–265
    Valued policies, 264–265
Number of occurrences, 40
Progressive losses, 222
Proximate cause, 237–253
Residual market mechanisms, 150
Sample homeowners policy, 183–209
Subrogation, 266–273
Sue and labor clauses, 236–237
Trigger of coverage, 217–223
World Trade Center, 40

PUBLIC POLICY AND INSURANCE
Automobile insurance, household or family exclusion, 657–658
Disability insurance, 421–429
General discussion, 94–105
Intentional acts coverage, 95–99, 98–99
Punitive damages coverage, 95–99
Time limits on accident/dismemberment claims, 99–105

PUNITIVE DAMAGES
Bad-faith actions against the insurer, 93, 94
Liability insurance for punitive damages, 98–99

RATES AND RATEMAKING
Collective ratemaking, antitrust challenges, 159–182
Contingent commissions, 73
Coordination of multiple coverages, 685
Discrimination by sex, 142
Driving experience, 135–138
Genetic discrimination, 141–142
    Standard of review, 128, 131
Rate rollbacks, 133
Sex discrimination, federal law, 142
Standard of review, 128, 131

REAL ESTATE SALES (MISMATCHED OR DOUBLE INSURANCE)
Generally, 282–289

REASONABLE EXPECTATIONS OF THE INSURED
Estoppel rationale, 53, 61–62

RECIPROCALS
Generally, 2

REGULATION OF INSURANCE
Armstrong Investigation, 108–109
Contingent commissions, 73
Federal regulation
    Antitrust regulation, 109–111, 157–168
    Credit Default Swaps, 171–173
    Discriminatory rate classification, 138–142
    Interstate commerce power, 107–111
    McCarran-Ferguson Act, 109–111, 157
National Association of Insurance Commissioners (NAIC), 111–113
National Conference of Insurance Guaranty Funds, 123
State guaranty funds, 111–157
State regulation of insurance
    Generally, 111–157, 159–160
    Antitrust law (state regulation), 168
    Solvency assured, 113–117

REINSURANCE
Duty of utmost good faith, 721–728
"Follow-the-fortunes" clauses, 728–745
Insolvency of insurers
    Generally, 745–751
    Cut-through clauses, 750
    Insolvency clauses, 745–751
    Reinsurer's right of set-off, 751–759
Reinsurance facility, 149

REMEDIES (AGAINST THE INSURER)
Bad Faith breach, 81–94, 390–398
Compensatory damages, 81–94, 390–399
Punitive damages, 93, 396

RESERVATION OF RIGHTS NOTICE
Generally, 581–585

RESIDUAL MARKET MECHANISMS
Automobile insurance, 149–150
Liability insurance, 150
Malpractice insurance, 150
Property insurance, 150
Workers' Compensation insurance, 150

RISK
    Generally, 3–4
Risk allocation, 4
Risk pooling, 4
Risk transfer, 3

SAMPLE POLICIES
Automobile insurance, 638–650
Directors & Officers Liability Insurance, 538–554
Homeowners insurance, 183–209
Liability insurance, 437–454
Property insurance, 183–209

SEPTEMBER 11, 2001
    Generally, 1
Contra proferentem, 40–41

SETTLEMENT OF CLAIMS
Bad-Faith in settlement, 614–615
Duty of settlement
    Generally, 609–617, 624–630
    Duty of excess insurers to primary insurers, 624–630
    Duty owed to insureds, 609–617
    Duty owed to reinsurers, 745
Exhaustion, 618–624

SOCIAL FUNCTIONS
Generally, 5

SPECIMEN POLICIES
"Stacking" uninsured motorist coverages, 706–710

STANDARD FORM INSURANCE POLICIES
Generally, 33–40

STANDARD MORTGAGEE CLAUSE
Generally, 274

STOCK INSURANCE COMPANIES
Generally, 2–3

SUBROGATION
    Generally, 266–273, 415–421
Equitable and contractual subrogation, 266–267, 418
Equitable subrogation and the duty to settle, 624–630
Health insurance and tort recovery by subrogation, 418–421
Property insurance, 266–273
Uninsured motorists insurance, 701

SURPLUS LINES
Generally, 151

TENANTS AS IMPLIED CO-INSUREDS
Generally, 277–282

THEFT LOSS
Forcible entry requirement, 54–58

THIRD PARTY INSURANCE
Generally, 183

TIME LIMITS ON ACCIDENTAL INJURY CLAIMS
Generally, 99–105

TITLE VII
Generally, 142, 154

TRIGGER OF COVERAGE
Exposure theory, 470–471, 475–476
Injury in fact theory, 469–477
Manifestation theory, 472–473, 476
Occurrence clauses construed, 473–474

UMBRELLA COVERAGE
Generally, 617

UNDERWRITING
    Generally, 7–8
Profit and loss, 128–129

UNINSURED MOTORISTS INSURANCE
Generally, 693–710
Arbitration, 701
Contact requirement, 701–706
Forms of coverage, 701
Moral hazard, 706
Multiple coverages, 706–710
Plain-language UM coverage, 701
"Stacking" coverage, 706–710
Statutory requirement, 701–706
Subrogation, 701
Underinsured motorists insurance, 700

USE OF VEHICLE
Generally, 665–669

VACANCY EXCLUSIONS
Generally, 259

VALUED POLICIES
Generally, 264–265

VENDOR-VENDEE PROBLEMS
Mismatched and double insurance, 282–289

WAIVER
Generally, 74–78

WARRANTIES
Breach of warranty, 9–14
History of warranties, 13–14
Lord Mansfield's Rule, 13–14
Materiality of breach, 14–16
Mitigating doctrines, 15–16
Regulation of warranties, 15–16

WORLD TRADE CENTER
Generally, 40